P9-DYZ-359

ALSO BY JANE BRYANT QUINN

Smart and Simple Financial Strategies for Busy People

Everyone's Money Book

THE CLASSIC
BESTSELLER

Completely Revised
for the *New Economy*

JANE
BRYANT
QUINN

MAKING
THE MOST
OF YOUR
MONEY
NOW

Simon & Schuster
NEW YORK · LONDON · TORONTO · SYDNEY

This publication contains the opinions and ideas of its author. It is sold with the understanding that neither the author nor the publisher is engaged in rendering legal, tax, investment, insurance, financial, accounting, or other professional advice or services. If the reader requires such advice or services, a competent professional should be consulted. Relevant laws vary from state to state. The strategies outlined in this book may not be suitable for every individual, and are not guaranteed or warranted to produce any particular results.

No warranty is made with respect to the accuracy or completeness of the information contained herein, and both the author and the publisher specifically disclaim any responsibility for any liability, loss or risk, personal or otherwise, which is incurred as a consequence, directly or indirectly, of the use and application of any of the contents of this book.

Simon & Schuster
1230 Avenue of the Americas
New York, NY 10020

Copyright © 1991, 1997, 2009 by Berrybrook Publishing, Inc.

All rights reserved, including the right to reproduce this book or portions thereof in any form whatsoever. For information address Simon & Schuster Subsidiary Rights Department, 1230 Avenue of the Americas, New York, NY 10020

This Simon & Schuster hardcover edition January 2010

SIMON & SCHUSTER and colophon are registered trademarks of Simon & Schuster, Inc.

For information about special discounts for bulk purchases, please contact Simon & Schuster Special Sales at 1-866-506-1949 or business@simonandschuster.com

The Simon & Schuster Speakers Bureau can bring authors to your live event. For more information or to book an event contact the Simon & Schuster Speakers Bureau at 1-866-248-3049 or visit our website at www.simonspeakers.com.

Designed by Paul Dippolito

Manufactured in the United States of America

1 3 5 7 9 10 8 6 4 2

Library of Congress Cataloging-in-Publication Data
Quinn, Jane Bryant.
Making the most of your money now : the classic bestseller / Jane Bryant Quinn.
      p.   cm.
Includes index.
1. Finance, Personal.   2. Investments.   I. Title.
II. Title: Completely rev. for the new economy.
      HG179.Q57   2009
332.024'01—dc22   2009032610

ISBN 978-0-7432-6996-4
ISBN 978-1-4165-5352-6 (ebook)

Previous editions of this work were published as *Making the Most of Your Money* in 1991 and 1997 by Simon & Schuster, Inc.

For Carll

Contents

Money and Me

No one is born with a mind for personal finance. I certainly wasn't. I came from a family that handled money prudently, but I understood that only in retrospect. We didn't talk about it. Everything I learned about money, I learned by watching, reading, doing, and—yes—making some awful mistakes.

I'd love to tell you that I embraced my mistakes because they taught me so much, but I'd be lying. I hated making those mistakes! Still do. The only upside is that, after going wrong myself, I understand how easy it is to get off track—especially when money is short or when so-called financial experts are whispering into your ear. I also learned, through trial and error, what the better choices are.

I started out fine as a money manager, teenage division. On my sixteenth birthday, I took the bus to city hall in my hometown, Niagara Falls, New York, to apply for working papers. That afternoon I interviewed with the head of the public library, who not only hired me for afterschool work but gave me my favorite job title ever: I was a "page" in a building full of books. I spent some of my earnings (not a lot; we weren't big spenders at Niagara Falls High School) and put the rest in a savings account to help pay for college.

At college, I got a check from my parents to supplement what I'd saved. I watched my pennies, balanced my checkbook, and never overdrew. In those days we couldn't get credit cards, so I wasn't put to the plastic test. Summers, I clerked in a grocery story and waitressed at Howard Johnson's. (I never learned the trick of balancing a fully loaded serving tray on one hand, held above my head. I was always terrified that I'd drop four hamburger specials with Cokes and fries down the customers' necks.)

Finally I got the summer job of my dreams: reporting stories for the *Niagara Falls Gazette*. I wasn't on the front page. It was more like, "Jane, go to the Friday greenmarket and update the table of vegetable prices." But I was a *reporter.* I had a desk, phone, and ID card to prove it.

My financial *oops* moments started when I got out of school and went to work at a consumer newsletter in New York City. For one thing, I didn't save. I spent every dime and never looked ahead. One year when I unexpectedly had extra income taxes to pay, I had to take out a loan. I lived the paycheck-to-paycheck life.

Lucky for me, a colleague at work dropped by one day to tell me I was an idiot (his word!) not to have joined the company automatic-savings plan. "I can't afford it," I whined. "Yes you can," he said. "Have 5 percent taken out of your pay automatically, and you'll never notice." I did, and he was right. I was still living paycheck to paycheck, but suddenly, I was saving money along the way. The money wasn't much (I wasn't earning much), but I'm grateful to this day for his having taken the time to tell me I was being dumb. I've been devoted to automatic savings plans every since.

I didn't have a lot of other financial options during my twenties. I married young, had a beautiful baby right away, and money was tight. It got tighter at twenty-five, when I found myself broke, divorced, and struggling to pay rent in a city that isn't for sissies. Young journalists didn't earn much, especially if you were of the female persuasion. In those bad old days, there was something called the "female discount." If a man and a woman held the same type of job in the company, the woman was paid 30 percent less—and it was legal. At my job inter-view, the discount was figured out right in front of me, on an adding machine. Total humiliation—but I was stuck. Thank goodness for the feminist movement, which eventually put an end to overt wage discrimination—although not in time to help me with the rent.

I survived by pleading for discounts on nursery school fees (the wonderful headmaster said yes) and scrambling for freelance jobs I could work on after putting my son to bed. Those were tears-in-the-pillow years, and bills I didn't open because I knew I couldn't pay them right away. It's the only time I've ever run up credit card debt and haven't forgotten the scare. To this day, I pay my bills in full on the day they arrive.

But except for my checkbook worries, life was great. My son was growing. At work, I was learning how to report and write, and starting to specialize in consumer finance. The more I interviewed financial people, the wider my eyes grew. I realized that I could learn this stuff. It wasn't magic, it was all based on simple common sense. I'd had no idea.

Fast-forward in time. I got better jobs and earned more money. I married again. We rented a house for a while and finally found the resources to build our own. I felt back on track.

With some money to spare, I ventured into investing and that's when the oopses really started. I opened an account with a stockbroker—a friend of my dad's—and asked for advice. He started calling me with new stocks to buy and suggesting that it was time to sell old ones, in order, he said, to diversify. After a couple of years, it hit me that he was making money on commissions but I wasn't getting anywhere, so I took my money back. At about that time, another broker put an important chunk of my husband's savings into a single can't-lose stock. You know the rest of that story! We were stupid and inexperienced, what can I say?

By then, my reading and reporting had led me to low-cost index mutual funds. Whew, just in time. I've kept them to this day without a moment's regret. (You'll learn to love them too—see page 745.)

But let's face it, index funds get b-o-o-o-ring. A girl ought to own something interesting, right? Gotta make a killing. At that time, I was editing an investment newsletter and talking to Wall Street gurus all the time. They must know something special about making money. Otherwise, why was I interviewing them?

There's no point going into all the sad details. Here's what I got out of my super-guru advice: an oil well in Ohio that came up dry and a top-performing mutual fund that lost 80 percent of its value because it owned too many of that era's hottest stocks. All the way down, its brainy manager urged me not to sell.

I even went local, in hopes of getting in on the ground floor of something big. A neighbor and former executive of a blue jeans company had a smart new idea for making jeans that fit all figures. I was all too right about the ground floor. That's where we stayed, as the seed money dribbled away.

In my heart, I knew better than to write those checks. I'd reported extensively on oil-well partnerships and how the fees ate you up, even if you were lucky enough to hit some oil. But I was dazzled by the guru—a regular source for me—who touted the Ohio well as something special.

The mistaken mutual fund investment is even more embarrassing. I knew it owned highfliers, but I was so impressed by the manager's smarts (or what sounded like smarts) that I figured he'd sell those zoomy stocks at their top and switch to the next Great Investment Game when it came along. Wrong. Soooo wrong. As I've learned, almost no fund manager can do that successfully (and probably you should delete the word *almost*).

About my neighbor, what can I say? It was a completely dumb move that my accountant advised against—but the jeans were so cool. (They ought to have been, considering what I paid!)

Did I mention that I bought some gold coins near the 1980 peak?

All my mistakes came from turning off my common sense and BS detector and letting a salesperson or silly enthusiasm run my mind. Happily, I never had too much money at stake, so I could ramp up my savings again. But, gee, I wish I'd kept it all in index funds.

By this time, I had left my job at the investment letter and started freelancing. I quit because I got a promotion but wasn't given the same title held by the job's previous occupant—a man. I got a lesser title, not to mention lesser pay. Sound familiar? Those were still the bad old days when women couldn't catch an even break.

As it turned out, leaving that job was *not* one of my mistakes. In fact, it's the best thing that ever happened to me professionally. To earn money, I wrote my first book on personal finance. I started a syndicated newspaper column for *The Washington Post,* thanks to the head of the syndicate, Bill Dickinson, who was willing to gamble on an unknown. His belief in me changed my life. At first it wasn't clear that the column would succeed (Jane Bryant Quinn? the newspapers asked. Who's that?). I still have in my files the names of the nineteen papers and their open-minded editors who bought the new column and gave me my chance.

When the column caught on (250 papers eventually came on board), one thing led to another. I started a column for *Newsweek* magazine, added CBS-TV (morning and evening news), and wrote the first edition of the book you're reading now. But I've never forgotten the feeling of launching out on my own—the thrill of a high-wire act and the nail-biting wait to see if I'd make it to the other side.

Freelancing taught me yet another lesson. When you work for yourself, your investments ought to be more conservative. No employer was contributing to my retirement plan. If I got hit by a truck, my savings were my only safety net. So I had to invest more carefully. I've always held a higher percentage of bonds, compared with stocks, than I would have if an employer were funding my 401(k).

Fast-forward again, to another hard-learned lesson—this one on long-term care insurance. When LTC policies were first introduced, many of them were poor. They low-balled their premiums, bumped up the price later, put unexpected limits on coverage, and sometimes used fine print to deny payments due. Then the products improved and my husband and I applied. My husband was turned down because, by then, he had some health issues. One day he had a debilitating stroke and the cost was all mine. Would those earlier LTC products have paid? Maybe, but maybe not; they were generally nursing-home contracts and I wanted to care for him at home. Still, it's never a smart idea to put off buying life, health, disability, and long-term care insurance that you know you need. Buy it now while your health is good. One bad diagnosis renders you uninsurable overnight.

When I became a widow, I bought a house in haste. That's one of the things I've always told others not to do. I righted myself and last year had the joy of remarrying. Money matters in life, but what matters more is holding yourself open to happy surprise.

After you've read a list of my financial crimes, you might wonder why I'm writing a personal finance book! First, because I'm a lot smarter now. Second, because I hope to help you avoid some of my own hard lessons and make good choices right from the start. It's pretty easy to avoid my mistakes once you've been alerted to them. And third—the most important thing—to abolish the myth that you have to be born with a math book in your mouth to be good at making decisions about your personal money.

I'm terrible at math; I always have been. Personal finance has nothing to do with math. It's all about understanding simple principles (such as automatic savings), knowing where to find the advice and tools you need (in this book, I've rounded them up for you), choosing plain-vanilla financial products (they've proven to be superior to everything else), and ignoring the America's Great Financial Marketing Machine. In a lifetime of studying personal finance, I can say with confidence that roughly 97.23 percent of the highly touted financial products that you read and hear about will make other people rich; they won't make you rich. The products and strategies that *will* make you rich are in these chapters.

A trusted adviser who won't be identified here once suggested that I invest with Ezra Merkin, a prominent financier. "No home runs, just a steady 10 to 20 percent a year using puts and calls," the adviser said. I begged off. Not my style. Years later, it turned out that Merkin's miracles came from investing with the notorious Bernie Madoff, the Ponzi guy. (I still trust that adviser in his area of expertise—but not his investment advice!)

I dodged the Madoff bullet not because I suspected fraud but because—by now—I have rules for myself. Investments have to be simple so that I can understand them perfectly. I won't pay high fees—they're your first sign that a product is poor. I stick with things like mutual funds whose prices are published daily, online, and can't be fudged. Mystery systems of puts and calls don't fit the bill.

Developing simple rules is one of the secrets of managing money well. You create a list of what works for you and apply those rules to each new idea that comes along. If the idea fits, I consider it. If not, I don't even bother investigating it. For investing, my rules are: mutual funds, not individual stocks; passive investing (index or target retirement mutual funds); strict diversification between stocks and bonds related to age (110 minus your age is the maximum percentage you should risk in stocks); regular rebalancing, to keep the stock/bond diversification on target; low costs, which keeps me out of all those dubious, expensive annuities; and investments whose price I can follow publicly, in the newspapers or online. In other words, b-o-o-o-ring. For thrills, I go to the horse races. I want my investments to be about as interesting as watching paint dry.

This book explains all these rules, and other rules, about savings, credit, mortgages, and insurance. With any luck, they'll steer you around my mistakes, or at least keep your bumps to a minimum!

At this writing, we're also in the midst of a once-in-a-lifetime economic earthquake. Important products such as health insurance, credit cards, retirement plans, and college loans are up for change. I've caught as many of those changes as I could before this book went to press. You can check for updates on my Web site at www.janebryantquinn.com.

But the details aren't as important as the overall concepts—eternal commonsense concepts—that you'll find here. You can apply these rules to new products as well as to the existing ones. Pay down debt, hold down fees, keep all your insurance plans simple, choose plain-vanilla mortgages, stick with simple investments, and tune your BS detector to "high." I've made mistakes in my time but in the end I got it right, and so will you. Every day, I'm cheering you along.

Jane Bryant Quinn
New York

BUILDING YOUR BASE

If I could have lunch with anyone, whom would I choose? Shakespeare, for sure. Cleopatra, to see how compelling she really was. Sojourner Truth. The historian Henry Adams. Jon Stewart (Jon, call me). Archimedes.

Okay, Archimedes isn't someone you would think of right off the bat. But I have a special feeling for the Greek mathematician. Aside from his theoretical work, he constructed ingenious mechanical devices. He showed that great weights could be moved with small effort, provided that the lever was long enough. "Give me a place to stand," he said, "and I will move the world."

Our world could stand a little shove, especially the world of money. Each new generation staggers forward under the weight of old ideas. We "know" too much that isn't true, or isn't true anymore. This is a pressed yet hopeful time (as I would explain to Archimedes over sandwiches). The stock boom lies behind us, and so does the real estate boom. Peering forward, we wonder where to light next. Our minds need moving, as well as our money.

That's a job for a lever. This book was written to help you find a place to stand.

Finding Your Financial Self

Where You Stand on the Money Cycle

**The finest of all human achievements—
and the most difficult—is merely being reasonable.**

All of our deepest beliefs about money are formed in the years when we grow up. We learn the great lessons of our era and set out to put them all to work.

But time is a trickster. Just when you think that you've learned all the rules, some hidden umpire changes the game.

Think about the Depression Kids. Those woeful years left a legacy of fear. Forever after, the generations marked by the 1930s saved compulsively. A loan made them feel sick to their stomachs. They took no risks. When the Great Prosperity swelled around them, they mistrusted it. They knew in their hearts it wouldn't last.

Now think about the Inflation Kids, raised in the 1960s and 1970s. They saw in a flash that a dollar saved was a dollar lost because inflation ate it up. A dollar borrowed was a dollar saved. You could use it to buy a car or a stereo before the price went up. They learned to love debt and couldn't change.

Then came the Bubble Kids of the 1980s and 1990s—years when stock and bond values soared, real estate boomed, and everyone thought it was going to be easy to get rich. Even after the bust, they didn't save much, because they still trusted "the market" or "home equity" to rebuild their wealth automatically. Can they change their approach to money any better than earlier generations could?

The new turn of the wheel—the 2008 financial bust—is bringing us the Struggle Kids. They endured the Great Recession, with jobs hard to get, layoffs and wage-cuts common, foreclosures and bankruptcies wiping families out, investments unreliable, health care expensive, and global interconnections that no generation has grown up with before. They're saving more and spending less. What will their orthodoxies be? Can we all find a better place to stand? On the answer to those questions, everything depends.

A Cycle of Spending and Saving

Money comes and goes in your life at different times. Mostly goes, when you're young. Those are the spent years. Maybe the misspent years. But never mind. As you grow older, the urge to save creeps up on you. Here's the typical cycle of wealth:

Ages 20 to 30. You establish credit, buy your first furniture and appliances, take out your first auto loan, learn about insurance and taxes. Maybe (here I'm dreaming) you save a little money, in the bank or in company retirement accounts. Retirement accounts are money machines for young people because you have so many years to let them grow untaxed. By the end of the decade, you cohabitate or get married, maybe have a baby, buy a house. (You save for a house the old-fashioned way: by borrowing some of the down payment from your parents.) Entrepreneurs start a business.

Ages 31 to 45. You don't know where your money goes. Bills, bills, bills. College is a freight train headed your way. Maybe (here I'm dreaming again) you start a tuition savings account. Money still dribbles into retirement savings, but only if your company does it for you—by taking it out of your paycheck before you get it to spend. When you're pressed, you open a home equity line of credit and borrow money against your house. If you haven't started a business, you think about it now. This is also a good time to get more education. Invest in yourself and hope for a payoff.

Ages 46 to 55. You *do* know where your money goes: to good old State U. At the same time, you get the creepy feeling that maybe you won't live forever. You thrash around. You buy books about financial planning. You have an affair. When all else fails, you start to save.

Ages 56 to 65. These are the fat years. You're at the top of your earning power, the kids are gone, the dogs are dead. Twenty percent of your salary can be socked away—which is lucky because you will need extra money for your children's down payments when they buy a house (kids never really go away). Consider long-term care insurance.

Ages 66 to 75. How golden are these years? As rich as your pension, Social Security, and the income from the money you saved. Start out by living on the first two. Let the income from savings and investments compound for a while, to build a fund for later life.

Ages 76 and Up. Quit saving. Spend, spend, spend! Forget leaving money to your kids—they should have put away more for themselves. Dip into principal to live as comfortably as you deserve. This is what all those years of saving were *for*.

When You Fall Off the Cycle

You say you can't find your place on the cycle? That's no surprise. Almost no one lives exactly to order anymore. There are a million ways of getting from birth to death, and they all work. If you fall behind financially during any decade, you'll need a plan for catching up.

You Have Your Children in Your 30s. It seemed like a smart idea at the time: diapers tomorrow but never today. No one told you that, in your 50s, you'd be paying for college just when you were trying to save for your own retirement. (And even if they'd told you, you'd never have believed that you would ever be that old.) You might have to choose between sending your children to a low-cost college and shortchanging your own future. Maybe your children will have to pay for their education themselves. The moral, for those who can think ahead: save more in your 20s, using the discipline of tax-deferred retirement plans. These plans penalize you for drawing money out, so you're more likely to leave it in.

You Get Divorced and Start Over. Divorce costs you assets and income, with the greater loss usually falling on the woman. She can rarely earn as much money as her ex-husband takes away. For the man, a new wife and new babies might mean that college tuition bills will arrive in the same mail as the Social Security checks. Unless you're rich or remarry rich, divorce is a decision to cut your standard of living, sometimes permanently.

You Don't Marry. You lack the safety net that a second paycheck and an in-home caregiver provide. On the other hand, there's usually no other mouth to feed. You can start saving and investing earlier than most.

You're Married, with No Children. You've got nothing but money and plenty of it. You are one of the few who really can retire early, not just dream about it.

Life Deals You an Accident. A crippling illness. Early widowhood. A child with anguishing medical problems. A family that has always saved can scrape through these tragedies. A family in debt to the hilt cannot.

You're Downsized. That's today's euphemism for getting fired. The money in your retirement plan goes for current bills. Your next job pays 30 percent less, with no health insurance or retirement plan. But you can still secure your future by downscaling your life to match your income. There's honor at every monetary level of life.

You Get the Golden Boot. A forced early retirement. Sometimes you see it coming, sometimes it blindsides you. You get a consolation prize in a lump sum payout or a higher pension for a retiree of your age. But you lose 5 to 10 years of earnings and savings. This risk is the single strongest argument for starting a retirement savings program young. At your age, a new job will be hard to come by, but you can't afford to retire for real. So you do project work, part-time work, and unexpected work such as clerking, to pad out your early-retirement check.

Memo to All Workers: Employers don't care that you've worked hard and late, that you haven't been sick in a dozen years, or that every supervisor you've had thinks you're hot stuff. They ask only: What have you done for me lately? Is your job essential to business today? Are your skills the right ones for business tomorrow?

Few people "hold a job" anymore. Instead we have talents that we sell to employers for various projects, some longer term than others. In this kind of world, nothing is more important than continuing education and upgrading skills.

Who Needs What When

The number of financial products on the market today—bank accounts, insurance policies, annuities, mutual funds—I estimate conservatively at two zillion point three (2.3Z). Most of them nobody needs but buys anyway because some salesperson convinces you to. In fact, you need only a few simple things, matched to your age, your bank balance, and your responsibilities. The rest of this book tells you how to choose them. Here I offer a general framework for your thinking.

Young and Single

Admit it: you are living your life on hold. Cinderella, waiting for Prince Charming. Peter Pan, not wanting to grow up. You are serious only about your work (or finding work!). Everything else is temporary. There is nothing in your refrigerator and nothing in your bank account. "Wait until I'm married," you say. But what if you don't marry? Or you marry late? Looking back, you'll see that you lost ten good years. Your future starts now. As a young person you should:

- *Establish credit with a low-cost bank card.* Practice on one card before getting two. Debt tends to rise to the highest allowable limit. If you're in college, apply for a bank card before you leave. Banks give credit faster to students than to job-seeking young adults. (They count on the parents to save their kids' credit rating by paying off their debts.)

- *Get disability insurance coverage if your employer offers it.* It pays you an income if you're sick or injured and can't work. How will you afford the premiums? By not buying life insurance.

- *Get health insurance if you don't have a company plan.* I know you're immortal, but buy a policy anyway, just in case you should be a teeny-weeny bit mortal and need an operation or a splint. No one wants a charity patient. If you can't afford a policy, maybe your parents will buy it for you. They would probably pay for the splint, so buying your health insurance is really a way of protecting themselves. Under health insurance reform, a policy would be mandatory.

- *Invest in your own education and training* even if it means more student debt. Your earning power is your single greatest asset.

- *Start saving money.* Put away 10 percent of your earnings. I hear you saying "I can't do it." So sneak up on it: start with 5 percent, then move up to 7 percent. You can get to 10 percent within the year. Where should the money go? For starters, part to a bank account and part to a retirement plan.

- *Start a tax-deferred retirement plan:* an Individual Retirement Account (IRA) or a savings plan through your employer. Put the money into stock-owning mutual funds and leave it there.

- *Rent, don't buy an apartment.* You don't yet know whether you're ready to put down roots. Except in unusual boom years, like the ones at the turn of the twenty-first century, it's hard to make money on real estate that you'll hold for only a short time—say, less than four years. Resale prices for condominiums and cooperative apartments typically lag behind those for single-family homes. At this point in your life, the money you'd spend on a down payment is better invested somewhere else. Buy only when you have a place you expect to live in for many years.

- *Buy property insurance if you have valuable possessions.* You especially need it for business property if you work out of your home. But you don't need it for furniture if your apartment's style is Modern Attic.
- *Make a will* unless it's okay for your parents to inherit everything. If you die will-less, that's where your property will probably go.
- *Create a power of attorney, a living will, and a health care proxy.* That's basic protection in case you meet with a horrible accident that leaves you alive but not alert. Someone has to act for you, both financially and medically, and you should pick those people yourself.

Older Singles

You might be your own sole support for life, but don't let that scare you into playing your hand too conservatively. Stocks do better than bank accounts or bonds over long periods of time. For financial self-defense, you need:

- *A good credit record*—good enough to be approved for a mortgage or a business loan.
- *Enough education and job training* to keep your income moving up.
- *Good health and disability insurance.* The older you get, the greater your risk of illness or injury. When you pass 60, consider long-term care insurance. You don't need any life insurance unless someone depends on your income for support.
- *A home of your own.* Living will be cheaper and expenses more predictable if you own a house or apartment free and clear when you retire. Keep your home-owners insurance up to date.
- *A habit of saving.* Try for 15 to 20 percent of your income. No, that's not too much.
- *A retirement plan:* pension, company tax-deferred savings plan, Individual Retirement Account, Keogh plan, or Simplified Employee Pension (SEP) for the self-employed. Get more than one plan if you qualify. Fund everything to the max.
- *A mix of investments in your retirement plans:* some U.S. and foreign stock-owning mutual funds; some Treasury, tax-exempt municipal, or other bonds.
- *An interest beyond your regular job*—a pastime or charity. It may open the door to a second career.
- *A will, a living will, a health care proxy, and a durable power of attorney.*
- *A good attorney or other surrogate who will manage your money if you can't do it yourself.*

Married Couples

You have a lot of responsibilities. Your mate needs security if you die. Children have to be set up too. After that, the big question is how to handle the family money. You need:

- *A cost-sharing system.* If you are a two-paycheck couple, will you split the bills or pool your money in one account? If you are a one-paycheck couple, will you start a savings account for the nonearning spouse? Financially speaking, there is no best way, only your way.

- *Credit cards in the names of both spouses,* or separate cards—at least one in each of your names. A wife without joint responsibility for the debt, or a card of her own, could have her cards yanked if her husband dies or leaves. And vice versa, of course.

- *Disability insurance.* Every income-earning person needs it, to cover lost paychecks (and maybe home health care bills) if you become too sick or disabled to work.

- *Health insurance.* Don't go without it, especially between jobs. When you're out of work, you're under a lot of stress, which can lead to accidents and poor health. Working couples should try not to duplicate benefits in their company health plans.

- *Life insurance.* If your family depends on your income for support, you need life insurance. If your family can get along without your income, you don't. Working couples with no kids may do fine with whatever group term insurance they get from their companies. But you'll need much more coverage if children arrive. Buying insurance on a nonearning spouse is a luxury purchase. Buying it on a child is a waste.

- *A will,* so that beneficiaries will inherit exactly as much as you intend.

- *A power of attorney,* so that someone can manage your finances if you can't.

- *A living will and health-care power of attorney,* in case you fall into a permanent coma and don't want to spend years on life support. You need a surrogate to speak for you, or your living will might be ignored.

- *A premarital agreement,* if you want to limit what your spouse will collect at divorce or inherit at your death. These agreements are used mostly by people of vastly unequal wealth, the previously divorced who swear that they won't be "burned again," and older people with children from previous marriages to protect. There are postmarital agreements too, for arrangements you wish you had made earlier.

- *Your own home.* It should be an acceptable investment if you own it long enough. It's also a form of forced saving and a cheap way to live in retirement, once you own it free and clear. Keep your homeowners insurance up to date.

- *Regular savings.* Sprinkle 10 percent of every check among ready savings, his-and-hers tax-deferred retirement plans, and college savings. Come to think of it, sprinkle more. You'll never catch up with college costs on a mere 10 percent. Be sure to fund both spouses' retirement plans. Some couples waste a tax deduction by forgetting to fund a plan for a spouse who has only modest earnings.
- *Job skills.* A spouse without them is asking for trouble, even if he or she is home with the kids. Life is not fair. Death or disability occurs. Breadwinners lose their jobs. Not all spouses love each other until the end of time. As the poet said, "Provide, provide."
- *Long-term care insurance* once you pass 60.

Blended Families

Life gets expensive when both bride and groom come with children attached. You need everything that any other married couple does, plus extra protection for stepchildren. Check:
- Whether all the kids are covered by health insurance.
- Whether you want to change your will to include the stepchildren.
- Whether you need trusts to ensure that the children of your former marriages inherit the property they're due.
- Whether all the kids will have enough money for college.

Younger Widows and Widowers, and the Divorced

Maybe you're just plain single again. More likely, there are children to support. It's harder alone. You'll need a substantial safety net:
- *Buy as much disability insurance as you can get.* If you can't work and can't support your children, the family might break up.
- *Don't be without a family health policy for a moment.*
- *Buy a lot of life insurance* if your children's future depends on you. Stick with low-cost term insurance and cancel it when the kids grow up.
- *Write a will,* especially to name a guardian for your children. Add a living will, a health care proxy, and a power of attorney.
- *Call Social Security.* An unmarried child under 18 or 19, or a child disabled before age 22, whose mother or father is dead, can get a monthly Social Security payments on that parent's account. So can a widowed person (including a divorced spouse whose ex-spouse dies) if his or her child is disabled or under 16.

- *If you're divorced, report your new status*—in writing—to everyone who gave you credit and cancel all joint credit cards. You don't want your ex-spouse's new charges to show up on your personal credit history. (You'll still be responsible for the past debts that you contracted together.)

- *If you're widowed,* maybe you want to report your new status to credit granters. Then again, maybe you don't. If the card was based on two incomes or on the income of the spouse who died, you may not be able to keep the card unless you can prove that you're creditworthy. If the family credit history is good and you have an income, the card would doubtless be reissued. But if you have only a small income, it might not be. In that case, nothing in federal law stops you from keeping your old card and keeping mum.

- *Find work.* Or find better work. Train for a higher-paying job. You can't afford to coast.

- *If you collect child support,* take out a term insurance policy on your ex-spouse (this should be part of your divorce agreement). The insurance proceeds will make up for your lost child support if he or she dies.

- *Save money even at the cost of your standard of living.* Maybe you will remarry, but you can't count on it.

- *Consider trading down to a smaller house.* Keep your homeowners insurance up to date.

- *Own a home*—your current house or a smaller one—if you're rooted in place. Otherwise hang loose and rent on a short-term lease. Your next life may lie somewhere else. Get renters insurance to protect good furniture from fire and small, expensive objects from theft.

- *Take no quick advice about money.* Not from your brother. Not from your friends. Above all, not from anyone selling financial products. Salespeople love widows for their ready cash and their presumed dependence on a sympathetic ear. Keep your money in the bank until you've learned something about managing it and know exactly what you want to do.

- *Don't automatically turn your life insurance proceeds into an annuity.* Inflation will gradually wipe out the value of a fixed monthly income. You might want to take a lump sum instead and invest it conservatively.

Older Widows, Widowers, and the Divorced

You have great freedom if your children are grown. Your life can be reconstructed from the ground up. Your checklist includes "cancels" as well as "buys":

- *Cancel your life insurance.* Use the money to add to your savings and investments.

- *Cancel your disability insurance* if you have retired and no longer get a paycheck.
- *Keep your health insurance.* At age 65, get a Medigap policy or join an HMO that will cover what Medicare doesn't.
- *Call Social Security.* If you worked at least 10 years, you're owed a retirement benefit on your own account, starting as early as age 62. Alternatively, you're entitled to benefits based on your spouse's account. You can collect whichever is higher. The widowed are entitled to benefits on their late spouse's account as early as 60 (50 if you're disabled) unless their current earnings are too high.
- *Study up on money management.* If you've never handled investments before, this is the moment that nature has chosen for you to learn. In the meantime, keep your money in the bank. Don't give it to anyone else to manage until you've learned a lot about money yourself. You have to be able to follow what your "expert" is doing. Otherwise your money might be expertly "managed" away.
- *Write a will or change your old one.* A living will and a health-care power of attorney grow even more urgent as you age. You need someone to speak for you if you become incapable.
- *Write to your late spouse's (or ex-spouse's) company immediately after the death or legal separation.* Better yet, write in advance. You may be due some employee benefits, including up to three years of health insurance at group rates. The employer is supposed to notify you about the health insurance but doesn't always do so. If you don't apply for the policy immediately after losing your coverage as a spouse, you won't be able to get it at all.
- *Find work if you need it,* perhaps through a temporary help agency.

Sort of Married

More than single but less than married, you have only to change the locks to "divorce." You need:

- *Separate bank accounts.* Contribute to common bills in proportion to your earnings. If one of you earns only 30 percent of the total, that person should pay only 30 percent of the expenses. It's not fair to hit him or her for 50 percent.
- *Separate property.* One buys the lamps, one buys the couch, so that ownership is clear.
- *Written agreements for property bought together.* What happens to it if you split up? If one of you dies?
- *A will, to be sure that the other gets—or doesn't get—what you intend.* If you have no will, everything will go to your family, not to your partner.

■ *The same health, disability, and living will protection that you'd give yourself as a single person.* If you both work, you need no life insurance unless there are children. If you decide that one of you won't work, buy a policy to protect the partner at home. In a few jurisdictions, a domestic partner—straight, lesbian, or gay—might be covered by the other's employee benefits plan.

These lists tell you generally what you need. The rest of this book tells you how to get them. As you read, you can construct your own financial plan, chapter by chapter—adding, subtracting, revising, updating—one step at a time.

The Ultimate Wish List
What You've Got and Where You're Going

Need rises with income. What was out of the question when you made $30,000 becomes urgent at $60,000 and indispensable at $100,000.

Your own financial plan starts with a wish list. Write it all down, every single thing. A speedboat. A week in Barbados. State U. for two children. Enough money to retire early. Forget that you can't afford it. Maybe you only think you can't. The whole reason to have a financial plan is to focus on what matters most and work out a strategy for getting it.

So get out a yellow pad and a pencil, or set up a "Life Goals" file on your computer, and start dreaming. On the left side of the pad or screen, write "What I want." On the right side, write "When I want it"—next summer? In three years? In the middle, write "How I get there from here." That middle column is the terra incognita that this book will fill in. You are going to develop some real numbers and a real timetable so you won't still be dreaming five years from now.

Once you've listed all your material wants, stare off into space and think. Even if you can have it all, the cost of getting it might be an extra job, working nights and weekends, working to a later age than you'd intended, or hanging on to a job you hate. Is it worth it? Or would you rather take that speedboat off your wish list?

When reflecting on this question, take another piece of paper (or open a new file) and write down your personal goals. Don't kid yourself. If money and status are important, say so. Do you want to write a book by the time you're 30? Start a business? Spend more time with the kids? Move to the country? Become a top officer of your corporation? Change careers? Give more time to charity? All the things you care about most are likely to affect how much money you'll have, which in turn will shape your financial plan. The planning process asks you to set priorities and make trade-offs.

The plan you finally develop may not work—at least, not exactly. Some things may go better than expected, others may go worse. You may fall behind schedule. You may filch money for a new car that should have gone into the education fund.

But the point is, you'll know it. You'll see the hole in your kids' tuition account and figure out how to make it up. The reason financial plans succeed is almost stupidly simple. It's their specificity. Instead of vague hopes, you have hard targets—something concrete that you're working toward every year. Once you see it, you can get it.

Your Basic Security Package

Back to your dreamy goals. I know you've remembered to list "Barbados vacation." But one or two other things might have slipped your mind, without which your prettier plans might be undone. Here is the basic security package that also has to be on your list:

1. Life insurance. Do you have enough? If you die, your spouse or mate needs enough to support himself or herself. Your children need support and education. Part of that money will probably come from the surviving spouse's earnings. You need enough insurance to cover the rest. For how much life insurance to buy, see chapter 12.

2. Disability insurance. Most people are covered if they die. But what if you fall off a ladder, break your back, and live? That's the risk nobody thinks about (or wants to). You need two levels of disability coverage: (1) for a short illness of 6 to 12 months, during which you'd try to keep your way of life intact, and (2) for a permanent disability, usually requiring a drop in your standard of living. For how large a policy you need, see chapter 14.

3. Health insurance. You probably get it from the company you work for. If not, call an insurance agent, BlueCross BlueShield, or a health maintenance organization. Long-term care policies are improving rapidly, but they're not yet for younger people. Shop for this coverage when you pass 60. See chapter 13.

4. Repaying debt. It's pointless to save money at 5 percent interest while you're still supporting a Visa card habit at 18 or 26 percent. Pay off the Visa first. Often, the best use of savings is to pay off the debts that are costing you more than your savings earn. For ways of saving more money, see chapter 9.

5. Owning a home. How much do you need for a down payment, and how will you raise it? The lucky ducks go to the Daddy Bank. Failing that, you will have to throw every resource you have at the problem. For ways of finding the money for a home of your own, see chapter 17.

6. College. How much will college cost when your children reach 18, and how long do you have to accumulate the money? Four years at the average public college, for a student living in the state, might cost as much as $84,000, starting in 2009 (assuming annual increases of 5 percent). For the average private college, it might be $170,000 (before tuition discounts). The most selective and expensive schools top $40,100 *a year*. You'll find a list of college savings and investment plans in chapter 20.

7. Fun and games. Put some luxuries on your list. A new kitchen. An RV. A trip to Europe. August at the racetrack. Estimate what they will cost (except for the racetrack, where you'll make money, right?) and when you will want them. Chapter 8 tells you how to fit them into your plan.

8. Retirement savings. How much will you need to retire on? A younger person hasn't a clue. Too many incalculables exist in the economy and your personal life. Still, you ought to make a start. By your late 40s, the picture should be coming clear. For the book on retirement planning, see chapter 29.

For your pains, you'll wind up with a daunting list of expenses:

1. The price of more life insurance.
2. The price of a disability policy.
3. The price of health insurance if you don't have a company plan.
4. The extra monthly payments needed to zero out your consumer debts.
5. How much you'll have to save each month for a down payment on a home.
6. The net cost of your children's college (after any student aid) and the length of time you have to raise the money.
7. The price of anything special you want for yourself and how long you have to save for it.
8. The amount of savings you'll need for a decent retirement.

Some of you are starting out at the top of this list; others are already partway down. In either case, the total may look unattainable, but I promise you it's not. It's like running a marathon: you do one mile at a time until you finish.

Finding the Money

Winning a lottery would be nice. Maybe you could marry rich. An inheritance is dandy, the drawback being how you get it.

Windfalls aside, there are only three ways of getting the money you need to underwrite a financial plan: culling current income, taking loans, and using the gains from your savings and investments. But everything ultimately springs from income, which sets up your savings and pays off your debts.

No plan will succeed if you live to the brink of your income and beyond. You must hold back something for savings and investments. "No way," you say? It takes $50,000 just to pay the grocer? Sure, but only if you build your life that way. Every single one of us can look down the street and see someone living as well as we do on $5,000 less a year than we make. That's $5,000 we could be saving every year and still hold up our heads in the neighborhood. Only by living on less than you make will you ever be able to live on more than you make.

Keeping Score

Start your plan by figuring your present net worth. Recalculate it once a year. These figures, and the changes in them, will show you a lot of interesting things:

- *Whether your debts are under control.* Is your indebtedness growing faster than the money you're saving?
- *How well you're investing the money you save.* Does your investment account keep up with the market? Or does it fall behind?
- *How much money you could lay your hands on in an emergency.* Do you have enough readily salable assets to help you through a bad patch, or are too many of your assets tied up?
- *Whether you need more life and disability insurance.* What income could you get from your assets compared with how much you need to live on?

To find your net worth, add up the value of everything you own (your assets), figured at what you could reasonably sell each item for. Then subtract everything you owe (your liabilities). The remainder is your net worth. It's the money you'd have if you converted all of your salable property into cash and paid off your debts. If you owe more than you own, you have a negative net worth, and maybe an ulcer. ("I'm going to be a millionaire," a gambler friend of mine used to say. "I'll die owing a million dollars." He came close.)

Your aim is to raise your net worth over time, through a combination of new savings, sound investments that recover after market setbacks, and fewer loans.

Just as important, you need a good balance between assets that are tied up, such as your house, and assets that can quickly be turned into cash.

The parts of your net worth that are always on tap are your *quick assets*, such as cash, mutual funds, stocks, bonds, and life insurance cash values. You fall back on your quick assets in an emergency.

The parts that might take a long time to sell are the *slow assets*, such as most real estate. Don't load up on slow assets until you have plenty of quick assets on tap.

Some of your slow assets are effectively frozen. That would include your home, if no buyer wants it right now, an interest in a limited partnership or other

YOUR NET WORTH

Date _____

WHAT YOU OWN (ASSETS)	AMOUNT
Quick Assets	
Cash in checking, ready savings, and money market mutual funds	$ _____
Other mutual funds	_____
Stocks, bonds, government securities, mutual funds	_____
Publicly traded partnerships	_____
Other easily salable investments	_____
Money due you soon for work you've done	_____
Life insurance cash values	_____
Precious metals	_____
Easily salable personal property: jewelry, silver, cars	_____
Restricted Assets	
Certificates of deposit if they have early-withdrawal penalties	_____
Retirement accounts: IRAs, Keoghs, tax-deferred annuities, company savings accounts, deferred salary	_____
Current worth of your vested pension if payable in a lump sum	_____
Stock options	_____
Slow Assets	
Your home	_____
Other real estate	_____
Art and antiques	_____
Other valuable personal property: furs, boats, tools, coins	_____
Restricted stock, not readily salable	_____
Limited partnerships, not readily salable	_____
Money owed you in the future	_____
Equity value of a business	_____
Total Assets	_____

WHAT YOU OWE (LIABILITIES)	AMOUNT	INTEREST RATE
Current bills outstanding: this month's rent, medical bills, insurance premiums, utilities, and so on	$ _____	_____
Credit card debt	_____	_____
Installment and auto loans	_____	_____
Money borrowed from family members	_____	_____
Home mortgage	_____	_____
Home equity loan	_____	_____
Other mortgages	_____	_____
Student loans	_____	_____
Loans against investments, including your margin loans	_____	_____
Other loans		
Income and real estate taxes due	_____	_____
Taxes due on your investments if you cash them in	_____	
Taxes and penalties due on your retirement accounts if you cash them in	_____	
Total Liabilities	_____	
Net Worth (assets minus liabilities)	_____	

investment that can't be sold easily, money owed to you at some point in the future, and a lump sum due from your pension plan. Mentally, you might also add a pending inheritance, although it doesn't belong on your personal balance sheet until it's actually yours.

Yet another part of your net worth is restricted in that it can be reached only by paying a penalty. This includes most unmatured certificates of deposit, tax-deferred retirement plans, and tax-deferred annuities if you're younger than 59½.

When figuring your net worth: (1) You don't have to know the exact value of everything. A ballpark estimate will do. (2) To find out what your individual bonds are currently worth, ask your stockbroker to price them for you. They will bring more or less than face value, depending on market conditions today. To price bonds yourself, check Investinginbonds.com. (3) Sherlock Holmes couldn't ferret out the value of limited-partnership shares unless they're traded publicly. Ask your stockbroker whether he can sell them and for how much. If no one is biting, list the shares at zero. When the partnership dissolves, thank the gods for every dollar you get back. (4) In a pinch, you could sell your cars and jewelry. But you won't, so they're not truly part of your usable net worth. You need to know their current value only to keep them well insured.

Patching Your Safety Net

Optimist: "This is the best of all possible worlds."
Pessimist: "That's right."

So far, you've been thinking like an optimist. You're worth more than you thought! Your pencil is flying! Your stock options will pay off your loans, and then you'll be on easy street! All it will take is a few more years.

But what if you don't have a few more years?

Here's where the average plan comes a cropper. How would your family manage if you died? How would you live if you had an accident and couldn't work anymore? There would be some income from your spouse's earnings, Social Security, disability insurance (if you were clever enough to have

---

YOUR SURVIVOR'S USABLE CASH

Date _____

	AMOUNT
Assets	
Quick assets (not counting life insurance cash values, one of two cars, and personal property)	$ _____
Restricted assets	_____
Slow assets (not counting your house and personal property that your spouse would want to keep)	_____
Proceeds from life insurance	_____
Total Usable Assets Left for Survivor	_____
Liabilities	
Loans against insurance policies	_____
Death costs, including funeral and estate administration, up to 5 percent of assets	_____
Taxes, including final income tax return and estate taxes if you're wealthy enough to owe them	_____
Total	_____
Money Left for Survivor (usable assets minus liabilities)	_____

bought it), and so on. But probably not enough. You'd also have to live on your savings.

To measure the real strength of your position, you have to look at your net worth in another way. How much cash would be available to you or your family if you had to marshal all of your assets to live on?

Start with the figures you just reached and assume three things: (1) you (or your survivor) would not sell your house, one car, and personal property; (2) all other slow assets would be converted to cash; (3) your restricted assets would be freed up for use.

You need a large enough nest egg so that when your savings are combined with other sources of income, your dependents will have enough to meet their expenses. If your savings fall short, fill the gap with more life insurance. If your household depends on two paychecks, do these calculations twice—first assuming that the husband dies, then assuming the death of the wife.

If you think that your family would move to a smaller house at your death, they would net some money from the sale of the house you own now. Add those funds to their assets.

Disability is another story. There's no life insurance payoff, so your usable assets are much smaller. I've shown few liabilities in the table below because

YOUR USABLE CASH IF YOU'RE DISABLED

Date _____

	AMOUNT
Assets	
Quick assets (except for one car and personal property)	$ _____
Restricted assets	_____
Slow assets (not counting your house and any personal property you want to keep)	_____
Total Usable Assets	_____
Liabilities	
Taxes on funds you withdraw from retirement accounts	_____
Uninsured medical bills (make a guess)	_____
Total	_____
Money on Tap (usable assets minus liabilities)	_____

you can't predict your lump sum expenses. Even the size of your uninsured medical bills is a question. You have three ways to prepare for a disability: get a better disability insurance policy, save more money, or invest better.

Use this same calculation for early retirement.

There is one more way of measuring your personal security: Do you have enough quick assets to cover all the bills coming due this year? That would give you a 12-month breathing space if you lost your job. Figure it this way:

1. How much has to be paid on your debts over the next 12 months? Call this your current debt: $_____.

2. How large are your quick assets, not counting personal property and life insurance cash values? Call this your ready money: $_____.

3. Your ready money should be greater than your current debt. If not, you are living with a lot of risk. As time passes, your ready money should grow larger and larger than your current debt.

Roundup Day

Once a year, sit down with your spouse or mate (if you're single, sit down with yourself) and see where you stand. Go over everything. Are you spending too much? Did you save enough money? Should you change your investments? Did your net worth improve? Do you need more insurance? What financial goal will you shoot for in the next 12 months? What personal purchases would you like to make?

I call this annual accounting Roundup Day. A good time for it is the week after New Year's, when things are usually slow. Another good time is the week you do your income taxes, when every money nerve is tingling. Working couples need this day to tally their separate savings and investments, and show their spouses what's happening with their 401(k)s. Spouses who don't handle the family money need this day to keep in touch. Everyone needs this day to gloat over triumphs, fix mistakes, and start the next year fresh.

How Much Is Enough?

You don't have to get richer every year. At some level of personal security, all you need is enough growth to keep your after-tax assets even with inflation. Knowing when to quit and go fishing is just as important as knowing when to keep your shoulder to the wheel.

My job is to help you grow wealthier and more secure. But not everyone is so lucky. Accidents happen. Investments fail. Companies fold. So here's a heretical thought: If your income dropped, would that be so bad? Would it be so terrible to live in a cheaper place with fewer clothes and luxuries? People who earn $5,000 less than you live happy lives, and so do people who earn $5,000 less than *they* do.

I wish you every increase, but if the gods frown, there are worse things in life than having to step down.

I Have It Right Here Somewhere

The Right Way to Keep Records

(Don't go away. I'm still looking.)

Okay, I confess.

Sitting here, right now, I can't remember the name of my life insurance company. The keys to my safe-deposit box are in my office, but I'm not sure where. In the pile of papers on the floor to the left, I think there's the booklet explaining the changes in my group health insurance. In short, I am often a slob about my own financial records.

But I am reforming. Writing this chapter has embarrassed me into reorganizing the scattered Quinn financial files. And take my word for it: when you finish this kind of job, you feel new, as if you had shined all your shoes and cleaned up the cellar.

With good records:

You Can Find Things. I estimate 84 hours saved per year, right there.

You Can Remember What You Have. Did you sign that power of attorney? Did you fill in the form that lets you take money out of your mutual fund by phone? Now you'll know.

You Can Remember What You Don't Have. No, you didn't sign that power of attorney, because you kept misplacing it. Now that you're putting your records together, you'll get it done.

You Can Save Money for Your Heirs. They will be able to find things too, without paying a lawyer to do detective work for them. They won't shake their heads and mutter "What a mess."

You Can Feel Terrifically Smart and Well Organized. You Will Know That If a Ceiling Fell on Your Head This Very Moment, Your Heirs Would Get Every Dime That Was Coming to Them. Sometimes a deed, contract, or bankbook is hidden away and never found. Ditto for old stock certificates, records of small brokerage accounts, and retirement savings accounts left with a former employer. After several years, unclaimed money passes to the state (page 28). Lawyers tell story after story about stumbling across a stray piece of paper that entitled a widow to money that she didn't know anything about. Think of the number of widows who throw those pieces of paper out.

Where to Keep Records

Invest in a file cabinet. It doesn't have to be steel; cardboard works fine. You can tuck a two-drawer cabinet under a table. Or use it as a table (put a round piece of plywood on top and cover it with a cloth). Don't put it in the attic or behind the ice skates in the closet under the stairs. Unless your cabinet is so handy that you practically trip over it, you'll put off filing your records, which means that your system will fall apart.

Eventually back tax returns and old bank records will overflow your file drawers. Don't compulsively save everything with your name and a dollar sign on it. Some records can be thrown away (see "What to Keep, Where to Keep It, What to Toss," page 29). Put beloved old statements that you can't part with into labeled boxes. Keep them in the attic or on a closet shelf.

What? You had a fire? I forgot to tell you: invest in a fireproof home safe or bank safe-deposit box for records that are a pain in the neck to replace. Or buy a service that keeps online records in a server off-premises.

A home safe should be rated for fire resistance by the Underwriters Laboratory. You need a class 350 safe, which protects paper documents against high heat for at least a half hour and perhaps up to four. If you keep computer records on CDs, you'll need a class 125 safe. An unrated metal box with a lock won't do anything except keep curious children out; in a fire, the heat would scorch to ashes any documents inside.

These safes, incidentally, won't stop a jewel thief for a moment; they're only for papers. You might as well write the combination on the top to save the burglar the trouble of whacking off the lock. To protect valuables at home, you need a much more expensive vault. For items that you consider irreplaceable, rent a safe-deposit box.

Safe-deposit boxes are normally rented from a bank, although they are increasingly being offered by credit unions. Small boxes, for holding papers, photographs, and a little jewelry cost around $15 to $50 a year. For a lot of valuables or your magnificent hubcap collection, the bank has larger boxes at a higher price.

Sometimes there's a waiting list, especially for the bigger boxes. As an alternative, you might look at a private vault company. It charges more than banks but is supposed to follow bank security procedures and may even offer 24-hour access—handy for dropping off your diamonds after the ball. If you have something to hide, it will interest you to know that most private vaults let you open an account under a false name (banks require identification). On the downside, private vaults may not provide all the security that customers were promised. Many have gone bankrupt. Personally, I wouldn't go near one.

When you rent a safe-deposit box, you sign a card. The bank or vault will also need the signatures of anyone who you think should have access to the box: your spouse, your executor, a business colleague, a friend. Every time you visit your diamonds or hubcaps, you sign again so that your signature can be checked. It takes two keys to open the box, yours and the bank's. You get two copies of your own key. If you lose one, no problem; it costs maybe $7.50 to $10 to replace. But it might cost $100 if you lose both. The bank doesn't keep a copy of your key, so it has to drill into your box and start you out with a brand-new lock. Give your cosigners a key only if you want them to be able to enter the box at any time. If you want them to enter it only in an emergency, keep the second key yourself but tell them where it is. (Note that the person who holds your power of attorney does not have access to your box unless he or she is on the signature card.)

What to keep in your safe-deposit box depends mainly on how hard the item is to replace. Most financial documents, such as insurance policies and cemetery deeds, can be replaced pretty quickly; you might put a copy in your box, for reference in case of fire, while keeping the original at home. But reverse that procedure—copy at home, original in the box—for documents that take a long time to procure or will cost you a fee. This category might include birth and marriage certificates, divorce papers, military records, the deed to your house, and citizenship papers. Few people have stock certificates or paper bonds anymore, but those that exist should be kept from harm. So should signed notes for any money you're owed. Safe-deposit boxes are also good repositories for personal treasures such as old family photos, lists of the contents of your house (to prove what you owned, in case of fire or theft; digital photos can be stored online), the master list of your financial documents (page 42), and heirloom jewelry you don't wear. Keep your own list of what's in your box in a file at home, so you won't forget.

Unfortunately, nothing in this world is 100 percent secure, not even safe-deposit boxes. If a thief breaks in, the bank or vault company is not responsible for your losses unless you can prove negligence. Federal deposit insurance isn't responsible either. It covers only your deposit accounts. But your homeowners or tenants insurance should pay up to the limits of your policy (page 533). After a theft, you have to prove what you kept in the box, which is not always an easy job. Keep receipts, appraisals, and photos, including a photo of your box with the valuables in it. Put items that could be damaged by water (a flood or a burst municipal pipe) into ziplock bags or plastic containers.

When you rent the box, ask the bank who will have access to it after your death. Almost all the states give ready entry to anyone on the signature card who also has a key. If the cosigner has no key, the bank will drill the box. Anyone not on the card needs proof—for example, a *letter of testamentary*—that he or she is an heir who's allowed to remove property. If your will is missing and your representative wants to search the box for it, he or she will need a search order. Ideally, someone with signature authority should also be present. To simplify life for your heirs, keep your will at home and give the executor a signed copy (the executor is the person who makes sure that your will's provisions are carried out). If you have a cemetery deed, keep that on hand too.

If you and your spouse or mate keep separate boxes, give each other access, just in case something happens. Important! Tell your heirs and executor where the box is and where you keep the keys! Lots of property is lost because relatives haven't a clue where to look for a box in your name. If you keep a home safe, note the combination to the lock in your personal-money file.

You might also consider a waterproof emergency flight bag, kept on a bedroom shelf. Ask yourself what you'd need if you had to evacuate your house in a hurry because of a hurricane, flood, or fire. Pack that bag with your critical records and mementos: a copy of your homeowners insurance policy, your birth certificate, some wedding pictures. That way, you won't have to stop and think if you smell smoke in the middle of the night. Just pick up the bag and run. Include photos of what's in your home. Hurricane victims, for example, have received thousands of dollars extra from their insurers when they were able to prove exactly what they owned.

Do you really need a safe-deposit box? Few of us have documents that are truly irreplaceable. If you don't need your box for other items—heirloom jewelry, gold coins—you might decide that the annual fee isn't worth it. If the worst happens, you'll face the nuisance of replacing your birth certificate, citizenship papers, and so on, but many people consider that a risk worth taking. As an alternative to a safe-deposit box, consider scanning your important documents, filing them in your computer, and backing them up.

Keeping Records Online

Set up folders on your computer for your bank statements, credit card statements, bill-pay accounts, scanned documents, and other records you keep online. File them faithfully and *back them up*! Without a backup, those records will fry when your hard drive fails (as it inevitably will). You can use a second hard drive, a small flash drive, or a service that backs up your records at another location. Some banks market online storage as a "virtual safe-deposit box." Make paper copies of documents you need to keep for tax purposes and file them with your tax records.

You Didn't Lose It, You Forgot It. Now What?

Money—billions of dollars of it—is mislaid in America every year. People move and don't leave a forwarding address. They forget to give their new address to every institution holding money due them. Sometimes they don't know they're owed money. Sometimes they get dotty. Maybe they die without leaving the well-organized records that you're about to create, and their heirs can't find all the property.

The federal government is holding an estimated $20 billion worth of uncashed Treasury securities and savings bonds; unclaimed Social Security benefits, civil service retirement checks, tax refunds, veterans' benefits, and refunds for mortgage insurance premiums owed to many home owners who prepay Federal Housing Administration (FHA) loans; and property left on federal land. The states hold perhaps $10 billion in unclaimed bank and brokerage accounts; Individual Retirement Accounts and other pension savings; paychecks and dividend checks; funds left in unused prepaid tuition plans; refunds from telephone and electric companies that people failed to collect when they moved; uncashed money orders and cashier's checks; unused gift certificates; contents of unclaimed safe-deposit boxes; and life insurance policies that the heirs never knew about.

Every state's unclaimed-property law is a little different. But in general, a bank or other private company, including nonprofits, can't hold dormant funds for more than three to five years.

Your bank account or mutual fund is considered dormant if you've made no transactions for several years and don't answer mail about the account.

Untended savings accounts are especially vulnerable. So are safe-deposit boxes that your family doesn't know about.

Dormant funds held in private hands are eventually transferred (escheated) to the states. The states list the missing owners in newspaper ads, usually in obscure publications. They may also try to find you through telephone directories, credit bureaus, and motor vehicle records. Some states try harder than others.

You can reclaim your property no matter how many years have passed (except in New Hampshire, which confiscates money after three years). When stocks, bonds, and mutual funds go to the state, they're usually sold after three years and the proceeds retained.

To see if you're due any money held by a state, go online to the National Association of Unclaimed Property Administrators (NAUPA) (www.unclaimed .org or www.missingmoney.com), where you can link to all the state unclaimed-property offices. If you're not online, you can get online help at your local library. Most of the states list the names of everyone they're holding money for. Check for your own name in every state where you've ever lived. While you're at it, check for your parents (including those who have died) and your adult children. Recheck every couple of years to see if anything new has been added to the list. If you find your name, follow the instructions on how to claim the property. States often pay interest on reclaimed interest-bearing accounts, such as bank deposits, but not on other funds.

Unfortunately, there's no unclaimed-property office for money held by the federal government, nor do the feds try to track down missing owners. If you're lucky, you'll get a letter from a private tracing service saying it knows where some federal money is stashed that probably belongs to you. The price of retrieving it runs around 30 percent of the recovered funds (the service might ask for 50 percent, but when you call, you can usually talk it down). People sometimes get sore at these services because they think they charge too much. But if it weren't for their efforts, you wouldn't get any money at all. Never pay up front; that's not a legitimate request. Pay only when money is produced.

What to Keep, Where to Keep It, What to Toss

Clarity, clarity. A filing system should be so logical that anyone who opens the drawers can find exactly what he or she wants. Label every folder, choosing titles that are sensible, not cute. If a financial document doesn't fit exactly into one of the categories you have already, start a new file for it. Keep weeding out documents that don't matter anymore. No sense sending your heirs on wild-goose chases. Most of these documents can be kept at home in a simple filing cabinet. There's an outside risk of losing documents to a fire or flood, so for supersafety, choose a fireproof home safe or safe-deposit box.

Your Will

You have one, of course. A good-looking, clever, glowing social success like you wouldn't be so dumb as to go without. The only reason I even put chapter 6 in this book (it's about writing wills) was because that was the only way to get from chapter 5 to chapter 7. Chapter 6. It's on page 95. Just in case.

It is simple and safe to leave the will with your lawyer, keeping a copy for yourself. On your copy, put the lawyer's name, address, and phone number. One drawback—if you see it that way—is that your family might feel forced to use that particular lawyer to handle your estate. They don't have to. They can retrieve the will and pick a different lawyer. If you think that would embarrass them, keep the will yourself. Another drawback is that your lawyer might die. Be sure there's someone in the firm who will inherit his or her files.

If you keep the will yourself, a safe-deposit box is okay, provided that you know it won't be sealed at death and your cosigner can get into it without any trouble. If your only cosigner is your spouse, however, you run the risk of dying together. It might take some time for your remaining heirs to get the will, which is needed to confirm the executor and start settling the estate. You also might put your will into a fireproof safe, giving the executor a copy.

If you don't keep your will at home, put a note in your file telling your heirs where to find it. Whenever you make a new will, destroy the old one along with all copies.

Your Durable Power of Attorney

This is a piece of paper that says, "The named person can act for me, in all financial matters or in certain matters that I have specified here." The empowered person might be able to manage your money, sign checks to pay your bills, or sell your real estate.

Keep the power of attorney at home, in a filing cabinet or a fireproof home safe, as long as the person you named knows the combination. Give that person a signed copy for safekeeping. (I assume that you trust your deputy; otherwise you wouldn't have given him or her the power.) Don't put this important document into your safe-deposit box. Your deputy can't get into it if you become mentally incapable, which is just when the power of attorney might have to be used.

Your Living Will, Health Care Proxy, and Uniform Donor Card

Your living will is a piece of paper that says, "If I'm in a permanent coma, pull the plug," or "don't pull the plug," depending on how you feel about it. The health care proxy names the person who will make sure that your wishes are carried out. This deputy can also make other medical choices if you're temporarily incapable of deciding for yourself. You should give your deputy written permission to see your medical records. If you want other friends or family members to see your records, put that in writing too.

A lawyer can draw up these documents for you. Or fill in the free forms you'll find at Caring Connections (www.caringinfo.org) or Legaldocs (www.legaldocs .com). Be sure you get them witnessed, as required by the laws of your state. The forms you find on the Web will explain what to do.

Keep these papers in your filing cabinet or fireproof home safe where people can find them. Give signed copies to the people who will make these ultimate choices in accordance with your wishes: your spouse or partner, your child, a friend, your doctor (page 126).

If you want to donate any of your organs after your death (please say yes; they're of no use to you and may save another person's life), fill in a Uniform Donor Card and keep it in your wallet. Tell your family of your intent. If that dreadful day should ever come, you'll have made the decision for them.

Life Insurance Policies

Keep them in your safe-deposit box only if the bank assures you that, under state law, your beneficiary can get to them immediately. Include all correspondence affecting the policy, such as change-of-beneficiary notices or proof that ownership of the policy has been transferred to someone else. The insurance company should have those records too, but there's a risk that it might lose track. Add the name, address, and phone number of your insurance agent. If you keep the policies and correspondence at home, put copies in your box or scan them into your computerized records, just in case.

In the same file, include a note about any life insurance you have through your employer and how to claim it. Also, file your receipts for mortgage-life and credit-life insurance if you've bought any. These policies pay off your loans if you die. If your executor doesn't know about them, he or she will waste money by paying the debts out of your estate.

You may have some other forms of coverage that your executor should know about. For example, if you charge a travel ticket to a credit card, it might generate $100,000 or more of life insurance if you die during the trip. You might also be covered for accidental death and dismemberment, whether you travel by plane, train, bus, or ship. Ditto if your accident occurs in an airline terminal or while traveling on public transportation to or from the terminal.

The government will cancel your guaranteed student loans or PLUS loans (Parent Loans for Undergraduate Students) if you die or become permanently disabled.

There may be government benefits if you ever served in the armed forces. Your surviving spouse or minor children should also get a $255 death benefit from Social Security.

Credit union members sometimes have small life insurance policies linked to their savings accounts.

If you belong to the American Automobile Association (AAA), you might be covered if you die in an auto accident. Not all clubs offer this protection, however, and coverage varies according to the type of accident.

Other clubs and organizations may also offer small policies as part of your membership package.

Clues to any payments of this sort should be kept in your life insurance file.

Health, Disability, and Long-Term Care Insurance Policies

Keep the insurance policy or the booklet explaining it in your file cabinet, so you can check it whenever you want. As backup, put the names of your health insurer, the policy numbers, the phone number of your company's employee-benefits office, or the name of your insurance agent on your master list. Also, keep the booklets explaining your benefits under Medicare or Medicaid.

If you're arguing with your HMO or insurance company about what should be treated or which bills should be covered, put everything in writing and keep copies. You'll need these records for an appeal or a lawsuit.

A disability policy or long-term care insurance can also be kept on file. Add the name of the insurer and the policy numbers to your master list.

Homeowners, Tenants, and Auto Insurance

You usually get a new policy every 6 or 12 months, but don't throw the old ones out right away. If someone was injured on your property or in your car 18 months ago and develops back pains from a previously undiscovered crack in a spinal disk, you'll want to be able to prove that you were insured at the time (especially if you've changed companies). Your insurer should have all the records, but you need backup, just in case. Furthermore, the language of insurance policies changes over the years. It could be important to know exactly what you were covered for when an injury occurred.

Keep current policies on file and old policies in a box somewhere. State statutes of limitations normally run for two or three years from the time the medical problem is discovered, so you could be sued for an injury three years after it happened. When your liability has expired, you can throw the policies out.

As usual, put the names of these insurance companies, the policy numbers, and the name of your insurance agent on your master list. File information on how to make a claim. If you bought special riders for valuables such as furs, art, jewelry, and silver, include appraisals of their current value or sales slips showing what you paid for them.

Monroney Labels

A *what*? Who's Monroney? He's an otherwise obscure U.S. senator who, in 1958, helped create the label you get on a new car listing all its features, serial number, and other important data. These labels come in handy when you need information for insurance claims, recalls, and resales. Drop them into your auto insurance file.

Household Inventory

I'm not your mother. I don't care that your room is messy and you don't write, but you still haven't done your household inventory, and how many times do I have to tell you? I know it's boring. I know that you started out in the living room, put down your pencil while you made some coffee, and never got any further. That's because you were using a pencil. The simple way is to use a camera. Take pictures of every room, every open closet, every open drawer. If you're using a video camera, comment on anything especially valuable. Keep sales slips for expensive purchases. Otherwise you'll have to compile an inventory of all your possessions from memory if your house burns down. Get appraisals on your antiques, art, rare books, furs, good jewelry, silver, and special collections. Some will need special insurance riders.

Put the appraisals, pictures, and sales slips in your safe-deposit box or scan them into your computer records. If you use a home safe instead, stash copies at a friend's house in case your safe isn't quite as fireproof as promised.

Personal Papers

Anything that you need to prove who you are, how long you've been around, and what you're entitled to needs to be carefully filed—some items in a file cabinet, others in a home safe or safe-deposit box or scanned into your computerized records. The important papers would include your birth certificate, marriage certificate, all documents relating to separation and divorce, military service records, proofs of citizenship, adoption papers, diplomas, licenses, passports, permits, union cards, Social Security card, and family health records such as vaccinations and dates of operations. Keeping an expired passport makes it easier to get a new one. Don't stash your military records before checking with the service to be sure that its dates agree with yours. If the service has them wrong and your survivors don't realize it, they might not get all the benefits they're due. Military service organizations send out newsletters about benefit changes; save those, too.

As a general strategy, keep at home anything you'll need to produce for employment, insurance, or government benefits. Choose safer storage for records that are rarely used or hard to replace. You might consider a safe-deposit box for originals, while keeping copies at home.

Tax Records

Yes, I know. You accidentally added the veterinarian's bill to your deductible medical expenses. How long does the Internal Revenue Service (IRS) have to catch and fine you? Three years, during which time you'd better keep not only your tax return but all supporting data. After that, you're in the clear and can toss the return, unless the vet is the least of it. The government has six years to audit you if you underreported your income by more than 25 percent. If it pursues you for fraud, or if you filed no tax return at all, there is no statute of limitations; you can be hit for back taxes anytime.

If you lose your federal returns, you can get copies covering the past 10 years. You pay nothing for an IRS transcript (a computer printout showing what was on the original return). For actual copies of the returns, or returns for earlier years, you're charged $39 each. Request Form 4506 for copies and Form 4506T for transcripts. For state returns, ask the state what's available. These are just the returns themselves, of course, not the data proving your right to the deductions.

In many cases, you should keep returns longer than the typical four years (the year you filed plus three more). For example:

Keep the returns and supporting documents that show any investment losses you're carrying forward and tax deductions taken on limited partnerships.

Keep the returns that show any contributions you made to a traditional Individual Retirement Account that were not tax deductible (page 1055). When you start withdrawing money, you'll need these records to establish how much of each IRA withdrawal is tax exempt. Leave a note for your heirs telling them to watch out for this. If they don't know you made those contributions, they may inadvertently pay taxes on the whole amount.

If you qualify for a company pension, consider keeping every single return you file, together with your W-2 forms. Companies don't always keep accurate records of how long you worked and how much you contributed to your retirement plan, especially companies that merge or are sold. You may need your tax returns and W-2s to prove what you're due when you leave your job.

In fact, it's worth keeping all your returns if you have the room. You can ditch the supporting documents, but it's nice to have the returns on hand if one of your employers didn't report your earnings to Social Security, reported an incorrect amount, or reported it under the wrong Social Security number. The returns also protect you from claims that, in some past year, you never filed returns at all. At this writing, the IRS is developing a service, "My IRS," that will let you review your returns and other personal business online.

Paycheck Stubs

If you trust your employer to add up your annual earnings correctly (as I do), you can throw your pay stubs away. But sometimes they contain important information that isn't included on your year-end W-2, such as the number of hours worked. If your union or employer keeps poor records, you may need your pay stubs to prove your eligibility for pension and welfare benefits. The stubs also make it simple to claim unemployment pay. Freelancers should keep all payment receipts for the year. Compare them with the 1099 forms you get, to make sure that your clients reported the payments correctly. Then you can throw the receipts away.

Employee Benefits

They've gotten so complicated that companies often publish them in loose-leaf notebooks. File everything. Keep the annual statements on the status of your pension, profit-sharing, salary deferral, or retirement savings plans so you can follow their progress. Keep employment contracts in your home file, with a copy in your safe-deposit box or the office of the lawyer who negotiated them.

Retirement Plans

Add to your master list the numbers and locations of all your retirement accounts: Individual Retirement Accounts, Simplified Employee Pensions, 403(b)s, 457s, Keoghs, company plans. Keep the plan documents in your file cabinet along with the annual reports showing how your investments are doing. Keep records of any loans you took against your plans and loans repaid. An unpaid loan may cost you a tax penalty if you leave the job, and you'll want to be sure that your employer's records are right. Finally, keep withdrawal records. Throw them out when the withdrawals show up on the annual statement of your account.

Bank Records

Canceled checks come in many forms these days. You might get the actual checks with your monthly statement; miniature pictures of the checks; or lists of the checks, delivered with a statement online. The miniatures and online statements are easy to file. If you get the checks themselves, keep the ones you might need for tax or insurance purposes. You might keep other checks too, for three years or so. You never know when they'll come in handy. Here are seven good reasons to have them on hand:

1. If you want to make a budget, old checks are a road map to what you've been spending.

2. The IRS might disagree with your version of life and ask for proof. Canceled checks can sometimes stand in for receipts in substantiating tax deductions (although usually the IRS wants receipts).

3. Old checks show the names of the people you've done business with and might want to find again.

4. It's easier to collect in full on a property insurance claim if you can show the company what you paid for your rugs, furniture, and other damaged items.

5. Your ex-spouse might claim that you missed some child support payments. If you didn't, your canceled checks will prove it.

6. You might have to prove to one of your creditors that a bill was paid. For this purpose, keeping checks for six months should be enough.

7. If you're one half of an unmarried couple and own property jointly, the checks prove what you paid for, which could be important if you split or your mate dies.

If you also have loans or certificates of deposit, keep the most recent statements showing their status. Old ones can be tossed. When you make new deposits, keep the receipts until the monthly statement comes in, so that you can check that they were entered correctly. Keep loan agreements; when the loan is repaid, throw out the agreements but keep the final closing statement. File any records for open savings accounts. Keep copies of letters that confirm the instructions you gave about your accounts or CDs, including beneficiary statements. Keep all disclosures you receive from the bank about its fees and interest rates so that you can check any changes you question. Note your PIN (personal identification number), lest you forget.

Receipts for Paid Bills

In Your File Cabinet. Keep receipts for every expense that is tax deductible, along with the checks or credit card statements showing that you paid. The IRS prefers both if you're ever audited.

In Your Fireproof Safe or Safe-Deposit Box. Keep receipts for high-cost purchases such as furs and antiques. They'll prove your claim if you have to dicker with the insurance company after a fire or theft. Also, keep statements that show you no longer owe money on past debts such as mortgages, closed credit card accounts, old cell phone contracts, and private loans. That protects you if the company ever claims that you never paid.

In a Box on Your Bureau or Desk. Keep receipts for gifts until you know that you won't have to take them back (if asked, many stores now put "gift receipts" in the box, so that recipients can return things themselves). If you pay in cash, keep the receipt long enough to be sure that the item is in good working order. Throw other receipts out. Your canceled check, debit-card entry, or credit card bill is normally proof enough of payment.

Medical and Drug Bills

Submit them all to your insurer. They'll be rejected until you have met the annual deductible, but unless you submit them, your insurer won't know when reimbursement should start.

File copies of all unreimbursed bills for the year. Expenses exceeding 7.5 percent of your adjusted gross income are deductible on your tax return. You might qualify for this write-off if you've been very sick or are poorly insured. If you get no tax deduction, throw the bills away.

Keep any bills that you and your insurer are arguing about, along with copies of all the letters you write and receive and notes of telephone calls.

Monthly Credit Card Statements

Check every one as soon as it comes, to be sure that every bill is actually yours. A thief needs only your credit card number, not the card itself, to buy goods and charge them to your account. Paper bills are easy to check; get in the habit of reading through the purchases when you open the envelope. If you're billed online, however, it's all too easy to pay without checking the statement, especially if you've arranged for automatic payments. Put a recurring alert in your computer's calendar, telling you to read the bill.

Add to your file on homeowners insurance any statements that show the price of something particularly expensive. Keeping the rest of your statements is optional. Personally, I hang on to them for two years. Who knows when an item charged and paid for will erroneously pop up on my bill again? Who knows what will break and need returning—and how else will I remember the store? Who knows when I'll want to look up the name of that great Cajun restaurant in Biloxi? Back bills also help you track your spending and draw up a budget. But if you never use these records, toss them. For tax purposes, you need to keep records only of business purchases.

When you take something back to a store, you'll get a return receipt. Keep it right where you open your mail, to remind you to check that the money was actually credited to your account. When it is, throw the receipt away.

Deeds, Titles, Title Insurance, Surveys

Records of purchase, property descriptions, and proofs of ownership—including the title to your car—belong in your fireproof home safe or safe-deposit box, or scanned into your computer. Copies are available if you lose the originals, but it's simpler to protect the records you have.

If you inherit property, keep any evidence of what it was worth when you got it. You'll need it to figure the gain when you sell.

File any records of legal proceedings, current tax assessments, and—if you're in a condominium or planned community—rules of the property owners' association. If you rent, file a copy of your lease.

Debts

In the file cabinet: your mortgage, bank loan records, contracts for installment purchases. No problem if a fire burns them up. Your creditors will remember. They'll even have copies.

But paid-off debts are another story. Get a receipt for the canceled note and keep it in your safe-deposit box. Proof of payment is especially important when you borrow money from an individual. He or she may note the debt in his or her records and forget to erase it. The heirs might ask you (or your survivors) for payment. The receipt shows that you're clean.

Instructions and Warranties

File the operating instructions for any equipment you buy. File warranty information. File maintenance contracts.

Money Owed to You

Keep the note in your home safe or safe-deposit box. Keep the repayment records in your file cabinet. When you get all your money back, cancel the note.

Note any refundable deposits, to the electric company, the phone company, your landlord. When you move, you're entitled to get them back.

Household Help

If you have an employee, keep proof that you paid all applicable taxes: Social Security, unemployment, disability, and any other tax your state requires. Keep a copy of the W-2 form you give your employee each January.

Your Phone File

If you keep track of your friends' names, addresses, and phone numbers in your computer, be sure the list is backed up. Your appointments too. If you keep these records in a book, photocopy it every few months. I lost a book once, unphotocopied. Never again.

Your Computer

Back up your files! If your computer is password protected, note the password in a separate file in your filing cabinet. E-mail critical information to another computer—say, in your office—in case a virus destroys both your computer and your hard drive backup. You also can use an Internet storage service that keeps your data in a remote location. Beware free storage services. In the past, they've tended to go out of business, taking your backups with them. A service you pay for will be more dependable.

Investments

Your safe-deposit box, fireproof home safe, or files of scanned documents are the right place for the following items:

Paper Stock Certificates. They're rarely issued anymore, but you may have inherited some. At home, keep a list of their names, denominations, certificate numbers, and CUSIP (Committee on Uniform Securities Identification Procedures) numbers, so you can remember—and refer to—what you have. Take great care with your paper securities: It's costly and time consuming to replace them (page 803). Records of new purchases are almost always held by your brokerage firm, which is simpler and safer.

Your Right to Stock Options or Deferred Compensation. These are payments that your heirs might overlook.

Paper Bonds. All new U.S. Treasury securities exist only as blips in the mind of a computer, so you have no actual certificates to store. Most corporate bonds and municipals are also issued this way, but store any certificates you have. Also, store any paper U.S. Savings Bonds. In your home file, keep all your purchase records, including a list of the bonds' denominations, serial numbers, and issue dates. You may need them to prove your ownership if an interest or principal payment goes astray.

Gold, Silver, or Platinum Bars or Coins.

The Names and Account Numbers of Your Mutual Funds and Unit Trusts (on Your Master List).

Your home file is the right place for:

Informational Material You Get from Your Mutual Fund or Unit Trust. Keep the original prospectus and sales literature. They tell you what you bought, how to redeem shares, and the services offered to investors. Keep any letters that say the fund has changed its rules. Keep the fund's annual reports. They show its performance compared with the market in general—a valuable history when you're deciding whether to hold or sell. Keep your year-end statements, showing purchases and sales. You needn't keep all the interim statements and reports.

Your Brokerage House Agreement and Annual Statements. Keep all confirmations of trades. You have to know exactly when each security was bought and sold, the price, and the commission you paid in order to figure out your income tax. Add up your commissions once a year to see what you're paying for the account. (Commissions usually appear only on your "confirms," not on your annual statement.)

The Original Prospectus and Sales Material for Any Initial Public Offering You Own. If a deal goes bad and was misrepresented, your prospectus could help establish grounds for a lawsuit. Also keep the annual reports that chart the investment's progress.

Take notes of all conversations you have with your broker. Put all your instructions in writing, including follow-up letters after a phone conversation. Keep copies. If you get into an argument about how the broker handled your account, these records can support your case.

If you're a casual investor betting your money on a broker's say-so, there's no point cluttering your file drawers with the periodic reports sent by the companies whose stocks you own. But at least look through them before tossing them out. Maybe you'll learn something. If you're really following the company, keep the annual reports in your files.

Rental Properties

For reference, keep a couple years' worth of income and expense records in your current files. Older receipts belong on the shelf with your back tax records.

Business at Home

There you are, in the spare-bedroom-turned-office, trading currency futures for all the parents at your day care center. You know that you can write off your telephone expenses (a separate phone line is best) against the potloads of profits you're making. But what else? For a home-based business, take a lesson from an accountant on how to keep track of income and expenses and what your tax deductions are. For example, you may be able to depreciate that part of the house that serves as your office. You might also be able to write off a portion of what you pay to heat, light, clean, and insure your house (page 184). So you'll need to keep all those bills and canceled checks. Keep current bills in the filing cabinet and old bills with the tax records. Carry a business diary or PDA to record tax-deductible expenses for travel, entertainment, supplies, and so on. The IRS gets dark under the eyes when your diary reads as if you composed it just in time to make the audit.

Trust Documents

Keep the originals with your lawyer or in a safe-deposit box. Put copies in your files.

Charities and Gifts

Keep copies of pledges to charities and the letters that acknowledge your contribution. Keep canceled checks showing how much you gave. Keep the appraisals on donated property. If you do volunteer work, keep track of the miles you drive on the charity's business. They're tax deductible.

Put notes about important gifts to friends and family members in your safe-deposit box if the gifts will affect the size of your estate tax or keep the peace in a squabbling family.

Bankruptcy Records

I hope you never find yourself in bankruptcy court. But if you do, keep careful records of all the debts that were discharged. Creditors have a nasty habit of trying to collect debts you no longer owe.

In Case of Death

Keep a last-wishes file. Include the cemetery deed if you have one, material for your obituary (relatives often get things wrong), final instructions about your funeral if it matters to you, and a copy of your living will if you don't want to be kept alive by extraordinary means. Tell your relatives and executor about this file and where to find it. President Franklin D. Roosevelt made detailed notes about how his funeral was to be conducted and put them in the White House safe. They weren't found until after he was buried.

Safe Deposit Box Key

Drop it into a toolbox. Keep it with the handkerchiefs. For obscurity—the usual fate of a key to a safe-deposit box—those places are as good as any. In my dreams, however, I see the key resting in your top desk or bureau drawer, labeled, with the bank's name attached (what's the good of a key if your survivors don't know which bank to take it to?). I see a note on your master list telling everybody where it is. Ditto for the combination to the lock on your home safe.

The Master List of Where Everything Is

Record the results of your masterful filing system in your computer or on a couple sheets of paper and leave this master list in your home file for your executor and heirs. Put a copy in your safe deposit box. List:
- Your insurance policies and insurance agents
- Employee benefits and the phone number of the office that handles them
- Bank accounts and any particular banker that you deal with
- Where to find your safe-deposit box and keys
- Where you keep your will or living trust and the name of the lawyer who drew it up
- Your executor or trustee
- Where other trust documents are
- Where all your personal papers are
- Your brokers or investment advisers—names, addresses, and phone numbers
- Your accountant

- Where to find your securities and retirement accounts
- Where your tax records are
- What properties you own and where the deeds are
- Your debts and any money owed you
- Your Social Security number and that of every family member
- Your important computer passwords
- Where you've hidden your home safe and what the combination is
- Where you keep your emergency flight bag, if you have one
- A list of all your credit cards—account numbers and emergency telephone numbers—in case your wallet is stolen and you have to cancel them
- Where your last-wishes file is

Finally, photocopy everything in your wallet: ID cards, driver's license, health insurance card, and other items you carry for reference. That makes them easier to replace.

4

Your Basic Banking

Banking in the Internet Age

**Good bankers are nice,
but great online services are even nicer.**

When you look for a bank, you're looking for services, convenience, and price. Your options are small banks, big banks, online banks, and credit unions.

Internet banks, with no actual buildings, and the online, or "direct," services of traditional banks, are a huge win for savers (page 45). They pay top interest rates on savings accounts and certificates of deposit. Their checking accounts also offer higher rates.

Small, community banks win on personal service, both for individuals and small businesses. They usually charge lower fees and pay higher interest rates than big banks do. They're also in a better position to restructure mortgages that are in trouble. Some of them specialize in trusts and other financial services for the well-to-do. I *love* community banks.

Big banks win on convenience, thanks to their wider network of ATMs, longer list of financial products, and better services online. They might even let you use your cell phone to pay your bills. But they kill you with fees.

Credit unions win on niceness, community feel, and caring about their members' financial well-being. In general, they offer better interest rates and lower banking fees than the competition. If you can't join through your employer, you might find one that serves your city or region. Anyone can join the Pentagon Federal Credit Union (www.penfed.org). For other possibilities, check the Web site of the Credit Union National Association (CUNA) at www.cuna.org; write to CUNA at P.O. Box 431, Madison, WI 53701; or call them at 800-356-9655. Some credit unions offer a limited fare: only checking accounts (known as share draft accounts), savings deposits, and consumer lending. Others also provide mortgages, credit cards, online banking, and stockbrokerage at a discount. Check that the credit union carries federal deposit insurance (see the National Credit Union Administration's credit union directory at www.ncua.gov/data/directory/cudir.html). Around 3.5 percent of them still carry private insurance, which, as previous banking debacles show, can buckle under pressure.

Savings and loan associations used to specialize in mortgages, but that was many years ago. Now they're like small or large banks, with similar services for consumers.

Banklike services can also be had at large brokerage firms through their asset management accounts (page 51). But those are best used as convenience accounts for investors. For everyday transactions, most people need a bank.

The New, Improved Choice: An Internet Bank

If you want a basic savings account, there are two ways to go: a traditional bank, where your money will earn a pittance; or an Internet bank, which will pay you more. That's a no-brainer. Go online!

You open the account online and transact your business there. You can also access the account by mail or phone and speak to a service rep if you have a problem. The rules are simple: no fees, no minimum deposits, no complicated accounts, no bank lines, no time wasted driving back and forth to see a teller. *And* your savings will earn a lot more money.

You can link your Internet savings account to the checking account you already have at a traditional bank. That lets you move money back and forth with the click of a mouse. Consider having your paycheck deposited into your Internet savings account automatically. To pay bills, move some of that money into your checking account as needed. There might be a two- or three-day delay before the traditional bank credits your checking account with the cash, but so what? You're earning interest on cash that would otherwise lie fallow. If you'd rather send your paycheck to your traditional checking account, set up an automatic savings arrangement. Have a fixed sum of money transferred to your Internet account every time your paycheck comes in.

Checking accounts are the next step for Internet banks. They're in their infancy but are sure to grow. As with savings accounts, there are no monthly service fees, no minimum deposits, and high interest rates, compared with those paid by traditional banks. You get overdraft protection if you authorize a check for more than you have in the bank; your only cost is the interest you pay on the amount you borrow to cover the bill. There's no delay when transferring money from Internet savings into Internet checking, so you can pay your bills immediately. The technology is a little different from that of online bill-paying at traditional banks. You don't get a checkbook. Everything is paid electronically or with debit cards. Still, it's easy and will earn you extra money on your funds.

Where to Go for Internet Banking

At this writing, the majors include EmigrantDirect, EverBank, ING Direct, and UnivestDirect. Traditional banks that offer high-rate Internet-only savings accounts include First National Bank of Omaha (FNBO Direct), HSBC Bank (HSBC Direct), and Citibank (Citibank Direct requires you to have a Citi checking account too). High-rate savings are also available at certain brokerage firms such as E*Trade Financial and Charles Schwab. At this writing, free high-rate checking accounts can be had at ING Direct and HSBC Direct, with more to come.

Most Internet banks also offer a range of other banking services: certificates of deposit, Individual Retirement Accounts, mutual funds, credit cards, auto loans, mortgages, and home equity lines of credit.

Note that these are all pure Internet accounts. A Citibank Direct customer has to handle his or her business online (or by mail or phone) and doesn't have access to the branches. But why would you want it? It's easier to bank from home at whatever hour suits you. The service is as good as or better than you get from traditional banks. If your paycheck is deposited into your account automatically and you pay your bills online, you rarely have to visit a bank branch. This way of doing business also makes you a cheaper customer to serve, which is why you can earn higher interest rates.

Checking accounts and some of the savings accounts come with ATM cards. Internet customers of a traditional bank can use its ATMs free. ING Direct, which has no ATMs of its own, offers free use of Allpoint ATMs, found in stores and at smaller banks. At other ATMs, you pay the ATM owner $1.50 or $2 per transaction. The Internet banks all reimburse you for at least $6 in ATM charges every month, and sometimes more.

Some people worry that Internet banks are vulnerable to hackers. But banking environments have been highly secure. An Internet bank is no more vulnerable than the online bill-paying services of traditional banks, which millions of customers use. If a hacker broke into a bank's database, the bank would reimburse you. If the bank goes out of business, your deposits are protected by the Federal Deposit Insurance Corporation (look for the FDIC label on the banks' Web sites or check it yourself on the FDIC Web site, at www3.fdic.gov/idasp, or call 877-275-3342).

Don't confuse Internet banks with traditional banks that have simply moved their usual services online. The traditional banks still charge fees for various types of checking or savings accounts, require minimum deposits, and charge if you fall below the minimums. True Internet banks—the direct banks—ditch the service fees and pay high interest rates.

Opening an Account at a Traditional Bank

Don't just drop in and wait to see someone who's free. Avoid a long wait by making an appointment with the person in charge of opening new accounts.

Before going to the meeting, check the bank's financial products and fees online or pick up the brochures that it stocks by the front entrance. Read them to see what services you might want. Make a list of questions.

At your meeting, go through your questions one by one. Ask for a list of the bank's fees for various services, including all the costs associated with its checking accounts, savings accounts, and credit cards (they may also be listed online). Ask how long it holds checks you deposit before you have access to the money (page 56). If you write checks against your deposits too soon, you'll be charged $20 or $30 for having nonsufficient funds (the bank calls it an NSF fee).

Explain to the banker the kind of customer you expect to be. How much money will be flowing through your checking account. What services you might need. Find out whom to call if you have a question or need some help. Talk about any loans you might want. A home mortgage or home equity line of credit? Money for starting a business? What does it take to get a lower interest rate on loans and a higher rate on savings?

Take the measure of the person you're meeting with. Is he or she helpful? Knowledgeable about the bank's products and services? Willing to answer your questions in detail? Ready with good ideas? Interested in getting your business? A banker who starts out gruff, impatient, vague, supercilious, or ill informed will not improve with time—and what is tolerated in one bank officer will be tolerated in others. Go to a place that makes a better first impression.

Compare the fees, interest rates, and services offered by at least two institutions—say, a big bank and a small one. Each represents a statement of business philosophy. High-fee banks are likely to charge even more in the future; low-fee banks are dedicated to holding down overt costs. Banks that pay high rates on savings have effectively announced that they'll always be competitive; banks that pay low interest won't be. Those are messages to pay attention to.

Don't be swayed by the various types of investments the bank is selling. You can usually do better somewhere else. You should make your decision based on its banking services alone.

Which Checking Account?

No need to wander through the wilderness, wondering which of a half-dozen checking accounts is best. If you're a customer of a traditional bank, your choice hangs on a single test: what is the lowest average balance you will leave on deposit every month? If it's small, get a checking account that pays no interest. To earn interest, you have to maintain an average of $2,600 on deposit, depending on the bank, according to the latest checking study by Bankrate.com, which surveys interest rates nationwide. (You can earn interest on as little as $1 if you use an online bank—see page 45.)

By law, banking institutions must use the *average daily balance* method of figuring your minimum balance. This takes the amount you have in your account each day and averages it across the entire month. If you keep $5,000 there for 29 days and on the 30th day write a $5,000 check, that month's average balance would be $4,833. In arriving at your average daily balance, some banks will count both your checking and your savings deposits.

Some 218 small credit unions still gyp customers with low-balance accounting. Here, the credit union looks only at the lowest point in your account that month. If you held $5,000 for 29 days and then emptied your account, the credit union would call your monthly balance "$0." You would earn no interest. Worse, you might pay a fee for falling below the minimum balance. Ask about low-balance accounting before deciding to join.

Besides interest rates and minimum deposits, look at the schedule of fees: monthly fees, fees for each check you write, fees for dropping below the minimum balance or bouncing a check, fees for checking your current balance, fees for using another bank's ATM, and others. Don't let your banker's hand be quicker than your eye. A checking account might deliberately carry a low monthly fee or no fee at all in order to make it look cheap to price shoppers. But the bank might recoup by charging you extra for processing checks. Banks are required to give you a full list of fees. Ask for it before opening an account.

You want an account that pays the highest interest rate possible on the average balance you can afford to keep, while not breaking your back with extra fees. So look around. At GoodGuy Bank, your checking deposits might earn $75 a year. At BadGuy Bank, exactly the same account might cost $150 even counting your interest earnings. In general, smaller banks charge lower fees and require lower checking account balances than larger ones. Here's an idea of what's around.

If You Keep a Low Balance and Write Your Account Down Almost to Zero Every Month, Look at

No-interest checking. The majority of accounts require no minimum balance and charge no monthly service fee. Where monthly fees and balance requirements exist, they're low. You earn no interest on the idle money in the account.

If You Maintain a Sizable Minimum Balance in Your Checking Account, Look at

Interest-Paying Checking. You earn a wee interest rate on your idle balances—at this writing, less than 0.5 percent. There are usually no monthly fees if you maintain a minimum balance in the $2,500 to $10,000 range, depending on the bank. Otherwise you might pay $10 or so per month. At some banks, the amount of interest you earn and the fees you pay vary from month to month, depending on the size of your balances or the amount of business you do.

No-Interest Checking Plus a Bank Money Market Account. Why keep $2,500 on deposit earning 0.5 percent or less? Instead choose no-interest checking and park your $2,500 in the bank's money market deposit account (page 219), where it will earn more.

Bundled Accounts. Your interest-paying checking account may be "bundled" with other banking services, such as discounts on loans or a quarter-point interest bonus on various savings deposits. You get the whole package for a single monthly fee or no fee at all, depending on the size of your combined checking and savings deposits.

If You Write Only a Few Checks Every Month, Look for

Basic, Lifeline, Student, or No-Frills Checking. These accounts are for people who keep superlow average balances (as low as one penny) and write just a few checks a month. If there's a fee, it's small. The first 8 to 12 checks or withdrawals may be free, with fees of 35 cents or more for each check over the limit (if you write a lot of checks, you should be in regular checking). This simplified service is offered by about half the banks, although it may be restricted to students or the elderly.

Express Checking. You do all your banking business by personal computer, phone, and ATM. If you need a teller, you pay a fee.

Protect Yourself Against Overdrawing Your Account

It's easier than ever to overdraw. You're not only writing checks against your account, you're also taking money from ATMs, making purchases with debit cards, and arranging for certain bills to be paid automatically every month. What's more, the checks you write can be turned into digital images and sent to your bank for payment overnight. A supercareful person will get all these payments and withdrawals into the check register on time. But it's easy to slip, and when that happens, checks may bounce. To avoid high bounced-check charges, set up one of these three backup systems:

1. Link to Your Savings Deposits. If you accidentally overdraw, the bank will take the extra money out of your savings—either regular savings or a money market deposit account. There may be a $5 or $10 fee for each transfer.

2. An Overdraft Line of Credit. The bank lends you money to cover the check or withdrawals. You pay interest as long as the loan is outstanding and, sometimes, an annual fee of $15 to $25. Some banks lend only in $50 increments, so if you write a check for $1 too much, you'll have to borrow $50 to cover it. There may also be a transfer fee. Monthly repayments may be deducted from your account automatically.

3. Link to Your Credit Card. Overdrafts will be charged as a cash advance. You'll pay a fee each time ($3 or so), plus the card's high interest rate.

What About Bank "Courtesy Overdraft Protection" Plans? Your bank might advertise that it automatically covers overdrafts for accounts in good standing, up to a certain amount—say, $300. You'll pay $20 to $35 for every item covered. The amount owed, plus fees, is deducted from your next deposit. Sometimes there's an additional fee of $2 to $5 for every day that you don't repay the loan. This "courtesy" is usually offered "free" as a part of the package, and you can see why. It makes a ton of money for the banks! Reject it. Instead, choose one of the three alternatives above.

When Can a Bank Say That a Checking Account is "Free"?

A free account has no monthly maintenance fees, no per-check fees, and no fees for falling below the minimum balance. But there can be plenty of other charges: for ATM use, bounced or stopped checks, printing checks, balance inquiries, and a few other minor items.

Alternatives to Checking Accounts

Asset Management Accounts. These are for active investors who want an easy way to keep track of their cash. They generally combine a money market account (which doubles as an interest-paying checking account) with a brokerage account and a credit or debit card. With asset management accounts:

- Your cash earns a higher interest rate than you'd get from regular interest-paying checking (although less than you generally get from a bank money market deposit account).
- You can draw on your money with a special checkbook or a debit card (checks may have to be written for a certain minimum, such as $250).
- You might get a credit card, which can trigger a loan against any stocks you own.
- A single monthly statement shows all your investment and banking transactions.
- All dividends and interest are automatically reinvested.
- You might get access to your funds through an ATM network.

Some accounts offer an automatic bill-paying service and let you arrange to have your paycheck deposited electronically.

The minimum deposit for asset management accounts (including the value of your stocks and bonds): $1,000 to as much as $25,000. Annual fees run from zero to $125. These accounts are offered by a few big banks, brokerage houses, some mutual funds, and a few insurance companies. When you're not with a bank, you may have to wait up to 15 days for the checks to clear.

Money Market Mutual Funds. These too are normally for investors. Rates of interest change daily but are usually higher than those on the banks' interest-paying checking accounts. The funds that offer checking (about half of them do) charge lower fees than banks and zero for falling below the minimum balance. You can arrange to have your paycheck deposited directly. For more on money market funds, see page 220. Most won't cash checks smaller than $100 or $250, so you'll still need a bank account.

The drawbacks to using money funds as checking accounts: You may not have access to ATMs, deposited checks will be held for up to 15 days before you can draw against them, and you can't get a line of credit.

Paying Bills Online

At most traditional banks, you can pay your bills online—a huge convenience. You enter the names and addresses of the companies or people you owe money to. If it's a company, include your account number. When the bills come in, you just call up your payee list, enter the amounts you owe, click, and pay. Payments to big companies usually go electronically. Otherwise the bank will mail a paper check, so you can pay a friend, a small business, your sister, anyone. The account can be programmed to pay certain bills automatically every month. You can also transfer money from one account to another. Some banks charge a fee for online bill paying, but most don't.

Online bill paying is a godsend if (like me!) you hate balancing your checkbook. All your deposits and online payments show up on your computer screen when you access your account. That gives you a running daily tally of most of the money in your account. Occasionally an item you buy with a debit card might not register right away, so it's worth checking those receipts against the sums debited from your account. You also have to keep track of the few paper checks you might still write by hand. As long as you can keep a cash cushion in your account, however, online banking makes checkbook balancing obsolete. Whew!

Online payments may also save you money. Some companies charge $1 to $5 a month for mailing paper bills. You avoid this fee if you arrange to have the bills paid automatically through your bank account.

One warning when you pay online: The debit will show in your checking account immediately, but the actual payment won't be sent right away. Some banks make the payment in a couple of days; others take as long as a week. If your bank delays sending out checks, pay your bills as soon as they arrive. If you hold your bills for a couple of weeks and the bank adds a week for processing, your payment may arrive late and incur a late charge. (Even if your bank takes a week to pay, by the way, it will probably credit your checking account with interest until the cash actually leaves the account.)

Money management online: The next step for online banking will be personal financial management. Some banks already show you all your accounts, including your mortgage, on a single page. They may break down your expenses by tax category or provide a budgeting tool. You can even link to your other financial institutions, such as brokerage or mutual fund firms, and manage those accounts through your online bank portal. Other possibilities: an online check register where you can enter checks you write by hand, thus keeping your bank balance up to date; daily downloading of your credit card charges, so you'll always know how much of your income you've spent that month; online spending alerts if you go over your budget for certain types of expenses; and similar options.

Can you switch banks? Changing banks gets more complicated once you've established online bill-paying accounts. But don't hesitate if your bank has been giving poor service or hiking your fees. Some banks have "switch kits" to walk you through the procedures. An increasing number of banks will even handle the switch for you, to make it easier to move.

How about paying bills online through each company's individual Web site? Why would you bother? You'd have to click on several sites and remember a pile of passwords. When you pay through your bank, it's just one password, all the time.

How about letting utilities and other regular billers take what they're owed from your bank account automatically every month? Absolutely not. It there's an error, it takes a while to get your money back. If you cancel the payments, the companies may keep drawing on your account for several months more. Set up these automatic payments yourself, through your bank account online. That lets you stop payments at any time.

How about paying through a dedicated bill-paying service? No point. These services charge monthly fees, while your bank's service is usually free.

How safe is banking online? Plenty safe. Banks are *extremely* careful about their security systems. The breaches you hear about involve mostly credit or debit cards and corporate or government data, not bank data. Millions of people successfully bank online through traditional services and Internet banks. If a hacker gets into a bank system and steals your money, the bank will pay. If a fraudster steals your PIN and writes himself a giant check, you're liable for no more than $50, as long as you tell the bank right away.

Paperless Banking

Internet banks don't send out paper statements. Traditional banks urge you to cancel your paper statements and let the computer keep track of everything for you. One problem: your online account may show transactions back for only 6 months (online banks may show 12 months). The bank can retrieve older payments, but it will take a few days and you may be charged a fee. That's a problem if there's an audit or transactions are questioned. If you have a traditional account, I'd suggest that you keep paper statements and file them for at least 6 years. At an Internet bank, I'd print out or download a statement every month and file that.

If Your Bank Fees Are Too High

Join the crowd. Everyone's screaming. That's one of the reasons they're moving to purely Internet banks—to avoid the fees.

If you prefer traditional banks, you may be able to cut your costs. When you opened your checking account, you probably looked only at how much interest you could earn. Now you know that the best account is the one that carries the lowest fees.

To find that account, start by analyzing your recent bank statements. Circle every fee to see how much you're spending each month (it could be as much as $300 a year) and list what all the fees were for. Then make a written summary of the way you use the account. How many checks do you write per month, and what do they cost? How often do you use a teller or ATM (and does your bank charge you for it)? How low does your monthly balance go? How many incidental services do you use? How large are your savings deposits there? How much interest have you earned on your interest-paying checking, and does it exceed the fees you pay?

Armed with this information, sit down with a bank employee and say that you'd like to find ways of lowering your fees.

■ *Maybe you have an interest-paying checking account but your balance keeps falling below the required minimum.* That might cost you $10 or more each time. You'll save money over the year by choosing free no-interest checking.

■ *Maybe you write so few checks that you can manage on a no-frills account.*

■ *Maybe your fees will drop if you keep more deposits in the bank.* If you have a CD somewhere else, move it to this bank when it matures.

■ *Maybe you're tapping your account through another bank's ATM.* That usually costs more than using your own bank's machines. Big banks have ATMs everywhere. If you're at a small bank, see if it has a "selective surcharge" deal that lets you use the ATMs in a particular network free.

■ *Maybe you pay ATM fees to check the balance in your account because you don't keep your check register up to date.* You might even find yourself overdrawing month after month. Switching to online banking could save you money because you'd always know how much cash you had on hand. (So would keeping up your check register, but I don't want to ask too much.)

■ *Maybe you haven't noticed that your account limits the number of debits you're allowed each month.* You can eliminate overage fees by staying within the rules.

■ *Maybe it costs less to pay by debit card or automatic electronic transfer than to pay by check.* Automatic transfers work for any regular monthly payments: mortgage, rent, auto loan or lease, condo maintenance, life insurance premiums, utility bills, and regular monthly investments.

■ *Maybe your bank offers online banking from your home computer* at a lower price than banking in person or by mail.

■ *Maybe it's cheaper to have your paycheck deposited electronically or to accept a checking account statement* in lieu of canceled checks.

■ *It's doubtlessly cheaper to switch to a credit union* if there's one you can join (page 44) and it has the services you want.

■ *For sure, it's cheaper to buy checks from a commercial check printer rather than through your bank*. Three to try: Checks in the Mail (www.citm.com or 800-733-4443); Deluxe Checks (www.deluxe.com or 800-335-8931); and Checks Unlimited (www.checksunlimited.com or 800-210-0468).

Two Final Points

1. Banks have to tell you 15 or 30 days in advance when they're raising a fee, depending on the product. But the notice might be written in fine-print Sanskrit, which means that you'll probably throw it away. Prudence dictates that you read all bank notices and get a translation when you don't understand them. If you don't bother, check your statements periodically for new fees that you may have missed.

2. Banks charge wildly different fees! Your bank may be expensive compared with the competition. You might be able to cut your fees in half simply by comparing prices and switching to a cheaper bank. Small banks and credit unions usually charge the least. But a few big banks have eliminated all nuisance fees for customers who keep balances of $2,000 or more.

How to pay the lowest fees the easy way: choose an Internet bank. Or have I said that before? Also look at credit unions and small community banks.

Test Your Banker's IQ

A good banker should be able to answer all nine of the following questions. If you get a blank look—or a gentle drift of oral fog—ask again. You're entitled to a clear and simple statement that makes sense. If you don't understand what the banker is saying, don't blame yourself. Blame the banker, who probably doesn't have all the facts and is covering up. If you had $10 for every "expert" who wasn't, you'd be rich.

1. Ask: With interest-paying checking, what does the banking institution pay interest *on*? By law, it must pay on the money that's in your account at the end of each day. That's "day of deposit to day of withdrawal." But some pay on each check from the day you put it in. Others pay only on the *collected balance,* which means you get no interest until the check has provisionally cleared. That usually takes one or two days but sometimes more.

Some banks advertise more than one rate, depending on the size of your deposit. They might pay 1.5 percent on balances up to $1,000 and 2.7 percent on larger amounts. But what exactly does that mean? There's a good way and a bad way to figure it.

Say, for example, that you deposit $2,500. You might get 2.7 percent on the whole amount, usually called a *tiered rate*. That's good. Or you might get 1.5 percent on the first $1,000 and 2.7 percent only on the remaining $1,500, usually called a *blended rate*. That's bad. In fact, it's a clip job. Avoid blended rates.

2. Ask: What is the penalty for falling below the minimum balance? The fee might exceed the interest that your account is likely to earn. If you can't be sure of maintaining the minimum balance, switch to an account with a lower minimum—for example, a no-interest-paying account.

3. Ask: What fees might you have to pay with this account? You should get a list, including charges for maintaining the account, processing checks, bouncing checks, using an automated teller machine, using a human teller, buying checks printed with your name and address, confirming your current bank balance, buying certified checks, stopping payment on a check, transferring funds by telephone, and depositing checks that turn out to be no good (called deposit item returned—see page 58).

4. Ask: Will the bank reduce the interest rate on your loans if you keep a checking account there and allow the loan payments to be deducted automatically?

5. Ask: If you invest in a certificate of deposit or take out a loan, will the bank eliminate the fees it charges for your checking account? Most institutions give their better customers special breaks. Some tie-in deals, however, are not worth having. You might save yourself a quarter point on an auto loan by taking out a certificate of deposit. But that's no bargain if cheaper auto loans are available somewhere else.

6. Ask: If you sign up to have your paycheck deposited directly in your account, will the bank waive the fee? Some banks offer lower monthly fees or free checking for direct deposits.

7. Ask: What's the cost of protecting yourself against a bounced check? Get all the fees for overdraft protection—whether linked to your savings account, credit line, credit card, or the bank's so-called courtesy (or high-fee) plan.

8. Ask: When you deposit a check, how long do you have to wait before being able to draw against the funds? By law, your bank has to tell you exactly what the rules are. People with new accounts usually have to wait longer than people whose accounts have been at the bank for two or three years.

9. Ask: If you choose paperless statements, how long does the bank keep the record of your past transactions (for tax purposes, you want seven years) and what does it cost to retrieve your past records?

How Fast Will the Bank Clear Checks You Deposit?

There you stand, like a kid with his nose pressed against a pet store window. Your money is romping behind the glass and you can't get at it. Any checks you deposit may be held by your bank for a specified number of days. Fortunately, most institutions offer one-day clearance for almost all checks deposited to well-established accounts. But they're allowed to hold checks longer and you need to know the outside limits.

Under federal law, banking institutions normally must give you access to at least $100 of your deposit on the next business day (not counting Saturday, even if the bank is open) and must clear the rest of your deposit on a specified schedule (with some quirky conditions here and there). All the following limits apply to checks deposited to your account before the bank's cutoff hour—generally, noon for ATM deposits and 2:00 p.m. for deposits made in person. Add one business day for checks you deposit after the cutoff. The general schedule:

1. One business day for federal, state, and local government checks, electronic payments (like direct deposit of a paycheck or Social Security check), postal money orders, cash, personal checks drawn on the same bank, cashier's checks, and certified checks. To get one-day access, certain checks have to be deposited in person or sometimes on special deposit slips. Ask about this if your timing is critical.

2. Two business days for local checks.

3. Five business days for out-of-town checks.

4. For cash or checks deposited on a business day (not Saturday) in the bank's own ATM: one business day for U.S. Treasury checks; two business days for cash, local checks, cashier's checks, and state and local government checks; and five business days for out-of-town checks.

5. For cash or checks deposited in an ATM not owned or operated by your bank: five business days.

6. On checks you mail to the bank: one business day after receipt by the bank for U.S. Treasury checks; two days for cashier's checks, postal money orders, and local checks including the checks of your own state and local governments; five days for out-of-town checks.

Is a bank ever allowed to hold checks longer than usual? Absolutely. It needs at least some weapons against the risk of fraud. Expect a delay in drawing against deposited checks if:

1. You're a brand-new customer. The bank gets 30 days to take your measure, during which time you might have to wait longer than usual for checks to clear. But on the next business day, even new customers can draw on the first $5,000 of funds from a government, cashier's, or travelers check, or from deposits made electronically. So if you move, transfer your bank account by wire. If you bank entirely online, you won't have to transfer your account at all.

2. You repeatedly overdraw your checking account or are redepositing a check that bounced. In this case, a local check can be held for 7 business days and an out-of-town check for 11 business days.

3. You deposit more than $5,000 in checks in a single day. Part of your money will be released on the normal schedule; part can be held up to 6 business days longer.

4. The bank has "reasonable cause" to think that something is fishy. This covers such things as suspicion of fraud, suspicion that the account holder is going bankrupt, or concern that the check is too old to cash.

These rules all apply to withdrawals by check or to cash withdrawals through a human teller. Limits are also allowed on cash withdrawals through an ATM. Limits on cash withdrawals are always allowed for security reasons, through tellers as well as through ATMs.

The Most Hated Bank Fee in America

It's the fee known in bank jargon as deposit item returned (DIR). You may be charged a DIR when you get a check, deposit it, and then learn that it bounced. You are blameless. You had no idea the check wouldn't clear. Nevertheless, the bank nicks you for an average of $6, with some banks going as high as $10 (large banks charge more than small ones). If the DIR drops your account below the minimum balance, you're charged a fee for that too.

In most cases, the checks aren't truly bad. The writer just made a math mistake in his or her check register, forgot to enter past checks, or thought a paycheck would clear faster than it did. When the check is resubmitted, it's usually good. Still, the innocent party pays. If you're hit with a DIR, call your bank and ask it to cancel the charge. It sometimes will.

How Fast Will Your Bank Cash the Paper Checks You Write?

Faster than you think possible. If you give a check to a major retailer, it may be scanned into the banking system right from the store and debited from your account before you get home. Never count on having a day or two of "float" before your checks are cashed. Treat your checkbook as if it were a debit card.

What You Need to Know About ChexSystems and SCAN

You probably never heard of ChexSystems. But you're on its blacklist if you ever mismanaged a bank account. Banks report people who dupe them in some way. Maybe your account was overdrawn, the bank closed it, and you never paid what you owed. Maybe you withdrew $100 through an ATM, then closed your account before the bank learned about the $100. Maybe you didn't realize that you got $100 too much. But your intentions don't matter. If you beat the bank out of money, it will report you to ChexSystems. When you try to open a new account somewhere else, you'll be denied. If you pay the old bank what you owe, it's supposed to add that fact to your file. Even so, a new bank might refuse to take you on. Black marks stay on your ChexSystems report for five years, unless the reporting bank asks that it be removed.

The Shared Check Authorization Network (SCAN) is a similar database used by retailers and other businesses that accept checks. They scan your check against the names of people who have bounced checks and not made good. The database also shows whether your bank account is still open. If you appear to be passing a bad check, the retailer won't take it. Unpaid checks stay on the system until the retailer reports them as paid or otherwise resolved. If you don't pay, you stay on the record for up to seven years.

If you think there's been a mistake or you don't know what you've done wrong, go to Consumer Debit Resource (www.consumerdebit.com/consumer info/us/en/scan/report/index.htm) for information on how to order your reports. You can print order forms to mail or fax. Or call ChexSystems at 800-428-9623 or SCAN at 800-262-7771 (have your checking account number and driver's license number ready).

More Check Facts

To cash checks at a branch other than your own, get a signature card.

When you endorse a check (that is, sign your name on the back), it becomes as good as money and can be cashed by anyone who finds it. To prevent that, endorse it with instructions: "Pay to the order of Amanda Smith" or "For deposit only." When accepting an endorsed check from someone else, ask him or her to write "Pay to the order of [you]," so that if you lose it, neither of you will be out the money.

Endorse checks on the back, at the left-hand end, in the first inch and a half of space. If your signature is anywhere else, the bank may ask you to sign again. Most checks now carry a line to show where your signature goes.

Technically, a check may be good for years. But in practice, the bank might refuse any check that is more than one year old. That is, if the bank notices.

If you write a check and wish you hadn't, call your bank and ask it to stop payment. Your account should be flagged right away, but you have to follow up with written authorization, usually by filing a stop-check form. The cost: $18 to $32. A stop payment lasts for a limited period of time but can be renewed. If the check slips through, the bank takes responsibility for it. The stop-check form should spell out the rules.

You can arrange for regular, automatic transfers from your checking to your savings account. Interest earned on your certificates of deposit can be deposited into either account.

If someone forges your signature on a check and the bank cashes it, you are entitled to 100 percent reimbursement. It doesn't matter that you failed to report that your checkbook was stolen (although you should have). It doesn't matter that you kept your checks with your credit cards, which carry your signature. In most cases, it is the bank's absolute responsibility to guard against forgery. Some banks blame you and refuse to pay, in which case you should write directly to the bank's president and to its state or federal regulator.

You have a responsibility too. If you don't report a forgery within 14 days after the bank mailed your statement and fraudulent checks continue to be cashed by the same person, the later losses are all yours.

Use a *certified check* when the person you're paying wants a guarantee that the check will be good. The bank certifies that the check will be paid by withdrawing the money from your account when the check is issued. A *cashier's check* can be used by people with no checking account. You give the money to the bank, and it issues a check on its own account. Banks, money order companies, and the post office also issue money orders, payable to specific people. Keep all receipts. They're your only proof of payment. File them as if they were canceled checks.

If you have a checking or savings account that you haven't touched for a while, check into its status. Some banks stop paying interest on quiescent accounts. Some even start charging fees. You can usually return to claim an old account, but you won't receive any interest for the years it lay dormant or get back the fees that you were charged.

If your bank accounts lie untouched for three to seven years (and sometimes longer, depending on your state), the money will be turned over to the state treasury (page 28). Ditto for property in safe-deposit boxes, certificates of deposit, even property held by the bank in trust. The bank, saving and loan (S&L), or credit union first has to try to reach you by writing to your last known address and putting a notice in a local newspaper. The state may have to advertise too. If you don't show up, the money goes. You (or your heirs) can get it back by going to the state with proof of ownership. But only a few states pay interest on the accounts they've held.

If you owe the bank money and haven't paid, it can generally dip into your other accounts—savings; checking; sometimes even a trust account, depending on the trust document—to satisfy the debt. Some states put modest limits on which accounts can be seized for what. Federal law prevents banks from taking money to satisfy a disputed credit card bill. But otherwise you are at risk for your own unpaid loans and any loans that you cosigned.

Balancing Your Checkbook

Good news: you don't have to. The Rockies won't crumble, Gibraltar won't tumble, if you take the bank's word that your balance is right. It's important that your written check register comes close enough, so you don't overdraw or fall below the minimum balance the bank requires. But what's a $1.26 discrepancy among friends? If you're allergic to arithmetic, bank online, where you always have an automatic running tally of your balance. If you're still in the pencil-and-paper age, here's the minimum you can get away with:

■ *Enter every deposit and withdrawal on your check register as you go along,* not forgetting your dealings with ATMs, direct deposits such as paychecks, bills paid automatically through electronic transfers, and money withdrawn when you paid for something with a debit card. (For more on debit cards, see page 276.)

■ *When the statement comes in, check every deposit and withdrawal against your check register* to be sure there aren't any errors or alterations. If you wait a year or more to report a mistake, the bank might not make good.

■ *Note each check that was cashed.*

■ *If you have an interest-paying checking account, add the interest the bank paid that month to your checkbook balance.* Then subtract all the fees. (These items show on your monthly statement.)

Assuming that nothing feels wildly out of line, it's okay to leave it at that—even if your bottom line is a little different from the total the bank reports. I don't always trust a bank to enter checks correctly, but I do trust its addition. (My own addition isn't so hot.)

Every six months or so, purge your math errors. Take the current balance as reported by your bank, add all new deposits, subtract all uncashed checks, enter the result as the new balance in your checkbook, and start over. If the error seems large, take your checkbook to the bank and ask for help.

Mind you, I don't recommend that you leave your checkbook a mess. But getting it in perfect balance isn't the Oscar of good financial planning.

Automated Teller Machines

The ATM is McBanking at its easiest. You insert a card and punch a few buttons. Instantly, you're in touch with your bank account to confirm your checking account balance, withdraw or deposit funds, or, at some machines, switch money from one account to another. Banks hook up their ATMs to national and international networks, so funds are available when you're out of town or traveling abroad. I've given up traveler's checks; I travel with only cash and an ATM card.

Most banks don't charge you for using their own ATMs. If you reach your account through another bank's ATM, that bank will claim a fee—usually in the $1.50 range. The ATMs in retail stores may cost $2 or $2.50. Abroad, you'll be charged up to 3 percent. Deposits are usually free (but not always). You'll probably be charged even if all you want is to check the balance in your account or get a cash advance on a credit card.

If the Big Attraction of ATMs is Convenience, the Big Risk is Crime. When you slip your card into an outdoor ATM, you're a sitting duck for a cruising crook. He knows that you've just picked up some cash. If he has the time, he might force you at knifepoint to tap your account for even more. Then he might steal your car and drive away.

ATM crime is growing, although no one knows by exactly how much. Banks don't like to report it for fear of scaring you away. Also, full disclosure of the risks of using ATMs might give victimized customers stronger grounds for suing the banks to recover their losses. So the bankers keep mum.

Under the Electronic Fund Transfer Act, your bank has to reimburse you for all but $50 of an unauthorized withdrawal, provided that you report the loss immediately. So you're covered if a thief swipes your card and drains your account. You are also covered if you're persuaded by a gun in your back to empty out your account. Some institutions have tried to avoid paying customers in this situation, but the law says that you're owed.

It is not at all clear, however, that the bank has any liability for your losses if you're knocked on the head as you're leaving the machine. Customers have sued their banks, but most of the cases are settled out of court. In at least one case, a bank argued successfully that the customer was himself negligent for using a poorly lighted ATM at night. Here's how to play it safe with an ATM:

- *Don't use ATMs at night, even if they are located on bank property.* A survey by the Bank Administration Institute discovered that most ATM crimes take place in the evening between seven and midnight, on bank premises.
- *Don't use ATMs in isolated areas at any time.*
- *Don't use ATMs that are badly lit or readily accessible to a quick-hit thief in an automobile.*
- *Don't be the only person at an ATM.*
- *Don't use ATMs that are hidden by shrubbery.*
- *Don't use a drive-up ATM without first locking your car doors.*
- *Don't use ATMs that lack a permanent surveillance camera that could identify an assailant.* (During a Florida lawsuit, it was discovered that although a sign at an ATM said the machine was under surveillance, no camera existed.)
- *Don't write your personal identification number (PIN) on your ATM card.* The PIN tells the bank machine that you're really you. If your card is lost, that number is an open door into your account.
- *Don't give your PIN to a stranger.* If the stranger claims to be a cop or banker, he's lying. No one but a crook would ask.

What about relatives and friends? If you give them your PIN so they can use your account and they take more money than they should, you have to swallow it. The bank won't pay. Ditto if your daughter finds your PIN and writes herself electronic checks. Change your PIN if you want to rescind someone's access to your account.

For Fast, Fast, Fast Relief

When you have to get money to someone in a hurry, a check might serve if it's delivered fast. Use a commercial overnight delivery service or the post office's Express Mail. If the recipient has nowhere to cash the check or doesn't have time to wait for the check to clear, use one of the following quick-delivery systems:

1. An ATM card. If the recipient has a card, you can put money into his or her U.S. bank account. It can be withdrawn at a cash machine, here or abroad. Abroad, you'll get the wholesale rate on your currency exchange.

2. Postal money orders sent by Express Mail. You can count on rapid delivery only within the United States. International money orders are governed by country-to-country agreements and may take four to six weeks to arrive.

3. Western Union. Call 800-325-6000 or go online at www.westernunion.com. By phone, you can charge up to $10,000 on your Visa, MasterCard, Discover Card, or debit card. Online, the limit is $999.99 to $2,999.99, with Visa, MasterCard, or your debit card. Or take cash (sometimes a cashier's check is okay) to a local Western Union agent. Some agents, and the 800 service, are available 24 hours a day, 7 days a week. Cash can be transferred within the United States, to Puerto Rico, and to more than 190 foreign countries in 15 minutes or less. Funds wired elsewhere usually take at least 2 business days because delivery goes through local banks. The recipient can pick up the money at any Western Union agency. For the address of the closest one, ask the local agent or the 800 operator.

4. MoneyGram. It will transfer cash to more than 170 countries, for pickup within 10 minutes. To find a nearby location, go to www.moneygram.com or call 800-MONEYGRAM (for Spanish, call 800-955-7777). You can also send money through an online account. The limit is $500, charged to your Visa or MasterCard, or $899.99 if you're debiting your bank account.

5. The U.S. State Department. It's the agency of choice if your son was robbed in Bangladesh. In an emergency it will send cash within 24 hours to any American embassy or consulate for a fee of $30 per check. All you have to do is get the money to the State Department, using Western Union, bank wire, overnight mail, or regular mail. For details, call Overseas Citizens Services at 888-407-4747.

6. Your bank, for big-money transfers within the United States. It can wire money to another bank for pickup the same day or one day later. But mistrust banks for international transfers. Unless the foreign bank pays a lot of attention, a transfer that ought to take a day can take a month.

Ask what identification the recipient will need in order to pick up the money. Usually two proofs are required, such as a passport and a driver's license. Sometimes he or she will also need a code word or authorization number that you furnish.

Slowly, banks are looking into quick-money transfers for smaller amounts. Ask if you can get a check delivered overnight. If you're sending money to another of the bank's customers, ask if you can make an instant transfer from your account.

To Get Extra Money When You're Out of Town. If you run short of cash or traveler's checks or your wallet is stolen, there are several ways to rescue yourself:

1. **Get someone at home to send you money,** using one of the techniques just described.

2. **If you know your Visa or MasterCard number,** call Western Union at 800-325-6000, charge your card for up to $2,000, and send money to yourself.

3. **If at least one of your cards wasn't stolen** (just in case, travelers with two cards should keep them in two different places), you have some choices. Your ATM card will plug into one of the national (and international) ATM networks. You can generally withdraw $200 to $600 a day from your account at home. You might also be able to get a cash advance against your credit card or overdraft checking. Transaction fee: usually $20 to $30. Many ATM webs have toll-free numbers that you can call to find cash machines wherever you go.

The leading credit cards, such as Visa, MasterCard, and the various cards from American Express (Blue, SkyPoints, and so on), offer loans against their lines of credit through ATMs or banks—domestic and foreign—affiliated with the card's sponsor. You pay the cash-advance interest rate plus fees. Amex's charge cards work through the company's Express Cash service. If you have a green card, you can use an ATM to tap your bank account for up to $1,000 a week. Gold card holders can get up to $2,500 a week; platinums, up to $10,000 a month. Fee: 3 percent, with a $5 minimum. (The ATM owner will probably charge you something too.)

4. **Take some checks when you travel.** Many stores, hotels, and restaurants accept personal checks from tourists. American Express holders can cash personal checks (up to certain limits) at any Amex office, as well as at some hotels and airlines.

Which Savings Account?

For savings, choose an online bank. They're paying top interest rates on accounts opened with as little as $1 and charging no monthly fees. You reach your savings by debit card or by transferring money to a checking account, either at the online bank or at your current account at a traditional bank. The banks vary the rate, depending on market conditions. At this writing, the high-paying banks with no fees and no minimum-deposit requirements include EmigrantDirect,

HSBC Direct, and ING Direct (see p. 46). Some traditional banks such as Citibank may also offer online savings at high rates. Online banks also offer high-rate certificates of deposit.

At most traditional banks, however, your options aren't as good. The savings accounts are generally of two types:

Regular Savings, for Small Accounts. You need minimum deposits in the $200 to $500 range. Interest rates are low. You're charged fees for falling below the minimum, and they may exceed the interest you earn. Some charge no fees as long as your account stays above the minimum, but you'll earn a barely visible interest rate. There might be free accounts for kids.

Money Market Deposit Accounts. They pay higher rates on minimum deposits of around $1,500 and up. Rates rise if you keep more money there, but they're still not competitive with the online accounts. You get unlimited deposits and withdrawals, although each withdrawal might have to exceed a certain minimum amount. These accounts can also be used to pay a few bills. You're allowed up to six preauthorized transactions a month, three of which can be checks to third parties (the others can be automatic bill paying or checks written to yourself). You'll be charged monthly fees if your deposit falls below the minimum. Your account is FDIC insured.

Savers tend to use money market deposit accounts because they're there. But a smarter buy is often a money market mutual fund (page 220). Mutual funds pay around 0.5 percentage point more than bank accounts when interest rates are low and as much as 3 percentage points more when rates are high. At this writing, they're competitive with the savings accounts online. One risk: mutual funds are *not* federally insured. (For more on money-fund risk, see page 220.)

Certificates of Deposit. You commit your money for anywhere from 6 months to 10 years. Some institutions set fixed terms, such as 1 or 2 years; others let you pick the exact number of days, weeks, or months you want. Normally, the longer the term, the higher the interest rate. For CDs too, online accounts tend to beat those at traditional banks.

You normally pay a penalty (of 1 to 6 months' interest, and sometimes more) for withdrawing funds before the term is up. But don't let that scare you out of choosing a CD. If you're forced to break it before maturity and pay the penalty, so be it. That won't be the first bit of money you've frittered away. The chances are, however, that you'll keep your CD for the full term and earn more interest than you'd have gotten from a regular savings account.

High-Yield CDs. Some traditional banks offer higher yields than you'll find even at Internet banks. You can locate them through Bankrate.com (look for the "100 Highest Yields" page). Typically, they require minimum deposits of $1,000 and up. There's no need to worry about the safety of high-yielding institutions. As long as they're covered by the FDIC, you won't lose any money.

To make a long-distance deposit in a high-rate bank or S&L, call the institution that interests you and ask for the deposit forms. Or get the forms online. You can mail the bank a check or transfer money directly from your present bank.

Broker-Sold CDs. The major stockbrokerage houses sell CDs, not at top rates but at rates above average. The bank pays the sales commission, not you. The minimum investment is generally $1,000. One hitch: a broker-sold CD can't be cashed in before maturity, which could be as long as 20 years. If you need the money early, the broker will put it up for sale and try to get you a reasonable price.

Which Type of Savings to Choose? Pick money market or regular savings account for cash you might need at any moment. Pick a CD for cash you have to keep safe but won't need immediately, such as your daughter's tuition for next year or money you're saving for a new house.

Yield Shoppers Beware: Advertised high yields are sometimes good for only 30 or 60 days, after which they drop. For a reality check, always compare the annual percentage yield (APY) with those of competing CDs.

Truth in Savings

By federal law, banking institutions all have to figure their interest rate yields in a standard way. That's disclosed in an annual percentage yield. Always use APY to compare two interest-paying bank accounts. No matter what else the advertisement may say or how often your deposit compounds, the bank with the higher APY is paying more on your checking account or savings deposit.

Laddered CDs

You can earn the highest possible interest on CDs, without surrendering easy access to your money, by using a simple strategy called "laddering." Here's how it works, assuming an initial pot of savings of $6,000:

You start out by splitting that money among bank deposits of varying maturities: $1,000 into a money market account, for cash on hand; then $1,000 each into 1-, 2-, 3-, 4-, and 5-year CDs (or different maturities, depending on what you find). Normally, the longer the maturity, the higher the interest rate.

One year later, your first CD will mature, paying $1,000 plus interest. If you don't need the cash, reinvest it in a new 5-year CD, which pays a higher interest rate. You can risk putting money away that long because in another year your next CD will mature—once again, giving you cash on hand. If you still don't need the money, it too goes into a new 5-year CD.

If you do this each time a CD matures, all your money will soon be earning 5-year interest rates. Yet a $1,000 certificate will come due every 12 months, providing ready cash if you need it. Result: you will earn much more on your money without having to tie it all up for 5 years at a throw. You could stretch out this ladder by using 1-, 3-, 5-, 7-, and 9-year CDs.

Some mutual fund companies offer a fund that ladders CDs for you.

Designer CDs

Hungry bankers and brokers respond to every fresh scent on the wind. Show them a new market, a new worry, a change in the economic outlook, and they will design a certificate of deposit to match. Not all banks offer exotic CDs. Those that do may call them by different names than I have used. But if these ideas interest you, watch for them in the newspaper, TV, and online ads, in bank windows, or in communications from your broker. The better the deal, the larger the minimum deposit the institution may want. Always compare the annual percentage yield with those being offered by standard CDs of the same term. Sometimes the designer CDs pay less. Also, check the maturity date. Some investments that look like 1-year CDs actually lock up your money for 15 or 20 years.

Liquid CD: if you think you might need some of the money before maturity. You're charged no penalty for early withdrawal of some or all of your funds.

Bump-Up CD: if you expect interest rates to rise. If that indeed happens, the bank will—at your direction—raise the rate you are earning on your CD once or twice during its term.

Step-Up CD: also for people who expect higher rates. This CD pays less now but guarantees higher rates in the future. It's especially important to compare a step-up's APY with those for fixed-rate CDs of the same term. Step-ups offer dazzlingly high yields in, say, their final 3 months. But on average, they may pay less than a plain-vanilla CD.

Variable-Rate CD: again, for people who expect higher rates. Your interest rate rises and falls with the general level of rates. Buy it only if there's a guaranteed floor below which the interest rate cannot go. The rates on some variable CDs rise and fall on a preset schedule, over time.

Market-Linked CD: This is a complex investment product, not a bank product. Beware its many risks.

Bitter-End CD: if you know you can last for the full term. You get a bonus for keeping your money in the CD for a full 5 years.

Zero-Coupon CD: if you want to make a gift of money look extra good. You put down a small sum now, at a guaranteed interest rate. It will grow to equal the CD's larger face value in a given number of years. Each year's increase in value is taxable, even though you get no cash payout. So zeros are best kept in a tax-deferred retirement account. Always ask for the annual percentage yield and compare it with those of regular CDs of the same maturity. Some institutions clip you a little on their zeros.

Jumbo CD: if you (or a group of investors) have more than $100,000 or $250,000. Banks pay higher interest rates on large amounts of money. But choose a safe institution. If your bank fails and the government can't find a buyer for it, your deposits over $250,000 may not be fully reimbursed.

Tax-Deferral CD: if you're chiefly interested in deferring your tax. This 12-month CD is bought at a discount in the current calendar year, to mature next year. No interest is paid until the CD matures, which puts all of your income into the next tax year.

Callable CD: Beware this broker-sold CD. It pays a slightly higher interest rate than a regular CD of the same term, but if interest rates go down the bank can redeem it, leaving you to buy a new CD at a lower rate. If rates rise, the bank will not redeem the CD. The broker will sell it for you if you want to cash in, but probably for less than you originally invested. These CDs may not mature for 15 or 20 years. The broker might offer you a "1-year noncallable," but that's not a 1-year CD. It's a 10- or 15-year CD with one year of call protection, meaning only that the issuer can't take it away from you in the first year.

Absolutely Not CDs

Are you looking for higher interest rates than CDs will pay? Some banks sell an instrument called a *subordinated debt note, lobby note, retail debenture,* or similar term. When you buy it, you are lending money to the institution, unsecured. Lobby notes don't carry federal deposit insurance. If the institution goes broke, your investment will probably be worthless.

Banks that peddle these notes may not be in the greatest financial shape. Not only are you shafted if the institution fails, you are also shafted if it succeeds. The fine print in a lobby note usually allows the bank to redeem it before the full term is up. So you might lose the high interest income you expected.

Other financial institutions also offer high-rate notes—for example, the Demand Notes sold by GMAC Financial Services or the Interest Advantage notes from Ford Motor Credit Company. Like bank notes, they're backed only by the company itself. You gotta have faith.

When Your CD Matures

When you open a CD, ask the bank what happens when the certificate matures. What instructions does it need regarding what should be done with the CD's proceeds, and how soon does it need them? Can you give instructions now? All this information will be in your CD contract but it's important that you understand it exactly.

Each institution handles things a little differently. Normally, there's a short grace period after maturity—maybe 7 to 10 days but sometimes as little as 1 day—during which the bank waits to hear from you. Do you want the money invested in another CD or moved to another account? Interest may or may not be paid while you're making up your mind. If the grace period expires and you haven't told the bank what to do, your money will probably be reinvested in another CD of the same term. If you then decide that you want the cash, you might be able to break the CD without penalty. On the other hand, you might not.

Banking institutions have to notify you shortly before your CD matures. But keep track of the payment date yourself, just in case there's a slipup. Don't leave your decision to the last minute. The bank might want written instructions, and you'll have to allow enough time for them to arrive.

Other Bank Products

Banks also sell mutual funds and tax-deferred annuities. They note when your CDs are coming due and call you with a sales pitch. You might visit with someone you think is a banker and never learn that he or she is actually a broker angling to sell you a product and earn a commission. Your friendly teller might have to refer you to these brokers in order to keep his or her job. The tellers earn commissions or bonuses too.

At some banks you will get a full and fair explanation of annuities and mutual funds. But don't count on it. All too often, the operation reeks of deceptive sales tactics. How bad are they? *American Banker,* an industry trade paper, once sent reporters posing as mutual fund customers into ten banks. Reps at eight of those banks "forgot" to mention that mutual funds aren't federally insured; only a few of them disclosed fees; most downplayed the investment risk; some illegally forecast specific (and double-digit) gains; and one even suggested that mutual funds were like CDs but with higher yields.

Similar surveys using "mystery shoppers" keep turning up similar results. Some customers don't realize they've bought mutual funds or annuities, don't understand the risks, and find out too late that there's a stiff penalty for withdrawing money before several years have passed. In one case I'm familiar with, a 92-year-old man was sold an annuity with withdrawal fees lasting until he was 99. He thought he was buying a high-rate CD.

According to federal guidelines, banks are supposed to:

- Tell you that mutual funds and annuities aren't backed by the bank or by federal deposit insurance.
- Tell you that the performance of mutual funds and annuities isn't guaranteed.
- Tell you that your interest and principal may be at risk.
- Sell in an area clearly separate from the rest of the bank, with no FDIC signs anywhere near.
- Sell you investments appropriate to your age and financial circumstances.

Industry guidelines add that all sales commissions, surrender charges, and other fees should be fully disclosed.

Should you invest with banks? To help you decide, see chapter 22 (mutual funds) and page 1072 (fixed-rate tax-deferred annuities).

Test Your Banker's IQ, Again

1. Ask: How often does interest compound? Compounding means that the bank adds the interest you earn to your account and then pays interest on the combined interest and principal. The more often your interest is compounded, the more money you make. Daily or continuous compounding (they're just about the same) yields the most, followed by quarterly compounding, then semiannual, then annual. With "simple" interest, there is no compounding at all. What difference does it make? Plenty. At 6 percent interest, compounded daily, your savings are worth 14 percent more after 10 years than if you had earned only simple interest. Compounding is included in the annual percentage yield. At equal rates of interest, an account that compounds daily or continuously will have a higher APY than one that compounds any other way.

2. Ask: How often is interest credited to your account? Most banks that compound interest daily do not actually give you the money until the end of the month or the end of the quarter. So then ask: What happens to that last bit of interest if I close my account before the end of the period? Normally, you will lose it even though the bank claims that it's paying you right to the day of withdrawal.

3. Ask: What is the annual percentage yield on your savings? This yield takes all kinds of mathematical quirks into consideration, not only interest rate and frequency of compounding but also such technical details as how many days the bank counts as a year. (Some banks use 366 days, others use 365, still others 360. For reasons only Computerman would believe, 360 yields more interest.) The higher the APY, the better the deal.

Table 1.

COMPOUND INTEREST: THE MAGIC MONEY MACHINE

A $10,000 Deposit at 5 Percent After

Compounding Method	1 Year	5 Years	10 Years
Daily	$10,513	$12,840	$16,487
Monthly	10,512	12,834	16,470
Quarterly	10,509	12,820	16,436
Semiannually	10,506	12,801	16,386
Annually	10,500	12,763	16,289
Simple interest	10,500	12,500	15,000

Source: RSM McGladrey.

4. Ask: What is the periodic payment rate? That's the rate the bank applies during each compounding period when figuring how much interest you have earned. Knowing it, you can check the bank's calculations to see if it paid you properly (that is, if you're into decimals). Mistakes are not uncommon. A good bank will give you its periodic payment rate and show you how to use it.

Fixing Bank Mistakes

Cash

How many times have you cashed a check in a hurry, then walked away without counting the money? Maybe you think the teller is always right. Maybe you are intimidated by the line of grumpy people behind you. But if you count the money at the bank door and find that you're $20 short, you might be stuck. Tellers aren't allowed to hand over extra money on a customer's say-so. After all, you could have slipped the missing $20 into your pocket before you went back to the teller's window.

Rule 1. Count your money before leaving the window. If you discover an error later, give your name, address, and account number to the manager. If the teller winds up the day with the right amount of extra cash, you'll be reimbursed.

Deposits

Tellers sometimes err when crediting deposits—for example, entering $100 when you actually put in $1,000.

Rule 2. Double-check every transaction for accuracy before leaving the window. If you mail deposits, check your paper or online statement. What if the teller credits $1,000 to your account when you gave him or her only $100? Don't spend the money. The mistake will be found, and in banking, there's no finders keepers.

Automated Teller Machines

ATMs goof, just as people do. They shortchange the occasional customer, giving you $80 when you asked for $100. Sometimes they accept cash and checks without crediting them to your account.

Rule 3. Never deposit cash in an ATM. It's impossible to prove how much you put into the envelope, so losses are sometimes hard to recover. Checks are easier to find or replace.

Rule 4. Report mistakes right away. Some banks install telephones next to their ATMs for that purpose, although they may be answered only during banking hours. When you call, leave your name, address, account number, the amount of the loss, and the location of the ATM; then put the same information into a letter. You will have to wait until the accounts are balanced, but if the machine is over by the sum that you reported, you will get your money. At the bank's own ATM machines, the error might be fixed at the end of the day. But it will take an extra day or two (and sometimes weeks) if you used an ATM at another bank.

Deposit Slips

It always astonishes me to see the trash baskets near ATMs overflowing with deposit receipts. If the deposit is entered wrong, would those customers know it? (I don't remember the exact amounts of the various checks I get.) With-drawal slips are also dumped—by people who aren't balancing their checkbooks, I guess. But what if there's an error?

Rule 5. Keep all deposit and withdrawal slips until your bank statement comes in to be sure the transactions were entered correctly.

Certificates of Deposit

Your bank might automatically renew your CD when it expires even though you told it not to.

Rule 6. Keep a copy of the instructions you gave when you opened the CD and mark the due date on your calendar. If an error is made, hustle to correct it. Too long a wait may cost you your chance to get your money out.

Federal Deposit Insurance

If your bank fails, it will pay right away—usually the next business day.

Don't believe investment advisers who try to steer you away from banks with the claim that, if the bank closes, you'll have to wait 99 years for your money. And don't waste your time searching through subclauses, thinking you'll find a loophole in your coverage. The federal government will restore 100 percent of your insured account, and fast. This applies to all insured institutions—banks, credit unions, and savings and loans.

During the 2008 credit crunch, Congress raised the deposit insurance ceiling to $250,000 from $100,000, which covers almost everyone. At this writing, it's scheduled to return to $100,000 in 2014, but who knows? Maybe Congress will decide to keep the higher amount.

You can find the current insurance limit at www.fdic.gov/deposit/index.html.

Your deposits are entirely safe up to that amount—and more, depending on how the accounts are held. Safe in a failing bank. Safe in a bank that pays cockeyed interest rates. Safe even with a crook or incompetent at the institution's helm. So don't worry, be happy, and collect the highest interest rates you can find.

To estimate how much insurance you have on multiple accounts in the same institution, use the FDIC's easy calculator at www2.fdic.gov/edie/index.html. You get the full amount of coverage on *each* of the following accounts or groups of accounts:

1. All the accounts in your name alone, added together, including any accounts in the name of a business you own as sole proprietor.

2. Each account that you hold jointly with different people. The FDIC splits joint money evenly among the account holders. Then it adds up each holder's money to see how much is insured. As an example, say that the ceiling is $250,000 and that you own three joint accounts—one with your spouse for $350,000, and an $80,000 account with each of your two adult children. For the first account, the FDIC assigns $175,000 of coverage to you and $175,000 to your spouse. You're also assigned half ($40,000) of each of the two $80,000 accounts, leaving each child the other half. Your spouse's and children's money falls under the $250,000 umbrella, so their shares would be fully insured. But your share totals $255,000. That leaves $5,000 uninsured.

The FDIC lumps together all accounts held jointly by the same people, such as a checking and savings account owned by a married couple, and gives you each the maximum coverage. When the insured ceiling is $250,000, joint accounts are covered up to $500,000.

Some couples try for double coverage by shuffling the names on the accounts—listing one as husband/wife (with the husband's Social Security number) and the other as wife/husband (with the wife's Social Security number). Nice try, but it doesn't work.

You may *not* have joint coverage if you put a small child's name on a checking or savings account. A child under 18 cannot legally make withdrawals, so he or she isn't a true co-owner. If the FDIC discovers that the child is a minor, all the money in the account will be assigned to you.

3. Each "in trust for" account or "payable on death" account held for a member of your immediate family—child, spouse, grandchild, siblings, and parents. These are the accounts to use for minor children, among others. There can be multiple owners and multiple beneficiaries, each with his or her own FDIC coverage. For example, say that the ceiling is $250,000 and you and your spouse open an account in trust for each of your three children. You're insured for up to $1,500,000: $250,000 for each beneficiary of each account owner.

4. Your bank deposits in retirement plans containing investments that you control—including Individual Retirement Accounts, Simplified Employee Pensions, Keoghs, and individual 401(k) plans. If you have several self-directed plans in the bank, these deposits are lumped together as if they were a single account and insured up to $250,000.* (Note that the FDIC covers only deposits, not other bank products in retirement plans, such as annuities and mutual funds.)

5. Your share of retirement plan deposits that are managed by your company—say, a traditional pension plan or a company-run 401(k). Each person's interest in the fund is normally insured for up to $250,000, assuming that the bank meets certain capital requirements for safety and soundness. If it doesn't, the FDIC insures the fund as a whole for $250,000. That gives each participant much less protection, but so far this harsh provision of the law has been applied only once.

It takes a bit longer than usual for retirement plans to recover insured deposits after a bank failure. The FDIC has to get the plan's records to determine how much of each account is covered. But you will always get up to $250,000 back. The same would be true of your share in a jumbo CD purchased through a stockbroker.

6. Living trusts, including in-trust-for accounts, held at a single institution. If your combined living-trust deposits are worth up to $1.25 million and you have five or fewer named beneficiaries, each is insurable for up to $250,000. This covers the vast majority of depositors. If your combined living-trust deposits are worth more than $1.25 million, with more than five named beneficiaries, the deposit is insured for at least $1.25 million and perhaps more. The calculation is complicated, so use the FDIC's calculator at www2.fdic.gov/edie. At this writing, the maximum insurance for living trusts is also scheduled to return to $100,000 per beneficiary in 2014, but that may change.

7. Irrevocable trusts, established for the same beneficiary by the same grantor. They're added together and covered up to the full amount. The bank's records have to identify each beneficiary's interest, so talk to the bank about what it needs.

8. Each account owned by a partnership, corporation, or unincorporated association, such as a union, home owner's association, or fraternal organization. These funds are insured separately from the funds of the principals or the members.

---

*That's a permanent ceiling. It is not scheduled to revert to $100,000 in 2014.

To find a sound bank, check the free Safe & Sound ratings at Bankrate.com. Banks are rated from five stars (best) to one star (weakest). There are problems with these ratings. They cover only the most recent quarter for which Bankrate has data. The situation might have deteriorated since. And crooked institutions dress up their financial statements so that they'll look better than they really are. Still, you can't hide all traces of a skunk in a rose garden. If you have any doubts about your bank, check the ratings for several quarters to see if they change.

If your institution fails, it's a nuisance but not a disaster, provided that you're covered by federal deposit insurance. The FDIC has several options for moving your money, safely, out of an insolvent bank. Here are the three most common ways:

The First Way: The dead institution is sold to or merged with a live one. Both insured and uninsured deposits are transferred to the new institution intact, giving you immediate access to all your funds. Your old branch continues to operate, but under a new name. Outstanding checks clear as usual, but the interest rates on your old account aren't guaranteed. High-rate CDs may be knocked down to a lower rate immediately. If you don't like the new terms, you can close your accounts and cash in your CDs without penalty.

The Second Way: No one wants to buy the dead institution, but another bank takes the insured deposits. They're transferred immediately. So are the insured portions of multiple accounts, such as retirement accounts held in a single name. Your old branch reopens as a branch of the new institution. Checks clear as usual, but the interest on high-rate CDs may be reduced. Dissenters can move their accounts to another institution without penalty. If your bank fails on a Friday night (the usual situation), your insured deposits should be available the following Monday.

The Third Way: No one wants any part of the dead bank. The institution fails and stops paying interest. Checks no longer clear. Typically, the bank closes on a Friday and opens on Monday to pay off the insured depositors. If you go in person, you may be able to pick up your money right away. Otherwise, the FDIC will start mailing out payments within a day or two. The majority of accounts should clear in the first week. Almost all of them clear within four weeks.

A few accounts, however, will face delays. If the institution's records are bad, you might have to prove what your account was worth. Company retirement accounts may need sorting out. If you bought a share of a jumbo CD through a stockbroker, the broker has to show who the CD's owners are.

What Happens to Uninsured Deposits? They stop earning interest and become a claim against the failed bank. There's no telling how much you'll recover. The bank's assets have to be sold, with the proceeds parceled out pro rata among the uninsured depositors. Whatever you recover will mostly be paid in the first year, although additional payments may dribble in over the next several years.

Customers should take four precautions: (1) Check each statement to be sure that the bank has entered all your deposits correctly. (2) Keep copies of pertinent correspondence with the institution and your most recent statements. (3) Deposit less than the insured amount in each covered account so that, even with the interest received, you will never exceed the ceiling. (4) Ask your bank whether your deposit meets all of the technical qualifications for FDIC coverage.

For additional information on deposit insurance, call 877-ASK-FDIC; look online at www.fdic.gov/deposit; or write to the FDIC's Division of Supervision and Consumer Protection, Deposit Insurance Outreach, 550 Seventeenth Street NW, Washington, DC 20429.

Never Rely on State or Private Deposit Insurance. This includes the private insurance carried by some credit unions. If just one institution collapses, customers often make a run on other institutions that the fund insures, even the sound ones. That may force them to close too. The only safe bet is Uncle Sam.

What Happens to Your Loans When Your Bank, S&L, or Credit Union Goes Bust? You keep making the payments to whoever takes over the loan portfolio. In almost all cases, no one can force you to refinance on different terms as long as your payments are up to date. For anyone behind on a loan, the jig is up. Bad loans often go to the FDIC's Deposit Insurance Fund, which will want a settlement or else.

What Happens to an Unused Credit Line? It may be sold to a new institution as is. If no institution buys the credit line, however, it will be terminated.

What's the Smartest Way of Setting Up Bank Accounts?

Use a convenient bank for your checking account, with acceptable minimum deposits and interest rates and well-located ATMs. Keep enough money there to lower the service fees you're charged. But for savings deposits, choose an online account or buy a CD by mail from one of the nation's high-rate institutions. The extra percentage point you will earn is worth the stamp.

Do You Need a Traditional Bank at All?

That's a question worth asking in this Internet age. Direct online banks offer attractive, high-interest savings and checking accounts. Mortgages can be had online or from any traditional financial institution. Ditto home equity loans, student loans, auto loans, and credit cards. If you handle all of your banking business online or by mail or phone, you're a cybercustomer already. It's a pain to switch accounts to a new bank. But if you're opening your first account or moving to a new bank in a different town, consider the purely online option. It's simple and lower cost.

Poolers, Splitters, and Keepers

Who Should Own the Property—Me? You? Us? Them?

**To the question of who should own the property in your
household, no answer is right. But then again, no answer
is wrong. Who ever said this was going to be easy?**

Get out your yellow pad again and some more pencils. Write down all the serious property and assets you have: house, bank accounts, cars, mutual funds,
stocks, bonds, beach house, other real estate, insurance policies, gold coins,
whatever. Who owns each asset? Whose name is on the deed, title, account, or
purchase order? Whose money bought it? Is it yours alone or is it held jointly? Is
that okay, or should it be owned in some other way? You can keep the property
or share it. You can give it away. With a trust, you can give it away and still keep
it. (Like the economics of the oldest profession in the world: "You got it, you sell
it, you still got it.")

Federal estate taxes used to have a bearing on who owned what, but now
they matter only if you have a superhigh net worth (page 1190). For everyone
else, ownership depends on personality and circumstance. Almost every choice
has its good and bad points.

One for the Money

Whether you've never married (or partnered) or were formerly married, your
singleness defines the rules. You are a *keeper* because you can own everything
yourself, no fuss, no muss. All you need is a reliable friend or relative to hold
your durable (or springing) power of attorney (page 125) and your health care

proxy (page 126). That person could write checks on your bank account, manage your investments, and deal with your doctors if you were incapable (say, in a coma after an auto accident, God forbid).

That's when you're young. When you age, you may not be quite so independent and might wonder if sharing ownership could solve some problems. For example, you might think about giving half your house to your son and his family if they will live there with you. Or you might put your niece's name on your bank account if she helps you do your taxes and pay your bills. If your son is a good egg and your niece is a doll, co-ownership can work.

But what if your son gets a new job and moves? The house might have to be sold to give him the money to buy a new one. What if he gets divorced? His half of your house might have to be divided with his ex-wife. What if your nice niece nicks a bit of your money? A co-owner of a bank account can take every penny unless you specifically require both signatures for withdrawal, which, for daily bills, gets tiresome. You can sue a co-owner for withdrawing more than he or she deposited—but the last thing you want late in life is to get tangled up in lawsuits with your relatives.

You can escape from a co-owned bank account that you've come to regret just by taking out your money. But it's a lot harder to get back your house once you've given half of it away. With a house, you might also get into a fight over who should live there or how much to spend on repairs.

Then there's the fairness issue. A joint owner with the right of survivorship gets the property, regardless of what it says in your will or trust. Say, for example, that your will leaves everything equally to your daughter, Tammis, and son, David. Then you add David to your bank account. He gets every penny of it when you die. You have cut Tammis out. By naming a joint owner, you took your bank account out of your will, and Tammis won't be able to touch it. The same is true for anything else you put in joint names with a right of survivorship. The other owner or owners walk away with the prize.

There's a way around the bank account problem: both of you sign a notarized agreement that the joint ownership is for convenience only, not for inheritance (in many states, that's called a *convenience account*). But this might not work. If David keeps his mouth shut, the bank might give him the money anyway. Or his creditors might move in on the account. Why run the risk of having to start a lawsuit or stirring up trouble among your heirs? Give David a power of attorney to manage your affairs but hang on to the ownership yourself. Or open an *agency account* if your bank offers one. It lets you authorize someone else to write checks on your account without making that person a joint owner. For more on powers of attorney, see page 125.

As an alternative to co-ownership, consider a "pay on death" arrangement for your bank savings, investment accounts, and, in some states, real property deeds. With POD accounts, the property is yours for life but transfers to the named successor when you die.

Two for the Dough

A married couple is a pushme-pullyou, a two-headed animal with two minds of its own. You have to figure out how to pull together.

When You Both Have Paychecks

Poolers put all the money into a common pot. *Splitters* keep their own separate accounts. Which one you choose is a matter of soul, not finance. Poolers think that sharing, including financial sharing, is what a marriage is all about. Splitters hold to their own independence within the marriage. The previously married often split but sometimes pool. The first-time married often pool but sometimes split. Working couples might do either. It's so unpredictable that even your best friend might surprise you. Over time, and if the marriage goes well, splitters usually turn into *spoolers*—splitting some, pooling some, and growing less antsy about who pays for what.

The challenge for poolers is the checking account and the ATM/debit cards. How do you know how much you have in the bank when both of you draw from the same account at different times? To keep your finances organized, you can:

- *Pay all bills online, where each of you can see the balance all the time.* That's the easiest.
- *Write no checks away from the checkbook.* Use credit cards instead (you can earn points and miles), then pay bills by check or online at the end of the month.
- *Use checks backed by carbons, if you each want a checkbook.* Return all copies to the central checkbook. When you use the ATM, return the receipts to the central checkbook and enter your withdrawal.
- *Faithfully bring back every debit card receipt,* if you use the card to make purchases, and enter the withdrawal.
- *Walk around with two or three checks.* When you use one, enter it into the check register.
- *Keep a big balance in the checking account to prevent overdrafts.* Or sign up for overdraft protection (page 50).
- *Let just one of you handle the bills.* The other hangs on to two or three checks and reports whenever one is used. As in:

She: "Honey, I need more checks."

He: "How's that? You still have two."

She: "No, I'm out."

He: "What did you write the last two for?"

She: "Didn't I tell you?"

He: "No."

She: "Oh."

It's the only truly romantic system. Once a month you kiss and make up.

Poolers usually have some separate money, probably in retirement savings accounts. There is also something about an inheritance that often resists the impulse to share. But the house, the savings, and the investments are kept routinely in joint names, even if just one of you makes all the investment decisions.

The challenge for splitters lies in keeping track of who pays for what. As in:

She: "I bought the groceries for two weeks running."

He: "But I got your laundry and paid the sitter."

She: "But you already owed me two sitters from last month."

He: "Those sits were short, so they just count for one."

You never finally kiss and make up because you never figure it out.

For clarity, you can:

- *Keep three checking accounts: his, hers, and ours.* Each pays into the "ours" account for common household bills or for the children. You can contribute even or uneven amounts, depending on what each of you earns.
- *Where earnings are unequal, split expenses accordingly*—say, 60 percent him, 40 percent her. Apply these percentages to the income taxes too.
- *Split all expenses right down the middle,* even putting down two credit cards when you eat out. (No kidding. I know a couple that does this.)
- *Make a list of "his" and "her" household expenses* and take turns treating each other to dinners out.
- *Toss receipts for cash payments into a box and settle up when the box overflows.* Use the same box for "loans" you make to each other.
- *Write memos about property bought together, spelling out who owns what percent.* Each of you should sign. Your amount of ownership might be based on how much of the price you contributed. Or you could make the ownership 50–50.
- *When it comes to major financial decisions,* splitters should make them together. You are still a single financial unit, regardless of how you handle the money.

I've lived under both arrangements—pooling and splitting—and gave up splitting pretty fast. It's a financial nuisance in a settled relationship and creates small resentments that are a waste of a couple's time and love.

Then there's the Old Dispensation: the wife's paycheck is "hers" while the husband's is "ours." I hold with this arrangement only if the husband is well paid and the wife is truly earning peanuts. Otherwise they're in it together, and both should contribute.

If Only One of You Has a Paycheck

Splitting is Out. Pooling is In. Your basic contract is money-for-services, and everything tends to be jointly owned. If all the property is in just one name and you divorce, the courts are supposed to treat it as mutual marital money, although sometimes the homebody gets short shrift. If the husband keeps bank and investment accounts in his own name, the wife should have her own funds too. Fairness requires that some of the husband's assets be shifted into her name. (It reminds me of what my grandmother used to call "garter money": "Pin two dollars to your garter, dear, and if he reaches for it, take a taxi home.")

When Older People Remarry

Your friends will be enchanted, but don't be surprised if your children aren't. It's usually not the "pater" they worry about but the patrimony. If your new spouse gets your property after your death, he or she is free to cut your children out. Even if you own assets separately, state laws dictate that your surviving spouse should inherit one-half or one-third of them.

To prevent this, you need a prenuptial agreement (see page 146)—truly important for marriages later in life. You agree in advance not to inherit each other's property but to leave most or all of it to your respective children or other beneficiaries instead. To provide for each other, you might take out life insurance policies or make each other the beneficiary of policies you own already. Or you might agree that you each get the income from the other's property for life, with the children getting the principal after the death of the surviving spouse. A premarital agreement also settles your rights in case of divorce. One thing it cannot limit: any legal responsibility you have for each other's long-term care. That will depend on your state's Medicaid rules. Talk to lawyers about a prenup (you each should have your own). The lawyer will have some good ideas.

If You Owe an Estate Tax

You have a high-class problem. If you're married, you can lower that tax by using *bypass,* or *credit shelter, trusts* (page 122), one in each spouse's will (or in each spouse's living trust). To make bypass trusts work, however, husband and wife have to own property separately, as community property, or as tenants in common without right of survivorship. Again, see a lawyer. Bypass trusts can't be funded with property that is jointly owned.

Partners and Housemates

You are probably splitters. Each handles his or her personal expenses, and you work out a system for paying joint bills. A 50–50 split is fair only if your incomes are roughly equal. If one of you earns two-thirds of your combined income, that person should assume two-thirds of the rent and two-thirds of the grocery bills. Otherwise the one with the smaller paycheck is subsidizing the other. If there's going to be any subsidy at all, it should be from the richer to the poorer, not the other way around. If one of you leaves a job to keep house for the other, consider a written agreement for temporary support if the relationship fails. That gives the at-home partner a financial cushion during the months he or she is searching for a job again.

Longtime partners drift toward pooling some of their money, especially cash used for household expenses. But for property that is complicated to unwind, separate ownership is best.

If you buy a piece of real estate together, do it as *tenants in common* (page 86). Write an agreement for sharing expenses: how you'll divide the taxes, insurance, and mortgage payments. What happens if one person quits paying his or her share? If the relationship fails, how will you get your money out? Will you put the house on the market and divide the proceeds according to the percentage each person put up? Will one person buy the other out, and if so, which? How will you determine the price? If one of you dies, will his or her share be willed to the other, or would a written contract be a safer choice? (Remember that minds, and wills, can change.)

A lawyer should draw up these agreements (preferably two lawyers, one for each of you). You'll never think of all the contingencies yourself. You should also have the contractual right to force the sale of the house if you're having to shoulder more of the cost than you bargained for.

By all means consider a full *cohabitation agreement*—the prenup for unmarried couples. It spells out your obligations—or lack of them—to each other. What, exactly, does each of you own? What will each of you contribute to the partnership? If you split, how will you divide the assets and household goods? Is either of you entitled to ongoing support? After a split, a partner who quit working to take care of the home might be able to sue for palimony or for a share of your business if he or she contributed to its success. The only way to prevent such claims is for each of you to waive those options in writing. Look at the sample cohabitation agreement at FindLaw (www.findlaw.com). For a fuller discussion, get *Living Together: A Legal Guide for Unmarried Couples,* written by three attorneys, from Nolo publishers (www.nolo.com or 800-728-3555).

If your state lets you legalize your union—be it a marriage, civil union, or domestic partnership—you'll have virtually all the legal rights of a spouse. If you split or divorce, alimony is possible, and the property normally has to be divided roughly in half—again, unless your cohabitation agreement says otherwise.

Parents—married or not—are obligated to support their minor children, no matter what their written agreement says.

Four Ways to Own Property Together

Joint Ownership with Right of Survivorship

The owners (there can be more than two) hold the property together. If one dies, his or her share passes automatically to the other owner (or other owners), usually in equal parts. This form of ownership is for married couples, for any two people who live together and need a convenient household account, and for truly committed unmarried couples. It protects gay couples whose relatives might attack a will. Your contribution to the joint account can be attached by your creditors, but your partner's share can't.

To put something in joint ownership, you list it as such on the deed, title, or other ownership document, specifying "with right of survivorship." That's important. Otherwise it might be argued that you held the property only as tenants in common (see below).

Joint ownership isn't an inescapable trap. You can generally get out of it—although not always easily—even if the other owner objects. The ways of doing this vary, depending on your state's laws. When a jointly owned property is sold, the proceeds are normally divided equally. If you all agree, however, you can make an unequal division. (Gift taxes might be due if one owner gives the others part or all of his share.)

Tenancy in Common

This is a good way to own a beach house or snowblower with a friend. Married couples use this method when they want to leave their share of a co-owned property in trust. So do unmarried couples who can imagine an end to their relationship.

Each tenant in common has a share in the property, although not necessarily an equal share. You can sell or give away your share at any time. In the case of a house owned in common, for example, your partner could sell his piece to his brother, and suddenly you would have a new roommate. If the owners fall out, one might buy the other's share. Or one could file a partition lawsuit that might force the property to be sold.

You can pass your share of a co-owned property to anyone at death; it doesn't automatically go to the other owners. If you die without a will, your share of the property will be distributed to your relatives, according to state law. So write a will.

Tenancy by the Entirety

This arrangement, for married couples only, must be established in writing (a properly worded deed will do it) and is recognized by twenty states. It's similar to property owned jointly with the right of survivorship but gives each of the owners more protection. Neither of you can divide the property without the other's consent. In many cases, it's protected against one spouse's creditors (assuming that only one spouse signed the debt). If you divorce, it's automatically split 50–50.

Community Property

Nine states (Arizona, California, Idaho, Louisiana, Nevada, New Mexico, Texas, Washington, and Wisconsin) have community property rules for married couples. They declare that property acquired by either spouse, with money earned during the marriage, is owned by both, regardless of whose name is on it. This rule affects anyone who ever lived in a community property state. Even if you move away, your community property keeps its character. It is always 50 percent owned by each spouse (although, as a practical matter, this ownership right can be lost if you don't document it when you move to a non–community property state). The portion of a private pension earned during a marriage is usually community property, but Social Security isn't.

During life it is hard to dispose of your half of the community property without the other's consent. At death, things change. If your state lets you hold your half of the property with right of survivorship, it goes to your spouse. If not, you can generally leave it to whomever you want; it doesn't have to go to your spouse. Unlike jointly owned property, community property goes through probate (that is, unless you hold it in trust or use some other probate-avoiding mechanism allowed by your state). For more on probate, see page 129.

All the states have slightly different rules about what is not community property. They generally exempt inheritances, gifts, and property acquired before marriage. Most (but not all) states exempt property acquired before moving to the state. However, in order for separate property to stay solely yours, it has to be kept apart from the property you own together. If you inherit money and want to maintain sole ownership, put it into a bank account or other investment in your own name. If you mix separate property with community property, it may join the community whether you mean it to or not.

You can get out of community property if you'd rather hold your assets in some other way. Each state runs its own escape routes. For example, you might make a gift of your community property interest to your spouse. You might sign an agreement specifying what is community property and what isn't. In most of the states (but not all), you can annul the community property rule with a premarital or postmarital agreement. Non–community property can be owned separately or jointly, as you prefer.

Why Most Married People Love Joint Ownership

1. It makes marriage a partnership; share and share alike.

2. When one of you dies, the other automatically gets the goods. No doubts, no delays, no tears, no probate.

3. The other owner can't wheel and deal the money away. As a practical matter, most joint property cannot be sold or borrowed against unless both of you sign.

This applies especially to real estate and securities registered in your personal names. Securities held in the name of a brokerage house ("street name"— see page 801) are another story. It normally takes only one of you to buy and sell, even if the account is jointly owned. Similarly, mutual funds usually allow either of you to make telephone switches. But be it a mutual fund or a brokerage account, neither of you should be able to take the money and run. A check for the proceeds of any sale will be issued in the joint names. (This doesn't prevent some spouses from forging the other's signature!)

Your most vulnerable property is a jointly owned bank account, which your spouse can easily clean out.

4. In divorce, a joint owner is a more formidable force. Under state laws, the marital assets are supposed to be divided fairly, without regard to who holds title. But possession might still be seven-tenths of the law. If you hold the property or at least have your name on it, your bargaining position is stronger than if you don't.

5. Out-of-state property passes to the other owner, without probate in that state. This saves your survivor some time and money.

6. Say there's a debt that you're not responsible for, such as a judgment levied against your spouse. If he or she dies, those creditors usually can't collect a dime from joint property. During your spouse's lifetime, however, joint property is vulnerable—to what extent depends on the laws of your state. You get the most protection in a tenancy by the entirety (page 87).

Why Some Married People Hate Joint Ownership

1. If one of you splits, he or she can clean out the bank accounts and safe-deposit box. You can file a lawsuit to get back what's yours, but the effort might cost more than it's worth.

2. Some investments can't be sold if one of you is too sick or senile to sign the papers or too sore to cooperate. A durable power of attorney solves the sick-or-senile problem. The second is all yours.

3. You can't set up a bypass trust to reduce your estate taxes if your property is jointly owned with a right of survivorship. So if you're wealthy, this form of ownership costs you money. However, joint property can be *disclaimed* into a bypass trust. You disclaim an inheritance when you refuse to accept it. If you're disclaiming for tax purposes, federal law gives you nine months to decide. The inheritance then passes to the next person or people in line, perhaps in trust.

4. Your kids might lose money if you marry more than once. Say you put all your property into joint names with a new spouse—and die. That spouse gets everything and can cut out the children from your previous marriage. Don't assume that your new spouse will do the right thing by your kids. The spouse may have his or her own children, who might want the money kept in their part of the family and will pressure an elderly parent to comply. Separate property plus a prenup make things simpler for everyone.

5. Joint property can be tied up for a long time in divorce because it often can't be sold until both spouses agree to sign. Separate property can be sold anytime you want unless a judge ties it up during a contested divorce.

6. In community property states, you'll save taxes by choosing community ownership rather than joint ownership. When an owner dies, any taxable capital gains on the property are erased. This applies to only one-half of joint property but all of community property.

Joint Property for Unmarried People?

The Weak Case in Favor

1. It passes automatically to the other without a will and without probate. This is a strong case only for committed couples—for example, gay and lesbian couples whose families disapprove of the relationship and might challenge a will. A carefully drawn will usually can't be broken, however, except by a surviving spouse who wasn't left the share of the property required by state law.

2. It's a sign of good faith.

3. It's convenient. A mother and daughter living together might want a joint account for household bills.

The Strong Case Against

1. If you want to take your property out of joint names and the other person refuses, you may have the devil's own time getting it back. Only bank accounts are simple to reclaim. You just take the money out (unless . . .

2. . . . the other person got there first. Either owner can empty a joint bank account. You'd have to sue to get your money back.

3. You might need both signatures to sell an investment or to cash a check for the proceeds of a sale. What if your ex-mate gets sore or leaves town?

4. Say you put your investments in joint names with your son, who manages them for you. His business goes broke. His half of your property could be attached to pay his debts. (He can manage your money just as well with a power of attorney or through a trust.)

5. Assume the same story, except that your son gets divorced. Part of your property might go to his ex-wife.

6. Same story, only you have two sons. When you die, Son One inherits your investments, and Son Two gets nothing. Joint property usually goes to the surviving joint owner, cutting other beneficiaries out. (A few states might allow you to designate that your joint account will go half to Son One and half to Son Two or your other beneficiaries.)

7. The relationship might end but not joint ownership. For example, say that you and a partner own a house together. Even if the partner buys you out, you're still on the mortgage and are fully responsible for the debt. Only the lender can release you, and the lender may refuse to do so. If your partner (ex-partner) quits paying the mortgage without your knowledge, the default will show up on your credit report. Ditto any liens that your ex's creditors put on the house. If the bank comes after you for the mortgage payments, you'll be supporting your ex-partner's real estate investment and getting nothing in return—unless a written agreement allows you to force the sale of the house to recover the money you put up.

8. If you're rich enough to owe federal gift and estate taxes (page 120), you can trigger a tax liability when: (1) Stocks or real estate go into joint names, and the owner doesn't pay for his or her half share. (2) The noncontributing owner takes money out of a joint bank account or U.S. Savings Bonds. (3) One of you dies. All joint property is taxed in the estate of the first owner to die except for anything that the survivor can prove he or she paid for. These rules, incidentally, apply only to joint owners who aren't married. Most married couples[*] can give, or leave, each other property without paying federal gift or estate taxes. At this writing, you can also give away $13,000 annually, tax free—$26,000 for gifts made with a spouse—to each of as many people as you want. (This exemption may change when the estate tax rules do—page 120.)

In Either Case . . .

Own your cars separately. If you cause an accident and are hit with a judgment that exceeds your insurance, your other property can be attached—and so can the property of the car's joint owners. If you own the car alone, no one else will be affected.

If There's a Child . . .

He or she may have rights to property and support provided for in law.

Ownership in Same-Sex Marriages, Registered Domestic Partnerships, or Civil Unions

Federal tax law doesn't recognize these unions, but states that authorize them do. In these states, you have the same property, inheritance, and state estate tax rights as traditional married couples, so check all the ways of owning property together, listed above.

---

[*]Married same-sex couples can't take advantage of federal gift and estate tax rules. As long as the Defense of Marriage Act stays in effect, these apply only to heterosexual couples.

Should Your Kid Own It?

That's a close call. Congress wiped out most of the tax break that used to encourage parents to shift investments into their children's names. Today, a small amount of the child's *unearned* income—interest, dividends, and capital gains—passes tax free, and an equal amount is taxed at the child's own rate. The rest is generally taxed in the parents' bracket for dependent children under 19 years of age or dependent, full-time college students under 24. (For the latest unearned-income amounts, see Publication 17, Your Federal Income Tax, at www.irs.gov.)

The tax break still works for children who save the money until they grow up. Any interest or dividends they earn may be low enough to fall into their own tax bracket. If they don't go to college and start supporting themselves, they can sell at age 19 or older and pay the capital gains tax in their own bracket, which may or may not be lower than their parents' bracket.

It's another matter if the child goes to college and will need this money for tuition. Investment proceeds are taxed in the parents' bracket. Families saving for college are far better off with 529 plans (page 667), where investment income and capital gains can pass tax free.

If you do want to make a money gift to children, it has to pass through the following four wickets:

1. You won't need the property back. This isn't Ping-Pong. Whatever you give your child is his or hers to keep.

2. You have the sort of kid who won't take the money and blow it. Gifts are generally given under the Uniform Transfers (or Gifts) to Minors Act. At age 18 or 21, depending on state law, the property will belong to the child unless it's protected by a trust or some alternative, such as a family limited partnership (ask a lawyer about that one).

3. The small tax savings are worth the loss of flexibility.

4. You think that your child won't be eligible for much college aid. Eligible students get larger grants or loans if the savings are in the parents' name rather than the child's name (see page 686).

There are better and worse ways of giving money and property to a child under 18. Here are your choices:

1. Outright ownership. You hand the money to the child with a ribbon around it. That's okay for a $100 birthday present or a $50 savings bond at a bat mitzvah. But don't do this with larger sums. Sometimes access to the money is too easy: the child can cash out bank accounts or savings bonds whenever he or she wants (although you could hide the bonds!). With stocks and real estate, on the other hand, access is too strict: it's tough, sometimes impossible, for your son or daughter to sell the property while underage.

Some people think they have given money to a child by opening a bank account in trust for him or her. Not so. You still own the money and pay taxes on the interest. It doesn't pass to the child until you die.

2. Joint property. Forget it. Putting property in joint names with a child is even worse than giving it outright. You can't sell the whole property without the child's consent. If the child is underage, he or she usually can't give consent without the agreement of a court-appointed guardian. You still owe taxes on at least part of the income. If you die rich enough to owe estate taxes, the entire property can be taxed in your estate (depending on your state). The only joint property that you can liquidate easily is a joint bank account. But that doesn't even count as a gift, or save you taxes, unless the child withdraws the money.

3. College 529 plans. If you intend that the money be used for higher education, 529 plans (page 667) are the ticket. The money accumulates tax deferred and can be withdrawn for college expenses tax free.

4. Uniform Transfers to Minors Act. In the states that have passed it, UTMA makes sense for substantial gifts intended for purposes other than higher education. Cash, stocks, mutual funds, bonds, real estate, and perhaps even insurance policies can be given to an adult acting as custodian for the child.

The custodian—typically, your spouse, the child's parent, or some other close relative—manages the money and can spend it for the child's benefit. Most states require the remaining money to be distributed to the child at age 18 or 21, although some have extended the time period.

States without UTMA have the older but similar Uniform Gifts to Minors Act (UGMA). With UGMA, however, you can't transfer real estate or other complex types of property.

Gifts under UTMA or UGMA pass with no muss and no fuss. Your bank, mutual fund, stockbroker, or insurance agent can give you the papers and tell you where to sign. In fact, it's almost too easy. Without legal advice, you might make a gift that you'll regret.

Don't name yourself custodian. If you do, and you die before the child becomes a legal adult, the money will be included in your taxable estate just as if you hadn't given it away.

5. Trusts in the child's name. To give a child a large sum of money, see a lawyer experienced in trusts. A true gift has to be an *irrevocable trust*—meaning that you can't change the beneficiary, cut the child out, or take the money back. These trusts can do almost anything you want: accumulate the income or pay it out; pay out income but not principal; or hand over the money at whatever age you think your child will be grown up. (No, don't wait until 50; if the child doesn't grow up earlier, he or she never will.)

Don't use trust income for the child's support, and be sure that the trust so specifies. Support is your legal obligation. If the trust picks up your obligation—by paying for your child's food and clothing—that income can be taxed back to you.

So here's the big question for well-to-do parents: Can trust income be used to pay for private school or college? In divorce courts, education is increasingly considered a legal obligation for parents with money. But so far, there has been no tax attack on the many trusts that pay your child's school and college bills. Parents should not sign a contract to pay tuition if a trust is involved. However, it's okay for them to sign as trustee.

Should a Living Trust Own It?

Maybe. A lot of people set up living trusts, principally to avoid probate. They shift the property out of their own names and into the trust, naming themselves trustee. But probate isn't the black hole it used to be. Most states have simplified their laws, making the process pretty straightforward. You'll find a discussion of probate and living trusts in chapter 6. That will help you decide whether having a trust is worth the cost and paperwork.

My view? These trusts are suitable only for a small group of people. If you're not among them, don't waste your money.

6

Willing Makes It So

Wills and Trusts—For Everything You Can't Take with You

**The three immutable facts: You own stuff.
You will die. Someone will get that stuff.**

Please write a will. I'm on my knees. Just do it, *please.* Your family will praise your sainted memory. It will settle their minds and settle the arguments (or most of them). The people you care about will think of you as someone loving and fair. (A sense of fairness trumps all when an inheritance hangs in the balance.)

If you don't write a will or set up your property so that it passes directly to its proper new owner, the result may not be fair. You'll have lost your right to choose. Instead your state will distribute your property, following rules already written into law. Your state means well, but it's not too clever, brooks no appeal, and makes no exceptions. Various relatives will get pieces of your property, but no one else—and no one will get more than the state-allotted share, even if it's unfair. Depending on the state, a spouse can get the short end of the stick.

You don't want this to happen—or I hope you don't. Yet many people who know better don't write wills or living trusts and are not moved by the risk of leaving a mess behind. Maybe they don't intend to die. Neither do I, but I have a will anyway, just in case.

While I'm here on my soapbox, let me also nag at those of you whose wills or trusts are out of date. Old wills, written before your income went up, before family members married, divorced, or died, or before laws changed, can wreak just as much havoc as no will at all.

Making a will is so engrossing that it beats me why anyone has to be dragged to it. As you assign your computers to Barbara and your antique table to Jeff, you imagine their gratitude. You feel like God; you arrange everything.

I've heard plenty of excuses for not writing a will. To answer some of them: You can write a will even though your financial affairs are a mess. You don't have to have your property appraised. Neither the witnesses to the will nor the beneficiaries have any right to know what is in it. Your property isn't locked up in any way. You can change things as often as you want. You won't suddenly drop dead.

Without a Will . . .

- *If you're married, not all of the property may go to your spouse* (depending on state law). It may not go to your registered domestic partner, either.
- *If you have children, or no children but a living parent, they may inherit some of your money, leaving your spouse with too little to live on.* Grown children will receive their money directly. The money inherited by younger children will be guarded by a court-appointed conservator. If your spouse is conservator, he or she will be able to use it only for the children's support. The court will have to approve certain expenditures and may require an annual accounting.
- *A court will choose the conservator of your minor children's property.* Your spouse will be named, if he or she is alive and competent. If not, some other relative will step in—maybe not the one you love best.
- *If the child will inherit money, a fight might break out among your relatives* over who should care for the child and control his or her inheritance.
- *There probably won't be a trust to take care of your young children's inheritance.* Trusts are useful because they let you decide, among other things, when the child should receive the money: for example, at age 25 or later. Without a trust—just a state-appointed conservator—the children gain control of their money at 18 (sometimes 21, depending on state law). If they're not ready for the responsibility, too bad.
- *Adopted children might get nothing.*
- *Stepchildren get nothing, even if they're close to you.*
- *Neither do your friends or your partner.*
- *Your grown children might battle in the courts.* They might also fight with a second spouse or the second spouse's children.
- *Part of the family might be cut off from the family business.*
- *A closely held business might have to be sold fast* if the estate isn't permitted to run it.
- *You can't leave your favorite things to your favorite people.*
- *You can't leave a contribution to a church or charity.*

- *Your disabled child might inherit money,* disqualifying him or her from government aid.
- *Everyone will be sore at you.*

If you're married, wills sometimes seem to be beside the point. You simply put all the property into joint names so that your spouse will inherit. But
what if you die together in an accident? Who gets the property then, and how
will any children be taken care of? You wouldn't go out at night and leave your
youngsters without a babysitter. Why would you go out forever and leave them
without a guardian? If you have no children and the wife dies five days before the
husband, everything may pass to his relatives, leaving hers out, or vice versa

If you're	And die without a will, your property will go
Unmarried, no children, parents living	To your parents. In some states, they have to split it with your brothers and sisters.
Unmarried, no children, parents dead	To your brothers and sisters. If you were an only child, to your next of kin.
Unmarried, with children	To your children, but probably not to stepchildren. The court appoints a guardian for your minor children and their funds.
Unmarried, no relatives	To the state.
Married, with children	Depending on the state and the size of the estate, all to the sur-viving spouse or part to the spouse and part to the children. The spouse may get one-third to one-half of your separately owned property, part or all of the community property, and all of the joint property you held together.
Married, without children	Depending on the state and the size of the estate, all to the surviving spouse or part to the spouse, part to your parents, and perhaps even part to your siblings. The spouse may get one-half of your separately owned property, part of all of the community property, and all of the joint property.
Registered domestic partner	The same intestacy rights as a married person in most but not all of the states that permit this legal arrangement.
Single or married	Any property jointly held with another person, with right of survi-vorship, goes to that person. Property with a named beneficiary, such as an insurance policy, pay-on-death account, or IRA goes to that beneficiary.

(the exact number of days depends on state law or what it says in the will). If you die together and are worth more than the estate tax exemption as a couple (page 120), your estates will owe federal taxes that could have been avoided if you'd drawn a will with the proper trust.

Single people may not care that everything goes to their parents. But it takes a will (or living trust—page 130) to include a friend, a partner, a roommate, a church or charity, or, in most states, a sibling. A will is especially important for live-in couples, straight or gay. If your parents hate your way of life or aren't fond of your partner, they may vent their anger on the survivor, seizing property he or she ought to have. They might take it even if they like your partner, because they got greedy. People surprise you when money is at stake.

Innocents think that even without a will, property passes to the person who most ought to own it. How mistaken they are! What's "right" under state law may be all wrong for your family and friends. Laws vary, but the following table gives you a general idea of what could happen if you die intestate (without a will). For your state's specific rules, see www.mystatewill.com.

What Passes by Will?

For many of us, surprisingly little passes by will nowadays. Here is what happens to some of your major assets, whether you have a will or not:

- *All joint property with rights of survivorship goes to the other owner or owners.* This includes a home in joint names.
- *Property with a named beneficiary goes to the person named.* This includes your life insurance, U.S. Savings Bonds, Individual Retirement Accounts, tax-deferred annuities, and bank accounts held in trust for others. Employer plans such as 401(k)s go to your spouse unless he or she waives that right—in which case, the money goes to whomever you name.
- *Property disposed of by contract goes to the person named.* For example, you might state in writing that your house goes to a daughter or son who takes care or you in your old age. To make it binding, your son or daughter should sign it. Unsigned, it amounts to no more than a handwritten will, which your state may or may not accept.
- *Property put into a revocable living trust goes to the beneficiaries of the trust.*
- *The usual sort of personal property that we all own—the clock, the sugar bowl, the TV set—is usually divided by private agreement without a will,* assuming that no one in the family lodges a formal protest. Many states even let you transfer title to an automobile without cranking up the probate machine.

What property does pass by will? Any asset that you own individually (including your half of community property and property held as tenants in common—page 86) *and* does not have a named beneficiary. If everything is held jointly or goes to a named beneficiary, there may be nothing left to pass by will. If there are just trivial amounts, no probate will probably be required. But remember: you may own property you know nothing about, such as a big legal settlement paid if you died in an accident. Your will directs where that will go.

What If Your Will Says One Thing but Your Property Deeds and Beneficiary Forms Say Something Else?

This happens all the time and can be a tragedy for heirs. You may assume that your will takes care of everything. But it does *not* apply to joint property or property with named beneficiaries. If the names on those properties don't harmonize with the intent expressed in your will, tough luck. The people in your will lose out.

It's oh, so easy to make mistakes. For example, you might say in your will, "Divide my estate equally between my beloved children, Patty and Bob." Later you put Patty's name on your bank account so that she can help you pay your bills. When you die, the account will probably go to Patty. Too bad for Bob. To avoid this, give Patty your power of attorney. That frees her to write checks for you without being on the account. On your death the remaining money will still be split between Patty and Bob, as you intended. Another option is a convenience account, if your bank offers them. Patty can write checks, but any money left in the account will be divided according to the terms of your will.

Here's another mistake that could devastate your heirs: you might leave your Individual Retirement Account to the wrong person. For example, say that your will leaves the IRA to your spouse. But years ago, before you married, you named your sister as beneficiary of the IRA and never got around to changing it. If you die, your sister gets the money; your spouse is cut out. (When you married, you should have told the IRA trustee—the bank, mutual fund group, brokerage firm, or insurance company—to send you a change-of-beneficiary form by the speediest mail.)

And again: your will might set up an estate tax–saving trust for the benefit of your children, to hold, say, $3.5 million of your assets. But your major asset is your mansion, which you keep in joint names with your spouse. You also have a life insurance policy naming your spouse as beneficiary. When you die, your spouse gets the mansion and the life insurance. There may not be enough in your probate estate to fund the children's trust. Several thousand dollars' worth of estate planning will have gone down the drain, along with the tax savings you'd hoped for. (You should have kept at least $3.5 million in your separate name or named your estate the beneficiary of your life insurance.)

And yet again: if you open a new brokerage account, the broker may advise you to name a "pay on death" beneficiary in order to avoid probate. All the money in that account would go to the person named, regardless of what it says in your will. This too could wreck a lot of careful planning.

The lawyer who prepares your will should quiz you about all the assets you own to see how they're held, what they're worth, and whether you have named beneficiaries. You may be advised to change the beneficiaries of insurance policies and retirement plans to make the will work the way you want. If you write your own will (see page 103), these complicated ownership questions will be entirely in your hands. If you slip up, you may leave some family members less than you intended. That could sour relations among your children for many years.

If Virtually All of Your Property Is Disposed Of in Other Ways, Why Bother with a Will or Trust?

Several reasons:

- *To name a personal guardian for your minor children and a conservator for any money they inherit.*
- *To name a trustee to protect your children's inheritances until they can manage their own affairs.*
- *To dispose of property you didn't expect to own.* This especially affects married couples. Say that a husband with no will inherits from his wife. If he himself dies soon thereafter (perhaps because they were both in the same auto accident), the property and the children will be left in the arms of the state.
- *To dispose of any property you get after your death.* You actually can get rich posthumously. For example, if you die in an accident, a jury might bring in a big judgment payable to your estate.
- *To avoid fierce family arguments over who gets the beloved painting of Uncle Carll.*
- *To dispose of your half of jointly owned property* if both you and the other owner die in the same accident.
- *To make sure that your probate-avoiding tactics work.* If you set up a living trust, you need a *pour-over will*. It guarantees that any property you forgot, or that comes to you after your death, will be added to your trust.

The "I Love You" Will

This is the basic will for married couples. You each leave everything to each other and, if you both should die, in trust for the kids. Simple, clean, and cheap. Complications arise only if you have kids from an earlier marriage who may need protection; you have kids with special needs; or you're wealthy enough to owe estate taxes.

An I-love-you will for singles leaves everything to a partner or to a few other named beneficiaries. It couldn't be easier.

Do You Need a Lawyer?

Strictly speaking, no. You can draw up your own will. But a lawyer who represents himself is said to have a fool for a client. I think the same about people who, having assets to leave behind, still handwrite their wills and stick them in desk drawers.

Centuries of tradition and legal precedent stand behind the formalities of wills. The words are precise (if often legalistic) to avoid ambiguity. The procedures are as orderly as a ballet, to make it irrefutably plain that these indeed are your intentions. Homemade documents, which are clear to you, may be so vague to others that your heirs (if they squabble) have to get a reading in court. The will may even be thrown out and your property distributed according to state law. Books and computer programs exist that guide you through writing a valid will, but they take a lot of time and study. A lawyer should charge a modest fee for a simple I-love-you will (plus a living will, health care proxy, and durable power of attorney), although you can pay in the thousands for a document that is complex. The first meeting, to discuss objectives and fees, ought to be free—so make that phone call! You have nothing to lose.

Here's why you need an attorney:

To Say Exactly What You Mean. If you leave money to "Ada and her children," do you mean "Ada, if living, and if not, to her children"? Or do you mean "divided in equal parts among Ada and her children"? Or "one-half to Ada and one-half to her children"? Who knows? Depending on the state, Ada and her children may become joint owners, Ada may get the income from the property for life, or Ada may be able to occupy the land for life, with the children inheriting it after her death.

To Advise You on How to Hold Your Property: Jointly? Individually? In trust?

To See That the Names on the Property Agree with Legacies in Your Will.
I've said it before, and it's so important that I'll say it again. Here's where many
estates get fouled up. Your will says one thing, but the names on your property
say another. For example, take a will that divides the property equally among
three children. For help with money management, however, the parents put one
child's name on the securities account. That child will inherit the whole account
plus one-third of everything else. The other children will be shortchanged.
Lawyers watch out for this.

To Clue You In on Your State's Weird Inheritance Laws. For example, if
you leave someone a house with a mortgage on it, your estate might have to
pay off the loan unless you specifically indicate it shouldn't. Your spouse may
be entitled to the family home unless he or she waives that right. If one of your
children witnesses the will, he or she may not be able to inherit.

**To Reduce Estate Taxes If Your Estate Is Larger than the Federal Estate
Tax Exemption** (page 120). Even smaller estates may be subject to taxes at
the state level.

To Provide for "Advancements." Say that you're leaving your money to all
your children equally. But one child needs financial help to pay for his own children's college or to buy a house. You can treat the money as an advance against
his inheritance, if the will so provides. You attach a schedule to your will, showing how much that child received. When you die, that amount is subtracted from
his or her inheritance, preserving your original goal of giving all your kids the
same amount.

**To See That Your Heirs Are Not Robbed of Their Share of Your Closely
Held Business.** Unless someone agrees in writing to buy out your interest, the
business may be worthless to the family you leave behind.

To Ask Questions That Might Not Occur to You. For example, do you want
your executor to post a bond to ensure that he or she won't misappropriate the
assets? If you chose a family member as executor, you probably won't want him
or her to have to pay. But your will must specify that no bond is needed.

Another example: If one of your adult children dies before you do, who should
inherit his or her share of your property? Do you want it to go to your child's
children (your grandchildren)? Do you want it to go to your late child's spouse?
If your will simply leaves your property to your "surviving children," and one
child dies before you do, the money will go to your other children, cutting your
deceased child's children out.

To Deal with the Questions Surrounding Assisted Reproduction. For example, if you've stored frozen embryos, do you want the surviving parent to be able to produce a child after your death? If you served as a surrogate womb for an infertile woman and your will leaves your money to "all my children," does that include the child you bore for someone else? What about a child born of a donor's sperm? If a large trust is involved, a swarm of children with the right DNA might show up—none of whom you meant to share in your property. Betcha hadn't thought of complications like these! In 2008, the Uniform Law Commission established rules for sorting out these claims but it will take time for the states to adopt them. In the meantime, state courts are struggling with some weird cases. You can head off potential trouble in your will.

To Suggest Smart Strategies for Doing Right by Your Heirs. Tell your lawyer everything; your feelings about your family, what worries you about your kids, whether you expect quarrels among your heirs (sibling quarrels, or fights with a second spouse and stepchildren), and what you hope to accomplish with the money you leave behind. Disclose all your assets, debts, and any income you expect to leave behind. Your lawyer will have good ideas about how to mobilize your money to leave your heirs well supported and, if possible, at peace.

To Make Your Will Challenge-Proof. All the formalities have to be followed. You need the right number of witnesses, all of whom can testify—if required—that you knew you were signing your will, that you were competent to do so, and that the signature on the will is yours. Where there's no contest, your will is *self-proving*. It's admitted to probate without any testimony from witnesses.

Homemade Wills

You don't believe me. You think you're smarter than a lawyer and don't see why you should pay him or her to complicate your life. So . . .

You Handwrite a Will, Sign It, Date It, Leave It Unwitnessed, and Put It in Your Desk Drawer. Is it valid? Yes, in about 30 states; no, in the rest. The bad news for lawyerphobes is that you have to ask a lawyer what your state allows. Some require that every word be handwritten; others might accept your handwriting on preprinted will forms; others will throw out an unwitnessed will.

Even if the will is good, its terms may be fuzzy. That won't matter as long as your heirs agree on where you wanted your money to go. But if they disagree, your "will" could set off a terrible fight. People who boast that they've done their own wills wouldn't be so smug if they saw what could happen later.

You Type a Will, Sign It, Date It, and Put It in Your Desk Drawer. At this writing, it's invalid in all but three states (Montana, South Dakota, and Colorado), and it's not even foolproof there. It is not considered a handwritten will. To validate it, you need the signatures of the right number of witnesses. And both you and the witnesses have to follow certain procedures, required by your state, for creating a valid will.

You Get Witnesses. You must be sure to follow the rules. The witnesses may have to see you sign or hear you acknowledge your signature to them. You may have to tell the witnesses that this is your will. You may have to see the witnesses sign, or they may have to sign in the presence of one another. Some states and courts will accept a will with minor technical flaws as long as no one challenges it (the "harmless error" rule). But others won't, and there's no way you can tell in advance. Who witnesses the will may also be critical. Many states put limits on what a witness can inherit. A few states don't let a witness inherit anything.

You Type a Will, Sign It, Date It, and Get It Notarized. This way of legalizing a will was approved by the Uniform Law Commission in 2008. Your state has to adopt it, however, for it to become effective.

You Fill In the Standard Do-It-Yourself Will Form That a Few States Provide or That You Find Online. These forms are fine, in theory, for simple wills ("everything to my spouse" or "everything to my children"). But they don't allow for many choices. Like a typed will, they need witnesses. If you misinterpret the instructions and make a mistake in getting the will witnessed, it probably won't be valid.

You Tell People Orally What You Want. Not accepted in many states. In others it's a valid will only if you're in imminent danger of death, not much property is involved, and several witnesses hear you. Some states allow only soldiers in combat to have oral wills. If you survive longer than a certain period, your oral will evaporates.

You Videotape Yourself Reciting Your Bequests. You do not have a will. A tape generally has no formal standing in law, although a court might recognize a particular set of bequests as valid. A videotape of you signing the will, however, can prevent unhappy relatives from charging that you were too woolly-headed to make decisions.

You Prepare Your Will Online, Providing a Digital Signature. At this writing, electronic wills are legal only in Nevada, and you have to jump through hoops to be sure that the will can't be hacked. Consult a Web-savvy lawyer.

You Get a Book on How to Write Your Own Will and Follow the Instructions. If you're patient, and read the directions carefully, there aren't too many mistakes in the book, and your affairs are truly simple, maybe it will work. Daredevils might consider Quicken WillMaker Plus by Nolo, the leading publisher of do-it-yourself legal materials. It covers both wills and living trusts. Order online (www.nolo.com) or by phone (800-728-3555). You might also try LegalZoom (www.legalzoom.com). You fill in a form online and receive a will in the mail.

But even with guidance, you're better off not writing your own. In simple situations, the cost of a lawyer is surprisingly small and worth every penny. If your situation is more complex, look for a lawyer who specializes in wills and estates. The more a lawyer sees of what can happen in a family after a death, the more sensitive he or she becomes to how exact a will has to be.

Joint Wills

A *joint will* is a single will for two people, usually a husband and wife. They might each leave all the property to the other, and to the children equally when the second spouse dies.

I believe in sharing secrets, sharing beds, and sharing property—but not in sharing wills. Don't do it. A joint will can be hard to change without the consent of your spouse. The surviving spouse might not be able to change it after the first spouse dies. And it might not qualify for the marital deduction—the provision in the tax code that normally lets you leave everything to a spouse, free of estate tax. That would be a disaster for people wealthy enough to owe estate taxes.

Naming an Executor

The executor—known in many states as the personal representative—sees that your will is carried out. It's a tiresome, detailed, time-consuming, thankless job. You're doing no favors for the person you name. All the property has to be tracked down and assembled (no easy job if you didn't keep good records). Creditors notified. Heirs dealt with tactfully. Arguments settled. Bills and taxes paid. Property appraised and distributed or sold. Investments managed until they can be distributed to their new owners. Final accounting to be made to the heirs and, perhaps, to the courts.

The executor usually works with a lawyer who handles the technical details, so you don't need an expert in estate law or high finance. You need virtues that are much harder to find. An executor has to be willing, reliable, well organized, honest, responsible about money, fair minded, and sensitive to the worries of the heirs. The usual practice is to ask an able heir (or friend) to do the job. If you name a professional executor—a bank or a lawyer—include a family member as coexecutor, just to keep things moving along. Get permission before putting down someone's name. If money is misspent or errors made, the executor can be held personally responsible.

Friends or family members usually don't ask for compensation. But you should specify this in the will; otherwise they may claim the commission allowed by law, even though you expected them to serve for nothing.

When banks or attorneys are executors, however, they may charge, and charge, and charge—sometimes by the hour, sometimes a fixed fee, sometimes a percentage of the assets in the estate that goes to probate. Your estate will pay less if you keep the executorship at home and let your family hire a lawyer by the hour or by the job. Executors should shop for lawyers, asking more than one what they'll charge. Like any other businesspeople, lawyers cut fees for jobs they want and that they know are up for bid.

In a state with simplified probate laws (page 129), legal fees will be lower because there are fewer court procedures. Your family may not even need an attorney. The job might be easy enough to do themselves. Most states now have instructions online. Alternatively, your executor can go to the courthouse and ask the clerk of the probate court what's involved or have a onetime conference with a knowledgeable lawyer. Very small estates might not have to go through probate at all.

Who Gets the Andirons?

"How nice. Mommy Dearest left me a nice, round one million dollars—but what did you say? Sandy took the andirons? They were supposed to be mine! I'll sue!"

And so it goes. Personal property usually goes to a surviving spouse. If there is none, it's often divided equally among your heirs, leaving it to them to decide exactly who gets what. If your heirs fall out, money may not be the issue. They're more likely to fight about all the things that can't be split: the music box, the opal earrings, the antique pool table.

To avoid this, talk with your kids about which of your personal items matter to them the most. You may be surprised. They might not value the furniture you inherited from your own mother but love sentimental items of lesser monetary worth. When two people want the same thing, discuss it with them and broker a trade-off (Sue gets the Oriental rug, but Diane gets the bracelet *and* the brooch).

Once the main items are settled, make named bequests; the andirons to

Sandy, the feather boa to Sarah. The easiest way is to put your desires in a separate letter attached to your will. You can then change your mind about the andirons without having to reexecute the will itself. In some states this letter has the force of law if your will states that you'll leave a letter and if the letter is properly written. For example, it should be signed and dated, and say specifically that you want these particular people to get these particular items. In other states, you're simply depending on your family and executor to cooperate.

The letter might also tell your heirs which items are of special value. Identify paintings, prints, and craft items picked up on your travels. If you collect Batman comics or Japanese netsuke, leave the name of a dealer who might buy them back. Guns should be left to a person who can possess them lawfully.

For all the items not worth naming individually, suggest to your kids that they do a round-robin, each picking something in turn. You might name a third party to distribute items the kids can't agree on.

Leave some information about items of sentimental value. "I bought that wonderful green silk pillow in Thailand on our twenty-fifth anniversary trip." And the history of family heirlooms: "The dried flowers in the brass and glass paperweight came from your great-grandmother's wedding bouquet." Your kids will be glad for the notes, to help them remember the provenance.

Blended families need to be especially sensitive to deep feelings of ownership. Take a family where the mother died and the father remarried a woman who had children of her own. On her death, the kids from the first marriage will probably want to inherit china or other items that their biological mother owned. So consider which side of each family the property came from when distributing even ordinary goods.

Talk with your children about other ways of distributing the personal property.

If you carry insurance on special items, such as a gun collection or an antique car, ask your insurer to make it available to an heir for a certain period. Then state in your will that the policy follows the gift. This protects the valuables from the time you die to the time the heir collects them and gets insurance of his or her own.

Pets (or "heirdales," as rich dogs are called by Lawrence Waggoner of the University of Michigan Law School) are not allowed to inherit money. In a majority of states, you can leave a trust for their upkeep as long as the trustee is willing to carry out its terms. But the trust might not be enforceable if the trustee you name doesn't want to bother. You might also leave a friend a bequest on condition that he or she adopt your pet. Either way, confirm with your trustee or friend in advance.

Settling Shares

Unequal shares, to people who feel that they ought to be equals, become an eternal thorn in the side. Aunt Emily's last revenge on an irritating nephew is to leave him only $1,000, while his brother gets $2,000.

For the sake of family relations, equal shares are politic, with a few exceptions. If you've already put two kids through college and have one to go, that child deserves something extra for his education. He shouldn't have to spend his inheritance on a college degree that, for everyone else, was financed out of family funds (see page 118 for a trust that can help with this problem). If one daughter married in lace and pearls, the other should be able to afford the same. If one adult child is rich and the other poor, you might all agree to help the one who really needs it (although beware of divorce; a rich child may be suddenly poor if his or her marriage breaks up).

When one child is treated differently from the others, you're setting up a potential will challenge. Angry, the snubbed one may claim that the other siblings influenced you unduly. So leave a letter with your will, explaining why you made the choice you did. Even better, tell the whole family in advance.

Let the Sun Shine In

Don't keep your kids in the dark about the will. Explain the provisions, by letter or e-mail, especially if you're leaving them unequal shares. (It's important to say it in writing; they might forget or misinterpret a mere conversation.) Clarify how much you're leaving to charity or to people outside the family. Matters get especially touchy when stepparents and stepchildren are involved. If one of your heirs feels left out, he or she might challenge the will—in which case the lawyers will "inherit" the estate. So talk, explain, listen, adjust, and talk again. It's the unexpected that sends families into a tailspin, making enemies of steps and siblings who might otherwise have gotten along. As long as they all understand what you're doing and why, they'll probably accept it, happy or not. And if you can make them happy with just a few changes, all the talk-talk was time well spent.

One caveat: There's no need to tell your kids how much they might inherit. They'll start spending that money, mentally, and feel cheated if the bucks aren't as big as they expected. Instead, tell them that the ultimate size of your estate depends on a lot of things—how long you live, whether you'll need long-term care, how well your investments do, how much you'll spend in your retirement years, and circumstances unforeseen. Warn them that, in the end, there might not be a lot left to parcel out. Your "sunshine policy" has to do only with the fairness of the shares everybody gets.

Picking a Guardian

If you and your spouse both die, who better than Grandma to look after the minor children? The answer to that question is: practically anyone you can think of. Grandma paid her dues. She shouldn't have to gear up for child rearing all over again. Furthermore, if your parents are named guardians, you are setting up your children to lose a mom and dad all over again.

A brother or sister is a better choice. So is an older, married child, a cousin, or a close friend who shares your values and way of life. Of course, the guardian should be willing to undertake the job. If you name a friend instead of a family member, spell out your reasons in your will. The family might challenge your choice, and you want the court to understand your thinking.

If your children are old enough to understand the question, ask them where they'd like to live if anything happened to you—and let them in on what you decide. Don't be afraid to raise the issue. Children are often better able to cope with thoughts of dying than adults, maybe because to them death seems so remote. The older the child, the more important that he or she be part of the decision. Guardians raise the child, decide where he or she lives and goes to school, give medical consents, and influence the child's values and decisions.

Besides a personal guardian for your children, you need a "property guardian," or conservator, to manage their inheritance. That would be a trustee, if you've left the money in trust, or a custodian, if it's left to the kids directly.

Consider whether you want the same person to exercise both the personal and financial functions. If your loving brother offers the perfect home but is an airhead about money, pick someone else to look after the child's property. You don't need a financial genius, just a conscientious person with common sense who is financially well organized and knows how to get good investment advice. He or she also has to get along with the child's personal guardian. The guardian will need a regular allowance to help support the child, plus expenses for special items such as summer camp. You don't want quarrels. It's important that the child not be a financial burden on the guardian.

If you're divorced, the personal guardianship of the children normally goes to your ex-spouse, as long as he or she wants it. A court will step in only if the parent is clearly unfit (say, a drug addict) or has legally abandoned the child. If you don't think your ex-spouse is interested, name someone else and explain in your will why you made that choice. Your ex-spouse still gets first crack. But your candidate should come in ahead of all other contenders. You don't have to name your ex-spouse the protector of the child's money if you think he or she is financially irresponsible. But the keeper of the money should be able to get along with your ex and willingly pay out the funds the children need.

If you're putting off naming a personal and financial guardian, consider this sad story. A few years ago, four people battled for the guardianship of a toddler whose parents were killed in a boat explosion. The contenders: an uncle, an aunt, a cousin, and a friend. What made the child so popular? A potential multimillion-dollar wrongful death settlement from the boat company. Too bad the parents hadn't picked the guardians themselves.

Ways to Leave Money to Young Children

1. Use the Uniform Transfers to Minors Act (UTMA). UTMA accounts accept gifts left to the child in your will as well as gifts during your lifetime. The funds are left to an adult, who acts as custodian for the child. The law determines how the money can be spent and invested. The funds go to the child when he or she reaches 18 or 21 (higher, in some states). UTMA works well when the legacies are small.

2. Use the Uniform Gifts to Minors Act (UGMA), if your state doesn't offer UTMA. Under UGMA, you may have to make the gift during your lifetime rather than by will. The custodian manages the funds until the child reaches 18 or 21.

3. Leave the money in a trust that your will establishes (a testamentary trust). This is the best solution for sums over $100,000 or so. It's also best for property that starts small but will grow substantially over the years. Your trustee—a relative, friend, or bank—manages the inheritance and pays it to the child according to your instructions. He or she can dole out income and principal as needed for the child's education and living expenses. The remainder is turned over to the child at the age you set. You can provide that the child gets the money all at once or in installments—say, at ages 25, 30, 35, and 40. You might make the child cotrustee at, say, age 23. That allows him or her to share in investment decisions without yet having to handle the money alone.

A trustee can be told to withhold payments if it seems to be in the child's best interest. I think of this as the "crisis clause." Do you want the child to have the money if he or she has just joined a religious cult and will give it every penny? If he's mired in a nasty divorce? If she's abusing drugs or alcohol? Maybe the child has a gambling habit or has proven to be a spendthrift. The crisis clause protects children from themselves.

Most parents set up a single trust for all the children. If one child has big medical bills or hasn't been to college, those expenses can be paid out of common funds—just as they would have been if you had lived. Typically, the trust document will provide for all the money to stay in trust until the youngest child reaches, say, age 25. Then the trust dissolves, and everyone gets his or her appointed share. (At your death, however, a nominal payment might be made to the older children. If some children are quite a bit older, they might get a larger disbursement).

4. Name a legal conservator for the children's funds. This is the option for people who don't use UTMAs, UGMAs, or testamentary trusts. It the least flexible. State law determines what can be spent on the children and what investments can be made. The conservator makes an annual accounting to the court. When the child comes of age—at 18 or 21, depending on your state—he or she gets the money.

Leaving Property to a Partner

Since families may mistrust these relationships—especially gay and lesbian ones—the loving couple can't be too careful. After the death of one, his or her parents might make a strong effort to carry everything away. If you want your mate to get your money, you need a will. And spell out specifically why you chose your partner to inherit rather than your family: "Mickey, who has lived with me faithfully for seven years . . ."

Leaving Property to a Registered Domestic Partner

Federal tax laws don't recognize registered domestic partnerships, civil unions, or same-sex marriages. Neither do the laws governing Social Security or the inheritance of retirement plans. You're in the same boat as any other pair of lovers.

But you generally do get equal treatment under the laws of the states that permit your union. Most of them let you inherit from a registered partner who died without a will. If your partner did leave a will but you weren't mentioned in it, you may be able to inherit one-third or one-half of the probate estate, just like any other spouse. At this writing, states with domestic partnership, civil union, or similar laws include California, Colorado, the District of Columbia, Hawaii, Maryland, Nevada, New Jersey, Oregon, and Washington. Same-sex marriage is legal in Connecticut, Iowa, Maine, Massachusetts, New Hampshire, and Vermont (although the Maine law faces a voter challenge).

Redo your estate plan if you move to another state. Your new state generally won't recognize same-sex unions contracted elsewhere. If you registered as a domestic partner in Oregon, you'll have to do it again in New Jersey. At this writing, only New York and the District of Columbia recognize same-sex marriages performed in other states. Rhode Island recognizes Massachusetts marriages.

Divorce gets even more complicated. If a same-sex couple marries in Massachusetts, then moves to Florida and splits up, their relationship is in limbo. You can't get divorced in Florida because it doesn't recognize your marriage. And you can't get divorced in Massachusetts because you don't live there. Eventually, states will recognize each other's laws, but for now, you need a lawyer who specializes in same-sex estate planning and has some creative ideas.

How to Ruin a Relationship

Your nieces Kathy and Martha love your antique grandfather clock, so you leave it to both of them. Your 1957 red Thunderbird with tailfins goes to your two grandsons. Three of your children inherit the beach house.

Is this generosity? Will it bring the new owners together in an orgy of sharing? Not likely. You may have created a monster that will eat your family up. Your nieces, once in perfect sympathy, may well fall out over whose turn it is to have the clock.

Few people can reach perfect accord over what to do with mutually owned property. Their personal and financial situations are different. So are their attitudes. If Martha moves to a distant state and takes the clock with her, how will Kathy get her share back? If your older grandson is a demon driver and wrecks the car, can the younger one force him to put it back into prime condition? What if the beach house needs a new roof but one of the owners can't afford to pay? What if one owner wants to sell?

Anything that can't be divided cleanly should either be left to one person or sold and the proceeds split.

More Will Facts

Execute only one copy of your will. If you sign more, the court will hold up probate until they're all found. For extras, make photocopies.

Have your will checked when you move to a new state. A properly signed and witnessed will is usually valid everywhere. But ownership rights differ from state to state, which might make a difference to how your property is held.

Two ways to cancel a will: (1) The only sure way is to make a new one, specifically revoking all wills and codicils (legal additions to wills) that have come before. (2) You can tear up your old will or mark it "revoked and canceled," with the date and your signature. But do so in the presence of several witnesses (*young* witnesses, who aren't likely to die before you do) and say specifically that this will is no longer valid. Otherwise an heir might argue successfully that your executed will is merely missing. A photocopy in the lawyer's keeping might then be accepted as a valid will, even though you meant to revoke it.

You should keep old wills, even if they have been canceled. If questions arise about the new one, the old will gives your heirs some guidance about your original intent. Even more important, if the new will is ruled invalid, the prior will comes back into effect. In general, it's better to have a prior will rule the disposition of your property than to become subject to your state's intestacy laws. So mark your old will "superseded" and keep it in your file.

The only way to make a small change in a will is to execute a formal codicil, amending it. Don't ink out an old provision or insert a new one. In a few states and with some provisions, that might work; in most, it doesn't. Any change should be signed, dated, and witnessed according to your state's procedures. Otherwise the court will ignore the change or revoke the entire provision. Extensive changes might invalidate the entire will.

Say you leave your spouse money, get divorced, and die before you change your will. Does the ex-spouse collect? Generally, no. The rest of the will is usually valid, but your ex-spouse will be cut out. However, exceptions exist, so change your will as soon as the divorce negotiations get under way. If you don't change your will and die when you're legally separated but not divorced, your spouse will collect. Even if you do change your will, your spouse will collect his or her legal share (page 114) if you haven't yet divorced.

If you're getting divorced, immediately drop your spouse as beneficiary on your life insurance policy, employee benefits plan, IRAs, Keogh, 401(k), and revocable trust. If you don't and die, most states allow your ex-spouse to collect even if you have married again.

If you're in a registered domestic partnership or civil union, your partner may have the same rights to your property as a spouse. For example, registered partners may have "spousal" rights if you die without a will.

Say you leave half of your property to "my dear children, Justin and Matthew" without adding "any future children." Then Heather is born, but you die before changing your will. Has she been disinherited? No, but how much she gets will depend on your state. She might get exactly what the other children do. Or she might be given what she'd have received if you had died without a will—which could be more or less than the other children inherit. The same is true for an adopted child. Unless specifically mentioned, a stepchild is out.

Say you get married but your will still leaves everything to your pals. Is your spouse disinherited? No. State law dictates that he or she get at least something from your estate. But it may not be as much as you want. Moral: execute a new will while the "I dos" are still on your lips.

Say you get married and regret it. Your will leaves nothing to your spouse. Tough luck. Your spouse will still collect something. His or her minimal inheritance depends on state law. For a short marriage, it might be $50,000; for a long one, half of all of the marital assets. Or one-third to one-half of the late spouse's assets, regardless of the length of the marriage. Or the deceased spouse's own share of the community property. The spouse is taken care of first. The bequests to the rest of the heirs are reduced proportionately.

A spouse won't inherit, however, if you both sign a valid prenuptial contract to that effect, disclosing all assets in advance. You can write a postnuptial contract, too (page 149).

When leaving money to charity, check that you have the legal name and address. Many charities have similar names and might mount a fight over the bequest. Name an alternative charity in case the first one is out of business or no longer qualifies as a tax-deductible recipient.

If your estate will owe taxes, consider directing that the people who will receive small cash gifts and items of personal property inherit them free of tax. All the taxes will then be paid from the balance of the estate.

If you own homes in more than one state, establish one of them as your legal residence by voting there, paying taxes there, listing that address on your credit cards, getting a driver's license in that state, and so on. Otherwise both states might try to tax your estate. Real estate, such as a vacation home, is taxed in the state where it's located.

You can disinherit a child in every state except Louisiana. Your will should state specifically that you are leaving that child no money or property, or leaving a nominal sum such as one dollar.

Small bequests are usually stated in dollar amounts, such as "$1,000 for my friend Susan, if she survives me." But it's generally better to state major bequests in percentage terms rather than in dollar amounts. Consider what might happen if you leave $30,000 to each of three nieces and the remainder to charity, expecting the charity to get a large share. If the stock market crashes and your estate winds up with only $90,000, your nieces will get theirs and the charity will get nothing. So instead say "40 percent for the charity and 20 percent for each of my three nieces." Alternatively, provide that cash gifts be reduced proportionately if they exceed a certain percentage of the estate.

Your will can forgive debts. In a community property state, however, you may be able to forgive only half of the debt. Your spouse would have to forgive the other half.

Some reasons to change your will: (1) a big rise or fall in your net worth; (2) a new child, by birth, adoption, or marriage; (3) marriage, separation, or divorce; (4) a child's marriage, separation, or divorce; (5) a child's college graduation; (6) the death or disability of an heir; (7) an illness in the family that may go on for life; (8) changing financial circumstances in your family or a child's family; (9) a change in the state of a family business; (10) a change in the property or inheritance laws.

Are you holding investment real estate? If your heirs aren't capable of managing real estate, leave a letter for the executor giving all the details about the investment, what it should be worth, and who is most qualified to sell it.

If estate taxes will be due and your estate is made up mostly of illiquid real estate, leave enough life insurance to cover the bill. When considering how large a policy to buy, remember that the policy itself may increase the value of the estate (although there are ways of getting it out of your estate—see page 121).

Does your net worth depend on a closely held business? Get buyout agreements with your partners, enough life insurance to cover estate taxes, and agreements to protect your family's interests. Otherwise the business might prosper while your heirs get nary a penny.

All of your property doesn't have to be distributed right away. You can set up trusts in your will and instruct the trustee to hold the property until your children are older, distribute just the trust income, or distribute property to some beneficiaries and not to others. Whatever you want.

Five grounds for challenging a will: (1) a procedural flaw such as an unwitnessed change in the text; (2) age (the will was made when the person was still a minor); (3) undue influence or duress (the will was signed under pressure); (4) fraud (the person thought he or she was signing a letter or contract rather than a will); (5) mental incapacity (the person was too senile to have made or changed his or her will). But you have to raise your objection quickly. If you miss the deadline set by your state, you won't be allowed to make your case.

Sexism and Wills

It lingers on. Fathers may leave less to their daughters than to their sons. Daughters may be shut out of the family business. Wives may not be consulted. Money for a wife or daughter may be left in trust, forcing them to live on a trustee's dole for the rest of their lives. The wife might even have agreed to the trust because she took no interest in investing while her husband was alive. But when a wife becomes a widow, things change. She often discovers the lovely little secret that conservative money management isn't hard. She may come to resent her dependency on a trustee or bank trust department.

In the case of a longtime marriage, especially a first marriage, all questions about what happens to the money when the husband dies should be resolved on the side of the widow's freedom to act. The husband should add a trust to his will only to minimize estate taxes, not to "protect" his wife from making her own decisions about her money. If she decides that she'd rather not, she can give it to a bank trust department herself. But the issues may be different with second marriages, especially second marriages later in life. Each spouse may want to leave money in trust for the children of a former marriage.

Sexism affects males too. The will might leave all the jewelry to daughters. But a son might like some too, to give to his spouse or to his own daughter, eventually. The same might be true of china and other household goods.

Divorce and Wills

As soon as you separate, consider changing your will, living trust, health care proxy and power of attorney. At this point, you probably don't want your spouse or registered domestic partner (or any of their relatives) involved in your affairs. Your new will should limit the amount that your spouse or partner can inherit to the minimal share required by the state. After the divorce, your ex can be removed from the will entirely. Also change the beneficiaries of your life insurance and Individual Retirement Account. The eventual divorce agreement may require that you continue a certain amount of insurance or divide your IRA, but you can make changes at that time. You cannot change your 401(k) until you're actually divorced. Until then your spouse will inherit unless he or she formally waived those rights.

If you don't take your ex-spouse (or ex–registered domestic partner) off these accounts and die, what happens? That depends on state law. In general, here are the rules.

- *Your will.* Most states automatically remove an ex-spouse from an old will. If you still want your ex to inherit, write a new will saying so. Ex-partners are removed too, as long as you've been through your state's legal "divorce" process.

In a few states, however, your ex can inherit from an old will that you failed to change. A new spouse could collect up to one-third or one-half of the money that passes under your will, but your ex would get the rest.

- *Your life insurance.* Most states automatically remove an ex-spouse or official ex-partner from an old life insurance policy. But again, some don't.
- *Your 401(k).* It will go to your ex unless you change the beneficiary form or remarry. If you've remarried, it automatically goes to the new spouse. If you want someone else to inherit, the new spouse will have to waive his or her inheritance rights. (Domestic partners and married same-sex couples don't have the same rights as heterosexual couples. That's because 401(k)s are ruled by federal law, which doesn't recognize these relationships.)
- *Your living trust.* A few states automatically take your ex-spouse or partner off your trust. But a majority let him or her inherit, if you haven't changed its terms. A new spouse or official domestic partner may be entitled to one-third or one-half of the trust assets, depending on the state.
- *Your Individual Retirement Account.* It usually goes to the named beneficiary. If that's your ex-spouse, there's usually no way around it, even if your spouse waived all rights to your property as part of the separation agreement.
- *Your power of attorney and health care proxy.* Hospitals, doctors, and financial institutions probably won't accept the decisions of an ex if the rest of the family objects. But better to be safe than sorry.
- *Your trustees.* An ex may or may not be automatically removed, depending on state law. But it may be harder for your heirs to remove a member of your ex's family if you didn't do so yourself and he tries to hang on to his position.

Moral: Change your beneficiaries, proxies, and trustees! You'll leave a super-unhappy family if you don't.

Wills That Leave Money in Trust

A testamentary trust is set up by your will. Instead of leaving money directly to the beneficiary, you leave it in trust, to be managed by a trustee. Funds can be paid out for various purposes. At some point, the trust dissolves and the money is distributed. This differs from a living trust (page 130), which holds property during your lifetime. A testamentary trust doesn't come into existence until you die. Some of the uses of a testamentary trust:

The Trust Can Hold Money Until a Child Grows Up (page 110). You might want to maintain the trust into adulthood, to protect it from a spendthrift child, keep the inheritance in the family, ensure that the money is professionally managed, or for other reasons. But don't be a dead hand from the grave, holding on to the child's inheritance for years. By the time they're 30 or 35, the children should be able to get the money and take their chances. You can give the trustee the right to withhold the money in unusual circumstances, such as drug addiction, mental or financial incompetence, or a pending divorce. In that case, design the trust to give the child at least some input into decisions about investments and distributions.

The Trust Can Equalize Inheritances. Say that you've put two children through college, and there's one still to go. Their joint inheritance can go into a group trust. The trustee manages the money and pays the youngest child's tuition. When that child is 23 or 24 (plenty of time to get an undergraduate degree), the trust can terminate, with the money disbursed to all three children equally.

The Trust Can Save Estate Taxes. If your net worth exceeds the federal estate tax exemption, talk to a lawyer about how to cut the tax. There may be state taxes due on even smaller sums. Trusts are just one solution. Often, you can cut taxes without using a trust (page 120).

The Trust Can Manage Money Left to a Spouse. A trustee runs the money. The spouse receives the income and, if needed, payments out of principal. When the spouse dies, the remaining money goes to whomever is named.

The spouse can serve as his or her own trustee, with a backup trustee who takes over if there's a need. He or she might also be cotrustee with a family member, bank, lawyer, or investment adviser. In some cases, the bank or family member might be sole trustee.

The spouse should be able to change trustees if the relationship isn't working. But don't lock up all of a widow's money in trust. Maybe she didn't take much interest in investing while her husband was alive, but in widowhood she might turn into a demon money manager. I've seen it happen. Name her as cotrustee or leave her free to run at least part of her funds as she pleases.

The Trust Can Provide for Mentally or Physically Disabled Children. State and federal programs cover basic medical and residential care for children who need it, but only if the child has almost no money. This presents parents with a dilemma: Money left to the disabled child will be consumed by the institution. But without that money, the child will get only bare-bones support.

Middle-income parents may feel that they have little choice. They leave their modest assets to their healthy children and let the handicapped one get government aid. In this case, you should specifically disinherit the disabled child (and tell your relatives to do likewise). Your healthy children should be willing to provide any extra comforts that their institutionalized sibling needs.

Higher-income parents, however, might set up a trust, often funded by life insurance. The disabled child, who possesses little or no money, can qualify for government aid, while the trust supplies extra maintenance and support. But the wording is critical to ensure that the government can't break the trust (words such as *health, welfare,* and *support* are usually no-nos). Some states have their own "special needs trust" laws. For advice on getting a well-drafted trust, call your local Arc of the United States (find it at www.thearc.org or 800-433-5255). Ask for the names of lawyers experienced in your state's public assistance laws. The Web site also links you to its "Family Resource Guide" series, published for about half the states, explaining the benefits available there.

The Trust Can Ensure That the Children of a Prior Marriage Will Inherit. If you leave all your money to a second spouse, he or she can do absolutely anything with it. For example, your spouse can leave it all to charity or to his or her own children from a prior marriage, cutting your children out. A trust prevents this. You can give your second spouse an income for life while guaranteeing that your children will ultimately inherit the principal.

Whatever you do, don't lock your heirs into an estate planner's prison. It's not worth saving the taxes if your trust will completely inhibit your family's freedom to act.

Choosing a Trustee

The average trust does just fine with an individual trustee—a spouse, family member, friend, lawyer, accountant, or business associate. His or her powers are outlined in your will or in the trust document. Fundamentally, you want the trustee to do what you would have done had you been alive, including hiring investment services. So you really have to believe in this person's morals and motives—and the morals and motives of a successor, if he or she should die.

Give your trustee wide latitude. You don't know what's going to happen 10 or 20 years hence and shouldn't try to guess. Write a letter to all the trustees (including successor trustees), with copies to all beneficiaries, explaining what you want the trust to accomplish and what the money can be distributed for. That way everyone understands exactly what you have in mind.

Your risk is that the trustee will slip. His or her judgment may go. The trustee may steal, or disapprove of one of your children and deny that child funds, or decide not to follow the terms of the trust when distributing the property, or grow senile, or become disabled. Trustees don't have to account to a court for their actions, as is required of the executor of a will. It's difficult to curb a willful trustee or one who plays favorites in the family. Your will or trust document should provide for a substitute if the family demands it or when the trustee passes a certain age.

If your spouse is trustee, he or she will need a cotrustee. Your spouse can take up to $5,000 or 5 percent of the estate each year (whichever is larger), but that's normally the limit. Only a cotrustee can make larger distributions. State laws vary on a spouse's powers, but your lawyer will know the rules. Assuming that you trust your spouse, he or she should be given the power to change the cotrustee.

The alternative to having a friend or relative as trustee is naming a bank or trust company. There you get a professional money manager and experienced estate administrator who won't move away and won't steal. If your family hates its trust officer, it can ask the bank for another one. But this choice has some drawbacks too. The bank charges money. It takes only larger trusts for personal management (generally $250,000 to $500,000 and up). It is often too busy to take an interest in the family, although this can be solved by naming your spouse or another relative cotrustee.

Always put an escape clause in the document so that your heirs (or their guardian, if they're minors) have the option of moving the trust to another bank or trust company. The new trustee shouldn't be related or beholden to any person with the power of removing him or her.

Require your trustee to make an annual, audited accounting to your family and other heirs. That allays suspicions, helps trustees avoid temptation, and can catch something fishy that might be going on.

Avoiding Estate Taxes

The value of your property at death is called your estate. The federal government collects a tax on large estates but not on midsize or small ones.

At this writing (summer 2009), the amount of the estate tax is up in the air. A law signed by President George W. Bush abolished the tax for 2010, then reinstated it for 2011 and later, at a much higher cost to families of midsize wealth. Almost certainly that nonsense will not prevail, but I had to ship off this manuscript before I found out what happened.

One rule hasn't changed: you can leave any amount of money to your spouse, estate-tax free. My best guess for your other heirs: they'll inherit under something similar to the 2009 rules. That gives them up to $3.5 million free of federal tax. (Some states tax smaller amounts.)

If your net worth isn't likely to exceed $3.5 million (or whatever exemption is set for 2010 and beyond), a simple "I love you" will is all you need. But if you're over that limit, stay close to your lawyer for the next couple of years to be sure that your will or trust is always up to date. With good legal advice, you can cut the tax bill without mishap. Among the attorneys' bag of tricks:

1. Make gifts while you're alive. Up to $13,000 a year can go to each of as many people as you like, tax free. (That sum includes small gifts such as $50 at Christmas.) If your spouse joins in the gift, you can give up to $26,000, even if it's all your money.

You can also give as much as $60,000 to a 529 college savings plan ($120,000 if you and your spouse both give—see page 667 for details).

Larger gifts will eat into your federal estate tax exemption; they may even trigger gift taxes during your lifetime if you give away more than $1 million. But in most cases, no payment is due until after you die. The rule is: a gift is taxable only if its value, when added to the value of your estate at death, turns out to exceed the current estate tax exemption. Even if the gift will lead to taxes, the cost may be worth it. If you give, say, $30,000 in cash to a son who'll buy stocks, the gains will accumulate in his name instead of yours—saving you income taxes and maybe estate taxes too.

2. Give away your life insurance policy. Give it to your spouse, your child, or an irrevocable trust. That takes the proceeds out of your estate unless you die within three years of making the gift; then the proceeds, and taxes, come back. You can even continue paying the premiums, although if you do, they could become a taxable gift to the new owner. (To minimize the gift, use what's called a Crummey power. I'll leave it to your lawyer to explain that one.) As an alternative, the new owner can pay the premiums.

The new owner can change the beneficiary, withdraw the cash value, or even cancel the policy. If you give the policy to your spouse and then divorce, tough luck.

If your spouse owns the policy, his or her will should leave it to the children or another beneficiary. Otherwise, if your spouse dies first, the policy might come right back into your estate. If your spouse leaves the policy to your children in trust and you're the trustee, it could also be taxed in your estate. (You see why I told you to consult a lawyer.)

If your spouse owns the policy, he or she should be named beneficiary. If you make the children the beneficiaries and you die, the IRS may say that your spouse made the children a taxable gift of the insurance proceeds.

To give away an individual policy, ask the insurance company for an assignment form. You can also give away a group policy that you hold through your employer. Term policies, in particular, make terrific gifts because there's no cash value, so no gift tax can be imposed.

3. Marry. No estate tax is levied on property given or bequeathed to a spouse. When the spouse dies, any money exceeding the estate tax exemption can be taxed in the spouse's estate when he or she dies—unless, of course, the spouse remarries and passes the tax deferral on.

4. Create a bypass trust. Married couples can avoid a tax when the surviving spouse dies by creating his-and-her trusts (sometimes known as credit shelter trusts or bypass trusts, because they bypass estate taxes). These trusts can each hold assets worth up to the current estate tax exemption. That money generally goes to the children, although the spouse can have some or all of the income from the trust and access to the principal for life. The children can also be given some or all of the income. Here's how this strategy usually plays out if the husband dies first and the law exempts $3.5 million from tax (reverse it if the wife dies first):

　　a. The husband dies.

　　b. Up to $3.5 million of his assets goes into a bypass trust for the children and the wife. This money passes estate tax–free because it's protected by the husband's federal estate tax credit.

　　c. The wife gets the income from the trust for life, plus the right to receive funds directly from the principal if needed. That's a key point. She always has access to all of the money. It's never locked away from her.

Additionally, the trust can allow her to take out $5,000 or 5 percent of the value of the trust each year (whichever is larger), without asking the trustee and without paying any tax. If she wants even more of the principal, the trustee has to agree. But that shouldn't be a problem as long as the husband names a sympathetic trustee and makes it clear that his wife should be given whatever she wants. In some states, the husband can name the wife trustee. The trust document should broadly provide that the money be used for her happiness and general welfare.

　　d. After benefiting from the trust for many years, the wife dies. All the remaining money in trust is distributed to the children, tax free.

　　e. The wife leaves the children another $3.5 million, sheltered by her own estate tax credit.

　　f. A total of $7 million (or more, if the value of the first trust has grown) has been left to the kids free of federal estate taxes. That's at least twice the amount that the kids could otherwise get untaxed.

For this to work, each spouse has to have enough assets to fund a trust—held in his or her separate name, in both names as community property, or as tenants in common without rights of survivorship. If you own everything jointly, your tax-saving trust won't work. If your house is a substantial part of your net worth, consider owning it as tenants in common (see page 86). Your half of the house (or the spouse's half) can then become part of the trust.

Take special care if you're putting Individual Retirement Accounts or other tax-deferred retirement savings into a bypass trust. Such a trust must be drafted in a particular way. If it's not, your spouse loses the right to stretch out the payments from the retirement fund over his or her lifetime. Instead the money would have to be received—and taxed—all at once.

What if you're worth just a little over $3.5 million and don't want to decide in advance whether to put money into a trust? Your spouse can assess the situation after your death and, if it seems smart, disclaim (refuse) any part of the inheritance. Your will can provide that any disclaimed money would go into a trust. A beneficiary has a limited period of time within which to disclaim: nine months from the date of death for federal tax purposes; longer, in some states, if you want to disclaim for reasons other than saving tax.

What if you're in a second marriage and your spouse is about the same age as your children? Give them some money when you die. Otherwise they may never see it.

Warning: Older wills often tell executors to put the maximum amount of money allowed by law into the trust. But the new maximum is so high that it might take most or all of your assets. That would leave your surviving spouse completely dependent on trust income for his or her support. Also, that old language might trigger an unnecessary state tax. Instead, name a dollar figure for the trust or use flexible language allowing the executor to decide the amount.

Further warning: Some states levy taxes on estates worth less than $3.5 million. Bypass trusts can still work, but the drafting becomes more complicated.

5. Disclaim. Let's say that your uncle Bill died and left you some money. But you're well off, and your son in college is next in line to inherit. You can say no to the bequest, letting it go directly to your son. That saves your estate from paying taxes on that money when you die. A spouse might want to disclaim a payout from a late spouse's 401(k) plan and let the money go directly to the children if they're the alternate beneficiaries.

6. Give money to charity. Money given—or left—to charity reduces your estate, hence your estate tax. See page 141 for information about charitable trusts.

7. Start a family limited partnership. This arrangement lets parents and children, as well as other relatives, own assets together. Over time you gradually raise the children's stake in the assets. The earlier they possess them, the more of the assets' capital appreciation will be moved out of the parents' estates. That will lower their tax. Typically, the parents are the general partners, which gives them the right to make decisions about the assets. The children are limited partners with no voice in management. They sign buy-sell agreements so that the other partners can buy them out if they want to quit. (Those shares are the children's, by the way. The parents can't take the assets back.) Family limited partnerships are usually used to hold business interests and real estate. A couple needn't go to this trouble, however, if their joint estate will probably be worth less than the federal estate tax exemption. Also note: Future changes in tax laws might make these arrangements less attractive.

When to Ignore Estate Taxes

It isn't graven in stone that you have to avoid estate taxes for the sake of your heirs. You come first. Don't give away so much property or put so much in trust that you or your spouse will become dependent on others, even if they're your own children. They're lucky to be getting anything from you at all and have no right to grumble if extra estate taxes are due.

Whatever you decide, don't undertake your own tax planning. To explain all these concepts, I have made a meadow out of what is actually a briar patch. Only an experienced estate-planning attorney can walk you through unscratched.

When Are Inheritances Paid?

Probate can go quickly when your lawyer hustles, the courts are efficient, there aren't a lot of distant heirs to notify, and no one challenges the will. A will might be admitted to probate anywhere within a couple of days to a couple of months after the death and declared valid almost immediately. A surviving spouse can generally start taking reasonable sums from the estate right away in order to meet living expenses. Life insurance is paid out pronto. So is jointly owned property, in most cases. If months pass and nothing happens, it probably means that your lawyer or executors aren't paying attention, not that the property is somehow "stuck in probate."

Some executors start distributing the property without delay. Others distribute part of it but hold on to the rest of the assets for four to twelve months, which is the time generally allowed for creditors to file claims against the estate. Stocks, cars, and bank accounts can be distributed as quickly as you can get a new name on the title. Other property—real estate, for example—takes longer to transfer because of the paperwork or the need to sell at a reasonable price. Valuable personal property often can't be divided until it's appraised, unless all the beneficiaries agree on who gets what.

Executors usually hold back a little money until the final tax return is accepted (if there's a deficiency, the executor is personally responsible). The average estate might be fully distributed in six months to a year and a half. Large estates can take several years—not because probate delays things but because the property is complex. It would take just as long to distribute it from a living trust with no probate involved. In some states, trustees as well as executors are liable for unpaid bills and taxes, so they're careful to get these obligations paid before distributing all the money to heirs.

Granting the Power, Durably

Everyone needs a backup, a person to act for you if you're away, if you're sick, if you get hit by a car and can't function for a while, or if you grow senile. That means giving someone—a spouse, mate, parent, adult child, or trusted friend—your power of attorney. A lawyer can get this document together in a jiffy. It's probably in his or her word processor and just needs printing out. Young people need a power of attorney as well as the old. Your agent is known as your *attorney-in-fact.*

Limited powers of attorney grant narrow rights, such as "Christopher can write checks on my bank account to pay my bills while I'm out of the country for six months." *Ordinary* powers of attorney give broader powers over your finances. But both limited and ordinary powers expire if you become mentally disabled, which is exactly when you'll need the help the most.

So protect yourself against doomsday by asking a lawyer to draw up a *durable* power of attorney. It lets someone act for you if you're judged senile or mentally disabled, if you fall into a coma, or if illness or accident damages your brain. As long as you are mentally capable, you can revoke a durable power whenever you like.

The person who holds your power of attorney could, theoretically, exercise it at any time, even if you're healthy. He or she could sell your investments and clean out your bank account. But that's not as easy as it sounds. Banks and brokers normally check on what has happened to you before accepting a power of attorney. Besides, you wouldn't give the power to someone you didn't trust.

Be sure to execute copies of the durable power—maybe even three or more. Most institutions want to see an original, although they'll make photocopies for their files. (But don't sign too many; they may be hard to retrieve if you want to revoke them or change a name.)

In some states, you have to execute new durable powers every four or five years to show that your intention holds. Insurance companies and financial institutions probably won't honor an old power. A few won't honor any power more than six months old or any power not written on their own forms, unless a lawyer leans on them. In my view, that's harassment, but they sometimes do it, and you might be stuck. Always ask your bank, broker, or insurance company what its policy is, so you'll know for sure that the power you've signed is going to work. If they dig in their heels when you're too senile to make decisions, your attorney-in-fact will have to apply to the court for a guardianship. No institution can refuse to obey a court-appointed guardian, but it's outrageous that any should push the issue this far. Fortunately, few do. Some states have laws requiring financial institutions to accept valid powers of attorney.

If you'd rather not trust anyone until you absolutely have to, write a *springing* power of attorney. It doesn't take effect unless you become mentally incapacitated and the document defines exactly what that means. For example: "I shall be deemed to be disabled when two physicians licensed to practice medicine in my state sign a paper stating that I am disabled and unable to handle my financial affairs." The same language can be used to determine when your disability has passed. Springing powers are cumbersome, however, and an extra complication for financial institutions.

How do you cancel a durable power of attorney? Tell the person holding it that he or she is out; get all signed copies of the power back; destroy the copies, preferably in front of witnesses; where there are duplicates, write to the institutions holding your money telling them not to accept that person as your agent.

How do you maintain your family's trust in your agent? Require that he or she make an annual accounting of what's being done with your money. That relieves suspicion and protects the agent too.

A Living Will and Health Care Proxy

Anyone who has seen a dying or permanently comatose person hooked up fruitlessly—sometimes painfully—to life support machines understands the issue of the right to die. As long as you're conscious, you can make your own medical decisions, including the decision to refuse treatment. The problems arise when you're unable to speak for yourself. Many of the patients attached to respirators and food-and-water tubes without hope of recovery have been forced to it by state law or custom. If they could speak, they'd say stop, but no one is authorized to pull the plug. Life "support," in these cases, is merely delaying death rather than truly sustaining life. In several states, there's a movement to require artificial feeding unless the patient—specifically and in writing—said no.

Your best hope of avoiding this fate yourself is to sign an *advance directive*. It includes a *living will* dictating the kind of treatment you want if you're terminally ill and cannot speak for yourself. You also need a *health care agent* or *proxy* or *durable health care power of attorney*. They name an agent to do two things: (1) See that your end-of-life decisions are carried out. (2) Make medical choices for you when you're not dying but are in no condition to make them yourself. Lawyers advise that you name two stand-ins to act for you in case one isn't around at the critical moment. To avoid inaction or delay, either one should be able to act alone.

All the states recommend specific living-will language. For free forms, go to Caring Connections (www.caringinfo.org) or Legaldocs (www.legaldocs.com), Be sure to specify your exact wishes, especially as to withholding or withdrawing treatment, tubes for delivering food and water, and a respirator. If you spend time in more than one state, write an advance directive for each. They may have different rules. In some right-to-life states, it can be hard for your proxy to withdraw food and water unless your directive conforms exactly to the wording in state law.

Even with a living will, your wishes might not be carried out without court enforcement. A son might say, "I don't care what my father thought he wanted; go ahead and treat him," and the doctor probably would. Your best hope of avoiding this is to talk with everyone in a position to influence your treatment: spouse, children, siblings, doctors, and the person or people named in your health care proxy. Discuss exactly what you'd expect, under varying medical circumstances. Let them ask you hypothetical questions about your end-of-life care. For a good guide to these discussions, read the "Consumer's Tool Kit for Health Care Advance Planning" on the Web site of the American Bar Association (www.abanet.org/aging).

What happens if you suffer a situation—permanent coma, brain-crushing accident, terminal illness that takes your reason first—and have no living will? In 39 states and Washington, D.C., written legislation permits family members or a legal guardian to "stand in the patient's shoes" to make the life-or-death decision that the patient would probably make were he or she able to do so. Case-by-case court decisions or sympathetic doctors may lead to the same result in other states, although you can't count on it. The issue might have to go to a hospital ethics committee, which could put families through a difficult question-and-answer session. The problem is that family members might not agree, as in the famous Terri Schiavo case, in which her husband fought with her parents over removing life support. In New York, no surrogate decisions are supposed to be accepted unless there's "clear and convincing" evidence that the patient—while still functioning—expressed a wish not to be kept alive artificially. That's a high standard that theoretically can't be met unless you leave a written document, although some doctors quietly fudge the rule. California, Michigan, and Wisconsin apply a "clear and convincing" standard in cases where helpless patients do not have a terminal illness and are not in a permanent vegetative state.

An advance directive is the clearest expression of your intent. The lawyer who drafts your regular will or living trust will include it as part of the package.

If You Prefer Life at Any Cost

You may feel that you want to be kept alive regardless of the terminal state of your disease, any pain that additional treatment might cause, or the risk of living in a comatose state for many years. The National Right to Life Committee (www.nrlc.org) has free state-by-state "Will to Live" forms, telling your doctor to resuscitate you if your heart stops, provide all life-preserving treatments, and prescribe and maintain artificial feeding and hydration. Many doctors would be reluctant to provide all treatments to someone who's comatose or unconscious and terminally ill, so, again, you'd need someone to insist. Will to Live forms also leave a space for you to say that treatment can be ended if your death is imminent.

For Access to Information

Sign a letter giving your health care agent the right to talk to your medical providers about treatments and billings. Otherwise your agent may be denied critical information, due to the workings of the federal privacy law. If you want your adult children or any others to have access to your medical records, sign separate letters for them.

Adult Guardianship—How to Prepare

We think about guardians for our children. But who will take care of us if our mental powers decline? If you haven't prepared, your children or other relatives might have to go to court to have you declared incompetent. An adult with money could even be the target of a custody suit, as various relatives vie to get you and your checkbook under their control.

To keep this from happening, draw up a *Nomination of Guardian* or *Nomination of Conservator* form, permitted in many states. In it, you name the person or people you want to be the guardian of your person, your property, or both, if you become incompetent. Specify what "incompetence" means—for example, if two doctors agree that you can no longer handle your affairs. Be sure that the guardian is willing to take the job. The document can be handwritten, but your signature has to be notarized.

Alternatively, you might choose a living trust, if it makes sense to have one for other reasons. The trustee you name can start making decisions for you under specified conditions—for example, if two doctors say that you're unable to handle your affairs—without a court proceeding.

Wills Versus Living Trusts

A huge industry exists in America peddling the false idea that everyone needs a living trust. Trusts are flogged via seminars and cold-call telemarketing by lawyers, insurance agents, and financial planners, all of whom will make a few bucks (in fact, more than a few) if you set one up. Deceptive selling is widespread. Many people believe, for example, that only living trusts will lower your estate taxes, when, in fact, you get exactly the same savings from wills. Many more people believe that probate means disaster, which isn't true either. So before I talk about trusts, let me talk about probate.

Slaying the Probate Myth

"Avoiding probate" is one of the big reasons that people give for investing in living trusts. They hear tales that probate leaves you poor. Your property gets stuck in the courts. Lawyers bleed the estate. In the old days, this was sometimes true, but it's not anymore. Bad probate is the exception, not the rule.

Probate means "prove." It's the system that ensures that your will is valid and that your property passes to the person who is supposed to get it. Nowadays, most of the states offer simplified probate,* especially for small estates or estates in which everything goes to the spouse. There may also be speedy procedures for estates that aren't contested—meaning most of them. Odds and ends of personal property, including a car, rarely have to go through probate. They're divided as your will directs or by private agreement among your heirs. Families can even handle the paperwork themselves; just go to the probate court and let the clerk tell you what to do. Or a lawyer can handle it for you. With simplified procedures—meaning little or no court oversight—the lawyer shouldn't charge

---

* Here are the states that, at this writing, have instituted the Uniform Probate Code or similar forms of simplified probate procedures: Alabama, Alaska, Arizona, Colorado, the District of Columbia, Georgia, Hawaii, Idaho, Illinois, Indiana, Maine, Maryland, Michigan, Minnesota, Missouri, Montana, Nebraska, New Jersey, New Mexico, North Dakota, Pennsylvania, South Carolina, South Dakota, Texas, Utah, Washington, and Wisconsin.

too much (show the lawyer this sentence!). In fact, it shouldn't be any more than he or she would charge to help you handle a living trust when the owner dies.

Many of the stories you hear about being "tied up in probate" involve disputed property, delays by banks and brokers in getting the title changed, or disputes with insurance companies over old policies—none of which has anything to do with the courts. It may also have taken a lot of time to find all the property if the deceased didn't keep good records. You'd face exactly the same problems and delays if the assets were in living trusts (especially because people may forget to transfer all their assets to the trust). Sometimes the probate courts are indeed the baddies, but usually they're not. The trustee of a living trust can sometimes be a baddie too. So can some of the lawyers who promote living trusts. I've heard them tell older people, "If your estate winds up in probate, your lawyer can't go to the bathroom without court approval." Not true. Simply not true.

This is not to say that you shouldn't consider a living trust. They have their uses. It's just that avoiding probate for reasons of cost and complexity usually isn't one of them.

What Is a Living Trust?

The trust transfers property ownership from you as an individual to you as trustee. *You* no longer own it; it's owned by the trustee, who happens to be you. (It's like a fun house mirror where you see yourself in every glass.) Some states require at least one other trustee. You and your spouse or partner can be cotrustees, or you can name an outside trustee.

As trustee, you run the money just as if you still owned it in the old-fashioned way. You can invest it as you like, use income and principal, leave the money to whomever you want, change beneficiaries at will, even revoke the trust altogether. In short, you have the same control as you'd have if you were leaving your property by will.

You name one or more successor trustees to manage the money if you become incapable and to distribute the assets when you die. These can be changed, too. If someone other than you is trustee and he or she won't follow orders, you can fire that person and install someone else if the trust document allows it. As long as you're competent, you're completely in charge. Because you can change or cancel the trust at any time, it is also called a *revocable trust*.

For the trust to be effective, it has to hold all of your property that would otherwise go through probate. You will no longer own your home directly; instead you'll hold it as "Eric F. Jordan, trustee of the Jordan Family Trust dated February 5, 2009." Ditto for your securities, business interests, cars, and most other assets. From a paperwork point of view, it's like going through probate before you die. (Note that transferring real estate into a trust terminates your title insurance in most states; talk to your insurer about how to keep the coverage going.)

When you buy additional property, such as a new house or more mutual fund shares, they also have to be bought in the name of the trust. Checks for these purchases have to be signed "Eric F. Jordan trustee [etc.]" and be issued from the trust's bank account. You report your trust's taxable income on your regular Form 1040. Los Angeles attorney Charles A. Collier, Jr., suggests that you set up a bank account outside your trust for routine bills and transfer money to it as needed. An outside account lets you pay bills without involving your trust. It also saves you from having to disclose the language of your trust to banks or other sources of credit. An outside account won't trigger probate as long as it contains a small amount of money or is held jointly with a spouse or another co-owner.

Only the property held in trust can be distributed by your successor trustee after you die. The document should include an assignment of all property to the trust.

Many people start a trust on a salesperson's say-so but never deed their property to it or set up a trust bank account. If that happens to you, you'll have wasted your money on the legal documents. You effectively have no trust at all. Or you have some property in trust and some outside it, meaning that you have to go through *both* probate and trust administration!

Property not held in trust is handled under the terms of your will and usually goes through probate. To simplify matters, your successor trustee and the executor of your will should be the same person.

Why You Might Want a Living Trust

1. To avoid probate, if that matters to you. When property is to be distributed according to the terms of a will, the will goes first to probate court. The court certifies the will as valid and empowers the executor to distribute the property. Certification can take a few days to a couple of months. By contrast, property held in a living trust goes to the beneficiaries when you die, without pausing in the probate court. A trustee can start distributing property right away. Still, distribution can be delayed for reasons other than probate. Deeds have to change hands, assets valued, and tax forms filled in. The trustee will want to collect and pay all debts. With larger estates, the trustee may want to hold back some or all of the assets until he or she settles income tax and estate tax questions with Uncle Sam. In short, it may take the same amount of time to clear the estate, whether the property passes by trust or by will.

2. To have someone on tap to handle your money if you're incapacitated. You might be ill. You might have grown permanently vague. The cheapest and easiest way around this problem is to give someone a durable power of attorney, to manage your property when you can't. A financial institution will want to check the power's authenticity before your agent can act. It might make your agent jump through hoops if the power is many years old. It also might not let your agent do risky or unusual things with your money, such as buy derivatives or invest in stocks on margin.

Trustees have more latitude. Institutions can't refuse someone who succeeds you as trustee of your living trust (although, again, it will take the time to check). And the trustee can do whatever he or she wants with your money as long as it's covered by the language of the trust. So pay attention to the powers you're giving.

The trust should specify when your trustee is allowed to take over your affairs. Give yourself a lot of latitude, so that the trustee doesn't step in too soon. You should be free to throw money at a gigolo, retreat to an ashram, or hunt for gold in Alaska if that's what appeals to you. The law lets you waste your assets however you like as long as you *know* that you may be doing something dumb. Only when your mental capacity goes, as determined by independent doctors, should your trustee be empowered to take over the money.

3. To handle real properties out of state. Your will has to be probated in every state where you hold real estate unless you hold it in joint names or in trust.

4. To handle closely held business interests, rental real estate, large stock portfolios, or other complex properties. A knowledgeable trustee can keep all your business interests functioning smoothly until they're sold or otherwise disposed of. The trustee can also manage the property if you're disabled or on vacation for an extended period of time.

5. To test the ability of a professional money manager. If you intend to leave money managed in trust for heirs, it makes sense to give the managers a trial run. You turn over the trust to a bank trust department or investment-management firm, while you remain trustee. They will also manage your money independently of a trust. The advantage of the trust would be to have the arrangement in place in case you died or became mentally disabled.

Banks take almost any sum of money. Small amounts (and large ones too) can go into pooled accounts that work like mutual funds. Amounts exceeding $200,000 to $300,000 can usually be managed individually if that's what you want. Make sure that you're able to switch to a different money manager if you don't like the personal treatment you get or the investment results.

6. To defend against relatives who might challenge your will. Trusts can be challenged too—for example, if you can be shown to have been senile when you dictated a new beneficiary. But they're generally harder to break than wills. All the relatives don't even have to be notified of the terms of the trust. Some states let you use living trusts to disinherit a spouse, who would normally be entitled to a substantial portion of your estate. Disinheriting a spouse is contrary to public policy, not to mention dad-gum mean, but it's done.

7. To keep matters private. Wills are public documents, and therefore, in many states, so is the inventory of your estate. Trusts are normally private.

8. To try to avoid creditors. In some states, funds in a living trust that haven't been pledged to secure a debt might not be available to pay your creditors after your death. But this common-law protection is crumbling. For the best protection against the creditors of a deceased spouse, use tenancy by the entirety (see page 87).

9. To simplify the process of leaving money to young children. Your will can set up a testamentary trust for your minor children, but it's under the supervision of a court. Living trusts escape that scrutiny (although you have to trust the trustee).

10. To try to minimize family fights. If your family doesn't get along and you plan to leave less (or nothing) to relatives who won't take it lightly, a trust might make it easier to get your wishes done. Disgruntled relatives can challenge a trust just as they can challenge a will, but it costs them more to do so. Also, trustees generally have more discretion than executors, and trusts are harder to break.

Living Trusts Do *Not* Save Taxes

They're not unique vehicles for cutting your income taxes or estate taxes. Many people erroneously believe they are, because a living-trust salesperson told them so. But as long as you control the property, it will be income-taxed to you and treated as part of your taxable estate. Your living trust can contain other trusts that reduce or eliminate estate taxes. But those tax-avoiding trusts can also be put into a will. In short, living trusts have no significant tax advantages. If you buy one for tax reasons, you've been steered wrong.

Will a Living Trust Save You Money?

No, in jurisdictions with reformed and speedy probate procedures, such as those under the Uniform Probate Code (see page 129). Typically, trusts cost more than wills up front because of all the legal work. Probate may cost more after death, for the same reason. The total bill may not be much different in either case. If you choose a trust, you'll still need a will to handle any property that accidentally—now or in the future—gets left out of the trust. You'll also need a will to name a guardian for your young children. That's something a trust can't do.

Yes, in jurisdictions where the probate courts deserve to be shot. There, legal fees are high. Happily, most of these states have made reforms. A lawyer who's a friend can tell you about the local courts. Or call or visit the court clerk and ask: (1) Are there simplified probate procedures? (2) What are they? (3) To what kinds of estates do they apply? You may also find this information on your state's Web site. Even a state plagued with delays may have some streamlined jurisdictions.

In states that set maximums on how much a probate lawyer can charge, some lawyers try to treat the maximum as a fixed price. But many of their competitors charge less and advertise that they do. You can often negotiate a lower fee.

More Living Trust Facts

Each state has its own rules and taxes affecting trusts, so see a lawyer if you move. Your trust document should specifically allow for a change of state so the laws that govern the trust can change too. Otherwise the laws (and taxes) of your former state apply unless you get a court order allowing a change.

There's a lot of legwork involved in transferring property into a trust. Your lawyer will prepare the new deed for your real property, as well as transfer letters for assets held by your bank, broker, and other financial connections. But you'll have to follow up or else pay your lawyer to do it. Be sure to check with your title insurance company before transferring real estate into the trust. If you don't, the insurance may lapse.

Don't make the trust the beneficiary of your 401(k) or Individual Retirement Account. If you died, that whole sum of money might go into the trust and be taxed right away. By contrast, a spouse or other individual beneficiary can roll the 401(k) into an inherited IRA and take payments over many years (page 181). That spreads the taxes out. Some 401(k)s include a special provision allowing a direct transfer to an inherited IRA for the benefit of a trust. But the plan could change its rules at any time, so relying on this angle is generally not a good strategy.

You can name the living trust as the beneficiary of your life insurance policy. The proceeds would then go into the trust to be distributed as you directed. Before doing this, however, married people should ensure that a surviving spouse will have plenty of ready cash in case there's a delay in getting the trust paid out.

Your trustee can take over your financial affairs if you become disabled, so the trust should specify what "disabled" means. For example: "I shall be deemed to be disabled when two physicians licensed to practice medicine in my state sign a paper stating that I am disabled and unable to handle my financial affairs." The same language can be used to determine when your disability has passed and you can handle your money again.

To change the terms of a living trust, you prepare a written amendment. Don't scratch in the changes on the trust document; they won't be accepted. In some states, the amendment has to be signed and, maybe, witnessed just like a will. But in most states, a notarized signature will do.

A married couple should ask an experienced estate-planning lawyer (not a lawyer or insurance agent who's hard-selling trusts) whether they need one trust or two.

In community property states, it's common to have a single trust document for all the property. Each spouse's separate property interests are segregated within the trust. At the death of the first spouse, the trust divides into multiple trusts.

In other states, dual trusts are more common, so that each of you has more freedom to act. With a single trust, you both may have to agree on changing the beneficiaries or other terms of the trust unless the document specifically permits only one of you to do so. Ditto with investment decisions. Ditto the decision to withdraw your property from the trust or revoke it if you split. In some cases, joint trusts create strange tax consequences that you need an expert to expound. It's best that each of you has his or her own trust.

To revoke a living trust, you have to retitle all the trust property in some other name. It's legwork, legwork all over again.

If a couple's joint trust is revoked, the assets might be distributed 50–50 unless the trust document provides for a specific uneven split. If one of you puts in 70 percent of the assets and the other puts in 30 percent, you might want to provide for a 70/30 split in case of dissolution.

If you have an individual trust naming your spouse as beneficiary and you separate or divorce, remove the spouse's name immediately. If you die, a separated spouse can inherit; in some states, so can a divorced spouse. (By contrast, a divorced spouse generally cannot inherit under your will, even if he or she is still named as beneficiary.)

You normally need a will to appoint a guardian of your minor children. State law might allow you to use some other document, but check with a lawyer to see if a living trust will meet the requirements. It may not.

If your trust owns a certificate of deposit and it matures, the payment must be made into a bank account opened in the name of the trust. Ditto for any proceeds from the sale of real estate or securities.

A successor trustee who takes over from you must distribute the income and principal as the trust requires. You can give your trustee the discretion to distribute unequally among the named beneficiaries if that seems like the right thing to do.

All the trust's property doesn't have to be distributed right away. You can instruct the trustee to hold property until your children are older, or distribute just the income, or distribute property to some beneficiaries and not to others. Whatever you want.

Check "More Will Facts" on page 112. Many of those rules apply to trusts, too.

For a discussion of wills versus living trusts, see page 139.

Choosing a Trustee

If you go for a living trust, your toughest decision will be choosing a trustee who'll step in if you or your spouse can no longer serve. Trustees don't have to account to a court for their actions, as do the executors of a will. They might ignore your wishes. If there's a dispute, it's harder to take a trustee to court. So it's superimportant to find someone who's reliable.

A dependable grown child will see to your welfare but might have bad financial or investment judgment. An undependable grown child might loot your assets.

A business associate or lawyer might be good at managing your money but help himself or herself to it.

A bank or brokerage house has investment experience, won't skip out or steal, and will handle the paperwork. But institutional trustees are expensive and may not knock themselves out to keep you happy.

Cotrustees often work well—a family member and a bank or investment adviser. But again, you pay.

In the end, you can only go for integrity and intelligence and keep your fingers crossed. Make your wishes crystal clear, so that the trustee—and everyone affected by the trust—knows what's allowed. And, of course, provide a method for kicking out a trustee whom the family doesn't like.

Don't Try to Save Money by Setting Up a Trust Without Using an Experienced lawyer. Books with tear-out forms for doing trusts or do-it-yourself computer programs are not your friends. You might misunderstand the instructions, which are complicated and often incomplete. You might fill in ambiguous forms ambiguously. Without your knowing it, the forms may be unsuited to your purpose. You might miss an important angle that specifically affects your family. You might be working with a defective or out-of-date do-it-yourself book. You might think you've put property into trust when you haven't because you didn't transfer the title to yourself as trustee, or you might not understand which assets need to be retitled. You risk making the same kinds of errors with bequests that are made with homemade wills (page 103). I beg you to see an experienced tax- and estate-planning lawyer. I am down on my knees. If it's worth having a trust, it's worth doing the job right.

If you insist on doing the job, consider the Quicken WillMaker by Nolo, the leading publisher of do-it-yourself legal materials. It covers both wills and living trusts. Cost at this writing: software on CD, $49.99; downloadable software, $39.99. Order online (www.nolo.com) or by phone (800-728-3555). Helpful as these are, however, I wouldn't touch them myself. I'd rather have an experienced lawyer do it.

The Poor Man's Living Trust

Here's how to get the advantages of a living trust without actually setting one up:

1. To ensure that there's someone to manage your affairs if you become incapable: Give a trusted relative or friend your durable power of attorney (page 125). But check with all the institutions you do business with—bank, broker, mutual fund group, insurance company. Some will want the power written on their own form or will have other antiquated rules.

2. To make it easier for your surrogate to manage complicated property: Set up a *standby living trust* containing only a token amount of property. If you ever become mentally incompetent, the person holding your durable power of attorney could activate the trust, put the rest of your property into it (if the durable power so authorized), and arrange for it to be properly managed. At your death, it would go to the heirs you designate.

3. To pass important assets to heirs without going through probate: Put property into joint names with right of survivorship. Name specific beneficiaries for your insurance policies, Individual Retirement Accounts, 401(k)s, real estate, and investment accounts. Just make sure that the named beneficiaries match the beneficiaries named in your will.

4. To pass bank accounts to heirs without going through probate or naming a joint owner: Set up accounts "in trust for" or "payable on death" to one or more beneficiaries. In many states, you can do the same with stockbrokerage accounts, mutual fund shares, and deeds (those accounts are referred to as *transferable on death*). In all cases, control stays with you—to change the invest-ments, change the beneficiary, even cancel the account by taking every penny out. You haven't made a gift, so the income is still taxable to you. The beneficiary can't touch the money until you die. But at death, the account passes directly to the beneficiary without going through probate. One possible drawback: when you die, the beneficiary gets the money immediately, ready or not.

Risks of Probate-Avoidance Techniques

1. A joint owner might take your money and run or die a week after you do, leaving the assets to be probated in his or her estate. A child named as joint owner, to help you manage your money, may feel entitled to some of the assets on the side.

2. Naming individual beneficiaries for each of your assets might leave one of your children with less money than another. Even if they have equal amounts at the start, changes in the investments' value or withdrawals from one account but not another could disadvantage one of your children in the end. If you leave everything by will, it's easier to divide the estate evenly.

3. A do-it-yourself living trust might not work out if it wasn't properly set up and managed. Lawyer-drawn trusts need, well, a lawyer.

4. Even with a trust, it can take a year or more to settle an estate. That's because actual probate—the court procedure—usually isn't the problem. The delays arise when you try to get property appraised, get ownership transferred into new names, and pay all the income and estate taxes—all of which have to be done whether there's a trust or not.

They're Out to Get You

Squadrons of insurance agents are knocking on doors all over the country, using high-pressure tactics to sell one-size-fits-all living trusts, at too high a price, to people who often do not need them. Battalions of lawyers are holding seminars, especially in retirement areas, claiming that trusts will solve all life's problems, up to curing the common cold. They're telling you lies. Typically, they lead you to think that probate costs tens of thousands of dollars more than trusts (in fact, probate can be cheaper than the trusts these phonies sell); that only trusts can lower your estate taxes (not true; there's no tax advantage to trusts over wills); that probate will tie up your estate for years (not true, as long as your family isn't fighting over the remains); and that if you become incompetent, only a trust

(*continued on page 141*)

Table 2.

WHICH TO CHOOSE: A WILL OR A LIVING TRUST?

On balance, most people will do fine, and save money, with just a will. Living trusts are suitable only in a minority of cases. Here's a checklist to help you decide which is the best for your particular circumstances. Read the footnotes carefully. The answers you seek aren't simple ones.

Objective	Will	Living Trust
Save estate taxes	Yes	Yes
Save income taxes	Barely[1]	No[1]
Make charitable gifts, directly or in trust	Yes	Yes
Make annual tax-free gifts	Yes	Usually[2]
Save money up front	Yes	No[3]
Save costs at death	No[4]	Usually
Clear the way for speedy distribution of property after death	Often[5]	Yes
Actual speedy distribution of property	Sometimes[6]	Sometimes[6]
Keep your affairs private	Sometimes[7]	Usually[8]
Provide for continuous management of small-business interests	No[9]	Yes
Provide for continuous money management after your death	No[9]	Yes
Duck your creditors	No	Sometimes[10]
Provide for your money to be managed if you become incapable	Usually[11]	Yes
Provide for personal matters to be handled if you become incapable	Yes[11]	No[12]
Stop a challenge to your bequests	No[13]	No[14]
Avoid out-of-state probate	No[15]	Yes
Avoid paperwork	No[15]	No[16]

[1] Probate estates get a $600 income tax exemption, can choose a fiscal year that defers taxes, and can deduct income set aside for future distribution to a charity. A living trust gets only a $100 income tax exemption, must use a calendar year, and gets the charitable deduction only when the gift is made. It offers no income tax benefits that can't be matched by a will.

[2] Gifts made from trusts within three years of death might be included in your estate unless you use so-called Crummey powers (for these, see a lawyer).

[3] It costs more to set up a living trust than to prepare a will—maybe by $1,000 or more. A trust requires a backup will plus the paperwork for transferring property into the trust and setting up the trust's books. Also, you still need a durable power of attorney.

[4] Probate usually costs more because of court expenses, but not necessarily a lot more—perhaps just a few hundred dollars. In a few states, money-grubbing lawyers and antique court practices do indeed run up the fee. Your defense is to use an attorney who bases his or her fee on the work involved rather than a flat percentage of the value of the probate assets. In many other states, however, especially those that have adopted the Uniform Probate Code, streamlined probate procedures let the family settle many estates with zero legal costs. If you

consult a lawyer about transferring property into new names and preparing tax forms, it shouldn't matter whether the property is in trust or in an estate: your bill should be the same.

[5] Executors of wills have to wait until their formal appointment, which takes anywhere from three days to three weeks or more, depending on the court. After that, distributions can begin. Trustees don't have to wait at all if their names are already listed on the trust document.

[6] Executors usually wait until the debts are assessed, bills paid, and taxes wound up, although adequate amounts may be distributed promptly to a spouse or a child needing cash. It's the same for trustees in states where trusts are liable for debts. In other states, trustees may act more quickly; that is, they may try. To get property into the names of new owners takes the same length of time, whether it's being distributed from a trust or a probate estate. When people speak of being tied up in probate, they often mean that it's taking forever to get title to what they've inherited. That's the fault of the bank or broker responsible for making the name change or of a dilatory executor, not of the probate court. A trustee can be dilatory too.

[7] With probate estates, many states require that an inventory of the assets and debts be filed with the court. Others don't. Few of us have to worry about nosy neighbors running down to the courthouse. But this may be an issue for people in the limelight or business owners who don't want their competitors to know their true financial position. Trusts normally don't have to file an inventory. If it does have to be provided, you can request that it not be a matter of public record.

[8] Unless the trust is contested. If real property is added to a trust, the title company might require the trust instrument to be publicly recorded.

[9] Trusts set up in wills can handle or distribute business interests and provide continuous money management for such purposes as dispensing income to spouses or disabled children. But the trustee has to be appointed by the will and then get geared up to act (unless he or she has already been handling your affairs via a durable power of attorney). In the meantime, your executor usually has the authority to handle your business interests. Trustees of living trusts may already be on the job, although they too will have to get geared up unless they've been acting for you already.

[10] This is a pretty inglorious intent, but in some states, unpaid creditors can't attach the assets in a living trust. In other states, they can. They can definitely go after assets in a probate estate and in some states may be able to file against the trust if the probate assets aren't sufficient. The executor can be personally responsible for unpaid bills. One reason for delay in distributing probate assets is that the executor wants to be sure that all the estate's bills are paid.

[11] The will itself doesn't do this, but it's no hindrance. Your lawyer usually arranges for money management as part of the will-writing process. You'll sign a durable power of attorney, naming someone to act for you (your attorney-in-fact) if you're too sick or senile to act for yourself. Some banks, insurers, mutual fund companies, and brokerage houses are a pain about powers of attorney. They won't recognize them unless they're written on the institution's forms (or on forms legislated by the state). Trustees, by contrast, can't be denied. One wrinkle is that, with a living trust, incapacity has to be confirmed (maybe by a doctor; the trust will specify the rules). Attorneys-in-fact are empowered to act without this step. Assured continuity of management is especially important for people with no family member to handle their affairs.

[12] A trustee can't deal with questions involving Medicare, Medicaid, retirement plan transactions, family matters, and tax matters, and can't go into the safe-deposit box unless his or her name is on the signature card. All these things can be done, however, by an attorney-in-fact under the durable power of attorney prepared with wills. Neither attorneys-in-fact nor trustees can normally make gifts of your property unless the documents specifically allow it. In some states, the attorney-in-fact can make annual gifts if you previously established the pattern.

[13] Wills are broken for technical errors or because you're shown to have been too gaga to know what you were doing. But you can include a no-contest clause, removing a bequest from anyone who challenges your will.

[14] Technical errors in trusts rarely sink them completely. And because living trusts are typically in effect for some time before your death, it's hard to prove you were incompetent when you set them up. In some states, you can include a no-contest clause, removing a bequest from anyone who challenges your trust. The legal period for filing claims against a trust may be longer than for a will.

[15] Property you own in another state will undergo probate there unless it's jointly owned or in trust.

[16] It will take a lot of personal effort to get your assets transferred into your living trust (unless you have your lawyer do it, which runs up your fees). Banks, brokers, and other institutions may demand a copy of the trust to be sure they're dealing with a legitimate representative. (You shouldn't have to produce the whole trust; your lawyer will normally prepare an abstract showing the first page of the trust, the signature page, and the pages that list the trustees and enumerate their powers.) You'll have to transact business in the trust's name, which sometimes gets complicated. At death, both trustee and executor must, among other things, gather information about the assets, get real property appraised, value closely held business interests, round up and pay all outstanding bills, decide whether assets should be sold, transfer assets into new names, decide when assets should be distributed, make a final accounting to beneficiaries, and file final tax returns. Executors face the extra step of filing the will with the court and complying with any other court rules.

can save your family from a troubling court procedure to appoint a guardian (you can prepare for this with a durable power of attorney instead of a trust).

For a true comparison of wills and trusts, see the table above. If you decide that you do want a trust, don't buy it from one of these slick salespeople. You're likely to get a shoddy product that doesn't meet your family's particular needs—and you'll be overcharged to boot. Go to a lawyer experienced in both wills and trusts who'll examine all your assets, question you closely about your family's needs, and draw up the best document to serve them.

Charitable Trusts

If the tax code didn't exist, America's charities would have to invent it. Generous donors start with a personal sense of mission, but it doesn't hurt that gifts for good works are, within limits, written off on your tax return.

Planned giving is especially appealing. It's a six-step program for making gifts and strengthening your retirement income too. Here's how it works: (1) You donate cash savings to the charity, or stocks or land that have appreciated in value. (2) You win substantial tax breaks. (3) The charity invests your money for growth. (4) Now or in the future, the charity starts paying you (and perhaps your spouse or another person) a lifetime income. (5) When the last beneficiary dies, the charity gets the remaining money. (6) If you want, you can replace some of the money you gave away by using your tax savings to help buy life insurance to leave to your heirs.

These gifts are irrevocable. You cannot get your principal back. But you'll enjoy the following tax savings:

- *You sidestep the capital gains tax on appreciated property.* Say, for example, that you made a huge profit in stocks or land but now want to switch to a more conservative income investment. If you sell, the federal tax forceps will extract a portion of the gain. But if you give the asset to a charitable trust and the trust sells, it generally pays no tax. It can reinvest all the money and use it to pay you an income for life.

▪ *You create an immediate tax write-off.* The size of this deduction depends, among other things, on your age and the amount of income you want to receive.

▪ *You lower your estate taxes.* A charitable gift reduces the size of your estate, saving federal taxes if your net worth exceeds the federal estate tax exemption.

A complex estate requires the expensive services of lawyers, accountants, trust companies, money managers, and expert insurance planners. But for gifts on a more modest scale, the charity can do most of the work and will usually absorb the expense. When you cast your bread upon the waters, here are the ways to guarantee that you'll get some of it back:

The Charity's Pooled-Income Fund, for donors seeking conservative growth. It's similar to a mutual fund and pays you a pro rata share of its earnings. Your income will rise or fall depending on investment performance. Minimum investment: usually around $5,000 to $10,000.

A Gift Annuity, favored by older retirees. It pays a fixed income, guaranteed for life and partly tax free. The size of your payout depends on your age. The older you are, the bigger your check. Warning: If the charity's investments fare poorly, your promised income might not materialize.

A Deferred Gift Annuity, favored by younger and middle-aged donors. The gift grows in value for several years before the fixed payments start.

A Charitable Remainder Annuity Trust also pays a fixed income. Minimum investment: usually $50,000. Payouts can be higher than with gift annuities. But if the trust runs out of money, your income stops, whereas gift annuities always pay.

A Charitable Remainder Unitrust, the chief object of affection of inventive lawyers and donors alike. Minimum: usually $50,000. Your income varies, depending on how the investment grows. Payout rates are based on the trust's entire market value, running from 5 to about 8 percent. Savvy investors choose the lower number. It gives them the largest tax write-off plus bigger payouts over time because more money stays in the trust to grow.

A Spigot Trust, the star of the show. Minimum: usually $50,000, invested in a tax-deferred variable annuity. This unitrust lets you turn your income on and off. For example, you might forgo payments in the early years while the trust's investments build. Later on, you can withdraw extra money to make up for the years you missed. By law, the trust pays out only income, not principal. But in most states, your trust can define income broadly to include your capital gains. Spigots can help fund a wedding, add to a retirement plan, or pay future income to a child.

One warning about a unitrust, including the Spigot: Your actual payout depends on its annual investment performance. Take a $10,000 unitrust with a 5 percent payout to the donor, invested in Standard & Poor's 500-stock index. If the market rises 20 percent in the following year, you'll get $6,000. If it falls 20 percent, you'll get $4,000. As the poet said, everything depends. All that's certain are your tax savings and the pleasure gained from your charitable act. For a true giver, just the latter is enough.

A Charitable Lead Trust, for people who want to leave their money to their children. The charity uses the income while you're alive. At your death, the principal goes to your heirs.

Donor-Advised Funds. You give to a charitable fund and get the tax benefits right away. The fund invests your money, which can grow for years. When you're ready, you tell the fund to make gifts to various charities of your choice. Funds are run by some 650 community foundations that advise on gifts to local charities; find them at Community Foundations (www.communityfoundations .net). Four popular commercial funds: Fidelity Charitable Gift Fund ($5,000 minimum), Schwab Charitable Fund ($10,000 minimum), T. Rowe Price Program for Charitable Giving ($10,000 minimum), and Vanguard Charitable Endowment Program ($25,000 minimum).

The Writer's Malpractice Avoidance Paragraph

Writers are licensed only by the First Amendment. We can be as pigheaded and opinionated as the vocabulary allows, but we don't practice law. This chapter should give you a general understanding of wills, living trusts, and estate planning. But in practice, the field is pocked with traps that you've never heard of and wouldn't believe if you did. So when I write, "See a lawyer," I really mean *see a lawyer.* That's the only way to do this right.

7

All in the Family

Twelve Checklists for Life's Milestones

**Learn from the mistakes of others.
You won't live long enough to make them all yourself.**

A Premarital Checklist*

1. Talk money. It's the last taboo. Get a loaf of bread, a jug of wine, and your net-worth statement and make an afternoon of it. What does each of you earn (the *real* figure, not what you claimed when you were trying to impress)? Are there any other sources of income, such as a trust? Do you have savings and investments—how much and where? How have those investments done over the past three years? Are you putting money into a retirement account? Do you own real estate? How big are your debts—student loans, mortgages, credit cards? Lay out the credit cards in your wallet and your latest statement from each; big debts are something embarrassed spenders sometimes try to hide. What's your personal credit score (page 266)? Has either of you ever gone bankrupt? Failed to pay income taxes? Do you owe back taxes? If there's a small business, how's it doing? (Look at the statements showing revenues and expenses for the past three years and get a running explanation. Then ask about business debts for which your dearly beloved may be personally liable.) Full disclosure is required. Bring a copy of your latest credit report and maybe a second jug of wine.

2. Talk money management. In a two-paycheck marriage, who pays for what (page 82)? One bank account or two? Merged money but with separate

---

* This applies to those entering civil unions and registered domestic partnerships too. Like spouses, you're taking on legal responsibilities.

accounts for money you can spend as you like? How will you pay off the debts you come into the marriage with? Will you invest separately or together? Look at each other's investment statements for the past three years, especially if one of you buys and sells stocks. What were the actual gains and losses, and should the investment approach be changed?

3. Talk jobs. What are your prospects and goals? Does one of you want to return to school, and how will you pay for it? After the marriage, will one spouse quit work? How about after a baby is born? How might you feel if the other changes his or her mind? (You can't predict feelings but should discuss it anyway.) If you'll work and have children, how will you handle child care?

4. Talk debt. How do you handle it? If one of you has a black belt in credit card shopping, while the other wants to pay only cash, there may be trouble ahead. Ditto if one of you pays bills on time while the other is always late. Marriage won't change either of your credit scores, even if one of you changes your name (your new name will be listed as an alias on your old account). Nor will anything change if you're made an authorized user on your partner's account. But if you apply jointly for credit—say, to get a mortgage—one low score will bump up your interest rate, even though the other score is solid gold. You're both liable for any bills run up on a jointly held credit card. In the nine community property states (page 87), you're generally responsible for all the debts of the marriage, even those racked up on a separate card.

5. Talk life insurance. Who needs it and how much (page 336)? You may have some automatic coverage from your company. If you die, is that enough to support a dependent spouse? If not, buy more coverage right after the wedding. Two-paycheck professional couples may not need extra life insurance until they buy a house or have a baby, because each would be self-supporting if the other one died.

6. Talk health insurance. Will you keep separate policies (if you're both lucky enough to have them), or should you consolidate? What maternity benefits are paid if there's a pregnancy? At some companies, one spouse can drop health insurance entirely and choose another benefit instead.

7. Talk savings. Be idealistic; assume that you'll have some. How much can you put away each year, and how will you do it? Go for automatic payroll deduction if your company provides it. Fund to the max any retirement plan where the company matches the contributions you make. Agree to start a plan (page 1028) if you haven't already.

8. Talk commitments. Does one of you have an aging parent or disabled child or sibling to care for? Is one of you paying alimony or child support, and, if so, how much and for how long? These will effectively become joint responsibilities, even though you personally don't owe the other's child support payments, so walk in with your eyes open. An older man marrying a younger woman will probably have to postpone his retirement, especially if there are children. That younger woman can expect to nurse him through his last illness and maybe spend many years as a widow. A younger man marrying an older woman might also have nursing duties in his future.

9. Talk houses. If you each own a house or condominium, where will you live? What would be the tax consequences of selling one of them (page 1154)? If you don't have a house, do you want one, and how do you think you might raise the down payment?

10. Talk name. Either of you can keep your last name or change it. If you make a change, tell Social Security, all your creditors, and anyone else with whom you do business; if you don't, just leave things as they are. No law requires a Mr. and Mrs. to have the same name. But a Mrs. with her maiden name should check her Social Security account (page 1095) every three or four years to be sure each year's earnings were credited. Sometimes the IRS fails to pick up your maiden name from the joint tax return, and your Social Security credits fall into a black hole.

11. Talk education. Say that the woman agrees to put the man through medical school if he will then put her through law school. Will he put his promise into writing?

12. Talk prenuptial agreement. You don't need one if you each come into the marriage with minimal assets and no expectation of a large inheritance. You'll build your financial life together, as well as your emotional one. If the marriage falls apart, you'll wind up with a roughly even split. That's a fair result. If your dearly beloved wants you to sign away that result in advance—well, I'm a New Yorker, and I say "fuggedaboudit." That kind of prenup is the enemy of love.

Here's a contrary argument: even if you have no assets, you might consider a prenup saying, "If we divorce, we split all assets acquired during the marriage 50–50." Again, that's normally what a court would decide. Such a prenup saves you the cost and effort of fighting over money when you're going to wind up with 50–50 anyway.

It's another matter when significant assets are at stake. Then you have to think about whether you want to share those assets with your new spouse in case of divorce or death. If you do nothing, the spouse will get at least his or her legal share—typically, half the marital assets at divorce and one-third to one-half of your estate at death. A prenup changes that. You can sign away all rights or settle on a larger or smaller share. Or exempt some assets from the pot and split the rest of them 50–50.

In a bad prenup, one partner plays the bully, the other plays the martyr, and then they wonder why their honeymoon isn't a joy. Sometimes an agreement is presented on the eve of the wedding, under the threat that the bully won't show. The other should always call that bluff. Better to learn the bad news now than to start a marriage with a mortal wound. A nice way of putting it is "I'm sorry, but I couldn't sign an agreement that's unfair to me and to our future children." And who knows? Maybe the bully will repent. If he or she won't—well, you've learned that your partner is a rat, and in time to back away. In good prenups, the partners discuss the possibilities—what about existing children, what about future children, what about family businesses, how will each of them live if the other dies or decamps—and sign something with which they're both comfortable.

Don't try to write the prenup yourselves. It's too important for amateurs. You each need a lawyer to advise you on every proposal's pros and cons; one lawyer can't ethically help you both. Experienced lawyers will know ways of melding clashing interests. In a second marriage, for example, what if a wealthy groom wants all of his property to go to his kids, while the bride wants her kids to get at least something out of the relationship? One solution: the husband could buy a permanent life insurance policy on his life or hers, payable to the wife's children. What if an heiress had a bad marriage and doesn't want to risk her money the second time? One solution: the sum left to the groom could increase if the marriage lasts. Another important issue is the retirement account. By law, one spouse has a right to the other's 401(k) and other non-IRA retirement benefits. That right can be waived but not before marriage. In the prenup, you'd agree to sign the proper waivers immediately after the wedding.

Whatever you expect from the prenup, start the negotiation early. It almost always takes longer to resolve issues and deal with new ones than you originally thought.

A prenup is a dandy arrangement when:

- Both parties want it, and both parties think that it is fair.
- Both parties have enough income to live comfortably on their own.
- Both parties want to preserve their own wealth for the children of their previous marriages.
- One of you has a closely held business or partnership interest and doesn't want to lose part of it in divorce.
- One of you will inherit a lot of money and use it to improve your joint standard of living.
- The spouse in the weaker financial position is guaranteed a decent settlement.

- Neither spouse is left high and dry without an income from any source.
- A one-sided deal, if you accept it, self-destructs or phases out after the marriage has lasted a certain number of years.
- The agreement covers only money, not where to live or who washes the dishes.

You have to disclose all your assets, so the partners know exactly what they're getting and what they're giving up. No fraud is allowed. If those conditions are met, a prenup is almost impossible to break—even if you were bullied into signing. The judge will say, "You made your bed . . ."

Very important! The prenup should deal with what happens if one of you dies, not just with possible divorce. Say that in their 30s, Becca and Peter earn about the same and agree that neither will inherit from the other. Over the next happy 40 years, Peter's earnings and assets soar while Becca eventually stops working. Then Peter dies. Under the (now-forgotten) prenup, Becca gets nothing; she's a bag lady at 75. A prenup that says "at divorce, we get only the property we entered the marriage with" might also say "same thing at death," "full inheritance at death," or "partial inheritance at death"—whatever seems best. And of course, the prenup can be changed at any time if you both agree.

13. Talk long-term care. Older people marrying have to consider the question of long-term care expenses. In the prenup, each of you might agree not to claim the other's assets. But if one of you enters a nursing home and doesn't have enough personal assets, the other might have to pay, under state laws regarding spousal support. A prenup can't get rid of this obligation. To protect your finances, each of you should agree to buy long-term care insurance.

14. Talk priorities. What matters most in your life? House? Children? Jobs? Savings? Reducing debt? Travel? Care of a parent? Fun? Each of you might draw up a plan for the next five years and then compare plans. You might be surprised by how differently the other thinks.

15. Talk over what you've learned. What will you do about any differences that arose? How will you resolve the arguments? Don't paper them over; they'll come back. This is the time to start handling them, with love. Some problems can be solved, such as agreeing on a schedule for repaying debts. Others, such as different investment styles, may have to be managed for life. But thanks to the money talk, there should be no surprises after you say "I do." Already, you're ahead.

A Postmarital Checklist

1. Redo your will. Or make one.

2. Change the beneficiary on existing contracts if you want your spouse to inherit. Do this for life insurance, pension plans, annuities, living trusts, and Individual Retirement Accounts. If your spouse has agreed not to inherit your 401(k) and other retirement plans, ask the plan for the waivers that have to be signed (page 1038). In fact, have the papers ready to sign as soon as you've both said "I do."

3. Set up a joint financial file (see chapter 3). You each should know where the other's personal records are.

4. Consider a joint bank account. It's useful for household expenses, even if you keep separate his-and-hers accounts for personal spending.

5. Give each other a durable power of attorney (page 125). That lets each of you act for the other in an emergency. Also, give your spouse the right to make medical decisions for you if you're unable to make them yourself. He or she will probably be on the spot if a crisis occurs and will have your best interests at heart.

6. You might want a postnuptial agreement at some point in the future. The happily married might want to change the prenup's terms. A postnup is especially useful for couples who grow wealthier than they expected. For example, take a wife who starts a business that turns out to be successful. She might want to be sure that she retains all the stock if the marriage breaks up (her husband could give up his stock rights in return for cash). Or take a husband with children from a previous marriage. He might now be able to leave them all his property without impoverishing his wife. Like a prenup, a postnup has to be signed after full disclosure of what the property is worth.

A New-Baby Checklist

Before Your Pregnancy

1. Check your medical insurance. You might have been covered for pregnancy from the day you (or your husband) were hired. Then again, you might not be. You need to find out what your plan will pay. Individual insurance may require a 12-month waiting period, starting the day you buy, before maternity benefits start. A health maintenance organization typically covers most of the cost of a routine birth. Other plans pay the "reasonable and customary" charge in your area, minus the deductible. If your doctor charges more than the plan deems "reasonable," it comes out of your pocket. You'll be covered up to your plan's limits for cesarean sections, other surgical procedures, and neonatal costs if the birth is premature.

2. Check your other employee benefits. You may find some gems. For example, if your company employs 15 or more people and covers its workers with disability insurance, pregnancy will be treated the same as a disability. You might get payments for 90 days or more if your pregnancy is complicated and you have to stay home.

You and your spouse are also entitled to at least 12 weeks of unpaid family leave if you work for a company with 50 or more employees in the local office, have been there for at least 12 months, and work at least 1,250 hours a year. Some states allow even more leave and mandate it for smaller companies too. You keep your group health and disability coverage while you're gone, although it's up to your employer whether to continue your group life insurance, accrued vacation time, and other benefits.

When you return to work, you get your old job back or an equivalent job with the same pay, benefits, and terms of employment, including seniority. That is, unless you're in the top 10 percent of your company's pay range. In that case, your job doesn't have to be held, although companies will doubtlessly accommodate a valuable executive. While you're at home, by the way, no additional seniority or pension credits build.

You can take family leave not only for newborns but also when you adopt a child, accept a new child in foster care, or have to nurse a close relative.

3. Save money. In most cases, you'll have to pay part of the medical bill yourself. Even if you don't, most insurance policies don't pay a dime until after the baby is born. Your doctor, however, might require you to pay as you grow. Some insurers offer interim payments to consumers in these situations.

If your company offers a flexible-spending account (page 421), put away some money toward the pregnancy bills. That's a way of getting a tax deduction for your share of the medical expenses.

During Your Pregnancy

1. Buy more life insurance. That's not just a baby you're getting, it's bicycles, braces, and a college tuition bill.

2. Obey your health plan's provisions. You might be required to attend prenatal classes or join a maternity managed care program. If you don't, your insurer might pay less of the bill. You may also have to get special permission for certain procedures such as amniocentesis or ultrasound or else pay for them yourself.

3. Find out what your health plan pays for routine births, then ask your doctor if he or she will charge no more than that amount. Usually not, but you just might be surprised.

4. Call the hospitals in the area and make an appointment to see the birthing facilities (that is, if you're not in an HMO that requires you to use a certain hospital). There's a lot of competition for maternity business. Some hospitals offer package plans: bedroomlike birthing rooms, prenatal exercise classes, and a candlelit meal with your spouse.

5. Find out how long your insurer will let you stay in the hospital. Normally, it's two days for a routine birth and four days for a cesarean. Any extra days are on your tab unless your health plan agrees that you need to be in the hospital longer.

6. Think carefully before choosing a separate birthing center instead of a hospital's birthing rooms. Centers may charge half the price and are great for women with normal deliveries. But they lack high-tech operating rooms and intensive care facilities. If something suddenly goes wrong, you're zipped to a hospital, but how long is the ride? Ten minutes? Fifteen? That's not good enough.

Take my friend Judy, whose second baby got into trouble at the very last minute. Her doctor slammed her wheeled bed into the operating room and did a cesarean in two minutes flat. Being in a hospital saved her baby's life. Or take my friend Angela. Right after the normal delivery of her third baby, she started to hemorrhage. She might not be alive today if, five minutes later, she hadn't been in the operating room, stanched and sewn up. Some birthing centers are built right into hospitals, which is another matter. But if you're a few minutes away and something goes wrong, the lives of both mother and baby are on the line.

7. Women with paying jobs should be frank with their companies about what will happen next. Some new mothers go right back to work within a few weeks. Some want part-time jobs while their children are small. Some aren't yet sure what they want. It's not fair to your boss to delay a decision or keep mum about what your plans really are. If you'll want a part-time schedule for two or three years, be up front about it. A growing number of companies make such deals with valuable employees.

8. Write a will or update the will you have. You'll need a guardian, both for the child and for the child's inheritance, in case you die. Otherwise the court might name someone you'd never have chosen had you been alive.

After the Birth

1. Notify your health plan of the new arrival within 30 days or else the baby might not be covered on your family plan. If you have an individual health plan, you'll have to buy family coverage. If your baby is diagnosed with a serious or chronic illness and wasn't signed up for your family plan in time, the plan may reject the child.

2. Be sure you'll have family health insurance if one parent quits work to take care of the child. If that parent carried the family coverage on his or her employee plan and no other plan is immediately available, ask about COBRA benefits. When a company has at least 20 employees, a worker who leaves can keep that group health plan for up to 18 months at his or her expense (29 months if the worker or a dependent is disabled). But you get this insurance only if you ask for it within 60 days of leaving your job, so don't miss the deadline.

If it's unlikely that the working parent will have a company plan, start shopping immediately for separate family coverage. You'll want to buy it while you're all insurable. If, God forbid, one of you falls sick, you might not qualify for coverage you can afford once your COBRA benefits run out.

3. Start saving for college. It's not a moment too soon.

A Day Care Checklist

1. Don't kid yourself about the cost. Children aren't cheap at any age. Working parents might pay 10 to 20 percent of their income for day care, with infant care the most expensive and hardest to come by.

2. See what your company has to offer. Some companies run an information service about the day care centers in town. Some subsidize places for employees' children. Some provide flexible employee benefits, with day care as an option. Some help with emergency care when your regular sitter calls in sick. A few even run a center of their own. If your company has its head in the sand about child care, form a committee, find out what forward-looking companies are doing (the Internet can help), and make a proposal to management.

3. If your company's flexible-benefits plan includes day care, take it. You're one of the lucky ones. Part of your pretax salary (up to $5,000) goes into a special day care account. The company often contributes too. That account is then used to pay the babysitter's bills. This is the cheapest way of paying for day care, because you are using pretax dollars.

4. If both parents work and you have no flexible-benefits plan, use the child care credit on your income tax return. You can also claim the credit if you're a full-time student or incapacitated. You subtract from your income taxes a portion of your child care expenses: day care, babysitters, day camp, even the price of room and board at boarding school. Tax credits are normally available for the care of children under age 13.

Note: You cannot use both the child care credit and a company flexible-spending plan. You have to choose. In general, the flexible-spending plan is better if you earn more than $30,000.

5. Here are your day care choices, ranked by cost:

- *Your own full-time housekeeper or nanny.* Sleep-in help costs about the same as someone who works from nine to five. Besides salary, plan on paying for health insurance, half or all of the Social Security tax, unemployment taxes, workers compensation in some states, and a paid vacation.
- *Day care centers.* They cater principally to toddlers and up.
- *Family day care.* This describes a neighborhood mother who takes care of several children in her own home. Infants are more likely to be accepted here.
- *After-school care for older children.* You might find it at day care centers or in the neighborhood. You should pay no more than half the cost of full-time care.
- *Grandma.* But give her a break if you can. She has already raised one set of children. Why should she be saddled with another?

6. Some things to look for in a day care center or a family day care home: a state license if one is required; a stable workforce; clean, happy children; plenty of clean, appropriate toys; a safe place to play, indoors and out; an organized daily child care plan; friendly people; at least one adult for every four infants and one adult for every six toddlers; references, so you can ask other parents how they like the center; organized games rather than care-by-TV; after-hours care if necessary; a connection with a doctor or nurse for medical emergencies; your own child's attitude—does he or she seem to be having fun?

7. Be prepared for the taxes owed on a nanny's wages. You don't have to withhold state and federal income taxes if you'd rather not, but you *must* pay Social Security and Medicare taxes for every employee to whom you paid cash wages of $1,500 or more per year or $1,000 or more per calendar quarter. Of the 15.3 percent due, you pay half. The other half is deducted from the nanny's wages. If you pay both halves, the nanny's half must be added to her taxable income for the year. At the end of the year, you provide the nanny with a W-2 form showing wages earned and Social Security taxes paid.

You also owe federal unemployment taxes if you pay an employee more than $1,000 in a calendar quarter.

All these taxes are paid annually as part of your personal tax return. To be sure you have the money by April 15, ask your own employer to increase your tax withholding. If you're self-employed, increase your quarterly estimated tax payments.

If you don't pay these taxes, it might become a public issue if you're ever a candidate for a cushy political job. Even if you're not, your nanny might rat on you to the IRS.

Ask your state about its own nanny taxes for workers compensation and the unemployment fund. These taxes might have to be paid quarterly. You also must pay quarterly if you withhold federal income taxes from an employee's wage.

A Checklist for Kids' Allowances

When parents teach their children about money, their questions center on technique. When should an allowance be paid? What should I let my kids do with their savings? Should I pay them for doing chores around the house?

But technique isn't nearly as important as the values you communicate. All your cash transactions with your kids tell them what you feel about money. If you're uncomfortable talking about it, your children may not learn what you intend.

There's no right or wrong way of teaching children good values and sound financial habits. Different families make different choices. What's most important is for parents to agree. Only then can they send consistent messages to their children. Kids need to develop four key skills: setting priorities, managing on a budget, saving for a goal, and the value of work. Here are some ideas for you to play with:

1. Pay allowances early, starting as young as age 6 or 7. How large should the payment be? Large enough for your children to think they have money to squander but not so much that you'll be upset when they do. Surveys show that children who get no allowances receive roughly as much money from their parents as children who do. But those on a regular "paycheck" learn more about managing money. Children under 14 should be paid once a week. Consider paying older children biweekly or once a month, to give them more experience in managing money over time.

2. Tie the allowance to the purchases you want your children to be responsible for. At 7, they might buy their own candy, sodas, hair ornaments, or toy cars. At 12, their movies, video games, and school lunches. At 15, their iPod downloads, plus a twice-a-year lump sum clothing allowance (excluding basics such as underwear and socks). At 18, their cell phone bills and gasoline.

Their allowance should cover the reasonable cost of a kid-friendly standard of living but no more. If your daughter blows $100 on designer jeans, she might have to turn off her phone for a while. Parents shouldn't ride to the rescue. If a child runs out of money, let him stay financially grounded until the next allowance day. If the child continually runs short even though spending prudently, you're probably not paying enough. Your money management lesson won't come through if the child sees that budgeting won't work.

3. Many parents tie allowances to chores. Some put price tags on specific jobs and pay for performance every week. Some provide basic pay plus extra money for nasty chores such as taking out garbage. Some give weekly pay with a side agreement on what the child is expected to do. Your choice will depend on your principal goal. Are you teaching your children to manage money? Or is the objective to show them that they don't get something for nothing?

4. Consider a three-tier system for allocating your children's cash: one jar for spending money, one for savings, one for religious services or charities. Savings work best when a child has a specific objective, such as a jacket that costs more than you're willing to pay. Consider paying "interest" on the money by adding a nickel for every dollar left in the savings jar each week. As for charities, many families tithe, putting 10 percent of their income toward good causes. Children should be encouraged to choose a cause of their own.

5. Treat the supermarket as a school. Give the kids a grocery cart, a list, and $30, and see how far they can make their money stretch. Send them searching the aisles for goods that you have cents-off coupons for. Ask them to pick the best buys.

6. Don't lie to your kids. Make a clear distinction between what you can't afford and what you don't think is worth paying for. If they still want it, let them save for it. If it violates your principles, just say no.

7. By their midteens, start giving your kids a sense of what life is like by having them pay the family bills for two or three months. Sit down together with the bills and show them how to write checks to pay for the family's utilities, mortgage, rent, phone, water, doctors, and credit cards. They'll find it instructive to see how fast the bank balance drops. They'll also start getting a better idea of how much it costs to live.

8. Don't shell out for practically everything your kids want or need. That teaches them nothing except dependency, not to mention the fine art of wheedling. They need to make choices within budget limits to learn adult skills. If they want more than their allowance can buy, they should find a part-time job. Children will spend unlimited amounts of their parents' money, given a chance. They're much more careful with their own.

9. Use cash. Don't put young kids on your credit cards as authorized users or provide them with prepaid debit cards. They need to learn how to allocate real dollars before they can transfer those skills to plastic. Consider plastic after age 16, to introduce them to credit while their spending is still under your supervision.

A Checklist for Domestic Partners

1. Keep all property separate at the start. You don't know how long this relationship will last. If one of you is wealthy, consider a cohabitation agreement (see page 85) to avoid demands for palimony if you break up.

2. Decide how to divide the household bills. Typically, you'd contribute according to your income. If you bring in 40 percent of the mutual income, you'd pay 40 percent of the household expenses.

3. Provide for individual savings. You each should be saving separately for retirement. If your joint lifestyle is so expensive that the lower earner can't save, your arrangement is unfair. Either dial back your lifestyle or agree that the higher earner will assume a higher portion of the daily expenses.

4. If you buy a house together, agree—in writing—what will happen if you separate. Do you sell the house and split the proceeds? Does one partner buy the other out, and how do you set the price? What happens to the furniture? If you sell to your partner, he or she should get a new mortgage. If you keep the old one, you'll still be on the debt, making you responsible if your ex-partner fails to pay. Lawyers should work on this agreement—yours and your partner's—to be sure you haven't overlooked something important.

5. If you own assets together, such as real estate or financial investments, think about how to title the property or account. Joint property with a right of survivorship? That means the account will pass to the other if one dies. As tenants in common without a right of survivorship? That lets each of you leave his or her half to whomever you please—to your partner or to someone else.

Unmarried couples can't file joint federal tax returns. If you own property as tenants in common, each of you gets a percentage of the tax deductions, depending on your individual contribution to the purchase price. You can't write off a higher percentage, even if you pay the whole bill yourself. If you own the property jointly with a right of survivorship, however, one of you can choose to pay the mortgage and take all the deductions.

The financial institution will issue your year-end tax documents, such as the amount of interest paid, in the name of the first person listed on the mortgage.

So name the higher earner first if he or she will be making the payments. That simplifies things for the IRS. If you're splitting the mortgage interest payments, put a note on your tax return giving the name and Social Security number of the person paying the other portion.

6. See if your employer gives health benefits to domestic partners. Most don't, but the number that do increases every year. To qualify your partner, however, you might have to agree to be financially responsible for him or her—raising the palimony risk. You will also owe taxes on your partner's benefits. Because of the tax cost, it may be cheaper for your partner to buy health benefits separately.

7. If you want to leave property to your partner, have a lawyer draw up a will or living trust. This is no time for a do-it-yourself document, especially if your family doesn't like your partner. A will or trust that you write yourself is often easy to attack. If a court knocks your partner out (or if there's no will or trust at all), your property goes to your parents, siblings, or other close relatives. Families may turn away even from partners they liked.

While you're getting a will, get a durable power of attorney naming someone to act for you, financially, if you can't act for yourself. Maybe your partner is the right person, or maybe it's someone else.

You'll also want a health care proxy (page 126), allowing someone to deal with your doctors if you're unable to speak for yourself. That's usually your partner, because he or she is the person on the spot. If you have adult children, the proxy might ask your partner to consult with them before authorizing treatment in nonemergency situations.

8. What's the deal on children? If there are any, will both of you agree, in writing, to provide financial support? Will there be custody and visiting rights? Or does the child "belong" to one of you exclusively? The laws on these points are tricky and unreliable. Some states allow a same-sex partner to adopt the other's child, other states don't. Some enforce visiting rights, others let the birth parent take the child away. Rules vary for heterosexual and same-sex couples, so talk to a lawyer about what you can do contractually. Parents—birth or adoptive—are always required to support their children, but a contract can make it easier to collect. You definitely need an agreement if there's only one parent (for example, if one of a lesbian couple went to a sperm bank), because your partner could walk out, leaving you on the hook and the child in a hole. If your partner wants to keep your child if you die, he or she may have to adopt if your state allows it. Otherwise the court may give the child to one of your relatives if he or she applies, even though you named your partner the guardian in your will.

A Checklist for People Who Might Be Laid Off, but Then Again Might Not

1. Secure your home. Refinance if you can get a better interest rate, to minimize your monthly mortgage payment. Take a fixed-rate 30-year loan for its certainty and flexibility. If your job turns out to be secure, you can always accelerate payments if you want to repay on a shorter schedule.

2. Secure your life insurance. Your company may give you a certain amount of free term insurance, plus the option of buying more through payroll deduction. But you generally can't take term coverage with you when you leave your job. If you had to keep that policy—say, because you became uninsurable on the private market—you'd have to covert it to individual cash-value coverage, and believe me, that doesn't come cheap. It's smarter not to buy extra coverage through payroll deduction. Use that money to buy term insurance outside the company, which gives you a policy you can keep no matter where you work. The outside policy might even cost you less.

3. Secure your credit lines. If you're a home owner, open a home equity line of credit but don't borrow against it. This will become your safety net if you're fired and need quick cash. If you're carrying credit card debt, start a ferocious plan to get rid of it. You don't want to face stiff monthly payments if you're out of work.

4. Control your spending. Look for ways to cut back before a job loss or salary reduction forces your income down. Living on 10 percent less than you make isn't downward mobility, it's common sense. For help on financial planning after you've lost your job, see page 1103.

5. Increase your ready savings. When you cut back on your spending, increase your savings. You're aiming for six months' worth of basic living expenses in the bank. If you're carrying credit card debt, take care of that first and increase your savings after that.

6. Pursue retirement savings. Keep on putting money into your retirement account. Contributions reduce your taxes, give you hope for the future, and may include company matching funds. In order of importance, funding your tax-deferred retirement plan comes even before paying down consumer debt. If you leave your job, don't cash in your 401(k), 403(b), or government 457 account—that's tax suicide. You'll owe income taxes on the entire sum plus a 10 percent penalty if you're under age 59½. Instead roll it into an Individual Retirement Account, where it remains tax deferred. If you're short of money for current bills, withdraw cash from the IRA as needed. You'll pay taxes and penalties only on the dollars you take out.

A Preretirement Checklist

For detailed discussions of some of these questions, check the chapters on health insurance, investing, financial planning, and the two chapters on retiring. Here's the quick checklist:

1. **Will you have health insurance?** It's dangerous not only to your health but to your wealth to retire without. If you're thinking of moving to another city and you haven't reached 65 (Medicare age), check first on whether you can get health insurance there.

2. **Do you have enough income and savings to support yourself for the rest of your life?** Don't try to figure this out yourself on a spreadsheet or a yellow pad. If ever there were a time to see a fee-only financial planner (I emphasize, *fee-only*—page 1176), this is it. The planner will run your financials and tell you what kind of lifestyle you can afford. You need to establish a spending plan and figure out whether you'll have to work part-time.

3. **How should you handle your company retirement plan?** If you have a pension, a fee-only planner can help evaluate whether to take the money in a lump sum or as an income for the rest of your life. With 401(k)s, decide whether to leave the money in the plan for now or roll it into an Individual Retirement Account.

4. **How should you invest your savings?** As the shattering stock market crash of 2008 showed, you need bonds as well as stocks and enough cash to see you through several years of expenses without having to sell any of your investments.

5. **What will you *do*?** Maybe you'll be happy basking in Florida and bemoaning the price of oranges, but maybe not. You need at least the start of a plan to make a life—and with different friends. The friends of your work days will fall away. They still love office gossip. Your mind will be in a different place.

6. **If you're married, will you both retire together?** If not, it's even more important for the spouse newly at home to find an occupation. Work, hobbies, charities, *something*. You'll get testy sitting on the sofa all day, waiting for your spouse to come home. Your spouse won't like it, either. And by the way, guys (it's usually guys who aren't aware of this little point), a spouse at home owes the breadwinner some housework, including errands, laundry, and grocery shopping. If you can't handle that, don't retire.

7. **If you do retire together, how will you manage this new relationship?** Each of you needs something engaging to be involved in and enough self-sufficiency to find it.

8. **If you're single, where is your support group?** Look for relationships

that will help you transition from work to leisure—clubs, interests, and friends of your own age who will be retiring too.

9. Where will you live? If your budget requires you to downsize, will you stay where you are or move away? A new city requires some real-life testing before you actually move. Vacation there for a couple of years. Try to meet some people. If you attend worship services, do you like the temple, church, or mosque? What clubs, cultural activities, political groups, or charities might you get involved with? Think about living close enough to your children to make regular visits possible.

10. How will you deal with the loss of status, if you always identified yourself closely with work? How about loss of income? There are many ways of living well but not necessarily as well as you did when the paychecks were coming in. You're the same useful person you always were, but you might have to fight a feeling of being cast aside. The world always belongs to the younger generation, but civic institutions are nourished by the older generation, who have the time for them.

11. What's Plan B? You might get along fine for several years and then hit a wall. Stocks might crash. One of your children might desperately need help. A major illness could eat up your reserves. You should always have a general idea about what you're going to do if you can't afford your lifestyle anymore. Reducing spending is always at the top of the list. You might also sell assets such as a second car or second home, get a part-time job, take out a reverse mortgage, rent a room to a boarder, or sell your house and rent an apartment. There are many possibilities, as long as your mind is open to them. If you've thought about them in advance, making the decisions will be easier, emotionally.

12. For a start on your new life of Saturdays, how about hitting the paperwork? This is the moment to reorganize—your will or living trust, health care proxy, investments, old photographs, and computer files. While you're at it, clean the attic and basement and paint the front hall. You're moving into a new phase. Might as well start clean.

An Elder Care Checklist

1. Don't swoop down on a capable parent. Most older people are perfectly able to manage themselves. In fact, their finances may be in better shape than yours. When you start seeing signs that help may be needed, don't go overboard. Ask them if there's anything you can do to make their lives easier or help them maintain their independence. It might be enough to find a good home health care service or make a suggestion about certificates of deposit. Respect your parents' wishes; don't push them around. If your parent loses track of the bills, however, worries obsessively about money, or writes a check every time a phone scammer calls, it's time to take more responsibility. When one parent dies, keep an eye on how the other handles the finances. Find out where your parent keeps all the financial records in case you have to step in fast.

2. Don't miss any tax write-offs. If you support (or help support) a parent, you may be entitled to a dependency exemption. If your parent lives with you and you have to hire in-home help so that you can go to work, you get the tax credit for dependent care (it's the same as the child care credit).

3. Check your employee benefits. If your company employs 50 or more people in the local area, the same law that gives new parents family leave (page 150) gives you time off from the job to care for a parent who has a serious health condition. If there's a flexible-benefits plan, you can generally arrange to pay for elder care with pretax dollars (it works like child care; see page 152). A few companies even offer elder care referral services or emergency in-home care as an employee benefit.

4. Call the Eldercare Locator (800-677-1116), sponsored by the U.S. Administration on Aging and several nonprofit senior citizen groups, or consult it online at www.eldercare.gov. The locator sends you to a community agency, which tells you how to locate elder care services such as adult day care, senior citizen lunch groups, home-delivered meals, home health care, chore services, financial aid, legal services, hospice programs, and transportation. The local agency may also be able to find you a care manager, who will visit your parent, assess any health and homemaking needs, and suggest services that can help. There may be a waiting list for assessments, but give it a try.

Also try the Office for the Aging in the capital of the state where your parent lives. It will refer you to a local Area Agency on Aging (AAA) or other assistance agency for free booklets and advice. For other local organizations, check the Web. Also check the Yellow Pages under "Elderly" or under your city's government listings.

For tons of free advice, visit the Family Caregiver Alliance (FCA) at www .caregiver.org. It offers an excellent booklet, "Handbook for Long-Distance Caregivers," among many other publications and fact sheets. The alliance can also steer you toward government benefits that your parent might be eligible for. Another source: the National Association of Area Agencies on Aging at www .n4a.org.

5. Square away the finances. If you're going to handle your parent's money, you'll need a durable power of attorney (page 125) and the authority to write checks on his or her account (page 125). Or perhaps you might become the trustee of your parent's living trust. Arrange for the pension and Social Security checks to be paid directly into your parent's bank account. Bills should be sent to your address, billed to a credit card, or paid automatically from a bank account. Reorganize investments to produce maximum income with minimum risk. Find all the financial documents (stocks, deeds, savings bonds, life insurance policies) and personal documents (birth certificate, marriage license, military discharge papers). Cancel the life insurance policy if it's no longer needed. See to the income taxes and get your parent an up-to-date will. These matters are best settled while your parent is sound of mind. If confusion descends, so may suspicion about money and an instinct to shut you out. A mentally incapable parent won't be allowed to make a new will.

6. Make a safety check of your parent's house. Are the lights bright enough (older people need extra illumination). Can you get rid of throw rugs? Should the doorsills be removed (they're a major cause of falls)? Does your parent need a stool in the tub, a higher toilet seat, a stair elevator? A cell phone with large buttons and emergency numbers programmed in?

7. See to your parent's health. Make sure that he or she eats. Help arrange regular medical checkups. If you can, see that the doctor's orders for taking pills and other medications are carried out. If your parent moves slowly, suffers pain, or forgets things, don't write it off as old age. Many such problems can be corrected.

8. Deal with Medicare. This is a kindness that will qualify you for sainthood. At 65, people have to decide which prescription drug plan to choose (Medicare Part D), whether to join one of the Medicare Advantage programs (Medicare Part C), or whether to stay with Original Medicare and buy a Medigap policy. These aren't easy choices. It helps to have a third party join the discussion and share the research. Some older people stick with a plan they chose in the past because it's the easiest thing to do, when they could save money by switching to another plan.

You also can help with Medicare claims. Your parent pays part of the bill, so it's essential that the provider enter the claim correctly. If Medicare rejects a bill, you can appeal, but the process is annoying and time consuming. If large bills pile up, consider hiring someone to check them for accuracy and get them paid. You'll find local help through the Alliance of Claims Assistance Professionals (www.claims.org) or Medical Billing Advocates of America (www.billadvocates.com).

Ask your parent to sign a letter of authorization, enabling you to speak with his or her medical providers. Otherwise the privacy laws may prevent you from getting information about treatments and billing. You may need a letter for each of the doctors individually.

Seniors with low incomes and few assets qualify for Medicaid. Anyone who deals with Medicaid is in the first ring of archangels.

If your parent has private insurance, ask the carrier how to become a patient advocate. That lets you receive bills, pay premiums, and handle appeals.

9. Shoot down the scams. The elderly are to crooks as meat is to hyenas. Some older people will send money to every "charity" that asks, pay to enter sweepstakes that offer "free gifts," make expensive calls to 900 numbers, succumb to hard sells at free-lunch seminars where unethical salespeople peddle high-cost annuities and inappropriate living trusts, or fall for fast-buck investments offered by phone. These seniors aren't stupid, they're just trusting and perhaps so lonely that they enjoy talking with con artists (often "sympathetic" women) by phone. They may be in denial about what's happening or too embarrassed to tell you about it.

So keep in close touch with your parents, ask about new people, especially financial people, entering their lives, and watch the checking account, if that's possible. Maybe you or a neighbor can help your parent go over the mail (lots of junk mail for contests or sweepstakes shows that he or she is on a sucker list).

If you spot a problem, don't accuse your parent of doing something foolish, just work to solve the problem. Consider delisting your parent's phone number. You can stop most telemarketing calls by visiting the National Do Not Call Registry at www.donotcall.gov. A local senior service agency might help with fraud.

Older seniors are especially vulnerable to dishonest caregivers. Before hiring one, check his or her background using a service such as ChoiceTrust (www .choicetrust.com). Suspect a big problem if the caregiver starts limiting access to your parent or your parent seems to have grown quiet and frightened.

10. Get help from willing neighbors. Line up a teenager to mow the lawn, weed the garden, and shovel snow. Arrange for a neighbor to check on your parent if he or she doesn't answer the phone when you call. Line up someone to run the little errands that you can't if you live far away. Offer to pay a caregiver who will drop in, shop, do a wash, and fix a meal.

11. Make yourself a list of your parent's current support system: doctor, lawyer, banker, broker or planner, insurance agent, church or temple, neighbors, friends.

12. Consider a private care manager. This new and rapidly growing field is peopled with nurses, social workers, psychologists, and self-styled gerontologists. For a fee in the $300 to $800 range, they'll visit your parent and make a report. For additional fees ($80 to $200 an hour, depending on the region), they'll find home health workers, recommend nursing homes, pay regular visits, and handle emergencies. Your first stop for referrals: local nursing homes, doctors, and hospital social service offices. Second stop: the National Association of Professional Geriatric Care Managers. Members pay $245 to join and have to meet certain professional standards. To find the names of members in your area as well as advice on choosing one, go to www.caremanager.org.

Warning: This field is totally unregulated. So talk to the care manager in person and check every claim on the résumé to see if it's true. Interview at least three of the care manager's clients, get a written plan of action for your parent, nail down costs, and don't choose anyone who rubs you wrong. Don't allow the caregiver access to your parent's checking or investment accounts—set up a separate account for daily expenses.

13. Keep good sibling relations. When an adult child is the caregiver, he or she might make free use of the parent's money, maybe even transferring it to a hidden personal account. It's okay for a family caregiver to receive a decent wage but not to steal! The caregiving sibling should make annual financial reports to the rest of the family, including current copies of the parent's bank and investment accounts. This deters potentially dishonest siblings and protects honest ones from suspicion.

14. Consider assisted living. Maybe your parent would like to move to an apartment in an assisted-living home, where nursing care is available too. You can visit the homes and make suggestions.

15. Don't shrink from the nursing home or assisted living decision. This may be your best option if your parent can't manage alone, can't afford a companion, can't find a home-sharing arrangement, and—for any number of reasons—can't move in with a family member. Make the same decision for a parent who already lives with you if his or her physical or mental problems exceed your ability to cope. Nursing homes are not snake pits. Although some are indeed mediocre, you'll also find some excellent places where the patients are clean, cheerful, mentally and physically active, and watched over by caring staffs. Ask a doctor, nurse, or the social service worker at a hospital for recommendations and visit them all. Don't feel guilty about it! Many parents who fight the idea find a nursing home or assisted living home congenial once they've settled in and made some friends. And even if they don't, some things can't be helped.

16. Bring up the question of a living will and health care proxy (page 126). What is your parent's opinion about artificial life supports if he or she is terminally ill?

17. Collect information for the obituary. Many families put out wrong information because they're hazy on the details of their parents' lives.

A Divorce Checklist

1. Follow the money. Modern divorce is not about who's the meanest or who slept where. It's mainly about children and money—how to split up any property and what to allocate for alimony and child support. The financial division won't be fair unless all the income and property are on the table.

If you don't know much about your spouse's finances and fear that he or she won't pay, go ahead and snoop. Any financial document can be a clue to income, assets, and debts. Also, comb the computer. Look for:

• *Online links to banks, brokerage accounts, mutual fund companies, and other financial connections.* Clone the computer's hard disk.

• *Your spouse's payroll stubs.* They show whether money is being deducted for savings and retirement accounts.

• *Life insurance policies.* What's the face amount, and how large is the cash value?

• *Current statements for any retirement plan held by your spouse:* Individual Retirement Account, Simplified Employee Pension, Keogh plan, 403(b), 457, 401(k), and company pension and profit sharing.

• *The most recent state and federal income tax returns.* Try for returns from at least the past five years. If you can't find copies, get them from the IRS or the state tax office. You have an absolute right to copies if you filed a joint return. There's no charge for an IRS transcript (that's a computer printout showing what was on the original return) of your filing for the current year and the past four years. Call 800-829-1040 or make your request on Form 4506-T (you can print out the form at www.irs.gov—just enter its number in the Search box). For actual copies of the returns, plus returns from earlier years that are still on file, send Form 4506. You'll be charged $39 for each return.

• *A copy of all financial statements filed for all recent mortgages or business loans.* Again, you have an absolute right to copies of anything you cosigned. If you don't want to mention divorce, tell the lenders that you're updating your personal financial statement and have lost the original. Look for large chunks of money leaving the account.

• *A copy of the will.* It may list assets you'd forgotten about. The lawyer who drew up the will may have a specific list of assets and liabilities.

• *Copies of appraisals* on the house, furnishings, and jewelry, done for insurance purposes.

- *Deeds, bank statements, check registers, loan documents, credit card statements, mutual fund reports, statements from stockbrokers, statements of employee benefits, insurance policies.* These not only document assets, they also help establish your marital standard of living.
- *Claims to future income, such as potential royalties and stock options.* You may need a specialist to establish the value of complex investments such as options and hedge funds.
- *A copy of your credit report, which will show transactions on jointly held accounts.* Some credit bureaus will also send your spouse's report, so you can look for separate accounts. But don't ask to have your spouse's report sent to a different address; the credit bureau won't do it.
- *A list of all your debts, secured and unsecured.* They too need to be divided. Even if your spouse takes them as his or her obligations, you remain liable to the lender for payment if you signed the application.
- *Evidence of any money that you brought to the marriage.* If you kept it in a separate account, it should be wholly yours. If you mixed it with marital assets, it's up for splitting. But it might change the split from the typical 50–50 to 60–40 in your favor, thanks to your extra contribution.

Each spouse should have a copy of all these financial records. Neither one of you should spirit them away. If one of you plays nasty, so will the other. You'll throw away money on court battles and wind up testing the limits of your mutual capacity to hurt.

2. Don't hide assets from your spouse. It's not only mean, it can be illegal. If you're caught and the divorce is in court, you might have to pay whatever it cost for your spouse to uncover the deceit. As a penalty, you may even have to forfeit the property. And you'll blow your credibility with your lawyer and the judge. (Unfortunately, outside court, a spouse with money can make life tough for a spouse without it.)

3. Hire an investigative accountant if your spouse owns a business or you believe that he or she is hiding assets. Your divorce attorney should know where to find one. Wholly owned businesses are especially notorious for shielding income and assets from public view. One accountant who specializes in divorce cases says that underreporting deprives spouses (usually wives) of 20 to 50 percent of their rightful share of property and support. You need someone with a well-developed sense of the absurd to examine your spouse's business tax returns and to press for documents that show more fully what the business earns. (Sorry, but you've nothing to gain by vindictively calling the IRS. If your spouse underreported personal income and you signed the joint income tax return and benefited from the tax evasion, the IRS generally holds you equally liable for the taxes owed. There's something called "innocent spouse relief" that lets you off the hook, but it's hard to qualify for. Go to www.irs.gov and search for Publication 971 for details.)

If you worked in your spouse's business—even if unpaid—document what you did and the hours you worked. While you're working there, ask for a fancy title, such as vice president. Evidence of your contribution and position may raise the payout you receive. In many states, however, any ownership interest you get in the business as part of the divorce wipes out a separate payment for unpaid work. If your relatives helped your spouse get started, prepare to prove it—that may get you more money too.

4. Protect your flanks. You'll need personal money to tide yourself over the months it takes to reach a settlement, so start putting part of each paycheck into a separate account. You might move half of the cash in a joint bank account into your separate name. But don't be greedy. Take only your share, explain what you've done, and take over part of the bills. Once the divorce is under way, disclose exactly what assets you have.

Next, tell your stockbroker, investment adviser, and mutual fund companies, in writing, not to sell jointly owned investments unless your signature is on the order. Tell your banks that your signature is needed for withdrawals from your joint accounts. Tear up any power of attorney that gives your spouse power over your assets, and tell your banks and brokers, in writing, not to accept any copies. Consider destroying any health care proxy (page 126) that gives your spouse the right to make medical decisions for you and putting that power in other hands. Open your own safe-deposit box and keep your valuables there. Don't cosign any new loans with your spouse.

Photocopy the latest credit card bills so it's easy to tell who's responsible for any future spending.

Write to your creditors and close joint home equity credit lines and credit card accounts (registered mail, return receipt requested). Also state that you won't be responsible for future debts added to the card. Tell your spouse what you're doing, by the way; it's bad form to leave him or her with a card that some clerk at a cash register will confiscate. Closing the cards is normally in both spouses' interest unless it leaves one of you without credit.

If you alone signed the credit card application, making your spouse an authorized user, you can cancel your spouse's card while keeping yours intact. If you both signed, however, the account will be closed and you'll each have to apply for a new card.

When an account is closed, some creditors may require that any existing debt be paid in full. If you don't have the cash, you and your spouse could divide the joint credit card balances and transfer them to your separate cards. If debt is left in a closed joint account, you're both responsible for paying it—on time and in full.

When you decide which of you should pay the mortgage and the auto loans, ask the lender how to transfer the debt into that spouse's name alone. There's no guarantee, however, that the lender—especially a mortgage lender—will agree. If you can't refinance the loan into a single name, you'll both remain responsible for it. If neither of you pays, it will be a blot on both your credit reports.

Start a child care diary, noting which of you fulfills the children's various daily needs. It may be helpful in a custody battle, although that kind of warfare hurts the children above all.

If you have no income of your own, you're at a disadvantage. Every nonworking spouse needs personal savings for emergencies like this. You might be able to stake yourself by pulling cash from a credit card or home equity line of credit. But don't be surprised if your spouse refuses to make monthly payments on those loans. You're better off applying to the court for temporary support. Be prepared for a fight if yours is a difficult divorce. Temporary-support hearings can be as intense as a full trial.

5. Count on a reasonable share of the reported property if there is any. In community property states, assets acquired during the marriage are normally divided in half. Spouses fight over which those assets are and what they're worth. In other states, the division turns on the length of the marriage and each spouse's contribution, professionally or in the home. The law calls for "equitable" division regardless of fault; in practice, that comes pretty close to equal division. Inheritances and assets owned before marriage usually stay with the spouse they came with, as long as they're kept in separate names. The same may be true for rents and profits from premarital assets as long as they haven't been mixed with marital assets. Unwinding such assets is tricky. You need an expert.

6. Don't forget the pension. In many marriages, the only assets are the house and the pension or retirement savings. Spouses are generally entitled to a share of each, although not necessarily a half share. When you both have retirement savings, both plans—his and hers—will be on the table. If one plan is a traditional pension, your lawyer should call in an expert to check its value, propose the best method of division, and be sure the rules are followed. If you can get only a future allocation from the pension plan, not a current payout, you might prefer to take property of equivalent worth. Here's what you generally can expect:

• *Individual Retirement Accounts and Simplified Employee Pensions are divisible, tax free, at the time of divorce, with a written agreement or court order.* Your portion can be transferred into an IRA in your own name, with no current taxes due. You can tap the IRA for instant cash, but that triggers income taxes plus a 10 percent tax penalty if you're under age 59½. (If you divide the IRA or SEP before divorce and then decide to stay together, the transfer will be taxable.)

• *Company 401(k) plans, including the employer's contribution, are generally divisible at divorce with a court order.* You can take most of the payout options the plan offers: a lifetime annuity, payment over 10 or 20 years, or a lump sum distribution. If you cash out right away—again, pursuant to a court order—you'll owe income taxes but no 10 percent penalty. If you want to keep the tax deferral, you can roll the lump sum into an IRA, but any later withdrawals will be subject to the 10 percent penalty. Attorney Marcia Fidis of Pasternak & Fidis in Bethesda, Maryland, advises that you figure out how much cash you'll need from the plan, take that immediately, and roll the rest into an IRA.

Alternatively, you can transfer your portion of your ex's 401(k) into your name and keep it invested in the plan's mutual funds. If you want the money later, you can usually take it, subject to the 10 percent penalty prior to age 59½. Some plans make you wait for payout until your ex leaves the job or reaches age 50. Check all the rules before deciding.

The same rules that apply to 401(k)s also apply to your company's profit-sharing plan, if there is one.

• *403(b) retirement plans, typically held by teachers and employees of non-profit institutions, and government 457 plans,* can also be formally split as part of the divorce agreement and rolled into IRAs. Whether you can leave the investments where they are depends on the plan. Your lawyer should contact the plan's custodian to find out what your options are.

• *Traditional pensions,* known as defined benefit plans, can be divided in one of two ways:

With a *shared interest,* you get part of your spouse's pension when he or she retires, as well as a survivor benefit if he or she dies before retiring.

With a *separate interest,* you can start getting pension payments even if your ex has not retired (although you'll probably have to wait until he or she passes the plan's early-retirement age—typically, 55 and up). This is usually the better choice. Your share of the pension might be payable in a lump sum, which can be rolled into an IRA. More often it's paid as a monthly income over your lifetime. Your checks come directly from the plan. They don't pass through your ex's hands. Some of the smaller pension plans may give you a lump sum at divorce instead of waiting for retirement.

If your spouse has stock options, an excess benefits plan, a supplemental benefits plan, or any other *nonqualified* plan, negotiate for a share of it too. (A plan is nonqualified when the company makes no current benefit payments but promises the full amount when the employee—usually an executive—dies, retires, or leaves the job.) But whether or not you can get your share of these valuable plans directly from the company depends on the plan's provisions and state law. They're not governed by court orders. If the plan won't pay you directly, the divorce agreement has to require that your ex pays you these benefits when he or she receives them.

Be sure that your lawyer gets a copy of all the pension and other benefit plans, so that he or she can see what's possible.

• *Non-IRA plans for the self-employed or partnerships, commonly called Keoghs, follow the rules for 401(k)s or for traditional pensions,* depending on the type of Keogh.

To nail down a share of a 401(k), 403(b), 457, profit-sharing, or pension plan, you need something called a *qualified domestic relations order (QDRO),* issued by the court. (The order has slightly different names if it's served on a government plan.) It spells out exactly what you will get. Well-drawn orders also state how the payment will be figured (including whether you get interest on the amount) and what you get if your ex should die. A QDRO must be approved by the pension-plan administrator as well as the court, to be sure that it follows all the plan's rules. If it doesn't, the plan will not pay, no matter what the divorce agreement says. Be sure that the QDRO is signed at divorce. Otherwise your rights might be jeopardized.

The QDRO makes you a plan beneficiary. Well in advance of the divorce, your lawyer should get you a summary of how the plan works along with a current benefits statement. After the QDRO is delivered to the plan administrator, you're supposed to start getting annual statements. Unfortunately, plans often neglect to send statements to ex-spouses. Your lawyer should get your name on the list when the QDRO is approved. Otherwise send a certified letter to the plan administrator, citing your right to information under the Employee Retirement Income Security Act (ERISA) (the pension law), Section 105. (Government pensions aren't covered by ERISA.)

7. Don't forget the professional degree. Remember the PhT (Putting Hubby Through)? If the wife worked in order to get her spouse through medical or law school, she may, in some states, be entitled to share in the income likely to be produced by that degree. And vice versa, in the case of a PwT. But you may have to show actual dollars spent, such as a cosigned student loan. Alternatively, the court may take your whole marital history into consideration when awarding support, without focusing on who did what for whom.

8. Divorce is a shock and a tragedy for your kids even if they know you're not getting along. They worry that the split was their fault, they'll have to move away, they'll have to choose between parents and not see the other one again, or that their custodial parent will be poor. They'll feel loss, anger, anxiety, and depression. You'll make things worse if you criticize your spouse or try to recruit the kids to your side. Custody battles are horror shows. You'll find lots of free advice on the Web to help you minimize their stress. Try Helpguide.org (www .helpguide.org/mental/children_divorce.htm) or Children and Divorce (www .childrenanddivorce.com/id2.html). Also, browse the online bookstore sites. The American Bar Association publishes *What Your Children Need . . . Now!*, available at www.abanet.org or 800-285-2221.

9. Don't expect permanent alimony. Spouses with decent paychecks get no alimony. Spouses with tiny paychecks or none at all may get only temporary support while they go back to school or learn a job skill. This can be tragically unfair to middle-aged homemakers, who will probably have a hard time finding well-paid work. If the marriage lasted more than 10 years, however, the court may order alimony when the other spouse can afford to pay. In several states, older women with long-term marriages have a right to support for life. Even so, the wife's standard of living usually falls after a divorce, while, over time, the husband's improves. (Increasingly, a dependent husband gets temporary or permanent alimony from an employed wife, but bias against male dependents still prevails in many courts.)

If you're not working or are working part-time, start gearing up as soon as divorce enters the picture. Look for a job, see a career counselor, go back to school, refresh your career skills (using marital assets to make yourself more employable). Some spouses think they'll cut a better deal if they come into court looking poor. But that's a myth, says Pasternak & Fidis attorney Linda Ravdin. Instead it lets your ex-to-be (who doesn't love you!) argue that your future earning power is, say, $80,000 a year—and what does a judge know about it? If you can show that you've applied for work and can't expect to earn more than $35,000, you should get a more realistic settlement.

10. Parents without physical custody should expect generous child visi-tation rights. Both courts and lawyers have grown more sensitive to the rights of noncustodial parents, typically fathers. Custody of young children still tends to go to the mother, by family agreement. But fathers are pursuing and winning more cases, especially if the mother wants to move to another state. Mothers who will put their children in day care while they work also have weaker claims, as do mothers with low incomes and gay or lesbian parents (although some states now bar discrimination based on sexual preference). Joint custody, where parents share the child's time, is becoming more common. Joint *legal* custody— where parents share decision making—is now the norm. You have to learn how to talk to each other.

11. Parents with custody should get adequate child support. Federally mandated child support guidelines direct how much of a parent's income has to go toward maintaining the children. Some states look only at the income of the noncustodial parent, others look at the parents' combined incomes. If your current award is below the guidelines, you can get it raised.

In one interesting twist, a mother with a job who decides to quit and stay home with her children might not be able to get extra child support. The court may base her expected financial contribution on what she could have earned had she stayed at work. Her ex-husband wouldn't have to pay more just because she decided to give more time to the kids. The same rules would apply to the husband if he took a lower-paying job to try to reduce his support obligations.

You might try to negotiate cost-of-living adjustments (COLAs) for long-term child support payments, so that your young children's standard of living won't fall. If you don't have a COLA in your divorce agreement, ask your state's Child Support Enforcement agency about getting the payments raised to today's guideline levels. You should find the phone number on the Web or under the state or county listings for social service agencies.

What if your ex doesn't pay? Call the state Child Support Enforcement agency. The state can also help you trace a parent who has skipped. To apply for help will cost you $0 to $25. If you're not on welfare, states charge $25 a year for their legal and collection services.

All states will enforce a court order to withhold child support payments (and sometimes alimony) from a parent's paycheck. They can also tap your ex-spouse's state and federal income tax refunds. Some states will order a spouse to pay through a court trustee to simplify collection. The process of obtaining an order, however, is often slow. It's especially hard to nail a parent who deliberately moves around.

Even if your ex doesn't pay, you're not allowed to withhold visiting rights. Conversely, the law doesn't allow you to withhold payments if your ex is making it tough for you to see the kids. Custody and support are two separate parts of the agreement.

How well these rules work depends on where you live. Some states have terrific child support procedures and a large enough staff to keep up with the new cases coming in. Many other states, however, are desultory and understaffed. Nevertheless, try the public child support office before paying the large sum that a private lawyer would want.

The government publishes an excellent free booklet titled *Handbook on Child Support Enforcement.* Get it online from the Office of Child Support Enforcement (OCSE) at www.acf.hhs.gov/programs/cse. You're most apt to collect your child support if you're on good terms with your ex-spouse and he or she sees the children regularly.

What if there's a change in financial circumstances? The court might lower child support if the change is substantial—say, the paying parent loses his or her job or suffers a large decline in income. If the same thing happens to the receiving parent, the court might order child support to be increased. The change could be temporary or permanent.

It takes a substantial change to modify an alimony agreement. Some agreements even state that alimony can't be modified. Property settlements usually are cast in stone unless you can prove that they were obtained through fraud or duress. The same is true of contractual agreements to pay for college education.

12. Reach an agreement on who will pay for college. Child support in most states stops at age 19 or high school graduation, unless the parents agree to continue. A few states continue it to 21 or 22, or as long as the child is in school. Some dependent wives elect to give up other financial support in exchange for a college agreement (get it in writing). Others don't, trusting the husband to see that the kids get a good education.

When it comes to awarding financial aid, schools ignore what the court papers say. State colleges and universities tend to base awards on the income of the custodial parent (and stepparent, if there is one). By contrast, most private colleges and universities base financial aid on both parents' incomes (including stepparents), regardless of whom the child lives with.

13. Don't borrow against your house if your marriage isn't going well. Your house is often your major asset. What happens if a wife (for example) agrees to cosign for a home equity line of credit and her husband (for example) takes the money and spends it? Her share of the home equity has been reduced, and she might not be able to get it back. In a case like this, the judge should order the husband to repay, but you can't assume that's going to happen. Take a big loan only if you're sure that you'll both be there to pay it off. If the marriage looks shaky, you'd be smart to freeze or cancel the credit line. Either one of you can usually do so unilaterally.

14. Negotiate where you'll live. The custodial parent may have to agree not to move to another city, so the other parent can have ready access to the children.

15. Don't hit below the belt. Don't cancel all the joint credit cards unless your spouse has a card of his or her own (or can qualify for a new one). Assure your spouse that, during the divorce negotiation, you'll continue to cover the household bills that you've always paid. Don't hide or destroy financial records. Don't hijack valuables out of the house and claim they've been lost. Don't steal money. Integrity not only facilitates divorce, it also helps the children recover. Remember that divorce, unlike marriage, really does last until death do you part.

16. Hire a lawyer who believes in settlement. A peaceful solution can keep you out of court, hold down your costs, and leave your relationship reasonably cordial. When looking for a lawyer, talk to friends who have been divorced for a while and have some perspective on what they went through. Meet with the lawyer before you proceed. It's important to like the person who represents you.

Don't hire a "bomber" who gets his or her kicks by hanging up your spouse by the thumbs. It may feel good at first but, in the long run, will hang you too. Bomber tactics lengthen the negotiation, tempt you into dishonorable acts, ruin any hope of an amicable relationship after the divorce, and fatten the lawyers' bills. Don't hire a bomber even if your spouse has one; they'll play well-rehearsed war games at your expense. Just be sure that your own lawyer is a specialist in divorce. Bombers eat general practitioners and corporate lawyers for lunch.

The same lawyer should never represent both you and your spouse. In theory, this could work if the split is amicable, both parties can support themselves comfortably, you're in perfect agreement about who gets what property, and no children are involved. Even so, most lawyers would think it unethical. You each need separate representation.

What raises the price of divorce is arguments. The more you quarrel over property, the more you struggle over payments, custody, and visiting rights, the more you delay, prevaricate, and punish each other, the more you'll pay. You'll wind up spending your kids' college educations on lawyers' fees. Try to put together some ground rules for conduct even before you see your lawyers.

Mediation services exist to help resolve differences between you and your spouse. The mediator—usually a mental-health professional rather than a lawyer—meets with the couple to help them resolve their differences. If you go this route, see a lawyer first, so you'll know your legal rights and the tax issues involved. You should also check in with the lawyer before major agreements are reached. Mediation-cum-legal-advice should be cheaper than letting your lawyers do all the work. But beware the mediator who strong-arms an agreement by beating on the more compliant spouse. If you agree to a poor or misguided settlement, it may be too late or too difficult to start negotiating again. Mediation won't work if one spouse is a bully, won't cooperate, won't disclose assets, lacks good faith, or consults with a bomber on the side.

A newer approach is *collaborative law.* The couple and their lawyers sign an agreement to reach a negotiated settlement. The lawyers agree to withdraw from the case if the couple winds up in court, so they have no incentive to encourage their clients to ask for too much. Everyone bargains together until they have a deal. For more information about the process, check the Web site of the International Academy of Collaborative Professionals (IACP) (www .collaborativepractice.com).

Try Divorcenet.com (www.divorcenet.com) for the names of mediators and collaborative-divorce lawyers in your area.

17. Get tax advice right from the start if there's a lot of money at stake. You need to know what's deductible and what's not and what the after-tax value of your settlement will be. For example, if you accept highly appreciated stock, you'll pay taxes when you convert it to cash, so it won't be worth as much as you thought.

The same could be true of your home. When a house is sold, couples are normally allowed to take the first $500,000 in profit tax free; singles get the first $250,000. But to claim that big tax break, you have to have lived in the house for at least two of the past five years. If you sell earlier, you're taxed on the entire gain. Warning: the spouse who moves out risks losing his or her share of this tax break if the divorce negotiations drag on for years. To protect yourself, draw up a written agreement saying that the absent spouse is "deemed" to be still living there. You can write this yourselves, informally.

If the house is worth less than the debt against it, you'll have to negotiate how to share the loss.

Discuss who gets the dependency deduction normally awarded to the parent with physical custody of the child. That parent can waive the deduction and give it to the other. Such an exchange makes sense if the noncustodial parent is in a much higher tax bracket.

The child care credit can be taken only by a custodial parent who hires the care so that he or she can work. If the wife has the child, the husband might pay the equivalent of child care expenses to her directly, in the form of deductible alimony; she would then pay for the care and take the credit on her return.

If one spouse starts paying "faux alimony" to the other—in advance of a formal separation—put the agreement in writing. That makes the payments tax deductible. They're not deductible if you simply write checks based on a verbal agreement. You don't need a lawyer to arrange this; just draw up something between yourselves.

18. Get financial planning advice right from the start. How much will you need to support yourself? Do you really want the house, or are the mortgage and maintenance too much for you to carry? Is your spouse proposing that you get the risky investments while he or she keeps the safe ones? Can you live on the settlement that's proposed, not just this year but 10 or 20 years from now? A good financial planner can help you think through these and other issues during the negotiation. For more information, check the Institute for Divorce Financial Analysts (IDFA) at www.institutedfa.com. You need a planner, attorney, or accountant knowledgeable about divorce tax rules.

19. If you work for the federal government, get an attorney familiar with its benefits. Ex-military, foreign service, and civil service spouses qualify for a variety of benefits, depending on how their divorce is structured.

20. Do it yourself, with help. In some states, lawyers have published do-it-yourself divorce guides. They work best for working couples who are ending their marriage politely, with minimal assets and no children to consider. But before you make the settlement final, pay a visit to a lawyer just to be sure that you haven't overlooked anything important.

21. Don't lose your health benefits. Wives are no longer dropped automatically from their husbands' company health plans, and vice versa. If the company employs at least 20 people, you can stay in your ex-spouse's group plan, at your own expense, for up to three years. This is called your COBRA benefit. To arrange it, notify the employee benefits office, in writing, within 60 days of your legal separation or divorce. Pay the premiums on time! If you're late, an insurer can drop you like a hot potato, with no grace period and no reinstatement.

If you can't afford the premiums, you might try to get your spouse to pay as part of the divorce agreement. You normally lose COBRA coverage if you remarry and come under your new spouse's insurance or get a job that covers you with another plan. Your ex's plan would have to keep you only if you're ill and there's a waiting period before the new plan covers your preexisting conditions.

22. Get life insurance on your spouse for as long as alimony or child support payments are due. You need an inexpensive term insurance policy that runs out when the obligation does. To be sure that the policy stays in force and that you're the beneficiary, own it yourself and make the premium payments. Your spouse can reimburse you through regular support payments (put this in the divorce agreement).

23. Collect all your Social Security benefits. You are generally entitled to benefits on your ex-spouse's account, provided that the marriage lasted for at least 10 years. Social Security looks first to your own account to see how high your personal benefits are. If you'd collect more as an ex-spouse, that's what you'll get. Here's when you can stake a claim on your ex's account:

a. *For retirement benefits:* (1) You're at least 62, haven't married, and your ex-spouse is also on Social Security. (2) If your ex is eligible for benefits but not collecting them, you can still collect as long as you've been divorced for at least two years.

b. *For survivor's benefits, after your ex-spouse's death:* (1) You're 60 or older, or 50 and disabled, and haven't remarried. (2) You're any age, unmarried, and caring for the deceased worker's child who is disabled or under age 16. In this case, you can collect even if you were married for less than 10 years. (3) You remarried after age 60 but are entitled to a better Social Security benefit from your ex-spouse's account than from the account of your new spouse.

c. *For disability benefits:* (1) You're at least 50 and unmarried. (2) You're permanently and totally disabled under Social Security's hard-nosed rules. (3) Your disability started before age 60 and no later than 84 months (seven years) after the latest of the following two dates: the month the worker died *or* the last month that you were entitled to parental benefits on the deceased spouse's record. (4) You remarried but did so after age 50 and after becoming disabled. In this case, you can still collect from your ex's account if that payment is more than you'd get from the account of your new spouse.

What if your ex-spouse remarries? Both you and the new spouse are eligible for exactly the same benefits. Neither of you takes one dime away from the other. But you may reduce others' benefits if you're caring for your ex's child who is under 16 or disabled.

What if you remarry and then divorce? You can return to the benefits owed from the account of your first ex if they're better than what you'd get from the second ex.

24. Don't take a note from your spouse for money owed if you can help it. If there's no option, see that it pays a competitive interest rate and is guaranteed by a performance bond or a lien against property. You need some easy way to collect in case he or she declines to pay or files for bankruptcy.

25. Don't challenge a premarital or postmarital agreement unless you can truly show that you were defrauded into signing or that, by failing to disclose some significant assets, your spouse led you to a wrong decision. Judges are reluctant to revoke these contracts except for a very good reason. It usually does no good to argue that the contract is "unfair." Presumably, you knew that when you signed it. (A few states do look at the contract's fairness but will change it only in egregious cases. It's not egregious enough to be a multimillionaire whose homebody wife gets no assets, only child support. She signed on to that deal, and it's her loss.)

26. Change your beneficiaries. As soon as you separate, redo your will. Name someone other than your spouse as beneficiary of your savings account, mutual funds, brokerage account, Individual Retirement Account, 401(k), life insurance, will, living trust, and any other assets. Be sure that these changes are made by the time the divorce is final. If you don't get around to updating these documents and you die, your ex may inherit your money even if you've remarried and started a new family. Some states take your ex off some of these beneficiary forms even if you forget to do it yourself. So do most insurance companies. If you don't take your ex off your retirement plan, however, the ex gets the money, even if he or she waived it in the separation agreement.

27. Browse the Web for help. You'll find tons of resources at sites like Divorcesource.com (www.divorcesource.com), Divorcenet.com, and Nolo publishing (www.nolo.com). I especially like one of Nolo's books, *A Judge's Guide to Divorce: Uncommon Advice from the Bench.*

28. Do it right the first time. Except for child support, custody arrangements, and court-ordered alimony, divorce agreements usually can't be reopened unless both of you want a change.

A Checklist for New Widows and Widowers

1. Get multiple, certified copies of the death certificate—perhaps 20 or more. This chore is usually handled by the funeral director. You'll need the copies for claiming insurance proceeds and Social Security benefits, and for transferring property into new names.

2. Find the will and any trusts. Decide whether to handle the estate yourself or to hire a lawyer to help. If there's an outside trustee, talk to that person about how the assets should be managed.

3. Find any life insurance, including company insurance, and put in a claim immediately. An insurance agent or lawyer can help, or call the insurer for instructions. Don't make an irrevocable decision about how to handle the policy's proceeds until you've had time to think about your financial affairs.

4. Inventory the safe-deposit box.

5. If you're covered under your spouse's company health insurance, find out immediately about keeping the policy. Under the so-called COBRA rules, most companies that employ at least 20 people have to keep you in the plan, at your expense, for up to three years (page 424). But you must notify the company, in writing, within 30 days of your spouse's death. When you hear from the health insurer, you must say yes to the policy within 60 days. If you're not protected by COBRA, you may be able to convert the group policy into individual coverage. If you buy family coverage through an individual non-group policy, tell the insurer that your spouse is dead. Your insurance premium will drop.

6. Find the rest of the assets: deeds, securities, bank accounts, contracts, partnerships, retirement accounts, annuities, deferred salary, stock options from previous employers, money lent to a third party. And the liabilities: mortgages, personal debts, business debts. Go through the checkbooks, bank statements, and your spouse's personal computer files for clues to property you didn't know about.

7. Pay all bills on time if they relate to your personal life. You don't want to lose your good credit history or have a credit card withdrawn. Bills for a business operated by your spouse should go to the person handling that side of the estate.

8. Claim any benefits you're entitled to: Social Security parental, survivor's, or disability benefits, railroad retirement, civil service, veterans, travel accident insurance.

9. Call your spouse's employer to see how much money is due, and follow up with a letter. There may be company life insurance, deferred salary, stock options, retirement funds, commissions, a bonus, or accrued vacation pay. Labor unions may pay benefits too. If your spouse died from a work-related injury or disease, you may be entitled to payments from worker's compensation.

10. Inspect all your spouse's papers and don't throw anything away. They may relate to assets or liabilities you knew nothing about. If the papers are in disarray, promise yourself that when you die, your family will find everything in order.

11. If your spouse owned a business, be sure that the administration is in competent hands. Consult with the business's attorney and accountant.

12. If your spouse died in an accident, talk to a lawyer about whether you have a legitimate claim for wrongful death.

13. Reconsider your will or living trust, or draw one if you haven't. Give someone your durable power of attorney (page 125) and your health care proxy (page 126). Change the beneficiaries of your IRA, life insurance, 401(k), investment accounts, and other assets.

14. Make no irrevocable decisions! Don't sell the house, change your investments, invest in a business, or give your insurance proceeds to a financial planner to manage. Keep your cash in a bank and your hands in your pockets until the emotional storm has passed. You'll make better decisions once you've had time to assess your situation.

An Inheritance Checklist

1. Do nothing at first. Let the deeds, securities, and bank accounts be transferred into your name. Then make a plan.

2. List the holes in your safety net and use your inheritance to fill them. If you don't have health or disability insurance, get it now. If you haven't been able to afford the full contribution to your company's 401(k), step up your payroll deductions. Pay off credit card debts. Set aside money for your children's college education. Buy a house if you've been renting, provided that you can handle the carrying costs.

3. Don't blow the money (or blow no more than 5 percent). Your inheritance may be your last, best hope of living well when you retire. What to do with your luck depends on the size of the windfall and how well fixed you were before. Assuming that the money is important, here are some thoughts:

- *A modest inheritance*—up to $75,000 or so. Invest for retirement and your children's education. Your life won't change, but you'll feel more relaxed.
- *A moderate inheritance*—up to $500,000. You can afford some big vacations and new living room furniture, while still padding your retirement and education funds. But don't quit your job unless you have a lot of money of your own.
- *A major inheritance*—up to $2 million. You might be able to flee the office, depending on your age. Or you might change careers or do nonprofit work.
- *A megainheritance*—$2 million or more. Money like this often comes with a team of advisers to help you make decisions. If not, get your own. You can live larger than you do now, or work less. But $2 million ain't what it used to be. To make sure it lasts for life, an heir in middle age should spend no more than 4 percent of the money the first year, then increase the draw by no more than the amount of inflation each year after that. On $2 million, that's $80,000 plus annual inflation increases. Nice, but not a Bentley budget.

4. Get advice if you've never handled a large lump sum of money before. Avoid planners and brokers who earn commissions on products they sell. Find a fee-only planner (page 1176) who will steer you toward sensible, low-cost investments suitable for your specific goals.

5. Don't play investment wizard. Just because you have money doesn't mean that you suddenly know how to pick winning stocks. Money can vanish on bad investments even faster than if you spent it on fast cars and boats, with less to show for the expense. If you want to try playing the market, fine—but do it with just a small amount of your inheritance. Stash the rest prudently in well-diversified mutual funds.

6. Don't keep a particular stock just because Daddy loved it. Its time may be over. Design an investment plan for the future, not for the past. And remember: daddies make investment mistakes just like everyone else.

7. Think about future costs before using the money to buy a big house in a more expensive neighborhood. All your living expenses will rise, not just this year but every year in the future. Maybe your inheritance is large enough to cover them. If not, you may be setting yourself up for trouble.

8. Consider keeping the inheritance in your name alone. If you divorce, this money won't have to be divided with your ex. If you put it in joint names or joint investment accounts and get divorced, you'll kiss half of it bye-bye.

9. Know the tax rules when you inherit an Individual Retirement Account. Handled right, you can keep the money growing tax free or tax deferred for the rest of your life. Handled wrong, you'll be taxed on the entire sum in the year you receive the money. *Many* brokers and planners don't know the rules! If they mismanage the paperwork, you'll owe the tax. Here's what to do:

• *If you're the spouse of the deceased*, have your late spouse's IRA retitled in your name so the money can continue to grow untaxed. Or roll the money directly into an IRA that you already have (your late spouse's IRA trustee should write a check to your IRA trustee).

With traditional IRAs, taxes are deferred until you take money out. If you don't need the money, you can defer withdrawals until you reach age 70½. With Roth IRAs, you're never required to make withdrawals. If you do, the money generally comes tax free. (For more on the difference between the two types of IRAs, see page 1047.)

Do *not* take all the money out of the IRA and put it into a personal account. That would make the IRA money taxable all at once.

• *If you're not the spouse of the deceased*, open a new, "inherited IRA," titled with your name, the name of the deceased, and the date of death. For example, if Dana inherits from Jesse, the IRA would be titled "Dana, as beneficiary of Jesse, IRA, deceased November 5, 2009." The inherited money is transferred directly from Jesse's old IRA to Dana's new one, without passing through Dana's hands. If Jesse left several heirs—Tyler, Hudson, and Maisy—the IRA could be divided in thirds. Again, each should be titled with the name of the beneficiary, Jesse's name, and the date of death.

If you inherit a traditional IRA, you'll have to withdraw (and pay taxes on) at least enough money each year to deplete the IRA over your lifetime. You can withdraw larger amounts, of course, but anything you leave in the IRA will grow untaxed. The same rules apply to Roth IRAs, except that the withdrawals are tax free.

Here are three things a nonspouse beneficiary should *not* do: Do not transfer the inherited IRA into an IRA titled in your name alone—for example, "Dana's IRA." Do not have a check for the IRA proceeds made out to you for redeposit into an inherited IRA you set up. Do not have the money deposited into a taxable bank or brokerage account. All three actions strip you of your tax shelter. You'll have to pay taxes on all the money right away. If you were misadvised, tough luck. This is one genie that you can't put back in the bottle.

• *If there's no named beneficiary,* the tax shelter vanishes fast. Say that Jesse died and simply left his IRA to his estate. If he died prior to age 70½, his heirs have to withdraw all the IRA money within five years. If he died at 70½ or later, the IRA payout can be stretched over Jesse's remaining statistical life expectancy (or taken earlier, if that's what the heirs want).

• *Know the rules for inherited company retirement plans* such as 401(k)s, 403(b)s, and 457s. Spouses can roll the money into an Individual Retirement Account. Other heirs can roll it into an "inherited IRA"—following the rules above—provided that the plan allows it. If the plan doesn't allow it, you have to cash out of the plan within five years and pay the tax. (For an excellent book on tax planning with IRAs, see *The Retirement Savings Time Bomb . . . and How to Defuse It* by Ed Slott.)

A Checklist for Starting a Business at Home

1. A good accountant is a must. You need to know how to keep your books, what's tax deductible, and what employee benefits your business can legitimately pay for.

2. Open a business bank account. Mixing your business with your personal money makes it harder to track your business profits and to do your tax returns.

3. Get a separate business telephone. If you're not there, let the call jump to an answering machine (it's not professional for your kids to answer). Turn down the ringer when you "leave the office." A surprising number of people today leave orders at midnight, expecting to reach a machine. The entire cost of this telephone is tax deductible.

If your home phone is also your business phone, you cannot deduct the standard cost of the first line into the house—only the added business costs, such as call waiting and business-related long-distance calls. You'll also have to document your business use of the telephone.

4. Start a Web site. Your current customers expect you to have one, and new customers will find you there. Let them leave Web orders for you, paying by credit card or through a commercial payment service such as PayPal.

5. Apply for a merchant card, which lets you take customers' credit cards when you make a sale. Banks normally don't give merchant cards to home-based businesses unless they have a long track record. But you may be able to qualify after a year or two. To find a vendor, type "small business merchant account" into a Web search engine.

6. Get a vendor number from your state (in most cases, you apply to your state's retail sales tax division). That enables you to buy goods wholesale instead of retail, which is a huge money saver. On goods bought for resale, you often pay no sales tax (check the rules of your state).

7. Prospect for health insurance if you're not covered through a spouse. Perhaps there's a group you can join that offers coverage to members; a professional association or your local chamber of commerce. Some insurers sell "group" policies for groups of one. But you'll have to show that you're running a real business and have been at it for a while.

Another angle is to hire your spouse, then set up a tax-deductible medical reimbursement plan (your accountant does it for you). The plan can't include you directly; it's only for your employees and their dependents. You get coverage as a dependent of your employee-spouse. With this plan, you don't buy insurance. Instead your business reimburses—and tax-deducts—your employees' out-of-pocket medical, dental, and psychiatric expenses. That includes any health insurance premiums you pay, the deductible and copayments in a group plan, and any bills not covered by insurance. If you have employees other than your spouse, the plan has to cover them too. This works for all types of small-business arrangements except S corporations.

8. Check your business insurance coverage. You probably have inventory and business equipment to protect; you're also potentially liable if a client is injured on your property or by using your product. For a craft business, your basic home owner's policy may be enough. If you have a lot of computer equipment, you might add a rider that raises the basic coverage limit. There are separate policies for more elaborate business needs, including liability coverage.

9. Check your local zoning. Some neighborhoods or apartment houses don't allow any home businesses, no matter how unobtrusive. Others rule out businesses that put up signs or attract traffic. If you're out of compliance, it takes only one unpleasant neighbor to shut you down, so keep quiet about your home office if you don't have to troll for customers locally. If your business isn't a nuisance and your neighbors support you, you can ask for an exception (a variance), even where the law is against you. But you might not win.

10. Get a separate business computer with software to track your orders and expenses. If you mix home and business use, you'll have to document the time you spend on business and write off only that portion of the computer's cost. You also don't want your kids and their friends playing with the machine that you use for business, just in case one of them is accident prone. Install a good backup system for your computer's hard drive, and *use it*!

11. Find out what business licenses you'll need. Also check your business tax obligations. You'll have to make estimated quarterly income tax payments, including the Social Security and Medicare tax on the self-employed.

12. Keep records of your direct business expenses, including equipment, magazine subscriptions, advertising, office supplies, the wholesale cost of any products you resell, employee wages (including wages paid to your spouse and kids), office furniture, business travel, a business car, and business entertainment. Your business driving is deductible at a flat rate per mile plus parking and tolls, but you have to document the miles driven. That means a driver's diary showing the date, purpose, and mileage of each business trip. You can also deduct a portion of your car loan interest or the cost of the lease.

If your expenses exceed the income from your business, as they doubtlessly will at first, you can write off those costs against income you have from another job or your spouse's job. That lowers your total taxable income and hence cuts your tax. Your home business becomes a tax shelter.

As a general rule, however, your business has to turn a profit in three years out of the first five. If it doesn't and you're audited, the IRS will probably rule that it's not a real business, it's just a hobby (although you might be given a grace period if you're seriously trying to make a go of it).

With a hobby-business, you can still deduct expenses up to the amount of your net business income. But you're not allowed to tax-deduct additional losses, so your tax shelter goes bye-bye. What's more, all prior tax shelter deductions will be disallowed. You'll owe back taxes, interest, and penalties. The best way out of this squeeze is to close your unprofitable business. That usually leaves you with most of your past deductions, although you have to repay any write-offs you took for accelerated depreciation. Start-up businesses probably shouldn't take accelerated depreciation, just in case.

13. Set up a deductible home office. It can be a room or a portion of a room, but it must be used exclusively and regularly as your primary place of business.

Otherwise it won't qualify for a tax deduction. There's zero write-off for an office that doubles as the dining room table.

The size of the deduction depends on the percentage of floor space used. If your office takes up, say, 10 percent of your house, you can write off 10 percent of your mortgage interest or rent, homeowners insurance, home maintenance such as house painting, and the bills for heat, electricity, trash removal, and a home security system. You can also depreciate your office space.

There's a limit, however. Most home office write-offs can't exceed your net business income. So you get zip if you're running at a loss (the exception: you're allowed full write-offs for real estate taxes and mortgage interest). Unused home office deductions can be carried forward and deducted against profits in the future. For more on taxes, go to www.irs.gov and download Publication 587, *Business Use of Your Home*. Some other useful IRS publications: 334 (on small business taxes), 463 (on travel and entertainment), 535 (on business expenses), and 917 (on business use of a car).

14. Don't try to tax-deduct your vacations. Only business trips are deductible. It's legit to combine a business trip with a vacation. To deduct the cost of travel, however, you have to document that the trip's primary purpose was business. Visiting suppliers for a day or having a couple of job interviews is not enough to turn a week's vacation into a business trip. At best, it lets you deduct one day of hotel bills, meals, and some taxi fares. Business conventions are deductible, however, even if you spend the afternoons on the golf course. To tax-deduct a spouse who accompanies you on any trip, he or she has to be an employee of the business and have a legitimate business reason for being there.

15. Hire a babysitter, even if for only a half day. A lot of women start a business at home so that they can be with their children. But you can't keep your customers and a three-year-old happy at the same time. Home workers often need child care, just as office workers do. And speaking of kids, tell your spouse not to interrupt you unless the house is on fire.

16. Hire your older kids and pay them tax-deductible wages instead of an allowance. No Social Security taxes are owed if they're under 18 and your business isn't incorporated. If their wages are low enough, they won't owe income taxes either. But they have to do real work and be treated as real employees. That means preparing W-4 forms for tax withholding even if you don't withhold, filing quarterly 941 forms showing wages paid to family employees; and issuing annual W-2 forms. Otherwise their wages may be disallowed on audit.

17. Set up a retirement plan. In 2009, you can put up to $5,000 of your earnings into an Individual Retirement Account if you're 49 or younger and $6,000 if you're 50 or older. Starting in 2010, contributions will rise with the inflation rate. If you hire your spouse to keep the books or do other part-time work, he or she can start an IRA as well. For that matter, even the kids who work in your business can start IRAs to help tax-shelter the money they've earned, although they'd want some pocket money too. (Or let the kids keep the cash and fund their IRAs out of your own money.) If your business gets bigger, you might start a more significant retirement plan (see chapter 29).

18. Avoid the prepackaged businesses that are flogged in get-rich seminars, on the Web, and on cable TV. The promoters tend to overcharge for the books, manuals, disks, tapes, and computers they sell you. They overstate your chance of success. They may also encourage you to tax-deduct personal expenses, which could lead to a nasty audit. Your best shot is a business that grows out of a past job or a hobby you like and are good at, and where you can make the professional contacts you're going to need.

FINDING THE MONEY

Most people don't come to financial planning until they have some extra money. They start with the question "How should I invest?"

You should start earlier. The right question is "How will I get the money that I will then wonder how to invest?" You need a way to acquire cash.

You can win your kitty in a lottery. You can hope to marry well. You can wait for the ground to open before you and a delicate hand to thrust $100,000 into your waiting wallet. Or you can cull the money from what you earn. Save it or borrow it. You are the source. If you do something, you'll have something. If you do nothing . . . (finish the sentence yourself).

The earlier this idea hits you, the wealthier you can be. Time is as much a money machine as earning power. Funds put away when you're 25 are worth far more than funds put away at 40, which in turn are worth more than funds put away at 55. So don't just sit there. Read.

A Spending Plan
That Works

How to Take Charge of Your Money—At Last

**If all of us had every dime that we've wasted in our lives,
we'd be a nation of millionaires.**

Make yourself a spending plan. Not for discipline, not for tidiness, not because your mother told you to. Make it for your own sake. That's the only way to coerce your money into doing what you really want. I've lived with spending plans, and I've lived without. I come back to them every time I'm in a pinch.

A spending plan always works. It captures the cash that slips through your fingers, unnoticed, every day. It discriminates between what's important to have and what you buy because it's there. It rescues you when your income falls short. It lets you save money painlessly, and that's the truth.

A plan is an active strategy for getting wherever you want to go. It starts with a general idea: "I want to live better." "I want to get out of debt." "I want to invest more." "I want to retire early." Then it breaks up that dream into small, specific, everyday actions that you can accomplish one by one.

Plans have to be written down. And they need simple measuring posts to show how you're doing. Imaginary plans that you follow in your head will always be no more than that: a walking dream. They won't get you anywhere.

To start, take this test: write down where your money went last month. Don't do it from memory; use your checkbook, credit card bills, and online bank account for reference.

Compare the result with your take-home pay. Odds are that you can't account for all the money. In fact, there will probably be a substantial gap between what you earned and what you can remember spending—money that seems to have gone up in smoke. Some of it did.

Here's another test: Of all the things you bought last month, how many could have been put off for 30 days without doing any harm? And then put off for another 30 days? You probably could have postponed quite a bit. In fact, now that you think of it, some of what you bought may not be worth the debt you're carrying.

Now for the final test: How inviolate, really, is your "fixed-expense" list? Can you cut your taxes, pay less for insurance, refinance your mortgage to get lower payments, find a cheaper apartment, sell your second car? (Spending $15 on taxis every working day might cost $3,600 a year, a fraction of the price of owning, insuring, gassing, and repairing an automobile. And think of the savings if you took a bus.) If you paid off more debt, you would reduce your interest payments, giving you more cash in hand.

I am not advising that you lower your standard of living. Good financial planning starts from where you are and makes things better. On the other hand, neither should you feel locked into your current way of life, no matter how immutable the bills may seem. There are, as a science fiction writer would say, alternative realities. And you are going to find them.

Truth in authoring compels me to say that this process carries another name. An awful name. Budgeting, the dreaded *B* word, smelling of shortages, self-denial, and regret. A b _ _ _ _ t seems to say, "I can't afford the things I want," and on that depressing thought, good intentions usually founder.

A spending plan, on the other hand, says, "You can get what you want just by figuring out how to do it." It's a positive step that allows for choices and new ideas. It puts you in control.

Seventeen Reasons to Have a Spending Plan

1. To find out what you're spending money on. Few of us know.
2. To extract more money for savings and investments.
3. To figure out how to quit a job, move, build a house, have a baby.
4. To get out of debt.
5. To show the spouse who doesn't pay the bills where the money goes.
6. To live on your income.
7. To prepare for big expenses such as college, a new house, a major vacation, a face-lift (that's probably not covered by your HMO!).
8. To retool your life after losing a job or a spouse or becoming too sick to work.

9. To keep money from slipping through your fingers.
10. To determine the minimum income you can live on, so that you can handle a cut in earnings, erratic paychecks, a divorce, a period of retraining for a different job, early retirement.
11. To know how you'll handle unexpected expenses.
12. To be able to buy what you want.
13. To prepare for harder times.
14. To make the best use of the money you get in better times.
15. To get the whole family pulling in the same direction.
16. To put a tool in your hands that can change your life.
17. To put your new financial plan into action. (Which plan? The one you're developing as you read this book.)

Three Reasons Not to Have a Plan

1. You're rich enough to buy anything you want and still have plenty of money left over.
2. I forgot the other two.

A Free List of Excuses for Ducking This Job

1. Making a spending plan takes too much time. It will take no more than a weekend of thinking, research, and erasing what you just wrote down, followed by a few minutes every day for a month or so. In the beginning, you'll spend an hour or two once a month to see how you're doing. After that, it's just as easy as spending money without a plan.

2. I won't keep it up. But you might. Most people do, once they decide they want better control of their money, because this is the only way to get it. As soon as your plan is up and running, there's not a lot more to do.

3. I don't want to live in a straitjacket. You won't. Your plan will move and breathe. If it pinches, you can change it. It will always include a provision for buying some of the things you really like, so you won't feel deprived.

4. I hate arithmetic. So do I. So what?

5. None of my friends does it. Too bad for them.

6. I budget in my head. And all your good intentions run out your ears. You're sure that you have an extra $55 this month for a turtleneck sweater. Then you discover that you can't pay the dentist. Besides, I'm not asking you to budget, I'm asking you to plan.

7. I'm too tired, too young, too old, too busy, too poor, not poor enough. My husband, wife, daughter, parakeet won't cooperate. It won't work, can't work, would drive me bananas if it really did work. I'm too dumb, too smart, too short, too tall, too fat, and can't give up smoking. You can always think of reasons not to take charge of your life. But if you don't mean to change, why did you waste your money by buying this book?

How to Begin

Write down all your cash expenditures every day for a month. And I mean everything. Carry a notebook in your pocket or purse so that no expense will slip away. Start with "Monday, April 8" and go on to "Tuesday, April 9." Day by day by day.

Some things may seem too trivial to bother with. Coffee, newspapers, flowers, an apple. But look at it this way: if you saved $5 every day for a year, you'd have $1,825. That would fund part of an Individual Retirement Account or give you a nice week in Maui watching whales. Small expenses are not trivial.

During this month, make no effort to change your spending habits. You're simply taking a snapshot of how you live now.

Take an afternoon to go through your checkbooks, bank statements, and itemized credit card statements for the past six months. List the size of your regular monthly bills: utilities, mortgage, rent, car payments, day care. Make a separate list of your intermittent expenses: clothing, life insurance payments, birthday presents, car repairs, dentist bills.

Some spending is hard to reconstruct. Maybe you've been throwing out old credit card bills. Maybe you haven't been noting on your checks exactly what the money was for. When your records are bad, it might take two or three months to learn where all the money goes.

Once you've got the information, organize it into categories, showing how much you spend every month. Mortgage. Rent. Gasoline. Car lease. Laundry. Groceries. Drinks. Books. Cosmetics. Gasoline. Bus fare. Credit card debt. Tennis. Haircuts. Restaurants. Pets. Children's clothes. Your clothes. Doctors. Real estate taxes. Movies. The more precise, the better. You need a detailed picture as a starting point.

Construct a chart of how you spent your money, month by month, over the past six months. Assume that the walking-around expenses that you recorded in your notebook will always be the same.

Now write down your monthly income, minus federal, state, and local income taxes, Social Security taxes, and any other automatic deductions due to employment, such as union dues. Include all your income: wages, annuities, pensions, dividends, interest, rents, everything.

Compare your spending with your income, and don't panic if you're in the red. That's what a spending plan will fix.

The snapshot you took may surprise you.

Many people learn that, except for credit card repayments, they are spending less than they earn. They're short of money only because they are doing battle with old debt. Once they pay it off, they'll have a substantial sum to invest.

Others are astonished at how much they are spending on particular items— health clubs, books, fast-food restaurants, beauty salons, tools, fishing, shoes. You must spend money on yourself; otherwise your spending plan will be too disheartening to stick with. But maybe you can pick one thing and cut down on others. Exercise with weights at home, use your library card, make your own hamburgers, ski cross-country instead of downhill. That will free up cash for something else.

It's not unusual to discover that you are better off than you thought. Fear often arises from ignorance. Once you take an organized look at your situation, you might see that your worries have no basis in fact.

On the other hand, if you really are in trouble, you'll learn by how much.

Above all, you'll finally find out where the money goes, because most of us don't have a clue. With that snapshot as a guide, you are ready to channel some of your spending in new directions.

The Truth About the "Latte Factor"

Plenty is written about the "latte factor." If you're paying $3.50 every day for expensive coffee to drink at work and cut it out, you'll save $910 a year toward a retirement plan. But c'mon, you still want coffee. Cheap coffee costs $1.50, so you've really saved only $520 while hating it every minute.

I'm not dissing the small stuff. It's important, too. But the latte factor isn't your problem. The question is, what shops do you pass to and from the coffee shop? Do you walk to a bus or subway and see the perfect pink handbag in a shop window? Do you steer your car toward an electronics shop for a bit of gear? Whether you go to a workplace or not, what else are you buying while you're running personal or household errands? Male or female, your eye can light on a dozen spending ideas. Stores, catalogs, online shopping sites, TV shopping— everything tempts. *That's* what to worry about. Everyone can get a little sloppy with cash, and it's smart to notice. But what's squeezing you is the big stuff that you ladle onto your credit card.

What Do You Really Want?

First, you want to know what you're redirecting your spending for. What do you want from your money that you're not getting now?

Maybe you need to be out of debt. Maybe you need college money, for your children or yourself. Maybe you want to build a rainy-day fund or save for a down payment on a house. Maybe you want to get serious about a retirement fund.

Your goal won't always be the same. The important thing right now is to focus on a limited and specific objective that you can achieve.

Write it down at the top of your spending plan. "Goal: Save an extra $100 a month." Or "Goal: Put an extra $100 a month toward paying off the Visa card." Take that money right off the top of every paycheck. Then rearrange the rest of your spending to fit within the income that's left.

Drawing Up Your Plan

The plan (page 196) will look very much like a b _ _ _ _ t, but it differs in four ways:

First, you enter your current goal at the top of the page. That will be funded every month before you pay any other bills. Don't even give it a moment's thought. Set the money aside and then start to juggle. Just having that goal transforms a b _ _ _ _ t into a *plan*.

Second, start a column called "Current Spending." Here you write down what you've been spending in every category. This is your benchmark; the money habits you have now, which you want to change.

Third comes your "Spending Plan." Play with your income and expenses and write down where you'd like the money to go.

Fourth comes the payoff; the column called "Actual." Once a month, enter what you actually spent in each category. If you're spending more than you planned for telephone bills or sports, you may have to strengthen your resolve. On the other hand, maybe your telephone goal was unrealistic and should be changed. After several months you'll arrive at a plan you can live with. Then it becomes a habit.

Some Technical Matters

Start with a six-month plan to see how it works. One year is too long for someone just learning where the money goes.

Make your categories specific. For example, instead of lumping all your medical expenses together, create separate columns for Doctor, Dentist, Therapist, Medicines, Veterinarian. Instead of Utilities, write Water, Electricity, Heat, Telephone. The categories in the sample Spending Plan on page 196 are just suggestions; most plans contain many more. If you'd rather plan by computer instead of with pencil and paper, you'll find plenty of downloadable budgeting kits and forms on the Internet at modest prices. One to try: the *Quick & Easy Budget Kit CD.*

To cut spending, squeeze a little something out of every category rather than slashing just one or two. Even if you're trimming just $10 or $20, that's money you'll have for something else. Don't eliminate whole categories; in most cases, you'll be kidding yourself. Above all, don't wipe out all the things that make you the happiest. You need to get some fun from your money, to have the incentive to carry on. Every member of your family also needs a personal playpen.

It helps to enter your spending at least weekly so that you won't lose track. Subtract each week's expenses from the budgeted monthly amounts so that you'll know how much you have left. At the end of the month, carry forward to the next month the money unspent in any category. For example, if you budgeted $100 for entertainment and spent only $80, start out next month with $120. If any category gets bigger and bigger each month, cut back your targeted spending there and add the funds somewhere else. If most categories come in on target but a couple always fall behind, go over your budget again and trim.

When a bill is paid quarterly, budget for one-third of it every month. For the first two months, that money stays in your checking account; in the third, you'll have enough for the payment. If you're an irrepressible spender, write a monthly check for one-third of each quarterly bill and deposit it in your savings account or transfer that amount from your online checking to online savings. If you don't see the money, you won't spend it (I hope).

Handle clothing the same way. Budget a certain amount every month and let it build up. Some months you'll exceed your plan, but over a year it should even out.

Unexpected expenses, such as car repairs or an operation for a sick dog, should be listed in their proper categories so you'll know how much you've spent. But you cannot specifically budget for them. Instead put some money for these bills into a modest reserve fund every month.

You will have some bothersome spending overruns. Don't quit; just try again. Spending plans don't prohibit splurges. They merely show you—graphically— that for every extra purchase you make, you have to cut spending in another category or go further into debt. We're talking choice. It may take a while for your real desires to overcome your trivial ones.

SPENDING PLAN

Month _____ , 20 ____

Total income _____

Special goal _____

Reserve fund _____

Expenses	Current Spending	Spending Plan	Actual				
			Wk. 1	Wk. 2	Wk. 3	Wk. 4	Total
Savings							
Mortgage/rent							
Heat/light/water							
Telephone							
Life insurance							
Health insurance							
Disability insurance							
Homeowners insurance							
Auto insurance							
Auto loan							
Credit card payments							
Back bills							
School/college							
Child care/support							
Groceries/drinks							
Clothing							
Doctor/dentist							
Veterinarian							
Gasoline							
Bus/subway/taxi							
Restaurants							
Entertainment							
Sports/pastimes							

Expenses	Current Spending	Spending Plan	Actual				
			Wk. 1	Wk. 2	Wk. 3	Wk. 4	Total
Books/magazines							
Repairs/upkeep							
Housecleaning							
Personal care							
Laundry							
Charitable contributions							
Furniture							
Birthdays/holidays							
Vacation							
Walking-around money							
TOTALS							

Add up your spending every month to see how you're doing. Juggle the categories; some will be high, others will be low. But it shouldn't take long to develop a framework. If you overspend in one area in April, you'll have to find a place to compensate in May.

Spending Plans for Working Couples

Some couples pool their money. A single, unified spending plan is all they need.

Other couples keep their paychecks separate. They might need three plans: one each for husband and wife to keep track of their personal expenses and set their personal saving and spending goals, and one for shared household expenses to which each contributes.

Can Anyone Love a Decimal Point?

Some people love keeping records to the penny, and may the God of the Green Eyeshade be with them. Others manage quite nicely by rounding off. Rounding off a lot. A lucky few don't even care if the columns add up as long as they're (probably) not too far wrong.

Keep your accounts however it suits you. The objective is mainly to *keep accounts.* You'll learn more from setting up detailed budget categories than you will from struggling over the math.

Ways to Cut Spending

To get more money for something you want, you have to spend less on something else. That's all there is to it. You can climb the highest mountain, consult the wisest wizard, and you'll get the same answer.

You can borrow the money, but then you'll have even less to spend because there's another loan to repay. That's like having another mouth to feed. Too many mouths, and pretty soon you are really poor.

Everyone finds different ways to save. But here are some surefire places to look:

Bury your credit cards. Charge nothing. Interest payments will then melt away. (Okay, charge something, but not much.) Shop with a debit card instead.

Declare a new-clothes moratorium until your present wardrobe is paid for.

Quit smoking. You'll save on cigarettes, life insurance, doctor bills, breath sweeteners, and soap to rub off the yellow stains.

Rent, don't buy, things you rarely use. Or split the cost with a neighbor (half-half on the snowblower and all repairs).

Buy toilet paper labeled Toilet Paper. Buy peanut butter labeled Peanut Butter. If you hate the generic stuff, switch back to the higher-priced brand names, but try the cheap ones first.

Shop with a list and stick to it. No impulse purchases, unless—

—unless there's a terrific sale. Then buy by the carton. You say you can't be bothered saving $7.50 on tuna fish in bulk? Do you realize that you need $250 in the bank to earn $7.50?

Own an economy car. It runs on economy gas, with economy insurance and economy repairs. Make that a used economy car.

Save gasoline by piling up errands and running them all at once.

Save on heating and air-conditioning bills by improving your insulation and eliminating drafts.

Use up your savings to get out of debt. Only losers pay 18 percent on their credit cards so they can keep earning 3 percent on their bank accounts.

Never pass up a garage sale. (But pass up most of what's there. It's hard to believe what people buy at garage sales and then chuck into their own garages.)

Don't trust any bills, especially those that are computer generated. If you take the time to check for errors, you'll find a lot of overcharges.

Stop subscribing to magazines you don't read. That not only saves you money, it also saves the space next to your bed or chair where they pile up.

Refinance any high-rate loan. But use a home equity loan to eliminate credit card bills only if you're swearing off your credit cards. Otherwise you'll run up your credit cards again, winding up with two debts where there used to be one.

Serve punch and hors d'oeuvres at parties rather than drinks and dinner. People drink less punch because the cups get sticky.

Learn to love your neighbors. With them, you can pool services such as babysitting and transportation. You can even swap skills: you do my taxes, I'll paint your garage.

Track down all local resale shops, discount centers, and factory outlets.

Vacation at off-season rates. The sun is just as hot the week before Memorial Day as the week after.

Sell something that's expensive to keep, such as a second car that you don't use regularly to drive to work.

Call your mother in the evening, at cheap rates. Better yet, write, don't call. Or don't write. Maybe she'll call you.

Rent DVDs instead of going to the movies. Or get a library card and borrow DVDs.

Maintain your car properly so you can keep it longer.

Eat more meals at home.

Ask your doctor to write prescriptions for generic drugs.

Look for cheaper insurance. You can probably find a company that charges less than you're paying now. Take a larger deductible on your fire and auto coverage. Cancel collision insurance on an old car.

Make the gifts you give. Or perform a personal service instead of purchasing a thing.

Look for cheap entertainment. Museums. The zoo. Parks. Walks. Library books. Picnics. Parades. Friends.

Do your own home repair, car repair, sewing, painting. I reupholstered a chair in my attic furniture days, and it came out fine.

Pay cash for gasoline instead of using a credit card. You might save up to 5 cents a gallon at many service stations.

Eat more meatless meals. They're good for you.

Switch to lower-watt bulbs in all but your reading lamps.

Exercise at home instead of at a health club. Or join a Y.

Shift your credit card balances to a lower-rate card, then use the interest savings to pay down the debt.

Clip cents-off coupons. There's no point throwing them out with the trash.

E-mail your friends and your kids instead of calling long distance.

Join a home-swap network for cheaper family vacations.

Find new uses for things instead of throwing them out. Start seedlings in the cutoff bottoms of milk cartons. Twist newspapers into cylinders for kindling. Maintain a useless-objects shelf for items that might be reclaimed someday. The handier you are, the more money you'll save.

When you think you're at rock bottom, with all of the air sucked out of your budget, go back for one more try.

But . . . none of these ways to use money is right or wrong. Your spending reflects your values, just as my spending reflects mine. There's no ideal budget or ideal percentage of income to put toward this or that. Your goal is to live within your income your way.

If All This Talk Falls on Deaf Ears

Maybe you don't budget because you think you're okay. Every month you meet all your bills and even have some dinners out. But then a big expense comes along, such as a vacation, and you don't have the money to pay for it. So you put it on a credit card, and, bit by bit, your debt builds up.

You aren't saving money because you can't resist spending what's in your checking account. And you can't bear to rein yourself in by writing down every little expense. Ugh, ugh.

For you—a budget refusenik—the best strategy is to spirit some cash out of sight (unseen means unspent). Do it by setting up three accounts:

1. Create a retirement investment account and add money to it on a regular schedule. If you're lucky, your employer will deduct money from every paycheck automatically. Second choice: have your bank deduct money every month from your checking account and ship it to a mutual fund. There you can invest it in an Individual Retirement Account, SEP-IRA plan for the self-employed, or an ordinary investment account. Third and weakest choice: write your own check to a mutual fund each month. (Maybe writing your own checks will work, but you know from experience that any money in your checking account will often be spent on other things.)

2. Create a big-bill account at your bank or credit union. A simple savings account will do. It's for bills that turn up now and then, such as quarterly life insurance premiums, vacations, estimated taxes, holiday presents, household repairs. Go through your bank and credit card statements for the past 6 to 12 months to gauge what you're spending annually on these things. Then divide the total by the number of paychecks you get every year (by 12 if you're paid monthly, 26 if you're paid biweekly, 52 if you're paid weekly). Write a check for that amount every time you're paid, and immediately deposit it into your big-bill account. Or transfer the money from checking to savings online. Or have the money transferred automatically. When those bills come in, you'll have the cash to cover them. This takes some fine-tuning but works well. It's the closest to true budgeting you'll have to do.

3. Maintain your usual checking account for other expenses. Your paychecks go into this account. Money comes out for your big-bill account and your retirement account. All the rest is yours to spend on your regular household bills. You won't need a budget for this money. You'll continue your old habit of spending everything that you see in your checking account. But you'll spend less than you did before, because there's less money there. It will happen automatically, without your even thinking about it.

What? You say you don't believe me? You can't possibly save because you have too many bills? Just for fun, try this: Put 5 percent of every paycheck into your savings account as soon as the money arrives. Then get on with your usual life. You'll find that nothing will change! You'll still be living paycheck to paycheck, except that now you'll be saving 5 percent. Hiding money from yourself, and then cutting spending without knowing how you did it, is the only true magic in personal finance. Once you see that it works, gradually raise your savings to at least 10 percent. You'll become a believer, just like me.

4. You might object that if you put money into savings, your spending *won't* drop—you'll just run up your credit cards. That happens only to people determined to bankrupt themselves. Most of us simply trim our spending to match the money available. You won't even know what it was you didn't buy—only that, for the first time, your savings are building up.

When There Really Is No Money

When you're truly living on a wing and a prayer, it is fruitless to look for meaningful budget cuts. You'll have to increase your income in some way. A second job. A better job. A session of night school, to qualify for a different line of work. A sideline business run from home. Selling stuff on eBay.

If those routes aren't practical, try for a job with better employee benefits. A company puts money into your pocket by paying most of your doctor bills as surely as it does by giving you a raise.

How Long, O Lord?

Keep up your monthly budget for as long as it takes to get more from your money. By then you should know how to do it without always putting pencil to paper. Your spending caps will be imprinted in your mind.

As your goals change, however, you may need new spending plans to achieve them.

Your first year's aim might be quite modest: "Reduce by half my credit card debt," achieved by doubling payments every month. Having succeeded, you'll get more ambitious: "Carry no debt and build a cash reserve fund." Then you'll move on to: "Save 10 percent of my income."

Along the way you'll have minigoals, such as "Buy a living room rug." Or "Spend a long weekend in New York and go to the theater." Write these goals down, allocate money to them, and check them off as you succeed.

Sometimes you force a goal on yourself—for example, by buying a house. Meeting your mortgage payments then becomes your first priority. All the rest of your spending shrinks.

Once you have a plan that works, there may be no reason for keeping monthly accounts. Start over again, however, if:

- Something in your life changes.
- You begin to feel that you're losing track.
- You notice that you can't meet expenses without putting down a credit card and stretching out payments; that means you're spending more than you earn.

Special Problems with Irregular Incomes

Neat monthly spending plans may sound hopeless to people without a regular paycheck: freelancers, project workers, consultants, small-business owners. But you can do it easily. Start with the premise that your total income is more predictable than when your paychecks will arrive. And budget this way:

Estimate, conservatively, what you're likely to earn this year. Guess your monthly income by dividing by 12. Develop a regular monthly budget based on that estimated income. Whenever a fee comes in, put it in the bank and spend it according to your plan. If there's money left over, leave it alone; it might be awhile before another check comes in.

If you fall short that month, you might have to dip into overdraft checking or run up some debt on your credit cards. If this happens more than once, reconsider your basic budget. You may be living higher than you can afford. When another check comes in, your first priority should be getting rid of that debt. Then build a reserve fund of three to six months' living expenses in a bank or money market mutual fund. With a fully funded reserve, you can start putting extra money into personal consumption and longer-term savings and investments. You also need at least three months' reserve in your business account. When you're flush, set up a home equity line of credit, also for emergency cash.

If, after a few months, it appears that your income will fall short for the year as a whole, revise your spending plan downward. If you're doing better than expected, revise it upward or save the surplus. Whenever you dip into your reserves, replace that money before doing extra spending of any kind.

Many workers with regular paychecks also have irregular total incomes because part of their pay comes from bonuses or incentive plans. In this case, draw a budget based on the pay that's guaranteed. Your bonus can pay for next year's extras: additional investments, a vacation, new furniture. Don't go into debt in the current year, expecting a bonus to bail you out. You might not get as big a payout as you'd hoped.

All workers with irregular incomes should hold their fixed expenses down. This year might rain money. But if you move into a bigger house, you might not be able to keep up the mortgage in a drought.

Planning When Taxes Aren't Withheld

People paid by fee, with no income taxes withheld, are true heroes if they make it to April 15 without spending any of their tax money. You have to pay estimated taxes every quarter. But it's all too easy to fall behind. If you're too far behind, you'll owe a penalty on top of the tax.

How to solve this problem? Look at last year's tax return to see what percentage of your total income went for taxes. Take that percentage off the top of every check you get. Earmark it for the government and tuck it into a savings account. Only your net spendable income, after taxes, should land in your checking account.

Planning for a Raise

Will you gross an extra $3,000 this year? If you spend it all, you'll be worse off than you were before. A $3,000 raise might leave only $1,900 in the bank after state and local income and Social Security taxes. Spending the gross puts you into debt, which is why so many people feel poorer and poorer as their incomes rise.

Anyone allergic to saving money should regard a raise as a main chance. Just pretend it didn't happen. Keep on living the way you did before, and put that extra money in the bank. Or buy one thing and save what's left. Many companies these days give bonuses instead of raises. That's an easy chunk of money to save (if you haven't spent it in advance).

Planning After Being Fired

At first you may panic, especially if you've never lost a job before. You're spending every penny you make. How can you live on a nickel less? This very month the bank will foreclose. Your creditors will cart off your furniture. You'll join the homeless. Your children will have to live on a grate.

Not so. You have far more financial resilience than you imagine. Here's what to do:

1. Find out how your ex-employer can help. A firm that employs 20 people or more has to offer to keep you in the group health plan for up to 18 months, at your expense. You generally have 60 days to decide, from the day you're notified about the option. Sign up, unless you can be insured immediately under a spouse's plan or find cheaper insurance somewhere else. Also, ask if a severance check can be paid in monthly installments; if you take it all at once, your tax bracket might jump. Consider leaving your 401(k) with the company, as long as you can tap it anytime you want. You have troubles enough without fretting over finding a place to invest those funds. You can move the money when your life is more settled and you're able to make long-term decisions again.

2. Draw up a bare-bones spending plan. Cover the mortgage, car loan, utilities, gasoline, food, life and health insurance, the minimum on credit card bills, and the expenses of looking for another job. At first, budget only for these. Put all other bills aside. Job-hunting expenses, by the way, can include a golf club membership; it's important to keep up all of your social and business contacts. If you can't continue your company's health insurance plan, ask your insurance agent for a low-cost, high-deductible policy. If you carried your life insurance through your ex-employer, buy some low-cost term coverage. Your family can't afford to have you go without.

3. Add up what remains of your regular income: a second paycheck in the family, union benefits, interest from savings, dividends, unemployment insurance. Don't reject unemployment payments. Many white-collar workers are ashamed or afraid of standing in unemployment lines. But times have changed. Whole echelons of middle management have been laid off. Your ex-employer pays taxes to ensure that you get some financial support between jobs, and you should take every nickel due. You'll find your peers in line behind you.

4. Compare your remaining monthly income with your bare-bones spending plan. If you can cover your basic bills, you're in good shape. If not, write down how much more money you're going to need each month.

5. Add up all your lump sums of money: a final paycheck due from your company, severance pay, savings, investments (leaving out the money in a tax-deferred retirement account). A portion of this cash reserve can be used each month to fill the gap in your spending plan. Your goal, at this point, is to find a way to cover your essential bills for at least nine months—longer if you think that your job hunt will be a tough one. If you have to sell stocks or mutual fund shares, dump those with losses first.

6. If you have enough income left over after covering bare-bones expenses, allocate it to other expenses.

7. Try to reduce the expenses that look immutable but might not be. For example, if your child is in day care, private school, or college, tell the school about your financial emergency. You'll rarely get a moratorium on payments, but you might be offered more scholarship aid or a low-interest loan. Take the same approach to any other service that you feel should not be interrupted, such as dental procedures or children's music lessons.

8. If you need more cash, borrow it—provided that your situation is temporary. Take loans against your credit cards, home equity line of credit, securities, and insurance policies. But don't clean yourself out. You may need some money to relocate.

9. Don't take cash out of retirement accounts unless absolutely necessary. Ideally, you will leave your 401(k) with your employer for now, so it can be managed efficiently. Or roll the money into an Individual Retirement Account to avoid current taxes and penalties and keep your investment building up. But you might not have the luxury of keeping retirement savings whole.

If you have to make withdrawals from a tax-deferred plan, you'll owe income taxes on what you take. There's also a 10 percent tax penalty in the following situations: on withdrawals from an IRA if you're younger than 59½ and on withdrawals from a 401(k) or 403(b) if you left the company when you were younger than 55.

You can duck the 10 percent IRA penalty by setting up a withdrawal plan that will pay you a steady monthly income based on your life expectancy (page 1064). The withdrawals must continue for at least five years and until you reach 59½. After that, you can stop and let your IRA build up again. But avoid doing this if you expect to be reemployed soon. You don't want to be locked into monthly withdrawals for years after it's necessary.

Best advice for handling your tax-deferred plan while you're unemployed: move a portion of your investments out of stocks and bonds and into the plan's money market mutual fund. You don't want to risk losing money in the market if you might need this cash to pay your bills. If you do have to tap your retirement account, draw from the money market fund and take only as much as you need each month. That holds down taxes and penalties. When you get a job again, you can put what's left of your money market investment back into stocks and bonds.

If you know for sure that you're going to need some of the money in your 401(k) or 403(b), and you're between 55 and 59½, you might as well take it out of the plan immediately. That avoids the 10 percent penalty. If you roll your 401(k) into an IRA and then take some money out, the penalty is due.

10. Do not pay what you can't afford to pay! That sounds obvious, but it's a basic rule of survival that laid-off workers violate all the time.

Don't use your severance check to pay off your credit card debts; conserve that cash and pay only the minimum each month. Make no payments on postponable bills if doing so means that you'll run out of money within a few months. Write to your doctor that you'll pay in the future with interest. Let the school tax slide and accept the late-payment penalty.

At the start, keep current with your credit cards and mortgage in order to keep your credit history clean. Some employers check the record when they vet you for a job.

If months drag on with no sign of work, you'll have to reconsider your credit card expenses too. Nonpayment hurts your credit rating. It also raises your interest rate, which makes it harder to get out of debt when you're earning money again. This tactic is strictly last resort. Still, it's far more important to keep the lights on, the telephone working, gas in the car, and food on the table.

When you don't pay, however, you must tell your creditors what you're doing. Write each one a letter explaining that you have been laid off and cannot currently cover your bill. But say that you will, absolutely, resume making payments in full (including interest and late charges) when you get work. Another approach is to say that you will pay $5 or $10 a month as a token of your good faith. You might also add a note to your credit file explaining that unemployment has temporarily hindered your ability to pay.

Some creditors will take this deal. If they don't respond, or if only their computers respond by sending another bill, set up a telephone appointment to discuss your debt. If you don't find work in a couple of months, write or call again. This keeps the creditors informed and reassures them that you're not going to skip.

Hold to your position even if your creditors bluster, threaten to ruin your credit rating, or claim that they'll sue. Keep on explaining your situation in reasonable language. Say that you're out of work; say that you'll pay eventually; say that you can't pay now or can pay only $10 a month. Don't cave in, even if your account is turned over to a bill collector. Your main priorities are to hold your life together and keep your job search going. When you find a job, you can work out a repayment plan. Consider working with a credit counselor (page 288) to get you through this bad patch. They can put a stop to the nasty phone calls.

11. If three months pass without a job nibble, talk to the company that services your mortgage. You might have to take a home equity loan, using the proceeds to keep your mortgage current. If you have no equity the lender might agree to accept only interest payments for a few months, letting the principal coast. In 2009, the government established some mortgage forbearance programs. To see if you're eligible, go to www.makinghomeaffordable.gov. There are also special programs to help you refinance your home at a lower rate.

12. Try to bring in some extra income. Sign up with a temporary-help agency. Pitch for consulting jobs. Accept project work and temporary executive spots (sometimes they lead to full-time jobs). Advertise your services in the neighborhood: typing, carpentry, accounting, day care. If your spouse doesn't work, now is the time for him or her to start. Ask your teenagers to pitch in with after-school jobs.

13. There's no item 13 on this list. It's unlucky, and you need all the luck you can get.

14. Be cautious about starting or buying a business. With your severance and 401(k) plan in hand, you might buy a franchise or start your own small business. But unless you choose carefully, you could lose the last stake you'll ever have. Work in the business for a year before deciding whether to buy. Or investigate it exhaustively by visiting outlets—or similar businesses—over a wide geographical area—and talking to successful franchisees.

15. If you don't find work and see that your money won't last, it's time to rethink your life from the ground up. Look for cheaper housing. Move to an area where living costs are lower. Consider jobs at a much lower salary. Tell your children they'll have to leave college for a while or transfer to a school they can pay for entirely with their earnings and student loans. Consider bankruptcy (see page 289). Reach these decisions before you start borrowing from relatives. My reasoning here is tactical, not moral. Your relatives are normally your ace in the hole, the only people who might help you finance a new start in life. So try to tap them last, not first.

Spending and Your Financial Plan

A spending plan is the visible evidence of financial planning at work. The other chapters of this book help you make strategic choices. The spending plan executes them.

9

Saving More Money

Patented, Painless Ways to Save and Where to Save It

**The 1980s worshiped spending. The 1990s worshiped debt.
The twenty-first century belongs to the saver.**

It seems like only yesterday that savers were dorks. They kept piggy banks. They drove last year's cars. They fished in their change purses for dimes while the superstars flashed credit cards.

Today values are changing. The new object of veneration is not money on the hoof but money in the bank—and the dorks have it. The more you save, the freer you become, because time is on the saver's side. Compound interest floats all boats.

Like most people who make their own money, I started out living paycheck to paycheck. I could cover my bills (most of the time). But I "knew" that I couldn't afford to save, so I didn't bother. Even had I bothered, my small $20 or so a week wouldn't have seemed worth the effort.

Some years (and many lost $20s) later, I learned I was wrong. Anyone can put money aside, at any level of income. You just have to do it. Of all of the New Era's new virtues—daily jogging, eating bran, going green—saving money is the simplest and the least demanding of your time and attention. Savers can lie in a hammock all day lapping ice cream and still feel good about themselves. As for the value of a tiny $20 a week, take a look at the table on page 215.

A financial plan is grounded in savings. That's how you get enough money to pay off your debts and accumulate an investment fund.

How much should you save? The answer comes from ancient times: you tithe. It was learned generations ago—and is still true—that most people can save the first 10 percent of their incomes and hardly notice. I can't tell you why it works, only that it does. Tithing seems to collect the money that otherwise would go up in smoke (it's 9:00 a.m.; do you know where yesterday's $10 is?). On a $40,000 paycheck, you can save $333 a month, $4,000 a year. On $60,000, shoot for $500 a month, $6,000 a year. On $100,000, save $833 a month, $10,000 a year.

I hear you, I hear you. You say you can't do it. Your rent is too high, your bills are too large, your needs are too great, your credit lines are too long. None of those things is actually an impediment, but it will take you a while to see it. So start by saving only 5 percent of your income. Take that money off the top of every paycheck, and live on what's left. What will happen to that pile of monthly bills once you start putting 5 percent aside? They will be paid! You'll still go to the movies and put gas in your car. Your standard of living will be unchanged. Those savings pick up dollars that leak through your fingers unseen. The rest of your life goes on exactly as before.

You say you don't believe me? Fine. Try it and prove me wrong. When you find out it works, raise your savings to 7 percent. I predict that you'll be at 10 percent within the year.

If you're already tithing to your future, take a moment to feel superior. What's life without a touch of smug?

What Are You Saving Money For?

A savings account isn't something to hang on the wall and stare at, like a Rembrandt. You're not hoarding. You're preparing to use your money in a different way.

Refer, please, to your spending plan (chapter 8). It says that your current goal is to pay down debt. Or have three months' living expenses in the bank. Or $2,000 more in a college account this year. Or $5,000 for long-term investments. Or $1,000 to play the slots in Vegas, where you'll really make some money. Tithing, or semitithing, is how you're going to raise your stake.

Here's how to accomplish it:

First, write down how much you're going to save (5 or 10 percent of each paycheck).

Second, write down how long it will take to reach your goal. At $250 a month, you'll have your extra college money in eight months. You'll have college money *and* Las Vegas in 12 months. (Tip: It's easier to save $59 a week than $250 a month. The smaller sum sounds more doable, even though it comes to the same amount in the end.)

Third, note each future $250 (or $59) payment on your calendar and check off every one you make. That may sound hokey, but it's a strong motivational tool.

Every time you turn to a new week or a new month, there's a written reminder to keep up your resolve. Saving money is easier if you see it climb toward a specific end. It's like polishing the car; you feel that you've accomplished something.

Fourth, when you've reached your goal, give yourself a little present. Then start the process all over again.

Should You Build Up a Bank Account Instead of Paying Off Consumer Debt?

No, no, and again, no. Repeat after me: paying off debt is a form of saving. In fact, debt repayment is one of the most lucrative ways to save. It's nuts to keep money in the bank at 3 percent interest while carrying credit card debt at 18 percent. You are losing 15 percent a year on that deal (the 15 percent cost of the debt minus the 3 percent earned on the bank account). Take most of your money out of the bank and reduce the debt. If you need quick cash, you can borrow against your card, but in the meantime, you're saving yourself a mountain of interest.

Using savings to pay off debt is one of the simplest, fastest ways of setting your finances aright. It's also a fabulous use of your money. Your return on investment equals the interest rate on the debt. When you make an extra payment on your 18 percent credit card, for example, you're getting an 18 percent return, guaranteed. If you pay down a 24 percent debt, you're getting a 24 percent return, guaranteed. No other investment can offer the same.

You may find it hard to accept this truth. Money in the bank is so comforting. Haven't you read that everyone should keep three to six months' worth of expenses in an emergency savings account? Hardly anybody does, but the books all say that's the right thing.

Not this book—at least, not while you carry debt. You do indeed need three to six months' worth of basic expenses on tap in case of illness, job loss, or other emergency. A year's worth of expenses would be even better. But you can protect yourself nearly as well with 12 months' worth of borrowing power on credit cards or a home equity line. (I say "nearly" because borrowing builds up an obligation, while taking money from savings doesn't.)

For mathematical proof that this strategy works, assume that you have $1,000 in the bank earning 3 percent, a $1,000 credit card debt at 18 percent, and no extra fee for taking a cash advance. Here's your position, under various scenarios:

First, assume that no emergency comes up. You might:

■ *Leave your $1,000 in the bank.* You're losing 15 percent a year—the 18 percent cost of the debt minus the 3 percent gain from the savings account.

■ *Use your $1,000 to pay off the debt.* Instantly, you've *earned* 15 percent (the 18 percent you gained by eliminating the debt minus the 3 percent you lost by giving up the savings account).

Second, assume that, after a year, a $1,000 emergency comes up. You might:

■ *Take the $1,000 you kept in the bank.* Your cost: 15 percent (the price of not having used that $1,000 to reduce your debt).

■ *If you used the $1,000 to reduce your credit card debt, you can borrow the money back.* Cash advances are expensive so you might have to pay an interest rate of 22 percent. But subtracting the 15 percent you saved by reducing debt, your net cost is just 7 percent.

You'll probably want to keep a little quick cash in the bank, but don't try to build a larger account until your high-rate debts are paid off.

Here's another version of the saving-versus-borrowing question: "I need a new gallimawhatsis. I have enough money in the bank to pay cash. Should I use that money or take a loan instead?" One argument favors the loan: you will be forced to repay the money, whereas no one will grump if you leave a hole in your savings account. But a better argument favors cash: taking money from savings is the cheapest way to buy. Once you've made the purchase, make regular payments into your savings account (just as you'd have made regular payments on the loan) to replace the money you took out. As long as you're capable of saving money, you don't have to worry about using your savings from time to time.

I'd vote differently if your savings cache came from an inheritance, a life insurance payoff, or a lottery ticket, and you've never been able to save by yourself. In that case, consider the loan. Preserve that precious windfall for college tuition or your old age. The interest you pay, unnecessarily, is the price of lacking discipline.

Saving Versus Investing

Savings are, by definition, *safe.* You can turn your back and they won't escape. When the stock market crashes, they're unalarmed. Every time you look, they've earned more interest. You're never going to lose a dime.

Investments, by contrast, put your money at risk. Good investments yield much more than savings over the long run. But you have to put up with losses too.

Savings will not make you rich. Only canny investments do that. The role of savings is to keep you from becoming poor. They're your security. Your base. They preserve your purchasing power. With enough savings tucked into your jeans, you can afford to take chances with the rest of your money, and with your life.

Should You Invest Rather Than Pay Down Debt?

These are tricky calculations and depend on your options. My priorities look like this:

1. Invest in a tax-favored retirement account (chapter 29). If you have a 401(k) with a company match, put in as much as you need to capture the match in full. Then . . .

2. Pay off high-rate consumer debt. It gives you the highest guaranteed investment return you'll ever earn. Then . . .

3. Build an emergency cash reserve for personal security. I call this your Cushion Fund. Cash savings don't earn high interest rates but help ensure that you'll always be able to pay your basic bills. Then . . .

4. If your kids will go to college, start college investment accounts (chapter 20). Aim to accumulate half the probable cost, planning to pay the rest out of current income and student loans. You might get a tuition discount too. Then . . .

5. Return to your tax-favored retirement investments. Start putting in the maximum the law allows. If you're already at the max, invest in regular after-tax accounts.

Is It Better to Prepay Your Mortgage or Use Your Extra Cash to Invest?

That depends on your age and the interest rate. Here's how to look at it:

1. If you're young or in early middle age, it's more important to contribute to a tax-favored 401(k), Individual Retirement Account, or other retirement plan. If you're contributing the maximum, open a regular, taxable investment account. Over the long run, they'll be the better investment.

2. If you're approaching retirement, it's important to get your mortgage paid off. If you can't, plan on selling the house and buying something smaller for cash when your paycheck stops. The easiest way to live in retirement is in a mortgage-free home.

3. If you're paying a punishingly high mortgage interest rate, prepay your loan as fast as you can. You need to accumulate more equity so that you can refinance into a loan with a lower rate.

The Best Years of Your Life . . .

. . . are when you're young. At least, they're the best years for saving money. The sooner you start, the more time your savings have to grow.

Typically, young people turn a deaf ear. "I'm too broke," they say. "I'll save when I'm older." But later money won't earn you nearly the return that early money does.

You want proof? Take a look at the startling table on page 215, prepared by the late Professor Emeritus Richard L. D. Morse of Kansas State University. It compares early savers with savers who start late.

The Early Saver deposits $1,000 a year for 15 years at 5 percent compounded daily. Then she stops. Having put in a total of $15,000, she leaves her stash alone to build.

All during that time, the Late Saver spends every dollar he earns. In the sixteenth year, he gets religion and starts saving $1,000 a year, also at 5 percent. Forty years later, he has put up a total of $40,000. But he hasn't caught up with the Early Saver—and never will! He can go on depositing $1,000 a year until the fourth millennium. At 5 percent interest, the Early Saver (although still depositing no more money) pulls further ahead of the Late Saver every year.

If the Early Saver's money compounds at 8 percent, thanks to a growing stock market, the gap grows even larger. It pays to start saving at any age, but young is best.

How Long Does It Take to Double Your Money?

For a close estimate, use the rule of 72s. Divide 72 by the yield you expect to earn. The result is how long it will take for your money to double. At 5 percent, your money will double in roughly 14.4 years. At 8 percent, it takes 9 years.

Twenty Patented Painless Ways to Save

1. Pay yourself first. That's the oldest financial advice in the world and one of those things you can't improve on. Take a slice of savings off the top of every paycheck before paying any of your bills. If you pay your bills first and save what's left, you'll always be broke because there is never anything left.

2. Bill yourself first. Keep stamped envelopes, addressed to your bank, in the same drawer as your bills. Send the bank a fixed check every month to deposit into your savings account. Or keep a "bill" for your savings account with

Table 3.

AND THE WINNER IS . . .

	Early Saver	**Late Saver**
	Depositing $1,000 a Year at 5%	**Depositing Nothing**
Year 1	$ 1,051	$0
Year 5	5,824	0
Year 10	13,301	0
Year 15	22,903	0
	Depositing Nothing More	**Depositing $1,000 a year at 5%**
Year 16	$ 24,077	$ 1,051
Year 20	29,407	5,824
Year 25	37,758	13,301
Year 30	48,482	22,902
Year 35	62,251	35,230
Year 40	79,931	51,060
Year 45	102,631	71,384
Year 50	131,779	97,482
Year 55	169,205	130,990

Source: Richard L. D. Morse.

the bills you pay through your bank account online. "Pay" it as if it were just as pressing as keeping the mortgage current—and in fact, it is. If you're paid irregularly, save a fixed percentage of every paycheck.

3. Get someone else to save for you (Part One). Your bank will transfer a fixed sum of money every month from your checking account into savings or a mutual fund.

4. Get someone else to save for you (Part Two). You'll never find a better savings machine than your company's payroll deduction plan. A fixed amount of money is taken out of every paycheck, so the cash never hits your checking account. What you don't see, you don't miss—and you don't spend. The money normally goes into retirement savings accounts.

5. Do coupons turn you on? Create your own Christmas club or vacation club. Decide how much money you want 12 months from now, divide it into 12 equal payments, and make "coupons" to remind you to keep up the monthly deposits. Or make 52 coupons for weekly payments. You could call it a Down-

Payment-on-a-First-Home Club or an I'll-Send-Junior-to-College-If-It-Kills-Me Club.

6. Save all dividends and interest when you don't need this money to live on. If you have a mutual fund, those dividends should be reinvested automatically. If you keep stocks with a stockbroker, have the payments swept into a money market fund for reinvestment.

7. Don't spend your next raise. Put the extra money away, even if it's just $20 a week. The more money you earn, the more of it you should set aside. Toward late middle age, you should be saving 15 to 20 percent of your income, at least.

8. Quit spending your year-end bonus in advance. Save it instead. At the very least, quit spending more than your net bonus after tax.

9. Save all gifts you get in cash, even small ones. Nothing is too small to save.

10. Pay off your mortgage faster by doubling up on principal payments every month. You'll build equity sooner, which is a form of saving. You'll also spend much less on interest payments.

11. Quit buying books (except, of course, for this one, which no prudent saver should be without!). Get a library card instead.

12. Refinance your credit card, auto, or other high-interest loans at a lower interest rate. You might be able to shift your credit card balances to a cheaper card. If you're disciplined, transfer the debts to a home equity line of credit; the interest is tax deductible if you itemize deductions. Use the money you're saving on interest payments to reduce your debts even faster.

13. Don't trade in your car as soon as the loan or lease is paid off. Make repairs if you have to and keep it for a year or two longer. Save the money you were spending on monthly car payments.

14. Pay cash for everything by shopping with a debit card. You will spend less because it's harder to part with cash than to put down a credit card.

15. Take $5 out of your wallet every day and put it in a coffee can. That's $1,825 a year—a good start on funding an Individual Retirement Account.

16. Take a part-time job and save all the income.

17. Let the government withhold extra tax money from your paycheck and save the refund.

18. Pay off your credit cards, then save the money you're no longer spending on interest charges.

19. Trim your spending by 5 percent, then trim it by another 5 percent. Best way to trim: put 5 percent of your income into savings and live on what's left.

20. Save early and often. The sooner you put some money away, the longer it has to fatten on compound interest. Saving money young is a painless way of saving more.

Plus Seven Tax-Blessed Ways of Building a Retirement Fund

1. Join the company retirement savings plan. Your basic contribution escapes current taxes and will accumulate tax deferred. What's more, these plans often give away money free. The company matches your contribution—say, $1 for every $2 you put up. That's a 50 percent return on investment, instantly and at no risk. There's no better deal in the entire U.S. of A. You may also be able to add a nondeductible contribution that can accumulate tax deferred.

2. Join your company's stock purchase plan. You run the risk that the stock will fall. But over long periods, your investment should do better than a savings account. (One warning: Don't let more than 5 percent of your net worth accumulate there. It's risky to bet your future principally on one stock. From time to time, sell some of the stock and diversify into other investments.)

3. Sign up for an Individual Retirement Account. Make monthly payments so you won't have to scramble for money when the deadline for contributions looms. For more on IRAs, see page 1047.

4. Don't spend the lump sum distribution you may get from your retirement plan when you leave the company, even if it's small. You generally have three investment choices: leave it in your ex-employer's plan, roll it into an Individual Retirement Account, or roll it into your new employer's retirement plan. If you spend it, you'll lose the value of your early saving years, and pay taxes and penalties besides.

5. If it takes a contribution to join your company's pension plan, make it—even if you're young. If you leave early, you'll get your money back plus everything your money earned. You'll also get some or all of your company's contribution, depending on how fast it vests.

6. Start a tax-deferred Simplified Employee Pension or individual 401(k) if you're self-employed or earn self-employment money by moonlighting (page 1043).

7. Consider a tax-deferred annuity, but *only* if you'll hold the investment for at least 15 or 20 years (page 1071). If you hold for a shorter period, the expenses and eventual taxes will add up to more than the taxes you originally saved.

What Your Savings Have to Earn

Say that inflation is running at around 3 percent. And say that you're earning 5 percent in a five-year certificate of deposit. What's the effective return on your money after state and federal taxes? Probably pretty close to zero—either just above it or just below, depending on your tax bracket. You may have preserved your purchasing power, but you haven't increased it, or not by much.

I'm not knocking a break-even result. The basic job of a bond or a bank account is to keep you from falling behind. But you won't achieve even this much protection unless you avoid low-rate deposits.

The table below gives you some guidelines. Find the current inflation rate at the left, then look across to the column showing your federal income tax bracket. Take the interest rate shown and raise it a little to compensate for state and local taxes. That's the minimum rate that your money has to earn to keep the value of your savings from eroding.

Where to Keep Your Savings

Don't automatically think "bank." That's only one of many choices. To find the right place to keep your savings safe, start with what you want from your money and work back. You need: (1) at least the break-even yield that you've just found and (2) access to the money when you need it but not a day sooner. Funds you

ARE YOU GETTING AHEAD?

At this rate of inflation	You need to earn this rate of interest to break even in the following tax brackets				
	15%	25%	28%	33%	35%
1%	1.20%	1.33%	1.39%	1.49%	1.54%
2%	2.35	2.67	2.78	2.99	3.08
3%	3.53	4.00	4.17	4.48	4.62
4%	4.71	5.33	5.56	5.97	6.15
5%	5.88	6.67	6.94	7.46	7.69
6%	7.06	8.00	8.33	8.96	9.23
7%	8.24	9.33	9.72	10.45	10.77
8%	9.41	10.67	11.11	11.94	12.31

Source: David Kahn, RSM McGladrey, Inc.

won't want until next year can be invested differently from—and more profitably than—funds you're going to use next week.

For Savings You'll Need Immediately

(I mean right now. Or a week from Friday. Within three months, at the very most.)

Hold this part of your cash cache to a minimum because ready money earns less interest than money invested for longer terms. I'd include only:

1. Funds that you know will be spent very soon, such as a down payment on a car you'll buy this month or an ongoing renovation of your home.

2. Your permanent floating emergency fund. Don't let this fund get too large. Keeping $10,000 in a passbook account—just in case the house should burn, the world explode, or your hair drop out—is dumb. Into the dailiness of life, costly emergencies rarely fall. If one does, you can always retrieve your money from wherever you stashed it. A quick-cash fund of two months' basic expenses should be plenty. Savings do better when stored at higher rates of return or used to reduce debt.

3. Money waiting to be invested in stocks, bonds, or real estate.

Four Places to Keep Short-Term Money:

Money Market Deposit Accounts at Banks Online. There's no better place. Online MMDA accounts are handy, they're government insured, and they pay higher interest rates than you'd get from traditional MMDA accounts in the very same banks. There's no minimum deposit and no annual fee.

Money Market Deposit Accounts at Regular Banks. You earn a floating interest rate that is loosely tied to the general level of market rates. (And I mean loosely. When other interest rates go up, banks are slow to raise the rate on money market accounts. But they drop rates enthusiastically when other interest rates go down.) You can take out money whenever you want, although only six transactions a month can be with third parties and only three of those by check. Minimum balances fall in the range of $500 to $2,500. You'll pay a penalty if your account drops below the minimum. (You may find no minimum at a few banks but probably a higher fee.)

The downside? The low interest rate. It rarely meets the break-even test. Your savings may lose value after counting inflation and taxes. If the bank charges fees, you'll lose even more. The only hope of maintaining your money's purchasing power is to search out an institution that pays high interest rates on money market deposits. Do it by checking "100 Highest Yields" at Bankrate .com (www.bankrate.com) or, BankingMyWay.com (www.bankingmyway.com). During the credit crunch of 2008–2009, bank money market accounts often paid higher rates than their nearest competitors, money market mutual funds.

Passbook Accounts. These pay even less than money market accounts. Skip them unless you're below the minimum for a money market account and want to stay with a traditional bank.

Money Market Mutual Funds. Money funds offer a somewhat better chance of breaking even. In normal times, the average fund pays around 0.5 percentage point more than the average bank money market account when interest rates are low and as much as 3 percentage points more when rates are high. During the credit crunch, however, banks often paid more.

Like any other mutual fund, a money fund is a basket of various types of securities—in this case, low-risk investments that earn short-term interest rates. The Securities and Exchange Commission (SEC) limits taxable money funds largely to U.S. Treasury securities, insured bank certificates of deposit, and top-grade commercial paper (short-term loans to creditworthy corporations). Tax-exempt money market funds, for people in higher tax brackets, invest in the short-term securities of states and municipalities, and local authorities that maintain sewers, water, and so on. All these investments usually mature within a brief time—a day, a week, three months, six months.

In theory, money market mutual funds are worth $1 a share, all the time. They don't rise in value in good markets or fall in bad ones. They generally credit you with dividends daily (and pay them monthly), passing along whatever the fund is currently earning. Your minimum investment: $2,500 or $3,000, depending on the fund. Some require $5,000 or more. You can write an unlimited number of checks on the fund, generally for a minimum of $250 or $500. A few process $100 checks. You pay no penalties for low deposits, although many funds will cash out your shares if your balance falls below a certain minimum, such as $500 or so.

But . . . money funds, including the money funds sold by banks, don't carry federal deposit insurance. So although the funds are extremely safe, they're not perfectly safe. In 2008, the giant Reserve Primary Fund got stuck with worthless commercial paper from Lehman Brothers, an investment bank that suddenly failed. Share values at Primary dropped to 97 cents a share—a shock called "breaking the buck." Investors fled similar money funds and didn't return until the U.S. Treasury stepped in to offer temporary insurance.

Back in 1989 and 1990 some corporations defaulted on their commercial paper, posing a potential loss to a few money funds. In 1994 a sharp rise in interest rates damaged a handful of funds invested in the riskiest sort of derivatives—complex investments whose market value isn't always clear. No one lost money. Those funds were sponsored by large financial institutions that dipped into their pockets to make investors whole. Reserve Primary wasn't owned by a financial institution and couldn't make good. I still think that money market funds are safe enough, but only if they're owned by major institutions that can afford to support the $1 price.

Money funds come in various types:

- *The supersafe.* They invest only in U.S. Treasury bills and buy no Treasury derivatives. In general, investors earn less than they would in other funds. An exception could be an investor in a high-tax state such as California, Massachusetts, or New York. Dividends paid by Treasury funds are exempt from state and local taxes. As a result, they may net you more than funds invested in taxable corporate securities, especially if the Treasury fund has low expenses.
- *The plenty safe.* These mixed funds buy Treasury securities and corporate securities too. They usually yield 0.25 to 0.5 percentage point more than pure Treasury funds, so you're gaining $12.50 to $25 a year on a $5,000 investment. In my opinion, mixed funds are safe enough. Tax-exempt money funds, invested in short-term municipal securities, are plenty safe too.
- *The probably safe.* The highest-yielding money funds buy corporate securities and follow slightly riskier strategies. Reserve Primary Fund strayed into this area. So far, it has been the only one to lose money for investors, but it probably won't be the last. If you buy a high yielder, be sure that it's sponsored by a major financial institution that will step in if anything goes wrong.

Regardless of the type of fund you're interested in, don't break your neck hunting for the highest payer. There's always a different name at the top of the list, depending on each fund's holdings and how fast it responds to daily changes in interest rates. I'd use six criteria in choosing a fund:

1. Are its expenses low? You'll find the answer in the prospectus, in the table that shows all the fees and expenses. Managers who charge 0.5 percent of assets or less have a good shot at being top performers. Fees of 1 percent or more usually mark the funds that do the worst. Some funds with low expense ratios levy separate service charges, such as $2 per check or $5 per telephone transfer. If those fees were figured into the expense ratio, the fund would show a slightly higher cost. Some funds waive part of their fees temporarily to produce a competitive yield. When fees return to normal, your yield will drop. In general, large money funds are more cost efficient than small ones and ought to cost you less.

2. Does it fit your purse? You should have no problem meeting the fund's minimum balance and check-writing rules.

3. Is it handy? If you invest with a particular mutual fund group or stockbrokerage firm, you'll probably use the firm's own money fund as a place to park cash.

4. What's the fund's average maturity—meaning, how long does it take for its average investment to come due? The shorter the term, the less risk the fund takes. Under proposed SEC rules, average maturity generally can't exceed 60 days. (An average of 75 days is also under discussion.) Most funds post even shorter terms.

5. Does the fund belong to a major financial organization—a mutual fund group, a large brokerage house, an insurance company? This is your equivalent of deposit insurance. So far, these money fund sponsors have always paid for their mistakes rather than saddle their shareholders with a loss. A fund without major sponsorship, such as Reserve Primary, might not be able to cover a major error's cost.

6. Are you comfortable with the fund's investment policies? Safety is the watchword here, but that means different things to different people. You might want a fund that buys only Treasury bills. In a broader-based fund, you might want certificates of deposit only from the soundest banks and a limited amount of commercial paper.

As for derivatives, some of them aren't particularly dangerous. Others can lose an unexpected amount of value when interest rates suddenly change.

How do you find out what a money fund buys? There's only one way: read the prospectus. For safety, a suitable disclosure is, "This fund does not invest in derivatives." Funds that devote many paragraphs to derivatives may be running more risks than even the managers realize.

Funds that consistently pay higher yields than the competition are the ones taking higher risks. And why would you take any risks at all? On $5,000, the difference between 3.5 and 3.1 percent comes to $20 a year. Big deal. If you've got $5 million, that 0.4 percent is worth a tidy $20,000—but short of that, why mess around?

A note about tax-exempt money market funds: Some people will do anything to beat Uncle Sam out of a few bucks, even if it costs them money. They buy a tax-exempt fund even if they'd do better in a taxable one. Look at a tax-free fund only if you are in a middle or high federal tax bracket (at this writing, 25 percent and up).

Here's how to figure whether you'll net more money from a tax-exempt fund than a taxable one: Subtract your combined state and federal tax bracket from 1.00. Divide the result into the current yield of the tax-exempt fund you're looking at. The result is your break-even point. If you can find a taxable fund paying more than the break-even point, buy it.

For example, say you're in the 25 percent bracket and are considering a fund that yields 2.5 percent. Subtracting 0.25 from 1.00 gives you 0.75. Dividing 2.5 by 0.75 gives you 3.33 percent. A taxable fund paying more than 3.33 percent will yield you more, after federal taxes, than the tax-free fund.

Four alerts:

1. A general tax-exempt fund includes the securities of many states. Your state may tax the interest on out-of-state bonds, making these tax exempts less attractive.

2. Single-state funds exist for states with higher taxes (California, Ohio, New Jersey, New York, Maryland, and Pennsylvania, among others). Your dividends should be entirely tax exempt. You take on slightly more risk, however, because you're not diversified.

3. U.S. government money market funds include a mix of government securities, only some of which are state tax–exempt. Your fund should tell you what's reportable in your state.

4. Some state and local securities are considered *private purpose*. That subjects them to the alternative minimum tax, as long as it survives. Ask about this if you're in an AMT bracket (you know who you are!).

Beware of look-alike money market funds! They yield more than regular funds because they're invested in the securities of a single company, such as Ford Motor Credit Company or GMAC Financial Services. At this writing, the Ford and GMAC notes are paying the interest due, despite their ties to the shrinking auto industry, but the notes are worth much less than you paid. Money funds need to be diversified to be acceptably safe—or, like bank money market accounts, they need to be federally insured. Check the money fund industry's current average yield at iMoneyNet (www.imoneynet.com), and be suspicious of any "money account" that pays more.

Beware of "enhanced" cash funds! They're diversified, but they invest in securities maturing in up to a year instead of super-short-term 30- to 60-day securities. If interest rates rise, the enhanced funds may lose money—not a lot, but enough to notice. Enhanced funds are fine for people who want to take a little risk in the hope of earning a higher return. But they're not for savers who intended to keep their money safe.

Beware any investment that claims to act like a money fund while paying a sharply higher yield. That was the promise of the complex instruments called auction rate securities. They yielded high returns for 20 years. Then the market froze and investors couldn't get their money out. Don't play games with money fund look-alikes. For liquid savings, stick with the real thing.

For Savings You'll Need for Sure in Six Months to Five Years

Here I count everything from college tuition due next fall to the down payment on the house you hope to buy the year after next. You can't risk losing a penny of it, so you can't afford to play around. On the other hand, neither should these funds nap in a low-interest savings account. By choosing a guaranteed investment that pays a higher interest rate, you'll pile up savings faster.

Most of you will agree with me about keeping six-month money safe. But five years sounds a lot further away. Why not invest in stocks for growth? Here's my argument: Stock prices rise and fall. For money you'll absolutely need, it's the "fall" you have to worry about. If you have the bad luck to invest just before stocks go into a decline, you'll lose some of your principal, which could be disastrous if that money is needed to pay a specific bill. Since 1929, it has taken investors an average of nearly four years to get even again after a major stock market drop, assuming that dividends were reinvested.

If you're more adventurous, you might decide to keep only two-year money totally safe. Since World War II, the average stock market dip and recovery took just over two years. Still, the second longest dip and recovery on record started in August 2000 and lasted until October 2006—more than six years. And then the market fell again, with years of recovery still ahead! How much risk are you willing to take with money you *must* have within a shorter period of time?

Four Places to Keep Medium-Term Money:

Certificates of Deposit. With a CD, you put your money in a bank or credit union for a fixed term. You normally earn a higher interest rate than you would in a bank money market deposit account.

Some people hate CDs because they feel that their money is locked away. But it's not. You can break into a certificate anytime you want before maturity. The worst that can happen is that you'll pay an interest penalty. Big deal. That's nothing compared with the interest you lose by keeping too much money in a low-interest savings account. If you balance risk and reward, CDs are a shoo-in. Most savers will not face an emergency need for cash. You'll hold your CD to maturity and earn more interest along the way. Note that CDs at online banks usually pay more than those at traditional banks.

Institutions may offer standard terms for CDs, such as 6, 12, or 30 months. Some let you pick whatever term you like. Normally, the longer the term, the more interest you earn. For how to get higher interest through laddering CDs, see page 67.

U.S. Treasury Securities. A Treasury security is the fruit of federal deficit spending. When the government spends more money than it collects in taxes, it has to borrow to make up the difference—and it borrows from you, by selling you Treasuries. You are actually lending money to Uncle Sam for a fixed period, earning interest all the while.

To buy Treasuries, go online to TreasuryDirect (www.treasurydirect.gov) and set up an account. You can do it in five minutes flat. If you aren't online, write to the nearest Federal Reserve Bank (they're listed on page 229) for the forms you need. The job is not exactly a brain buster and there are no charges to pay when you buy direct from the Fed. Still, I can hear some of you groaning. If this sounds like too much work, a bank or a stockbroker will buy Treasuries for you for a fee. Or you can buy a TIPS mutual fund (see page 226).

What's your reward for becoming a Treasury investor? In most states, an instant break on your income taxes. The interest you earn on U.S. Treasury securities, while taxed at the federal level, cannot be taxed by states and cities. So you might earn a higher after-tax return than you'd get from the average certificate of deposit.

The minimum investment for Treasuries is $100. The yield is set through public auction by the big institutions that put in bids. When you buy directly from the Federal Reserve, you piggyback on what the institutions pay. You'll find the auction dates at TreasuryDirect.

Which Treasuries to buy depends on when you'll want the money:

Treasury bills mature in four weeks, three months, or six months. You send the Fed a certified check for the bill's face amount or authorize a direct payment by your bank. Immediately after the auction you get a *discount* payment back, representing the difference between the face value of the bill and the lower auction price. At maturity, you're paid the face value. Your profit is the difference between the two. For example, say you send $1,000 for a six-month bill that sells for $950. The Treasury sends you $50 back. At maturity, your T-bill pays $1,000, for a $50 profit.

There are two ways of measuring your return on investment. The newspaper stories generally highlight the *discount rate,* which compares your profit ($50) with the bill's face value ($1,000). By this measure, you've apparently earned 5 percent.

But that understates what you've really earned. After all, you didn't put up the full $1,000. In this example, you invested only $950. A $50 return on $950 comes to about 5.3 percent. That's called the *coupon-equivalent yield* and is the true measure of your return. Use it to compare the profit in Treasury bills with what you might get from alternative investments, such as bonds and CDs. You'll find the coupon-equivalent yields on the Web site TreasuryDirect.

T-bills let you play income tax games. If you buy a security today that matures in the next calendar year, your interest income falls into that year, so you defer the tax you owe. Note that your taxable profit is not the discount check that the Treasury sends you right away. It's the profit you make when the bill matures.

Treasury notes mature in two, three, four, five, seven, or ten years. Different maturities are auctioned at different times (you'll find the dates at Treasury-Direct). Just authorize a withdrawal from your bank account for the face amount of the notes you want, or mail a check. Immediately after the auction, you will usually get a few dollars back because the notes sold for a hair less than their face value. Only one yield is reported (there's no coupon-equivalent yield to worry about, as with Treasury bills). Interest is paid on your full investment twice a year.

When choosing Treasury notes, pick a maturity that coincides with the date you'll want to use the money.

Treasury Inflation-Protected Securities (TIPS) are issued for terms of 5, 10, and 20 years. They protect both your principal and interest from inflation. Your principal rises by the percentage change in the consumer price index (the increase is compounded daily and added to the value of your bond every six months). The interest rate is fixed, but it's paid on a rising amount of principal, which means that your income, in dollars, increases too. If inflation rises by 1 percent, the value of your TIPS will also rise by 1 percent.

Your principal's increase in value is taxable in the current year, even though you don't get the money until the bond matures or until you sell before maturity. For this reason, investors prefer to hold individual TIPS in tax-deferred retirement accounts. Most TIPS mutual funds work differently. They pay out the gain in your principal in monthly or quarterly installments, so you have cash in hand when your taxes come due.

Initially, TIPS pay a lower interest rate than you could earn on fixed-rate

Treasuries, but they'll pay more if inflation rises faster than people generally expect. For help in choosing between TIPS and fixed-rate Treasuries, see page 929.

Shorter-term zero-coupon Treasuries can be good ways to save over four years. A *zero* is a Treasury note bought for less than its face value. It pays no current interest (also called the "coupon"). Instead you buy the note for less than its face value. Every year the interest builds up within the bond until it reaches face value at maturity. For example, you might pay $865 (before sales commissions) for a zero that will be worth $1,000 in five years. That's an annual compound yield of 4.8 percent.

Zeros are sold by stockbrokers and banks, not through TreasuryDirect. Just be sure that you can hold the note until its maturity date. You may lose money if you have to sell a zero before maturity.

What's nice about zeros is that they reinvest your interest at the same rate that you're earning on the bond itself. With the zero just discussed, for example, you earn 4.8 percent on every interest payment. With other bonds, you're paid in cash and have to reinvest the money yourself. Small payments (if not spent) will probably land in a bank account or money market fund, where they'll generally earn much less than you're earning on the bond itself.

What's bad about zeros is that you're taxed every year on the interest that builds up, even though you don't physically receive the money. If you're younger and will want the cash at maturity, you'll have to grin and bear it. If you're older and can wait for the cash until after age 59½, buy your zeros in a tax-deferred retirement account.

A four-year zero-coupon Treasury is a reasonable bet for your teenager's education fund. Buy one when the child is 14 years old, to cash in when he or she reaches 18. Your money is safe, and the earnings should compound at a reasonable rate of interest. (For younger children, don't buy zeros, buy stock-owning mutual funds—see page 845.)

Long-term zeros are another story. Like other Treasury bonds, they're generally wrong for short-term savers. When interest rates rise, zeros lose value faster than other bonds do, which can hurt you if you have to sell before maturity. For more on zeros, see page 945.

Treasury bonds have the longest maturities, generally up to 30 years. They're auctioned in the same way as Treasury notes, with interest payable twice a year. I mention them here only to be orderly. Long-term Treasuries aren't the right place for savings you might have to tap. If you sell them before maturity, you'll be exposed to the hard, cold winds of the open market, where your bond might bring less than you originally paid. The newer inflation-indexed Treasuries don't vary in price as much as conventional Treasuries, but they pay a smaller current income. For ways to use long-term Treasury bonds, see page 921.

— How to Buy Treasuries —

There's no such thing as a physical Treasury certificate. Your purchase is recorded. You get a statement. But you don't get the thing itself to hold in your hand because there is no "thing itself." A Treasury certificate has become a concept in the mind and a byte in the computer.

You can buy Treasuries online at TreasuryDirect, through a Federal Reserve Bank (page 229), or through a commercial bank or stockbroker. Which to choose depends on the kind of investor you are. (Note that TreasuryDirect is only for personal investing. You can't buy for your Individual Retirement Account.)

Savers: Buy Through the Fed When you buy online or through the Fed, you pay no fees or commissions on securities held to maturity. Every penny you earn in yield is yours to keep. The system, called TreasuryDirect, is entirely Web based. Older accounts, now called Legacy Treasury Direct, can still be handled by mail.

With TreasuryDirect, you open an account with the Federal Reserve, which keeps track of all your transactions. You'll be asked for your bank's nine-digit American Bankers Association routing transit number. That's the mystery number on the bottom of any check or deposit slip. Usually it's on the left; your account number is on the right.

To buy, you authorize the Treasury to withdraw the money from your bank account. Your interest earnings can be paid electronically into your bank or mutual fund account. Ditto the proceeds when your securities mature. If you'll want to reinvest, check the date when the proceeds will be paid. Tell the Treasury to return to your account that day and withdraw the money again for a new purchase. You can also have the proceeds parked in a non-interest-bearing Treasury security (called a certificate of indebtedness), waiting for reinvestment.

Investors with legacy accounts still have to send a tender form and certified check for their purchases. However, you can arrange for your maturing Treasury bills to be reinvested automatically, for the same term. You may find it convenient to convert from a legacy account to the new TreasuryDirect, so that you can operate entirely by Web.

If you want to sell a security prior to maturity, you have to mail a form to the Chicago Federal Reserve Bank (page 229), which will get three price quotes from dealers and sell for you at the highest bid. The fee for this service: $45.

Speculators: Buy Through Banks or Stockbrokers A speculator buys and sells long-term Treasury bonds, hoping to earn a profit from changes in interest rates. This means selling securities before they mature and at a moment's notice. Only commercial banks or stockbrokerage firms do that. They also let you order by phone and will lend you money against your securities. Sales commissions: a minimum of $15 to $60 every time you buy or sell. Online brokers may let you buy large amounts of Treasuries free.

FEDERAL RESERVE BANKS

P.O. Box 55882
Boston, MA 02215
617-973-3000
www.bos.frb.org

33 Liberty Street
New York, NY 10045
212-720-5000
www.newyorkfed.org

Ten Independence Mall
Philadelphia, PA 19106
215-574-6000
www.philadelphiafed.org

P.O. Box 6387
Cleveland, OH 44101
216-579-2000
www.clevelandfed.org

701 East Byrd Street
Richmond, VA 23219
804-697-8000
www.richmondfed.org

1000 Peachtree Street, N.E.
Atlanta, GA 30309
404-498-8500
www.frbatlanta.org

230 South LaSalle Street
P.O. Box 834
Chicago, IL 60604
312-322-5322
www.chicagofed.org

P.O. Box 442
St. Louis, MO 63166
314-444-8444
www.stlouisfed.org

90 Hennepin Avenue
Minneapolis, MN 55401
612-204-5000
www.minneapolisfed.org

1 Memorial Drive
Kansas City, MO 64198
800-333-1010
www.kansascityfed.org

2200 North Pearl Street
Dallas, TX 75201
214-922-6000
www.dallasfed.org

101 Market Street
San Francisco, CA 94105
415-974-2000
www.frbsf.org

It makes no sense at all to use brokerage firms for small orders of short-term Treasury securities. The commission might slash your yield by 0.5 percent on a six-month T-bill. On larger purchases or on longer-term securities, however, brokerage fees don't take such a big bite.

Buying Zero-Coupon Treasuries They're bought through stockbrokers. But some firms clip you for a higher price than you should pay. They trap you by quoting a dollar figure—"only $865 for these bonds"—without telling you what the bonds are priced to yield. That might saddle you with an unfairly low rate of return.

A smart investor buys through a discount broker. Ask for both the dollar price and the net yield to maturity after sales charges, which is what the bond pays over its full term.

For Savings You Won't Need for Five Years or More

Risk part of it in the stock market or other growth investment—the amount depending on your age. Otherwise, you'll never get ahead of inflation and taxes.

But you might want to keep even some of your long-term money absolutely safe. For this purpose, two suggestions:

Five-Year Certificates of Deposit or Treasury Notes, Continually Reinvested. They should roughly preserve your purchasing power, provided that you reinvest all of the interest as well as the principal. You're buying for only five years at a time, so you'll probably be able to hold each note until maturity. That's important, as you might lose money if you have to sell before the notes mature. You can ladder Treasury bills and notes just the way you do certificates of deposit (explained on page 67).

U.S. Savings Bonds. Savings bonds, although issued by the U.S. Treasury, are not what investors know as Treasury securities. Treasuries pay competitive interest rates and can be bought and sold on the open market. Savings bonds don't and can't. They're a special type of bond, sold principally to small investors. You pay no fees to buy or sell. You cannot lose money on savings bonds regardless of general market conditions.

Savings bonds come in two types: (1) The traditional Series EE bonds, which pay a fixed rate for the life of the bond, and (2) Series I bonds, whose yields adjust for inflation. They pay a low fixed rate, good for the life of the bond, plus a floating rate linked to the consumer price index. The floating rate changes every May 1 and November 1. Interest on both types of bonds is compounded semiannually and credited monthly. I bonds usually yield more than EE bonds, but not always.

The government limits how much you can put into savings bonds every year. At this writing, it's just $5,000, for a bond with a $10,000 denomination. Fixed-rate Treasuries or TIPS pay higher interest rates, but savings bonds have some special virtues:

■ *You can earn these rates on a very small amount of money.* The cheapest bond costs $25 ($50 if you buy through payroll deduction).

■ *You can tax-defer the interest* until the bonds are finally cashed in or until they reach their final maturity.

■ *You receive no money until redemption, so you can't go out and spend the interest.* Savings bonds (as well as zero-coupon bonds and TIPS) force you to save.

■ *If you bought savings bonds after December 31, 1989, and use the proceeds to cover tuition for qualified higher education,* you might pay no income tax on the interest you earn (page 678).

There are four ways of buying savings bonds, with different rules.

1. You can buy online through TreasuryDirect. You won't get a paper bond. Instead your purchase will be held in your electronic account. With investments over $25, you can buy to the penny; for example, you could get a bond worth $70.45. Interest is paid on the purchased amount.

2. You can buy paper bonds through most banks and some credit unions. You'll receive the bond in about three weeks. Paper bonds are sold in denominations of $50, $75, $100, $200, $500, $1,000, $5,000, and $10,000, at a 50 percent discount from face value. The $100 bond costs $50; the $500 bond costs $250. Each month's interest is added to the bond's redemption value. Since December 11, 2001, paper EE bonds bought through banks have been stamped "Patriot bonds." That's just a name. They're the same as any other EE bond.

3. You can buy through a payroll savings plan if your company offers one. There are plans for both paper and electronic bonds through TreasuryDirect.

4. You can check a box on your tax return, asking that your refund be paid in savings bonds instead of in cash.

No matter how you buy, the interest rate will be the same. You must hold the bond for at least 12 months. After that, you may cash it in whenever it suits you. As with other Treasury securities, you owe only federal income taxes on the interest you earn, no state and local income taxes.

Plan to hold for at least five years. There's a three-month interest penalty on bonds redeemed within that period. If you sell after the first five years, you'll get whatever the bonds have earned since the month you bought. If you hold for 20 years or more, the government offers a guarantee: your EE-bond investment will—at minimum—double in value. That gives super-long-term holders a base rate of 3.5 percent, and higher if long-term interest rates stay above that level. For a recorded announcement of current savings bond interest rates, call toll-free 800-US-BONDS. Or visit the Web site TreasuryDirect.

— Savings Bond Maturities —

Here's a subject that's widely misunderstood. Unlike certificates of deposit, savings bonds do not have to be held until a particular maturity date. You redeem them at your convenience, receiving whatever they're worth at the time.

This misunderstanding arises because of the way that paper EE bonds are sold. You buy at a 50 percent discount, paying $50 for a $100 bond. So you naturally might think that you have to hold until your bond is worth $100. Not so. You have no idea when it will be worth $100 because that depends on what happens to interest rates. At the very worst, you'd get $100 after 20 years because that's your government guarantee. But the bond might reach $100 in value sooner than that. In any event, none of this matters. You just cash in the bond when you need the money and get all your principal back plus any interest due. You do not have to hold for 20 years.

Here are the maturities for savings bonds and what they mean:

1. Original maturity. This is the maximum time it will take for a paper bond to reach its face value. For newly issued bonds, that's 20 years, even though they may actually reach face value sooner.

2. First extended maturity. This lasts for 10 years after the original maturity date.

3. Additional extended maturities. Older bonds with original maturities shorter than 10 years get an additional extension, allowing them to pay interest for 30 or 40 years.

4. Final maturity. This is the date after which the bond will no longer earn interest. On newly issued bonds, the final maturity—printed on the face of the bond—is 30 years away. Here are the final maturity dates for all other bonds (note that the oldest of these are no longer earning interest):

Series E bonds issued earlier than December 1965—40 years after their issue date

Series E and EE bonds and Freedom Shares issued after November 1965—30 years after their issue date

Series H bonds issued between 1959 and 1979—30 years after their issue date

Series HH bonds issued since 1980—20 years after their issue date (new Series HH bonds are no longer being issued)

5. Maturities on bonds bought through TreasuryDirect. They're a flat 30 years, with no complications.

Don't hang on to old savings bonds that aren't paying interest anymore! Cash them in and get the money. Ask older family members whether they have any

E bonds stashed away and check the dates. When an E or EE bond reaches its final maturity, all the unreported interest becomes taxable even if you don't turn it in. Here are the dates for the bonds no longer earning interest: those issued between May 1941 and May 1963 and those issued between December 1965 and May 1973. Americans now hold more than $12 billion in bonds that are no longer earning interest! Savings Notes, also called Freedom Shares, are also no longer earning interest.

— Some Angles to Savings Bond Investments —

■ **An individual can invest up to $5,000 in a calendar year in each series (EE and I) and in each format (paper and electronic).** That's a total of $20,000 or $40,000 for two co-owners. Paper savings bonds bought as gifts aren't included in your annual limit.

■ **Bonds earn interest from the issue date, which is always the first day of the month you bought.** If you buy a bond on the last day of the month, it will be backdated to the first day. Interest on new bonds is credited every month.

Interest on older EE bonds—those bought prior to May 1, 1997—is normally credited every six months. You earn more money by cashing them just after the crediting date rather than just before. You can find that date at TreasuryDirect.

■ **To find out what your bonds are worth today,** go to the pages for EE or I bonds at TreasuryDirect. Click on Redeem and look for the Savings Bond Calculator.

■ **You can redeem just part of a bond** if its face value is at least $50 for Series E bonds, $75 for Series EE or Series I, and $1,000 for Series H or HH. For example, a bond worth $1,000, with an accrued value of $700, can be turned in for $700 in cash and $300 in bonds. The new bonds will have the same issue date as the old one did.

■ **If you buy a savings bond in your own name, you control it completely.** If you name a beneficiary on an EE bond, you can change the beneficiary whenever you want just by filling in Form PD 4000 (available at TreasuryDirect or from many of the agents who issue savings bonds). The rules are different for the older, Series E bonds. With them, the beneficiary has to agree to being removed by signing Form PD 4000.

■ **If you buy a savings bond in joint names, both owners have to agree to any changes.** But either one of you can cash in the bond and the other doesn't have to know. Whoever holds it, controls it.

■ **The person whose money bought the bond is called the principal co-owner, and all the income should be taxed to him or her.** If both of you contributed, there is no principal co-owner and taxes should be allocated according to what percentage each of you paid. As a practical matter, however, the tax is usually paid by the person who redeems the bond.

■ **If you buy a paper bond as a gift, you don't need the recipient's Social Security number; you can use your own.** Gifting is more complicated, however, through TreasuryDirect.

■ **If the bond is a gift, the interest is taxed to the person receiving it.** In theory, the purchaser should sometimes pay the tax. For example, the interest is taxable to you if you buy a bond as a gift for a child and name yourself co-owner. Nevertheless, if the child grows up and redeems the bond, the 1099 will be issued in the child's name.

■ **The interest earned on savings bonds is normally tax deferred.** But children who own bonds and are in low (or zero) brackets should not defer. Report the interest now, when little or no tax will be due, rather than wait until the child grows up. To get this easy tax break on bonds bought this year, file a return for the child showing how much the EE bonds gained in value (your bank or credit union may have this information; you can also use the Savings Bond Calculator at TreasuryDirect). No further tax returns have to be filed for those particular bonds as long as the child owes no tax. In any year the child does owe a tax, his or her return will have to report that year's gain in the EE bonds' value.

What if your child deferred income taxes in the past and now wants to pay them currently? In the year that you switch, all past gains must be reported.

What if the child has been paying taxes currently and now wants to defer (deferral is smart for children who have enough unearned income to be taxed in their parents' bracket—page 91)? File Form 3115, Application for Change in Accounting Method, with the child's tax return for the year you want the change to start.

Keep copies of all the child's tax returns. When the bonds are cashed in, you or your child must be prepared to prove which gains were previously reported. Otherwise the IRS might conclude that the child owes taxes on all of the profits.

■ **Bonds may be held by the trustee of your trust.** But the trust can't be co-owner or beneficiary.

■ **What if you die holding savings bonds?** Your executor or trustee has two tax choices:

1. *All the income to date can be reported on your final tax return and the taxes paid.* The beneficiary who receives the bonds should then be taxed only on the income earned from that point on. To avoid being taxed on the full amount at redemption, however, the beneficiary must have a copy of the tax return to prove how much was previously paid.

2. *The bonds can be passed to the beneficiary as is, with all the tax deferred.* When the beneficiary redeems, he or she pays the entire tax.

■ **When one owner dies, a co-owner takes over the bonds automatically.** But they should be reissued in the surviving owner's name (or in the name of the surviving owner—named first—plus a new co-owner). If you inherit a savings bond that was issued to someone else, you can also have it reissued in your name or in your name plus a co-owner.

On reissue, the bond's final maturity remains the same, interest accumulates as usual, and no taxes are due. However, you can't have a bond reissued if it's close to its final maturity. Such bonds must be redeemed.

To redeem a bond after a death, or have it reissued in a new name, a beneficiary has to produce a death certificate. A co-owner can redeem without a death certificate but will need it for reissue.

If you inherit a bond and die without having the former owner's name removed, your heirs will have to produce two death certificates—yours and the former owner's—before they can redeem the bonds.

Co-owners can redeem their bonds at any bank that handles that business. If you inherited someone else's bond, however, you have to redeem through a Federal Reserve Bank or the Bureau of the Public Debt (page 237).

■ **If you die without a will, your family will have to suffer a mess of paperwork** (Form PD 5336) before your savings bonds can be passed to a new owner. So don't.

■ **If you co-own bonds that cannot be found after the other owner's death, file a lost-bond claim with the Bureau of the Public Debt and have them reissued.** You may discover that the other owner cashed them without telling you.

■ **For a reissue form (PD 4000), ask a bank that handles savings bond sales, call the nearest regional Federal Reserve bank, or go online to Treasury-Direct.** The forms are fairly simple. If you have a question, call the nearest Fed. Your bank might also help you—sometimes free, sometimes for a fee.

■ **What if you want to give away a savings bond?** Don't have it reissued in the new name. If you do, you'll owe income taxes currently on the accumulated interest even though that interest won't actually be paid out. Years later, when the recipient redeems the bond, all the interest will be taxable unless he or she can prove that part of the tax was already paid. These rules also apply if you're the bond's principal co-owner (listed first on the bond's face) and want to reissue it solely in the name of the other owner.

The best way of making the gift is to add the lucky person to the bond as co-owner. There are no tax consequences. The co-owner can cash in the bond whenever he or she wants, deferring taxes until that time. There's also no tax if you remove the second co-owner's name or have the bond reissued in the name of the trustee of your trust.

- **What if you marry and change your name?** You don't have to get your savings bonds reissued. When you cash them in, just sign the bond with both your maiden name and your married name.
- **What if you buy a bond and it comes with your name spelled wrong or the wrong date on it?** Don't fix it yourself. You cannot redeem a bond that has been altered. Return it to the place that issued it and get the error fixed.
- **You're not allowed to borrow against your savings bonds.**
- **If you lose a bond, it's easy to replace** as long as you know its face value (denomination), issue date, registration number, and the name or names in which it was issued, their addresses, and their Social Security numbers. Photocopy each bond you own or list the critical information. Keep these records in your safe-deposit box or fireproof home safe.
- **If you don't keep good records, the Treasury may be able to trace the bond for you, especially if it was issued after January 1974.** All those savings bonds have Social Security numbers on them. What's lost can be found if the Treasury knows the Social Security number of the first owner named on the bond.

Older bonds sometimes carry Social Security numbers too. If not, the Treasury can't hope to trace ownership unless it knows the bond's serial number or the name on the bond and that person's address when it was bought.

A lost bond can be replaced at no cost to you. If you're replacing a partly burned or mutilated bond, send the Bureau of the Public Debt the remains. The form used for replacement is PD 1048, available online or from many commercial banks, a regional Federal Reserve bank (page 229), or the Bureau of the Public Debt. Replacement takes anywhere from 8 to 24 weeks.

If you replace a bond and the original turns up, it must be surrendered for cancellation. The government won't let you cash the same bond twice. If you try, you'll find out that Big Brother knows.

If you're in a payroll deduction plan, you can buy fractions of bonds. For example, you might have $25 taken from every paycheck and credited toward the $50 cost of a $100 bond. After two payments you should be issued your bond. Arrange to have the bonds mailed to you and check that the amounts are right. Your only proof of purchase is normally the deduction shown on your pay stub, and it's up to you to check that you received what you paid for. To simplify the job, buy a full bond with each deduction rather than a fraction of a bond. If your bonds don't arrive or you get the wrong denominations, query your payroll department, which should initiate a claims procedure.

- **Any bank authorized to sell EE bonds can also cash them in for you,** although some redemptions, such as those by a guardian or trustee, may have to be handled directly by the government. Try to redeem at a place where you're known, such as your own bank. If you're not known, you will need documentary identification—a picture driver's license, an employee card with your picture on it—and may be limited to redeeming only $1,000 worth of bonds per day.
- **Your accumulated bond interest becomes taxable when you cash in the bonds.** So if possible, don't redeem them in a high-earning, preretirement year. Wait until well after you retire, when your income may have dropped.
- **A tip on older savings bonds, bought prior to May 1, 1995:** these bonds have interest rate guarantees ranging from 2.5 to 4 percent. Don't cash in an older bond without ascertaining its guarantee. It may be earning more than any other fixed-income investment you own. To check the guarantee, consult TreasuryDirect's online "Table of Guaranteed Minimum Rates and Original Maturity Periods."

— Where to Get Information on Savings Bonds —

You can't rely on banks to answer your questions on savings bonds correctly, even if they handle them. The program is complex and the clerks may not be fully trained. You should go online to TreasuryDirect or get information brochures to research the bonds yourself. The Bureau of the Public Debt answers questions, handles problems, and mails out forms. You can order forms online or write to the Bureau's Division of Customer Assistance at P.O. Box 7012, Parkersburg, WV 26106.

For a question about paper savings bonds, call the Savings Bond Processing Site. There are two numbers: 800-245-2804 and 800-553-2663.

If you don't want to dig through all the numbers yourself, you can buy a personal savings bond report from SavingsBonds.com (www.savingsbonds.com). It tells you about each bond you own—interest rate, current value, maturity date, and so on. If you're cashing bonds in, it will advise you on which ones to redeem first (those paying lower interest rates) and when to redeem them, to capture the final six-month interest payment. The Web site also contains plenty of free information.

You can get a similar report from the Savings Bond Informer at P.O. Box 11721, Monroe, MI 48161, or call 800-927-1901. If you want to look before you buy, the Informer will send you a free example.

I also recommend the Informer's valuable reference book on how the bond program works, *U.S. Savings Bonds.* It was published in 1999 but comes with an update on all the latest changes, strategies, and interest rates. Cost: $19.95.

Saving Money in a Life Insurance Policy

When you buy cash-value life insurance, you buy a kind of savings account that builds up over many years. But there are two fatal drawbacks to this form of savings: (1) Very little money normally accumulates in the early years. (2) To get at your money, you generally have to borrow it, paying interest as you go. If you choose the money fund option in a variable-life policy, the annual fees will virtually wipe out your yield. I'm all for good insurance, and, in a few cases, a cash-value policy may be exactly what you want. But if savings are your primary interest, look somewhere else.

When to Stop Saving

When you're young, you have to learn how to save. When you're old, you have to learn how to stop. Many older people deny themselves comforts because they're afraid to spend the money they have so carefully put aside.

Past a certain age, it's time to spend your children's inheritance, to give yourself the decent retirement you deserve. In chapter 30, you'll find guidelines on how to spend your money without running out.

10

Kicking the
Credit Card Habit

Learning to Live Without Consumer Debt

**The new macho is paying cash. It says that you're
flush enough not to take plastic seriously.**

Why do you need a fistful of credit cards? They're heavy. They make your wallet bulge. They cost money. You can't remember how much you've charged on them. Now that even the hoi polloi carry platinum, prestige lies in flashing a plain-vanilla card. For an even bigger thrill, pay cash.

As a status symbol, the fancy credit card is finished. It's now just a transactions workhorse and having too many of them says that you're dumb. Assuming, as I do, that you want to get out of debt and build some savings, plastic ought to serve a single purpose: convenience. You put it down instead of writing a check or paying cash. At the end of the month, you pay the bill. The whole bill.

Not that you're perfect. You'll still stretch the occasional bill over two or three months—maybe during holiday seasons or after a vacation. But your goal is to never charge more than you can easily repay. In a slowdown economy, savings are more important than ever.

How to Get Rid of Consumer Debt

It's so simple that I'm almost embarrassed to mention it: *Don't borrow anymore.*

That's all there is to it.

Say to yourself, "Today I am not going to put down a credit card for anything." When you buy something, pay cash, use a debit card, or write a check.

Tomorrow say the same thing: "I am not going to put down a credit card for anything. I am not even going to borrow ten dollars from a friend." Take it slowly, one day at a time. It's like stopping smoking. You'll be nervous at first; you won't see how it's possible to live; you'll suffer relapses and sneak a new debt or two. But when you get up every morning, renew your pledge. To make it easier, quit carrying credit cards.

I hear you saying, "I can't get along without a credit card!" Of course you can—at least, most of the time. You can pay by check or debit card. You can buy your Starbucks with cash (they still take it, you know). You may have to show a credit card to rent a car. But when you bring the car back, pay the bill by debit card or personal check.

If you object that you can't pay by debit card or check because you don't have enough money in the bank, you're missing my point. When you don't have the money in the bank, don't buy. If you find that you have to put down plastic, use an American Express green, gold, or platinum card. They're not credit cards, meaning that you can't stretch out payments. You have to pay your bill in full by the end of the month. (Okay, there's an annual fee for using these cards, but when you need discipline, Amex is it.)

Once you stop using credit cards, three things will happen:

1. You will buy less—and whatever you do buy will probably be a less expensive model or make. Studies have found that people spend more when they pay with plastic because it doesn't feel like real money. When it *is* real money, you're more sensible.

2. Your total debt will shrink rapidly. By paying off back bills and not adding new ones, you leave yourself pots of extra money to apply to debt reduction. You're also paying less interest, a big saving right there.

3. You will grow incredibly smug. You're the first on your block to get out of debt. Others will follow, but you'll be the first.

I'm not against credit cards. They're easy to use. They're handy. If your card has no annual fee and a 20-day interest-free grace period for paying your bills, you're getting free monthly loans. What I'm against is buying more on your credit cards than you can pay for at the end of the month.

Once you've fought your way out of debt, you can start using credit cards again, but only for the convenience of not carrying cash. Your days of debt are done. A big expense may sometimes drive you over the limit. A flat-screen TV. A llama. A hot-air balloon. Whenever you limp home back in debt, recite your mantra: "From now on, I'm not going to put down a credit card for anything." Stick with it until you're free again.

Rehab in Seven Steps

Haphazard repayment—the minimum on this card, an extra $100 on that one—progresses so slowly that you'll get discouraged. After a few months, you might give up. What you need is a total debt repayment *plan*, and here it is:

1. List each of your loans: how much you owe (most people don't know), how much you're paying every month, and any fees. Total it up.

2. Restructure your debt to reduce the interest cost. You might apply for a card that offers zero interest on transferred balances for the next 12 months (most cards charge a 3 percent balance transfer fee; look for an offer with no fee or a fee capped at $50 or $75). Use that grace period to pay off the debt. Just be sure that once the zero-rate period passes, your new card will carry the same, or a lower, interest rate than you're being charged now.

Alternatively, consolidate your consumer loans on a low-rate credit union loan or home equity line of credit. This works *only* if you've brought your spending under control. If not, you'll run up the debt on your credit cards all over again, giving you double the consumer debt you had before. Compulsive spenders should not consolidate their loans. It just digs them into a deeper hole. If you borrow anyway, draw up a plan to repay the debt in three to five years.

If mortgage interest rates have dropped, consider refinancing the mortgage and taking a large enough loan to repay your consumer debt. Important: use the money you're saving on interest costs to make extra mortgage payments, to reduce the total amount you owe! Otherwise you're merely stretching out the cost of your sweaters, iPods, and gas grills over 30 years—not a good strategy at all.

It doesn't hurt to ask your current lender to lower your interest rate—saying that otherwise you'll give up the card. It's a long shot, but sometimes you might catch a break.

3. Make one-shot reductions in your loan balances. You might run a yard sale and use all the proceeds to pay off debt. Or sell off a few shares of stock you inherited. Or use your savings, if you have any. It's smarter to chop debt than to hoard a low-rate savings account. (But keep on adding to your retirement account because those contributions lower your tax.)

4. Increase your monthly debt reduction budget, even if it's only by a small amount. Small amounts make an enormous difference. Say that you owe $8,000 at 18 percent interest, on which you're paying the bare minimum: 2.5 percent of the balance each month. You start out at $200 a month and pay a little less money in each subsequent month (that's because you're paying 2.5 percent of a declining balance). On this schedule, it will take 30 years to get out of debt!

Now let's say that you pay a fixed $200 each month. That will get you out of debt in just over five years, saving an enormous $7,306.34 in interest. If you added just $50 a month—paying $250 each time—you'd be debt free in less than four years and save $8,634.87 in interest. (A lot of people find these calculations, and others like them, too astonishing to be true. But they *are* true. Honest. Check it at Bankrate.com's calculator called "The True Cost of Paying the Minimum.")

5. Keep on paying the same amount each month, even though your loan balance goes down. The faster you pay off principal, the more interest you save and the faster your total debt declines. Once you've erased the highest-rate loan, start on the next highest—still paying the same fixed amount (or more!).

6. Pay the monthly minimums on your lower-rate loans while putting the rest of your available money toward the highest-rate loan. The size of the loan doesn't matter, only the size of the interest rate. The faster you knock off high-rate debt, the faster your burden will decline.

7. Work your way down the list, debt by debt. To keep yourself motivated, you have to take satisfaction from the process. Post your payment schedule on the refrigerator and check each one off. Or give yourself a quarterly reward for staying on the wagon.

8. If you wiped out your credit card debt by taking a home equity loan, don't imagine that you're home free. You've just transferred your debt from one piece of paper to another. Pay off your new home equity loan on the same schedule you'd have used to pay off your credit cards (use the Bankrate.com calculator to figure it out). You'll be out of debt even faster because this loan carries a lower interest rate.

9. Don't pay big bucks to get rid of debt. Tons of "debt elimination" services lure you by Web, mail, and phone. They're costly (just another debt) and may not do the job. For most of us, repaying loans doesn't require expert advice, just a simple, methodical program like the one outlined above. If you can't repay all your debts, set up a program through a dependable consumer credit counseling agency (page 288).

Credit Cards Versus Charge Cards

Visa, MasterCard, Discover, and American Express Blue and Optima are credit cards. You can charge up to a certain limit and carry most of the debt forward from one month to the next. Interest is levied on the unpaid balance.

No central organization sets the interest rates and charges on MasterCard and Visa cards. Each issuing bank determines its own, so costs vary widely. There are wonderful cards and rotten cards, depending on the deal.

Department store cards are credit cards too, but they usually have a lower credit limit and a higher interest rate. It usually pays to use your bank card instead of the store's card unless the store offers discounts to frequent shoppers. When you shop, you may be offered 10 percent off on that day's purchases if you'll apply for a store card. Don't do it unless you'll really use it.

American Express's classic Green, Gold, and Platinum cards and Diners Club are charge cards. You pay the full bill at the end of each month, although some credit is allowed. For example, you can stretch out payments on airline tickets or other big-ticket items charged to American Express. Unlike most credit cards, charge cards carry annual fees.

What's the Best Credit Card?

The best cards charge no annual fee and offer low interest rates to people who carry debt. My general advice is to own just two cards: (1) a convenience card, for bills that you'll cover by the end of the month. Buy all perishables, such as restaurant meals and gasoline, with this card, as well as all other items you know you can pay for immediately; (2) a low-interest card, for major purchases that will take several months to pay for. Charge only items that will last a long time, because those are the only ones worth paying interest for.

The trouble is, that advice is too simple. Low-rate cards can turn into high-rate nightmares if you're just one day late in paying your bill. What matters nowadays is how you handle your card—do you keep its up-front, honeymoon terms, or will you fall into one of the costly traps that the banks lay for you?

Trap 1: Interest Rate Outrages

Card companies play around with interest rates today. You think you've signed up for one rate—in fact, you've got it in your budget—when suddenly you're charged more. That's another reason to avoid consumer debt. It almost always turns out to be more expensive than you thought. In 2009, President Barack Obama signed the Credit Card Accountability Responsibility and Disclosure Act (Credit CARD Act), which eliminates some of the abusive practices. Unfortunately, it applies only to purchases made in February 2010 or later, so consumers with older debt can still be taken advantage of. What's more, plenty of bad practices remain. Here's what to watch out for:

- *"Fixed" interest rates.* "Fixed," my grandmother's left foot! When you sign up for this card, you assume your rate won't change. That makes you just the kind of sucke—um, *customer*—the bank wants. In the fine print, you'll find a statement saying that the bank can change rates, fees, and other terms whenever it wants and for any reason. And be assured, it will. Starting July 1, 2010, the fine print has to specify how long this so-called fixed rate will last.

- *Variable interest rates.* The majority of cards today charge variable interest rates on your revolving balances. *Variable* means that the rate changes in line with market interest rates. Typically, you pay a certain number of percentage points over the bank's prime rate (the prime is the benchmark lending rate). For example, you might pay prime plus 5.99 points. If the prime is at 8.25 percent, your card will charge 14.24 percent; if the prime rises to 10 percent, your card will charge 15.99 percent. If the prime rate drops, your rate should too— although there's a floor below which it's not allowed to go.

Generally speaking, applicants with impeccable credit histories can get no-fee cards charging 2 or 3 percentage points over prime. A decent history gets you 5 or 6 points over prime. Anyone with a heartbeat and a mailbox can get a card charging 8 percent or more over prime. The bank can change these point spreads whenever it wants.

When the prime changes, the bank won't necessarily change your interest rate right away. Some change rates monthly, others change them quarterly. The bank might also pick the highest rate during any 90-day period, which extracts extra dollars from its customers. It's all there in the fine print.

- *Teaser rates.* These are the superlow rates that card issuers dangle when they're trying to sign you up. They last no longer than a few months, then jump to the standard rate. Sometimes they cover only balances transferred from another card, not new purchases. When you're choosing a card, the standard rate is the one to evaluate, as well as the possible default rate (see below). Your best long-term bet: a low-rate card, even if it lacks a spiffy introductory offer.

- *Mystery rates.* Practically all cards today are actually offering mystery rates, not the interest rate you see in the ad. The bank may trumpet that a rate is "as low as" 7.9 percent. But that's only for applicants with top credit scores (page 266). When you receive your card, you may find that you'll be charged a much higher rate. The gyp is that you can't find out until you apply, which makes it impossible to compare the true interest rates available to you in the marketplace. This is *totally* unfair. In fact, banks may deliberately market to people with poorer scores—dangling a low rate but knowing that applicants will be issued only high-rate cards (they call this practice *downselling*). Your credit limit also might be lower than you expected (page 255).

- *Default or "penalty" rates.* These also give the lie to the low rates that you see in ads. Every card has a default rate that it charges people who make mistakes. Were you one day late in paying your bill? Your interest rate might rise. Were you one day late a second time? It will jump again. Did you accidentally charge more than your credit limit? Up the rate goes. Ditto if you pay the bill with a check that bounces. Did you take a new card because it offered you zero interest on your debt for the first 12 months? A late payment will bounce your zero rate up to the card's high rate on cash advances—and higher if you misbehave again. Even worse, the rate will be charged retroactively, from the time you got the card.

Penalty interest rates are running anywhere from 23 percent to 41 percent, with no end in sight. (They're disclosed in the fine print; check "Terms and Conditions" or "Pricing and Terms" if you're card hunting on the Web.) It's cheaper to borrow from the Mob. Starting in February 2010 penalty rates can be charged only on new purchases, not on older purchases that you're carrying on your card. That is, unless your payment is more than 60 days late. In that case, the bank can charge the high default rate on your older purchases, too.

Also starting in 2010, banks have to cancel any new penalty rate added to your card if you've made on-time payments for six consecutive months—so be sure to do it!

While you're paying penalty rates, charge nothing more. Concentrate on reducing your debt. If you can, find a card that offers you a better deal.

Reminder: if you pay late or go over the credit limit, there is also a fee. So you're hit twice.

- *Residual interest.* Never heard of this? Neither had I until a reader questioned the math on his credit card statement. He had been carrying a balance and, in February, paid it in full (he thought!). In March he found an additional and unexpected charge on his card. It turns out that the interest clock had kept running from the time he paid the bill until the time the payment was credited to his account—in his case, seven days more. That's *residual interest,* another cheat. Not all banks charge it (check the fine print in the credit card agreement). To avoid it, you have to call the bank and ask how much you'll owe, say, seven days from now, and pay that amount, not the lower amount shown on your bill.

- *Daily compounding.* Banks used to compound the interest on credit cards monthly; now most of them do it daily, which costs you more.

- *Higher rates on cash advances.* You're charged 23 percent or more for drawing on your credit card for cash.

Trap 2: The Conflagration of Fees

Why do so many banks offer cards with no annual fee? Because they know that you'll look at that cost before signing up. By dropping it to zero, they make the card appear "free." In fact, they'll be charging you even higher fees, in ways that you might not notice until too late. A sampling:

▪ *Late fees.* Pay just one day late, and you might be charged anywhere from $15 to $39 (with $49 on the horizon). Your interest rate might go up too (see above). At many banks, cardholders with small balances pay more than those with large balances. (Some banks now offer to send payments to your creditors overnight, for a fee that's less than the late charge would be.)

▪ *Over-limit fees.* Every card carries a credit limit. That's the total amount of money you're allowed to charge. In the past, the banks cheerfully let you exceed your limit and hit you with a $29 to $39 fee each time. They also used over-limit mistakes as an excuse to charge you a penalty interest rate. You had to pay.

On new accounts, however, you have a choice. You can't be charged over-limit fees unless you agree to accept them. Some banks are dropping the fees. Others might urge you to accept, so they can keep mining you for profits. The fee will be sold as an over-limit "protection" plan. My advice: Just say no. You'll save yourself fees and the risk of incurring a high penalty interest rate. If you try to buy something that exceeds your limit, the transaction probably won't go through, but so what? You should always carry at least one credit card with lots of charging power. If the first card won't work, use the second one. Having credit limits is a wonderful discipline. They motivate you to keep a closer eye on what you spend.

▪ *Balance transfer fees.* When you transfer a balance, you're typically charged 3 percent of the amount (with many banks at 5 percent). That's $300 to $500 on a $10,000 debt. A few banks charge no fees. Some will waive the fee if you call and ask—so always call. Some cap the fee at $30, $50, or $75. Never accept a zero-rate balance transfer offer without checking on the fees.

▪ *Fees for cash advances.* You might pay 3 to 5 percent with a $10 minimum. That's on top of the higher interest rate banks charge for a cash advance.

▪ *Fees for paying with a check that bounces.* These run up to $34.

▪ *Fees for inquiring about your credit limit.* That's a particularly neat trick. You're charged if you exceed the limit and charged if you ask how close to the limit you've come. You might even be charged for paying off your card in full.

▪ *Foreign transaction fees.* You might be charged an extra 1 to 3 percent for shopping abroad. The fee could even apply to foreign items bought online.

▪ *Slamming fees.* Your bank may have added something extra to your account that you didn't agree to buy, such as credit life insurance, rental car collision insurance, and other extras. Watch for these on your monthly bill and cancel them fast if you don't want them.

Trap 3: "Convenience" Checks and Cash Advances

They come in the mail from time to time. Your bank sends convenience checks, with the suggestion that you use them for some pressing bill (or pressing want). Need a vacation? Want a new computer? Just write a check. What's not to like? Here's what:

- *The interest rate.* Convenience checks are cash advances. Banks charge higher rates for cash than they do on credit card balances. You could easily pay up to 28 percent.
- *The fee.* There's usually an up-front fee, amounting to as much as 5 percent of the cash advance. That's $50 on a $1,000 advance, plus the higher interest rate. Counting rates and fees, the effective interest rate on short-term loans can top 100 percent.

Rewards Cards—Are They Worth It?

With a rewards card you earn "points" based on the amount of money spent. You can use those points to buy airline miles, catalog purchases, or earn cash back. The cards are worth it if there's no up-front fee and you pay off the balances every month. Even if you carry balances, rewards cards are good as long as you don't pay a higher interest rate than you would on a regular card. Always compare offers before making a choice—some cards give three points for every dollar spent, others give only one point. Some get good ratings from consumer groups, others don't. Get all the details at CardOffers.com (www.cardoffers .com). I like airline miles, so I carry a rewards card and use it to charge everything in sight. If you're not a traveler, choose a cash back card that will send you a check equal to 1 or 2 percent of your purchases. What about using your points to buy catalog merchandise? Forget it—the goods are often overpriced. Instead redeem your points by asking the card issuer to send you a check.

Some rewards cards, however, cost more than they're worth. They carry annual fees or charge higher rates of interest than plain-vanilla cards, making them losers for people who carry balances. Airline cards generally charge higher rates than general-purpose rewards cards from Visa and MasterCard. You're better off with lower-rate cards whose points can be used on several airlines.

What's more, rewards cards are tricky. You may earn points for everyday purchases but only for a limited amount of spending each month. Points may not be awarded for shopping at discount stores, department stores, convenience stores, or online. Cash back cards may pay the full amount only on spending that exceeds $3,000 in any year. Your points may expire if you don't use them. Airline points can be hard to use because of high demand and limited numbers of free seats. If you pay late or go over your limit, you might lose your rewards that month. The bank can change the rules at any time. So know your card's rules to get the most bang for your plastic bucks.

How to Handle Your Card to Keep Costs Down

The rules are simple:

1. Pay your credit card bill as soon as it arrives. That way, you won't forget it and won't risk its being slowed in the mail. If your payment is one day late, you can be bumped to a sky-high interest rate, even if it's your first offense. You might schedule automatic monthly payments from your bank account, if you're sure that you'll always have enough money available.

2. Don't take cash advances or accept convenience checks. They're superexpensive, which makes them harder to repay.

3. Don't charge any more than 50 percent of your credit limit on any card. If you do, your bank might decide you're a greater risk than it thought and increase your interest rate. It affects your credit score, too.

4. Don't apply for another card when you already have several in your wallet. More cards make you look like a higher risk, especially if you apply for two in a row. This includes applying for a zero-interest card in order to transfer expensive balances. You'll do yourself no good if that zero-rate card causes rates on your other cards to jump.

5. If you take a zero-interest offer, squeeze your budget to repay the loan during the interest-free period. That's what it's for. And don't use the new card until the zero-interest time frame expires. If you do, you'll run up a new interest rate bill on all your purchases.

6. Carry only one rewards card. If you own several cards—for airline miles, cash back, and catalog purchases—you may not accumulate enough points on any one program to make it worthwhile. Also, pay the bill in full each month. That's the only way your "gifts" will be truly free.

7. Don't pay only the minimum. That will never get you out of debt.

8. Don't carry balances at all! Isn't that what this chapter is all about?

Finding a Low-Rate Card

To find a good credit card, try CardTrak.com. It lets you sort cards by various categories, such as "No Annual Fee," "Low Rate," and "Low Intro/Promotional Rate." Look for low rates with no annual fee. Check these listings against CardOffers.com, which gives short, useful reviews of what customers get—costs, rewards, perks, and brief discussions of a card's pros and cons. If you need spending discipline (and don't mind paying an annual fee), choose the classic Green, Gold, or Platinum American Express card. It's useful to know that you *have* to pay the entire bill at the end of each month.

Who qualifies for the low rates you see in the ads? People who: (1) carry a reasonable amount of debt relative to their incomes—no more than 40 percent tops, including the mortgage; (2) always pay on time; (3) have at least two active accounts that have been in use for a year or more; (4) use only part of their available credit, with balances on no more than four accounts; (5) have worked at the same company and lived in the same place for a couple of years; (6) had no credit problems in the past; (7) have high credit scores—generally, 720 and up (page 266); (8) are U.S. citizens; and (9) haven't opened another credit line recently.

The last point—no new credit lately—eliminates a lot of people who think of themselves as good credit risks. Here's why: Whenever you apply for credit, the lender inquires about your payment history. That inquiry shows on your credit report. If you have just refinanced your house at one bank and applied for a new credit card at another one, your credit report will show that two lenders asked about you. The report doesn't say whether they accepted you or turned you down, only that they asked.

But that makes a low-rate lender's computer a tad suspicious. It might assume that you're suddenly loading up on credit for purposes it doesn't know about. You'll get a card but at a higher interest rate than you expected.

So you need a strategic plan for getting a low-rate card. First, pay down your current debts. Second, if your wallet is thick with cards, cancel the ones you're not using much. (Your canceled cards will still show on your credit report because they're part of your history, but the accounts should be shown as closed.) Third, let at least a year go by without applying for any new loans or accepting a higher credit limit on your remaining cards.

You may have read that you shouldn't cancel unused cards because that will lower your credit score. That's true in the short run if you're carrying a lot of debt on the cards you use regularly. But if you reduce your debt and then cancel the extras, you'll be okay—in fact, better than okay (for details, see page 268).

Why Are You So Popular?

Your mail and e-mail are full of offers from bankers begging you to take a new credit card. It's not your good looks that attract them. It's not even your income. It's your gorgeous pile of debt.

These banks buy lists of names from credit bureaus. For traditional cards, they typically want people who have no more than five or six cards already, are carrying debt on most of them, and pay their bills on time. You may be choking on your debts. You may be paying just the minimum on every card you have. You may be taking cash from one card to pay off another. That doesn't matter. As long as you're not a late payer, these banks want to reel you in. Some even go after people who have ten cards or more.

Most banks also offer a line of cards with high interest rates and low credit limits. They're marketed to people who habitually pay late (think of those fat late-payment fees!), overspenders (think of the fees for going over the credit limit!), and bankrupts. They can even get lists of these unlucky people. A certain percentage of defaults is built into the rate they charge, so that they can make money even from people who can't keep up with the bills.

Spendaholics imagine that as long as the bankers keep offering them credit, they must not be too deeply in debt. They think that the credit machine will flash *TILT* when they go too far. Not likely. Banks will happily dig you into a hole and charge you for the shovel. If you go broke, that's your lookout, not theirs.

How to Avoid Trouble!

If you don't want the credit bureaus to sell your name to credit card and other direct-marketing companies, just tell them so. Call 888-5-OPTOUT to remove your name from the major bureaus' lists for five years. It's not clear, however, that these calls are always honored. To take your name off the lists permanently, you have to write. That means hunting around on their Web sites for the special opt-out address. At this writing, here are the permanent opt-out addresses for the big three: Equifax Credit Information Services, P.O. Box 740241, Atlanta, GA 30374; Experian Consumer Services Department, 901 West Bond, Lincoln, NE 68521; and TransUnion Name Removal Option, P.O. Box 505, Woodlyn, PA 19094. You have to write to just one of these bureaus; it will spread the word to the other two.

Cards for People with Poor Credit or No Credit History

If your credit score falls below 660 or so (out of 850 tops), you probably won't be able to get a regular card even at a high interest rate. Ditto if your credit history is scant. Instead banks advertise special cards for poorer risks, and they're making a fortune at it. The worst of the issuers don't even care if you can't pay. During the months that you struggle to keep up, they extract enough money from you—in high interest rates and superhigh fees—to more than cover their losses if you eventually give up and default.

In general, people with poor credit shouldn't go looking for more debt. You're already finding it hard enough to pay your bills. But there may be reasons to have a functioning Visa or MasterCard—for example, to rent a car. If you're shopping for credit, there are three possibilities—one best, one middling, one so awful you should stay away:

The Best: A Secured Card

With secured cards, you make a cash deposit into an interest-earning savings account. In return, the bank gives you a Visa or MasterCard. The card's credit limit will typically be 100 percent of the money you've left on deposit. If you deposit $300, for example, you can charge $300 worth of goods. If you always pay on time and never go over your credit limit, you can graduate to a regular card in a year or two. At that point, the bank will return the money you put up as a security deposit, along with the interest it earned. If you don't pay on time, however, the bank will use your security deposit to collect what it's owed.

Ask your own bank or credit union about a secured card (it's sometimes offered even if not advertised). Or check CardTrak.com and CardOffers.com. In general, you'll need a certain minimum income (often $12,000 but sometimes less), a job, a verifiable address, and a phone number. There's usually no credit check. You'll probably pay 24 percent and up on unpaid balances, plus annual fees in the $30 range. Only a few banks offer secured cards, but they're the best choice if you think a card is essential and are sure you won't overspend. (If you blow this card too, your debt mess will be even worse.)

The Middling: A Prepaid Card

This is a form of debit card. You load it up with cash from your bank account (or other sources, such as Social Security) and use it wherever debit cards are accepted, including online and at ATMs. Each purchase or ATM cash withdrawal reduces the amount of money stored on the card. When it runs out, you can't buy anything more until you load up the card again. Some cards offer overdraft protection—at a price. To check your card's current balance, call the issuer or look up your account on the issuer's Web site. Some cards let you check the balance on an ATM.

Prepaid cards don't help (or hurt) your credit score because these transactions aren't reported to the major credit bureaus. They simply give you a card to flash around. If you lose the card, it's like losing cash—you're out the money. If you want to return an item bought with a prepaid card, you might get a store credit rather than cash returned to your card.

The main thing to beware is fees, which jump out at you from every side. The better cards charge maybe $10 for the setup, $5 a month, $2 for using an ATM, and assorted smaller fees. The terrible ones charge a $60 application fee, a $90 processing fee, $7 a month, $15 in a month you don't use the card, and $15 to cancel the card, in addition to incidental fees (yikes!). And there are plenty of offers in between. The high-fee cards may lure you with the possibility of a cash advance, which—if you get it—will almost certainly be smaller than advertised. Check all the offers at CardTrak.com and CardOffers.com, reading the "Terms and Conditions" to find the best.

If you have a bank account, it's cheaper by far to open a checking account and carry a Visa or MasterCard ATM/debit card.

If you can't get a bank account because of previous problems, you have three choices:

1. **Prepaid cards that let you add cash to the card** by money order, through Western Union, or by bringing cash to participating banks for loading onto your card. Some employers put wages on prepaid cards. Cards might accept Social Security payments and tax refunds too.
2. **Prepaid cards replenished with deposits at major retail outlets.** These cards may carry a Visa, MasterCard, or Discover logo.
3. **Disposable prepaid cards,** such as telephone cards, that you buy with cash and throw away when the money is gone.

As usual, it's important to read the fine print (terms and conditions). You might not be able to use your card at gas pumps (you'll pay inside the station instead), and there may be daily spending limits. Each card is different, so pay attention—especially to the fees! Choose only a card that discloses its fees *before* you fill in the application, not after.

The Awful: An Unsecured "Subprime" Card

People with poor credit may not have $300 to put up for a security deposit or may not want to. So it sounds like a terrific deal to be offered a Visa or MasterCard at a decent interest rate and with a credit limit "up to $3,000."

It's a hoax. When the card arrives, your credit limit might be only $250. And then come the fees: "program" fees, account setup fees, participation fees, annual fees. The Credit CARD Act of 2009 limits these fees to no more than 25 percent of your credit line in the first year, but even that is shocking. More fees will arrive in later years, including over-limit fees if you allow them. These subprime cards are a travesty—stay away from them. They won't help restore your credit, as the ads claim; they'll almost certainly plunge you even deeper into a hole.

Finally, *never* pay in advance to get a credit card. People with poor credit may jump at "no questions asked" offers of credit carrying fees of $100 to $200 up front. Trust me—you'll never get the card or will get a prepaid card that you have to fill up with money yourself. Advance-fee scams proliferate faster than the government can stamp them out. It's up to you to protect yourself.

Comparing Cards: What You'll Learn if You Read the Disclosure Box

Read the disclosures? Is Quinn nuts? All that stupid fine print and sentences written by Philadelphia lawyers?

I know what you mean. But if you read slowly, the sentences almost parse. The disclosures tell you pretty quickly which cards are worth getting and which are pickpockets in disguise. There's a disclosure box on the back of every credit card application and on the card's Web site (click on "Terms and Conditions" or "Prices and Terms"). Starting July 1, 2010, you'll get a new summary table, providing more disclosures about rates, penalties, and terms. Here's what to look for:

- *The interest rate.* What's the promotional rate for new buyers? What's the standard rate after the promotional period passes? The card may show several rates: a low one for top credit risks and higher ones for everyone else. Banks with variable rates will tell you how many points over the prime rate (or other rate) the bank charges. The box should also show the rate on balance transfers, cash advances, and the default rate if you don't pay on time.

- *The grace period.* Most cards give you 20 days before charging interest if you're not carrying any unpaid balances. Some give you 25. But others are cutting back to 15 days. A few have no grace period at all, charging you interest all the time on everything you buy. There's no grace period at all for cash advances or for new purchases if you're carrying forward a debt from the previous month.

- *The minimum finance charge*—the amount you have to pay even on small balances. Get rid of small balances right away.

- *The annual fee.* Convenience users seek out no-fee cards. But sometimes the fee is waived for the first year only or waived only if you charge a substantial amount.
- *Other fees.* The disclosure should lay out all your fees—for balance transfers, wire transfers, late fees, fees for going over your credit limit, and fees for taking a cash advance. Some cards charge a onetime cash advance fee plus a much higher interest rate than the standard rate that's applied to purchases. Other cards have no fee and charge the same rate for everything.
- *International transactions.* What will you be charged for using your credit card abroad? (Hint: *lots.*) But you usually get a better exchange rate than if you cash a traveler's check or exchange your dollars at a bank, a currency kiosk, or your hotel.
- *Total cost.* This one's an eye-opener. Starting July 1, 2010, your monthly bills will show, in dollars and cents, how much you've paid in interest for various types of transactions since the start of the year. You'll also get a year-to-date total for fees. When you see them added up, you might decide that credit isn't worth its cost. Anyway, that's what I hope you decide.

The Cardholder Agreement

Once you've signed up for the card, you'll get the full cardholder agreement laying out all the terms that the early disclosure didn't mention. Hardly anyone reads this agreement. But if you protest a fee or change in interest rate, expect the issuer to tell you that it's in the contract.

How to Get Your First Credit Card

Students in college used to be bombarded with credit card offers. But too many 18-year-olds were signing up for multiple cards, running up debt, paying late, and wrecking their credit histories. When they stepped out into the world, they were already thousands of dollars behind.

As a result, I used to say, "Don't take a credit card for the first couple of years. Run your life with a checking account and an ATM/debit card while you're learning how to manage money and live within your means."

Now I think differently. The Credit CARD Act of 2009 requires people under 21 to qualify for cards just like everyone else. Their credit limit is based on their income, which for most students will be low. At this writing, it's not known how the card issuers will define "income." It might include the allowance that many students get from their parents. Nevertheless, credit limits will be low, too.

Often, young people won't qualify without a cosigner. Usually, that's a parent, who's now in a position to restrict the child to a single card. Cosigners for students also have to approve any increase in the credit limit, in writing.

With controls like these, students can't get into too much trouble. So it pays for them to get a credit card early and start building a credit history. When they graduate, they'll have three or four years of credit-card and bank-account history, which will help them lease an apartment or get a car loan at a decent interest rate. (Assuming, of course, that they pay on time and don't exceed their credit limit!)

The picture is a little less clear for the parent who does the cosigning. If your child doesn't pay the bill, the delinquency shows on your credit report. If you trust the child, go ahead and sign, but ask for copies of the bills so that you can be sure they're paid. Once children are well established, they can cancel the cosigned card and get one entirely on their own. Any debt on the old card should be either paid off or transferred to the new one.

If you're not a student or can't get a cosigner, start your credit life with a checking account at a bank or S&L. When you've had a steady job and address for a few months, go to a major retailer (one that will report your payment history to a credit bureau) and apply for a charge account. At the start, you'll be given a low line of credit but that doesn't matter. Once you prove your reliability, you'll be able to charge more. Finally, apply for a Visa or MasterCard—just one. You'll pay a higher interest rate on unpaid balances than people with long credit histories do, but bide your time. Keep your credit nose clean, and apply for a second card after three or four years. At that point, you should get a better deal.

What if you're a widow or widower? You can go on using the credit cards you have already. As long as the cards were in both your names, you have a credit history of your own—even if none of the cards was in your name alone.

A Credit Card Fact Sheet

- *Your credit limit is the total amount you can borrow*—by making purchases, transferring balances from other cards, or taking cash advances. It includes fees and finance charges. Ads for cards may promise credit lines "up to $10,000," but you typically won't get anything close to that amount—first, because you're a new customer, and second, because high limits go only to people with top credit scores. As you use the card successfully, your limit will rise, probably automatically. In fact, it may rise to more than you can handle. To avoid temptation, you might tell the bank to reduce your credit line, not increase it! During the 2008 credit crunch, many lenders slashed customers' credit lines, like it or not.

If you accidentally exceed your limit, you could be charged a stiff over-limit fee and the bank might raise your interest rate. So look at your statement every month to see how much of your borrowing power you've used up. It's dangerous even to run close to your limit because a fee or interest rate charge could push you over. To maintain a good credit score, you shouldn't use more than 50 percent of the credit you have available.

Some card companies set you up for over-limit fees by refusing to raise your limit but issuing a new card instead. Now you have two cards with low limits, giving you double the chance of owing penalty fees. Don't accept the second card! It's trouble. Demand a single card and don't opt into the game of over-limit fees (page 246).

- *A few cards require that you take a cash advance when you first sign up,* so you start out with a $2,000 debt. Avoid them.

- *Having too many credit cards may prevent you from getting other loans,* even if all your payments are up to date. That's because each of your cards has a line of credit that you could borrow against at any time. A lender will ask: Could you carry your debts if you borrowed against every card to the max? If not, you'll be denied another loan or get it only at a high interest rate. How do lenders know how big your credit lines are? They check your credit report at the credit bureau.

- *Ask the issuer of your lowest-rate card how to use its credit line to pay off balances on other cards.* Some issuers will want the list of your debts and will handle the payoffs themselves. Some will accept telephone requests. Some will send you a convenience check or a pack of them. Before you act, check on the interest rate and fees.

- *You canceled the credit cards that you don't use, but have you looked to see if the cancellation took?* Some lenders keep on reporting your account as open even after you close it. There's only one way to find out: get a copy of your credit report (page 260) and look. If the card isn't shown as closed (using a designation such as "paid satisfied" or "closed by the customer"), call your former creditor and find out what it takes to get your name off its files. Then follow through in writing.

- *If you don't use a particular credit card for a year or two, the bank might yank it.* They have no interest in customers who cost them money—in this case, the expense of printing bills that say "Balance due: $0." A card cancellation, by the bank or by you, nicks your credit score, although it will build back up. If you want to keep the card, use it every six months or so.

■ *You might be offered a bank card that carries the name of your college or union or a favored charity.* My question: has the group bargained for the best deal for its members, or has it taken the best deal for itself? Most organizations think "me first." They get perhaps 0.5 percent of whatever you charge on the card, or 25 cents per transaction, or a bounty for everyone who signs up. You'll pay the price in a higher rate or fee. Accept a bank card only on competitive terms. If you want to support your college or a charity, give money directly and take a tax deduction.

■ *You are not responsible for your spouse's debts that occurred before the marriage or occurred during the marriage for purposes unrelated to it.* For example, you wouldn't have to pay if your spouse sneaked off to Las Vegas and put the trip on his or her personal credit card. But you're generally responsible for marital debts that are considered "necessaries" or purchases made by one spouse as "agent" for the other. You're also responsible if you cosigned the debt or the credit card (including the credit card used for the Vegas trip).

■ *Keep a list of all your cards (or photocopy them)* so that you can call pronto if your wallet is lost or stolen. You're liable for no more than $50 per card if it's used by a thief. Most issuers charge you nothing at all (page 279).

■ *Do you plan to pay for an ongoing service by having the company debit your bank account automatically?* Consider giving the company your credit card number instead. If there's a dispute and you cancel the service, automatic debits may take a while to stop. But you can get a credit card payment reversed by reporting it as an unauthorized charge (page 280).

■ *Don't jump at a creditor's offer to let you skip a month of payments.* All you're doing is running up extra interest charges for the month you didn't pay.

■ *If you marry and change your name, change it on your credit cards too.* Always use the same name when you apply for credit to help keep your credit history all together.

■ *If you're carrying unpaid balances, send in your payment as soon as you get the bill.* You're being charged interest every day, so the sooner you pay, the less your debt costs.

■ *You think you're paying the stated rate on your credit card?* Guess again. After monthly compounding, an 18 percent card actually costs you 19.65 percent. You might also have no grace period and daily instead of monthly compounding. All this raises your effective rate.

■ *Don't buy credit card life insurance to pay off the balance if you die unless your health is so poor that it's the only coverage you can get.* These policies are outrageously expensive for the benefit you receive. Ditto credit card disability and unemployment insurance, which offer very limited protection.

- *When you pay with a Visa, MasterCard, or American Express card, you shouldn't have to present any identification.* The merchant will check the validity of the card electronically or by telephone and check the signature on the card against the way you sign the bill. You can be asked for ID if you've forgotten to sign your card or asked for your address if you order by telephone. Otherwise you shouldn't have to prove anything. The card companies all guarantee payment on cards that have been properly checked.

At any rate, those are the rules. Some merchants do check, and it's hard to override them. There are exceptions for suspicious circumstances, which some merchants stretch. Ill-trained bank card personnel may tell you, erroneously, that merchants can do whatever they want. If a merchant insisted on your ID, report the incident to your card's customer service center. With Discover Card, however, merchants can check IDs at will.

- *You're running some risks if you tell your credit card company to bill you electronically instead of by snail mail.* You'll get an e-mail notice. Still, you might forget the bill is there and neglect to pay it on time. You might miss important messages about usage and fees. Bills are usually archived for only a few months, so you can't check on old transactions unless you print out paper copies each time or save the bills on your computer. None of this may trouble you. But think about it before giving up that monthly paper bill that comes in the mail.

- *Three good sites with more information on credit cards and other issues:* Consumer Action (www.consumer-action.org), Consumer Federation of America (CFA) (www.consumerfed.org), and the Consumer Information section of the Federal Trade Commission (FTC) Web site (www.ftc.gov). For books, I'm especially fond of *The Ultimate Credit Handbook* by the consumer debt expert Gerri Detweiler (she answers consumer question on her blog, at www.gerridetweiler .blogspot.com).

- *Here's a useful tip from a reader:* "While on a trip, I started having trouble with my ATM card. At first it worked erratically in the ATM machines, then not at all. It turned out that I had a magnetic clasp on my billfold, which demagnetized my card. I had never heard of that." Neither had I, but now all the other readers will!

What Happens if You Don't Pay Your Bills on Time?

Every lender has different rules for handling delinquents, but here are some general answers.

- *What if I pay my credit cards late?* Just one late payment will cost you a fee in the $35 to $40 range. It nicks your credit score but won't affect your access to decent cards. Two or more add a fee each time and can raise the interest rate on your unpaid balances to 30 or 40 percent. Late payments show on your credit history. If you apply for a mortgage, the lender may demand an explanation for any late payment within the past two years.

■ *What if I miss a payment?* After the first month, you'll get a letter or phone call from the bank. At that point, or one month later, your interest rate will increase. If you still don't pay, your charge privileges will be suspended. New cards are suspended more quickly than older ones. If you try to use the card, it will be rejected at the cash register.

■ *Will the lender restructure my debt?* Sometimes, if your problem appears to be temporary and not of your making. Banks understand sudden unemployment but have no sympathy for people who overspend. If you think your cash shortage won't last long, talk to the bank before you become unable to make the minimum payment. You might be offered lower payments, or no payments, for a few months. If you're truly desperate, the bank might settle for less—say, 50 or 70 cents on the dollar for unsecured credit. Skipped payments are usually reported to the credit bureaus, but at least you won't be dunned. Banks don't always offer a hand. Still, you might as well ask.

■ *If my credit card is suspended, can I get it back?* Usually yes, as long as you pay enough to bring your card up to date. But you'll pay a much higher interest rate. If you rack up two or three 60-day payment gaps or don't pay for three months or more, your account will probably be revoked. You might still recover your card by making back payments. But the bank may reduce your credit limit, perhaps leaving you too little credit for business travel. Your slow payments or suspension will show on your credit report.

After three to six months of skipped payments (each bank has its own rules), your account will be reported to the credit bureau as a charge-off—meaning no-pay. Even if you eventually repay, that lender is unlikely to restore your card. When you think you can pass a credit review, go to a different lender.

■ *Why bother repaying if I already have a charge-off on my credit record?* You can't remove this credit blot by bringing your account up to date. It will stay there for seven years, warning other creditors to beware. But the record will also show if you eventually paid (check your credit report to be sure). Making payments gives you a better shot at new credit than if you let the delinquency stand.

■ *Will the lender sue?* That depends on how much you owe, what assets you have, and where you live. Some states make it easier than others for a creditor to win a lawsuit and collect. The cost of filing a suit is also an issue; one county might charge $60 and another $160. One bank might sue for as little as $1,000 in a procreditor state if you have assets and the cost of the lawsuit is less than it hopes to recoup. At another bank, the lawsuit trigger might be $2,500. More likely, your account will be sold to a collection agency that will drive you nuts with dunning calls.

■ *Can I keep the one or two credit cards that are up to date even though I've stopped paying others?* Usually, yes—but not on the same terms. Most lenders check their customers' credit reports every month, every quarter, or when a card is renewed. If you're delinquent on other bills, it will increase your interest rate. Some banks will suspend your card even though you're still making payments on time. You probably won't get your charge privileges back until you bring all your debts up to date.

■ *If my credit cards are taken away, what should I do?* Start repaying past debts, perhaps through a local office of the Consumer Credit Counseling Service (for an office near you, call 800-355-2227). The initial consultation is free. For more on counseling services, see page 287.

Your Credit Report

All the credit card companies, finance companies, and major retailers report to at least one of the three major credit bureaus: Experian, Equifax, and Trans-Union. They send data once a month showing who paid bills on time and who didn't. They also collect information from bankruptcy courts and debt collection services. The three bureaus operate separately, so they may not all have exactly the same data. Here's what shows up on a typical credit report:

1. Your name and the variations you've used on credit applications (such as "Hallee Jones" and "Hallee M. Jones"; then, after marriage, "Hallee Smith"), current and previous addresses, Social Security number, driver's license number and the state where it was issued, year of birth, current and previous employers (this list may not be complete), and the name of your spouse if you have one.

2. Your bank cards, retail charge accounts, installment loans, home equity lines, first mortgage, and when each account was opened. Also, the type of loan—revolving, education, auto.

3. Whether your last payment to each creditor was on time or late and, if late, by how much. (Creditors pay more attention to the past two years than to your earlier history.)

4. Current account balances, the highest amount that you're allowed to charge on each line, and the largest amount that you've ever owed to that particular creditor.

5. The status of your account—current, past due, or charge-off.

6. The amount that's past due.

7. The latest you ever paid on that account and how many times you've been delinquent.

8. Any special problems with your account—for example, that goods were repossessed or that a bill collector had to be called in.

9. Court actions such as liens, judgments awarded to creditors, bankruptcies, foreclosures, wage attachments, accounts in collection, and delinquent child support payments being tracked by the state.

10. Your legal relationship to the account: Are you jointly responsible? Individually responsible? A cosigner? Who else is responsible for paying?

11. Past accounts paid in full but now closed and closed accounts that were not paid in full.

12. Whether you've put a statement on the record in a dispute with the lender.

13. The names of the companies that have looked at your account. Your copy of the report includes companies that sent you promotional mailings in the past year, current creditors that are monitoring your report, companies that vetted your report for employment purposes during the past two years, and companies checking you out because you solicited credit. (The companies checking you for credit see only the inquiries from other potential credit granters made in the past two years.)

On the personal side, credit bureaus know only what you've put on the application when you requested credit. It reports what you do for a living but not how much money you make. It doesn't know if you're divorced or have nine kids or drink or have an arrest record or your age or what color you are or what interest rate you're paying on other cards. It does not make credit decisions. It simply reports your payment history to lenders who are thinking about giving you money. The lenders make their own judgments about whether to take you on. One lender may love you and give you a huge credit line; another one may turn you down. If you misrepresented something on your credit application, that will show up on your credit report too.

Most people have good credit. All you need is a steady job with a history of paying bills on time. If you tend to pay late, the interest rate on your unpaid balances will rise, but you won't be kicked out of the credit system. Lenders get rich on people who pay late! It's not smart to apply for new credit at a time when you're behind. But once you've caught up for a couple of years, you should be able to get new credit on decent terms.

Here are the few things that may cause a lender to turn you down for a regular card:

- You already have a lot of credit cards, with large credit lines and a lot of debt.
- You had to be chased for payment by a collection agency.
- You were sued for money owed.
- There's a lien on your property.
- A creditor closed one of your accounts.
- You went bankrupt.
- You have been applying for a lot of credit lately. (Maybe you're in trouble? Maybe you're going to charge up a storm and go bankrupt?)

None of these black marks means that you won't get a card at all. Subprime lenders stand ready to give you a card that carries outrageous fees and may get you even deeper in debt (page 252). Best advice: Don't look for more credit when you're already in trouble. Clean up past problems so that you can start over on reasonable terms.

Negative credit information, including the history of closed accounts, stays in your file for 7 years. Positive information can be reported indefinitely. *Wage earner plans* (Chapter 13 under the bankruptcy code, page 289) may be wiped out after 7 years, but straight bankruptcies will weigh down your record for up to 10 years. Bankruptcies go onto your credit report shortly after you file and will stay there even if you change your mind.

You should check your credit report from time to time to be sure it's accurate. Checkups also alert you to identity theft. Reports are available free from AnnualCreditReport.com (www.annualcreditreport.com)—one a year, from each of the three major bureaus. You can get three at once; alternatively, order from one bureau in January, another in May, and the third in September, so you'll be current all year. Each credit bureau also offers its own "free" report, but only if you buy other services, such as your credit score (see below) or a pricey monitoring service ($9 to $15 a month) to tell you when notable changes occur in your report or score. In general, monitoring isn't worth it because new accounts aren't entered right away. Monitors don't know if new purchases were made by you or a thief, nor can they tell you whether your Social Security number is being used by someone with a similar name. Newer services troll the Internet to hunt for misused Social Security numbers, but it's not clear how effective they are. If you've suffered identity theft or worry about it, forget about monitoring. Instead add fraud alerts to your accounts or freeze your access to credit (page 272). And watch for changes yourself on your free reports.

You also get a free report if you ask for it within 60 days of being turned down for credit, an apartment, insurance, or a job based on something the report says. The rejection letter will tell you where to write or call. Free reports can also go to victims of fraud; people on welfare; and unemployed people who are looking for work.

Married people should ask for reports listed under their personal names and Social Security numbers (Elias Smith and Laurie Smith, not Mr. and Mrs. Elias Smith). If you use just one name (the Mr. and Mrs.), you'll get only one credit report, so lenders won't be looking at both of you. There's no such thing as a joint report. Transactions arising from joint accounts are reported twice, once to the husband's account, once to the wife's. Note that you cannot get your spouse's history, only your own.

Your report will come with a form for reporting errors. If you find one, note it on the form, make a copy, and mail the original back to the credit bureau. The bureau must check the disputed information with the creditor. If it can't be verified within a reasonable time (around 25 days), it should be deleted. Request a report from all three major bureaus (Equifax, Experian, TransUnion); they may share the identical mistake.

Unfortunately, your creditor might not bother to check the facts. Its "investigation" may merely verify that its records match what the credit bureau shows. You'll have to go mano a mano with the creditor, presenting evidence that you're right. Once you've proven your case, the creditor will send the credit bureau a correction. The credit bureau will also accept certain evidence from you directly—for example, canceled checks proving that a debt was paid or a receipt showing that a disputed item was indeed returned.

When your name is cleared, check your report at each of the three major credit bureaus, and ask those bureaus to send fresh reports to the smaller bureaus they sell information to. Sometimes this job is only a headache. Sometimes it's a nightmare.

If any correction is made in your credit report, the credit bureau has to send a corrected copy to any creditor who received it in the past six months and any employer who received it within the past two years.

If you find a mistake on one credit report, get your free reports from the other two bureaus too. You might have a file in each, and they don't always share corrections.

You can't sue a creditor for making a mistake. Lawsuits are possible, however, if the creditor doesn't correct a mistake or reinserts erroneous data in your file. Creditors also have to report, and your credit history has to show, when an account is in dispute and if you closed an account voluntarily. If you need a lawyer, look for one who's familiar with the complex credit laws. One source: the National Association of Consumer Advocates (NACA) (www.naca.net).

Why It's Important to Fix Mistakes

Nowadays, even minor errors can make a difference. They won't prevent you from getting credit but may increase the interest rate you're charged. Take a single, erroneous "slow-pay" report. That might raise your credit card rate from 12 percent to 19 percent. A major mistake, such as showing a tax lien against you that belongs to someone else of the same name, may cut you off from credit during the months it takes to straighten out the mess.

How You Can Help Prevent Mistakes

1. Always use the same version of your name when applying for credit: say, Dolly P. Green, never using Dolly Green, Dolly Patricia Green, or D. P. Green.
2. Always list your past addresses so the credit bureau can keep the links together.
3. If you're a Jr. or a II or III, always include that fact, so your report won't be confused with that of someone else in your family.
4. Always give your Social Security number.

Six Special Reasons to Check Your Credit Report

1. You are applying for an important loan, like a mortgage. An inaccurate credit history might keep you from getting it or raise your interest rate.

2. You are separating from your spouse and want his or her new transactions off your personal credit record.

Write to all your creditors, closing joint accounts and asking for a new account in your name alone (tell your spouse you're doing it so that he or she can write for a personal card at the same time; it's vindictive to leave a spouse with an invalid card). Three months later, get a copy of your credit report. It should show your joint accounts as closed *by the consumer* (not closed by the creditor). If it doesn't, tell each of the bureaus that the joint accounts are listed in error. At the same time, go back to the creditors and demand a correction.

The closed accounts will remain on your report as part of your credit history. You're both still responsible for any debt you contracted jointly. If neither of you pays, the blot will show up on both your reports. For this reason, it's safer to move all joint debt to separate cards.

3. You've paid off a court judgment against you for money owed. Your credit report may carry the judgment. You want to be sure that the record shows the judgment paid.

4. You've had a dispute with a store and refused to pay a bill. You and the store cannot reach agreement, so you're reported as delinquent.

You are entitled to put a 100-word explanation into your credit report. Call each of the three bureaus in case they all have files on you. The report will summarize your side of the story or list the type of dispute by code number. Warning: This procedure may help in face-to-face credit situations—say, if you've applied for a mortgage or a personal loan and can tell the lender more about the dispute. But if you apply for a credit card and are checked by computer, your explanation will normally be ignored. If the issue is resolved, the adverse data has been removed, or seven years have passed, be sure to remove the explanation.

5. You have been harmed (turned down for credit, rejected for insurance or a job) based on information in a credit report. The lender has to tell you the name and address of the bureau it used. That bureau will send you a free copy of your report as long as you ask for it within 60 days, plus the names of everyone who got the report in the past 6 months, plus the form for challenging erroneous information.

6. You had a dispute with a lender over whether a bill had been paid, and the dispute was resolved. It's important to be sure that the bill no longer shows on your credit report. Sometimes lenders don't remove the item and sell it to a debt collection service. Your credit score will plunge and you'll be dunned endlessly for money you don't owe. Check, check, and recheck at all three bureaus until your report is clean.

Your Credit Score

Lenders use computer models to identify the borrowers who are most likely to repay their debts on time. We all get points for the various items shown on our credit reports, such as how long we've used credit cards, how often we pay on time, and how much we owe. Certain lenders may add other items, such as how long we've been at our current job. The total of all our points is called a credit score.

The most commonly used credit scores today, computed by a company called Fair Isaac, are known as FICO scores. You have three FICO scores, computed from your credit history at each of the three major credit bureaus. They're similar, so knowing one FICO is usually enough. The three bureaus also advertise scores that they have developed themselves, but they're not worth buying. Creditors don't use them; they use only FICOs.

What's a good score? That's something lenders decide for themselves, but in general a top FICO would be 740 or higher (out of 850). In the high 600s, you can still get a conventional mortgage or credit card, although at a price. Below 620, you're probably subprime, with poor credit options. Below 550 . . . well, you don't want to go there. Interest rates and fees are lowest for those with the highest scores and rise as your score drops.

Scores change as new information arrives each month. If you were running at 740 and then put the cost of new living room furniture on your card, the added debt will drop your score a few points, but normally not by enough to put you into a different category of risk. As you pay off that debt, your score will rise. Each lender chooses a cutoff score for applicants, depending on the kinds of customers it wants. You're the ideal applicant everywhere if:

- *You have held your job for a while.* (Lenders assume that you aren't going to be fired, although that's hardly a certainty anymore.)
- *You own your home.* (Owners are less transient than renters.)
- *You've lived in your home or rented your current apartment for a while* (proving that you can handle the payments).
- *You hold just a few credit cards and always pay on time.*
- *You carry balances on your card rather than paying in full each month* (card companies love debtors best). But the balances rarely exceed 30 percent of your available credit and usually run lower than that.
- *You have reasonable debts and credit lines compared with your income.* (A high income isn't required, just evidence that you live within your means or not far beyond it.)
- *You haven't recently applied for other credit or run up major new debts* on the cards you have.
- *You carry more bank cards than department store or retail cards.*
- *You've led a spotless credit life:* no delinquencies, no charge-offs, no liens, no bankruptcy.
- *You work in a field considered steady.* Teachers are more desirable than farm owners because farms can go bust; doctors are more desirable than lawyers because lawyers worry less about being sued.

It's crucial that your credit report be accurate, because it's the basis of your scores. An error can affect the interest rate you'll have to pay. Check your report for things such as debts you've repaid that still show as open or accounts belonging to an ex-spouse.

If you've just moved, keep on using the bank cards you have already. This isn't the moment to apply for a card with a lower rate. Don't ask for new credit (except, perhaps, a department store charge card) until you have been at your new job and new address for a year.

If you're turned down for credit, lenders have to say why. The rejection letter might list several items you scored low on. None is the deciding factor, and some may be incomprehensible (how would you interpret the following explanation: "Recently active or lack of bank, retail, or finance accounts"?). You're entitled to a free credit report from the bureaus the lender relied on, so you can check them for accuracy. If just one of your low-scoring items had been higher, it might have lifted you above the line.

Don't Apply for a Lot of Credit All at Once

Every time a potential lender pulls your credit history, that inquiry shows on your record. Some lenders automatically turn down anyone with three or four inquiries—say, for a mortgage and new credit cards—over a short period of time. Apply for just one card, and build a good credit history on it. Then apply for a second (following the strategy of owning two different types of cards—page 243). After that, get another card only if it's better than one you already have. Don't take cards you won't use or keep too many cards.

There's one exception to the inquiry rule: for people rate shopping for a mortgage or auto loan. All the inquiries you make within a 14-day period will count as just one application, so do your shopping all at once.

How to Improve Your Credit Score

Check your score a year before applying for an important loan such as a first mortgage. Improving it by just a few points might speed the approval process and reduce your interest rate by a half percent or more. Here's how to do it.

- *Check your credit report for errors* that might have lowered your score.
- *Pay down the high balances on your cards.* This alone can improve your score pretty fast. Shifting balances from one card to another doesn't help. Creditors look at your total debt.
- *Pay all bills as soon as they come in,* to be sure that none slips past its due date.
- *Pay off back bills;* they don't go away.
- *Pay more than the minimum* on your accounts.
- *Pay your balances in full each month.* It's a myth that scores are higher for people who carry debt (although credit card issuers might solicit perennial debtors, for the interest revenue they bring in).
- *Two cards are better than one.* If you own just one, your credit history may be too thin.

- *Don't open new accounts* (except to get that second card).
- *Never go over* your credit limit.
- *If you have loans from a credit union, ask if it reports your payment history to all three credit bureaus.* Many of them don't. If yours isn't reporting, and you're paying on time, that good behavior won't show on your record. If your credit union doesn't report, you'll need credit cards or loans from another source to build a credit history.
- *Increase your credit limit.* By increasing your limit, your current debt becomes a smaller percentage of the total credit available to you. That raises your score. But if you spend to that higher limit, your score will tumble again—*and* you'll have a bigger debt.
- *Borrow from banks rather than finance companies.* Customers of finance companies are generally thought to be slightly poorer risks.
- *Use credit cards instead of debit cards* and pay off the balance every month.
- *Be sure that the credit bureau removes any adverse information that's older than 7 years and bankruptcies older than 10 years.* This should happen automatically, but sometimes credit bureaus slip up.
- *Avoid cards that don't report your credit limit to the credit bureaus.* In cases like this, scorers will treat your highest balance as your limit. That makes it look as if you've run up a lot of debt on that card, hence reducing your score. At this writing, Capital One is the largest issuer that doesn't report credit limits.
- *Get separate credit cards for any business you run.* Business charges generally aren't reported on your personal credit history.
- *Canceling unused cards won't raise your credit score.* In fact, it will lower the score if you don't reduce your other credit card debts. (That's because having fewer cards increases the ratio of your debt to your open credit lines.) Your score shouldn't change, however, if you cancel cards and substantially reduce your outstanding debt at the same time. It you have lots of cards, reducing their number will improve your credit standing, over time.
- *Never cancel your oldest card, and use it now and then to keep it current.* Longtime accounts mark you as an experienced user of credit, which lenders like.
- *Become an "authorized user" on someone else's card.* By sharing the card, you share its credit history although you don't get the same credit score. Authorized users are typically teenagers or young adults added to a parent's card, or a new spouse added to the other's account.

Don't Give a Nickel to a "Credit Repair" Firm

Their ads imply that they can wave a wand over a bad credit history and bring you out smelling like a rose. They can't. If there are errors in your record, you can fix them yourself. True information cannot legally be removed.

Some credit repairers harass credit bureaus, challenging even items that are correct. Their strategy is to question more items in your record than the bureau can verify within the time limit, so it will have to expunge derogatory facts. But credit bureaus will resist. They don't have to follow up on frivolous challenges. They might not deal with a particular credit clinic at all. By law, clinics aren't allowed to charge you until they've delivered the goods. If you pay up front, you're waving bye-bye to your cash.

New Uses for Your Credit Score

When you get instant credit at a department store or instant approval for an auto loan, the lender is dialing up your credit score. It's increasingly being used to judge mortgage applications, approve small-business loans, and check on job applicants. A number of insurers check a similar, credit-based score before selling you a homeowners or auto policy (it predicts how likely you are to cost your insurer more in claims than you pay in premiums). Who knows where scoring will spread next? More than ever, you need to keep your nose clean and periodically check the accuracy of your credit report.

Some lenders mine your credit accounts to see where you've been spending money. A 2008 lawsuit filed by the Federal Trade Commission charged that a particular subprime card issuer lowered credit lines for customers who used their cards to pay tire-retreading shops, massage parlors, billiard halls, and marriage counselors. The FTC didn't object to the fact that the issuer was monitoring its customers' behavior—only that it didn't tell them so. As data mining grows more common, more scoring systems may peek into your private life. It's an unsettling trend.

How to Buy Your Credit Score

Unlike credit reports, FICO credit scores aren't free. You have to buy them, and the selling organizations try to get you to purchase much more besides. At this writing, one FICO score from Equifax or TransUnion costs $15.95 from myFICO (www.myfico.com). Experian sells its own report for $15 at www.experian.com but it's not the FICO score that lenders use. All three credit bureaus sell a "3-in-1" score, which packages their credit scores with pricy add-ons such as debt analysis, credit monitoring services, and your current credit report (they think you don't know that you can get your credit report free). For general purposes, one FICO is enough. Any correction you make is supposed to be shared with the other bureaus. Buy all three FICOs only if you want to be sure that all three reports are error free before you apply for a mortgage or other important loan.

As for the credit-monitoring services, they tell you whether new accounts have been opened in your name. Cost at this writing: $9 or $10 a month. That's pretty pricey. If your identity has been stolen, a service may get you that information a little sooner than you'll discover it yourself, but the damage is already being done. Besides, a lot of ID theft comes from using numbers stolen from your current cards, not by opening new accounts. Those worried about ID theft would do better to freeze their accounts, so that no new loans or cards can be taken without your personal say-so (page 272).

Scores for People with No or Little Traditional Credit History—Immigrants in Particular

FICO offers lenders an Expansion FICO score that gleans information from payday lenders (they give high-interest loans against your next paycheck), rent-to-own stores, and companies with files on people who bounce checks. If you've used these banking and buying services and handled them responsibly, your history will help you get a traditional loan or credit card. But if you paid late or are constantly in debt to payday lenders, your credit will go down the tubes. In general, payday loans and rent-to-own services charge such high interest rates that you shouldn't use them at all. Instead establish a bank account and try for a retail credit card or gasoline card to build a traditional credit history. Getting an auto loan helps too.

The Expansion FICO score also reports data from Payment Reporting Builds Credit (www.prbc.com), a site that gathers data principally on rental payments but also on other recurring bills that aren't reported to the traditional credit bureaus. You have to sign up to be part of PRBC.

Investigative Reports

When you apply for a big life insurance policy, the insurer wants to know more than whether you pay your bills. It wonders whether you've told the truth about where you work, whether you've ever been caught driving drunk, and whether your hobby is skydiving. So it will turn to one of the bureaus that specialize in gathering personal information. Some employers do the same. You give permission for the investigation when you sign the insurance or job application form.

Who is the chief source of information for this type of report? Usually you. The investigator calls you up and asks you some questions. Your neighbors may also be called, or a former employer. The interviewer has to identify himself and his purpose. Before answering, write down the interviewer's name and get a place to call to check up on him.

These reports are not kept very long because the information goes stale. They may be junked after just 90 days (although they'll stay in storage for six months, in case a consumer requests disclosure). If you're turned down for insurance or charged more than the basic rate, based on information in an investigative report, you have a right to see and challenge it. The bureau can withhold just two things: (1) the names of the people who gave the information and (2) the nature of any medical information that may have been given directly to the insurer or potential employer without being copied into the bureau's files.

The Credit Nightmare: Identity Theft

Identity thieves masquerade as you. They get your name, address, and other identifying information, which is available from dozens of legal and illegal sources. Then they open fraudulent accounts in your name or change the address on your credit cards and take over accounts you already have. They run up huge bills and leave you with the mess. Creditors may not believe you when you say that you didn't make those purchases. Bill collectors may dun you. Liens may pile up on your property. Because of your apparent debts, you may lose your access to credit, be rejected for jobs and apartments, even be subject to arrest.

One way the thieves operate is to steal credit card offers from your mailbox or place of business. They apply in your name but with a different address. The credit card and all subsequent statements will be sent to that false address. They sometimes get a card even if they give a wrong Social Security number. You'll know nothing about it until you get the first dunning phone call. How to avoid this? Get your name off the marketing lists that credit bureaus sell (go to www.optoutprescreen.com or call 888-5OPTOUT).

There's a hitch: you can take your name off only the lists drawn from personal credit information, which are sold for credit card solicitations. Credit bureaus can continue to sell so-called header information (the identifying items at the top, or head, of your credit report, such as name, address, and even Social Security number), whether you approve or not.

Another way thieves operate is to "phish" for data. You may get an e-mail message, apparently from your bank, broker, or other financial company, asking you to update your records. It might even tell you there was a break-in and that—for safety's sake—you must confirm your personal information. The site looks like the one you normally do business with. If you provide the information, however—bank account number, credit card number, Social Security number— it goes right into the hands of crooks. How to avoid this? *Never* provide personal information in response to an unsolicited Web or telephone request. True financial institutions don't ask.

How else can thieves get you? By stealing your wallet and hoping it contains your ATM PIN number and Social Security card. By hacking into your computer if you do online banking in a wireless hot spot. By breaking into a large computer—say, at companies that process credit cards, retailers, universities, or the federal government—and stealing millions of numbers at a time. By buying data from careless credit bureaus. By bribing employees who have access to data. And that's just a start. No matter how careful you are personally, you're potentially at risk from companies and institutions that handle your information. Your mother's maiden name and your Social Security number may already be circulating on the Internet.

Does online banking increase the risk of identity theft? Only if you use your computer in wireless hot spots where a hacker can grab your passwords. Otherwise bank links are generally safe. If a crooked employee lifts money from your account, the bank will make good. Consider receiving your bank statements by Web rather than by mail, since thieves can raid mailboxes.

Does buying goods online increase your risk? Possibly, if you buy from a "shop" that turns out to be a front for collecting personal data. But stick with well-known companies and you'll be reasonably safe. Besides, you can't save yourself by ordering only by phone or even by going into stores. All credit card data will probably be stored in a central place. A successful hacker can grab the numbers, no matter how you purchased the goods.

How to Prevent Identity Theft

1. Put a security freeze on your credit account—the surest protection I know. It prevents anyone (you included) from opening new accounts in your name without your say-so. If you want a new account yourself, just contact the credit bureau and lift the freeze temporarily.

The rules on freezing your reports vary according to state law. Check your state at FinancialPrivacyNow.org, a site run by Consumers Union. If your state has no law, you'll be subject to the credit bureaus' rules. The bureaus can charge up to $10 for imposing the freeze and another $10 for lifting it (some states cap the fees at $5 or less). A freeze might be free if you've been a victim of identity theft. To prove it, however, you'll have to provide a police report showing that you made a formal complaint.

The credit bureaus require that you ask for the freeze by mail. To unfreeze your account temporarily, you'll need to call or make an online request using a special PIN number that the bureau sent. At this writing, the process may take up to three days, so if you plan to apply for a loan or open a new credit card account, call the bureaus in advance. Some states are passing "quick thaw" laws requiring bureaus to take just 15 minutes to unfreeze accounts.

You may not be able to use a debit card to rent a car or pay for a hotel room if you freeze your reports. But a credit card will work.

To set up a security freeze, check each bureau's Web site (by typing "security freeze" into its search engine) to see what information they want. They won't accept you if you miss one little thing. Here's where to write:

Equifax Security Freeze
P.O. Box 105788
Atlanta, GA 30348

Experian
P.O. Box 9554
Allen, TX 75013

TransUnion
Fraud Victim Assistance Department
P.O. Box 6790
Fullerton, CA 92834

One chink in this armor: A security freeze stops thieves only from opening new accounts in your name. They can still steal the numbers on cards you own already and run up bills.

2. Don't carry critical information, such as your PIN, in your wallet. If the wallet is stolen, close your credit card account immediately. If there were checks in your wallet, close your bank accounts too. Call any one of the three credit bureaus and put a "fraud alert" on your account (Equifax: 800-525-6285;

Experian: 888-397-3742; TransUnion: 800-680-7289; the bureau you call is supposed to notify the other two). Fraud alerts last for 90 days. During that time, creditors are supposed to verify your identity personally before opening new accounts, and the credit bureau is not allowed to sell your personal information. You're also entitled to a free credit report from each of the bureaus (but you have to ask for it).

3. Ask that your credit reports show only the last four digits of your Social Security number. The credit bureaus are required to comply.

4. Don't give out personal information to people who call or who send apparently "official" e-mail notices. If you did so accidentally, call the credit bureaus and impose a fraud alert.

5. Don't store your financial passwords in your computer, especially if it's a laptop that you carry around.

6. Shred or tear up financial records before throwing them out.

7. Check your credit report regularly. This won't prevent theft but can catch it before it goes too far.

8. If a company informs you that its data bank has been breached and offers to monitor your credit report, accept (as long as you don't have to pay). Most breaches don't result in identity theft, but you never know. Freeze your accounts!

What to Do if You're a Victim

1. Tell the credit bureaus to impose an instant fraud alert, take your name off marketing lists, and send you your free credit reports. Check all your transactions and accounts and notify the bureau, in writing, which ones aren't yours. Check that the bureau has your correct name, address, and Social Security number. Close all accounts that have been tampered with.

2. If you live in a state that allows it, freeze your accounts. If not, tell the bureaus that you want a long-term (seven-year) fraud alert. For this you'll need a police report.

3. Report the thefts to the police and get an official identity theft report. Some police departments may try to brush you off, but persist. You often need that report to start the process of clearing your name. If the local police won't comply, try the state police.

4. File an ID Theft Affidavit with the Federal Trade Commission (www.consumer.gov/idtheft or 877-438-4338) if new and unauthorized accounts have been opened in your name. The affidavit can be included in the police report. You should also send copies to the three credit bureaus and each of your creditors, along with the statement of rights that the FTC provides. Phony accounts shouldn't show on your credit report while they're being investigated, and bill collectors aren't allowed to dun you.

5. Ask your creditors what you have to do to get the phony accounts or unauthorized charges off your record. Follow up with a dated letter (certified mail, return receipt requested) saying that you're a victim of identity theft and enclosing copies of the proof the creditor wants. Include a copy of the police identity theft report and the ID Theft Affidavit you filed with the FTC. The affidavit includes a list of the creditor's obligations; among other things, it has to stop reporting phony accounts to credit bureaus while the dispute is being investigated. Keep copies of everything you send. Keep a list of the names and phone numbers of everyone you speak with and the date you called. This will be a long campaign.

6. Call the courthouses that have reported cases against the fake you, and follow up with letters. This will be an even longer campaign.

7. Don't cancel credit cards that haven't been affected. It will be hard to get new credit as long as your reputation is under a cloud.

8. For expert guidance, check the FTC's identity theft Web site (www .ftc.gov/bcp/edu/microsites/idtheft). It includes sample letters to send to police departments, creditors, and credit bureaus, information about your rights, and action plans.

Retail Debit Cards

Almost everyone carries a retail debit card today. It's your ATM (automated teller machine) card with a Visa or MasterCard logo attached. Your bank might call it a cash card, pocket check, check card, convenience card, or similar name. Paying by debit is the electronic equivalent of writing a check, so you're effectively paying cash. In an ATM, the card "debits"—withdraws—money from your bank account. When used for a retail purchase, the card authorizes the bank to pay the bill from your account immediately. You can pay in one of two ways:

1. You slip the card into a terminal. After the clerk adds up your purchases, you punch in your personal identification number (PIN) and zap the payment out of your account. You can ask for more money than you owe; the clerk will give you the overage in cash.

2. You use the card at a store or restaurant anywhere in the world that accepts Visa or MasterCard credit cards. There are no terminals and no PINs; you simply sign for the purchase. When it reaches your bank, it registers as a debit.

A cash management account at a major stockbrokerage house also provides a debit card. Your account presumably contains cash waiting to be invested or parked there for convenience. If you use the debit card to make a purchase, payment is made from the money fund account.

Some consumers don't use their debit cards except at ATMs. They prefer to put down credit cards and pay by the end of the month, before running up any interest charges. But for people struggling to get their spending under control, debiting helps limit impulse buying.

Every time you use your debit card, enter the amount into your check register to keep track of how much cash you have left. Or check your balance online.

Debit Rewards Cards

Many debit cards now include rewards points for airline miles or catalog purchases. They're typically not as generous as those given by credit cards but at least offer a little something back. Some users, however, are losing their points because they don't know how to collect. Here's what you need to do:

At terminals where you enter your PIN, the screen asks you to tap either "debit" or "credit." If you tap debit—the logical thing to do—you do *not* get rewards points! You have to tap credit so the transaction runs through the credit card system; that's the only system that handles points. Your transaction will still be handled as a debit when it reaches your bank, but now your rewards will be registered too.

You face no complication when you sign for a purchase without entering your PIN. In that case, the points come automatically.

When You'd Use a Debit Card

1. **You're swearing off credit cards but want the convenience of paying with plastic.**

2. **You don't want to carry a lot of cash.**

3. **You don't want to bother carrying your checkbook or hauling out identification to get your check approved.**

4. **You don't want to run the risk of paying interest on your purchases,** as you might if you paid with a credit card and couldn't cover the full bill at the end of the month.

5. **You want a plastic way of making small purchases without adding them to your credit card and triggering extra interest** that month.

6. **You're learning financial discipline.** Debit cards encourage you not to

spend more money than you have in the bank. You can add overdraft protection—loans to cover your purchases if you overdraw. But psychologically, you'll hate to see those loans on your balance sheet and will hasten to pay them off.

What about the float? When you write a check, you imagine that you have a couple of days before it clears, during which time your funds could still earn interest. Unfortunately, your imagination has run away with you. That float is gone at major stores. They can "cash" a check immediately by sending your bank the information on your check electronically. You're asked to sign a receipt, and the store will hand back your check, noting that it has been paid. You might as well use your debit card.

The Downside of Using Debit Cards

1. More banks are adding fees to certain types of transactions. If you swipe your card, press "debit," and enter a PIN, you might be charged 10 cents to $1.50 each time. There's usually no fee, however, if you swipe your card, press "credit," and sign for the transaction—so always take this approach. Your purchase will still be handled as a debit, and you've saved some money.

2. There's less theft protection with debit cards. If a thief steals your credit card, the law says that you generally can't be forced to pay any more than $50 of the bill. Most banks waive even that small penalty. No such law protects people whose debit cards are stolen and used for retail purchases. As a practical matter, however, both MasterCard and Visa say they'll treat you the same as their credit card holders if your account is in good standing. That means you shouldn't be charged for transactions where the thief signed for the purchase or used your card on the Internet. (For more on your legal rights, see page 279.)

3. MasterCard and Visa protect only Internet or signature transactions. If a thief uses your PIN—for example, to withdraw money from your account at an ATM—it's up to the bank to make you whole. You have to explain to the bank how your card might have been misappropriated—maybe because you lost your wallet or used your card in an ATM that had a funny look (some thieves install "card skimmers" over regular ATMs, especially abroad; the skimmers read your card number and PIN). But you might not know how the theft happened if someone stole your numbers by looking over your shoulder while you were at the ATM. The bank is supposed to assume you're telling the truth about the loss, unless it can prove otherwise. If the bank resists, send a formal complaint letter to the Office of the Comptroller of the Currency, Customer Assistance Group, 1301 McKinney Street, Suite 3450, Houston, TX 77010, or fax 713-336-4301. For more information about the complaint process, see www .occ.treas.gov/customer.htm.

4. If a debit card thief empties your bank account, you might bounce some checks. The bank should restore the money stolen from your account, but that takes several days. In the meantime, bouncing checks may create a late payment in one of your credit card accounts and a blotch on your credit record. How much could be stolen? All the cash in your account plus any credit line the card will access.

If you lose a debit card linked to a brokerage account, the thief can spend all the cash you're holding there, plus the value of your margin account (that's up to half the value of your stocks and stock-owning mutual funds, and even more for bonds).

5. Payments by debit card don't help you build a credit record, although you're probably using a credit card too. That will keep your record up to date.

6. You can't stop a transaction the way you can stop a check.

7. If you buy something that's defective and pay by debit card, you have leverage if the seller won't replace it. Visa and Mastercard let you rescind the payment. You can't rescind, however, if you paid with any other type of debit card. For extra safety, don't use a debit card for Internet, toll-free number, or catalog purchases.

8. If you use a card—either debit or credit—at gas stations, hotels, and car rental agencies, the seller typically puts a hold (a "block") on your account for a larger payment than you'll probably authorize. For example, they might block $50 of the money in your checking account when you fill up at the pump, even though you spent only $30. New Visa rules require gas stations to lift the block on the money you didn't spend within two hours ($20, in this example). MasterCard stretches that to 24 hours or the next business day. At this writing, however, hotels and rental car agencies might maintain the block for several days. Why do they do it? Because, at the start of the transaction, they don't know how large the bill will be (will you drive the car an extra day or return it on time?). They want to be sure you have enough cash on hand.

Starting July 1, 2010, credit-card holders cannot be charged an over-the-limit fee if the reason they ran over their limit was a hold or block on their account. But there's no such break for people who use debit cards. Debit card users who are close to the limit in their checking accounts may find those accounts completely frozen, causing outstanding checks to bounce or triggering an expensive bounce protection plan. To avoid long blocks from hotels or car rental companies, pay with a credit card. If you use a debit card, ask how large the block will be and when it will be removed.

What if You Overspend with a Debit Card?

It's easy to do. In the past, banks alerted you if your purchase was for more money than you had in your account. Some wouldn't even let the transaction go through. Now, however, they've realized that debit card holders are ripe for milking. They allow you to exceed your balance, up to a ceiling such as $300, and charge you for it. Typically, you'll pay $20 or $30 for every so-called courtesy overdraft, and maybe a $5 fee for every day the debt is outstanding (the $300 ceiling includes the fees). Automatic overdrafts take unfair advantage of consumers who don't keep track of their accounts to the penny. At this writing the Federal Reserve is considering rules that would let you opt out of them.

There are three better ways of protecting yourself from bounced debits: (1) Link your checking account to your savings account, so that overdrafts will be paid with your own funds. There might be a $5 transfer fee. (2) Take the bank's overdraft line of credit, paying maybe $15 a year plus a high rate of interest as long as the overdraft is outstanding. (3) Link overdrafts to your credit card, where they'll be paid with a cash advance. Any of those options is better than courtesy overdrafts or bouncing a check.

College students are increasingly being offered prepaid debit cards in lieu of credit cards. The student or parent puts money onto the card, which the student can use until it's gone. Then the card is loaded up again. The upside to prepaid debit cards: It's all but impossible to incur an overdraft and run up fees. Students won't graduate thousands of dollars in debt. The downside is that prepaid debit cards don't help you build a credit history and they're loaded with fees.

Your Rights When You Pay . . .

. . . With a Credit Card

Unauthorized use: Here's what you have to pay if your credit card is stolen and charges are run up: *Nothing* if you reported the loss to the bank before a fraudulent charge occurred. *Up to $50* for charges run up before the theft was reported to the card issuer—and banks usually waive even that small fee. *Nothing* if you still have your card but your number was used fraudulently—for example, in a mail-order transaction or a transaction over the Internet. This covers both business and consumer transactions.

Billing Errors: You're fully protected against consumer billing errors. Check all your bills—paper and electronic—for the following common mistakes:
- You get someone else's bills.
- You're billed for something you didn't buy.
- You paid the bill and shouldn't have been charged any interest.
- The bank sent an electronic payment in the wrong amount or sent a payment that you had canceled.
- An item that you returned was never credited to your account.
- When a store finds its mistake, it doesn't rescind the interest you were charged.
- You're not charged for an item you bought. (That's an honesty test; would you tell?)
- You're charged twice for the same purchase. (Now would you tell?)
- The bill was mailed to your old address; by the time you got it, finance charges were due. (But you have to have given the lender the correct address at least 20 days before the end of the billing period).
- Your bill was mailed too late to reach you before the clock started running on finance charges.
- The item you ordered arrived broken and hasn't been replaced, but the bills (and finance charges) keep coming.
- The goods never came.
- The goods came but in the wrong color or quantity, and you sent them back.
- You refused to accept the goods on delivery.
- The bill contains an arithmetic error.
- An unauthorized person used your card.

Many credit card bills don't include copies of your receipts. Instead you get a simple list of purchases, with the stores sometimes shown under a corporate name you're not familiar with. Keep all receipts until the bills come in. That makes it easier to find mistakes.

To solve a billing error under the Fair Credit Billing Act, notify the credit card issuer immediately in writing that a problem exists. A phone call won't preserve your rights.

The card issuer has to receive your letter within 60 days of the date your credit card statement was mailed. Send the letter to the address designated for billing errors, not the address where you pay your bills. Keep a copy of the letter. For safety, use registered mail with a return receipt requested, and keep a copy.

Give your name, address, and account number, a concise description of what's wrong (with copies of supporting documents), the date of the error, and the dollar amount in dispute. Just give the facts; don't moan and groan all over the page.

The card issuer has to acknowledge your letter within 30 days of receiving it and resolve the problem within 90 days. In the meantime, you can withhold payment for the item and the creditor can't report you as delinquent. Any other charges on your bill, however, must be paid as usual.

If you turn out to be right, the disputed charge and any finance charges related to it will be taken off your bill. That's called a *chargeback*. If the merchant claims the charge was valid, you can ask for supporting documents. If the merchant supplies them and you still disagree, you have three choices:

1. *Pay the bill, including any late charges.* This keeps a black mark off your credit record. You can sue the merchant for recompense.

2. *Don't pay, be reported as delinquent to the credit bureau, and risk being sued by the card issuer.* Send a statement of your side of the story to the credit bureau, to be included in your file (although, frankly, that won't help you much; statements don't improve your credit score).

3. *Don't pay, assert that you received defective goods or services, and ask your credit card issuer to rescind the charge.* If the issuer agrees that you were taken advantage of, it will charge the payment back to the merchant's bank, and you won't be reported as delinquent. This strategy will succeed, however, only if you meet all of the qualifications listed next.

Defective Goods: You might not have to pay if you received, and returned, consumer goods or services that weren't what you ordered, came too late to be useful, or were defective in some way. You're also protected if you never received the goods but were charged for them anyway. To go this route, however, you have to meet the following tests:

- *You used a credit card issued by the same store* you're having the dispute with, or . . .
- *You used a bank card such as Visa or MasterCard or a charge card such as American Express.* In this case, the item in dispute must have cost more than $50. You also had to have bought it in your home state or, if not, within 100

miles of your mailing address. (Some card issuers typically waive the 100-mile rule.)

- *You purchased by phone, mail order, or the Internet from a company that advertises in-state or sent material (such as a catalog) to you there.* Whether these transactions occur in-state depends on state law, but they normally do.

- *You made a good-faith effort, in writing, to resolve the issue with the merchant (unless the merchant is out of business).* Keep copies of all correspondence with the merchant, including copies of e-mails and follow-up notes sent to confirm a phone conversation. Best advice: follow the rules prescribed by the Fair Credit Billing Act (see www.ftc.gov).

- *You're complaining about a consumer purchase,* not a purchase for use in a business.

- *You haven't yet paid for the item or haven't paid in full.* Card issuers can erase outstanding bills, but they don't retrieve cash from the merchant's bank account.

Make your claim in writing (not by phone), supported by evidence that you tried and failed to resolve the dispute. The card issuer must investigate. Until the argument is resolved, the issuer cannot close your account or report you as delinquent, although it can note on your credit report that the payment is in dispute.

You're allowed to withhold payment only on that one transaction. Keep making payments on anything else charged to the card.

If the card issuer takes your side in the dispute, it will charge the disputed payment back to the merchant's bank. The unpaid amount, plus any finance charges, will be removed from your account. But you won't recover any money you already paid.

If the card issuer concludes that the fault is yours, it may report you as delinquent. If you still don't pay, it can turn the bill over to a collection agency. You, in turn, may assert any consumer rights you have.

... With a Cash Advance Check Written Against a Credit Card

You get full protection against unauthorized use and billing errors. But you can't force a chargeback if you received defective goods or services.

... With a Debit Card

Unauthorized use: If fraudulent charges are run up, here's what federal law says you owe: up to $50 as long as you tell the bank about the loss within two business days of discovering it; up to $500 if you let 3 to 60 days go by before reporting the problem. If you wait more than 60 days after getting a statement showing the fraudulent charges, you'll generally owe $50 plus everything charged to the card from 61 days on. Only a few states put lower limits on how much you can lose.

All this is irrelevant for most holders of MasterCard and Visa debit cards. Those issuers promise you zero losses on transactions that you sign for (but not on PIN transactions). There's a caveat: your account has to be in good standing and you have to report the problems promptly. Otherwise the issuers can charge you as much as the law allows.

Billing Errors: You get roughly the same protection that you would with a credit card.

Defective Goods: Your level of protection depends on which card you have. With a Visa or MasterCard debit card, the bank will give you chargeback protection on defective goods and purchases that never came or that came too late to be of use. With another debit card, it won't.

. . . With Visa or MasterCard Prepaid Cards

These issuers promise to treat you the same as the holders of their debit cards. It's not required by law, however, and some issuing banks may balk.

. . . With Other Prepaid Cards

If you lose the card, you're generally out the money, whether it's used by a thief or not.

. . . With a Check

If a thief cashes one of your checks and you sign an affidavit of forgery, the bank will pay. So you're fully protected.

If you regret your purchase, you can ask the bank to stop the check. You'll have to follow up your telephone call with a written stop-check order (by mail or e-mail when you bank online). There's usually a fee. If the check slips through anyway, it's the bank's responsibility.

Credit Discrimination

You can't be denied credit solely on the basis of color, race, religion, sex, age, marital status, national origin, or the fact that you're on welfare. If you are turned down for a loan or a bank card, it is probably because:

1. You don't have enough income.
2. You don't have a steady job history.
3. Your debts are too large relative to your income.
4. You don't have a credit history.

Wives and Credit

Many married women apply for credit based entirely on their own incomes and think it's pure discrimination if they're turned down. It's probably not. They simply haven't focused on how large their debts really are.

Take a wife who cosigns a mortgage with her husband. If he skips out, that obligation becomes hers alone. It would probably overwhelm her resources.

She doesn't think about that debt as long as she's well married, but her creditors do. If she tries to get credit based on her income alone, the lender will set off that mortgage against her paycheck and conclude that she can't carry any more loans. The same would be true for a married man who couldn't meet the mortgage payments were it not for his wife's salary.

Learning this, some married women wonder how they will ever get credit "in their own name." But they already *have* credit in their own names as long as the accounts they hold with their husbands were applied for jointly. At the credit bureau, all transactions will be reported in her name as well as his.

Married couples usually apply for credit jointly in order to get the benefit of both incomes. When a married person applies separately, it's usually for a business loan. A bank can ask you for a cosigner, but it can't demand that the cosigner be your spouse. What if your spouse has an interest in the property you're putting up as collateral? The lender can require the spouse to sign a waiver allowing the property to be seized if you don't pay, but that's different from cosigning the loan itself. As a practical matter, however, your spouse is usually your best cosigner.

If you're widowed and your credit cards were granted partly on the strength of your spouse's income, the lender can require you to show that you're still credit worthy. That is, if the lender finds out. Best advice: keep mum, and keep on using your cards. It's essential, however, that you keep paying your bills on time. If you're too distraught to open the mail and write checks, find someone who can do that for you.

The divorced can't help revealing their status when they close joint accounts and ask for new cards in their own names. If your payment record has been good, creditors will generally issue you a card without question. But they're entitled to put you through a credit check all over again. The lender must consider alimony as part of your regular income unless there's evidence that it's not being paid.

On a marital card, a spouse can be either jointly responsible for the debt or an authorized user, with the other spouse solely responsible for payment. You normally want to be jointly responsible, assuming that your spouse isn't a spendthrift. That way you'll share your spouse's credit score. If you're merely an authorized user, you'll get a lower score. Still, that doesn't necessarily work against you. Lenders say that authorized-user scores also work well, to predict how responsible a borrower you'll be. How do you find out what your status is? The easiest way is to get a copy of your credit report, which will tell you who's responsible for each account. How do you change your status? Write to the lender and request it. The lender may agree or may require you and your spouse to reapply for credit jointly.

If your spouse is a deadbeat, his or her bad habits will taint your own credit-worthiness unless you can show that you lead a more responsible financial life. One possible way to do this: get a bank card or store charge card in your name (a friend or parent may have to cosign it), keep it solely for your own use, and keep the bills up to date. You can show that account as proof of your personal reliability. Similarly, buy a car yourself (or with a cosigner) and make all the payments on it—in full and on time. It will show on your credit history as your own debt. Finally, don't cosign any of your spouse's loans or credit cards. If circumstances allow it, you should cancel the cards and credit lines that you've cosigned already.

Older People and Credit

Older people often feel that they're being discriminated against. More likely, it's that their clean lifestyle doesn't fit the profile of a good credit risk. Here are several eye-opening cases that were supplied to me by the AARP:

- *Ray G., age 71, retired businessman,* was refused a Visa card because of his "limited credit experience." His mistake: when he retired, he paid up everything, dropped all his credit cards, and started living on cash. Six years later, when he wanted a credit card to travel with, he no longer had sufficient credit history.
- *Martin K.* couldn't get a Discover card because he had too many other cards. That made him sore because nine of his cards he never used, but how was the

lender to know that? If you have accumulated a lot of cards over the years, get rid of all but two or three of them.

▪ *Evelyn L., 75 and widowed,* was turned down for a card because she had no credit history. She had always paid cash for everything, a way of life handed down to her by her parents. In old age, she wanted a credit card for catalog shopping but couldn't get one.

The moral of these stories is to get a card when you're young, working, and laden with debt—the very customer the lenders want. Keep that card for when you retire or are widowed, even if you don't use it very often. The time may come when you'll want it again, and it's hard to recover your credit once you've given it up.

None of the turndowns just cited were illegal. They were all based on legitimate credit criteria, not on age. But consider the following stories:

▪ *Marjorie W., 68,* bought a travel trailer on an installment contract. Later, the dealer called and canceled because the finance company wouldn't lend more than $6,000 to someone over 65.

▪ *Robert M., 72,* was denied a loan because his bank wouldn't lend to anyone over 70.

▪ *Martha P., 71,* was rejected by a finance company because she didn't qualify for credit life insurance.

All of these lenders broke the law. You cannot be turned down for credit solely on the basis of age. Nor can a lender set different terms for older people than for younger people in the same situation. A lender is allowed to consider age only if it makes a proven difference to creditworthiness. For example, if a 75-year-old applies for a 30-year mortgage, a bank might legitimately ask about his or her future cash flow or request a larger down payment. But the senior can't be turned down if the loan would be granted to a younger person with the same income and assets.

What can an older person do if he or she no longer has a credit history? Ask a major store where you shop for a charge account. Use it for a while and then ask for a credit card where you bank. The card might carry a higher-than-average interest rate, but that doesn't matter. You're going to pay all your bills on time, right?

Tip: Older people should consider putting a security freeze on their credit accounts (page 272). You're not likely to be opening new accounts and the freeze will protect you from some forms of identity theft.

If You Can't Pay Your Bills

Don't hide. Don't cry. Don't shove unopened bills into a drawer. Don't have your cousin tell the bank that you've gone to Sicily for the summer. That won't help. Someone—probably a bill collector—will find you and you'll be in more trouble than you were before.

What's your biggest problem when you can't pay your bills? Money, you say. I say it's fear. You're sure that everyone will point and sneer. Your son will be kicked out of Boy Scouts. The police will hang you up by your thumbs. But nothing like that is going to happen. You're not Jack the Ripper. You don't beat up babies or set fire to cats. All you did wrong was to buy more things than you can pay for right away. That's an error in judgment or change in circumstance (maybe you lost your job), not a sin. You will pay eventually, and your errors will be forgiven.

If you can't pay your credit card bills, call your lenders and tell them so. You'll need to negotiate a payment plan. To do this you need: (1) a spending plan showing how much money you need to live on (page 189); (2) a repayment plan showing how much you can spread among your creditors every month; (3) a specific offer for each creditor, as in "I will pay you $50 a month and clear up this bill in two years." If your situation is dire, offer your unsecured creditors a settlement—say, 50 cents on the dollar.

Each creditor will want more. But if you hold firm and keep making the payments you've decided on, they should eventually accept the deal. If someone threatens to sue, don't ruin your rehabilitation plan by trying to accommodate him. Keep on talking, keep making your payments, even go to court. No judge will order you to pay more than you can afford, and your creditors know it. Your strengths are three: the lender would rather stretch out payments than write them off, it's cheaper to talk than to hire a debt collector, and the interest you pay is compensation for the delay. If you're talking to a debt-collection service, make them an offer for only part of what's owed. If you wait long enough, they'll eventually accept.

If you can't handle these negotiations yourself, or if you're such a spend-aholic that you find yourself hurtling toward bankruptcy, nonprofit credit counselors can help. Lenders might even direct you to a counselor rather than accept the spending plan you drew up.

Professional counselors give you moral support. They help you develop a budg—, er, I mean, a spending plan. They talk to your creditors and get them to waive late fees, accept smaller payments, and reduce your total debt, provided that you stop using the cards. Once the size of your debt is pared down, you'll usually be enrolled in a debt management plan. You'll pay a lump sum into a trust account each month (be sure it's a trust account, separate from the funds belonging to the counseling firm!). The counselor will divide your payment among the creditors who agreed to join the plan. Note that this is not a debt consolidation loan, it's simply a convenient, one-stop way of getting your creditors paid off.

Nonprofit counselors charge modest fees and work with you in person, by phone, or over the Internet. Their basic budget consultation is often free and may be all the help you need. If you enter a formal debt repayment plan, they charge enrollment fees of up to $75, monthly fees in the $10 to $50 range, and zero for clients with low incomes. They normally handle only unsecured consumer debts such as credit card bills, not business debts or secured debts such as mortgages or car payments (although some offices will negotiate lower payments on mortgages too).

For the name of a local nonprofit counseling agency, ask the debt collection office of your bank or credit union; your city's department of social services; the National Foundation for Credit Counseling (NFCC) (www.nfcc.org or 800-388-2227 for an office near you); or the Association of Independent Consumer Credit Counseling Agencies (AICCCA) (www.aiccca.org or 866-703-8787). You can work out a repayment plan over the Internet, by phone, or in person. Talk to at least two different services to see what they offer and what they charge. Low-cost counseling services are funded by credit card companies, whose interest it is that you pay as much as possible on your debt. But you and your creditors have the same goal: to rescue your finances before you fall into bankruptcy.

Don't be afraid to ask for help. Thousands of people share your problem. Counselors have seen it all and consider it their job to haul you out of the pit.

Do *not* pay a firm that offers to straighten out your debts in return for a percentage of what you owe. Do *not* sign up with a service that takes your first monthly check as payment, in addition to monthly fees. Do *not* assume that a "nonprofit" is always a good guy. Hang up the phone if you feel that you're getting a hard sell or extravagant promises of relief or if the counselor is vague about the fees. Don't believe Internet ads telling you that debt clearance is easy. Stick with counselors on the NFCC or AICCCA rosters.

What About Your Credit Score? Accounts that were behind when you entered counseling will still show as behind and drag down your score. But as long as you keep up your payment plan, you shouldn't suffer any further damage. Some creditors flag your account if you're in counseling, but that doesn't affect your

FICO score. When you complete the program, some creditors will "re-age" your file, showing that all payments are up to date.

If Negotiation Doesn't Solve Your Problem, Consider Bankruptcy. There are two ways to go:

1. Chapter 13, known as the wage earner plan. It stops your creditors from hounding you and lets you keep your property while you start on a formal, court-approved plan to pay at least part of your debts over three to five years. Make this choice if your troubles are temporary—for example, you were out of work but now have a job with money coming in. The plan lets you catch up on mortgage payments, which may be your key concern.

Your only choice might be Chapter 13 if your income appears to be high enough to cover at least some of your debts. The law measures your current monthly income against your state's median income for a family of your size. If you're above the median, a means test will be applied. Certain expenses and debt payments will be subtracted from your income. If there's enough left to pay some bills, you'll have to enter a wage earner plan. For a calculator that helps you find out whether you're destined for Chapter 13, see LegalConsumer.com at www.legalconsumer.com.

2. Chapter 7, for people too deep in the hole to climb out. Most of your unsecured debts will be canceled, such as credit card and medical bills. You might or might not be able to keep your house or car, depending on their value and your state's law. You'll definitely lose them if your mortgage and auto-loan payments are not up-to-date.

Get good legal advice from a bankruptcy specialist. It's risky to read a book and try to do it yourself because you might miss something of advantage to you. For details on your state's bankruptcy rules and how much property you can exempt, see BankruptcyInformation.com (www.bankruptcyinformation.com).

Certain debts normally cannot be discharged, although there are some exceptions to the rules. These debts include student loans, child support, alimony, most taxes, loans you didn't mention on your bankruptcy petition, criminal fines, loans granted on the basis of untrue financial statements, and court judgments for certain damages, such as an accident you caused while driving drunk. You also can't get out of loans taken just before bankruptcy to buy luxury goods and services (that's the "no-last-minute-BMW" rule) or big cash advances (the "no-last-minute-Caribbean-vacation" rule). If you owe money to a relative or friend, you can't pay it off if that leaves your other creditors empty-handed (the "no-rescue-for-brothers-or-cosigners" rule).

Before entering either type of bankruptcy, you're required to receive budget and credit counseling.

Go bankrupt before you go broke! It's painful and humiliating even to consider bankruptcy, let alone join that crowd in the courthouse corridor, waiting for your name to be called. Normally, I'd say suck it up, cut your spending, and repay your consumer debts. But that's not always possible, especially if you've been out of work for a long time or have huge uninsured medical bills.

Most families, honorable to the end, struggle longer than they should. By the time they give in, they've lost assets that they could have used to start over again. That defeats the point of bankruptcy—to stop the self-blame and hopelessness that go with bad luck and give yourself a second chance.

The right time to go bankrupt is when you're financially stuck but still have assets to protect. For example, it's a mistake to tap your retirement accounts to make minimum payments on monstrous bills. IRAs and 401(k)s are largely protected in bankruptcy, as is most of your child's 529 college savings account. That money is your future. Leave it alone and use credit cards for your necessities. Card issuers know that some of their customers will fail. That's why they charge elephant fees.

Your health is your future, too. You're doing your family no favors by forgoing medical treatment because you can't pay. Bankruptcy eliminates medical as well as consumer debt.

Bankruptcy can even help you save your home, especially when its value has dropped and your mortgage is under water. You're allowed to keep a limited amount of home equity in most states. If the house is worth less than the mortgage plus your home equity exemption, you can file for Chapter 7 bankruptcy, wipe out your consumer debts, and still keep your home, provided that your mortgage payments are up to date. If your house is worth more than the exemption, however, or you're behind on your payments, it will likely be sold.

You can use Chapter 7, the most popular type, only once in eight years. So before you file, draw up a "no kidding" plan for living on your income when you're finally clear. If you're out of work, try not to go bankrupt until you have a new job and can see what's ahead of you.

Don't try to preserve your house if you're going broke. Stop making payments, stay there while foreclosure is under way, then move out and rent. If the mortgage is under water, you're already functionally renting because you have no equity. In theory, many states allow mortgage lenders to chase you for the sum still owed after the house is sold. But that's rare. Lenders know that you probably can't pay.

Foreclosures stay on your record for seven years and bankruptcies for ten. If you reestablish good bill-paying habits, however, you may get decent credit even sooner. And you'll start fresh, which is what bankruptcy is about.

Tax Note: If your creditors forgive part of your debt, the IRS will treat that amount as taxable income. You'll receive a Form 1099-C. It's reported as "other income" on your tax return. The IRS may negotiate a lower payment, however, if you're insolvent or broke. You do not owe taxes on debt discharged in bankruptcy. Through 2012, you also owe no tax on up to $2 million in mortgage debt on your principal residence that was canceled as part of a mortgage restructuring or foreclosure.

Gyp Note: Creditors are finding unfair (even illegal) ways to force you to pay debts that bankruptcy supposedly wiped out.

One ploy: They offer you a new credit card if you'll agree to pay what you owed before the bankruptcy. Don't agree! You'll find other cards.

Another ploy: They won't remove your discharged debt from your credit report, arguing that no law requires it. You might not be able to get a mortgage or other loan as long as the debt still shows. They're trying to force you to pay the old debt, even though you don't owe it anymore. To fight, write to the creditors, with copies of your bankruptcy papers. If you're ignored, get a lawyer to write. Sometimes that helps. Sometimes you're still ignored by these disreputable debt collectors, which, by the way, include some supposedly blue-chip banking names. Reject their wickedness. Don't pay.

Yet another ploy: They sell your debt to vulture collectors who harass you and your relatives until you pay. That's illegal too, but it happens all the time. Your legal so-called remedies are to write a letter telling them to stop, which they might thumb their noses at. Or to sue, within a year of the illegal action. Or to send a complaint letter to the Federal Trade Commission, Consumer Response Center, 600 Pennsylvania Ave NW, Washington, DC 20580, or via the Internet at www.ftc.gov (click on "Consumer Protection," then on "File a Complaint"). The FTC collects data on abuses but won't *do* anything for you.

How to Tell You're in Trouble

Quit buying on credit if:

1. You can afford to pay only the minimum on your credit cards every month, and even that's a stretch.
2. You have to charge purchases that you used to pay for in cash.
3. You took a debt consolidation loan and now you're running up fresh debts.
4. You can't save a dime.
5. You look forward to the junk mail, hoping that a new bank will be careless enough to offer you a credit card.
6. You're taking cash advances from one card in order to make minimum payments on another.
7. You can't pay your basic bills on time.
8. You're being dunned.
9. You get turned down for credit.
10. You don't even want some of the things you buy.
11. Your friends can't figure out how you manage to live so well.
12. Without overtime or moonlighting, you'd lose your house, your car, and your kids.
13. You're taking cash advances for daily expenses such as food and rent.
14. You borrow $50 from the guy in the next office until the end of the week. You borrow $500 from your brother.
15. You don't open an envelope that you know contains a bill.
16. When you buy on credit, you always choose the longest time period to repay.
17. Your debts are rising while your income is going down.
18. You can never pay off your credit cards completely.
19. You put off paying by fiddling your creditors—putting the bill for the dentist in the envelope addressed to the doctor, and vice versa.
20. You bounce checks.
21. You don't know exactly how much you owe and avoid finding out.
22. You get scared about money in the middle of the night.
23. You don't dare tell your mother or your spouse—or, sometimes, yourself.

Credit card issuers have developed sophisticated systems for identifying borrowers who are likely to default. They call it behavior scoring. Here are six of the warning signals that creditors look for:

1. You pay only the bare minimum every month.
2. You make partial payments.
3. You started falling behind on your payments soon after opening an account.
4. You have taken the maximum cash advance.
5. Your account balance always grows; you can't ever seem to pay it off.
6. You have periodic bouts of late payment.

If this describes you, your number one job is to get out of debt. Only then can you start getting rich.

When to Hock the Farm

All the Best Ways to Borrow Money to Invest

**The rich didn't get that way by saving pennies.
That's only what they tell their biographers.
They made their fortunes on borrowed money.**

Don't borrow to spend. Occasional debt on a credit card never hurt anybody, but permanent indebtedness to support an implacable spending habit is a staggering waste. A loser's game. At 18 percent interest, you are paying an extra $18 for every $100 you spend. Why would you want to throw that much money away? You're living rich while growing poor.

But don't be shy about borrowing to invest. That's how people get rich. They use OPM—Other People's Money—to build something of value for themselves. Here are the classic steps to wealth: First, shed consumer debt. Second, build assets through home ownership, saving money, and investing. Third, borrow prudently against some of those assets to invest for even more net worth.

What Is Investment Debt?

Investment debt is money you borrow to acquire an asset that, with luck, might rise in price. You're gambling that the price increase will more than cover the loan's cost. You hope to be left with a profit after selling the asset and paying off the loan.

A mortgage is the most ubiquitous form of investment debt. A college loan comes second—an education is an investment because it builds your earning power or the earning power of your children. A loan to start or buy into a business can multiply your money many times if the business succeeds. A car loan supports both your earning power (you drive to work) and your investment program (by buying a car with borrowed money instead of cash, you're left with more earnings to stash in a tax-deferred retirement account). Even a debt consolidation loan is worthwhile if it lowers the interest you have to pay and you don't run up your debts again.

Borrowing to invest in stocks, however, is a high-risk proposition. If you're feeling crazy, you can borrow against other stocks to do this (page 310). But never buy stocks with money borrowed against your house or your retirement account. They're the building blocks of your security.

The critical test of the value of any loan is that the money you borrow not disappear (say, into lizard-skin shoes or gear). It should be used in some way to maintain and improve your wealth.

How Much Investment Debt Can You Afford?

When you borrow to invest . . .

1. You can afford any debt that will support itself. Can you rent out a duplex for enough to cover its costs? If so, and if you have savings to cover the mortgage in case something goes wrong, and if you like being a landlord, go ahead.

2. You can afford any debt that you can easily repay out of personal earnings. If your job is secure, up to 40 percent of your income can be committed to monthly repayments, including mortgage repayments. When you borrow against your salary, however, you should generally be making a liquid investment—that is, an investment that's instantly salable at the current market price. If you lose your job and you're pressed for cash, you can dump the investment and eliminate the debt. Mutual funds are liquid. Second homes aren't. When you finance a second home out of earnings, you should either be dead sure of your job or have enough savings to carry the mortgage for a year or two if your income falls.

3. You can go into debt to make an illiquid investment as long as you have a substantial amount of liquid securities or money in the bank. Say, for example, that you borrow to buy a piece of land that you intend to subdivide and sell as separate building lots. Then you lose your job. The land may not be salable except at a giveaway price. But your lender (that stone-hearted bean counter) thinks you should keep on making monthly payments anyway. How will you manage? No sweat, as long as you have a lot of cash or stocks that you can liquidate. If you don't, never finance an investment like this. You'll be playing dice with your solvency.

The Money Stores

When you want a loan, don't put on the sackcloth of a mendicant and approach your banker on bended knee. You are a customer in a money store. Everyone wants your business if you're a good credit risk. You can negotiate terms just the way you negotiate a new-car price. Bankers expect borrowers to be choosy and are astounded when they're not.

In any city, the most costly lender may charge anywhere from 2 to 6 percentage points more than the cheapest one. A poor credit risk may have to accept those terms; a good one doesn't.

Your search for a loan should start with the online lenders such as E-Loan (www.eloan.com) or LendingTree (www.lendingtree.com). They often have the lowest rates and fees and disclose them in full (no surprises when you close!). You can handle the entire transaction online or speak with the lender over the phone. Next, consider a credit union if you can find one to join (page 44). Finally, look at banks. In general, smaller institutions charge lower rates and fewer fees than large ones and may be more willing to negotiate. You might also get a discount by borrowing from your primary bank (although online lenders might even beat the discounted rate). At a bank, always make an appointment to see a loan officer; don't just wander in off the street. Innocents wander; smarties prearrange.

Make a list of the things you want to know: annual percentage rate, fees, down payment, monthly payments, repayment schedule, interest rate options, and, on variable loans, your risks if interest rates rise. Ask: "Is that the best you can do?" "Will you cut a quarter point off the interest rate?" "Will you lower the points I have to pay up front?" If it's a big personal loan, ask: "Can I borrow at less than the prime lending rate?" (That's the bank's benchmark rate.) Then say, "Thanks very much, I'll think it over," and leave. You can negotiate with online lenders just as you can in face-to-face situations. Larger loans (say, $50,000 and up) get better terms.

Check two online lenders against what a bank or credit union will offer. If your favorite bank has a higher interest rate than the others, tell it what the competition is doing. If it wants your business, it will come down. You'll get the best rate if you have at least two lenders bidding for the loan.

If you don't qualify for an online or bank loan on the best terms, you shouldn't be borrowing to invest. You're simply not solvent enough to take the risk. Consumer finance companies lend to people with lower credit ratings, but they charge higher interest rates and fees. They may want your house as collateral, even for very small loans. If you take a series of small loans, you'll find fee piled on fee, making borrowing hugely expensive. That's no way to get rich.

Borrowing Against Your House

It may sound uncharacteristically wild of me to suggest your home as a source of risk capital, but that is the principal source that many of us have. If you think you can profit by borrowing money against your home, it's worth a try. But *only* if you can comfortably carry the larger mortgage; and *only* if you're sure of your income; and *only* if you've applied the rules of sound investing (chapter 21); and *only* if you expect the investment to appreciate by more than your net interest cost; and *only* if you're not gambling on stocks; and *only* if you wouldn't be devastated if your house declined in value or the deal flopped. That's a lot of "onlys."

You borrow against your equity, which is the difference between the value of your home and the mortgages you carry. It's the cash you'd realize if you sold the house and repaid the bank.

Generally speaking, people feel more comfortable tapping their homes for real estate investments than for stocks. For example, you might use your equity to finance a rental property. Well-chosen real estate usually won't lose half its value in a year the way that stocks can (unless you bought into the bubble, a once-in-a-lifetime wreck). A home is also a good source of college money: an investment in future earning power.

But—if your outside investment goes sour, you lose the money and can't repay the loan you took against your home, you're stuck with higher monthly payments for the duration of the mortgage. If your life goes sour—you get sick or lose your job and can't make those mortgage payments—you forfeit your home. Think the new investment through with care before financing it with money borrowed against your house.

Second Mortgages: A Traditional Loan
Versus a Home Equity Line

The loan of choice today is a second mortgage, also called a second trust, which pledges your house as collateral. It has become standard issue, like a car loan or blue jeans. Practically everyone has them, for one purpose or another. They come in the form of a loan with fixed terms or a home equity line of credit. Some lenders also give second mortgages on condominiums and mobile homes.

Home-equity loans are a child of the tax laws. You can tax-deduct the interest on a second mortgage up to $100,000 (although the loan can't exceed your home's fair market value). By contrast, you get no deduction at all for interest paid on auto loans, some student loans, credit card debt, and personal loans.

Second mortgages come in two main types:

A traditional second mortgage works just like a first. You borrow a lump sum of money and pay it back over a fixed term, usually 10 to 20 years and sometimes 30 years. The interest rate may be fixed or variable. The minimum loan runs in the $40,000 to $50,000 range. Good credit risks can borrow online or from a bank or credit union. Marginal credit risks should try for a Title I Property Improvement loan insured by the Federal Housing Administration (FHA) and offered by a limited number of banks. Go to the U.S. Department of Housing and Urban Development (HUD) (www.hud.gov) for more information on these loans, as well as for the names of FHA lenders in your area.

Borrowers, however, have fallen in love with a different kind of second mortgage: *the home equity line of credit.* It's a loan tailor-made for our self-service times. Instead of borrowing a fixed amount of money, you arrange for a fixed amount of borrowing power (typical minimum: $5,000 to $10,000; maximum: $100,000 to $500,000), available over the next 10 to 15 years usually at a variable interest rate. During that time, you can take a loan anytime you want, with no further approval from the bank.

Different lenders provide different ways of tapping your home equity line. You might use a special check, put down a credit or debit card, attach the credit line to your regular checking account, make a phone call asking that funds be transferred into your account, or make transfers online. There may be a minimum initial draw, such as $5,000, and minimums of $250 or $500 for subsequent draws. You pay interest only on the money that you actually use.

How fast you repay a home equity loan is often up to you. Depending on the lender, you can generally choose to:

1. Pay interest and a portion of the principal each month, erasing the loan over 5 to 20 years.

2. Pay only the interest for 5 to 10 years. After that, you might renegotiate the loan terms, continuing to pay interest only. Or you might have to start reducing the principal at a big jump in monthly costs.

3. Make fixed monthly payments even though you have a variable-rate loan. When rates rise, you may be paying less than the interest due, which ramps up the size of your loan and costs you extra money. *Not advised!*

4. Pay substantial amounts each month to clear up the loan as fast as you can. If this is your plan—and it's a good one—get a loan without prepayment penalties. Some lenders charge $500 or so for accounts paid up within the first 2 or 3 years.

Whichever payment method you choose, a home equity loan is payable in full when the house is sold.

Home equity lines are offered by online lenders, commercial banks, mortgage banks, credit unions, consumer credit companies, finance companies, and even some large brokerage houses. Online lenders and credit unions often have the best terms. Finance companies have the worst.

Note that your borrowing power isn't guaranteed. Any lender may reduce or freeze your credit line if your home's value falls.

Should You Take a Home Equity Line or a Traditional Second Mortgage? A traditional second mortgage is all discipline. Your interest rate is usually fixed, so the loan won't cost more if rates go up. You cannot easily add to the loan— no temptation there. It's a good way to borrow for a single purpose, such as redoing the kitchen. It's the right loan for people on limited budgets. And it's a good defensive loan in a shaky marriage. The money goes toward something you both want, and there's no other borrowing power on tap. This loan is the wrong choice, however, if you want to be able to borrow in the future, at various times.

For multiple loans, go for a home equity line of credit. Once you've opened the line, you can borrow against it whenever you want. It's the right choice for meeting a series of needs, such as college tuition for the next four years. Most lenders charge variable interest rates—typically at a margin of one to three percentage points over the prime interest rate. So your monthly payments can rise and fall. This loan is safest for people with comfortable incomes who won't faint when rates go up.

Which is Cheaper, a Traditional Second Mortgage or a Home Equity Loan? That's hard to tell. You can't necessarily compare their annual percentage interest rates (APRs) because they're figured differently.

On a fixed-term second mortgage, all the financing fees are considered part of the APR. That's the loan's true cost. On a home equity loan, however, finance fees are not included in the APR. Some home equity lenders don't charge any finance fees, in which case their APRs are true. When lenders do charge fees, the APRs understate the loan's true cost.

In general, both the interest rates and closing costs on fixed-term second mortgages are higher than on lines of credit. But not always. To compare these loans, list all their costs: their interest rates, any financing fees (application fees, points, and loan origination fees), and any service fees (for title search, survey, appraisal, credit check, legal work, and so on). Most home equity lines charge nothing up front but typically levy annual fees of $50 to $75. The few loans with high up-front fees may not be worth their cost.

Should You Finance a Car with a Home Equity Loan or an Auto Loan? Unfortunately, you can't necessarily compare their annual percentage rates of interest to see which is the better deal. Up-front fees are figured into the APR for the auto loan but not for the home equity loan. The comparison is fair only if the home equity lender doesn't charge any fees. Otherwise that loan costs a little more than it appears.

The auto loan might be cheaper if you can get a super-low-cost promotional loan. Otherwise the home equity loan should be cheaper because you can tax-deduct the interest.

Should You Take a Home Equity Loan to Pay Off Your Credit Card Debt?
I can think of two reasons to say yes and four to say no. First, the positives:
- *It's almost always smart to substitute low-cost debt for high-cost debt, and home equity loans cost less.* The money you save can be used to reduce your home equity debt or to raise the amount you contribute to a tax-deferred retirement account.
- *Furthermore, home equity interest is tax deductible on loans up to $100,000 if you itemize deductions.* There's no tax write-off for credit card interest. (There's also no write-off for home equity interest if you use the standard deduction.)

Now the negatives:
- *Most credit card debts are paid off within about 15 months.* That holds down the interest bill. On home equity lines, however, loans usually linger much longer. Some people treat them as permanent debt to be paid off when the house is sold. So despite the lower interest rate, a home equity loan might cost you more.
- *You might borrow against your home to clean up your credit card debt, then run up your credit cards all over again.* That gives you double the debt you used to have.
- *With so much home equity at your fingertips, you might shop up a storm.* Your home value could vanish in a mad afternoon at the mall.
- *When you don't repay your credit card debt, the lender duns you and may sue.* At worst, this ruins your credit record. But if you don't repay home equity debt, you can be foreclosed. For this reason, you shouldn't pile all your consumer loans onto your house, regardless of the tax advantage. In an emergency, you need some loans you can duck.

Bottom line: It's fine to refinance non-tax-deductible consumer debt with a home equity loan if you pay it off fast and resist new debt. Otherwise forget it. To spendaholics, home equity lines are a doomsday machine. For calculators that will help you decide whether to consolidate debt, go to www .mtgprofessor.com.

Should You Consolidate Debt By Refinancing Your First Mortgage, or Should You Take a Second Mortgage to Do the Job? When making this decision, don't rely on the advice of a lender or mortgage broker. They may tell you to refinance because that earns them the biggest commission. You need to determine which will cost the least over the years you expect to be in the house. To help you do this, check the calculators at Mtgprofessor.com. In general, the refi will be better if you can lower the interest rate that you currently pay. If not, the second mortgage is usually the better choice. Your calculation also has to consider costs such as closing fees and mortgage insurance, as well as the number of years you expect to be making payments. You do yourself no good if you lower your monthly payments but stretch them out for so many years that you raise the total interest cost.

Should You Borrow If You Plan to Move? This is the downside nobody thinks about. When you sell your house, you have to pay off your first mortgage and the home equity loan. That leaves you less cash to put down on your next home and may stop you from trading up. If your home drops in value to less than the amount of the loans against it, you won't be able to move unless you have extra cash on hand to repay the bank.

If you think you'll move in four or five years, buy your car with a separate auto loan and leave your home equity alone.

Should You Agree to a Home Equity Line If Your Marriage is in Trouble? Absolutely not. And tell the bank, in writing, to freeze any lines that you already have. When you're married, it takes only one signature to originate a home equity loan. One spouse could borrow up to the limit of the line and spend the money, yet you're both responsible for the debt. A divorce-court judge ought to tell the spouse who took the money to pay it back, but you can't count on that.

How to Use Home Equity Lines

1. **Don't open a larger credit line than you really need.** If you apply for a credit card, the lender will check your credit report to see how much borrow-

ing power you have already. A large, unused home equity line shows that you could add substantially to your debts. As a result, your card may carry a higher interest rate.

Banks usually lend a maximum of 75 to 80 percent of the value of your house, minus the amount remaining on your first mortgage. On a $200,000 house with a $120,000 first mortgage, for example, you could get $30,000 to $40,000 more. If your income seems too low to carry so large a debt, the bank ought to lend you less. Some lenders, however, stretch you right to the edge of your income and beyond. It's up to you to say "Enough."

In the past, a few lenders let you borrow up to 100 percent of equity. Homeowners came to grief when prices fell and they owed much more than their homes were worth. Don't be tempted to borrow more than 75 percent of your home's current equity value. You *must* leave a cushion for yourself in case conditions change.

2. Compare costs before deciding on a lender. You probably look mainly at the interest rate. But there's something even more important, called a *margin*. That's where the real money lies.

On a typical home equity loan, the interest rate floats one to three percentage points above the bank's prime (or benchmark) lending rate. Those one to three points are the margin, or spread. Higher margins are good for the lender and bad for you.

As an example, say that the prime rate is 5 percent. You're offered prime for six months (the teaser rate), then prime plus a margin of two percentage points—7 percent in all. A competing loan goes for half a point under prime, or 4.5 percent, but with a 3 percent margin. After the teaser period, the competing loan will cost 7.5 percent. If you look only at the interest rate, the second loan seems more attractive. But adding the margin shows the first loan to be the better bet. The lower your credit score, the higher the margin you'll pay. Poorer risks might be charged prime plus 5.5 percent or more.

Lenders often won't disclose the margin unless you ask. So ask!

Most lenders charge no up-front closing costs, so normally there's no reason to take a loan that levies them (for example, points, application fees, and other charges). There's usually an annual fee in the $75 range. There may also be transaction fees or fees for closing your credit line within the first two or three years. Ask about them.

Some equity lines come with fixed interest rates. They cost about 0.5 percentage points more at the start than variables do. You might be allowed a one-time rate cut if the general level of rates declines. You might also be able to convert a variable-rate loan to a fixed-rate loan after a certain number of years.

Always look for discounts. There may be an interest rate discount for dealing with the bank that services your first mortgage or a discount for making monthly automatic payments from your bank account.

3. Check the caps. There's usually no limit to how much your rate can jump in a single year. The maximum rate on your home equity loan could be as much as 18 percent or more. In short, these are pretty risky loans. Find out how your monthly payment would change if rates went up. Some lenders have introduced reasonable annual and lifetime caps, so ask about them.

Where there's a ceiling, there's sometimes a floor. Your rate might not be allowed to drop below 5 or 6 percent. If the general level of rates goes much further down, however, you can usually refinance.

4. Read the fine print. Lenders use tiny type for information that they don't care if you overlook. So do yourself a favor: put on your glasses and read through the loan agreement.

You'll probably learn that your credit line can be reduced or frozen if: (1) you don't pass continuing credit checks, (2) the value of your house goes down, or (3) interest rates have risen above the cap. You'll discover any prepayment penalties. You'll learn when and how your interest rate adjusts, what all the fees are, when your credit line expires, all the repayment terms, and whether you'll face a single large payment when the loan ultimately falls due. On credit lines opened since November 7, 1989, most of the terms are guaranteed. But not always, so check!

When a lender freezes your home equity line, the letter will tell you the reason for the action and how to appeal. If your credit score fell, build it up again and ask for your line to be reopened. If the value of homes in your city have declined, have your own home reappraised—maybe its price has held up. If your appeal fails, try for a lower credit line instead of a total freeze.

5. Ask about the bank's policy on subordination. That's a big but important word. A second mortgage is always subordinated to the first, meaning that if you can't pay and your house is sold to cover the debt, the holder of the first mortgage gets his money first.

Let's say that mortgage rates have dropped and you can now get a new first mortgage at a lower rate. The bank that holds your home equity line has to subordinate its loan to the new mortgage you're taking out. Usually, that's a routine bit of paperwork, perhaps costing you a modest fee. But some banks won't do it, which locks you into the mortgage you have currently. If you see this in a home equity loan agreement, don't sign! There are plenty of other home equity lenders around.

6. Repay early and often. Lenders encourage you to take 10 or 20 years to repay. But stretching out your loans over that length of time is a sucker's game. If you use your home equity line to buy a new car every three years and make only the minimum payments, you could find yourself paying for your present car plus the four previous ones all at once. That's a lot of money down the drain.

Fit your payment schedule to the purchase. Get rid of a debt consolidation loan in a year and a half. Clean up an auto loan in three to four years. Don't let a home improvement loan hang around for more than seven years. Reduce a loan that is carrying a successful investment, so that you'll have the equity to make more investments.

7. Beware the call clause. Lenders reserve the right to *call,* or force you to repay, a home equity loan that might be in trouble. This could happen if you miss some payments or if you endanger the bank's interest in the house, perhaps by not keeping it in good repair. Exactly what can trigger a call will be outlined in your loan agreement. The moral: back up your home equity loans with liquid investments. You should be prepared to make six months of payments even if you're out of work.

8. Don't be tempted to reborrow. If you've paid off your loan, the lender will do everything possible to get you into debt again. You'll get blank checks in the mail at holiday or tax time, when you just might want some extra money. You'll get marketing calls that offer special interest rate deals. Hang tight. Hold that balance at zero.

Lenders also market to people who have almost used up their credit lines. Borrowers in that position often start to repay. "Egad!" say the banks, "We don't want that!" Suddenly, you'll discover that your line has been raised by $5,000 or $10,000, so you can easily borrow more. Thwart them by repaying anyway.

9. Don't bet against the real estate market. If house prices in your community are getting beaten up, stay away from home equity loans. If you take a big loan and then need to move, you might blow your entire equity in paying off your mortgages and covering the real estate broker's commission. You'll have little or nothing to put down on another house. What if you can't sell the house right now and decide to rent it out until the market improves? Your home equity contract might not allow it. Check it out. Home equity loans are safer in better times.

It's Okay to Borrow Against Your House When

- *You put no consumables, such as parties or clothes, on the credit line.* Put these on a credit card and pay them off in the same month.

- *You use the line to consolidate expensive credit card debt* and repay the loan fast.
- *You use it for unavoidable consumer debt,* such as buying a car, and repay it fast.
- *You use it for major investments:* education, home improvements, or buying property that you can afford to hold. These investments should yield more than the cost of the loan.
- *You don't run up other loans* on top of those on your home equity line.
- *You can handle the payments comfortably.* If your income drops, you can sell assets to repay the loan.
- *You have other sources of cash* to help make a down payment on a new house if you move.
- *You hate and fear home equity lines.* You worry when you use them. You treat them like time bombs.

It's Wrong to Borrow Against Your House When

- *You love home equity lines.* They're mother's milk. You feel wealthy when you use them.
- *You borrow to support* your consumer spending habit.
- *You will stretch out the loans for many years,* paying jillions of dollars in interest.
- *You think of the loan as a permanent debt,* not to be repaid until you sell your house.
- *Your job is shaky.*
- *You're borrowing to make an investment* but have chosen rotten investments in the past.
- *You'd be left with so little equity* that if you sold your house and repaid all the loans, you couldn't afford the down payment on a new house.
- *You will need your home equity pretty soon* to pay for your children's college.
- *You can't repay if your income drops,* except by selling the house.
- *Home values in your area are going down.*

Refinancing Your House

When you refinance, you get a new first mortgage and use the proceeds to pay off the old one. You'd normally do this in order to get a lower interest rate. If your house has risen in value, you can take a larger mortgage than you had before and use the extra money for other investments.

If you're going to tap your house for funds, you have two ways to do it: refinance with a larger first mortgage or add a second mortgage—either a fixed-term loan or a home equity line of credit. To choose, compare the following:

Up-Front Costs. Refinancing usually carries higher up-front costs. Fees run in the area of 1 to 2 percent of the mortgage amount, although your own lender may do the job for less.

Interest Rate. Refinance if you can get a lower interest rate. If the rate will be higher and you still want to raise money, take a home equity loan instead. The home equity loan will carry a higher interest rate, but it's paid on a smaller amount of money. That should make the combined loans cheaper than if you had refinanced the whole amount.

Flexibility. You can't beat a home equity line. You borrow periodically rather than in a big lump sum and pay interest only on the money you actually take.

Term. When you refinance, you start your primary mortgage from scratch, with payments typically lasting for 15 or 30 years. Home equity loans usually run for shorter terms, so you pay less interest in the long run.

Risk. How fast and how high could your monthly payments rise if interest rates go up? Your risk is higher with variable-rate home equity loans. Minimum monthly payments change immediately, and rates can run much higher than on first mortgages.

What You Can Tax-Deduct on a Refinancing

1. Interest on any new mortgage loan that equals your existing loan plus up to $100,000.
2. Interest on any new loan that equals your existing loan plus the cost of a home improvement (if you are borrowing to finance that home improvement) plus $100,000.

Both of these rules apply to your primary house and to one vacation house. A cabin, condominium, mobile home, and even a sleep-in boat can count as a house.

These rules are also subject to a cap. You can't deduct mortgage interest on loans higher than $1.1 million on your regular house and vacation house, combined. If you borrow more, however, and use the extra money to start a business or make investments, the interest may be deductible as business or investment interest.

Up-front points paid to the lender when you refinance normally have to be deducted over the life of the loan, with this exception: if part of the loan is used to improve your principal home, you get an immediate write-off for the points attributable to that portion of the loan.

Borrowing Against Your Cash-Value Life Insurance

When you have cash values in your life insurance policy, you can borrow against them. The money stashed in your policy keeps on earning interest. But an amount equal to your loan may earn interest at a lower rate.

That loss of interest raises the cost of your loan, so you're paying more than you realize. Instead of the 6 percent or so that your policy states, your actual loan rate can be 8 or 9 percent.

To see how to figure the true rate of interest on a loan against a universal-life insurance policy, see the example that follows. The footnotes show you how to adjust for loans against whole-life or variable-life policies.

Typically, the agent will claim that you're paying 1 or 2 percent. Untrue. The cost of a life insurance loan is about the same as a home equity loan. The difference is that policy loans aren't tax deductible.

Borrowers normally don't pay the interest out-of-pocket (although they could). Instead they add each year's interest to the loan, raising the amount they've borrowed. The policy's death benefit will be reduced by the total owed.

As an example, say that you have a policy with a $100,000 death benefit and borrow $30,000. Initially that leaves $70,000 for your heirs. Each year the cash value will rise by the premiums you pay and the interest your money earns, but it will decline by the insurance charges and the unpaid interest on the loan. If you keep that loan for many years or increase your borrowing, you may tear the policy apart. The net cash value may decline to the point where it can't support the insurance benefit anymore. You'll have to start repaying the loan or else let the policy lapse. If the policy lapses, you'll generally owe taxes on the amount by which your loan exceeded the premiums you paid. The tax bill can be a shocker if the loan was large.

Ask your insurance company or agent for a computer-generated policy illustration showing what might happen to your cash values and death benefit over your life expectancy, with and without the loan. That tells you whether your policy can last and how much you'll leave for your beneficiaries, assuming current interest rates. Get a new illustration from time to time.

If you borrow to invest and the investment earns less than the true rate of interest you're paying on the policy loan, you've made a mistake. Counting both

Figuring the True Rate of Interest on a Universal-Life Insurance Policy Loan

The Method	An Example
1. Find out the stated loan interest rate that the policy guarantees.	Your policy loan rate is 6 percent.
2. Find out what rate of interest the insurance company currently pays on your cash values. Typically, you're earning about the same as you would on a Treasury bond.	Your company credits 6.25 percent on cash values.
3. Find out what interest rate the company pays on any cash values you borrow against. It will usually be the policy's minimum rate, say, 4 percent.	If you borrow $5,000, the insurer credits $5,000 of your cash values with an interest rate of only 4 percent.
4. Subtract the reduced rate of interest earned on the cash you're using as collateral from the interest the insurer pays when you haven't borrowed (item 2). The difference shows you how much interest you are losing.	You are earning 4 percent on $5,000 in cash values, instead of 6.25 percent. That's a 2.25 percent loss.
5. Your true borrowing cost is the stated rate of loan interest plus the interest lost on your cash values.	Your $5,000 loan costs 6 percent plus the 2.25 percent loss of interest—8.25 percent in all.
6. *The agent might say that your loan's "true cost" is the difference between the loan interest you pay and the interest your cash value earns.*	*The agent claims that the true cost is only 2 percent: the 6 percent loan rate minus the 4 percent the insurer is still crediting to your policy.*
7. *THAT'S PURE BALONEY.*	*The true rate is 8.25 percent, as explained.*

For Whole Life Policies: Find out what the policy's dividend will be if you borrow and if you don't. You can get this information from an agent or from the insurance company. Add the difference between those two dividends to the amount of interest you'll pay to get your true borrowing cost. Divide the cost by the size of the loan to get the percentage rate. You'll have to do that every year. If your dividend will remain unchanged, then the policy loan rate is indeed your cost. Old whole-life policies (roughly, those issued prior to 1980) charge a loan rate of 5 to 6 percent. Newer policies may charge 8 percent or a variable rate.

For Variable Life Policies: An amount equal to your loan is transferred out of your separate investment account and into the insurer's general account. Find out the difference between what you pay on the loan and what your cash will earn in the general account. Add that to the policy loan rate to get your true borrowing cost.

the investment and what remains of the policy, your heirs will get less than if you had left the policy alone.

It often doesn't occur to people to repay their policy loans. That's another mistake. You improve your financial position by taking a lower-earning asset (say, a 5 percent bank account) and using it to repay an 8 or 9 percent policy loan. Repaying is the financial equivalent of investing, tax free and risk free, at the effective policy-loan rate. Put another way, you're earning a true 8 or 9 percent by repaying the loan.

If you do tap a universal policy for funds, leave enough money there to be sure that your insurance will stay in force for the rest of your life. If you take out too much, the policy may expire before you do. Your insurance company or agent can tell you where the withdrawal limits lie. As usual, the policy's death benefit will be reduced by the amount you withdraw.

For more on cash-value policies, including the question of whether to take withdrawals instead of loans, see page 379. Withdrawals from universal-life policies reduce the death benefit without running up interest charges.

Borrowing Against Certificates of Deposit

The bank will lend you money against your CDs. But do you really want that loan? Would it be smarter to cancel the CD, pay the early-withdrawal penalty, and use cash for whatever you want to buy?

To answer this question, use your handheld calculator and your common sense. Figure out how much interest you'd pay on the loan; compare it with the money you'd lose by cashing in the CD (you'd lose your after-tax interest earnings plus the early-withdrawal penalty). Then . . .

1. Take the loan if it costs less than cashing in the CD.
2. Break the CD if it earns less than you'd pay for the loan (which is usually the case).
3. Take the loan even when it costs more, if the CD is from an inheritance or other onetime source of money and you'd never be able to save such a sum yourself.

Loans against CDs aren't as cheap as the lenders make them out to be. Say that your banker offers you a 6 percent car loan, when your CD is earning 4 percent. The banker might say that you're paying only 2 percent "real" interest (subtracting the interest you earn on the CD from the interest you pay on the bank's auto loan). That appears to be a better deal than, say, a 3 percent promotional loan being offered by an auto dealer down the block. But it's not! To prove it, apply the banker's "logic" to the auto loan. If you keep the 4 percent CD and pay the car dealer 3 percent, you're gaining 1 percent "real." The auto loan costs less.

To find the cheapest loan, ignore net-cost gimmicks and compare each loan's annual percentage rate: the bank loan versus the auto loan. The lower the APR, the less it costs. If you use the cash in your CD to reduce or eliminate the loan, that's the cheapest strategy of all.

Borrowing Against Stocks, Bonds, and Mutual Funds

Loans against securities are called *margin loans*. You usually borrow from a stockbroker, although banks are in this business too. You can borrow up to 50 percent of the value of stocks listed on a stock exchange, well-diversified mutual funds, some over-the-counter stocks (*over-the-counter* means that they aren't sold on formal exchanges—see page 867), and listed convertible bonds; up to 75 percent of the value of listed corporate bonds, up to 85 percent on municipal bonds, and up to 95 percent on Treasury securities. Your brokerage firm may set its own limit at something less than these maximum amounts. You generally need an account with a discount stockbroker to borrow against no-load mutual funds (those are funds with no up-front sales charges).

Margin loans are usually used to buy securities. With just $10,000 cash, you can borrow enough money to buy up to $20,000 worth of listed stocks or $200,000 worth of U.S. government bonds.

But you can borrow against your securities for other purposes too. Interest rates on margin loans run 1 to 4 percentage points over the broker call rate, which is what banks charge brokers for their money. You don't have to make any loan repayments. The interest compounds in your brokerage account, payable when the securities are sold.

There are two major risks with margin loans:

1. Interest charges and sales commissions can easily eat up any profit you make on your securities.

2. If your stocks drop too far in price, the broker will ask for more collateral in the form of cash or securities. That's what's known as a *margin call*. If you don't have the money, some of your securities will be sold to cover the debt. You usually get a margin call if the value of your interest in the securities, net of the debt, shrinks to 30 or 25 percent of the market price.

Thousands of Investors Take Margin Loans Without Knowing What They've Done

Here's how that happens: The monthly statement from your broker may show, in one corner, your "borrowing power." The broker encourages you to use the money to buy a car or take a vacation. (The firm earns a nice piece of change on these loans.) He or she forgets to tell you that it's not an ordinary loan. Suddenly the market drops, and you get a margin call. You have to repay part of what you borrowed or lose some of your securities. But you've spent the money and haven't got any extra cash, so you have to sell some of your stocks.

There goes some retirement money down the drain.

If you borrow from your broker, don't do it for spending money. Borrow only to buy more securities in hopes of increasing your net worth, and don't hold the margin loan for long.

Loan Costs Can Demolish Your Profits

After paying loan interest and brokerage commissions, you might earn less on a margined investment than if you hadn't borrowed at all. This true story is best told by example.

Say that you have $5,000 to spend on a $50 stock. You can buy 100 shares for cash. Or you can buy 200 shares, putting up $5,000 and borrowing another $5,000 from your stockbroker. If the share price rises by $5, the cash investor grosses $500, or 10 percent. The margin investor makes $1,000, grossing 20 percent on his or her original $5,000. Wow! Gimme a loan.

But what if you hold your margined position for a year? You'd pay $500 on a loan that charged 10 percent interest. You paid your discount broker maybe $13 in sales commissions (more at a traditional brokerage firm). That's $513 in costs, subtracted from your $1,000 profit, for a net gain of $487—a 4.87 percent return on $10,000 invested. Compare that with the unmargined investment: a $500 profit minus $13 in sales commissions for the same $487 gain, but a fatter 9.7 percent return on a $5,000 investment, and with less investment risk. So maybe the loan isn't such a hot idea. For it to work, you need either large gains or fast ones, so you don't have to hold the margined position very long.

On the downside, margin loans are poison. Still using the same example, assume that the share price drops by $5. The cash investor loses 10 percent, but the margin investor loses 20 percent plus the extra commission and interest expenses. If the price drops by $12 a share, the margin buyer has to put up more money or be partly sold out.

Do You Really Want to Borrow Against Your Securities?

Yes, if you're a proven success as an investor and will use those loans to compound your winnings. *Yes,* if you're able, temperamentally, to sell losing stocks quickly. *Yes,* if you know the cost of your loan and will balance it carefully against your potential for profit.

No, if you're a new or uncertain investor, because you'll probably go wrong. *No,* if you're a long-term investor rather than a quick trader. *No,* if it wouldn't occur to you to borrow unless your stockbroker suggested it. *No,* if you're borrowing to take a vacation or buy a car; that simply consumes the investments that you are laboring so hard to build. *No,* if you're dabbling in mysterious investments that you only faintly understand. Some of the biggest losses in the crash of 1987 were taken by investors who borrowed against stocks to pyramid stock-index options. They didn't have a clue what they were doing. Many wound up losing far more money than they invested.

Borrowing Against Your Smile

Collateral is property you put up to guarantee or secure a loan. Stocks, certificates of deposit, automobiles, and real estate can all be used as collateral. The lender will grab them if you don't pay.

An *unsecured loan* is given on the strength of your paycheck and credit history. If you don't pay, the lender can only sue. The interest rate is higher than on secured loans, and the repayment period often shorter. For these reasons, these are *not* suitable sources for investment loans (although many an entrepreneur has bootstrapped himself or herself with credit card advances!).

The line of credit tied to your credit card is the commonest source of unsecured loans. The lender gives you the right to borrow up to a certain amount—maybe $1,500 to $10,000—whenever you want. You get the money by slipping your card into an ATM, writing a "convenience check," visiting the bank, or asking the bank (online or by phone) to transfer the cash to your checking account. There's usually a 2 to 5 percent transaction fee, and you'll probably have to borrow in multiples of $10 or $25. Interest rates are high—often 25 percent, not tax deductible! Credit card advances are handy for sudden emergencies, but clear up these expensive loans as fast as you can.

For a cheaper bank loan, ask about a personal credit line attached to your checking account. That might cost you 9 or 10 percent, and 8 percent at a credit union.

If you have a good salary and a high net worth, you might qualify for "personal banking." Someone is assigned to your account, and it's his or her job to make you happy. Whatever you need—loans, brokerage services, certificates of deposit, Treasury securities—your personal banker makes it work. Interest rates are negotiable. High-income clients can usually get a better deal than anyone else because they bring the bank more business.

How much you can borrow unsecured depends on your salary and the value of your assets, such as savings, investments, and real estate. It's not illegal to puff your net worth a bit by taking an optimistic view of the value of your house. But if you borrow more than you can handle, you're the loser in the end.

Borrowing Against Your Retirement Fund

It's a lousy idea to borrow against your retirement plan for spending money. But borrowing to make an investment—a solid, well-considered investment—can work. Stocks and bonds are usually available within the plan, so you wouldn't borrow to buy more of them. But you might want to borrow to buy real estate or invest in a business.

A loan from a retirement plan does not necessarily deplete your assets. Sometimes it enlarges them. Follow me through an optimal transaction, and I'll show you how.

1. You borrow money from your retirement plan and invest it.

2. You pay interest on the loan, at 1 to 3 percentage points over the prime rate. That interest payment usually goes right into your own retirement account, so you're paying interest to yourself instead of a bank. If your retirement fund had been earning 6 percent on the money you borrowed, and you pay 9 percent on the loan, your account has just picked up an extra 3 percentage points.

3. You repay most loans over 5 years, in regular monthly or quarterly amounts. As I see it, that's a form of forced saving. If you borrow to buy a principal residence, your monthly payments are amortized over 10 to 30 years, depending on the plan. Loan repayments are usually deducted automatically from your paycheck.

4. Your retirement fund gets its money back plus interest. Meanwhile, the money you borrowed is (one hopes) prospering in your outside investment. It has to earn at least enough to cover the extra income taxes this loan will cost.

Your Tax Cost

One drawback to loans against retirement plans is the extra tax you pay. The loan interest normally isn't tax deductible. Neither is the money you use to repay principal. So that money is taxed twice: once when you earn it and use it to make loan repayments into the plan and again when you retire and take it out of the plan. Put another way, you put after-tax money into the plan, and it's taxed again when you take it out.

Loan interest is deductible only if it meets the following two tests: (1) you borrow your employer's contributions, not yours (the employer would have to segregate these funds, and few do); and (2) the money is used for a deductible purpose, such as running your small business or making an investment.

Your Investment Cost

Sometimes your retirement plan is earning more than the interest charged on loans. Then the loan creates a loss. For example, say your retirement investments yield 10 percent, but you'd pay only 9 percent if you borrowed the money out. That's a 1 percentage point loss, which would compound over time. The loan's true cost becomes 10 percent (the 9 percent loan rate plus the 1-point drop in yield). You might find a bank that charges less.

It's unlikely, however, that all of your plan's investments earn the same high rate of return. If you borrow, you can arrange for the loan to come from the lowest-earning assets.

Borrowing from Your Plan Makes Sense as Long As

- *The plan charges a lower interest rate than you could get at a bank,* counting both the direct loan rate and any loss your plan takes by lending to you rather than making other investments. A home equity loan will almost always be better than a retirement plan loan because interest on home equity loans is tax deductible.
- *You pay a higher interest rate on the loan than your plan is earning on its investments.* That way you are adding assets to your plan.
- *Your outside investment earns enough to cover its tax cost,* plus something extra to compensate you for the risk you took.
- *You'll be with the company long enough to repay the loan.* If you quit or are fired, a few companies let you continue the payments as scheduled. More likely, you'll have to repay the loan immediately. If you don't, it's treated as a withdrawal. You'll owe income taxes on the remaining loan amount plus a 10 percent penalty if you're younger than 59½. Retirees may be allowed to repay on the original schedule, even if others aren't.

Here's How Much You Can Borrow from the Plan

1. Up to 50 percent of the assets in your company savings or profit-sharing plan or $50,000, whichever is smaller. If you borrow any more, it will be treated as a taxable withdrawal.

2. If your plan is worth less than $20,000, you may be able to borrow up to $10,000 as long as the loan is adequately secured.

With Keogh plans, you can borrow if you're an employee but not if you own the business or are self-employed. With Individual Retirement Accounts, you cannot borrow at all.

For more on retirement accounts, see chapter 29.

Your Tax Deduction for Interest on Investment Loans

You're going to hate this. The deduction is so complicated that it makes no sense for me to try to explain it. For the gory details, ask an accountant or get a current tax guide. I'll just give you the gist.

If you take out a loan to make an investment, the interest is deductible to the extent that you have net taxable income from investments (after deducting your expenses).

Say, for example, that you collect a net of $1,500 in dividends and interest. That allows you to write off $1,500 of interest paid on loans that were taken to make investments. If you pay more investment-loan interest than you receive in investment income, the extra can be carried forward and deducted in future years.

More on Tax Deductions for Interest on Loans

What if you borrow money and do two things with the proceeds: buy some stocks and buy a car? The interest on the money used to buy stocks falls under the investment rule—deductible to the extent that you have net investment income. The interest on the money used to buy the car falls under the consumer loan rule—not deductible at all. Are you still with me? If not, call a tax preparer.

What if you borrow against your house? The interest is fully deductible as mortgage interest as long as you stay within the loan limits (page 306). The interest on larger loans can be deducted as investment interest if you use the money to make other investments.

What if you borrow to buy tax-exempt municipal bonds? The interest on such loans is never deductible.

What if you borrow to fund an Individual Retirement Account? No interest deduction is allowed.

What if you borrow to buy investment real estate? The interest is deductible against your rents, as well as against income from limited partnerships and other tax-shelter investments (check the tax guides for the *passive activity* rules). If you have a vacation home that you rent out, larger amounts of interest are sometimes deductible (page 605).

What if you borrow to start or expand your own business? All the interest is deductible as a business expense.

What if you borrow from your retirement savings plan? You get no tax deduction for interest on any part of an unsecured loan attributable to your own pretax contributions plus the money your contributions earned, or for money commingled with money your employer put in. But you do get a write-off if you borrow for a deductible purpose and take money that the employer contributed. See if you can specify that those are the funds you want. Some companies let you put up home equity as collateral, which makes the interest on any loan deductible.

What if you contributed after-tax money to your company plan? You can borrow against it for a deductible purpose and get the write-off.

What if you borrow from your retirement savings plan to buy a principal residence? The interest is deductible only if you put up your house as collateral for the loan. Some company plans let you do this; most don't.

What if you're a key employee of the business (generally, an owner or an officer) and borrow from the company savings plan? You get no interest deduction, no matter what you invest in.

How to Ensure That You Get Your Proper Interest Deductions. When you borrow money for more than one purpose, don't put all the loan proceeds into the same bank account. Keep separate checking accounts for personal borrowing (which is nondeductible), business borrowing, and investment borrowing.

Say, for example, that you take a $50,000 bank loan to buy a car for your own use, a computer for your business, and some stock. Put $28,000 for the car into your regular personal account, $2,000 for the computer into your business account, and $20,000 for the stock into an investment account. That makes it clear how much interest is deductible on each part of the loan.

Don't put all the loan proceeds into your personal checking account. If you do and wait more than 15 days to buy your business computer or make an investment, some of the loan may be treated as funding your normal living expenses. That will reduce your loan interest deduction.

I'll stop here. The actual rules are even more complicated than I've suggested. It's madness to have to pay for extra bank accounts just to keep track of your tax deductions. Even thinking about it can drive you nuts.

Auto Loans

Car dealers love you when cars aren't selling well. On certain models, they'll offer the lowest interest rate on the block—as little as 0 to 5 percent on two- to three-year loans, sometimes up to five years when manufacturers want to "move the metal." When dealers and manufacturers are fat, their interest rates rise. Then the best choice might be a home equity loan.

Always compare the two types of loans after tax. Your payback schedule is more flexible on a home equity loan and you can deduct the interest if you itemize on your tax return. On loans from any other source, there's no potential write-off.

If you don't want to borrow against your house (or don't own a house), find out—before you car shop—what interest rate you can get from an online lender or your own bank or credit union. Compare that with what the dealer offers when you're ready to buy. Dealers usually have competitive rates, especially for buyers with good credit ratings.

For an online financial calculator comparing different ways of financing a car, go to one of the auto sites such as Cars.com (www.cars.com) or Edmunds.com (www.edmunds.com).

Many dealers offer only fixed-rate loans because that's what customers prefer. They let you budget for the same payment every month.

Variable rates are available too. Consider them only if you can get the loan for at least one percentage point less than the cheapest fixed-rate loan around. You deserve a lower payment for shouldering the risk that rates will rise. A variable-rate loan will be cheaper if interest rates decline, stay level, or rise just a little bit. But these loans have no caps, or high caps, so you'd be hurt if rates took a sudden jump and remained on that new plateau.

If you do choose a variable-rate loan and interest rates rise, one of two things will happen: (1) Your monthly payments will go up but probably not by very much. On a $20,000, 5-year, 7 percent loan, an increase to 10 percent would cost you an extra $29 a month. (2) Your payments will stay level, but the term of your loan will be extended. Taking this same example and assuming that the rate rose after the first 12 months, you'd owe an extra 6 months' worth of payments.

Some lenders add upfront fees (documentation or loan fees) that raise the effective cost of your loan. Compare each loan's annual percentage rate (APR) to see which is cheapest. Rates can vary by one to two percentage points within the same metropolitan area.

When you borrow to buy a car, you usually need a down payment. But not always. The finance companies owned by some manufacturers may lend you the entire amount if you have a good credit history. Some lend more than your cost to help cover the amount still owing on a prior loan or lease. You can also find large loans at some banks. Expect to pay one to three percentage points more than you would for a regular loan.

Auto Loans for Poorer Risks

You're no longer poison if your credit history shows a bad patch, you've only recently been employed, or you've already borrowed a heap of money. Instead you're a "subprime borrower."

A few credit unions give subprime auto loans. So do some of the nation's largest banks. But your best source may be the auto dealer. You'll pay a higher rate of interest than prime borrowers do, and there may be a higher down payment. You won't be able to bargain the car price down quite as far. But you'll get a loan. After a year, recheck your credit. If you've paid all your bills on time and are steadily employed, you may be able to refinance at a lower rate.

Your current lender is the first place to go to refinance. It will want to keep you as a customer.

Now for the Nub of Your Decision: How Many Years Will You Carry the Loan?

The longer the term, the lower the monthly payment and the easier it is to buy today's expensive cars. Auto finance companies owned by manufacturers may let you borrow for five and a half to six years, or even seven years for a luxury car and a customer with a top credit rating. Some banks and credit unions also go to seven years on luxury cars. On a $30,000 loan at 7.5 percent, you will pay $206 less a month by stretching the loan to six years instead of holding it down to four. The downside is that the longer-term loan costs you an extra $2,530 in interest.

To hardened spenders, interest costs are a yawn. So I'll give long-term borrowers something else to worry about. (What good is a personal finance book that doesn't give readers something to worry about?): *A long-term auto loan may prevent you from trading in your car as soon as you'd like.* Why? Because you're "upside down"—the industry's term for owing more than the car is worth.

Most auto loans of five years or longer are typically upside down for the first 36 to 40 months, unless you made a substantial down payment of 15 percent or more. Then they straighten up. Gradually you build equity value. That equity gives you a trade-in allowance when you buy a new car.

But if you want another car before 36 to 40 months have passed, there's nothing to trade with. You have *negative equity.* Your car's net value is less than, or not far above, zero.

Ideally, a car should be financed over the number of years you expect to drive it. If you like a new car every three years, buy it on a three-year loan. If you took a longer-term loan and still want to trade after just three years and your loan is upside down, you have three choices:

1. Find the cash to get out of the old loan. You have to pay the difference between the loan balance and the trade-in value. Your savings take a hit, but your debts don't balloon.

2. Roll your negative equity into the loan you take to buy the new car. Effectively, you're now carrying two auto loans instead of one. That's expensive and not worth it except for a very good reason—for example, because your old car is a maintenance nightmare or guzzles too much gas. If you take a home equity loan, work on paying it back over 4 years or so. Stretching it out to 10 or 15 years puts you even deeper into the hole.

3. Shine up your old car. Keep it tuned up, with the brakes lined and the oil changed. Do what it says in the owner's manual. Make small repairs as they come along. Swallow a big repair if you have to. Stick with the car until it's paid for or until you have enough equity to make a trade. This option gets my vote every time. Your car can run reliably for 100,000 miles or more.

Financing a Used (Oops—"Preowned") Car

Nowadays, a used-car loan may cost about the same as a new-car loan, or only slightly more. Lenders have learned that four- and five-year-old cars have plenty of life left in their engines. There's also a wealth of good cars coming off three-year leases.

Lenders aren't the only ones to notice. Increasingly, people with good credit ratings are turning to the "preowned" market for luxury cars or second and third cars for the family. The best loans go to the best credit risks who buy expensive, newer-model cars. The older the car, the lower its price; and the lower your credit score, the higher the interest rate a dealer will charge.

You should finance the car over the number of years that you expect to drive it and no longer. That's because it will have lost much of its value by the time you're ready to give it up. You don't want to be paying interest on a big loan to carry a car worth only $2,000 in the marketplace.

In most cases, your best financing choice will be a home equity loan, especially if you itemize on your tax return. Just be sure to schedule payments at a rate that will repay the loan in full by the time you're ready to junk the car. If you don't own a house or have no spare equity in your home, start your search for a Car Loan With An Online Lender Or A Credit Union.

What's a "Certified Preowned" Car? It's a car in good condition with average mileage or less, inspected and repaired by the dealer and carrying a manufacturer's warranty. Not all cars advertised as certified meet these tests. The key is the warranty. If you pay for it separately, it's merely an extended service contract. In true certified programs, the warranty comes from the manufacturer and is included in the price.

Pay Cash or Take Out a Loan?

It's cheaper to pay cash if you have the money. It also feels good not to have the monthly debt.

But some auto dealers (who make money on car loans) have come up with a clever, computerized gimmick to bamboozle customers into thinking that loans are a better deal.

For example, say you have $10,000. You can put it into a certificate of deposit earning 5 percent interest or use it toward buying a new car. The dealer may argue that it's smarter to choose the CD and take out a 7 percent auto loan.

Here's the dealer's four-step "proof":

1. If you leave your $10,000 in the bank for four years, you'll earn $2,155 in interest, pretax.

2. A four-year, $10,000 auto loan will cost $1,494 in interest (the interest is less than you think because it's paid on a declining loan balance).

3. So by keeping the CD and taking the loan, you're apparently $661 ahead.

4. Furthermore, the dealer croons, debtors do even better when the loan's term is up. Say the car is worth $5,000 at trade-in. If you bought for cash, you effectively have $5,000 in hand. But the borrower supposedly has an amazing $15,661—adding together $5,000 from the trade-in, the $661 gain in interest, plus the $10,000 still in the bank!

Before you decide that the road to riches is paved with auto loans, sit back and think a minute. There's something the dealer didn't mention. How are you going to repay the $10,000 loan?

If you take the monthly payments out of your bank account, your $10,000 in savings will be wiped out before the loan is entirely repaid.

If you make the monthly payments out of personal earnings, you'll be giving up $11,494 (the interest and principal repayments) that you could have saved or invested. Either way, the loan costs you more than paying cash.

So pay cash if you have it. Then take the equivalent of the monthly payment, which you're *not* spending on the auto loan, and use it to replenish your savings. At the end of the term, you'll have your car and more than $10,000 back.

I'd vote for the loan, however, in one of four circumstances:

1. Your fat savings account was a windfall—a gift, an inheritance, a winning lottery ticket—that you'd never be able to replace.

2. You have credit card debts. You'll save more money by using your cash to pay down those high-rate loans.

3. You need a ready savings account. Never tie up all your cash. Save something for unexpected expenses.

4. You haven't been funding your retirement plan to the max. Save for retirement first, even if it costs you interest on an auto loan.

The same arguments apply to the question of whether to make a large down payment or a small one, if you have the choice. Make a small down payment *if* you'll use the extra money for one of the four purposes above. Otherwise make a large down payment.

Should You Lease Instead of Buy?

For the poor of pocketbook but rich in taste, auto leasing is hard to beat. You can drive out of a dealer's lot on four of his classiest wheels for a small up-front deposit and lower monthly payments than you'd owe on most auto loans. Payments are lower because you're not financing the car's entire cost.

Briefly, here's how leasing works:

You negotiate a car price (the *capitalized cost*). The leasing company subtracts the amount it expects to get for the car on resale after you turn it in (the *residual value*). You have to pay only the difference between those two prices (the *depreciation*). As an example, consider a $30,000 car with an expected resale value of $12,000. If you lease it, you pay only $18,000 of principal—the difference between its $30,000 price (including various fees) and its turn-in, or residual, value. That reduces the amount you have to pay each month. You're still charged implied interest (the *rent charge*) on the full negotiated price. But out-of-pocket costs are far lower than if you'd financed the car at its full $30,000 price.

Leasing isn't for everyone. Here's what to consider when making your decision.

You Shouldn't Lease If

- *You expect to keep your car for many years.* If you lease for a while, then buy when the lease runs out, you'll usually pay more than if you purchased the car up front. This isn't always true, but it's true often enough.
- *You hate monthly payments.* Loan payments eventually stop, but lease payments never do. It's like burying your grandfather in a rented suit.
- *You're hard on your cars, driving them many more miles than average.* The excess-mileage charge on a lease may raise its cost to more than you'd pay on an auto loan.

But Consider a Lease If

- *You have no car to trade in and not enough cash for a down payment* (although many lenders give no-down-payment loans).

- *You have the cash down payment but can—excuse me, will—put it to work earning more than 10 percent a year,* says Randall McCathren of BLC Associates in Nashville. That's actually easy for many people. You can earn more than 10 percent on your money just by paying off credit card debt that is costing at least that much in interest.

- *You want lower monthly payments.*

- *You want a more expensive car than you could afford otherwise.*

- *You're trading in your car in the fourth year of a six-year auto loan and owe more than the car is worth.* You can't afford to pay off your old loan and make a down payment on a new car too.

- *You want to drive a new car every two to four years* and don't mind having permanent monthly car payments.

- *You make plenty of money and want someone else to worry about keeping your car in good repair.* For an extra fee, the lessor will do all the maintenance and lend you a car to drive while yours is in the shop.

- *You're looking for business tax breaks.* Business use of your car is deductible whether you lease or own. But because of quirks in the tax law, business lessees can typically write off more of the cost of the car than owners can.

- *You want to reduce your state's sales tax.* In most states, you're taxed only on your monthly payments, not on the car's full purchase price.

- *You want a guaranteed trade-in price,* so you don't run the risk of seeing your car's market value drop by more than you expected (14 mpg gas-guzzlers, anyone?).

Which Is More Expensive, Leasing or Buying?

This depends on two things: (1) the car's final value when you turn it in. That would be the residual value if you leased; it's the trade-in, or resale, value if you bought. (2) the effective interest rate you paid—the *implicit lease rate* on a lease or the annual percentage rate on a loan. Counting all fees, the implicit lease rate is usually higher than the auto loan rate, making leasing more expensive. But the leasing company may guarantee a final residual value that turns out to be higher than you could have gotten on a resale.

Over the past 10 years, leasing often turned out to be cheaper than buying because certain cars lost value (depreciated)—for example, 14-mpg gas guzzlers. If you bought those cars, you took a beating on their trade-in value. If you leased them, you benefited from the higher residual value that the leasing company guaranteed. The company took the resale loss instead of you.

Two Circumstances When Leasing Will Be Cheaper

1. It's cheaper to lease when the automaker subsidizes the transaction. In this case, the implicit interest rate in the lease will be less than you'd pay for an auto loan, and the lessor may increase the residual (resale) value that it guarantees.

There's no way to tell directly when a lease is being subsidized, but the dealer can calculate the implicit lease interest rate for you. You can then compare it with the interest cost of taking a loan. As for whether you're getting a subsidy on the depreciation rate, you'll have to take the dealer's word.

2. It will have been cheaper to lease if, at the end of the lease, the car's market price is lower than its guaranteed residual value. By rolling into a new lease, you'll have saved yourself the cost of trading in the car for less than you expected. If you want to own the car, the company might let you buy it at its current, low market value rather than at the higher value specified in the lease. You can't know in advance, however, whether your lease will work out in this lucky way.

When Buying Will Be Cheaper: You pay lower interest on your loan than the lessor offers, and your car maintains (or improves on) its expected future market value.

How to Get the Most Future Value Out of a Car, Whether You Lease or Buy: Choose a car that tends to depreciate less than similar vehicles. In the view of *Kelley Blue Book*, that's one in a popular color (silver, white, gray, black); optional equipment that's typical for the car (say, automatic transmission, not manual transmission); and attractive extras such as leather seats or an audio system with MP3/iPod compatibility (or whatever the latest in music is in the year you buy). Gas-efficient cars do better than the competition.

A Definition That People Leasing Cars Need to Know

The "money factor"—a number that dealers typically use to calculate the monthly charge. It's a decimal, such as .00292. The higher the money factor, the higher your monthly payment. As a broad generality, you can multiply the money factor by 2,400 to approximate an annual interest rate. It's not exact, but it gives you a good idea of what you're paying for the money.

Types of Leases

The leasing process is pretty simple. You typically make one month's payment up front plus a refundable deposit roughly equal to one month's payment, and drive away. On subsidized leases, or if your credit is less than sterling, the lessor may want a down payment too—usually 5 to 10 percent.

On a *closed-end lease,* your basic costs are fixed. At the end of the term, you can usually buy the car you've been driving at a guaranteed price or turn in your keys and get a new one. You can lease the same car a second time if your first lease ran for two to four years. Almost all consumer leases are closed end.

On an *open-end lease,* which is generally offered only for business use, you pay less per month. Your final cost, however, depends on the car's resale value. If it sells for more than the leasing company expected, you may get a refund. If it sells for less, you pay the difference.

On both types of leases, you buy your own auto insurance. You're responsible for general maintenance unless you buy a maintenance contract. You'll generally owe an extra 10 to 15 cents a mile for driving more than 12,000 miles a year. (Watch this excess mileage charge; some lessors hit you for 20 or even 25 cents on more expensive vehicles.) There are extra charges for excessive wear and tear, such as cracked glass, lost trim, bald tires, torn seats, and deep dents. Look for an itemized list in the lease. The leasing company decides how much wear is excessive and generally will not overreach. If you get sore, your dealer won't send new customers the lessor's way. Some lessors build the cost of $500 to $1,500 of excess wear into the leasing price; others sell it separately as an option.

Don't Lease the Car for a Longer Period Than You Expect to Drive It. Some drivers go for 5-year (or even 66- and 72-month) leases because of the super-low monthly payments. The dealer might even say there will be no problem breaking the lease if you want to switch to a brand-new car. But there *will* be a problem. You generally face an "early termination deficiency" for the depreciation that you haven't paid for yet. It could be 5 to 10 percent of capitalized cost or more (at least $1,500 to $3,000 on a $30,000 car). The dealer might be able to roll the debt—called *negative equity*—into your next lease, but not always.

The formula for determining the balance of your lease payoff will be printed in your contract, probably in Sanskrit. To avoid that cost, drive the car for the lease's full term.

What Happens If Your Leased Car is Stolen or Wrecked? That's usually counted as an early termination. Your auto insurance will cover the car's market value. But in most cases, money will still be owed on the lease. Major lessors typically offer *gap insurance*, which covers your portion of the loss. Don't drive away without it.

Check the Lease's Fine Print If You Think That You Might Move Out of State. A few leasing companies charge an extra fee if you do. A few make you convert the lease to a loan. Tell your car dealer that you want a national lessor that doesn't care where you live.

Tips for Getting the Cheapest Lease

1. **When you start talking lease, the dealer will offer you "$XXX a month."** That's usually based on the car's full list price, which is more than you ought to pay. Before talking monthly payments, bargain down the price of the car. That gives you a lower lease price, too. To be sure you're getting that lower price, check the car's capitalized cost on the lease contract. (Note that you won't be able to bargain very much if you're buying an advertised "manufacturer's special.")

2. **You can lower the lease cost by making a down payment up front.** But a smarter use of that money may be to lower your credit card debts. Credit cards ding you for higher finance costs than you pay in the lease.

3. **Ask to see more than one lease contract; every dealer has access to several different sources.** Compare all fees, such as the *acquisition fee* for acquiring the car and the *disposition fee* for selling it. They're not the same at all companies.

4. **If you'll drive more than the standard 12,000 miles a year that leases usually allow, buy excess mileage in advance.** For example, you might arrange to drive the car for 15,000 miles. That's cheaper than paying for an extra 3,000 miles when you turn the car in.

5. **A growing number of credit unions offer cheap leases** to their members.

6. **Leasing companies are required to make standard disclosures on their leases.** That makes it easy to compare one lease with another, to see which offers the better terms. *Always* comparison shop.

7. **At the end of the lease, find out the market price of the car.** If it's substantially higher than the guaranteed residual value, don't passively turn the car over to the dealer and lease or buy a new one. Instead ask for a turn-in value higher than the guaranteed residual. The dealer might treat the extra value as a down payment on your next car or even give you cash. If the dealer refuses, consider buying the car. You could resell it yourself or trade it to another dealer for a better lease.

If the market price is lower than the lease's residual value, here's a different strategy to consider. Ask to buy the car at its current, lower value. If the dealer says no, turn in the keys and buy a car just like it that's coming off someone else's lease. You'll get the lower price.

8. Sometimes you're offered a chance to extend your lease for another two or three years. Compare this with the cost of leasing a new car. When there are factory-subsidized deals, the new car may be cheaper.

Leasing a Used Car

Er, I mean a preowned car, which is the idiom that dealers prefer. Originally, companies offered leases only on luxury preowned cars. But now they'll lease almost any car that's no more than four years old and hasn't been driven more than 60,000 miles. Formerly, used cars came with 30-day limited warranties at best. Today's cream puffs are often "certified" by the manufacturer as being completely reconditioned. They even come with another two- or three-year warranty good for up to 100,000 miles.

Compare the price with the cost of leasing the same car new. Used cars don't get manufacturers' incentives, so the lease might save you only $20 to $50 a month. For that price, you might prefer something new.

Dirty Lease Tricks Some Dealers Play

1. You bargain the car price down, give the dealer your old car, and make a down payment. But the dealer still bases the lease on the car's list price, not on the lower price you negotiated. If this happens, all the money you put toward the new car has effectively been stolen. To protect yourself, ask for a printout of the lease contract before signing and check it for the car's capitalized cost. That should reflect the list price, minus the discount you negotiated, minus the value of any car you traded in, minus any rebate the dealer is offering, minus your down payment, plus taxes and such incidentals as fees, rustproofing, and maintenance agreements. Your lease payments are based on the capitalized cost. Federal law requires the dealer to tell you the capitalized cost, although he has to itemize it only if you ask. Fortunately, most leasing companies now require itemization in their contracts—so read the contract.

2. You intend to buy a car, but after the negotiation, the dealer gives you a lease to sign instead. You're told it's a special, low-priced deal. You don't notice it's a lease, because the salesperson's hand covers up the heading on the contract. The lease is based on a high car price. When you discover the deception and protest, the salesperson claims that you always knew you were leasing the car. To avoid this, take the documents home and study them before signing. Your intended car won't go away. At the very least, hold the documents in your hand and read them before signing. Dealerships have waiting areas that you can use.

3. You're attracted to a lease with an especially low monthly cost. But it's cheap only because the allowable mileage is low; you might be buying just 10,000 miles a year. If you drive another 5,000 miles a year on a four-year lease, you might owe $3,000 when you turn the car in. To avoid this, estimate realistically how much you drive and cover it in advance. A 10,000-mile allowance gives you only 27 miles a day. A 12,000-mile allowance gives you almost 32 miles. A 15,000-mile allowance gives you 41 miles. If you're faced with a big mileage bill at the end of the lease, it may be smarter to buy the car instead of turning it in.

4. You're overcharged for wear and tear. When you turn the car in, the dealer says "no problem." But after it's been wholesaled, you get a large bill. If you don't pay, it goes on your credit history. To avoid this, most leasing companies mail out a detailed description of what counts as excess wear. You can also have your car checked by their third-party inspector (not the dealer) just before the lease ends, to see what you might be responsible for. They'll conduct the inspection in your presence. If there is indeed excess wear, you can use their cost estimate to decide whether to make repairs yourself or buy the car and keep on driving it.

What's the Cheapest Lease?

When comparing leases on the same car, shoppers usually look only at the monthly payment. That can mislead you. It doesn't take into consideration the amount you paid up front. For a true comparison, look at "Total of Payments"—the top-right disclosure box on the lease contract. The lease with the lowest total payments is the best deal.

If you plan to buy the car at the end of the lease, add the total payments to the end-of-lease purchase price. The car with the lowest total cost is the best deal.

Buying or Leasing a Car Online

Simplify your shopping and (maybe) find a better deal by buying your car online. You negotiate the price on new and used cars by e-mail, which gives you more time for thought. Most of the online services ask you to fill in a form, detailing the make and model you want as well as any special add-ons. The site forwards your request to dealers in your area, who respond with offers. You take the negotiation from there. Your options include Autobytel.com (www.autobytel

.com), Cars.com, Edmunds.com, and Kelley Blue Book (www.kbb.com). Taking another approach, CarsDirect (www.carsdirect.com) prenegotiates with local dealers and offers you a single, no-haggle price on the car you want. Finally, auction sites such as PriceGrabber.com (www.pricegrabber.com) put the specs of the car you want online, where local dealers can bid for your business.

If you have the time and interest, you can e-mail competing dealers yourself. Choose the car you want, draw up an exact list of the desired equipment, and ask the dealers for a bid. They have staff on hand to respond to e-mail buyers. It's a terrifically efficient way of finding the best deal in your area.

If you want a lease, try online sites such as LeaseCompare.com (www.lease compare.com). They'll show you three different offers as well as put you in touch with a local dealer who might want to bid even lower. If you think you paid too much for your current lease, you might be able to refinance it on better terms at LowerMyLease.com (www.lowermylease.com). New leases can be had on cars that are less than four years old, without your having to turn in the car and pay early termination fees. To find leases subsidized by the carmakers' finance arms, go to Edmunds.com, enter the car you want, and then click on "incentives."

Do You Really Need Your Own Car?

In a big city, with public transportation, maybe you don't need to own. Look into car sharing, through companies such as Zipcar (www.zipcar.com). You pay a monthly fee for the right to reserve a car and drive it for a specified period of time—a few hours or a few days. Drivers usually have to be at least 21 years old with a good driving record. On college campuses, the minimum age may be 18. The deal includes insurance, so you don't have to buy your own. If you already own a car, Zipcar can give you access to a second vehicle for someone else in the family to drive.

How to Lower Your Interest Charges on Loans

1. Pick the right lender. Credit unions and direct online lenders often charge less than banks offer at their branch offices. Competing lenders may be as much as 2 or 3 percentage points apart in rates, which is discoverable only by people who price-shop.

2. Pick the right annual percentage rate (APR). Don't look only at the interest rate. Look at the APR, which usually counts up-front fees as well as the interest itself. (Exception: the APR on home equity loans excludes any up-front fees, so this type of loan costs more than it first appears.)

3. Pick the right time period. The longer the term, the more expensive the loan because the rate is a little higher and you make so many more payments. If you're doing something constructive with the money, such as investing in a retirement account, never mind the longer term. But on depreciating assets such as a car, keep the term as short as possible.

4. Put on the squeeze. Many borrowers don't realize that lenders compete. If bank A will give you a fixed rate loan at 7.6 percent and you tell that to bank B, dear old bank B may counter with 7.4 percent. If it's an auto loan, the dealer may chime in with 7.2 percent if you're a good credit risk. This happens only to borrowers who price-shop. If you're borrowing a lot of money, you might get a quarter point off your interest rate just by asking for it.

5. Avoid traditional installment loans. They're often front-end-loaded (the fine print will say that they're computed by the *rule of 78s*). You pay a higher interest rate in the early months than you do in the later ones, which penalizes you if you pay off your loan ahead of time. You also get no benefit from making extra principal payments along the way.

The better loans charge the same interest rate every month (*simple interest*). Given two loans with the same annual percentage rate, the one charging simple interest will cost less over the life of the loan than the one computed by the rule of 78s.

How can you tell if you're offered a simple-interest loan? The installment agreement will say that the interest is figured "on a simple-interest basis." Be sure to check.

6. Don't buy credit life, disability, or unemployment insurance from the lender. These policies sound like a good deal. They cover your minimum monthly payments for a certain length of time if you're disabled or unemployed. If you die, they pay off the debt up to the maximum stated in the policy. Some also pay the policy maximum if you become totally disabled. The maximum may be less than your total debt.

These policies are expensive, and their coverage can be full of loopholes. What does it mean to be disabled if the condition is temporary? Are some conditions not covered? Are you considered unemployed only if you qualify for unemployment insurance? (That's the usual case.) Do you have to be working full time? Do they cover the self-employed? (Usually not.) Fall afoul of the fine print and the policies won't pay. There's usually a 14- or 30-day waiting period before they pay on unemployment or disability claims, by which time you may be back to work. Even if they accept your claim, they make the minimum payment for a limited period of time (a few months to two years). After that, you have to pick up the debt again.

Some lenders hide the fact that they're selling you insurance. They call it a "payment protection plan" or some similar name. But it's credit insurance all the same.

The price of credit insurance is usually rolled right into your loan, so you wind up borrowing—and paying interest on—your insurance premiums. It's a costly system that often enriches the loan officer personally. At some banks, he or she earns a commission on the sale.

Sometimes the lender adds this coverage automatically and asks you to sign. That's called "sliding the policy." The lender hopes you'll say okay just because the paperwork is done. But don't submit to that kind of pressure. By law, this insurance is optional. Tell the lender to redo the contract, leaving the insurance out.

What's the alternative to this type of insurance? Buy term life insurance (page 343) to pay off your debts at death—it's *much* cheaper per $1,000 of coverage than credit life. Cover minimum payments during a bout of unemployment with your personal savings, spouse's earnings, or unemployment pay. If you're temporarily disabled, you may get disability payments from your employer. Credit disability insurance is no help to the permanently disabled because it pays so little and for such a short period of time.

Does credit life insurance ever make sense? Only if your health is so bad that you can't qualify for term life insurance.

Your Personal Financial Statement

For a big loan, a lender wants a financial statement and, often, copies of three years of income tax returns. What do you earn? What's the value of your house, your other real estate, your savings accounts, your stocks? How much do you owe? Put down everything you can think of, including any bonuses due. How much you can borrow depends on what you earn and what you're worth.

During the 2002–2006 real estate bubble, bankers were making mortgages without proof of income—so-called liars' loans. You could claim whatever income you wanted, and the banks charged a higher interest rate for letting you get away with it. But those loans came to grief. (Why am I not surprised?) Now lenders want to know the facts.

If You're Turned Down for Credit

It's getting rarer to be turned down for credit. Lenders take you but charge a higher interest rate. If you *are* turned down, they have to say why. If it's because of something they saw in your credit report, get a copy of the report and check it for errors (page 265). If it's because your credit score is too low, there's no easy fix. But the turndown letter should mention some things that weighed against you, which, over time, you might be able to fix. If the lender is a local bank or credit union, make a date to talk. There might be something you can do immediately.

Never give up. If one lender won't take you, another one might. Lenders that charge higher interest rates take borrowers with lower credit scores.

Cosigners

A cosigner is best defined as a saint, an idiot, or a parent. If your child can't get an auto loan, credit card, or apartment lease based on his or her credit alone, you might be asked to cosign the application.

The moment you do, that loan is just as much yours as your child's. Its payment history goes on your credit report. If your kid doesn't pay the bills on time, your credit record shares the black mark. If the child defaults, you are shown as having defaulted too—a sin that will put you into credit hell for seven long years. It does no good to argue that you didn't know your child wasn't making payments. You're expected to keep track.

You're liable for every nickel of a debt that you cosign. The lender may not even bother pursuing the original debtor or collecting the security that the debtor pledged. As cosigner, you can be asked for the money immediately, in cash. Many children can be trusted not to wreck your credit report, but others can't. To them, even a saint might say no.

If you say yes, tell your child or other cosignee about the risk you're going to run. He or she may not realize that the payments will show on your credit report. Ask to be told immediately if the debtor can't pay. And don't yell about it, or the child might be afraid to tell you. From the start, ask the lender to send you a copy of each monthly bill.

If you find out too late that the loan is in delinquency, take over the payments immediately. Then contact each of the three major credit bureaus to see if you have a credit file there. If so, add a statement to your record explaining why the payments were late.

Credit card issuers ignore the personal statements in credit reports. But if you apply for a mortgage or a personal loan, the lender may see the explanation and give you a chance to make your case.

Doomsday

What if the world falls apart? Your income drops, your spouse gets fired, you can't pay your bills, your children are crying, and you have to give away the dog? With all these overhanging risks, isn't it dangerous to borrow to invest?

Not if you follow sound principles. First, make suitable investments (chapter 21). Second, construct an escape hatch for yourself.

To save yourself if hard times strike, your investments should meet one or more of the following tests:

1. They must be liquid, meaning that they can easily be sold to pay off your debt. Mutual funds are liquid. Vacant lots are not.

2. If not liquid, your investments should yield enough income to carry themselves. If you buy a condominium to rent out, your tenant's rent should cover the mortgage, taxes, monthly maintenance, insurance, and other expenses, plus 5 to 10 percent for emergencies. That saves you from having to unload the condo at a giveaway price if your personal earnings drop.

3. Any investment that is not liquid and not yielding enough income should be backstopped by liquid investments. For example, if you buy a rental property that isn't covering its costs, you should have enough money in mutual funds or in the bank to support the property and cover your living expenses for 12 months. If you don't have this much liquidity, don't make such investments. They're too risky for you.

4. The value of your investment shouldn't fall below the size of the debt that's carrying it. If its price declines, put it on the market while you're still ahead. Sell it as soon as you can and pay off your loan.

Debt isn't a free pass to the high life. Overused, it can bankrupt you. But well used, debt is one of the building blocks of wealth.

YOUR SAFETY NET

Insurance is a protection racket. Everyone hates to pay the price.

But until you are well enough insured, you might as well have no assets at all. Everything you own is a hostage to fortune. Sickness or accident could leave you a pauper.

I know. I hear you. It's never going to happen to you.

The funny thing is, I've never met anyone "it" was going to happen to. So who are all those people in the hospitals, the wheelchairs, the funeral homes? Who are those stunned families staring at smoking ruins? Visitors from Mars?

A classic story for personal finance reporters is the interview with unfortunate souls who found out what "it" really feels like. They deliver a lecture that might be generically entitled "What You Should Do Right Now So You Won't End Up a Wreck like Me."

Here is that lecture.

The Money on Your Life

What Kind of Life Insurance? How Much Is Enough?

Life insurance is full of more angles than a hardware store. Maybe that's why grieving widows are handed small checks when they could have been handed large ones.

Here is the single most important thing to know about life insurance: *It is not for you!* It's for the people you'll leave behind. You pay for it; they use it. Wear that principle like an amulet, to ward off nonsense. If you're not leaving anyone behind—and don't want to leave a special bequest to a charity—you don't need life insurance.

The second rule is to *keep it simple.* Life insurance can be numbingly complicated. Clients often turn off their brains and surrender their judgment to the very agent or planner who brought on their coma in the first place. Clean and easy policies are the surest. Fancy tax-dodging or investment deals make money for the agent but may not do the job *you* want.

The third rule: *be a cheapskate.* If you want to show off your spending power, do it in a way that counts—like, say, 10 carats. For insurance, find a low-cost policy from a high-quality company.

For most people, the coverage that best fills the bill is *term insurance.* It's cheap and simple, with nothing in it for you but the knowledge that you've done the right thing. Term insurance pays off if you die prematurely. That's all. No gimmicks, no tax games, no investment values, no stock market risk. Just a check—and a large one—paid to the people who depend on you.

Traditional term is for younger people. "Permanent" term, known as *no-lapse universal life,* is for older people who find that they need coverage for longer periods than their term insurance allows.

All other forms of coverage—known generally as *cash-value insurance*—

contain a savings element that raises your out-of-pocket outlay. The debate over whether cash values make good investments is long past. They don't. What they give you is forced savings that yield a conservative rate of interest if, and only if, you hold for 15 to 20 years or so. That gives you options if your income falls short in later life or your real investments fail.

Who Needs Life Insurance?

1. You're young and single, with no dependents. Forget life insurance or go with whatever free life insurance you get from your employer. Instead buy disability coverage (chapter 14) and add to your retirement account.

Ignore an insurance agent who advises you to buy coverage because premiums are lower for the young. If you don't need insurance, you'd be wasting your money. It's like buying a tennis racket just in case, 10 years from now, you might want to learn the game.

Besides, insurance premiums rise so slowly that waiting doesn't matter much. If you buy a $500,000 20-year term policy at age 35 instead of 30, you might pay an extra $15 a year. Big deal. Cash-value coverage costs much more, but you shouldn't be buying that anyway.

An agent might also argue, "Buy now just in case you develop a dread disease, become uninsurable, and then discover a need for insurance." You might just as easily marry a zillionaire and not need life insurance at all. The odds of either are small. What's more, we all have limited budgets. When you're setting priorities, unneeded life insurance should fall to the bottom of the list.

2. You're older and single, with no dependents. Maybe you never married. Maybe you're a widow whose children have left home. You need no insurance. Cancel any term policies and use the premium money for retirement savings instead. If you have cash-value coverage, look into selling it to a life settlement company (page 398), surrendering it for cash, or donating it to a charity and taking the tax deduction. Alternatively, you could convert it to a paid-up policy for a smaller face amount so that you won't have to pay the premiums anymore, and name a charity or your children as your beneficiary.

3. You're single, with dependents. What happens to those dependents if you die? If you're a divorced parent and the children would go to the other parent, you don't need life insurance if the other parent can afford to take care of them. If not, keep the policy for the children's education and support. Your lawyer, financial planner, or insurance agent can help you make sure that the money goes to the kids, not to your ex, perhaps by leaving the proceeds in trust for them. Keep the policy too if the children will go to one of your relatives.

Orphans shouldn't arrive like beggars, cup in hand. You may also need life insurance if you're supporting an elderly parent. You can cancel the coverage when your parent dies.

4. You're a DINK: a double-income couple with no kids. You might not need insurance. Each spouse could be self-supporting if the other died. Buy coverage only to keep the survivor from falling to a lower standard of living.

5. You're an OINK: a one-income couple with no kids. The working spouse needs life insurance to support the spouse at home.

6. You're young marrieds with children. You need insurance, a lot of it. Those kids have to be raised and educated, and it's not cheap. But you probably need the coverage only until they're on their own. Then this portion of your insurance can be canceled.

7. You're having or adopting kids at an older age. You need insurance, just as a young parent does, and it will have to last into your 60s or 70s. Go for term insurance—probably 20- or 30-year term—to get the coverage you need. The policy should be convertible to good cash-value coverage in case you'll need a reduced amount of insurance into later age.

8. You're a spouse with kids, who doesn't work outside the home. Insurance on your life is generally misguided. You have no income that has to be replaced. You and the children will be more secure if the breadwinner fully insures himself or herself and uses any extra money to add to savings and investments. People who favor homemaker insurance say that the coverage is needed to pay for day care and housecleaning if the breadwinner is left alone. That's fine, but only *if* you have small children, and *if* the breadwinner truly couldn't afford day care (remember: the household is saving money by not having any expenses for you, including, perhaps, a second car), and *if* the breadwinner carries enough insurance to cover you and the kids in full. Full insurance on a breadwinner is rare. So I continue to believe that homemaker insurance should be a low priority. Buy it only if the breadwinner truly couldn't afford child care, and cancel it when the kids are old enough to take care of themselves.

9. You're retired. You need insurance only if your retirement planning failed and your spouse couldn't live on the Social Security, pension, and savings that you'll leave behind. If your spouse dies and you're short of money, cancel the coverage or sell the policy (page 398), which will save you the cost of the premium. Keep a cash-value policy, however, if you have enough money to live on and want to leave a larger estate to a charity or your kids. You can restructure it so that you don't have to pay premiums anymore.

10. You're a kid. Insurance on a child, including a teenager, is a waste of money. What secures a child's future is life insurance on the parents and a college savings fund. Some parents are persuaded to save for college in a cash-value kid insurance policy. But the cost of the needless life insurance slashes your return on investment. For a far larger college fund, put the money into a 529 plan (page 667), arranging for automatic monthly contributions from your bank account.

11. You own a business. Either you or the company will doubtlessly need a policy on your life. For sole owners, the impetus may be to cover the debts that they signed personally or to pay estate taxes. (You may want a trust to own the policy, to hold down taxes by keeping the proceeds out of your estate.) A co-owner may want to be able to buy his or her partner's share of the business if the partner dies or becomes disabled. Talk to your lawyer about a buy/sell agreement funded by life and disability insurance. Don't leave your spouse and kids to a business partner's tender mercies, no matter how friendly you are now. The business might never make a cash distribution or declare a dividend. You need the insurance to be sure that your family gets a payoff.

12. You're rich. Life insurance can help pay your estate taxes. On the other hand, the taxes can be paid out of your liquid investments so you don't need insurance after all. On the third hand, your investments may be illiquid (real estate, a small business), so your estate will need the insurance to provide ready cash. You might even want the policy so that you can leave an even larger estate to your heirs. Take your pick. To keep the insurance proceeds out of your estate (lest they raise your taxes even more), put the policy into an irrevocable trust.

13. Your job is covered by Social Security. You automatically have "free" insurance that covers an older spouse, a spouse caring for young children, your children, even parents you support (page 339). Don't forget about this when estimating how much more coverage you should buy.

How Much Insurance?

If you need it at all, you probably need plenty—almost certainly more than you have now. And you can afford it. Low-cost term insurance can be slipped into almost any spending plan.

In fact, buying it is the easy part. The hard part is knowing how much to buy.

I've seen rules of thumb about how much life insurance you need: 8 times income, 10 times income, 15 times income, depending on how heavy the thumb. None of them is exactly right, because so much depends on how old you are, whether you have children, what your spouse earns, and how much money you've saved.

Table 5.

THE QUICK-FIX INSURANCE PLANNER

If You Die	Your Money		My Example
1. Your family's annual cost of living	$ _____		$80,000
2. Your family's annual income from:			
• Social Security*	$ _____		$15,000
• Spouse's earnings	$ _____		$30,000
• Other (except income from investments	$ _____		0
TOTAL	$ _____		$45,000
3. Your family's investment income:			
• Your investment capital, from page 18	$ _____		$100,000
• Multiply by what your capital might earn pretax: 5%? 7%?	× _____		5%
RESULT: your family's annual income from current savings	$ _____		$2,500
4. Your family's annual budget gap: Add the totals in steps 2 and 3 and subtract them from line 1	$ _____		$32,500
5. To fill that budget gap:			
• Turn to Appendix 4 to estimate your spouse's life expectancy.	___ years	45	
• Turn to the table on page 1110† and find the column that shows what you think your money can earn (use the same percentage you chose for step 3)	___ %	5%	
• Looking down that column, find your spouse's life expectancy or something close to it. Look across to the left to see what percentage of capital your spouse can withdraw annually to make the money last a lifetime.	___ %		3.5%
• Divide line 4 by the percent your spouse will withdraw annually.			
RESULT: the additional money needed for living expenses	$ _____		$928,571
6. College fund for the children (page 624)	$ _____		$200,000
7. TOTAL LIFE INSURANCE NEEDED	$ _____		$1,128,571

* For two small children. This drops to zero when the children pass age 18 or 19.
† Assuming a 3 percent inflation rate. For other inflation rates, see Appendix 2.

If you want to make it simple, the Consumer Federation of America (CFA) recommends at least eight times income for a married couple with two small children. It assumes that, if a parent dies, the policy's proceeds will be invested conservatively, the surviving family will spend both income and principal, and the family will also collect Social Security survivor's benefits. It doesn't include a specific college fund. For college, add an additional flat amount.

At the other end of the scale, go to Term4Sale.com (www.term4sale.com), which provides free online insurance quotes. Its Income Calculator shows that you need 15 times income to provide your family with benefits over 20 years, adjusted for inflation but not counting Social Security. You'll also find calculators at the Web sites for Teachers Insurance and Annuity Association—College Retirement Equities Fund, or TIAA-CREF (www.tiaa-cref.org) and Choose to Save (www.choosetosave.org).

On page 339 you'll find a Quick-Fix worksheet pegged to your personal income and assets. It takes a little calculating, but that's why God made Excel (and yellow pads). Start with your family's probable living expenses after your death. Check with Social Security to see the size benefit your family might get (my example assumes two young children). Be conservative when figuring your return on investments, to account for market fluctuations.

When only one parent works, he or she should carry all the coverage. When both parents work, split the coverage proportionately: if the wife earns 40 percent of the family income, she should carry 40 percent of the coverage, leaving the remaining 60 percent to the husband. The cheapest way to cover the lower earner may be through a rider on the policy of the higher earner.

Your Social Security Insurance

Most people think of Social Security purely as a retirement plan. But your payroll tax also pays for life insurance and disability coverage. There's a lump sum death benefit of $255, plus monthly payments to dependents. To find out how much your family would get, see page 1096. Here's who could collect on your Social Security account after your death:

1. A surviving spouse age 60 and up, or 50 and up if he or she is disabled. Divorced spouses are covered too if the marriage lasted at least 10 years. A spouse or divorced spouse who remarries can still collect on the first spouse's account if that's a better deal than the new spouse's account.

2. A surviving spouse who's caring for your child who is under 16 or was disabled before age 22. An unremarried divorced spouse caring for your child is covered too regardless of how long the marriage lasted.

3. Unmarried dependent children under 18, or under 19 if they're still in secondary school.

4. Parents 62 and older who received at least half their support from you.

The Great Debate: Term Insurance Versus Cash-Value Coverage Versus No-Lapse Universal Life

Term insurance is pure protection, like fire insurance or auto insurance. Its sole function is to support your family if you die. You can buy large amounts of coverage for modest amounts of money—and big policies are what your spouse and children need. Most breadwinners are seriously underinsured, partly because they're wasting their limited budget on cash-value coverage. Only with term will you be able to protect your family well.

Most term policies last for a certain number of years at a fixed price. Then the protection ends. If you still need coverage, you can re-up for another term at a higher price. At late ages, you usually don't need life insurance anymore, so you can let the policy run out. If you do need protection, you can convert your term policy into no-lapse coverage (page 352) at a reasonable price. Conversion rights usually end at age 65, 70, or 75, depending on the policy.

Cash-value insurance comes in two parts: (1) an insurance policy and (2) a cash account. You pay a large premium compared with the premium for term insurance or no-lapse universal life. Most of the extra money goes into the cash account, which builds up tax free or tax deferred. You can hold the policy for life with no increase in premiums, provided that the policy is property structured. If you die, the insurance company uses the cash in the policy to help make the payment to your beneficiary.

If you need money later in life, you can tap the cash by taking a loan against the policy. The loan reduces the size of your death benefit, but if you're careful you can maintain at least some coverage (for loan management, see page 307). Some cash-value policies let you make withdrawals, the way you'd take money out of a bank account. If you cancel or sell the policy, you can put the cash value (net of any loans, surrender charges, and taxes) into your pocket.

No-lapse universal life resembles permanent term insurance. You get coverage for life at a very low premium compared with cash-value insurance. But these policies don't have much in the way of cash value, so there's no money to tap in older age.

Consumers Versus Life Insurance Agents

Agents sell term policies because the public wants them. But they're trained to push you toward cash-value insurance too. That's where the money is: in sales commissions and profits for the company. Agents will urge you to buy a cash-value policy along with your term. Over time, they'll try to convert your term into cash-value coverage. If you don't want to pay the high premiums for cash values, they'll pitch you on no-lapse universal life. The sales pitch will sound persuasive, of course, so you need to be armed.

Here Are Some Answers for When the Agent Says . . .

"Term premiums are wasted because you have nothing to show for them in the end." Wrong. You've had years of protection and that's what you paid for. Would you say that you've wasted the money you've paid for fire insurance because your house didn't burn down?

"Term is like renting. Cash value is like buying." And some things it's smarter to rent, like life insurance.

"Term insurance is an illusion. Hardly anyone collects on it." Hardly anyone collects on fire insurance either. Term insurance is meant to be canceled when the need for protection no longer exists. When you think about "collecting" from your own life insurance, you are thinking, What's in it for me? *Then* the agent has you and can sell you anything.

"You will need permanent life insurance eventually, so you might as well buy it now." Any life insurance policy, including term insurance, is "permanent" if it lasts until you die. If the agent means, "You will always need life insurance until you die of old age," the answer is "nonsense." An insurance policy replaces earnings if you die prematurely. When you retire, you have no paycheck to replace. You'll be living on your pension, your savings, and Social Security—all of which can continue to pay your spouse after you die. Older people often cancel or sell their cash-value policies so they won't have to pay the premiums anymore.

You will need life insurance into old age only if: (1) You had children at a late age and will need insurance money to help support them. (2) You've retired and don't have enough savings for your spouse to live on if you die. (3) You're worth a lot of money and want insurance to cover the estate taxes on illiquid assets that can't easily be sold. (4) You want to leave extra money to your children or a charity tax free and can afford the premium cost.

When you're younger, you don't know if any of these things will become true. If it turns out that you do indeed need continuing coverage, you can wait until your term insurance is nearly finished and convert it at that time. You don't have to add a permanent policy in advance.

"You should start converting your term insurance into a permanent policy so that you'll never be without protection." Same answer.

"You will need insurance in middle age to protect your family. Term insurance is too expensive then." If you use one of the price-quote services on page 348, you can find reasonably priced term insurance even in your 60s or 70s. If your health deteriorates and you don't qualify for new coverage, you can convert your expiring term policy into some form of permanent insurance. That's the time to do it, not before.

"Cash-value policies force you to save for old age." Here again, the agent wants you to think, "What's in it for me?" By putting yourself first, you put your spouse and children last. The rule is: protection first, savings later. If you can afford all the term insurance you need—10 or 15 times your income—and will have some money left over, put it into a retirement account, a college fund, or a mutual fund. Insurance "savings" aren't good enough.

"I can sell you a policy that will be paid up at sixty or sixty-five. You'll then have a permanent policy with no more premiums due." Even if true, so what? This kind of coverage costs you big bucks in the early years. You're prepaying for something you may not need. Besides, at 60 you may discover that the premiums don't end as promised. The agent may have steered you wrong.

"Buy term, but add a small cash-value policy just in case you'll need it later." Hmmm, another appeal to "just in case." Why don't you buy a parachute just in case you decide to jump out of a plane? What's the point of an expensive $50,000 or $100,000 policy? A smarter choice is to buy term insurance that's convertible into cash-value coverage at a later date if the need arises.

All About Term Insurance

How Much Cheaper Is Term Insurance?

The table on page 344 shows dramatically how much more coverage you get for your money with term insurance. I'm showing lower-priced $500,000 non-smoker policies for people in excellent but not perfect health, in the Midwest. Prices vary from state to state and from day to day, so you won't pay exactly what I've quoted here. But you get the idea.

Employee Term Insurance

Increasingly, life insurance is being sold through the workplace, and it's often a good deal. Employers may provide a certain amount of coverage free (typically,

Table 6.

SAMPLE YEARLY PREMIUMS FOR A $500,000 POLICY

	20-Year Term		Cash-Value	
	Male	**Female**	**Male**	**Female**
Age				
30	$360	$290	$2,080	$1,750
40	500	420	3,100	2,600
50	1,200	870	4,700	4,000
60	3,100	2,100	8,000	6,500

one and a half times salary). Employees are offered the chance to buy more, paying the premiums through payroll deductions. Your company might provide group coverage, open to everyone regardless of health status; or individual coverage, for which you have to take a health exam.

Before loading up on term insurance in the workplace, however, do two things:

▪ *Check the price against what you can find on a price-quote service (page 348).* Policies bought elsewhere may be quite a bit cheaper, both for young people and for healthy older people. After age 50, term insurance bought on the open market is usually a lot less expensive than group term. Group coverage is terrific, however, for people in poorer health.

▪ *Find out what happens if you leave your job.* There are two possibilities: (1) You have a *group individual* policy. It can follow you wherever you go, at no increase in premium. (You have to exercise this option within 30 days of leaving the company.) (2) You have *true group* coverage. If you want to keep it when you leave the company, you'll have to convert it to an individual policy—usually to cash-value coverage. You can convert regardless of health, so conversion attracts people who can't get insurance somewhere else. For that very reason, the premiums are high and the benefits often limited. You don't want to get stuck with this as your only option. If you can't get group individual coverage, don't buy your life insurance at work. Buy from an outside insurer instead.

Note that any free group insurance given to workers or retirees generally can be reduced or eliminated by the company. Nothing is guaranteed. It's reasonable to expect that the coverage will continue, but don't stake your family's future on it, especially if you're an early retiree. Be sure you have coverage that you know you can keep. Your coverage may terminate if you stay on the job past age 70 or 75.

Other Group Term Coverage

Apply a sniff test to group coverage offered by trade groups, professional associations, alumni associations, and fraternal orders. Sometimes it's good; sometimes it's not. Professional associations often slant their coverage toward younger people, offering them much better rates, relatively speaking, than older people get. If you're middle-aged, in good health, and don't smoke, you should be able to find a cheaper policy elsewhere. Check the rates your association offers against what you can get through a quote service (page 348).

Be sure that you can take your policy with you if you resign from the group, regardless of your health at the time. If you can't, buy your coverage somewhere else.

Individual Term Insurance Policies

There are two types of individual coverage: level term and annually renewable term.

Annually renewable term (ART) is renewable for life without a health exam. Every year, the premium goes up. In the first two or three years, it's cheaper than level term. After that, it gets more expensive. For this reason, it's not sold much anymore. Three companies still offer ART: National Life of Vermont, Northwestern Mutual Life, and TIAA-CREF.

The value of ART is its guarantee. You can keep the policy for as long as you need it, up to age 90 or more. It's hugely expensive at later ages, so, in real life, you wouldn't let it run that long. If you discovered that you needed insurance for life, you'd convert your ART to cash-value insurance in late middle age. The three companies that sell ART are the bluest of blue chips and offer excellent conversion options. This, combined with the lifetime coverage guarantee, makes ART worth paying extra for.

Level term dominates the business. You pay a fixed premium for a certain number of years—typically, 10, 15, 20, or 30. At the end of the term, the policy will lapse. You're hoping that, when the policy's guaranteed premium runs out, you won't need life insurance anymore.

But what if you do? Maybe you married late and have young children. Maybe you lost your savings through bad luck or bad investments and have to keep working to support your spouse. The answer is to buy more insurance when your level term policy ends. You have three choices—two of them affordable and one for desperation only:

1. If you're in good health (or good enough): Shop for new level term insurance. You'll have to pass a medical exam and pay the appropriate premium for someone your age. You can find a policy that will cover the number of additional years that your family will need protection.

2. If you're in poor health: Convert your level term policy to permanent insurance. You'll be offered whatever types of conversion policies the company has on its shelf at the time. There's no medical exam. You'll pay more than you were paying for term but you can limit the cost by buying a smaller policy. A smaller policy should work because you're older and don't need as many years of protection as you did before. Good timing is important! You must convert within the time period that the policy allows. Check this with your insurance agent or read the policy yourself. If you wait too long, you lose your chance.

Don't convert too early. Say, for example, that you have a heart attack halfway through a 20-year term policy. Your agent might urge you to switch to cashvalue coverage right away. But why? If you die, your heirs will collect on your current term policy. If you live, you might be considered a better risk 10 years from now than you are today. (But switch if you accidentally bought a policy whose conversion privilege lapses after the first 10 years. It's important to keep your coverage going.)

3. If you're in poor health and missed your chance to switch to permanent insurance coverage: You can renew your expiring level term coverage without a health exam but only at an incredibly high premium (called the *reentry* premium). Worse, the cost will jump every year, by large amounts. This is worth doing only at death's door. If you know you'll need coverage well into the future and see that you won't be able to pass a health exam, convert your term policy to cash-value coverage while you still can.

When You Buy Term Insurance . . .

Choose the Right Term. Choose a policy that will last as long as you think you will need the coverage. If you're starting to have children, for example, and hope to send them to college, a 20-year policy probably isn't long enough. Look instead at 30-year term*. The annual premium will be higher, but you've nailed down coverage that should last through their college years even if your health goes bad. Conversely, if you're 50, your term policy is expiring, and your youngest child is in his or her teens, maybe a 10-year policy will do. If, at 50,

---

*Some experts argue against 30-year term. They expect term premiums to fall and say that you overpay when you lock yourself in that long. I say that you shouldn't bet on shorter terms if you'll need coverage this long, even if it comes at a higher price.

you haven't yet saved enough to help support your spouse if you die, look at a 20-year policy. The need is all.

You might also ladder your protection. Divide your total insurance coverage among a 10-year, a 20-year, and a 30-year policy. When the first 10 years are up, consider whether you still need that portion. If not, let it lapse. If so, re-up to a new term policy for the length of time you want.

Look at Your Conversion Choices. Your term policy should be convertible into permanent insurance right up to age 70 or even 75. That allows you to switch your policy into one that lasts as long as you live, at a level premium, if you still need insurance and couldn't pass a health exam. Some policies provide conversion rights only for the first few years—say, the first 5 years out of a 20-year term. Skip them. You need a longer conversion period because you don't know what the future will bring. And skip a policy that offers you just a single option at conversion. You want several options, including cash-value and no-lapse coverage. If you'll need to convert, do it toward the end of the policy's term. There's no point in paying higher premiums until you know you have no other option. And remember: you won't need as much insurance at a later age.

If you do decide that you need insurance for life, don't automatically convert the term policy you have. If you're insurable, you might find less expensive coverage through another company.

Make It a Nonsmoker Policy. Save money. Quit smoking. Nonsmokers live longer than smokers and pay around half as much for their term insurance. To most insurers, you're a nonsmoker if you've avoided the weed for two to five years.

Look at the Guarantees. Be sure that the premium is guaranteed for the policy's full term. The policy should also be renewable without a health exam.

Find a Low Price!

Will the Real "Low-Cost" Term Policy Please Stand Up?

All term insurance does not cost the same, as some people think. The price differences among companies are huge. You can save hundreds, even thousands, of dollars by spending 10 minutes comparison shopping on the Web.

As an example, take a 40-year-old man, a nonsmoker in excellent health, buying a 20-year term policy worth $500,000. A low-priced insurer might charge him $450 a year. A high-priced insurer might charge $625—and for exactly the same product! The older you get, the wider the spread. Why would anyone pay the higher price? Because he or she didn't shop. Or because the agent claimed that the higher price was worth it. That's baloney. You can get excellent service at top-rated companies that charge consumers less.

Different companies might also assign you to different health classes. If that 40-year-old were knocked down one class, from "preferred" to "standard plus," premiums would range from $600 to $840.

When comparing premiums on level term, don't look only at the cost going in. Ask how much you'd pay if you wanted to convert to a cash-value policy at or near the end of the term (page 347). That price isn't guaranteed, but it gives you a general idea of how competitive each particular insurer is.

Also, ask what you'd pay to renew your current term policy without having to pass a health exam. You'll be shocked by how high the premium (called the reentry premium) is. Fortunately, people rarely pay it. The majority of policyholders are still insurable, so they can shop for new coverage at competitive rates. If you're not insurable, you can convert your term policy to a smaller cash value policy (page 346). The high reentry premium is your final fallback position if all else fails.

How to Find a Good, Low-Cost Term Policy. Go to a free online quote service and enter your information. Your age and health status are run through a data bank. Out comes a list of policies to consider, along with their premiums and the insurers' safety ratings (the quote services offer only higher-rated companies).

The policies won't necessarily be America's cheapest, only the cheapest of those that the quote service follows or does business with. If you check with two or three of these services, however, you'll get a pretty good list to pick from.

Every few years, run yourself through the computers again (in fact, do it now). If you stay in good health, you'll probably find something cheaper every time.

Insurance quotes are free of charge. To buy the policy, however, you have to use an insurance agent—either an agent connected with the quote service or a local agent that the service will suggest. It may turn out that you were too optimistic (or pessimistic) about your state of health, and the final quote will be different than you thought. If you're bumped from preferred rates down to standard rates, go to the quote services again to find the company with the best standard-rate policy. It's no cheaper to buy online, by the way. Any given policy costs the same, whether you buy through an online insurer or across the kitchen table.

The best online service: Term4Sale.com. It sifts through some 125 insurance companies, including the low-loads (low commission costs), to find the best quotes. There's some good consumer information here too, and no agent will call. If you want to buy a policy, the site will send you the names of three local insurance agents to choose from.

Other services, such as AccuQuote (www.accuquote.com) and Insure.com (www.insure.com), sell through their own agents by phone or online. You have to supply your phone number, so an agent may call.

Three low-load insurers give free quotes online without asking for your phone number: Ameritas Life Insurance Corp. (www.ameritasdirect.com), SBLI (www.sbli.com), and TIAA-CREF. They'll also sell you a policy online or by phone. (Of these three, only TIAA-CREF is available in every state.)

Is Return-of-Premium Term a Good Buy? No. It's a shell game—great for the agent, who earns a higher commission, but of dubious value to the family you're trying to protect.

Return-of-premium term promises to pay all your premiums back at the end of the term, provided that you're still alive. It sounds like free insurance for 20 or 30 years. To get this "free" insurance, however, your premiums might be 50 percent to 150 percent higher than you'd pay for regular term.

What's the result? If you die, you've simply overpaid for life insurance, big time. If you drop the policy early, you may or may not get a small portion of your premium back—and you will still have overpaid for the limited years of coverage you got. If the policy's higher cost reduces the total amount of insurance you can buy, you have shortchanged your family. At your death, they'll get a smaller payout than they need. This is a classic case of thinking about yourself ("What's in it for me?") rather than thinking about the risk to the people you love best. On paper, it might be a good deal *if* you still buy enough coverage for your family, *if* you don't drop your policy, *if* you live, and *if* you wouldn't have used that extra premium to add to your retirement account. That's too many ifs for me.

Your Premium and Your Age. The older you are, the more you pay for life insurance. But at later ages, you usually need less coverage and for shorter terms, so you can probably still afford to buy what you need. At 60, a man in excellent health might pay just $1,400 a year for a $200,000, 10-year term policy. If he still needs $500,000 (late marriage, young children), he might get a 20-year policy for $3,000. In short, there's enough level term around to cover people of all ages who might need it, always provided that you stay in decent health.

Your Premium and Your Health. The size of your premium depends on the state of your health. The best rates go to "superpreferred" and "preferred" risks. But even if you're rated "standard-plus" or "standard," term insurance is cheap. A $500,000 25-year standard policy might cost a 40-year-old man as little as $1,035 a year.

What kills you is smoking—speaking only financially, of course. A smoker policy would cost our guy $2,605 a year. Your price also jumps if you're overweight, have high blood pressure or high cholesterol, a chronic condition such as diabetes or a history of depression, or have endured assorted specific ailments such as a blood clot in your leg. The insurer will send a paramedic to your home or office for a blood test, urine test, and blood pressure reading. If you've had health problems, you may need to take a more extensive physical exam and provide a statement from your doctor. People in tricky health need a life insurance agent who specializes in finding coverage for "impaired risks." I don't know how often they actually get a break on a policy for a client, but they might as well try.

You can get small amounts of insurance—maybe $25,000 to $150,000—without a medical exam. But that doesn't mean that the insurer doesn't care about your health. You still have to answer questions about your medical history, medications you take, and any conditions you're currently dealing with.

Tell the Whole Truth on Your Application!
Don't misspeak or let the insurance agent misspeak for you. Insurance companies will test your honesty by getting their own medical tests, asking for reports from your doctor, and checking your history with the Medical Information Bureau (MIB) (page 483). They look at *everything,* even minor ailments that hardly seem worth mentioning. They'll also ask about your parents' and perhaps your siblings' health.

What happens if a deception slips through? If you die during the first two years that you hold the policy, the company might check your application against your medical records at the time. It may even assign an investigator. If it finds a misstatement that could have caused the insurer to turn your application down, it can cancel your coverage posthumously. Your beneficiaries will get back all the premiums you paid but will lose the large lump sum you intended them to have. If you last at least two years, however, the policy will pay.

Mortgage Life Insurance
Do you want to leave your survivors a house free and clear? If so, get enough coverage to repay the mortgage as well as pay all the rest of your family's expenses. There are two ways to go.

1. Buy mortgage life insurance from the lender. It's a term policy whose cost can be bundled into your monthly mortgage payment. If you die, the proceeds pay off your loan.

Sound good so far? Now watch me trash it. First, this coverage can be shockingly expensive. Second, it locks your survivors into using the policy to pay off the mortgage loan. Maybe they'd rather use the money for something else. Mortgage life is worth considering only for smokers and people in poor health who can't get life insurance elsewhere at standard rates. (And even then, compare prices before settling for the lender's policy.)

2. The better choice is regular term insurance, which is generally cheaper than what the mortgage lender has to sell. You might take level-premium term for a period lasting at least as long as the mortgage will. If you die, the proceeds go to your survivors, not to the lender. They decide what to do with the money. Maybe they'd rather keep on making mortgage payments and use the insurance money for other expenses instead.

Credit Insurance

Credit insurance is packaged with specific loans, such as car loans, installment loans, and second mortgages. It usually pays the remainder of the loan if you die; a certain number of minimum monthly payments if you're disabled and unable to work; and a certain number of minimum monthly payments if you're laid off and collecting unemployment insurance. Read the fine print! These policies are riddled with limitations and exceptions. For example, you may have to be out of work for 30 days before you can collect on the disability and unemployment policies. They're also expensive, compared with the amount of protection you actually get. It's against the law to pressure you into buying this coverage, although lenders may try; they make a lot of money selling credit insurance. If you want your debts paid off at your death, skip these high-priced bits of insurance and buy more term insurance instead.

I make one exception:

If you're otherwise uninsurable, credit insurance might be worth the price. There's no health exam, although a few simple health questions may be asked and the insurer might require that you be actively at work. In some states, credit insurers can refuse to pay if, within six months of the policy's start-up date, you die from an illness that was treated or diagnosed in the six months before you bought. Some insurers collect medical information from people taking out policies larger than $20,000 to $25,000. Payment can be denied if you hide your true physical condition and die within two years.

Miscellaneous Insurance

Keep a note in your life insurance file if you qualify for any of the following payments, so that your survivors will know where there's money to collect:

1. Credit unions sometimes provide up to $10,000 in free insurance, depending on your account balance.

2. If you charge a travel ticket to a credit card, it may generate $100,000 or more of free life insurance. You might be covered for accidental death and dismemberment whether you travel by plane, train, bus, or ship. Ditto if your accident occurs in an airline terminal or while traveling on public transportation to and from the terminal.

3. You might have bought some credit insurance when you took out a loan.

4. Employers may provide up to one and a half times your salary in free life insurance.

6. Some retirement systems also provide benefits.

All About No-Lapse Coverage

No-lapse universal-life insurance* lasts for life. The size of your premium and your death benefit are guaranteed—you set 'em and forget 'em. Its selling point is its low, low premium cost compared with cash-value coverage, the only other form of permanent insurance. If your term insurance is running out and you find that you still need protection into older age, no-lapse is the right type of policy to choose. It's not for younger people. You shouldn't even consider no-lapse until you're reaching retirement age.

How much cheaper is no-lapse? A lot. The premiums usually can be half as much as you'd pay for a whole-life policy with the same face amount of insurance protection. As an example, take a man, 45, in excellent but not perfect health, buying a $1 million policy. His guaranteed premium for traditional whole life might run in the $20,000 range, per year. For $1 million of no-lapse, he'd pay only $8,000. No-lapse premiums undercut those on straight universal life as well.

Why is no-lapse so much cheaper? Because you get almost nothing in the way of guaranteed cash values. There may be zero cash in the early years. If you cancel the policy during that time, you'll get nothing back at all. After five years or so, cash values rise for a while. In your older age, they retreat again. You don't build retirement savings inside this policy, and the death benefit normally will not increase. Effectively, it's a guaranteed-premium term policy that lasts for life.

---

*These types of policies are sometimes called *guaranteed universal life* or *universal life with secondary guarantees.*

You have some choices with no-lapse universal life. You can pay a level premium for the policy's entire term. You can pay less at the start and more later on. You might be able to stop payments for a while and then start them up again. Whatever you decide, the policy's internal costs will be locked in when you sign the contract. As long as you follow the program, the death benefit is guaranteed.

Don't start with no-lapse when you have a family to protect. Begin with a large term insurance policy, making sure that it's convertible to a variety of permanent options, including no-lapse, just in case. If you still need coverage when the term runs out, shop for another term policy—again, with a no-lapse conversion option. If you still need coverage when the second term runs out, no-lapse (or whatever similar policy takes its place 20 or 40 years from now) will probably be your best choice.

You can roll one or more existing cash-value policies into a no-lapse universal policy in a tax-free 1035 exchange. The cash in those older policies glides into the new policy, minus any fees. (Just make sure that the transfer doesn't subject your cash value to an agent's large, first-year sales commissions!) At first, the cash account in your new no-lapse policy might grow a bit, depending on current interest rates. Eventually, however, it will decline and run out. That won't affect your premiums or death benefit. Even with a zero cash value, no-lapse benefits are guaranteed.

When Would You Use No-Lapse Universal Life?

■ *You're older, your term insurance is running out, and you find that you'll need coverage for life.* If you're insurable, shop for a no-lapse policy. If you're not insurable, convert your current term policy to no-lapse, if that's an option, which you can do without a health exam.

■ *You're older and own several small cash-value policies, purchased at various times, and are still paying premiums.* You can roll them into a single paid-up no-lapse policy in a tax-free exchange. The no-lapse policy will preserve your cash values, minus any charges. The death benefit will be smaller, but there are no more premiums to pay. (Note: As an alternative to no-lapse, consider a rollover into a single paid-up cash-value policy. The no-lapse will give you more insurance, for the price. The cash-value policy will preserve more of your cash.)

■ *You own a variable universal or straight universal policy that is underfunded (page 362).* Unless you put up more money, the policy won't last for life. You can roll it into a no-lapse policy—either a smaller, paid-up policy with no more premiums due, or a larger policy with the premiums and death benefit guaranteed. The premiums will probably be lower than those you're paying now.

When Would You Not Use No-Lapse Universal Life?

- *You're young.* This is no time to spend a bundle on what amounts to high-cost term insurance. Buy regular low-cost term instead.
- *Don't buy unless you're certain that you can keep the coverage for life.* There's no cash surrender value, so if you cancel, you'll get nothing back. A canceled no-lapse amounts to nothing more than superexpensive term insurance. No-lapse is for people who can afford the premiums without strain or who buy it as a paid-up policy that they won't have to think about again.
- *Don't buy if you might need more savings as well as insurance in your later age.* No-lapse doesn't build cash values. Look at a whole-life policy instead (page 358).
- *Don't buy if you want to keep your options open.* What happens if the beneficiary dies and you don't want the coverage anymore? What if you divorce? A canceled no-lapse policy is a ton of money down the drain.

Possible Risks. At this writing, no-lapse coverage is pretty new. It doesn't have a track record yet. Here are some points to think about:

- *If there's any cash value in the policy and you borrow against it, you lose your guarantees.*
- *It's possible that it won't turn out to be no-lapse after all.* You get the guarantee for life as long as you've paid enough premiums to support it. The fixed premiums in your contract are supposed to do the job. It's not clear what might happen, however, if the insurance company miscalculates or you change your premium schedule.
- *Some no-lapse policies lock you into payment premiums for life.* Other designs let you stop or reduce your premiums as long as there's a cash balance in your account.
- *Some insurance experts worry that the premiums on no-lapse policies are being set too low.* If the companies don't build enough reserves to cover their guarantees, the policies—and maybe the companies—could become unprofitable. Your guarantees ought to be good but, in times of economic stress, you never know. There may be wrinkles in these contracts. It's not clear whether in an insolvency these policies are protected by the state guaranty funds (page 403).
- *No-lapse is being sold aggressively to replace older cash-value policies.* That's not good. It's often better to hang on to the insurance you already have (page 385). You can't help but worry about insurance that comes with hype.

All About Cash-Value Insurance

The premium you pay for a cash-value policy goes into a pot that's divided three ways. Part of it pays for insurance coverage. Part covers the insurer's expenses, including sales commissions. Part goes into a tax-protected cash fund. Over time, the cash fund grows. Cash-value coverage has two main appeals:

First, you can hold the policy, at the same level premium, right into old age. That's a time when term insurance grows impossibly expensive—if you can buy it at all. You'll want coverage in older age if: (1) you expect to be working and have a spouse or child who will depend on your income; (2) you didn't build enough savings to protect your spouse if you die; (3) you want to leave your heirs or a charity a sizable pot of money free of tax; (4) your estate will owe taxes at your death and you want them paid out of life insurance proceeds rather than out of the estate itself.

The second appeal of cash-value insurance is the tax-protected "savings" that accumulate inside the policy. You can think of them as a form of forced savings. Your return on investment should roughly equal that of bonds, provided that you hold the policy for 15 or 20 years. You might (might!) earn more than bonds if you buy variable universal life—page 364.

Normally, your insurance savings support your policy's death benefit. You can tap this money yourself, however, if you find that you need extra cash. There are four ways of doing it: (1) You can borrow against the savings. The interest you owe on the loan accumulates inside the policy. (2) With universal policies (page 360), you can also withdraw the cash value directly. (3) With whole-life policies, you can often withdraw the paid-up additions (page 358). (4) You can surrender the policy and collect the cash value. At surrender, you'll owe taxes, at ordinary income rates, on anything more than the sum of the premiums you paid. (The tax can be large.)

When you remove money from a policy, it reduces your death benefit—meaning a smaller payout for your beneficiaries. If you take out too much, the policy can collapse, leaving you with no coverage at all.

Here's the bottom-line question: If you don't need a cash-value policy for other reasons, is it worth buying one for the forced savings element? Or should you buy only term insurance and invest your money somewhere else?

In most cases, that's a no-brainer: Buy term insurance and invest elsewhere. Fill up your tax-deferred retirement accounts. Start a Roth IRA, where all the earnings are tax free. Buy mutual funds, which are taxed at the low rate for capital gains. At this writing, dividends enjoy low tax rates too. If you find that you need permanent insurance in your later age, buy no-lapse universal life.

I see only one set of facts that makes investing in cash-value policies plausible: (1) You can afford the full amount of insurance that you need to protect your family. This usually means buying term coverage along with the cash-value policy. *And* (2) you're young enough so that the cash values will have 20 years or more to build. *And* (3) you think that you'll probably need coverage into older age. *And* (4) you are certain that you can afford to keep on paying the higher premiums on cash-value coverage. *And* (5) you want to build a cash account inside the policy, to insure against the chance that you might need that money in later age. *And* (6) you know how to monitor the cash value, so you don't withdraw so much that the policy collapses.

How many cash-value insurance buyers meet all those conditions? Not many, I suspect. When they don't, they're buying an expensive policy they don't need and probably won't use. At some point they'll cancel it, losing most of the money they put up.

P.S.: Here's a possible up-and-coming use for cash-value insurance: it might be a substitute for buying long-term care insurance (page 468). A few companies are structuring policies or adding riders to pay benefits for both life and continuing care. You might buy a policy paid up at 65 or 70. If you die, your beneficiary gets the life insurance payout. If you enter a nursing home or need home care services, you could use up to 100 percent of your death benefit for expenses. For the policy to be an effective hedge against long-term care costs, however, you have to put *a lot* of money into its cash values. (You can also buy long-term care riders on regular policies, but they're not as comprehensive.)

When You Buy Cash-Value Coverage, Get the Most Cash You Can!

Oddly, buyers don't appreciate the cash values they're paying extra to own. There may be *no* cash in your policy after the first year. It all goes to pay sales commissions and other marketing expenses. In the second year, a tiny bit of cash appears, and a modest amount in the years after that. If you cancel the policy in these early years, as a majority of buyers do, you pay a surrender charge and recover little or nothing of the money you spent. It would have been cheaper—much cheaper—to own term insurance all along.

There are two ways of buying insurance that give you higher cash values in the early years. You can choose low-load (low-commission) products—see page 371. Or you can buy blended policies—page 372. If you drop these types of policies early, you'll get at least a decent amount of money back. Low-load policies also have no surrender charges. If you keep low-loads or blends into older age, you'll have higher cash values to tap in retirement and a higher death benefit too.

Why do consumers settle for low-value insurance? Because they don't shop around and don't understand the importance of getting high cash values in the policy's early years.

Why do so many consumers cancel cash-value insurance early? Because they discover they can't afford it, or decide that they should have had term coverage all along, or are talked into buying a new policy by a different agent. If you're going the cash-value route, take the time to find the best.

When you're buying a policy, the agent will give you a policy illustration, showing how your cash value accumulates. (The cash value might be called the "account value," the "accumulation value," or something similar.) Ignore it! It doesn't represent the actual savings you have in your policy. If you cancel your coverage during the first 10 to 15 years, your cash value will be reduced by a surrender charge, which is often quite large. So look for the *surrender value* in the illustration. That's the real amount of cash that you've built up.

Don't Mistake the Premium You Pay for the Policy's Cost

The cost is the expense of insuring you every year plus the company's overhead and profit. The premium is merely the money that you choose to put in. At the start, your premium may indeed cover all your costs. If costs rise, however, your premium may be too low. Some agents deliberately suggest a low premium to make the policy look low cost compared with others on the market. That's a sham. Too low a premium in the early years sets you up for rising premiums in the future.

Get the Right Life Expectancy

The insurance industry updated its mortality table in 2001 to account for our longer lives. That should mean lower premiums, on average. Some companies, however, are still using the old table, compiled in 1980. Before buying, ask your agent if the company is using the 2001 CSO Mortality Table to set its premiums.

Types of Cash-Value Policies

Cash-value policies come in three* main types: *Traditional whole-life insurance* is guaranteed. You'll get the promised death benefit as long as you pay the fixed

---

*You can argue that no-lapse universal life is also a form of cash-value coverage. I put it into a separate category because it's not designed to deliver cash.

premiums in the contract. *Straight universal life* can be guaranteed, provided that you pay a "guideline" premium. *Variable universal life* is not guaranteed. You may be required to put up more money to keep the policy in force. Here's the scoop on all of them.

Traditional Whole-Life Insurance

These policies are marketed to people who want guarantees. You pay a fixed premium every year, up to age 100 (increasingly, up to age 121). You can choose to pay larger premiums up front so the policy will, contractually, be paid in full by a certain age. You earn guaranteed interest on your cash values. You know for sure that when you die, your beneficiaries will get the policy's face value. The best whole-life policies pay dividends. They're sold by the large mutual life insurance companies and a few others.

What percentage return will you earn on the money you invest in a whole-life policy? Beats me. The insurance company usually doesn't reveal how much of each whole-life premium goes to cover the cost of insurance and overhead expenses, so you can't tell what you're earning on the rest of your funds. Most likely, your policy will earn little or nothing in the first couple of years, due to sales expenses. In later years, the rate will rise. Over 20 years, good whole-life insurance should earn as much as a quality corporate bond, tax deferred.

It's possible to get a whole-life policy that's not guaranteed, if you want to pay a lower premium and count on dividends to make up the difference. But the very reason to buy whole life is to set everything in stone.

The Joy of Dividends. The dividends paid on whole-life policies by mutual insurance companies are a terrific bonus. You can use them to buy *paid-up additions* (PUAs)—tiny paid-up policies added to your original policy. That increases your cash value and guaranteed death benefit every year. PUAs are also a highly efficient way of buying more insurance. The agent earns no commission on each addition, so all of your dividend dollars go for family protection.

Alternatively, you can use the dividends to reduce the premiums you pay.

Dividends are declared once a year, on your policy's anniversary date. If you surrender the policy before that date, you'll lose your share of that year's dividend. So don't. A few companies promise *terminal dividends* if you hold the policy for 15 or 20 years. They may be worth waiting for.

Dividends aren't guaranteed, so you can't be sure how much insurance they'll buy in the future. But any additions are a good deal.

Some things to know about whole life:

- *If you reach retirement and want to stop paying premiums,* you can use the cash value to buy a smaller "paid-up" policy.
- *If you don't want the policy anymore,* you can cancel it and pocket the cash value. If you're 65 or older, you may be able to sell it to a private investor for substantially more than you'd get from the cash value. See page 398. Both transactions are potentially taxable.
- *If you want to take cash out of the policy,* you can often withdraw the accumulated paid-up additions. You can also take a policy loan (page 379).
- *You will be docked if you cancel the policy.* Hidden charges in the early years can slash your cash surrender value to a number too low to mention in polite company. ("Oh, c'mon, say it," urges New York fee-only life insurance adviser Glenn Daily.* "You can lose one hundred percent of the money you put up.") Don't buy whole life unless you can afford to keep it.

You can buy a whole-life policy that's not entirely guaranteed—a risk that traditional buyers should watch out for. For example, you might plan to have the policy paid up at age 65, based on the current dividend scale. If dividends fall, however, you'll have to pay premiums for a longer period than you intended. This is the same sort of "vanishing premium" problem you can confront with universal life (page 360). If you've had the policy for a while, ask your agent for a computerized policy illustration, to be sure that it's on track.

You can improve your policy's cash surrender value by buying a blend (page 372)—a mix of whole life, dividends, and term. The advantage of blends is that they cut your costs. However, the policies aren't entirely guaranteed.

Some insurers currently pay higher dividends than the market can sustain. That's fine for now. But as part of the sale, the agent will show you a policy illustration with today's high dividends projected 20 and 30 years into the future. That paints far too rosy a picture. Be sure that the projection also shows what will happen if the dividends drop to current market rates or less. You should focus your attention on the parts of the policy that are guaranteed.

Variable whole-life insurance and *interest-sensitive whole-life insurance* offer a guaranteed death benefit. Your cash values, however, are linked to the performance of the stock and bond markets. If they underperform, your premiums will rise. If you don't pay the premiums, the policies will be canceled. These types of whole-life insurance are more expensive than traditional whole life. There's absolutely no reason to buy them.

---

*Daily's free booklet, *Life Insurance Sense and Nonsense: For People Who Don't Mind a Little Complexity,* can be read at GlennDaily.com (www.glenndaily.com). Click on "Publications."

Who Should Buy Traditional Whole-Life Insurance? It's the policy of choice for anyone buying cash-value coverage. That's because it can offer certainty, with no investment risk. You pay your money, get a guaranteed death benefit, and accumulate a guaranteed cash value. Guarantees are what you buy life insurance *for.* The premium normally stays the same throughout your life, although you can pay more and stop the premiums at an earlier age. You might get higher cash values and a higher death benefit, depending on the policy. But you'll never get less than the guarantee.

Buy your whole-life policy from a mutual insurance company, so you'll earn the dividends. This type of insurance isn't as glamorous as universal life, but it has performed better over time.

Universal-Life Insurance

Before I start explaining, a warning! Universal-life insurance is complicated! You may not understand all the risks in a policy you buy. Your insurance agent may not understand them either. Your policy needs constant attention to be sure it stays in force.

Okay, on to the details.

These policies are flexible. They're marketed to people who want options. You decide how much premium to pay, subject to specified minimums and maximums. If you pay enough, your policy can be guaranteed to last for life and build substantial cash values. If you pay too little, your policy will eventually lapse. Your choice of premium dictates the result.

How do you decide how much premium to pay?

1. The insurance agent will give you a "guideline" premium. It should be high enough to guarantee that your coverage will last for life. This is the best and safest choice.

2. You can put additional money into the policy if you're using it as a tax-protected investment. It will earn interest at whatever rate of return the policy is currently yielding (to find out how much, see page 362). If you die, however, your beneficiaries may or may not get this extra money, depending on the policy option you choose (see below). There's a limit on how much money you can put in and still get favorable tax treatment—ask your agent what the maximum is (page 374). You pay a new sales commission on every "deposit."

3. If you're watching every dollar, you can put in a little less than the guideline and still have a policy that's reasonably safe.

4. You can put a lot less into the policy if money is tight right now. But in this case, you'd have to pay more in the later years to keep the policy alive.

5. You can vary the size of your premiums, paying more this month, then skipping the next three months. In theory, that's an advantage; in practice, it will probably lead to a policy that will fail because it's starved for cash.

What happens if, in any month, you don't pay a high enough premium to cover the current cost of your insurance protection? The insurer will take the missing payment out of your policy's cash value. If you consistently pay too little, your cash value will decline and the policy will eventually collapse. You'll lose your coverage and might owe income taxes too.

Buyers of universal life can also choose how large a death benefit they want their premiums to buy. You generally have two options:

Option A: Your death benefit stays level. Your policy's earnings go into extra cash value. This option gives you more insurance coverage right now for the money you put up. Don't put any extra money into your policy if you've chosen option A. If you die, your heirs will get only the death benefit, not the death benefit plus the extra cash you put in.

Option B: Your death benefit rises. Your beneficiaries get the policy's face value plus the cash value, which normally goes up every year. You get less coverage for a given amount of premium, but you gain an inflation hedge. If you dump extra money into an option B policy, those funds will earn a tax-deferred return and go to your family tax free at death.

Option B gets expensive at later ages. Your premium may have to rise. Best strategy: Start with Option B if you want to be able to put more money into the policy. Later switch to option A. If you start with option A and want to switch to option B, you'll have to pass a medical exam, because option B increases your coverage.

In either case, your family will get no less than the policy's face value, provided that the insurance remains in force.

You can take money out of a universal-life policy without borrowing against it. Instead you make a "partial withdrawal," usually paying a $25 fee. Ask the insurance company whether any part of the withdrawal is taxable. The answer depends on actuarial calculations. There also may be surrender charges. For deciding between loans and partial withdrawals, see page 379.

You'll pay substantial surrender charges if you drop the policy before 10 to 15 years have passed. What looks like a large "investment account" could be cut in half, or worse, if you give up the policy too soon. There may be a partial surrender charge if you reduce the policy's face value.

How Much Is Your Policy Earning, Really???

Universal-life policies disclose the interest rate that you're earning on your policy's cash value. You get an annual statement showing how much interest you earned, how much was withdrawn from your policy to cover costs, and how much your savings fund increased.

But, but, but . . . the stated rate tells you next to nothing. A high stated interest rate can be undercut if the insurer charges extra for expenses and for the insurance portion of the policy. Furthermore, interest rates change. Actual rates will be lower, or higher, than the insurance company projects. In recent years, they've been substantially lower, and large numbers of policies have collapsed. You are guaranteed only the company's minimum; typically 3 percent (4 percent on older policies).

Never compare the iffy advertised interest rates on life insurance savings with the guaranteed interest rates on bonds or bank accounts. They don't compute. You can't even compare one insurer's interest rates with another's because the companies subtract different amounts from your cash value to cover their costs.

Anyone with a Universal Policy Should

- *Pay the full guideline premium needed to secure the policy for life* even if interest rates decline. If you can't afford it, at least pay enough to keep the policy going under current interest rates. If you can't afford that, universal life is not for you. Your policy will eventually lapse, costing you all the money you put in and leaving your family without protection. You'll be better off with term insurance from the start.

- *Call your insurance agent if you're not paying the guideline premium.* You want to know whether your policy is still on track or if you'll have to put more money in. The agent should give you an *in-force*, or *current*, illustration. It shows what will happen to your cash value and death benefit over the next 30 years or so if interest rates and your premium payments stay the same.

Bore in on the policy's current and future cash value (it might be called the policy value, account value, accumulation value, or something similar). It should always be going up, not down. If the illustration shows it declining in some future year, you're not paying high enough premiums to keep the policy going. Shrinking cash values should always be treated as a red alert!

- *Check the annual statement that the insurance company sends you.* At the end, you should find a sentence disclosing how many years your policy will remain in force if you (1) pay no more premiums or (2) keep paying premiums at the originally scheduled rate. If the policy will obviously lapse before you do, call your agent to see what your options are. If you can't find that disclosure on your annual statement, call your agent and ask for it. Don't dally, and accept no excuses. You must find out if your insurance is running down!

■ *Don't be lulled by the policy's guarantees.* You may have a guaranteed interest rate of 3 or 4 percent on your cash values, but you could be earning less than that after expenses. Your guaranteed death benefit is good as long as the policy is in force, but if the cash value sinks there's no guarantee that the policy won't expire.

■ *If interest rates go up, a sinking policy might recover.* But don't gamble. Check it out.

■ *Buy a term insurance policy as a backup,* in case the universal policy doesn't work out.

Who Might Be in Trouble with an Older Universal-Life Policy Right Now:
(1) Anyone who bought when interest rates were higher and who isn't paying a higher annual premium. (2) Anyone with a loan on a policy or who has taken a withdrawal. (3) Anyone who has skipped premiums or is paying less than originally planned. (4) Anyone who's paying less than the guideline premium. (5) Anyone who bought with a single lump sum and hasn't added money since.

**If Your Policy Is in Trouble and You Still Need Insurance,
What Should You Do?**

1. Find out how much money you'll have to add to bring the policy up to speed. The sooner you get the answer, the less it will cost.

2. See if you can save the policy by switching from option B to option A (page 361).

3. If there's a loan against the policy, consider repaying it. That may put your policy back on solid ground. You can repay with the proceeds of a partial withdrawal from the policy if you don't have other cash. Be sure to specify that the money you're adding should be used to reduce the loan. If you just send in a check, it will be treated as a premium, and a sales commission will be deducted.

4. Restructure the policy to a smaller face amount. You might have to pay a partial surrender charge. Unless you're in poor health, however, shrinking your coverage is better than pouring cash into a larger policy that will eventually lapse.

5. Let the policy gradually run down. You'll be insured for as many years as it lasts. Quit paying premiums if you're in poor health and think you might die before the policy lapses. Morbid, I guess, but good advice.

6. Cancel the policy and take back whatever cash value is left. This may be the worst choice. There may be a surrender charge. You will also owe income taxes if you receive more cash than you paid in premiums. If you need more insurance, consider keeping your universal policy and adding some term insurance.

7. If you've lost money on the policy, you can transfer the remaining cash value to a tax-deferred annuity. The built-in loss will tax-shelter some of the annuity's future investment gains when you draw out the money (page 368). This strategy won't fix your life insurance problem, but it at least salvages something. (Be sure to buy a low-cost annuity— page 1087.)

— Where to Get Help —

In theory, you can call the insurance agent who sold you the policy in the first place. In practice, that agent may no longer be around. There's a huge turnover in this business. The new agent in the office you used will probably want to sell you a new policy rather than help you with your old one. But who knows? Maybe you'll luck out.

Before making any changes, contact the excellent life insurance service run by the Consumer Federation of America (read all about it on page 373). For just $75, actuary James Hunt will evaluate your policy and make some suggestions. I cannot praise this service enough! Hunt could save you thousands of dollars, not only on this policy but on any future cash-value policy you might consider buying.

After All These Warnings, Who Might Buy Universal Life? Someone who wants cash values and can easily afford the guideline premium. Someone who will monitor the policy every three years to be sure it's working out. Someone who can afford to pay higher premiums if necessary. Someone working with a financial planner who will adjust the policy's premiums and death benefit for you as your circumstances change. Someone who didn't read about the simple virtues of a traditional whole-life insurance policy, back on page 358.

Variable Universal-Life Insurance

Repeat warning! Variable universal life (VUL) has all the complications of straight universal life and then some. Insurance is supposed to protect your family from risk. Variable policies add risk. The 2000 stock market collapse left thousands of VUL buyers in the hole, and the 2008 collapse did it again.

A variable policy ties your death benefit and cash value to the investment performance of stocks, bonds, or money market securities. You can vary the premiums you pay, just as you do with straight universal life. What's different is that you get to choose what your policy will invest in. You're offered a variety of *subaccounts,* which are similar to mutual funds. You pick one (or several) and can move your money among them at will. What rings buyers' bells is the chance to invest in stocks. The assets behind other life insurance policies are invested mainly in mortgages and bonds. Variable policies give you a shot at higher growth.

When your investments do well, your cash value rises. If you chose option B for policy earnings (page 361), your death benefit rises too. When your investments do badly, however, your cash value falls. Your death benefit also falls unless you add more money to the policy—in a lump sum or in higher premium payments. (Under option A, your death benefit might rise or fall in the future but not right away.)

Some policies offer a guaranteed minimum death benefit for a limited number of years to keep the policy from lapsing if the stock market drops soon after you buy. This feature usually involves an extra cost.

Your cash values, however, are never guaranteed. In good markets, they'll rise; in bad ones, they'll fall. If they fall too far or for too long, your insurance policy will collapse.

Over 20 or 30 years, you assume that the value of your policy has nowhere to go but up. But how far up? Not as much as you might think. That's because of the policy's costs. The internal charges levied against variable policies tend to be higher than those on other forms of cash-value coverage.

Take one typical bull market contract earning 10.2 percent on its cash value, analyzed by the consulting actuary for the Consumer Federation of America, James Hunt. After five years, the policyholder had a negative investment return (−8.7 percent), principally due to the up-front sales charge. After 10 years, the policy still returned a net of just 4.8 percent; after 15 years, 6.6 percent; after 20 years, 7.3 percent. Even in good markets, these policies don't reward you enough for the investment risk you take.

Over the past 10 years, these policies haven't rewarded you at all! Back in 1999, insurance agents were predicting that VUL policies would earn 12 percent a year. By 2009, U.S. stocks had earned less than 1 percent a year. You're losing big money, after costs.

At this writing, the returns on new policies are being projected at 8 percent a year. But showing average future returns is highly misleading. First, who knows what the market will do? Second, your policy's success depends on what happens year by year, not over the long term. Say, for example, that the market averages 8 percent over 20 years but loses money during the first 5 years. Those first 5 years can wipe you out.

VUL investments earn you even less after tax. If you owned these same mutual funds outside your policy, any gains would be taxed at the low capital gains rate. If you ever surrender the policy and take the gains, you'll pay the higher ordinary income rate. Opting for higher taxes doesn't strike me as a good idea.

The one exception I might make to my general dump on VUL is TIAA-CREF's no-commission policy. Its insurance charges are low and you can invest in the company's own mutual funds, which are inexpensive too. You should plan on holding the policy for life so that the proceeds will pass to your heirs tax free.

If You Own VUL, It Might Be Collapsing Under You, Even As We Speak. To maintain your death benefit for your family's protection, your VUL has to yield a certain investment return after costs. Ten years of bad markets almost certainly put you way behind. You will probably have to add money if you want to keep the policy going. In the previous section on straight universal life insurance, I discussed—at length—how to find out if your policy is in danger and what it would take to save it, so I won't repeat it here. Go to page 363 and follow the same steps. Consult with the expert life insurance service provided by the Consumer Federation of America.

If You Buy Variable Universal Life, How Should You Invest?
- *Pay the full guideline premium.* That reduces the odds that you'll have to pay higher premiums later. Remember, nothing in VUL is guaranteed. If you can't afford the guideline premium, your investment—and your insurance—will be at serious risk. All the caveats that apply to straight universal life apply to the variable version too.
- *Low- and medium-yield investments are a waste of money in VULs,* even if you use them for only part of your policy's cash value. Money market returns have virtually no chance of raising (or even maintaining) your death benefit, after subtracting costs. Neither do returns from bonds. Bonds yield about the same as an investment in regular life insurance, so you'd get nothing in return for paying a variable policy's higher costs.
- *If you're going to bet on variable universal life, go all the way.* Put all your money into a pure stock index fund and leave it there. Don't even bother with an asset-allocation fund, which invests in a mix of stocks and bonds and moves the money around as markets change. If you don't want to hold stocks for the long term, don't buy variable insurance.

- *Buy through a financial planner, not through a general agent.* VUL pays big up-front commissions but small commissions in the later years. There's little to motivate an agent to keep track of the policy and suggest investment changes. A planner who's giving you continuing service on other matters will review your insurance policy from time to time.
- *Buy this insurance only if you can afford to pay large premiums.* The insurer might levy $8 a month in fees in addition to all its other costs. That batters investments of just $50 or $100 a month. Costs are more reasonable if you're investing, say, $1,000 a month. Before signing up, ask the agent to give you a *written* list of all costs. They're buried in various places in the prospectus (variable policies come with a prospectus). If you just ask about costs verbally, the agent may not "remember" them all. There are substantial surrender charges if you give up the policy before 10 to 15 years have passed.
- *You can use the policy's earnings* to build either the maximum cash value or the maximum death benefit, just as with regular universal life (see options A and B, page 361). That is, if the market goes up.
- *Buy a backup term insurance policy,* just in case your VUL fails.

Why Would You Buy VUL? Because you're blinded by the belief that anything linked to stocks has to do well in the long run. You don't realize how deeply costs bite into your returns. You need superior stock market returns over a long holding period for this investment to do better than other forms of cash-value insurance. If you plan to hold for 20 years or so and can afford to raise your premiums when the stock market lags, you have a shot. Maybe.

It can't be said often enough! If you buy universal or variable universal coverage, pay the high "guideline" premium. Otherwise your "permanent insurance" might lapse when you're 50, 60, or 70, leaving you without the protection that you spent your youth paying for. With VUL, it might lapse anyway. Find out *now* how long your current policy is actually going to last. Call your agent or insurance company for a current illustration. Go to the last page of your most recent annual statement, where a universal policy's lapse date may be disclosed. Check your policy's viability with the Consumer Federation of America (page 373).

Second-to-Die Insurance

These policies are for well-to-do married couples who want extra cash to cover the estate tax. No tax is generally due when the first spouse dies because the second spouse inherits. It's only when the second spouse dies that the government takes its cut.

Enter second-to-die insurance, also called *survivorship life*. It insures both lives but pays off only at the second death. The premium is lower than if you bought separate cash-value policies, one for each.

This policy should probably be transferred into an irrevocable trust so as not to be taxed in your estate. After the second death, when the life insurance pays off, the trust uses the proceeds to buy assets from the estate. That provides the estate with the money it needs to pay the tax. Don't rely on an insurance agent to structure this arrangement for you. See a tax attorney who specializes in estate planning.

Second-to-die policies can be whole life, universal life, or variable universal life. If you choose a universal policy, be sure to pay the guideline premium, so that you don't run the risk that the policy will lapse. For safety, these policies should be overfunded rather than marginally funded.

Also, look at your options if you divorce. If you're insurable, it's best to cash in your second-to-die insurance and make other arrangements. If you're in poor health, you should be able to split this policy in two without having to pass a health exam or pay sales commissions on two new policies. There may be taxes and fees, however, and some companies impose a surrender charge on the original policy. Large premiums are usually involved in second-to-die insurance. You should be looking at low-loads (page 371) and well-funded blends (page 372) that provide the safe level of premiums you want at a lower cost.

How to Defer Income Taxes When You Cancel a Policy

When you cancel a policy, you'll be paid the cash value it contains minus any surrender charge. You'll owe income taxes on the amount of the payout that exceeds the premiums you paid. On older policies, that tax can be quite large.

To defer the tax, roll the cash you receive into a tax-deferred annuity (technically, it's called a tax-free 1035 exchange). The money can be invested in the annuity's various mutual funds. You won't be taxed on your gains until you take the money out.

The 1035 route works even better on policies that show a loss. Your loss is the difference between all the premiums you paid and the piddling amount of cash value you got back. When you roll the cash value into the annuity, document that loss. It will tax-shelter an equal amount of future gains on your annuity investments when you eventually take the money out. If the cash coming out of your policy isn't enough to buy an annuity, you can add money from other savings.

Only the insurance company can certify the loss. The annuity company won't accept it on your say-so, so there's some nuisance paperwork. Your new insurance company should handle it for you. To keep this transaction tax free, the money has to go directly from the policy into the annuity, without passing through your hands first.

You can't use this strategy if your policy has no cash value after subtracting the surrender charge. In that case, you'll just have to swallow the loss.

I have many reservations about variable tax-deferred annuities (page 1084). But for this purpose, they're ideal. Choose a low-cost annuity from Vanguard or TIAA-CREF.

Can You Trust Computer-Generated Life Insurance Proposals?

Yes, for term insurance. No, for cash-value policies. Well . . . maybe some cash-value illustrations are okay, but the problem is that you can't tell the good ones from the bad ones.

Illustrations are neat rows of columns attempting to show what your policy will be worth 30 years or more into the future. But you can't predict what the company's cost-of-insurance charges will be or where interest rates will go. You also don't know if the agent has lowballed the premium to make the policy look more competitive.

Illustrations are useful to people who know how to interpret them. They're also a way of explaining how a product works. But they can easily mislead you, leaving you with the impression that that's the way your policy will work out.

With life insurance, the only thing you can count on are the guarantees written into your contract. Everything else is speculative. If you own universal life or variable universal life, which don't guarantee your premiums and death benefits, get a new illustration every three years to see if the policy is still on track.

If you're buying cash-value insurance, there are four things the illustration can help you with:

1. Look at the difference between the premium you paid and the *cash surrender value* in the policy's first year. That's the amount you're paying that year in sales commissions and other marketing expenses. You pay continuing commissions in future years, but the first year is the big one. *All* of your premium might have gone toward selling expenses, leaving you with nothing in your account. Tell your agent that you want a "blended premium" (page 372) that will leave your account with at least 50 percent of the premium you paid. With a low-load, you might keep 80 percent of your premium.

2. A separate column will show you cash values, or account values, or accumulation values, or somesuch. That's not real money. It's what builds up in the policy if you don't touch it. If you want your money out, the column showing the cash surrender value is the only one that counts.

3. Look at the columns showing how your cash value grows. One column projects your gains based on current interest rates or assumed stock market gains. The other shows the minimum you're guaranteed. The cash in both those columns should rise every year if you want the policy to last for life. If the cash starts going down in the future, your policy will slowly run out. You'll have to raise the premium to be sure that your coverage will last.

4. Look for any zeros or blanks in the columns that project your future death benefit and cash value. Their meaning is simple. They show that in those years, your policy will have lapsed, collapsed, exploded, gone up in smoke, given up the ghost. There's no more insurance. In the plan proposed, you're not paying a high enough premium to keep the policy going.

5. When you're considering buying a policy or replacing one, the illustration can help you get expert advice. Send it to the actuary for the Consumer Federation of America, James Hunt (page 373). He'll advise you on whether it's a good buy.

What You Should Know About Selling Expenses

The expenses of selling the policy—also called loads—are deducted from the premiums you pay. Some deductions are direct, such as a fixed percentage of each premium. Some are indirect, such as surrender charges if you quit. Most policies charge both.

For agent-sold cash-value policies, sales expenses normally run from 70 percent to more than 100 percent of your first-year premium and 5 to 8 percent of your renewal premiums for 2 to 10 years. That load covers the salesperson's commission, a percentage payment to the manager of the sales office, an override for office and training expenses, fringe benefits for agents, and other marketing costs.

A few universal policies have no front-end load, only a back-end load or surrender charge, which you pay if you drop the insurance within the first 10 or 15 years. An agent might call this no-load insurance. It is not. The agent gets an up-front commission, paid by the insurance company. The company recoups its cost by charging you higher policy expenses every year or by paying lower interest rates on your cash values.

Sales expenses for low-loads (page 371) come out of the policy itself rather than being deducted from your premium up front. They usually come to less than 20 percent of your first-year premium and 2 to 3 percent of subsequent premiums. Those are the policies you want.

Three Ways of Buying Permanent Insurance at a Lower Cost

The Low-Loads

Low-load policies eliminate sales commissions to insurance agents. As a result, most of your premium payments go into the policy itself. You'll get some combination of reasonable premiums, higher cash values, and higher death benefits than regular agent-sold policies offer. Low-loads are available to buyers of universal life, variable universal life, and second-to-die insurance.

An insurance agent might try to convince you that low-loads are shams. He or she will show you a policy with a lower premium than the low-load charges and claim that it's less expensive. It's not! The true cost of a policy shows up in its future cash values and death benefits, and that's where low-loads shine. They have larger cash values in the early years than agent-sold policies do. As a result, their investment values and death benefits build up much faster. Also, the low-load typically has no surrender charges. If you cancel it early, you'll get most of your premium payments back. Contrast this with the pittance you get after quitting an agent-sold policy early.

Where to Buy Low-Loads. Two* main companies sell them. You can't apply online because cash-value insurance is too complicated. Instead, decide on the type of policy you want (they're explained in the previous pages) and call the companies for free quotes. One of them may be more competitive than another at your particular age. To compare their policies directly, ask for a universal-life proposal with the same premium and death benefit. The policy with the higher cash value after 10 or 15 years, wins. The low-load companies:

- *AmeritasDirect.com*—for universal life, variable life, and second-to-die. Ameritas also sells full-commission products through insurance agents, so be sure you don't buy one of those by mistake.
- *TIAA-CREF.org*—for universal life, variable life, and second-to-die.

---

*USAA Life Insurance Company sells low-load policies but directs its marketing only to military families. Go to www.usaa.com or call 800-531-8722.

Blended Premiums: The Low-Cost Way to Buy from Agents

Blends are the cherished little secret of consumers in the know. They let you buy life insurance at a lower cost than you'd normally pay.

A blend is a package of policies. It includes some whole-life coverage, some term insurance, and, at mutual companies, some paid-up additions, although these divisions won't be apparent to you. All together, they add up to the death benefit you want.

The savings come from the commission structure. Commissions are lower on the term insurance portion and minimal on the paid-up additions. You might save 80 percent on commissions, or 5 to 10 percent of your total premiums.

Because agents earn lower commissions when they sell a blend, they don't go out of their way to offer them. Most agents don't even know how they work. Blends are usually sold to customers of fee-only insurance advisers or buyers of large cash-value policies, whose agents have to be competitive.

You can use the savings you get from blends in one of two ways:

1. The blend can lower your premium—the most popular choice. When agents compete for your business, they usually do so by showing how little you have to pay for a large amount of coverage.

When you lower your premium, however, blends carry a risk. You're counting on earning enough on your cash values to support the policy. If that doesn't happen, your policy will gradually unravel. To save it, you'd have to increase your premiums or pay them for more years than you intended.

To avoid this risk, buyers who want to save money up front shouldn't cut their premium very far—say, no more than 10 percent below what they'd pay for straight whole life.

2. The blend can be used to build cash values faster than usual—another way of lowering costs. You pay roughly the same premium as you would for straight whole-life insurance, but the savings in commissions go directly into your policy. You'll have more cash values to tap in your retirement years.

With either choice, the death benefit stays level for several years and then starts going up. Eventually it should exceed the death benefit you'd get from straight whole life plus paid-up additions.

For the best buy in blends, tell the agent you want a mix that contains the largest possible amount of term and paid-up additions. That puts the maximum amount of money at work for you.

Blends are available for both whole-life and universal-life insurance. The universal policies don't have paid-up additions, so they blend just whole life and term.

Where to Buy Blends

Any insurance agent can structure a blend. He or she just has to want to, and most of them don't. Fee-only financial planners tell me that the agents for North-western Mutual Life are especially cooperative, so that's a place to try. Blends are typically offered on larger policies, not on small ones.

Otherwise I know of only one insurance brokerage firm that routinely structures policies to hold commissions down: Low Load Insurance Services in Tampa, Florida. The firm works only with fee-only financial planners, but readers of this book can use it too. Go to www.llis.com, click on "Quote Request" and then on "Universal Life" or "Survivorship Universal Life" (second-to-die), the only types of permanent insurance you can apply for online. Fill in the form after entering my name—Jane Bryant Quinn—in the "advisor" space. You'll get a quote on a policy at the guideline premium (for lifetime payments) and a 10-pay premium (if you want to pay in full over just 10 years). There's a case manager to provide advice, answer your questions, suggest options, and steer you through the purchasing process. If you're interested in variable universal life or no-lapse universal life, call the LLIS directly at 877-254-4429. (P.S.: I get nothing out of this except the pleasure of knowing that you'll get expert help.)

No-Lapse Universal Life (page 352). You pay low premiums for life and can buy a policy from any agent. No-lapse is an excellent buy if the reason you want insurance is to pay estate taxes or guarantee that a permanent dependent (say, a disabled child) will always have financial support. Don't buy, however, if you want the option of turning your insurance policy into cash later in life. No-lapse doesn't build cash values.

The Best Advice in This Book About Buying Cash-Value Life Insurance!

Are you confused about insurance policies? Are you wondering whether to buy a particular policy, keep a policy you have, or surrender it for cash? The answer is right at your fingertips—and at low cost. Have the policy analyzed by the expert service EvaluateLifeInsurance.org (www.evaluatelifeinsurance.org), offered through the Consumer Federation of America. Your expert is actuary James Hunt, formerly the insurance commissioner of Vermont. He'll study the economics of the policy, tell you what it's earning (if anything), and make recommendations. His advice could save you thousands of dollars, not to mention the gain to your grieving family if you die.

Among the questions Hunt can answer: (1) Should you buy a particular cash-value policy or choose term instead? (2) Should you keep a policy you own or surrender it? (3) Should you switch from your current policy to a new one that an agent is pitching? (4) Of two or more competing policies, which is the better buy?

For a proposed new cash-value policy, ask the agent for an illustration. That's a computer projection of the policy's future premiums, cash values, and death benefits. For a policy you already own, ask for a current or in-force illustration. Hunt's Web site gives more details on what, specifically, the illustration should include. Send your request, plus the illustrations and a check, directly to James Hunt, 8 Tahanto Street, Concord, NH 03301. Don't send the policy itself.

How much does this excellent service cost? Almost nothing, compared with the benefit you get. At this writing, Hunt is charging $75 for the first illustration and $55 for each additional illustration submitted at the same time. For variable and second-to-die policies, you pay $85 for the first illustration and $55 for each additional one. Make out the check to the CFA Insurance Group.

Single-Premium Policies: A Great Investment for Some People

You are exactly the right person for a single-premium cash-value life policy if you (1) are over age 59½ (or soon to be), (2) are well fixed financially, (3) have a big chunk of money that you don't need and plan to leave to your heirs, but (4) want a fallback in case you should need that money after all. If you nodded your way through all four points, read on.

These policies are also called *modified endowment contracts* (MECs). You put up a lump sum of money—as little as $5,000 but more often $50,000 to $100,000. You get life insurance plus a large pool of cash values, the amount depending on the company, the type of insurance, and your age.

Assuming that you hold the policy until you die—which is what you intend—your beneficiaries will receive a big payout, tax free. If it turns out that you need the money after all, you can borrow against the policy or withdraw cash directly. There's a downside with MECs: the loan or withdrawal will be treated as taxable income, up to the amount of money that the policy has earned. If you are under age 59½ and not disabled, you also pay a 10 percent penalty.

Still, these are good investments for wealthy people who don't expect to borrow against them or withdraw any funds. If you find that you need some of this money and have to withdraw it and pay a tax, so what? You are probably still leaving more for your heirs than if your money had slept in another conservative investment. A top policy, often recommended, is Northwestern Mutual's Single Premium Life.

Warning: Agents aren't always interested in selling MECs because the commission is low (around 3.5 percent). Instead they might suggest a regular whole-life or universal-life policy, not structured as a MEC. That might sound good because you don't risk owing taxes if you make withdrawals. However, you'll pay a large chunk of your investment in sales commissions. Always look at the difference between what you put into the policy and what your first-year cash value is. In a MEC, most of your money will stay in the policy where it can be used to increase the death benefit for your kids. In a fake MEC, the agent swallows a large part of the cash.

Riders to Your Policy

A rider is a policy benefit that you purchase separately. Here are the most common ones.

Waiver of Premium—pays your insurance premiums if, before a certain age (usually 65), you've been totally disabled for six months. It's a worthwhile buy unless you have ample coverage from a separate disability income policy (see Chapter 14). Ask what the insurer means by "disabled." Typically, the rider is triggered if you can't work in your own occupation for the first two years and then only if you can't work in any occupation for which you're fitted by education and training.

Accidental Death Benefit—pays off in the unlikely case that you die in an accident. People buy it like a lottery ticket, but it's not worth the price.

Cost of Living—raises your death benefit annually in tandem with the consumer price index, without your having to take a health exam. If there's a charge for the rider, it's a waste of money, in the opinion of the Consumer Federation of America. For better protection, buy paid-up additions (with whole life) or take option B (with universal life).

Guaranteed Insurability—lets you buy more insurance, at your current health classification, without taking a health exam. You have to buy certain amounts at certain ages; if you skip a buying opportunity, you don't get it back. This rider is generally available only to people under 40 and usually with cash-value policies (not term insurance). It becomes valuable only if (1) your health gets so bad that you can't buy normal coverage and (2) you think you might need substantially larger amounts of life insurance. CFA advises you to forget the guaranteed insurability option. If you expect to need more coverage in the future, buy it now in the form of extra term insurance.

Term Insurance—attached as a rider to a cash-value policy, to provide extra coverage for you or your spouse. Most of these riders are expensive. Go to Term4Sale.com to check them against the policies you can buy somewhere else.

Kid Insurance—attached as a rider to a cash-value policy, to provide a payment if the child dies. In my book (and this *is* my book), it's an unnecessary expense. The coverage offered by this rider normally ends when the child marries or reaches 18 or 25, but you may still be paying for it years later, as part of your regular premium. You have to ask to get the charge removed. If you bought the child his or her own policy, the insurer may automatically charge the child high smoker's rates when he or she reaches 18 or 20. Nonsmokers have to call to get the lower premium they deserve.

Paid-up Addition—uses your policy dividends to buy new insurance. A terrific choice.

Six Ways of Handling Insurance Policy Dividends

You get dividends with whole-life insurance, rarely with term insurance or universal life. Use your dividends to . . .

1. Buy small paid-up additions to your whole-life policy. This is my favorite use of dividends for people with families to protect. The paid-up additions give you extra insurance without deducting any sales charges. There's no medical exam, so your coverage can grow even if your health declines.

2. Take the money in cash. It's not taxed unless you have a modified endowment contract (page 374) or in the unlikely event that the dividends you take in cash exceed the premiums you paid.

3. Reduce your annual premium.

4. Reduce your policy loan.

5. Buy extra term insurance, good for one year. You may have to sign up for this option in advance.

6. Open a savings (or *accumulation*) account with the insurance company, where your dividends will accumulate and earn interest. You can use this money whenever you want, although you can't always get it fast. At your death, it passes to your beneficiaries. The dividends aren't taxable, but the interest is. Because of the taxes, this is generally a poor choice. Some agents suggest it, however, for a devious reason: they plan to call you in a few years and persuade you to use this money to buy more insurance. What a bum deal! If you simply buy paid-up additions (strategy 1), you avoid any taxes, eliminate sales commissions, get more insurance to leave to your family, and earn more on the money you invest.

Paying Premiums

With whole-life insurance, it's cheaper by far to pay premiums annually. If you pay monthly, quarterly, or semiannually, you're charged a high and *undisclosed* interest rate, typically running from about 7 to 25 percent (and occasionally higher—the known record is 51 percent). That makes your insurance much more expensive than you thought.

With universal insurance, you pay premiums anytime you want, with no effective interest charge. Sometimes, however, there's a processing fee of up to $2 for every payment, which punishes you for making a lot of small payments.

Virtually all premium payments are subject to the usual sales charges and premium taxes.

Incontestability

Once you've held your life insurance policy for two years, it's generally impregnable. Your survivors get the payoff even if you made misstatements on your application. If you misstated your age, the payout will be adjusted to reflect how old you really were. Tell your beneficiaries where to find proof of your age in case a mistake is made on your death certificate.

Suicide

Your survivors get no payoff if you kill yourself within two years after taking out the policy (the exact time limit depends on the policy and state law). The insurer merely pays your premiums back, sometimes with interest. But after that, you can swallow poison or jump out a window, and your survivors will collect in full. Aren't you glad you asked?

Paid-up Policies

A paid-up policy is (1) cash-value coverage (2) guaranteed to last for the rest of your life (3) with no further premiums due in cash. This idea appeals to many people. They'd like to quit paying premiums when they retire or when they start sending their children to college. To reach this blissful state, they pay extra-large premiums for 10 or 15 years and then stop. From that point on, a true paid-up policy carries itself. All further premiums are paid from the policy's own dividends, earnings, or cash values.

My question is, why would you want to do this? It feels good psychologically to know that premiums will end. But financially, it's dumb to pay current expenses (your insurance premiums) with tax-sheltered dollars (your policy's dividends and earnings). You're also suppressing the growth of your policy's death benefit and cash value. The death benefit might actually decline.

Taxwise investors who own attractive policies pay premiums out-of-pocket and let their insurance savings grow.

Besides, how certain is your policy's paid-upness? With both whole life and universal life, you can get a rock-solid guarantee but only by paying a high enough premium during the policy's early years.

Many buyers think they're paying enough but they really aren't. Your agent may say that your premiums will "vanish"—that is, be paid up—after a certain year. But he or she may have based that conclusion on the policy's current dividends or interest credits. If they decline, your policy will be underfunded in the year you expected it to be paid up. If you have a whole-life policy, you will have to keep paying premiums or else the policy will lapse. With universal life and variable universal life, you can stop paying premiums, but because your policy is now underfunded, it may lapse before you die. To avoid this problem, tell the agent that you want to fund the policy right up to the guaranteed level. *That's* paid-upness.

Premium Financing—A Big Mistake

When agents want to sell you life insurance, they look around to see where your money is. Often it's in your house. So here's the deal, they say: take a home equity loan and buy insurance. Interest on the home equity loan is deductible, interest earned on the policy's cash value is tax free, so you're ahead.

What can go wrong? Everything. Interest on your home equity loan could rise. You may need to borrow for other reasons but have already spent your home equity on your insurance policy. The value of your policy may decline. You may decide that you can't afford the policy's premiums anymore and find that you can't surrender it for enough to repay the equity loan.

In other forms of premium financing, you put up the policy as collateral for a loan from a bank or other lender and pay interest currently. It may look good, as long as the interest rate paid on your cash value is high. If rates fall, however, this deal goes upside down—your loan costs more than your policy is earning. Stay away from these schemes. If you need more insurance, buy a term policy instead. If you don't need insurance, why would you even listen to these guys?

Policy Loans

You can borrow from the insurance company, using the cash value of your insurance policy as collateral. If you die without repaying the loan, the loan proceeds and all the compounded interest are deducted from the death benefit. So your survivors get less.

Life insurance loans are often said to be cheap, cheap, cheap. That is absolutely not true. A loan that your agent says costs you "only 2 percent, net" might actually be costing 8.5 percent. To see how this works, see the full explanation on pages 307 through 309.

Universal and variable universal policies give you the option of taking money directly out of the cash value rather than borrowing against it. There's a fee—maybe $25. Check to see if there's also a partial surrender charge. Your death benefit is reduced by the amount withdrawn, but you save yourself the loan interest cost.

How do you decide whether to take a loan or a withdrawal from a universal policy? Take a loan if you intend to put the money back into the policy. You can use your premiums for loan repayments if you want. Make a withdrawal, however, if you don't intend to put the money back. You can probably take a substantial amount before incurring income taxes (taxes are due if your withdrawals exceed the premiums you've paid). Just be sure that you don't withdraw too much. You need to keep enough cash in the policy to keep it from falling apart.

Borrowing if You Read That Your Insurance Company Might Be Put into Receivership

Borrow, borrow, borrow every dime you can before the regulators move in. In every insurance company collapse so far, policyholders' cash values were slashed, but no one tried to collect on any outstanding loans. There's a risk that

that attitude might change. But so far, loans have proven to be a way of getting some of your capital out.

What if you read that your company's financial strength rating is being cut (page 406)? Don't worry about it. Ratings fall and rise all the time, and hardly any insurance companies fail. Don't be scared into switching your life policy or annuity to another insurer (and paying surrender costs and new commissions). On the other hand, if you're buying a new policy, look for one with top ratings, not one that's currently having trouble.

Why You Should Repay an Insurance Policy Loan

Many people don't. The loan sits there for years, costing ever more in interest. You may even lose track of the size of your debt. When you die, however, your family will learn how much you owe. The loan plus the compounded interest will be subtracted from the death benefit they get.

If you have the money, it's smart to repay a policy loan, especially if the loan keeps you from earning higher dividends or interest on part of your policy's cash value. When you die, all that money returns to your heirs, and you've saved them a lot of interest expense. If you can't repay the loan, restructure it. Create a smaller policy—smaller death benefit, smaller cash value, no debt— and save yourself the future interest payments. One exception to this advice: you wouldn't want to restructure if you're liable for a large surrender charge, or you'd create taxable income.

Quitting

If you cancel a cash-value policy that you've had awhile, you'll get some money back. There are four things you can do:

1. Put the cash in your pocket. You'll owe income taxes on any gains (page 402). If you quit before 10 or 15 years have passed, you may owe surrender charges.

2. Use the cash to buy a smaller, paid-up insurance policy. It can sit there for life without your putting any more money in. This is an excellent option if you want to stop paying premiums while retaining your insurance policy investment.

3. Convert the policy to term insurance. You'll be covered for as long as the money lasts. The price of this *extended term* option is usually high, so choose it only if you're ill and think you won't outlive the benefit. Otherwise buy a new term policy from a low-cost company.

4. Exchange it (in a tax-free 1035 exchange) for a tax-deferred annuity. For more on this option, see page 368. You can also do a tax-free exchange to a better insurance policy, but be sure that the new policy is really better. Agents use the tax-free gambit to get you to switch—to anything—so that they can collect a commission.

What If You Just Stop Paying Premiums?

With whole life, one of three things could happen: (1) Money might be borrowed from your cash value automatically, keeping your policy in force. When the loan limit is reached, your policy lapses. (2) If there's no automatic loan provision, your insurance stays in force for 31 days after the date the unpaid premium was due. If you die during that period, your survivors get the full payoff minus the missing premium. If you live, the policy lapses. With both (1) and (2), you get any cash value the policy contained. (3) The company might apply your cash surrender value to an extended-term policy, which covers you for a certain number of years. The premiums are high.

With universal life, the insurer automatically takes money from your cash value to cover the cost of insurance and other charges. You're insured until your cash value has been used up. After that, you have nothing left.

Collecting

When cashing in a policy or collecting its death benefit, there are usually four ways of taking the money. Don't lock your beneficiary into any of these options in advance. You can't predict which one will work out the best.

1. A lump sum. The company writes the beneficiary a check.

2. Interest only. You park the proceeds with the insurer in an interest-paying account. That's a good place for money that you're still deciding what to do with, provided that the insurer pays more interest than you'd earn in a bank or money market mutual fund. Check it out.

3. Installment payments. The insurance company pays you in regular installments of interest and principal. You can arrange for a fixed amount per month or for payments over a fixed period. You'll want a competitive rate of interest and the right to change the size of the payments when it suits you.

4. A life annuity. This method of payment guarantees you (or you plus a spouse or other beneficiary) a fixed and guaranteed monthly income for life. You can also arrange for payments to go to a beneficiary if you die before a certain number of years have elapsed (typically 10). But inflation will wear down fixed payments that last for much more than 10 years. You wouldn't want the bulk of your money in an annuity unless you're, say, over 75. Nor would you choose an annuity if you're in poor health, because you might not live long enough to collect very much.

You might want an annuity, however, if you intend to cash in a policy that contains a large taxable gain. A tax-free exchange, into the annuity, spreads the gain and the taxes into the future. For more on annuities, see page 1071. If you don't do an exchange, keeping the policy would be a better tax choice.

Best tip on this page: Before converting your insurance proceeds into a lifetime annuity with the same insurance company, check what other insurers are offering at www.immediateannuities.com. Some companies pay much more per month than others (page 1129). If you buy from the company that wrote the life insurance policy, check that your monthly payment is fully guaranteed. Some companies guarantee only a minimum payment, with the rest of your income linked to the size of the company's dividend.

Rating You for Risk

You don't smoke? Good news. You will live longer and get a break on your life insurance rates.

Insurers rate you by health risk, based primarily on medical testing and family history, plus other factors such as high-risk employment or pastimes. You might be superpreferred, preferred, standard-plus, standard, or impaired. The categories cover both smokers and nonsmokers, but in any group, smokers pay more. Next step for accepting or rejecting applicants or raising their premiums: genetic testing, unless Congress outlaws it. (It has been outlawed for health insurers but not for life insurers.) And the step after that? Only immortals need apply?

Find out exactly what health categories the company has and where you stand. At most companies, preferred is only second best—something you may not realize. If you're in good health and are rated standard instead of preferred, see if there's a way out. These classifications are idiosyncratic and vary a lot from one insurer to another. Shoppers using an agent should ask him or her to try different companies. Sometimes the first company will move you up in class to close the deal. (It might also be a high-cost company.)

If you're buying a term policy through a quote service and get a standard rating at the company you chose, see if you can do better at one of the other companies on your best-buy list. Alternatively, enter your data into the quote service again, this time listing yourself as standard. You might find a company offering a better quote than you got before.

You will and should pay more, however, if you've recovered from cancer, a heart attack, or other serious health problems, experienced various mild but chronic conditions, come from a family that has a history of disease, or go sky-diving on weekends. You're what the industry calls a rated risk. People with recent cancer or heart problems probably won't be able to get life insurance at all.

Most companies nowadays put every applicant through a blood and urine test. Besides disease, they look for evidence of hard drugs, liver damage that can reveal a problem drinker, and nicotine in the blood of people claiming not to smoke. If your condition is suspect, they may order more tests. They also check your reported medical history at the Medical Information Bureau.

Here's What to Do If You're a Rated Risk

1. Challenge any data you think is wrong. There may be an error in your file at the Medical Information Bureau (page 483). The insurer has to tell you if you're turned down for coverage or charged a higher premium due to something on your MIB report. If you write to MIB within 30 days, you're entitled to a free summary of your report.

2. Don't meekly accept a higher premium on an individual policy. Shop around. One company might quote a high, "impaired" premium to a person with high blood pressure. Another, believing that the condition is under control, might give that same person a standard rate. Most quality companies have several reinsurance outlets to which they'll refer your case for quotes. Ask whether this was done and what kind of rating you received. Note: Your agent should speak directly with the underwriters of the various companies to get a preliminary offer. Insurers are automatically rejecting cases that have been shopped around. You want to know what your two best possibilities are before making a formal application.

3. Don't work only with the captive insurance agent of a single company. Go to an independent agent too. If each of them knows that the other is bidding for the business, they'll both work a little harder for you.

4. Look for trade or professional groups you can join. There's usually a medical questionnaire, but you may be charged less than you would for an individual policy.

5. Try to buy extra coverage through your employer.

6. If your health has improved, shop around again for coverage. A person who had a stroke five years ago, with no further symptoms or recurrence, might get a new policy at a standard rate. The same might be true five years after a heart attack or after being cured of certain types of cancer.

7. You may have access to credit life insurance as long as you're not on your deathbed. You might, for example, buy a car on credit and insure the loan. If you die, the insurance company will pay. But credit life policies are growing more restrictive, so don't buy without checking the health requirement and the limitations on payment (page 351).

8. If you can't get normal insurance, even at a higher price, look at no-turndown, "guaranteed issue" policies that take all comers. You can sometimes buy up to $25,000 in coverage just by signing a check. But don't expect a terrific deal. These policies are priced to include the obese, people with HIV, and other uninsurables, so they're hugely expensive for the benefit you get. What's more, you have to live for a while before your beneficiary can collect in full. If you die within two years of purchase, some policies merely repay your premiums plus interest (unless you die in an accident). Other policies pay graded benefits: 10 to 30 percent of the death benefit if you die in the first year, 25 to 60 percent in the second year, and full payment from the third or fourth year on.

Small burial policies are sometimes touted to seniors at, say, $10 a month. That buys maybe $1,000 in coverage for a 65-year-old and less as you get older. At age 70, your coverage might drop to $700. By 71, you'd have paid a total of $720 for coverage worth only $700. After that, every month you keep that foolish policy, you're losing money.

Healthy People Should Stay Away From No-Turndown Insurance. You may be tempted by a flyer you get in the mail or an ad you see on TV: instant coverage for a mere $6.95 a month. Don't respond. The same money can buy you much better coverage somewhere else.

Women and Risk

On average, women live longer than men, so they get lower life insurance rates. For term insurance, finding a good rate is easy—just use a quote service such as Term4Sale.com. For cash-value insurance, it's harder. Some insurers charge close to the male rate, others charge quite a bit less. Most insurance is sold to men, so it's hard to know how well an agent knows what's available for women. You have to do a lot of shopping around, especially if you're 40 and up.

Montana is a special case. It has unisex rules that average women's rates with men's. As a result, women pay more than they'd normally have to for life insurance and less for health and disability insurance. Residents can buy cheaper life coverage out of state, but only from companies not licensed to do business in Montana. That diminishes your consumer protection.

Life insurance bought through employers also carries unisex rates. Women will probably do better with a quote service for term policies, a low-load policy for cash value coverage (page 371), or an insurance agent.

Should You Switch Policies?

The easiest way for an agent to generate a commission is to get you to drop your current cash-value policy and buy something else. The industry calls it *replacement.* The new policy might look grand, with bells and whistles belling and whistling, but the commissions and other expenses will come right out of the tax-protected values that your old policy built up. Your new policy has to pay much higher interest or dividends than your old one did just to bring your investment back to where it was before the switch.

Some switches make sense; others don't. The insurance agent is supposed to give you a full, written explanation of why the new policy is better than the old one, but the details may be scant. Before replacing a policy, run the proposal past the policy analysis service offered by the Consumer Federation of America at EvaluateLifeInsurance.org (page 373). See what the service recommends.

Here Are Some Switches to Consider:
- *You have a term insurance policy and find another one with a lower premium.* That's a no-brainer. Switch. In fact, you should check term insurance rates every few years to see if you can find cheaper coverage. You're most apt to find lower rates if you're in tip-top health.
- *You're older, still need insurance, but don't want to pay the premiums on your cash value policy anymore.* You can restructure your current policy in various ways, such as turning it into a smaller policy with all the premiums paid up. If you want more insurance than restructuring allows, consider switching to a no-lapse policy (page 352).
- *You own several small cash-value policies.* You might get a better return by consolidating them into one larger policy, provided that the sales commission doesn't eat up your cash.
- *You own a paid-up policy that earns no dividends.* It might contain enough cash value to buy a new paid-up policy for the same face amount, with some money left over for an outside investment.

- *Your cash-value policy is greatly overpriced or yields a substandard rate of return, according to an evaluation by the Consumer Federation of America.* You might get higher cash values and better performance by switching to a low-load policy or blend. Universal-life policies are particular candidates for replacement if you're in good health and you've held the policy long enough so that the surrender charge no longer applies.
- *You're older, still in good health, and have owned your cash-value policy for 20 years or more.* Because we're living longer, on average, insurance costs have declined, especially for people in your age group. You might find a policy that's a better deal even after paying acquisition costs.

Here are switches to avoid:
- *You have a cash-value policy. The agent suggests that you use the policy's cash to buy a second and larger policy.* Don't do it. You destroy your policy values to pay the agent a commission. If you need more insurance, buy term.
- *You have a whole-life policy and are using the dividends to buy paid-up additions to your coverage. The agent suggests that you use the dividends to buy a new policy instead.* Same answer as above.
- *You have a dividend-paying policy, and a salesperson shows you that universal life, without dividends, is better.* That's a trick comparison. Dividend-paying companies have higher premiums but return part of those premiums as a dividend at the end of the year. The agent may make the comparison without counting the dividend. In general, the major dividend-paying policies have outperformed universal life. Policy values get even better after the 10th year, when sales commissions usually terminate. Says actuary James Hunt of the Consumer Federation of America, "Never replace a Northwestern Mutual policy, no matter how old it is." To fee-only financial advisers, Northwestern is the gold standard.

Here are the switches that may or may not be a good idea, depending on circumstances:
- *You trade in a modest cash-value policy for a larger amount of term insurance.* This makes sense for families that need more coverage but can't afford it unless they give their old policy up. But term insurance doesn't cost very much at younger ages. You can probably keep the cash-value policy and add term on the side. Two good reasons for keeping the policy you've got: (1) You've already swallowed the costs. From here on, it will probably earn a decent tax-protected return (unless it's a midget, in the $5,000 range). (2) You may need coverage in old age, when your term insurance will have lapsed. If yours is a whole-life policy, you can use the dividends to buy additional, paid-up insurance, giving

your family more protection every year. Another alternative to switching: turn your cash-value policy into a smaller, paid-up policy. You'll owe no more premiums and its cash value will continue to build tax free. Buy more term insurance on the side.

■ *You have a cash-value policy and trade it in for term insurance plus a mutual fund.* That is a wise choice if it lets you invest more money in a tax-deferred retirement plan such as a 401(k). If you're investing outside a retirement plan, however, everything depends on the mutual fund you pick. A well-diversified no-load stock fund should outperform an insurance policy, but a bond fund might not. Even for the stock fund to work, you have to make regular investments over 10 or 15 years, so sign up for the fund's automatic monthly investment plan. If you abandon the automatic investing plan, you'd have been better served by keeping the cash-value policy.

■ *You have an older cash-value policy and an agent suggests that you switch to a newer and "better" one.* Sometimes a good idea but often not. You've already paid the premiums and commissions. If you switch, you'll pay them all over again (just what the agent wants!). Some older policies are earning 6 or 7 percent on your cash values, tax deferred—you wouldn't want to give that up.

When this switch is proposed, look at the cash surrender value in your old policy. It is probably going up. Estimate what it will be in a year and compare it with the first-year surrender value in the new policy. The difference is your first-year cost. And of course, your costs multiply because there's less money in your policy to grow. If you need more insurance, consider adding coverage rather than canceling the policy you have.

■ *You bought an insurance policy that you thought was guaranteed, and now you find it isn't.* You have to put up more money to keep the policy in force and don't want to or can't afford it. You can keep the policy but restructure it into something smaller. Or you can swallow your loss and find something that really is guaranteed. Candidates for a switch might be people who bought variable universal life at a stock market peak and are looking at significant losses. Check the current and future surrender charges before making your move. It might be worth holding the policy for another two or three years if the surrender charge is going to drop sharply.

■ *You bought what you thought was a tax-deferred retirement savings account but it turned out to be life insurance.* If you cancel, you get only a smidgen of your money back. Possible solution: exchange your policy for a low-cost tax-deferred annuity (page 368) in a tax-free 1035 exchange. You take a loss, but that loss can probably be carried over to your annuity, where you can use it to tax-shelter future gains of an equivalent amount.

▪ *You have been paying your premiums with money borrowed against your policy's cash value.* The policy is costing you interest every year. What should you do?

1. You can die. Not recommended.

2. You can pay off the loan. If you can't pay it quickly, pay your premiums out-of-pocket and use each year's dividends to reduce your loan. The money paid into the policy may earn a competitive, tax-protected interest rate. With universal or variable universal insurance, use your premiums to reduce the loan.

3. You can do a tax-free exchange to another policy in the same company or in a different company. It might offer the same face value but a lower cash value and lower loan, or a lower face value and no loan at all. You have taxable income, however, when a switch reduces or eliminates a loan.

4. You can cancel the policy. If the money you receive, plus any policy loans you've taken, exceeds the premiums you paid, you'll owe income taxes on that excess amount. You could use the net proceeds to buy a substantial term insurance policy covering the years of your family's highest need.

Approach with Caution (Suspicion!) Any Policy Comparisons Shown You by Agents Who Want You to Switch

There are a dozen ways to mislead you, and laypersons can't possibly spot the lie. Every day, agents churn the assets in somebody's cash-value insurance policy in order to earn a sales commission. They may claim that they're doing you a good deed by getting you extra life insurance. But they're raiding your cash values too. Too many Americans are innocently turning in policies they should keep.

If a new agent is proposing the switch, show it to your old agent. He or she may pick it apart. On the other hand, your old agent may see this as a replacement opportunity too.

When you're replacing one policy with another, that fact should be marked on your new policy's application. Check to see that it is. If the application doesn't say "replacement," assume that the sale is in some way disreputable. Otherwise the agent wouldn't be hiding it from the company. You also should be given a comparison between your old policy and your new one.

If your old policy pays annual dividends, find out when the next dividend is due. Replace the policy *after* the dividend is paid; otherwise you'll lose it. It could amount to several thousand dollars.

Walk away from an agent who warns you not to tell your old company that you're replacing the policy or asks you to sign forms that are not complete. Something's wrong.

Finding a Life Insurance Agent

This subject makes my heart sink. Yes, there are some splendid life insurance agents in the United States. And yes, they can do valuable work for you.

It's just that when I interview agents in the course of writing articles, I run into a lot of problems. Some agents don't know a lot about their policies and bluff. Some agents have been trained to mislead and are too thick to know it. Some agents know it and don't care. Some agents say they'll shop the market for you and don't. Some agents resist new information and ideas. Some agents assume that everyone needs to buy something, which isn't true. Some agents mean well but are sincerely and honestly wrong. Some agents have blind spots. Some agents will say anything to close a sale. Some agents are your brother-in-law, and you feel stuck.

On the other hand, some agents study for years to become technically competent, search out the best policies and strategies, care deeply about the ethics of their business, go to bat for you with the company, solve pressing problems, encourage you to buy only what you need, keep your life insurance program up to date, research your questions to find the best answers, and help you squeeze the most out of every dollar you invest—for example, by selling you blends (page 372).

I don't know how to find one of these smart, straightforward insurance agents. You ask around. You interview. You work with a fee-only financial planner who refers you to agents who provide low-load policies and blends. You try the following techniques to light a lamp against the dark:

1. Find your agent yourself. Don't take someone who cold-calls with a proposal, or comes with a reference from a friend that he or she just sold a policy to, or "happens" to bump into you on the street. There's small chance that these prospecting agents will be the smartest ones. Instead ask your business associates, accountant, or lawyer who they think are the best life insurance agents in your community and why. You want someone who's been in the business at least 10 years, who works at it full-time, and who represents large, high-quality companies. Agents with a Chartered Life Underwriter (CLU) designation have given the field more serious study than other agents. Chartered Financial Consultants (ChFCs) have combined life insurance studies with financial planning.

2. Interview at least two agents. Take a list of questions and consider their answers. You might ask: Where did they go to school? Where did they work before, and how do they happen to be selling insurance? Do they do business with just one insurance company or several? What kinds of policies do they like and why? How often do they attend continuing education seminars, or, better yet, do they teach them? How do they develop an insurance proposal? What roles do they think life insurance should play in a financial plan? What system do they have for keeping policies up to date, and who would service the business if they suddenly died? How are they paid—fees, sales commission, bonus compensation, trips and other rewards for achieving high sales? Tell the agents that you expect to be told what they'll earn on the proposals they make to you—will they agree? Will they give you blended policies that reduce commissions? What are the names of two or three clients you could talk to?

If the agent resents any of these questions, or fudges, or doesn't seem smart, or sounds like a know-it-all, move on to the next name on your list. Some agents resist disclosing commissions by saying, "I don't ask how much money you make, so you shouldn't ask how much I make." That's completely misleading. You're not asking for their annual earnings, you're asking for the price of the product they're selling. You're entitled to know.

While you're there, by the way, notice if the agent asked about you: your situation, your attitude toward insurance, what you're looking for. This should be a two-way interview.

3. Check up on what you've heard. Talk to the clients: Are they happy about everything? Any tips on working with the agent? If the agent sells variable life, he or she should have an employment and complaint file at the Central Registration Depository run by the Financial Industry Regulatory Authority (FINRA; for details, see page 817). Check it out. If the agent told you anything different about his or her past, bail out.

4. In the end, you'll pick an agent who feels right to you, but the conversation you instigated will, subtly, help you choose.

When you present yourself as a client, write down your general objectives and your attitude toward insurance and investments. Give a copy to your agent. Keep notes of your conversations with the agent and copies of all correspondence. Ask that all proposals be in writing, including any assertions about the policy that the agent makes. Keep all sales literature and all policy illustrations. If something goes wrong, this paper trail may help you get some money back.

Many financial planners also sell life insurance and earn commissions. All the caveats about insurance agents apply to these planners too.

Using a Fee-Only Insurance Adviser

If you're buying a large cash-value policy or tax-deferred annuity, or considering dropping one, get advice from a fee-only insurance adviser. These unbiased specialists charge only for their time; they don't sell insurance or earn commissions. Their job is to help you figure out the best solution to your particular insurance problem, tell you whether or not your current policy is worth keeping, and direct you to the blended or low-load products that will do the job.

Fee-only advisers typically charge $250 to $350 an hour. That may sound pretty stiff, but it's a good deal for people who need large amounts of cash-value coverage. All in all, you might pay the same no matter which way you go. With the agent, there's a high commission. With the adviser, there's the fee plus the low commission you'll pay on a low-load policy. Three things are different, all of them important: You pay the adviser in cash, whereas the agent's commission is hidden in the policy—hence, is probably higher then you think. The adviser might tell you *not* to buy, which can be worth a thousand times the fee you pay. And with the adviser, you're getting unbiased advice.

I know of only a handful of fee-only insurance advisers in the United States. You'll find their names at www.GlennDaily.com (yes, he's one of them). Click on "Glenn Daily," at the top of the page, and scroll to the bottom for the names of six others. Some of these advisers handle disability and long-term care insurance too.

Using a Fee-Only Financial Planner

Fee-only planners also charge for their time. They don't sell insurance, so they're not biased by commissions. Their job is to figure out how much insurance you need, not necessarily to analyze policies you already have. A few of these planners may have insurance expertise, but, more likely, they'll give the business to an agent who has agreed to provide low-loads or blends.

Warning: Plenty of insurance agents have their business cards reprinted to read "senior planner," "insurance adviser," or "actuarial consultant." They may present themselves as "fee-based," which sounds like "fee-only" but isn't. Most of their income actually comes from sales commissions. They may even duck the word *insurance* and sell their policies as college- or retirement-savings plans. If your "adviser's" proposal shows a policy with little or no cash value in the first and second year, you've got a plain old commissioned salesperson pulling the wool over your eyes.

Rotten Games Some Agents Play

In recent years, some of the country's largest insurers paid huge fines because some of their agents sold cash-value life insurance in a deceptive way. They did it to earn sales commissions and didn't give a fig for the people whose financial security they wrecked. Despite the fines, these practices continue. You might run into the following schemes by agents for almost any insurer:

Churning (or Deceptive Replacement). You have a cash-value policy. A new agent calls and suggests a "free policy review." Or your old agent calls with a "routine update." Surprise, surprise—the agent finds that your policy should be replaced with one that he or she claims is better. When you replace, however, you pay the sales commission all over again. You also wind up with less cash value than you had before. Existing policies should almost never be replaced (page 385).

Piggybacking. You're especially vulnerable to piggybacking if you have a small policy with a relatively high cash value. An agent calls and says, "Would you like more insurance for the same premium you're paying now?" Sure you would. But the agent is lying. The cost of the additional insurance is borrowed out of your policy's cash value, which reduces the death benefit and may harm the policy down the line. Your cash value is further reduced by the commission the agent earns.

In a variant of this fraud, the agent says, "Would you like a second policy at a low bargain price?" If you say yes, you'll be paying full price but in a hidden way. The few extra dollars you're charged per month will cover only part of the new premium due. The rest comes from loans against your original policy's cash value. Eventually the first policy's cash value will run out. At that point you'll lose your coverage unless you can start repaying your loan and/or increase—substantially—the regular premium you pay. If you complain to the insurer, the agent will claim that you knew exactly what you were doing.

Vanishing Premium. You buy a whole-life or universal-life policy that you believe will be paid up in a certain number of years. To achieve this, you pay a larger-than-normal premium. Once you've built up a certain amount of cash value, you don't pay any more premiums out-of-pocket. The policy's dividends or earnings are supposed to pay them until you die.

But the agent "forgets" to tell you that if interest rates drop, the cash value won't grow by enough to do the job. To keep a whole-life policy, you'll then have to pay premiums for many years more—a serious problem if you're retired and don't have much income to spare. With universal life, you can indeed stop paying premiums on the target date but will probably have to resume in the future.

With variable universal insurance, the proposal will show the policy paid up based on a high return from stocks. If stocks don't do that well, you'll have to keep on paying.

A good insurance agent will explain exactly how paid-up policies work (page 378) and whether you're running any risks. If there's a problem, he or she will alert you early so that you can adjust your plan. A bad agent lets your insurance planning fall apart. If you're looking at a paid-up proposal, ask for illustrations showing how the policy would work if interest rates dropped by 1 or 2 percentage points.

Retirement Plan Scam. The agent approaches you with a so-called tax-deferred retirement plan. It may have a name that sounds like Individual Retirement Account—for example, "individual retirement benefit." The agent speaks of "deposits" or "contributions" and the tax-deferred buildup in your "savings plan." He or she may mention in passing that some death benefits are involved, but you get the idea that they're marginal. You think you're buying a tax-deferred annuity when, in fact, it's a straight cash-value life insurance policy.

If you need retirement savings but don't need insurance, this purchase wastes your money. What's more, the whole sales presentation is illegal—illegal not to disclose that you're buying life insurance; illegal to pretend that your payments are contributions to a retirement account. If you have all this in writing, you ought to be able to get your money back.

Nursing Home Insurance Scam. See above. It's the same subterfuge under a different name. Older people are cheated into buying life insurance, thinking they're buying a policy to cover nursing home expenses. The policy may indeed cover some of those costs, but the buyers are also paying for life insurance that they don't need. They'd get much more protection from a pure long-term care policy.

College Savings Scam. See above. Same cheat, only this time the policy is presented as a college savings account.

The Surrender Squeeze. The agent sells you a policy that will pay you "tax-free income" when you retire. But it's not really income, it's a loan against your cash value. After you've borrowed a certain amount of money, you may owe more premiums to keep the policy going. If you don't—or can't—pay, the policy will fail. If the policy fails, you'll owe a big tax bill. The money you've borrowed, in excess of the premiums you paid, becomes taxable income. So that's the squeeze: it's expensive to keep the policy and expensive to cancel it. So much for your "retirement income."

How Can You Protect Yourself, with All These Bandits on the Prowl?

Ask any agent who makes a policy proposal to make it in writing. Most misrepresentations are oral, hence deniable by the salesperson. A written document—in full sentences, not just the columns of numbers in the policy illustration—should reduce outrageous claims and preserve your legal rights. It should address the particular need the insurance is supposed to fill, describe the policy in full, explain how dividends (if any) will be used, state whether cash values will be used to cover premiums, explain the uncertainties of a vanishing premium plan, and say whether or not the insurance is guaranteed to last for life.

If the agent is replacing a policy you currently own, state laws require that he or she compare the two policies and disclose the pros and cons. Piggybacking—using the cash value in the policy you own in order to buy an additional policy—is a form of replacement that also triggers the disclosure laws. Keep your notes and all the written material in an insurance file. Be sure that the policy illustration contains all the pages (each one will be numbered; for example "2 of 12"). Ask the agent to explain the illustration, and make your own written notes on the pages so you'll remember. If your policy goes wrong, all this documentation may help you get your money back.

In addition, don't sign any form that contains blanks or has boxes that are left unchecked. Always read the annual policy statement you get from the insurance company. If something looks wrong—less insurance than you thought you bought or a loan you didn't know about—address it right away. First ask the agent about it, following up in writing. If the agent says, "Oh, the company got it wrong," be suspicious. Write directly to the company president (certified mail), enclosing a copy of your letter to the agent and asking for an explanation. You can find the president's name and address on the company's Web site. If you get no answers, write to your state insurance department (find the address at www .naic.org, the Web site for the National Association of Insurance Commissioners, or NAIC). States differ greatly in their response to consumer complaints, but it can't hurt to write, and it might help. Keep copies of the letters or e-mails you send or receive.

How to Get Some Money Back If You've Been Scammed

It's hard. Insurance companies are tough nuts. You need proof, and here are six ways to get it:

1. Check your original application, which should be in the back of your policy. One question reads, roughly, "Do you intend to borrow against, surrender, or discontinue any existing insurance?" or "Is this replacement insurance?" If the agent said no, when in fact you gave up a policy or borrowed from your present insurance to finance additional coverage, that's fraud.

Your own bank and tax records can help prove that a replacement occurred. For example, the agent may have canceled policy A, sent you a check, then had you write a new check for policy B. Or you might have rolled policy A into policy B.

2. Check the sales material (you kept it, right?). Was the sales proposal enclosed in a retirement plan or college plan binder? Was the policy called an investment rather than life insurance? Were your premiums called contributions or deposits? That's evidence of deception. Did the agent prepare his or her own sales material that embellished the official insurance company brochure? Do you have a written statement from the agent, saying how the policy worked? Do you have the policy illustration?

3. If you didn't realize that loans were being taken against your policies, ask the insurer's customer service or customer relations office for a copy of the loan authorization document. Check the signature carefully. The agent may have forged it by tracing your signature from another document. You might also have signed the form in blank for another purpose, not knowing that the agent planned to check the box authorizing loans.

4. Write to the customer service or customer relations office of the insurance company for a copy of the agent's report that accompanied your application for insurance. The agent may have falsely said that your policy wasn't a replacement. If you were piggybacked, ask for a copy of the withdrawal and loan history on your older policy or policies and the payment history on your new one. They will show payments matching up—proof that replacement occurred.

5. Check the original policy illustration—the pages with columns of numbers showing how the policy works. Did the agent use the right health class? Does it show a policy for a preferred nonsmoker when in fact you were rated a standard risk? It might pay to have the illustration examined by a fee-only insurance adviser for angles you can't recognize yourself.

If you've been ripped off and can prove it, what should you ask for? If you were churned from one policy to another within the same company, ask for your original policy back, with all loans canceled and all past dividends credited. Ditto if you were piggybacked. Victims of investment scams should ask for their money back plus interest so they can invest in something else.

Vanishing premium schemes are harder to fix. Insurance companies won't listen unless you have hard evidence that the agent gave you a guarantee (for example, maybe the agent wrote on your policy illustration "paid up in *X* years"). You'll probably grind your teeth and keep on paying. Try to restructure these policies if you can't pay the full premium. Ditto if you were churned into another insurance company, which makes it impossible to restore what you formerly had.

Forget the "Private Pension Plan"

Should you buy a universal-life or variable universal-life policy for retirement savings, even if you don't need the insurance? For sure, say many insurance agents, who'd sell to a corpse if it had any money.

Their rationale for the so-called private pension plan goes like this: The cash in a life insurance policy builds up tax deferred. You can take out a certain amount of money tax free at retirement. After that, you can start taking tax-free loans to supplement your other retirement income. When you die, your heirs get the policy's cash value (minus withdrawals and loans) tax free. The tax advantage more than offsets the money you paid for the unnecessary life insurance. The agent will have an illustration, showing how beautifully this works out.

But it doesn't. It's a fake. The agent's sales pitch fails to consider several things:

1. If you don't buy insurance, what will you do with the money instead? Would you put it into a tax-deductible company retirement plan where the company matches your contribution? If so, that's a deal absolutely nothing can beat. If the agent gives you an illustration showing that life insurance is better than your 401(k), something is missing. Like maybe the company match.

What if your company doesn't match your contribution? It's still smarter to fatten your retirement plan than to buy a life insurance policy, given comparable investments. On the surface, this doesn't seem to be so. You have to pay taxes when you take savings out of a retirement plan, while insurance cash values can be taken or borrowed tax free. In real life, however, it's dangerous to use any more than 70 percent of your policy cash values (see item 3, below), while every dollar of your retirement plan money is on tap.

Besides, you might put the money into a Roth IRA. All those proceeds come tax free.

2. If you buy the insurance, will you invest the maximum annual premium to build up the highest possible cash value? If not, this scheme will probably blow up in your face. To make the sale, the agent might quote you a low annual premium, counting on policy dividends or earnings to build the necessary cash values. But if the stock market or interest rates fall, your cash value will grow more slowly than planned and might start to decline. Your "private pension" would gradually erode unless you put substantially more money into the policy. If you decided not to, the cash value might decline so far that the policy would lapse. You'd have paid for insurance you didn't need and lost your "private pension" too.

3. Do you understand that policy loans can blow up in your face? Once you've borrowed substantial amounts from your insurance cash values—that's your "tax-free retirement income"—you're locked into keeping that policy for life. If you drop the insurance, part of the money you've borrowed will become taxable income. Your tax bill could be large—maybe more than you could afford to pay. The same thing will happen if you borrow so much and live so long that the policy eventually lapses. To be on the safe side, you should borrow no more than 70 percent of the cash value, which may mean no more borrowing from about age 80 on. At that point, you'd still be paying your premiums, but your "tax-free income" would end. A Roth IRA or other savings plan, by contrast, could be tapped until any age—and with no premiums to pay.

When illustrated on paper, a private pension can be made to look better than a tax-deferred retirement plan—but that's only because the illustration is twisting something or leaving something out. This is a risky program that could ruin your finances in the end. So forget it.

Insurance Alive

It's a pity that the only way to collect on your life insurance is to die. Such a pity that the industry has come up with a product that pays off while you're still alive.

It's a "living benefits" provision. Some insurers let you withdraw part of your policy's face value if you're struck by one of a half-dozen dread diseases (stroke, terminal cancer, AIDS, Alzheimer's, heart attack, kidney failure) or dread operations (cardiac bypass, organ transplant). Others pay if you're diagnosed as having only 6 to 12 months to live. Yet others supply monthly benefits for the rest of your life if you enter a nursing home. This is not a policy loan. You receive actual tax-free death benefits in advance—either a portion of the policy's face value or almost all of it, depending on what your insurer allows. When you die, your beneficiary gets whatever is left.

Living benefits are available with many cash-value policies, some term policies, even some group policies. Some insurers add these benefits to every new policy sold, at no extra charge; some have applied them to older policies retroactively; some charge nothing extra but require you to ask for the benefits when you buy; some charge for the benefits separately; some charge nothing up front but impose a fee when the payout is taken. Many people don't even know that they have living benefits in their cash-value life insurance policies.

Who might be interested in living benefits? (1) Those at risk of getting a fatal disease that runs in the family. (2) Middle-agers who worry about serious illnesses. (3) A small business that could use the policy to buy out a partner who's terminally ill. (4) Older people concerned about nursing home expenses. A nursing home living-benefits rider is cheaper than buying separate nursing home insurance, but it doesn't deliver the same level of support.

The drawback to living benefits is that you can't use the same life insurance dollar twice. If you draw out money for the cost of a final illness, the policy will pay your survivors less.

Getting Money Out of an Unwanted Policy

Are you 65 or older? Got a life insurance policy you don't need? Not feeling too well these days? You may be able to sell your policy to an investor for cash up front. Maybe that's a good idea, but maybe not. You might part with a valuable policy unnecessarily and incur taxes that you didn't expect.

I'm talking about the *life settlement* industry, which appeals to older people seeking ready cash.

If you have an insurance policy you don't want anymore, you have two tested ways of cashing in. You can surrender it to the life insurance company and receive a modest payout. Or you can do a life settlement.

With a life settlement, you sell your policy to an investor who will pay the premiums while you live and collect the proceeds when you die. Investors will offer you more—usually substantially more—than the insurance company will. You generally qualify if you're 65 or 70 and up and have some sort of health problem. You'll have to take a health exam. A little bit of doddering helps.

A life settlement makes sense if you truly have no need for any more insurance—no beneficiary who could use the money, no charity you want to give the policy to, no business purpose, no estate taxes to fund. All you want is to dump the policy and receive as large a payment as possible. You don't care that a total stranger will profit from your death. You don't worry that your policy might wind up in Tony Soprano's Individual Retirement Account. (Settlement brokers promise not to reveal your name and address to the investor, but it sometimes happens anyway.)

Policy sales are taxable. You owe ordinary income tax on the amount by which the policy's cash value exceeds the premiums you paid. Any settlement money you receive in excess of the cash value may or may not be a capital gain. The IRS hasn't ruled on this, so your accountant decides.

Most life settlement investors want whole-life and universal-life policies with face amounts of at least $250,000 to $500,000. A few accept amounts as small as $50,000. You can sell a term policy if it's guaranteed renewable or can be converted into universal life. There's less interest in variable life.

The amount of money you're offered for your policy will depend on your life expectancy as well as such things as the premium amount and how old the policy is. Investors like policies bought some time ago, when you were in better health. They don't want you to live too long. They have access to your medical records, so they can keep track of whether you're alive or dead.

Life settlement brokers earn rich commissions for placing policies—up to 35 percent of the policy's purchase price or perhaps 5 percent of the face amount. That makes them aggressive. They're persuading some older people to sell policies they should keep.

For example, take an older person whose heirs still need insurance protection but who can't afford to pay the policy's premiums anymore. It may seem as if there's nothing else to do but sell. Not so. There's a much better option: Start paying the premiums from your cash values. If you die, your beneficiaries will get the net policy proceeds. If you live, you can sell the policy a few years later, when the cash values have run down. In the future, you'll have a shorter life expectancy, which means that you will be able to sell at a higher price than you'd get today (grim arithmetic, but that's how it works).

With some policies—say, an older universal-life policy with a large surrender charge—you might be able to sell for enough to buy a new and better policy for the same face amount.

To learn more about selling a policy, go the Web site of the Life Insurance Settlement Association at www.thevoiceoftheindustry.com. It takes you through the process step by step.

New York Life Insurance Co. has developed another way of getting money out of a policy that you no longer need. It's a loan called Access Plus, available to its own policyholders in 22 states and the District of Columbia. You keep the policy and borrow against the death benefit. The loan can be larger than your cash value, and no taxes are owed. At death, your heirs get the policy's face value minus the amount of the loan and the interest due. In general, it's for people whose life expectancy is between 1 and 10 years. You will probably see more of these types of arrangements in the years ahead.

Should You Invest in Life Settlements?

No! Stay away! They can yield high returns but the risk is over the moon. If the insured person lives longer than expected—maybe because he or she is healthier than was advertised or new medications are developed—your gains on that policy might shrink to zero. You might even have to put up more money to pay the premiums. You can buy into a pool of policies, but the fees are high and, again, you can get stuck. If the investment goes bad, there is usually no way out. The industry suffers from hype and fraud. The large institutions that buy most of the life settlement policies can afford the risk. The little guy can't.

What About Viatical Settlements for the Terminally Ill?

These are life settlements too, but the sellers are terminally ill. In most cases, they're expected to live no more than a year. Some investors accept policies from sellers with as few as five years to live, but the longer the probable life span, the less money the seller is going to get. A doctor certifies the life expectancy.

If you're thinking of investing because viaticals are "safer," I have just two words: new drugs. Ten years ago, agents sold policies owned by people with HIV on the assumption they would die soon. Well, along came transcriptase inhibitors and—wonderfully—infected people didn't die. The investors who bought their policies may be paying the premiums on them to this day.

What about the people who *do* have short expected life spans and are looking to their insurance policies to raise money for care? If you're one of them, look at your other options first. Your first step should be to preserve any medical coverage you have. If you're insured at your job and your company employs at least 20 people, you can continue the coverage for 18 months at your expense. Second, turn to your disability income policy (you bought one, of course). Third, apply for Social Security disability benefits. Fourth, see if your income is low enough to qualify you for Medicaid.

After that, your choice depends on whether you have dependents to take care of. If not, sell the policy—there was no point buying it in the first place. If you do have dependents, try to keep it. Cover your bills by using your savings, selling other assets, or using your policy's loan or living-benefits provisions (page 397). A loan or a small withdrawal will leave some insurance for your family. A high withdrawal might net you more than you'd get from a viatical sale.

Last choice is selling your policy to a viatical company. Three points: (1) You can sell just a portion of your policy, keeping the rest of it for your heirs. You can also keep the benefit paid for accidental death. (2) Different companies offer different prices, so you should shop diligently. Take the time to fill out several applications. Many thousands of dollars ride in the balance. (3) If your life expectancy is two years or less, you can receive the money tax free.

Warning, if you're on Medicaid: selling the policy might give you so much money that you're disqualified from government programs for low-income people. Balance the gain against the cost of losing your Medicaid insurance.

Should You Accept Payment for Taking Out a Life Insurance Policy?

Beware, beware. Older people are being tempted by what amounts to a fraud on the insurance company. It's a deal known as *stranger-initiated life insurance* (STOLI), and it works like this:

A salesperson approaches a wealthy person in the 70-to-80 age range and asks if he or she is willing to take out a large life insurance policy. A speculator group will pay you a tidy sum up front for the favor and lend you the money to pay the policy's premiums too. You wait two years, to get past the period when the insurer can normally revoke the policy. Then you sell the policy to the speculators for (one hopes) considerably more than the amount you need to repay the loan, loan interest, and expenses. The salesperson earns a huge commission, perhaps including a percentage of the profits on the sale. The speculators may sell it to someone else, also at a profit. The final owner (usually a life settlement company) is gambling that you'll die before it has to make too many premium payments. They'll be checking on you regularly. Do you have palpitations? Maybe a cough? During the first two years, you name your family as beneficiaries. When you sell, the investors will name themselves.

In theory, a STOLI transaction can put extra money in your pocket, plus provide you with two years of "free insurance." In practice, there are costs and major risks.

The up-front payment is taxable income. When you sell the policy, the proceeds are taxable too (whether as ordinary income or capital gains isn't clear). If you find that you need more life insurance for your family, you probably won't be able to get it—your STOLI insurance will have used up all the coverage that an insurance company will allow. If you die within two years, your beneficiaries have to repay the money that the investor group advanced, at a high interest rate and perhaps with penalties. If you live, the policy may not sell for anything close to what you were promised when you signed up. The legal agreements you sign are complex and may contain risks that you didn't know about. For example, if the speculators can't resell your policy for as much as they expected, they might be able to sue you for the balance, or sue your estate, on the grounds that you misled them in some way. Some tax professionals think that the "free" insurance may turn out to be a taxable benefit. If, after two years, you turn over the policy to the speculators and walk away from the loan (an option, if the policy doesn't sell for enough), the forgiven loan may be taxable income, too.

Finally, insurance companies won't sell STOLI knowingly. You might have to say on the application that you're taking this policy for your own benefit—which, in this case, would be fraud. If you die and the company discovers the fraud, it might refuse to pay, even though the policy has passed the two-year mark. Your heirs might have to sue. In the meantime, they still have to repay the money the speculators advanced and probably fight off a lawsuit from them too. Why expose yourself to these risks for a few extra bucks, especially when you're already well-to-do?

A dozen states have passed laws against STOLI, and others have them under consideration. If you're asked, don't participate. There's quicksand ahead.

Insurance and Taxes

Here's everything you didn't want to know about the taxes due on your life insurance.

The dividends paid on whole-life policies are not taxed if you reinvest them in more insurance (paid-up additions—page 358). You also pay no tax on the interest or earnings when they're credited to your cash values in universal-life or variable universal-life policies.

If you hold your dividends in a separate account at the insurance company and they earn interest, the interest is taxable.

You can withdraw dividends or other earnings from your policies tax free until they equal the premiums you paid. Any withdrawals in excess of the premiums you paid are taxed as ordinary income.

You can borrow against most insurance policies tax free. The exception: single-premium policies issued after June 20, 1988, as well as certain other policies that allow a fast cash buildup. They're known as modified endowment contracts (page 374). You owe taxes on loans or withdrawals from this type of policy up to the amount that the policy has earned. You're also taxed on money you receive by pledging these policies as collateral. There's a further 10 percent penalty unless you've reached age 59½, become totally disabled, or are taking substantially equal withdrawals over your expected lifetime or the joint lives of yourself and a beneficiary.

Partial withdrawals of cash values from universal policies may be taxable. You'll have to ask the agent about it. There are actuarial calculations.

Beneficiaries pay no income tax on the policy proceeds they receive.

Any policy that you own at death is part of your taxable estate. But the estate will not owe a federal estate tax on the policy's proceeds if you're worth less than the current estate tax exemption or your estate is going to your spouse. State inheritance taxes may be due on smaller estates.

Normally, no estate taxes are due if, before you died, you gave the policy to someone else, such as your children or a trust. If you die within three years of making the gift, however, the policy proceeds will still be counted as part of your taxable estate.

If you cash in the policy, you'll owe ordinary income taxes only on that portion of the payout (plus loans and loan interest) that exceeds all the premiums you paid minus any dividends not used to buy more insurance. If you cash in a variable insurance policy, any stock market gains from your policy investments are treated as ordinary income, not capital gains. Always ask about your policy's tax status before you surrender it.

You can transfer gains and losses to a new policy or a tax-deferred annuity tax free (page 368).

Stick with Super-Safe Companies

Buying life insurance is an act of faith. When you die—in 30 or 40 or 50 years—you expect some young kid, not yet born, to process your claim and send your family a check. In general, that's been a good bet. But occasionally, insurance companies fail.

State life and health guaranty funds swing a safety net under your insurance benefits—but the net is far from perfect, and you could suffer loss. If your company fails, here's what might happen:

■ *Your state's guaranty fund will step in and transfer the policy to a new insurer, usually at its full face value.* In the larger insolvencies, however, policies often take a haircut of 5 to 15 percent in both their death benefit and cash value.

■ *There are minimum guarantees.* In most states, you're protected for as much as $300,000 in death benefits and could receive more if the failed insurer has enough assets. A few states protect you up to $500,000. Cash values are usually protected up to $100,000. That cash will almost certainly be frozen while the bailout is being arranged, in order to protect the acquiring company against a run. It might be years before you can draw all the money out without paying a penalty (with exceptions, if you can show a special hardship).

- *Your policy's terms may change.* Going forward, your premiums could rise (or fall), your cash values might not accumulate as fast as they did before, and dividends could be slashed or eliminated. But your health status won't change. If you were a preferred risk before, you're still a preferred risk, even if your health has deteriorated.

- *If your policy's terms are materially changed,* you'll probably be offered the option of taking its liquidation value in cash (a court will determine the amount). You could then apply for new coverage from another company, assuming that you're still insurable.

- *If your company fails and no other insurer will take over your policy,* it will be administered by the guaranty association, subject to the $300,000/$100,000 coverage caps. The association will continue to look for a new insurer. It will probably continue the policy you have but in some cases might issue a replacement.

- *Tax-deferred annuities and annuities yielding monthly payments are usually covered for their current value up to $100,000.* If your annuity is worth more than that and the insurer's assets don't cover the whole amount, the annuity's cash value will be reduced. If you're receiving monthly payments, they'll be cut too. The uncertainties could last for years.

- *Health insurance policies will be moved to a new carrier* if one can be found. Any policy not guaranteed renewable (usually, group health) will probably be canceled. Claims in the pipeline will be covered, subject to a $100,000 cap. (Some states allow up to $500,000 in medical claims.) If you're embarking on a costly treatment, you'll have to pay the excess yourself. You'll also have to hunt for a new policy, which—until reform kicks in—may be unobtainable if you're ill. The new company will look at your current state of health, not how healthy you were when you bought the policy you had before.

- *You're usually protected for up to $300,000 (or $500,000) for all claims combined.* If your insurance company fails and it holds both your life insurance and your annuity, $300,000 (or $500,000) is all you'll get.

- *The guaranty associations don't cover pure variable policies* such as variable universal-life insurance or variable annuities, the value of which is linked to investments. They're held in a legally segregated account. In theory, that should protect them from a general failure of the firm.

- *Hybrid products are another matter;* for example, variable annuities with guaranteed minimum death or income benefits. At this writing, there has never been a failure involving hybrids. If the guaranteed portion is backed by the insurance company's assets, the guaranty funds would step up. The level of your protection depends on how the contract is written.

▪ *Not all guaranty funds cover the same things.* They have different rules for covering out-of-state policyholders; different rules about people who move to the state and hold policies from companies not licensed there; different rules for annuitants; and different rules about covering guaranteed investment contracts held in company retirement plans. How well you're protected depends on where you live.

▪ *For detailed information on what's protected in your particular state,* go to the Web site of the National Organization of Life & Health Insurance Guaranty Associations (www.nolhga.com).

Even if your insurance company doesn't fail, a weak balance sheet could mean lower dividends and skimpier cash values in the years ahead. So buy only from a company with high financial strength ratings from at least two of the four insurance rating firms: A. M. Best, Fitch Ratings, Moody's, and Standard & Poor's. If a company has a good Best rating but a zinger from Moody's, its agents may disseminate only the first. So here's how you can check all of an insurer's financial ratings yourself:

1. Go to the ratings services directly. You can get free ratings by registering at www.ambest.com, www.fitchratings.com, www.moodys.com, and www.standardandpoors.com.

It's not enough to know that an insurer is rated, say, A+. You need to know how high A+ stands in that particular rater's system. At A. M. Best, it's the second rating down. At Standard & Poor's, it's the fifth rating down ("good," not "excellent"). You can see each rater's ranking system on the next page.

2. Send for the special ratings issue of the Insurance Forum, P.O. Box 245, Ellettsville, IN 47429 ($25, at this writing), issued every September. It shows all the financial strength ratings of about 1,300 U.S. and Canadian life and health insurance companies issued by the four firms. The *Forum* also publishes a watch list of companies that you might reasonably have some concerns about and lists almost 200 companies that conservative insurance buyers should find attractive.

Here are the ratings that the *Forum*'s editor, Joseph Belth, defines as high:

• *For extremely conservative consumers:* A. M. Best, A++; Fitch and S&P, AAA and AA+; Moody's, Aaa and Aa1.

• *For very conservative consumers:* A. M. Best, A++ and A+; Fitch and S&P, AAA, AA+, and AA; Moody's, Aaa, Aa1, and Aa2.

- *For conservative consumers:* A. M. Best, A++, A+, and A; Fitch and S&P, AAA, AA+, AA, and AA–; Moody's, Aaa, Aa1, Aa2, and Aa3.

High ratings aren't a guarantee of good consumer value. They tell you only that the insurance company is financially strong—not how well it treats its customers.

Should you reject a company with less than the very top rating? No. Of some 2,000 life insurance companies in America, only a small number have failed. But I wouldn't stray far from the top, because you don't have to and because the consequences could be severe.

If your company slips in the ratings, then slips again, ask for a written explanation. It's costly to swap policies, but at some point you might decide that you're willing to pay the price. Weaker companies may not treat their policyholders as well.

Here's a real shocker: You may have no control over which insurer ultimately owns your insurance policy or annuity. You might shop diligently for a blue-chip company, only to discover that that company may be able to transfer your policy to any other insurer it wants without your written permission. The company may "ask" your permission by sending you a formal document written in Sanskrit. In most states, it's assumed that you've said yes if you don't reply.

Table 7.

THE INSURANCE RATING SYSTEMS*

Rank	A. M. Best	S&P	Moody's	Fitch
1	A++	AAA	Aaa	AAA
2	A+	AA+	Aa1	AA+
3	A	AA	Aa2	AA
4	A–	AA–	Aa3	AA–
5	B++	A+	A1	A+
6	B+	A	A2	A
7	B**	A–	A3	A–
8	B–**	BBB+	Baa1	BBB+
9	C++**	BBB	Baa2	BBB
10	C+**	BBB–	Baa3	BBB–
11	C**	BB+**	Ba1**	BB+**

* Lowest ratings not included. The ratings in each rank are not necessarily equivalent to one another.
** At this rating and below, *The Insurance Forum* puts the insurance company on its watch list.

Only two states require a personal yes. Some policyholders have been transferred to companies that ultimately failed.

If you get a letter saying that your policy is being transferred, check the new company's financial strength rating. If it's not up to snuff, write a letter to your present company saying that you won't go. You have this option in all states. Some insurers disclose this option, others don't. If you refuse to go, the new company will administer your policy, but your former company remains responsible for its policy obligations.

When All Is Said and Done, How Would I Buy Life Insurance?

I'd start with low-cost term insurance, expecting to cancel it when I retire or when my kids are grown and my spouse is self-supporting. I'd find the insurer through an online quote service.

If I had some employee coverage, a small cash-value policy, and a family, I would hastily buy more term insurance to protect them.

I'd build up investments somewhere else—in retirement funds, mutual fund portfolios, Roth IRAs, and Treasuries—to guarantee my security.

I would not buy life insurance on any of my children.

If, later in life, it seemed that I still might need insurance after 65, I'd buy permanent insurance. If I needed it just for another few years, I'd choose low-load or blended whole life or universal life funded at the guideline premium. If I needed it for life (to pay estate taxes, say), I'd buy no-lapse universal life. If I were in poor health, I'd get those policies by converting my term insurance.

If I had a universal policy, I'd check it every three years to be sure that I'm putting enough money in.

If I wondered whether my cash-value policy was worth keeping, I'd have its rate of return checked by James Hunt at EvaluateLifeInsurance.org. I'd check any proposed new policy too.

I'd pay the premiums on my life insurance policy even in hard times. I owe it to the people who depend on me.

13

The Health Insurance Lottery

Paying More, Getting Less, Rooting for Change

America's wasteful way of paying for health care is breaking down. We spend almost twice as much per person as other wealthy countries do, yet we leave people uninsured or so underinsured that they go without care they need. Change is in the air—again. But true health security isn't in the offing yet.

Health care is an American obsession. Can you get a job with medical benefits? If you have one, will your benefits be cut back? If you're on your own, how much insurance can you afford? What if you're sick and uninsured or underinsured? Will medical bills force you into bankruptcy?

It's shocking that—in so rich a country—we even have to ask ourselves questions like these. But we do, as long as our current patchwork system (or so-called system) lasts. Health security has been for people in other developed countries, not for us.

At this writing, President Obama is driving toward reform—he and Congress are hashing out options for covering more of the uninsured and giving you equal access to individual policies regardless of your health. You will probably be required to buy a package of basic benefits, or your company might be required to give it to you. For updates on health reform, check my Web site at www.janebryantquinn.com.

Whatever happens, most of it won't take effect for about three years, so the rules in this chapter still apply. Even after the proposed reforms, you will still face the same, two-pronged insurance world you see today—group plans subsidized by your employer and individual policies that you buy yourself (or with a government subsidy). Costly, inefficient private insurance will continue to dominate health care for people under 65, until "reform" is reformed again.

If you don't have health insurance, you don't have—can't have—financial security or independence. A single, unexpected health event can blow you out of the water, taking your savings and future income with it. Some lucky people have access to good coverage. Others skate by even with poor insurance, thanks to their good health. Unlucky people founder, which is why I call our American health system a lottery. How you fare depends on chance.

Even with good insurance, we're paying more out-of-pocket every year. We're asking our doctors what treatments cost and skipping some of the care we need. It tests your ingenuity to find decent coverage and health care at reasonable costs. I hope that this chapter will give you some ideas.

Which Type of Policy Do You Want (Or Can You Afford)?

There are two ways of buying insurance in our American lottery system, the easy way and the hard way. Easy: you get subsidized employer coverage, Medicare, or Medicaid. Hard: you buy individual coverage and pay for it yourself. Here are the types of comprehensive (major medical) coverage available in the employer, individual, and Medicare markets:

- *Health Maintenance Organization (HMO).* An HMO has doctors—both generalists and specialists—on staff or in a network, and those are the only ones you see. It's linked to specific hospitals and pharmacies too. You pick a primary physician (your "gatekeeper"), who's responsible for all your care. He or she will refer you to a specialist in the HMO if you appear to need one. If you need an unusual type of care that the HMO normally doesn't offer, you may be referred to an outside specialist at no extra cost, but that doesn't happen very often. HMOs normally cover out-of-network care only in emergencies, and "emergency" may be narrowly defined. If you go to an outside doctor, hospital, or clinic without a referral, you generally have to pay the entire bill.

HMOs are the lowest in cost of the traditional comprehensive or major medical plans. The majority of them serve only employer plans or Medicare, but some of them take individuals too. You pay a fixed monthly fee (the premium) for all services, including preventive care, and perhaps a small additional fee (the co-pay) for an office visit. The doctors often share your medical history on an HMO intranet, which reduces paperwork.

A good HMO, with a large number of doctors to choose from, is a great buy, especially for people on limited budgets. The main drawback: you may have to fight for a referral to a specialist. Only your gatekeeper-doctor can open the door to an appointment. (Note that some HMOs now call themselves EPOs, for Exclusive Provider Organization. It's all in the marketing.)

- *Point of Service (POS) plan.* This is an HMO with an exit door. You choose a primary physician to supervise your care and get all the usual HMO services. But you're also allowed to see any outside doctor, without a referral. The POS will pay something toward the outside doctor's bill, but you'll have to pay a substantial amount of it yourself. This type of plan is good for someone who will generally stay within the HMO network but is willing to pay extra to have access to other docs if there's a dispute about care.

- *Preferred Provider Organization (PPO).* Here, you choose any doctors you want within the PPO's network, which is usually large. There's no gatekeeper. You can see a specialist at any time. In addition to monthly premiums, you're charged a co-pay for every visit or a specified percentage of every doctor's bill— less for doctors in the PPO network, more for those outside the network. PPOs are the most popular type of plan because of their flexibility. They're also more expensive than an HMO or POS, so they're for people who can afford to pay for maximum choice.

- *Catastrophic coverage.* These PPO policies carry the lowest monthly premium, but that's because they cover the least. You can choose any network doctor you want. The drawback is that you pay the first $2,500 to $10,000 in annual costs yourself—the amount depending on the deductible you choose. When the plan does kick in, it may cover less of each medical bill than the low-deductible plans do. Check the amount you're expected to pay out-of-pocket each year. If you get really sick, your personal expenses might be large.

Catastrophic coverage appeals to people who think they won't get sick (the young and invincible) or people who can't afford a more comprehensive plan. They provide three things: (1) A lower monthly premium. (2) Protection against a giant cost, such as cancer treatments or surgery after a serious auto accident. (3) A discount on the medical bills that you have to pay yourself. You get all the discounts negotiated by the PPO—up to 50 percent off each doctor and hospital bill and lower costs for prescription drugs. Many parents buy catastrophic policies for adult children who can't afford their own coverage. If anything happened to your child, you'd probably step in to help, so the policy protects you too.

- *Consumer Directed High Deductible Plan (CDHDP).* This is a high-deductible PPO that comes with a tax-free Health Savings Account. You or your employer deposits money into the savings account, which can be used for the medical bills that you pay yourself.

These plans are governed by federal rules, which dictate how much you can put into the account each year and the maximum out-of-pocket you'll be required to pay. If you use the money for anything other than medical bills, you pay taxes on the earnings plus a 10 percent penalty if you're under age 65. At 65 you can use the money for other things, paying taxes but no penalty. (Also, at 65 you can no longer contribute to an HSA.)

CDHD plans may pay in full for preventive care, such as Pap smears and annual physicals, without counting the cost toward your deductible. See what your plan considers "preventive." It may include certain prescription drugs that you take for maintenance.

In general, these plans work well for healthy, high-income people who don't have a lot of medical bills, can afford to pay the bills they do get out-of-pocket, *and* will deposit the full amount into the tax-free savings account every year. If you put only small amounts into savings, you may pay more in account fees than you earn in interest. (For fee comparisons on HSA accounts, go to the Vimo Web site at www.vimo.com/hsa.)

Be wary of these plans, however, if someone in your family is seriously or chronically ill. They'll probably cost you more than a PPO after counting all your out-of-pocket costs.

■ *Fee for Service (FFS).* These old-fashioned *indemnity* policies barely exist anymore in the under-65 world. There's no network of doctors and no cost control. You go to any doc you want, and the insurance company will pay a fixed dollar amount, according to a schedule set forth in the contract. Sometimes it pays a percentage of what it decides is the "reasonable" fee. You pay the rest.

FFS costs run so high that few working people buy these types of policies. Unfortunately, they are enjoying a revival in Medicare, thanks to conservative politicians who want to privatize the system. Medicare FFS costs the government (that is, we the taxpayers) much more per person than traditional Medicare. Worse, FFS plans are too often missold to older people (page 457).

■ *State High-Risk Pools.* These plans take people who can't get coverage through the private insurance market. Premiums may be 125 to 200 percent of the standard cost and often for more limited benefits.

How Much Will Your Health Insurance Cost?

This varies tremendously by your age, the state you live in, the type of coverage, the deductible you choose, your age and gender, and your health.

For individual policies that you buy yourself, start with eHealthInsurance (www.ehealthinsurance.com). Enter a few bits of data, and you'll get quotes from insurance companies that sell in your area. Those quotes are all for people in good health. If you have health issues, you'll pay far more.

But monthly premiums are only the tip of the iceberg. When you click on the details of the policies, you'll see that those with lower premiums require higher up-front deductibles and co-pays. If your health is good, a low-premium policy saves you money. If you or someone in your family gets seriously ill, that same policy could blanket you with cost-sharing bills you can't afford. So choosing a health plan is like entering a lottery too. Whether you win or lose depends on what happens to your health.

Here's a list of the typical costs found in company plans and individual insurance. When comparing two policies, write these costs down. Then compute what you'd have to pay if you had a horrendous medical bill. That's the true test of any plan: your potential, annual out-of-pocket cost.

1. The premium—the fee you pay each month for the policy itself. Family plans cost more than single coverage. Employers typically subsidize part or all of your coverage and often pay something toward the cost of insuring your children and spouse. The rest of the premium you pay out of payroll deductions.

Plans in the individual market may charge about the same as company plans but offer fewer benefits for the money.

2. The deductible—the amount you pay for health care in a single year before the insurance plan kicks in. In large employee plans, there's usually no deductible for HMOs (where there is, it averages about $500). Deductibles at PPOs average $750 for in-network doctors and $900 for those out of network. High-deductible plans may require you to pay the first $1,800 or more.

In individual PPOs, buyers are choosing $2,000 to $5,000 deductibles. The higher the deductible, the lower your premium but the more you pay if you get sick.

3. The co-payment or co-insurance—the amount you pay toward each medical service. It might run in the $10 to $30 range for every visit to a doctor at an HMO or an in-network doctor at a PPO or consumer-directed plan. If you go outside the network, you might pay 30 to 50 percent of the bill, up to a specified out-of-pocket maximum (the *cap*).

4. The annual maximum—the most you have to pay out-of-pocket in any year for your covered medical bills, after meeting your deductible. In employer plans, it typically runs from $1,500 to $3,000 for singles and $3,000 to $5,000 for families. In individual plans, the annual maximum depends on the deductible you choose.

Once you reach the max, your plan pays your covered expenses in full *but only for the rest of that year.* When January rolls around, your deductible and out-of-pocket obligations start all over again. A few health plans have no annual maximum; avoid them if you can.

5. The lifetime maximum—how much the plan will pay toward all of your medical bills over your lifetime. Employer plans, most HMOs, and one-third of the PPOs and consumer-directed plans have no lifetime maximum. If they do, it's usually $2 million or more. Lower limits may apply in certain conditions.

In individual plans, lifetime maximums hover in the $3 million to $4 million range, although low-cost plans might offer as little as $500,000—not nearly enough for a single serious illness, let alone a lifetime. Some plans set lifetime limits for certain treatments or conditions, such as infertility treatments or major organ transplants. Most maximums may be eliminated by insurance reform.

6. Rules for specific treatments—plans may put dollar caps or treatment limits on certain services. For example, there may be a max of 10 visits to a chiropractor or 20 to a speech therapist. Anything more you pay yourself. Many of these rules arise from state mandates that require insurers to cover certain conditions. Dental work is usually covered only if needed after an illness or accident.

7. Services not covered—things you have to pay yourself. Every plan has a list of what's not covered. Some typical examples: cosmetic surgery, routine physicals, hearing aids, reversal of sterilization, routine dental care, or experimental procedures (the insurer gets to decide what's experimental).

8. The cost of choice—relevant to HMOs. They have an approved list of doctors you're allowed to see. You might occasionally be referred to someone outside the plan. Otherwise, going outside the network will cost you a higher co-pay or percentage of the bill—perhaps even all of it.

9. The gender cost—especially relevant to women. Younger women (under 45 or 50) typically have more claims than younger men, so they usually pay more for individual health insurance. A lot more. Their premiums may run 35 to 40 percent higher, even without maternity coverage. Employer plans, however, charge unisex rates, if they cover 20 workers or more.

10. The bad-health cost—group plans have to charge everyone alike, regardless of their age and health. Individual policies, however, rate you on both. Your premium rises every year as you grow older. If you make a lot of claims, your premium will rise even more. Insurance companies shaft the sick, unless the reform bill makes them stop.

11. Dental insurance—offered as an add-on to the medical plan. It covers certain types of routine dental care, up to specified (usually low) limits.

The Insanity of Medical Pricing

In PPOs and consumer-directed plans, insurance companies pay by the visit or procedure. Different insurers pay doctors different amounts for exactly the same service. Each insurer also differentiates among doctors, paying some more than others. Only the big boys—for example, a major local hospital or large medical group—can negotiate a better financial deal for themselves. Doctors in small practices have to take whatever the insurer offers. The main reason that docs drop out of particular plans—or out of health insurance entirely—is that the company doesn't pay them enough to cover their costs (including the cost of endless phone calls to collect the money they're owed). The plans set the rates that in-network doctors can charge for each service, including your portion of the bill. Out-of-network doctors are paid the "usual and customary" charge (which may be low). If the doctor charges more than that, you have to pay the additional amount.

When you're shopping for a policy, you don't know how your insurance company's payments to its network doctors compare with those of other insurers. If your plan pays more, more doctors will accept it—but you'll pay more to the doctor too, because you owe a percentage of the cost.

The Insanity of Wrong Incentives

There's growing evidence that people with high-deductible or catastrophic plans are skimping on medical care because they can't afford the out-of-pocket cost. They're forgoing mammograms, prostate exams, and cholesterol screenings, failing to fill prescriptions, and skipping doctor visits to monitor heart disease and diabetes.

Ideologues say that making people pay for more of their personal bills will hold down general health inflation. There is no evidence—zero, nada—for that claim! Instead people may be buying less of the medical care they need, leaving them sicker in the end. Insurance companies have noticed. Many high-deductible plans now pay for physical exams, immunizations, maintenance drugs, and preventive care. The ideologues, however, are still singing the same old stupid, mistaken song. (Have I made myself plain?)

The Insanity of Billing the Broke

If you're uninsured, you have the honor of being billed at the highest rates in medical-dom. Health insurers negotiate discounts for their policyholders. Those who can't afford insurance are expected to pay full freight.

People who claim that the uninsured get free treatment in emergency rooms have no idea what they're talking about. Uninsured patients receive high, undiscounted bills, work out payment plans that may last for years, borrow against their homes to make their payments, get chased by bill collectors if they fall behind, and may eventually have to go bankrupt. On whose planet would you call that *free*?

If you're underinsured due to high deductibles, you at least get the PPO discount. But if your plan calls for you to pay up to $10,000 a year out of a modest salary, you still may be on the ropes. You too are borrowing against your house, raiding your retirement account, or running up credit card bills to take care of your children or yourself. In surveys, both the uninsured and underinsured say that they often put off needed health care or medications—even for chronic illnesses or when they're in pain.

People with good insurance complain when their co-pay goes up. I know. I've complained too. But until health reform begins, we need to be thankful that we have decent protection at all.

What a Good Policy Should Cover

Don't ever assume that everything is covered. It isn't. Inexpensive policies don't pay much at all, no matter what the advertising says. For true protection, you need a comprehensive, major medical policy. Here's what it should cover:

- *The cost of basic hospital services.* This includes a semiprivate room, board, emergency room, nurses, intensive care, medicines, ambulance services, X-rays, and lab tests. If you take a private room, the extra cost is generally yours (unless your plan determines that it's medically necessary).
- *The cost of surgery, including surgeons, assistant surgeons, and anesthesiologists—provided that they're in your network.* Your surgeon probably is because you asked in advance. After the operation, however, you may be shocked to discover that the anesthesiologist, whom you met just moments before counting down to sleep, won't accept your insurance and sends you a separate bill. So might a radiologist or a doctor in the emergency room. Your plan covers these services, but you may be forced to pay an out-of-network deductible and co-insurance. That's totally unfair. You don't pick the doctor who reads the CT

scan and shouldn't be blindsided by his or her high cost. A handful of states have banned the practice. It ought to be condemned everywhere.

■ *The cost of outpatient care.* Take a good look at this section of your policy. Many procedures that used to require hospitalization are now "cut and run," with short hospital stays. To prevent infections and other ill effects, your insurance should provide good home health support.

■ *Part of the bill for home health care* that is ordered by your doctor.

■ *Good coverage for children, including stepchildren and foster children if you're responsible for their support.* Check how long they can stay on your family policy. Typically, they're covered up to age 19 if they're not full-time students and anywhere between age 21 to as much as 29 if they're unmarried and in school. Some states let them stay on your plan up to age 26, even if they're not in school, if they depend on you financially. For your state's rules, go to the Kaiser Family Foundation's Web site (www.statehealthfacts.org). Click on your state, then on "Managed Care and Health Insurance," and then on "Dependent Coverage." (Note that these rules don't apply to big companies that self-insure their plans.) Children with mental or physical handicaps who can't support themselves should be covered permanently, as long as the disability occurred while they were still on your policy.

Children generally lose coverage under a family plan if they marry. When they become ineligible, however, they may have the option of remaining in the plan at your (or their) additional expense—temporarily or permanently.

Find out what happens if the child goes to school part-time or drops out for a year (see page 432 for more on student policies). Notify your insurer or plan sponsor in writing if you're responsible for children who live elsewhere—for example, children who live with a former spouse.

■ *Care for an infant from the moment it is born.* By law, a newborn or newly adopted child has full health coverage on your employee family plan *provided that* you tell the insurance company about the birth within 30 days. Don't fail to do so, especially if the child is born with a medical problem. If you add the child after 30 days have passed, you might have to cover the cost of the birth problems yourself. The insurer might wait for 18 months before adding the child to your plan. Most states have adopted similar rules for the family policies you buy in the individual market.

■ *Most doctor bills*, in full or in part.

■ *Part of the bill for convalescing in a nursing home* after you've been in the hospital.

■ *Part of the cost of prescription drugs.* Typically, your co-pay is arranged into three tiers: $10 or $15 for generic drugs, $25 or so for favored brand-name drugs in the plan's formulary, and $50 or more for nonfavored brand-name drugs. The insurer might cap its payments at $1,200 to $3,000 a year. There's usually a discount for ordering your maintenance drugs through the plan's mail-order program. It may be even cheaper to buy from a U.S. or Canadian mail-order pharmacy.

Some plans have "Tier 4" pricing for the expensive specialty drugs that treat illnesses such as hepatitis C, multiple sclerosis, and rheumatoid arthritis. You have to pay a percentage of the cost, up to $100 or even $350 for every prescription. Plans change their drug coverage every year, so even if there's no Tier 4 pricing when you sign up, it may be imposed later on. (Have I mentioned that it's past time for drug-pricing reform?)

When buying prescription drugs, don't assume that all pharmacies charge the same. Some are much more expensive than others. At this writing, Walmart and Target offer many generics for as little as $4.

■ *Part of the treatment for mental illness, drug abuse, and alcohol abuse.* Starting January 1, 2010, companies that offer this coverage have to provide it on an equal basis with coverage for physical illness if they have more than 50 employees. Smaller companies and individual policies, however, may require higher co-pays, coinsurance, or annual limits, depending on your state. Some policies don't cover mental illness at all.

■ *Most of the cost of incidental expenses*: physical therapy, oxygen, medical devices, and so on.

■ *Part of the cost of work done by oral surgeons—for example, for impacted teeth— or dental work needed as a result of an illness or accident.* But the usual things that dentists do, such as crowns, root canals, and fillings, aren't included in a medical plan. Some of that cost should be covered if you buy a separate dental plan.

Don't Accept a Simple Sales Brochure

A health plan brochure may imply that everything is covered and let you find out later what's not. By law, members of group plans are entitled to a summary plan description, telling you how the plan operates, what's covered, what you have to pay, and your rights as a plan member. If the plan changes, you'll get a summary of material modifications. If benefits are cut, you'll get a statement of material reductions in benefits within 60 days. Keep all these documents on file in case there's a dispute. If you're buying an individual plan, read the policy itself and direct any questions to your agent.

Preexisting Conditions—Can You Get Coverage?

In general, a preexisting condition is a medical problem that was diagnosed or treated—or was manifestly obvious—during a specified period before you bought the policy. Traditionally, insurers have been able to restrict or refuse coverage to people who have had health problems in the past.

Under health insurance reform, insurers would be required to take all comers. Even before the full law took effect, subsidies might be available to help some people join high-risk insurance pools. Nevertheless, many of you will still face the 2009 limits on preexisting conditions. And even when these cruel rules are eliminated, insurers might be able to limit expenditures for certain expensive illnesses or find other ways of making your life hard.

If you have such an illness or someone in your family does, it's important to know whether you qualify for coverage and when the plan will start paying the bills. Here are the 2009 rules, from the federal Health Insurance Portability and Accountability Act (HIPAA):

Group policies: Health plans, including association plans, can impose a waiting period before any benefits start. Generous plans start your coverage right away or within 30 days. Others may impose longer waits.

If you previously had health insurance for at least 12 months and sign up for the new group plan as soon as you are eligible, preexisting conditions have to be covered as soon as other benefits begin. Your previous insurer will give you a certificate of creditable coverage, showing how long you've been insured. That's a valuable document. Be sure you keep it.

If you were covered for less than 12 months, the group plan can wait before covering preexisting conditions but, in any case, no longer than 12 months from your employment date. (Those periods can stretch to 18 months if you didn't join the health plan right away.)

Maternity benefits, however, always start when general benefits do. So do benefits for newborns and children placed in your home pending adoption, provided that you enroll the new child in your health plan within 30 days.

To come under this federal law, businesses need at least two employees. If you're self-employed, consider hiring your spouse, full-time, for management or bookkeeping jobs to create a group of two. Around 18 states give various forms of protection to the self-employed, ruling that they're "groups" of one.

Plans can impose longer waiting periods or refuse to cover preexisting conditions if you previously had no health insurance of any type. You're defined as having no insurance if you lacked coverage during the previous 63 days.

Employers generally offer an annual open enrollment period toward year-end. Once you've chosen a plan, you have to stick with it for a year. If you lose other health coverage or acquire a new dependent, such as a child or a spouse, you or your dependent is entitled to join the plan right away under special enrollment. You have to make that election within 30 days.

No plan guarantees coverage for everything. Insurers can exclude certain illnesses or cap payments for them, provided that they treat everyone alike.

Individual policies: By 2009 law, you're entitled to buy individual insurance, including coverage of preexisting conditions, if you meet *all* of the following three conditions: (1) You're coming off 18 months of continuous group coverage without a 63-day break and you have a certificate of creditable coverage to prove it. (2) Your most recent coverage was under an employer group plan or COBRA (page 424). (3) You're not currently eligible for COBRA or for a group or government health plan such as Medicare or Medicaid. Depending on your state, you'll be offered the coverage through an individual insurer or a special high-risk pool. There's a hitch, of course. In most states, there's no cap on what you can be charged. Your "guaranteed" policy may be unaffordable.

If you lack that magic 18 months of insurance, you are *not* entitled to coverage for preexisting conditions in most states. That means trouble. Health screening can be astoundingly rigorous. The insurer might: (1) Refuse to cover a particular condition for a certain period of time. If little Eric has had two sinus infections this year, future infections might not be insured until he has been symptom free for 12 months. (2) Refuse to cover a specific condition permanently. Two sinus infections might rule out that ailment for any coverage, ever. (3) Charge you more money. Mild high blood pressure, for example, may cause your premium to soar. (4) Reject you entirely. People who have had, say, diabetes, heart disease, or epilepsy probably will be turned down. You might not even get coverage if you've ever had psychological care, including—would you believe it?—marriage counseling.

Health underwriting is getting tighter every year. If you're financially capable of buying insurance, do so now, before barriers get even higher.

A handful of states require insurers to accept everyone regardless of health, even if they had no previous coverage. A few even prevent them from charging the sick a substantially higher premium. Both these rules are a godsend for people who otherwise couldn't get health insurance at all. With any luck, health insurance reform would extend these requirements to all the states.

Dependents: The rules on preexisting conditions apply equally to your spouse and children. For example, say that you divorce and your ex-spouse has a health problem. If your ex was previously in your health plan, he or she has the same right to buy new insurance as you do.

General Health

Except for preexisting conditions, you're generally covered in group, association, or individual plans as soon as you buy or within 30 to 90 days. If you don't sign up for a group plan as soon as you're eligible, however, you'll be subject to health screening. You may be turned down, and will have to wait until the next open enrollment period.

The Federal Nondiscrimination Rules

These 2009 rules apply to group plans but not to individual plans. Group plans cannot reject you on grounds of poor health, medical history, a history of domestic violence, too many previous claims, or disability as long as you sign up within 30 days of joining the company. Nor can they charge you higher premiums than others pay. However, they can exclude specific medical problems such as cancer, as long as they do it for everyone. Or they might cap the payments allowed for specific illnesses.

Some states apply similar nondiscrimination rules to individual health insurance policies, but most don't.

Domestic Partners

Some large companies extend health insurance to domestic partners as well as to spouses. Unmarried heterosexual couples account for most of the people who make use of this benefit. Only spouses, however, get their group insurance tax free. For partners, it's treated as taxable income. Correction: only *some* spouses get tax breaks. Married same-sex couples aren't recognized under federal law.

Genetic Testing

A federal law passed in 2008 prohibits employers and insurers from discriminating based on genetic information. It affects all health plans: federal, state, and private, including Medigap. The law also covers hiring and firing and brings genetic information under the health privacy laws. By all means get tested if you're at high risk for any inherited illness that's curable if caught in time, but be aware that it will land in your written medical record. The law protects you, but you never know. (Note that the law doesn't cover long-term care insurance or disability insurance.)

Finding Out About Your State's Health Insurance Rules

The Kaiser Family Foundation runs a terrific Web site called statehealthfacts .org. Call it up, click on your state, and you'll find all the special rules affecting your state's plans. What benefits are mandated? What are your patient's rights? What consumer protections are required in individual and small-group plans? What are the rules for the high-risk pool? What special tax rules exist? Does the state have better rules on guaranteeing coverage than the feds provide? It's all right there.

For another source, go to the site run by the National Association of Health Underwriters at www.nahu.org. Click on "Consumer Information," then on the "Healthy Access Database," then on your state. You'll find all the rules for small groups, COBRA, HIPAA portability, individual coverage, the high-risk pool, and lower-income programs such as Medicaid and the State Children's Health Insurance Program. SCHIP is a lifesaver for parents with modest incomes who seek low-cost coverage for their children. Find your state's program at Insure Kids Now (www.insurekidsnow.gov).

Company Plans

Companies of all sizes are cutting back—and they're going to cut some more. You're getting fewer choices, higher deductibles and co-pays, and higher premiums, especially for family coverage. There's an explosion of interest in consumer-directed plans, which shift more of the up-front expenses of chronic or continuing illness onto employees. In fact, they're the only plans that some companies offer. Small employers are finding it harder to offer health insurance at all. The smalls pay more per person for coverage and may not have access to the same benefits offered to larger groups. (Under health insurance reform, all but the smallest companies might have to offer coverage or subsidize individual coverage for their employees—see my Web site for updates.)

If Both Husband and Wife Have Employee Plans and You Don't Have Children: You each should insure yourself with your own company. That's usually the cheapest route. With children, you want a single family plan. Choose the better of the two, after comparing their costs and benefits point by point. The unused plan can then be dropped.

If Your Company Offers a Medical Flexible Spending Account, Use It! You make payroll contributions into the account, pretax. Then you tap it to pay your qualified, unreimbursed medical bills, including the deductibles and co-payments on your insurance plan. If you're in an HMO, you can use it for doctors outside the HMO network. There's one risk: any money left in the account at the end of the year reverts to the company. So don't deposit anything more than what you're sure you'll use. If you deposited too much, look for things to buy at year-end: prescription sunglasses, a supply of prescription or over-the-counter drugs, dental work. Your company will tell you what counts as a qualified medical expense.

If Your Company Offers a High-Deductible Plan as One of Its Options, Should You Choose It? It will probably come with one of two types of savings accounts attached:

• *A Health Reimbursement Account (HRA).* This account is funded entirely by the company. You can use it to pay the qualified medical expenses that you're responsible for, usually including the deductible, co-pay, and coinsurance. Your employer decides what's qualified. To be reimbursed, you submit a claim form to the company, with a supporting receipt. It might take weeks to get your money, but the payment is tax free. Some plans now come with debit cards for paying the bills.

There's no actual money in an HRA. Your employer merely promises to pay up to a fixed amount per year. If you don't use the full amount, it carries over to the following year. Any unused money stays with the company if you leave your job, although you might be able to use it to pay the premiums on a COBRA plan (page 424) or a retiree insurance plan.

• *A Health Savings Account (HSA).* This tax-free account has to follow federal rules. Both you and your employer can contribute up to the maximum allowed. The money is usually managed by a financial institution, and interest or other investment gains accrue. If you leave the job, you can take the savings with you. An HSA can be used for a variety of medical, dental, and vision expenses that you pay out-of-pocket for yourself and your dependents (but not for your health insurance premiums unless you're unemployed). You usually pay with a debit card. "Smart" debit cards are being developed, to tell the difference between paying for a prescription and buying shampoo. On average, companies put less money into HSA plans than into HRAs, so an HSA will cost you more out-of-pocket.

Who should choose a high-deductible plan? Consider it if you're young and healthy and your children are well too. The low monthly premium will save you money and, presumably, you won't have much to pay out-of-pocket for medical bills. If the company also contributes to a tax-free savings account on your behalf, so much the better. Or add money to the account yourself, through payroll deduction. Some high-deductible plans don't come with savings accounts attached but still might be attractive, thanks to the low monthly premium.

If you get sick, however, or one of your children does, a high-deductible plan can cost you more than you'd pay for a PPO. Before choosing the plan, add up everything that you might have to pay out-of-pocket if a serious illness strikes (there's usually an annual maximum). If you couldn't pay those bills, the policy is a gamble. In an employer plan, however, you can usually switch to HMO or PPO coverage at the next open enrollment period, so you're not stuck permanently.

Anyone with a lot of medical bills should steer away from high-deductible plans. Older workers are more likely than younger ones to be upended by a nasty health surprise. Be cautious, too, if you're pregnant, just in case the baby is born with medical problems.

As part of your open enrollment decision, your company should give you a rundown on all the plans it offers: premiums, coverage, and your out-of-pocket costs. Unfortunately, some employers offer only high-deductible plans.

An HSA as a retirement account? Healthy higher-income people are turning these tax-free savings accounts to another use. They pay their medical bills out-of-pocket and contribute the maximum to the HSA. As it builds in size, they transfer it from a savings account to an investment account. The account grows tax deferred. At 65, when the investor is on Medicare, the HSA money can be used for any purpose, as long as you pay taxes on the earnings. You've changed a health savings account into the equivalent of an Individual Retirement Account. My only question is, why would you want to use this money for other things? You'll have plenty of medical bills in the years ahead. If you use the HSA to pay them, your earnings will pass entirely tax free.

An IRA rollover to an HSA? If you have an Individual Retirement Account, you can roll some of the money into your HSA and use it tax free to pay medical bills. It's a onetime option, and you can move no more than the maximum HSA contribution allowed that year. To avoid paying taxes and, maybe, penalties, have your IRA administrator arrange the transfer.

Multiple Employer Welfare Arrangements (MEWAs): These plans are established by trade associations and other entities and offered to small-employer groups. Employees pay the premiums, an insurance company may administer the plan, and the employers pay the medical bills. The plan might buy loss insurance to cover bills that are especially large. In the past, some MEWAs have set premiums too low to cover future claims. If they fail, you, your company, or both are stuck with any outstanding medical bills. MEWAs aren't covered by the state health insurance guaranty funds (page 447).

Leaving Your Company

If You Have Group Health Insurance and Are Leaving for a New Job That Also Offers Coverage: You will be covered immediately (including your preexisting conditions), as long as you've had at least 12 months of continuous group coverage. Health insurance reform might eliminate the 12-month rule.

If You Leave Your Job, Don't Come Under a New Employee Group Plan, and Your Company Employs 20 People or More: You can buy individual insurance if you qualify. If not, you can keep your old plan for a while at your own expense. Extending your old plan is known as a COBRA benefit because it was created by the Consolidated Omnibus Budget Reconciliation Act of 1985. To get it, you generally have to apply within 60 days of being notified about the option. You're allowed up to 18 months of continued coverage if you quit, are laid off, have your hours reduced to something less than the coverage threshold, and even if you are fired (as long as the firing wasn't for "gross misconduct," whatever that is). Widows, widowers, and the divorced can stay on their former spouse's plan for up to three years. So can dependents whose spouse switched from company coverage to Medicare. You pay the group health premium plus 2 percent. If you chose an expensive company plan while still employed and now would prefer a cheaper option, you have the same right to switch that current employees have. Newborns and newly adopted children can be added to your family coverage as long as you notify the plan in time (usually within 30 days).

COBRA lapses early if you find a new job that covers you with group health insurance. Don't let COBRA go, however, until your new policy's waiting period expires. You can also continue to call on COBRA if it covers an illness that your new policy excludes.

If you leave your job because you're totally disabled, you can keep the group plan for up to 29 months. This right also clicks in if you go on COBRA and are disabled within 60 days. Disability protection doesn't come cheap. After the first 18 months on COBRA, you can be charged as much as 50 percent above the normal group health premium—an expense that you probably can't afford. If you go on Social Security disability and you're under 65, you're eligible for Medicare. But there's an unconscionable two-year wait for Medicare, during which time you may use up your savings to pay for medications. Reform! Reform! Once you get Medicare, you may or may not have early access to Medigap coverage, depending on your state. You can definitely get Medigap at 65.

Make Sure You Get the Paperwork on Time! The insurance company is required to notify you about your COBRA option. It also has to send you a Certificate of Creditable Coverage, showing how long you've been insured. You need this paperwork in order to buy new coverage without passing a health test, and you need it in time to keep your coverage continuous. When I left an Aetna group plan, I had to wrestle the plan to the ground (with the help of my former employer) to get the documents. So watch this carefully. You don't want to be sandbagged by a tardy customer service rep.

If You Leave Your Job, Worked for a Company with Fewer Than 20 Employees, and Don't Have a New Job Yet: Preserve your future insurability by maintaining your health insurance without a break of more than 63 days. Consider an individual high-deductible plan, which is a good, low-cost stopgap. You're not entitled to COBRA because your ex-company is too small. Nevertheless, a few states require the old plan to keep you for 3 to 18 months, at your expense. Alternatively, your company plan might be convertible into individual coverage without a health exam. If it's an HMO, the conversion plan may be pretty good. If it's a PPO, conversion may be more expensive and provide you with limited benefits. Still, that's a better option than a state risk pool if that's your only other way of staying insured.

If You're Insured Through an Association Group Plan: COBRA doesn't cover group plans established for members of an association (although it may cover that association's direct employees). But any group plan member—in an association, small firm, or large firm—has portability rights. You can get new insurance under 2009 rules, even for preexisting conditions, if you've had group coverage for at least 12 months.

If you're leaving your company to start your own business, see page 429 for your health insurance options. If you're retiring early, see page 430.

If You're Buying Your Own, Individual Insurance

My condolences. It's hard to find comprehensive health insurance at a decent price, especially when you have a family. In 2006 the Commonwealth Fund studied adults ages 19 to 64 shopping for individual policies. Nearly 90 percent of them never bought a plan. A majority couldn't find affordable coverage. One-fifth were rejected or charged more because of their health or had a medical problem excluded from coverage. Even if you find an affordable plan, you're not necessarily well insured. On average, people with individual policies pay 43 percent of their medical costs themselves, according to the Kaiser Family Foundation, compared with only 22 percent for people in employer plans. You will probably be required to buy coverage under health insurance reform. It remains to be seen how well the new rules can actually control costs.

When you do find a policy, you have to expect its premiums to rise rapidly, especially if you develop medical problems. You can lock in the price of your insurance for just 12 months. After that, you'll get annual increases based not only on your age and the rate of medical inflation but also on the number of claims made by everyone in your insurance pool and even on your individual health. If you have a heart attack and run up a lot of bills, your premium may rise by a larger amount. The insurer is trying to price you out. Most states limit how much your premium can jump if your health goes bad. Still, you'll find that the policy becomes harder to pay for just when you need it the most.

You must make every sacrifice to buy good health insurance. I've heard too many stories about families wiped out by a breadwinner's cancer, a newborn's deformity, a paralyzing automobile accident. The uninsured and underinsured use doctors less than the insured (putting off care they need), aren't screened for breast, cervical, or prostate cancer, don't get continuous treatment for chronic conditions, go to the hospital sicker, and are more likely to die when their illness is serious.

And please, apply for coverage while you and your family are still in good health! If you wait and develop an ailment of some sort, you'll pay more for your coverage until decent health insurance reform clicks in.

Once you've got a policy, it's guaranteed renewable. The insurer can't cancel it unless you fail to pay premiums, you leave the association through which you carried the coverage, or the insurer quits doing business in your area.

The Best Buys and the Cheapest Ways In

■ *Buy insurance through an association.* Many organizations—professional groups, trade groups, even political action and social responsibility groups— offer health insurance to members. Group coverage generally costs less than individual coverage, but not always. Compare both the price and the benefits with what you can get on the individual market.

You'll have to answer some health questions for both yourself and your dependents. The policy may exclude certain serious or chronic illnesses or limit how much is paid for them.

There are some drawbacks to association health insurance:

First, the policy may be canceled. Usually the association finds another insurer, but sometimes it doesn't. The new insurer generally picks up all the old policyholders, but it doesn't have to. Individual policies, by contrast, normally aren't canceled.

Second, the price of association insurance may climb steeply from year to year. Most state regulators don't review rate increases in advance as they do for individual coverage.

Finally, be suspicious of pitches for association policies that arrive unsolicited. They sound terrific up front but are probably riddled with unfair exclusions. Some groups are phony. They're peddled by con men who disappear when you start filing medical bills. Always Google the name of the association along with words such as *complaint* or *lawsuit,* to see if anything turns up.

Ask what happens if you leave the association. Sometimes you can keep the plan with no change in premium, sometimes you can convert to a more limited plan, sometimes you have to abandon the coverage entirely.

- *Call a local HMO.* HMOs are generally cheaper than traditional plans.
- *Get comparative price quotes.* At this point, you'll want to work with an insurance agent who specializes in health insurance. You can find the names of people in your area on the site run by the National Association of Health Underwriters (www.nahu.org). The agent knows what's available in your state and can explain the pros and cons of various types of policies. The price is the same whether you use an agent or not, so you might as well benefit from his or her expertise. Don't shop based only on the monthly premium. Plans with low premiums limit the benefits they offer. You might also check eHealthInsurance (www.ehealthinsurance .com) for quotes from companies that operate in your state. And check BlueCross BlueShield. Apply only to the company most likely to take you. A rejection looks bad on your record.
- *Be sure to enlist an agent if you're in poor health or someone in your family is.* An agent has the best chance of finding you a decent offer.
- *Consider taking a big deductible and co-pay.* The more of the bills you'll cover yourself, the lower the monthly premium. In some states, individual policies are routinely sold with deductibles of $2,500 or more. But get a policy that caps the total you have to pay each year. Otherwise the expenses might run away with you. If an illness strikes, you might pay more in deductibles and co-pays than you saved by buying a policy with a lower monthly premium.
- *If you choose a consumer-directed high-deductible plan, open a health savings account on the side.* That lets you cover your uninsured expenses tax free.
- *Talk to your doctor.* If he or she knows that you're paying for regular care yourself, you might get a discount. Also, ask that all prescriptions be for generics unless there's a strong reason to stick with the brand name.
- *Quit smoking.* Insurers charge nonsmokers less. And while you're at it, lose weight and bring your blood pressure under control. With better health, you'll see a doctor less often and might move into a lower-cost insurance class.

- *Consider hospital/surgical coverage.* It's much cheaper than comprehensive coverage because it insures only hospital bills and the various costs of surgery, not your regular doctor bills or bills for the care of chronic conditions. I'd rather have major medical insurance with a big deductible. Still, these policies are better than nothing. If you buy one, be sure that it covers outpatient surgery, which is increasingly used today.
- *Send all medical bills to your insurer even though they're below the deductible.* Your coverage will click in as soon as the bills you report exceed your deductible. If you don't send in bills or have your doctor submit them, you may accidentally pay more than you ought. The deductible will be levied once a year. If you have a family policy, the deductible should be satisfied by the bills of just two or three of you. And by the way, file bills on time. Most insurers won't pay if you file 18 or 24 months late.
- *Buy short-term coverage.* Some insurers offer short-term policies to new college graduates to carry them over from school to work. They're also good for students who drop out of school for a while and will lose coverage on their parents' plan, or people who are between jobs. Short-term health insurance typically lasts for 6 or 12 months and may not cover preexisting conditions, pregnancy, substance abuse, illness while you're traveling abroad, or mental health. If you're allowed to renew the policy, any ongoing health problem may be classified as a preexisting condition and ruled out.
- *Talk to your parents.* Young people in low-paying jobs have a hard time paying their rent, let alone their health insurance. Feeling immortal, they often go without, even skipping a policy offered by their employer. Parents shouldn't let that happen. If your child got sick or has a terrible accident, you would probably raid your retirement savings to help. So buying your kid a health insurance policy protects your own financial plan.
- *Consider no-frills coverage.* Some insurers are marketing cheap, cheap limited-benefit plans to young people who normally couldn't afford a policy. The premium—maybe $30 or $60 a month—doesn't buy you much. You get discounts on generic drugs and a limited number of doctor visits, but your annual deductible runs as high as $7,500. It's insurance you'll barely notice unless you have a catastrophic health event—and then you're covered, up to a lifetime limit of $1 million or $2 million. That's better than going bare.
- *Check into medical tourism.* You can get top-notch, low-cost surgery in India, Thailand, Belgium, Singapore, and other countries with first-rate doctors and hospitals. Internal U.S. medical tourism works too. Hospitals in Oklahoma or Wichita may perform surgical procedures for two-thirds less than they'd cost in Boston and San Francisco—especially if you'll pay cash. Healthplace Amer-

ica (www.healthplaceamerica.com), which works with employers and insurance companies, lists 10 U.S. cities where you might get good surgery cheap. Boston-based Healthbase (www.healthbase.com) arranges for medical tourism in the United States and abroad. Also check the Medical Tourism Association (www.medicaltourismassociation.com). Some U.S. health insurance companies are even setting up subsidiaries abroad.

- *Ask about the State Children's Health Insurance Plan (SCHIP).* In families with modest incomes, the children may qualify for low-cost coverage through SCHIP. The most efficient way to cover your family might be by combining SCHIP for your child with a high-deductible policy for yourself.

- *Follow the rules.* You often need preauthorization for elective surgery and various expensive tests; otherwise the plan might not pay. Emergency surgery usually has to be reported to the insurer within a day. You'll need special approval to spend an extra day in the hospital. If you don't follow all the rules, you may have to pay the bill yourself.

- *Educate yourself.* Two good sites on the Web for learning more about health insurance are HealthCareCoach (www.healthcarecoach.com) and HealthInsuranceInfo (www.healthinsuranceinfo.net). The latter gives you all the insurance rules for your state and lists any state-subsidized plans that people with middle incomes might qualify for.

Coverage for the Self-Employed

You might find a group policy that's cheaper than an individual plan, especially if you have a health problem. Here are seven places to look:

- *Your local chamber of commerce may have plans for sole proprietors or small groups.* So might a professional association that you can join.

- *The Small Business Service Bureau* (www.sbsb.com) sponsors plans for members in many states.

- *The AARP* offers coverage to people 50 and up.

- *Fourteen states permit "group" plans for groups of one.* Check it out at statehealthfacts.org (click on "Managed Care & Health Insurance," then on "Small Group Guaranteed Issue"). In other states, you might create a group of two by establishing a formal business and hiring your spouse to do bookkeeping or marketing.

- *The Freelancers Union (www.freelancersunion.org) has its own health insurance company* in New York State and offers coverage through Golden Rule Insurance Company in 30 other states, for people in certain occupations.

- *Go to eHealthInsurance (www.ehealthinsurance.com).* You enter your zip code, age, gender, smoker status, and whether you're a full-time student, and back come premium quotes from the plans for which you might qualify. You'll see several marked "for the self-employed." But don't let them fool you. These quotes are only for people in the very best of health. When you contact the companies, you may be given a higher rate.

- *Work with an experienced health insurance agent* (for names in your area, go to www.nahu.org). It won't cost you anything extra, and you'll get the benefit of the agent's expertise.
- *Go to HealthInsuranceInfo (www.healthinsuranceinfo.net),* run by the Georgetown Health Policy Institute. It gives state-by-state info on the programs available to small-business owners and people who have been rejected for coverage.

Coverage for Early Retirees

Retirement planning usually focuses on "the number"—how much money you'll need to afford the kind of retirement you want. For early retirees, there's a second question, potentially even more important: Will you have health insurance to carry you to 65, when you finally come under the protection of Medicare? Without it, your health, your savings, and your standard of living are at serious risk.

Who will pay the medical bills if you're cut adrift? Increasingly, they fall on the shoulders—that is, the bank account—of the retiree. The number of large employers offering health benefits to retirees dropped to 31 percent in 2006 from 66 percent in 1988, according to a survey by the Kaiser Family Foundation and Hewitt Associates (at this writing, these are the latest numbers available). In 2007 it was offered by only 4 percent of companies with fewer than 200 employees. Companies are also raising early-retiree premiums faster than they are for plans that cover new retirees 65 and up.

It's dangerous to go bare. A study published in *The New England Journal of Medicine* evaluated adults who were 51 to 61 in 1992. Those without insurance were almost three times as likely to suffer a decline in health in the following five years as those who were insured. Another study looked at uninsured people arriving at Medicare age with hypertension, diabetes, heart disease, or stroke. They were sicker than insured people with the same diseases, saw doctors more often, and required more hospitalization.

Going without insurance is also dangerous to your financial health. Bankruptcies are soaring among older people. In 1991 only 8.2 percent of bankrupts were 55 and older. By 2007 that number had almost tripled to 22.3 percent.

Insurance reformers are targeting early retirees in particular. New rules could make policies easier to get and, with luck, more affordable. Until then, don't even think of retiring (if you have a choice) until you know you can fill the health insurance gap. Freedom doesn't feel free when you know that a bad diagnosis—for you or your spouse—could wipe you out. When trolling for health insurance in your 50s and early 60s, here are some places to look:

▪ *Join your spouse's plan if he or she has benefits.* Be sure to check the enrollment dates. You usually have only 30 days after your retirement for signing up.

▪ *Find a new job that provides benefits* (not easy in your mid-50s or early 60s). You might consider teaching. You'd be doing good work for the country and getting health insurance too. Other government jobs and hospital jobs usually offer coverage. See what's available for part-time work. Corporations such as Home Depot, Wal-Mart, and Costco cover part-timers, although there are waiting periods before benefits begin.

▪ *Look for individual coverage with the help of an insurance agent.* Start the search before you commit to early retirement, to see what you qualify for. You might even decide not to retire until you're closer to Medicare age. Maybe your employer will let you cut back your hours by just enough to keep you in the medical plan. By law, people who leave group plans are entitled to buy insurance, regardless of health, if they follow the rules (page 424). But you can be charged so much that you can afford only limited benefits.

▪ *Use your COBRA benefits.* If you find that you don't qualify for standard coverage, file for COBRA benefits when you retire. They're good for up to 18 months, at your expense. When the end of COBRA is in sight, go for the best deal you can find, even if it's a limited-benefit high-risk pool.

▪ *Go into business for yourself.* You might find a one-person group policy that beats the cost of individual coverage. In states that require two employees to create a group, hire your spouse.

▪ *Move to Maine, Massachusetts, New Jersey, New York, or Vermont.* Those are *guaranteed issue* states. Insurance companies have to take you, at not-unreasonable rates, regardless of health. There are those northern winters, of course, but at least your pneumonia will be paid for. With the right insurer, you can go south for a couple of months and take your coverage with you. Note that some of these states open their enrollment windows only once a year for a limited period. Insurance reform should let you buy coverage in any state.

▪ *Buy a high-deductible policy.* Deductibles even as high as $7,500 or $10,000 are worth it, although you might not think so if you're buried under annual medical bills. These policies do two things: They protect you against a catastrophic illness. They also put you into the PPO network, which gives you the network discount of up to 50 percent on your medical bills—including the bills that you have to pay yourself. Those savings reduce the effective cost of the policy you buy.

▪ *If you plan to retire in another state, or even another part of the same state, plot a health insurance strategy first.* The options available in your new state or city will depend on your health and the type of coverage you have now.

If you're in an HMO, you'll lose access to care unless the HMO has facilities in your new town. You'll have to apply for a new policy from scratch and risk being turned down or charged a much higher price. If your HMO is part of an employer plan, switch to a PPO before you retire. PPOs are more apt to be portable.

If you're in a company PPO that gives benefits to retirees, and it's a national plan, you may be able to carry it to your new state. Your new doctors would still be considered in-network, although your premiums and co-pays would almost certainly change. If it's not a national PPO, you'd probably be able to keep it, but you'd have to pay your doctors out-of-network prices. That's too expensive over time.

If you're in an individual PPO, ask your insurance company whether you can transfer the plan to your new city. It all depends on your plan. BlueCross BlueShield, for example, says no—you'd have to apply for a new plan and go through medical underwriting all over again. Aetna says yes for its Aetna Advantage plan, which operates in 30 states. Your new Aetna plan would differ from your old one, due to different state requirements, but you wouldn't be treated as a new applicant.

Make your move in time to establish a relationship with a doctor before you reach Medicare age. He or she will usually keep on seeing you after you switch to the government program. It can be hard to start up with a doc when Medicare payments are all you have to offer.

Student Plans

Most family policies include full-time college students (page 416). If your child goes away to school, however, your plan may not cover local doctors and hospitals or may require you to pay the high deductible applied to out-of-network providers. It might be inconvenient to get a physician referral or authorization for a test.

Colleges and universities offer health plans at reasonable costs, and you should probably take them. Policies vary widely. There may or may not be coverage for sports injuries, allergies, and prescription drugs. Major medical insurance may be capped at a fixed amount, such as $250,000, or $100,000 per illness or injury. It will probably exclude the hazards of youth, such as injuries sustained during a student riot.

Be sure you know what happens when the student is temporarily out of school. There may be a fee for continuing coverage during the summer vacation or any semester that the student takes off. If you drop the coverage over the summer and start it again in the fall, any limit or waiting period on preexisting conditions could start all over again.

Maternity Benefits

Group plans have to cover pregnancy on the same basis as any other medical condition. A few states require that all individual policies include maternity benefits too. They may also be offered at HMOs. But most individual policies exclude pre- and postnatal care and normal deliveries unless you purchase a special maternity rider, or require a separate deductible of $5,000 or more.

Should you buy the rider? The only people who buy are those who intend to use it, so there's no true insurance pool. The rider is expensive. Basically, you're giving the insurance company a little more than your delivery will cost so that the company will pay the bill when it arrives (and make a profit, besides). There's typically a 6- to 12-month waiting period before benefits start. The payment might amount to only $2,500 in the first two years but $5,000 if you have your baby in year three or four. There may be large deductibles and coinsurance.

The least expensive way to pay for a normal delivery is to cover it yourself. Ask the doctor how much the delivery will cost, then start paying him or her that amount on a monthly basis.

You do need insurance for complications of pregnancy, including emergency cesarean sections. But that's normally included in your major medical policy even if you don't buy maternity coverage. The policy also should cover premature babies, illness in newborns, and birth defects.

If you leave one group plan and join another, your pregnancy cannot be treated as a preexisting condition. The new policy has to cover it.

32 Ways of Saving Money on Medical Costs

We're paying more of each medical bill ourselves, in high deductibles and co-pays. Here's how to hold some of those costs down:

1. Join an HMO and see only the doctors on the list.

2. Use the low-cost walk-in clinics at stores like CVS, Walgreens, Publix, Target, and Wal-Mart for minor ailments, flu shots, and cholesterol screening. They're staffed by a nurse, no appointments are necessary, prices are posted, and wait times are short. They accept most major health insurance policies.

**3. For emergencies that aren't life threatening (a broken finger but not

chest pains), try a stand-alone urgent-care clinic. There's a doctor on staff, it's open evenings and weekends (maybe even 24/7), and will be cheaper and faster than the service in a hospital emergency room.

4. Don't rush to the doctor every time you feel sick. A lot of illnesses go away by themselves. See if the doctor or nurse will give you advice by e-mail on follow-up care, drug side effects, and similar issues that shouldn't require an office visit. Use the e-mail option cautiously, however. Your doctor should ask the same questions by e-mail that he or she would ask in an office visit, to be sure that your symptoms don't suggest something more serious.

5. Tell your doctor, hospital, or dentist that you're paying out-of-pocket and ask for a discount.

6. Switch to a dentist who's part of your PPO network. Many dentists haven't bothered affiliating with a plan, so you may be paying at out-of-network prices. Major insurance companies such as Aetna, Cigna, and WellPoint offer dental discount plans for services from network dentists.

7. Check yourself regularly for breast cancer, testicular cancer, and lumps on your skin.

8. Pay for costly medical procedures up front, in cash. That might earn you a discount of 10 percent.

9. Use generic drugs unless there's a good reason not to. For the best buys in drugs and other valuable consumer information, go to Consumer Reports.org's "BestBuyDrugs" at www.consumerreports.org//health//best-buy -drugs//index.html.

10. Buy from the discount pharmacies at places like Wal-Mart or Costco. They usually charge much less for prescriptions than your local mom-and-pop, or even the chains.

11. Buy at a discount through your health plan's mail-order service. You'll also find discounts online at both U.S. and Canadian pharmacies. The government isn't intercepting small amounts of prescription drugs shipped from abroad. Online pharmacies approved by the National Association of Boards of Pharmacy will display the seal of VIPPS (Verified Internet Pharmacy Practice Sites).

12. Try store-brand over-the-counter drugs. They're cheaper than brand-name remedies and often just as effective. Or just as ineffective, as the case may be. They may be cheaper from online pharmacies too.

13. Split your pills. Large doses generally cost the same as small ones, so buy the large dose, equip yourself with a pill splitter, and make your money go twice as far.

14. Snag as many free samples of a prescription medicine as your doctor will part with.

15. Ask for discounted medications. The Partnership for Prescription Assistance (www.pparx.org) links to more than 400 programs that offer free or discounted medications to people in financial need. Your doctor might know of a free source for your particular drug.

16. Use your company's flexible spending plan to pay medical bills (page 421).

17. Stay insured, even if it means taking a $15,000 deductible. When you leave a group plan and apply for new, individual coverage within 63 days, the insurance company has to take you. If you wait for more than 63 days, it can require a waiting period for covering certain conditions, refuse to cover those specific conditions, or (until insurance reform) turn you down entirely.

18. Buy your own crutches or other medical equipment after a hospital stay. You'll find them for less than the hospital will charge.

19. Ask your doctor for the names of the anesthesiologist, radiologist, or other specialists who will be involved in your surgery and check with your health plan to see if they're in the network. If not, tell your doc to find someone else so that you won't be charged out-of-network rates.

20. Compare hospital prices. There's a wealth of price and performance data on the Web site of the federal Centers for Medicare and Medicaid Services. Go to www.hospitalcompare.hhs.gov. You'll see what Medicare pays for various services, which should help you benchmark your own costs.

21. Check your health plan's Web site, to see if it provides information about the cost and quality of various medical providers. Two leaders in this new performance-disclosure field: Aetna and Cigna.

22. Recheck your employer plan options every year, during the sign-up period, to see if there's a plan with a better offer. The key to your real, potential cost lies not in the monthly premium but in the deductibles and co-pays.

23. Have your recent X-rays sent to a new doctor or dentist. That should save you the cost, and risk, of being X-rayed again.

24. See if your health plan requires prior approval before you undergo expensive tests or elective surgery. Without approval, it might not pay.

25. Know your plan's rules by heart. What will it cost you to see a doctor who's not in the network? If you're rushed to an out-of-network emergency room, how soon must the plan be notified? (It might not pay the bill if your family calls too late.) If you take sick out of town, what's the procedure for getting permission to see a doctor at in-network rates? (Put the info on a card and keep it in your wallet.)

26. Read the explanation of benefits you get from your health plan. It should show you the amount that was billed and the discounted amount that the plan actually paid. If you owe a percentage of each bill, your percentage should be figured on the discounted amount, unless your contract specifically says otherwise.

27. Learn how to take care of your illnesses yourself, and follow your doctor's directions to the letter. A large percentage of the people readmitted to the hospital soon after being discharged have to go back only because they didn't follow doctor's orders.

28. Report overbilling and other forms of Medicare fraud to the program's fraud hotline: 800-HHS-TIPS. Any money Medicare saves leaves more money in the till for beneficiaries like you.

29. Recheck your Medicare drug plan every year. You're looking for a plan that covers all the drugs you use and charges a lower monthly premium. For the plans available in your area, go to the Medicare Prescription Drug Plan finder at www.medicare.gov.

30. If you're on Medicare, get doctors who accept assignment. That means they charge no more than what Medicare will pay. You still pay your annual deductible and a 20 percent share of each doctor bill. But you don't have to pay any excess charges. The vast majority of doctors accept assignment today.

31. E-mail your doctor. Many health plans now pay doctors for handling medical problems online. The "appointment" is shorter and you pay less. Use this channel for routine illnesses that your doctor has treated you for before.

32. Lose weight. Quit smoking. Drink less. Eat right. Wear seat belts. Exercise. There is no doctor bill so cheap as the one that you don't incur in the first place.

Three Ways Providers Are Making You Pay More

1. Do you know what's in your medicine cabinet? Maybe not, but the health insurance industry does. The companies collect data from the pharmacy benefit managers that process consumer drug claims. If you apply for coverage, they can find out in an instant which drugs you've taken in recent years. From that, they construct a "pharmacy risk score." The higher your score, the higher your premium is likely to be. If you're taking the "wrong" drugs, you might be turned down. In one known case, a patient on Prozac for menopausal hot flashes was turned down for health insurance because Prozac suggests depression. She wasn't depressed, and her doctor supported her appeal, but she was rejected anyway. How can anyone wonder why we need reform?

Two companies, Milliman IntelliScript and Ingenix MedPoint, provide the data. If you're denied or charged extra based on something in their reports, you have to be notified, given free access to your report, and offered a chance to correct any errors. But your Prozac may count against you nonetheless.

2. Did your hospital give you a wallet biopsy? Hospitals are buying software that lets them check your credit score and the size of the line of credit that's still open on your credit cards. Your low income might normally qualify you for charity care or a low-income discount. But if your credit score is high, the financial office might conclude that you have money squirreled away somewhere. Poof, your discount is gone. You might also be required to pay if the hospital finds that you have available credit on a credit card. There are cases of patients being told to max out on their MasterCards or they wouldn't get treatments, or ordered to tap a meager 401(k). And here's a new one on me: Hospitals also might refuse treatments to lower-income people who bought a high-deductible health insurance policy. They figure that the deductible will be too much for you to pay.

3. Do you know if you financed your dental care with a high-interest loan? Some dentists, doctors, and hospitals who used to let patients pay over time without high interest are now steering them into high-risk installment plans. You might think you're signing a simple promise to pay the hospital over several months. Instead it's a contract with GE Money CareCredit, CapitalOne Healthcare Finance, ChaseHealthAdvance, or Citi's Health Card. Interest rates are reasonable until you're late on one payment, and then they may jump to as much as 28 percent.

From a health provider's point of view, these plans are great for business. Financing encourages you to go for expensive treatments, such as tooth implants and cosmetic surgery. If you know what you're signing and the treatment is optional, it's your funeral. But these plans are also being pushed on patients who need appendectomies and chemotherapy and are told that this is the only way they'll be allowed to pay. Doctors as shills for high-interest finance companies? Promoting the medical equivalent of subprime mortgages? Stop the world, I want to get off.

Questions to Ask When Choosing Among Plans

HMOs, PPOs, and POS plans all come under the heading *managed care.* They limit your choices in some way to deliver health services at a lower cost. You can ignore their limits if you're in a PPO or POS plan, but you'll pay for it in higher medical charges. When choosing among several plans, the first thing you look at is the out-of-pocket cost. But there are other things to think about:

- *How good is the plan overall?* Find out how it stands with the National Committee for Quality Assurance, which accredits and rates commercial, Medicare, and Medicaid health care plans. At www.ncqa.org, click on "Report Cards" and then on "America's Best Health Plans," a ranking of more than 600 plans done in collaboration with the magazine *U.S. News & World Report.* At NCQA's "Health Plan Report Card," on the same Web page, you can enter the names of health plans you're considering, to see where they stand. Only about one-third of the plans are accredited. They're your best choice.

■ *How old is the plan?* Avoid new ones. They need time to test their treatment guidelines and line up decent rosters of doctors.

■ *Which doctors are available?* An HMO can't be any better than the doctors it uses. See if you recognize the doctors on the list. You're generally allowed to change primary-care doctors if you don't like the one you started with. If you want a particular doctor, find out if he or she is accepting new patients. A wide choice of doctors doesn't necessarily make that plan the best. Plans with high-quality reputations are often those with a central clinic and a closely knit group of salaried doctors working together to find the best treatment for each disease.

■ *Will the doctor answer questions by e-mail or phone?* You shouldn't have to make an appointment for minor matters.

■ *What happens nights and weekends?* Presumably, a duty doctor will answer your call. Where should you go for emergency care?

■ *Does your primary doctor take patients from several managed care plans?* If not, you may have to switch doctors if you change your job or if your employer changes plans. This is one of the more annoying aspects of today's medical system. A job switch or plan switch may require everyone in your family to develop new medical relationships, even if they're in the middle of a course of treatment. PPO plans solve this problem by letting you go to doctors out of network. You'll at least be able to finish your treatment (although at a higher cost) before signing up with a new doc.

■ *How easy is it to see a specialist?* At HMOs and POS plans, you have to see your primary-care doctor first and let him or her assess the problem. The problem might be solved right there. If not, a specialist may be ordered. Some primary docs will skip this step and refer you to a specialist by phone—a big time-saver. A few HMOs even let you see specialists in the plan without prior permission. But the specialist will have to get an okay from your primary doctor before prescribing a course of treatment. In PPOs, you can go to any in-network doc you want without needing to be referred.

■ *Which specialists can you see?* PPOs have a wider choice of in-network specialists. HMOs restrict you to their own. Some HMOs let you seek out doctors with national reputations if yours is a complicated case. Others, however, may force you to use a less expensive surgeon who doesn't have as much experience in the type of procedure you need. Appeals are allowed, but it may take a while to resolve your claim and you may be in no condition to wait. In difficult cases, you need a representative to go to bat for the treatment you need.

■ *Are the drugs you need on the plan's formulary?* That's the list of drugs it's willing to pay for at the contract price. Formularies change, but if you start out with an approved drug, you'll have a good case for keeping it if your doctor agrees. Some plans may require you to try another drug to see if it works before letting you use a drug that's not on its list. Don't object. If it turns out to work and costs less, you're ahead.

■ *Which hospitals are on the list, and do you have a choice?* Managed care plans will generally list the best hospitals in the area. But they don't necessarily let you go there. The best may be reserved for more serious illnesses. Otherwise you may be sent to a less costly place. Find out if you have access to a major medical center if you or a family member needs unusually complex surgery.

■ *How conveniently located are the doctors, hospitals, physical therapy centers, pharmacies, and other services?* You don't want to have to drive to the other side of town when there are perfectly good services nearby.

■ *What if you're traveling and get sick?* Managed care plans cover emergency screening and stabilization provided by nonnetwork doctors and hospitals. Once you've been stabilized, however, they have to call your plan, generally within 24 or 48 hours. If they treat you further without getting permission, an HMO plan probably won't pay. A PPO will pay out out-of-network rates.

A murkier question is how the plan handles urgent but nonemergency care. What if you're visiting your mother and your son gets a terrible earache? What if you're on a business trip and wake up with chills, a high fever, and a sick stomach? BlueCross BlueShield launched a national network in 1996 and started adding international hospitals in 1997, so there might be an approved doctor nearby. An HMO might tell you to call the plan before leaving town to get the names of approved medical groups in the cities you're visiting. As long as you call a preapproved group, your HMO will cover the bill at the network cost.

But what if you don't call before each and every trip (and who would?)? To get the network cost, you have to call the HMO from wherever you are and describe your symptoms to the person staffing the medical-advice line. Based on what you say, you'll be told to go to a local clinic, call a local medical practice, or take two aspirin and see your doctor when you come home. If you see a local doctor without permission, it's usually on your nickel. Here's where a PPO or POS has an advantage. You can see any doctor, as long as you're willing to pay the out-of-network charge.

Losing important prescription medication can be an emergency. If your plan calls an out-of-network pharmacy to order the prescription, you'll probably have to pay cash and put in a claim for repayment when you get home.

■ *What's an emergency, and who decides?* If you think you're in a situation that threatens your life or health, you can rush to the nearest emergency room even when it isn't part of your health plan. The cost should be covered at in-network rates. If the bill exceeds what your plan considers "reasonable," the hospital can charge you for the additional amount.

But what if the pain in your chest turns out to be indigestion rather than a heart attack? Managed care plans are supposed to pay for out-of-network care if a prudent layperson might reasonably believe that there is a need for immediate medical treatment. With perfect hindsight, however, the plan may reject the bill—a pretty cynical way of saving money. When you call your plan, by the way, note the time of the call and the name of the person you spoke to. Some plans have denied payment because they said that the patient never called.

■ *What if you spend part of each year at a second home?* You need a plan that has in-network affiliates in both places.

■ *How does the plan handle preexisting conditions?* Find out if you'll be covered right away for ailments that you and your family have had recently. There may or may not be a waiting period. If you need medical equipment, ask what's covered and how often it can be upgraded or changed—for example, new wheelchairs for a growing child. Ask if any illnesses are excluded from coverage completely.

■ *What is the plan's policy on superexpensive treatments such as organ transplants?* There's usually a wishy-washy assurance that they're covered if appropriate. You can't be sure what's "appropriate" until you're actually there. Insurance companies won't pay for treatments considered experimental, but there's a lot of discussion about what that means. Use a search engine to check on your proposed plan, adding keywords such as *lawsuit, complaint,* and *arbitration,* to see if any stories turn up about denial of care.

■ *How much coverage is offered for mental illness and substance abuse?* Starting in 2010, employer plans with more than 50 employees have to cover them on an equal basis with other medical conditions. But the federal law doesn't cover individual plans. Some plans may cover them equally; others may grant a patient no more than a handful of visits to a psychologist or psychiatrist. If you or your child has a drug or alcohol problem, you may be allowed only seven days in a treatment program.

- *Do you have all this coverage information in writing?* What salespeople say over the phone or in person may be different from the plan's actual rules. The rules rule every time.

Appealing a Managed Care Decision

Health insurance doesn't cover treatments that are experimental or medically unnecessary. Sometimes, these decisions involve a lot of shouting and tears. If the plan rejects a treatment that your doctor supports, you can request a formal internal review. The plan will give you a booklet outlining all the steps. Normally, an answer is required within 30 days. Urgent-care cases are handled within 72 hours. The reviewers have to be people who didn't make the original decision. If the plan still says no, you might pay for the treatment yourself and then bring a claim for reimbursement. You can assemble additional information to support your claim.

If you've exhausted your appeals and you work for a big company that self-insures its plan, you can go to court. That's expensive, however, and your chance of winning is small. Under the law, the court can consider only one thing: Did the plan make a reasonable decision based on the information before it at the time? Maybe there's research to support your side but you didn't know how to find it. Maybe the plan didn't make a thorough investigation. Tough luck. No new evidence is admissible in court.

If your plan is backed by an insurance company, 44 states and the District of Columbia provide independent medical review boards to hear your complaint. Some boards hear all complaints; others take only specific disputes. Typically, the plan might be refusing to pay for certain drugs or tests, access to mental health professionals, hospital admissions, new types of surgeries, or medical equipment. A study by America's Health Insurance Plans found that the boards supported the health plans about 60 percent of the time and the patients, 40 percent of the time.

If you have a dispute, it's important to present the strongest possible case, starting from the time you (or your spokesperson) appear before the first review board. Your objective is to show that you need the treatment and that it's covered by the plan. In urgent cases, it's hard to round up all the information you need within the short time allowed, but do what you can. If you lose, work up a stronger case for the next review board. Ideally, here's how to arm yourself:

- *Immediately ask for a written explanation for why you were turned down.* The reasons should be specific, not vague. "The surgery is experimental" isn't good enough. It should say, "It's experimental because . . ."

- *Ask for the actual language from the plan's master document on which the plan based its decision to turn you down* (the language in your plan handbook is only a summary). If the wording is vague, demand the specific definition the plan relied on—for example, what does "experimental" mean? (The wording might be so broad that many accepted treatments could be called experimental if the plan so chose.)

- *Supply additional paperwork.* Denial of coverage might arise from a simple mistake—for example, the plan might think that you hadn't gotten prior authorization for a treatment when in fact you had. You doctor will help you straighten this out by confirming that his office asked. Many cases are won this way. The paper record has to be complete.

- *If you're clashing over a serious medical issue—say, whether you should be allowed to see a specialty surgeon who's out of network—you'll need a lot of support from your doctor's office.* Consider hiring a medical expert to help you assemble the evidence (try AMFS at www.amfs.com). Assume there will be a biased report on the other side. The expert's job is to overcome it. You might also consult a lawyer on how to prepare your case.

- *Ask for the credentials of the people who are investigating your case.* If it's a cancer treatment, it should have been evaluated by the appropriate oncologist. You should receive a copy of his or her final report so that your medical expert can look for inaccuracies and holes.

- *Demand any reports the plan gets from third-party experts, as well as their credentials.* You're entitled to know the full case against you.

- *You need to rebut the plan's arguments point by point, and your documentation should be overwhelming*—medical papers, proof of how often the treatment is used in your kind of case, proof of its efficacy, proof that it's the best possible treatment in your case, several supporting witnesses. If you eventually go to court, the evidence presented during your appeal may be the only information you'll be allowed to submit.

- *Follow all the plan's appeal rules.* Handle everything in writing, keeping copies for yourself so you'll be able to prove what you said and did. If you have a telephone conversation about the problem, note when the call came, the name of the person you spoke with, and what was said.

- *Try to stay cordial and businesslike.* Your spouse's life may be at risk, but, to the appeals board, this is simply *a contract dispute.*

If the plan says no again, many patients stop. In life-threatening situations, they pay for the treatment themselves if they can dredge up the money. Or their condition gets so bad that the plan finally acts. Or they die. The patient or family may sue to recover any money they spent on the treatment. But you can use only the record you made during the appeal, which may or may not be sufficient.

You can see in a flash how cruel these rules can be. The patient's family may rush the appeal because the condition is critical. If they later sue for payment, their hasty presentation might prevent them from getting their money back, even if they were in the right.

In less critical situations—for example, getting a larger wheelchair for a growing child from a plan that says it will provide just one—persistence may pay off. Dig deeply into the language of the plan. Call, write, submit opinions from outside doctors, have a lawyer write, referring specifically to the section of the plan you think applies. The meek may inherit the earth, as the Scriptures say, but they won't get anywhere with their health insurance plan. You have to be a pain in the tail. Your objective is to show that the contract does indeed cover the treatment, drugs, or medical equipment your doctor says you need.

When it's an employee plan, your state insurance department usually won't intervene (although some do). Go to your company employee benefits office and pound the table. See the company president if you can, or write an internal memo. Rally other employees round. Noise may help. Some consumers get lucky by writing to a newspaper or television reporter who covers consumer or health care issues, or to their state representative. Publicity may help too. But don't bad-mouth your company, especially on a blog. Accusing your boss does *not* help and could even cost you your job.

Can You Sue a Managed Care Plan for Malpractice if Stingy Medical Treatment Led to Death or Permanent Disability? No, if it's part of an employer plan. You can sue the doctors. But the plan itself can normally be sued only in federal court and for just one thing: mistakes in deciding whether the plan should pay a particular medical bill. If you win such a case, all you get is the cost of the benefit you erroneously had to pay yourself plus attorney's fees. For example, say that your late wife was sick and the plan wouldn't authorize a blood test. She gets sicker, you pay for the test yourself, and it reveals a disease that has now progressed too far to treat. You can sue only to recover the $350 you paid for the test plus, if you're lucky, "reasonable" attorney's fees. You cannot bring a malpractice suit. You cannot get damages for negligence, bad faith, or wrongful death. What's more, your burden of proof is higher than for malpractice suits. Justice aside, alas, these cases are rarely worth bringing at all.

There are exceptions. You can sue if you joined the plan as an individual rather than as part of an employee group. Ditto if you're in an employer plan offered by a state government, church, or church-related group. A different law, which is more patient friendly, covers federal employees, but they first have to go through an internal appeals process. Decisions that reach court review are rarely overturned.

Some Health Plans Require That Disputes Be Settled by Arbitration. That's faster and cheaper than bringing a lawsuit and can produce a fair award. But the way the panels are constructed generally favors the health plans. Get a medical adviser and a lawyer to help with your arbitration too.

Don't Waste Your Money On . . .

One-Disease Insurance (such as coverage specifically for cancer or heart attacks). The odds are against your lucking into the one disease that you insured against. Put your money toward broader coverage that protects your general health. If I can't talk you out of buying, check the exclusions carefully. These policies are cheap because they don't cover a lot.

Hospital Daily-Pay Insurance. This policy pays a fixed number of dollars per day if you enter the hospital—often in the $200 to $600 range, with a little extra for intensive care but no coverage for maternity. That barely scratches the surface of your real daily cost. What's more, you might not even be hospitalized for more than two or three days. You're paying a lot for virtually nothing.

Limited-Benefit Coverage. These policies could mislead you into thinking you have more protection than is actually the case. For example, the agent might say that you have $2 million in lifetime coverage. You might not be told that your hospitalization "protection" pays only room and board, not the medical and surgical costs. Your medical "insurance" might pay no more than $5,000 annually for outpatient care—pretty useless if you're diagnosed with a serious disease. There may be high co-pays or caps on doctor visits. These policies are sold by some big-name companies as well as by smaller companies whose agents go door to door. How can you guess that these limited policies might not cover your actual bills? They're much cheaper than regular insurance. *Always* ask what the limitations are. You're better off with a policy with a high annual deductible than with one that won't help you with big bills.

Medical Discount Cards. Ads for these cards appear on TV and in your e-mail or are delivered over a fax machine. They claim to offer discounts on bills from thousands of doctors, dentists, and pharmacies in their national network, at a cost of a mere $65 to $100 a month. Usually they're scams. When you present the card to health providers, they've probably never heard of it. Don't buy a card unless you've asked your providers whether they accept it.

Accident Insurance. It pays medical bills that result from an accident, not an illness. But why would you think that your biggest risk in life is falling off a ladder or being hit by a truck? Only 4.5 percent of deaths are accidental. When such deaths occur, they often give rise to a lawsuit, a form of "insurance" you carry at no charge. Put your money toward comprehensive coverage that includes both accident and sickness.

Celebrity Insurance. Run, run, run, when you hear a celebrity hawking health insurance on TV or get a pitch by mail or e-mail. All you can be sure of is that the policy won't cover what you think and costs too much for the limited benefits offered. The celebrities who promote this stuff should be ashamed of themselves.

Double Coverage. An insurance agent might urge you to add a cancer policy or hospital policy to the health insurance you already have. The appeal: "This gives you an extra payment when you need it." Or "This fills the gaps that your other policy doesn't cover." You might better say that it fills the gaps in the insurance agent's personal income. The best way to get extra money is to build up your own personal savings. Cheap hit-or-miss insurance is always a waste.

The Death Spiral

Buyers of individual or small-group coverage may run into an odious method of pricing health insurance. It's known, appropriately, as the "death spiral" and could cost you your health insurance when you need it most. Here's how it works.

You buy a health insurance policy, carefully checking to be sure that it's guaranteed renewable. You've now joined a specific pool of people who are sharing risks. Most members are healthy and make few claims. Their premiums more than offset the payments made to members who are sick. A constant infusion of new, healthy members makes the pool work.

But many health insurers don't keep these pools open to new blood. After 12 to 36 months, they may close your pool and start a new one, issued on a new policy form. As the people in your pool age, the number and size of their claims go up. Your insurer shows this "bad experience" to the state insurance regulator, who may approve premium increases over and over again.

Pretty soon your pool's healthy members start dropping out. They switch to newer, cheaper pools, offered by that same insurer or by some other insurance company. That's when the death spiral begins. The members left behind are in poorer health, which drives up your premiums even more. Slowly, the sicker people leave too because they can't afford the price.

As long as you and your family remain in excellent health, you can jump to cheaper policies. But someday one of you may fall ill, and that's when your personal death spiral starts.

There are two other ways an insurer might play this game. If it's insuring an association, it might offer new, low-cost coverage to the healthier members every year, leaving sicker members in older policies with rates that will soar. Or it might maintain several risk pools and move all of its higher-risk people into the same pool.

I can't give you six easy tips for avoiding this crime against the public. It can be stopped only by state regulators and health insurance reform. Your best hint of trouble is the policy's premium. Given similar benefits, the policy with the lowest premiums is apt to start death-spiraling first.

Is Your Health Insurance Safe?

If your insurance company falters, your state's insurance commissioner will step in to see if the business can be rehabilitated or if another insurer wants to buy the business. If so, your policy should survive, although its provisions might change. If not, the insurer will be declared insolvent and liquidated and its policies transferred to another insurer.

Each state has a guaranty fund to provide continuing coverage and pay claims, including claims on long-term care policies. About 15 states pay at least $100,000, 19 cover $300,000, and most of the rest cover medical claims up to $500,000. Some states have tiered coverage—$100,000 for general medical claims, $300,000 for long-term disability, and $500,000 for hospital/surgical major medical. There are other variations. Look up your own state's limits at the Web site of the National Organization of Life & Health Insurance Guaranty Associations (www.nolhga.com).

If the failed insurer was providing group health plans, they'll typically be canceled on the next renewal date. Your employer will have to find new coverage somewhere else. The guaranty funds will continue individual noncancelable plans, collecting premiums and paying claims until they can find an insurer to take them off their hands. A few state guaranty associations cover HMOs, but most of them don't. Not all BlueCross BlueShield plans are covered, nor are Multiple Employer Welfare Arrangements (MEWAs), although some of these plans may be backed in other ways.

Will you have to pay any medical bills that exceed what you'll collect from your guaranty fund? That depends. Maybe the failed insurer has enough assets left to cover the claim eventually. Maybe the medical group or hospital had a *hold harmless* deal with the insurance company, agreeing not to bill the patient for any money unpaid by the insurer or plan sponsor. Maybe the state will step in and tell everyone to shut up. Failing that, you'd be responsible for the bill.

Fortunately, health insurers rarely fail. But prudent shoppers stick with companies that are rated AAA, just in case.

Some Health Plans Are Crooked

When people are desperate for affordable health insurance, crooks oblige. They peddle "group health insurance" at low prices, but it's actually a Ponzi scheme. They take in "premiums," pay small claims, stall on large ones, and eventually vanish. You know they're gone when the druggist won't fill your prescription and your doctor turns your bills over to a collection agency. The sad truth is that comprehensive health insurance doesn't exist at a moderate cost. If you're offered such an impossible dream, here's what to do:

1. Call your state's insurance commission or check its Web site. If the company isn't licensed to do business in your state, it's a fraud. Walk away from the sale *and* from the insurance agent. If your employer replaces its old health insurance with a new plan that's low cost, check out that policy too. Lots of con men prey on small companies that want policies for their employees.

2. Skip any cheap policy that claims to give generous benefits through a large provider network. They attract desperate people, but what's the use if they don't pay?

3. Don't trust a "professional association" or "union" plan without checking to see if it's licensed. Sellers of fake insurance often create sham associations or unions as a cover.

4. Beware the drug discount cards sold by phone, mail, fax, and on the Internet. For a monthly or annual fee, you'll be promised discounts of "up to 80 percent" on medical and drug bills. But your actual savings may come to little or nothing, after fees. Often, the doctors and drugstores don't even know about the card. Some fraudsters pretend to represent Medicare and offer you what appears to be a cheap Part D drug plan. Medicare drug discount plans are *never* sold that way.

What If You or a Member of Your Family Gets Sick and Is Uninsured?

Until insurance reform kicks in, you've got problems. The uninsured get sicker than others before being treated, receive less care for chronic illnesses, aren't routinely screened or tested for disease, and get virtually no preventive care. They die earlier of diseases that could have been cured or arrested if they'd had equal access to medical services. Emergency rooms will treat you. Then they'll send you a bill that you probably can't afford. The underinsured run this gauntlet too, but it's worse for those with no coverage at all.

So listen up. If you're healthy, buy insurance! *Buy it now!* If money is tight, take the cheapest major medical policy you can find—say, one with a $10,000 or $25,000 deductible. It protects you from the Really Big One and gives you the PPO discount on ordinary bills.

Here are your limited choices, if health problems bar you from regular coverage. For particulars, ask an insurance agent.

■ *A handful of states require insurers to take everyone, without charging them extra for their higher risk.* The states: Maine, Massachusetts, New Jersey, New York, and Vermont. Health insurance reform might extend this rule to every state.

■ *Some BlueCross BlueShield plans and some HMOs have open enrollment periods.* They'll take you, regardless of health, but preexisting conditions may not be covered for 6 to 18 months. Some diseases may not be accepted, period. Your premium will usually be high, although some states limit how much the insurer can charge. Open enrollment at HMOs may be limited to small businesses and the self-employed.

■ *You or your spouse might try for a job at a company with a group policy.* These plans take all comers, including dependents who are seriously ill. You may have to wait up to 12 months before the insurer will cover those particular bills, but so what? At least it's *future* health insurance. Some plans exclude certain illnesses or cap their coverage, not just for new employees but for everyone.

■ *The State Children's Health Insurance Program provides low-cost coverage to uninsured children from families with modest incomes.* For your state's rules, go to www.insurekidsnow.gov. You may be uninsurable, but your kids can get help. Sign them up!

■ *Try an independent insurance agent.* You might get lucky. Some insurers are more liberal than others about accepting certain kinds of health risks. For the names of nearby agents, go to the National Association of Health Underwriters Web site (www.nahu.org).

■ *If your state has a health insurance pool for high risks, check it out—with this warning:* You may have to pay 125 to 200 percent of the standard price, with a high deductible, substantial co-payments, and modest lifetime benefits. But at least you're protected from most catastrophic costs. To qualify, you generally have to have lived in the state for 30 days to 12 months and been turned down by one or two private insurers. Some medical conditions, such as cancer or AIDS, let you into the pool immediately. In a few states, there are waiting lists for coverage. At this writing, Florida's pool is closed.

■ *Your doctor may know of a program for uninsured people in need of expensive prescription drugs.*

■ *The healthy dependents of an unhealthy worker can buy their own insurance through many associations*, BlueCross BlueShield, or another private insurance company.

You have almost no choices if you're uninsured because you can't afford a policy. You can:

■ *Hunt for a job that offers group health coverage.*

■ *If you were formerly insured, see if your doctors will cut you a break.*

■ *Scour your city for free clinics and other social services.*

■ *Use the hospital emergency room sparingly.* It will bill you. You can work out a payment program if your finances permit.

■ *Partnership for Prescription Assistance (www.pparx.org)* links with more than 400 programs that offer free or discounted medications to people in financial need.

■ *Be as well as you can*—lose weight, don't smoke, eat right, exercise.

■ *Marry someone who has benefits.* (Immigrants talk about green card weddings; Americans, about health insurance weddings.)

■ *If you've run up huge medical bills, consider bankruptcy.*

■ *Pray that you'll last until 65 before a serious illness strikes.* You can fall into the arms of Medicare and, finally, get help.

Dependent Spouses and Children Without Their Own Medical Coverage

Everything here applies equally to men. But dependent coverage is overwhelmingly an issue for women and children.

If you are covered under your husband's employee group plan, you risk losing your health insurance if he separates from the company plan or separates from you. That can happen if he dies, if you divorce or legally separate, if he retires and lacks retiree health benefits, or if he goes onto Medicare. If you have a job with benefits, you can quickly switch to your own company's policy. If not, you should start checking your options right away.

Your First Step If You're Losing Coverage: Find out what it will cost to buy an individual plan (or a family plan, if you have dependent children). Work with an independent health insurance agent, with a backup call to your local Blue-Cross BlueShield and any HMO that sells individual coverage. The list that starts on page 433 will give you some other ideas. Remember to check each policy's full out-of-pocket costs, including deductibles and co-pays, in addition to the monthly premium.

If Your Spouse's Company Employs 20 People or More and You Have a Group Plan: You're usually allowed to stay in the employee plan for up to three years at your expense. This is known as your COBRA benefit. You're charged the group premium plus 2 percent. That's a high price—probably more than an acceptable individual policy will cost. But you'll get better coverage per dollar than individual policies offer.

To stay in the group, you must: (1) Make sure that your spouse's company notifies the insurer about your eligibility. Notification has to be made within 30 days from the day your spouse dies or goes onto Medicare, or within 60 days of your divorce or legal separation. Call the company yourself if you think that your spouse might not. (2) Watch for a letter from the insurance company asking if you want to continue. You have 60 days to say yes. If you miss any of these deadlines, you're dropped from the plan without the right of appeal. (3) Be sure to check on the date that your group insurance will expire. That's the date that you want your COBRA benefit or a different plan in place. It's important not to leave a gap in your medical coverage.

Your grown children can stay in the group for up to three years after they get too old for formal family coverage. To keep them enrolled for those extra years, alert the plan within 60 days of each child's cutoff age. Some plans will keep them even after COBRA expires.

Your COBRA coverage ends as soon as you (or the child) qualify for another group plan—for example, if you get a job with employee benefits. But if you have an illness that the new plan won't cover or won't cover right away, your old plan will keep on paying the bills.

If you haven't joined another group plan by the time your COBRA benefits end, you come under the *portability* rules (page 418). You should have access to at least two individual health plans without passing a health exam and with no waiting periods for preexisting conditions, including pregnancy. These might be plans from other insurers, your COBRA plan converted to an individual policy, or a state risk pool. There is, of course, the usual hitch: you may not be able to afford the premiums. Again, check my Web site for updates on insurance reform.

If Your Spouse's Company Employs Fewer Than 20 People and You Have a Group Plan: You don't get COBRA benefits, but state law may require the plan to keep you anyway. If you've had at least 18 months of group coverage, you have the right to buy an individual policy with no health exam and no waiting period for preexisting conditions, including pregnancy.

If Your Family Carries Its Own Individual Coverage: You can keep the policy if your spouse dies. In fact, your premiums will go down because the policy now covers one less person. Many new widows and widowers don't realize this and keep on paying for health insurance at the old rate. As soon as you tell the insurer about the death, however, any overpayments should be refunded. Also, ask for a lower premium as soon as your children leave school and are no longer covered under your policy.

If you divorce or legally separate and your spouse keeps the policy, you'll lose your personal health insurance. The children can still come under his or her plan as long as he or she agrees to it. Coverage for you might be part of the divorce agreement. If not, consider the cost when working out what you'll need to live on.

If Your Spouse Is Retiring and Will Have a Retiree Plan: You can continue on the plan as a dependent.

Help for Those (Like Me) with Paperwork Phobias

And you thought the government was bureaucratic. Have you filled in any private-insurance claims lately? Probably not if you're in an HMO. You face no paperwork there as long as you stick with its approved physicians. Ditto in a PPO. Large-group plans are handled automatically, with the bills going to the insurer directly. In the Medicare program, the doctors submit the claim forms for you. Sometimes they'll handle claims for Medigap coverage too.

But you face paperwork, big-time, in individual PPOs, POS plans, and Medigap or small-group plans if you go out of network and have to handle the claim yourself. You may also have to battle Medicare if the local claims administrator incorrectly rejects a bill.

If everything works right, you fill in the insurance form, attach your doctor's medical report, and send it in. Back comes a check in the right amount. Or the doctor gets the check directly.

What can go wrong? Your doctor might put down the wrong code number for your illness, resulting in an incorrect payment or an outright denial. If you took two children to the same doctor on the same day, the insurer's computer may decide that one of the claims is in error. Forms might come back requesting more information. Forms might get detached, so write your name and policy number on every piece of paper. You might need a special form for prescription drugs. If you're dealing with two insurers—one for doctor bills, one for hospital bills—they may fight over who should cover expenses related to both. You might make a simple mistake on the form, such as transposing two numbers. (Tip: Fill in a blank form with care and make multiple photocopies of it. Use a copy for every claim.)

Most of all, you might lose track of your expenses. People often save medical bills at home, intending to send them all in at once as soon as they equal the plan's up-front deductible. But some might be misplaced, causing you to pay more than you should. If you submit medical bills after a year or more, they may be refused. The time limits for making a claim will be spelled out in your policy.

Instead, send in a claim for every covered bill even though you know that you haven't yet met the plan's deductible. The insurer keeps track of those bills and knows to the penny when the deductible is reached. Another reason to send in claims that you know won't be paid: you might need your plan's official denial in order to submit the bill to another insurer or have it paid from your company's flexible spending account (page 421).

With just a tiny amount of patience, you can handle a few claims a year. But a serious illness can pile up so many bills from so many doctors that filling in claim forms and tracking payments becomes an overwhelming burden. Bills may not be paid because you're too sick to put in claims. A helper may not have the time to take care of a sick person and handle the paperwork too.

You may know a punctilious person who will take over the claim forms for a fee. If you have a small business, maybe your bookkeeper will do it. Or a wonderful child. Alternatively, hire a claims specialist. These professionals can help you track what's owed, catch billing errors, wipe out late-payment charges, and fight when payment is denied. They handle Medicare claims too. For the names of experts in your area, go to Medical Billing Advocates of America (www.bill advocates.com) or the Alliance of Claims Assistance Professionals (www.claims .org). They may charge flat fees, hourly fees, a percentage of the claims collected, or some combination of the three. One thing they can't do: rescue any payments denied you when you don't follow the health plan's rules.

Medicare, Old and New

You have health insurance at 65. You may complain about it, argue this or that point, grumble with your doctor, but in the end . . . *you have health insurance.* National, single-payer, government-run health insurance. Only younger people have to struggle with payments or go without.

You qualify for Medicare if you've met the work requirement for Social Security benefits (40 quarters of work) or if you're on the account of someone who qualifies. The latter group includes spouses, unmarried ex-spouses whose marriages lasted at least 10 years, widows and widowers, and parents who got half their support from a Social Security–eligible child who died or became disabled.

You can go on Medicare earlier than 65 if you've been receiving Social Security disability payments for two years or if you have lost the use of your kidneys.

Until a few years ago, Medicare was a pretty simple program. You hit 65, you signed up, you got benefits, end of story. Now it's complicated, with many options and some wolves in the forest trying to eat you up. Here's what you need to know.

Medicare Comes in Four Parts

Part A helps cover hospital bills and bills for skilled nursing homes, hospice care, and a certain amount of home health care. You have already paid for this coverage in your Social Security taxes, so you get it automatically at 65, at no extra cost.

A tiny percentage of people don't qualify automatically for Part A—for example, those who haven't met Social Security's work requirement. But it's easy to get in. You are eligible for Part B (below). As soon as you buy Part B, you're allowed to buy Part A. For those with official poverty-level incomes, Part A will be paid by your state Medicaid program.

Part B is optional. It carries a monthly premium, which the government deducts from your Social Security check. Multitiered premiums started in 2009, with one rate for the average retiree and higher rates for those with higher incomes. Part B helps cover, among other things, doctor bills, outpatient surgery, emergency room treatment for patients not admitted to the hospital, X-rays and CT scans, some laboratory tests, durable medical equipment (such as wheelchairs and hospital beds), mammograms, Pap smears, screening for diabetes and colon cancer, physical therapy, speech therapy, and some outpatient treatment for mental health care.

When you register for Medicare Part A, you're asked if you also want Part B. For 96 percent of you, the answer is yes—absolutely yes. But a few people should say no and enroll at another time. Here's how to decide.

You Will Need Part B If . . .

- *Medicare is your sole, or principal, medical insurance.*
- *You are moving from an active-employee plan to a retiree group plan that is still subsidized by your employer.* Your medical benefits stay pretty much the same. But at 65, your company pays only the bills that Medicare doesn't—and the plan assumes you have Part B. Some companies pay the Part B premium for you.
- *You're covered under your spouse's retiree plan and you're 65 or older.* Dependents typically get the same coverage as the retiree, so you too will need Part B.
- *You have individual health insurance.* At 65, drop it and switch to Part B for your medical bills. If yours was a family plan and your spouse is younger than 65, keep the private policy but only for your spouse. That will cut its cost.
- *You have no other health insurance.* You depend entirely on Medicare to pay your covered medical bills. If you're at the official poverty level, your state Medicaid program will pay the Part B premium for you.
- *You're 65, still working, and have a comprehensive company medical plan.* In some plans, especially small ones, your coverage might switch to *Medicare primary.* All your bills will go to Medicare first, and the company will pay what's left (after the usual plan deductibles). The plan might pay your Part B premium. The same is true for a spouse who is 65 and up and covered on your plan.
- *You're 65, still working, have a company medical plan with high deductibles, and face large medical bills.* Part B will pay the portion of the bill that the company plan won't cover, after the usual Medicare deductibles.

If you fall into one of these groups, sign up for Part B when you get Part A. You can enroll during a seven-month period—three months before you reach 65, your birthday month, or three months after. The premiums for late enrollees go up 10 percent for every year of delay.

If you'll want Medigap insurance (page 465) you normally have six months to buy it—at standard rates, regardless of your health—beginning on the first day of the month you turn 65 and are enrolled in Part B. If you dally, that no-excuses opportunity is lost. If you apply later and have a health problem, some states allow you to be rejected. Or your premium will rise.

If you'll want a Medicare Advantage plan (page 456), you have seven months to buy it at standard rates—three months before you turn 65, your birthday month, and three months after. You can also join later, during an open enrollment period (page 462).

Skip Part B (for Now) If . . .
- You're still working and have employee medical insurance.
- Your spouse is working, and you can go on his or her medical plan as a dependent.

But don't fail to sign up for Part A! It doesn't cost you anything and gives you extra coverage. Any hospital expenses not paid by the company's insurance (including deductibles and co-payments) can be submitted to Medicare—an ace in the hole that younger people don't have. You are subject to the usual Medicare deductibles. But after that, the government picks up any eligible bills that your health plan doesn't.

If you skip Part B at 65 for the reasons just discussed, be sure to sign up for it as soon as you leave work. If you wait longer than eight months after leaving your group plan, you'll pay extra for Part B and won't be able to join until the next Medicare open enrollment period.

When you finally leave your job and join Part B, you have the same six months in which to buy Medigap insurance at standard rates, regardless of your health, and seven months for a Medicare Advantage plan (page 456).

Parts A and B, Together, are Known as Original Medicare and are the way most retirees choose to receive their benefits. You can go to any doctor who takes Medicare. He or she sends in the reimbursement forms. You receive a report of what's paid (the explanation of Medicare benefits) and the amount the health provider is allowed to bill. When the bill comes, you write a check.

Part C, also known as Medicare Advantage, includes a variety of plans funded by Medicare but owned and operated by private companies. Medicare pays Advantage plans more per head than it pays for people in Original Medicare. Part of that extra money goes for overhead, marketing, and profits. The rest supports slightly better benefits than original Medicare offers. This varies by plan.

Medicare Advantage plans are controversial. They use up the Medicare trust fund faster, and lean on the taxpayers more, because of their higher cost. But they're favored by people who would like to see the system privatized. Most likely, Congress will cut back on the higher payments made to Advantage plans, which would reduce the extra benefits they offer. Until then, however, you may like what you see—especially the plans where the premiums are very low.

All Advantage plans cover the services offered by Parts A and B. You get additional benefis (lower co-pays, extra days in the hospital, annual checkups, vision care, and so on), varying by plan. They usually include Part D, for prescription drugs, at a relatively low premium. To know how much more you are getting (if anything), you have to lay out each plan's list of benefits, costs, and limitations and compare it with the plan you have now—either Original Medicare (plus Part D and, perhaps, a Medigap policy) or the retiree plan that your company subsidizes. As you might guess, the differences are often subtle and hard to quantify in dollars and cents. Also, they change from year to year. Tip: don't give up a retiree plan. It's almost certainly the best.

When considering an Advantage plan, you may have turn up your BS detector. Insurance agents earn commissions for signing up people. Abusive sales—cheating, lies—have been reported. The insurance companies are imposing mere oversight, and, in 2008, Medicare wrote new marketing rules. Still, you probably shouldn't trust the salespeople. When presented with a plan, wait a few days, think it over, and ask your doctor if he or she accepts it. Review the Summary of Benefits to see what's covered. Don't sign on the spot, especially if the salesperson gets pushy. One favorite lie: "Sign here, but only to receive more information." Bosh. If you sign, you join and will have to put a lot of effort into unjoining.

Here are your Advantage choices:

- *A Medicare HMO.* You can go only to the doctors and hospitals on the plan's list, except in an emergency. A single primary physician will be in charge of your care and refer you to specialists you need. If you're comfortable with the doctors, this arrangement works fine and usually costs less than other plans. It doesn't work fine, however, if you don't realize that you've joined an HMO. If you use your old doctor and hospital and they aren't in the network, you'll get big bills that Medicare won't pay. HMOs don't cover you if you spend part of the year in another part of the country. If you want an out-of-network specialist, you'll have to pay for it yourself.

■ *A Medicare PPO.* A large network of doctors, hospitals, pharmacists, and other providers belong to these plans. You can go to any of them you want without a referral from a primary physician. A PPO could make sense if your usual doctors participate (check it out). If the price is right, it may even be worth changing doctors; you'll probably have a longer list to choose from than you'd get in an HMO. You're allowed to go outside the network, although it will cost you more. You may be out of network if you live part of the year in another city or state.

■ *A Plan with a Medicare medical savings account.* These plans started in 2007 and haven't gained much traction. They mimic consumer-directed high-deductible health plans and are complicated. In a year when you have only a few medical expenses, you might pick up some extra money from the Medicare-funded savings account. If your expenses are average to high, however, you'll have to pay more out-of-pocket before Medicare kicks in. At 65 or older, why would you want that risk?

■ *A Medicare special needs plan.* This manages the care of people with chronic or complicated illnesses who live in nursing homes or are also eligible for Medicaid.

■ *A Medicare private fee-for-service plan (PFFS).* This profitable plan is hot, hot, hot among private insurance companies. Its agents have been especially guilty of rotten sales tactics—for example, signing up patients with dementia, falsely telling people they had to switch because Original Medicare was closing down, or presenting PFFS as a Medigap policy to supplement their company retiree plans. Some older people have been enrolled without knowing it, discovering the switch only when their pharmacist refused to fill a regular prescription. In 2007, the government stopped seven big companies from marketing PFFS plans until they cleaned up their act. In 2008, Congress prohibited certain sales tactics, such as door-to-door sales, free-lunch seminars, and cold calls.

PFFS resembles Original Medicare in that you can go to any doctor or hospital you want, if they'll accept the payment the plan offers. There's no such thing as in-network or out-of-network care. What's different is that the insurance companies, not the government, decide how much of the cost you will have to pay. The monthly premium may be low, but you could be charged more (or less) than other plans charge for hospital stays, home health care, or expensive drugs. Here's what you won't learn from the salespeople pushing happy brochures:

• *Your doctors might not accept this plan, even if they participate in general Medicare.* They might accept payments for some services but not others. Check it out before signing up. They can bill you an extra 15 percent if the plan allows it. (Doctors are allowed that extra 15 percent in original Medicare, too, but rarely charge it.)

• *Signing up for PFFS automatically removes you from the plan you have already.* You can switch back to other Medicare plans, but if you left a retiree plan that your company subsidizes, you probably won't be able to get back in.

• *Whether the plan saves you money, compared with other plans, will depend on the benefits offered and the services you use.* In general, you pay less in the years that you're healthy. In years that you require more expensive services, you could pay more. For example, the co-pay for a visit to a specialist may be much higher than that of a visit to your internist. However, there is usually an annual out-of-pocket limit on your costs.

What if you were misled into buying a Medicare Advantage plan? You can call Medicare and ask for retroactive reenrollment into the plan that you had before (including Medigap). At that point, your old plan will pick up any qualified bills that your rejected Advantage plan left unpaid. Certain government retiree plans might also take you back at the next enrollment period. Private-sector retiree plans probably won't. Starting in 2011, the government will tighten its control of private fee-for-service plans. They might evolve into something closer to PPOs.

Part D of Medicare covers prescription drugs. It's a private insurance program, funded by the government and enrollees, with many companies participating. There's no basic plan like Original Medicare. Instead you have to search through the many plans available in your area to find one that covers the drugs you need at a reasonable cost. If you enroll in a Medicare HMO or PPO, a drug plan will generally be included in your premium. The same is true for some PFFS plans.

If you're on Original Medicare, you buy a drug policy separately. Here's how Part D works:

▪ You pay a monthly premium, depending on the plan. At the start, you pay the entire cost of your prescriptions until you've met an annual dollar deductible. After that, the plan kicks in, paying part of each prescription's cost. You pay the rest in the form of a co-pay or coinsurance. (Some plans have no deductibles.)

▪ The plan continues to help with your drug bills until you and the plan, together, have spent a certain amount. Then there's a coverage gap, known as the "doughnut hole." In the gap, you normally pay all the drug costs yourself (some plans cover certain generics). For most people, that's the end of their coverage for the year.

▪ If your drug bills are high, however, and you spend another fixed amount, you'll emerge from the gap back into the *catastrophic* portion of the plan. From that point on, you're charged only a small co-payment for each prescription until the end of the year. When January rolls around, your deductibles and coinsurance start all over again.

How do you choose a drug plan? Go to www.medicare.gov.

First, look up Part D in the online booklet *Medicare & You.* You'll find an illustration showing dollar amounts for the current deductible and the doughnut hole. Each plan's doughnut hole may be a little different, but this gives you the general target.

Then start researching the plans that are available in your area, using the site's cost- and service-comparison tool. There are two tools: one called Medicare Prescription Drug Plans (for the stand-alone plans), the other called Medicare Health Plans (for the Advantage plans, many of which include prescription drugs).

In either location, enter your zip code and the list of prescription drugs that you take regularly. You'll be shown all the plans that offer those particular drugs, along with the plans' monthly premiums, the annual deductible, the estimated cost of using that plan to buy your drugs (based on your premiums and what you might pay for generics), the estimated cost if you use the plan's mail-order service, the number of pharmacies available locally, whether the plan pays for any generics when you're in the coverage gap, and a Medicare quality rating for the plan itself. All these facts make it easy to zero in on some sensible buys.

Once you have your list, click on each plan's name for additional information. You'll see what each is apt to cost once you've passed the deductible period. The more generics you use, the less likely you are to fall through the doughnut hole.

If you're not comfortable using the Internet, you can get the same help by calling Medicare at 800-633-4227. A representative will take your information and mail you a comparison of the various plans. For personal advice, call your State Health Insurance Assistance Program (SHIP), which has volunteers available. The Medicare rep will give you SHIP's phone number, or go to www.medicare.gov and click on "Find Helpful Find Phone Numbers and Websites" and then on "Related Websites."

You can enroll by phone or online. The plan will send you a card to use at your pharmacy. If you take only a couple of drugs, choose the cheapest possible plan. If your personal formulary is complicated, look for a plan that covers everything (brands *and* dosages). If that plan doesn't exist, talk to your doctor about substitutes. All the plans give you incentives to use generics—for example, by cutting the co-pays or reducing your deductible. They may require you to try a generic or low-cost brand name before okaying a more expensive version (that will be noted under "Step Therapy" when you click on a plan's information page).

Drugs are usually arranged in tiers. Your co-pay might be only $5 in Tier 1 (for generics), $25 in Tier 2 (for favored brand-name drugs), $50 or more in Tier 3 (for drugs not on the favored list), and 25 percent of the cost for specialty drugs in Tier 4. You want a plan that puts your brand-name drugs no higher than Tier 2. If you take Tier 4 drugs, your doctor may have to attest that the prescriptions are medically necessary.

Part D provides an "extra help" program for people with lower incomes. If you qualify, your prescriptions may cost you no more than $1 to $6 each.

So much for the first year on your drug plan! Every October your plan will send you information on changes: a higher premium, different co-pays, changes in its list of drugs. Some plans have been raising premiums by 10 to 20 percent. So . . . go back to Medicare.gov to look for something better. The open enrollment period runs from November 15 to December 31. If you see a plan that provides your medications at a lower cost—in premiums and co-pays—sign up for it. You'll be disenrolled from your old plan automatically. In about a week, the new plan will send you a letter of acknowledgment that you can use at your pharmacy as proof of coverage, starting January 1. It will be followed up by a membership card.

Should You Sign Up for Part D If You Don't Use Many Drugs? Yes, because you never know when you'll get sick and might need expensive medications. Waiting is certainly an option. If you join Part D later, your monthly premium will rise, permanently, by about 30 cents for every month of delay, starting from the first month you became eligible. That's not a large charge for coming into a plan a year or two late. On the other hand, the cost could be huge if you suddenly need a suite of drugs and have no insurance coverage.

When to Sign up for Medicare

If you took early Social Security retirement benefits (age 62–65): You'll be enrolled in Medicare automatically at 65. You'll get a notice when coverage starts. If you don't want Part B, check the appropriate box on the notice and send it back.

If you qualify for Social Security's disability benefits: You'll get Medicare two years after receiving your first disability check. (An unconscionable wait for disabled people who can't work and earn a living! Only people with Lou Gehrig's disease, amyotrophic lateral sclerosis, get Parts A and B automatically in the month their disease begins.)

If your kidneys fail: Sign up immediately. You'll get benefits 3 months after the start of dialysis at a medical facility or right away if you're in a self-dialysis program. Transplant patients get benefits the very month they enter the hospital.

If you're 65 and about to retire: Sign up for Medicare when you apply for Social Security. Do it during the 3 months before your 65th birthday. That way you'll be covered from the month of your birthday on. If you sign up in your birthday month, your Part B coverage starts the first day of the following month.

If you're 65 and still working: Sign up for Part A (and Part B if you want it) during the 3 months before your 65th birthday and no later than your birthday month. The same is true for a spouse covered under your plan.

If you worked past 65, stayed in an employer plan, and have just retired: Join Part B in the month that you retire or up to 3 months before. That way you'll be covered as of that month. If you join during the following seven months, you are covered from the first day of the month after the month you enroll. The same rules apply to a spouse who is covered by your plan.

Don't miss your Medicare sign-up dates! If you do and get sick, here's what happens:

1. You're normally okay on your Part A hospital bills. Anyone 65 or older who has met Social Security's work requirement can sign up for Part A at any time. You also get it if you haven't met the work requirement but are receiving Social Security benefits on the account of someone who has. If you apply late, your coverage starts six months prior to your sign-up date and picks up your qualified medical bills for that prior period. If you forget to enroll and then enter a hospital, you or your representative should fill out a statement of intent to file for Medicare benefits. That's considered an application and you'll be insured (although a formal application must be made within six months). If no statement of intent is signed at the hospital and you die, Medicare won't pay.

2. There will be a gap in your Part B coverage if you don't enroll during the three months prior to the month you turn 65. If you sign up during your birthday month or the 3 months after, you'll have to wait 1 to 3 months before your coverage starts. Any bills incurred during that period won't be paid. If you enroll later, you won't have another chance at Part B until the next general enrollment period. That's January 1 through March 31 of each year, with coverage beginning the following July 1. Your premium will be 10 percent higher for each 12-month period when you could have been enrolled but weren't.

3. No surcharges apply if you (or your spouse) work past 65, are covered by a group health plan during that period, and join Part B during the eight-month period starting the month you leave the plan or leave your job, whichever comes first. If you miss that special enrollment period, you'll have to wait for the next general enrollment and pay the 10 percent surcharge for being late.

Can You Disenroll from Medicare If You're Going to Live Abroad? Part A doesn't matter. You're in it automatically and it doesn't cost you anything more. Part B is another matter because you pay for it monthly. You can file a form and disenroll. But if you ever come back to the United States and want Part B again, your premium will be 10 percent higher for every year you could have been enrolled but weren't.* The reenrollment window is January 1 to March 31, with benefits starting on July 1. There's a penalty for rejoining the Part D drug program too.

When Can You Change Medicare Plans?

Open enrollment for changing any Medicare plan starts on November 15 and concludes on December 31. You can switch to a new Medicare Advantage plan, a new Part D plan, or Original Medicare. Your new coverage takes effect on January 1.

You can also make a switch between January 1 and March 31, but only to a new plan of the same type—meaning that you can't add or subtract a drug plan. If your Advantage plan has drug coverage, you can switch to Original Medicare plus a Part D plan, but not to an Advantage plan without drug coverage. Your new coverage starts the first of the month after you make your selection.

If you switch to Original Medicare, you can also enroll in a Medigap plan.

What Medicare Doesn't Cover

I haven't listed in detail all the benefits that Parts A and B provide. The Centers for Medicare & Medicaid Services (CMS) publish a dandy booklet, *Medicare & You,* which comes to you, free, every fall. You can also get it from Social Security at 800-633-4227 or as a download from Medicare.gov. What's more important is that you understand the gaps in Medicare that you have to pay yourself. In Advantage plans, the gaps vary by plan, so ask the salesperson

---

*There's an exception for international volunteers.

to spell them out. I've listed the ones in Original Medicare below (for the specific dollar costs, see Medicare.gov). You can plug some of these holes with a Medigap policy if you want to. All told, older people are covered for virtually all of their bills for medically necessary services, including a "Welcome to Medicare" physical, free if you take it within six months of joining Part B.

What you pay out-of-pocket when you're on Original Medicare:

1. You pay an up-front deductible when you're hospitalized. It's applied to every *benefit period,* which roughly corresponds with a spell of illness and rises a little bit every year. Once you've paid the deductible, you're covered in full for 60 days. If the need for hospital treatment continues, you pay part of the bill for the 61st day through the 90th day. After another deductible, you requalify for 90 days of coverage again and again, as long as each new hospital stay qualifies as a different benefit period.

2. After 90 days in the hospital during any single benefit period, you start dipping into what's called your *lifetime reserve days.* You get 60 of those, of which you also pay a portion. Once they're used, they're forever gone, but hardly anyone faces this long a stay today. You'd almost certainly be moved to a skilled nursing home.

3. For doctor bills and other medical services, Medicare establishes a fee schedule that varies slightly from one part of the country to another. You pay a small deductible every year. After that, Medicare pays 80 percent of the scheduled fee for that particular treatment, and you pay 20 percent. To take an example, say that $500 is the scheduled fee. Medicare pays $400, and you pay $100. In certain hardship cases, doctors may waive your share.

Most doctors charge no more than the Medicare maximum. They're called *participating* doctors, or doctors who *accept assignment.* At your very first meeting, make sure the doctor participates. Some states require docs to abide by the Medicare fee.

A few doctors insist on billing more. If you insist on seeing them, you'll have to pay the excess charge. In Original Medicare, however, they can't charge more than 15 percent above the scheduled amount (10 percent in some states). Using this example, a procedure that normally costs $500 can't be billed for more than $575. Medicare's payment toward such a bill would stay at $400 (80 percent of the scheduled fee). You'd have to pay $175. Check the explanation of Medicare benefits form that you get after every claim to be sure that the doctor didn't charge more than the allowable amount.

4. Medicare pays for "appropriate" treatment that is "medically necessary." It might deny payment for treatment that it doesn't think you need. If a decision goes against you or you think you haven't been reimbursed properly, you can and should appeal below.

5. You're insured for up to 100 days in a skilled nursing home if you're there to recuperate after spending at least 3 consecutive days in a hospital. After the 20th day, however, you pay part of the cost.

6. Important! Medicare doesn't cover the cost of long-term custodial care—for example, for people with Alzheimer's disease or who need daily help with such things as eating, dressing, and bathing. The Medicaid program pays for patients who have no substantial income or assets. If you don't qualify for Medicaid, consider buying long-term care insurance (page 468).

7. You're not insured for prescription drugs. For this you have to buy Medicare Part D.

8. Among the excluded odds and ends are: routine physicals (other than one when you first enter Medicare), eye and hearing exams, glasses, hearing aids, private-duty nurses, medical bills you incur while traveling abroad, most immunizations, dentures, routine dental and foot care, and homemaker services. Some of these can be covered through a Medicare Advantage plan.

A warning: When you go to the hospital for surgery, you may think that you've controlled your costs because your doctor accepts what Medicare will pay. But the radiologist or anesthesiologist may not accept it, which you won't realize until you get their supercharged bills. For these docs, you're a captive patient; they don't have to compete for your business by charging a "Medicare-reasonable" price. To me, the whole arrangement smacks of monopoly profits. The hospitals should not allow it. Your own doctor should not allow it. You should be able to assemble an entire team that accepts Medicare assignment.

Another warning: Hospital outpatient departments are allowed to charge you a co-pay of anywhere from 20 percent to 40 percent of Medicare's approved charge—probably more than you expected. For the same service at an ambulatory surgical center, your co-pay would be only 20 percent. For certain colon cancer screening services, the co-pay at hospitals is 25 percent.

Appealing Medicare Denials

When your doctor or hospital puts in a claim, it is usually paid. Sometimes, however, Medicare turns it down. There may be simple bookkeeping reasons—for example, the doctor's assistant may have entered the wrong code for the treatment. Alternatively, Medicare or your Advantage plan may think that the service isn't covered or didn't mesh with the diagnosis. The doctor will bill you even if Medicare doesn't pay. If the problem can't be solved administratively, you may want to appeal.

If you're in Original Medicare, your appeal rights are printed on the back of the explanation of Medicare benefits or the Medicare summary notice you receive. For a detailed fact sheet, go to www.medicare.gov/publications and look for "Rights and Protections." You'll find a lot of terrific how-to information at www.medicareinteractive.org, run by the Medicare Rights Center. Just enter "appeals" in the Search box.

If you're in a Medicare Advantage plan, the insurance company will follow Medicare's prescribed appeals procedure, reviewable by an independent board that works for Medicare. There's a similar appeals system for challenging a Part D plan that won't provide you with a specific prescription drug or won't provide it at a low, discounted cost.

For all appeals, you'll need your medical records, supporting information from your doctor, and any other helpful material that you can dig up. Follow the rules to the letter, don't miss the deadlines, and don't let anyone discourage you. Thousands of people win their cases.

Plugging the Medigap

If you're in original Medicare, how will you cover the expenses that Medicare doesn't? A retiree health plan may plug the gaps, if you're lucky enough to have one. Medicaid pays the bills for many low-income people. Medicare Advantage plans fill some of the gaps but not all of them. For everyone else, the answer is a Medicare-supplement policy, popularly known as Medigap insurance.

Medigap policies are sold by private insurers. You cannot be rejected for reasons of health or charged a higher than normal premium if you apply for Medigap within six months after turning 65 and joining Medicare Part B. You also get guaranteed admission under several other circumstances. For example: (1) You joined a Medicare Advantage plan at 65 and, within 12 months, switched to Original Medicare plus Medigap. (2) You started out with Original Medicare and Medigap, switched to an Advantage plan, then switched back again within 12 months. In this particular case, your free pass is limited to your old Medigap plan and just a few others. (3) You started out with Original Medicare plus a union or employer group plan (including retiree or COBRA coverage) that filled in the gaps in Medicare, and that coverage is ending.

At this writing, Medigap insurers can refuse to pay for preexisting conditions during the first six months the plan is in effect, if you did not have prior coverage. But some of them pay anyway.

Medigap policies cannot be used with Medicare Advantage plans.

The Standard Medigap Plans

Medigap policies come in different standard forms. Each one has a different benefit mix—from bare bones to rich—but the mix doesn't change from one insurer to another. So the companies are competing solely on service, reliability, and price. All the policies aren't available in every state or from every insurer. Three states—Massachusetts, Minnesota, and Wisconsin—have standardized policies of their own.

When you join Medicare Part B at 65, you have six months in which to buy Medigap insurance at standard rates, regardless of your health. Once you have the coverage, Medigap policies are guaranteed renewable unless you don't pay your premiums or materially misstate your health status on your application.

Medigap insurers set their prices in different ways. Some fix your premium based on your age when the policy was bought (*issue age*). Others charge everyone the same (*community rating,* required in certain states). Yet others raise your premium as you age (*attained age*). To me, attained age is a form of bait and switch. You're lured with a low starting price. Once you're locked in, your premiums rise steeply. When you reach your 80s, the premiums may become a serious burden.

When buying Medigap insurance, ask the agent for a policy with a premium that is fixed for life—and be sure that's specified in the contract. Such coverage will cost more at the start, but you'll be able to budget for it and will probably pay less over a lifetime. (One caveat: premiums can rise if your state approves a general increase for all the company's policies in that particular book of business.)

If you're in poor health and didn't sign up for Medigap during those six open months, some insurers will still accept all comers. Also, check with your state's insurance department. Some states require the Blues and HMOs to accept all applicants during open enrollment periods.

Whatever you do, buy from a company with high safety-and-soundness ratings (page 405). Reject any insurer whose literature implies that it's somehow connected with Medicare or Social Security. The government does not sell Medigap insurance.

It's illegal, by the way, for an agent to sell you more than one Medigap policy or to sell Medigap to someone in an Advantage plan. If you buy a new policy, you're supposed to sign a statement saying that you plan to cancel the old one. Be sure to do so as soon as your new coverage takes effect.

After you sign, you have 30 days to change your mind. If you regret your move, mail back the policy and ask for a premium refund (registered mail is a good idea).

Under a program called Medicare Select, you can buy many of these policies at a lower premium. In return, you have to stay within a network of certain doctors, hospitals, and clinics. As you get older, however, your premium may rise. At 65, Select costs less than a regular Medigap policy from the same insurer (although it may not be the cheapest plan on the market). By 75, Select policies often cost more.

If Your Income Is Low. You don't have to buy your own Medigap coverage. The Medicaid program may cover similar services, or it may buy you one of the Medigap policies. Two other state-run options exist for low-income people: the Qualified Medicare Beneficiary Program, for the old or disabled whose incomes are at or below the poverty level; and the Specified Low-Income Medicare Beneficiary Program, for the elderly just above the poverty level. Apply to the state Medicaid office to see if you're eligible.

A Little-Known Gap in Medigap. If you're under 65 and on Medicare because you're disabled or suffering from kidney failure, you can't buy Medigap except in the handful of states that require insurers to take all comers. Some states make coverage available in their high-risk pools.

Paying Claims. Your Medicare carrier will handle both your Medicare and Medigap claims if your doctor accepts Medicare assignment and indicates on the Medicare form that you want all the payments made to him or her directly. You'll get an explanation of Medicare benefits form explaining what was paid and what you still owe, if anything.

Should You Really Buy Medigap Insurance?

With any insurance, *first-dollar coverage* is expensive, relative to what you get. "First dollar" means no deductible. The insurer picks up the bill from the very first dollar you owe—for example, the annual deductible for doctor bills. A basic rule of insurance is that you should pay those first dollars yourself.

Another rule is that it's not worth insuring expenses that are likely to occur, because the cost of insurance may be roughly what you'd pay anyway. With first-dollar coverage, for example, all you're doing is paying those medical bills in advance with administrative costs and a profit built in for the insurance company.

Insurance should cover dangers that are plausible but remote and would impose a terrible burden if you had to shoulder the cost yourself. Most of the holes that Medigap policies plug aren't very large. Assuming that you enter retirement with a decent amount of savings, I could argue that you don't need Medigap at all. Your money is better spent on long-term care insurance. Long-term care is more than a gap in your Medicare coverage—it's a crater. That's the kind of risk to insure.

Retiree Group Coverage

These wonderful plans are becoming an endangered species. (Don't you wish you could put them on a "protected" list?) In companies that still offer this benefit, your group plan may transform itself into supplemental Medicare coverage when you retire. You'll have to sign up for Medicare Parts A and B, but your company may cover most of the Part B premium cost. The policy will probably cover the gaps in Medicare listed on page 463, plus such extras as home care, payments for prescription drugs, and perhaps dental care. There are no waiting periods or exclusions for preexisting conditions.

Check the booklet that describes your costs and benefits, including those for your spouse. It will almost certainly state that the company has the right to change the plan. I call this the "maybe not" clause, as in "I'm paying your medical bills today, but tomorrow, maybe not." Thousands of retirees have discovered this clause already. Benefits are being shaved, annual premiums raised, and, in some cases, policies canceled altogether. As long as you have it, hang on to it. If you lose your retiree plan, you still have Medicare Parts A and B and can buy Part D and Medigap or a Medicare Advantage plan.

Long-Term Care (LTC) Insurance

Long-term care policies address themselves to a new insurance market: a generation of Americans fearful not of dying too soon but of living too long. These policies pay for custodial care if you're no longer able to manage yourself—because of Alzheimer's, perhaps, or because an illness or accident makes it hard for you to perform the simple activities of daily life.

Today the vast majority of long-term care, including insured care, is given outside nursing homes—in your own home, an adult day care facility, or an assisted-living community. Families typically step up. At this writing, home health aides clock in at around $20 an hour. The median cost of a private unit in an assisted living community is about $36,000 a year. If a nursing home is the only answer, the price is averaging $76,000 a year. Before you gasp, remember that a nursing home is essentially a medical cruise ship. It provides room, board, entertainment, laundry, social services, nursing, and personal care, every day, for life, at a cost that runs lower than you'd pay for a quality Holiday Inn. That doesn't make it affordable, but at least puts its charges in perspective.

What is your chance of needing long-term care? Roughly 6 out of every 10 people who are 65 will need it at some point in their lives, although not necessarily in a nursing home. About 4 out of 10 will enter a nursing home for at least a short stay. Of those 4, about half will stay for a year or more, with the odds much higher for women than for men.

LTC insurance is expensive and difficult to get if you're not in excellent health. It's mainly for people with upper-middle incomes and assets. Married couples should make every effort to buy a policy. It helps preserve the standard of living of the healthy spouse if one of them takes sick.

For single people, the question is more complicated. On the one hand, you're free to use your money to pay for your own long-term care, so you might prefer to add to your savings rather than buy an LTC policy. If you're a widow or widower, consider canceling any coverage you already have. On the other hand, you might think that your assets aren't sufficient to cover your home care or nursing home care, in which case a policy would be useful. You might also want a policy if it's important to leave more money to your heirs.

If you're not in this upper-middle group, LTC insurance will probably cost more than you can afford. For long-term care, you'll rely on your family, neighbors, church, temple, or various social services for support. If you have to enter a nursing home, you'll turn to Medicaid.

Medicaid and LTC

Medicaid is a medical social services program funded by the federal and state governments and administered by the states. It steps in when you need custodial care and don't have the money to pay for it. Each state's program is a little different, but they have the same objective: they want you to pay as much as you can for care without leaving your spouse destitute.

Your Medicaid application is handled through the nursing home you choose (or that's available to you). You have to disclose your income and assets.

If you're single with no dependents at home, you're generally expected to use your money to pay for your care. When the money runs out, Medicaid will start paying the bills.

If you're married and only one of you is sick, a certain amount of income and assets is set aside for the healthy spouse. Anything over that limit has to go toward the nursing home bill.

Medicaid looks at your financial history for the past five years, to see if you gave away any of your income and assets. If so, you will have to wait for a period of time (as much as five years) before Medicaid will pick up your bills.

Couples worry that the spouse at home will be impoverished by the other's care. But the various Medicaid exemptions protect people with average incomes and assets. Here's what the healthy spouse is usually allowed to keep: the family home, all the furnishings, a car, a term life insurance policy, his or her Individual Retirement Account, a few lesser assets, some additional savings (ranging from around $25,000 to $100,000, depending on the state), and all the income received in his or her sole name (or a modest part of the income payable to the spouse in the nursing home). For most 70-year-old couples, that covers everything. The ill spouse will be able to receive Medicaid right away, with little or nothing taken from the spouse at home. If you're single and one of your children lived with you and took care of you, the house and furnishings also can be preserved.

That's a very general account. States have all sorts of special rules. If possible, you should save enough money to pay for at least six months of care before applying to Medicaid. Private-pay patients have access to much better nursing homes and in more convenient locations. If you enter as a Medicaid patient, the only open bed may be in a home that's many miles away.

For home care, middle-income people struggle by themselves or with the help of free social services. Very few Medicaid programs offer any help. For full-time custodial care, however, you can get financial aid.

LTC Insurance for Those Too Rich for Medicaid

If you've piled up a lot of income and assets, you're expected to pay for your care yourself. That's where LTC insurance comes in. Large companies may offer it as a group benefit, which is a terrific option. Otherwise you need to sort through the various types of individual policies. In some cases, individual coverage might be cheaper for a married couple in good health than their company's group plan.

When Should You Buy? The younger you are, the cheaper it is. If you buy at 50 and hold for 35 years (to age 85), you'll pay less than if you buy at 75 and hold for 10 years, even counting what that early money could have earned if invested elsewhere. Furthermore, you generally can't buy a policy unless you're in reasonably good health, so the longer you wait, the greater the risk that you won't be insurable. Among applicants 50 to 59, 14 percent are rejected on grounds of health, the American Association for Long-Term Care Insurance reports. That number almost doubles for applicants 60 to 69 and rises to 45 percent for people in their 70s. (This doesn't count the number of people in less than perfect health who have to pay higher premiums.)

On the other hand, you can't count on keeping those low premiums you copped at 55. When insurance companies get more claims than they expected, as has been happening with LTC, the policies become less profitable. They can't raise the price on individual policies, but they can—and are—raising prices on whole books of LTC business. In your 70s, you might learn that to keep your coverage, you have to pay more.

The size of the premium you pay will depend on the benefits you buy. At 50, you're probably looking at $700 to $1,200 a year for individual coverage if you're in tip-top health. At 70, it's $4,000 to $5,500, if you can get coverage at all.

Which Type of Policy Should You Choose? There are two types of policies. *Indemnity* policies pay a flat daily amount, regardless of your cost of care. You might choose anything from $50 to $250 a day. No proof of expenses is required once you've qualified for benefits, although your health will be checked from time to time. *Reimbursement* policies pay a percentage of the actual cost (often 100 percent), up to the daily maximum you bought. Reimbursement plans may require more medical paperwork but are generally less expensive. (They're also more likely to produce wrangles over claims.)

How Much Coverage Can You Afford? Estimate how much you could afford to pay for long-term care from your 401(k), Social Security, and other sources of income and savings. Compare that with a nursing home's actual daily cost and insure yourself for the difference. If you could pay $50 a day and the home costs $200, you'd want to be covered for $150 a day. If you can afford it, cover yourself for the full amount. (You might get away with less expensive home care, but always insure for the worst.)

Next consider how long you're willing to wait before benefits begin. The longer the wait (called the "elimination period") the lower the monthly premium. A 90-day wait might require you to pay $20,000 before the policy kicked in. But your premium might be 10 to 20 percent lower than if you took a 30-day wait, depending on your age. Most new LTC policies don't pay at all unless your disability is expected to last at least 90 days.

Leaving aside short stays of three months or less, the average nursing home stay appears to be somewhere around three years. Around 10 percent of the patients stay five years or longer. A five-year benefit costs 15 to 20 percent more than a three-year benefit. A lifetime benefit adds another 25 to 50 percent more.

Whether to buy a three-year, five-year, or lifetime benefit depends on how you want to handle your personal finances. If you enter a nursing home and out-live the policy, you'll have to spend your own money, which may be okay with you. If it's not, buy a longer-term policy. If both the insurance and your personal savings run out, the nursing home keeps you for whatever Medicaid pays.

Policies may have dollar caps rather than time limits. The higher the cap, the higher the premium you'll pay. An unlimited cap covers you for life. A $250,000 cap might last three years, depending on what local nursing homes charge, and cost about half as much. Some policies have both time and dollar caps.

An important question for your LTC agent, rarely asked: How does the LTC insurer calculate how fast you're using up your benefits? Some policies pay for a specified number of days, even if your expenses on some of those days were small. The better policies go by dollars, covering you until a specified dollar pool has been depleted.

If you're married, consider a joint policy. You can buy a pooled or shared-care benefit that covers you both for much less than the price of two individual policies. Unmarried couples qualify too. Divorce tip: If a split is imminent, buy the LTC policy first. At divorce, you're entitled to two separate policies and can probably keep the discount you got.

What Should the Policy Include? Read the policy carefully when it arrives— and I mean the actual contract, not the short sales brochure. Some literature waffles; some salespeople misspeak. You have 30 days during which you can revoke the insurance and get a refund. Here's what you want to see in a long-term care policy, in black and white:

1. Comprehensive coverage. Your policy should click in if you're suffer-ing from Alzheimer's or a similar brain disease, or if you're unable to per-form at least two of the following activities of daily living: bathing, dressing, toileting, continence, eating, and transferring (for example, from your bed to a chair). Some policies count only five of those activities, perhaps leaving out bathing. Yet the ability to bathe yourself is often the thing that goes first. Restrictive policies may not pay until you fail three of the tests.

Check what the insurer means by "unable to perform." Some policies won't pay unless you can't perform those activities without help. Less restrictive policies pay if you merely need supervision. If the policy is vague, benefits are easier to deny.

Also find out if you're covered for nervous or mental disorders other than those traceable to an organic disease such as Alzheimer's. Most LTC policies exclude them. They also exclude coverage for drug or alcohol addiction and attempted suicide.

2. Payment for care in any licensed facility: a nursing home, assisted-living facility, adult day care facility, hospice, or any other approved setting. Avoid policies that limit you to particular types of places. You and your doctor should be able to decide on the best venue. You should also be covered for every level of care: skilled, intermediate, custodial, medical, and therapeutic.

3. A home care option. Most nursing home policies offer riders for certain types of home care. The annual home care benefit should equal at least half of the money available for a nursing home. Some policies set up one benefit for nursing homes and a separate one for home care. More flexible policies give you a pot of benefits that can be used in any qualified setting—home, community, or nursing home. The latter type of coverage is more expensive, but the dollars may go further and you're provided with more choices.

If your budget is limited, buy only nursing home coverage. That's the potentially catastrophic cost. Home care is a lovely extra, but only if you can afford it.

Some people do exactly the opposite: they buy LTC policies for home care only. But you're deluding yourself if you think that your policy's limited benefits will keep you home indefinitely. Any condition that triggers home care coverage will probably land you in a nursing home, and sooner rather than later. You'll then be stuck with paying for your care yourself.

4. An inflation option. This is chiefly for younger buyers. If you choose a $100 benefit at age 50, what will that buy when you're 80? Sweet nothing, that's what. You need an inflation rider—and, unfortunately, it's the most expensive rider on the list. A typical rider adds 5 percent to your benefit each year. That can be a simple 5 percent or a compounded 5 percent. The latter costs more but is also worth more. You might also have the option of linking your benefit to the consumer price index, although at this writing it's rising much more slowly than health care costs.

Some policies build in inflation costs. They're more expensive to start with, but the monthly premiums typically remain fixed. Other policies give you the right to buy future inflation adjustments. They're less expensive at first, but they cost much more when you start adding coverage at later ages. The choice will be dictated solely by your pocketbook. Older buyers—say, in their late 60s—may not want to bother with inflation protection. Their policies are already expensive enough.

5. Level premiums. If you buy at age 55, paying a "guaranteed" premium of $1,200 a year, you want that $1,200 to last for the life of the policy. In theory, it will. In practice, the insurer (with the state's permission) can raise prices on all LTC policies of that class if they're not profitable enough. Buyers should be prepared to pay more to keep their coverage in force. Some policies specify that your premiums will rise as you age, but that's a risky deal. By the time you reach 70, you may not be able to afford your coverage anymore, and that's when you'll need it the most. As a rule of thumb, your LTC premium shouldn't exceed 6 percent of your retirement income.

6. Waiver of premium. You should be able to stop paying premiums when you start collecting benefits or if you've collected benefits for a certain period of time. The waiver should cover home care as well as nursing home care.

7. Preexisting conditions. Most group policies accept all comers, regardless of health, but won't cover preexisting conditions right away. A preexisting condition is generally defined as an ailment you had in the six-month period before joining the plan. After a six-month wait, those ailments have to be covered. Some plans offer more liberal terms or even accept you with no wait at all. Others may exclude people with certain conditions, such as a previous stroke. Individual policies, or group policies with health questionnaires, don't have waiting periods for preexisting conditions. But they may exclude coverage for certain illnesses or refuse to accept you, period.

8. Lapse protection. Loss of memory is a leading reason for needing nursing home care. Unfortunately, one of the things you might have forgotten to pay is the premium on your LTC insurance. To protect yourself: (1) Ask the company to notify at least one friend or family member, and preferably three, if your policy is being canceled for nonpayment of premiums. (2) Tell those friends and relatives about the company's reinstatement rules, which will be printed in your contract. Where there's memory lapse, your insurer will usually restore your coverage if no more than five months have passed—assuming that your relatives get the back premiums paid. (3) Arrange for your premiums to be paid automatically through payroll deduction or from your bank account.

9. Nonforfeiture benefits. Skip them. They provide a limited amount of long-term care if you let the policy lapse after a certain number of years—so it looks as if you're "getting something back" for the premiums you paid. No, you're not. This rider is hugely expensive. You're better off using the money for almost anything else.

Cutting Your Costs. LTC premiums have been rising by 20 and 25 percent, as people live longer and make more claims than the insurers expected. Not surprisingly, sales aren't strong. To attract new business, especially from the 40-ish crowd, insurers are offering pared-down policies at lower costs. Here's what's out there:

- *Policies that let you start small.* You might buy an LTC benefit of, say, $100 a day. You may be able to increase it in the future without taking a health exam.
- *Policies with co-pays.* There's an up-front deductible. After that, the policy covers only 80 percent of your qualified expenses.
- *Flat-pay policies.* If you qualify for benefits, you get a check, no matter where you're getting care or how much it costs.

Buying LTC Through Your Employer. Jump at an LTC policy offered through your company. You may get a discount compared with what's on sale in the individual market. The insurer will usually accept people in less than perfect health, if you sign up within 30 days of being hired. That doesn't mean everyone, however. There are some knockout conditions—for example, a recent stroke, use of a wheelchair, or AIDS.

Your spouse might also be able to buy, but not on a favored basis. He or she will probably have to pass a health exam. Group plans don't provide discounts to couples, so if both of you are buying and you're both healthy, check the company's offer against what you could buy independently. Spousal discounts can run as high as 40 percent.

Ask what happens when you leave the company. You want to be sure that you can take the policy with you at no increase in price. If you can't, buy your LTC coverage somewhere else. You want it to stay with you for life.

If your employer switches to a new LTC insurer, stay with the old one if you can. That way your premium won't go up. If you switch to the new insurance company, you'll probably have to pay more because you're older now. In some cases, however, the new insurer will let you keep paying the old rate.

If you bought your plan through your spouse's employer and your spouse dies or splits, you're entitled to continue coverage on your own.

Some professional associations provide LTC coverage too. There's usually a nominal discount and simplified health underwriting.

LTC Insurance Versus Medigap. When people start Medicare at 65, they often buy a rich Medigap policy to plug the holes in their government insurance. But Medigap covers a lot of bills that you could probably pay yourself. By contrast, a stay in a nursing home could wipe you out. If money is tight, consider LTC coverage first. More extensive Medigap coverage should be lower on your list if you buy it at all.

A Special Note to Late-Marrying Couples. Long-term care may become a mare's nest when an older couple marries and they each have children with a former or deceased spouse. Their respective children expect to inherit from their parent. At a certain point, in fact, they start thinking of their parent's money as their own. If one of you enters a nursing home, the other may have some financial responsibility—and, trust me, your kids won't like it. You're spending *their* money on a second spouse. You can't get rid of the LTC responsibility by writing a prenuptial agreement. I have no particular solution to this problem but thought I'd mention it so that you can think about it.

Tax Breaks for LTC Insurance

■ *Part of your premium payment qualifies as a deductible medical expense, whether you buy employee coverage or an individual LTC policy.* For individuals, the size of your write-off depends on your age and rises every year to reflect increases in health care costs. To make use of this tax break, however, you have to itemize deductions. You will also need high medical expenses. Qualified expenses can't be deducted unless they exceed 7.5 percent of your adjusted gross income.

■ *If your LTC policy reimburses you for your actual expenses, you get those benefits tax free.* That assumes that your policy is *tax qualified*, as almost all new plans are today. If you're paid a flat per diem rate, the benefits are tax free up to a fixed amount. Your deduction can exceed that fixed cap if your actual medical expenses do.

■ *When you spend your own money on long-term care, it can count as a tax-deductible medical expense.* You can write off qualified home care and community care expenses as well as nursing home expenses. If your income is low and your uninsured LTC expenses high, this write-off could even eliminate your taxable income for the year.

■ *Various types of state and federal tax deductions are available to small businesses that buy LTC insurance.* Check them out at the Web site of the American Association for Long-Term Care Insurance (www.aaltci.org). The site has good consumer information, too.

Choosing an LTC Insurer

Benefits vary so much that two policies cannot be compared by price. Ask your insurance agent to show you what two or three different companies offer so you can get a feel for the kinds of choices you might make. Rates and acceptable health conditions also vary from one company to another.

Whatever you do, pick a company with top safety ratings (page 405) that appears to be firmly committed to selling LTC insurance. This business has shown itself to be pretty risky. Companies come and go. An unusually low-priced policy may be canceled after just a few years, leaving you high and dry. At this writing, companies considered committed to the business include Genworth, John Hancock, MetLife, Mutual of Omaha, Prudential, and Unum. To find an experienced agent, go to www.aaltci.org and click on "Find a Local Long-Term Care Insurance Professional." Also consider a large membership group such as AARP, which connects you with an insurance agent.

While we're on the subject of reliability, let's deconstruct that lovely phrase "guaranteed renewable," which almost all new policies are. This means only one thing: the insurer can't cancel your policy individually unless you stop paying premiums. But it can abandon the business in your state entirely, and there goes your "guarantee." That's why it's so important that your company be devoted to LTC insurance. You need to believe that someone will say "Yes, ma'am" 30 years from now when your granddaughter calls to activate your benefits.

LTC Alternatives

- *Buy a combination LTC policy and life insurance policy.* This product is for people with a large sum of money that they don't need for current retirement income. You buy a single-premium life policy. If you need long-term care, you get up to 100 percent of the death benefit in cash, tax free. If you die without using any or all of the benefit, the policy's proceeds go to your heirs, also tax free. The portion of your premium that funds the LTC coverage counts as a deductible medical expense.
- *Buy a combination LTC policy and deferred annuity.* This is for people in poorer health who can't buy life insurance at a reasonable price. You dump money into the annuity, which accumulates tax deferred. Money pulled out for long-term care will be tax-free. If you die, the earnings are taxed when your heirs inherit. If you already have a deferred annuity, you can switch to a combo in a 1035 tax-free exchange.

- *Buy a disability policy that turns into long-term care insurance when you retire or at a specific age, such as 65.* There are a few of these in the marketplace.
- *See if your existing cash-value life insurance policy will let you draw on some or all of the policy's face value to help cover nursing home bills.* But do this sparingly. Your family may need the policy proceeds if you die.
- *Take a reverse mortgage on your home* (page 1156) and use that to help pay your nursing home bills.
- *Join a continuing care or life care community.* This is LTC insurance by another name. The community provides medical care, home care, and social services. You pay a large up-front sum plus a monthly maintenance fee, which will rise as the cost of maintaining the community does. You also agree to pay other costs that may be assessed in the future. To be accepted, you have to be able to live independently. You move into a house or apartment, as you choose, and carry on with your life.

If you start to fail, you move to more supervised quarters that include home care. If that's not enough, you move to the community's nursing home. The community will also have close ties to a nearby hospital. With some contracts, you prepay for certain amounts of nursing care; with others, you're guaranteed access to care but pay for each service that you use.

When considering these arrangements, don't judge only by the living quarters or activities. Take a good look at the home care apartments and nursing home to see if they're really of the quality you want. Talk to some of the residents, especially the sick ones. Be sure the facility is accredited by the Continuing Care Accreditation Commission sponsored by the American Association of Homes and Services for the Aging (AAHSA).

Among the other things to check: the audited financial statement (is the line labeled "fund balance" or "net assets" in the black?); written assurance from an actuary that the community is on a sound financial footing; a history of the community's rise in monthly fees (if the fees aren't keeping up with inflation, that may portend a big rise in the future); any lawsuits against the community; the occupancy rate (if the rate is falling, why?); and your financial options if you decide to leave. A lawyer should read the contract and explain it to you before you sign. You'll find a list of communities and tons of tips and advice at AAHSA's Web site (www.aahsa.org). You can also telephone 202-783-2242 for a free list of accredited communities plus a brochure on how to evaluate them.

Don't Count on Being Cared for by One of Your Adult Children, in Your Home or Theirs. What with jobs, grandchildren, mobility, illness, and divorce, your children may not have the time, energy, or resources to take up the burden of your care. They will love you. They will worry about you. They will supervise. But if you guilt-trip them into doing it all themselves, you may hurt their marriages or their health, cost them their jobs, cause them to turn down a job promotion, or spark tension between the caregiver and the rest of the siblings who pop in only on holidays. It's better to spend your savings on LTC insurance or nursing home bills and leave the kids nothing than to leave them money in a cup of bitterness.

The Medicaid Ploy

If you're poor, with a modest income and few assets, the Medicaid program will cover your nursing home bills. It's taxpayer supported and administered by the states.

If you have upper-middle-class assets, you'll have to spend some of them on your own long-term care. In general, here's what's likely to happen:

For single people: You'll probably sell your house and put that money, along with your other savings and income, toward your nursing home bills. Once your savings are gone, Medicaid will pick up the cost for the rest of your life. If you give your money to your heirs to try to avoid supporting yourself, Medicaid will penalize you by refusing to cover your nursing home bill for up to five years (and perhaps longer, in the future).

For married people, when only one of the couple needs custodial care: The healthy spouse keeps certain assets, depending on the state. The rest of the money has to be spent on the nursing home. If that portion of the money runs out, Medicaid pays. For what the healthy spouse is allowed to keep, see page 470. Middle-class couples generally find that all their assets are protected. Upper-middles, however, have to spend some of their savings on the nursing home.

That makes them unhappy. They want to keep more of their money for the spouse at home or for their heirs. Enter the "poverty makers": eldercare lawyers who teach you how to look poor on paper even when you're not. Their objective is to help you hide or sequester your assets—through hidey-holes, giveaways, and trusts—so you won't have to pay for your own long-term care. Your kids get your assets, and we, the taxpayers, pick up your costs.

To my mind, this is a cynical misuse of a public program, so I'm not going to tell you how to do it. There's nothing illegal about Medicaid planning; it's simply unethical. Often, the parents don't want to take this course. They're pushed into it by their kids.

Here's the ethical approach: provide for your future yourself! You can:

- *buy long-term care insurance;*
- *buy one of the combo life insurance/annuity/LTC products;*
- *tap your home equity with a reverse mortgage;*
- *use the Partnership for Long-Term Care program,* at this writing, available in about 20 states. You buy an LTC policy that lasts for a certain period of time. If you continue to need care, you can apply for Medicaid without having to spend any more of your personal money.
- *pay your own nursing home bills as long as you can.* If your income and assets fall below a specified minimum, Medicaid will step in. You'll stay in exactly the same nursing home (although you might have to move from a single room to a double). You'll get the same care you got before. And because you started out as a private-pay patient, you'll be in a higher-quality home than if you had gone the "false poverty" route. Sometimes the state will put you on Medicaid while you're alive, then recoup the cost from your estate after you die.

Haven't you always told your kids that they should support themselves, not run around looking for a handout? The same goes for you at the end of your life. Medicaid is for people who earned modest amounts of money and couldn't possibly have built a huge pile of LTC cash. Those who do have a pile should pay their own custodial bills, not hit up the taxpayers for support. End of sermon. Amen.

Getting Paid

The vast majority of health insurance claims are faithfully paid. But then there are those unhappy few.

Usually these are claims with a problem at the edge. Maybe there's a technical question about whether the insurance applies. Maybe there's evidence that might be construed as fraud even when it's not. Maybe the company wants to improve its profits by toughing out every marginal case.

In denying marginal claims said to fall outside the plan, an insurer initially has little to lose. You might give up and go away. You might not find a lawyer willing to help, if the claim is small. If you do find a lawyer, the insurer can usually settle—and settlement might take a year or more. You might even die (although your heirs might sue).

If you have an individual or association plan, complain to the state insurance department before getting a lawyer. That might help settle your problem, at no cost to you. If that fails and you think your insurer is dealing in bad faith, see if you can get a lawyer interested. The law is on your side if: (1) The language of the policy is unclear, or (2) the terms of the policy could reasonably lead you to think you were covered, and (3) you told the truth on your application. Nor will the law let you be stripped of your coverage on a technicality, such as missing the date for filing the claim. (If you have an employee plan, however, you'll be bound by rules that make it almost impossible to win—see page 440.)

The tragedy is that while you're arguing, a family member lies desperately ill with no one on hand to pay the bills. Without guaranteed payment, hospitals, doctors, and therapists may be reluctant to rally around.

No one can predict when an insurer might turn tough, refusing treatment or denying claims. But here are some precautions to take.

Before signing up for individual coverage, get an explanation for every single little thing you don't understand. That's one of the services that insurance agents are paid for, so spend as much time as you need. Put notes in the margin of the contract or sales literature to remind yourself of what the agent said (he or she may misstate, which could be important evidence in an administrative hearing or in court). If you don't like what you see in a new policy you've bought, you have 30 days to return it and get a refund.

Pay special attention to the exclusions, including the unstated ones. For example, the policy may cover treatment in a "skilled nursing facility." By inference, this means no coverage in other types of nursing homes. You want a policy that covers you everywhere.

Check the definition of a dependent. Are your 18-year-old children covered automatically, or will you have to prove that they haven't become independent adults? Is your college student covered even though he or she is studying part-time? It might not occur to you to think about your kids in the context of long-term care, but bad things have happened on snowy ski slopes.

If you're buying employer-sponsored coverage, the booklet that explains the benefits is effectively your copy of the contract, although you can be ruled by definitions in a master copy that you've never seen.

If your claim is denied, get a written explanation for why the company turned you down. Ask for specifics, not generalities. Check the reasons against the language in your policy. If the language can be read in another way and you have an individual or association plan, you may have a case. Write to the person who heads the insurer's claims department (call the company to get the name). That sometimes stirs someone to take another look at your case. Talk to your insurance agent, who has an interest in keeping you happy. The state insurance department might also be able to help, unless you're in an employee plan (some states help with employee plans too). Complain, complain, complain. Nothing will happen if you don't.

Keep complete records of your claim, starting with the medical bills and doctor's report. Keep copies of letters. Note the dates and purpose of telephone calls, whom you spoke with, and what was said. Follow up those calls with a short letter. This strengthens your hand if you have to sue. It might show bad faith on the insurer's part.

The Trap of Post-Claims Underwriting

Here's a shameful practice that should be banned by health insurance reform. It's called post-claims underwriting or "recision." The company trumps up reasons not to pay a valid but expensive claim.

To *underwrite* means to evaluate you as a health risk. You fill in a questionnaire and take blood tests when you apply for a policy. The insurer uses this information to decide whether to accept you and, if so, to set your premium.

When you pay premiums, you naturally assume that you're insured. But if you develop a high-cost illness, the company—even a big-name company—might try to kick you out. It will go back over your application and your health records with a magnifying glass, looking for some little thing you failed to mention. If they find a "material omission," they will reject your claim, return your premiums, and say you misled them—even if the omission was a simple oversight and has nothing to do with the illness you have now. To take an example—you might have forgotten to mention the heart palpitations you had during a stressful, long-ago divorce. You haven't had them since and never thought of them as a "health condition." Now you need heart surgery. A bad-faith company may dig up those old palpitations, claim that you lied on your application, and refuse to pay.

The contract typically says that insurers cannot challenge your policy after two years have passed, except for fraud. But they can call a material omission fraud, and they get to define a "material omission."

In some states, this practice is illegal. A national reform bill would make it illegal everywhere. Until that happens, however, here's what you can do:

■ *Tell the whole truth on your health insurance application.* You're kidding yourself if you get health insurance under false pretenses. When you file a claim, you'll find that the policy isn't worth the paper it's written on.

■ *List everything—every operation, every illness, every medication you take or have taken, every physical condition, even athlete's foot.* Don't listen to an insurance agent who says, "No one needs to know that." Remember, any significant medical facts may already be on file at the Medical Information Bureau (page 483). Check your MIB file to see what's there.

■ *If the agent fills in the application, make that sure he or she does it right.* Some agents put "no" where they should put "yes," so that the company will accept you. If your claim is rejected later, it's no skin off the agent's nose. He or she will claim that the error was yours. It's essential that you read the application. Don't sign if it's incorrect.

■ *When you get your health insurance policy, a copy of your application should be attached.* Check it for accuracy. If you find a mistake, notify the company in writing and ask for an answer in writing. The agent might say over the phone that the mistake doesn't matter, but it might matter very much when you file a claim.

■ *If you're currently covered, don't exaggerate an illness in order to claim an insurance payment.* Your doctor might agree to call a routine office visit "flu," but if you change insurers, three cases of "flu" might put you into a high-risk pool. "Flu" might even be excluded from your next policy altogether.

Your Medical History

Few people have ever heard of MIB, formerly known as the Medical Information Bureau. But if you've applied for individual health, life, or disability income insurance, the insurer may have checked with MIB before it decided to write the policy.

MIB exists, first, to catch people who falsify their insurance applications. If one insurer learns that you've had a heart attack, that information goes to MIB. If you approach another insurer and fail to mention your heart condition, MIB will tell the tale.

But the truthful may run into trouble too. Doctors who examine you for insurance coverage will add to your record any health information that they think is relevant to life expectancy. Usually it is—but sometimes the information may mean little or nothing. A squiggle in an EKG may be well within the normal range, but the doctor may have sent the insurer a brief, coded description of it as part of the report. The insurer will transmit it to MIB. If you apply for more coverage, a future insurer might rule out anyone with an EKG report on file. You may be in perfect health, but the insurer won't take you at low, preferred rates. Instead you'll be asked to pay the higher, standard rate.

By law, you have to be told that your MIB file influenced the adverse decision. You can get a free copy, check it for accuracy, and challenge anything you believe to be mistaken. MIB then contacts the insurer that submitted it. The insurer is supposed to make a "reasonable effort" to check with its medical source and "appropriate efforts" to contact other sources you suggest. If the report turns out to be wrong or incomplete, it's deleted or amended. If the insurer stands by the report, you can add a statement of dispute. You can also ask an insurer to reexamine you and have a doctor write a letter on your behalf. If your condition has changed, your MIB file can be amended, although the original information may remain. New reports added to the system, including updates of old ones, stay in the system seven years.

MIB keeps files on about 19 million people who have applied for individually underwritten insurance during the past seven years. Its reports provide brief codes that show specific illnesses, overweight and underweight, high blood pressure, pertinent X-rays and lab tests, suicide attempts, psychiatric disorders, a family history of certain diseases, drug addiction or alcoholism (confirmed by the applicant or a medical source), and any other risk information that the insurance company considers relevant to health or longevity. A nonmedical category notes reckless driving records, participation in hazardous sports, amateur flying, and applications for much more life insurance than seems warranted. This kind of material comes from your application and from private insurance investigators (You authorize investigations and MIB searches when you sign an insurance application.) Disability insurers use MIB to find out if you're carrying policies that you didn't mention on your application.

Nothing in the file is verified by MIB. That's left to the insurer and you. If you're simply checking your file and haven't been turned down for insurance, call MIB at 866-692-6901 for a free copy of your consumer file. Additional copies or requests made by mail cost $10.50. For more information, visit www.mib.com. What will happen to MIB's files under health reform remains to be seen.

Coda

Health care anxiety floats through our lives—finding a job, losing a job, getting married, getting divorced, moving, having children, retiring early, or just plain paying the premiums on the policies we're lucky enough to have. Medical bankruptcies are soaring. People who never got behind on a bill in their lives are turned into basket cases by hospital debts they cannot pay. Parents are skipping needed medical care so they can afford to take their children to the doctor. That's wrong, wrong, wrong.

At this writing, it appears that changes will be made, but not enough of them. Some people will still be uninsured, and even more will be underinsured. Policies may be hard to pay for and benefits limited. Costs will continue to soar, eating up our earnings and tax money.

Americans have always bragged that we have the best health system in the world. We don't. We have an inhumane lottery with winners and losers, divided by wealth and chance. Powerful political and health establishment forces keep our costly, inefficient system in place. How many more of us have to struggle to pay for decent health care before we're strong enough to storm the joint?

14

Disability:
The Big Black Hole

The Risk That Everyone Forgets

**You insure your house, your car, even your
old couches and chairs. But you forget your
single biggest asset: your earning power.**

You plot. You plan. You save. You invest. Then you fall off a roof (or your spouse
does), wind up in a wheelchair, and your entire financial plan falls apart. You go
through your savings like a buzz saw. Your comfortable standard of living goes
down the drain.

All because you forgot to insure your earning power, which is your most
valuable single asset. If you're sick, you have health insurance. If you die, your
family can cash in your life insurance policy. But disability falls between the
cracks. You're alive—in a bed or a wheelchair—and have no money coming in.
You need disability insurance, which sends you a check when you can't work.

Are you just about ready to skip this chapter because you can't afford to
buy? Not so fast! There are new kinds of policies today, more reasonably priced
than the old ones were. Coverage is also streaming into the workplace, where
employees can buy for one-third the price of individual insurance and without
passing a health exam.

For single people, not rich, disability coverage is a must. You have no spouse
to support you if you can't work and don't have an independent income. Buy
for sure if there are inheritable, disabling diseases in your family, such as cystic
fibrosis or multiple sclerosis.

Whether married people need disability coverage depends on each spouse's
income and assets. If you had no paycheck, could your spouse's salary support

the family, including the extra costs of your disability (home care or more physical therapy than your insurance will pay for)? Are you certain that your spouse could keep working rather than tending to you? Alternatively, could you live on your savings for many years? If so, you don't need the insurance. If not, you need it badly. In many two-paycheck families, husband and wife should each carry a policy. There are policies specifically for nonworking spouses if there's no spouse rider on your group policy.

What Disability Insurance Does

It pays you a monthly income if, due to illness or accident, you're not able to hold a suitable job. The younger you are, the lower the premium you pay.

You insure for a specified dollar amount, such as $2,000 or $3,000 a month. The checks typically last until age 65 but can stop earlier or later, depending on the policy. If you buy new coverage after 60, you're usually entitled to benefits for only three to five years.

Younger people should increase their coverage as their incomes rise. The price of each addition depends on your age at the time. A health check will be required unless you bought a rider letting you forgo it. When looking for more coverage, check your current company first. It's also more efficient to deal with a single company's claims department. If you're offered a much better deal by another insurer, however, take it.

When you're not in excellent health (a "rated risk"), your insurance will cost you more—if you can buy it at all. On policies bought outside the workplace, underwriting is pretty strict. Here's where there's no substitute for an experienced, energetic agent. Some insurers are less restrictive than others. The agent should try several companies to see what kind of deal you can get.

There are many variations to disability coverage, as will be explained. Shoot for coverage that—together with any other corporate or government benefits—gives you a minimally acceptable income. If you have extra money to spend, put it into savings and investments rather than super-rich disability benefits. You're more likely to retire healthy than retire sick.

Your Automatic Coverage

Almost every worker has a source of at least some disability pay:

There's Workers Compensation, for work-related injuries. Disability payments vary widely from state to state. The maximum is 66.6 percent of your pre-disability gross wages or 80 percent of your take-home pay, up to a specified ceiling. Employers buy workers comp for their employees; the self-employed have to buy their own.

There's Social Security Disability Insurace, if you worked long enough to be eligible for coverage or are eligible on your spouse's account. But you have to be so pulverized, physically or mentally, that you cannot work in any substantial job (there's a limited exception for the blind). Your checks don't start until you've been disabled for five full months. Furthermore, your doctor has to expect your disability to last for at least a year or to end in your death.

Social Security applies these rules strictly, sometimes too strictly. You may have to appeal (ideally, with the help of a lawyer) to collect the benefit truly due you. About two-thirds of those who apply for benefits are turned down the first time they apply, generally because they're judged fit for some kind of work. Of those who appeal and whose cases are reviewed by the Social Security Appeals Council, however, nearly two-thirds are accepted. If you carry a private disability policy, the insurance company may pay the legal costs of challenging a turndown. Anything you get from Social Security usually reduces the monthly amount that your private insurer pays.

To find out what benefit you and your dependents can expect to collect, see page 1096. Beneficiaries get annual cost-of-living increases, which protect their purchasing power. After 24 months on Social Security disability, you qualify for Medicare.

There's Veterans Insurance, if you can trace your ailment to something that happened while you were on active duty with the armed forces. Low-income veterans who are totally disabled and who served during periods designated as wartime can get benefits even for disabilities that are not service related.

There Are Disability Funds in Several States, including California, Hawaii, New Jersey, New York, and Rhode Island, plus Puerto Rico. They pay sickness benefits for a limited number of weeks to people disabled off the job.

There's Employer-Paid Coverage, generally limited to large and medium-size companies. You may get short-term sick pay and long-term disability pay at no cost to you, you lucky duck.

Workplace Policies: Coverage You Can Afford

Disability insurers have discovered America. Previously, they sold principally to business executives and high-earning professionals. Now they're noticing everyone else: middle managers, midlevel professionals, small-business owners and employees, technicians, skilled clerical and white-collar workers, gray-collar workers in high-tech manufacturing plants—the vast middle market that needs disability coverage too.

This new group, however, can't afford the fancy individual policies that doctors and lawyers buy. So the trend today is toward stripped-down coverage sold through the workplace, where it can be delivered at a lower cost. Your premium rises as you age. A ballpark price might be $20 to $25 a month for someone in his or her mid-30s buying a disability policy worth $1,500 a month. In your mid-40s, you might be charged $30 to $35. Women and men are charged the same. That makes it a great buy for women, who would otherwise pay much more for their coverage than men. Some large employers provide this coverage free.

Workplace disability insurance, including unisex pricing, is available for groups as small as three, as long as they work in the same location. There are four ways that coverage might be delivered:

1. The company pays for everything.

2. The employer offers the plan but employees buy the coverage themselves through payroll deduction. Everyone in a given age range is charged the same.

3. The employer gives everyone a basic benefit regardless of health—usually covering 50 percent of the worker's pay. Workers have the option of covering another 10 or 15 percent of their pay at their own expense. To buy these supplements, you may have to pass a health exam.

4. The employer adds disability pay to a pick-your-own benefits plan. Employees receive a fixed number of credits and use them to choose the benefits they want. Some plans offer two levels of disability coverage. You can insure for either 50 or 70 percent of pay. The higher amount is available no matter how much disability coverage you have outside the company plan.

In big firms, you usually don't have to pass a health exam if you sign up for coverage as soon as you join the company. You will be examined, however, if you apply at a later date. If you're found to have a health problem, the company might turn you down. Alternatively, your policy might contain an exclusion for a disability caused by the illness you're known to have.

In all these plans, you probably won't be covered immediately for preexisting conditions, defined as ailments you've known about during the past 3 or 6 months. Benefits generally don't start until you've been free of that problem for at least 12 months.

Some employers offer short-term disability ("sick pay") for 3 to 12 months. The payments vary widely—maybe 100 percent of pay for 2 months, then 60 percent for the rest of the period. Maybe 75 percent of pay for 6 months. It all depends on what the company chose for its plan.

If you're sick longer, you'll qualify for long-term disability, often payable until you're 65. Typically, you get a fixed percentage of salary, up to a cap of perhaps $8,000 to $10,000 a month (this calculation may or may not include your bonuses and commissions). Your disability income will be reduced by certain other payments, including Social Security, workers compensation, and any pension that your company pays. There may be partial benefits if, despite your disability, you're still able to work part-time.

Here's what to expect from quality plans: coverage for both injury and illness to age 65; coverage for both total disability, when you cannot work at all, and partial disability if you can work part-time.

Here's what you might get from lesser plans: coverage only for total disability. If partial disability is included, it might last for only a few months. You might be covered to age 65 after an accident but only two to five years after a disabling illness. Even so, limited, affordable coverage is better than no coverage at all.

Your company might offer group disability coverage or individual plans. Group coverage usually isn't portable, meaning that you can't keep it if you leave your job. A few plans let you convert from the group to an individual policy with the same insurer. But conversion policies offer limited benefits at a humongous price. You'd buy one only if you were otherwise uninsurable.

Ideally, your company will offer individual coverage or an individual policy that supplements your group insurance. Individual policies cost more than group plans, but they're fully portable. You can take them with you when you change jobs, at the same price you were paying before (or perhaps just a little bit more). This lets you continue your protection, at what's still a bargain price, often to age 65. You don't have to worry that your next job might not offer disability coverage; or that your next group policy might not cover you for 12 months; or that you might become uninsurable; or that you can't get coverage because you're self-employed; or that you might be unemployed for a while. Your old workplace policy will carry you through. If yours was a supplemental policy, coverage can usually be increased.

Portability isn't always perfect. Some insurers don't allow you to keep the coverage if your employer switches to another group insurer. Some terminate if you're eligible for another employer's plan, even if it's not as good as the one you have.

If your workplace plan isn't portable or you think its benefits are poor, use the information starting on page 494 to price an outside policy. It will cost you more, but you'll have it regardless of what becomes of your job or health. You can also buy partial-disability coverage if your workplace insurance pays only when you're totally disabled. Don't fail to take the workplace coverage, however, if outside policies are too expensive.

If you're disabled, go over your plan with a magnifying glass. You don't want to lose benefits by violating some technical provision. Will the plan pay if you work part-time before switching to total disability? Will it resume payments if you return to work and find that you can no longer handle the job? What exactly is the definition of disability?

Association Insurance

Another source of cut-rate disability coverage is a trade or professional association. Some policies take everyone; others screen out only the worst risks (people with HIV, cancer, or a history of heart attacks); others screen for additional health or working conditions. Premiums increase as you age.

How much you pay may be linked to your health when you first apply. It may also depend on whether your association offers a group or individual policy. Those in mediocre health will typically pay more for individual coverage than for group.

Ask whether the coverage is portable (see the discussion on page 490). Some contracts let you keep your policy if you leave the association; others don't.

Before buying association coverage, check its definition of disability. Sometimes the price is low because the policy doesn't offer much. Also, talk to a disability insurance agent. You might be able to do better with an outside plan. It's especially important to check the alternatives if your association offers coverage that isn't portable.

A plus for some associations: they might insure members who work from home. Some associations, such as the Freelancers Union (www.freelancers union.org), specialize in insurance and other services for home-based entrepreneurs. Group coverage at large associations usually charges unisex rates, which makes the policies especially cheap for women. Individual policies charge women more.

Individual Coverage

This is coverage that you buy yourself, without employer sponsorship. It might be your only coverage, or it might supplement employer coverage. Individual policies are sold by insurance agents and are generally more comprehensive than workplace or association insurance. Translation: they're expensive. Prices vary tremendously, depending on the insurance company and the benefits you choose. A man in his mid-30s might pay $35 to $44 a month for every $1,000 of disability income he buys. In his mid-40s, he might be charged $57 to $71. Women in that age range might pay from 30 to 50 percent more. (It's no surprise that most policies are sold to men!) Unlike workplace insurance, premiums on individual disability policies don't rise as you age.

Until the early 1990s, agents concentrated on selling cushy, Cadillac coverage to business executives and professionals. But nowadays, leaner policies are coming on line for people who don't want to spend as much.

How much you personally would pay depends not only on your age but also on your health, your sex, the state you live in, the insurer you choose, the benefits you want, your smoking history, and your job. The lower your occupational risk (based on industry claims data), the lower your cost and the better your benefits may be.

The lowest prices go to people with clean-hands jobs such as college professors and accountants. Their illness and accident risk is low. When disabled, they're usually eager to recover and get back to work. Retiring on disability pay would bore them stiff.

Some clerical workers, by contrast, aren't offered affordable individual coverage because, when disabled, they may not be motivated to return to their jobs. Blue-collar workers have two strikes against them: presumed low motivation and the increased risk of industrial accidents.

For a general idea of how risky a client you're thought to be, check the sample classifications below. If you're in class 5, you might pay as much as 20 percent less than if you land in Class 4. So ask your agent to show you alternatives from the top companies. Different companies reach different conclusions about where a particular job belongs.

Individual disability insurance is sold to classes 5, 4, and 3. For the rest, individual coverage is effectively unaffordable.

Class 5. Big-business executives; selected professionals, such as accountants, architects, lawyers, pharmacists, and college professors.

Class 4. Doctors, dentists, technicians, and selected middle management. Most insurers have dropped doctors with invasive or surgical practices to class 3.

Class 3. Surgeons, small-business management, white-collar and selected gray-collar workers, supervisors, skilled clerical and technical workers, real estate agents, and teachers.

Class 2. Sales clerks, unskilled clerical workers, barbers, and pink- and blue-collar workers whose jobs involve some manual labor.

Classes A and B. The all-but-untouchables: skilled workers in risky jobs (carpenters, bricklayers) and workers in heavy-lifting jobs (porters, baggage handlers).

If You're Self-Employed and Work at Home. Almost all carriers offer comprehensive policies to self-employed people who work at home if they go to client locations or have clients visit them at their home offices some of the time. A few will offer it even if you don't leave the home on a regular basis for work.

If You're Uninsurable. You might want to accept the package of life and disability insurance that comes with credit cards, auto loans, personal loans, and mortgages. That coverage is pocked with exclusions (read the fine print; page 351), but it's better than nothing.

If You're Female. You're at a big disadvantage. Women make more claims than men (for example—surprise, surprise—pregnancy-related claims), so they're charged higher premiums by insurers that establish rates by sex. At 30, you might pay 60 percent more than a man of the same age; at 40, it might be 40 percent more; at 50 (postpregnancy), 25 percent more. A few companies charge unisex rates, which give women a break. Ask your insurance agent to find them. Workplace and some association plans also offer unisex pricing. (In Montana, unisex pricing is mandatory for all insurers doing business there.)

How Much Coverage Do You Need?

You need enough insurance to feel that you and your family would be okay if you couldn't work. You're shooting for a decent standard of living—not grand but decent.

To put that into dollars and cents, go back to page 21, where you figured how much money you'd have in the kitty if you became disabled. (What? You skipped that calculation? This proves my point about needing insurance: you never know when you'll get caught.)

Estimate how much monthly income your kitty might throw off. Add that to your other sources of income, such as spouse's earnings, company-paid disability benefits, and Social Security. If that's not enough to pay your bills, including the extra expenses connected with being disabled, fill as much of the gap as you can with disability coverage from your company or an insurance agent.

Insurers won't knowingly sell you a large enough policy to replace all your income. That destroys your incentive to work. Instead they'll restrict your coverage to a portion of what you earn. A person earning $500,000 might be able to replace less than 40 percent of his or her earnings with insurance benefits. At $60,000 in income, you'd be able to replace nearly 70 percent. Your effective income is higher, however, because these benefits aren't taxable (page 500).

What if you go for 100 percent coverage by buying individual policies from two different insurance companies? You won't get away with it. Insurers always ask whether you have any other coverage, so you'd have to lie. To test your truthfulness, they can run your name through the Medical Information Bureau (page 483), which keeps track of the policies you apply for. They also can telephone your employer.

What if you try to get extra coverage by overstating your income? The insurers will ask for your tax returns. You'll be offered only the amount of insurance you qualify for.

What if you're currently overinsured but only because your income dropped? Your insurer probably won't pay more than 100 percent of your previous earnings. Your benefit would be scaled back and some of your premiums returned. One exception: if the policy is noncancelable, it will pay the specified monthly benefits regardless of your current earnings.

What if you're overinsured because you added a big workplace policy to a preexisting individual policy? The insurers might pay even if your total coverage comes to more than 100 percent of your pay. More likely, your group plan will pay you less, so your disability income won't exceed what you earned before your illness or accident.

How to Get the Best Value

Your budget for disability insurance is probably limited, so weigh all the following options carefully. You're not looking for bells and whistles. The objective is a policy that meets your reasonable needs—no less, no more.

Fixed Premiums Versus Rising Premiums. An excellent buy for people on a limited budget is an annually renewable disability income (ARDI) policy. It works very much like yearly term life insurance. The premium starts low and increases a little every year. By contrast, a traditional disability policy charges more when you first buy but fixes that price for the policy's entire term.

ARDI makes sense for younger professionals and businesspeople who in the past may have felt that they couldn't afford disability policies. Depending on your age, you might cut 25 to 50 percent off your initial cost.

Your gamble is that, as the price of the policy rises, so will your income. That's a pretty good bet. ARDI's modest extra cost each year shouldn't be a strain. In early middle age, however, ARDI starts getting pretty expensive. You'll want to drop the policy or convert to fixed-price coverage. If you're insurable, don't convert without checking out the competition. Another insurer may offer you a better price.

A few insurers offer step rates—lower rates in the first few years, when your earnings are low, then a jump to a single, higher rate in later years. Step-rate policies cost more than ARDI at the start but less as the policy ages.

Noncancelable Versus Guaranteed Renewable. *Noncancelable* is a comforting word. It means that your policy's benefits can't change, premiums can't rise, and the company can't cancel it. It's renewable every year on exactly the same terms.

Most companies no longer offer noncancelable insurance or offer it with more limited benefits than they used to. Instead they're pushing *guaranteed renewable* coverage. Here your benefits can't change, but the company can raise the premium—not on your policy individually but on the entire policy class.

Guaranteed renewable policies cost 10 to 20 percent less than comparable noncancelable coverage, but you're taking a price risk. If claims are higher than projected, the insurers can ask the state regulators for a premium increase— and they'd doubtlessly get it. Insurers could even manufacture the grounds for a premium increase if they wanted their older—hence riskier—policyholders to drop out (see "The Death Spiral," page 445).

Shorter Term Versus Longer Term. Policies that pay benefits for just two or five years are inexpensive and will cover a lot of grief. But what if you're one of the unlucky 14 percent who become disabled for five years or more? You and your family need protection against the very worst that can happen, so try to arrange for payments right to age 65—at which point you'd pick up Social Security retirement pay and maybe a pension. (If you're already on Social Security disability, you're switched to its retirement program at 65 with no change of benefit.)

A few insurers offer policies that pay benefits for life if you're disabled anytime up to age 65 or 70. But you pay through the nose. Lifetime benefits are strictly a luxury buy for people with a high current income who aren't saving much of it. They'd be smarter to put their extra money toward retirement savings instead.

In real life, many people cancel their disability insurance earlier than 65. They may retire early. Or they may accumulate enough net worth to guarantee an income even if they couldn't work, which means they no longer need disability coverage.

Depending on your purse and your occupation, you might not be able to get coverage to age 65. In that case, take the longest period available or that you can afford. Even a five-year policy is better than nothing.

Don't keep paying disability premiums after you retire. It's a waste of money. Consider long-term care coverage instead.

If you're still working after 65 and in good health, you might be able to renew your coverage to age 70 or longer, but at a high price. It's probably not worth it.

High Benefits Versus Low Benefits. Don't save money by buying less disability income than you actually need. The policy either supports you when you can't work or it doesn't—and if it doesn't, your financial plan isn't worth a tinker's damn.

Insurers set a maximum that they'll cover you for. The more you make, the lower the percentage of income they'll provide. Some companies offer higher maximums than others, so ask your insurance agent to shop around.

If you have substantial income from interest, dividends, and capital gains, you won't be able to buy as much disability insurance. The rules on this point vary from company to company. Some might restrict your coverage if your unearned income exceeds 10 percent of your earnings. Others reduce your eligible earnings by up to $30,000 in unearned income. The working rich can't buy disability insurance at all. They don't need it. They'll live on their capital if they have to quit going to the office.

What if you can't afford as much coverage as you need, all the way to 65? Insurers recommend that you buy the monthly benefit you require for as many years as you can.

"Own Occ" Versus "Any Occ" Versus Income Replacement. Here we come to the all-important definition of "disabled." What are the terms under which your policy pays?

Some pay if you can't perform the duties of your own occupation ("own occ"). For example, a surgeon becomes disabled if he or she loses a finger. Traditional own-occ policies pay full benefits even if you take up another line of work. A nine-fingered ex-surgeon could collect disability even while holding a full-time administrative job at an HMO. These "double-dip" policies, however, are going the way of the dodo. More common (and less costly) own-occ coverage says that, if you can't work in your own occupation but choose to try another, the income you earn will be considered in calculating the size of your benefit. But you aren't required to retrain if you'd rather not. To strengthen your claim to benefits, define your occupation in as much detail as you can.

An "any-occ" policy pays only if you can't work at any occupation that reasonably fits your education, experience, and training (with a similar income level implied). If a nine-fingered surgeon is well enough to hold an administrative post at an HMO, he would no longer be considered disabled. The checks would stop whether or not he found a job. That's a big weakness in this type of coverage. You're subject to the judgment of the insurance company. Many policies combine these two definitions, giving you own-occ coverage for the first two to five years, then switching you to "any occ."

An income-replacement policy insures your income rather than your occupation. This is generally the most cost-efficient choice. You're covered for a certain level of income. If you can't work at all, you get your full insured benefit. If you can work at your own job part-time or handle a lower-paying job for which you are reasonably suited, your policy pays the percentage difference between your lower earnings and your insured benefit. As an example, say that you're earning 60 percent of what you did before. Your policy will pay 40 percent of your disability benefit. That protects the insured portion of your income, regardless of what job you hold. With an income replacement policy, the insurer can't cut off your checks if you choose not to take up another line of work.

Income replacement won't pay a business owner who keeps on receiving an income even if he or she is unable to work. On the other hand, the policy continues to pay if you're a fee-paid professional who returns to work but can't rebuild a client list immediately. (In the latter case, an own-occ policy could also help if it has good transition benefits—see page 500.)

What's the best choice? Own-occ with residual benefits (see page 498) or income replacement. If your occupation is pretty general—say, business executive—own-occ coverage may not buy you anything extra. If you can't function in your own occupation, you probably can't function at all. In that case, income replacement would be the better choice.

Long Versus Short Elimination Period. This is the waiting period before benefits begin. The longer you're willing to wait, the lower the premium you'll pay. A one-month waiting period makes no sense; you'll surely be able to cover your bills over so short a period. Instead consider any period between three and six months. A three-month wait might cut your insurance premium by 50 percent. A six-month wait cuts it by 60 percent.

Coordinate your coverage with any sick pay or short-term disability benefits that you're entitled to. If your employer will pay short-term benefits for six months, your personal, long-term policy could pick up from there.

If your budget requires you to choose between a higher benefit and a longer waiting period, take the longer waiting period. You can always scramble for money over the short term. It's the long term you have to worry about.

Do You Want Residual Benefits? Absolutely, with both an own-occ or any-occ policy. Without resid, these policies pay nothing if you're able to work part-time. With resid, you're paid if you're still able to work but your illness or accident leaves you unfit for the schedule you kept before. Maybe you're working only part-time. Maybe you had to switch to a less taxing, lower-paying job. Residual benefits help fill the gap between your old, high salary and your current one.

A true resid pays a pro rata portion of what you're insured for, depending on how much money you earn. Say, for example, that your policy carries a maximum benefit of $4,000 a month. If, after a stroke, you can work part-time earning 60 percent of your previous income, you'd get 40 percent of your disability benefit, or $1,600. Resid also should pay if you never were totally disabled but were gradually overcome by an illness that put you partly out of commission.

Instead of resid, some policies pay what they call "partial" benefits. That might be 50 percent of your full disability benefit, regardless of how much you earn. But this payment usually doesn't last very long, and you may be eligible only after a spell of total disability. A few policies pay partial benefits for a period of time, then switch to residual.

Many own-occ and any-occ insurers include this coverage automatically; others sell it separately, as a rider; a few don't offer it at all. Depending on the company, you're generally considered partly disabled if, because of your health, you lose more than 20 percent of your former income.

When you're on resid, you'll probably have to report your income every quarter (for those on straight salary) or perhaps every month (if your income varies), so the insurer can pay the proper percentage amount. Your insurer may also want to check your tax returns. If you have an income replacement policy, you also have to disclose your earnings periodically.

Some less expensive policies make fixed-dollar payments for partial disability—for example, $1,000 a month regardless of what you can earn. But these payments usually stop after 6 or 12 months.

Do You Want the Waiver of Premium? Yes, for sure. It lets you stop paying for your insurance if you become disabled. Most policies bundle it into your basic coverage, but sometimes you have to buy it separately.

In theory, you shouldn't need a waiver. Your disability income should be large enough to cover all expenses, including your insurance premiums. In practice, however, waiver of premium is a surer thing. It's especially important if you own a guaranteed renewable policy, the price of which could rise.

Do You Want Inflation Protection? Yes and maybe. *Yes* to predisability protection—built into some policies, sold separately with others. When sold separately, it's generally an inexpensive option. Your insured amount rises by a certain percentage every year for a specified number of years. If you don't want to pay for the increased amount in any given year, you can decline it. Once you're disabled and start getting benefits, however, your payments are fixed.

Maybe to postdisability protection. This rider adds inflation protection to your disability benefit. Some insurers let you pick a fixed annual increase once you start receiving checks. Others link your payouts to the consumer price index. A built-in 3 percent increase might raise your premium by 10 percent. I call this a "maybe" because, although it's nice to have, other benefits would be higher on my list. Buy it, however, if you can afford to.

Do You Want a Future-Purchase Option? Only if you can afford it and expect your earnings to rise by much more than the general inflation rate. It lets you add coverage at specified times in the future, even if a change in your health status makes you otherwise uninsurable.

The right to buy more insurance without a health exam is built into some of the more expensive policies. Separately, it may cost 5 to 15 percent of the policy price, depending on your age and the company. Each time you exercise this option, you'll pay the premiums for your age at the time.

If you take this rider, use it. Add to your policy on a regular basis. A future-increase option generally expires somewhere around age 55 or earlier. Don't fail to update your policy in that final year.

If you don't choose this option and stay in good health, you can still increase your disability insurance as your income rises. But you'll have to pass a medical exam.

Do You Want a Reducing Term? This is a neat solution for people who need extra coverage for a specific period. Say, for example, that you're buying a business and agree to pay the owner over eight years. As security for the payments, the owner might ask you to carry both life and disability insurance. You can buy coverage that expires on a date you name, which in this case would be the date that your debt is supposed to be paid up. The policy should piggyback on a regular policy that keeps you and your family protected too.

Other Policy Provisions. Some of these are built into your basic policy, some are sold separately. Every company is a little different. Consider all your options but don't waste your money on minor stuff.

• *Rehabilitation payments.* Your policy will pay for rehab in order to get you back to work. It should also train you for a new job and pay for mechanical aids that help you function at the office. But it won't finance any rehabilitation if it's clear that you'll never be able to work again. Expect your disability insurer to be in close contact with your doctors and your employer.

• *Transition and fallback benefits.* Disability income normally stops when you return to work. But what if your old job turns out to be too much for you? What if it takes a while to rebuild your former income? What if you lost a bonus by being away from work? The policy should cover any losses due to your disability, support a home-to-job transition plan, and resume paying benefits if it's clear that you'll have to train for something else.

• *Integration with Social Security and other plans.* This sensible provision saves you quite a bit of money. If you go on disability, the insurer reduces your payment by any disability benefits that you receive from Social Security, workers compensation, the military, or a state disability fund. Your total payment doesn't change. It simply comes from different sources.

• *A Social Security rider.* Comes with policies that sell lower benefits. The rider pays you extra if you're not disabled enough to qualify for Social Security payments.

• *Limited "soft" coverage.* A growing number of insurers limit benefits for ailments that can't be measured objectively, such as back and muscle pain, headaches, repetitive stress disorders, and chronic fatigue syndrome.

• *Presumptive disability.* A lottery ticket. You are presumed to be totally disabled if you lose the use of any two limbs, eyesight, speech, or hearing. Full payment is due even if you go back to work full-time. Generally, this isn't worth paying extra for. If you really are disabled, the basic policy will pay. If you aren't, you shouldn't collect.

• *Accidental death and dismemberment.* Another lottery ticket that hitches a bit of life insurance to your coverage. But it pays only if you die or lose a limb in an accident, not if you die after an illness (the more likely case).

• *Hospital income.* You get a certain number of dollars per day while you're in the hospital. This provision may not be worth a lot. Modern medical practice tries to keep you out of the hospital or sharply limits your stay.

• *A premium refund.* A way that some insurers make money by appealing to your greed. Under this rider, you may get some or all of your premium back after 5 or 10 years if you've made no claims or only a small claim. The insurer might even project that you'll earn a high rate of interest on the money. But that rate vanishes if you have a period of insured disability or if your group of policies is less profitable than the insurer expected. For this dubious gamble, you might pay an extra 50 percent or more. Don't be tempted. Put that money toward strengthening some other part of your disability coverage.

• *New designs.* Insurers are trying to broaden the market for disability coverage. A Unum life insurance policy, for example, has a rider option for long-term care. It lets you draw a percentage of the life insurance benefit to help cover the cost of a nursing home, assisted living, home health care, and adult day care, if you're so disabled that you need it. A MassMutual policy replaces the retirement contributions you lose during years when you're totally disabled and cannot work (the money goes into a taxable trust, but you can manage the investments). Watch for other new ideas to emerge.

Make Careful Comparisons Before You Replace an Old Noncancelable Policy with a New One. Your old policy may have a more generous definition of disability than the new one you're being offered. If you need more coverage, consider adding a second policy. Treat your first one as the treasure it is.

How to Shop

Companies vary widely in what their policies cover and what risks they accept, so disability insurance isn't something you can buy yourself. You'll need an insurance agent or a full-service financial planner to explain the options. If you can't afford a regular policy, ask about annually renewable coverage (page 494). And be sure that the company is rated A or higher for safety and soundness.

Readers of this book can access an excellent firm, Low Load Insurance Services in Tampa, Florida, that normally works only with fee-only financial planners. Its specialty is finding good coverage at a competitive price. Go to www .llis.com/quote_request.shtml, click on "Disability," enter my name—Jane Bryant Quinn—in the "advisor" space, and fill in the form. Or call 877-254-4429. You'll get a quote on a disability policy plus a case manager to provide advice and help you with the application. LLIS also offers you term and permanent life insurance. (P.S., I earn nothing from making this recommendation.)

Preexisting Conditions

When you fill out your application, you have to disclose all past and present illnesses. The insurance company will either (1) cover them at the policy's regular price, (2) charge you a higher price, (3) restrict your benefit, (4) refuse to cover a particular ailment, or (5) refuse to cover you at all. If any restriction is applied, ask your insurance agent to try again. Sometimes, a little pressure—or checking with some other insurers—can lead to a better result.

Don't lie about your illnesses, physical or mental. The insurer will check your health history through the Medical Information Bureau (page 483). It may also check with your doctors. If you're seeing a psychologist or psychiatrist, disclose it—especially if you have a preexisting mental health condition and even if you're in therapy just for general enlightenment. If you leave something out, the insurer can use it against you when you make a claim.

Once your policy has been in effect for two years (three years in some states, including California), the insurer normally shouldn't deny payment based on errors of fact in your application. If you put down the wrong age, payments will be adjusted to match your real age.

But the two-year limit doesn't protect you if the error involved your health history. The insurer will investigate. Your claim can be rejected on grounds of fraud if you failed to list a pertinent illness that would have affected the insurer's decision to accept you. The insurer decides what's pertinent.

Warning: many insurers are aggressive about this! Even trivial ailments not listed (acne, in one famous case) could be used to deny a claim and cancel your policy. You might win your case in court, but who wants to go through all that? If you are turned down, ask the insurer to specify in writing why, exactly, your claim fails to meet the contract's terms. These decisions are often subjective. You need an answer specific enough to help a lawyer judge your case.

Income Taxes

You pay no tax on disability income from policies that you buy with your own after-tax money. Most workers compensation isn't taxable either. Nor is income from state disability funds (unless the payments are in lieu of unemployment pay). But income from employer-paid plans is fully taxed. Up to 85 percent of your Social Security disability income can also be taxed, depending on how much other income you have.

What if your employer gives you a basic disability policy and you supplement it by buying coverage through payroll deduction? If you become disabled, the company-paid portion of your benefit is taxable; the rest isn't. Fortunately, you don't have to figure this out yourself. The insurer will send you a 1099 form every year.

Who Can You Trust?

You're counting on this insurance company to pay you a check many years in the future. But for some companies, disability coverage has been a money loser. Who can you trust to stick around?

Unum specializes in disability insurance. The top diversified companies include MassMutual, Northwestern Mutual, Guardian, Life Insurance Company of America, and Principal Financial Group. In low-load individual coverage: USAA Life. The leaders in employee group coverage include Unum, MetLife, and Hartford Life.

Many companies, especially the smaller ones or the ones with small disability portfolios, are wrestling with the question of whether to stay in the market at all. Some of them sell the policies of other insurers. Some put their names on policies that other insurers develop and manage.

If your company decides to drop its disability business, two things could happen. It could service its existing policies, although perhaps not as well as it did before. Or it could sell its policies to another insurer. In that case, keep track of when your premiums are due, just to be sure you're not lost in the shuffle. If you don't pay your premiums, for whatever reason, your policy will expire. For simplicity, you can have the premium deducted automatically from your bank account each month.

It is rare, but not unknown, for a company to "neglect" to send renewals to policyholders who had claims in the past and might again. This practice, sometimes called "starring," is illegal. If you think it has happened to you, complain to the state insurance department.

Look for companies with top ratings for safety and soundness (page 405). If insurers run into financial problems, they sometimes start treating policyholders badly, denying or delaying claims. You might be pressed to accept a modest lump sum instead of years of benefits.

Follow the rules exactly when filing a claim. A company may turn you down just because you didn't fill out the claim form properly, or failed to follow complex claim procedures, or missed a deadline. You're especially vulnerable if you have an aggressive insurer who thinks you won't sue.

Talk to your doctor before filling in the form the insurer sends, which seeks a description of how disabled you are. The questions may be phrased to tilt the answers the insurer's way. Be sure that your doctor understands your job's physical and mental requirements so that he or she can judge accurately whether you're able to perform.

If you have any trouble collecting, call a lawyer right away. You can check online for lawyers who specialize in disability insurance claims. Also, write to your state's insurance department (find it by going to www.naic.org).

Most claims are paid in good faith, but there's bad faith in the industry too.

Don't Leave Home Without It

If you have to work for a living and have no disability insurance, you effectively have no financial plan. Everything you own is held hostage to your continuing ability to get up in the morning and catch a bus. That's no way to live. Buy as much coverage as you need or afford. Fit it into your budget the way you do any other necessity, and get on with your life.

The Driving Dream

The Search for the Best and Cheapest Auto Insurance

**If you hold your car for four years or so and
have a teenage driver, it can cost you more
to insure the car than it did to buy it.**

Auto insurance is a toll bridge over which every honest driver has to pass. Policies cost the most in cities and suburbs. That's where most of the cars are and, as night follows day, most of the accidents. But even in the wide-open countryside, the price of coverage is steep.

Insurance is expensive for a lot of reasons:

- Cars are complex and costly to repair or replace.
- Streets are more congested, so people bump into each other more often.
- Medical and other costs keep going up.
- There are more lawsuits and higher settlements in injury cases.
- Some badly designed no-fault laws encourage litigation rather than discourage it.
- By law, insurance companies are allowed to exchange price information, so they don't always compete as much as they should.

New approaches to risk evaluation are reclassifying many drivers. People who once would have been "preferred risks" now are labeled "standard risks" and charged a higher premium. Many formerly standard risks are dropping down to substandard, where they must pay even more.

Some companies consider your level of education and type of occupation as part of their underwriting. This raises rates for people in certain types of jobs (the list isn't publicized) and with less formal training. That's a nasty approach, in my opinion, and unfair to good drivers who didn't finish school or land a job that the insurer doesn't approve of, but it's legal.

Insurance premiums follow cycles. For a few years, underwriting standards loosen; premiums are flat and sometimes fall. Then profits get dinged and all the companies tighten together. Rates may shoot up for two or three years, then settle into a new plateau.

The good news, at this writing, is that insurers are competing for the very best drivers, in the statistically safer parts of the country, by reducing their rates. There are ways to reduce your auto insurance costs, about which more below. But how you insure against an auto accident—and what you yourself can expect to recover—depends on where you live.

Fault Versus No-Fault

If you live in a "fault" state and are hurt in an auto accident that is the other driver's fault, you collect from his or her insurance company. That presumes that the other driver has insurance, which may not be the case. Many of the country's most reckless road hogs don't bother with coverage, even in states that supposedly require it. Tens of thousands of drivers simply can't afford it. You have to buy uninsured-driver coverage to protect against this risk.

If you luck out and the other guy does have insurance, the policy might be too small to cover all of your injuries. You can sue for a larger amount, but it won't do you any good unless the driver is rich enough to pay. Moral: make sure that you're hit only by a millionaire.

If you caused the accident, the other guy doesn't have to pay. Your own liability insurance pays for the person you hit but not for any injuries you sustained. If you're only partly at fault, state law dictates to what extent each policy pays.

The fault system does produce occasional huge judgments. You can sue not only for medical costs and the wages you lost while out of work but also for "pain and suffering," which is where the big money lies. But it's a lottery. You collect only if (1) the other guy has enough insurance and personal assets to cover a judgment and (2) the accident was at least partly his fault. Many injured people get much less than they deserve or nothing at all.

Lawyers love fault laws because they make so much money on lawsuits. But fault systems probably cost you money in higher insurance premiums and can't be relied on to help you if you're truly hurt. Pure no-fault is better, but whenever it threatens to be enacted into law, the lawyers spend huge sums of money to defeat it. They try to persuade the voters that fault laws are good for them.

When that fails, they lobby to water down no-fault so it can't achieve its goals. Most of us live in fault states.

If you live in a no-fault state* and are hurt in an auto accident, your own insurance company pays your medical bills and lost wages up to a certain ceiling. You collect even if the accident was entirely your fault. So everyone with auto insurance is protected, not just people who luck into the "right" kind of accident.

If your injuries are bad enough or your medical bills are high enough, you can also go to court and try for a pain-and-suffering award. There, fault rules apply: you don't collect unless you can prove that the other driver was at least partly at fault.

Three states—Kentucky, New Jersey, and Pennsylvania—offer you a choice: either fault or no-fault insurance. If you choose fault, however, you have to pay more for it.

One state, Michigan, pays for property damage under its no-fault rules. The rest address only bodily injury. Consumer advocates consider Michigan's law the best in the country. It combines unlimited medical and rehabilitation costs for an injured person with tough standards for limiting lawsuits.

No-fault can save money and slow down the rise in auto insurance premiums, but only if lawsuits are restricted to serious cases such as death, disfigurement, or severe impairment. Five states pursue no-fault seriously, in the view of Jeffrey O'Connell, the father of no-fault insurance and professor of law at the University of Virginia: Michigan and New York, closely followed by New Jersey, then Florida and Minnesota. In the rest, even people with modest medical bills are allowed to sue. The natural result: accident victims run up their medical expenses so that they can get into court, and no-fault's potential savings don't materialize.

In either type of state, your insurer will investigate the case, handle the settlement negotiations, defend you in a lawsuit, and pay any judgment against you up to the limit of your policy. If the judgment is larger, you have to cover the excess amount yourself.

What Kind of Coverage Do You Need?

Liability for Bodily Injury—
Absolutely Essential and Required by Law

It protects you if you're sued for injuring someone in an accident, including pedestrians and passengers riding in your car. The policy pays the victim's

---

*At this writing, Florida, Hawaii, Kansas, Kentucky, Massachusetts, Michigan, Minnesota, New Jersey, New York, North Dakota, Pennsylvania, and Utah.

medical costs, loss of earnings, and pain and suffering. You're also protected if someone is injured by a family member driving your car, a friend who is driving your car with permission, or a family member who is driving someone else's car with permission.

How much liability coverage should you carry? That depends on how you look at it. I offer three angles of vision:

1. Protect your assets. That means buying enough insurance to cover your net worth, on a bet that you won't be sued for a higher amount. If you don't own much besides your car, you'd buy only the minimum that your state requires— maybe $20,000 for every person injured, up to a cap of $40,000 for the whole accident (expressed as 20/40). If you own a home, you might want $100,000 for each person injured, to a maximum of $300,000 per accident (100/300); or $300,000 per accident without regard to how many people are hurt. The wealthy might want $500,000 to $1 million worth of coverage or more.

But how good is this strategy, really? You can be sued for more than your insured amount, and you're not off the hook just because the judgment exceeds your net worth. You can be ordered to pay out of future paychecks for years and years. Your earning power is an asset that needs to be protected too.

2. Protect yourself. If you're hurt by a driver who's uninsured or underinsured, you can be paid by your own auto policy, even above any no-fault limit. But only a handful of states let you purchase more protection for yourself than for the other guy. A $20,000 cap on your liability insurance (the maximum the insurer will pay the other guy) normally means a $20,000 cap on the amount of protection you can buy against uninsured motorists (the payment you and your family can receive). By pumping up your liability coverage, you're also protecting yourself.

3. Protect the injured. Drivers have a social and moral obligation to everyone else on the road. If you damage a life, you should pay for it. That means buying a substantial insurance policy—at least $100,000/$300,000—even if you don't have a lot of assets to protect. Higher liability limits may not even cost very much.

Liability for Property Damage—
Essential, and a Little Extra Doesn't Hurt

This pays for any damage you do to someone else's property. Buy at least enough to cover a car—say, $30,000, or $100,000 if you're tempted to veer into BMWs. But what if you hit a bus or a storefront? Costs can climb pretty fast. Some extra protection usually doesn't cost very much.

Medical Payments—Offered in Fault States but Not Essential

This coverage picks up the medical and funeral bills of anyone injured in your car, without regard to who caused the accident. It covers your family if they're hurt as pedestrians or while riding in another vehicle, including a taxi or a bus. It covers an elderly friend who stumbles while getting into your parked car and breaks her hip.

But it offers less protection than meets the eye. Your auto insurance will normally cover only the bills that your health insurance doesn't pay, which may not be very much. Those injured in your car may also have health insurance. If they want more money, they'll sue for it whether or not you have medical-payments insurance. Many people skip this coverage or buy $2,000 per person just to plug the deductible in a health insurance policy. If your health insurance is skimpy, beef up that policy, not this one. If you have no health insurance or limited insurance, however, medical payments coverage is a must.

In no-fault states, medical payments are tucked into your basic auto insurance policy.

Personal Injury Protection (PIP)—A No-Fault Fixture

You're covered for (1) your own medical bills up to a stated limit; (2) part of your lost wages; (3) funeral expenses; (4) in some states, replacement services—for example, a babysitter hired while a mother is in the hospital.

How much you ultimately collect depends on your state. Often the ceiling is $10,000, but there are states above and below that level. There may be a low ceiling on each doctor bill. You can usually fall back on your health insurance if no-fault doesn't pay enough of each bill, but that depends on your state. Ask if you can choose between using your no-fault and health insurance policies.

To lower the cost of your personal injury protection, see if your medical bills and lost wages can be paid primarily by your regular health and disability insurance. If so, you can buy less PIP. It becomes no more than a backup system for expenses otherwise unpaid. Some insurers also let you save a few dollars by signing up for a PIP managed care plan.

If you have no health insurance, or limited insurance, PIP is a must.

Collision—Essential for New Cars and for Drivers Who Have a Substantial Auto Loan; Worthwhile as Long as Your Car Has a Reasonable Market Value

This portion of your policy covers repairs to your own car, no matter who caused the accident. If you borrow the money to buy the car, as most of us do, collision coverage is mandatory. If the car is totaled, the insurance will repay the loan.

The price of collision insurance depends on the size of the deductible. That's the amount you pay toward each repair before the insurance policy kicks in. Deductibles typically range from $250 to $1,000. The higher the number, the lower your insurance costs. If the accident wasn't your fault, your deductible may be covered by the other driver's policy.

Collision insurance is generally written to cover your particular car's *fair market value*, defined as its *book value* (as determined by standard tables), minus any unusual wear and tear, minus a charge for unusually high mileage. The insurer won't give you a penny more. So compare the premium you pay with what you'd get if the car were totaled. Drop coverage on cars so old or damaged that their value is nominal. What's nominal? Any loss that leaves you philosophical instead of sore.

Comprehensive—Essential for New Cars, Useful for Older Ones

This pays for damage to your car from fire, earthquake, flood, vandalism, hail, pets chewing the upholstery, and the odd stone thrown up from the highway. It also covers theft and perhaps the use of a rental car after a theft. (Removable tape decks, CD players, and other expensive equipment might be covered by your homeowners policy or by a special rider to that policy.) Deductibles typically range from $100 to $1,000; the higher the deductible, the cheaper your insurance. Windshields may be insurable separately, with no deductible.

Comprehensive insurance covers the car's fair market value, which generally declines with time. Many drivers keep their comprehensive coverage even after dropping collision, because comprehensive tends to be cheaper. Still, the insurer won't pay anything more than the car is worth.

Uninsured and Underinsured Motorist— Required in Many States; Essential for Your Own Protection

This pays the cost of your injuries and those of the passengers in your car if you're hit by (1) an uninsured driver who's at fault, (2) an at-fault driver whose small insurance policy won't cover all your damages, or (3) a hit-and-run. It also covers lost wages. In some states, you might even be reimbursed for damage to your car. In no-fault states, uninsured-motorist coverage clicks in if you're injured badly enough to sue. You can collect from this policy on top of your no fault personal injury protection.

Why bother with uninsured-motorist coverage (you might ask) if your life, health, and disability policies already protect your family, cover your injuries, and pay you an income if you're disabled and cannot work? Because these policies rarely cover all your expenses. Uninsured-motorist coverage helps with the inevitable extra costs, such as support systems if you become disabled. It also gives you the right to sue for pain and suffering if you didn't cause the accident or were clipped by a hit-and-run.

As a practical matter, most Americans have little or no disability insurance, insufficient life insurance, and limited health insurance. Under these conditions, it's well worth spending money on uninsured-motorist protection.

Towing and Service/Rental Car Reimbursement—A Toss-In

If you have an accident or your car breaks down, you're covered for the towing cost and the labor charges for repairs. You might also receive $15 to $20 a day to rent a car while yours is being repaired. Some policies now include these items as part of the regular premium you pay. If they're extra, the cost is minimal. If you belong to an auto club, these benefits probably duplicate what you have already. Don't cover yourself twice.

Umbrella Insurance—Worthwhile to Protect Your Assets

An umbrella policy covers liability judgments that exceed the limits of your auto and homeowners policies. Typically, you have to carry $250,000 worth of liability on your auto insurance and $300,000 or so on your home. After that, you can insure for up to $1 million or more. Umbrella insurance is generally priced according to the number of cars you own. Some companies will add a $1 million rider to auto and homeowners insurance.

Umbrella coverage may defend you not only against claims of damage or personal injury but also against libel and slander (unless you're a professional writer or broadcaster), false arrest, invasion of privacy, and similar charges that spoil your day.

More Ways to Save Money on Auto Insurance

- *Compare prices.* Here lies your single biggest shot at saving money. In any city or any zip code, some insurers charge twice as much as others for exactly the same coverage.

Insurers don't advertise price, so you have to hunt for those that are lower cost. No single company always has the best rates. Each one prices differently, in different places, for different kinds of customers.

For quotes, begin online at sites such as InsWeb (www.insweb.com), Insure .com (www.insure.com), Esurance (www.esurance.com), and InsureOne.com (www.insureone.com). Enter the coverage you want. You may have to give your name, phone number, and e-mail address to get quotes, but it's a convenient, easy way of getting a good range of comparisons. It helps to keep a special e-mail address for online shopping so that junk doesn't pile up in your personal account. Some quotes come instantly, others a couple of days later. A few companies sell online with no call from an agent. Some familiar companies, such as Allstate, Amica, Geico, Progressive, and State Farm Insurance, aren't on the Web comparison sites. You have to log on to them separately.

With these prices in hand, ask an independent insurance agent if he or she can do better for you. Sometimes the agent can turn up a lower rate, perhaps from a regional company or a company that's especially competitive for drivers of your age and sex. At the very least, the Web quotes tell you whether your agent is offering a competitive price.

Good drivers who live in New Jersey should try New Jersey Manufacturers Insurance Company in West Trenton. If you're 50 and up, check the AARP (formerly American Association of Retired Persons) in Washington, D.C., which offers coverage to members, spouses, and certain driving-age children through The Hartford insurance group (at late ages, you may have to pass a medical exam). Anyone connected with the United States military should try USAA in San Antonio, Texas (800-531-8722). USAA insures present and former military officers, including their spouses, widows, and widowers. Their grown children can buy from a USAA subsidiary, which charges somewhat higher rates. Active-duty enlisted personnel and their families qualify too.*

Most of these insurance companies will check your credit score before they'll provide you with a quote, whether you inquire through an agent or online. That won't affect your credit score. The scorekeepers ignore all insurance-related inquiries.

Rate isn't everything, of course. You also want your claims handled promptly,

---

*For auto insurance, USAA accepts commissioned or warrant officers and their families from all of the uniformed services, including the U.S. Coast Guard, the National Oceanic and Atmospheric Administration, and the U.S. Public Health Service; also, foreign service officers of the U.S. State Department, special agents of the FBI and the U.S. Treasury Department, and officer candidates. The program for enlisted personnel includes the National Guard and Selected Reserve who have a current, active relationship with the armed forces.

fairly, and without any hassle. Amica, in Providence, Rhode Island, for example, which sells by phone to better risks, may not be the cheapest in your zip code but is widely considered to give excellent service. Ask your friends how they like their own insurers. Some states publish data on customer complaints. You'll also find it on the website of the National Association of Insurance Commissioners (www.naic.org; click on "Consumer Information Source").

When you find a good company that's substantially cheaper than the one you have now, consider a switch. But don't leave for penny-ante savings. Insurers may give special treatment to their longtime policyholders. For example, after an accident, they may be less likely to increase your premium. If you do switch, don't let your old policy run out until you've held the new one for 60 days. Sometimes an insurer will accept you as a policyholder, then reject you later—perhaps after finding something on your credit report that it didn't like. You don't want to get stuck.

- *Check your credit score* (page 265). Fix any errors that might be pulling it down. Insurers charge at much as 50 percent more to people with poor scores.

- *Tell your insurance company or agent about any changes that could lower your rate.* For example, you should pay less when (1) the young driver in your family graduates from college and leaves home; (2) you retire and stop using your car for commuting; (3) you start carpooling or move closer to your place of work; (4) you install an antitheft device; (5) you move to a city that's less accident prone or from the city to the suburbs or the country; (6) you have a birthday— some insurers reduce rates for people 55 and up who take a defensive driving course; (7) you marry; (8) you divorce, and your ex-spouse (who has all the speeding tickets) stops using your car.

- *Reshop for a policy every couple of years.* Any of the changes in the circumstances just listed may get you a better rate from a different company than your current one. It doesn't cost anything to check around and could save you hundreds of dollars a year. But don't think that approaching one or two agents constitutes "shopping around," says J. Robert Hunter, director of insurance for the Consumer Federation of America. You'll miss many good companies that don't work with agents, such as Amica, Geico, and USAA.

- *Your state may have an auto insurance buyer's guide showing what various auto insurance companies charge.* To find your state's insurance Web site, go to www.naic.org/state_web_map.htm. The guides give you a start but can be misleading, due to the complexity of auto insurance pricing.

- *Don't buy your collision and comprehensive coverage from the lender who finances your car or any insurer he or she recommends.* That's going to be high-cost insurance. Count on it.

▪ *Raise the deductible on your collision insurance from $250 to $500 or from $500 to $1,000.* You'll pay 10 percent less for the policy if you eat the smaller bills yourself. Odds are, you'll save more in premiums than you'll ever pay out-of-pocket in costs.

▪ *Drop collision insurance on an older car.* The insurer won't pay any more than the car is worth (page 510). Get an appraisal from an auto dealer.

▪ *Buy a car that's cheap to repair.* Your insurance agent can tell you which cars are money eaters and which aren't.

▪ *Buy a safe car.* Safety ratings are listed for many models by the Highway Loss Data Institute, part of the Insurance Institute for Highway Safety (www.iihs .org). In general, more claims are made on smaller cars than on large ones.

▪ *Don't drink or smoke.* Some insurers give discounts to clean-livers.

▪ *Earn a discount by insuring all your cars with the same company and by buying your homeowners or tenants insurance there too.* But shop first for the cheapest insurer. Even with a discount, high-priced policies are no bargain.

There may be additional discounts for young drivers who take driver education or an online safety course; teetotalers; nonsmokers; graduates of defensive driving courses; senior citizens; students with good grades; families whose teenage drivers go to school more than 100 miles away (so they can't get at the car!); cars parked in a garage or off the street; low-mileage cars; drivers who carpool; cars with air bags; cars with four-wheel, antilock braking systems; and cars with antitheft devices. Geico offers discounts to active and retired members of the military in 40 states. AARP provides discounts to members.

▪ *Describe exactly how your car is used.* A car driven for pleasure costs less to insure than a car used for everyday commuting. The insurer Progressive (www .progressive.com) offers a behavior-based option for people who drive safely, less often, and at lower-risk times of day. It monitors your habits through a small wireless device installed in your car.

▪ *In a no-fault state, people without a job—for example, retirees—may be able to drop the portion of their personal injury protection that covers loss of wages.* Keep it, however, if your spouse has a job.

▪ *Pay the premium all at once.* It costs more to pay in monthly or quarterly installments. Alternatively, set up automatic monthly payments through your bank. That should be cheaper than having to write a check once a month.

▪ *Drive safely.* Your rates soar if your record shows convictions for drunk driving, "chargeable accidents" (meaning that they're at least partly your fault), or a couple of speeding tickets.

▪ *Shop for the best risk classification you can get.* Many insurers are effectively raising premiums by rating more drivers as standard risks rather than preferred risks. Standard risks pay anywhere from 10 to 60 percent more, depending on the company. Every insurer may rate you a little differently, however. If you have a good driving record, ask your agent to try for a company that will consider you a preferred risk. If you've been classified as substandard, look for an insurer that will take you as a standard risk.

■ *If you're turned down for coverage because of your driving record, look for a better option than your state's high-risk pool.* Many companies are taking a second look at substandard drivers. You might have had a speeding ticket in the past couple of years or an accident that was partly your fault. In the old days, that could have dumped you into your state's assigned-risk pool for drivers who couldn't get insurance anywhere else. Now, however, you might find private coverage at a lower cost.

■ *Reform.* If your bad driving record tags you with a higher premium or lands you in a high-risk pool, work at keeping your record squeaky clean. After three years, shop again. A different company might take you at a better rate. Sometimes, however, it takes seven years or more to escape your foolish past. A drunk driving conviction may not be escapable.

■ *Look for group auto insurance plans.* They're offered through many large employers, teachers' associations, credit unions, and others. You get premium discounts and may be able to pay by payroll deduction. (But compare prices at other insurance companies before signing up.)

■ *Move.* Low insurance rates give you yet one more reason to avoid big, crowded cities. You can generally save $1,000 or more by living in a small city, a suburb, or deep in the country. Your rates may go up, however, if you move from Wyoming to a country town in, say, Pennsylvania, because Pennsylvania's rates are generally high all over.

■ *Avoid gimmicks.* If you buy "accident forgiveness" coverage, your insurer promises not to raise your premium the first time you're in an accident that's your fault. But ask the agent how much your regular premium would rise if you did indeed cause a crash. For careful drivers, the annual premium for the forgiveness insurance probably isn't worth it. For sloppy drivers, the policy might not pay. You may have go accident free for three years before it's possible to make a claim. Forget about "new-car replacement" insurance too. You're covered only if the car is totaled.

Ways to Save When There's a Young Driver in the House

■ *Share your car with your teenager (if you can stand it).* When teens have their own cars or drive your car more than half the time, they're "principal drivers." Your premium will rise by 50 to 100 percent. Teens cost less when they're "occasional drivers," using your car less than half the time. They also cost less if they drive a safe, older car with no collision insurance.

- *Tell your agent when your child is away from home and not driving the car.* Your premium should drop if he or she is away at school and driving the car only during short vacations. But be sure to tell the agent when the child returns. You don't want any arguments about coverage if there's an accident.

- *If your child has his or her own car, consider insuring it in the child's name instead of yours, even if that costs more money.* It might save you from being roped into a big liability judgment if your child causes a tragic accident. The child's name should also be on the title and registration.

- *Ask about policies targeted at the children of their adult policyholders.* Fireman's Fund Insurance Company, for example, offers a Youthful Driver program for kids who are buying their own insurance. Drivers up to 27 can piggyback on their parents' policies, earning the same premium discounts that their parents have. State Farm provides discounts to drivers up to 25 who complete a Steer Clear safety program and complete a log of their driving habits. Safeco Insurance Company of America's Teensurance program cuts the premium if you install a Safety Beacon GPS device in your child's car that tracks the car's whereabouts and can disable the engine if your child stays out too late or drives too fast.

- *Don't change insurance companies when your teenagers are within a few years of driving age.* You're better off with the status of long-term policyholder, just in case the the kids have a fender bender.

Think About Which Small Claims to Make

Some claims generally don't affect your premium. For example, you're normally not held responsible for physical damage paid from your comprehensive coverage, such as a windshield broken by flying gravel or accidents caused by animals. Other small claims, such as a bumper dinged by an unknown driver in a parking lot, count against you, even though it wasn't your fault. You might get away with one or two dings, but after that, your rate will rise. Insurers look more at the frequency of claims than how much they have to pay. Ask your company for a detailed statement, in writing, of which claims make your rates go up. That should ease your mind about reporting other kinds of claims. If you've decided not to report claims under $500 or $1,000, raise your deductible to that amount.

For rating purposes, insurers generally look at your record over the past 3 to 5 years. You might have loyally held the policy for 30 years, but two claims in 2 years might put up your rates anyway.

Buy Quality

Not all insurance companies survive. Some go broke, sending their policyholders scrambling. The industry supports state insurance guaranty funds, to make sure that the claims of all policyholders will eventually be paid (page 521). But they're not necessarily paid right away. A truly large bankruptcy might hold up claims for quite a while. So why tempt fate? Buy from a company highly rated for solvency (page 405).

Get It Right

Check a new policy for accuracy as soon as it arrives. A number of policies come through with mistakes: wrong amounts of coverage, a child left off the list of drivers, a discount forgotten. If you don't catch the error, you won't have the coverage you expected.

Don't lie on your application! The insurer will run your name through the state motor vehicle department to check whether you're licensed, what marks you have on your license, and how many licensed drivers live at your address. It will also check the Comprehensive Loss Underwriting Exchange (CLUE) in Atlanta or a similar service, where insurers report the claims you've made over the past seven years. If you say you've never filed a claim but CLUE turns up three, the door is going to be slammed in your face. The insurer can also check the claims record of every driver at your address.

If you're turned down for coverage or charged a higher rate based on information from a claims reporting service, you have to be told and given the service's name and address. Go to ChoiceTrust (www.choicetrust.com) to order a free copy of your record, to be sure it's correct. (Click on "Review Your FACT Act Disclosure Reports.") CLUE also wants to sell you an "insurance score," but knowing your credit score (page 265) is enough. The report may show claims for a particular vehicle before you owned it. If you haven't filed a claim against your auto or home owner's policy in the past seven years, you'll probably have a clear report.

Can You Be "Fired" by Your Insurer?

Absolutely. Every six months, your policy normally comes up for renewal. At that time, the company might blow you off or shift your policy to a related insurer that accepts higher risks. Maybe you've had a couple of speeding tickets. Maybe you've put in one claim too many. Maybe the company is withdrawing from your state. If it won't renew, see if another company will pick you up. Otherwise you'll have to join the state's high-risk pool, where your coverage will come at a much higher rate.

When you first apply for a policy, the insurer generally has 60 days to evaluate you. After that, you can't be canceled before the policy's renewal date unless you didn't pay your premium, your driver's license was suspended or revoked, or you made a deceptive statement on your insurance application.

What If You Have So Many Speeding Tickets or Accidents That Insurers Don't Want You?

All 50 states have assigned-risk pools for careless drivers. Your insurance agent can get you a policy. You'll pay dearly for it, but the coverage is worth it. It will protect you from losing everything you have if you hurt someone seriously in a crash. You can work your way out of the pool by keeping your record clean.

What to Do if You Have an Accident

Keep this list in your car's glove compartment, just in case:

1. **Attend to any injuries.** Have someone call an ambulance and the police.

2. **Move your car to a safer place,** if it can be driven, in order to prevent further damage. Warn oncoming traffic away from the wreck.

3. **Get the other driver's name, address, phone number, license number, vehicle registration number, and insurance company, and give him or her yours.** Look at his or her license to see if there are any restrictions that weren't being observed (wearing eyeglasses, for example). If the car is registered to someone else, get that person's name and address.

4. **Get the names and addresses of witnesses** and their statements of what they saw. This is especially important if you think you weren't at fault. If they won't talk, get the license numbers of their cars. Get the names and badge numbers of the police who arrive on the scene.

5. **If you think the other driver was drinking,** insist that you both take a breath test.

6. **Jot down your recollection of how the accident happened,** including the speed you were traveling at. Note weather conditions, time of day, and any hazardous conditions. Describe the area, writing down exactly where you're located. Fresh impressions are compelling in court.

7. **Don't sign anything unless required to by the police.** Don't admit guilt

or shared guilt. Don't say that your insurance will cover everything. Don't say how much insurance you have.

8. Ask the police whether you should report the accident yourself, and if so, how and where.

9. Call your insurance agent and tell him or her what happened. Summarize the evidence you have. Don't rely on the other driver's promise to pay; that might not last long. Report even small accidents if someone was injured. That injury might turn out to be serious. You risk losing coverage for that accident if you don't report promptly.

10. If you or any of your passengers were injured in any way, even bruised, see a doctor.

11. Cooperate with your insurance company on filling in forms and making reports. But don't make a quick, final settlement with your own company or with the other driver's. Injuries that don't seem serious at first may worsen with time.

12. If you're struck by a hit-and-run driver, tell the police within 24 hours. If you don't, you might lose your insurance coverage for that particular incident.

13. If you're sideswiped and worry that the other driver is trying to force you over in order to rob you, keep going, if you can, and find a police department. Call your insurer from there. Normally, you shouldn't leave the scene of an accident. But if you did so because you felt unsafe, your insurer will cut you some slack.

14. Keep records of all expenses connected with the accident, such as lost paychecks or the cost of renting a car until yours is fixed. In a no-fault state, your company might pay. In a fault state, the other person's company should reimburse you if the accident was his or her fault.

15. If the accident was serious, talk to a lawyer about what happened to get a handle on your rights and what your damages might be. Beware of any offers from your insurer. They may be based on a computerized personal injury service called Colossus or a similar program. In theory, the claims agent enters the facts of your case into the colossal computer, which then spits out the "proper" settlement. Proper, my eye. You can't expect fair treatment from a black box, especially a big one. Assume that the black box is lowballing and ask a lawyer to evaluate your case.

When to See a Lawyer

The following claims will be paid immediately without a lawyer's intercession: in no-fault states, your own medical bills and lost earnings and those of everyone in the car with you; in fault states, only the medical bills that are paid through your own health insurer or through the medical-payments coverage you carry on your auto insurance; in both kinds of states, car repairs, if you carry collision insurance.

You will need a lawyer: in no-fault states, when the injuries are serious enough to warrant going to court; in fault states, when the accident was serious. You'll want an evaluation of the settlement proposed by the insurance company.

The insurance company will defend you if you're sued. But if you bring the lawsuit, you'll need a lawyer of your own. He or she should have long experience in trying personal injury cases. At a first meeting (which might be free or might cost a flat fee), the lawyer will advise you whether the case is worth pursuing. Sometimes it is, sometimes it isn't. If you go ahead, you typically pay the lawyer nothing if you lose and a fixed percentage (usually one-third, plus expenses) if you win. If the insurance company has already made you an offer, a lawyer might be persuaded to take one-third to one-half of anything extra he or she can get.

Collision claims are usually negotiated between you and your company without legal intercession. A good insurance company inspects the car, tells you to get an estimate of what it will cost to repair, and promptly pays its share of the bill. No muss, no fuss. If you have to use the insurer's repair shop, don't sign a release until your own mechanic has examined the work. If something was overlooked, the insurer should fix it.

And then there's the other kind of insurer: a footdragger, a corner-cutter. Don't blindly sign a piece of paper accepting the insurer's estimate as the full cost of the repair. Get a second opinion from your own mechanic. And be sure to have your mechanic check the work. If the estimate or the repair was insufficient and the claims adjuster balks, invoke the arbitration clause contained in many auto insurance contracts. When it's all over, find a better insurance company.

If your car is totaled or stolen, the insurer is supposed to pay fair market value. If the offer is too low, get signed statements attesting to your car's actual value from auto dealers in your area. With those statements in hand, make a pitch for more. You never get what you don't ask for.

If you think you're being taken, go on the offensive. Complain to your insurance agent, the state insurance commissioner (copy to the president of the insurance company), and your local consumer office. Ask a lawyer to write a letter on your behalf to the insurance company's president. Tell your insurance agent that you're pulling all of your policies—auto and homeowners—out of the company. Sometimes pressure works.

If the accident was the other person's fault, your company will go after his or her insurer and collect your property damage claim in full. You will already have been paid if you carry collision coverage, but your company will have subtracted the deductible. Once your insurer has been reimbursed, it owes you the deductible too. Don't forget to ask for it.

Is Your Insurance Policy Safe?

Auto and homeowners insurance policies are covered by the National Conference of Insurance Guaranty Funds (www.ncigf.org). State limits vary, but you're usually insured for up to the limits of the policy or $300,000, whichever is less. You're protected only for claims in the pipeline. If your insurance company fails, your policies will be canceled. You will have to scramble for coverage somewhere else.

Rental Car Insurance

When you rent a car, the rental agency offers to sell you insurance to cover accidents on your trip. In many cases, you can decline it. You get the same or better protection from your personal auto insurance or perhaps from the rental car insurance attached to the credit card you use.

But there are holes in your personal or credit card coverage. If you don't know the rules and decline the rental agency's trip coverage, you may be driving uninsured.

You do want to decline that coverage if you can. It's shockingly expensive. Take the collision damage waiver, which protects you if the car is damaged or stolen. It costs somewhere between $9 and $19 a day. Adding $1 million in bodily injury coverage if you hit someone, and modest amounts of property damage and medical payments, you might pay $133 to $266 for a one-week trip. *And* the coverage may be void if you caused the accident by speeding or driving drunk, or if you were on an unpaved road.

To avoid this expense, ask your auto insurance agent whether your personal policy covers you when you drive a rental car. If the answer is yes, ask about the limitations (and double-check them in the policy itself). For example, there may be no collision or theft insurance on the rental if you don't carry it for your own car too. The policy might not pay if you're on a business trip rather than driving for pleasure. You're generally not covered in foreign countries. If you have coverage, it may last only for 15 to 31 days. If you have an accident on day 10 but don't turn in the car until day 32, you're not insured. For long rentals, see if the rental car agency has any special deals.

If you're driving a rented car on company business, your employer probably insures you. Ask about it. The company might refuse to pay, however, if you have an accident while using the rental car for personal purposes.

If your personal or company policy doesn't cover your rental car, you have another option. Certain credit cards will protect you against damage or theft for a limited number of days if you use that card when you pay for the rental. They may also cover any deductibles under your regular auto insurance.

But, again, there are limitations, and they vary, depending on the bank that issued your card. At this writing, Visa, MasterCard, and American Express permit rental car insurance only on gold cards and higher. You're usually insured only for standard cars and minivans carrying up to eight passengers, not luxury cars, larger vans, or sport vehicles driven off road. American Express cancels your insurance if you're two months behind on your bill.

If there's an accident, you risk losing your credit card coverage unless you follow certain procedures. You must call the credit card company—not the bank that issued the card but the card company itself—within a limited period. There's a special phone number, one for the United States, another when you call from abroad, which you should keep in your wallet.

If you don't know your car insurance rules, call your auto insurer or credit card company and get a list of them in writing. Check back from time to time to see if they've changed. If there's any doubt at all, buy the rental car insurance. You don't want to be caught out.

If you don't own a car, rent frequently, and don't get much liability insurance from your credit card company, consider buying "nonowned auto liability insurance" from your insurance agent. Over the year, it may cost less than you'd pay if you bought from the rental company each time. This coverage pays only what you owe other people if you cause an accident that injures them or damages their car. You still have to buy the rental car company's collision coverage, to protect yourself against the cost of paying for the car you're driving if it's stolen or damaged.

Fitting Your Coverage into Your Financial Plan

Spend your money on high-liability coverage so that any reparations you owe will be paid by the insurance company, not by you personally. Good auto insurance protects your personal assets and future income just as surely as a good investment plan does.

16

Fire! Theft! Wind! Flood!

Protecting Your Home and Everything in It

**Without enough insurance, you're betting your
savings that nothing bad will happen. I'd rather
bet a few extra bucks that something might.**

I have a friend whose house burned down. Luckily, he'd increased his home-owners insurance just a few months before. Unluckily, he'd made the mistake of pegging his coverage to the resale value of his house. He figured that, for insurance purposes, his house was worth what he could sell it for, minus an estimate for the price of the foundation and the land.

A lot of people make that mistake. The resale value of your house is often less than the cost of rebuilding it from the foundation up—and rebuilding a house is what homeowners insurance is all about. The limits on my friend's policy turned out to be too low. His error cost him plenty.

Home owner or tenant, you're living in a dream world if your property isn't fully protected. It doesn't matter that you've drawn up a nice financial plan. It doesn't matter that you're saving money and living smart. One pretty day, you might come home from work and see nothing but fire engines and flames. In a few shocking hours, your house is gone. And so are your savings if you don't have enough homeowners or tenants insurance to make good the loss. You'll have to start building up capital all over again.

Some people deliberately play the odds. It's rare for a home to be totally destroyed so they don't insure for the full rebuilding cost. Sometimes they feel they can't afford it. But a financial plan is only as sound as its backup systems. When you insure something for less than 100 percent, you are holding your savings hostage to luck. If your coverage slips below 80 percent of cost, which it easily might, even your lesser losses may not be fully insured (page 530).

What Type of Policy Do You Want?

Whoever said "A person's home is his or her castle" (it was said that way, right?) knew what he or she was talking about. Your home deserves "castle" coverage because it's worth that much to you.

Each insurance company has a slightly different contract, but all policies follow the same broad outlines (except in Texas, which has special forms; page 527). Buy the best you can afford, and recheck your coverage every couple of years or when you build an addition or make a major renovation.

Policies on the following forms will repair or replace covered structural losses up to your policy limit, provided that you keep your home sufficiently insured (page 529). You're covered for the cost of living in a hotel, motel, or mobile home while your own home is being rebuilt, as well as for your liability to anyone injured on your property except for family members. You are not covered for the cost of normal maintenance. Your furniture, clothing, and other personal property are typically insured for 50 to 75 percent of the amount of insurance on your home. So if you carry a $300,000 limit on the house, the contents are insured for up to $150,000 or $225,000.

How much are you paid for each loss? Less expensive policies cover *actual cash value,* which means replacement cost minus depreciation. If your house burns down, you don't get the full rebuilding cost; the insurer deducts something to account for the fact that you had an older house, and you have to plug the repair gap with your own income or savings. Ditto for used furniture: you're paid its secondhand value, not the cost of replacing it. So you're not as well protected as you think.

If possible, upgrade your coverage to *replacement cost.* That way you'll secure the full cost of replacing your home and restocking your personal belongings, up to the dollar limit of your policy. To get replacement cost coverage, you must insure for at least 80 percent of what it would cost to rebuild (page 530), but that's still too little to protect you. Insure for 100 percent of the rebuilding cost. Add inflation protection, to raise your coverage every year in line with an average of local building costs.

Even better, go for *guaranteed replacement cost* coverage or some variant of it. This pays for costs that exceed your policy's face value. Most policies have ceilings, such as 20 or 25 percent above the policy limits. For example, on a $200,000 policy, you might be covered for as much as $250,000 in replacement costs. For more on guaranteed replacement cost coverage, see page 529.

The Basic Policy Forms

■ *Broad coverage* (HO-2) insures some 16 or 18 risks to your home and personal property, ranging from fire, wind, and living in the path of a volcano to burst pipes and a short-circuited electrical system. It normally covers the actual cash value of your loss, although you usually can upgrade to replacement cost (see page 525).

■ *Special coverage* (HO-3), the most widely sold, costs just a little bit more than HO-2 but is a better deal. On the house itself, you're protected from all risks except a few that are specifically excluded, such as earthquakes, floods, sewer backups, and wars. Check your policy for the exclusion list. A few high-end insurers provide all-risk coverage for personal property too. Usually, however, your personal property is insured for the 16 or 18 specific risks included in an HO-2. HO-3 typically offers replacement cost coverage but lets you upgrade to guaranteed replacement cost.

■ *Tenant's coverage* (HO-4) protects against 16 or 18 risks to your personal property, although a few insurers give you all-risk protection. You can also get coverage for built-in improvements you make to the apartment, your liability to anyone injured there, your potential liability if you negligently cause an accident that damages the landlord's or other tenants' property, and living expenses if you have to move out while your apartment is being repaired. (For more on personal property, see page 536.) Most insurers put roommates—be they lovers or just friends—on a single policy.

■ *Condominium and cooperative apartment coverage* (HO-6) protects your personal property and any part of the structure you own or are responsible for. You can insure against 16 or 18 specific risks, but an all-risk policy is better. Show your insurer the condo agreement, which stipulates what you're responsible for. Sometimes the condo or co-op insures the unit as it was originally built, so you have to insure only the changes (yours and those made by previous owners); sometimes you have to insure everything from the bare walls out. Normally, only 20 percent of your policy's face value can be used to make repairs on your own additions or alterations. If you've renovated your unit, consider boosting this part of your policy.

The building itself, the common areas, and the owners' common liability should be covered by insurance bought by the condo or co-op board. But consider buying your own unit loss assessment coverage. It pays if your condo or co-op suffers damage or loses a lawsuit for which it was underinsured, requiring the unit owners to kick in.

■ *Unique or old-home coverage* (HO-8) is for hard-to-duplicate houses such as Victorians or true Colonials. They'd be far too expensive to replace in their original form. So instead of basing your coverage on replacement cost, most policies insure only for the home's market value. In a few states, insurers have to pay actual cash value (replacement cost minus depreciation) if that comes to more than the market value. Your coverage might also be defined as *modified replacement cost.* It replaces carved oak banisters, plaster walls, and fancy hardware with the building materials commonly used today.

Your house is usually insured only against the limited risks commonly used for HO-1 policies. That leaves out burst pipes and faulty wiring, which older homes are especially subject to. You might not even get replacement cost coverage (page 533) for personal property or for lesser losses, like those from a kitchen fire. Nor can you usually insure your personal property for more than 50 percent of the policy's face value. HO-8, in short, is mediocre but sometimes the best that you can get.

Some insurers impose HO-8 coverage on older houses that aren't unique. This can be a sign of illegal discrimination. An old house in the suburbs might get an HO-3, while the same house in a less desirable urban area might be offered only an HO-8. HO-8s are more expensive, per $1,000 of coverage, than HO-3s, so you're paying more for less.

Replacement policies do exist for rebuilding old or historic homes in their original form, but they're superexpensive.

■ *Mobile homes* are generally covered by a costlier form of HO-2 or HO-3. You can cover the home for its replacement cost (the price of a new home) or for its actual cash value (the market value of your older home). *Total loss* policies let you insure for a fixed dollar amount, which may or may not cover your home's replacement cost.

■ *In Texas,* coverage comes in three basic forms: HO-A insures against 8 classes of risk to your home and its contents, paying only their actual cash value or the cost of repair. HO-B insures against all risks to your home except those specifically excluded, and 12 risks to personal property. On the home, you get replacement cost coverage; on contents, you get actual cash value. HO-C covers all risks to both home and personal property except those specifically excluded. Premises are covered at replacement cost or actual cash value, whichever is greater, and contents at actual cash value. With HO-B and HO-C, you can buy replacement cost endorsements for the contents of your home (an endorsement modifies your coverage). Many other endorsements are available, including—at some companies—guaranteed replacement cost. There are variants of HO-B and HO-C for tenants and condominium owners. Mobile home owners generally buy a variant of auto insurance.

■ *One-form coverage* (HO-W), introduced by State Farm, abolishes all the separate HOs. There's a single contract, with coverage linked to how much of your home's replacement cost you choose to insure. If you cover 100 percent, you get superprotection; in a total wipeout, payments can even exceed the policy's face value (page 529). If you cover 80 to 99 percent of replacement cost, your losses will be replaced, in full, up to the policy's face value. At less than 80 percent, your loss is repaired up to the policy's face value but with common building materials, perhaps of lower quality than you had before. Your premium is adjusted depending on your insurance percentage and amount.

■ *Basic coverage* (HO-1) is a dinosaur. I list it last because it's no longer sold by most insurers. Where available, it typically covers only 11 or 12 specified risks to your home and personal property, leaving out such common happenings as burst pipes, falling tree limbs, and sudden leaks from an air-conditioning system. Some policies cut you down to 8 or 9 risks, excluding vandalism, glass breakage, and theft. The latter coverage is usually reserved for remote or one-season cottages that are uninhabited for months at a time. Buy HO-1 only if it's all you can get. It covers the actual cash value of your loss, although you might be able to upgrade to replacement cost.

Your Inflation Protection

Some policies today come with automatic inflation protection. At every renewal, your policy's face amount goes up, in line with an index of area construction costs. Naturally, your premium goes up too. But that's better than having a major fire and finding that you're underinsured. A few insurers let you decline this inflation guard. Don't.

There's no guarantee, however, that these increases will hit the mark. Your coverage may rise too slowly, leaving you more exposed than you had thought. Or it may rise faster than local building costs, forcing you to buy more insurance than you need. So even with an inflation guard, get a replacement cost appraisal every few years, to be sure you're still on track. And be sure to report any additions or renovations to your insurer.

For superprotection against inflation and other price risks, get *guaranteed replacement cost coverage*. It promises that if your house is destroyed, the insurer will repair or replace it in virtually every detail, even if the cost exceeds the policy's face value. If the house was custom-built for you, the insurer might even pay the same architect and interior designer to supervise the reconstruction. This coverage saves your skin if you're underinsured because you and your agent underestimated your rebuilding costs. It's especially valuable for homes that might be caught in a widespread disaster, such as a wildfire. When a lot of homes need rebuilding at once, builders inflate their prices.

Some insurers don't offer guaranteed replacement cost coverage on houses more than 25 years old, houses worth significantly less than the cost of rebuilding them, or unusually detailed and expensive homes. The latter might find coverage, however, through companies that cater to the carriage trade. Some insurers offer what they call *extended extra replacement cost* or an *increased insurance amount.* Here your payment is capped at 20 to 50 percent over the policy's face value. You may have to negotiate how much over face value the company is going to pay. To claim this coverage, you typically have to start rebuilding within six months of the loss.

To get guaranteed replacement cost coverage, you have to insure for 100 percent of the expected rebuilding cost. The face value (and price) of your policy will rise automatically every year, in line with the general increase in construction costs. If you improve your home in some way, you have to notify the insurer so that that extra value can be covered too.

From time to time, the insurer may reevaluate the cost to rebuild. Don't accept a big increase that seems unjustified. You're required to cover only the cost of reconstruction today. If you think the insurer overestimated costs, take your case to your insurance agent or get a replacement cost appraisal of your own.

Warning: The local building code may have changed since your house was put up. Guaranteed replacement cost policies typically pay for repairing your house but not for bringing it up to code. Ask about an *ordinance* or *law endorsement,* which covers needed code improvements too.

How Much Insurance Do You Need?

In my opinion, your policy should equal 100 percent of your home's rebuilding cost. You can't go by market value, which includes the land as well as the house. You need to know what it would cost to rebuild from the ground up. In the super-high heat of a fire, even the foundation may be damaged.

You'll get the best answer from a builder or appraiser (tell the appraiser you want building costs, not market value). Alternatively, you could use your insurance agent's rules of thumb. If the agent steers you wrong, however, and you find out too late that you're underinsured, the problem is entirely yours.

Guaranteed replacement cost coverage keeps you fully insured for the right amount. Second best is automatic inflation protection. Third best is to use your insurance company's worksheet every time your policy comes up for renewal to figure out how much more insurance you need to buy.

You'll probably have to increase your coverage even though housing values fell. No matter how bad the real estate market, building costs generally rise.

What Happens if You're Insured for Less Than the Full Replacement Cost?

That depends on how much less.

- *If you're covered for 80 percent or more of replacement cost,* your insured losses are normally paid in full up to the limits of your policy. Say, for example, that your home's replacement cost is $200,000 and you're insured for 80 percent, or $160,000. If a fire in the kitchen costs you $10,000, your insurer will pay the entire bill, minus the deductible. (A few companies require 90 percent coverage before smaller losses will be paid in full.) If the house burns to the ground, however, you collect only $160,000. *Please* insure your home for 100 percent of replacement cost.

Many home owners think they can't afford 100 percent coverage. But you probably can if you increase the deductible. The average person files a claim only once in every 8 to 10 years. It's better to pay for smaller repairs yourself than to get less money than you need to rebuild your home from scratch.

- *If you're covered for less than 80 percent,* you will not collect in full on any loss, even a small one. On a kitchen fire that costs $5,000 to fix, you might get $4,000 or less. The exact amount will depend on the age of the house and the payment formula used. People who insure for less than 80 percent are gambling that the worst won't happen. I think you're nuts. But maybe you know more about the future than I do. At the very least, keep your policy at 90 percent of replacement cost. That ensures full coverage for anything but a catastrophic loss and avoids philosophical discussions with your insurer over whether your coverage met the crucial 80 percent test.

You don't have to rebuild exactly what you had before. You don't even have to rebuild in the same location, depending on the policy provisions. If you decide not to rebuild at all, you can simply take the money (usually the actual cash value).

What's Covered, What Isn't

Policies differ. So do state laws governing what has to be covered. The depth of your protection depends on what your policy says, so be sure to read the list of covered items. Here's a general look at what it might include.

■ *Detached garages, sheds, driveways, fences, and other detached structures,* typically insured for 10 percent of the coverage you carry on your house.

■ *For home owners*—trees, shrubs, and plants worth up to 5 percent of the policy's face value, with a maximum of $500 per item. For renters or condo owners, it's 10 percent up to a $500 maximum per item. They're not protected against storm damage, only from theft, fire, lightning, vandalism, and so on.

■ *The contents of a house*—typically covered for 50 percent of the policy's face value. Some insurers have raised that limit to 75 percent. You're insured for losses both at home and away from home, including things stolen from your bank safe-deposit box.

■ *Water damage that's sudden and accidental,* from burst pipes, air conditioner leaks, or a flood in the basement. You're also covered if accidental damage to the roof lets in the rain, and for the havoc wrought by firefighters' hoses.

■ *The cost of protecting your home against further damage or loss*—for example, boarding up broken windows or gaps in the wall that a fire burned through.

■ *Reasonable living expenses if you have to move out* of your house while it's being repaired. Ditto if the authorities move you out of your house because of direct damage to a neighbor's house by a peril that your policy insures against. For example, your company would pay your hotel bill if the police or fire department prevented you from going home because your neighbor's house was on fire. You're covered only for extra expenses (restaurant meals), not expenses you'd normally incur (groceries). Reimbursement is generally limited to 20 percent of rebuilding costs. Insurers set limits on how long these payments can last.

■ *Lost rent if you rent out part of your house and those quarters become uninhabitable* because of a fire or other insured damage. But you don't get the full amount; the insurer deducts the business expenses that you normally would have incurred.

■ *Removing debris* from your property.

■ *Up to $2,500 if your fire department charges for calls.*

■ *Medical payments coverage,* for the minor medical bills of visitors or employees hurt on your property or injured by your family or pets away from home. If your dog bites the window washer, you can send your insurer the doctor bill, and maybe he won't sue. Typically, you're insured for up to $1,000. For a few bucks more, you can raise that to $5,000.

■ *Theft or damage to the personal property* of a guest or a domestic employee.

■ *Up to $1,000 for a loss to your condo or co-op building* if your owners' association assesses you for it. You can beef up this coverage if you want.

- *Up to $2,000* in cash, stored-value cards, or other legal tender.
- *Damage done by your pets* to the person or property of others.

Different policies have different exceptions. But in general, here's what might be ruled out:

- *A separate structure* on the property that's used as a business office or rented out.
- *Losses due to a power failure* from a source outside your home.
- *Water damage not arising from an accident.* That includes floods, tides, sewer backups, and seepage from groundwater. You can buy a separate endorsement to cover backups of sewers or drains.
- *Losses from mold or other fungi.* You might have limited protection if the mold arises from damage that's covered, such as a burst water pipe. Otherwise buy a separate mold rider.
- *Losses from neglect*—for example, property that's stolen because you walked away from a partly burned home without boarding up the windows.
- *Damage you deliberately do yourself.*
- *Earthquake,* except by special endorsement.
- *Ice or snow damage* to awnings, fences, patios, and swimming pools.
- *Vandalism* to houses left vacant for more than 30 days, depending on the policy.
- *Frozen or burst pipes* in a house you've left unoccupied without maintaining the heat or draining the pipes.
- *Damage from settling or cracking* in foundations, pavements, or patios.
- *War.*
- *Normal wear and tear.*
- *Damage done by birds, rodents, insects, or your own pets* (although the policy will repair your porch if it collapses due to hidden insect damage).
- *Smoke damage* from nearby factories or agricultural smudging.
- *Claims on policies obtained by misrepresentation or fraud.* So don't lie if you're asked whether your dog bites or whether you've had any previous losses.
- *A continuous leak* from the plumbing, heating, or air-conditioning system (you're covered only for sudden leaks).
- *Nuclear explosion*—although if you're nuked, the exclusions in your home owner's policy will be the least of your troubles.

Covering Your Personal Property

Clothes, furniture, and other personal effects are normally insured for up to half the face value of your home owner's policy. A few companies insure them for 75 percent. With a $200,000 policy, then, you get $100,000 to $150,000 worth of personal property protection. There are fixed maximums for special items such as jewelry and furs (page 537). You can increase your coverage by buying endorsements (to raise particular policy ceilings) or floaters (for special items such as jewelry). You may also have $500 of credit card coverage in case a crook gets your card number and it costs you some money.

If you're a renter or own a condominium or cooperative apartment, you are insured for the full value of your personal property.

Your policy covers damage or a theft reported to the police. It protects property in your home, temporarily out of your home (say, when you're carrying it in your handbag), or with one of your children at school or college. You're generally not covered, however, for personal property that you merely lose or break. There has to be vandalism, theft, or an accident that you or your family didn't cause. If you accidentally break someone else's valuable property, however, the policy should pay.

What are you covered for per item? In standard policies, less than you think.

Standard Reimbursement

When your insurer reimburses you for an item, you normally get its actual cash value—officially defined as its replacement cost minus depreciation. In other words, its value as used property, not new.

Your fire-damaged living room couch may have cost $1,200, but that was five years ago, before it was clawed by your cat and used as a trampoline by your kids. Its actual cash value, as priced by standard insurance formulas, might be only $650. The additional cost of a new couch will come out of your pocket.

Almost everything new loses value over the years: furniture, clothing, electronics, cameras, carpeting. Your insurer will repair the damaged item or reimburse you for its actual cash value, whichever is less. But you won't get the money you need to buy something new. To refurnish your house after an expensive loss, you need replacement cost coverage.

Good antiques, on the other hand, should increase in value as the years go by. Your basic insurance will generally cover their current appraised value, even though it's higher than when the policy was new. But you'll have to prove your claim with a proof of purchase, a new appraisal, a picture, and other details about the items. The insurer can also decide to repair an item rather than replace it.

Replacement Cost Reimbursement

If you can afford it, this is definitely the coverage of choice. You get whatever money you need to start over from scratch. If your $1,200 couch goes up in flames, you might collect $1,800 because that's what it costs to buy a couch of similar quality, new. The insurance company will also make repairs if the item can be restored to its original condition.

Only replacement cost coverage can restock your closets, rooms, and china cabinets after a major wipeout. The only articles not covered are those that are obsolete and in storage (your old Schwinn bicycle) and articles not in working condition (the broken TV set in the back bedroom).

Where possible, the insurer sends you an actual replacement of the item. If you know the make and model of your TV set, for example, the insurer will send you another one or one very similar. These goods are purchased at a discount. If you want cash instead—say, to put toward a larger-screen TV—the insurer gives you only the discounted price. That's more than you'd get with a regular policy but less than full retail value. Where standard replacements aren't possible, however, you get the full retail price of the substitute.

Standard Limits on Valuables

In standard policies, insurers pay a fixed, maximum price for the theft or covered damage to certain items, no matter how large your total coverage is. The typical limits: $2,500 for silverware, goldware, pewterware, and gold and silver plate; $200 for all bullion coins, rare coins, cash, and gold, silver, or platinum bars; $1,000 for all securities, deeds, manuscripts (which might include rare books), tickets, letters of credit, accounts, evidence of money owed you, and stamps; $1,000 for boats and their trailers, furnishings, equipment, and motors; $1,000 for other trailers; $1,000 for grave markers; $2,000 for guns; $2,500 for business property on the premises; $250 for business property away from the premises (such as a laptop computer stolen at an airport); and $1,000 to $2,000, collectively, for the theft of jewelry, watches, gems, and furs.

These limits apply to valuables in your bank safe-deposit box as well as to property kept at home. To raise your coverage, read on.

Blanket Coverage

For a small extra payment, you can raise the limit on most of the categories just listed. For example, you might want to cover $10,000 worth of jewelry without listing all the items, but with a $2,500 limit per item. If something is stolen, you'd report the loss, substantiate its value, and collect. No proofs of ownership are required in advance, but you'll need them if you make a claim. So keep sales slips and take pictures of your valuables or get appraisals, just in case.

Scheduled Coverage

Particular items of special value should be individually insured. Have each one appraised and listed separately: sterling silver flatware, $5,000; mink coat, $6,000; Dream Diamond, $7 zillion. If any scheduled item is stolen or damaged, the insurer pays its scheduled value, with or without a deductible, depending on the policy. You're also paid for items that you merely lose. But there may be no coverage for accidental breakage unless you buy extra coverage.

Other valuables, such as antiques, collectors' items, fine china, guns, musical instruments, or golfing equipment, don't have to be scheduled to be fully covered. You can insure them for their actual cash value (including any appreciation in value) right along with your other personal property.

The Advantages of Scheduling Your Valuables

1. They're covered if they merely disappear. If they're not scheduled, there has to be a likelihood of theft.

2. They're protected against practically all forms of damage, not just the 16 or 18 listed in your regular policy. This includes accidental wine or ink stains on an Oriental rug.

3. If they're included in your basic policy, they might push the value of your personal possessions above the policy's maximum limit. It's often cheaper to schedule a few items than to raise the ceiling on your total coverage.

4. You won't have to haggle with the insurer over whether you really owned the items and what they were worth.

The Disadvantages of Scheduling

1. It costs extra money.

2. You're covered for no more than the exact amount of the appraisal. If your Picasso lithograph was listed at $2,500, that's what you'll get—even if the appraisal is old and the lithograph is worth $4,000 today. Had it not been scheduled, you'd have gotten its current market value minus the policy's deductible.

3. You may wind up paying for insurance that you don't really have. Say, for example, that you scheduled your mink for $5,000. It's now three years old and worth only $3,500. If it's stolen, you'll normally get only $3,500, even though it's insured for more. Solution: Buy replacement cost coverage for scheduled items. You'll then be paid the full value that they were insured for.

All scheduled items should be reappraised regularly so they won't be under-insured. Special items you don't schedule need to be appraised only once and their pictures taken. If they're damaged, their value can be updated based on the work that was done before.

Count the Risks

You're insured only against the specific risks listed in the contract—as few as 9, as many as 18. A few insurers sell all-risk coverage, which actually should be called *almost* all-risk. It leaves out things such as floods, war, and wear and tear. But only all-risk coverage protects you against paint dropped on the carpet or wine stains on your pink velvet love seat. Ask your company about cigarette burns. Some cover them under the "fire" clause in your basic policy; others pay only if you buy all-risk insurance. Also ask about breakage: what's covered, what isn't? You pay for minor damage, under your deductible.

If a guest damages your property, his or her policy might pay under the property damage clause or the liability clause.

What May Not Be Covered

Policies vary on this point, but here are some likely examples:
- Lost pets or damage pets do to your property (although if your neighbor's dog knocks over your Ming vase, the neighbor's policy might pay).
- Aircraft.
- Boats, except in limited circumstances.
- Most motorized vehicles and the equipment, radios, or tape decks in them, unless they're parked on your property. (But you're usually covered for off-road vehicles that service the premises, such as lawn mowers, or that assist the handicapped, such as motorized wheelchairs.)
- The property in a room you rent regularly to someone not in your family.
- Records and data pertaining to your business.
- Theft of materials from a house under construction.
- Items that disappear, without the likelihood of theft.
- Breakage, unless it's vandalism.
- Loss of a gem from its setting.
- Marring.
- Wear and tear.

Ask about any special items in your home. A computer. A satellite dish antenna. A wine cellar. A coin collection. Ask about family members. Does the policy cover your mother who lives with you? Clarify your coverage before any damage is done.

When You Don't Replace

What if a spare camera is stolen from your house and you don't want to buy another one? At the very least, you'll be paid its current, flea market value (replacement cost minus depreciation). If you carry replacement cost coverage, there may or may not be limits on what you can collect. Some policies pay full cost whether you buy or not; others pay up to a ceiling, say, $1,000.

When Your Lost or Stolen Property Is Found

You can give it to the insurer and keep the money. Or you can keep the property and give back the money. It's your choice.

Upper-Crust Coverage

Some policies (HO-5s) are specifically aimed at the well-to-do. You get replacement cost coverage on both your house and its contents. You get protection against all risks. In addition, there might be:

■ *Higher payments for valuable items.* For example, jewelry and furs may be covered up to $5,000, silverware up to $10,000, and guns up to $5,000.

■ *Coverage for damage from a power outage* in your neighborhood.

■ *Tarping your house* right after a hurricane.

■ *Free fire protection consultations in wildfire areas* and brush-cleaning services at a discount. They might spray the roof with fire retardant if you're near the path of a wildfire.

■ *Coverage for food lost* when the power to your freezer went out.

■ *A bit of liability coverage for a small, part-time business* run out of your house. The policy might also pay toward replacing data lost in an accident to your personal computer.

■ *Coverage for damage from the backup of a sewer or drain*—not included in the average policy.

■ *Higher limits on your coverage for personal liability.*

■ *Recompense, up to $2,500, for the cost of changing the locks* when your keys are stolen.

■ *Medical treatment for pets* injured in a covered loss.

■ *The additional cost of rebuilding a damaged or burned-out portion of your house* to meet the standards of a new building code.

■ *"Green" replacements.* When you have losses, the policy will upgrade you to energy-efficient Energy Star appliances, lighting, and heating and cooling equipment.

■ *Reimbursement for items not obviously stolen but simply missing.*

■ *Homeowners, auto, and umbrella insurance,* bundled together for a single package price.

You can get much (but not all) of this upper-crust coverage by increasing the limits on your regular policy or by buying endorsements. Which choice to make depends on what you need. Ask the insurance agent to make a list of all the extras in the higher-cost policy. Cross off the ones that aren't essential. When you've pared down the list, find out what it would cost to add those extras to a standard policy. There's no point buying more insurance than necessary.

Even with upper-crust coverage, you may have to schedule valuable items such as silverware, jewelry, and furs.

Liability Insurance

This is your "banana peel" coverage. You're protected if someone—not a family member—slips on your banana peel, breaks a leg, and sues. You're covered for injuries on your premises. Your family members (and pets) are also covered for their actions (or bites) away from home. Some states require that you carry workers compensation to cover domestics, painters, gardeners, and other full-time or occasional employees. You're also covered if you negligently damage someone else's property—for example, if your wheelbarrow gets away from you on a slope and smashes into your neighbor's new Mercedes.

Only unintentional damage and injuries are covered unless the perpetrator is under 13. So you can't slash your neighbor's tires in a driveway dispute and expect your insurer to replace them. But it will pay in full if your small daughter hits your neighbor in the eye with a rock.

What if that same daughter, at 14, vents her emotions by deliberately setting fire to your neighbor's porch? The property damage won't be covered, but injury to your neighbor might. Your lawyer (you'll need one!) will argue that, although your nasty daughter meant to scorch the porch, she didn't intend to send anyone to the hospital for smoke inhalation, so the injury was unintentional—hence, insured. Right now, some policies pay if a court holds a parent financially responsible for children's evil deeds. Other policies don't.

If your dog bites the United Parcel Service driver, your insurance pays. If the dog lunches next on the driver for Federal Express, it pays again. But at that point, the insurer may cancel your policy, refuse to renew it, or try to exclude the dog (I say "try to" because it's not clear that such an exclusion would stand up in court). In some states, courts can levy extra, punitive damages after a second bite—your punishment for keeping a dangerous dog. Those extra damages might not be covered by your insurance. After a dog bite, find out what your liability could be if the sweet pooch bites again. Some insurers won't sell policies to owners of so-called vicious breeds: pit bulls, akitas, Dobermans, and others.

Your basic policy probably includes $100,000 of liability coverage. That's not much, especially if you own a swimming pool. For a small additional fee, you can have $300,000 of coverage or even $500,000. Some companies take you up to $1 million.

Alternatively, you can buy *umbrella insurance,* which covers losses in excess of the limits on both your homeowners and auto policies. You're required to carry certain minimums on your basic policies, maybe $250,000 on auto and $300,000 on your home. After that, the umbrella goes up. The ceiling can be $5 million or more. The insurance might also cover your liability if you're charged with invasion of privacy, false arrest, libel, or slander. Average price: $200 to $300 a year.

Not Covered Might Be:

- *Employees and clients if you run a business from home.* Ditto if you run a child care service. Even that Federal Express driver bitten by your dog won't be covered if he or she was delivering something for your business. For business risks, you need separate business or child care insurance.
- *Aircraft.*
- *Injuries from most boats and motor vehicles* (they have to be insured separately). But off-road vehicles such as golf carts and dirt bikes might be covered. Ditto small boats or boats parked in your yard.
- *Claims by one family member against another.*
- *Damage to your own property.*
- *Any disease that someone catches from you.*
- *Damage done by a leaking water bed* to an apartment you rent, unless you cover the bed with a special endorsement.

If you're sued, your insurance company not only pays the damages up to the limit of your policy, it also covers all the legal costs of reaching a settlement or going to court.

Flood Insurance

Your policy probably doesn't insure you against floods. If flooding is a risk and your community has met federal flood prevention standards, most home owners can insure themselves—for home and contents—through the government's National Flood Insurance Program (NFIP). For information, see an insurance agent. In 2009 the most you could insure for was $250,000 on a house or condominium and $100,000 on its contents. There's normally a 30-day wait before your coverage takes effect, so don't put off applying until you hear the waters rising. There's no waiting period, however, if you apply and pay for a policy in connection with a mortgage loan.

Consider buying flood insurance even if you live in a low-risk area. The feds say that 25 percent of all flood loss claims are filed by home owners living in places considered low to moderate risk. To determine your risk, go to Flood Smart.com (www.floodsmart.com) and type in your address. Some high-end insurers such as Chubb and Fireman's Fund will piggyback additional coverage onto your government policy. They even offer complete replacement coverage in low-risk areas.

If you've ever received federal disaster insurance after a flood and don't buy this coverage, you won't qualify for disaster aid again.

Earthquake Insurance

Insurance companies may sell earthquake insurance as a separate policy or as an endorsement to your homeowners policy. Deductibles run from 2 to 20 percent of the home's insured value. In California, most residential policies are placed through the California Earthquake Authority (CEA), with a 10 or 15 percent deductible, no coverage for outbuildings and pools, only $1,500 for living expenses while your home is being repaired, and no more than $5,000 (above the deductible) for replacing your home's contents. Higher coverage limits are available, for a price. Some California insurers may offer modest wraparounds to cover certain losses that CEA-approved policies don't.

Find out if you live near a geological fault (there are some in states other than California). If so, consider buying this coverage. Premiums are lowest for policies on wood-frame houses, which can sway with a quake and aren't too expensive to rebuild.

What's the very best earthquake insurance? Move to Dallas, where the earth doesn't move.

Hurricane Coverage

Home owner's policies normally cover wind damage except in places where windstorms are especially bad—for example, along the Gulf and South Atlantic coasts. There you may need special beach or windstorm coverage. Beach plans help protect coastal properties against wind and water damage during hurricanes. Wind plans protect only against hail and windstorm damage.

Some companies "shoreline," meaning they don't write beach policies at all. Others insist on a large deductible if you're damaged in a hurricane rather than an ordinary windstorm. As a condition of coverage, you may be required to take special steps, such as adding shutters, to better protect your house against wind.

The devastation wreaked by major hurricanes in recent years has led many insurers to quit insuring homes along the coastal areas in many states, including Massachusetts and New York. Those that do offer coverage have raised their premiums in shore communities by as much as 100 percent! Increasingly, people with moderate incomes are selling shore homes and migrating inland because they can't afford the policies.

For Rejectniks

Thousands of home owners in inner cities, high-risk coastal areas, wildfire zones, or along earthquake faults find good policies hard to get. Only a handful of companies may offer insurance at all. Those that do may provide bare-bones coverage or charge a painfully high price. Still, buy the best coverage you can. Losing your home will cost you more than paying a high premium for insurance. It's a rock-bottom rule of real estate: never buy a property you can't insure.

If one insurer rejects you, try another. They have different rules for accepting applicants. But you might not get coverage anywhere if you haven't paid your property taxes for a couple of years, if a past policy was canceled because you didn't pay your premiums, or if your house has been vacant for a while.

If you're switching companies, keep your old policy for a month in case your new company reneges. For example, the new company might back away because of something it sees on your credit report.

People who can't get normal homeowners or tenants coverage or are offered it only at a prohibitive price generally have access to risk pools organized by the state. These are bare-bones policies too. You buy them through insurance agents. They include:

- *Fair Access to Insurance Requirements (FAIR) plans*—available in 32 states and the District of Columbia, for protection against such perils as fire, rioting, wind, hail, smoke, and theft. Some offer beach and hurricane coverage. A few include crime insurance. The plans typically assess the state's insurance companies to help pay claims.

■ *Policies from state underwriting pools*—for broad-based coverage in areas where individual private insurers have pulled out. But even the state pools are writing rules to exclude high-cost properties, such as million-dollar beach houses in most vulnerable hurricane zones, unless they can't get coverage anywhere else, at any price.

■ *Policies from private companies that the state subsidizes*—to insure high-risk properties that couldn't otherwise get coverage. Some states require participating insurers to take over policies that are currently in the state risk pool.

■ *The surplus line or nonadmitted market*—for coverage not offered anywhere else. These companies, such as Lloyd's of London, lie outside the jurisdiction of state insurance regulators. Typically, they're for people needing unusually large amounts of coverage or coverage in high-risk areas. If you take this turn, read all the fine print and follow the rules to the letter. You may have gotten a credit for having hurricane shutters, but you won't get paid if you didn't get the shutters up in time.

Insurance on a Home Business

More than 20 million people are believed to work from home at least part-time. A fire, a burst pipe, or a tornado could wreck not only their living quarters but also their livelihood. A lawsuit brought by an injured customer or employee could wipe them out financially. A thief might vanish with their computer or inventory.

Some self-employed people think that special business insurance will cost more than they can afford. But you might find bare-bones coverage for computer equipment for as little as $25 to $50 a year as an endorsement on your homeowners policy. More comprehensive coverage might cost around $100 to $400.

Home-business insurance is an industry in transition. New types of policies are being developed, targeted at the new workplace's special needs. So when looking for comprehensive insurance, it's important to speak with a couple of different agents. Some can offer more inventive policies than others. Here are your options:

1. Your current homeowners or renters insurance. You may think that your policy already covers the contents of your home office, but that's not necessarily so. It typically protects only $2,500 worth of business equipment and a $250 loss off premises (for example, if a pickpocket lifts your cell phone). The equipment is insured against the risks named in your homeowners insurance, such as fire, theft, windstorm, and so on, but not flood—that comes under federal flood insurance—and not if your toddler dumps his spinach into your laser printer. There's no protection against business lawsuits and no income replacement if your business shuts down because of damage to your equipment or home.

Nevertheless, simple homeowners insurance may be enough for a one-person craft or service business. Read your policy to see what's covered. Strictly speaking, a business computer is often excluded. But if you also use it for games, balancing your checkbook, and other personal matters, the insurer may accept it as covered personal property.

2. Endorsements to your homeowners or renters insurance. You can usually raise your home-business coverage limits to protect equipment worth up to $10,000 or $15,000, and $1,000 or $1,500 off premises, at very low cost. There may also be endorsements for limited types of liability, such as injury to customers on premises or damage you accidentally do when calling on customers or setting up at craft fairs. But you don't get protection against broad business risks such as false advertising or product liability. To qualify even for limited liability coverage under an endorsement, your business might have to be *incidental*, meaning very small. Liability protection for home day care is written separately.

3. Stand-alone home business policies. You get more comprehensive coverage for liability and equipment than beefed-up homeowners policies offer. They also reimburse you for the loss of important papers and records. Some cover the income you lose if your home has been so badly damaged by a fire or other disaster that you can't do business there, plus the cost of temporarily locating elsewhere.

Ask the carrier that insures your home what it offers for home businesses. For a specialist in home businesses, try RLI Insurance Company in Peoria, Illinois. Among other things, you get coverage for anywhere from $5,000 to $100,000 worth of in-home business equipment ($1,000 to $50,000 off premises); $300,000 to $1 million worth of business liability protection for personal injury and property damage (although there's a long list of exclusions); and loss-of-business income for up to 12 months if a fire or hurricane shuts down your office at home. Prices run from $170 up.

4. Business owner's policies. These policies cover the works for businesses with more than one location. You're covered for loss of equipment, inventory, computer files, business property, cash up to $5,000 or $10,000, a broad range of business liability risks, and off-premises losses of equipment worth $15,000 or more. You get all-risk protection, meaning that you're covered for any loss not specifically excluded. If there's a fire in the warehouse where you store inventory, you put in a claim. These policies also reimburse you for 12 months of lost income if your business shuts down because of damage to your home plus the cost of setting up shop in a new location. Stepped-up coverage may cost $1,000 a year and up.

5. Automobile insurance. If you're using your car on business, let your agent know. And beef up your liability coverage. Clients don't take kindly to being injured in accidents.

The Inventory

Make a day of it—maybe a rainy Saturday in March. Lay in plenty of diet soda. Plenty of chocolate bars to keep up your energy. Photograph everything in your house. Open every drawer, every cabinet, every closet, and take pictures from a close enough range to show all the contents. Make overall views of your rooms and what's in them. Take close-ups of special items such as good china, Waterford crystal, and antiques. Don't forget the cellar, attic, and garage. When it stops raining, take pictures of the outside of your house—the landscaping, driveway, sidewalks, toolshed, pool.

Old-fashioned film works well (if you can find a place to develop it). When the pictures come back, you can describe the items briefly on the back. With digital pictures, label the most important ones. Put down the model numbers and prices of any costly items and when you bought them.

Go to KnowYourStuff.org (www.knowyourstuff.org) for free software that lets you keep your inventory online. You can import your digital pictures into your online list. E-mail the list to another location, to protect it in case your house burns down.

If you have a video camera, use it instead. Talk about each item as you show it, recording the model and price.

The inventory is your guarantee that you'll collect all the protection you paid for. With it, you can make a full list of all of your losses. Insurers will generally accept a list reconstructed from memory. But you'll never recall every single item, and those little things add up. Pictures also show the quality of your furniture and prove that your modest home really did contain an antique Oriental rug.

Keep a copy of the inventory—along with sales slips for the more expensive items and any appraisals or descriptive material about them—in your safe-deposit box or at the house of a relative or friend. You'd be chagrined if these records burned in the same fire that destroyed everything else.

Total up the rough value of everything you own. It's probably double what you thought. When buying property insurance, most people focus only on their few expensive pieces of furniture. But what drives up the price of refurnishing a house are the pencils and potholders, jackets and mittens, baseballs and house-plants. Your family's clothing alone may be worth $10,000 or more.

Appraisals

All special items should be separately described and appraised: furs, good jewelry, antiques, paintings, Oriental carpets, rare books, special collections, and so on. Take pictures of them in relation to other things in your home to prove they were there. To find an appraiser, ask your insurer, a local jeweler, and a furrier, look in the Yellow Pages, or search online. Keep the pictures and appraisals in your safe-deposit box.

The first appraisal is the most expensive because everything has to be written up. After that, you can coast. The only appraisals that have to be updated regularly are those for the items that are separately scheduled (see page 535). Leave everything else alone. When something is stolen or damaged, just give the insurer the description, the picture, and the original appraisal. The appraiser will update the value for you. The only reason to reappraise everything is to run a check on whether you have enough personal property insurance to cover all of your possessions.

Finding a Good, Low-Cost Insurance Company

Compare prices! In any city, the most expensive insurer may charge 50 percent more than the least expensive for the very same policy. Many consumers don't realize this or don't take it seriously. You might waste hundreds of dollars if you can't be bothered to shop around.

There are four sources of homeowners insurance: (1) Companies that sell only by phone or e-mail, such as Amica in Providence, Rhode Island (www.amica .com or 800-242-6422), specializing in better risks, GEICO in Washington, D.C. (www.geico.com or 800-841-3000), and AARP (for members only). Anyone associated with the U.S. military should call USAA in San Antonio, Texas (www .usaa.com or 800-531-8722—see page 512). (2) Companies that sell exclusively through their own agents or their own Web sites, such as Allstate, State Farm, and Progressive. (3) Companies available through general Web sites such as

Insure.com, InsWeb.com, esurance.com, and InsureOne.com. (4) Companies that sell through independent agents. These agents work with several carriers, although they usually specialize in two or three.

Prices vary depending on your circumstances and where you live, so the same company may not be the cheapest for everyone. Amica and some other insurers pay a dividend at the end of the year, so their true cost is lower than it seems (although dividends aren't guaranteed).

I like checking Web sites because you can get so many quotes. Be sure you give each company the same information, so that the quotes will be comparable. Quotes should come to your e-mail. Sometimes an agent will call; tell him or her that you're gathering quotes and will return the call if you're interested. Price shopping on the Web takes a little time but gives you a good look at the competition. It's also a reality check on what an agent might tell you. Both agents and Web sites will check your credit report before proffering a quote, but that won't affect your credit score. The scorekeepers ignore all insurance-related inquiries.

Price isn't everything, of course. You also want your claims handled promptly, fairly, and without any hassle. Ask your friends how they like their own insurers. Some states publish data on customer complaints.

Other Ways to Save Money on Homeowners and Tenants Insurance

1. Buy your auto, homeowners, and umbrella policies from the same company. You may get a package deal.

2. Install deadbolt locks, smoke detectors, a fire extinguisher, and burglar alarms. You get a 5 percent discount if your house is protected.

3. Pay annually. It's cheaper than paying semiannually or quarterly.

4. Raise the deductible. The standard deductible is $250, meaning that you pay the first $250 of any claim. The price of your policy goes down if you take a $500 or $1,000 deductible, but the saving may be only $50 or so. Ask yourself whether such a small price cut is worth the risk.

5. Quit smoking. Many insurers give nonsmokers lower rates.

6. If you have a second home, place both homes with the same insurance company. That way you pay only once for liability coverage.

7. Retire. Many companies charge retirees less than workers because they're more likely to be home during the day.

8. Call your state insurance department. A few states help you price-shop by publishing booklets that compare what various companies charge.

9. Buy a recently built house. Discounts are often available for insurance on newer homes.

10. Don't automatically take any coverage offered through your company's payroll deduction plan. It's not always cheap. Compare prices before signing up.

11. Build or rebuild your house right. Some insurers give discounts to coastal homes with storm shutters, shingles that are nailed down rather than stapled, and roofs that are strapped to the walls. California homes may need fire-retardant roofing.

12. Don't overinsure! You might be paying for more coverage than you can use. Check it out if you insured your house for its full market value or something close to it. Your purchase price covered the land as well as the house, and there's no point insuring your yard against fire and theft. Get a replacement cost appraisal of the value of the house versus the value of the land, and cover only the cost of rebuilding the house. If you're paying your insurance premiums through your mortgage lender, you'll probably need a letter from the appraiser if you want to reduce your homeowners coverage.

13. Don't underinsure. Lower coverage costs less up front but will leave you stranded if you have a major loss.

14. Check your credit report for accuracy (page 260). Most insurance companies now consider credit scores when deciding whom to cover and how much to charge. Pay bills on time. A couple of missed credit card payments may result in higher insurance costs.

15. Think twice before filing a small claim. Insurers can look up how many claims you've filed by searching automated claims history databases, such as the Comprehensive Loss Underwriting Exchange (CLUE) or the Automobile Property Loss Underwriting System (A-PLUS). If you file more claims than average (more than one in every 8 to 10 years), you may be labeled high risk (experts call this the "use-it-and-lose-it" syndrome). You might be turned down for coverage or not renewed by your current carrier. The reports also cover how many claims, if any, have been made on your house in the past seven years, including claims by previous owners. That shows the insurers whether the house has structural or other problems. Too many claims on the house can put your rates up too. You can't order a CLUE report on a house you want to buy, but you can ask the seller to get it for you.

Order a free copy of your CLUE report from ChoiceTrust.com at www

.choicetrust.com (click on "Review Your FACT Act Disclosure Reports"). CLUE also wants to sell you an "insurance score," but knowing your credit score is enough (page 260). For your free A-PLUS loss history report, call 800-627-3487.

16. Buy a house near a fire hydrant. You'll pay less than your neighbors at the other end of the street.

17. Clear the brush around your house if you're in a wildfire zone. In California, some insurance companies require a cleared area of as much as 1,500 feet.

Which Claims Put Your Premium Up?

A good insurer lets you make every weather-related claim you deserve. Your premium shouldn't go up just because you've had repeated damage. After some bad storms insurers may raise rates generally in your area, but that will happen whether you make claims or not. A few insurers, however, do raise individual rates after two or more weather-related claims, so ask about it. You may have to make your house more wind- and storm-resistant as a condition of continued coverage.

If you have too many fires or thefts, however, your insurer might conclude that you're a careless person (or a cheater). It might raise your premium or deductible, or even cancel your coverage. Ask your agent about your company's rules on this point. Many companies won't accept you if you've made several claims of this kind on other insurers.

Don't Lie.

When applying for new coverage, you'll be asked about past claims. As a double check on your truthfulness, the insurer will run your name and address through the Comprehensive Loss Underwriting Exchange (CLUE) or a similar service, where insurers report the claims you've made over the past five years. If you "forget" to mention a claim that CLUE reports, the insurer may decide that you can't be trusted and turn you down.

If you're rejected for coverage or charged a higher rate based on information from the claims-reporting service, you have to be given the service's name and address. Write or call for a free copy of your record to be sure it's correct. It may list claims made from that address before you owned the house.

The Public Adjuster

As you're standing in the street, staring at the smoking ruins of your house, someone may shove a card into your hand. It's a public adjuster. He or she helps you evaluate your losses and bird-dogs your insurance claim. The fee: 10 to 15 percent of what you recover.

Some people figure it's worth the price to have the adjuster round up proofs of value and handle the paperwork needed to process a claim. But you shouldn't need an adjuster to get a fair settlement.

Your insurer or agent will give you advice on filing the claim. In the normal course, you'll be paid in full without having to hire a consultant. If you don't agree with your insurer's appraisal, you can get one of your own and demand a referee. If you do decide to turn to a public adjuster, make sure that he or she is licensed by your state and ask for references. Base the fee on the extra money the adjuster gets for you, beyond what you were originally offered.

What to Do After a Loss

1. After a fire or storm damage, board up the broken windows in your home so that the remaining property can't be stolen. Your insurer will pay for it.

2. After a theft, notify the police.

3. Call your insurance agent.

4. Make a list of everything you lost, approximately when you bought it, and what you paid for it (or smugly produce the inventory you made in advance). The insurer will help you estimate current cash value.

5. Keep a list of all your expenses.

6. Get estimates for repairs.

7. Don't sign any contract to work with a public adjuster until you've first tried working with your insurance company. But if the company squeezes you, get help.

8. If anyone is injured, don't take the blame without first calling your insurance company.

Buy the Best

Some homeowners insurance companies have gone broke, and more will in the future. Your policy is covered by the National Conference of Insurance Guaranty Funds (www.ncigf.com), but you're usually insured for no more than $300,000 and perhaps only $100,000, depending on your state. You're protected only for claims in the pipeline. If your insurance company fails, your policies will be canceled and you'll have to search for coverage somewhere else. Save yourself the grief. Buy only from an insurer that has high ratings for safety and soundness and that is licensed in your state.

Trust No One

When you get an insurance policy—any policy—double-check it to see that you got what you ordered. Large numbers of policies come through with mistakes: wrong amounts, wrong endorsements, wrong types of coverage. When you put in a claim and find you're not covered, it's too late to argue.

YOUR OWN HOME

Once upon a time a big wind flattened the flimsy homes made of sticks and straw that had been ruining the neighborhood. The gentry moved in and property values went up. The third little pig, with the house of brick, grew fat and prospered. He took a second mortgage and then a third. He thought he could live on his house for the rest of his life. Next thing he knew, the wolf was at the door.

In 2006 the housing bubble popped. Prices went down. Home equity melted away. People started to worry that owning a home would no longer raise their standard of living. For this (we asked ourselves), we're cleaning the gutters, painting the shutters, paying the taxes, and feeling broke?

Most likely, we won't see a housing boom again for many, many years. Price appreciation will revert to "normal": slow annual gains, roughly tracking the general inflation rate. As an investment, stocks will probably outperform homes. But so what? A home of our own is still the rock on which our dreams are built. It's a state of mind, our piece of the earth, the place where a family's toes grow roots. It's where the flowers are ours, not God's.

17

A House Is a Security Blanket

. . . Even If It Doesn't Make You Rich

**Home ownership is your only hope of living
"free" when you retire. Rent goes on forever.
Mortgage payments eventually stop.**

A house may not be your best investment in the decade ahead. If the price drop starting in 2006 taught us anything, it's that real estate doesn't always go up. Over the time that you own your particular house, its value might rise, fall, or stall. You can't predict.

But there are reasons other than profit for owning a home. You get tax deductions on mortgage interest and tax-free capital gains. You're landlord free. You know the deep contentment of holding a spot of ground that others can enter by invitation only. You won't lose your lease. You can renovate to suit. Your mortgage payments build a pool of usable savings that you otherwise might not have. A house is collateral for a loan. House payments often cost less than rent, after tax.

As a home owner, you have three principal goals. First, to choose a mortgage you know you can afford. Second, to grow your home equity, which you can use to improve your house or trade up to something better. Third, to pay off the mortgage so that, by the time you retire, you'll own a home free and clear.

Smart home owners cherish their home equity. Defined, it's the difference between your home's market value and the balance owed on your mortgage. If the house is worth $350,000 and you took a $300,000 mortgage, you have $50,000 in equity. The greater your equity, the richer you are.

There are three ways for equity to grow: (1) The magical way, during real estate booms. Home prices rise because eager buyers bid them up. (2) The usual way, in normal times. Home prices rise modestly, while you lower your mortgage by paying down your debt. (3) You improve the property in some way. Most home owners benefit from all three.

There are four ways of losing home equity: (1) Home prices fall. Times have changed and buyers aren't willing to pay as much as you did. (2) You borrow more money against your home by refinancing into a larger mortgage or taking a second mortgage, such as a home equity loan. (3) You let the property fall into disrepair. (4) Worst case—you run into financial trouble or the mortgage rate jumps up, you default on the monthly payments, and you lose the property.

During real estate booms, people get careless with their home equity. They throw it away by taking serial loans against the house and spending the money. Or they take an interest-only mortgage, never paying down the principal. They assume that rising home prices will replace the equity they're destroying themselves. This works in boom times. But in normal times, when home prices are flat or rising only gently, you have to put money into repaying your mortgage to see your wealth increase.

19 Ways of Buying Your First Home

1. Save money for a down payment. People are doing it every day. No video toys. No dinners out. A cheaper apartment than you really could afford. A second job. A bigger savings account in place of a vacation. Down payments are higher today than they were in 2006 and 2007, but home prices are lower, so it's easier to start than you think.

2. Visit the Mommy-and-Daddy Bank. Many adult children nowadays rely on their parents to lend or give them part or all of their first down payment. A parent who's a gambler might even cosign your mortgage loan. (The M&D Bank may have to tell the lender, in writing, that the down payment is a gift.)

3. Move. If you can't afford a house near Washington, D.C., or Los Angeles, think about Wisconsin or Tennessee. Think about it when you're young and looking for your first job, because that's often where you'll buy your first home.

4. Commute. The further into the exurbs you're willing to go, the cheaper the houses, although the more expensive the gasoline that gets you to work. Maybe you can telecommute.

5. Buy an older house. It might cost 15 to 20 percent less than a newly built house for the same floor space. The down payment will be lower too. You'll have to spend some money repairing or updating the house, but at least you're in.

6. Buy a wreck. If you can stand living in a construction site for a year or two and are handy with tools, you can buy a wreck cheaply and fix it up.

7. Lower your consumer debt. The less debt you carry, the better the terms you can get on a mortgage.

8. Make a deal with the seller. Ask if he or she will lower the price by enough to cover your closing costs. If you can't get a big enough mortgage to pay the asking price, maybe the seller will take what you have and let you pay the additional money over one to three years. To guarantee payment, you'd give the seller a second mortgage or deed of trust against the house. (Be sure to disclose this arrangement to the bank.)

9. Get a low-down-payment loan backed by private mortgage insurance. In their dreams, lenders want 20 percent down, but they take less when you qualify for private mortgage insurance, as most borrowers do. If you quit paying and the house goes to a foreclosure sale, the insurer covers the lender's loss. With this guarantee, the lender may accept 10 percent down or even less, depending on the size of your income and market conditions.

Your insurance premiums are usually bundled into your monthly mortgage payment, although sometimes the first-year cost has to be paid up front. The price depends on the type of loan and how much money you put down. Some insurers charge a fixed annual rate on the loan's declining balance. Others charge roughly 0.3 to 0.9 percent of the original loan balance for the first 10 years, then perhaps 0.2 percent in subsequent years. There are dozens of permutations, including slightly higher rates in markets where housing prices are going down.

During the real estate boom, lenders offered an alternative to private mortgage insurance, known as a "piggyback loan." You were given a first mortgage for 80 percent of the property's cost and a second mortgage, at a higher rate, for most of the rest. At this writing, piggybacks aren't available anymore, because they ramped up the lenders' risk. If they return, you'll need to compare the cost of both options. Piggybacks might be less expensive if you'll pay off the second mortgage fast. In other cases, mortgage insurance could be the better choice.

10. Get a low-down-payment mortgage insured by the Federal Housing Administration. You can put down as little as 3.5 percent of the market price. At this writing, FHA insurance costs 1.5 percent at closing, which can be borrowed from the lender and repaid over the mortgage term. There's also a premium tacked onto every monthly payment: 0.25 percent for loans of up to 15 years and 0.5 percent for longer loans. On loans that closed after January 1, 2001, your insurance is automatically canceled when your equity reaches 22 percent, as long as you have made payments for at least five years.

FHA loans are offered chiefly by mortgage banks, including online lenders, but they're also available at some commercial banks and S&Ls. If a lender's Web site offers loans with "little or no money down," they're almost certainly FHA loans or loans guaranteed by the U.S. Department of Veterans Affairs (see below).

For other leads to FHA lenders, go to www.hud.gov, click on "Search," and then on "Lenders." Borrowing limits are usually set county by county and cover homes that are modestly priced. They were raised sharply in 2008, to help homeowners refinance during the mortgage crisis. At this writing, here are the maximum loans for single-family homes: $271,050 in lower-cost areas up to $625,500 in very-high-cost areas. The limits may change, either up or down. For the latest, see the FHA's Web site www.fhaoutreach.gov or check the Yellow Pages for a HUD-certified real estate agent in your area. For the loan limit in your area, go to MortgageLoanPlace at www.mortgageloanplace.com. For home buying and mortgage advice, call HUD's Housing Counseling Hotline (800-569-4287) for a counselor in your area or visit www.hud.gov/fha.

11. Get a mortgage sponsored by a housing finance corporation such as Fannie Mae (the Federal National Mortgage Corporation) or Freddie Mac (Federal Home Loan Mortgage Corporation). Down payments run as low as 3 or 5 percent. To find a Fannie lender, go to the Fannie Mae Web site (www.fannie Mae.com), click on its site map, and scroll down to "Find a Lender Search," or call 800-7-FANNIE (800-732-6643). Fannie also backs no-down-payment loans offered to rural residents of modest means through USDA Rural Development (formerly the Farmers Home Administration).

12. Get a no-down-payment loan guaranteed by the Department of Veterans Affairs. You can usually borrow as much as the house is appraised for, up to a certain limit—$417,000 in 2009 (this number rises annually; limits are higher in certain high-cost counties as well as Alaska, Hawaii, Guam, and the U.S. Virgin Islands). For county-by-county limits, go to the Web site of VALoans. com (www.valoans.com).

The up-front fee for a no-down-payment VA loan is 2.15 percent for regular military and 2.4 percent for Reserves and the National Guard. For regular military, that drops to 1.5 percent if you can afford a down payment of 5 percent or more and 1.25 percent if you can put 10 percent down. For Reserves it drops to 1.75 percent and for the Guard to 1.5 percent. This fee needn't be paid in cash; you can include it in the loan. For more information and a list of VA-approved lenders, go to www.homeloans.va.gov.

VA loans are generally made through mortgage banks, including online lenders, although S&Ls, commercial banks, and credit unions may offer them too.

Generally speaking, you qualify if you're a veteran, on active duty, and have served at least two years, or, under certain conditions, are an unmarried surviving spouse. At this writing, VA loans also go to people who have done six years in the Selected Reserve, including the National Guard. Reservists pay an extra 0.25 percent up front. For details, check www.homeloans.va.gov or call your regional VA office.

13. Sell any stocks or mutual funds you own that aren't part of your tax-deferred retirement plan. Put the proceeds into your down payment.

14. Borrow part of the down payment from your employee retirement savings account, if the plan allows it. For details, see page 313. The interest you pay on the loan goes back into your account.

15. Borrow part of the payment from your bank. Take a loan against the credit line on your bank credit card or write a check against your overdraft checking. This choice should be desperation only, to wrap up a deal. You'll want to repay this high-interest loan as fast as you can.

16. Buy a house in a foreclosure sale or through a real estate agent who handles foreclosures. There are no big bargains. But you might buy for 5 or 10 percent less than the price of a similar home that wasn't foreclosed (page 575).

17. Check the cost of buying from a builder in a new development. Builders often sell on flexible terms. One example: a *buydown*. The builder might pay the lender $5,000 or so to reduce your mortgage payments for one to three years. That will help you qualify for the loan. Alternatively, the lender may offer to cover the first two mortgage payments or pay closing costs and fees in return for charging you a higher interest rate.

Don't waltz into this deal without asking how much it's going to cost. You may have to pay list price on the house rather than bargaining it down. You may have to use the builder's mortgage affiliate, who won't come cheap. And what will the mortgage cost you once the buydown period passes? Always compare the builder's offer—rates, fees, costs, points—with what you could get from a Web lender or other outside sources. If you get a better offer, the builder may sweeten his or her deal too.

18. Shop. Interest rates and fees vary more widely than you realize, especially in tight markets. You might find a lender that charges 1 percentage point less on a fixed-rate loan and more than that on an adjustable loan. Smaller, local banks are offering good deals. Here are the top sites for comparison shopping online: the major banking institutions—Bank of America, CitiMortgage, Chase Home Mortgage, and Wells Fargo—and Internet lenders (page 570) that meet the pricing transparency standards of Jack Guttentag, professor of

finance emeritus at the Wharton School of the University of Pennsylvania (www
.mtgprofessor.com).

19. Lease with an option to buy. This approach faded during the years when
anyone with a pulse could get a mortgage loan. It's now coming back because
buyers with shaky credit can't borrow and sellers are having trouble getting
their price.

With an option, you pay a nonrefundable fee (perhaps $3,000 to $5,000) for
the right to buy the house in one to three years at a stated price. You move in
as a tenant, paying more than the normal rent. The fee plus the extra rent is
credited toward a down payment. When it comes time to buy, you get your own
mortgage for the remaining money owed. To find one of these deals, ask a real
estate agent, look for lease-option ads in the newspaper or online, or check the
classifieds under "Rentals." People renting out houses would sometimes rather
sell. Don't sign a lease option without having a lawyer go over it to be sure it's
fair. Sometimes it's not.

Do a lease option only if you're sure that you can get a sufficient mortgage
when the option comes due. That means prequalifying yourself with a lender
(page 560). The lease option should be viewed solely as a way of accumulating
a down payment. If you can't get a mortgage when the time comes to buy, your
option will expire, and you'll lose the extra money you paid. (You might recover
something, however, if the option price is less than the house's fair market value.
Before the option expires, advertise it for sale. An investor might respond.)

Why Your Credit Score Matters

The mortgage interest rate you're offered will depend on your credit score (page
265). For the best rate, you have to score above 740. A 700 score is almost as
good. As your score drops, rates and fees go up, and the amount you're allowed
to borrow goes down. Below 660, rates rise a lot, and you're offered fewer types
of loans. Below 620, you're "subprime" and may not be able to borrow at all.
Your lender will check your credit score as part of your mortgage application and
mail you the result. To qualify for a better mortgage, get the debt on your credit
cards down to less than half your total credit lines, take out no new cards, and
pay your bills on time, every time. Subprime borrowers might still be accepted
by the FHA or VA.

When couples with different FICO scores apply for a mortgage, the lender
uses a middle range. If one of you is subprime, however, you'll be stuck with a
higher interest rate. Consider applying in the name of the person with the better
score, if his or her earnings will support the loan.

How Large a Mortgage Can You Get?

How much you can borrow depends on both your credit score and the size of your current debt. Find yourself below, to see the maximum monthly mortgage payment that lenders typically think you can afford. That helps you target a price range for the houses you should be looking at. Just because you can borrow this much, however, doesn't mean that you should. It's important to keep your loan within your comfort zone.

▪ *If you have a high credit score, a solid income, and some investments,* lenders usually allow you to spend up to 30 percent of your stable, monthly gross income on home-owning expenses (principal and interest on your mortgage debt, home-owners insurance, and incidentals such as condominium fees). Up to 45 percent of your income could be committed to total debt, including housing expenses, alimony, child support, and payments toward long-term consumer debt (defined as loans lasting for more than 10 months, including car loans or leases, installment debt, and credit card debt). If you're self-employed, these ratios apply to your net income after expenses. If you depend on year-end bonuses, part of that bonus might be considered "stable" income.

▪ *If you have an average credit score, with an acceptable credit history and sufficient income,* lenders may want you to spend no more than 25 percent of your income on basic housing expenses, with a maximum of 33 to 40 percent on total debt.

▪ *If you're applying for a special lower-income loan,* you're allowed up to 30 percent of your monthly income for housing expenses and 35 percent for total debt. Ratios can be higher on loans insured by the Veterans Administration or the affordable housing loans backed by the Federal Housing Administration.

▪ *Sometimes lenders are willing to exceed these percentages,* but they're doing you no favor. Bigger loans let you buy a better house but also require monthly payments higher than you can really afford. Larger homes cost more to heat, light, and repair. If you move to a pricier neighborhood, you may feel the need to own a fancier car or throw expensive birthday parties for your kids. Consider all the costs before choosing a house that requires you to borrow more than the guideline amount.

▪ *Most lenders no longer offer "stated-income" or "stated-asset" loans— otherwise known as "liar's loans."* With these loans, you merely stated your income or assets and the lenders didn't check. They simply charged a higher interest rate to cover the loan's expected risk. Not surprisingly, a high percentage of them defaulted. Now you usually have to provide full documentation to get a mortgage loan. That not only protects the lender, it protects you from borrowing more than you can reasonably pay. In some cases, however, a self-employed person with good credit and a sizable downpayment might still be able to borrow on a stated-income basis.

- *If you want to know whether you can borrow enough to buy a particular house,* ask to be *preapproved* for a mortgage loan. To win preapproval, you fill in an application and have your credit checked. The bank may also verify your income and assets. If you pass, you'll get a letter telling you the maximum you can borrow at current interest rates (assuming no change in your financial condition). This helps you target a price range for shopping and gives you an edge over other bidders who haven't yet been approved for a loan. You can get preapprovals from many lenders free on the Web, through a mortgage broker, or from a local lender directly. Some lenders charge for preapprovals and refund the cost if you go through with the loan. But why pay if you don't have to?

You can also be *prequalified.* That's a free estimate of how large a loan you might be able to get, based on your financial data but with no income verification or credit check. Using the Web, you could collect several estimates. Local lenders may prequalify you too, at no charge. Preapproval, however, is more exact.

- *If you're checking out mortgages on Web sites,* keep in mind that the monthly payments you see cover only principal and interest. You'll also owe real estate taxes and premiums for homeowners insurance. Those expenses are usually bundled into the amount you pay the lender each month. The lenders hold them in escrow and make the tax and insurance payments for you.

If You Have a Choice, How Much Money Should You Put Down?

- *A larger down payment gives you a smaller loan and lower monthly payments.* If you put down 20 percent or more, you'll get a lower interest rate and better terms. Choose a large down payment if you want to hold down costs; if you're determined to pay off the mortgage as fast as you can; if you have an irregular income and feel safer with lower monthly payments; or if you would otherwise fritter away your spare money. Higher down payments can yield handsome investment yields, thanks to your savings on interest costs and fees. To calculate this, go to the Mortgage Professor's Web site (www.mtgprofessor.com), click on "Calculators" and scroll down to Calculator 12a.

- *A smaller down payment sticks you with a larger loan, higher monthly payments, and a higher interest rate.* Why do it if you have a choice? I can think of only two good reasons: (1) You want enough cash to fix up and furnish your new home. (2) You'll use your extra cash to reduce a mound of credit card debt.

- *Should you choose a smaller down payment so that you can invest the rest of your money somewhere else?* Not a good idea. The cost of this choice is far higher than people realize. That's because lenders charge higher interest rates and fees to people who put less money down. To make up for that extra out-of-pocket cost, the cash return on your outside investment has to be surprisingly large—typically, equal to your higher mortgage rate plus about 5 percent. Say, for example, that you could have borrowed at 6 percent, but your lower down payment raised your rate to 6.25 percent (plus higher fees). To make up for those extra costs, your investment would have to earn about 11.25 percent, and that's just to break even! You'd need an even higher return to make a profit.

Skimping on your down payment almost never makes sense. An investment in your mortgage when you buy your house is one of the smartest ways that you can use your money.

- *Should you put zero down?* Today, you can do this only with VA loans, or near zero with FHA loans and some loans backed by Fannie Mae. But you lose flexibility and may face higher costs. If interest rates fall, you won't be able to refinance because you won't have enough equity in your home. If you want to sell, you might not net enough to repay the mortgage, after subtracting 5 or 6 percent in sales commissions. Having equity in your home is one of your safety nets. Save for a down payment. It's one of the best things you can do for yourself. If you buy with no money down, make higher monthly payments to build equity as fast as you can.

Special Warnings to Subprime Borrowers

If your credit score is poor, you're classed as a *subprime* borrower. That costs you a higher interest rate, if you can borrow at all. After the housing bubble burst, most lenders stopped giving subprime loans. But they'll eventually come back. If you're offered such a loan, here's what to watch for:

- *Are you really a subprime credit?* Some mortgage brokers steer clients to subprime loans when they could have qualified for something better. The brokers earn higher commissions on subprimes. Before accepting a subprime verdict, consider visiting a bank directly or applying for a loan on the Web (page 572). You might get a better deal.
- *Even if you start as a subprime borrower, you don't have to stay in that category.* Make your interest and principal payments on time for two or three years, then see if you can refinance into a higher-quality loan.
- *Subprime loans normally carry prepayment penalties.* You'll owe a fee if you

refinance within the first three years or so. So be sure that you'll be able to carry your mortgage for at least that period of time.

• *Beware of rising interest rates.* Before saying yes to this mortgage, ask the broker to show you any built-in rate increases over the next five years and what the monthly payments would be. How much more would you pay if rates in general rose by 1 or 2 percent? If you can't afford to pay more each month, you might default and lose the house.

A Technical Phrase You Can't Ignore: Negative Amortization

Negative "am," as it's called for short, is a high-tech, death-defying, money-eating system for owing more money every time you make a monthly mortgage payment. *Amortization* is the payment schedule by which you reduce a loan to zero over a fixed number of years. *Negative amortization* means that instead of going down, the amount of your loan goes up.

You run into negative am whenever your monthly payments aren't large enough to cover all the interest due. As an example, say that you're paying $1,000 a month on a floating-rate mortgage whose rate goes up. You now owe an extra $50 in interest, but your mortgage contract lets you keep paying only $1,000. The missing $50 is added to your loan principal, so now you owe more than you did last month. Your interest cost rises too, because of the larger loan. The lender will let your debt increase by a certain amount. After that, you'll be required to make much higher monthly payments on a schedule that will reduce the loan to zero.

The mortgages known as *option ARMs* (page 564) often mire you in negative am. So will any other mortgage whose payments stay level while the interest rate is allowed to float. At this writing, these dangerous mortgages aren't being offered anymore, but plenty of old ones are still outstanding. If you find yourself with negative am, raise your monthly payments to climb out of it.

Finding the Right Mortgage

There are dozens of choices on the mortgage menu, all with different rates, different terms, and different fees. Here's how to decide what's best for you.

Traditional Adjustable-Rate Mortgages (ARMs)

With traditional ARMs, the interest rate and monthly payment change periodically—up or down—in line with the general level of rates. So far, they've proven to be low cost. An ARM with an annual adjustment might start at 1.5 or 2 percentage points under the cost of a fixed-rate loan—a valuable saving. Even if interest rates rise, the ARM will probably cost you less over the next three or four years. An ARM would cost more than fixed-rate loans if rates rose and didn't fall, but rate rises rarely last longer than a couple of years. Over a full interest rate cycle, ARMs could easily cost the least. Among their advantages: you don't have to pay fees for refinancing when interest rates fall, because ARM rates fall automatically. (For the specific questions to ask about ARMs, see page 565).

When to get a traditional ARM: (1) You need the lower monthly payment in the first year to buy the house you want. (2) You've looked at how payments might rise in the future and can handle them when they come. (3) You won't panic when payments rise, because you have faith that they'll fall again. (4) You expect to own the house for only four or five years (short-term owners should go for the cheapest ARM they can find). (5) You have plenty of money or plenty of confidence that your income will rise.

Fixed-Rate Mortgages

With these mortgages, you're safe. Your monthly payments are fixed for as long as you hold the loan. If rates rise and stay high, you've got a terrific deal. If they fall, you can refinance at the lower rate (page 580). Fixed-rate mortgages make the most economic sense when they're priced within one percentage point of an ARM's *regular* interest rate (not the discounted "teaser" rate given during the ARM's first year or so).

When to get a fixed-rate loan: (1) The size of the payment doesn't stop you from getting the house you want. (2) You want to lock in your mortgage payments because you can't count on earning a higher income in the years ahead. (3) You couldn't afford your house if your mortgage payment rose. (4) The thought of rising mortgage payments scares you stiff. (5) You think current mortgage rates are unusually low. (6) You're near retirement, at which point your income will drop.

Hybrid Mortgages

These are great loans for borrowers who want to start with guaranteed monthly payments but can't quite afford the initial cost of a regular fixed-rate loan. With hybrids, you get a fixed rate for a specified period, often 3, 5, 7, or 10 years. Then the loan converts to an adjustable rate. You pay more per month than for a traditional ARM but less than for a straight fixed-rate loan. The longer the fixed-rate period, the higher your initial interest rate will be. Lenders refer to hybrids in shorthand. A loan labeled "5/1" gives you a fixed rate for five years, then switches to a variable rate that changes every year. A "7/1" loan fixes your rate for the first seven years. The first time the loan adjusts, the rate could jump by as much as 5 percentage points. Make sure that you understand the range of future possible rates before you sign. Also make sure your deal is guaranteed. Some hybrids let the lender change the terms if interest rates suddenly shoot up.

When to choose a hybrid loan: (1) You'll stay in the house for only a few years. In effect, you have a fixed-rate loan at a lower monthly cost. (2) You hope mortgage rates will fall, at which point you'll refinance. In the meantime, you want a mortgage payment that's guaranteed. If rates don't fall, you can still handle the payments. (3) You expect to be earning more money when the fixed term ends, so switching to a traditional ARM won't bother you.

Interest-Only (IO) Mortgages

For the first few years of an IO mortgage, you pay only the interest on your loan and nothing toward principal. You get lower monthly payments, but you're not reducing the debt. After 3 to 10 years (you choose), your payments jump to a level high enough to retire the loan over its remaining term. For example, say that you take a 30-year loan and pay nothing toward principal for the first five years. In the sixth year, you have to start paying enough to retire the loan over the remaining 25 years. That's called *recasting* the loan, and your monthly payment jumps—often by a lot.

IOs today are being written mainly on 30-year fixed-rate loans, at a much higher interest rate than you'd pay for a traditional loan. When IOs are written on adjustable loans, they also cost more than you'd pay for a regular ARM.

When to choose an IO loan: Hardly ever. You're looking at it only because you need a superlow monthly payment to qualify for the mortgage you want. That usually means you're buying a house you really can't afford. You're gambling that you can handle the basic loan (which will be a large one, relative to your income) and make sharply higher monthly payments when the time rolls around. IOs *always* cost more in interest, whether you hold them for 5 years or 30 years, because of the higher rate and because the loan principal stays high.

Mortgages Called Option ARMs, FlexPay ARMs, or Pick-a-Pay

Mercifully, these terrible loans are now off the market. But plenty of old ones are still around. They allow you to choose how much you want to pay each month, including a payment so small that it doesn't even cover the interest owed. That unpaid interest is added to your loan, so your debt goes up every month instead of down. Five years from the day you took this loan (and sometimes earlier), your options will run out. You'll have to start paying enough to retire the mortgage over its remaining term. You won't even be able to refinance if the value of your house is down. Anyone stuck with an option ARM should start paying enough every month to cover both interest and principal. Otherwise, you might be greasing a path to default.

Balloons

Balloon mortgages offer low, fixed payments for a specified period of time. After that, the entire loan falls due. First-mortgage balloons typically run for five to seven years. After that, the bank will usually refinance them at whatever rate is current at the time. You'll pay a higher rate, however, if your credit score has dropped or you've fallen behind on some payments. You won't be refinanced if your house is worth less than the amount of the loan. Before you borrow, be clear about your options at the end of the term and what fees and interest rates you might have to pay.

If you buy a house and give the seller a note for part of the payment due, that's a balloon. When it falls due, the seller will rarely extend the term. If you don't have the cash, you'll be expected to borrow the money somewhere else.

When to consider a balloon: (1) The seller offers this loan to help you meet his or her price and you're sure you can pay when the term is up. (2) The bank offers a balloon with very low payments—say, only the interest—for a fixed number of years. You expect to sell the house and repay the whole loan sometime before the balloon falls due. This assumes that the market value of your house will not decline. (3) If you don't sell, you're sure that the bank will let you refinance. But who can ever be truly sure? A balloon is a hazardous undertaking at any time.

All About ARMs

Take this checklist with you when you talk to the lender. Use it for hybrid mortgages too, because they'll eventually turn into ARMs.

- *What's the initial interest rate?* ARMs usually offer bargain starter rates called teasers. Typically, they're one or two points under the loan's regular rate. Some teasers last for only 1 month; others, for 6 to 12 months. Some (on hybrid loans) last up to 10 years. Every time your rate adjusts, it will rise toward the regular, nondiscounted rate (although the rise can't exceed a specified cap). During this short period, your interest rate can rise even if rates in general are coming down. Once you've reached the end of your teaser period, your payment will rise and fall in line with general market interest rates.

■ *What interest rate is my loan linked to?* Most mortgages today are tied to Treasury securities. Six-month ARMs rise and fall with six-month Treasury bills; one-year ARMs link to one-year Treasury bills. Over a whole interest rate cycle, a mortgage linked to short-term Treasuries should cost less and is the easiest to follow in the newspapers.

Other loans adjust twice a year in line with the London InterBank Offer Rate (LIBOR), which reflects Eurodollar borrowing rates. It tends to rise and fall more rapidly than Treasury rates do. In the West, mortgage rates might follow the cost-of-funds index (COFI) for savings and loan associations in the Federal Home Loan Bank Board's 11th District, which covers California, Arizona, and Nevada. The COFI changes slowly, so your payments don't rise or fall a lot, even if they're adjusted once a year. But the sluggishness of the cost-of-funds index means that it may still be going up when rates in general have turned down, and vice versa. Finally, there's also a cost-of-deposits index (CODI) that follows the interest rates that banks pay on three-month certificates of deposit. In practical terms, it doesn't really matter which index your lender uses—you'll have to take what you get.

■ *What's the margin?* When figuring your ARM rate, the lender takes the index it uses and adds a fixed number of percentage points called a *margin.* This is one of the most important things that consumers should shop for. To see how it works, assume that your margin is 2.5 points. With the Treasury index at 3 percent, plus a 2.5 margin, your interest rate comes to 5.5 percent. If Treasuries rise to 4 percent, adding the margin raises your rate to 6.5 percent. Borrowers with good credit should get a low margin over the index (2.25 points is very good). Borrowers with poorer credit pay a higher margin (3 points or more). If you're a good credit risk, be sure you get the low margin you deserve.

The margin doesn't matter during the months you have a discounted teaser rate (or the 3 to 10 years of fixed rates on a hybrid loan). It matters a lot, however, when your rate starts adjusting normally. Between two lenders linking their mortgages to the same or a similar index, the one with the smaller margin will cost you less (unless that lender blows it by charging higher fees).

■ *How often will the interest rate change?* Most traditional ARMs adjust your interest rate once a year. Some adjust every six months. Generally speaking, the more frequent the adjustment, the cheaper the mortgage over an entire interest rate cycle (including both rising and falling rates).

■ *What are the caps?* You want fixed, annual limits on what you'll have to pay in case interest rates go leaping up. If you took a teaser rate, your *first adjustment cap* is typically large—maybe as much as 5 percentage points. After that, the *periodic cap* dictates how much the lenders can add each year—typically up to 2 percentage points, no matter what happens to the underlying index. For example, say that market rates rise by 3 percentage points in the second year and stay there. Your mortgage rate will rise only 2 points the second year, then 1 point the third year. Alternatively, if rates rise by three percentage points and then fall back, your mortgage rate will rise 2 points the second year and then stay level or fall the third year, depending on how far the index drops. Over the life of the loan, your rate can't rise by more than 5 or 6 percentage points, usually measured from your low, initial teaser rate. Given two similar loans, choose the one with the lower caps.

- *After the initial interest rate period expires, what will I pay?* The lender should show you a range of possible future payments based on various changes in interest rates. Ask for an illustration of the worst case too. If you faint dead away, maybe you should look at fixed-rate loans instead.

- *What happened in the past?* Ask the lender to show you how a mortgage payment like yours would have fluctuated over the past 10 years, using real interest rates. If the payment gyrations of an ARM make you uncomfortable, consider a fixed-rate loan instead.

- *Is there a floor?* Some loans limit how far your interest rate can fall. All things being equal, look for a loan without a floor.

- *Is there a risk of negative amortization?* Loans with negative am sometimes allow your monthly payments to slip below the total amount of interest due. The lender adds the unpaid interest to the loan balance, so your loan amount goes up instead of down. Not recommended. You'll find plenty of ARMs without this catch.

- *How often does your monthly payment change?* You want it to change every time the loan's interest rate does. Otherwise you run the risk of negative amortization.

- *Can I convert?* Some ARMs carry the right to switch to a fixed-rate mortgage after a certain number of years without paying closing costs all over again. Lenders charge for this in various ways. Some add an up-front fee. Some tack an eighth or a quarter of a point onto your initial interest rate or an extra half point or more to the interest rate on your future fixed-rate loan. With charges like these, nobody's giving you a bargain. Since you can't predict whether you'll want to convert, this generally isn't an option worth paying for.

- *How can I check the rate?* If I had one dollar for every mistake a lender made when it adjusted an ARM payment, I'd be an instant millionaire. The bank may pick the wrong index, loan balance, or adjustment date; it might round the rate up when it should have been rounded down; a new loan servicer might get your loan terms wrong; principal prepayments might not have been credited properly. Small errors compound into large ones over the years. When you take an ARM, ask when the rate will be adjusted, how it's done, and how you can track the index that underlies your loan. Verify the rate whenever a change looks too big or too small or your payment rises when interest rates in general have been going down. Pay the most attention to older loans. Small errors grow into big ones over several years. Consumers can get refunds if they were overcharged on a paid-up loan.

You can check your ARM rate free at HSH Associates Financial Publishers (www.hsh.com), a reliable provider of mortgage information. Click on the "ARM Check Kit" on the left-hand toolbar.

On Points

In mortgagespeak, one point is 1 percentage point of the loan amount. For example, on a $100,000 loan, one point equals $1,000—to be paid in cash or added to the loan amount. Adding the fee to the loan saves you money up front, but you'll wind up paying two or three times that amount in interest costs.

There's a trade-off between the discount points you pay and the mortgage interest rate you're charged. The higher the points, the lower the rate, and vice versa. So what should you do: cut your interest rate by paying extra points or not? Here's how to decide:

- *Pay zero or minimal points* if you'll be in the house for only a few years. The points would cost you more than the higher interest you'll pay. Points also make no sense when interest rates are very low.
- *Pay extra points* if you'll hold the house for many years. A lower interest rate will save you money over the long run, especially when interest rates are high.
- *To compare the dollars and cents,* Web calculators help. There are two ways of looking at the question: (1) Over 10 years, will you save more money by lowering your points or raising your down payment? Test this at www.dinkytown .net, the site of KJE Computer Solutions of Minneapolis. (2) How long will it take for the savings from lower interest payments to offset the cost of paying higher points? You can test this at www.mtgprofessor.com, or Choose to Save, at www.choosetosave.org.

Short Term or Long?

A traditional mortgage runs for 30 years. Monthly payments are low, which is what younger buyers usually need. In the early years, most of that payment goes for interest, not principal. Over any holding period, 30-year loans cost more in interest than loans of shorter terms.

Among the middle-aged, buyers are choosing 15-year and even 10-year terms. Monthly payments are higher, but these loans build equity faster and minimize interest costs. They're a way of ensuring that you'll own your home free and clear by the time you retire.

The new 40-year mortgages offer especially low payments to the cash poor. They're more predictable than interest-only loans. You won't face a sudden jump in payments five years from now, as IO borrowers will. The downside (and it's a big one): You pay a high interest rate. When you sell, you'll have paid much more interest and built less equity than with a 30-year loan. I'd stay away.

How to Shorten the Term of Your Current Loan

Anytime you want, send in a larger monthly check than the amount that is actually due. The extra money will automatically go toward reducing your loan. Many lenders even have a spot on the monthly bill where you can note extra principal payments. Others suggest that you send a note with every larger check, so the bank will know there's no mistake. A disciplined way of prepaying is to add money every month. Alternatively, send a larger check whenever you can. Every dollar counts.

With a fixed-rate mortgage, your prepayments shorten the term of the loan. If you have an adjustable-rate mortgage, however, the bank may keep the term the same and lower the monthly payment you owe. To accelerate that mortgage, keep on paying the same monthly amount that you did before.

Note that making prepayments doesn't give you the right to skip a month. You still owe the basic monthly payment, no matter how far ahead of schedule you are.

For Maximum Flexibility, Take a 30-Year Loan and Repay It on a Faster Schedule

Take a 30-year loan. Then find out how large a monthly payment you'll have to make to get rid of the loan over 15 or 20 years, and pay at that rate. To decide how much extra you want to spend, use the calculators at www.bankrate.com, www.choosetosave.org, www.dinkytown.net, or www.mtgprofessor.com. I guarantee that the savings will amaze you. If there's a month when you're squeezed for cash, you can always drop back to the minimum payment the loan requires. Be sure that you get a loan without a prepayment penalty. The table on page 570 shows how much money shorter terms can save you on a $250,000 loan.

Table 8.

BIG SAVINGS FROM FAST REPAYMENTS

Loan Term	Monthly Payment*	Total Repaid	Savings over a 30-Year Loan
30 years	$1,500	$539,595	—
25 years	1,682	438,226	$56,369
20 years	1,791	428,859	109,736
15 years	2,110	379,736	159,859

* At 6 percent interest. Numbers are rounded.

Source: Mortgage Bankers Association of America. See calculator at www.homeloanlearningcenter.com.

Is It Worth Your While to Pay Off Your Mortgage Faster?

Usually, yes. Faster payments will:

- *Force you to save.* Otherwise that money might be frittered away.
- *Reduce the amount of interest* you pay over any period of time that you hold the loan.
- *Give you an attractive risk-free return on your money.* Prepaying a loan is an *investment.* The return on your investment equals your mortgage rate. As an example, prepayments on a 6.5 percent mortgage give you a 6.5 percent investment return, guaranteed. That's a better deal than you'd get from other safe, taxable investments, such as a bank or money market savings account.
- *Build your home equity faster.* That's especially important in a weak housing market, where rising prices aren't building equity for you.
- *Put you in a better position to trade up to a larger house.* When you sell, you'll have more money in hand to put toward your next down payment.
- *Ensure that you're mortgage free* by the time you retire.
- *Lower your cost of living,* if you inherit a bucket of money and put it toward reducing or eliminating your loan.
- *Get you a lower interest rate.* The rate on a 15-year loan may be a quarter or half point less than the rate on a 30-year loan.
- *Save you a small fortune* in interest payments.

It does not make sense to quick-pay your mortgage if:

- *You're carrying credit card debt that's costing you 12 to 28 percent or more.* By paying it off, you get a 12 to 28 percent return on your money. First get rid of consumer debt. Then accelerate mortgage payments, starting with any home equity debt.

- *You aren't investing enough for your retirement.* Maximize your 401(k), 403(b), IRA, or Roth IRA account before tackling your mortgage debt.
- *You don't have an emergency savings account.* Build this cushion fund first (page 213).
- *You have children and haven't been saving enough to help them with the expenses of higher education.* Start or add to your 529 investment (page 667).
- *Once you've taken care of your retirement fund, emergency savings, and college savings,* you're ready to prepay your mortgage loan.

One way to quick-pay painlessly is through a biweekly payment schedule. Instead of making monthly payments, make half a monthly payment every two weeks. Result: one extra full payment per year, which shortens the term of a 30-year loan to about 23 years. Lenders sell quick-pay plans, charging you $195 to $350 or more for the paperwork. That's a waste of money. Here's Jane's Free Biweekly Payment Plan: add 1/12th of a payment to your regular payment every month. You get the same result that you would with a useless commercial plan.

Another quick-payment scheme, called an *offset mortgage,* involves money transfers among accounts. Just watch the bouncing ball: (1) You open a home equity line of credit. (2) You borrow an amount equal to the size of your monthly payment from your home equity line and use it to reduce your mortgage balance. (3) You use your paycheck to repay the home equity line. (4) You pay your monthly bills by withdrawals from your home equity line. (5) All together, these transactions get money into your mortgage a little faster. If you spend your whole paycheck, you *might* save something in interest, depending on the home equity interest rate you pay. If you spend less than your total paycheck, your mortgage will shrink at a faster rate.

Naturally, this is sold as a package, for a price. It's complex and confusing, and you can't be sure how much you're saving (if anything). Skip it, and simply add money to your mortgage payment every month.

You may think prepayments don't matter because you expect to sell your house within just a few years. But they do. No matter when you sell, prepayments will lower your interest costs and increase your home equity.

Are you keeping your big mortgage because you "need" the tax deductions? Phooey. "Needing" deductions must be the most successful piece of financial propaganda that the industry has ever launched. Okay, you can tax-deduct mortgage interest. But your tax savings amount to only a fraction of the cost. You pay the rest right out of your pocket—money transferred from you to the bank.

For example, if you're in the 25 percent bracket, the write-off saves you 25 cents out of every dollar you pay in interest. The remaining 75 cents is pure expense. If you had no mortgage (or a smaller mortgage), here's what would happen to every dollar you *didn't* pay in interest: 25 cents would go for federal income tax and 75 cents would be yours to keep. Getting rid of a loan is pure gain.

How to Find a Good Mortgage

It's nuts not to shop. Some lenders charge lower interest rates and fees than others do. A percentage point saved on a 30-year, $200,000 loan is worth almost $64 a month.

▪ *Start with the Web.* Check rates at sites such as Eloan (www.eloan.com), which provides offers from competing lenders. Also, check the lenders that make loans directly and meet the conditions for being a full-disclosure, Upfront Mortgage Lender (UML), as laid out by Jack Guttentag, the Mortgage Professor (for details, see www.mtgprofessor.com). UMLs disclose all costs—including rates, fees, and other terms—and let you price your individual mortgage online. They don't necessarily have the lowest costs, but they're visible and guaranteed. Note that UMLs don't qualify you for loans, they only give you prices based on the information you supply. People with lower credit scores will have to pay higher rates. If you're not approved for a conventional loan, reapply for a loan backed by the FHA.

For comparison, you'll also find the largest mortgage banks online: Bank of America (www.bankofamerica.com); Chase Home Mortgage (www.mortgage .chase.com); CitiMortgage (www.citimortgage.com); and Wells Fargo (www .wellsfargo.com).

If you find a good rate on the Web, borrow there. E-lenders are fully equipped to handle their side of the paperwork by phone, e-mail, and local agents.

▪ *Ask a local bank, mortgage bank, savings and loan, or credit union.* You might prefer the experience of talking with someone locally. Often, local banks offer lower interest rates and fees. Once the loan closes, however, the bank will probably sell it to an investor somewhere else in the United States (or the world), so some other institution will be servicing it for you.

▪ *Ask a mortgage broker.* Mortgage brokers know all the lenders and the offers. Their job is to shop the market and find you a suitable loan at the lowest possible rate. They can be especially helpful if you're a first-time buyer, need an FHA or VA loan, have problem credit, or need other special services.

Getting a loan through a mortgage broker should cost exactly the same as you'd pay if you went to the lender yourself. Unfortunately, not all brokers play fair. Some of them overcharge in ways you don't suspect. For example, they might: (1) steer you into a higher-rate loan because it pays them a higher commission, all the time telling you that it's the best you can get; (2) quote you an extralow rate (even lower than you found on the Web) to get your business, then tell you (falsely) "the market has changed" and deliver a higher rate; (3) say they're charging you "one point" (1 percent of the loan) without disclosing that the lender pays them a second point, which is included in your mortgage rate; (4) claim "Our services are free," then put you into a high-rate loan that pays them an extra-high commission. *No* services are free. A study for the Department of Housing and Urban Development, published in 2008, found that borrowers pay an average of $300 to $450 more in fees when they work with a mortgage broker than when they borrow directly from the lender. At this writing, some lenders won't deal with brokers because so many of them brought in deceptive loans during the housing boom.

To be sure you're dealing with an honest broker, start by negotiating a fee. Then ask to see—actually *see*—the sheet that shows the wholesale interest rate and points the lender charges. The sheet might say "6 + 1," meaning 6 percent plus one point. You should pay that amount plus the broker's fee, and no more. The broker should put the fee in writing and agree not to add a percentage to any third-party charge, such as the appraisal.

Consider doing business with one of the people who call themselves an Upfront Mortgage Broker. They promise to find you the best wholesale rate you qualify for and to disclose all their fees. You'll find them listed at the Upfront Mortgage Brokers Association site (www.upfrontmortgagebrokers.org). If none is local, you can deal with some of them by phone or online. For other mortgage brokers, check the National Association of Mortgage Brokers (www.namb .org), the Web, the Yellow Pages, real estate brokers (some of whom have mortgage broker affiliates), and friends. Ask these brokers to follow the same fee-disclosure procedures that Upfront Mortgage Brokers do. If they won't, don't work with them.

Regardless of the type of broker you use, keep careful notes of your conversations, including the interest rate the broker says you'll get. Make a list of features you want in the loan, such as no prepayment penalty. Go down your checklist before agreeing to the loan. *Any* broker, including the Upfronters, can pull a fast one.

By the way, mortgage lending officers at the big banks can deceive you, too. They might put you into a more expensive loan when you could have qualified for something cheaper. That's why it's so important to comparison shop.

- *Ask your real estate agent.* He or she may know of a local lender with good deals. But back off if the real estate firm has an affiliated mortgage company. Your agent might pressure you to pop over to the next desk and apply for a loan. Don't sign anything until you've shopped around to find out what rates and fees are normal for someone in your situation. The mortgage you're being pushed toward might be high priced.

- *Apply through several sources*—a bank, a mortgage broker, a Web lender—to see what you can get. Shop, shop, shop! Multiple mortgage applications normally show on your credit history and pull down your credit score. But all applications made within a single 14-day period count as a single application, so you're okay.

- *Don't answer spam ads for low-rate mortgages*—they aren't from real lenders. At best, the spammers are collecting personal information to sell to middlemen who, in turn, will sell it to real lenders, who may want to offer you a loan. At worst, they'll use your information in some identity-theft scam.

Don't Get Soaked by Fees

Some lenders go crazy with fees and mortgage-closing costs because they know that consumers usually don't compare. Fees vary widely. The same $200,000 loan could cost anywhere from $2,000 to $10,000, depending on where you borrow. So shop for fees as well as rates. You want to be sure that an apparently low-rate loan doesn't come larded with extra costs. A typical list includes application fees, points, "origination fee" (that's an additional percentage point for making the loan), underwriting, document preparation, escrow, recording, wire transfer, lender inspection, appraisal, title insurance, payments to the mortgage broker, payments to the bank's lawyer, rate lock (the cost of guaranteeing your rate for a certain period of time), credit report, courier, "processing" (a shameless kitchen-sink fee), pizza, coffee, Gucci shoes (well, maybe not, but if they could . . .).

Lenders have to give you a "good-faith estimate" of their fees within three days of receiving your loan application. But an estimate isn't a guarantee. At the closing itself (or only 24 hours before), you might discover that fees have miraculously risen. At that point, all you can do is walk away or pay.

Some Web lenders bundle their fees into a single charge and guarantee it—a welcome development. Whenever consumers are able to make comparisons, fees soon decline. You'll also find some lenders who advertise that they have "no closing costs"; they've bundled those costs into the mortgage itself. I wish all lenders would do this, because it gives you just one number to compare—the interest rate—with nothing else to trip you up.

At the closing, you'll have additional costs, such as local transaction taxes, prepaid interest if your mortgage closes before the end of the month, and the price of any oil or propane that the seller left in the tank. You'll also owe *impounds*—your first monthly payments toward real estate taxes and homeowners insurance. Some lenders let you pay your taxes and insurance separately but may charge you for the privilege.

Random Mortgage Recommendations

■ *Don't sign an agreement to buy unless it includes a mortgage contingency clause.* That makes your purchase contingent on finding a loan. If you can't borrow enough money, the deal is off and you get your deposit back.

■ *To compare the cost of fixed-rate loans, look at the annual percentage rate (APR).* The APR includes points and certain other financing charges, and is always higher than the stated lending rate. But it doesn't include all your closing costs, so a loan that looks a tad cheaper could be a tad more expensive after everything is paid. To get the best deal, you still have to check the fees.

On adjustable loans, the APRs last only until the first interest rate change. They're useful for comparing two loans with adjustable rates but tell you nothing about what you'll ultimately pay.

■ *Here's the minimum your lender will need when you apply for a standard loan:*

1. The purchase contract for the new house and the sales contract if you sold an old one.

2. Banking information: names and addresses of your banks, bank account numbers, copies of your latest statements.

3. Employment information: employer's name and phone number, proof of earnings (pay stubs, W-2 forms), your two most recent tax returns.

4. If you're self-employed, balance sheets for your business and three years of business and personal tax returns. It will take longer to process your loan, and you may be asked for a higher down payment.

5. Names and addresses of all creditors and the amounts you owe. (This will be checked against your credit report.)

6. Proof of what you currently pay for housing, either mortgage or rental payments.

7. Proof of other assets you own, such as mutual fund or brokerage house statements and retirement fund reports.

8. Proof of a cash reserve—enough for the down payment, closing costs, and the first two or three mortgage payments.

9. A certificate of eligibility if you're applying for a VA loan.

10. A letter from the donor if you're using a cash gift for the down payment. (The bank wants to be sure it's not a loan.)

11. The mortgage application fee.

There will be more requests for financial data as the loan processor checks you out. In fact, it's going to drive you crazy. But button your lip and supply the data. If the application seems stalled, keep calling to try to move it along.

▪ *When a lender drags its tail and a deadline looms,* call the mortgage broker and ask about starting all over again. Some lenders can close loans fast, efficiently, and at no extra cost.

▪ *The lender will have the property appraised.* If the value turns out to be less than you agreed to pay, that's your problem, not the bank's. It will lend only on the appraised amount. You'll have to come up with more cash than you'd planned or get the seller to accept a lower price.

▪ *Some loans carry prepayment penalties.* They're typically added to loans with especially low up-front fees or low interest rates that will soon rise. The penalties usually apply only during the loan's first three to five years and only if you refinance (page 580) or prepay more than 20 percent of the loan balance in a single year; no penalties are levied on the prepayment strategies outlined on page 569. The upside of accepting a loan with a prepayment penalty is that you start with a lower monthly payment. The downside is that you effectively can't refinance during the penalty period if interest rates decline.

▪ *When the bank agrees to lend you money, the interest rate isn't guaranteed.* You'll get whatever rate applies when the loan is closed. If you don't want that uncertainty, you can *lock in* today's rate for 30 to 60 days. It's smart to do so. Rates bounce around, even in the midst of a falling or rising trend. They can vary as much as a quarter-point in a single day.

▪ *If you want to close on a new house before selling your old one,* your lender may give you a "bridge loan" to cover the cost. It's due in six months or a year, in a lump sum. If you need it extended, the lender will probably agree but at a cost.

▪ *When you take a mortgage, you'll usually be offered tie-in insurance*—life, disability, even unemployment insurance. If you lose your job or become disabled, your mortgage payments will be made for you for a certain period of time. If you die, the policy pays off the loan. Appealing as this sounds, it is generally a poor buy (page 329) and not nearly as comprehensive as it sounds.

▪ *Your monthly payment to the lender usually includes the cost of your home-owners insurance and real estate tax.* Those funds go into an escrow account from which the bank pays the premiums and taxes when they come due. The account may or may not earn interest, depending on state law. By federal law, lenders can collect just enough to cover the actual bills, with no more than a two-month cushion for unanticipated expenses. If your annual statement shows extra money in your escrow account, ask for it back. Escrow is required on loans sold to Fannie Mae or Freddie Mac. The Fannie and Freddie limits: $417,000 in most areas and $625,000 in certain expensive zip codes. These limits may change, either up or down. For the latest, check the FAQs at www.fanniemae .com. If your loan is larger than Fannie or Freddie will accept, the lender may let you handle your own insurance and taxes.

■ *Jumbo or nonconforming loans*—those too big for Fannie and Freddie— typically carry higher interest rates.

■ *Read all the loan disclosures.* Don't rely on the banker or broker to tell you how your mortgage works. He or she may miss something or "forget" to tell you something.

■ *When you pay off a mortgage, be sure the lender records that fact.* If the loan still shows, you'll have to clear it before you can sell or refinance. That's no more than a nuisance if you have all the documentation. If you don't, you'll have to pursue the lender or buy an expensive bond. If you gave a second mortgage to an individual (say, the person who sold you the house), get a letter stating that the note was paid in full. If that individual went to the courthouse and formally recorded the loan, you'll have to record the payoff too.

■ *Beware the simple-interest mortgage.* SIMs calculate interest every day. On traditional mortgages, interest is calculated monthly. Monthly mortgages typically give you 10 to 15 days after the due date to make your payment at no additional cost. With daily accruals, however, you get no such grace period. If it takes six days for your monthly payment to reach the bank and another two days for the bank to post it, an additional eight days' interest is taken out of your payment, with less applied to principal. Given two loans with identical interest rates, the SIM will cost you more unless you pay *before* the due date each month.

You won't know if you have a SIM unless the lender tells you. If your loan is sold, it may be converted to a SIM without your knowledge. Yet another nasty little package from your friendly lender.

Buying a Foreclosed House

Some get-rich-quick shows on radio or late-night TV sell you the dream of a bargain price on a foreclosed home with no money down. Fat chance. There's competition for the houses worth having, and lenders apply their usual down payment rules. Occasionally you can make no-cash deals with the Federal Housing Administration or Department of Veterans Affairs. But they generally want up-front money too.

Foreclosed homes are usually handled by real estate brokers, not by some shadowy office on the edge of nowhere. They carry a market price. If their prices are lower than those of similar, occupied homes, that probably means they need more fixing up (the previous owner might have trashed it on the way out). Bargain hunters often ask about foreclosures, so the better houses go fast.

Where you might get a break on a foreclosed home is the mortgage rate, if you can buy directly from the lender's own inventory. Ask to speak to the bank's *REO* (real estate owned) division and say that you are a serious bidder. Get a property list to see if there's something you might be interested in. An inspection can be arranged through a real estate agent. As part of your bid, tell the institution that you need a deal on the mortgage—maybe a lower rate for the first couple of years and zero closing costs.

For a list of the local foreclosed properties owned by Fannie Mae, plus the names of the brokers handling them, go to www.fanniemae.com and click on "Homes for Sale." Or write to the Fannie Mae Public Information Office, 3900 Wisconsin Avenue NW, Washington, DC 20016. For homes owned by Freddie Mac, check out www.freddiemac.com (there's no place to write). You'll also find foreclosures listed at RealtyTrac (www.realtytrac.com).

Buying a house at the foreclosure sale itself is a hazardous undertaking best left to professional investors (page 994). Sales occur or are canceled at the last minute; you can rarely inspect the home's interior before buying; you need someone to check on the liens and whether the title is clear (a mistake can wipe you out); the lender may demand a price that equals the mortgage amount, even if the house is worth less; if your bid is successful, the full price usually has to be paid by cashier's check on the spot. Home buyers shouldn't get involved in this. Wait for the lender to take the house and put it back on the market through a real estate broker (as usually happens). Then you can walk through the property, buy with clear title, and get a mortgage loan.

At the Mortgage Closing

Bring money. The lender is required to give you a good-faith estimate of all the closing costs within three business days of receiving your mortgage application. Before the closing, your lawyer, real estate broker, or escrow agent should give you the exact figure, although you typically won't get it until 24 hours before you have to sign—too late to walk away. Expect to pay anywhere from 3 to 7 percent of the loan amount—for title search, title insurance, survey, appraisal, credit check, loan origination fee, processing fees, legal fees, recording fees, home-owners insurance, mortgage insurance, and taxes. If you have only enough money to make the down payment, you can generally add your closing costs to the loan amount. In fact, you can get a "no cash" mortgage—no points, no fees, no closing costs—in exchange for a slightly higher mortgage rate.

When looking for a lender, compare closing costs as well as interest rates. Some banks and S&Ls extract much less from you than others.

Writing Off the Interest

On first mortgages, all interest is tax deductible up to $1 million. On second mortgages, including home equity loans, it's deductible up to $100,000. Those two loans can be bundled into a single mortgage, with the interest deductible up to $1.1 million.

You can spread your deductible interest over two homes (one a personal residence, the other a vacation or secondary home), but not over three or more. The loan has to be secured by the property itself, and you have to borrow within 90 days of making the purchase.

On a purchase, points are deductible in the year they're paid.

On a refinancing, points are deductible in the year paid only if the money is used for home improvements. Otherwise they're deducted over the term of the loan.

If you build a house, the interest on your construction loan is normally deductible for two years from the time you first break ground. This loan also must be secured by the property. You have to get the mortgage within 90 days of the finishing date.

You can deduct the portion of your monthly condominium maintenance fee that represents your share of the building's real estate tax.

It's Nine P.M. Do You Know Where Your Mortgage Is?

Probably not. The days are long gone when your banker kept mortgages in his vault.

Nowadays, banks sell most of their mortgages to private investors world-wide. You still might mail your monthly payment to the bank you borrowed from. But the bank only "services" the loan by processing your check, paying your real estate taxes and homeowners insurance, and sending the investor the rest of the money. For this, the bank collects a fee—but from the investor, not from you.

Your bank might also sell the right to service your mortgage. In that case, you should get two notices, one from your old servicer and one from your new one. Both notices have to give you the new servicer's name and address, the date you will start making payments there, toll-free numbers for both servicers in case you have any questions, information about any changes in the credit insurance package, and any new procedures for handling your escrow account. The terms of the mortgage itself will remain the same.

When servicers change, keep an eye on what happens to your tax and insurance payments. The servicer normally pays them from your escrow account. But if there's a hitch in transferring the account, a payment might be missed. You'll discover it when you get a notice in the mail from your city or the homeowners insurance company. If there's a penalty for late payment, the mortgage servicer has to pay it—provided, of course, that your own monthly payments were made on time. Sometimes the new servicer finds that your escrow account is short of money, in which case your monthly payments will rise.

There's a 60-day grace period after the change, during which you won't owe a late penalty if you mistakenly send your mortgage check to the wrong servicer.

All this assumes an honest servicer. Some servicers have found nasty ways to charge you more. For example, they might add flood insurance to your mortgage without telling you. Your usual monthly payment won't be enough to cover the increased cost. Suddenly you're in arrears. You start getting late-payment charges. When you protest, the servicer will claim that you were fully informed of the change and won't rescind the charges. In some cases, lenders have sent foreclosure notices because the record shows you behind for several months. That will be reported to your credit bureau too. Make it a habit to save *all* notices from your loan servicer. Inspect every bill to be sure it looks right.

When to Refinance

When mortgage rates skid, you can refinance at a profit. Take out a new, low-rate loan and use the proceeds to pay off the loan you're carrying now. If you need extra money, you can often take a larger loan with little or no increase in the amount you have to pay each month.

Some homeowners won't be able to refinance through the usual channels, because the equity in their homes amounts to less than 20 percent. Still, there's hope. A special government program provides refis to people with low or no equity and whose loans are owned by Fannie Mae or Freddie Mac. Check it out at Making Home Affordable (www.makinghomeaffordable.gov).

Borrowers should hit the refi phone the moment rates look attractive. If you dally, they may rise again. Six refinancing ideas:

- *Replace your current fixed-rate mortgage with a new fixed-rate loan.* That's a smart move as long as your savings—in interest costs or monthly payments—will outstrip the refinancing cost during the time you'll keep the house. Paper-and-pencil jockeys should be able to figure that out. For an online calculator, go to the Mortgage Professor's Web site (www.mtgprofessor.com) or KJE Computer Solutions (www.dinkytown.net).

- *If you like adjustable-rate mortgages, exchange your current ARM for a new one and glory in its low initial teaser rate.* You might save as much as 2 or 3 percentage points. You'll also lower the cap on how high your mortgage rate could be allowed to rise.

- *Switch your adjustable-rate mortgage to a fixed-rate loan.* A new ARM would be cheaper, but you may want the security of knowing that your monthly payments cannot rise.

- *Switch your 30-year loan for one with a 15-year term, perhaps at little or no increase in monthly cost.* A shorter term greatly reduces your interest expense.

- *Pay off a balloon loan ahead of time* if you see a regular mortgage rate you can afford.

- *Consolidate a first and second mortgage into a single loan* if the new rate will be below the weighted average of the rates on your existing loans.

You cannot save money by switching into a loan with a higher interest rate! The loan can be made to *look* cheaper. The lender can stretch out its term to give you lower monthly payments. But it's all baloney. Higher-rate loans still cost you more.

Even a lower-rate loan can cost you more if you stretch out the term. For example, say that you took a 30-year mortgage six years ago, so today you have 24 years left to pay. If you refinance (refi) into a new 30-year loan, you're stretching out your remaining principal payments for an extra six years. That's an extra six years of interest costs—not cheap.

You might think that refinancing into a longer-term loan doesn't matter because you won't keep it for 30 years. But it matters a lot. Ask the bank to show you how much interest you'd pay on both the old loan and the new one if you sold the house after, say, seven years. You might be surprised to see that the new loan isn't the money saver you thought.

If the bank doesn't let you refinance over exactly the number of years remaining on your old loan, go for the first available shorter term—say, 20 years. There's another option: take the longer-term loan but turn it into a shorter one. A 30-year loan can become a 24-year loan if you make slightly higher payments every month. Use a mortgage calculator to check this out.

Lenders typically charge the same fees on a refinancing as they did when you borrowed to buy the house. They're delighted to fold those costs right into the loan, so you're borrowing more. You'll also see "no-cost" refis, which carry a slightly higher interest rate (the costs are contained in the rate, rather than being listed separately). A no-cost might be cheaper if you plan to move pretty soon. But if you'll probably stay in the house for five years or more, it's best to take a lower-rate refi and pay the closing costs in cash.

Should You Do a Cash-Out Refinancing?

With a cash-out, you take a larger loan than you had before. You pay off the old mortgage and use the extra money for other things. The interest rate on a cash-out is a little higher than on a straight refinancing and the larger loan reduces your home equity. So you're incurring extra costs and spending down your wealth.

Whether a cash-out is smart depends on what you're taking the money for:

- *A new kitchen?* The down payment on a second home? A child's tuition? These are reasonable choices, provided that you can make the larger mortgage payments without strain.

- *Starting a business?* Have a fallback plan to protect your home if the business doesn't work.

- *Investing in stock?* You're trading a pretty secure investment for a riskier one, probably on a stockbroker's promise that over the long term you can't lose. You *can* lose. What's more, you need a higher return on investment than you imagine to exceed the cost of the refi's rates and fees. I like the stock market just fine, but invest with money you've saved on the side, not with your home equity.

- *Taking a really great vacation?* Please, no. You'll be paying for that vacation for the next 30 years.

- *Paying off your credit cards?* Okay, you're stealing a fortune from your future. You're relieved of your high monthly credit card payments, which gets you out of a short-term bind. The interest become tax deductible. But consumer bills that you should repay over just a few months or a couple of years are now stretched over 30 years, costing you interest every year. If you have to consolidate these bills, go for a home equity line of credit and pay it off as fast as you can. Also, switch to a debit card for all your shopping, so you won't run up your credit cards all over again.

What if you need money but mortgage interest rates have gone up? A cash-out refinancing isn't worth it if you'll pay a higher rate. Take a second mortgage instead. The rate will be higher on the second, but you'll be paying it on a smaller amount. That will be cheaper in the end. In bad housing markets, lenders may not allow cash-outs.

Warning: The interest on a large cash-out may not be entirely deductible. The IRS lets you write off all the interest on your original mortgage, up to a loan value of $1 million. But the rules change when you refinance. You're allowed to deduct only the interest on your original mortgage balance plus an additional loan of up to $100,000. The 1099 form you get from the bank will show all the interest paid. But depending on how much you borrowed, it may not all be a legitimate deduction.

What It Costs to Refinance

Talk to your current lender first. You may be able to recast your present mortgage for a low fee without going through a full-scale refinancing. If not, check the Web to see what's available. If your current lender can't beat the price, see a mortgage broker or borrow online.

Some lenders charge zero up front if you'll pay 0.25 or 0.5 percentage points over the going rate. This offer still might cost you less than you're paying now. Also, it effectively makes your closing costs deductible.

Expenses rise, however, if you want to take a larger loan. Then you're scrutinized—and charged—as if you were borrowing from scratch. Many Web sites, including those mentioned in this chapter, offer refinancing calculators to help you decide whether the savings are worth the costs. For short-term needs, it's cheaper to get a home equity loan that you'll pay off fast (page 297).

Canceling Your Private Mortgage Insurance

Private mortgage insurance terminates automatically on your personal residence once you've paid down your loan to 78 percent of the original value of the home. This usually takes 10 or 11 years, depending on the interest rate. Also, your payments have to be up to date.

You can request cancellation when you've paid down the loan to 80 percent of the home's original value, provided that your payments are up to date, the property hasn't declined in value, and you have no other loans against the home (such as a home equity loan). This applies to most loans made after July 28, 1999.

The insurance may continue, however, if you're considered to be high risk or you took the loan before July 29, 1999. For more information on loan cancellation, see the Web site of the Mortgage Insurance Companies of America,

MICA (www.privatemi.com), or the Mortgage Professor's Web site (www.mtg professor.com).

On older FHA loans, insurance may have to be carried for the life of the loan. The policy changed for loans closed after January 1, 2001. FHA insurance will terminate automatically under one of two conditions:

1. The loan is for more than 15 years, the mortgage is down to 78 percent of the home's original value, and you've held the loan for at least five years.

2. The loan is for 15 years or less, your down payment came to 10 percent or less, and your loan is down to 78 percent of the original value.

No monthly insurance premiums are charged for FHA loans with terms of 15 years or less if your down payment exceeded 10 percent.

If the lender that made the mortgage sold it to Fannie Mae, you might be able to drop the insurance earlier. Cancellation is possible if no payment was late by 30 days or more over the past 12 months or late by 60 days or more in the 12 months before that. You also have to meet one of the following conditions:

1. Your mortgage is down to 80 percent of the property's original value, the property hasn't dropped in price, and you've held the loan for at least five years. If the loan was a refinancing, you must have made at least 12 consecutive payments.

2. Your mortgage balance is 75 percent of what the house is currently worth, and the loan is at least two years old.

Fannie Mae also allows automatic termination on second homes and investment properties.

If the loan is held by Freddie Mac, you can cancel the insurance if you ask in writing, have a good payment record, and:

1. Your mortgage balance equals 80 percent or less of the property's current appraised value, and you've held the loan for at least five years.

2. Your mortgage balance is down to 75 percent or less of the home's current appraised value, and you've held the loan for at least two years.

3. You've made substantial improvements to the home, and your mortgage balance is 80 percent or less of its current value.

To request cancellation, go to the lender who's servicing your mortgage (that's the place where you send your mortgage payments). The servicer is required to follow Fannie's or Freddie's rules. You'll need an appraisal showing what the property is worth. Don't waste your money coming in with your own appraisal. You'll be required to use an appraiser who's lender approved.

Can You Cancel the Insurance Early if You Have a Home Equity Loan or Other Second Mortgage on the House?

Fannie and Freddie allow it, but the investor holding the mortgage may prevent it. Nevertheless, the rules on automatic termination still apply. You're off the hook once you've paid down your loan to 78 percent of the original value of the home.

You Cannot Cancel Mortgage Insurance if the Lender Bought It for You.

The price of the coverage is included in the mortgage rate you pay. To escape the cost of the insurance, you will have to refinance.

When You Sell

You don't have to pay the traditional 5 or 6 percent real estate commission. That's what the real estate broker quotes—sometimes even 7 percent. But many of them will negotiate. Brokers who stick to the higher commission will probably tell you they're worth every penny because they can get you more for your home. But there's no proof of that (it's like stockbrokers saying they'll find you stocks that go up). Plenty of fine and experienced brokers will take your listing for less and put the same effort into selling your house that the pricier ones do.

On the Web, you'll find discount brokers that will sell your house for as little as 4 percent or even 3 percent. That's a saving of $7,000 to $10,500 on a $350,000 house. Some traditional brokers boycott the discounters and won't show the houses they list—proof that they care more about protecting their income than helping their customers find homes. But the discount business is growing because home sellers want it and the discounters advertise widely enough to attract clients. Check sites such as ZipRealty (www.ziprealty.com), Help-U-Sell Real Estate (www.helpusell.com), and Assist-2-Sell (www.assist2 sell.com). They're not in all states but may be in yours. To see if there's an independent discounter nearby, enter words such as "discount real estate broker" or "4 percent real estate commission" in your Web search engine. Almost certainly, some will turn up.

How about selling the house yourself, without a broker? It's easier in a hot market than a cool one but works anytime for sellers willing to make the effort. On a $350,000 house, you'd save $21,000—a payoff worth working for. You don't have to put your own hand-lettered sign in the window. Web sites such as Owners.com (www.owners.com) and ForSaleByOwner.com (www.forsale

byowner.com) sell professional For Sale yard signs, a toll-free number for receiving calls, a listing on their own Web site (with pictures of your house), and a listing on the Multiple Listing Service (MLS) that all real estate brokers use. From the MLS, listings migrate to Realtor.com—a big break for do-it-yourselfers. People looking for homes nationwide tap into www.realtor.com, where your house can be seen along with the houses shown by brokers. There's pots of free info on the Web about pricing your house, preparing it for sale, and negotiating terms. If it doesn't sell, you can always try a broker later.

Should You Offer a Buydown?

When the market is slow, sellers look for little treats to offer buyers. One of them is a buydown mortgage. You pay the lender a lump sum in return for offering your buyer a lower mortgage interest rate for a short, fixed term.

That's cute but may be pointless. It's smarter simply to cut the price of your home by the cost of the buydown. The buydown's value accumulates over the life of a 30-year loan. If your buyers sell any earlier, as they almost certainly will, that "special deal" isn't worth as much. Buydowns appeal to sellers who don't want to admit that their house is worth less than they think. It appeals to buyers for whom lower monthly payments matter most.

If You Can't Sell, Should You Rent?

To begin with, *any* house can sell if you drop the price enough. We're talking here about people who don't want to do that, maybe because the house is worth less than the loan against it or because they think they can do better two or three years from now.

You can probably find a renter, but it's not so easy to make the arrangement actually pay.

To start with, the rent has to cover all your costs: principal, interest, insurance, taxes, repairs, a reserve for the unexpected, and a rental agent if you use one. The cost of your homeowners insurance will rise, and you'll need a big liability policy. Rents in your area may not be high enough for all that. If you're forced to pay some of the bills out-of-pocket every month, you're trimming any profit you'll eventually make on the house.

You'll probably have to borrow money for the down payment on your next house, which also adds to your cost.

If you rent for more than three years, you may lose the big homeowners tax break: no tax on the first $250,000 in profits for singles and the first $500,000* for couples. Instead, all your profits may be taxable when you eventually sell.

The value of your house may fall instead of rise or may not rise by enough to make the hassle of renting worth it.

You'll have to deal with tenants who may be complainers, pay their rent late, treat the house badly, or call at three in the morning for you to fix the toilet. Some don't pay at all and have to be evicted. Maybe these things won't happen. You could find dream tenants. But you never know.

When tenants leave, it may take a month or more to fix up the house, find potential new renters, and do background checks on them to be sure they're not crooks. In the meantime, you have to cover the ongoing costs.

Renting, in short, isn't a picnic, especially if you've moved away. Unless you're an experienced rental real estate investor, it's better to face facts, drop your price, sell, and move on.

Don't Wind Up a Tweener

These are people who buy a house before they've sold their old one and get stuck with their old one in a slowing housing market. They've got two mortgages, two home equity loans, maybe a high-cost bridge loan for the second down payment, and a dying bank account. The stress of living "in between" drives them to find renters—and to drink.

Best advice: don't buy until you've sold the house you have. You can put off the closing on your house for several months while you shop for something new. There are plenty of homes on the market, and prices aren't running away. You'll find something you like.

If your old house doesn't sell, drop the price. Your real estate agent can tell you what comparable homes in your area have sold for (the actual prices, not the asking prices).

If you feel that you have to buy because you're moving your kids to a new school, do it with a *contingency clause*. These clauses pretty much vanished during the real estate boom. Now they're making a comeback. Make the purchase contingent on selling your old house within a certain number of months. If that won't fly, agree that the seller can keep his house on the market with a promise

---

*Widows and widowers also get $500,000 if they owned the home jointly with their late spouses and sell within two years of the day that their spouse died.

to let you match a better offer if he gets one. If it comes, you can then decide whether to move into tweenerdom or to let the house go.

If you're a tweener already, look at your carrying costs and make a guess as to how many months this torture might go on. Cut the price of your old house by the amount of your carrying costs and see what happens.

When You Can't Pay Your Mortgage

Don't stick your head in the sand. If you foresee trouble—maybe because you've lost your job—act right away.

If you have equity in your home, use it to assemble a pool of cash. Take out a second mortgage or home equity line while your credit is still good. That could help cover your mortgage payments for several months or even a year, while you get back on your feet. You might also consolidate your credit card debt into a new mortgage if that will lower your monthly payments by enough to keep you afloat.

If think you'll never be able to pay, sell the house as fast as you can in hopes of getting some equity out.

If you have no equity in your home, you're under water (and I don't mean flooded). Your house is worth less than the mortgage against it. If you have to move and have enough savings, sell the house for what you can get and use your savings to cover the additional money you'll owe to the bank. This keeps your credit score intact.

If you can't afford your mortgage and can't sell for enough to cover your loan, none of your choices is good. You can:

- *Ask the lender for forbearance.* You might be offered reduced payments for up to six months if it seems likely that you'll soon be able to cover the arrears and return to a normal payment schedule. This could work if you lost your job but expect to start a new one pretty soon.

- *Ask for a loan modification.* The loan servicer (the place where you send your payments) recasts your loan. Unfortunately, you're not in control of the type of modification offered or whether you'll be given one at all. There are government incentives for recasting loans. Still, it's entirely up to the mortgage servicer.

Modifications come in five types: (1) Adding your past-due payments and late fees to your loan and recalculating the payment. You'll have to pay a little more each month. This helps only people who fell behind because of a job loss but now are working again. (2) Extending the term of the loan, which brings the monthly payment down a little bit. But you still might not be able to afford it. Don't do a deal that fails to ease your financial problem. (3) Reducing the interest rate. This does get the payment down, but loan servicers are reluctant to do it. Try for a temporary reduction with the rate rising gradually back to its original level. (4) Freezing the interest rate on a loan where the rate is scheduled to rise on a specified date. Many subprime loans were modified this way in 2008 and 2009, under pressure from the government and consumer groups. (5) Reducing the loan balance. For the servicer, this is a last resort.

Any distressed mortgage can be modified if the servicer is willing. To see if you're eligible for the government's hardship loan-modification program, go to the Web site Making Home Affordable (www.makinghomeaffordable.com).

Warning: Servicers hate to be bothered with loan modifications, even when pushed by the federal government. They might dicker endlessly, or "lose" your paperwork and never call you back. The institutions that invested in your mortgage might be roadblocks. So be persistent. Push, push, push. If you qualify under the government hardship program, provide copies of all the income and expense data that the servicer needs. If not, try to show that prices are still falling in your neighborhood, so it's in the investor's and servicer's interest to do a deal with you now. Show that you'll be able to make all future payments if the mortgage's terms are changed.

- *Use a Consumer Counseling Service* (page 288). They have lines into the servicer's distressed-mortgages unit and might be able to start you on the path to loan modification. While they're at it, they can help you figure out a budget and negotiate with other creditors.

- *If you have private mortgage insurance, see if the company will help.* PMI companies often offer "claim advances" to qualified customers, to help them bring their loans current. You probably qualify if you missed your payments due to an illness or a short bout of unemployment, and could get back on track with just a little help.

- *Do a short sale.* Find a buyer for your house at its current market price or only slightly less. The bank agrees to accept that amount and write off the rest of the loan. The failure to pay shows up on your credit report, but at least you're out from under.

Books and seminars often claim that short sales are an easy escape, but that's not so. Roughly, here's what happens: You make many, many calls to the lender to find the person in charge of short sales. The lender wants proof that you can't pay the mortgage (financial statements, tax returns) and that the house is worth less than the loans against it. There's an appraisal. You list the house with a real estate broker at market price, to attract some credible offers, or you find a private buyer who will pay close to the market price. The buyer submits a written offer. There's lots of back-and-forth with the lender over taxes, expenses, and loan arrears, often taking months. You may be pressured to sign a note for part or all of the deficiency, in which case it wouldn't be a true short sale. (Don't sign! If the bank threatens to foreclose, you can threaten to go bankrupt, which would cause the lender an even larger loss.) If there's a second mortgage on the property, including a home equity loan, you'll have to cut a deal with that lender too.

Please pay an attorney to check the short-sale papers to be sure that you're released from the full debt. If the fine print continues to bind you to the second mortgage or to the deficiency on the first, the lenders can sue for the rest of the money owed. Find out what the lender will put on your credit report. It should show the loan as satisfied, even if short.

■ *Do a deed in lieu of foreclosure.* It's like a short sale but without a buyer. The lender agrees to take back the house for what it's worth and write off the portion of the loan that remains unpaid. Here too the lender may try to get you to sign a separate note for the remainder of the payment owed. Don't. Be sure the loan will be reported as satisfied on your credit report. Your lawyer should check the agreement before you say "done."

■ *Accept foreclosure.* In general, the lender takes your house and settles for whatever it can get on resale, without pursuing you for the deficiency. But state laws differ. If you have other assets and the law allows, the lender might chase you for any remaining money owed. Some states prevent lenders from collecting deficiencies on the original mortgage but allow it if you refinanced or took a home equity loan. An attorney can advise you.

Beware the fees that servicers try to slap on! Judges are finding that they may make improper claims, add costs for vague reasons, fail to account for all the payments you made, levy improper late fees, and generally run up your bill. In one egregious case, a lender filed a claim for more than $1 million, but when the loan's history was examined, the borrower turned out to owe only $60,000. You need a lawyer to watch this too.

■ *Use jingle mail.* Pop the house keys into an envelope, mail them to the lender, and walk away. The lender will handle this as a foreclosure and show it on your credit report. If you have means, the lender might pursue you for any additional money owed. The odds are, however, that it will leave you alone.

■ *Use the special loss mitigation programs* available to people whose loans are insured by the Federal Housing Authority (FHA) or Veterans Administration (VA). Your lender is supposed to take action as soon as you default on a payment, to try to keep you in your home. Anyone with an FHA or VA loan should ask about them as soon as money runs short.

■ *Consider bankruptcy.* Chapter 13 stops foreclosure proceedings and lets you catch up with back payments over a reasonable period of time. You also have to make scheduled payments on your other bills. If you miss any scheduled payments, foreclosure proceeds. Alternatively, choose Chapter 7 if you have little or no equity in your home or if the amount of equity is protected under your state's bankruptcy act. You can shed the rest of your consumer debts and keep your house, provided that you're up-to-date on mortgage payments. For more on bankruptcy, see page 289.

Be warned that all these tactics stick like glue. Whenever you apply for a mortgage in the future, you'll have to disclose that you've used loan modification, short sales, deeds-in-lieu, or foreclosure to get out from under housing debt. You'll never be able to get terms as good as those offered to people who've never been in trouble with their loans.

Special tax note: With short sales, deeds-in-lieu, and similar arrangements, you pay the bank less than you actually owe. Normally, the amount of the loan that a bank agrees not to chase you for (the *deficiency*), plus any closing or commission costs that the lender paid, are treated as taxable income. Your lender reports it to the government on Form 1099-C. But Congress gave troubled home owners a break for tax years 2007 through 2012. You won't be taxed for debt of up to $2 million that lenders forgave on your principal residence. The debt has to have been used to buy, build, or improve your house, so home equity loans used to pay off credit cards don't qualify. To escape the tax on your deficiency, file Form 982 with your federal tax return.

Don't Hang On to a House You Can't Afford!

If you're behind on your mortgage and struggling with other bills, face the music early. Don't raid your retirement savings account to hang on to a house that's a lost cause. Sell it now. If you can't sell it, let it go into foreclosure. You'll be able to live there for a few months, rent free, while the paperwork gets done. Use the money you save on mortgage payments to pay your credit card bills and build a cash fund for your future. Move to rental housing. If your house is worth less than the mortgage against it, you're effectively renting anyway. If you ask, the bank might even give you $1,000 in moving money—known as "cash for keys"—as an inducement to take care of the house during the foreclosure process.

A great weight will lift from your shoulders when you let the house go. Look to the future and a lifestyle you can afford.

What if You Can Afford the Mortgage but Your House Is Under Water?

If you bought the house to live in, keep on making payments. Over time, its value should rise again. To build equity faster, put extra money into your mortgage every month.

If you bought the house as a speculation and want out, don't expect the servicer to give you a short sale or deed-in-lieu. The servicer wants to be paid. If you go to foreclosure or mail in the keys, expect to be pursued for the extra money owed.

Predatory Mortgage Servicers

Mortgage servicers are the people who receive your mortgage payments, record them, and distribute them to the investors who've bought your loan. They compute your interest rate changes on adjustable-rate loans and collect the payments for your homeowners insurance and real estate taxes. They manage defaults and pursue collections on bad loans. But some of them aren't happy with their legitimate profits. They've cooked up some neat little scams that, so far, no one has bothered to stop.

Some of them arise from sloppy practices, especially on subprime loans. Servicers buy and sell loans to one another and don't always transfer your entire record along with the loan. You may not be told about the change in a timely fashion, so you keep sending your mortgage payments to the servicer you had before. Your checks will eventually come back, but meanwhile, the new servicer docks you for a late or missing payment and deducts a penalty. You'll be recorded as delinquent. You might even get a foreclosure notice even though you've been paying on time.

That's just the start. Some servicers have been caught pocketing payments rather than posting them to your account. Some post them late, deliberately, and charge you a late fee. They may not pay your taxes on time, resulting in liens on your house. Many of them pile on huge penalties when payments are late. Just one late payment can generate so many fees that the borrower can't afford them—driving him or her into a foreclosure that never should have happened.

Another scam involves insurance payments. Servicers have been caught adding, say, expensive hazard insurance to borrowers' accounts without telling them. You keep making payments, but now they're not large enough to cover the mortgage plus the extra premium due. Does the servicer tell you? No, it puts your payments into a "suspense" account instead of applying them to your loan. You're marked as delinquent and penalized. After a couple of months, your payments may be refused and foreclosure begun.

You don't realize what's going on because servicers don't have to send you monthly statements. By the time your troubles bubble up, it becomes almost impossible to save your home. No one stops these servicers, no legislation gets passed, so they keep it up. When, oh, when will Washington start listening to consumer advocates again?

Watch Out for Scams

Always, always, crooks lie in wait to prey on folks in need. If you can't pay your mortgage and have equity in your home, scumbags will almost certainly show up, offering to "help." They're aiming to grab your equity for themselves. You're vulnerable because you don't want to sell the house and move. Here are some of the "deals" they may offer:

- *They'll sell your house, privately and temporarily, to a handy investor.* You'll get some cash up front and can stay in the house for a year. The investor promises to pay the mortgage in your name, to improve your credit score. At the end of the year, you can get a new mortgage and buy the house back.

- *They'll do a private "refinancing."* You agree to a "loan" at a lower interest rate and, in the process, turn over the deed.

- *You sign over your deed and make reduced payments for five years.* The scumbag says he'll invest your home equity, earning enough to top up your monthly payments and pay off the mortgage completely. After that, you'll get your home back free and clear.

Here's what actually happens: The scumbag does a cash-out refinancing at the highest possible amount, pockets the money, and vanishes. The lender forecloses.

There are variants to these schemes, but you get the idea. If you foresee that you won't be able to handle future mortgage payments, sell your house right now to capture the equity for yourself. Or use one of the strategies given on page 587. Don't call a "mortgage rescue" company you see in the newspaper or on the Internet. They're out to rob you blind.

Dumb Investment Ideas

A tap-dancing salesperson may advise you to take all the equity out of your house and buy a life insurance policy. Your home equity earns no return, they say. The cash buildup in an insurance policy comes tax free.

So much is wrong with this pitch that I hardly know where to start. You add to your costs by taking a maximum loan against home equity. The insurance is so expensive (fees you don't see) that it's hard for the gains in your policy to cover your extra mortgage costs. When you sell your home, odds are that the profits will also be tax free (singles get a tax-free $250,000 over the purchase price plus all improvements; married couples get $500,000). If you take too much cash from your insurance policy, it might collapse, hitting you with a tax bill you never expected (see page 307). With little or no home equity, you can't move, because you owe the lenders more than you'll get for your house.

There are plenty of similar dumb investment ideas. They all involve stripping your home equity to buy something else—usually something complex and expensive that will make only the salesperson rich. Say no. Just say no.

For Plenty More Mortgage Information

Check out these Web sites:

1. The Mortgage Professor's Web Site (www.mtgprofessor.com), the most comprehensive source on the Web for tutorials, consumer information, tools, and tips about the complex mortgage market. It includes eye-opening sections on how you can be skinned by lenders and mortgage brokers. Jack Guttentag (the "mortgage professor") also has written an excellent book called *The Mortgage Encyclopedia: An Authoritative Guide to Mortgage Programs, Practices, Prices, and Pitfalls.*

2. HSH Associates Financial Publishers (www.hsh.com) provides tidy primers on borrowing as well as articles on current developments and a search feature for loans. It also offers a series of useful "Homeowner's Guides."

3. For more educational tools, try Mortgage101.com (www.mortgage 101.com) and Mortgagex.com (www.mortgagex.com), and Freddie Mac (www .freddiemac.com).

The Great Condo Question

Condominiums and town houses are homes attached to each other. You own a unit, but you and your neighbors share common areas: lobbies, central heating, landscaping, a pool. Cooperative apartments are similar, except that you own shares in the co-op as a whole with the right to lease a certain unit. Monthly maintenance fees are levied on each owner to keep the common areas in good repair. You're also assessed for special expenses, such as replacing an elevator.

Condos and town houses have two big advantages: they cost less than comparable freestanding houses and require less personal upkeep. If your condo's roof starts to leak, you don't have to call the roofer or nail up shingles yourself, you have only to help pay for repairs. For the young, condominiums are often a first step into the housing market. For the old, they're a comfortable step back from the burden of caring for a house.

But check these drawbacks before you opt for condo or co-op living:

- *Condominiums typically rise less in value than freestanding houses and fall much faster when market conditions are poor.* You're far more likely to lose money on a condo than on a house. That's because buyers prefer new units where they can pick the rugs and appliances themselves. To sell, you may have to slash the price. Young people ready to trade up may find that they've built little or no equity. For some owners, condos become a trap.
- *The smaller the condo, the harder it is to sell for a profit.* Two-bedroom units sell better than one-bedroom units, which sell better than studios (studios barely move at all on the resale market). Town house condos do better than two-bedroom apartment condos.
- *Most lenders allow home equity loans on condos, but some won't take co-ops.* Co-op boards often limit the amount of financing you're allowed.
- *The condo developer might have lowballed the monthly maintenance fee.* You learn too late that it's going to cost a lot more than you thought to keep the building or development running. New condos might also have hidden flaws that will be expensive to repair.
- *The condo owners might be suing the builder for shoddy construction and other sins.* Check this out before you buy. Also ask if any special assessments are in the wind for improvements or major repairs.
- *If owners can't sell, they might move away and turn their units into rental properties.* As more renters come in, the character of the condo changes. Tenants don't treat the property as carefully as residents would. The absentee owners don't want higher maintenance fees because they can't recover the cost

by raising rents. If owners can't find tenants or earn enough rent, they might not pay their maintenance fees. That could force the condo onto a bare-bones budget—reducing services, deferring maintenance, and cutting property values. There may also be special assessments on the other unit holders to cover the bills. Banks generally don't give mortgages in new developments where tenants occupy more than 30 percent of the units or in older developments that are more than 40 percent rented, although exceptions may be granted. If you're an owner, that makes it tough to resell.

■ *Town house developments have long lists of don'ts:* don't paint your front door red, don't plant bushes by your front walk, don't use an outdoor clothesline, don't keep a large dog, don't, don't, don't, don't. These rules will be enforced by neighborhood posses who want to keep the grounds looking uniformly attractive. If you like red doors and large dogs, don't move in.

■ *Buildings converting to condo or co-op ownership may have hidden flaws.* If the present owner of your building proposes that you buy it, the tenants should hire a lawyer and engineer. You need to know what's wrong with the building (will it need a new roof? new wiring? at how much per tenant?); what it will cost to run the building well; what taxes you'll pay after conversion; and whether the title is clear. Will you own the land under the building or only the building itself? If someone else owns the land, what's to prevent him or her from jacking up the rent or, worse, not renewing the lease? With conversions, an insider's price is usually low, but it's no bargain if the building needs expensive repairs or the units aren't easy to resell. Unless you feel certain that the unit is a sound investment, try to stay as a renter and let the new owners handle the headaches. Or bail out.

■ *Each condominium development or co-op building is governed by a board of owners.* Your property values depend on how well the board members do their job. Do they enforce collections from people who don't pay their maintenance fees on time? Are they unafraid to levy higher assessments for essential maintenance? Can they settle disagreements about what amenities the building should invest in? Will they see that the building is always kept in good repair? Under an ineffectual board, a co-op or condominium can fall apart.

■ *If an owner doesn't pay his or her maintenance fee, the condo board generally has the right to foreclose.* But even then, the condo may not get the money it's owed. The proceeds of the foreclosure sale go first to satisfy tax liens and second to repay the first mortgage. Only then can the condo collect, and there may not be enough money left—especially on units that are fairly new or in areas where condo values have declined. The remaining owners may be assessed to cover the default.

■ *Buyers of cooperative apartments run similar risks.* You're on the line for the building's entire mortgage, tax bill, and upkeep. If your neighbors don't pay their share, you may have to kick in. A co-op, however, can generally evict an owner who doesn't pay and sell the unit on the open market. The co-op takes any money it's owed; the former owner gets whatever is left. To minimize defaults, co-op boards don't let you sell your apartment at will. The buyer's finances first have to be checked. If the board finds reason to object—personal or social as well as financial—you lose the sale.

The trend in town houses is away from condos. They're increasingly being built to sell as individual homes.

If You Want a Condo or Co-op, Here's Your Best Hope of Making Money on the Deal

- *Find a building where the units are almost entirely occupied by owners rather than by renters.* These buildings are usually better maintained. Beware the condo whose sponsor couldn't persuade enough tenants to buy their own apartments.
- *Buy a two-bedroom condo rather than a studio.* The larger units hold their value better because there are more potential buyers.
- *Stay away from small buildings.* If a 10-unit condo needs a new roof, each owner could face a whopping cost.
- *Buy where condos or co-ops are the normal form of ownership,* as in New York City or downtown Chicago. There, the prices behave more like those of individual houses.
- *Buy a well-kept, well-run older condo rather than a new one.* Its price will be lower and you don't risk the new-condo problems: careless construction, unfinished amenities, and higher taxes and maintenance fees than the salespeople said. The owners' association will be functioning smoothly, and there should be a sizable cash reserve for unexpected repairs.
- *Find a unit with amenities appropriate to the people who might buy from you:* good schools and a playground for young families; social spaces and bus service for older people.
- *Don't buy where you see new condos going up or space where the developer can build new ones in the future.* Most buyers choose new units when they can. You may not be able to sell your older unit unless you cut the price drastically.
- *Don't buy without reading all the condo documents* (murky as they are) to be sure that you understand—and can live with—the bylaws, the budget, and the rules.
- *When checking the budget, look for a sizable cash reserve for repairs.* If there

isn't one, take a walk. It shows that the building is poorly run. Ditto if there's no reserve for the cost of collecting maintenance fees from any owners who default. Ask about the delinquency rate: What percentage of owners aren't paying their bills? What is the board doing about it? A sound building assumes a certain percentage of deadbeats and budgets for it. If the budget assumes that everyone will pay, you're going to get a nasty surprise.

■ *Avoid a building or condo development with a lot of defaults or where more than 20 percent of the units are rented out.* Outside owners default at a much higher rate than owner-occupants do—and when others don't pay, you'll have to pick up the slack. A growing percentage of renters also means that the building will run down.

The Strategic Renter

In Some Circumstances, It's Smarter to Rent than to Buy

Maybe you have a rent-controlled apartment that's unbelievably cheap. These bargains are fading from the scene, but as long as you have one, keep it and use your extra money to invest.

Maybe you expect to move within three or four years. You'd probably lose money on a house if you bought and sold in such a short period of time.

Maybe you're young and single and want to be ready to change your life in a moment. Or you're newly divorced and haven't decided what you'll do next.

Maybe you're retired and want to sell your house. You could invest the proceeds and use part of the income to pay rent.

Maybe you see house prices slipping in your area and hope to buy more cheaply if you wait a year.

But for Long-Term Occupancy, Ownership Is Best

Home-price busts, as happened in 2006–2009, are rare. Over longer periods of time, you'll get a reasonable return on your investment even with housing prices only crawling up.

On paper, there's nothing wrong with investing your money in something other than a house—as long as you really do it and add money each month, as people repaying mortgages do. But to equal what you get from a paid-up house, you'll have to build a large enough fund to cover your rent from the day you retire until the end of your life. I don't see many pots that large. Whoever first said that a house was a security blanket wasn't kidding.

A Second Home
for Fun and Profit

The House That Doesn't Cost You Anything (Much)

**Imagine a house that helps pay for itself.
When you're not there it's making money and
lifting the mortgage from your back.**

As luck would have it, I wrote this chapter in my second home. My husband and I had a string of cottages on the ocean. We built them, rented them out, sold at a profit, and built again. We made some money and had a lot of fun. A vacation house that comes close to carrying itself is a dream property. It's always on tap for your own weeks off, and the renters help you pay the bills.

But you shouldn't think of a house like this as a true investment. It's more like owning a pleasure palace at a discount price. You'll almost never get enough rent to cover your costs, let alone make a profit. A portion of the cost, especially the mortgage payment and major repairs, is going to have to come out of your pocket. If property values rise enough, the house might make money after all. But to measure up as a good investment, the sale price has to be large enough to cover your previous annual losses plus interest, and deliver a compounded double-digit profit for each year you held. That's a tall order, rarely achieved.

Back when we built our vacation houses, the profit hurdle wasn't so high. We broke even on rentals after tax and made good money on capital gains. We got out of the game the first year we found that our costs, after tax, would exceed our rents. As a business proposition, real estate stinks if you need enormous capital gains to bail you out.

The one house we kept (and continued to put up for rent) wasn't quite at breakeven. From an investment point of view, we'd have done better with our money in a tax-exempt bond. But it's not much fun vacationing in a tax-exempt. It has a lousy view of the sea.

Maybe you can afford to keep a vacation home or condo without renting it out. But if you can't, renters are fabulous. They help you carry a place that you otherwise wouldn't own. You're not making money, but so what? Just a look out the window—at the mountains or the beach—proves that you came out ahead.

On the Other Hand . . .

Why do you want to *own* a second home? Lots of people (like me) have dandy rentals on the market. We're the ones who have to worry about cash flow, customers, and repairs. If you rent the same place every year, it can feel like home, and you haven't had to make a capital investment. Or you can pick the nicest and newest house each year. If you tire of that neighborhood, you can vacation somewhere else and let the owners worry about who's going to rent it next. You can enjoy my money-losing home while putting your own cash toward reducing college debt or building up a retirement account.

One plausible reason for buying is that you're not really investing, you're planning ahead. You expect to retire in that home, so you're buying it now and getting renters to help with the mortgage. But how do you know that you'll want to live there 15 years from now? Maybe the town will change. Maybe your opinions or health status will. Maybe you'll want a house big enough for grandchildren rather than a condo on a golf course. Maybe you'll want to be close to your kids rather than close to the beach. Retirement homes are best chosen five years or so before you actually retire.

If you really will vacation and retire there, it's great to get renters to help with the mortgage. But consider the home's resale potential, just in case you want to retire in some other place.

If You're Buying a Place That You Plan to Rent . . .

- *Buy an existing house.* If it has a vacation-rental history, so much the better. You'll know what your net costs are likely to be. If there's no rental history, ask a local real estate agent what you can charge and how long the rental season is. As a check on the agent, talk to one or two people who own rental homes nearby.
- *Buy a run-down rental house and fix it up.* You might be able to raise the rent and rent for a longer season than the previous owner did. I said you *might*. There's no guarantee that you'll succeed.

- *Buy an empty lot and pay for it as fast as you can.* Once the property is yours, put a house on it. You can get a mortgage for 75 to 80 percent of the combined value of the house and land. That's usually enough to build the house and furnish it.

- *Buy a condominium.* Older condos are usually cheaper than new ones and often just as nice. Ask a real estate broker to show you some places. If you refurnish, you might be able to get more renters. But condos are harder to rent and resell than freestanding homes. They don't rise nearly as much in value and may even fall while house prices are going up. Better to view yours principally as a vacation home, with renters providing a little income on the side.

New condo owners should get involved with the home owners' association. Spend a year on the board so you'll know how the condo operates and what costs are coming down the pike. If you sense a growing resistance to paying maintenance fees, you might want to sell before the development runs down.

Your Rental Success Depends on the Right Answers to These Questions

1. Is the house or condo in a known resort or vacation spot that's easy to get to? For a steady supply of renters, buy where vacationers already come. You need an infrastructure—advertising, rental agents, house cleaners, and service people who make quick repairs. Your home shouldn't be much more than half a day's drive from a major population center.

2. Is the place large enough? The rental trade leans heavily toward families. That means at least two bedrooms and preferably three. With four bedrooms or more, you'll tend to attract two families vacationing together. That may or may not mean higher rents but does create more wear and tear. You'll have more rentals if you allow dogs. I do and have never had any damage.

3. Are the house and property something special? Land on water—an ocean, a lake, even a lagoon—costs more than land elsewhere. But houses on water rent for a premium and rent for more weeks each season than equally good houses back from the beach. That extra income helps you cover the higher price. In slow real estate markets, property on water sells better than those with less interesting views (provided, of course, that beach erosion hasn't reached your front door).

In ski areas, houses with picture-perfect views of the mountains do better than houses overlooking the road. Golfers like villas overlooking the golf course. Bird-watchers like marshes. Windsurfers like bays. The best-renting condo resorts have classy amenities: pool, health club, beach. Within the resort, condos surrounded by green space rent better than those that back up on the supermarket road.

From a business point of view, homes back from the beach or with no mountain view are cheaper to buy, so check the market for lower-priced rentals. If demand is steady, you can purchase a modest place and still attract enough business to cover part of your cost. Regardless of price range, look for something a little special: a garden, a good layout, quiet woods in back. To bring in extra rent, you need an edge.

4. Is the house or condo well furnished? Today's affluent renters won't put up with early–Salvation Army furniture, lumpy mattresses, and campfire kitchens. They want comfort and will pay for it. So set up a convenient house with modern appliances, flat-screen TVs, good chairs and beds, plenty of lamps, and, for summer homes, air-conditioning—in the bedrooms, if nowhere else. Keep the pillows and shower curtains fresh, the grime out of the bathroom, and the screens in good repair. Your renters will repay you by returning year after year. You'll also get a steady trade from rental agents, who like houses that clients don't complain about.

5. Do you have a good rental agent? If you need only one or two rentals a summer, maybe you can find tenants yourself. Take pictures of the house or condo, inside and out, to show your friends, put on your Web page, or advertise on Craigslist. The Web might bring you renters from England or Japan.

To rent more often, you'll need an agent. Look for one who's well located on the main road, works at the business full-time, advertises widely, and is well known in the community. An agent keeps your house as full as its location, price, and condition allow, collects the rents, sends you the checks, cleans up between tenants, fields complaints, and arranges for small repairs. The commission: usually 15 to 25 percent of the rent.

Some condo resorts handle rentals themselves for commissions in the 50 percent range. That's a greedy price, even if it includes cleanup costs. But you may be stuck. Unless you rent through the resort, your tenants might not be allowed to use the clubhouse, golf course, and pool.

6. Can you rent for enough to cover most of your cash costs? Ideally, the rents cover everything. In practice, the net rents may cover only your operating costs—utilities, routine maintenance, replacements, and small repairs. You'll probably have to pay part or all of the mortgage and major repairs yourself. Before you buy, ask yourself: What can I afford to pay each month and each year? Can I really count on rentals to cover the rest?

If you must have extra income to maintain the house, you shouldn't buy at all. Your financial condition is too fragile for this kind of risk. If you decide to ignore that boringly good advice, don't take the salesperson's word that "rentals are no problem." Check the history of the property or properties just like it. Build in a safety margin. Could you carry the house if it rented for only half the time—or half the price—you expected? How long could you carry it if it were damaged by a hurricane, vandalism, fire, or a flood, and you couldn't rent for a while? Your homeowners insurance will probably cover lost rents if the damage was done by a peril that the policy covers. But you won't be paid immediately. Also, flood insurance doesn't cover lost rents.

You're at Risk if You Need Rental Income or Are Buying for Investment and You . . .

Buy in a Spot Where Few Tourists Come. You might love the house yourself. But don't expect to rent it much or sell it easily.

Buy a House That's Remote. Neither renters nor buyers will normally beat a path to your door.

Buy a Small, Dreary House or Run-Down Condo, Even in a Strong Tourist Town. Renters will avoid your property except when everything else is full. So will real estate agents, because their clients would complain. You won't attract many tenants even by dropping your rent. No vacationer wants to be stuck in a dingy living room with grumpy kids when it rains.

Buy a Condo in an Area Where Lots of Building Is Going On. The number of new rental properties may exceed demand. If the development has no rental history, you don't know what income you're likely to get.

Buy Land or a Condominium in a Development That's Not Fully Sold Out. As long as it's in business, the development company will hog all the renters and buyers who come to visit. It won't be easy to find someone to take your unit. That might not matter, however, if you're sure you can hold for many years and want to be sure that you get a condo on the beach.

Respond to a Postcard That Offers "Free Gifts" for Sitting Through a Sales Pitch. In the enthusiasm of the moment, you might buy a time-share property that you don't really want, can't rent, and can't resell at any price. Never, never, *never* respond.

Buying Country Property and Homes

Here come the city slickers, buying up country properties for a song. So how come the local yokels hum so happily when they sell? Because they know things that you don't about the hazards of making the property pay. I'll list just a few: (1) the boundaries may be uncertain, and you'll have to pay to establish them (Farmer John's old "deed plot" is not a survey); (2) the area may not be zoned, meaning that anything can be built right across the road; (3) toxic agricultural chemicals may have been buried there, which you'll be responsible for removing; (4) you may have to drill a well; (5) it may cost a fortune to bring electric power to your castle in the woods or to rewire an old farmhouse for computer, Internet access, and fax; (6) wetlands rules will complicate your plans to build near a lake, stream, or marsh; (7) there may be easements across the land for logging, riding, or utility poles; (8) it may take years to get permission to subdivide.

That's just for starters. When buying country property, you need a good local lawyer and real estate consultant to keep the yokels from giving you donkey ears.

Financing a Second Home

My first choice is a local lender. They know the properties, have a good fix on what they're worth, and understand the needs of buyers of second homes. Next check the Web (page 572). Compare those offers with what a local mortgage broker might suggest. Developers often offer financing for the lots, homes, or condos they have for sale. You put a small sum of money down and pay the rest over a specified number of years. Warning: that may be convenient but the terms aren't terrific. You can almost certainly save money by doing your financing elsewhere.

Loans on second homes are usually more expensive than those on first homes. Expect a higher interest rate and extra points. You might also have to put more money down.

Insuring a Second Home

For a quote on homeowners insurance, go first to the company that insures your primary home. It may take your second home at a discount. If not, see what a local insurance agent can do. Some vacation-home policies reduce premiums by (1) letting you choose less contents coverage than the typical homeowners policy includes (you probably keep fewer valuables in your beach cottage than in your principal home) and (2) offering less coverage for temporary living expenses (if your vacation home burned, you wouldn't have to live in a motel while it was being rebuilt). By contrast, you might pay more for fire and vandalism protection, because the home won't be occupied full-time.

Whichever policy you choose, keep your liability coverage high in case a renter is injured and sues. Don't let hazards linger. Repair the front steps, replace the bad lamp cord, stick nonskid pads on the shower floor.

See to your home's security. It will lower your insurance premium and increase your peace of mind. Ask a home security company to set up an alarm system that notifies the police or fire department if there's an intrusion or smoke in your home, puts a water detector bug on your basement floor, and installs a low-temperature alarm in case your furnace dies.

Don't buy a house that you cannot fully insure unless you're rich enough not to care. Theft and vandalism coverage might not be granted to remote cottages. Fancy beachfront homes might cost more to rebuild than the maximum $250,000 that flood insurance policies paid in 2009 (plus up to $100,000 for contents). Without insurance, a lot of your equity is at risk.

The Caretaker

You need someone to check the house regularly for storm damage and needed repairs. If there's no alarm system, the house also has to be checked for burst pipes, vandalism, a dead furnace, and other problems. If you put up the house for rent, the rental agent may provide this service. Otherwise ask for recommendations from other vacation-home owners in the area or a contractor you trust. Some possibilities: a neighbor who might want to make a little extra money, the handyman at a local apartment house or condo complex, or a local police officer or firefighter. You'll also want to keep the lawn cut and the garden weeded, so the house looks good.

The Tax God Isn't Overly Fond of Second Homes

Some of the rules that apply to your principal residence apply equally to a second home. You can deduct mortgage interest, property taxes, and casualty losses.

You lose your interest deductions, however, for a third house, a fourth house, and so on up. That is, unless they're business properties, in which case they operate under different rules (page 607).

You're taxed on your profit when you sell a vacation home. At this writing, the federal capital gains rate is 15 percent, plus any state taxes due. If you rented the house when you weren't there, you may owe extra taxes under the *depreciation recapture* rules (see your accountant about them). There's a strategy for reducing these taxes, used especially by new retirees: move into your vacation house for several years and sell it then. It will have become your principal residence and a portion of the gain can be excluded from tax. The exact amount of your tax-free gain will depend on how long you've owned the house, the number of years you rented it, and the number of years you lived there yourself.

But the Tax God Really Messes Around with People Who Take Renters

When you rent your house or condo to others, what's deductible depends on your income, your involvement with your rental property, and how much you use the house yourself. Here are the general rules.

Personal Residence

Your rental home is treated as a personal residence if you use it more than 14 days a year, or more than 10 percent as much time as you rent it, whichever is greater. Days you visit the home to make repairs and attend to your rental business are not counted as personal use. On the other hand, if you rent to a relative or friend at something less than the going rate, that is personal use.

All your expenses are allocated between business and personal use. If the house is rented 40 percent of the total number of days it's used, then 40 percent of the overhead—interest, taxes, utilities, repairs, maintenance, rental costs, depreciation—are business expenses.

When preparing your income taxes, you would normally:

1. **Figure the portion of interest and taxes that applies to your personal use** and deduct it along with your other itemized deductions on Schedule A.

2. **Report the rental income on Schedule E.** Deduct from it, first, the portion of interest and taxes that applies to the rental use of the property. After that, deduct the business portion of your insurance and maintenance costs. Finally, deduct depreciation. But your total allowable deductions cannot exceed your rental income. In most cases, that means that some expenses will go unused.

3. **If the business portion of your interest and taxes exceeds the rent,** the remainder can be deducted with your personal expenses on Schedule A.

4. **Other unused business expenses can be carried forward to future years.** If you hold the property long enough to pay off the mortgage, your rents

may start to exceed your current expenses. At that point, you can start deducting unused expenses from previous years.

There's a twist to the rules if you rent for fewer than 15 days. You don't report that rental income on your tax return, and you can't deduct any rental expenses except those for taxes and mortgage interest.

Business Property

Your rental home is treated as a business property if your own use amounts to no more than 14 days or 10 percent of the time that you rent it, whichever is more. You allocate expenses to personal or business use, just as you would if it were a personal residence. But in this case, you cannot deduct the mortgage interest and taxes for the short time that covers your personal use. On the other hand, you get a break when you want to sell. You can do a tax-free exchange for a different property (talk to an expert in commercial property transactions about this). If you sell at a loss, that loss is deductible from your ordinary income.

If a rental agent manages your house or condo: You can normally write off expenses only against your rental income or any income you're getting from other *passive* investments—meaning businesses where you're a silent partner. You will probably have excess expenses that can't be deducted currently. Just carry them forward. Unused expenses can be deducted from the profits on this or any other passive investment when you sell.

If you manage the property yourself or actively participate in the management: In general, this covers people who find their own renters, collect the money, and handle maintenance and repairs. You may be able to write off all the expenses, even if they exceed your rental income. That creates a tax shelter. Some of your ordinary earnings are protected from tax.

You qualify for this shelter if you meet one of the following tests: (1) Your adjusted gross income (not counting income and losses from other shelters) doesn't exceed $100,000. In this case, you can write off up to $25,000 in business losses, including depreciation. (2) Your income falls between $100,000 and $150,000. Over that range, the $25,000 deduction gradually phases out.

There's one exception: you will *not* qualify for tax shelter if your tenants, on average, rent your house for fewer than seven days at a time. In short, there is no tax break if you own a ski condo that attracts principally weekend renters.

Is It Better to Treat Your Second Home as a Personal Residence or as a Business Property?

If you're entitled to the $25,000 exemption (few are), it's better to have a business property. Ditto if you plan to buy and sell because you can do a tax-free exchange. Otherwise, flunk the business test by using the home more than 14 days. That way, you get an unlimited deduction for mortgage and taxes.

About Time Bombs—Oops, I Mean Time-Shares

If you can't afford a house and you can't afford a condominium, maybe you can afford a piece of a condominium.

That's a *time-share.* You generally buy the right to vacation in the same unit during the same week every year. If you buy a "floater," you can be put into any unit of the size you contracted for. Your basic cost might be $7,500 to $25,000. There are also monthly maintenance costs and special assessments. If you finance your purchase, you might pay as much as 16 percent interest, and it's usually not tax deductible.

The most desirable time-shares are in spiffy resort areas—on the beach, by a golf course, on the Mediterranean, or near Disney World—and in the high season. You can buy for cash or on terms. You have to pay regular maintenance fees to keep the property clean and in good repair. Some resorts find you a tenant if you can't use your regular week (you pay a rental commission of 25 to 50 percent). Or you may be able to swap, using someone else's unit in a different resort in return for letting a stranger make use of yours.

Time-shares are sold as "prepaid vacations"—locking in today's prices for the rest of your life. But that's not quite true. (These days, what is?) Your annual real estate taxes and maintenance costs will rise. Many resorts hit you with extra assessments—in the $500 to $1,500 range—for major improvements or repairs. It might be 10 to 20 years before owning the time-share actually becomes cheaper than renting the unit every year, even projecting an annual increase in rents. Will you still want to visit the time-share 21 years from now? *Really?*

If you do buy, stay away from the developer's mesmerizing (and misleading) sales pitches for new units. Older units cost less and may look just as good. See if there's a bulletin board listing resales, ask any unit owners you run into during your visit, check time-share Web sites (page 610—there are tons of time-shares for resale), or call a local real estate agent. If you see an older unit that you like, make a low offer. You can probably buy a time-share for 25 percent of the developer's price or less. Some people who bought for $15,000 will be thrilled to get out at $1,000—and they'll let you pay in installments too. Many time-shares are given away, just to get them off the owners' backs.

The So-Called Advantages (and the "Buts")

1. A time-share is a cheap vacation, especially for a family. (But renting a time-share unit is cheaper than laying out the money to buy it. You can rent at the same resorts that are trying to get you to buy.)

2. You see some of the same friends around the swimming pool every year. (But the same will be true if you always rent at the same time.)

3. You can swap for a time-share in other parts of the country or elsewhere in the world and get a unit of about the same quality, and in a similar season, as yours. (But you may not be able to swap for the places and times you want. That's especially true if your own unit isn't in a top-drawing location or the most desirable season. Renters, by contrast, can pick any kind of time-share they want—anywhere, anytime—without negotiating a swap.)

4. You can rent the time-share if you can't use or swap it in any year (assuming you can find a renter—not easy).

5. If you hold and use the time-share for 10 to 20 years, your regular vacations will probably cost less than if you'd rented every year. (But your vacation choices have been limited, and when you're finished with time-share living, you probably won't be able to get rid of your contract and its ongoing—and increasing—maintenance fee. When you add up all those later, unused years, you'll find that your vacations were very expensive indeed.)

The Definite Disadvantages

1. Unless you buy a good time-share—a desirable place, a desirable unit, a desirable week—you might not be able to make a good swap. You'll be stuck every year with the unit you have or a unit of indifferent quality, at an inconvenient time, in a place you might not want to be. If you own an off-season week, you generally can't swap for a week at a better time of year.

2. If the resort runs downhill in the future, you won't want to go there anymore—and neither will anyone else. If your life pattern changes and you don't use the time-share, you'll be paying for a vacation you no longer take. You cannot count on getting a renter when you're not there.

3. You're stuck with the contract if your lifestyle changes—for example, if you get divorced, if your spouse dies, and when you get older and don't want a family atmosphere anymore. The monthly maintenance fees and assessments keep on running (and rising!), whether you visit or not. These can be real burdens to widows or widowers who don't have the money to carry a unit they don't want and can't use.

4. You will almost certainly *not* make money on the time-share unit itself. The day will come that you'll be begging people to take it off your hands.

5. If you do manage to sell, you'll take a loss—probably a huge one. Even worse, the loss is not deductible. I suppose there are rare birds who do indeed sell time-shares at breakeven or at a profit, but I've never met one. Count yourself lucky if you find a buyer at all.

Getting out of a Time-Share

How I Sold My Time-Share would be one of the world's thinnest books. This deal is easy to get into but hard to get out of. Almost all the new buyers are grabbed by developers, not by individuals with units to resell.

The first rule of resales is to *slash your price!* Check the Web sites below to see the asking price of comparable units. Often, they're in the $500 to $1,000 range and probably sell for less. I've seen them on eBay for $1. Owners like these are effectively giving their time-shares away just to get out from under the monthly payments and special assessments. Here are some other ideas, but don't count on any of them to working for you.

1. Ask the developer. Sometimes they handle resales, but only in popular resorts where no more new units are being built. Typical commission: 25 to 50 percent. You might also be able to post on a bulletin board or list your time-share in the resort's newsletter.

2. Post an ad on the Web. You might be lucky enough to find some suck—, um, *buyer* there. Try eBay and Craigslist. Post on the free newsgroup sections of MSN, Yahoo!, and AOL. Go to specialized sites such as the Timeshare User's Group at www.tug2.net, which has lots of good consumer advice for time-share owners; MyResortNetwork.com (www.myresortnetwork.com); or Sell MyTimeshareNow (www.sellmytimesharenow.com). Post pictures of your unit. Offer extras, such as a free rental week to try it out.

3. Print some pretty for-sale flyers. When visiting your unit, pass them out to the people lounging by the pool. Maybe they'd like to add to the week they already own. Get 'em now, while they're still happy. You have a shot if the time-share is obviously a going concern, with assessments apparently under control.

4. List with a time-share resale broker in the city where your unit is located or on the Web. (Try to ignore the broker's chuckle when you ask what the unit will sell for.) You'll pay a commission if the time-share does indeed sell, but you should not pay an up-front fee. Be sure you understand what services will be provided. And don't expect any broker to sell a unit that's overpriced.

Some brokers take advantage of owners desperate to resell. They'll claim they have buyers and ask you for an upfront "listing fee" or "appraisal fee" of $100 to $500 or more. Your property will sit on the list indefinitely, you won't get a buyer, and you'll never see your money again. Other brokers will claim that they want to buy your time-share but require that you get an appraisal (from a company they control). You pay for the appraisal, but your sale never closes. Some offer to take your time-share off your hands if you pay them $3,500 or more. You pay but may find that the deed hasn't actually changed hands.

5. Look for a charity that accepts donated time-shares. Normally, it will accept only time-shares that can be resold quickly, which rules out the majority of donations. (If you could sell, you'd have done it yourself.) Some charities might list your time-share for a fee and accept the donation only if it already has a buyer (it makes money on the fees).

If your donation is accepted, you can generally treat it as a tax-deductible gift. But you can deduct only the time-share's fair market value, which, as you learned from trying to sell it, is pretty low. The chief value of the donation is to get it off your hands.

6. Some Web sites tout a unilateral *quit claim deed.* You deed the time-share back to the resort and walk away. But the resort doesn't have to accept the deed and almost certainly won't if you still owe money on the original purchase. It will list you as a deadbeat for not paying the monthly maintenance and report you to the credit bureau. It might take a time-share back, however, if all it would lose is the monthly maintenance fee and it thinks it can resell it. You have to negotiate this; you can't just walk away.

How can you get out of a time-share that you haven't been able to sell? You probably can't if you're only a year or two into the deal. If you quit paying, you'll be sued and your credit report will be wrecked. If you've paid for the unit, or almost paid, and decide to walk, you might not be sued for your annual fee or any remaining money due. But the default will still show up on your credit history.

Some developers will take the unit back if there's a lot of demand for time-shares in their resort. You get no money for the time-share, but at least you're off the hook. That would be a huge relief to widows or widowers who can't afford the payments.

If you can't get rid of the time-share and die, your heirs will probably inherit it. The time-share company may try to get the heirs to pay. But they weren't part of the contract and don't owe the company a dime. The heirs should simply ignore the contract. Let the unpaid fees pile up! At this point, you're past caring what's on your credit report.

Instead of Buying a Time-Share, Consider Renting a Unit at a Time-Share Resort

You can get a lovely place for far less than the weekly cost of a hotel or motel. Good rental time-shares offer one to three bedrooms, a kitchen, a living room, and access to lots of amenities: swimming pool, golf course, tennis court, and local entertainment. If you love the resort, you might go every year when the children are small. Or you might try other places. The important thing is that you're not tied down financially and not stuck with something you can't sell. When the kids grow up, you can say ta-ta to the family vacation and try something else. You can also rent condominiums that aren't used as time-shares. Condo resorts are usually top of the line. Just call a resort you're interested in or look for time-share rentals on the Web. Condo and time-share rentals direct from the owner should cost less than those offered through the office of the resort.

Resorts often offer vacations at a discount if you'll sit through a sales pitch for time-shares, aimed at getting you to buy *right now*. Expect the salesperson to tell you that time-shares are a terrific investment (they're not), that they "lock in today's vacation price" (not so—fees and assessments will rise), and that they're easy to resell (fat chance). Buy only if you know that you'll want to vacation at this resort, or others like it, for as many years as you can imagine, with your family or without, paying annual fees until the end of time. . . .

If You Still Want to Own a Time-Share, Don't Buy from the Developer

Buy from one of the tens of thousands of unhappy people trying to resell. Resales are available through the Web or through real estate agents. You might get a splendid unit at 75 percent or more off the developer's price. Some are free; all you have to do is take over the annual maintenance.

Before signing any time-share contract, go to Web sites such as Timeshare Trap (www.timesharetrap.com) and read about the experiences of people who've bought time-shares joyfully and then couldn't get out. Time-shares are far more complicated than they seem at the start.

If you still want to own, go through all the clauses in the contract and decipher the rules. What are the monthly maintenance fees? How often do they rise? What special assessments might (rather, *will*) you have to pay? What do you actually own—a deeded fraction of the property as a whole or a right-to-use contract for a specific time? (Right-to-use contracts eventually expire and can be reasonable buys if they're not far from their expiration date.) Can you sell to someone else (assuming you can find a buyer), or are resales prohibited? Do you get the same unit every year? If you're offered a "bonus week," when can you take it? What happens if some of your fellow owners stop paying their share of the costs (inevitable when they get soured on the deal)? What if someone is injured in your unit? What if the developer doesn't finish the project, leaving you without some of the promised amenities? How is the property owners' association run, and what are its rules? How does the time-share exchange program work—what does it cost, and what kind of unit can you expect in an exchange? If the exchange program works on the "point" system, how many points is your unit worth, how many points do you need to swap for units you'd like in other resorts, and, if you want to upgrade, how much do extra points cost? Who manages the property? (You want an independent company that's in the hospitality business, not a subsidiary of the developer.) Is your unit a "lockout" (meaning that you could divide it in two, occupy part of it, and put the other part into an exchange program)?

Don't buy from a resort that lures prospects with free gifts. Or from salespeople who imply that you're making a good investment. Or if you're told that "today only" there's a discount price. Or without taking home the sales contract and other ownership documents to read and consider quietly.

Stick with a nationally known company, of good reputation, whose resorts you have visited and liked and whose salespeople don't hustle you. If there is such a combination.

Fitting a Second Home into Your Financial Plan

Like a first home, a second home does double duty. It's a place to live and has elements of an investment. It forces you to save (assuming that prices hold up so that you can build equity). It costs you money as long as you own it, in interest, insurance premiums, taxes, improvements, and repairs. You hope at least to break even by selling the house for enough to cover the purchase price plus all those additional costs. If you're lucky, you might even sell it for more. If you're unlucky, you'll sell for less and can't sell in a hurry, except at a discount price.

When you own two homes, you need the protection of cash in the bank to pay the mortgages just in case your income stops. If you've tapped all your cash to buy the house, make it your top priority to build up your liquid savings again.

PAYING FOR COLLEGE

A friend and I were celebrating over lunch. He had just written his last tuition check. My husband and I had the end in sight.

"It's funny," my friend said. "For years, I was terrorized by the unimaginable price of college. The cost projections were appalling. How was I ever going to pay? I saved *some* money but not enough. When my daughter started filling out applications, I lived every day with a stone-cold fear.

"Then I borrowed some money through one of those college payment plans, and suddenly it was over. And it wasn't so bad.

"I suppose," he went on, "that if I hadn't been scared into saving some money, I couldn't have done it. But in the end, I lived."

I recount this story just to remind you that almost every child who wants to go to college gets there. Savings, earnings, loans, and tuition discounts foot the bill.

When your children graduate, life resumes.

Tuition, Room, and Board

The Matterhorn of Personal Finance

**Paying for college is a peak experience. No one
who has stood in those chill winds ever forgets them.**

College is worth it. Write that tuition check and repeat after me: college is
worth it. All of today's best jobs take smarts, and most of the lesser jobs too.
Your degree is an admission ticket to a range of options that others don't have.
You don't even have to pay a high price for college if you play your cards right.
Whatever you pay, your child (or you) will earn it back in spades. People with
bachelor's degrees earn 60 percent more, over their lifetimes, than people with
only a high school diploma.

Many families, pinched by tuition, dug that hole all by themselves. A survey
by student loan provider Sallie Mae found that some 40 percent of parents pay
no attention to costs when searching for a school! They've bought into the myth
that their child should choose the school he or she wants and then they'll figure out how to pay. That's approaching life's realities the wrong way. Early on,
your child should know how much you can afford to pay for education. You'll be
amazed at how fast he or she will "want" a school that's within your limits.

How Much? How Much?

That depends on the school you choose. Most state colleges and universities are
reasonably priced, especially for in-state students. Private colleges cost much
more. But higher-cost schools also have larger financial aid budgets and give
the biggest tuition discounts to people who don't otherwise qualify for financial aid. So don't assume that you can't afford the freight. Your price isn't the
sticker price, it's what you pay out-of-pocket after receiving any grants, tuition

Table 9.

STUDENTS PAY LESS THAN YOU THINK

Average Cost of Tuition and Fees, 2008–2009	But Did You Know That . . .
Private four-year: $25,143	Of the full-time students enrolled in private four-year schools, about 56 percent attend institutions that charge tuition and fees of less than $9,000.
Public four-year $6,585 for students who are state residents	Of the full-time students enrolled in public four-year schools, 43 percent attend institutions that charge tuition and fees between $3,000 and $6,000.
Schools charging $33,000 or more	These schools enroll only about 6 percent of all students.
Public two-year: $2,402	Of all full-time students, 25 percent attend public two-year colleges.

discounts, or student jobs that you can snare. Your job, as a cost-conscious parent, is to help find an attractive school that will make your child happy, while borrowing the least amount of money.

In the table above are some eye-opening facts from the College Board, the authoritative source of information on college costs. On the left, you see the average sticker price for various types of schools in 2008–2009 (get out the smelling salts!). On the right, you'll see that the averages are only part of the story.

So you have choices. You don't have to pay high tuition to get your kids a good education. What's more, your salary will rise in the years ahead, thanks to regular raises and promotions. By the time your child goes to school, costs will be higher, but your income will be higher too. Somehow, you and your child will find a way to pay.

Price, Quality, and Prestige

Here's a tale for our times. It's about two private colleges, Dim Bulb U and Wise Guy Tech. Both were down in the dumps because enrollment had fallen off. How could they attract more students?

Dim Bulb U cut its price to make its degree more affordable. The kids stopped coming, and its reputation sagged. Wise Guy Tech jacked up its price to

Ivy League levels, and students banged down the doors to get in. It added more services, upgraded buildings, and its prestige ballooned.

This story is true. Only the names have been changed to protect the guilty. Parents tend to equate price with quality. In the competition for students, schools have found that it pays to charge more. That's one of the reasons that private institutions cost so much—not to mention the price competition for top faculty, the need to keep the campus technologically up to date, country-club competition (lovely dorms, dining choices, weight-training rooms), modern science and performing arts centers, and continuing investment in program improvements. High prices bring in extra money from well-to-do students, which helps pay for the country-club campus they and their parents want.

Do you want to play this game? If so, keep on writing out those checks. If not:

■ *Consider a high-priced private college or university only if its educational program suits your child's wants and you can afford it without taking out big loans.* Do you know if it has an effective alumni network to help graduates get jobs? The school will cost less than it appears if you get a *merit award.* That's a tuition discount offered to talented students who don't qualify for much (or any) need-based aid (page 641).

■ *Apply to lower-priced private colleges.* They do a splendid job for the average student and for honors students too. Check out a wide range of schools to see what each offers in student aid. Many offer substantial merit awards to above-average students who don't qualify for much need-based aid.

■ *Apply to your state university, especially if your grades are good.* You'll get a top education, often at half the price. As the price gap widens between public and private education, talented students are streaming into the public universities, especially those with fine academic reputations. Increasingly, these schools are offering merit aid too.

■ *Consider state colleges, which should cost even less.* They vary in quality, however. In states that underinvest in education and let their classrooms crowd up (California is one), you may have to attend for six years or more to get all the courses that a particular major requires. Every extra semester costs a fortune and may deter you from getting a degree at all.

■ *Go to a school where the odds are high that your child will graduate in four years or less.* You can check the school's four-year graduation rate at College Results Online (www.collegeresults.org) before signing up. To find the number you want on the site, start with "Institution Search," which gives you the six-year graduation rate. At the bottom of that page, click on "View Comparison of Similar Institutions" and set the year at the top of the table for the four-year graduation rate.

- *Spend two years at a community college, than transfer to a four-year school.* Some community colleges are becoming low-cost four-year schools.
- *Get a degree online, or at least take some courses for credit online.*
- *Never tell your child, "Honey, you can go to any school you want," unless you're prepared to pay full freight.* When money is limited, talk about costs with the child well in advance. That brings the child into the financial decision and keeps his or her expectations running on a realistic track.

Should You Worship *U.S. News & World Report?*

The Holy Book for people seeking schools is the annual guide called "America's Best Colleges," published by the magazine *U.S. News & World Report*. It ranks the colleges based on a variety of hard data and also on "reputation," a more nebulous standard. Students and parents believe in rankings so fiercely that they'll fight for a school listed 51 over one that's "only" 50. Seeing this, the colleges struggle to improve their ratings, sometimes by manipulating the data that the magazine measures.

Critics complain that the Best Colleges list gives an unfair advantage to the wealthy, selective schools. They have a point. Here's why:

- *The "reputation" factor accounts for 25 percent of a school's ranking.* It's derived by sending questionnaires to college administrators, asking their opinions about their competitors. But how much can they really know, especially about schools in other states? They make give shrugs to a fine school that they've barely heard of. And what's to stop them from bad-mouthing a school they'd like to bring down a peg?
- *The rankings give extra weight to schools with large endowments, high faculty pay, and a high percentage of graduates who contribute to fund-raising drives.* That solidifies the rich schools' hold at the top of the list. It also puts private colleges ahead of the publics, based on factors other than educational excellence.
- *Schools get high grades for being "selective"*—meaning that they're so flooded with applicants, they can admit only a small portion of them. It's a self-reinforcing standard. More students apply to highly ranked schools, making them even more selective. This measure also favors private schools because the publics may be required to take any student from their state. Parenthetically, it encourages cheating. Schools may drop application fees and encourage mass applications by Web, which raises the number they can reject and increases their "selectivity" standing.

It's no accident that elite high-cost private schools dominate the Best Colleges list. Parents want their children to go to the "best" school possible, which makes it easier for ranked schools to raise their sticker price. The good news is that many of these schools discount their tuition by 50 to almost 70 percent for students who show financial need (although see page 622 for an explanation of what constitutes "need"—it's not as obvious as you think). The bad news is that only a tiny fraction of students will get in.

The Best Colleges list has had an unintended consequence: in order to move up in rank, the schools are competing harder for students with above-average academic records. They're offering large packages of financial aid, called *merit aid,* even if the student's family is well-to-do. Read all about it on page 641. Meanwhile, the purchasing power of Pell Grants for lower-income students is going down. High-ranked colleges are getting more segregated by economic class.

Is there a better way of judging schools than the Best Colleges list? Yes, but it isn't as simple as finding a single score in a magazine. What you really want to know, about any school, is how well it will teach your child to think critically, solve problems, and increase his or her understanding of the world.

The colleges want to know how to best to fulfill that mission too. So far, around 1,200 of them have participated in an annual National Survey of Student Engagement (NSSE), designed to discover how to improve the learning that's going on. You might call it a search for "best practices" in higher education, based on student interviews, with schools getting scored on how well they do. Most of the schools don't disclose their scores, but they do use them to improve the way they teach. The goals include seeing that students meet with an adviser at least twice a year, work with other students on projects, engage in research with a faculty member, have access to a year of study abroad, make class presentations, and serve an internship in senior year. *That's* college quality and what you should be asking admissions officers about.

When you go on college tours, take along NSSE's booklet *A Pocket Guide to Choosing a College: Are You Asking the Right Questions on a College Campus Visit?* You can download it from www.nsse.iub.edu. It will help guide your conversation with the admissions office *and* with your student guide. You'll miss an opportunity if you ask the guide only about student life. He or she is your best informant on the school's academic practices too.

So what should you do about the Best Colleges list? Don't imagine that those are the only colleges worth getting into. There are fine schools at the top of the list and fine schools further down. The funny thing is that most students love whatever college they wind up going to. So forget the beauty contest and ratings, just find a good academic, social, and financial fit. People at the top of their various professions come from all types of schools.

How Much of the Price Will You Have to Pay?

How much you pay depends entirely on where your child goes to school.

The basic aid package depends on such things as the size of your family, the age of the parents, the cost of the school, the number of family members in college, the avoirdupois of your monthly salary check, and, in some cases, family assets. A student judged able to pay in full for good old State U will qualify for financial aid at a private school.

But that's where the calculation starts, not where it finishes. College aid today isn't based entirely on need. Schools are courting the children of the middle and upper-middle classes by offering them large amounts of merit aid. To capture it, however, you have to apply to colleges strategically—maybe settling on one you never heard of before.

Lower-income people, by contrast, are having a harder time. They get income-appropriate tuition discounts and other grants but may find it hard to come up with the additional out-of-pocket contribution that most schools require. Nor do the students get an extra $100 a month from parents at home. As a result, fewer students from poorer families are showing up at elite schools, private schools, and leading state universities, even when their grades and SATs are good.

Traditional college aid is based on an eligibility calculation. There's one for federal programs (also used by most state colleges and universities) and a second one used by most of the selective private colleges. Conceptually, they work roughly like this:

1. Add up your family income and assets. The federal calculation omits the value of your home, retirement plans, and certain other assets. Most private colleges include at least some of your home equity and perhaps other assets too.

2. Subtract the money you need for the bare essentials of life (page 623) plus an allowance for taxes. Everything over that amount is considered "discretionary" income. A small portion (5.64 percent) of certain of your assets will be included in your discretionary money too.

3. Part of your discretionary money has to be spent for college. That's your "expected parental contribution." It's determined by a standard federal needs analysis used by all schools.

4. Look up the total price of the school your child wants—tuition, fees, books, room and board, transportation, college activities, personal expenses.

5. Subtract your parental contribution.

6. Subtract the money your child is expected to pay out of his or her income and savings.

7. The remainder shows your eligibility for aid, sometimes called financial need. Need is the difference between what you and your child are expected to pay and the college's total cost.

8. The college that accepts your child tries to fill your need (or most of it) with grants, loans, and student jobs.

On paper, that approach sounds reasonable. The college tries to make up the difference between what it charges and what you're expected to pay. If your family contribution is determined to be $12,000 and the college costs $18,000, you'll be eligible for $6,000 in need-based aid. If the college costs $40,000, you'll be eligible for $28,000 in aid. Your family contribution remains the same, no matter which institution you choose. The pricier the school, the better your chance of getting help.

But the joker lies in the calculation's second line: the amount of money you need to live on. No one cares about your actual bills. Instead, your income and assets are judged by a standard formula developed by the federal government. It assesses your need by playing a game of "let's pretend."

Let's pretend, it says, that you live on a budget that covers just the bare essentials for a family of your size (as estimated annually by the U.S. Department of Labor). That's your official living allowance. In 2009 it was $23,660 for a family of four. Anyone netting that much or less is assumed to be too broke to pay anything for school. But anyone with a higher net income is assumed to have discretionary income, some of which is expected to be available for college costs. If your actual living expenses are higher than the rock-bottom budget allowed, tough luck. You can't expect the college to make up for the fact that you decided to live so well that you couldn't save a lot for your child's education.

When the low living allowance is subtracted from your earnings, there appears to be lots of money left over, which the college will tap on a sliding scale. No matter that most of that money goes for locked-in expenses such as mortgage payments or auto insurance on two cars. The standard formula pretends that you really are living a bare-bones life. It concludes that you have much more money to spend on college than, from your point of view, is actually the case.

Most middle- and upper-middle-income families will be startled by the amount that the colleges expect them to pay, from savings, salary, and loans. That's why you should start saving now. It will protect you and your child from a lot of borrowing later. Even lower-income families will be pressed for as much as they can come up with.

Two things soften this picture. A huge pool of merit aid is available for students with better grades. If your child qualifies, that reduces the amount you have to pay. Also, some colleges cost much less than others. You should be able to find a place that matches your means.

The Bottom Line

The table below shows how much an average family was expected to contribute toward a college or university in 2009–2010, according to what's known as Federal Methodology. That's the government's way of calculating aid awards. It won't hit your contribution on the button, but you'll get a general idea. This calculation is based on financial need. The colleges may very well give you something more in merit aid.

Here's how to use the table, and how to update it for the current year:

- *Look for something close to your 2008* pretax *income on the left.* (What you're expected to pay for college generally depends on how much you earned in the previous year.) At this writing, 2008 data was the latest available.

Table 10.

THE PARENTAL CONTRIBUTION
(Use This as a Rough Guide to What You Might Be Expected to Pay)*

	Net Family Assets†							
	$25,000		$50,000		$100,000		$150,000	
Family Size:	**Three**	**Five**	**Three**	**Five**	**Three**	**Five**	**Three**	**Five**
2008 Income, Pretax								
$ 30,000	$ 531	$ 0	$ 566	$ 0	$ 1,886	$ 55	$ 3,217	$ 1,375
40,000	2,227	425	2,261	459	3,644	1,779	5,367	3,009
50,000	3,938	2,087	3,977	2,121	5,820	3,485	8,208	5,151
60,000	6,221	3,780	6,274	3,819	8,836	5,605	11,656	7,910
70,000	9,390	6,005	9,463	6,058	12,283	8,537	15,103	11,357
80,000	12,837	9,091	12,910	9,165	15,730	11,985	18,550	14,805
90,000	16,120	12,539	16,193	12,612	19,013	15,432	21,833	18,252
100,000	19,098	15,681	19,171	15,754	21,991	18,574	24,811	21,394
150,000	35,384	31,967	35,457	32,040	38,277	34,860	41,097	37,680

*Federal Methodology, 2009–10. Most private schools use a different calculation, called the Institutional Methodology. It counts more assets and generally (but not always) results in a higher family contribution.

† Excluding home equity, annuities, life insurance cash values, and retirement plans.

Source: the College Scholarship Service of the College Board.

■ *Read across to the column that best represents your current net worth, as the federal aid formula counts it:* the value of your savings, investments, and second home, minus your mortgage and other debts. Exclude the value of your principal home, family farm (if you live there), tax-deferred annuities, retirement plans, and life insurance cash values.

■ *For incomes between the amounts shown on the table, take a percentage estimate.* For example, with an $80,000 income, assume that you'll owe the midpoint between the amounts shown for $70,000 and $90,000.

■ *The figure in the crosshairs shows you roughly what the feds expect you, as parents, to pay.* If it covers the cost of the school that your child will attend, you can't expect any federal student aid. If it falls short, at least some federal aid should come your way.

■ *For 2010 and later years, guesstimate your payment this way:* Find your expected payment for 2009–10 and multiply that number by the subsequent percentage growth in average college costs.

■ *When you have more than one child in college, your expected family contribution is divided among them,* making each of them eligible for more aid. For example, if you have to pay $12,000 for one child, your expected contribution will be $6,000 for each of two.

■ *On top of the parental contribution shown here, a contribution is expected from student earnings.* There's a formula for calculating it (in 2008, it was student earnings, minus taxes, minus $3,080, with half of the remainder going toward the college bill). Other colleges expect a flat amount, such as $1,550 for the first year of school and $2,150 for each subsequent year.

■ *If your income is under $50,000 and you're eligible to file one of the two simple tax returns*—the 1040EZ or 1040A—the feds don't count your assets when figuring what you're expected to pay. But private colleges probably will.

■ *This table is for a two-paycheck couple, with equal earnings, income only from employment, and an allowance against net assets for two retirements.* The older parent is 45. They take the standard deduction on their 1040 tax return and have only one child in college.

A one-paycheck couple with exactly the same income and assets would pay slightly more than the table shows. That's because the family doesn't have as many work-related expenses. A single parent would pay even more because he or she is presumed to have lower living expenses than a two-parent family. You'll also pay more if you're under 45 or have just one child. Older parents pay less, as do parents with more children.

■ *To estimate what some private colleges and universities will expect you to pay, take 5 percent of your home equity and add it to the appropriate figure in the table.*

Some colleges also ask about the value of your retirement plans, salary-deferral plan, tax-deferred annuities, and life insurance cash values.

- *These amounts rise for people who take an education tax credit* (page 628).

For a More Exact Fix on What You'll Probably Have to Pay

Go to one of two free calculators: the Expected Family Contribution calculator at the College Board Web site (www.collegeboard.com) or FinAid's Expected Family Contribution and Financial Aid calculator (www.finaid.org). The earlier you start figuring your expected contribution, the better prepared you'll be when that day finally comes.

And There's More . . .

If yours is a typical college search, you'll spend serious money even before the fat envelope comes. There's the cost of SAT (Scholastic Aptitude Test) and ACT (American College Test) tests and maybe pretest prep courses. You'll take driving trips to some campuses and flights to others, if it's important. Some families hire counselors to help their children narrow their choices.

Many of these costs can be reduced. Your child will probably practice the SAT in school. For free online practice tests, go to Number2.com (www.number2 .com) and the College Board Web site. Private prep courses claim that they can add 100 points to your child's score, but that's in dispute. Your student may not even need a higher score—go to "College Search" at CollegeBoard.com, enter a school that interests you, then click on "SAT" to see the range of scores of the students it admits. Your child might be right in its sweet spot.

Good high schools have college guidance counselors, free. Most families find appropriate schools through their own research. There's plenty of information at CollegeBoard.com to help you and your child identify schools with the kinds of programs your child might want. Look, too, at the U.S. Department of Education's College Opportunities Online Locator, at http://nces.ed.gov/collegenavigator. Enter the type of program and school you want and some other identifying characteristics, and you'll get a list of schools that include some colleges you wouldn't have known about.

Private counseling might help if you have the money and your child remains confused, but you shouldn't need more than one or two sessions to create a plan. Two places to find consultants: the Independent Educational Consultants Association (www.educationalconsulting.org) and the Higher Education Consultants Association (www.hecaonline.org). Get a written list of services. Costs average $160 an hour and run to $300 in big cities and suburbs. No counselor can guarantee to get your youngster into an Ivy League school. You luck into that on your own. Their best service may be to direct you, gently, to schools within your ability range that you hadn't thought about.

College visits make sense, to help your child get the feel of big schools versus small schools, schools in cities versus schools in suburbs, and two-year schools versus four-year schools. Start with those within driving range. Take virtual tours of the rest. Consider transportation costs when choosing the schools that the child will apply to. Flights are expensive.

As freshman year draws near, you'll have to establish a monthly walking-around budget. You know about fees and books (used books, except in the greedy schools that force kids to buy new books and that, incidentally, profit on the sales). Students also need cash for personal items such as movies, hamburgers, college activities. The college will estimate personal expenses—maybe $150 or $200 a month at residential schools. You and your child have to agree what the limits are. For example, if you're paying for the dining room, the child shouldn't expect to receive extra money for eating out.

Strike a deal on plastic too. I like to start students with debit cards while they're learning how to manage money. Credit cards can come later, when they've conquered the concept of spending no more than they have in the bank.

If your child owns a car, leave it at home. Residential colleges are meant for walking. Ditch the gasoline and parking bills. Tell your student that you're going green.

After your child's first year, he or she might try for the post of dormitory adviser, which reduces your bill for board.

How Will You Pay?

You have five sources of funds:

Savings and Investments. This is by far the cheapest source of funds. When you save in advance, you cover part of the tuition with money you earn from interest, dividends, and capital gains. To see the tremendous boost you get from starting early on college savings, see the table on page 215. To boost your savings, use tax-favored plans (chapter 20).

Current Income. Spending current income reduces your personal options for as long as the college bills last. But at least it's over when it's over.

Loans. This is the most expensive source of funds because loan interest payments hang around your neck for years. Young college graduates can handle the payments if they get jobs commensurate with the amount they borrowed.

Otherwise they'll struggle. Parents who borrow more than a modest amount are mortgaging their future at a time when they may not have many working years left.

Work. The work-study program, a form of federal financial aid, is open to middle-income kids as well as those with lower incomes. It lets students earn part of their tuition by taking a school job. But the income allowed under work-study is limited. To earn more, a student will have to find a part-time job.

Need-Based Grants. Free money goes to students in the greatest need. But hardly anyone gets a totally free ride. Most eligible students get an aid package made up of loans and a work-study job, as well as a grant.

Merit or Non-Need Aid. These are tuition discounts offered to students from families with middle and upper-middle incomes. The amounts are larger than your official financial "need."

There are two types of tax credits (credits are deducted directly from your income tax bill, dollar for dollar). They benefit parents who can afford to pay the tuition up front and wait to collect the credit when they file their tax return. And they benefit parents who owe income taxes in the first place, not lower earners who owe only Social Security taxes.

The Hope Scholarship Credit—available during each of the first four academic years of school, to students enrolled at least half time. You get 100 percent of the first $2,000 you pay in tuition and fees and 25 percent of the second $2,000, for a total of $2,500 Those limits were raised for 2009–2010 and are expected to be made permanent (they'll also rise with inflation over time). You can take a Hope credit for each student in the family. If you don't owe enough in income taxes to make full use of the $2,500 credit, you can claim up to $1,000 in the form of a tax refund.

The Lifetime Learning Credit—available any year a student is in school, for an unlimited number of years. You get up to $2,000 (20 percent of the first $10,000 paid in tuition and fees). This credit is available for graduate students, adult education, and incidental study—say, a single course to improve your job skills. $2,000 is the maximum credit, no matter how many students you have in school.

Here are the eligibility rules for both of these education tax credits:
- *They're for you, your spouse, or your dependent child.* If you're divorced and claim your child as your dependent but your spouse pays the tuition, neither of you gets the credit.

- *They offset the amount you pay for tuition and eligible fees* (after deducting any grants) at qualified institutions of higher learning—trade and career schools, community colleges, and four-year schools. The Hope can also be used for course materials. You don't get credits for room and board.
- *Singles get the full Hope credit if their adjusted gross income is under $80,000.* Over that amount, the credit shrinks; at $90,000, it phases out entirely. Marrieds get the full credit up to $160,000; it phases out at $180,000. These are 2010 numbers. They rise with inflation every year.
- *Singles get the full Lifetime Learning credit if their adjusted gross income is under $50,000.* Over that amount, the credit shrinks; at $60,000, it phases out. Marrieds get the full credit up to $100,000, phasing out at $120,000. These ceilings also rise with inflation every year.
- *You can't use both credits at once for the same child.* But you can use different credits simultaneously for different children.
- *You have one more option: a tax deduction for tuition and fees.* The maximum write-off is $4,000, for singles whose adjusted gross income doesn't exceed $65,000 and for married couples with AGIs up to $130,000. If you earn more, there's a $2,000 deduction for singles with AGIs up to $80,000 and couples, up to $160,000.

You'd use this deduction in one of two circumstances: (1) You don't qualify for a Hope (perhaps because your student is in grad school) and you earn too much to take the Lifetime Learning deduction. (2) You want to improve your eligibility for student aid. This deduction is taken "above the line," as an exclusion from income, so it helps reduce the taxable income you report. It's available even to people who don't itemize their deductions.

- *When you claim your child as a dependent, the credits go on your tax return, not the child's.* When the student is independent, the student gets the credit if he or she pays the tuition.
- *Complicated rules dictate how the tax credits mesh with using 529 accounts and Coverdell Education Savings Accounts for college expenses.* See pages 677 and 679.
- *Finally, there's an interest deduction for student loans in repayment status.*

A Matter of Form(s)

Check the catalogs or the Web sites of the colleges that interest you to see which financial aid forms they want.

Every applicant has to fill in an FAFSA—a Free Application for Federal Student Aid. You'll find paper copies at high school guidance offices, at college financial aid offices, or by calling 800-4-FED-AID. Even better, fill it in and file electronically at www.fafsa.ed.gov. The built-in directions will help you answer all the questions accurately. Then go to the Federal Student Aid PIN Web site at www.pin.ed.gov for a PIN number that serves as your electronic signature. You can use this number to make corrections in the form and to renew your FAFSA next year.

For most state schools, state grant agencies, and some private colleges, the FAFSA is enough. Many private colleges and some scholarship sponsors, however, also ask you to complete a CSS/Financial Aid PROFILE provided by the College Board's College Scholarship Service. You can fill it in and file it at https://profileonline.collegeboard.com or call the CSS at 305-829-9793. Your high school guidance office or college aid office will have the form too. PROFILE asks questions about family assets, income, and expenses that the FAFSA ignores. You pay $9 to register plus $16 for each school that will receive the report. If you're divorced, the other parent may have to fill in a noncustodial parent form.

Contact every college and university that interests you, to see if the PROFILE is required. If not, ask if they use their own financial aid forms. There may also be a form for family-owned farm and small-business income. Some states require the FAFSA plus a special form for state-sponsored aid. Be sure you know what all the deadlines are. If you miss them by a day, you're usually toast.

Fill in the FAFSA even if your income is high and you don't expect college aid. Doing so gives your child access to low-cost unsubsidized Stafford loans (page 647).

Five Steps to College Aid

Step One

Get the FAFSA (see previous section) plus any other financial aid forms each college wants. The filing season for FAFSAs begins on January 1, so apply as soon after that date as possible. The Federal Student Aid Web site (www.fafsa.ed.gov) has worksheets, so you can be ready to click "Send" right at the top of the year. Don't drag your feet! Your aid application has to go through a processing firm before it's passed on to the college. Most colleges have early deadlines for having the material in hand, such as February 15. Early-decision students may have to file PROFILEs by October or November. Federal Pell grants (the government's leading grant program, page 639) and federal Stafford loans (the leading loan program, page 647) are always available to qualified students. But if you apply late, the money in other programs may be used up. A trough that was full in February may be empty by April. You want to get your nose in first.

The forms have the same grim feel as an income tax return. First you give personal data about yourself and your family. Then you put down all your taxable and nontaxable income. Next you add up certain assets—bank accounts, mutual funds, investment real estate. Then the student weighs in with his or her own income and assets. If the student is married, the spouse has to report too. (Families earning less than $50,000 and not required to file a 1040 income tax form or who receive means-tested government benefits such as food stamps can use a two-page FAFSA-EZ form.)

That's for federal aid. Many private schools also ask for home equity, the value of family businesses, and whether any relatives can be expected to help. You might be asked about any unusual expenses, such as private-school tuition for younger children or unreimbursed medical bills. (If the form doesn't cover these expenses, mention them in a separate letter. Mention any other circumstances that impinge on your ability to pay—for example, that one breadwinner had to quit work to take care of an ailing grandparent, or you have a child in graduate school, or you're carrying high debts because of a previous business failure or bout of unemployment.) Some forms ask about retirement plans, life insurance cash values, salary deferral plans, and tax-deferred annuities. These assets aren't taken into account when determining your eligibility for institutional aid, however, unless they're unusually large.

Leave no questions blank unless the form specifically tells you to. If something doesn't apply to you, write 0 (zero) where the answer should go. Otherwise the company that processes your form will have to check back with you, which holds up your paperwork. Be sure to enter the code number for every school and state-aid agency that should receive the report (the codes are at www.fafsa.ed.gov). If the form is filled in incorrectly, you'll get it back, which means that your schools might get it late.

Do your tax return early so you'll know how much you earned. That also simplifies the job of filling in the financial aid form, because many of the questions are keyed to lines on the 1040 or 1040A. (You don't actually have to file your tax return early if you don't want to; just fill it in and use the data to help you apply for college aid.)

If the W-2 form from your employer is late, don't wait for it. Make a close estimate of your income so that you can mail the aid form on time. Send the college your exact earnings later. You may be asked for your tax return as verification.

You may need help completing the FAFSA. That's the beauty of filing electronically—help notes and corrections are built right into the form. For help by phone, call 800-4-FED-AID. You also get online help when filing the PROFILE electronically.

Step Two

Watch your mail or e-mail. An aid-processing center is now analyzing your ability to pay. The FAFSA generates a personal Student Aid Report (SAR), including the all-important EFC—expected family contribution. That's the minimum the colleges expect you to pay toward school. Look for it on the SAR in the upper right-hand corner. It will say, for example, "EFC12500"—meaning that you'll have to come up with at least $12,500 this year, no matter where your child goes to school. An asterisk next to this amount means that the college will ask for verification of the income and assets you reported. If you're applying to a private college or university, the PROFILE result usually shows that you'll have to pay an even higher amount (although it could be lower too).

You should receive the SAR in about a week if you filed electronically; otherwise, within four weeks. If you don't, call the Federal Student Aid Information Center (800-4-FED-AID) and ask what's happening. If you filed a PROFILE, you should get an acknowledgment within three weeks, along with a report showing all the data on the form.

Check the data on the SAR and the PROFILE report to be sure that the processor hasn't made any mistakes. Return the form to the processor only if there's an error or if you want the report sent to some colleges that weren't originally on your list. Call the schools to be sure that the data were received.

Step Three

Wait to hear whether you're accepted by the school. If so, you'll get an aid package. The college's own office of financial aid establishes a cost of attendance for each student, depending on whether he or she is single or married, living in a dorm, an apartment, or at home, traveling to the school by plane or car, and so on. If you have extra expenses—say, medical expenses for a chronic condition—ask if the college will build them in. Some schools are generous, others stingy.

From that budget, the school subtracts the money that parents and the student are expected to pay. Any gap between the student's budget and your total family contribution is your "financial need." The school will offer a package to fill that gap, made up of grants from the federal government (including Pell grants for low-income students), state government grants, federal student loans, a work-study job, and money given by the college—some of it merit money, not based on financial need. The aid office decides which resources to tap and in what order.

A few schools accept the students they want, then fill their financial needs in full. If you're $18,000 short, that's what you'll get in aid. Lower-income students with strong academic records shouldn't hesitate to apply to costly schools. If they're accepted, they'll usually be awarded all the money they need.

Other schools won't accept you unless they can afford to provide all the aid you need. At these schools, your ability to pay is one of the factors the admissions office weighs.

Many schools give full aid to some applicants, while leaving others hanging. For example, a student with an $18,000 need may be offered only $11,000 worth of help. You go on a waiting list for the missing $7,000. If the money doesn't come through, you'll have to raise it yourself. The school might assume that you'll use an unsubsidized Stafford loan or a PLUS loan (for parents) to fill the gap (page 647). If you won't or can't, you'll have to turn to a high-cost private loan (not recommended) or choose some other school.

For a quick way of checking on a college's aid policies, see page 643.

Step Four

Accept, reject, or appeal. If you qualify for aid, your package will reflect how badly the school wants you. The greater its interest, the more you'll be offered in free grants. Students further down the list will be offered smaller grants and larger loans. Some elite schools provide financial aid entirely in the form of grants.

Call the school if the aid package is too small and you think that something has been overlooked. Maybe a parent died suddenly. Maybe a competing school has made a better offer and you're hoping your first-choice school will match it (maybe it will, maybe it won't). Any change that raises your grant and lowers your loan puts money in your pocket. Often, however, the package stands. It always stands if your only complaint is "I can't afford it." No one can afford it.

Step Five

If your aid package plus your income and savings aren't enough to pay for school, turn to unsubsidized federal Stafford loans and PLUS loans for parents. Last choice is a private student loan from a lending institution (page 650). These are high-rate loans, and they mount up. Your student might be happy to sign (and you might cosign) because the money comes easily. But the burden could be huge when you have to repay.

Step Six

Return to Go. Every year you have to suffer through this process all over again. Your eligibility for aid may change. The mix of loans and grants may change. If you filled in a FAFSA, you should get a partly preprinted Renewal FAFSA between late November and January 1. If you don't, call the college aid office and ask about it.

For Parents Only

What If You're Having a Fight with Your Kid and Refuse to Pay for College or Fill in a Financial Aid Form? The child is stuck. In almost all cases, the college won't award aid without financial information from the parents. Otherwise everyone would "fight"! To apply for aid without involving parents, students typically have to be 24 and up.

What If You're a Divorced or Never-Married Single Parent? If the child lives with you, fill in the FAFSA form. It asks only for your income, not the income of the other parent. You can receive federal aid and any applicable state aid too. State colleges and universities ask only for a FAFSA, so the child is good at all these schools.

Most private colleges will want to see the other parent's income too, before dispensing aid they administer themselves. This includes an ex who never took any interest in the child or a partner who dropped into your life, never married you, and then dropped out. If the second parent won't cooperate by filling in the Noncustodial PROFILE form or something similar, the child usually won't qualify for aid. One possible way around this problem: get a letter from someone closely connected with your family or your circumstances—say, your divorce lawyer, pastor, or rabbi—who can testify that other parent vanished and isn't involved in your child's life.

What If Your Child Lives with the Other Parent? If you don't have custody, you don't have to file a FAFSA. The federal government and state colleges and universities don't count your income when dispensing aid. But the private schools usually do. You'll have to disclose your income on the Noncustodial PROFILE form. If you refuse, the private schools generally won't give your child any aid at all.

What If You're a Stepparent? If your spouse is the custodial parent, the FAFSA wants to see your income too. The federal government considers your combined incomes when deciding whether the child qualifies for aid. The other parent isn't counted at all. What if you have a prenuptial agreement stating that you aren't responsible for your stepchildren's education? Tough luck. The government didn't sign off on your prenup. It expects you to ante up.

Most private colleges handle things differently. They do ask for information from the noncustodial parent. Their awards may be based on the incomes of the two biological parents, leaving the stepparent out entirely. Or maybe not. There's no sure rule. The decision may turn on how old the divorce is, whether the noncustodial parent has remarried, and how long the stepparent has been in the picture.

What If You Don't Want Your Children to Know How Much You Earn? Fill in the form electronically, sign electronically, and get a PIN. You can use your own e-mail address.

What If You Don't Want to Show Anyone Your Tax Returns? You may have no option. The college might insist on seeing tax returns as a condition of granting aid.

What If You're Unemployed or About to Be? Tell the financial aid office. Normally, colleges use last year's income when figuring what they expect you to pay. But they can use this year's projected income if you or your spouse is out of work.

For Independent Students

If you're an independent student, you can apply for aid based on your own income rather than that of your parents. The sons and daughters of the middle classes dream of "going independent" because that could qualify them for more help. But they rarely qualify. Students from low-income families, by contrast, might get more help if they file as dependents rather than as independents.

You are generally considered independent if you'll be 24 by December 31 of the year that the grant will be awarded. This is true even if you're living at home on your parents' dole and even if you're taken as a dependent on their income tax return. (When you're living at home, however, some schools may decide to count family income as part of your financial resources. This won't affect your eligibility for federal aid, but it will make it harder to qualify for the aid controlled directly by the college.)

If you're under 24, you're independent if:
- You're an orphan or ward of the court (or were a ward of the court until 18).
- You're a veteran of the armed forces or are on active duty.

- You're married.
- You're in graduate school.
- You have legal dependents other than a spouse.
- You're declared independent by a financial aid officer because of special circumstances.

One sure way of losing aid (for men 18 to 25): fail to register for the selective service. Federal aid goes only to men who have registered. FAFSA forms are computer matched against selective service lists to catch the forgetful or artful dodgers. You're supposed to register within six months of turning 18. You can do it by checking a box on the FAFSA. Late registrants aren't being prosecuted.

Where the Loopholes Are

You can manipulate the financial aid form in your favor. Of two families with exactly the same income and assets, one child may qualify for somewhat more assistance simply because the parents used all the available loopholes. Some of the measures are smart, and others are stupid. Here's a list:

1. Keep your college savings in your name, not your child's name. Smart. The schools count 20 percent of the child's assets as available to pay education costs but only 5.64 percent of the parents' assets (after exempting a certain amount).

2. Save in tax-favored college plans. Smart. Payments from 529 plans or Coverdell Education Savings Accounts aren't counted as income on the FAFSA form, although private colleges may consider them. If you have been putting money into a child's account via a Uniform Transfers to Minors Act, you can shift it, tax free, into a 529. A 529 plan maintained for your child by another relative, such as a grandparent, doesn't show up on the disclosure forms at all.

3. Don't touch the equity in your home. Smart. If you take a large home equity loan in preparation for four years of college costs, it becomes a cash asset that could reduce your eligibility for college aid. Instead draw on your equity only as needed for college bills.

4. Keep adding to your 401(k) and other retirement plans. Smart. You don't have to report their value on the FAFSA form. Only your current contribution is counted.

5. Avoid taking capital gains, starting from the year before college starts until your child's last year in school. Sometimes smart. If you sell an investment during this time period, the profit is counted as current income on the FAFSA form. It will weigh more heavily in the college aid formula than the value of unsold investments or the cash assets you have on hand. Sell any stocks that you'll need to help pay for college by your child's junior high school year. If you have a onetime capital gain—say, from selling inherited shares—tell the school about it. Many schools will leave it out of the calculation.

Avoiding a capital gain can be stupid, however, if you've lost faith in the stock. If its price declines, you could lose more in the market than you pick up in aid.

6. Get rid of cash savings by prepaying your mortgage or paying down a home equity loan. Sometimes smart. Home equity isn't counted when awarding federal aid. Some private colleges don't count it, either. You'll have gained nothing, however, if you have to borrow it back to pay college bills.

7. Get rid of cash savings by making an expensive purchase. Stupid. Instead of keeping $20,000 in the bank you might use the money to buy a car. Suddenly, you're $20,000 "poorer" on the FAFSA form. But this makes a negligible difference to your eligibility for aid. With luck, you might pick up $1,128 (5.64 percent of $20,000). But you might get no extra aid at all. And what if you find that you need that $20,000 to pay for school?

8. Manipulate your small-business income. Stupid, bad, and unfair. Farmers and small-business owners have a lot of holes for hiding income. This may work at state colleges that rely only on the FAFSA, but at private colleges, you may have to fill in a special small-business form asking about dividends and assets. Financial aid officers doubt claims that a family business isn't throwing off a living wage. They will definitely look at your tax returns.

9. Buy financial products that move your money into assets that don't have to be reported on the FAFSA form. Stupid, stupid, stupid. The game isn't worth the candle. The salespeople who rope you in are thinking only of the commissions they'll earn.

This ploy looks plausible because the federal aid form doesn't pry into all your assets. It asks about your bank accounts, stocks, bonds, mutual funds, investment real estate, vacation home, and family business, but not the value of your principal home, retirement plans, family farm, or—here's the kicker— money saved in tax-deferred annuities and cash-value life insurance policies. If you took $20,000 out of the bank and invested it in a tax-deferred annuity, that $20,000 would "disappear." You might get an extra $1,128 in aid.

There are so many drawbacks to using financial products to try to beat the system that I have to make a list:

- *You pay high (and hidden) commissions for tax-deferred annuities and life insurance.* Odds are, they'll be much more expensive than any extra aid you can pick up.
- *Your aid package depends mainly on the size of your income rather than*

the value of your assets. Only 5.64 percent of your assets are counted after deducting a general allowance ($50,000 or so, depending on your age and other factors).

• *You can't be sure that you'll get more aid.* A higher award isn't automatic. If you do get extra aid, it might come as a loan, not a grant. Your scheme will increase the interest that you have to pay.

• *When you buy tax-deferred annuities or cash-value insurance, you're putting your cash out of easy reach.* If you need extra money to help pay for college, you'll have to get a larger loan. If you try to take it out of your annuity or insurance policy, you'll incur penalties and maybe taxes, too.

• *Private colleges and universities have their own questionnaires that ask about these hidden assets.* So you might have bought that tax-deferred annuity for nothing.

• *The annuity or insurance policy may be a lousy investment.*

• *Manipulating your assets is unfair to the spirit of the student aid system.* Whether to do so is more than a financial issue. It's a conscience call.

How Is Home Equity Handled?

The state and federal governments ignore your home equity when awarding financial aid. Some private colleges do too. Most private colleges do take a look at it, however, counting it as one more parental asset. They'll usually want an estimate of your home's value now. They'll also ask for the price you originally paid and the year you bought it. Their aid formula applies a multiplier to your purchase price, reflecting the growth (or decline) in housing values in your part of the country. If your estimate is much lower than theirs, they'll ask about it. The schools are sensitive to the housing bust. They'll pay attention to evidence that a recently purchased house is worth less than you paid for it or that homes in your neighborhood are doing worse than the regional average. Many schools don't count your home equity's entire value; they'll take only a portion of it when developing your package of aid.

Were You Hoping to Use the Tuition Discount for State Residents?

You pay less if your child goes to a state college or university in the state where you live. A few states offer discounts to each other's residents. But you can't turn your child into another state's resident by subterfuge. Some students try it—say, by renting an apartment there, registering to vote, and getting a state driver's license. But the schools know these games and have tight rules about who qualifies as a resident, which may include proof of financial independence.

Tell the Truth on Your App!

About 30 percent of the federal forms are selected for verification against tax returns and other data. If you're caught lying, it will ruin your chances for any discretionary aid. "Every family has one opportunity to tell the complete truth," one aid officer told me. "If I catch anything, I put that application at the bottom of the heap and look at it again only if I have any money left." By contrast, aid officers can be tremendous advocates for students whose families play it straight.

Grant Me a Grant

A grant is the college subsidy of choice. It's free money. You don't work for it, and no one wants it back. Here's what's around:

- *For undergraduates, the largest single source of grants is Uncle Sugar,* most of whose money is reserved for people with low incomes. At this writing, the government's federal Pell grants run to a maximum of $5,350 for the lowest-income undergraduates. The size declines as family income rises. If your family earns $35,000 to $40,000, a Pell might provide no more than $400. Pells are generally available to full-time or half-time students at accredited academic, technical, or vocational institutions (this includes certain online courses). You apply for a Pell and all other federal aid automatically when you fill in the FAFSA (page 630).

- *Federal Supplemental Educational Opportunity Grants (FSEOGs)* are dispensed through college aid offices to especially low-income people who have no hope of raising other funds. Awards run from $100 to as much as $4,000 a year, with the biggest ones going to the truly poor. Like Pells, FSEOGs go only to undergraduates. You get one only if the school has FSEOG money (not all of them do), and if it decides to award it.

- *The Federal Work-Study program* (FWS) isn't exactly free money, because you have to take an approved job. But you don't have to pay anything back. Work-study, administered by the college aid office, is often open to middle-income students as well as the poor, and graduate students as well as undergraduates, if they have financial need. You work until you've earned your full award—say, $1,000—then the job is over. To earn more money, you'll have to find a different job.

- *The states make awards to residents going to in-state schools* (although some states offer reciprocity to one another's students). Most of them target students with financial need, but there's a lot of merit money too. For example, 14 states provide automatic awards to students whose grades average B or higher, regardless of financial need. Even rich kids can get them—in fact, well-to-do students get most of the money. Some of these scholarships provide full tuition and fees for four years at any state college or university, with a book allowance too. Others offer a flat dollar amount. These awards, combined with excellent state universities, add up to an offer hard to refuse.

- *Colleges make need-based grants in the form of tuition discounts.* Instead of charging you, say, the $12,000 EFC you're supposed to pay, they may settle for only $7,000. Before choosing a college, ask about its policy on aid renewal. Some schools shave their awards after the freshman year.

- *Special grants often go to scholars, musicians, and other students with unusual talents.* You can get these merit awards in addition to grants for financial need. You can also get them if your family earns too much to qualify for need-based aid. For more on merit aid, see page 641.

- *Schools may also have scholarships funded by alumni for students of a particular type.* They're usually listed on the college's Web page. If you think you might qualify, ask the financial aid office.

- *You can volunteer for AmeriCorps VISTA, working in nonprofit and community organizations for up to two years.* You'll earn a modest living allowance (about $12,500 a year) plus an annual $4,725 credit toward college costs (generally $2,362.50 if you work part-time). That credit can be used at any college or graduate school or to pay down federal student loans. For information, go to www.americcorps.org or call 800-94-ACORPS.

- *Federal TEACH grants go to students who promise to teach for four years in a high-need subject area,* such as math, science, or reading, at a low-income school. You can get $4,000 a year (up to $16,000) for undergraduate work and $8,000 more for graduate school. But read the fine print: If you don't fulfill the obligation, your grant is converted into an unsubsidized Stafford loan, with interest calculated from the day you received the money.

- *You can sometimes give yourself a grant equivalent by:*
  - *Going to a community college for two years at a low price, then transferring to a full-term college for your last two years.* Just be sure that all your course credits are transferable so that you won't have to stay an extra semester at the second school.
  - *Taking advanced placement courses in high school.* If the college gives you credit for them, you might get through school in seven semesters rather than the traditional eight. That saves you a bundle. Go to the college's listings at www.collegeboard.com to see if AP courses are acceptable.
  - *Using the College Level Examination Program (CLEP).* Many schools extend college credit to people who pass these proficiency exams. The col-

lege's listings at www.collegeboard.com tell you which CLEP exams are acceptable and what scores you have to have. For more on CLEP, see www .collegeboard.com/clep. Some schools also accept self-study programs known as DSST and ECE, but don't sign up for their courses until you check.

• *Living more cheaply off campus than on.* Or living at home for a couple of years.

• *Taking courses in the summer for credits that can be applied to your degree.* Enough of these courses might save you a whole semester.

• *Attending a college that lets you get your bachelor's degree in three years instead of four.* Conversely, avoiding colleges where only a small percentage of students graduate in four years (page 617).

• *Getting external college credits or full degrees by taking courses on the Web.* Many online programs are offered by colleges and universities that specialize in distance education. Traditional colleges are entering this business too. Some schools mix campus and online classes. For a summary of these programs, check out Monster Learning (http://edu.monsterlearning.com) or Peterson's (www.petersons.com). Beware diploma mills that take your money and give you useless courses. Online schools should be accredited by the same organizations that monitor well-known brick-and-mortar schools.

How Much Should You Work?

Work-study jobs, awarded as part of financial aid, require just a few hours a week. The more hours you add, the harder it will be to keep up your academic schedule. If your job prevents you from graduating in four years, you are probably adding to your costs, not reducing them. You might not even finish school at all—leaving you with debt but no degree. It's better to borrow than to run up your hours to 20 or 25 hours a week. If a salary is essential, consider cooperative education (page 660), which is structured to combine study with work.

Money Even for Rich Kids

Not all grants are based on financial need. Certain highly desired students can also find aid even if they come from well-to-do families.

Merit, or "non-need," scholarships are offered by colleges that want to upgrade the quality of their student bodies. They're buying brains and student leadership, just as the Big Ten universities buy quarterbacks. Tuition discounts can run to 50 percent or more. Private colleges and universities give the largest discounts, but the publics offer them too.

You needn't be a genius to qualify. At some schools, money is available to any student with a B average, a spot in the top third of his or her high school class, and above-average scores on one of the college testing programs

Certain colleges also make merit awards to students with special skills such as acting, music, science, or entrepreneurial activities. Some offer them to honor students attending a private college in-state. And, of course, there are always athletic scholarships—with more offered to women than used to be the case.

You won't find the nation's most prestigious colleges giving merit money. They attract all the talent they can handle. But private schools in the tier just below them are begging for brains. The same is true of public universities seeking to raise their national profile and smaller public colleges trying to upgrade their student bodies. If they can attract smarter students, they'll raise their ranking on the annual Best Colleges list published by *U.S. News & World Report*—the bible for parents hoping for better colleges for their kids.

Be sure to ask if the merit award is renewable. Some schools pay you to come but don't pay you to stay. Also, look for schools that have special honors programs, so your brains won't go to waste.

14 Ways of Improving Your Shot at Aid, Including Merit Aid

1. Don't ask for an early-admissions decision. Early-decision students have declared themselves. They want this school and no other. You've agreed to come, regardless of the size of the aid package you get. It improves your chance of admission, if that trumps all. On the other hand, it costs you your chance of finding something better somewhere else. Conversely, it's smart to apply for "early action" if the school offers it. You're telling the school that it's at the top of your list but you're open to other offers. You might get an excellent package to nail you down in advance. Early apps help at schools with rolling admissions policies too.

2. Apply to schools in pairs—say, two similar private colleges and two similar universities, preferably two that compete with each other for students. If you get a better award from your second-choice school, your first choice may be willing to match it. Always apply to at least one in-state public school so that any private colleges on your list know they're competing with something cheaper.

3. Apply to schools where you're in the top 25 percent academically. They'll want you more than schools that see you as marginal. So-called stretch schools are fine, but they're not going to offer you the biggest bucks. Look up each school on the College Search at www.collegeboard.com and click on "SAT." That will show you the range of scores on the SAT and ACT college entrance exams achieved by the students they admit. Also on that site, or on the school's own Web site, you might find the grade point averages of their entering freshmen.

4. Athletes should apply to schools whose teams are in their ability range. You don't have to be a top athlete to get an athletic scholarship, just better than average and an asset to the team. Write to the school's coach and have your high school coach write too, detailing your letters, victories, and value to the team. And remember: colleges need tennis and lacrosse players just as much as they need footballers.

5. Be so fabulous that you can get into the nation's most generous elite schools, including Amherst College, Bowdoin College, Davidson College, Harvard University, Pomona College, Princeton University, Stanford University, Williams College, and Yale University. Schools like these may fill the gap between your expected contribution and the college's cost entirely with free grants, not loans. It doesn't matter how much the family earns. Grants might go to people earning $180,000 a year or more. Other schools might also provide aid to families in this income range, especially if they have more than one child in school.

6. Go for the automatic tuition-and-fees awards offered in 14 states for students with B averages and higher. It's a low-cost ride to a top state university and a chance of graduating with little or no debt.

7. Apply, strategically, to the schools most likely to give you grants. These might include lesser-known private schools in a distant state, interested in diversifying geographically and looking for students with superior talents or academic abilities. Or state colleges eager to upgrade their student bodies. Or state universities trying to raise their profiles nationally. Or any school trying to raise its rank on the annual Best Colleges list published by *U.S. News & World Report.*

8. Check out the college's policies on aid, starting with the College Board's College Search. Enter the schools on your list and click on "Cost & Financial Aid." You'll see how much of the aid they award comes in the form of loans rather than grants and what they list as their students' average indebtedness at graduation. Some schools burden their students much more than others. You'll also see what, if anything, they offer in merit (nonneed) aid and for what reason—for example, "academics, leadership, music/drama." Then go to the school's own site for details. It might tell you what percentage of entering freshmen bag the awards.

The schools also disclose whether they fill their students' full financial needs or whether, on average, they fill only part of them. It's tough to attend a college that concedes you need $12,000 worth of aid but can afford to give you only half of it. You'll have extra costs even at schools that claim to fill 100 percent of their students' need. Remember, that's 100 percent of your *official* need—the calculation that assumes you're living in a bare-bones way (page 623). Your real need will almost certainly be higher. If you go, you'll need a parental PLUS loan, an unsubsidized Stafford loan, or—last choice—a private loan (page 650), on top of your school-approved student loan.

9. Apply to private schools as well as state schools. The state schools charge less but also have less money for grants and merit aid. You won't know which school will be cheaper until the aid packages arrive and you see how much more you'll have to borrow to pay the bills.

10. Make multiple contacts with the schools on your list—visit them, call for information, ask for an interview with local alumni, e-mail the admissions office with questions. The more interested you look, the more likely you are to be accepted and to get an award.

11. Look at the school's gender balance. Men are more apt to be admitted and get awards at private colleges where women are approaching 60 percent of the student body. Coed schools need to maintain some sort of gender balance to keep the guys' parents happy (although maybe the guys are happy as is!).

12. For academic merit aid, type "scholarship" and your combined SAT or ACT scores into a search engine—for example, "scholarship SAT 1100." The names of schools will pop up that are looking for *you*. Some of the awards are large. I found awards at lower SAT scores too.

13. Search for America's Best Colleges, the ranking published annually by *U.S. News & World Report*. It includes a list of schools that give the most merit aid.

14. For a rundown of the merit awards available at about 1,200 schools, send for the book *The A's and B's of Academic Scholarships*, at this writing $12 from Octameron Associates (www.octameron.com). Some are tiny grants, maybe $200 or $300. Others list at $1,000 or $2,000. A few exceed $35,000. On the Web, go to MeritAid (www.meritaid.com).

The Chimera of Private Scholarships

Computerized college scholarship services offer to tap you into a running river of private scholarships. "Don't let free money go to waste!" they trumpet on their sites. It sounds as if you simply have to dip in your hand to scoop them up.

My guess is that you'll come up dry. I tried three of the services in the name of a hypothetical high school senior, with these results: "Scholarship Search" at www.collegeboard.com served me 100 potential awards from various organizations. The first 50 I clicked on had nothing to do with the information I had entered (including awards for disabled students or members of the American Quarter Horse Foundation), so I wouldn't have qualified. I got discouraged and didn't do the second 50. FastWeb (www.fastweb.com) gave me 34 offers, falling into two general categories. First, essay contests, most of them asking students to write on various patriotic or free-market themes. Second, promotions, where you click to put your name on an e-mail advertising list and maybe win $25,000 (I'd call that a lottery). You also have to click through commercial offers as you go along. "Undergraduate Scholarship Search" at www.petersons.com gave me 427 possibilities. The few I clicked on didn't fit. All told, a waste of time.

Still, someone wins those lotteries or writes those essays. If you've filed your FAFSA, worked at finding state scholarships and merit aid, and crafted your college essays, you might spend an afternoon on these free services to see if anything comes up. Don't pay for computerized searches; they're money down the drain. Your best shot at winning money will be a local program. Check your parents' company or union, a community foundation, or a service organization such as Lions Clubs or Rotary International. Local contests have fewer entrants, and the organization will probably know you.

If you decide to compete for an award, ask the school how it would handle any money you won. Could you apply the whole amount to your expenses? Or will the college reduce your aid package by the extra money you now have in your pocket? Commonly, schools use the award to replace your work-study grant, so you won't have added to the total funds available for school. Instead, your winning essay will save you from working a few hours a week.

Scholarships and Taxes

Grants for tuition, books, fees, supplies, and equipment are tax free for students working toward a degree. But any money you get for room and board should be reported as taxable income. Ditto for grants or tuition reductions given in return for teaching or other services to the school. Research assistantships may be tax free, however, because you're helping only the professor, not necessarily the school.

Lend Me a Loan

The cheapest loans go directly to students, courtesy of the state and federal governments. Students can borrow without collateral, cosigners, or credit histories and don't have to pay until they get out of school. There are federal loans for parents too. Parent loans carry higher rates than students pay but are cheaper, by far, than loans from private lenders such as banks and Sallie Mae.

It's so easy to get private loans that some students sign up for them automatically if their government loans aren't enough. *Don't do it before checking out your other choices!* If a parent is involved, the parent should take a government loan to cover the financing gap or take a home equity loan with tax-deductible interest. If the student is going to be responsible for the cost, you can set up a formal repayment agreement—privately, between the two of you, or using a service such as Virgin Money (page 654). Turning your back on private loans is the only way to get the debt burden down.

Read This First!!!

Young students don't know much about living on a small income and juggling debt. A loan is just a piece of paper they sign today so that they can get back to the dorm. When they get out of school, however, they'll be in repayment hell if they borrow more than they can readily repay. If they enter a lower-earning profession, lose their job, struggle through divorce, choke on medical bills— anything that pares their income—student loans become a millstone that will drag them down for years. Students should judge their potential earning power before taking on big loans every year. As a rule of thumb, they shouldn't borrow any more than their likely starting salary. Better to go to a less expensive school than to run the risk of blighting their future with major debt.

Okay, these are all just words to kids who have never been on their own. So make this Web site—StudentLoanJustice.org (www.studentloanjustice.org)— required reading before you let your son or daughter accept the fat envelope from an expensive school and start signing up for loans. These are tales from students who had bad luck, economically, and whose student loans turned out to hurt or wreck their lives. Most students repay their loans successfully, but life is discouraging for those who can't. For your (few) rights when you're having trouble paying, go to the Web site for Student Loan Borrower Assistance (www.studentloanborrowerassistance.org).

Parents need to read these Web sites too. In most cases, student and parent loans, including private loans, cannot be discharged in bankruptcy. You're stuck with these obligations, and penalties are stiff. Borrowing may be necessary to get a college degree or certificate, but how much to borrow is a *choice*. Look at the probable cost of the schools you're considering over the next four years, add up the loans, see what you'll have to pay per month when the time finally comes, and ask: Am I out of my mind?

P.S.: When researching www.studentloanjustice.org, I accidentally typed in, "www.studentloanjustice.*com*." Guess what? That takes you to a site that advertises loans! If you overborrowed once, the lenders figure you'll do it again. There oughta be a law . . .

Keep Track of Your Debt

When you take your first loan, as a student, your school is supposed to counsel you about it—explaining the loan, the dangers of overborrowing, and the consequences of default. Take it seriously. This is your first venture into a world of potential worry—not just from education debt (a reasonable amount is worth it, to get a degree) but all the other kinds of debt that lie ahead.

Store all the information regarding your education debt in a single file, along with the loan documents. Keep a running total of what you've borrowed. Use FinAid's (www.finaid.org) Loan Calculator (Standard and Extended Repayment) to keep track of what your monthly payments will probably be after you leave school. Discuss with the financial aid office how much you'll probably have to earn to cover your living expenses and your loan repayments too.

Here are your borrowing choices:

1. Federal Stafford Loans—the government's primary college lending program. Staffords come in two flavors:

• *Subsidized Staffords*, for students whose FAFSA forms show that they're eligible for federal aid at the particular school they choose. The government pays the interest on these loans while you're in school and for the following six months. After that, you pay. At this writing, subsidized Staffords carry a fixed interest rate of 5.6 percent, declining to 3.4 percent in 2011–12.

• *Unsubsidized Staffords*, for students who need more money than they can borrow on the subsidized program or whose higher family income makes them ineligible for aid. You're responsible for the interest. You can put off making interest payments while you're in school, letting your debt compound. Or you can pay as you go (a sounder choice, financially). At this writing, unsubsidized Staffords cost 6.8 percent.

In either case, there's a loan origination fee of up to 2 percent (waived by some private lenders). Principal repayments don't have to start until six months after you leave school or start attending less than half-time. Monthly payments may be fixed or varied, depending on your repayment plan (page 656). Usual repayment period: 10 years, although payments can be stretched over as many as 30 years.

Staffords are available through many banks, credit unions, state loan guarantee agencies, college lending companies such as Sallie Mae, and about 1,200 institutions of higher learning. (The Staffords you secure through your school are called direct loans, meaning that they come directly from the government without using a bank as the source of funds.) You can use student loans at qualified career schools as well as for academic studies.

Apply for a Stafford as soon as your college accepts you—either through the college (for students whose schools are in the direct loan program) or through the lender you choose. You'll typically pay 2 to 4 percent in insurance and loan origination fees, depending on the lender (a few of them charge zero). You can pay it in cash or add it to the loan amount. Cash is better. If you add the up-front fee to the loan, as most people do, the cost compounds.

Check the table below for the maximum amount that you can borrow each year. Students who qualify for aid may be subsidized for only part of the maxi-

Table 11.

HOW MUCH UNCLE STAFFORD WILL LEND*

	Freshmen	Sophomores	Juniors	Seniors	Later Years	Maximum
Dependent undergraduates	$5,500	$6,500	$7,500	$7,500	$7,500	$31,000
Independent undergraduates and dependent undergrads whose parents don't qualify for PLUS loans	9,500	10,500	12,500	12,500	12,500	57,000
Graduate or professional students	20,500 in every year					138,500†

* The maximums include subsidized and unsubsidized portions.
† This figure includes your undergraduate Stafford loans. In certain health-education programs, you can borrow up to $224,000.

mum amount. These maximums are reduced for students attending less than full-time.

2. Low-income students might get a federal Perkins loan at only 5 percent interest. But you can't apply for it on your own. It's awarded by the college as part of a package of financial aid. Undergraduates can normally borrow as much as $4,000 a year, to a maximum of $20,000. Graduate students get $6,000 a year, to a maximum of $40,000 (minus any Perkins money they took as undergraduates). The government pays the interest while you're in school and for the following 9 months. Then repayments begin. Normally, you make payments over the next 10 years, although that period can be extended.

3. If federal student loans aren't enough, parents can borrow from the government too, under a program known as PLUS. You can borrow up to the total cost of your child's education, minus any student aid awarded. You do have to pass a credit check. A bankruptcy or foreclosure will exclude you—bad news for parents hurt by the housing bust. The government doesn't evaluate your debt load or your ability to repay, so use this largesse with care. (Graduate students can get PLUS loans too.)

PLUS loans for parents are available from private lenders at 8.5 percent or through colleges in the direct loan program at 7.9 percent. Loan term: 5 to 10 years, although payments can be extended. Fee: up to 4 percent. Repayments don't have to start until your child leaves school (you can also repay earlier).

4. Some states offer terrific loans at low interest rates. Out-of-state students might even qualify. The college financial aid office will know.

5. State college loan agencies may cut special deals with students who want to be teachers. If, after two years in the classroom, you can't stand the little darlings one moment longer, you can switch to another field without penalty.

6. If you're training for one of the health care professions, Uncle Sugar really rolls out the cart. You'll find loans for doctors, nurses, dentists, optometrists, public health officers, podiatrists, veterinarians, pharmacists, physical therapists, and others. Any medical or professional school will have a full list.

7. The college may lend you money directly, in the form of a private loan. It might even include its loan in your financial aid package. But don't take the college's private loan without checking other sources. You might get a better rate somewhere else. For example, it might be smarter for your parent to take a home equity loan or a PLUS.

8. The college will have a list of lenders it recommends. Look it over, but don't assume that they're the best you can get. In 2007, lenders were caught buying their way onto some of these lists. That's over, presumably. The colleges are being more careful and are a more reliable source of information than the Internet. Still, the schools may give higher priority to lenders whose systems they're connected with, even if those loans don't offer the best terms. They may even discourage you from looking elsewhere. Nevertheless, they're required to work with any lender you find.

9. Home owners should borrow against their home equity, which might carry even lower rates than PLUS loans (always depending on the market at the time). Interest rates are deductible, regardless of income. You have to start making monthly repayments right away, rather than waiting, as you can with PLUS. But prompt payments are a better strategy with PLUS loans too. They save you pots of money on interest in the years ahead.

10. Your college may offer a monthly payment plan or send you brochures for one or more commercial tuition management plans. These plans convert the twice-a-year lump sum payments required by many schools into 12 equal monthly installments. There may also be 5- to 15-year payment plans at variable interest rates. Tuition plans generally include life and disability insurance. If you die or become totally disabled, all the rest of your child's college bills will be paid in full. Two payment plans to consider: Academic Management Services, a Sallie Mae company (www.amsweb.com, 800-891-4203), and Tuition Management Systems at www.afford.com, 800-722-4867.

As a homemade alternative to tuition management plans, consider this: Pay the college bill by borrowing at the lowest interest rate that you can and make monthly repayments. Buy more low-cost term life insurance to guarantee your child's education if you die and pray that you won't become disabled. (If you do become disabled, your child will qualify for much more student aid.)

The Burden (and Pitfalls) of Private Loans

At many schools, federal student loans don't begin to cover the cost, even after counting your tuition discount. Your first stop should be a home equity loan or a PLUS parent loan, if a parent is contributing and can pass the credit check. The PLUS will cover the entire remaining cost, so you don't need a private loan. *Never* take a private loan without consulting first with your school's financial aid office. The school might be able to find you a better loan at a lower rate.

Private, or "alternative," student loans are offered by banks, credit unions, and student loan companies such as Sallie Mae. Interest rates are high unless you can get a cosigner, and then they're merely less high (although not as bad as credit card rates). They're also variable, so you'll pay more if rates go up—and without caps! If interest rates soar, your payments will too. You usually can put off repayments until you get out of school. Some loans may require payments monthly—either interest only or interest and principal. There may also be fees, subtracted from each disbursement you get. If you or your cosigner has a low credit score, you won't get a loan at all.

Unfortunately, you can't compare private loans simply by researching their sites on the Web. Lenders advertise their lowest interest rate, but *your* rate will depend on such things as your credit history, your cosigner, how much debt you have, and how far along you are in school. To find out what you'll be charged, you have to apply. If you apply to more than one lender to find the best deal, each one will query your credit history, which will nick your credit score by a few points (five points for one inquiry, and it runs up from there). Too many nicks, and you might have to pay a higher interest rate. It's a credit Catch-22.* Smart consumers search for low rates, but the price of too many searches might put your interest rate up.

The rates may confuse you. They're pegged to a variable interest rate index—either the prime bank lending rate (the U.S. benchmark rate) or LIBOR (the London Interbank Offered Rate—the rate at which banks lend to each other on London's wholesale market). The rate on your loan will be quoted at a certain number of points (the *margin*) over the prime rate: for example, LIBOR plus five percentage points. You might get LIBOR plus two points if you're a great credit risk or LIBOR plus eight points if you're not. Your margin is fixed for the life of the loan. The total rate floats up and down as the index changes.

Some evidence suggests that pegging to LIBOR will give you a lower cost loan, but you can't predict. FinAid shows you the margins at various lenders, but that's no guide to what you will pay yourself (note that the numbers aren't always up to date). Also, you have to look at fees. Lenders with high fees can advertise lower interest rates; lenders with low fees have higher rates. In other words, it's a mess. You can't figure it out.

And that's exactly what the lenders like. You *can't* figure it out, which means that you can't compare two or three offers without applying. Most students don't apply to several places (it's a pain). The big-name private lenders have an edge and they charge you for it. Rates and fees are highest at the best-known banks.

You might take a high-rate private loan without realizing it. That's because the lenders provide federal student and parent loans too. You might go to the

---

*Do students know the origin of Catch-22, from the World War II novel of that title? If flying dangerous missions made you crazy, you could ask to be relieved. But asking to be relieved of a dangerous mission is sane, so you'd be turned down.

bank for a Stafford. The bank will look at your costs, say that you're coming up short, and sign you up for a private loan too. They're both called "student" loans, so how would you know?

An estimated 20 percent of dependent students who have private loans *don't* have Staffords. Maybe they never filed the FAFSA form, which would have qualified them for Staffords. Maybe they mistook the bank loan for the Stafford or PLUS and signed up because it was so easy to get. Either way, they lose.

The lenders may advertise various rate incentives on their Web sites. For example, you might get 0.25 percent off your interest rate if you sign up for automatic repayments from your bank account and another 0.25 or 0.5 percent if you make every payment on time for the first two or four years. But roughly 90 to 95 percent of borrowers never qualify for the on-time break, maybe because they're unsure of their first payment date and miss it, or maybe because they're a day late one month because the mail was delayed. So don't let prospective savings like that influence your choice. When deciding on a lender, look only at the current rates and fees.

If parents are in the picture, students can duck private loans and ask their parents to borrow through PLUS instead. Students on their own, however, are usually stuck—and they'll get the highest rates.

Warning: A 2009 study by Student Lending Analytics, a firm that analyzes lending programs for colleges, found that many private lenders don't disclose all their fees. When your loan goes into repayment, you may be tagged with an unexpected service charge. In some cases, students have to sign loan contracts without knowing what the interest rate will be. The lender might also have the right to hike your rate if you pay late. For more gory details, go to the SLA Web site (www.studentlendinganalytics.com) and read the "2009 SLA Private Loan Series: The Promissory Note." SLA's Blog has lots of other useful information too.

Second Warning: Lenders solicit parents and students by making their private loans fast and easy. "No paperwork!" they promise, just money fast, with payments deferred. Sounds great, right? But if you skip the paperwork— namely, the FAFSA—you lose access to low-cost student loans. Those lenders are taking advantage of you. Some private lenders try to discourage you from getting Stafford and PLUS loans by telling you that their loans are better—for example, that they cover more of the college expenses or have more flexible repayment terms. Often these are false, deceptive, misleading, unethical, and a lie. Do I make myself clear?

Four Ways of Finding Better Rates on Private Loans

1. The only sure way: Apply to two or three lenders, despite the credit score risk, to see if one of them offers a better deal. Odds are, the nicks on your score will not push you over the line and into a higher interest rate category. Compare the interest rates, margins, fees, and penalty charges or rates in the fine print.

2. Check the ratings that Student Lending Analytics gives to the leading plans (www.studentlendinganalytics.com/ratings.html). The best plans earn four stars, the worst ones just one star. SLA also provides all the details on each lending program.

3. Go to FinAid at www.finaid.org. It has a list of private lenders, their range of fees, and the amounts you can borrow. It also shows you the formulas they use for setting rates (pegged to the prime rate or to LIBOR), with a link that helps you figure out what the minimum and maximum rates would be. This list isn't always up to date but gives you an idea of where to look.

4. Look for services on the Web that compare offers from lenders. The number of private lenders dropped during the 2007–2009 credit crash, and so did the sites that helped you find the better offers. But they'll rise again, so use your search engine to see what's currently around.

Should You Borrow from Your Company Savings Plan?

No—not even if the plan gives you better terms than you'd get from a commercial student loan program or from a bank. If you lose your job, the withdrawal turns into taxable income with, maybe, penalties too. If your child can't attend school unless you shred your retirement plan, he or she—and you—has chosen the wrong college. You shouldn't have to make such a sacrifice.

Who Should Borrow, Parent or Student?

Parents with above-average incomes should shoulder at least some of the loans. Giving your child an education is part of your parental duty. If you haven't saved enough, you can probably afford to borrow the full amount and repay out of future income. If paying the full freight will damage your ability to retire, your child should borrow too, but only with federal student loans, not with private loans (too costly!). If you haven't saved at all and are close to retirement age, however, you have thrown your children to the wolves. They will have to take on more of the expense. Parents can't risk new, big debts lasting 10 years or more at a time when their paychecks are going to stop.

Parents with middle incomes won't be able to help as much as higher earners do. You cannot afford to take big loans that would make it harder for you to save for your own retirement. You won't do your kids any favors by retiring broke and in debt. Your parental duty is helping your children find good schools that minimize loans, because they'll have to borrow most of the out-of-pocket cost themselves.

Children of lower-income parents should get enough grants to see them through most of their education, if they choose their schools carefully. Some student loans may be required, but, historically, these kids have been more wary of debt than kids whose families earn more.

Students should understand that borrowing is a *choice*. It's worth borrowing more to attend a clearly superior school, but not a lot more. It's *not* worth borrowing more when similar schools are just as good.

Be supercareful about borrowing to attend a for-profit trade or career school. They're generally expensive, and some of them don't train you well enough for you to get a good job. If you can't earn enough when you graduate, you can put off making full payments for a while (page 655), but the interest owed on the loan will mount. If you eventually default, you won't be able to get a student loan in the future, to attend a better school. Look at a community college before considering a for-profit school.

Loans the Hot Potato Way

One loan strategy is to borrow where it's cheapest, then shift the loan to the person who's going to repay. The student might take the maximum low-rate Stafford loan on the assumption that an affluent parent will eventually pay part or all of it off.

For the portion of the cost that the student will pay, the parent should still participate in order to hold down the future expense. You might take a PLUS loan or a home equity loan, then draw up a formal repayment plan that both you and your child sign. To elevate this transaction to the status of "real" loan, consider making use of Virgin Money (www.virginmoneyus.com). This company will prepare a formal loan document on whatever terms you and your child agree. The child makes repayments to Virgin, which deducts a $9 service charge and passes the net payment on to you. If the child doesn't pay, there are penalties, just as if he or she had borrowed from a bank. Cost of the contract: $199; $299, if you'll want to add additional loans.

Considering only cost, it's better to make this loan without putting Virgin in the middle. On the other hand, parents may be reluctant to force a stubborn child to repay. Virgin becomes the enforcer to be sure you get your money back. And if, in the end, you want to forgive the loan, you can.

Loan Consolidation: Yes or No?

Oppressed by the size of your student loan payments? Tired of writing several checks a month to repay your various loans? Not earning much money but no longer eligible for deferments or forbearance on payments? There's a way out: as long as you're out of school, you can consolidate your debt.

Consolidation takes all your government-backed student loans—all your Staffords and Perkins and any loans you've taken for studies in the health care professions—and packs them into a single loan with a single monthly payment. The new term is 10 to 30 years, so you lower the amount that you have to pay each month. PLUS loans can be consolidated too (except in the government's income-contingent plan, page 656). You can even "consolidate" a single loan. You don't have to put up any collateral or pass a credit check. Consolidation loans are granted on your signature alone.

Most private lenders stopped consolidating federal student loans when the credit markets crashed in 2008 (check the Web to see if they've resumed). But there's plenty of money available through the federal government's Direct Loan Consolidation plan (www.loanconsolidation.ed.gov, 800-557-7392). You get a fixed interest rate that's a weighted average of the loans you're consolidating. There are no fees. For details, go to the site's FAQs. The site also gives you a calculator, for figuring out what your new interest rate will be. You can prepay a consolidated loan without penalty.

If you consolidated your loans with the government once before, you can't do it again unless you have a new loan you want to add or you qualify for the income-contingent plan (below).

Table 12. Consolidating Student Loans

Size of Debt	Maximum Consolidation Term
Less than $7,500	10 years
$7,500–10,000	12 years
$10,000–$20,000	15 years
$20,000–$40,000	20 years
$40,000–$60,000	25 years
More than $60,000	30 years

Your Repayment Choices on Government Consolidation Loans

1. A standard repayment plan. You make fixed monthly payments of at least $50 to pay off your loan in 10 to 30 years, depending on how much you owe.

2. An extended repayment plan. This reduces your monthly payments by stretching them over a longer term. How long depends on how much you owe.

3. A graduated repayment plan. You repay over the same length of time allowed in the extended plan. But your payments start low and rise every two years, based on your total education indebtedness. This arrangement works well if your first job pays peanuts but your income gradually goes up. If it doesn't, you can escape higher payments by switching to another plan.

4. An income-contingent plan, for people with low earnings. Your payments are capped at 15 percent of your discretionary income, figured on the basis of income and family size. There's a variable interest rate. If you're still paying off the loan after 25 years, the government forgives the outstanding balance. It forgives the remaining loan after 10 years if you're working in an eligible public service job.

Private Lender Repayment Plans

At this writing, private lenders aren't consolidating most federal student loans. They might make you a special offer if they lent you $30,000 or more. But they'll try to talk you out of consolidating smaller loans. They might tell you (wrongly) that the government's direct loan consolidation program is no good.

Instead of consolidation, they'll offer you extended or graduated repayments on your individual loans. If you have large loans but a low income, they offer an *income-sensitive plan.* There your payments are pegged to the size of your monthly income. You can pay as little as 4 percent of what you earn and as much as 25 percent. Ask the lender what happens if your chosen payments don't cover the standard interest and principal due. The lender might lower the payment required by extending the term of the loan for a specified number of years. At a minimum, you will always have to pay the interest. You will also have to document your income annually so that payments can be reset.

Compare the private lender's offer with the government's direct loan consolidation plan, to see which one better meets your needs. Usually, the government makes you a better offer.

Private lenders do consolidate private loans. You're given a single payment in place of several payments on loans from separate lenders, but there aren't any special, income-sensitive repayment plans. You simply get a new loan for whatever term you can negotiate. If your credit score has risen—say, because you have a good job and have been making other loan payments on time—the new loan might carry a lower interest rate. It doesn't hurt to ask. You can release your cosigner too.

Don't Stretch Out the Loan Term Unless You're Desperate. Adding extra years to your loan means extra years of interest payments. You might still be paying off the cost of your own education when it's time for your children to enter school. You also lose any discount you were getting for making payments on time—although, if you're struggling with payments, you're probably not getting the discount anyway.

The Smart Way to Consolidate. Pack all your federal loans into a single payment and take the shortest term possible. Save money by paying off your loan in an even shorter period of time. There's no prepayment penalty.

Payments on Federal Loans Can Be Deferred or Forgiven

When loan repayments become a burden due to low wages, poor health, or some other personal problem, sometimes you can catch a break. *Deferment* lets you put off paying for a while. *Forbearance* offers low or no payments for a limited period of time to people with repayment problems who don't qualify for deferments.

Payments can be temporarily deferred if you:[*]

- *Return to school at least half-time.*
- *Study full-time in an approved graduate or postgraduate fellowship program.*
- *Receive services from a rehabilitation program for the disabled, full-time.*
- *Can't find work, even though you're job hunting.* Repayments can be deferred for up to three years, but you have to reapply for this deferral every six months.
- *Face economic hardship, as defined by the U.S. Department of Education.* One criterion: working full-time and earning less than the minimum wage. This deferment too can last for up to three years.
- *Work in a social service job that lets you cancel your student loans* (page 658; this is for Perkins borrowers only).
- *Are on active military duty during a war, other military operations, or a national emergency.* This applies to loans taken after July 1, 2001.

If you don't qualify for deferment but are having financial problems, you can request forbearance. Payments can be temporarily reduced or postponed if you:

---

*This applies to loans taken on or after July 1, 1993. Earlier loans have different rules.

- *Can't pay owing to poor health.*
- *Find that your payments on certain federal student loans equal or exceed 20 percent of your monthly gross income.*
- *Are serving in a medical or dental internship or residency, or in a position under the National Community Service Trust Act of 1993,* including AmeriCorps Vista (Stafford and Direct loan holders only).
- *Teach in a place that the government defines as short of teachers* (Stafford and Direct loans only).

PLUS Loans are eligible for deferral and forbearance too, under various conditions.

Your loan can be wholly or partly canceled if you:
- *Die.*
- *Become totally and permanently disabled.*
- *Go bankrupt, show a hardship that will prevent you from ever paying, and get a sympathetic judge.* The judge is key. In one courtroom, a married couple working in low-paying teaching jobs got their student loan discharged. In another courtroom, a cellist and music teacher didn't because the judge thought he ought to look for higher-paying work. In most cases, however, student and parent loans, including private loans, cannot be discharged in bankruptcy.
- *Enlist in the Army, Army National Guard, or Army Reserve.* If you sign up for certain types of military work, the U.S. Defense Department will forgive your loan for each year that you serve.
- *Lost a spouse or child in the tragedy of 9/11.*
- *Were cheated by a school that closed before you completed your course or falsely certified that you could benefit from the course.* This generally applies to dishonest trade and career schools.
- *Hold a Perkins loan and teach low-income or handicapped students; teach in a shortage area; work as a full-time nurse, medical technician, or law enforcement officer; provide services to high-risk children in a low-income community; provide early-intervention services to infants and toddlers; serve in the armed forces in an "area of hostilities"; or join AmeriCorps Vista or the Peace Corps.* Part of your loan is forgiven for each year you serve.

Do You Owe Interest During the Time that Loan Repayments are Postponed? *No,* if you defer a subsidized Stafford or Perkins loan. *Yes,* if you defer an unsubsidized Stafford or PLUS. *Yes,* if you've been granted forbearance rather than deferral. If you owe interest, you'll have a choice: make your payments monthly (even though your principal payments are deferred) or defer the interest too, adding it to your total debt. You'd be smart to keep paying interest monthly. Otherwise the total amount of your debt goes up and you'll face higher payments when the deferral ends. (If those payments are burdensome, however, you can consolidate for a longer loan term.)

Never Default!

If you stop paying your student loan . . .

- you'll be charged punitive fees so high that you may never get out of debt
- you can't get additional student aid until you've repaid
- a collection agent may pursue you
- your delinquency will trash your credit report
- your bad credit report will prevent you from getting other important loans, such as a mortgage
- your wages can be garnished
- if you work for the federal government, the payments may be withheld from your salary
- your income tax refunds may be held back. If you file jointly, so might your spouse's
- because this debt normally can't be discharged in bankruptcy, you'll be under its lash for life

Loan Rehabilitation

You can recover from a defaulted loan by entering loan rehabilitation. You're required to make a certain number of consecutive on-time payments. Once that's done, your default should be removed from your credit report and the other bad things listed above reversed. Cleaning up your credit report is supposed to be automatic, but sometimes the default stays on your record. Check your credit report and agitate if this happens to you.

Adult Students

Adults can apply for the same college aid programs that young students get. But there's a catch. Your application for federal aid (the FAFSA form) asks for your prior year's earnings and assumes that the same amount of money will be on tap for this year's costs. If you're quitting your job to go to school, you won't have that income anymore. Raise this problem with your school's office of financial aid. The school can ask the government to refigure your eligibility for aid based on your projected income while you're in school. The PROFILE form adjusts for this at the time you file.

Raising Money for Graduate School

As a parent, you're financially exhausted. Child One is through college; Child Two will be finished in two years. Retirement is within sight. Then Child One says that he or she wants to go to graduate school. Ouch.

Most parents assume that their financial obligations stop with the undergraduate degree. If the kid wants more education, that's his or her responsibility.

But try telling that to a university. Most of them look at parental income before granting any financial aid. Parents of graduate students aren't squeezed as hard as the parents of undergraduates. Still, your expected contribution may be high. If you won't help pay, your child might not be able to go.

How much aid is available depends on what your child will study. In medicine, law, and other well-paid professions, lower-income students get grants, but middle-class students and parents are expected to pay much of their own way. Borrow it or earn it, but don't look to the grad school for serious money. Your student is "independent" on the FAFSA form but not in the aid offices of the graduate schools.

Advanced science and engineering degrees, on the other hand, are heavily funded by scholarships and research assistantships, which are often awarded on merit, not need. The social sciences and religion offer administrative assistantships, such as being a counselor. The arts may give teaching assistantships. Parents are rarely tapped for PhD programs.

When hunting for a grant, start lobbying in the fall of the year before you'll go. Talk to the head of the academic department; that's the person who can hand out the paying positions. File your FAFSA on January 1 and start consulting with the student aid office. Also, consider cooperative education (see below).

What if a student still comes up short? The grad schools aren't entirely flint hearted. Some don't pursue the parents of students who have been self-supporting for three years. Some let stepparents off the hook. Every family should talk to the financial aid office to see if there's any wiggle room.

The Job Connection

Sometimes your job can lead to a grant. Employers may help pay for college courses or let you alternate between work and school. In the armed services, you can march for your money. Whatever the deal, you get an education at a fraction of the cost that other students pay. Here's what's out there.

Cooperative Education

A co-op student gets a job related to his or her field of study. Your salary pays a significant share of your college costs. Schedules vary. You might alternate semesters; one in school, one at work. You might attend classes in the morning and work in the afternoon. It may take five years to earn an undergraduate degree. Co-op programs are also offered by two-year community colleges and some graduate schools. Around 200,000 students participate. Check *The Best of Co-op Guide,* at the Web site of the National Commission for Cooperative Education, www.co-op.edu. It covers programs for both graduates and undergraduates. Octameron Associates publishes *Majoring in Success* ($8 plus $3 shipping, from www.octameron.com), on co-op programs, internships, and other work-study connections.

The Military Budget

Military scholarships come with the commitment to service. To compete for a two- to four-year grant from the Reserve Officers' Training Corps (ROTC), you need high grades and, usually, a tilt toward math, science, nursing, or engineering. ROTC isn't offered at every college. For information call the Army at 800-USA-ROTC (www.goarmy.com/rotc), the Navy and Marines at 800-NAV-ROTC (www.nrotc.navy.mil), or the Air Force at 800-423-7682 (www.afrotc.com).

If you enlist, the Army, Navy, and Air Force will repay part of your federal student loans (in the Navy, you also have to sign up for certain types of work).

You can get grants for courses taken at nearby schools or online during your off-hours.

To provide a future education for yourself, put $100 a month of your military pay toward a higher education fund during your first 12 months of service. After that, the Department of Veterans Affairs will help pay for your future education—at a college or career school, including online education—provided that you're honorably discharged. The size of your grant generally rises each year to match inflation. At this writing, here are the rules for 2009. For updates, check the Web.

- *If you stay in the service for fewer than three years and go to school full-time,* you'll get $1,073 a month for 36 months while you're in school (that should cover eight semesters, for a four-year course). For a hitch of three years or more, you can get $1,321 a month. You're also eligible for the higher amount if you do two years of active duty plus four years in the Selected Reserve or National Guard.

Your particular branch of service may add even more if you sign up for certain lines of work. If you contribute an extra $600 before discharge, your benefit as a full-time student rises by $150 a month. After leaving the service, you generally have up to 10 years to matriculate. If you don't go to school, you normally don't get your $100-a-month contribution back.

- *Under the Post-9/11 GI Bill, qualified veterans get up to 36 months of higher-education benefits* for tuition and fees (not to exceed the cost of the most expensive public institution in the state); books and supplies up to $1,000 a year; a housing allowance; and for some, a $500 relocation allowance. Because of the way the benefit formula works, the size of your grant depends on the state you live in. The benefit is good for 15 years after you leave the service.

- *Enlistments in the military reserve are attractive too.* For a six-year commitment, you qualify for education assistance worth up to $11,412 and get drill pay besides. You might also get called up.

- *The spouses and children of veterans may qualify for education benefits* if the vet dies or is permanently and totally disabled as a result of his or her service; dies from other causes while suffering from a service-connected disability; has been listed for more than 90 days as missing in action, captured by an enemy, or interned by a foreign government; or is hospitalized or receiving outpatient treatment for a permanent and total disability that is service connected and is likely to be discharged on account of that disability. In 2008 the government paid $915 a month for full-time students for up to 45 months. To qualify, children generally have to be 18 to 26. Spouses have up to 10 years to complete their training.

For current details on military education assistance, go the "Education" section of the Web site Military.com (www.military.com).

The Company Perk

Some employers pay part or all of the price of courses at local undergraduate or graduate institutions or training schools. Will you be taxed on the value of the company contribution? The answer is no if the company requires you to take the courses to maintain your current job. The company might also offer tuition assistance as an optional fringe benefit. Under that program, you can take any kind of course the company allows, whether it relates to your job or not (exception: sports and hobby courses, which do have to relate to the business in some way). The benefit is tax free up to $5,250.

For More Information on Raising Money for College

1. Go to www.collegeboard.com for a complete tutorial about the college process, including college planning, finding schools, SAT tests, applications, cost calculations, scholarships, and financial aid. You'll find the basics on more than 3,600 colleges, universities, and proprietary schools—majors, college costs, financial aid, sports teams, admissions, SAT scores, student housing, and special programs.

2. Go to www.finaid.org for a roundup of everything you could possibly want to know about financial aid, including scholarship sources, calculators to help you figure out your expected family contribution, advice from financial aid administrators, and links to Web pages for state aid agencies, federal student aid guides, and college aid offices.

3. Go to Federal Student Aid (www.federalstudentaid.ed.gov) for detailed information on government programs such as Pell grants and Stafford loans, as well as general information on college planning.

4. Send for Octameron Associates' *Don't Miss Out: The Ambitious Student's Guide to Financial Aid,* a sound strategic guide to finding and qualifying for student aid. Cost: $13 plus $3 shipping, from www.octameron .com. Octameron publishes many other books on specific kinds of aid, such as merit aid and aid to athletes.

5. Go to the site of Merit Aid (www.meritaid.com) for merit scholarships listed by state and school.

6. For a reference book, get *Peterson's College Money Handbook,* $32, available through bookstores or by calling Peterson's customer service at 800-338-3282. It lists more than 2,100 institutions, their expenses, the amount of aid on tap, the merit awards you can apply for, money-saving options (such as accelerated degrees, ROTC, co-op education, guaranteed tuition plans, and off-campus living), and athletic scholarships. A helpful chart gives parents a general idea of what they'll be expected to contribute to their children's education. Athletes should check *Peterson's Sports Scholarships and College Athletic Programs,* $27.95.

Don't Get Scammed!

One day you may get an exciting e-mail or snail mail. You have qualified for a scholarship! Just send $5 or $10 or $20 for processing costs. The announcement looks as if it came from the government. I guarantee you it's a fake. You never have to send money for a scholarship you've won. College aid never comes unsolicited.

Or the letter might say, "Your son, Rick, has been chosen as one of the students in your area to apply for grants through our college assistance program." It asks for your bank account number "so the money can be wired to you directly" or your credit card number "to verify who you are."

Don't believe a word of it or any pitch like it. It's a cheat.

What's Your Best Shot at Getting College Aid?

Lower-income kids are being pressed harder than they were in the past. The size of the Pell grant hasn't kept up with the increase in college costs. So use a barbell strategy. Apply to the nearest community college, which will probably be your lowest-cost option. Your Pell might even cover the tuition bill. At the same time, apply to a more expensive school with the type of program you want and within your ability range. It may offer you substantial aid based on need. If your grades and SATs are high, a state flagship college or private college may add enough merit aid to cover the entire freight. But remember, there are other costs: transportation, campus activities, personal expenses. Be sure that you can afford those too.

Middle- and upper-middle-income families should:

1. Find out what they're expected to pay for college and compare it with what you can afford. That will influence the range of schools you look at.

2. Look for schools that give more need-based aid in the form of grants rather than loans.

3. Check out schools that give merit scholarships.

4. Apply to schools in a different part of the country. Choose places where your academic record puts you in the top 25 percent of the applicant pool or the sports teams will consider you an asset. They're the most apt to offer you extra need-based or merit aid.

5. Go to a community college for the first two years.

6. Apply both to state schools and private ones. See which one costs the least, after receiving your aid package. Go to an acceptable school that will minimize your loans.

7. Go to a public college or university in your home state. Or check the schools in neighboring states to see if you can study there without paying a nonresident fee.

8. Apply to competing colleges or universities. Their aid formulas vary. If one school offers you more aid, the other might decide to match it.

9. Choose cooperative education. It gives you job training as well as academic training.

10. Ask the student aid officer to base your grant on your projected income rather than on last year's earnings. This is critical to families whose earnings will drop—for example, parents who lose jobs or adults who give up jobs to return to school.

11. Write a letter explaining any special circumstances that cause money to be especially tight in your family. This won't help with federal or state aid, but it might improve your college grant.

Grants are nice when you can get them. But, bottom line, you won't get through school without a lot of savings and loans.

The Best College Investment Plans

How to Beat the College Inflation Rate

If you play it too safe with your college funds, you'll never raise the money you need.

No one saves enough money to pay for higher education. It's not possible, when you're working to cover your monthly bills and trying to save for retirement too. But you *can* put away enough to avoid feeling suicidal when college draws near.

Here's how the college-money game usually plays out: You save some money toward the cost—one-third would be nice; starting early makes it work. Your child saves money too, from his or her paychecks and holiday gifts. Depending on your income and the school you choose, you might get a government grant and a tuition discount (more higher-income students get discounts than you may think). When enrollment time rolls around, your student gets government student loans. You pay the rest out of current earnings—yours and whatever your child can add.

Don't—please don't—plan on taking loans yourself. You won't want to carry a pile of extra debt into your retirement years. Your kids have plenty of time to repay education loans. You don't.

How to Start Saving in the First Place

Make your savings automatic. The sooner you start, the less college will effectively cost, because you'll be paying part of the bill with money that your money earned. To appreciate the astonishing value of early savings, look at the table on page 215.

When your child is still small, start making regular monthly payments into a college savings plan. Automatic deductions from your bank account are best. That gives college contributions as much importance in your budget as paying the mortgage or rent. If you get annual bonuses, throw part of that money into your education fund. That's also a good place to stash a tax refund. If one parent hasn't been working, he or she might get a part-time job with the net earnings slated for tuition.

The later you start to save, the more important it becomes to set aside money regularly and save every extra check.

Your financial fate also depends on the college you choose. Private schools, in particular, offer large tuition discounts to desirable students, even when they have no official financial need. You can find these schools on the Web and match your child to the places most likely to offer generous grants (page 644).

The more money you can capture from the school, the less you and your child will have to borrow. Still, education won't be free. You have to bring money to the table, not only for your child's future but for your own.

529 Plans: The Single Best Way to Invest

The simple, no-brainer way to save for higher education is through the tax-favored savings plans called 529s (named after the part of that tax code that created them). They're authorized by the federal government and run by every state but Wyoming. You deposit money into a plan, in a lump sum or through regular deposits, and name your child as beneficiary. Over time, the value of your fund will grow. When college rolls around, you tap it to pay for tuition, room and board, and other expenses.

529s provide two types of tax breaks:

1. All the money that you earn on your 529 investments—dividends, interest, and capital gains—passes tax free if you use the account to help pay for the child's higher education. All types of accredited schools count: colleges, community colleges, and trade or career schools. You can even use the money for adult education (page 677).

2. Thirty-four states and the District of Columbia give you a tax deduction or tax credit on your state return, linked to the contribution you make. You generally have to live in the state and buy the state's own plan. At this writing, five states* give you tax breaks even if you invest in another state's plan—

*Arizona, Kansas, Maine, Missouri, Pennsylvania.

an option that's expected to spread. Twelve states* may add a bit of matching money to the accounts of lower-income savers.

If your child decides not to go to college or to drop out, you can switch the account to another member of your family—including you, in case you ever want to return to school or take courses after you retire.† If you withdraw any money for purposes other than higher education, you owe income taxes on the earnings plus a 10 percent penalty.

There are two types of 529 plans: a prepaid tuition plan that I'll call the "prepaid" and a pure savings and investment plan that I'll refer to simply as a 529. Here's what you need to know when you're deciding between them:

The Prepaid Plan

Twelve states have plans open to new investors, usually for state residents only. I love these plans. They're supersimple, conservative, and designed to be certain. You put up money today to buy a fixed amount of tuition in the future. Buy four semesters now, and you'll get four semesters in 2020, no matter how high tuition has risen in the meantime. The Florida plan can also cover room and board.

The amount you invest in the plan is based on current costs (often a little bit higher so that the fund can build a reserve). When your child finally goes to school, the portion of his or her education that you paid in advance will be covered in full. The states limit the number of years you can hold the plan. For example, you might have 10 years after the child reaches 18 to use up the value of the tuition credits or switch them to another member of the family.

Prepaid plans cover any public college or university in your state. If your child goes to a private college or a college out of state, a sum based on the cost of an in-state school (or your payment plus an interest rate) will be transferred to the chosen place. If your child wins a scholarship that covers tuition and fees, most plans let you use the money for other education expenses.

Can you be sure the prepaids will pay when tuition time comes? Seven states‡

---

*Arkansas, Colorado, Kansas, Louisiana, Maine, Michigan, Minnesota, Pennsylvania (in its prepaid plan), North Dakota, Oklahoma, Rhode Island, Utah.

†Besides you, the "family" includes your children and stepchildren, grandchildren, siblings and stepsiblings, parents and grandparents (full or step), nieces and nephews, aunts and uncles, in-laws, family members' spouses (as long as they live with the family member), and first cousins.

‡Florida, Maryland, Massachusetts, Mississippi, Virginia, Washington. Also Ohio, whose plan, at this writing, is closed to new enrollment.

guarantee their plans, so they're totally safe. The other plans can ask their state legislatures for additional funding if their finances fall short. I'm confident that you won't lose money in a prepaid. Even if a state ends its prepaid plan or closes it to new investors, as several have, current investors will get full value for the money they've contributed so far. (The states that closed their plans did so because they turned out to be too good a deal for investors! Tuition went up at rates far higher than expected, while the stock market went down.)

Who should choose a prepaid plan? Buy if you want to feel that your child's future college tuition is guaranteed, no matter what happens to your job, your personal income, or the stock market. You're not looking for a growth investment with its scary ups and downs. You want certainty. You should also be reasonably sure that you'll continue to live in the state and that your child will attend a public college there.* Depending on the plan, either the owner or the beneficiary (or both) has to be a state resident. To see if your state has a plan, go to the Web site Savingforcollege.com (www.savingforcollege.com).

Important! If you buy, pay in lump sums (even serial lump sums) rather than sign up for an installment plan. Installments carry hidden interest rates in the 6 percent to 9 percent range, which will probably exceed the increase in future tuition costs. You gain nothing for your money.

The private college prepaid plan. More than 270 private colleges and universities belong to this plan, called the Independent 529. Credits for future tuition payments are on sale at slightly discounted rates. You can use them at any participating school. For details and a list of the schools, go to www .independent529plan.org or call 888-718-7878. You get no state tax deductions for contributions to this private plan. But all your investment gains pass free of federal tax.

The 529 Savings and Investment Plan

Here you get no guarantees. Instead you put your money into one or more of the plan's investment pools (mostly mutual funds). Over time, its value grows (you hope). You use the proceeds, tax free, for any of the direct expenses of higher education: tuition, fees, books, room and board, and any equipment required by the school. All accredited schools in the United States are eligible, as well as schools in some countries abroad, so you're not forced to stay in your home state. You can join another state's plan if you don't like your own.

---

*Alabama alone takes out-of-staters whose children expect to go to an Alabama school.

There's no limit to the amount of time the money can stay in the 529 so long as there's a named beneficiary who's a family member. Most states put no age limits on the beneficiary, either. If your child drops out of school, you can leave the money in his or her name, in hope of a change of heart. Or switch the account to someone else in the family, including one of your grandchildren. You can divide the account among several grandchildren. Even a newborn is a legal beneficiary.

Investment 529s aren't as cut and dried as the prepaid plans. You have a few choices to make, but they aren't complicated.

■ *Which state's plan should you use?* Look first at your own state's 529. It could be the best if its fees are low (page 675) and especially if it offers state tax breaks. Some states let you deduct a portion of your investment on your state tax return. A few even make a small cash contribution to your account if you're a lower-income saver. If the plan's expenses are high, however, or you get no state tax breaks, jump to a state with low fees and solid investment choices.

■ *How should you purchase the plan?* Buy your 529 directly from the state. That's called a *direct-sold plan.* It's free! You just fill in a form, pick your investments, and mail a check. States have information lines to call if you need help.

States also offer plans through stockbrokers and financial planners, called *adviser-sold plans.* Don't buy them. (I'm tearing my hair here!) Salespeople charge commissions (typically 5.75 percent) for every contribution you make to the 529, and the states charge higher administration fees because it's more expensive to handle investment accounts through brokers than to deal with you directly. Adding insult to injury, adviser-sold mutual funds are more expensive (and no better—maybe worse) than the funds sold directly through the state. After paying those extra costs, you almost never (say it: *never!*) save more in taxes than you pay in expenses.

Both direct-sold and broker-sold funds are listed on your state's 529 Web page. When pricing plans, be sure you're looking at the right one.

Beware this cynical broker ploy: You're buying a plan in, say, Ohio, which lets you deduct up to $2,000 in contributions on your state tax return. "Ah," says the broker, "Ohio's plan is terrible. It's got awful investment choices. I'm going to give you Maine's superterrific plan instead." Wow—are you ever grateful for that information! It's so good to hire brokers who have expertise! So you buy Maine. Needless to say, your broker earns a higher commission by selling that particular plan, and you lose your state's tax break. In several states, 80 to 90 percent of the investors come from out of state—not because those are better plans but because the brokers earn more by selling them. Never go out of state for a 529 without checking your state's tax deduction and comparing the cost of the home-state plan with the one that the broker suggests. (Also, check the low-cost plans I suggest below.)

■ *Should you buy through payroll deduction?* At a growing number of companies, you can ask that money be taken from your paycheck and invested automatically in a 529. I love payroll deductions but not necessarily this one. The plan the company chooses might not be based in your state, so you'll lose any state tax deduction available. If it is in your state, it's probably a broker-sold plan with higher 529 expenses. Compare the company's offer with what you can get directly from your state. If the state's plan is cheaper, set up your automated payments through your bank rather than through payroll deduction.

■ *Who can contribute to the plan?* Any warm body—grandparents, other relatives, friends, your children themselves, Santa Claus. Most states let them contribute to the plan directly. In some, they have to give the parents the money and let the parents deposit it. Wisconsin gives tax breaks to certain family members who contribute to your 529. Virginia lets you take a tax break for money contributed by other people. There's paperwork—you have to fill in a form, including the child's account number, and mail it with your check.

■ *How much can you contribute?* As much as you want up to $350,000 or more per child, depending on the state. Not that you intend to save that much by next Tuesday morning. You can start with as little as $15 or so per month. My point is that 529s aren't really limited, as so many other tax-favored savings plans are. With investment gains, your account could grow even larger than $350,000—enough for a lifetime of degrees for a large family. There's also no limit to the number of 529s that can be established for a single child. When there's more than one 529 account, however, you'll have to coordinate among yourselves, so you're not all paying the same bills. Double payments would make half of that money taxable.

There's a special tax angle here for wealthy contributors. You get a break on the federal gift tax when the money goes into a 529. In general, you can give $13,000 a year (in 2009) to any recipient, gift-tax free—double that for a married couple. If you're giving to a 529, however, you can make up to five years' worth of gifts in advance. That's $65,000 or up to $130,000, all at once. After that, you can't give the recipient any tax-free money until five years have passed. If you die within five years, some of that money returns to your estate. If you last longer, it's out of your estate and passes untaxed. Surprisingly, the gift doesn't have to be permanent. You can take it back, on payment of taxes and the 10 percent penalty on any earnings.

Don't put too much money into 529s. You might discover that you can't use it all, due to various other tax rules (page 678).

- *Who should own the 529?* Normally, a parent owns it. Register it in your name. You can then decide what to invest in, how much money to distribute, and who the beneficiary will be. On the federal aid application, it makes no difference whether the parent or child owns the 529. But you're apt to get more aid from the schools themselves if the account is in your name. Note that 529s normally don't accept joint owners; they want only one person in charge. If a grandparent is contributing money, consider holding the 529 in the grandparent's name (page 673).

- *Will the 529 reduce your college aid?* For some families, no. If your income is modest, no assets are counted, including 529s. All families get an asset allowance that's not counted, either. If your countable assets exceed those amounts, 5.64 percent of your 529 will be considered when figuring your child's federal aid. Translating that into dollars and cents, a 529 worth $10,000 will reduce your aid package by $564. The colleges may or may not follow the federal formula when dispensing their own aid. Most states don't count the 529 at all when awarding state grants. Remember that most "aid" comes in the form of loans. Anyone with savings, especially tax-free savings, will be a leg up.

- *When should you start saving?* As soon as your child gets a Social Security number. Keep saving right up to the last minute. In most states, you can contribute to a 529 when your child is 17, grab the state tax deduction, and immediately take out the money for tuition. Not bad.

- *What if your student gets scholarships and doesn't need the 529?* You can remove an amount equal to the scholarships from the 529, paying taxes on the earnings but no penalty. And, of course, you always can keep the account, naming a new beneficiary.

- *What if you move?* You can transfer your 529 money to another state's plan or leave it alone and open a second plan in your new state. A few states tax any earnings you transfer from your old plan into a new one—check it out before you switch.

- *What if your 529 shuts down?* Two states, Wyoming and Tennessee,* have shuttered their 529s because they didn't attract enough money to hold down costs. Other small plans might do the same. You can roll the money tax free into another state's 529. Wyoming currently partners with Colorado. If you don't do a rollover, you'll be cashed out—owing taxes and penalties on your gains.

- *Can you spend your way to college sayings?* A company called Upromise (www .upromise.com) offers a credit card with a college savings twist. You earn cash rebates worth up to 1 percent of the charges you put on the card (with a few

---

*Tennessee still has a prepaid plan.

merchants offering more). The rebates go into a cash account, from which they can be swept into a 529. At this writing, Upromise works with 18 plans—5 of them sold nationally, plus 13 state plans. The rebates are small, in dollar terms. They're not worth opening a separate 529 to get. But if the plan works with the 529 you have already, why not?

Let's Hear It for Grandparents!

If you're a grandparent who wants to help your grandchildren get an education, a 529 is a terrific choice. Register the plan in your own name with the grandchild as beneficiary. Money in grandparent 529s isn't counted on federal college aid forms, so it won't reduce whatever federal and state aid you might receive. Many private schools, however, do inquire and will count it as a resource.

If you choose a plan in your state, you'll get the state income tax deduction, if any. The money you give to the plan is out of your estate, but you can reclaim it if you run into unexpected expenses. By contrast, if you give the grandchild money through the Uniform Transfers to Minors Act, you can't get it back. If the parents live in a state that offers no tax deduction, they might want to put their own contributions into a plan that the grandparent set up. That keeps their money out of the federal college aid formula too.

When you create the 529, name someone to succeed you as owner if you die—the parent, say, or a trust if the account is large. That way, the money will remain tax protected for college expenses. If you have several grandchildren, set up a separate 529 for each.

Note that you can use your state's investment 529 even though your grandchild doesn't live in the state or plan to go to college there. Residency rules apply, however, if you want to start a prepaid plan.

There are other ways a grandparent can help.

For example, you can pay any amount at all for higher education, with no gift tax consequences, as long as the money goes directly to the school and is used to help cover tuition and fees. Some schools, however, will use a grandparent gift to reduce the student's package of college aid.

In that case, consider giving the money to the parent and letting the parent pay the bill. The parent doesn't have to mention it on the college aid form. You can make a tax-free gift of as much as $13,000 a year at this writing, or $26,000 if you're married. Alternatively, let your grandchild take deferred-payment student loans. After the last student aid application has been filed, start making gifts to help the grandchild pay off the loans. (You might leave your grandchild loan repayment funds in your will, in case you die.)

Don't give the money to the child, directly or through the Uniform Transfers to Minors Act. The schools assess 20 percent of a child's assets to help pay the bill, which will reduce his or her college aid.

Gifts made to grandchildren, including to a 529, can affect your Medicaid eligibility. If you enter a nursing home and have to turn to the government program for money, the authorities will look at your gifts over the previous 60 months. Gifts delay the date that you can apply for aid (page 470).

Fees, Fees, Fees—How Not to Get Rooked

Fees have been coming down because of competition among the states. Residents of the higher-fee states are jumping to better plans. To find all the costs, go to Savingforcollege.com. The range of fees is listed for every state's plans, both the direct-sold and the adviser-sold. You can double-check fees in the formal plan documents, available on each plan's Web site. Here's what to look for:

1. Fees charged by the state for running the program, expressed as a percentage of the value of your account. Look for a plan that costs 0.3 percent a year or less. Fees of 0.5 percent and up are just too high.

2. Fees charged by the managers who run the mutual funds in the 529s. The lowest-cost funds come from Vanguard, and they're only in the plans that you buy directly from the state. You might pay as little as 0.025 percent a year. By contrast, adviser-sold funds could cost 1 percent or more. That's a huge difference, compounded over time. Even worse, if you're paying 1 percent, the fee probably exceeds what you're saving in tax. In other words, you're losing money on the deal! The lower your tax bracket, the harder it is to break even on a high-cost 529.

3. Flat-dollar fees, charged by some of the states, for enrollment or to maintain your account. These fees take the largest bite out of small investments. States might waive them for state residents, large accounts, accounts receiving automatic contributions, or accounts invested in fixed-income funds.

4. Bundled fees. A few states quote you a single price, which covers both their own fees and the fees for money management. These tend to be plans with lower (although not the lowest) costs—typically, less than 0.7 percent a year.

Why Only a Low-Fee Plan Makes Sense

This is really important: you *must* find a low-fee plan with low-cost investment funds. Otherwise you're throwing away most of the value of the 529. A fee might look small in percentage terms compared with the return you expect from the plan's stock-owning mutual funds. But in dollar terms, it could easily exceed the amount of money you're saving in tax (see the proof on page 675). In the plan's safer, low-yield investments—the kind you use in the years just before your

How You Can Pay More for a 529 than the Taxes You Save

Assume that you have $5,000 in your 529 account, invested in bonds and earning interest at 5 percent. You make $250 for the year and save $62.50 in tax in the 25 percent bracket.

In a high-cost 529, your annual fees might come to 1.5 percent in state program fees and money management expenses. That means you pay $75. Your expenses are exceeding your tax savings by $12.50. Put another way, you're giving $12.50 to middlemen rather than keeping it for college tuition.

In a low-cost 529, you might pay just 0.3 percent. That's a mere $15 for the year. In this case, you'll be earning $47.50 in tax savings, net of costs. You have that much extra money invested for your child's future.

The comparisons look even worse if the $250 you earned came from a capital gain, taxable at 15 percent. The plan will save you $37.50 in tax. In the high-cost 529, your expenses exceed your tax savings by $37.50, so you're behind. In the low-cost 529, your savings exceed your expenses by $22.50.

In either case, your $250 of earnings accumulate tax deferred, so you're better off with a 529 than with a taxable mutual fund. But the low-cost plan is the better buy, by far.

child starts school—the fee in high-cost 529s could even exceed the interest you earn. Some of these states are profiteering. They should be ashamed.

Which states give savers the very best deal? At this writing, I have four favorites, and they all accept out-of-state investors. The cost quotes below combine each state's program fees with the management fees for the plan's lowest-cost direct-sold funds:

- *Ohio's CollegeAdvantage 529 savings plan,* for as little as 0.19 percent per year (www.collegeadvantage.com, 800-233-6734).
- *Illinois's Bright Start college savings program (Direct Sold),* for as little as 0.2 percent per year plus $10 for portfolios invested in index funds (www.brightstartsavings.com, 877-432-7444).
- *Utah's Educational Savings Plan,* for as little as 0.22 percent, plus $4 for each $1,000 invested up to an annual maximum of $15, waived for state residents (www.uesp.org, 800-418-2551).
- *Virginia's Education Savings Trust,* for as little as 0.31 percent, plus a onetime $25 fee (www.virginia529.com, 888-567-0540).

In the next group, I'd put the states that bundle their fees. The list, at this writing: California, Iowa, Michigan, Minnesota, Missouri, and New York. Oregon doesn't bundle its fees, but it's lower cost too. Louisiana's excellent plan is open only to its own state residents.

Have you noticed the difference between the direct-sold plans and adviser-sold plans? Look at the fees. Look at the mutual fund expenses. You're paying too much for advice.

Should you change the plan you have? Sure. Why not? If you've just discovered that you accidentally bought an expensive plan, and if your state tax benefits don't save it, there's no reason to stay. Roll your money into the 529 plan of another state. The new plan will tell you how to proceed. You have 60 days to receive the check from your old plan and deposit it into the new plan, in order to keep your tax breaks. Your old state may or may not charge a small exit fee. Warning: if you leave the plan, a few states charge you the equivalent of the state tax savings you've received. That's a dirty trick. If it's small enough, pay it and leave. If it's large, you're stuck.

How Should You Invest the Money You're Putting into a 529?

The plans offer several options, including an all-stock fund, a fixed-income fund, a mixed stock-and-bond fund, and several age-related choices. A few provide insured certificates of deposit.

For a smart, one-step, sleep-tight decision, choose an age-related fund. Its investments change depending on how old your child is. When the child is young, the fund will lean toward stocks for growth. As your child grows older, it will lean toward safer, fixed-income investments, so that you're sure to have cash when college expenses start. It happens automatically. You never have to worry about it.

Some age-related programs have gotten pretty fancy, letting you choose among three or more investment portfolios: aggressive, moderate, or conservative. The aggressive fund will stay substantially in stocks, even when your child approaches freshman year. That's okay for high-income people. If their stocks tank in the year the tuition is due, they can write the check out of other savings they have. But aggressive strategies are risky for people who'll definitely need their 529 plan to pay the bills. What will you do if the market drops and doesn't recover over the next four years? For true security, choose an age-based fund that will be mostly in cash and other fixed-income investments when your child turns 17.

If you don't want an age-related fund, you'll have to manage your own 529 account. You have several choices, including aggressive growth funds that look good on paper but will kill you if the market turns. (I remember people buying high-tech funds in Arizona's 529 just before the bubble burst.) You have to keep monitoring these funds. When your child is 15, you'll want a different mix of investments than those you chose when the child was 8 (page 682). Most plans let you transfer money from one mutual fund to another once a year.

A broker might steer you away from an age-related fund by claiming that he or she can pick investments that will earn higher returns. On that, you have no guarantee—but I do guarantee that you'll wind up with funds that charge higher fees. Note that your broker normally doesn't earn a new commission when you change investments in a plan. That probably means that he or she will lose interest in advising you as your child approaches the college years.

Bottom line: make college investing easy for yourself by choosing a prudent age-related fund. It provides timely money management automatically, with lower fees, and with cash on hand when your child goes to school. That's exactly the kind of help busy people need.

Making Withdrawals from Your 529

You fill out a form, telling the plan how much money you want. The plan will send it to you, to the school, or to the student, whichever you want. At the end of the year, ask the school for a form detailing that year's "qualified" education expenses (tuition and fees; also, room and board, for students attending school at least half time). Add the cost of required books, equipment, and supplies. Together, they represent your total expenses for the calendar year. In January, your 529 plan will send you IRS Form 1099Q, noting the amount of money you withdrew. If you took more from the plan than the amount of your qualified expenses, you owe taxes on those earnings (each withdrawal is partly principal and partly earnings). Hand over the whole mess to a tax preparer. If you really want to know more, get IRS Publication 970 and weep.

529s for Grown-ups

Your kids aren't the only ones eligible for a 529. You can use it yourself for your own future education. Maybe you're planning to go back to school when the children are older. Maybe you're looking forward to adult education classes after you retire. Maybe your child dropped out of college; you can name yourself beneficiary and use that money to train for a new career. No matter who in your family is going to school these days, you can use tax-free dollars to pay.

Where to Get More Information on 529s

The indispensable source is Savingforcollege.com. It summarizes all the plans, rates them for attractiveness, keeps up with the changes in each state, floods you with information, and offers useful tips. The College Savings Plans Network (www.collegesavings.org), run by state officials, also helps you compare one state's plan with another. It too has good information. You can screen plans for low asset-based fees and enrollment fees, but not other flat-dollar fees.

More Than You Want to Know About 529s and Taxes*

Here's a surprising fact: you might not be able to use all the money in your 529! That's because of the way the tax rules work.

The government hands out tax breaks like cupcakes to people paying for higher education. Tax-exempt savings in 529s are only the start. You also get tax deductions or credits for the tuition and fees you pay. But you can't collect one tax break on top of another. There's only one cupcake per customer. You're not allowed to use your prepaid plan or 529 to cover college expenses that have already been used to claim another tax deduction or credit.

That sounds simple, right? But what's simple to say isn't simple to figure out.

There are four different tax breaks parents might claim on their tax returns. Each of them "uses up" a different amount of college tuition. Your 529 savings can be spent only on expenses that haven't already been "used." Here's a summary of how these tax breaks work, using numbers for 2010. Check the Web for numbers in later years.

1. The Hope tax credit—good for the first four years that your child is in school at least half-time. If you meet the income test (page 628), you can lower your taxes by 100 percent of the first $2,000 you spend on the child's tuition and 25 percent of the second $2,000. The total credit comes to $2,500 per child but, to get it, you've "used up" $4,000 in college expenses. Anyone who takes the Hope credit on his or her tax return can use a 529, tax free, to cover only the expenses higher than $4,000. That first $4,000 has to be paid from other funds.

2. The Lifetime Learning tax credit—good during any year of higher education, even for single courses. As long as you meet the income test, you can deduct 20 percent of as much as $10,000 spent on tuition expenses (that's the total for everyone in your family who's studying that year). The credit itself comes to a maximum of $2,000, but it "uses up" $10,000 in tuition. If you take the maximum Lifetime Learning credit, you can use your 529, tax free, only for

---

*Don't bother reading this if your kids are still young. It's only for parents dealing with withdrawals now.

education expenses higher than $10,000. That first $10,000 has to be paid from other funds.

3. The deduction for tuition and fees—good for any year, even for students taking just one course. It's worth up to $2,000 or $4,000 in tuition costs, depending on your income. You get this write-off even if you take the standard deduction (to claim it, file Form 1040, not the shorter 1040A or 1040EZ). Again, there's just one cupcake per customer. The tuition deduction applies only to expenses not already paid by a 529 plan, a Coverdell Education Savings Account, or the tax-free interest from a U.S. Savings Bond. If you qualify for both the tuition deduction and the Hope or Lifetime credits, you have to choose between them. For undergraduates, the Hope generally works best.

4. The deduction for interest paid on student or parent loans—you can write off up to $2,500 in interest payments against your income. It applies to both government-backed loans and loans from private lending institutions for qualified educational expenses. You can't deduct interest on loans from relatives, a related entity, or a qualified employer plan. The students have to be independent and pay the loan themselves. They can't get the write-off if they're taken as dependents on their parents' return.

Here's an example of how these rules work: say that, after adjusting for any grants, fellowships, and tuition discounts, your school expects you to pay $15,000 cash. If you take the Hope credit, you've used up $4,000 of expenses that year. You can take only $11,000 from your 529 tax free. The rest of the money has to come from other sources. If you take the Lifetime Learning credit, you'll use up $10,000 in expenses. In that case, you can pay the school only $5,000 from your 529 tax free. If you pay any more, you'll owe taxes on it (the 10 percent penalty is waived).

Be careful of how much you take from the 529 in each *calendar year*. Take your tax-free limit in August for the fall semester and wait until January to take the money for the second semester. If you take it in December, the withdrawal will put you over the limit for the year, forcing you to pay a tax. Always take the January money after January 1.

If you don't empty the 529 when your child is an undergraduate, you can keep it for graduate school. It will come in handy for kids who want to be doctors or lawyers or get an MBA. In the sciences and liberal arts, however, they're apt to get fellowships that cover a substantial amount of the cost—again, reducing the amount of money you'll need from a 529. If you find that you've oversaved in a 529, name a new beneficiary for the remaining funds. You can even name yourself, in case you might want to take courses in the future.

For details on the tax rules, go to www.irs.gov and search for the government's explanatory guide, Publication 970, *Tax Benefits for Education.* The one-cupcake rules apply to Coverdell Education Savings Accounts and qualified U.S. Savings Bonds too. Whew.

Other Tax-Favored College Savings Plans

Other college savings plans offer tax breaks too, but to my mind, none is as good as a low-cost—emphasize *low-cost*—529. If you have any of these plans already, you can switch the money into a 529. Here are your options and why I generally rate them second best. (Okay, they're still best for some uses, which I note.)

A Coverdell Education Savings Account

A Coverdell works like a 529. You invest your money in mutual funds and the earnings grow tax free if they're used for education. Coverdells are convenient. You can usually open them at your bank. Contributions are limited to $2,000* a year for each child up to his or her 18th birthday (longer if the child has special needs). You get no state tax break on the money you put in, and higher-income people are excluded.† Any balance left in a Coverdell has to be used before the beneficiary reaches 30, although you can name a family member as a new beneficiary. If there's money left in the account or you spend it on anything other than education, you owe taxes on the earnings plus a 10 percent penalty.

If you started saving with a Coverdell, you can switch some or all of the money into a 529 for the same beneficiary, tax free.

You can use Coverdell money in a year you take the Hope or Lifetime Learning tax credits but, as with 529s, you can use it only for expenses not already covered by the credits (page 675).

The pluses: Coverdells are simple for savers who will never put away more than $2,000 a year. You can also use them for the expenses of private school,

---

*This is scheduled to drop to $500 in 2011 unless Congress changes the law. Check the Web for the latest.
†To set up a full Coverdell, your adjusted gross income must be $95,000 or less for singles and $190,000 or less for couples filing jointly. Contribution amounts phase out at $110,000 for singles and $220,000 for couples.

kindergarten through 12th grade, or equipment needed for public school, such as a laptop computer.* A 529, by contrast, is good only for higher education.

United States Savings Bonds

This tax break is attached to Series EE bonds issued since January 1990 and all Series I bonds. You can use the earnings, tax free, toward the cost of tuition and fees (but not books, room, board, and other expenses) for yourself, your spouse, or a dependent. There are two requirements. You have to have been at least 24 years old when you made the purchase. And your income has to fall within certain limits† in the year you cash in the bonds and pay tuition. If you think that your income will exceed those limits in the future, you have an out: you can cash in the bonds tax free if—in that same year—you (1) meet the income requirements and (2) contribute an equal amount to a prepaid tuition plan or a 529 savings plan for yourself, your spouse, or a dependent.

You have to buy the bonds in your own name or jointly with your spouse. They can't be owned or co-owned by the child, although the child can be the beneficiary. You can even buy them for your own education, in which case they have to be registered in your single name. You can't use these bonds for a grandchild's education unless the grandchild is a dependent.

Saving bonds are better buys than bank certificates of deposit because of their tax exemptions. They make sense for savers who can't stomach any risk at all, even though they probably won't keep up with the rise in college costs. (A better, college-inflation-protected choice is a prepaid tuition plan if your state has one and your child will go to an in-state school.)

Two warnings: when you cash in the bonds for college, they count toward your personal income for the year. That might put you over the income ceiling, which reduces your tax break. Also, you can't use earnings tax free to pay for expenses covered by other tax breaks (page 678).

If you plan to use savings bonds for college, be sure that you can hold them at least five years. Your interest rate is docked if you cash them in earlier. Buy them in smaller and midsize denominations so you won't have to redeem more than you need to cover tuition and fees (anything extra is taxable). And keep good records. You'll need the name of the school, the amount of tuition and fees, the date you paid, and exactly which bonds you used—issue dates, date

---

*This provision is scheduled to end at the start of 2011 unless Congress extends it.
†In 2009 the tax breaks are phased out for single people with adjusted gross incomes between $69,950 and $84,950 and couples between $104,900 and $134,900. These limits rise with the inflation rate.

redeemed, face values, proceeds, and serial numbers. To get your tax break, file IRS Form 8815. Form 8818 is helpful for keeping track of your redemptions.

The plus: If you don't use the bonds for higher education, you still get the earnings free of state and local tax (although you still owe a federal tax). For more on savings bonds, see page 230 and www.savingsbonds.gov.

An Individual Retirement Account

Your IRA is for retirement money. Normally, you owe income taxes plus a 10 percent penalty on withdrawals prior to age 59½. The penalty (not the tax) is waived if you use the money to pay for higher education. If you have a Roth IRA, you can withdraw your own contribution tax free at any time (page 1048). IRAs are on this list only because of that small college tax break. Don't use them—save the money for your later years.

The plus: There are no pluses to IRAs for college savers.

Managing College Money Yourself

As a practical matter, I don't know why you'd want to do this. You get no tax breaks for your efforts, and it's hard to imagine that amateurs will outperform professional money managers. You avoid the annual 529 fees, but that may not make up for the tax exemptions you lose. If you want to try it, however, you should follow the blueprint laid down by age-related 529 plans:

For Children Through Age 12

Choose a mix of U.S. and international stock-owning mutual funds plus a small percentage of bond funds for ballast. Invest faithfully, month after month, no matter where the stock market goes. Stocks normally beat other financial investments over 10-year time frames.

For Children 13 Through 14

Leave prior stock investments alone but deposit new savings into safe havens such as intermediate-term bond funds and longer-term certificates of deposit. By age 14, 25 percent of your college pot should be earning interest in secure investments. That's for your child's freshman year. Money you'll need within five years* should never be invested in stocks. Stocks may beat everything in the long run, but in the short run, they can kill you.

---

*Why did I pick five years? In hope that's a reasonable number that you might accept. I looked at how long it took investors to recover their money after every U.S. bear market since World

For Children 15 and Up

New investments should continue to go into something secure. Start switching some of the money currently in stock funds into bond funds. By age 16, half the money should be in intermediate-term bond funds.* By age 17, three-quarters should be secure, with the freshman-year money in bank deposits or money market funds. At 18, it should all be in bonds and cash. Your timing on these changes may vary because you won't want to sell stocks if the market is down. But over the critical four years before tuition is due, move your money gradually out of harm's way.

What If You Don't Start Saving Until Your Child Is a Teenager?

You've missed the safest part of your personal stock market curve. To buy stocks now is too great a risk. Choose bond mutual funds instead.

Parents who start saving very late and won't qualify for much college aid might have to borrow so much money for college that they can't afford to retire when they planned. Ditto for divorced men who remarry and start second families and women who have children in their late 30s or early 40s. Most likely, your children will have to shoulder much of the college cost.

Should You Sell Your Stocks When Your Child Is 16, Even If They're Doing Great?

Say that you have a whiz of a mutual fund that did 15 percent last year. Why not leave the money there, use PLUS loans for college, defer the loan payments until your child is out of school, then repay the whole amount out of the profits your zippy fund is going to make?

Sounds like a great idea if (1) you're willing to gamble that your stocks will go

---

War II. The average was 2 years, 10 months, with dividends reinvested. Prior to the 2000 stock market bubble, the longest was 3 years, 6 months (in 1972). After the 2000 bubble burst, it took 6 years, 9 months, for investors to get their money back, and the market immediately turned down again. Based on this most recent experience, you'd want to invest in stocks for children through age 11, and then start moving all your money into bonds, although that may be carrying caution too far.
*Since World War II, it has taken intermediate-term bond investors an average of 1.5 years to break even after a market decline of 5 percent or more, with bond interest reinvested. The worst bond market (the one starting in 1958) lasted about 2 years. So you're probably okay if you keep your bond funds until your child is 16. Then move the freshman-year money into short-term bond funds, money market funds, or bank accounts. Move out the sophomore-year money at 17, the junior-year money at 18, and the senior-year money at 19.

up by enough to cover the cost of the loan and give you a profit too; (2) you can borrow enough for college; and (3) you can afford the loan repayments if your mutual fund disappoints. On the whole, this is a gamble that only higher-income people can afford to make.

How to Pay for College and Save for Retirement at the Same Time

Ideally, you fund your retirement plan to the max and then start a separate college savings plan. You do it by holding your personal spending down. That's not so easy, however, for middle-income families. I've spoken with too many parents who barely save for retirement so that they can fund a modest 529 for their kids. They worry all the time that their kids' accounts aren't getting more.

I admire their hearts and their dedication to the children. But stinting on retirement saving doesn't do anyone any favors. If you don't have enough to live on, your kids will have to support you in your old age. Think of the number of people who complain about being in the "sandwich" generation, taking care of children and parents too. Those will be your children if you have to depend on them for food and rent.

Always save for retirement first. Fund a retirement plan to the max. If there's not enough left over for a college fund, here's your strategy:

1. Tell your kids to set their sights on a school of modest cost. It could be a state school or a private school that will give them a big tuition discount. Either way, the decision will depend on the finances, not on the beauty of a campus or where their friends are heading. Kids are practical. By telling them early, you're saving them from disappointment later.

2. Own a house. This didn't help families who lost their home equity in the housing bust. But new buyers or long-time owners, who managed their mortgages prudently, still have home equity to work with. Build additional equity by making larger mortgage payments every month. Those payments are earning a risk-free return equal to your mortgage interest rate. Having home equity gives you future tax-deductible borrowing power.

3. Don't open a home equity line of credit. It will tempt you to borrow. If you already have one, clean it up. Clean up your credit card bills too.

4. Set up a tax-deferred retirement savings plan (chapter 29). Sock every penny into it you can. Retirement plans are wonderful ways to save because your contributions are pretax. In company plans, your employer often matches part of your contribution. That's free money, not to be missed! What's more, the accumulated value of retirement plans isn't counted as personal wealth on the federal financial aid application, which might help your child qualify for a larger grant.

5. When your child goes to college, apply for financial aid. The child should take (and expect to repay) the maximum federal student loan (but stay away from private loans—page 650). He or she should also be working and building a savings account for spending money or food outside the college's meal plan.

6. Cut back your spending and contribute as much toward tuition as you can from your current earnings. Prepare for this by avoiding consumer debt.

7. If you need more money, borrow what you must but choose a school that doesn't require you to borrow a lot. Draw on your home equity line of credit. The interest is fully deductible on loans up to $100,000 (not that you would dream of borrowing that much). You can also take a federal PLUS loan for parents (page 649). Start repaying the PLUS loan monthly instead of letting it accumulate while your child is in school. You might get interest deductions on a PLUS loan too.

8. Keep contributing to your retirement plan for the employer match (if any) and the tax-deferred growth. If you can't contribute and pay the college bills, too, reduce your retirement contribution (but not below the amount you need to collect the full employer match). Don't make any withdrawals from your retirement plan. Leave that account alone to grow.

9. When your children are through college, use the income that formerly went for tuition to pay off your PLUS or home equity loans. As soon as possible, resume putting the maximum contribution into your retirement plan.

10. Result: You'll have funded your retirement plan to the max, all during your earlier working life. It will continue to grow while your children are in school, even if you lowered your contributions. You'll have a college debt to repay—but not too much, as long as you made a wise choice of school.

What Can Go Wrong with This Plan?

You might have a financial accident, like a foreclosure, which wipes out home equity and prevents you from getting a PLUS loan. Or you might be forced to retire early and couldn't afford to take on college debt.

In either case, it wouldn't have helped to reduce your retirement savings in order to fund a 529 college savings plan. True, you'd have a little money set aside specifically for tuition. That would be offset by the fact that you lost your salary and couldn't write checks to help cover the remaining costs. Fortunately, colleges give more aid to students whose parents have retired or suffer a financial setback. Even the most loving parent can't take care of everything.

Should You Put College Investments into Your Child's Name?

No. Giving assets to children used to create a tax break for higher-income families, but this loophole was all but shut down in 2008. Dependent children—defined as kids under 19 or full-time students under 24—can't be used as tax shelters anymore. Here are the current rules:

Children's wages are taxed in their own bracket. Unearned income—interest, dividends, and capital gains from assets held in the children's names—is treated differently. A certain amount of unearned income* escapes taxes or is taxed in the child's lowest bracket. The rest is taxed in the parent's bracket. This includes income from custodial accounts and accounts held in trust under the Uniform Transfers (or Gifts) to Minors Act.

If you have these kinds of accounts, consider shifting that money into a 529 college investment plan. You'll have to open a custodial 529, but the plans know how to do that. Also, you'll have to sell the investments, which may give rise to capital gains taxes. The plans accept only cash.

If Not Stocks, What?

Some parents worry about buying stocks for young children's college accounts. They feel safer with bonds. If you go that route, here's what you can expect:

1. Bond mutual funds: Not as risky as stocks but not totally safe either. You'll make some money when interest rates fall but take some losses when interest rates rise. (For more on bonds, see chapter 25.) In a 529, your return might keep up with the rising cost of college. Outside a 529, it probably won't, because of the taxes you'll owe on the interest every year. But it might not miss by much. If you buy bond funds, sell them two years before you're going to need the money and put the proceeds in the bank or a money market fund. You don't want to risk market losses during that final stretch.

2. Individual bonds—taxable or tax free—maturing around the time that college starts. Your principal is safe, but your interest, after tax, will probably not keep up with the rise in college costs. You'll receive semiannual interest pay-

---

*Adjusted annually for inflation.

ments, which you'll have to reinvest at lower rates. Don't buy bonds that you'll have to sell before maturity. You might lose money on the sale.

3. Zero-coupon bonds—maturing around the time that college starts. You effectively reinvest the interest at the bond's original rate (for more on zeros, see page 945). You'll need a stockbroker to buy individual zeros. Alternatively, consider American Century's no-load Target Maturities funds—taxable zero-coupon mutual funds invested primarily in zero Treasury bonds. At this writing, there are funds maturing in 2015, 2020, and 2025—good, secure buys if they happen to coincide with your child's college years. (Visit www.americancentury.com or call 800-321-2021.) Minimum initial investment: $2,500 ($2,000 for a Coverdell Education Savings Account). Federal taxes are owed on Treasury bond interest, but not state and local taxes.

4. Real estate: Some families invest in a one- or two-family home and rent it out as a way of building savings for college. In the year before the child matriculates, they plan to sell the house, put the profits in the bank, and draw on the money as tuition bills come due. Well . . . that worked for a while. Then, splat. Home values fell. Profits (and college savings) evaporated.

But you can't keep real estate lovers down. Parents are wondering whether that strategy could work today, now that homes are cheap. Answer: unlikely. Many rental houses are mediocre deals (page 986). The rent is too low to cover all your expenses, so it may cost you money to run the property every year. To make up those losses and earn a profit large enough to pay tuition, you'll need substantial appreciation after tax. I wouldn't take that bet.

Financial planners love to talk about buying a house in the town where your child goes to school, renting rooms to students to cover part of the mortgage, and paying the child a deductible salary to manage the building. That's neat on paper, but not too many of us have junior Donald Trumps sprawled on our living room floors. Forget it.

5. Bank certificates of deposit—absolutely safe, but no way to grow your money. Savings bonds are a better choice.

How About Life Insurance?

Don't Buy It If Your Primary Goal Is Saving Money for College

The pitch sounds convincing: "Buy a universal life policy as a college investment. The cash in the policy builds up tax deferred. At college time, you can withdraw, tax free, a sum equal to the premiums you paid. Premium payments are a disciplined way of building savings, and there's money for college if you die."

But how large a pot of savings do you build? After you pay the insurance premium and the sales commission, there's not much left for your cash account, especially in the early years (page 356). Agent-sold insurance policies typically don't yield returns as high as those you'd get on bonds until 15 or 20 years have passed. If cash for college is your prime interest, you'll do better with *any* other investment.

That's for straight universal life. What about variable universal life whose cash values can be invested in stocks? For college savings, that's even worse. Variable policies carry higher internal charges. To overcome them, you need high returns on stock investments over a long period of time—15 years or more. But college savers shouldn't stay in stocks that long. To avoid the risk of a market crash shortly before tuition is due, you'll need to switch your insurance investments out of stocks and into bonds and money market funds. Bad news: the low yields on those investments will be devoured by your policy's high costs.

What If You Need More Life Insurance as Well as College Savings?

Buy cheap term insurance and devote the rest of your money to mutual funds in 529 plans. Even term insurance plus savings bonds would be better than most life insurance savings, especially if the bond interest is tax exempt.

What If You Already Own Universal Life Insurance for Other Reasons?

You could—I suppose—consider using the policy for increasing your college savings. You're paying premiums anyway. If you added additional cash, it would grow at the policy's crediting rate (at this writing, 4 to 5 percent), tax deferred. When college rolls around, you could probably withdraw some of that money tax free (ask the agent how much you could withdraw without triggering a tax). Be sure there won't be a surrender charge. If you die, however, that extra cash you dumped into the policy would effectively vanish. Your heirs will get the policy's face value, not the face value plus the additional money you invested.

Variable universal policies are always a bad idea for college savings. The expenses are high, so the returns on your stock investments will be subpar. You'll get measly-to-zero net returns when you switch to bond funds and money market funds in the years just before you'll need the cash for college bills.

Whatever You Do, Resist Buying Life Insurance on a Child in Order to Build College Funds

It's a waste of money. Besides paying commissions, a good part of each premium goes for insurance that the child doesn't need. You're simply buying a benefit for yourself if the child dies. If the child doesn't die and you hold for 15 years or more, you'll have some cash in the policy that probably grew at a rate of 4 or 5 percent—a modest return for money invested over that period of time. If you hold for just 10 years, returns could be 3 percent or less. To get that cash, you have to cancel the policy, paying taxes on your gain and wasting the money you spent on the insurance part. Alternatively, you could borrow or withdraw the cash. If you take too much, however, the policy will eventually collapse, making the benefit taxable.

No reputable agent should sell a "college" policy on a child. If you already own one (and hence have paid the commission and expenses), it might have long-term value for your child as long as you *don't* use it for college. If you'll need it for college, however, cancel the policy, cancel your agent (which you should do anyway), and put the proceeds into a better investment.

Are You a Sucker to Save?

No, you're not. It's a myth among struggling college savers that they may be making a mistake. The more you save, they say, the greater your assets, so the less you'll get in college aid. The aid formulas penalize savers and reward spendthrifts.

There is some truth to that statement, but not much.

It's true that the greater your assets, the less student aid you'll get. But you need a lot of assets before your aid is docked, and even then it's not docked by much. The size of your student aid package is based almost entirely on your income, not your assets. Furthermore, every package contains loans. By saving less, you wind up having to borrow more.

Spendthrift families that don't save might pick up an extra $1,000 in grants and subsidized student loans. And then what are they going to do? They'll still owe the college a huge sum of money and won't have the savings to cover it. They'll be up to their necklaces in debts.

Truly, savers win the day.

STEP 6

UNDERSTANDING INVESTING

There's a secret to investing that cuts a path directly to the profits that you're looking for. The secret is simplicity. The more elementary your investment style, the more confident you can be of getting past bad markets and making money in the long run.

This insight isn't easy for investors to accept. Wall Street resembles nothing so much as a storybook Oriental souk, whose subtle vendors bow and beckon, urging this purchase and that. The goods are colorful and varied. The more intricate the investment package, the stronger the spell it casts. But it's stuffed with risks (and costs!) you couldn't even begin to imagine. This glittering merchandise almost always profits the vendors more than you.

And you don't need it! You can rack up a superb lifetime investment record with just a handful of simple, low-cost stock-owning mutual funds and a couple of bond funds. You can protect your retirement merely by owning the right percentage of bonds for your age. That's all you really need to know. Investing is easy if you buy the simple things and buy them well.

21

Drawing Up Your Battle Plan

Which Kinds of Investments Serve You Best?

**When you start, the jigsaw puzzle that's your
personal money lies in dozens of pieces, all jumbled up.
When you finish, the picture will be clear.**

For investment success, you need a concept; a framework on which to hang all the thoughts and suggestions that are constantly coming your way. Should you buy this mutual fund or that one? How do you choose between stocks and bonds? Which risks make sense and which don't?

There are logical answers to these questions, but only if you start with a sensible investment plan. Once you've drawn up that plan, the mysteries of money will become clearer. You'll see exactly the kinds of investments you ought to make. Just as important, you'll know which investments to avoid.

Your plan will not make you rich tomorrow. You're not betting the farm on the pipe dream of doubling your money overnight. Instead you're using your common sense to map a steady strategy for building wealth.

You Can Only Get Poor Quickly; Getting Rich Is Slow

I would write a get-rich-quick book if I could. Everyone (me included) dreams of learning how to beat Wall Street in three easy lessons and with no risk. But the schemes behind such books are usually a ticket to the poorhouse.

There are no easy ways to beat Wall Street. That's not even an intelligent goal. Thoughtful people buy the kinds of investments that will yield the combination of safety, income, and growth they need. At the end of the road, they will look back and see that they did well.

Your Personal Investment Policy

Everyone needs an investment policy. It's a written plan for making good choices in the financial markets. Professional money managers always work within a policy framework and so should you. Once in place, it will end your uncertainties about where to put your money and how to react when the markets bounce around.

Preparing an investment policy isn't complicated. In its simplest form, it's an asset allocation plan. You decide what percentage of your money to hold in U.S. stocks, international stocks, short-term bonds, long-term bonds, and cash. You don't make a wild guess or pick a sample allocation from a pie chart on the Web. You create a policy for yourself alone, based on what you're saving the money for and how much risk it's wise to take. This chapter will show you how to do it. As you work with the plan, you can make it more detailed—for example, deciding how much you want to put in emerging markets, within your international allocation.

An investment policy should always be written down. When the markets rise or fall substantially, you consult your policy and bring your investments back to their original allocation. You know that's going to work for you, over the long term, because it reflects your personal needs and goals.

First Principles of Investing

The first step toward better investing is learning what has worked in the past. These are the lessons that history teaches:

1. For building capital long term, buy stocks. You are taking only a modest risk. Over 15-year periods, stocks have almost always outperformed bonds and have left simple bank accounts in the dust. Sometimes stocks plunge, as you know all too well. But avoiding them isn't the answer. The answer is owning them in the right proportion, as this chapter will explain.

2. Buy stock-owning mutual funds, not stocks themselves. Funds diversify your investments and balance your risks. Picking stocks individually is a hobby, not a productive investment strategy for amateurs. You can't beat the market with a handful of individual stocks. If you try, you'll almost certainly wind up with a smaller retirement fund. You can't even trust "blue-chip" stocks. In the last recession, some famous ones collapsed!

3. Diversify. Although stocks usually win the race in the long term, you and

I live in the short term. That means we need buffers: investments that give our capital some protection in a year (or years) when the economy falls apart and stocks decline. You need different types of stock funds because the various sectors perform differently at different times. You need international stocks, as well as stocks based in the United States. And you need bonds, for income and stability. Sometimes, bonds do better than stocks for extended periods. A historic bull market in bonds began around 1980 and continued through two huge stock market crashes, in 2000 and 2008. Super-safe Treasury bonds outperformed stocks over that entire 30-year period. Talk about a surprise! Just when investors settled into "stocks for the long run," bonds turned out to have been the better choice. It seems unlikely that bonds will repeat that trick. At this point, I'd bet on stocks. But that's why you diversify—because you never know.

4. Control your risk. This means thinking, in advance, of the consequences of being wrong. A good example would be borrowing all your home equity on the assumption that home prices would keep going up. You weren't prepared, financially, when prices dropped. Good risk managers limit the size of their bets— whether on homes, stocks, or any other investment—so they won't be wiped out if the bet turns out badly.

5. Keep it simple. Plain-vanilla stock and bond funds will do the job. All the other stuff—options, hedge funds, cash-plus funds, whatever—usually leave you wiser but poorer.

6. Reinvest your dividends. If I do no more than make you appreciate dividends, this chapter will have done its job. An investor who put $100 into the Standard & Poor's 500-stock average on the last day of 1925, held until January 1, 2009—and spent all the dividends—would have earned $7,079. If that investor had reinvested all dividends, he or she would have had $204,526! That comparison is my all-time favorite financial fact.* Compounding interest and dividends is the investment world's strongest, surest force.

7. Rebalance. Once you set your investment policy—say, 60 percent stocks, 40 percent bonds—you should maintain that allocation. If your stock funds go up in value, sell some to get back to the 60 percent of your portfolio they should represent. If your funds go down, buy some to bring your stock allocation back up to 60 percent. That's called *rebalancing*. You'll read more about it on page 710. For now, it's enough to say that rebalancing can improve returns and minimize risk. It's one of the secrets of investment success.

8. Invest regularly. Use a portion of every paycheck to invest in your mutual

---

*Thank you, Ibbotson Associates, a Morningstar subsidiary.

funds. Don't worry about "bad" markets. Bad markets are good buys for long-term investors because stock prices are so low.

9. Forget market timing. Market timers try to sell when the stock market nears its peak and buy again when stocks bottom out. As if they knew. This game isn't worth the candle because you are so often wrong. On a percentage basis, stocks rise more often and much farther than they fall. So the odds are on the side of the people who stay invested all the time, rebalancing as they go.

A study done by the University of Michigan for Towneley Capital Management in New York makes this point perfectly. The researchers looked at the 42 years from 1963 through 2004. They found that if you were out of the stock market during the 90 best days—just 90 days out of 42 years—you'd have missed an amazing 96 percent of all the market's gains. Those magic days were scattered randomly over the entire period. One dollar invested in 1963 and not touched would have grown to $73.99. But if you had missed those 90 days, your dollar would have grown to only $2.70—less than you'd have earned from Treasury bills.

If you'd been on the sidelines during the market's worst 90 days, your dollar would have multiplied to a breathtaking $1,693.68. But if you think you can pluck those few days out of a 42-year period, I'd say you'd been spending too much time in the hot sun.

There's a name for timing gurus who claim to have consistently picked the market's peaks and troughs: they're called *liars*.

What's your best protection against market drops? Steady investing, reinvesting dividends, diversification, and rebalancing. It's important to buy when prices are low as well as when they're high.

10. Stick to your investment policy. One year you'll make money. One year you'll lose money. But time is on your side. Don't let impulse investing or sudden market changes shake you out of your long-term plan. Change your plan only if your personal circumstances change.

11. Have patience, patience, patience, patience. The urge for quick returns hurls you into lunatic investments—the financial equivalent of lottery tickets, with just about the same odds. Fear scares you away, even from sensible choices. A successful investor hitches a ride on the global economy's long-term growth.

How Risky Are Stocks, Really?

Having made such a strong pitch for buying stocks, I can hear the echoes coming back—"Yeah, but what about the bubble that burst in January 2000? What about

Table 13a.

HOW OFTEN DID INVESTORS MAKE MONEY IN MAJOR U.S. STOCKS?*

Holding Period	The Percentage of Times Stocks Made Money			The Percentage of Times Stocks Lost Money
	0–10% Gain	10–20% Gain	Over 20% Gain	
1 year	16%	18%	37%	29%
5 years	28%	47%	11%	14%
10 years	43%	52%	1%	4%
15 years	38%	62%	0%	0%
20 years	33%	67%	0%	0%

*Standard & Poor's 500-stock average, 1926–2008, compounded annually with dividends reinvested.

Source: Ibbotson Associates, a Morningstar subsidiary.

a market that made no net gain between 2000 and 2006?" What about the crash of 2008, which took the market back to price levels not seen since 1997?

Well, what about it? Those drops are temporary. No one knows what stocks will do tomorrow, but the evidence is clear as to how they'll probably perform over 15 years. You will almost certainly make money. In the 15-year period ending in April 2009—covering the market collapse of 2008 and the copycat collapse of early 2009—long-term investors still reaped 6.5 percent a year with dividends reinvested.

Table 13b.

HOW OFTEN DID INVESTORS MAKE MONEY IN MAJOR INTERNATIONAL STOCKS?*

Holding Period	The Percentage of Times Stocks Made Money			The Percentage of Times Stocks Lost Money
	0–10% Gain	10–20% Gain	Over 20% Gain	
1 year	15%	19%	42%	26%
5 years	49%	28%	15%	6%
10 years	57%	30%	13%	0%
15 years	36%	60%	4%	0%
20 years	20%	80%	0%	0%

*MSCI EAFE index (Europe, Australia, Far East), 1972–2008, compounded annually in dollars, with dividends reinvested.

Source: Ibbotson Associates, a Morningstar subsidiary.

Furthermore, you protect yourself against a decline in a single market, like the S&P 500, by owning other markets too. Take the period January 1, 2000, though the end of December 2007. The S&P went nowhere—up a mere 1.66 percent a year. During that period, international stocks, as measured by the MSCI EAFE index of stocks in developed countries (Europe, Australia, New Zealand, Hong Kong, and Japan) rose by 5.54 percent. You'd have improved your performance by owning both. They all dropped in the 2008 bust, but some recovered faster than others.

The tables on page 697 show the percentage of times that investors made money in U.S. and international stocks over various holding periods: 1 year, 5 years, 10 years, 15 years, and 20 years. The U.S. data start in 1926; the international data start in 1972. Here's what you learn:

1. In any 1-year period, stocks are dicey. You get the biggest gains if you hit them right. But you also risk the biggest losses.

2. Over 5-year holding periods, your chance of loss is small. Over 10-year periods, it is negligible. The most recent 10-year period was one of the few losers for U.S. stocks but not for international stocks—one of the many reasons to diversify.

3. Over 15- and 20-year periods, your chance of loss is zero, provided that you reinvest your dividends. (You *may* lose money, however, if you don't reinvest your dividends, a matter important to retirees who are living on dividends.)

4. The longer you hold stocks, the greater your chance of making money and the smaller your chance of losing it. During long holding periods, however, you'll suffer through several stock market drops. If you panic and sell, you won't get the superior returns that stocks can deliver. Best antidote: own a sizable cushion of high-quality bonds. They support your portfolio during bad markets, which can save you from your impulse to run. A written investment policy can help you too (page 694).

5. The longer you hold stocks, the greater your chance of earning an average return rather than a spectacular one. U.S. and international stocks turn out about the same. But they rise and fall at different rates and often at different times, so owning both will smooth your returns.

Yes, but . . .

What about Murphy's Law, which says that if anything can go wrong it will? Or Quinn's Law, which says that Murphy was an optimist? In living memory, stocks have had three especially bad patches so far.

First, they were trounced by bonds during the early, and deflationary, 1930s.

(The reincarnated among us will remember that bonds also rolled over stocks during the deeply deflationary 1870s.)

Second, in the inflationary 1970s, stocks (with dividends reinvested) finished modestly behind both corporate bonds and Treasury bills. Stocks hate superhigh inflation just as they hate severe deflation.

Third, in the postbubble 2000s, big-company U.S. and international stocks lagged behind bonds from January 2000 through mid-2009 (and maybe more; mid-2009 is when this book went to press).*

In most decades, however, stocks finished first, usually by a mile. They can do fine during modest inflation as long as prices aren't accelerating by more than 4 percent. And they're just as happy during modest deflations (although you have to go back to the nineteenth century for proof). That's why smart investors emphasize stocks, with a prudent, age-appropriate diversification into bonds just in case.

Even during a bad patch, stocks can be rescued by the dividends they pay. Take the period from February 1966 to January 1983—17 long years. Stocks rose and fell and rose and fell but never advanced much higher than 1,000, as measured by the Dow Jones Industrial Average. Investors earned *zero* in price alone. If they reinvested their dividends, however, they earned 7 percent a year. During that same period, long-term bond investors earned 4.3 percent.

Some Simple Arithmetic to Keep in Mind

Limiting losses is more important than many people realize.

When you ride stocks all the way to the bottom of a bear market, you wind up with fewer assets invested. That makes it harder for you to make up the money you lost. For example, say that you have $100,000 in stocks and the market drops 10 percent, leaving you with $90,000. To get even, you need an 11 percent gain. Now say that the market drops 25 percent, leaving you with $75,000. At that point, you need a 33 percent gain to return to $100,000 again. Recovering money lost isn't as cut and dried as some investors think.

You may also imagine that fast-rising "growth" stocks do better over time than boring stocks ("value stocks") that don't rise as fast. But growth stocks also fall farther when the market drops. When prices start up again, the boring-

---

*(Bonds also beat stocks for a 30-year period, 1979–2008, but that comparison isn't quite fair. Bonds were reaching the end of a long, historic bull market in 2008, while stocks were suffering a near-historic crash. Still, it shows the value of holding bonds, even during years when stocks appear to be king.)

stock holder has more money invested to catch the rise. At the end of a couple of up-and-down cycles, boring stocks usually win.

How do you beat this unhappy arithmetic? Don't buy and hold. Buy and *rebalance* as the market falls (page 710).

Your Risk Tolerance

When you open a brokerage account, you're often asked to fill in a questionnaire. It's supposed to tell the broker your tolerance for risk. Are you okay with aggressive investments that will plunge when the market falls? Or would you prefer something grayer and less exciting? Depending on your answers, a computer spits out an asset allocation that supposedly will suit your temperament to a T.

These questionnaires are bunk. You never know what your risk tolerance is going to be. When the market is rising, you've just had a promotion at work, or the sun is shining in a particularly lovely way, you may be inclined to bet the house. When the market falls, you've had a quarrel with your boss, or your kid got his third speeding ticket and your insurance premiums are about to jump, you may not feel like taking any risks at all.

So ignore whatever feelings are dominant today. Match your investments to your age (page 722) and to an assessment of what you'll need the money *for* (page 706).

How to Limit All Your Risks

Some investors stay out of stocks in order to keep their money "safe." But what does "safety" really mean? Bonds and bank accounts carry hazards that you haven't thought about. A fixed-income investment can eat up your future just as surely as if you had fed it to sharks. You have to understand your whole range of risks in order to make good investment decisions.

Of all risks, the most familiar is *market risk*—the risk of losing money in a bad investment.

Adjust for this by (1) diversifying your investments so that a single loss (even though temporary) doesn't leave a hole in your wealth, (2) buying only the boring old standbys such as diversified mutual funds, and (3) skipping the dizzy investment ideas that only a novice or maniac could love. If you're dizzy at heart, give yourself a small mad-money fund to play with. I'll wager that your boring investments come out ahead.

Everyone endures *economic risk*—the hit you take when the economy turns down. Adjust for this risk by minimizing investments that get bashed in recessions such as junk bonds and aggressive growth mutual funds. Those invest-

Table 14.

HOW INFLATION CHOPS YOUR REAL RETURNS

	Average Compounded Returns After Inflation*	
Investment	1926–2008†	1946–2008‡
30-day U.S. Treasury bills	0.7%	0.61%
Long-term U.S. Treasury bonds	2.68%	2.06%
Large-company stocks§	6.61%	6.47%
Smaller-company stocks‖	8.66%	8.47%

* Dividends reinvested but not adjusted for income taxes.

† Average inflation for the period, 3.01% a year.

‡ Average inflation for the period, 3.95% a year.

§ Standard & Poor's 500 index.

‖ Dow Jones Wilshire 500 index.

Source: Ibbotson Associates, a Morningstar subsidiary.

ments soar in good times and may give you better long-term returns. But you have to be willing to suffer larger-than-usual losses when business sags. Hold a percentage of your money in high-quality bonds, which usually do well when the economy flags.

Less well understood is *inflation risk*—the risk of losing the purchasing power of your capital. This is the monster that eats fixed-income investors for lunch. After inflation, a certificate of deposit, zero-coupon bond, or traditional Treasury security yields little or nothing. An inflation-adjusted Treasury may preserve your purchasing power before tax but not after tax. After years and years of saving, you come out with a pittance in real terms. Inflation can devour stock investors too, on the rare occasion that the stock market goes nowhere for many years.

Adjust for inflation risk by (1) not keeping large, permanent sums of cash in money market mutual funds and similar short-term investments; (2) avoiding an all-bond portfolio, even in retirement; (3) buying some Treasury Inflation-Protected Securities (page 407), which can at least preserve your capital pretax; and (4) putting at least some of your money into diversified stocks for growth. The table above shows how well (or how poorly) all the common investments survive inflation.

The consistency of long-term common-stock yields over inflation is nothing short of astonishing. The Ibbotson table above shows virtually the same returns over two different periods. Here's another calculation, from Jack W. Wilson and Charles P. Jones of North Carolina State University, using a methodology that covers more stocks: From 1926 through 2008, holders of large U.S. stocks earned 6.11 percent annually after inflation, with dividends reinvested (6.79 percent before the 2008 market collapse). From 1871 through 1925, stocks earned 6.62 percent—again, very similar. Based on this record, it's reasonable to expect that, 20 or 30 years from now, you'll show close to a 6.5 percent return over inflation, whatever that may be. Charles Jones gives one warning: in the past, dividends averaged 4 percent, which accounts for more than half of the historical return. In recent years, they've averaged around 2 percent, which could reduce your future gains.

There's *deflation risk*—not seen in the U.S. since the 1930s. The odds run against deflation, but if it occurred, cash and fixed-rate Treasuries would be a fine defense.

In our global economy, there's *dollar risk*. This affects investors who hold international mutual funds. The value of your fund can rise for one of two reasons: (1) Foreign stock markets do well because those economies are growing. Or (2) the dollar falls against foreign currencies. When the dollar falls, holdings of international funds are worth more, in dollar terms. Similarly, the value of international funds can fall for one of two reasons: (1) Foreign economies are doing poorly, so their securities are worth less. Or (2) the dollar rises against international currencies, meaning that your funds are worth less in dollar terms. The performance of your stock fund will always be a combination of these two elements—economic results and currency changes. Bond fund performance depends almost entirely on currency changes.

Some international mutual funds try to hedge their dollar risk so their funds will do well even if the greenback's value rises. But professional managers are no better than you and I at predicting currency changes, and hedging raises the costs investors have to pay. So don't bother looking for funds that hedge. Just diversify internationally and let the dollar chips fall where they may.

For market timers, there's *error risk*. Timers try to sell at market tops and buy when stocks are low. Often they get it wrong, losing money on both ends of the cycle. Their biggest risk is selling when stocks are partway down and waiting and *waiting* before they have the nerve to jump back in. By the time they decide to buy again, the market has typically turned around and moved up strongly. Historically, you lose more money by missing the upside than staying too long and enduring declines. Defend against error risk by not trying to time the market. Rebalance instead (page 710).

Bond investors face *interest rate risk*—the risk that interest rates will rise. When that happens, the value of your bonds or bond mutual funds falls and you lose money (or make less money than you expected). Furthermore, the income you're earning may no longer beat inflation and taxes. Adjust for interest rate risk by owning short- to medium-term bonds (maturing in maybe 2 to 10 years). When rates rise, these bonds don't fall as much in price as 20- or 30-year bonds.

Fixed-income investors also face *reinvestment risk*. Say that interest rates are rising and you have to choose between a one-year CD at 4 percent and a five-year CD at 3.5 percent. You decide on the higher rate. But when that CD matures, one-year rates may be down to 3 percent. That 3.5 percent you spurned last year is no longer available. You'd have made more money by going for the five-year CD originally.

Adjust for reinvestment risk in one of two ways: (1) Ladder your fixed-income investments. For example, you might own CDs or Treasury bonds maturing in one year, two years, three years, four years, and five years. Every year, when a CD or bond matures, reinvest it in a new five-year instrument. If interest rates have risen, you'll get a higher rate. If they've fallen, you'll still be getting high interest income from your existing investments, and you'll have another shot at higher rates the following year. (For more on laddering, see page 67.) Some investors ladder up to 10 years. (2) Buy a bond mutual fund. There is always new money coming into funds. When interest rates rise, the fund manager will be buying those higher-yielding bonds, whose high rates will help offset any decline in market value. What's more, you'll be buying higher-rate bonds yourself through your reinvested dividends.

You also face reinvestment risk if you hold a *callable* bond (a bond is callable if the issuer can call it in before maturity). Take a 30-year tax-free municipal bond that's supposed to pay 3.5 percent interest for another 20 years. If interest rates fall, the municipality will call in the bond after 5 or 10 years, and you can kiss that income good-bye. Adjust for this risk by buying munis with faraway call dates. For a tax-deferred account, such as an IRA, buy noncallable Treasury bonds.

Then there's *liquidity* risk. A *liquid* investment can be sold immediately, at market price, if you suddenly find that you need some money. An *illiquid* investment can't be sold fast except at a discount. Not all of your investments have to be liquid, but enough of them should be, to ensure you quick cash if you ever need it without having to take a loss. So what's liquid?

- *A money market deposit account at a bank.* You can get your cash at any time. Money market mutual funds are almost always liquid (although a large one failed in 2008 and froze its customers' funds).

- *A certificate of deposit is relatively liquid but not perfectly so.* You can always get the money, but it may cost you an early-withdrawal penalty.
- *Mutual fund shares are liquid.* You can sell at any time, at current market value. If there's an investing scare, the fund's price may be down, but you can still get your money out. In a true panic, your fund has the right to suspend redemptions or delay mailing your check for up to seven days, but I can't recall that ever happening in any mainstream fund.
- *Exchange-traded funds (ETFs) are liquid.* They're mutual funds that are traded on the major stock exchanges (page 785).
- *Individual stocks are liquid as long as they trade on the major stock exchanges.*
- *Gold bullion coins can be sold anywhere in the world but at a stiff discount from market price.* Gold ETFs, by contrast, can be sold right away at market price.
- *Retirement accounts are liquid in that you can usually cash them in.* But I count them as illiquid because of the tax cost and penalty of breaking into them too soon.
- *Small amounts of tax-exempt bonds are often illiquid.* No one wants to buy them except at a steep discount.
- *Real estate is generally illiquid.* It can take months to sell, and even then you might have to mark down the property's price.
- *Precious gems are hugely illiquid.* They're salable, but the dealer may not offer you anything close to what you paid or what you think they're worth.
- *Your own business is illiquid.*
- *Shares of the exotic new financial instruments that Wall Street invented in the 2000s may become so illiquid* in a market panic that they're completely unsalable. Moral: buy the simple stuff, not the fancy stuff.

Adjust for liquidity risk by balancing illiquid assets with liquid ones. Anytime you buy something, ask: What happens if I want to sell? Can I get my money fast? Can I sell at market price without taking a discount or paying a penalty? If not, how long might I have to wait for my money? You should have enough liquid assets to carry you for a year even if no other money is coming in.

A risk almost no one thinks of is *holding-period risk*—the chance that you'll have to sell an investment at a time when it's worth less than you paid.

Say, for example, that you've been saving for a down payment on a house and are keeping the money in a stock-owning mutual fund. Three weeks before you'll close on the house, the stock market drops. You lose 20 percent of your down payment, can't buy the house, and your marriage breaks up. That's holding-period risk.

Or say that you bought a 30-year zero-coupon bond (page 945) for your child's college education. When college begins, the bond still has 15 years to run. You have to sell it to pay the tuition, but the market is down, no one wants a single bond unless you'll chop the price, and you're stuck. That too is holding-period risk.

I like stocks if the holding period will last for more than 5 years *and* you can tap other funds in case stocks happen to be down when the need for cash arrives. I love stocks for holding periods of 10 years or more. But I hate and fear stocks for periods shorter than 5 years because you cannot count on getting your capital out.

I fear 30-year bonds for any purpose but speculation on falling interest rates (page 924). I hate any bonds that will mature well past the date when I know that I'm going to need the money.

To adjust for holding-period risk, match your investments to how soon you're going to want the funds.

• *Cash you'll need within 1 to 2 years belongs in a supersafe place.* Four possibilities: money market mutual funds, bank money market deposit accounts, short-term CDs, and short-term Treasury bills (page 225). They'll preserve your capital while offering some inflation protection. (On money funds, your inflation protection is the fact that interest rates can rise. On CDs and three- or six-month Treasuries, you can roll over your investments at a higher rate.)

• *Cash you'll need in 3 to five 5 years could go into a CD.* It might be okay in an ultra-short-term bond fund too, but for true security—with liquidity—I'd keep 3- to 5-year money in money markets too. When the credit bubble burst in 2008, one popular ultrashort fund dropped more than 15 percent in value. Not good for people who needed to get their money out.

• *Cash you won't need for 5 to 10 years should be invested for income with a modest tilt toward growth.* This is the window for bonds and mixed stock-and-bond funds (called equity income funds).

• *Cash you won't need for more than 10 years should be invested for income and growth.* It's always possible that the stock market won't rise over that period of time. For example, large U.S. stocks went nowhere from 1998 to 2008. But for well-diversified investors, the odds of success are high.

Don't forget *expense risk*. It's hard to make money if you're taking a chunk out of your assets to pay high expenses each year. The best predictor of mutual fund performance is cost—on average, the less you pay, the higher your net gain. Paying less than 1 percent is fine. Paying 3 or 4 percent, as you might for a variable annuity, is cutting yourself off at the knees.

I'd be neglectful if I didn't mention *idiot risk*. That's the risk that you will take an idiot's advice about money (including that of all too many Wall Street professionals) or get swept up in a fad and act like an idiot yourself. Don't kick yourself. We've all been there at one time or another. The trick is never to put a lot of money into anything you suddenly get excited about. No single investment should be large enough to endanger your standard of living if it goes wrong.

Finally, there's *investment book risk*. Many of the investment returns you see here are averaged over calendar years. The same is true for most articles in personal finance magazines. But there are zillions of possible holding periods, which may produce higher or lower returns. Sophisticated financial planners use something called a *Monte Carlo simulation*. It looks at thousands of random possibilities to help you assess the chance of achieving average, above-average, or below-average results. If you work with a financial planner (chapter 32), he or she should have this capability.

The Right Shoe for the Right Foot

You cannot escape taking some kind of risk, so the next thing to ask is whether your current range of risks supports or undermines your purpose. Here's a general guide.

1. **Use safe savings, with no market risk, for:**
   - A cash reserve equal to three to six months' basic living expenses
   - Accumulating a down payment on a house
   - Saving for a vacation or any other big expenses
   - The account you use to pay current and future bills, including taxes
   - College savings that are needed within five years
   - Any fixed expense that has to be met within five years
   - Protecting capital when you've lost your job
   - A parking place for money waiting to be invested elsewhere
   - Preserving any sum you dare not put at the slightest risk
2. **Use stocks for:**
   - Accumulating college tuition while your child is young
   - Building a retirement fund
   - Generating an income out of dividends and capital gains

(*continued on page 708*)

Table 15.

DO YOUR CURRENT INVESTMENTS
MATCH YOUR GOALS?

Your Short-Term* Goals	Your Current Short-Term* Investments	Appropriate Investments
$ _____	_____	Money market mutual funds
$ _____	_____	Certificates of deposit
$ _____	_____	Short-term Treasuries
$ _____	_____	Ultra-short-term bond mutual funds

Your Medium-Term† Goals	Your Current Medium-Term† Investments	Appropriate Investments
$ _____	_____	Short- and intermediate-term bonds and bond mutual funds
$ _____	_____	Balanced stock-and-bond mutual funds and equity-income funds

Your Long-term‡ Goals	Your Current Long-Term‡ Investments	Appropriate Investments
$ _____	_____	Stock-owning mutual funds, including aggressive funds
$ _____	_____	Intermediate-term bonds
$ _____	_____	Intermediate- and long-term bond funds
$ _____	_____	Diversified individual stocks
$ _____	_____	Real estate

* Up to 5 years.

† Up to 10 years.

‡ Longer than 10 years.

3. Use medium-term bonds for:
  - Adding to your income from interest earnings
  - Reducing the risk in your investment portfolio
  - A source of monthly money when you retire

4. Use long-term bonds for:
  - Speculating on falling interest rates
  - A deflation hedge

5. Use investment real estate for:
  - Building retirement savings over 10 years or more
  - An inflation hedge

To find out if you're carrying the right investments to support your personal goals, fill in the table on page 707.

First, list all your savings and investments, both inside and outside your retirement plan. Divide them into short term and long term. Then list your short- and long-term goals. Note that growth isn't a goal, it's a strategy. Early retirement and college tuition are goals.

When you're finished, the table may show a mishmash of investments acquired without thinking what goals they should serve. The money you're saving for a down payment might be in a bond fund instead of cash; your retirement savings may be in certificates of deposit. Later chapters will help you straighten all this out.

Shooting Craps

"But where's the fun?" you ask. "Where are the kicks, the highs, the joys of the chase? I want to have some sport with my money!"

And why not? So do I. Over the years, I have fallen in love with one oil well (dry), one new venture (bankrupt), one glamour stock (down 80 percent, which is when I learned about stop-loss orders), and one of the worst mutual funds in history. I did make some money on some of my fliers (including that mutual fund, which I dumped before it went too far down). But that's not the point. What matters is that I was gambling with play money, not with the bulk of my assets. My basic holdings were, and are, in a suitable range of sober investments for my old age.

I want you to get all the pleasure you can from the money you've earned. If that means rolling dice in a Wall Street crap game, so be it. Just don't throw around your kid's college tuition account or the life insurance proceeds meant to see you through widowhood. Fund your serious needs seriously. If there's anything left over, do whatever you want with it.

Animal Spirits

A bull market goes up. A bear market goes down. A bear market rally, when stocks rise only to fall again, is a dead-cat bounce. A crummy stock is a dog. If you waste your brains throwing money at the hottest stocks, you're a pig. No one who reads this book is a pig!

Asset Allocation: How to Do It, Why It Works

So far we've been matching appropriate investments and levels of risk with a whole range of personal objectives, short term and long. Now it's time to consider pure long-term investing, such as parlaying your savings into enough to live on when you retire. Here other kinds of matching schemes come into play. You are asking the question: What return do I need from my long-term investments? How much risk am I willing to swallow to try to get it? Do I even know how much risk I'm willing to take? (When stocks plunge, minds change!)

Enter the concept of *asset allocation.* To explain it, let me start with a tale of two investors, as told by Marshall Blume, professor of finance at the Wharton School in Philadelphia.

Fighter Jock puts $100 into stocks in August 1929, just before the Great Crash. Measured by the Dow Jones Industrial Average, with dividends reinvested, it takes him almost 16 years to get his money back.

Savvy Sal also has $100, but she puts $50 into stocks and $50 into bonds and maintains that 50–50 split. When her bonds are worth more than 50 percent of her capital, she sells some and buys stocks. When her stocks are worth more, she sells some and buys bonds. That's called rebalancing. She rebalances every month (Blume is measuring by the market averages here), always seeking to keep half of her money in each investment. In just six years, she recovers her original stake.

Notice what Sal did *not* do:

- *She did not sell all her stocks at the bottom* and give up the market for ever and ever.
- *She did not try to guess when the market would rise or fall again.* She just followed her investment formula.
- *She did not let herself be swayed by the news of the day.* Instead she invested for the long term.
- *She did not fail.* She beat Fighter Jock, who bought stocks and held them. And she beat the investors who fled the market and put their money in the bank.

Sal practiced asset allocation, which, simply put, means dividing your money among stocks, bonds, cash, and other kinds of investments. She also practiced rebalancing, which means keeping each type of investment at the same percentage you started with, even when the market changes. People don't pay a lot of attention to asset allocation and rebalancing. Yet they're the two key decisions that determine your investment success, not how smart (or dumb) you are at picking stocks or mutual funds.

"But wait," you say, "Sal was just lucky. What would have happened had stocks bounced right back after 1929?"

In that case, Fighter Jock would have done somewhat better. But from time to time, he'd have taken a big loss.

Sal would have taken occasional losses on her stocks as well as her bonds. But because she owned both, her total portfolio of investments would never have dropped as far as Jock's. Her long-term results would still have been fine, without as much fear along the way.

But the fact remains that stocks *didn't* bounce back after 1929. And Sal was positioned to handle that risk. Balanced portfolios did better after the 2000 bubble too.

Rebalancing: How to Do It, Why It Works

To rebalance means to keep your investment portfolio on an even keel. You want to hold roughly the same percentage of your money in stocks no matter what the market does. That keeps your account from getting either too risky or too conservative, too exposed to stock market declines or too conservative to grow. You're aiming for a steady course.

To start the process, you have to decide what your balance should be—how much in stocks and how much in bonds. As an example, I'll assume that you're putting 60 percent of your investment money into a stock mutual fund that copies the behavior of the market and 40 percent into a bond mutual fund that does the same. That's your home base. (Funds that copy the market are called index funds—see page 745.)

As market prices change, however, the ratio of stocks to bonds will change as well. If stocks zoom up, they might soon account for 70 percent of the value of your investment portfolio. You'll feel rich, but you'll also be in a riskier position. If the rally fails, you'll have more to lose. So you rebalance. You sell some of your stock fund (at a profit) and put the proceeds into your bond fund. That returns you to your original 60–40 split between stocks and bonds.

The next year, stocks might do poorly—dropping in value to only 50 percent of your portfolio. Your investments have now become too conservative, with too little money invested for growth. This time, you'd sell bonds and reinvest the proceeds in stocks to raise your stock allocation back to 60 percent.

You handle all the investments you own in the same way. If you start with 20 percent in an international fund and price changes raise its value to 25 percent of your money, you'd sell some of the shares to bring it back down to 20 percent and reinvest the proceeds in your U.S. stocks or bonds.

Rebalancing makes you a smart investor—much smarter than people who keep on chasing hot mutual funds. The chasers buy at high prices, then get disappointed and sell when prices drop, locking in a loss. Rebalancers do the opposite. You are selling at high prices (taking profits) and reinvesting in lower-priced assets that haven't done as well. Those slower performers will eventually go up, and you'll make money because you bought them cheap. Remember, the types of assets that were yesterday's losers will be tomorrow's winners. A faithful rebalancer buys tomorrow's winners automatically.

Rebalancing is also a smarter strategy than buy and hold. If you always stand pat in a falling market, you give away the profits you made when stocks ran up. You also lose the chance to buy more stocks at the bottom when they're cheap. Market timers try to guess at the magic moments to buy and sell—and over time, they're going to lose. Rebalancers practice a discipline that reaps some of the advantages of successful market timing without getting you into trouble.

Sometimes rebalancers kick themselves. The market shoots up, you sell some of your stock position, and prices go higher yet. Then the market declines and you buy some stock, only to see prices drop even more. "Hey," you say, "wasn't I supposed to cut my losses and let my profits run?" Sure, except how are you supposed to know when the run is over and when to cut? Rebalancing works *over time.* When you practice it faithfully, you'll look back and see that it steered you right.

How do you rebalance? That depends on where the money is:

1. In a tax-deferred retirement account such as a 401(k) or IRA, rebalancing is easy. You'd sell some of the shares you hold in the investment that went up and reinvest the proceeds in investments that lagged. You might be able to make the changes yourself online. Some plans can be rebalanced automatically. Or call the plan's customer service center. No taxes or penalties are involved. The service rep might even help you make your rebalancing calculations.

2. If you're investing outside a retirement fund, you should handle rebalancing in a different way. You don't want to sell investments that rise in value, because you'll owe taxes on the gain. So leave them alone and rebalance by adding extra money to asset that fell behind. As an example, say that you've been putting $200 a month into your investment account—$120 into a stock fund and $80 into a bond fund, for a 60–40 split between stocks and bonds. After a good year, your stocks are now worth 70 percent of your portfolio. To bring your investments back into balance, start adding the whole $200 a month to your bond fund until its value rises back to 40 percent of your total investment.

Rebalancing works best for mutual fund investors, who can easily sell shares in one fund and move to another. It works especially well for index fund investors (page 745), because your funds are clearly divided into different investment types. You know exactly which fund to buy and which one to sell when your portfolio falls out of balance. It doesn't work well when you own a portfolio of individual stocks. Deciding which stocks to sell or how much of each position to sell gets too complicated. Moral: get smart, use mutual funds.

There's no need to rebalance after every little wiggle in the stock market. Do it only if one investment misses its home-base target by more than 5 percent, up or down. Check your investments once a year to see if you should act. You can get help with these calculations if you keep track of your finances with the latest versions of Quicken Personal Finance and Microsoft Money. Both products offer rebalancing programs that will tell you instantly whether you ought to sell or buy and, if so, how much.

My Rebalancing Sermon

You'll hear me say over and over again that smart investing is easy. You save money regularly, set yourself an investment policy using mutual funds, and rebalance. End of story. But I have to confess that rebalancing can be hard—not mechanically but psychologically. You're selling stocks as their price goes up, when your every impulse is to hold or buy. If prices keep going up, you'll kick yourself for selling "too soon." The opposite happens on the downside. When stocks decline, you're supposed to buy. If you get scared and sell instead, you won't get the long-term advantage that this strategy brings.

Rebalancing takes discipline and courage. The only way to stand the strain is to hold a really deep belief that rebalancing works. To reinforce your belief, remember the stock market bubble. Wouldn't it have been nice if you'd sold some stocks when prices went sky-high? Wouldn't it have been nice to reinvest in bonds, which rose in value during the years that stocks collapsed? Rebalancing could have done that for you. It works over every stock market cycle, all the time.

The best idea: let someone else rebalance for you. Many 401(k) plans now have a rebalancing feature. You might be able to: (1) press a "rebalance" button online, to have your investments adjusted; (2) call the plan's manager and ask how to rebalance; (3) invest in your plan's target-date retirement fund, which rebalances your investments for you automatically; (4) choose a 401(k) managed account. The manager picks funds and rebalances for you.

You can also invest in target-date funds outside a 401(k)—in your taxable account or individual retirement account. For more on target-date funds, see page 846. To me, they're best buys. Anything that helps you rebalance will improve your returns over time.

Mutual Funds: Why They're a Smarter Buy than Individual Stocks

A mutual fund is a big pool of money, contributed by thousands of people just like you. The manager of that money invests it in stocks, bonds, or both. Your share in the fund gives you a tiny ownership interest in all the fund's investments. You're spreading your money around, which is the right thing to do. There are many different types of funds. I'll explain them and how to use them in chapter 22. Here I want to show you why they work so much better than buying individual stocks.

Mutual funds have three big virtues:

1. They make it easy to construct an investment policy. You can match the types of funds with the types of investments you want to hold. An easy call would be international stocks. Instead of hunting for specific foreign companies, you'd buy an international mutual fund. Or say you wanted to bet 10 percent of your money on U.S. stocks that are probably underpriced. Do you know which stocks those are? I don't. But you can buy a "value" fund that specializes in those kinds of companies. Successful investors start with an investment policy (page 694), and mutual funds make it easy to carry that policy out.

2. They make it easy to rebalance. If the U.S. stock market goes way up, you'll want to sell some of your position and invest the proceeds in an asset that has not performed as well—for example, bonds. If you own individual stocks, however, which ones would you sell? The ones that performed the best? A portion of all the companies you own? Who knows? If you own mutual funds, it's simple—just sell a percentage of your fund shares.

3. They save you from making huge mistakes. If you own a substantial amount of a stock that goes bad, it wrecks your performance. The right mutual funds (see chapter 22) keep you so well diversified that one bad company won't get you into trouble.

For some people, buying mutual funds goes against the grain. You think that your job is to find "great companies" and hold their stocks forever. But "great companies" don't necessarily last. The superstars of 1990 were has-beens by 2000. The leaders in 2000 soon saw their stocks collapse. In hindsight, you can always find stocks with wonderful long-term records. Going forward, however, you can't know which stocks will be the big winners (or losers) in the decade ahead.

Time Out for Theory

Even if you know that you're supposed to diversify your investments, maybe you don't know why. A lot of study has established several things:

1. Different types of investments tend to move in different cycles. Some may go up, while others go down. Some go in the same direction, but not at the same time or at the same speed. Some move by larger percentages than others. Owning different types of investments protects you from big losses in your total portfolio and can improve your returns.

2. When you buy isn't nearly as important as what types of assets you buy and how much you own of them. You can be all wrong on your market timing and still do well if you are properly diversified.

3. Market timing (which means buying before the market goes up and selling before the market goes down) is extraordinarily hard to do. The average investor won't guess right often enough to beat the investor who buys and holds. Most professional investors don't do much better. You definitely won't beat the rebalancer. The Forecaster's Hall of Fame is an empty room.

4. Almost no one, including investment professionals, "beat the market" over the long term. It's a waste of time to set that kind of standard for yourself or to invest with that phony goal in mind. It will lead you wrong.

5. You cannot predict which types of investments—known as asset classes—will do better over the next five-year period. U.S. stocks? European stocks? Emerging markets? Bonds? Treasury bills? Who knows?

These findings lead to the conclusion that you shouldn't break your head trying to predict what will happen to stocks, interest rates, or the economy. Don't seek truth in the financial press. Don't consult gurus. Don't be stampeded into the market, or out of it.

Instead focus on what you're investing *for* (page 707). Then split your money among the types of investments most likely to achieve that goal. And stick with them. Amen.

How to Mix 'n' Match

To minimize risk, you need a mix of investment types that rise and fall at different times or at different speeds. Each type is called an *asset class*. In the real world, no investments counter one another quite that neatly. Nor do they maintain their relationships consistently. In general, however, here's how the various assets move in relation to one another:

- Stocks behave differently from Treasury bills.
- Long-term bonds behave differently from short-term bonds.
- Gold stocks behave differently from other stocks.
- International stocks and bonds behave differently from U.S. stocks and bonds over the long term, although not necessarily over the short term.
- Real estate often behaves differently from stocks and bonds, although in specific regions of the country they can all behave alike.
- In a global crisis, the rules go out the window, but only temporarily. All the major asset classes collapsed together in September and October 2008. As they recovered, the benefits of diversification showed up again.

How to Choose Which Assets to Own

- *In case of unanticipated inflation, you want Inflation-Adjusted Treasury Securities (TIPS), gold, or money market mutual funds.* Real estate can work too, although very slowly over time. Commodities are wild cards. They often rise during inflationary times, but not always.

- *For anticipated (but moderate) inflation and economic growth, you want U.S. and international stocks.* You also want stocks during periods of mild disinflation, when consumer price increases are gradually going down. To diversify among U.S. stocks, you need mutual funds dedicated to small companies, large companies, value stocks (low priced and unloved), and growth stocks (earnings rising rapidly). For more on value versus growth, see page 874. To diversify among international stocks, you need funds in developed markets such as Europe and Japan and in emerging markets such as Brazil, India, and China.

- *In case of economic slowdowns, you want high-quality, noncallable long-term bonds*—which means Treasuries.

- *If we ever see actual deflation, with price levels falling, you'd want Treasuries too.* Stocks can do well during a moderate deflation, depending on what the economy does, but they get creamed during severe deflations.

- *To stabilize the value of a portfolio, you want cash equivalents (money market mutual funds, short-term Treasuries) and short- to medium-term bonds.*

- *To prevent weight gain, hair loss, acne, and wrinkles—and to confront an unknown future—you want a stake in all of these investments.* The exact mix, however, has to be matched to your personal needs (page 707) and will change over time.

- *To keep it simple,* you want to own most of these investments through mutual funds.

You have *not* diversified if you own 15 stocks. It takes a minimum of 50, spread carefully over many different size companies and types of industries, to approach a proper U.S. mix.

You have *not* diversified if you own five growth mutual funds. Those managers all pick the same kinds of stocks and they'll rise or fall in tandem.

You have *not* diversified if you own all stocks or all U.S. mutual funds, even if they're different classes of stocks.

Nor have you diversified if you buy a bond fund, a Ginnie Mae fund, and some certificates of deposit. These too are much alike.

At minimum, you need a mix of U.S. stocks, international stocks, and high-quality medium-term bonds. An investor with more money will add emerging-market stocks and commodities. Real estate also belongs in the pot. Beyond your own house, consider real estate investment trusts.

Two Important Lessons Learned from the Crash of 2008–2009

When the markets collapsed in September and October 2008 and again in February 2009, there was nowhere to hide. All the risky assets fell together—every class of U.S. and international stock, real estate investment trusts, commodities, gold, high-yield bonds, and corporate and municipal bonds. The only bright spot was U.S. Treasury securities.

You might assume from that dismal record that broad diversification isn't worth it because it doesn't protect you when the market drops. That would be the wrong conclusion. You shouldn't draw up a long-term investment strategy based on a once-in-a-lifetime (we hope!) global financial meltdown.

The right conclusion is that you should look at your investment portfolio in two ways: What helps you when stocks are moving up, and what protects you when stocks are moving down?

In rising markets, stock diversification pays. You should own large stocks, small stocks, U.S. stocks, international stocks, and emerging-market stocks. These various classes of investments rise at different times and at different rates of speed. If you invest in just one of them—say, U.S. stocks—you run the risk of choosing a market that doesn't do as well as the other ones. To keep the wind in your sails, you want to own all types of stocks, across the board.

In falling markets, however, all these classes of stock will plunge at roughly the same time. Your equity diversification won't help you at all. To limit your risk in down markets, you should own Treasury securities, cash, and very-high-quality corporate or municipal bonds.

It's not possible to guess when those random bad markets will come along. For that reason, your long-term investment portfolio should contain both diversified stocks *and* a permanent allocation to diversified bonds, in an amount appropriate to your age (page 723). Just be sure to make them *high-quality* bonds. High-yield (low-quality) bonds tend to fall in price when the stock market does, so they don't reduce your risk.

The second lesson is how to assess your exposure to risk. Typically, you measure risk by the length of your holding period—as I have on page 697. The longer you hold a portfolio of diversified stocks and reinvest the dividends, the less likely your chance of losing money over the entire term.

But it's a mistake to focus only on your investment's theoretical ending date—say, 15 or 20 years from now. That assumes you'll be able to withstand the occasional market crash prior to that date, which may not be the case. On the way to its (presumed) positive, long-term result, your portfolio might suffer several declines of 20 percent or more.

The longer you hold your stocks, the more likely it is that such a collapse will occur. Looked at that way, your stock market investment grows riskier, not safer, with time. If you hold too much in stocks, one of those crashes might drive you out of the market entirely or force you to lower your stock allocation to protect the money that remains.

That's another reason to leaven your stock portfolio with a hefty portion of bonds. During one of those temporary stock market drops, your bonds will keep enough of your money safe that you can afford to stay the course.

Picking Your Mix

Selecting an appropriate level of risk means more than choosing among stocks and bonds. Within any class of investment, some types of securities carry more risk than others.

Say, for example, that you're buying stocks to help fund a college education for your kids. A conservative investment would be a mutual fund that buys blue-chip, dividend-paying companies. An aggressive choice would be a fund that buys the stocks of small companies or companies in Southeast Asia.

If you want bonds, a conservative choice would be Treasuries, an aggressive choice would be junk bonds.

So you really have two decisions to make: (1) What mix of investments best suits your needs? (2) Within each investment class, how much risk do you want to take?

A Fixed Mix Versus a Flexible Mix. Within the Church of Asset Allocation, two theologies are at war. One says: fix your portfolio at whatever mix of assets is right for you and stay there until circumstances change (which is my view). The other says: keep changing the amount you hold of each type of asset, to focus on whichever market you think is the strongest.

With a *fixed mix,* you might own, say, 45 percent U.S. stocks, 25 percent international stocks, and 30 percent bonds. From time to time, you'd check your portfolio to see if it needs rebalancing. That means bringing everything back to the percentages that you started with. In general, you rebalance when your investment mix gets out of line by 5 percent.

With a *flexible mix,* you might decide that U.S. stocks will make up, say, 30 to 70 percent of your portfolio. When times look good, you'll put in 70 percent; when you get worried, you'll cut back to 30 percent.

Table 16.

FINDING YOUR CENTER: RISK VERSUS REWARD
#1 (U.S. Investments)

If You Own	The Average Return*	The Single Largest One-Year Gain	The Single Largest One-Year Loss
100% stocks [†]	12.6%	61.2%	−39.0%
90% stocks, 10% bonds [‡]	12.0	59.3	−35.3
80% stocks, 20% bonds	11.4	57.4	−31.6
70% stocks, 30% bonds	10.8	55.4	−27.9
60% stocks, 40% bonds	10.2	53.3	−24.0
50% stocks, 50% bonds	9.6	51.2	−20.2
40% stocks, 60% bonds	9.0	49.1	−16.3
30% stocks, 70% bonds	8.4	47.0	−12.4
20% stocks, 80% bonds	7.8	45.9	−9.1
10% stocks, 90% bonds	7.2	47.0	−11.0
100% bonds	6.6	48.9	−13.0

*From 1950 through 2008, compounded annually, dividends reinvested, portfolio rebalanced to the original investment mix at the start of every year.

[†] Measured by Standard & Poor's 500-stock average.

[‡] Ten-year U.S. government bonds.

Sources: Towneley Capital Management; Standard & Poor's Corporation, Global Financial Data.

Table 17.

FINDING YOUR CENTER: RISK VERSUS REWARD
#2 (U.S. Investments)

If You Own*	The Average Return	The Single Largest One-Year Gain	The Single Largest One-Year Loss	Measure of Risk†
100% stocks ‡	10.8%	52.6%	−37.5%	18.0
80% stocks, 20% bonds §	10.1	41.3	−28.7	14.0
80% stocks, 20% cash	9.8	40.8	−30.3	14.3
60% stocks, 30% bonds 10% cash **	9.1	30.5	−20.4	10.9
45% stocks, 45% bonds, 10% cash	8.4	24.5	−13.1	8.5
25% stocks, 40% bonds, 35% cash	7.1	20.8	−5.2	5.3
100% bonds	6.3	29.1	−5.1	6.3
100% cash	4.8	14.7	−0.9	2.9

* From 1950 through 2007, compounded annually, dividends reinvested, and rebalanced to the original investment mix at the start of every year.

† Standard deviation measures *volatility*—how fast these investments rise and fall over short time periods. High numbers mean sharp, rapid changes; low numbers mean fewer, small, changes.

‡ Measured by Standard & Poor's 500-stock average.

§ Medium-term U.S. government bonds.

** 30-day Treasury bills.

Source: T. Rowe Price.

In other words, you try to time the market, guessing when it will rise or fall. And not just one market but perhaps four or five of them, depending on how diverse your portfolio is. To me, this is a gambler's game. It adds greatly to your chance of loss. I'm a fixed-mix type of dame.

Your Reward, at Last

Tables 16 and 17 take some of the guesswork out of allocating assets among U.S. stocks, bonds, and cash. They help you decide how much risk you are willing to tolerate in order to earn a desirable return. The first table, covering stocks and medium-term Treasury bonds, was prepared by Towneley Capital Management, an investment advisory firm in New York City. The second table, for stocks, medium-term Treasuries, and cash, comes from the mutual fund company T. Rowe Price. Here's how to use the data.*

Read down the columns headed "The Average Return." They show the average long-term return you can expect if you hold the indicated mix of investments. When you see a return that looks good to you, read across to the "loss" column. There you'll find the largest percentage loss that that particular mix of investments has ever had in a single year. In table 16, for example, the all-stock portfolio with a 12.6 percent return once lost as much as 39 percent. You recover those losses in later years but must be prepared to suffer through.

If the loss looks too scary, read on down the column until you find a one-year loss that seems tolerable. Then look back to the first column to see what mix of investments you've chosen and what your average return is likely to be. If that return looks too low, rethink the size of the one-year loss that you're willing to risk (remembering that these losses are temporary).

That's investing in a nutshell. You are looking for the highest possible return commensurate with the risk you're willing to take.

The middle column, by the way, is strictly for fun. It shows the kind of luck you might have in a superior year, in both stocks and bonds. But it shouldn't enter into your investment decision. Long-term investors won't earn the single highest return; they will earn something closer to the average return.

These tables are pretax, so they're for people who are investing their retirement accounts. Your returns will vary if you're investing after tax.

The Risk/Reward Tables Carry Some Home Truths

For safety with minimal risk, don't choose an all-bond portfolio. Always include some stocks. For proof, look at table 16 and compare the portfolio fully invested in Treasury bonds with the one that contains 70 percent bonds and 30 percent stocks. The mixed portfolio had a higher average return and a smaller maximum one-year loss. Then look at table 17. The all-bond portfolio gives you poorer returns—and with more risk—than a portfolio combining bonds and cash with a modest amount of stocks. Diversification wins again.

For maximum growth potential, choose all stocks—at least for that portion of your money available for long-term investment. Stocks show the highest risk of loss in a single year but the biggest average gain over time. You'll want to take the risk, however, only when you're young and have a lifetime of paychecks in

---

*The returns on these tables don't match because the two firms use different methodologies. Towneley calculates 12-month periods from the start of every month. T. Rowe Price uses calendar years. But the investment conclusions are the same.

front of you. As you grow older and your future earnings potential shrinks, you should gradually shift money into bonds. Bonds provide your portfolio with the security you'll need as you reach midlife. (For more on bonds, see chapter 25.)

For growth with less risk, add bonds to the portfolio rather than cash. The risks are about the same, and bonds give you a slightly higher return. Cash belongs in regular, taxable accounts, for paying your future expenses.

Making You Whole

There's one more thing that you might want to know about investment risk—namely, your break-even time. Say that you hold stocks at a bull market peak and then a bear market slide sets in. You didn't rebalance (tut-tut), so you're stuck with holding your securities until they recover. How long will it take before you get your money back? The following table gives you the answer for every 15 percent decline since 1929. One column assumes that you reinvest all your dividends; the other assumes that you cash the dividend checks and spend them.

Table 18.

HOW LONG DOES IT TAKE TO GET YOUR MONEY BACK AFTER A STOCK MARKET* DROP?

Month the Bear Market[†] Started	Number of Months Before You Broke Even (Dividends Reinvested)	Number of Months Before You Broke Even (Dividends Not Reinvested)
August 1929	185	301
July 1956	12	26
December 1961	16	20
January 1966	14	15
November 1968	28	42
December 1972	42	91
November 1980	23	25
August 1987	23	9[‡]
June 1998	5	5
August 2000	81	74[‡]
Average	39	58
Average since World War II	24.4	33.7

* Standard & Poor's 500-stock average.

† Prices down 15 percent.

‡ In rare markets, reinvesting dividends hurts. So many shares are bought on the downside that it takes longer to recover. But you still have more money working for you, over time.

Source: Ibbotson Associates, a Morningstar subsidiary.

Two points to note: (1) I draw my personal risk assessments from the period since World War II. After 2008, the 1930s started looking more relevant. Still, the financial structure was different then. (2) Reinvesting dividends gives you an enormous payback, especially after long bear markets. Each reinvested dividend gains value in the subsequent market rise. With this strategy it usually takes much less time to get your money back.

What's Your Ideal Split Between Stocks and Bonds?

Take your age and subtract it from 110. The resulting number is the percentage of your assets that you should put into stock funds with the rest in bond funds. If you're 30, put 80 percent into stocks. At 50, hold 60 percent in stocks. At 70, hold 40 percent in stocks. And so on.

This rule of thumb accounts for the fact that you need more asset growth when you're young and more security as you age. It also gives you a money cushion when stocks decline. Even at younger ages, you might suddenly need some cash. Holding part of your investments in bond funds gives you something to sell if you urgently need money at a time when stocks are down. Bonds hold their value better than stocks, so you won't be forced to sell investments at a loss. For help in using this rule of 110 to get you safely through retirement, see page 1141.

Constructing Your Portfolio

You need to take a total-portfolio approach. Put all your assets in a pot, then divide them into the types of investments that serve your personal time horizon and control your risk. You'll find specifics on all these investments in later chapters. Here you're constructing your battle plan.

What follows are examples, not gospel!! Every investor is a little bit different as to wealth, health, income, expectations, needs, and financial responsibilities. Every investment adviser will have different ideas about how portfolios should be constructed. Every time period is marked by different tax laws, interest rates, and market conditions—all of which influence portfolio choices. But the suggestions below are reasonable frameworks with which to start.

When tracking your progress, don't look at just one of your investments. Your stocks might slide by, say, 10 percent, giving you a scare. But all types of investments rise and fall periodically. That's why you diversify, so you're not dependent on just one thing. If your stocks are down 10 percent but your bonds are up 3 percent and you have some cash, your total portfolio might be down by only 2 percent. *That's* the measure to go by.

Here are some portfolio suggestions for people of various ages. For more on the types of mutual funds to buy, see chapter 22. For bonds, see chapter 25.

A Young Single Person

1. Cash reserve—in a bank or money market fund.

2. Retirement account—as heavily into stock funds as you can stand. Consider target retirement funds, stock-index funds, value funds, growth funds, internationals, and emerging markets.

A Young Married Couple or Single Person with Children

1. Cash reserve—in a bank or money market fund.

2. Inflation hedge—a house and the stock funds in your college and retirement accounts. The value of your home should rise with the inflation rate once the bad 2006–2009 housing market rights itself.

3. College account—consider an age-based account in a tax-exempt 529 plan (page 664). When your child is young, the account is heavily into stocks. As he or she moves through the teenage years, it automatically switches toward bonds and cash. When tuition is due, you'll have no-risk money on hand. Follow this same system if you're handling your own investments, inside or outside a 529.

4. Retirement account—as heavily into stocks as you can stand. Consider target retirement funds, stock-index funds, value funds, growth funds, internationals, and emerging markets. For bonds, consider Treasuries, general bond funds and high-yield funds.

5. Deflation hedge—Treasury bonds with fixed interest rates.

A Middle-Aged Couple or Single Person with Children

1. Cash reserve—in a bank or money market fund.

2. Inflation hedge—a house, maybe a vacation house, the stock funds in your college and retirement accounts, and some inflation-protected Treasury bonds. The value of your home should rise with the inflation rate once the bad 2006–2009 housing market rights itself.

3. College account—consider an age-based account in a tax-exempt 529 plan (page 667). When your child is young, the account is heavily into stocks. As he or she moves through the teenage years, it automatically switches toward bonds and cash. When tuition is due, you'll have no-risk money on hand. Follow this same system if you're handling your own investments, inside or outside a 529.

4. Retirement account—consider a long-term mix of medium risk rather than high risk. Maybe 65 percent stocks, 35 percent bonds (you can't afford too much stock market risk in case there's a problem with your health or job).

For stocks, consider the usual suspects: target retirement funds, international funds, emerging markets, stock-index funds, and growth-and-income funds, but perhaps with more emphasis on the latter. For bonds, consider Treasuries, general bond funds, and high-yield funds. Outside a retirement account, use tax-deferred municipal bonds.

5. Deflation hedge—Treasury bonds with fixed interest rates.

A Middle-Aged Couple or Single Person with Children in College

1. Cash reserve—a paid-up credit card. (All your cash is in the hands of the college bursar! Your only emergency money is your credit line.)

2. Inflation hedge—a house, maybe a vacation house, the stock funds in your retirement account, and some inflation-protected Treasury bonds. The value of your home should rise with the inflation rate once the bad 2006–2009 housing market rights itself.

3. College account—in savings bonds, Treasuries, short-term bonds, or bank CDs timed to mature when semesters begin. An age-based account in a 529 plan should do this for you automatically if it's properly invested.

4. Retirement account—consider a long-term mix of medium risk (page 726) rather than high risk. For stocks, it's international funds, emerging markets, stock-index, and growth-and-income, perhaps with more emphasis on the last. For bonds, consider Treasuries, general bond funds, and high-yield funds. Outside a retirement account, use tax-deferred municipal bonds.

5. Deflation hedge—Treasury bonds with fixed interest rates.

A Young Retiree (55 to 65)

1. Cash reserve—enough money in a bank or money market mutual fund to cover 24 months of current expenses not paid by your pension and other regular income. Enough in a money fund, CD, or short-term bond fund to cover 4 more years of current expenses. (For more on retirement investing, see chapter 30.)

2. Inflation hedge—a house, maybe a summer house, your common-stock funds, and some inflation protected Treasury bonds. The value of your home should rise with the inflation rate once the bad 2006–2009 housing market rights itself.

3. Retirement account—a long-term allocation of moderate risk; say, 45 to 55 percent stocks and the rest in bonds. Consider stock-index funds, growth-and-income funds, value funds, growth funds, and internationals. For bonds, buy Treasuries, intermediate- and short-term bond funds, high-yield funds, or individual bonds. Outside a retirement account, use tax-deferred municipal bonds.

4. Deflation hedge—Treasury bonds with fixed interest rates.

An Older Retiree (65 to 75)

1. Cash reserve—enough money in a bank or money market fund to cover 24 months of expenses not paid by your pension, Social Security, and other regular income. Enough in a money fund or short-term bond fund to cover 3 to 4 more years of current expenses. For more on retirement investing, see chapter 30.

2. Inflation hedge—a house, maybe a vacation house, stock funds, and inflation protected Treasuries. The value of your home should rise with the inflation rate once the bad 2006–2009 housing market rights itself.

3. Retirement account—a long-term allocation of moderate risk; maybe 30 to 35 percent stocks with the rest in bonds. Consider stock-index funds, growth-and-income funds, value funds, growth funds, and internationals. For bonds, buy Treasuries, intermediate- and short-term bond funds, high-yield funds, or individual bonds and ladder them (page 67). Outside a retirement account, use tax-deferred municipal bonds.

4. Deflation hedge—Treasury bonds with fixed interest rates.

An Even Older Retiree (75 and Up)

1. Cash reserve—enough money in a bank or money market fund to cover 1 to 5 years of expenses not paid by your regular retirement income. Also, a firm determination to spend your principal as well as your income, if that's what it takes to live comfortably. To make your money last for life, see chapter 30.

2. Inflation hedge—a house, stock funds, and inflation-protected Treasuries. You've sold your vacation house and reinvested the proceeds for income and some growth. Why growth? Because you could easily live for another 30 years.

3. Retirement account—a stock/bond mix of medium risk, if you have enough pension and Social Security income to live on. Concentrate on stock funds that pay high dividends, such as equity-income funds. Buy intermediate- and short-term bond funds, or buy individual bonds or CDs and ladder them (page 67). Choose a low-risk portfolio, maybe only 20 percent stocks, if your current income is insufficient and you're dipping into principal to pay the bills. You can't afford the risk of losing money in a stock decline. For bonds, choose Treasuries, intermediate- and short-term bond funds, and laddered individual bonds. Outside a retirement account, choose tax-exempt municipals.

4. Deflation hedge—Treasury bonds with fixed interest rates.

What if all your retirement money is in company plans that don't allow the investment choices suggested in the sample portfolios? Your plan should at least

Pick Your Poison: High, Medium, or Low Risk

Short-term portfolio, for money needed within 2 years: 100 percent in cash—money market mutual funds, one-month Treasuries, or bank CDs.

Short- to medium-term portfolio, for money you'll want within 3 to 5 years: Low risk—30 percent cash, 50 percent bonds, 20 percent stocks. Medium risk—20 percent cash, 40 percent bonds, 40 percent stocks. High risk—10 percent cash, 30 percent bonds, 60 percent stocks.

Medium-term portfolio, for money you'll want within 6 to 10 years: Low risk—10 percent cash, 30 percent bonds, 60 percent stocks. Medium risk—10 percent cash, 30 percent bonds, 60 percent stocks. High risk—20 percent bonds, 80 percent stocks.

Long-term portfolio, for money you won't touch for more than 10 years: Low risk—60 percent stocks, 30 percent bonds, 10 percent cash. Medium risk—80 percent stocks, 20 percent bonds. High risk—100 percent stocks.

SOURCE: T. ROWE PRICE.

have a stock fund and a fixed-income fund. Given these choices, younger people should put most of their money into stocks—especially an index fund or target retirement fund if you're offered one. It doesn't matter that you might leave the company in five years; you can roll that money into an Individual Retirement Account and keep it invested in stocks. In early middle age—say, age 45—you might want 65 percent of your money in stocks. At 60, your stock allocation might drop to 50 percent (see rule of 110, page 722). These are only examples, but they indicate a direction.

Don't make the mistake of diversifying your retirement savings separately from your other savings. Conceptually, you possess a single sum of money, some of it in the retirement account, some of it not. Your diversification plan should be tailored to that sum of money as a whole. The investments outside your retirement plan can fill in the gaps that the plan doesn't offer.

For example, your 401(k) plan might restrict your stock investments to U.S. mutual funds, so use your outside money to diversify into an international fund. Alternatively, allocate higher investment risks to your retirement plan (because you won't touch that money for 20 years or more) and choose lower risks for the savings that you keep outside the plan (because that's Junior's college money, which you'll need 5 years from now).

You get the idea: count *all* of your money when deciding whether you're properly diversified. Married couples should consider both spouses' portfolios as a unit. You might run your money separately, but you're going to retire together, and your standard of living will depend on what's in the common pot.

How to Get Money to Invest

It's no mystery.

> Live on less than you earn.
> Invest the surplus.
> If that doesn't work, inherit.

The Enemies of Good Investing

Don't look to the stars, look to yourself, as the great playwright wrote. You read all this stuff about steady investing and nod your head. But in a bear market, you may forget your good intentions. Our attitudes and emotions tend to undermine the strategy we set. Mastering these emotions is just as important as mastering an investment discipline. Here are the most common mental errors:

1. Fear of loss. We're more alarmed by a minor loss than we're cheered by a major gain. To prevent these temporary losses, we panic and sell or invest more conservatively than we should. Antidote: become a rebalancer (page 710), to check your tendency to cut and run. To encourage growth investing, study the market's past performance. See how little you get from conservative income investments after taxes and inflation.

2. Short-term focus. If the mutual fund in your 401(k) loses money over 6 or 12 months, you might sell it and shift to something "safer." Conversely, you might leap into a fund that currently tops the performance list. Antidote: keep checking Morningstar (www.morningstar.com), the publisher of mutual-fund data, to see which funds are currently ahead. A fund that's hot for six months often cools in the next six months and vice versa. Once you've chosen a fund for good reasons (chapter 22), stick with it for 3 or 4 years unless the fund's management and objectives or your circumstances change.

3. Fear of making the wrong decision. With so many investments to choose from, some investors freeze. They leave their money in the bank or the fixed-income account in their retirement plan. They leave it in mutual funds that they know are unsuitable because they're afraid to change. They might hand it over to someone to manage without knowing much about the person they've handed it to. Antidote: this book, of course! Keeping your money in its usual place is a decision too—and often the *wrongest* one of all.

4. Fear of regret, also known as hindsight bias. You're afraid that you'll hate yourself in the morning. You should have bought that East Asian fund that rose 25 percent instead of the balanced fund that did only 10 percent. You should have switched to a money fund this year because stocks went down. Self-recrimination produces one of two effects: you do nothing, so you won't have to kick yourself around; or you desperately try to catch up by jumping into that East Asian fund (too late). Antidote: proper asset allocation and rebalancing. Simple and steady gets you where you want to go.

5. Reluctance to take losses. This is the reverse side of panic selling. We refuse to sell because that seals our doom. We can't help believing that a stock is worth the price we paid for it, so we hang on to losers, waiting for them to "come back." As long as we wait, we have hope. Selling buries hope, which makes us miserable. Antidote: take losses in December, when you can think of them as tax deductions. Or think of the sale as a "swap" for another investment you like better. Or sell just some of the stock today and sell more later if it keeps doing poorly.

6. Exaggerated hopes of gain. At bull market peaks, participants tend to believe that huge gains will continue indefinitely. They quit diversifying into bond funds and rush entirely into stocks. Then stocks collapse. Antidote: the tables on pages 719 and 721. Do you have enough conviction to hold if your investments drop by 40 percent or more? What if two bad years occur back to back? Diversified portfolios are the easiest to live with.

7. Illusion of control. We think we can make a stock do what we want just because we picked it. If it misbehaves, we find even more reasons to believe we were right and that the stock will come around. Antidote: keep a history of your losers as well as your winners. Look at the performance of the stocks you sold as well as the stocks you bought. It's humbling.

8. Seeing halos. We hand halos to people who seem to know what they're talking about—for example, brokers and planners who exude confidence. We award them extra points if they're good-looking, dress well, and went to a good school. None of this has anything to do with competence. Antidote: in your imagination, put a bag over their heads and listen only to whether they make sense. Check 'em out (page 817) and watch how they perform.

9. Deciding too fast. When facts and feelings come hurtling at us, begging for a resolution, we make mistakes. That's why good salespeople drop a bundle of information on you all at once. To escape the confusion, you're likely to sign up. Antidote: take the materials home and think about them. If the market is in an uproar, wait a few more days. You don't have to act fast. There's always another opportunity.

10. Succumbing to prediction addiction. You imagine that you know what will happen with stocks or any other investments. You search for "the next Microsoft." You buy stocks or mutual funds with great track records, sure that they'll keep on going up. If some of your bets pan out, the surer you become that nothing will go wrong. Antidote: gamble with only a small percentage of your money, leaving the rest of it locked up in a simple, well-diversified investment plan. If your gambling pot runs out, lesson learned.

How to Handle Investments After . . .

Marriage

If you have two retirement accounts, treat them as a single investment pool. Think about how much of your joint savings you want to allocate to U.S. stocks, international stocks, and bonds. Create an asset allocation and apply it to each of your 401(k)s. If 80 percent in stock funds is your ideal, each account should be 80 percent in stocks. Vary this only if one of you has better investments available. For example, one 401(k) may offer an international fund, while the other doesn't. That 401(k) would then contain your entire international allocation, while the other would be more heavily invested in U.S. stocks.

Anyway, that's the idea. Sometimes, however, couples can't agree on what should be in their 401(k)s. One of you wants to invest more conservatively than the other. You can maintain your total allocation by putting the more conservative investments in one of the 401(k)s and the aggressive ones in the other. If you stay married, you'll carry that total investment pot into retirement together. If you divorce, however, the spouse with the more conservative investments won't have done as well. That might be equalized in the final settlement, but then again, it might not.

If you've each been buying your company's stock (maybe because you get a special deal on the price), you are overexposed to risk. Periodically, sell some company stock and diversify into something else. If your company gives you stock as part of your 401(k), direct your personal investments elsewhere.

If you both have employee retirement savings plans, coordinate your investments. See what each company's plan has to offer, then decide where to put your money. Together, your retirement plans should reflect the mix of stock and fixed-interest vehicles that you find appropriate as a couple.

Review your marital asset allocation from time to time. As you get older, you'll want to make more conservative choices.

A New Baby

Keep up with your retirement investing. Any separate college fund should be in an age-based investment account in a tax-exempt 529 plan.

An Inheritance

Don't keep a stock just because Daddy loved it or because its price is up. Maybe Daddy was holding a rotten stock. Maybe it yields income when you need growth. Maybe it was his company's stock and he was sentimentally attached to it. Keep only those assets that fit your own investment plan. Everything else should be replaced.

A Divorce

Investments made jointly aren't necessarily right for singles. So rethink your portfolio from the ground up. You may have to live on some of the money that you took from the marriage, which means keeping a larger cash reserve.

A New Job

If you get a lump-sum payout from your former company's pension plan, roll it into an Individual Retirement Account or, if allowed, into the retirement plan of your new employer. That preserves its tax deferral. Divvy up the money among the same types of investments that you had before. Or use the IRA for investments not included in your new company plan—say, international or emerging-market funds.

A Stock Market Collapse

Think of it as a stress test for your investment allocation, not to mention your nerves. Plunging prices expose any mistakes you've made in your asset allocation. For example, say you had money in stocks that you're going to need for college tuition two years from now. In 2008, you learned the hard way that money you'll need within five years should be kept safe. Move what's left of your college money into the bank or short-term bond funds. Or say you recently retired but kept 70 percent of your money in stocks. Too much of your nest egg was at risk. You should shift more of it into bonds.

Don't wait for the market to "come back" before making changes. How do you know that each of your investments will "come back?" On page 707, you developed some rational asset allocations tied to when you're going to need the money you've invested. If you made some mistakes, figure out a better allocation and, gradually, redo your portfolio.

Unemployment

Roll a lump-sum payout from your retirement plan into an Individual Retirement Account in order to preserve its tax-deferred status. Invest the IRA in a money market mutual fund or money market deposit account at a bank. Wait a while before drawing on this cash. Withdrawals will cost you income taxes plus a 10 percent penalty if you're under 59½ (for a way of avoiding the penalty, see page 1064).

If you have other investments, sell them (or sell the ones that won't generate a big tax bill) and put the proceeds into a money market fund. This preserves your capital. You may need to draw on this money and can't run the risk of losing it in a stock market decline.

Live on your cash reserve (You have one, right? In cash or an untapped home equity line of credit?) and your other investments. If you don't find a job right away and your money runs low, make IRA withdrawals as needed.

When you get a job, use any remaining taxable savings to clean up debt. Anything left in your IRA can now go back into stocks and bonds.

Retirement

Don't shift all your money into bonds and money market funds. You will probably live another 20 or 30 years, and during that time even modest inflation can decimate fixed incomes. You need a substantial stake in stocks in order to grow enough capital for your later years.

A Windfall

Maybe it's a lottery ticket. Maybe a big royalty check. Maybe the proceeds of selling your house. First, put the money in a bank or money market mutual fund while you think about what to do. Second, ask an accountant what portion of your windfall you will have to pay in tax (keep that in the bank until next April 15). Third, attend to your obligations, such as paying off debts or setting up a college fund. Finally, study up on investments. Don't talk to a stockbroker or financial planner until you have a good idea of what you want. Salespeople can mislead the uninformed. If you plan to live on the money, invest it as if you were 65—even if you're younger. You'll need a conservative strategy to make the money last for life.

If your windfall is from an upcoming lump-sum pension distribution, don't lay a finger on the money until you've talked to a qualified financial planner (chapter 32). The size of your net proceeds will depend on the tax choice you make.

When—and When Not—to Be an Averaging Investor

You already know that you ought to invest part of every paycheck—for the good of your soul, for your future, and because your mother told you so. Steady investing keeps you from overinvesting when prices are high. And it disciplines you to keep on buying when stocks decline. Low markets are the equivalent of a bargain-basement sale.

In a seesawing market, monthly investing can make you more money than periodically investing large lump sums. That's because you are *dollar-cost averaging*. Your fixed-dollar purchase buys more shares when prices are low and fewer shares when prices are high.

Dollar-cost averaging gives you better returns when markets are zigzagging up and down. By buying more shares when the price is low, you wind up with a lower cost per share. It was a lifesaver in the late 1960s and 1970s, when stock prices rose and fell and rose and fell, never exceeding 1,000 on the Dow Jones Industrial Average. It worked again in the market cycle of 2000–2007.

But this technique is a loser in bull markets like those of the 1980s and early 1990s. When prices are moving steadily up, monthly investing gives you a higher average cost per share than if you'd been able to invest all your money at once.

When you're making retirement contributions through a payroll deduction plan, you have no choice but to dollar-cost average. Reinvesting all dividends is an averaging strategy too.

But say that you have a lump sum of money—from a retirement payout, an inheritance, or a life insurance policy. You have a choice: invest it all at once or dollar-cost average by investing it gradually over a year.

In most cases, you'll do better investing your money all at once. Stocks rise more often than they fall. The chances are two out of three that lump-sum investing will outperform dollar-cost averaging.

But then there's that fatal, final, one-third of the time when stocks will drop soon after you invest.

I think of dollar-cost averaging not as a way of making extra money but as a way of limiting risk. A lump sum invested gradually over 12 months saves you from being badly hurt if you happen to start investing just before a market drop. If you worry more about losing money than making it, this technique is for you.

Dollar-cost averaging is better done with diversified mutual funds than with individual stocks. The broad market always recovers, but certain stocks might not. If you choose a rotten stock, buying more shares on the way down would be throwing good money after bad.

Memo to the Nervous

Maybe you quake more easily than others. You know in your heart that stocks are the best investment in the long run, but the thought of owning them scares you stiff—especially after the price collapse in 2008.

Obviously, I'd like to change your mind. So try this: Put just a little money into a diversified, stock-owning mutual fund—maybe 20 percent of your savings. Pick a simple fund, like an index fund (page 745), and invest a modest sum every month for the next 12 months. Then forget about it. Pretend it isn't there. Five years from now, take a look at what you've got. Odds are, you'll have a good result, good enough to encourage you to put even more money in stocks. If I can divert even a small portion of your long-term retirement savings into the stock market, this book will have done its job.

But you have to promise to leave that investment alone. If you'll panic and sell the first time stocks drop, forget it. You don't belong in the market just yet. But do keep on reading, to learn more about how investing works. Willingness to accept stock market risk isn't necessarily a function of your personality. It may be a function of your knowledge. The more you learn, the more you'll come to understand that long-term stockholding isn't as risky as you thought.

Memo to the Nerveless

Some investors are fearless. They're not happy unless they're buying options on futures and borrowing against their house to do it. A reader once asked me what I thought about investing his son's college fund in a single high-flying stock. I said, "Not much." And he said, "But mutual funds are no fun." For him and his kin, this book will have helped if they speculate wildly with only part of their money (preferably a small part).

I'm not asking you to give up your habit. But for your family's sake, balance your high-wire act with investments that are reliably dull. Learning not to take stupid risks is equally a function of knowledge and experience. With luck, you'll learn your lesson while you still have some money left.

Clearing Your Mind

We've all heard stock market maxims that sound like ideas to live by. Mostly, they're ideas to lose money by—like these:

Listen to Your Gut; It's Usually Right. No, it steers you into buying when the market is high and selling after you've lost more money than you can stand.

You Get What You Pay For. No, no, no! Expensive investments slash your returns. Low-cost investments usually win.

You Can Beat the Market if You Try. Almost never. The market is like par in a golf game. Hardly any players can consistently beat par. Most of them fall behind.

Smart Investors Don't Settle for Earning Only the Market Average. Wrong again. See "par," above. Rising numbers of professional managers and institutions are *indexing* the core of their investments so that they'll match the market. The market does better than most managers, after costs.

Stocks Are Killers, You Should Buy Only ——— (fill in your favorite investment: real estate, bonds, commodities, gold, puppies, whatever). Big mistake. Over the long term, stocks have averaged higher returns than any of these alternative investments (not counting puppies, whose returns are bested only by kittens).

This Fund Did Great for the Past Three Years—Topped the Charts. All that means is that it owned the types of stocks that were popular then. In the next three years, different types of stocks will top the charts, and your fund will lag.

Brokers, TV Shows, Newsletters, Online Chat Sites, Friends Who Work at the Company Give Me the Inside Dope. Sorry, only dopes believe that. The big-time professionals and their computers get the news long before they do.

Only Unsophisticated Investors Use Mutual Funds. Nope. Many of the country's finest managers put even their wealthy clients' money into mutual funds, often index funds. I've know many managers who index their own money too.

I'm a Professional! I Got You Great Returns This Year! Don't believe it unless your planner shows you your personal returns compared with what you'd have gotten from index funds invested in U.S. stocks, international stocks, and bonds. Odds are, you did worse. Unless you check, you'll never know.

This Can't Miss. Yes, it can. A "can't miss" or "double your money" pitch gets you too excited to think straight.

The Outlook

Breathtaking bull markets—such as the one that started in 1982 and ran to 2000—are rare. Over that amazing period, stocks returned 16.6 percent a year. Historically, stocks have gained 9.5 percent annually. They perform badly, however, after bubble peaks such as those of 1929 and 2000. From 2000 to 2009, they lost money even with dividends reinvested.

Stocks will recover and go higher, but on their own, unpredictable schedule. Let me suggest some possibilities and how to prepare for them all.

We Have a New Bull Market—with prices recovering lost ground and heading for new highs. Your long-term retirement fund will grow, relieving some of your worries about the future. But stick with the asset allocation appropriate for your age. It's risky to throw extra money into stocks in hopes of "catching up."

We Might Have a Sideways Market for a While—with stocks rising and falling but not making much of a net advance. Dollar-cost averaging does well in a crab-walking market. So does a *fixed-mix* portfolio (page 718) that you rebalance continually—taking profits on the upside and reinvesting in assets that are underpriced. Buy and hold isn't much of a thrill. Bonds might do as well as stocks (they did better than stocks from 2000 through mid-2009, when this book went to press). Long-term stockholders have to look past the sideways years to the next true market rise.

Our Hopes Might Be Interrupted by Another Terrible Market—with stocks falling steeply again. That's why money you'll need within two years should always be kept in safe investments, such as certificates of deposit, Treasury bills and notes, or money market mutual funds. Money you'll need for sure within two to five years should be in CDs or short-term bond funds. Long-term investments that can gain when others fall include high-quality corporate and municipal bonds, Treasury bonds and notes, and maybe gold-stock mutual funds. But keep on buying stocks. You are locking them up at bargain prices. They'll pay well when the market eventually turns around.

We Might Have Stagflation—with business flat while consumer prices spiral up. Your defense would be gold (especially exchange-traded funds), commodities, money market mutual funds invested in Treasuries, inflation-protected Treasury bonds, and, as a hedge against a dollar collapse, foreign-currency bonds or bank accounts. Stocks advance during mild inflation but fall behind when inflation is severe. Bonds with fixed interest rates decline.

We Might Have a Deflationary 1930s Market—the market of your deepest dread. I rate this chance as low. But as long as you own cash and Treasury bonds, they'd be your safety nets. Incidentally, there were two bull markets in stocks during the 1930s for anyone who had the money to play. (Really. Check it out.)

We Might Have a "Normal" Market—with interest rates more or less steady and stocks gradually pushing higher, both in America and abroad. This case rests on continued international growth, low to moderate inflation, increased savings by the baby-boom generation, continued international investment in the U.S., and expanded world trade. Long term, the world has always gotten richer and stocks have always trended up. On a percentage basis, history says that you might as well invest for success.

What Makes a Good Investor?

To handle money well, you need a certain resilience of spirit. Peter Lynch, a former manager of the Fidelity Magellan Fund, looks for these qualities:

Patience
Humility
Flexibility
Persistence
Detachment
Self-reliance
Common sense
Open-mindedness
Tolerance for pain
Ability to admit mistakes
Ability to do your own research
Ability to ignore a general panic
Ability to make decisions on incomplete information
Ability to ignore gut feelings, because gut feelings are usually
wrong

22

How to Pick a Mutual Fund

Every Investor's Bedrock Buy

**I love mutual funds. Left alone to compound,
they're the surest way to wealth—but only if you're
sophisticated enough to keep them simple.**

There are two ways of investing: directly, by buying stocks and bonds through a brokerage firm, and indirectly, by buying shares in a mutual fund.

I'm for mutual funds, especially for stock investments. Bonds are a little trickier; sometimes you should go for individual bonds instead. But for long-term growth, a well-chosen stock fund will serve you better than any other financial investment. After a collapse like the one in 2008 to 2009, you might have sworn off funds forever, but it wasn't the funds' fault, and they'll be back. Stocks had near-death experiences in 1929–32 (down 84 percent), 2000–02 (down 45 percent), and 1972–74 (down 42 percent). In retrospect, those were all good periods to buy. The 2008–09 trough will be too.

Mutual Funds Defined

A mutual fund is an investment pool. You and thousands of other people put money into the pool, which a manager invests in a wide variety of securities. You'll find U.S. stock funds, bond funds, money market funds, international stock funds, commodity funds, real estate funds—literally something for everyone. There are even funds for people who don't want to bother picking funds. You own a share of all the securities in the pool.

Six Reasons to Love Mutual Funds

1. You can buy an index fund. Your investments are guaranteed to do as well as the market, minus fees—a promise that no other investment can make. When planners forecast the size of your retirement pot, they use "market" returns as your hoped-for gain. *Only* in an index fund (page 745) can you be sure of getting those long-term returns.

2. You can pick the level of market risk that you want to take: conservative, aggressive, or in the middle. By contrast, when you buy your own stocks, you generally have no idea how risky your total investment position is. That is, until the market drops.

3. You share in the fortunes of a large number of securities rather than owning just a few. If one stock in your fund goes bad, it doesn't endanger your whole portfolio. When you buy individual stocks, you're not diversified enough.

4. You can participate in the stock market's long-term gains, or the gains you expect in a particular industry, without having to think about which individual stocks to buy. Your mutual fund does that for you.

5. You can automatically reinvest your dividends and capital gains. Steady compounding doubles and redoubles your returns over time.

6. You can get full-time money management if you want a fund that tries to beat the market. I don't recommend this type of fund because managers so often come up short. But fund managers do better than stockbrokers or commission-based financial planners, whose job is to sell stuff, not to manage your money. Increasingly, brokers are simply selling mutual funds or their equivalent at a higher price than you'd pay if you bought one on your own.

But What About the Big Killings That Are Made in Individual Stocks?

What about them? Your neighbors who buy stocks would be lucky if they made a killing 1 time out of 20. In some years, they've probably done it more often—but everyone is a genius when the market is steaming up. Even in good years, your neighbors accumulate losers and mediocrities (which they don't mention). Counting losers as well as winners, I very much doubt that they do as well as the average mutual fund, especially if they don't reinvest all their dividends and capital gains. On the downside, an individual stock portfolio might drop by far more than the average mutual fund. Think General Electric, AIG, and Citigroup.

Some investors enjoy the sport of buying stocks directly. But I'd buy mutual funds first. And even if I played around with stocks, I'd use funds for my important, life-changing money.

There Are Three Kinds of Mutual Funds

Most investors today own traditional, *open-end mutual funds*—the type of investment you've known for decades. *Closed-end funds* (page 788) are for traders. The newer *exchange-traded funds* (ETFs—page 785) are a great improvement over the open-end funds sold by brokers but not necessarily better for people who choose their own no-load funds (funds without sales charges).

Open-End Mutual Funds

These are the traditional mutual funds that most people buy. The fund sells you shares, either directly—online or by mail—or through a brokerage account. Shares are priced at the fund's *net asset value* (NAV). That's the current value of all the securities the fund owns, minus liabilities, divided by the number of shares outstanding. Share prices rise or fall every business day. Each day's NAV is based on prices toward the end of the day—usually 3:00 p.m. or 4:00 p.m., Eastern time. You can buy and sell shares whenever you want, at that day's NAV.

Every year, investors receive a pro rata share of the dividends earned by their fund plus any net profits from the sale of securities. This income can be taken in cash or reinvested automatically in more fund shares. Payouts are called *distributions* and may be paid monthly, quarterly, or annually. (Fixed-income funds may declare distributions daily, even though they pay out on monthly or quarterly schedules.)

An open-end fund provides you with a prospectus, updated annually. It tells you what types of investments the fund makes, discusses the risks, presents the fund's past performance, lays out the fees, and explains the rules for buying and selling shares. Fund managers also send their shareholders semiannual and annual performance reports with a letter explaining why the fund behaved as it did.

Most open-end mutual funds are *actively managed,* meaning that individual analysts pick the securities that the fund owns. The fund compares itself with a *benchmark*—a particular market index that best represents the types of securities it buys. For example, a fund that buys large companies will benchmark itself against Standard & Poor's 500-stock index, which represents how well large companies perform. An active manager's success depends on whether he or she can exceed that benchmark with any consistency.

Passively managed, or *index,* funds don't depend on managers to pick stocks. They're designed to duplicate the performance of a particular index, such as the S&P 500 or the Wilshire 5000 index of smaller stocks. Index funds own all the stocks (or a representative sampling of the stocks) in the particular index they follow. Their manager's job is to handle the buying and selling so that the fund price and its index stay on track. Effectively, index funds become the benchmarks that actively managed funds have to beat, in order to claim success.

Up the Ladder of Risk

Here's a summary of the kinds of funds available, what they invest in, and what they hope to achieve. Note that they may or may not achieve their goals. I've started with the funds that carry the least market risk and, roughly speaking, advanced to those that carry the most risk. Use this list as a quick reference to check on the funds you read about. There are many other types of funds, with narrower objectives, but this at least gives you a look at the landscape. For a more detailed discussion of stock and bond funds, see chapters 24 and 25.

Table 19.

A MUTUAL FUND RATING CHART

Type of Fund	Risk Level	Investments*	Objective
Money market	Low	Commercial paper, certificates of deposit, Treasuries, and so on	Keep capital safe; earn current short-term interest rates.
Tax-exempt money market	Low	Very-short-term municipals	Keep capital safe; earn current short-term, tax-exempt interest rates.
Stable value	Low	Fixed income, guaranteed by an insurance company	Keep capital safe; offered only in 401(k)s
International money market	Mid–low	Foreign CDs, governments, and other short-term paper	Hope for higher returns than in U.S. money funds; reap gains when the dollar falls and losses when it rises.

Type of Fund	Risk Level	Investments*	Objective
Short-term bond, taxable or tax exempt	Mid–low	Government, corporate, or tax-exempt bonds, 1- to 5-year maturities.	Keep capital fairly safe; earn a slightly higher taxable or tax-exempt income than money markets pay; small risk of loss.
Intermediate-term bond, taxable or tax exempt	Mid–low	Government, corporate, or tax-exempt bonds, 5- to 10-year maturities	Earn a higher taxable or tax-exempt return than on shorter-term bonds; accept more gains and losses of principal; expect solid total returns long term.
Long-term tax-exempt bond	Mid–low	Tax-exempt municipals, 15- to 30-year maturities	Earn high tax-exempt income in return for more risk of loss if bonds are sold before maturity.
Ginnie Mae	Mid–low	Securities backed by a pool of government-insured home mortgages; uncertain maturities, usually not more than 12 years	Earn good income; get a periodic return of capital; accept risk of loss if interest rates rise.
Global bond	Middle	Bonds of U.S. and foreign companies and countries	Go for high bond income; win gains when the dollar falls but risk losses when the dollar rises; owns some U.S. bonds, which cushions the currency risk.
International bond	Middle	Bonds of foreign companies and countries	Go for high bond income; greater gains when the dollar falls, but greater losses when it rises.
Long-term taxable bond	Middle	Government or corporate bonds, 15- to 30-year maturities	Earn high current income, speculate on declines in interest rates; accept the risk of higher losses in hopes of getting higher total returns.

(continued on next page)

Type of Fund	Risk Level	Investments*	Objective
Income	Middle	Emphasis on bonds and dividend-paying stocks	Emphasize income, but get more growth than bond funds offer; limited losses when the stock market falls.
Balanced	Middle	Part stocks, part bonds and preferred stocks	Earn reasonable income; get reasonable growth; limited losses when market falls.
Zero-coupon bond	Middle	Discount bonds paying no current interest	Accrue high bond income; dividends reinvested at the same rate paid by the bond itself; a lucrative speculation on falling interest rates, but big losses when rates rise. Safe if held to maturity.
Equity income	Mid–high	Stocks that pay high dividends, like blue chips and utilities	Earn modest income; get good growth; risk of average loss when the stock market falls.
Growth and income	Mid–high	Stocks that pay high dividends and also show good growth	A little more growth and a little less income than equity-income funds pay; average risk of loss when the market falls.
Total Market	Mid–high	U.S. and international stocks allocated among all sizes of companies and risk levels	Maintain a fully diversified world portfolio.
High-yield bond, taxable or tax free	Mid–high	Low-rated and unrated (junk) bonds; municipals or corporates	Earn higher returns than other bond funds pay; good performance in economic upturns; higher risk of defaults; poor performance in recessions.
Asset allocation (fixed portfolio)	Mid–high	A mix of assets: cash, stocks, bonds, foreign stocks, and so on	Seek good growth and limited losses in any market.

Type of Fund	Risk Level	Investments*	Objective
Asset allocation (flexible portfolio)	Mid–high	A constantly changing portfolio mix, trying to emphasize the best markets at any given time	Seek good growth and limited losses in any market; risk of being in the wrong market at the wrong time.
Lifestyle	Mid–high	A mix of assets: stocks, bonds, cash	Create an asset allocation suitable to people of different ages and temperaments.
Convertible	Mid–high	Preferred stocks and bonds, convertible into common stocks	Earn higher yields than on common stocks but less than on bonds; hope for limited losses; less growth than in pure stock funds.
Fund of funds	Mid–high	Shares of other mutual funds	Earn average stock-market gains and losses; big risk of paying too much in management fees.
Stock index	Mid–high	Stocks picked to match the performance of a specific market as a whole	Earn average stock-market gains and losses.
Large-size companies (known as large caps)	Mid–high	Major U.S. and multinational firms	Buy the largest and best corporations that perform reliably over time.
Real estate	Mid–high	Stocks in real estate companies	An inflation hedge: risk of loss when this industry falters.
Target-date	Mid–high	Wide variety of stocks and bonds including internationals	Create a properly diversified portfolio that ages with you.
Absolute return	Higher	Long and short positions in commodities, debt, stocks, real estate, currencies, whatever	Mimic hedge funds; try to succeed in every type of market; mixed results.
Real return	Higher	Real estate, commodities timber, gold	Earn returns that exceed the inflation rate.

(*continued on next page*)

Type of Fund	Risk Level	Investments*	Objective
Market neutral	Higher	Matching long and short positions in stocks	Earn returns that beat the Treasury bill rate.
Medium-size companies (known as mid-caps)	Higher	Companies of medium size	Earn better returns than big-company stocks.
Global equity	Higher	Stocks of U.S. and foreign companies	Earn worldwide capital gains and losses.
Growth	Higher	Stocks whose earnings usually rise fast	Earn above-average market returns (one hopes); accept larger losses when the market falls.
Value	Higher	Unloved companies whose stocks are down	Buy stocks cheap and wait for them to recover; higher dividends than growth stocks pay.
International equity	Higher	Stocks of foreign companies	Earn international capital gains; bigger gains when the dollar falls; bigger losses when it rises.
Socially responsible	Higher	Stocks in "moral" companies—no nuclear, no pollution, no tobacco, and so on	Earn average growth; same risk of gains and losses as other diversified funds.
Aggressive growth (capital appreciation)	High	Shooting for the moon, with high-growth stocks, options, new issues, and so on	Earn above-average gains at the risk of above-average losses; minimal dividend income.
Asset allocation (globally flexible)	High	A constantly changing portfolio mix, focusing on several U.S. and international markets	Seek good growth and limited losses in any national or international market; a risk that the manager will bet wrong.
Sector	High	Stocks of one particular industry	For market timers, who hope to catch an industry's rising trend, then sell before stocks decline; not for investors who buy and hold; big risk of sudden loss.

Type of Fund	Risk Level	Investments*	Objective
Small-company growth; small-company value (known as small caps)	High	Stocks in the smaller companies traded on stock exchanges or over the counter	Achieve superior long-term gains relative to other growth or value funds; risk that high gains will be followed by periods of slower gains; above-average risk of loss; minimal dividend income.
Commodity	High	Metals, grains, oil, gas, livestock, etc.	Prepare for unexpected inflation, diversify into investments that behave differently from stocks and bonds.
Emerging-markets	High	Stocks in the more advanced developing countries	Invest in the world's fastest-growing economies.
Microcap	High	Stocks of teeny-tiny companies	Earn higher returns than the average small-stock fund—but be prepared to hold for a decade and endure a wild ride.
Gold and precious metals	High	Stocks of gold and precious-metal mines	A hedge against war, monetary turmoil, and, usually, unexpected inflation; gold stocks often go up when other stocks fall; big risk of loss.
Frontier market	Superhigh	Stocks in countries with newly developing capital markets	Invest in the riskiest countries, hoping for super returns, eventually.

* Some funds in these categories invest differently, but this is the general expectation.

All About Index Funds: Your Basic Buy

You can win at the stock-picking game by deciding not to play at all. Do it by buying an index fund, also called a passively managed fund. Indexers don't try to beat the market. They don't break their heads on stock analysis or economic trends. They don't scour the Web for the names of "genius" managers who are beating the market. They simply buy the stocks (or a representative selection of the stocks) that track a particular market index. With just a few index funds, you can create your own well-diversified portfolio, giving you growth for the future without exposing yourself to extra risk. Here's how index funds work and why they're so good:

To start with, what's an index? It's a way of measuring changes in price. You're probably familiar with the consumer price index, which tells you how fast or slowly prices are rising for consumer goods. A stock market index tells you how fast stock prices are moving and whether they're going up or down. Was it a happy day in the market, a ho-hum day, or a rotten day? The index knows.

The stock market index that you hear about the most is the Dow Jones Industrial Average. The Dow covers 30 large American companies. The change in their average price shows whether the market was strong or weak that day. When the Dow rises, the talking heads on TV will intone that "stocks went up." When it falls, "stocks went down."

If you're an investor, however, other indexes matter more. The most important is Standard & Poor's 500 (the S&P 500, for short), a composite of 500 leading U.S. companies. It contains many more stocks than the Dow, which makes it a superior way of tracking how well America's larger companies perform over time. The Wilshire 5000 index tracks the performance of smaller stocks as well as larger ones, so you get a picture of the market, overall. Other indexes track the performance of bond prices, international stocks, and the stocks of certain industries such as real estate. You can see at a glance whether their prices are up, down, or flat.

What's an index mutual fund? It's an investment designed to copy the performance of a particular market index. The best example is the S&P 500. An S&P index fund owns the stocks of those 500 companies. When the index rises 5 percent, an S&P 500 index mutual fund will also rise 5 percent, minus whatever the manager charges in costs. When you buy this fund, your money is invested in the average performance of America's major corporations.

There are index funds for every market you can think of. They're basically run by computer, which adjusts the fund's investments to match the way the market changed that day. Each fund does as well as its particular market overall, minus costs.

How are index funds different from other mutual funds? Most other mutual funds are run by people, not by computer. They're called actively managed funds because managers decide which stocks or bonds to hold. One manager may love Cisco Systems, so he buys a lot of it. Another may load up on Procter & Gamble, which she thinks will do even better. Only in hindsight will you know which one was right.

Professionals try to "beat the market"—meaning beat the returns on index funds. Believing (or hoping) they'll succeed, investors pay them higher fees. That feels like the right way to invest. You assume that the people who study the market full-time will produce superior results. But it's all mystique. I've run many, many long-term performance comparisons between index funds and the managed funds that compete with them. At most, I've found three or four individual managers—out of thousands—who beat the indexers over ten years.

You don't have to monitor your index funds. They don't need oversight the way that managed funds do. The manager won't change; the investment committee won't make a disastrous asset-allocation decision. Once you've settled on your asset-allocation plan, you can invest and forget.

What happens to index funds when the market drops? Index funds fall when the market does. Managed funds do too. But index funds never sink further than the market, as so many managed growth funds and emerging-market funds did during the long collapse of 2000 through 2002 and again in 2007 to 2009. The way to reduce your losses during the months when stocks turn down is not to look for a manager who will predict the downturn and outsmart it. That's a bad bet, as the record shows. Instead, own bond funds as well as stock funds, to provide some stability when bear markets strike.

Can managed mutual funds beat index funds? They can, but most of them don't. It's hard to beat the performance of the total market over time. A particular fund may do better than the index for three years or even five years. When you read that the Super Bucks Fund has been rising by 30 percent in years when the market in general just poked along, you may rush to buy. But Super Bucks will almost certainly fall behind the market over the following three or five years—often by a lot. It soared because it happened to focus on an industry that suddenly got hot: telecom, energy, banks, whatever. When those stocks cool down, the fund will fall. With rare exceptions, top funds don't stay on top, even with a talented manager at the helm. When you average their good years with their bad ones, they usually lag.

Countless studies have proved that point. Vanguard's low-cost S&P 500 fund, for example, has beaten the average big-stock manager decisively over 10-year, 15-year, and 20-year periods. Over some 5-year stretches, the S&P fund runs toward the middle of the pack, but once you reach 10 years, it usually moves to the upper quarter or higher. Remember, investing is a game of odds. You're not aiming for the top fund every year—that's an impossible goal. To be a winner, you simply need a fund that runs well above the average manager over the long term. That's what you can count on an index fund to do.

A few active managers have beaten the S&P over longer periods, even up to 15 years. But there's no way of spotting those outperformers in advance. The mutual fund you decide to buy (because it's hot today) will probably not be the one that tops the scoreboard a decade from now. What's more, the winners beat the indexes by no more than 1 percentage point or so, on average, while the multitude of losers underperform by a lot. Your drive to beat the market makes it likely that you'll fall behind.

One of my favorite studies* took the 15 largest actively managed stock funds of 1999 and compared their actual four-and-a-half-year performance with how they'd have done if their managers had hibernated over that period of time. You have probably guessed the result already: in 11 of those funds, the stocks that were owned in 1999 outperformed the stocks that the managers replaced them with. Instead of adding value, most of the managers subtracted it! A 2007 study concluded that investors, including institutions, spend around $100 billion a year trying to beat the market (counting fund fees, management costs, and transaction costs)—and don't.

In theory, active managers have a better chance of outperforming the indexes in certain niches, such as small-company stocks or developing countries. But over 10 years, that hasn't worked out either.

Why do active money managers lose, given all their resources and expertise? First, they can't guess—consistently—which stocks will beat the market. Second, they're constantly trading stocks, which runs up brokerage expenses. Trading might cost the fund up to 2.5 percent a year, which directly reduces your return. Third, they charge high fees. Counting trading and management expenses, an actively managed fund might have to do 3 or 4 percent better than the index, just to cover costs. Finally, their trading racks up taxable capital gains—another cost, if you hold the fund in a taxable account.

You hope that active managers will beat the market, which is why you pay their fees. But in most years, you're paying them to miss! To be worth your time, a manager has to do well enough to match the investment return you'd get from an index fund, plus cover his or her extra costs, plus cover the extra taxes that result from trading, plus give you a higher return on your money. Not very likely, even if he or she has superior stock-picking skill. Over time, you'll almost certainly beat them with a low-cost index fund.

If index funds usually beat managed funds, how come investors keep giving managed funds their money? Lots of reasons. The money managers talk a good game. They're the experts. You read admiring stories about them in personal finance magazines and online investment blogs—always the ones with terrific

---

*By Morningstar for *The Wall Street Journal*. "The Cost of Active Investing," by Kenneth French, finance professor, Dartmouth College.

recent records (recent losers don't get interviewed). Managed funds advertise "top performance," and advertising works. You can't help believing that today's best funds will stay on top—the continuing triumph of hope over experience. Everyone else buys managed funds, and you think they must know something. They're the funds that stockbrokers and most financial planners sell. When your hot fund cools, you assume that you merely made a wrong pick and should look for another, better fund. That's what the experts say to do.

Money managers and financial salespeople dismiss index funds. They remind you that indexing gives you "average" performance, and who wants to be just average? You want to beat the average, right? But most managed funds don't beat the average over time, even though they claim they can. Think about Chico Marx in *Duck Soup,* saying, "Who are you going to believe, me or your own eyes?"

Believe your own eyes. The research on index funds is right.

Besides, what does "average" market performance really mean? In the normal world, average means "middle" (ugh, probably mediocre). But not in the investing world. When you're looking at market performance, "average" is actually "high." The stock market average is like par in golf—the score that only the best players get. A few golfers beat par, but most fall short. Money managers can sometimes beat the market over short terms, but over the long term, most fall short. If your investment performance matches the market average, you're up there with the very best.

Indexing can get frustrating if you watch the market all the time. You'll keep seeing funds that do better, and you'll think you should be buying them instead. There are periods when a third or more of the managed funds may be ahead. But decades of data prove that the market is hard to beat. The funds that outperformed during the past five years will be different from the winners in the next five years. If you keep trying to guess the winners, you'll keep making mistakes (studies show this, too). Besides, you're busy! You want to ignore your investments while you live your life. In 20 or 30 years, you want to wake up, look at the size of your retirement fund, and say, "Wow." Indexing is a wow.[*]

If you'd like to join a chat room full of ardent indexers, go to the site run by Bogleheads.org (www.bogleheads.com), named for John Bogle, founder of

---

[*]If you'd like to read a whole book on the superiority of indexing and diversification, I have three to recommend: *Winning the Loser's Game: Timeless Strategies for Successful Investing,* by the investment consultant Charles Ellis; *The Only Guide to a Winning Investment Strategy You'll Ever Need: The Way Smart Money Invests Today,* by Larry Swedroe of Buckingham Asset Management, which manages money for wealthy people; and *Unconventional Success: A Fundamental Approach to Personal Investment,* by David Swensen, who has made a spectacular success of managing Yale University's endowment.

the Vanguard Group, the first fund company to offer index funds to the general public. It's an education in itself. For information on the leading index funds, see page 850.

Yes, but My Index Funds Collapsed When the Market Dropped!!

Index funds will do that, of course. But did you notice that actively managed mutual funds collapsed as well? In theory, managed funds should do better when the stock market drops because their genius managers will get you out in time. Ahem. In practice, the majority of them do much worse. The proper hedge against the dangers of the market isn't to shift to a managed fund. It's to balance your stock investments with bonds and cash, so you never have everything at risk. That's what chapter 21 is all about.

Different Types of Index Funds

In general, there are three types of indexing strategies:

1. Classic index funds. These are the original funds and the type that most people buy. They follow indexes that are weighted by *market capitalization.** In market cap indexes, each stock affects the index price in proportion to its market value. For example, take the oil stocks in the S&P 500. If they're popular and highly priced, they will carry more weight than less popular stocks. Index investors will be proportionately more invested in oils than in other industries. When the oils lose favor, their weight in the index will decline and so will that portion of your index investment. Other portions of the index—say, chemicals or pharmaceuticals—will rise to take their place. Almost all of the open-end index funds are based on market cap indexes. They reflect the average return on the money invested in that particular market.

Critics say that the classic index fund forces you to overinvest in high-priced stocks and underinvest in the lower priced stocks that are better bets. For that reason, they've structured new types of indexes that they think will yield superior returns.

2. Fundamental index funds. This is the group that's getting the most attention. Fundamental indexes are constructed with stocks that meet specific tests of operating value—for example, cash dividend payments, cash flow, total sales, and stock price compared with the company's book value. Such measures favor

---

*A stock's market capitalization, or "market cap," equals the price per share times the number of shares outstanding. Take IBM, with 1.34 billion shares outstanding. On a day when it's priced at $90, its market cap is $121.9 billion.

smaller companies and stocks with low prices relative to earnings (called "value stocks"). Historically, these two classes of stocks have often (but not always) outperformed other types of stocks, although they carry more market risk.

The fundamental indexes, known as the FTSE RAFI series, track various types of U.S. and international stocks. You invest through exchange-traded funds (ETFs—page 785). They don't follow the market as a whole, the way classic market cap indexes do. Instead, they're an investment strategy, tracking the classes of stocks that the sponsors of the indexes think will do the best. And maybe they will, but only time will tell.

3. Dividend index funds. These indexes were built by analysts who believe that dividend-paying stocks will outperform the market over the long run. You invest through ETFs, sponsored principally by the investment company Wisdom Tree. Evidence for the possible outperformance of dividend stocks isn't as strong as the evidence for the FTSE RAFI fundamental indexes.

The ETFs that track these new indexes have to buy and sell shares more often than traditional index funds do, in order to maintain a portfolio that meets the investment parameters. As a result, investors pay higher transaction costs and may receive more taxable capital gains than if they chose a traditional open-end market cap fund.

How to Pick Actively Managed Funds, If You Still Want to Try Them

Let's say you've bought my story and will use index funds for your core investing. But you want to invest at least some of your money in actively managed open-end funds—hoping to conjure up one of those wizards who might outperform. Here's how you go about it:

1. Read up. Get some specialized books on fund investing that will carry you past what you're learning here. *The New Commonsense Guide to Mutual Funds* by Mary Rowland gives you a quick roundup of investment tips. For a clear-eyed discussion of mutual funds that barbecues herds of sacred cows, pick up *Common Sense Mutual Funds* by John Bogle, the brilliant founder of the Vanguard funds.

2. Understand the jargon. A *growth fund* looks for stocks whose earnings are rising rapidly. A *value fund* looks for companies that have had problems (temporary ones) and whose stock prices have been beaten down. A *blended fund* buys both types. *Cap* is short for capitalization, which refers to company size. *Large-cap* stocks are big companies. There are *mid-caps, small-caps,* and *micro-caps.* As a group, small caps are riskier than large caps.

A *price/earnings ratio* compares the price of the stock with the company's earnings (usually, earnings over the past year). High P/E ratios (say, over 25) go with stocks and funds that are highly priced relative to earnings; a 15 P/E ratio is about average; a 10 P/E ratio is low—suitable for a value stock or a market in a mess. For more on P/E ratios, see page 873.

A *market timer* is someone who buys and sells shares based on a short-term forecast of what the market is going to do. If you think prices will rise, you buy. If you think they'll fall, you sell, hold the money in cash, and wait until you expect prices to go up again. As a way of making money, market timing almost never works. You're wrong more often than you're right.

A fund with *alpha* has done better than the market (that is, better than the particular market that it uses as a benchmark). Managers or strategies that outperform are said to *add alpha*.

A fund's *beta* measures how fast it rises and falls (its volatility) compared with the market. Generally, a fund with a beta higher than 1 is considered higher risk. A beta lower than 1 is lower risk. In theory, a high-beta fund should produce higher returns (note the word *should*).

The measures of any fund's alpha and beta aren't sure things. They change with time and shouldn't be used to forecast results. But the concepts are thrown around a lot, so you need to know what they mean.

3. Settle on an asset allocation. Decide how to diversify your assets, based on what you concluded from chapter 21. A reasonable mix would be large U.S. stocks, small U.S. stocks, international stocks, emerging-market stocks, and intermediate-term bonds. You can buy them in the form of index funds as well as in managed funds. Real estate stocks are included in U.S. index funds and will probably be in diversified managed funds too. So buy a separate real estate fund only if you want to make a bigger bet on that particular type of investment. You have *not* diversified if you buy three aggressive-growth funds. They may own different companies, but they'll all soar or plunge together. Quantity doesn't mean you're diversified, either, because the funds probably overlap. You can cover all the bases mentioned in this paragraph with just five funds. Seven would be plenty. As you will see, even seven good managers can be hard to find.

4. Go no-load. When you're picking funds yourself, stick with those without *loads* (sales charges): no front-end load, back-end load, or level load (page 766). All things being equal, you'll do better in no-loads because none of your money goes for sales commissions. No-loads also tend to have lower annual expenses than load funds do. Some leading no-load families include Dodge & Cox Funds, Fidelity, Harbor Fund, Longleaf Partners Funds, Oakmark Funds, T. Rowe Price, and Vanguard.

If your money is being managed by a fee-only financial planner, he or she will probably use no-load funds too. Planners usually charge 1 percent or less on top of the fees the mutual funds charge.

5. Go for seasoning. Don't buy brand-new funds. You have no idea how well they'll perform over the long term, even if the manager had a good track record with other funds. New funds often start with gorgeous records—not because they're in the hands of a wizard but because of the way that mutual funds are developed. A company may start a dozen funds to see how they go. Invariably, one or two will do well over the incubation period. Those are the ones that are subsequently offered to the public, at which point they may turn into very different animals. New funds are also started to catch investing fads—real estate, Internet companies, gold. It's proof positive that stock prices in that sector are already high.

6. Discover the many research tools that are readily at hand. Here's where you start developing short lists of potential buys—three or four funds in each of the asset categories for which you're aiming. Good information sources include:

• *Morningstar.com*—the leading source of information for both traditional mutual funds and exchange-traded funds (page 785). To find a fund, enter its ticker symbol into Morningstar's Search box. You'll get a free "Snapshot," containing, among other things, the fund's objectives, investment style, fees and expenses, past-performance stats going back as far as 10 years, tax-adjusted returns, SEC filings, technical measures such as alpha and beta, and its relative attractiveness to investors (the "star" rating—see a warning, below). Another way of getting to the Snapshot is to type the fund's name into a search engine and follow the Morningstar link. If you don't have a fund in mind, Morningstar offers lists of recent high performers for you to rummage through.

If you take a premium subscription to Morningstar, you'll get reams of additional data, analysts' opinions, fund search screens, asset allocation tools, newsletters, and access to a valuable tool called "Portfolio X-Ray." When you enter all your mutual funds into the X-Ray, it will tell you how much their holdings overlap each other. You may be less diversified than you think.

• *The performance, "best-buy" lists, tips, and news coverage found on the Web sites of the following magazines: Forbes* (www.forbes.com), *BusinessWeek* (www .businessweek.com), *Kiplinger's Personal Finance* (www.kiplinger.com), and *Money* (money.cnn.com) They recommend different funds because they make different evaluations, but any of these lists will do. Like all managed funds, these may or may not beat the market (usually not).

- *FundAlarm.com, a fun site to read.* It lists the mutual funds you ought to consider selling, called 3-Alarm Funds, and provides some selling rules.

You'll also find potential "sell" flags at Morningstar. Its mutual fund Snapshots shows "flow data"—money going into the fund (new purchases) and money coming out (redemptions). If redemptions exceed new purchases, the manager will have to sell shares and won't have new money to invest in better ideas. That doesn't necessarily mean that the fund's price will drop. The manager and the new purchases may recover. But it's a warning sign.

- *The Web sites of popular mutual fund groups* such as Fidelity, Vanguard, and T. Rowe Price. They provide tons of investor education and advice, as well as information on their various funds.

- *The Web site of a recommended fund.* Look at its investment objectives to see if they mesh with yours. Call up the most recent annual report and read the letter to shareholders to see what the manager thinks about the market and his or her own performance. Does the manager make sense? Do you understand the strategy? Then check the financial parameters: recent performance, average price/earnings ratio of the shares it holds, the percentage of assets held in different industry sectors, the minimum investment required, expenses, and other data.

7. Choose funds with low annual expenses. You'll find a full discussion of expenses on page 764, including the surprising bite that a "mere" 1.5 percent a year subtracts from your investment gains. (Hint: you lose a lot more than 1.5 percent.) Index funds from no-load companies have the lowest costs. To earn his or her fee, any fund manager has to deliver an investment return high enough to cover expenses *and* outperform a low-cost index fund, not just for a year or two but over a long period of time. That's a tall order, especially if the fees exceed the averages shown on page 770. (Note, by the way, that not all index funds are low cost. Expensive, broker-sold index funds ought to be outlawed.) At Vanguard, many of the managed funds have beaten their benchmarks over various periods of time, partly because of their low fees.

8. Check the minimum investment. Most funds require $1,000 to $3,000 to open an account. A few hold out for $10,000 and up. You can sometimes open an Individual Retirement Account for less. Once you've become a shareholder, funds might accept additional investments of as little as $50 to $100. Some funds, including T. Rowe Price, let you start with $50 a month as long as the money is deducted automatically from your bank account.

9. Look for managers who have been in place for at least five years. Managed mutual funds are run by people, not computers, and you need to know who those people are. Some of them have proven to be more skilled than others.

When the lead stock picker leaves a fund, it effectively has no record until the new manager shows what he or she can do. The fund's Web site will tell you who the manager is and how long he or she has been there. You're hoping for a wizard (even though, deep in your heart, you know that wizards don't exist). Tenure isn't linked directly to performance, but a manager who has been there awhile at least knows something about the research team and understands the fund's portfolio.

A few well-regarded funds are run by teams. In this case, a change in lead manager may not matter much, as long as he or she has been with the group a long time. When a fund claims to have team management, however, read that section of the prospectus with care. The investment method used by the fund should be clearly spelled out, and most of the team's major players should have been on board awhile.

A few funds, at families such as Harbor and Vanguard, farm out money to various independent managers. That's a good way of signing up the industry's leading lights.

10. Check for consistency of investment style. A fund's style is defined by the kinds of stocks it invests in. Again, your best source is Morningstar. It prepares "style boxes" for each fund, defining the way the fund behaves. Is it invested primarily in large, medium-size, or small companies? Does its manager lean toward value stocks, growth stocks, or a blend? You want to see consistency (Morningstar shows prior-year style boxes, going back as far as 10 years, at the top of each fund's detailed Snapshot).

If the fund has drifted into and out of different styles, pass it by. The managers aren't in control of their strategy or are spinning the public, neither of which is promising. For example, take a high-performance small-stock fund that is now buying mid-caps. It probably got more new cash from investors than it knows what to do with. So it's being pushed into the mid-cap arena, where it may not fare as well. And take a value fund with a mediocre record. If it buys some growth stocks in a rising market, it may outperform its peers and rise to the top of the value list, which is a cheat. Morningstar fights these games by classifying funds based on the way their securities behave rather than by the type of fund they claim to be.

11. Consider the fund's size. Its size should be congruent with its investment goals. Small-company funds tend to lose their character once they've passed $1 billion in size. Funds specializing in mid-caps can generally handle up to $5 billion. Big-company funds can be any size. As for bond funds, the bigger the better.

Managers sometimes announce that they're going to close their funds. That's no time to buy. You've effectively been told that the fund has attracted more new money than it can handle, which means that performance may fall off. Reconsider the fund when it opens again, provided that its larger size hasn't forced the manager to change his or her investment style.

In general, small-stock funds do better than large-stock funds, but not all the time. Sometimes one group outperforms the other; then their records reverse. The data suggest that the outperformance comes from small-stock value funds rather than small stocks in general, so you might consider focusing your small-stock allocation on the value group. Performance depends on the manager, of course—unless you're in an index fund.

Small-stock funds are more volatile than those that own large stocks. On average, they rise more in good markets, attracting a lot of hot money. They fall more in bad markets, causing trend-following investors to flee. You take more risk in a small-stock fund, hoping to bag a higher return.

12. Avoid funds managed by banks and brokerage houses. They have lousy records, and not just because their fees are typically high. They have major investment banking clients they want to please and initial public offerings to manage. Studies have shown that to win big future fees, banks and brokerage firms may stick their clients' stocks into their own mutual funds and private investment partnerships, including stocks that aren't doing well. You can count on banks and brokerage firms to put their own interests first.

13. Look at past performance. This is the tough one. Past performance doesn't predict future returns, and that's not just boilerplate. It's real. So what can you make of the performance data? Can they help you find one of the better funds?

To begin with, your quarry is always a manager, not a particular fund. So the fund's performance is relevant only if that manager is still there and his or her methods haven't changed. Otherwise the testing period has to start all over again.

Most investors rely on Morningstar, which rates most of the funds that have been in existence for three years or more. Funds get anywhere from one star (bottom rung) to five stars (tops), based on their past performance adjusted for risk. The categories—internationals, large-caps, real estate funds, and so on—are rated separately, so you see each fund's performance relative to its peers. A five-star international fund has done better than most other internationals over the rating period. Investors follow ratings slavishly. Most new investments pour into funds with four or five stars. Those are also the funds most widely advertised and promoted on the companies' Web sites.

Morningstar's research shows that five-star equity funds, as a group, slightly outperform four-star funds three and five years later. Four-star funds slightly outperform those with three stars, and so on down the line. But the average out-performance is very small—usually just a few tenths of a percent. For example, in a period when five-star U.S. equity funds returned 11.93 percent, the four-star funds returned 11.78 percent, a difference of just 0.15 percent. The one-star funds returned an average of 10.84 percent. Each "star" group has better and worse performers, but the stars can't tell you which ones they are.

There's something else interesting about these ratings. Over three and five years, *the top-rated funds fall to the middle of the pack.* As a group, they start out with five stars and wind up with three stars. That's consistent with every-thing else we know. Regardless of tenure, managers who produce positive, risk-adjusted returns for three years are not likely to repeat their performance in subsequent periods. They're on top when their favorite industries or stocks are hot; then they fall back, and other stock pickers take their place. The next generation of five-star funds could come from anywhere on the list.

So what good are the star ratings? Use them this way:

• *One-star funds are less likely to move up*, so that's not the best place to troll for good managers.

• *Five-star funds aren't likely to retain their ranking,* so that may not be the best pool to choose from either. If you buy, look beyond the stars.

• *Consider the three-star and four-star groups.* A three-star manager with five stars in his or her past might cycle back up when those types of stocks gain favor again.

• *Low-cost funds get better star ratings than high-cost funds.* That's probably because the high-cost funds take on more investment risk. They need higher returns to cover their expenses and still be competitive. Their strategy might be successful, but it's also more likely to fail. That's what risk is all about.

• *The best place to start would be a higher-rated fund with low costs.* Low costs are still the best predictor of long-term performance, Morningstar says.

14. Look at the fund's cumulative record and deconstruct it. The fund's Web page and its Morningstar Snapshot give you the average annual returns over five years, three years, and year to date, compared with an appropriate market benchmark. But even though it's nice to have beaten the market, that's not nearly enough. Maybe the manager had four poor years plus one huge year, thanks to some lucky stocks that put him ahead. So check the year-by-year performance—again, you'll find it on Morningstar. You'd like to see consistency compared with the benchmark, not wild ups and downs.

15. Look at how well the manager performed compared with his or her peers. Here again, Morningstar can help. The Snapshot shows the fund's per-formance relative to other funds in its broad category, as well as to the general market. Another great source is FundAlarm.com, a site that focuses on which funds are candidates for trash. Click on your fund, and you'll see how the manager stands, compared with the fund's most suitable benchmark, over the past one, three, and five years.

You can't expect a manager to beat the market all the time, but he or she should do well compared with other managers buying the same kinds of stocks. Skip any fund that hasn't kept up with, or exceeded, the average performance of its peer group for at least three years.

16. Check the fund's performance in down markets. For recent markets, that means 2000–2002 and 2008–2009

In bear markets, some funds drop further than the general market average and then spring back: small-cap growth funds, for example. Others go down less but may not turn up as fast—more descriptive of value funds. Think about which type of fund would make you happier. Daring investors love volatility; sharply declining markets let them buy funds cheap. Conservative investors hate excessive drops in price; they might be scared into selling near the bottom, which costs them their chance to recover their loss. Over the long term, supervolatile funds generally don't perform as well as steadier ones. They lose so much in down markets that it's harder for them to recover their previous peaks.

Will Your Performance Match the Fund's Performance?

Probably not. Investors usually don't do as well as the mutual funds they buy. The reason is simple. You buy, or add to, successful funds *after* they've started zooming in value, not before. You sell during mediocre years, before the fund picks up again. On a buy-and-hold basis, the fund's past performance could be fine. But because of the way you timed your investments, you might show a loss.

How far behind do individuals fall? You can find out at Morningstar.com, which keeps track of average investor returns. Go to Morningstar's home page and enter the name of a fund in the "Quotes" box. When the fund page comes up, click on "Total Returns" to get its performance record. You'll then see a tab for "Investor Returns." Click there to find out how well (or poorly) a typical investor did.

Investors have fared the worst in volatile funds where prices zoom and dip. One example would be the technology sector. In a particular 10-year period when those funds grew at an annual 6.4 percent, their average investor was *losing* 4.2 percent. Investors have fared the best in conservative funds, where returns are steadier. This group includes the giant, well-diversified stock funds as well as funds that buy both stocks and bonds.

What's the lesson? If you seek the thrill of aggressive funds, you should be prepared to stick with them during their poor years too. Otherwise you're more apt to lose money than gain it. Investors who will sell after a couple of poor years should choose more conservative funds. Over the long term, you'll make more money in a fund that you can buy and hold.

A contrarian's starting place. Hunt for managers of lower-cost funds who have done well against their peers in the past and whose investment style is currently cool, not hot. They've probably lagged the market for two or three years. The types of stocks they buy have been out of favor for a while but might be ready to come back.

Don't be driven by fund envy. Every month the personal finance magazines and Web sites heap praises on the Fabuloso Funds of the Moment. Unfortunately, they're almost never funds you own. If you buy them, they'll usually shine for a while, then fall off. That's because it's not skill that puts most of these fund managers on top. Their stocks or investment style just happens to be in vogue. When styles change, their stars will dim, and the magazines will fall in love with another set of funds. Screen a Fabuloso Fund just the way you'd screen any other. Magazine editors have to produce exciting new reading matter every month and don't know any more about the future than you do.

Buying a Newly Issued Managed Fund

Why would you bother? A new fund is a huge risk. Its manager may have hit home runs at his or her last fund, but these are new conditions and who knows how long it will take for the portfolio to shake down?

There are some possible advantages. A new stock fund starts small, so its winning picks will have more impact than they would on a bigger fund (ditto its losing picks, of course). The fund has a flow of fresh cash to leverage the manager's best ideas. In bull markets, these funds often have pretty good opening months.

Still, performance is a question mark. Unless you've screened the manager at his or her last position and think you have a wizard, stick with seasoned funds whose long-term records are spread out for all to see (page 763).

Buying a Mutual Fund at a Bank

Screen it as carefully as you would any other fund. Bank funds aren't safer or better. They are not government insured. They're not cheaper or smarter or more attuned to small investors. You can lose money; these are not CDs. They're just mutual funds with sales charges, competing for your money along with all the rest.

What About "Alternative" Funds?

Stocks went exactly nowhere after the tech bubble burst in January 2000. Correction: large-company stocks went down, then clawed their way back to a little above their previous peaks and then dropped again. Tech stocks never reached their previous peak. Real estate stocks bubbled and broke. Investors started talking about alternatives to stocks: commodities, currency futures, gold, and various hedge fund strategies.

A hedge fund supposedly protects you from market declines. Here are some of the strategies being offered to stunned and unhappy stock investors:

Market-neutral funds. These funds include *long positions* in stocks (where you profit if prices rise) and *short positions* (where you profit if prices fall). The two types of positions should be of roughly equal value and invested in similar industries. If the stock market rises, the longs are supposed to produce more gains than the losses you take on your shorts. If the market falls, the shorts are supposed to earn more than you lose on your longs. Some market-neutral funds exploit small technical anomalies among stocks, making quick and constant trades. In either case, the managers aim to make money in any market, with returns exceeding the Treasury bill rate.

Absolute-return funds. By "absolute," they mean that they're managed to produce returns that, specifically, are not linked to the stock market in general. They're the anti–index funds. They're managed to decline less in bad markets by limiting risk. In return for that protection, you earn less in good markets. Absolute-return funds use a variety of hedge fund strategies, including long/ short positions, commodity and currency speculations, international investments, real estate, managed futures, cash, bonds, and assorted derivatives. Some of these funds are marketed as being able to make money in any market, which I'd call deceptive and delusive. Ditto for funds that appear to promise specific returns over a designated time period. The proper function of these funds (if managed well) is to fall less than stocks do when the market declines.

Synthetic absolute-return funds. These are sold in the form of ETFs. They track average hedge fund performance at much lower cost than you'd pay to be in a fund itself. Two such: the Goldman Sachs Absolute Return Tracker fund and Natixis ASG Global Alternatives fund.

What's the record on these funds? So far, decidedly mixed.

At this writing, market neutral funds have done worse than Treasury bills and ultra-short-term bond funds. Even if they did a tad better from time to time, I have no idea why you'd want to pay for a complicated and expensive investment that aspires to the same returns you'd get from something simple and safe. My opinion: skip them.

Absolute-return funds, on average, lost less during the 2007–2009 carnage than all-stock funds. In that respect, they fulfilled their charter. Still, not all strategies worked, and expenses can top 4 percent. Hundreds of hedge funds collapsed during the market crash. For success, you depend absolutely on the manager's skill, which, as a practical matter, you and I can't figure out. A few of them are supergood (for a while, at least) while the rest just run up trading costs and expenses. If you want a diversification into an absolute-return fund, buy the ETFs of one of the synthetic funds that copy the sector's average performance. Unlike the funds, ETFs carry reasonable costs.

The Commodities Alternative

Commodity prices normally move on a different track from the prices of stocks and bonds, which is a plus for a diversified portfolio. At this writing, they're down. In recessions, demand for commodities falls. With recovery, however, they'll pick up again. As a diversifier, they're worth maybe 5 percent of the money that you normally allocate to equities.

The easiest way to invest is through an exchange-traded fund (page 785). Commodity ETFs buy futures (page 963), not the commodities themselves. They also buy Treasuries and borrow against them for leverage. These complications make them expensive to run, so fees are higher than you'd normally find in ETFs. But they're cheaper by far than commodity mutual funds, especially when you consider sales commissions. For information on appropriate ETFs, see page 852.

Vetting the Fund Prospectus

Read the prospectus before you buy! Sales literature is fine, but it takes a prospectus to clue you in to the fund's costs and risks. When investing, there's no avoiding risks, but you should understand the ones that you're about to take.

Prospectuses for the widely sold no-load mutual funds have become remarkably clear, so there's no reason to shy away from them. They're well presented and written in plain English. Sit down with a pen and underline the important points as you read. That helps you focus. Most of the key things you need to know are in early pages. Toward the end of the prospectus, you'll get more detailed information about fees, taxes, and all the special rules that affect buying and selling. For example, many no-load funds apply *frequent trading limitations:*

if you sell (say, to nail down a year-end tax loss), you may not be able to buy again for 30 or 60 days. Most load funds, by contrast, are happy to have you trade—it's a commission to the broker each time.

Also, ask for (or download) the Statement of Additional Information (SAI). That's part B of the prospectus. Most of the data there is probably not your cup of tea. But you might be interested in the list of directors and officers, their compensation, and whether the manager is investing in the fund. You want the manager to have a substantial amount of skin in the game (at least $500,000).

If a fund is still offering an old-style, clear-as-mud prospectus, it doesn't care much about its retail investors. You should take the hint. A complex or technical prospectus also suggests that the fund uses complicated investment techniques that entail more risk than you care to take. If you don't understand the explanations, this is definitely not the fund for you.

Mutual funds are allowed to give you a plain-English *summary prospectus*— just a few pages disclosing key facts: investment objectives, costs, risks, performance, investment advisers, and the top 10 holdings. Each fund will have to deliver the information in the same order, making it easier for you to compare them. For reaching an investment decision, the summaries will probably be enough. Still, you should get the full prospectus too, in case there's something about the fees or transaction rules that you want to look up or if a question ever arises. The summaries and the prospectus can be mailed, if you want them, or downloaded from the fund's Web site. Keep the original prospectus, along with the SAI, permanently on file, or bookmark them on your computer for future reference. You'll get a new prospectus every year to bring you up to date. If the fund makes any changes in its investment methods or objectives, you'll be notified separately.

Investors also get annual reports, which are also posted on the fund's Web site. Always read the fund manager's letter in the front of the report before you invest. It discusses the fund's performance during the previous year. The best managers are very explicit about what happened and why. I'd suspect a fund that gave me fog or boilerplate. Many no-load funds post previous reports, so you can track the manager's thinking over several years.

Prospectuses for no-load funds are available on the company's Web site too. Some load funds put up prospectuses, but many of them don't want you to look. They put up only sales material and tell you to call a broker for more information. If you do, ask for the prospectus and the most recent annual report before you buy. No matter how hard he or she pushes, look at the prospectus first and run its costs through the Fund Analyzer at www.finra.com (page 769).

When you read a prospectus, here's what you're looking for:

The Fund's Objectives

Read this section with great attention. What you see is (usually) what you get. Study the fund's objectives in light of the ideal portfolio you have designed for yourself. Will this fund fit in? Does it buy small stocks, invest for growth, emphasize income? Does the manager try to time the market, and is that what you want? If the fund has two objectives—say, income and growth—it won't maximize either one of them. But that mixed objective may be exactly what you want.

Some prospectuses speak for several funds, each with a different investment objective. Make sure you're reading about the one you want.

What the Fund Invests In

This section tells you how the fund expects to meet its goals. What will it buy? Just as important, what won't it buy? Some funds stuff everything into this section, to leave its manager free to go in any direction he or she chooses. That's not a good sign. Your intent is to buy a particular type of investment, not give its manager a blank check. A useful fund defines its style and stays within those limits.

To help you understand its investments, the fund may include little primers on such things as how the bond markets work and what options or derivatives are. Small growth funds often get their performance kick by investing in high-risk initial public offerings—something buyers often aren't aware of.

Special Risks

On the front of the prospectus, READ ANY SENTENCES SET IN CAPITAL LETTERS. That's usually a red alert. It might say, INVESTING IN THE SHARES INVOLVES SIGNIFICANT RISKS. Or INVESTORS ARE SUBJECT TO SUBSTANTIAL CHARGES FOR MANAGEMENT. Or whatever. A sentence in capital letters tells you there might be trouble or cost. The risks will be covered in greater detail inside the prospectus—a section you shouldn't fail to read. If you lose money and complain, you can count on the lawyers for the fund to say "We told you so."

How the Fund Has Performed

You'll see average annual returns for 1 year, 5 years, and 10 years (or since inception, if the fund hasn't been around that long). But these numbers don't tell you much. They're not compared with a standard market index, so you can't tell whether the fund has done better or worse than the market as a whole. To see the annual returns compared with an index, you have to look in the annual report, which—for no-load funds—is viewable on the Web site.

There's one important line in prospectus' performance table, however. It shows your returns after tax, with taxes figured in the highest bracket. When you're planning your future, it's important to work with after-tax returns, so you don't kid yourself into thinking you're richer than you are.

What Mutual Funds Cost

There are five types of costs: *direct sales commissions (loads)*, *marketing charges* (known as *12b-1 fees*), *money management fees*, *account maintenance* or *service fees*, and *overhead expenses*.

No-load funds charge no sales commissions and usually no 12b-1 fees (although occasionally there's a small fee of 0.25 percent). You buy them directly from the fund company or through a mutual fund supermarket (page 779). Annual money management fees vary from fund to fund. There may be $10 or $20 account fees on small accounts.

Load funds charge sales commissions, 12b-1 fees, overhead expenses, service fees, and, on average, higher money management fees than the no-loads do. You buy them through stockbrokers and commission-based financial planners.

The 12b-1 fees, overhead, and money management expenses (but not the sales commission) make up a fund's *expense ratio*—the ratio of costs to total net assets—also called the fund's annual operating expenses. Every investor pays a pro rata share.

As a result of the terrible market performance from 2000 through 2009, investors have been paying more attention to fees. There's been a general migration to low-fee fund groups by people who choose their own investments.

Fees have stayed high, however, in broker-sold funds. You may think that they don't amount to much because they're quoted as a small percentage of your total investment. But when measured against your investment gain, they actually take an enormous bite. In fact, the 2.5 percent you might pay for a broker's mutual fund advisory account can only be called confiscatory. Even a 1.5 percent fee burdens your returns. In a slow-growing market, only a low-cost fund—charging 0.5 percent or less—keeps you alive. See the proof in the table on page 765. Bond funds need low fees to make any headway at all.

You'll find the fund's loads and expense ratios in the fee table in the front of the prospectus. If you look at nothing else, look here. How many of the following costs will you have to pay?

(continued on page 766)

Table 20a.

COST OF A $10,000 INVESTMENT IN A FUND THAT CHARGES 2.5 PERCENT OF TOTAL ASSETS A YEAR

When the Market Rises	You Earn	You Pay*	Percentage of Gain Paid in Fees
20%	$2,000	$275	13.8%
15	1,500	269	17.9
10	1,000	263	26.3
5	500	258	51.6
1	100	251	Tilt†

Table 20b.

COST OF A $10,000 INVESTMENT IN A FUND THAT CHARGES 1.5 PERCENT OF TOTAL ASSETS A YEAR

When the Market Rises	You Earn	You Pay*	Percentage of Gain Paid in Fees
20%	$2,000	$165	8.2%
15	1,500	161	10.7
10	1,000	158	15.8
5	500	154	30.8
1	100	151	Tilt†

Table 20c.

COST OF A $10,000 INVESTMENT IN A FUND THAT CHARGES 0.5 PERCENT OF TOTAL ASSETS A YEAR

When the Market Rises	You Earn	You Pay*	Percentage of Gain Paid in Fees
20%	$2,000	$55	2.8%
15	1,500	54	3.6
10	1,000	53	5.3
5	500	51	10.2
1	100	50	50.0

* Fee assessed on average assets for the year.

† You paid more than you earned.

Source: the Vanguard Group.

A Front-End Load—an up-front commission paid to the salesperson. It's assessed on what the fund calls *A shares* and typically ranges from 4.5 to 5.75 percent. That's $45 to $55 for every $1,000 you put up, leaving you $955 to $945 to invest. Some funds, plagued by weak sales, are cutting their loads to less than 3 percent.

At any commission level, you get a discount for investing a lot of money at once. The levels where the discount applies are called the *break points*. For example, the commission might drop to 3.5 percent if you invest $50,000 or $100,000, 2.5 percent for $250,000, and 1.5 percent for $500,000. If you're going to put up, say, $100,000, but in stages, see if you can file a *letter of intent* giving you a reduced commission right from the start. When several people in your immediate family invest in the same family of funds, the fund might count everyone's assets to determine whether each of you has passed the break point.

A Contingent Deferred Sales Load—an exit fee, charged if you drop your fund within a specified number of years. For example, you might pay 6 percent if you sell the first year, 5 percent the second year, and so on. Six full years would have to pass before you could sell your shares without paying a penalty. Some funds assess the exit fee against your original investment. Others assess it against whatever the fund is currently worth, which raises your cost if the market goes up.

Shares with deferred sales charges are generally known as the fund's *B shares*. Some salespeople tell B-share customers that they're buying a no-load because there's no sales charge up front. That's a lie. The broker always gets a commission. You simply pay it in other ways—including higher 12b-1 fees (described further on). Before buying, be sure you understand how long you're going to be locked in.

A Level Load—an annual charge for sales commission and money management combined. Typically, it's 2 to 2.5 percent of the value of the account. There may also be a 1 percent front-end or back-end fee. Brokers usually call these *C shares*.

A 12b-1 Fee—an annual fee paid to cover sales expenses, principally the salesperson's commission for B and C shares but also advertising, marketing, and distribution fees. It ranges from 1 to 1.25 percent and is levied every year, eternally. Some firms, however, reduce it on B shares after five or six years. Load funds are the heaviest users of 12b-1 fees. By definition, a no-load can't charge a 12b-1 of more than 0.25 percent. A majority of no-loads don't levy this fee at all.

An Exchange Fee—levied by some fund families when you sell one fund and buy another within the group. It runs between $5 and $25 and is usually the only charge. You should not have to pay a sales load all over again.

A Money Management Fee—charged by every mutual fund, load and no-load, to compensate the managers who run the money.

Transaction Costs—the price of buying and selling securities. These include brokerage fees, market impact costs, and the spread. *Market impact* is the cost to the fund if a large order to buy pushes up the stock's price (or if a large order to sell pushes it down). The *spread* is the difference between a security's bid and asked price—page 867.

The more a fund manager trades, the higher these internal costs—all of which come out of your pocket. In some cases, trading costs exceed the fund's expense ratio! On average, they add almost 50 percent to the costs included in the fund's published expense ratio. That's another reason why active managers find it hard to beat the market index.

Index funds cost the least to run, because there's virtually no trading. Next lowest in cost should be U.S. bond funds, then U.S. funds that buy large-company stocks. Funds that buy smaller U.S. companies incur higher transaction expenses because they buy in the NASDAQ and over-the-counter markets, where spreads are wider. Global and international funds, especially those in emerging markets, carry the highest costs of all.

Transaction costs don't show in the funds' published list of fees and expenses. They're paid out of assets as a regular cost of doing business.

Service Fees—placed on smaller accounts. They amount to $10 or $20 a year on accounts smaller than $5,000 or $10,000, depending on the fund. They might be waived if you transact all your business online.

Other Fees—shareholder accounting, franchise tax, start-up fees, account maintenance fees, legal and audit fees, printing, and postage—you name it, someone is charging it.

Waived Fees—Some funds raise their returns and hold down reported costs by temporarily waiving some of their fees. Only the asterisk tells the tale. Say, for example, the prospectus shows an expense ratio of "1.25%*." Under the asterisk, you might learn that the full fee is 1.8 percent, but the fund manager is taking less for a certain period of time. In the future, the fund will try to recover any fees it waived in the past. When making a buying decision, go by the full fee, even if it isn't currently being collected. You'll have to pay it eventually.

Redemption Fees—penalties charged by some no-load funds for selling shares within a short time after buying them, typically three to six months. The fee usually runs between 0.5 and 2 percent and is meant to deter you from using the fund for short-term trading. Trading adds to fund costs and can make it hard for managers to execute their long-term strategies.

Hypothetical Costs in Dollars and Cents—A table in the prospectus discloses what you might pay over 1, 3, 5, and 10 years, in dollars and cents, for every $10,000 invested, assuming an investment gain of 5 percent a year. Stated this way, the expenses look too small to worry about—another reason that high-cost funds get away with noncompetitive charges. Sneak another peek at the tables on page 765 to remind yourself what you're really paying.

The Published Performance Data You See in Magazines Make Load Funds Look Better Than They Really Are. That's because those "best buy" lists usually compute performance without deducting the up-front or back-end sales charge. You're looking at gross returns, not the net to the investor. A load fund may look better before fees, but the no-load may beat it after fees. Morningstar shows returns adjusted for fees and the fund prospectuses do too.

Choosing a Sensible Way to Pay. (1) Buy a no-load. (2) Buy a no-load (yep, I repeated myself). (3) Buy an ETF if you're dealing with a broker. (4) Very last choice, if you're dealing with a broker: buy an open-end fund. Broker-sold open-ends offer A, B, or C shares, each type carrying a different level of fees. Here's what that alphabet is all about:

■ *A shares*—You pay an up-front sales commission and a small annual 12b-1 fee. This is usually the cheapest way of buying load funds for the average investor. Over time, what you save on annual fees will more than cover your up-front cost. The up-front commission declines if you are investing large amounts. I ran dozens of comparisons on the Fund Analyzer (page 769), using popular funds. A shares consistently came out on top—sometimes even in the very first year.

■ *B shares*—You don't pay an up-front commission, but there's a deferred sales charge if you sell within five or six years. There are no break points, so you don't get a discount if you're investing a large amount. You're charged a higher 12b-1 fee, which may or may not be reduced after five or six years. The dollar cost of a 12b-1 increases as your fund rises in value, so high 12b-1s take extra nips out of your gains. Brokers have sometimes missold B shares by telling customers they're buying a no-load fund (fat chance at a brokerage house!) or selling them to large investors who should have been given A shares for the lower commission. Some funds have quit selling B shares or sell them only with the approval of a supervisor.

- *C shares*—You pay no front-end or back-end load, but the annual 12b-1 is high and it never declines. For longer-term holders, this is the most expensive way to pay. C shares are cheaper than A shares only if you sell within five years or so, and why would you buy a load fund if you intended to hold for only five years? If you want to trade in and out of mutual funds, go with a no-load or an exchange-traded fund (page 859). C shares just waste your money. Some firms have quit selling C shares, too.

There's a Beautifully Simple Way of Comparing All These Fees and Share Classes with Just a Few Mouse Clicks. Go to the excellent Fund Analyzer at www.finra.org/fundanalyzer. Enter the names of the funds you're interested in and choose three to compare. The calculator shows how much each fund will cost you year by year for 20 years, assuming a 5 percent return, and how much you'd net each year if you redeemed your shares. You can compare a load fund's A, B, and C shares in the blink of an eye, to see the best way to buy. Or compare two competing target-date 2025 funds or two competing index funds. All the funds' fees are broken out. You'll see immediately how many more dollars a low-cost fund will put in your pocket. You can store the data on up to 50 funds for future reference.

The analyzer also shows you each load fund's break points and lists its other fees and terms, such as whether you can sell shares and then repurchase them at no sales charge within a limited period of time. You can use this calculator to compare exchange-traded funds too, or compare an exchange-traded fund with a similar, traditional mutual fund. It's a terrific tool.

Your Guide to Average Fund Expenses

Here is the average annual percentage of assets you pay for various types of open-end funds, both no-loads (no sales charges) and similar load funds. These expense ratios include all money management and overhead costs but no front- and back-end sales charges, so the load funds cost even more than it appears. Smart investors, in funds of any type, stay away from those that charge higher than average fees.

Making the Most of Your Money *Now*

Table 21.

COMPARE YOUR COSTS WITH THESE

	Average Annual Fees Charged by Pure No-loads (No Sales Charges)	Fees Charged by Funds with Front-end Loads (A Shares)	Fees Charged by Funds with Back-end Loads (B Shares)	Fees Charged by Funds with Level Loads (C Shares)
Stock funds				
Index	0.70%	1.02%	1.54%	1.69%
Growth and income	0.87	1.18	1.81	1.85
Equity income	1.01	1.21	1.89	1.89
Growth	1.17	1.38	2.05	2.07
Value	1.08	1.30	1.97	2.00
Small company	1.24	1.52	2.13	2.17
Real estate	1.11	1.43	2.08	2.12
International	1.20	1.51	2.18	2.21
Emerging-market	1.46	1.81	2.47	2.51
Balanced funds				
Stocks and bonds	0.63	0.84	1.53	1.53
Bond funds				
Tax-free municipal	0.60	0.84	1.52	1.52
General corporate	0.75	1.01	1.68	1.67
General government	0.68	0.91	1.61	1.62
High yield	0.85	1.06	1.72	1.75

Source: Morningstar, 2008.

The Portfolio Turnover Rate

This tells you how fast the fund manager buys and sells. An 80 percent turnover rate means that 80 percent of the portfolio's average value changes in a single year. Generally speaking, 20 percent is a low turnover rate for stock portfolios; 80 percent, about average; and 120 percent, high. Rapidly traded funds have high transaction costs. To compensate, they need superior returns. Among funds that make high-risk investments, a high rate of turnover might help *if* the manager can choose the right stocks. Among lower-risk funds, it generally hurts. As a general rule, high trading costs reduce returns.

The Financial Results

The financial tables show the fund's results per share, in dollars and cents, for up to the past 10 years. Some parts of the table won't interest you, but there are some nuggets here—especially the bottom line. Here's what to look for:

Net Investment Income (Loss)—shows what the fund is earning in interest and dividends, after expenses. Income funds will show larger dividends; aggressive growth funds, smaller ones. The fund has to pay out at least 98 percent of what it earns.

Dividends from Net Investment Income—your dividends per share. Income investors can look back to see how reliably the fund has paid. You can take this distribution in cash or reinvest it in more fund shares.

Net Realized and Unrealized Gains (Losses)—shows how the securities are performing. Aggressive growth funds may show larger capital gains; income funds will show smaller ones. Realized gains are distributed to investors. Unrealized gains remain in the fund.

Distributions from Realized Capital Gains—your share of the taxable capital gains. The fund distributes at least 98 percent of its net capital gains (after deducting losses). You can take this distribution in cash or reinvest it in more fund shares.

Net Asset Value, Start of the Year and Net Asset Value, End of the Year— shows the value of each share at the start and end of each year, after distributing income and capital gains. A common investor mistake is to think that the change in the net asset value equals the total return. It looks low, so you think that you're not doing well. But to figure your actual total return, you have to include all the distributions too—the dividends and capital gains. If they're reinvested automatically in new fund shares, multiply the number of shares you now own by the fund's net asset value. That shows you what your investment is currently worth. Do this at the end of each year to see how your investment has progressed.

Ratio of Expenses to Average Daily Net Assets—gives you a figure for operating expenses. This ratio should fall when net asset values rise. If it stays level or rises too, the fund isn't managing its expenses well.

Total Return—the payoff line. This tells you what percentage return the fund earned (or lost) in every fiscal year. Look back at the record. Does the fund bounce around a lot—a great year followed by a lousy year—or is it reasonably consistent? How high has it gone in a good year and how low in a bad year, and is the low okay with you? If the fund changed managers, can you spot a difference in the annual returns? Even if it didn't change managers, do the recent returns suggest that the investment method might have changed? One warning: you can't use these returns to compare the performance of two different funds. Funds have different fiscal years, so their returns may be shown over different time periods.

For the fund's return compared with a standard market index, see the annual shareholders' report. Sometimes it's in the prospectus, but usually not. You'll also find it at www.morningstar.com.

The Name of the Manager

Most funds are led by an individual money manager. The prospectus provides the manager's name and how long he or she has been there. For a manager with a short tenure, you also get a sketch of his or her business career for the past five years.

If the manager leaves, you must be informed. The change can be shown in the prospectus (check this when you get your new prospectus every year), or you might get a notice in your midyear report.

If your fund is run by a team of managers, it doesn't have to note when one of them departs. But except for index funds and money market funds (which don't have to disclose a manager's name), there's almost always a single shot caller. Check for managers' tenure, to try to judge whether the team has changed.

Here's What You're Still Missing

You know from the annual report how the fund performed, but you don't know how *you* performed. Your total return will be different from the fund's if you added money during the year (for example, by reinvesting dividends) or took money out. Maybe you earned more than the fund because you invested or withdrew at a lucky time. Maybe you earned less. Financial planners who manage your money will report your personal, annualized return, but the funds ought to tell you too. It's not a big deal to develop the software and give you an individual report. How can you plan for the future if you're only guessing at what rate your money is building up?

The Propaganda

With the prospectus comes sales literature. It shows you "the mountain"—the amount by which your investment would have grown had you been in the fund for many years. But each fund's mountain shows a different time period, so you can't compare one with another. Nor does the mountain show each year's percentage gain or help you spot the years when the fund didn't do as well as the general market average. In short, the mountain is there to impress, not inform. Go to www.morningstar.com or look at the annual report for performance data compared with a standard index.

The propaganda will also explain the fund's investment objectives and investor services. It's a good place to start, provided that you go on from there.

The Fund's Regular Reports

Read every communication from your fund's manager. This normally isn't boilerplate, it's serious stuff. All funds have to report semiannually; some report quarterly too.

These reports include financial statements for numbers mavens who understand them. They list what securities the fund held on the reporting date, for shareholders in a position to analyze them. The list isn't current. Some of those securities will have been sold before the report was even posted on the Web. But you can see if your manager really diversifies or if he or she makes big bets on certain industries.

The annual report has to show you how the fund performed relative to a standard market index. Some funds skip this step in the semiannual report, which gives their managers six months to string you along. (In this case, go to Morningstar. It knows.)

How Fund Distributions Work

A distribution is money paid out by a mutual fund to its investors. An *income distribution* (known as a dividend) comes from the interest and dividends earned on a fund's securities. A *capital gains distribution* is the net profit realized by selling securities that rose in price (after subtracting any losses). Common-stock funds generally make distributions once a year.

Before buying a fund, check its *distribution date*. If you buy just before a distribution (usually in December), you're buying yourself an extra tax. Say, for example, that a fund is selling for $10 a share. The planned distribution is $1 a share. After the distribution, the fund will sell for $9—reflecting that $1 was paid to shareholders. The fund has not lost money! Investors still have $10, but only $9 remains part of the fund's net asset value. The other $1 is in your pocket or reinvested in additional fund shares. If it's reinvested, the value of your fund account will go back to $10. Still, that $1 distribution is a taxable dividend. When you buy just before the distribution, you get that year's tax without profiting from the fund's gains.

The best time to buy is right after the annual distribution date. If you want to sell, consider waiting until after that date so you'll collect the dividends you've earned. That's especially important for investors selling at the end of the year, to nail down a tax loss. If the dividend will be paid on December 14, sell on the 15th, not before.

Stock funds often make distributions quarterly. Bond funds may declare dividends daily and pay them monthly, so timing your purchase isn't an issue. Money market mutual funds credit interest daily.

Even on stock funds, the distribution date doesn't matter if you own the fund in a tax-deferred retirement plan.

There Are Three Ways of Handling Distributions

1. Reinvest everything in more fund shares (the right option for anyone trying to lay a nest egg).

2. Reinvest enough of the distribution to preserve your capital's purchasing power (the right option for people who need income but will be living on their capital for many years). The rest can be withdrawn and spent.

3. Receive everything in cash (the right option for anyone deliberately eating up a nest egg—usually in late old age).

Automatic Monthly Investments

If I had my investment life to live over again, here's what I'd do: from the very first day I got a steady paycheck, I'd put money away regularly. If I couldn't do it through payroll deduction, I'd do it through automatic payments from my bank into a mutual fund. You can set it up yourself through your online bank account or ask the fund to set it up for you. Some funds let you start an automatic monthly investment plan with as little as $50 plus additions of only $25 a month. If you're eligible, your investment can go into funds held in a tax-deductible retirement plan. Otherwise, put it into a regular, taxable account. If you have a retirement plan at work, use your outside mutual fund account to buy types of investments that your company plan does not include.

I sure wish I'd done it. I got smart too late.

Mutual Funds and Retirement Plans

Almost all funds offer traditional and Roth Individual Retirement Accounts, Simplified Employee Pensions, and 403(b) plans. You can roll money out of a 401(k) at work and into a mutual fund plan tax free. You can also transfer money held at an old IRA to a new one at another fund company. The company will tell you how.

Taxes may be due, however, if you take money out of a regular, taxable mutual fund account and add it to your retirement account. Your shares are sold (for a taxable gain or loss), then reinvested in the retirement plan.

Managing Your Fund Account Online and by Phone

Sign up for managing your account online. It gives you instant access to your funds' performance—yields, dividends, net asset value, current values, account history, and recent transactions. Once you've made the arrangements, you'll be able to sell shares or switch from one fund to another just by logging on to your computer. The fund may waive fees on smaller accounts that are handled entirely online. You'll be able to transact business by phone, however, even if you don't register online.

When you're buying several funds from the same mutual fund group, include a money market fund. It's a useful place to park money in between investments or that you're going to need for other purposes. Ask for a checkbook attached to the fund, so you can use it as a bank account.

When you sell by phone or on the Web, you get the next price that the fund computes—usually its price at 3:00 p.m. or 4:00 p.m. Eastern time. The money is mailed or wired right away to your home address or a predesignated bank. (The fund has the right to put off sending the money for up to seven days, as it might in a market panic.) Alternatively, you can tell the fund to put the proceeds of the sale into your money market fund. To withdraw it, simply write a check against the fund.

For security reasons, you normally can't use the phone to change the bank to which the money is wired. Changes have to be made by mail, over a signature guarantee. But you can probably change your address, provided that you give enough identifying information.

What if your online account is hacked? The risk is small. Fund companies have gone to great lengths to keep their systems secure. Some online brokers say they'll cover your losses if someone breaks into your account and steals money. But that guarantee generally isn't good if you have no security software on your own computer or have shared your login or password with someone else. I handle my own fund accounts online because it's so easy, but I'm *very* careful about security.

Managing Your Account by Mail

If you're managing your account by mail and want to sell, don't just write a letter asking the fund to cash some of your shares. First check the prospectus (you kept it, of course); all the how-tos of buying and selling are in the back. Maybe a simple letter will do, provided that you list, exactly, the number of shares in the fund you want to sell. On the other hand, maybe the system is more complicated. There are two ways of redeeming fund shares, or switching from one fund to another, by mail:

On your signature only—offered by most funds (but not all of them). Signature redemptions are good for sums up to a certain limit, often $50,000. The money has to be switched into another fund at the group or paid to the account holder at the address of record or a predesignated bank. If more than one person owns the account, both signatures may be required. Normally, money market funds accept one-signature checks on joint accounts, up to a maximum set by the fund. It is possible, however, to set up the account so that both signatures are required.

With a signature guarantee—which means taking the sell order to a bank, brokerage firm, or credit union where someone can guarantee that the signature is yours. On joint accounts, you'll need guarantees for both signatures. Having your signature notarized isn't enough. Notaries merely check your identity and attest to the fact that they saw you sign it. Guarantors ensure that you're the person you claim to be. If you're not, the guarantor makes good the loss. Guarantees are normally required only for large transactions.

If you want to prevent a single joint owner from making withdrawals from the account, go for two-signature accounts with the added protection of a signature guarantee.

If someone forges your name, the fund (or its transfer agent) normally bears the responsibility. It may duck, however, by claiming it had no reason to doubt the check and that you were careless with your account. The same could happen with redemptions made by phone or online. Your security is that the check will come to you at your registered address. If someone robs your mail, forges your signature on the check, and cashes it, the responsibility shifts to the bank that took the check.

What If You and Your Spouse Hold a Fund Jointly and One of You Decides to Split? Or One of You Fears That the Other Will Split? Notify the fund by certified mail that both signatures will be required to withdraw or transfer money. This order can be entered by either spouse. If you can prove that the fund made an error in letting your spouse withdraw the money, the fund has to make good.

What If Your Spouse Forges Your Name, Gets the Joint Check, Forges Your Signature on the Check, and Cashes It? Your bank is responsible for restoring your half of the money. But you'll have to prove that your signature was forged (not easy, given the ease with which many husbands and wives sign each other's names). Your best defense is to notify the bank that you won't be signing any joint checks.

Read Your Online Mutual Fund Statements

Increasingly, online mutual fund statements are turning into planning tools. They may tell you how you've allocated your assets (big stocks, small stocks, internationals, and so on). They may give you tax information, telling you how much you've gained or lost since you bought the shares. There's a history of transactions—money in and money out. And, of course, you'll see the gains and losses over time. Use what you learn from these statements to make yourself a better investor.

Automatic Withdrawal Plans

These can be wonderful arrangements. They let you live off your capital while still keeping it invested for growth. Not all funds offer withdrawal plans, but the majority do.

When you're on such a plan, your fund sends you a check of a certain size every month or every quarter. You still have your dividends reinvested automatically. The fund simply cashes in enough shares to pay the regular income you want. If your check this month exceeds what the fund has earned, your withdrawal reduces your principal. If not, your withdrawal comes out of earnings. You can stop the checks or change the amount anytime you want. Stocks rise two-thirds of the time, so, over time, you're hoping for a regular income and a rising nest egg too. It helps if you're prepared to lower your withdrawals when the market drops.

To start a withdrawal plan, you usually need at least $10,000 invested. There's a minimum withdrawal and a small fee per check. Withdrawals might be made in one of three ways:

1. You can receive a fixed number of dollars—say, $400 a month. More shares will have to be sold when the market dips and fewer when the market rises. You can raise or lower the amount, usually once a year.

2. You can receive the proceeds from the sale of a fixed number of shares—say, 20 shares a month. You'll get less money when the market dips and more when it rises.

3. You can sometimes receive a fixed percentage of your fund investment—say, monthly checks paid at the rate of 4 percent of capital a year. You'll get less money when the market dips and more when the market rises.

Withdrawal plans that send monthly checks, handy as they are, sometimes add to your miseries at tax time because calculating capital gains can be such a pain. But these days most funds tell you your average cost per share. If your fund doesn't, make a single lump-sum withdrawal each year, put the cash in a bank or money market fund, and make your monthly withdrawals from there.

These plans aren't suitable for volatile funds. Apply them to more stable investments, such as balanced funds or equity-income funds. For a sense of how much it's prudent to withdraw, see chapter 31.

Should You Switch-Hit?

This is a game played by market timers. They buy shares in a no-load fund. When they think the market is going to fall, they sell the fund by phone or Web and move the proceeds into a money market fund. When they think stocks will improve, they move the money back. Often they're not thinking at all—they're just following the headlines or a newsletter guru.

As a long-term strategy, fund switching is a lousy idea. First, because few investors can time the market consistently, including the newsletters that cost you a lot of money. Second, because selling shares may trigger a capital gains tax. Switching can't even pretend to be viable except in a tax-deferred account. And third, because it limits the type of mutual fund you can buy. Index funds, along with many other no-loads, don't allow you to trade in and out. When you sell, you may have to wait for 30 or 60 days before you can buy back in. That may hinder your trading plans. Check on the fund's "frequent trading" rules, which are explained in the prospectus. (They're in the final few pages, where the fund lays out all its buying and selling rules.)

Some funds welcome traders, but they charge higher fees.

One-Stop Shopping

How do you put together an intelligent mutual fund portfolio without being overrun by paperwork? Two ways:

Be a Groupie

Buy all your funds from a single no-load mutual fund family. Not many are large enough to provide enough good funds for a decent asset allocation. But you could make a good mix at the three no-load giants—Fidelity, Vanguard, and T. Rowe Price—or, for load funds, American Funds. Just don't be a brokerage-house groupie. Brokers offer a variety of funds, but most broker-brand funds are mediocre, due in part to their high fees.

Shop the Supermarkets

Supermarkets are run by discount brokerage houses. They give you hundreds of no-load funds to choose among, all of which can be handled through a single brokerage account. There is typically no transaction fee. You may not even be charged for opening the account.

Each supermarket has a different set of funds, so check to be sure that it offers the ones you want to buy. Those not on the no-fee list may still be available for a fee, usually in the $25 to $50 range. You can use the same account to buy stocks, bonds, load funds, and any other investment the discounter handles.

Charles Schwab's OneSource (800-435-4000) lists 1,300 no-fee funds from more than 100 groups and provides a wealth of information services besides. Fidelity Funds Network in Boston (800-FIDELITY) is the only supermarket where Fidelity's no-load funds are offered without a fee. At this writing, its list also includes about 820 other funds from 113 no-load families. Vanguard runs a smaller supermarket: the FundAccess program, with 900 no-transaction-fee funds from 25 families. T. Rowe Price's Mutual Fund Gateway (800-638-5660) offers 415 no-fee funds from 49 groups. You can also buy fee-free funds at discounters such as TD Ameritrade and E*Trade. The only way to buy Vanguard funds without a fee is to call the company directly at 800-662-7447. For T. Rowe Price, call 800-638-5660.

Following the Price of Your Fund

Just log on to your fund's Web site or go to Morningstar to check funds from various families all at once. My best tip: don't follow the daily changes in price. That might make you nervous. Ideally, you will pick a handful of funds and vow loyalty. You won't flip through magazines hunting for younger, prettier funds. You'll turn off the TV whenever anyone threatens to tell you about the Dow. From this point on, you'll think about each fund once a year, when you get its annual report, read what its manager has to say, and check its progress against the market and similar funds. Change it only if you run into one of the problems listed on page 781. Otherwise file the reports and do something more useful than checking on how the market did. Making money is fine, but it's not a life.

How Safe Is Your Fund?

A mutual fund can't go broke the way that mismanaged businesses can. It's hard to loot because the securities are held by a third-party custodian, usually a bank. The fund's manager tells the custodian what to buy and sell but never gets his or her hands on the money. If your fund company goes bankrupt, its creditors cannot attach your assets. You can lose money in a bad market; you can be charged outrageous fees; redemptions may even be temporarily suspended if there's a run on the fund. But your sell order is always priced on the day it comes in. The fund cannot delay mailing your check for more than seven days.

Fraud is possible in any business, but people with access to mutual fund money must be insured. To my knowledge, no fund holder has ever been told, "Sorry, the money walked out the door."

When a fund becomes unprofitable to run, it is generally merged with a larger fund. If no one wants it, the securities will be liquidated and the proceeds distributed to investors. You pick up any capital gains or losses remaining in the fund if you owned it in a taxable account (that sometimes happens with a merger too). The fund's custodian will automatically withhold 10 percent for federal taxes (and perhaps something more for state taxes) unless you return a form specifying that you don't want taxes taken out.

It's a little more complicated if you hold the fund in an Individual Retirement Account. You'll be informed that money in the fund will be distributed to you, minus 10 percent for tax withholding, unless you transfer your investment to another fund within a short period of time. Don't dawdle. Do the transfer. If you wait for the distribution, you'll have to roll the money into another IRA fund within 60 days to avoid being taxed on the whole amount. Also, you'll have to come up with the 10 percent that the custodian held back. If you don't, that 10 percent will be treated as a taxable distribution.

When to Sell a Mutual Fund

Sometimes your fund won't do as well as its peer group. But if you chose the manager carefully, why be in a hurry to sell? Every manager goes through periods when his or her stocks are out of style. If nothing appears to have changed in the fund or the way the manager makes decisions, hold on—or buy more—and wait for its quality to show.

But patience isn't always a virtue. Consider selling when:

The Fund Lags the Average of Similar Funds for More than Three Years in a Row. Read the shareholders' report to see what the manager thinks went wrong. Sometimes there's an interesting reason to hang on to stocks that haven't been doing well. If that reason makes sense, you might decide to stick. If the annual report reads like an annual excuse, however, I'd bail. Maybe the manager's passion for stock picking has cooled. Maybe he or she is running too many funds or has taken on too many administrative duties. Maybe there's been a death in a family or a divorce. Maybe the fund company's executives are battling each other for control. You don't know what's happening—all you see is the result.

How can you find out if your fund has underperformed its benchmark? Go to www.fundalarm.com. This site shows how your fund has performed, relative to an appropriate benchmark, over the past one, three, and five years.

The Lead Manager Leaves the Fund. Sometimes a superb replacement is on hand, trained by the former manager. But that's the exception, not the rule. The new manager may have had a good record somewhere else, but you don't know whether it can be duplicated here. What's more, he or she may drastically change the types of stocks the fund invests in. In most cases, you should leave when the old manager does. FundAlarm.com keeps track of manager movements too.

The Fund's Investment Style Changes. It's important that managers play their own game. If they switch from small stocks to larger ones, or from U.S. stocks to internationals, a caution light should flash. If performance slows, the new game isn't working and you should start looking for a new fund. You can follow any changes in style by calling up the fund's past style boxes at www .morningstar.com.

Your Investment Style Changes. Something happens in your life to change the amount of investment risk you want to take.

Your Fund Is So Popular That It Has Swollen in Size. Many a small-fund manager with good results loses his mojo if too much money rolls in. Investing large amounts will push up the price of the smaller stocks that he knows well, and larger stocks run by different rules. Morningstar's style box will tell you whether your small-cap fund is now listed as a mid-cap fund. Not a good sign.

You Own a 3-Alarm Fund. FundAlarm.com lists the mutual funds it considers especially ripe for selling, calling them 3-Alarm Funds. If yours is on the list, think about it. The site gives your fund a risk rating too.

P.S. Don't dump a fund just because it hasn't done as well as the S&P 500. The type of stocks that your mutual fund buys may simply be out of style for the moment. Growth funds or value funds sometimes lag the S&P for a couple of years. Alternatively, your fund might have some other investment objective— for example, high income or limited risk. You should worry only if your fund lags other funds of its type. If your objective is keeping up with the S&P, buy an S&P index fund.

How Your Fund Is (Gulp) Taxed

Most mutual funds are making it simpler to fill in your tax returns when you have a taxable account. They give you the average cost of the shares you sold, which makes it easier to figure your capital gains. If your fund doesn't provide this, I'd make that one of my reasons to sell it. Funds that care about their retail shareholders help them with this tricky task. Here are the tax-reporting rules:

Reporting Dividend and Capital Gains Distributions

In January your fund will tell you how much you got last year (on a 1099-DIV form—one copy to you, one copy to the IRS). All you have to do is enter that income on your tax return. You owe taxes on the income even if it was automatically reinvested in new fund shares and even if the total value of your fund went down. If the fund sends you any other tax information, read it gratefully. Tax-exempt bond funds will tell you whether any of your dividends are taxable in your state.

Reporting Capital Gains and Losses

You owe taxes when you make a profit by selling fund shares for more than they cost. When you sell for less, you have a deductible loss. The cost of each share is what you paid for it (including the sales commission if it's a load fund). But different shares carry different costs because they were bought at different times. Your statements will tell you what price you paid for any new shares, including shares bought with reinvested dividends. If you're buying load funds from a broker and chose the A shares, the confirmation you get for each purchase will show the commission. Keep these confirms to remind you.

As time goes by, you will collect a huge pile of shares, acquired at a wide range of costs. When you sell a share, which one have you sold? Which cost do you use when figuring your gain or loss?

The easiest way to handle this problem is to go by the *average cost*. Most funds will tell you what it was, in your mailed or online statement. Remember to add any commissions that you paid.

If you're obsessed with spreadsheets, you can keep track of the cost of each batch of shares you bought. Then, when you sell, you can specify the particular shares that should go. You'd specify the shares that have risen the least in value, to minimize your capital gains tax. If you have any shares that dropped in value, you can sell them and use the losses to offset any taxable capital gains. You can also deduct up to $3,000 in losses each year against your ordinary income.

In any year when you sell shares, your fund will send you a 1099-B form for tax purposes. It shows the total amount you received for your shares, without indicating the gain or loss. Don't accidentally pay taxes on the whole 1099-B amount!

Most Mutual Funds Give You a Hand

Your statement will show your average cost basis for recent years, so you don't have to figure it yourself. The fund may also provide a booklet, mailed or online, explaining how to compute your tax.

Some funds don't bother, however, and very few have average cost data stretching back further than the 1990s. If you've had your account for many years, the best your fund can do is to supply you with records that you may have lost. (But ask for them early; there's always a rush.)

What If You Own an International Fund or a U.S. Fund That Also Buys Foreign Securities?

You face the same tax rules that govern any other mutual fund. In addition, the fund's year-end statement will show your share of any foreign taxes paid. You're entitled to either a tax credit or an itemized deduction for that amount. The credit is worth more, but trying to figure it out is a waste of a nice spring day. Take the tax deduction instead.

The Government Is Here to Help You

For the IRS's official word on how mutual fund holders should handle their taxes, go to www.irs.gov to download the free IRS Publication 564, "Mutual Fund Distributions," or call 800-TAX-FORM.

You Don't Have to Worry About Any of This Stuff If You're Taking Money out of a Tax-Deferred Retirement Account

All withdrawals are taxed as ordinary income, regardless of their source.

Tax-Managed Mutual Funds Are Designed to Minimize Taxable Distributions

In tax-managed funds, the manager buys shares and holds them rather than trading and taking capital gains. When selling seems prudent, gains are generally sheltered by realizing capital losses. Large untaxed gains build up inside these funds. If investors ever flee and the fund has to liquidate some stocks, you could face a pretty big taxable distribution. But tax-managed funds tend to be of the plain-vanilla sort that investors buy and hold.

Index funds linked to the S&P 500 rarely have capital gains distributions, so they're effectively tax managed too. But you get distributions from other types of indexed funds. For example, say that you buy an indexed value fund. When stocks move out of the value category, they'll have to be sold, which may result in net capital gains. The same is true of indexed growth funds and any other fund where the composition of the index often changes. In general, however, index funds distribute fewer taxable gains than you'd get from the average managed fund. The newer index funds, such as those based on fundamental indexes (page 750), distribute more capital gains too.

Exchange-Traded Funds

Exchanged-traded funds (ETFs) are mutual funds in a different garb. For some purposes, they're an excellent investment choice. As more people learn how to use them, their popularity will grow.

An ETF is a basket of securities, usually stocks, assembled by a sponsoring firm. It's treated as an individual stock, just like Intel, Cisco, or General Electric. It gets its own ticker symbol and trades on an exchange. As an example, take the Standard & Poor's Depositary Receipt, or "Spider," an ETF that tracks the performance of the S&P 500-stock index. Its ticker symbol is SPDR, and it trades on the American Stock Exchange. You buy and sell through a discount or full-service brokerage account, paying the usual brokerage commissions.

An ETF's market price rises and falls during the day. You can trade at any time. You can also sell short (betting that the ETF will fall in price), buy on margin (borrowing some of the money to buy), or trade with limit orders (automatic orders to buy or sell if the ETF reaches a certain price). That's not possible with open-end funds.

Like any other stock, an ETF has an *asked* price, which you pay when you buy it, and a *bid* price, which you receive when you sell. The difference between them is called a *spread,* and it's a cost. Popular ETFs, such as SPDR, have narrow spreads—usually just a penny or so. As spreads go higher, your costs go up. *Tip:* don't buy an ETF first thing in the morning. Its bid/asked spread tends to be wider then, which makes it more expensive than it should be.

ETFs offer a tax advantage over traditional open-end mutual funds. The managers of either type of fund have to distribute any net capital gains to their shareholders. An open-end fund might be forced to sell some shares at a gain in order to meet redemption requests. Those gains are distributed among all the remaining shareholders, who will have to pay taxes, like it or not, if they're investing with a taxable account. By contrast, there are no redemptions with ETFs, so your taxes aren't affected by what other investors do.

Still, there's a way that ETFs might also be forced to distribute taxable gains. An ETF follows a specific market index, which means that it has to change its holdings when the composition of the index changes. If the changes result in shares being sold at a gain, it will be passed along to you. Your broker can reinvest your distributions in new ETF shares, but will charge a commission. (There are no sales commissions for reinvesting in a traditional open-end fund.)

In either type of fund, you will also receive taxable dividends paid by the underlying stocks.

A few ETFs—for example, commodity pools—might be structured as limited partnerships. That complicates your tax returns because you have to file a K-1 partnership form. The annual taxable income will be passed on to you, just as it is in traditional mutual funds. Highly leveraged ETFs and ETFs that sell a particular market short can produce a lot of taxable income too. Always read the taxes section of the prospectus before you buy, to see what your tax liabilities will be.

Most ETFs are index funds. For individuals, the most popular ones are those that follow broad indexes such as the S&P 500 or NASDAQ's index of 100 leading nonfinancial stocks. You can also buy ETFs for segments of the index, such as small caps or mid-caps. New ETFs pop up during investment fads, such as ETFs for gold, energy, currencies, and real estate.

The financial industry has also created hundreds of weird new indexes for tiny sectors of the market, and designed an ETF to match. They're used mainly by hedge funds and other professionals to execute complicated strategies that may or may not be worth their cost. For you, they're lottery tickets, pure and simple.

You can buy ETFs for bonds as well as stocks. They could be used as a substitute for, or to fill in, a traditional bond ladder. Bond ETFs distribute interest payments monthly. ETFs for Treasury Inflation-Protected Securities distribute their annual, taxable increase in value (for TIPS, see page 929).

At this writing, there are only a few actively managed ETFs where the managers pick stocks and try to beat an index. Costs are higher for these funds, they might not beat the index, and they're likely to deliver taxable capital gains, even to people who haven't sold their shares. I don't see the point.

ETFs should trade close to the net asset value of the individual securities they hold, give or take a few tenths of a point. But in volatile markets, the spread can widen. During the 2008 credit freeze, the price of some high-yield bond ETFs dived as much as 26 percent below the net asset value of the bonds in the portfolio—a serious loss for people who sold (and a windfall for people who bought). That doesn't happen with open-end funds.

Comparing Costs: ETFs Versus Traditional Open-end Funds

ETFs charge lower fees than broker-sold funds and most of the no-load funds run by active managers. That's because they're index funds, which are cheaper to manage. They also spend less in marketing expense.

But the low-cost open end index funds from firms such as Vanguard and Fidelity generally charge even lower fees than ETFs. Also, you can buy them without paying brokerage commissions—another plus.

If you're interested in ETFs, buy only the ones that are linked to broad market indexes, exceed $100 million in assets, and show heavy trading volume every day. The oldest and cheapest is the "Spider" (SPDR) S&P 500 ETF, tracking Standard & Poor's 500-stock index. The next most popular is Power-Shares QQQ, tracking the NASDAQ index of 100 large nonfinancial companies (especially techs). Third comes iShares MSCI Emerging Market Index ETF, and then iShares Russell 2000 Index Fund of smaller companies (a favorite of hedge funds). That's plenty to start with.

Scores of niche ETFs are launched every year, most of which attract fewer than $10 million to $25 million in assets. At that level, their sponsors can't make money on them unless they charge high fees—in which case, why buy? They also trade at wide spreads, which isn't good for investors. Look for ETFs that hold at least $100 million and preferably $500 million.

Unpopular ETFs will eventually be shut down. When an ETF is liquidated, the sponsor sells the securities, deducts expenses, and returns the remaining proceeds to investors. Any gains are taxable at that time, unless you're holding the ETF in a tax-deferred account.

For current information on ETFs, including trading volume, performance, ratings, and other data, go to www.morningstar.com.

Who Should Buy ETFs and Who Should Buy Open-End Funds?

ETFs are good choices for people who buy through stockbrokers because they're so much cheaper than broker-sold open-end mutual funds, including broker-sold index funds.

If you buy no-loads, consider ETFs if you're investing large sums and expect to hold the ETFs for a long time. The sales commission is small, relative to the amount you invest, and annual expenses are low.

You don't want ETFs, however, if you're investing small sums, making regular monthly investments, taking regular withdrawals, or rebalancing once a year. In an ETF, each of those changes would cost you a brokerage commission. In an open-end fund, you can make the changes free. For more on using ETFs, see page 859.

You Can Use ETFs for Year-End Tax Selling. If you have a loss in an open-end mutual fund, consider selling and switching, immediately, to a similar ETF. That nails down the tax loss without taking you out of the market.

Vetting the ETF Prospectus and Annual Report

Some of the things you look for in open-end fund reports apply to the reports on ETFs as well. The up-front letter from management will discuss what's happened in the market. You can check your ETF's total return for the year, compared with the return of the index it tracks, and the net asset value (NAV) of its underlying securities. They should all be close. If there's a noticeable discrepancy between your returns and the gains or losses in the NAV, you're probably in an ETF that doesn't trade a lot. Individuals don't do so well in funds like that.

You might also check the ETF's P/E ratio (page 752), and think about whether the stock is expensive (sell some?) or cheap (buy some more?).

Check the portfolio turnover rate if you've been getting unexpected distributions of taxable capital gains. If it's running higher than 10 percent, you're tracking an index that makes a lot of changes each year. Maybe you'd be better off in an S&P 500 ETF, where distributions are rare.

Closed-End Mutual Funds

A closed-end mutual fund normally raises money only once, in an initial public offering (IPO). It sells a fixed number of shares and invests the proceeds. The fund is then listed on a stock exchange or NASDAQ, just like any other public company. If you want to own shares, you buy through a discount or full-service stockbroker, paying regular brokerage commissions.

The prospectus comes out only once, when the fund is first offered to the public. After that, buyers get regular shareholder reports. The securities in the fund normally never change.

Closed-ends specialize in bonds, especially municipals, and are purchased by investors seeking income. But there are closed-ends for practically every kind of security.

What a Closed-End Fund Is Worth

Closed-end funds have two relevant measures of value: (1) the current net asset value (NAV) of all the securities in the portfolio and (2) the share price of the fund on the stock exchange.

Typically, closed-end funds sell at something less than net asset value—known as a *discount*. Take, for example, the Skyrocket Fund, owner of securities worth $10 a share. You can probably buy it for $9 a share, a discount of 10 percent.

Sometimes, however, investors fall in love with a particular closed-end fund and bid up its price to something more than net asset value—known as a *premium*. If you bought the Skyrocket Fund at $11, it would be selling at a 10 percent premium

Premiums rarely last. When a fund sells for more than its net asset value, it is usually way overpriced. If you buy, your odds of losing money are high. Ideally, you should buy a closed-end at a discount and sell at a premium, raking in a

"I'll pay $9!"

Skyrocket Fund
Owns $10 worth
of stocks

"I'll pay $11!"

Discount buyer   *Premium buyer*

capital gain along with the dividends these funds pay. (Of course, you could also rake in a capital loss, depending on your investment smarts and luck.)

Most bond closed-ends use leverage (borrowed money) to juice their yields by an extra percentage point or two. They raise money in various ways—say, by taking on debt or issuing preferred shares. They pay interest on the debt or preferred shares at low short-term rates and use the proceeds to buy more long-term bonds, which normally earn higher rates. That increases the yield for the fund's common shareholders. Closed-ends can look like bond funds on steroids to investors hungry for higher returns. If interest rates fall, the value of your shares can jump.

Leverage increases the annual fee you pay. It also comes with big risks. If interest rates rise, your fund's market price will fall, and fall much faster than that of closed-ends that don't use leverage. The fund will also have to pay more interest on its leverage, which slashes its dividend payout to common shareholders. For a list of funds that use leverage, go to www.cefa.com, an excellent informational Web site maintained by the Closed-End Fund Association.

Smaller closed-end funds trade in thin markets, meaning that there aren't a huge number of buyers and sellers. That increases the volatility. An unusual number of buyers or sellers can move prices up or down, faster, and by larger amounts than you'd see in a larger fund.

Here's How to Play the Closed-Ends

First check the listing of closed-end funds on Morningstar (click on "Funds" and then on "Closed Ends" in the menu on the left). A list also appears in *The Wall Street Journal* on Mondays. You'll see each fund's net asset value and premium or discount. Make a list of the funds with the largest discounts.

Research a fund just the way you'd research a stock—for example, by getting its annual report, checking its Snapshot page on www.morningstar.com, reading Web stories, and so on. Screen out funds with new managers, high expenses, and suspect yields (if they're bond funds, see next section). Then check the history of each fund's price and net asset value, available on www.cefa.com. You want to know the fund's typical price range relative to net asset value. As an example, take the Skyrocket Fund again. You might discover that every time it sells for 15 percent below its net asset value, it rebounds to about 5 percent below, creating a capital gain. You'd buy whenever its discount reached 15 percent and hold it for appreciation.

Long-term buying and holding aren't typical of closed-end investors. More likely, they trade. They buy when the discount is deep enough—usually, 5 or more percentage points wider than the fund's average discount (that usually occurs in lousy markets). When the discount shrinks, they sell. They buy the fund back when the discount widens again.

Not all deeply discounted funds are good buys. The fund might own chancy or illiquid enterprises, past performance may be poor, or the dividend might be ripe for cutting. Many funds deserve their low price.

With Closed-End Bond (Income) Funds, You Have to Keep Your Wits About You. These funds often mesmerize investors by paying especially high distributions. Sometimes that's legitimate; a fund's yield will rise if its price goes to a discount and can be boosted with leverage. But sometimes the dividends are phony. Your big check may come partly from option income, capital gains, or the fund's own capital. That's called a *managed distribution*.

This flimflam hurts investors three ways: First, you are being deceived about the fund's actual yield. Second, a payout of capital means that the net asset value is being eroded, which will eventually drive the share price down. Third, when part of the "dividend" comes from sources other than investment income, that high payment is unlikely to last. Eventually the dividend will be cut, and the fund's share price will decline.

Always check on the source of the dividend payments before you invest. The CEFA Web site maintains a list of funds with managed distributions. The list shows the fund's yield from *income only* (which may be tiny) compared with the *distribution yield*—the total amount of all distributions, from various sources. Newspaper listings typically print only the distribution yield, which can mislead you.

With Closed-End Funds, You Have Three Ways of Making Money
   1. **The value of the securities it holds can rise.** Example: the Skyrocket Fund, with a net asset value of $10 a share, goes to a net asset value of $12 a share because the stocks it owns went up in price. You bought it at a 10 percent

discount ($9), and, in the market, that discount still holds. Your shares are now worth $10.80 (the new $12 NAV less 10 percent). Both the net asset value and the share price have risen 20 percent.

2. The discount can shrink. Example: the Skyrocket Fund stays at a net asset value of $10 a share, but investors get interested in its prospects and bid the price up from a 10 percent discount to a 5 percent discount. The $9 price rises to $9.50. The net asset value went nowhere, but investors gained 5.5 percent. Sometimes a discount even rises to a premium. Occasionally a closed-end fund switches to open-end, which eliminates the discount.

3. The value of the securities can rise and the discount can shrink— the best of all possible worlds. Example: the $10 Skyrocket Fund goes to a $12 net asset value and the discount shrinks from 10 percent to 5 percent. You bought at $9; now the shares are worth $11.40 (the $12 net asset value minus 5 percent). The net asset value rose 20 percent, but the value of your shares rose 26.6 percent.

Needless to Say, There Are Also Three Ways of Losing Money: The net asset value can drop, the discount can deepen (or a premium can drop to a discount), or both of those things can happen at once. The last is the worst of all possible worlds.

You could lose money even when the net asset value is going up. Take the Skyrocket Fund yet again, with a NAV of $10. Due to investor optimism, it's selling at a stock price of $12, a 20 percent premium. The market bids up the value of the securities it holds, and Skyrocket's NAV goes to $11. But sensing an end to the party, investors bail out. The market resets Skyrocket's price at a 10 percent discount. Your $12 shares are now worth only $9.90 (the $11 NAV minus 10 percent). So the NAV rose by 10 percent, but you lost 17.5 percent.

That's especially apt to happen to a fund selling at a premium, so smarties avoid premiums. Smarties are also familiar with the discounts at which their favorite closed-end funds usually trade. You can make money in closed-ends but not by blundering around. You have to be disciplined, buying funds only at steep discounts. If market prices are high and the discounts narrow, bide your time.

Three Tips on Investing in Closed-Ends

1. *Never* buy newly issued closed-ends. They contain a large, built-in commission for sales and organizational expenses. Buyers pay perhaps 4.5 percent over the fund's net asset value. The syndicate supports the price for a short time after the shares are listed. Then it lets the price go.

Your broker will claim that, this time, this fund will hold its premium price, which is what persuades you to buy. But the price almost always drops. Moral: buying a closed-end fund on the opening is usually buying into a loss. If you like the fund, wait for it to go to a discount. If it doesn't, forget it and buy something else.

2. *Never* buy closed-ends selling at a premium. You're paying more than the underlying bonds are worth. Eventually the price of the fund will drop to a discount, at your loss.

3. *Beware* funds selling at yields way above the market. Maybe there was a special dividend that won't recur. Maybe you're looking at a managed distribution. Maybe investors have driven down the price because they expect the dividend to be cut—not good for people seeking income.

Some Final Suggestions

Here's a strategy for people who crave both wealth and action from their mutual funds:

1. Put your faith in low-cost, open-end index mutual funds or target-date retirement funds (page 846). Use them as your core investments.

2. If you're using index funds, decide on an appropriate allocation between stocks and bonds, consistent with your age and goals. With your stock allocation, you can buy the universe by putting 70 percent of your money into Vanguard's U.S. Total Stock Market Index Fund (for large and small stocks) and 30 percent into its Total International Stock Index Fund. For your bond allocation, consider Vanguard's Total Bond Market Index Fund, a mix of quality and high-yield bonds of various maturities. In a 401(k) plan, hunt through the offerings for index funds that reflect these targets.

3. Make regular investments.

4. If you're in a target retirement fund, leave the money alone. These funds are no-brainers—perfect for busy people who want to invest intelligently while spending their time on their real lives. If you're in index funds, rebalance them periodically to keep to your original percentage allocation. Slow and steady is the way to wealth.

5. For action—if you really want it—use ETFs and the occasional actively managed open-end fund. Learn more about investing as you go along. Have yourself a ball. If your stock picks don't perform as well as your index funds— well, you know what to do.

23

Working with a Stockbroker

Where It Helps and Where It Hurts

**A stockbroker can make you or—
quite literally—break you. The less you know
about investing, the more breakable you are.**

What do you need a stockbroker for? Only if you want advice on buying individual stocks, bonds, mutual funds, exchange-traded funds, and other securities. The broker pitches investment ideas and finds information about securities that you suggest. When you decide to buy or sell, he or she handles the order.

I call them "brokers," by the way, but their firms have given them much fancier names. They're "financial consultants," "financial advisers," "wealth managers," "investment consultants," or "vice presidents." But their function hasn't changed, and they're still not investment professionals. They haven't gone to school to learn how to analyze stocks or market trends. They're salespeople. Their job is to sell you the firm's financial products. Period.

You can trade without a personal broker by using a discount brokerage firm (page 796). There you're talking to order takers who execute whatever you've decided to do.

Either way, a brokerage firm is the gatekeeper to the wider market. You can buy no-load mutual funds, Treasury securities, and a limited number of stocks yourself (page 834), but you need a brokerage firm for everything else.

What Brokers Are Not

- *Brokers are not financial planners!* They're not qualified to prepare a financial plan unless they've taken the courses that qualify them as a certified financial planner (CFP) or an equivalent. That doesn't stop them from sounding like planners when you first meet. They may talk to you about insurance, college savings plans, and your retirement objectives and advise you on how to meet your goals—even though they have no professional chops in the field. Their firms may offer "plans," drawn up by CFPs who work from a questionnaire that you fill out. But that's not a true plan. Brokers and the planners behind them are focused 110 percent on getting you to buy the products of the firm. To understand true financial planning, see chapter 32.

- *Brokers are not investment advisers!* Investment advisers register with the Securities and Exchange Commission or a state regulatory body, and make a variety of disclosures about their experience, training, investment strategies, and fees (page 1183). Brokers don't.

Most important, registered investment advisers (RIAs) have a *fiduciary duty* toward you! That means they're required, by law, to put your interests ahead of theirs. Brokers do not have a fiduciary duty toward their customers. They're required only to recommend *suitable* investments. What's the difference? I can illustrate it better than I can explain it. Say that you have young children and need help choosing a 529 college savings plan. A planner who is also an RIA will check your own state's plan. If it offers the typical range of mutual fund investments, plus a state tax deduction, it's in your best interest to buy it. The RIA will recommend it. A broker, by contrast, may persuade you to buy another state's plan, even though you'll lose the tax deduction. The other plan will pay the broker higher commissions. It's deemed "suitable" because it's still a 529, even though it's not the most tax-efficient way for you to save. In another example, brokers can recommend mutual funds that have fee-sharing relationships with their firms, even if their performance has been mediocre. Brokers can, and do, put their own interests and the interests of the firm above yours.

You may think of your broker as an investment adviser because he or she, well, advises you on investments. That's what makes this field so murky. Technically, the broker is acting only as your *agent*—making suggestions but buying and selling only on your say-so. The fine print in your brokerage contract will specify that you're in an agency relationship in a brokerage account, not an advisory account. You're supposed to know what that means (ha ha).

A few brokers are indeed registered investment advisers. Planners may be

RIAs, too. To find out, ask your broker or planner this: "Do you have a fiduciary duty toward me? And how do you define 'fiduciary duty'? Many brokers have no idea what it means. Or they might say yes, they have the duty, and then define it incorrectly (in which case, the real answer is no). If they don't want you to know, they'll try to evade the question. Persist, persist. You need to understand the nature of your relationship with your broker so you can evaluate the "advice." At this writing, there's a proposal to require brokers to become fiduciaries too, but there's strong opposition. For more on RIAs, see chapter 32.

Brokers Sell

When you open an account, the broker will (or should!) ask what your investment objectives are. You'll probably fill in a form disclosing your assets and evaluating your tolerance for risk (or what you think your tolerance is). The broker will respond with investment proposals. He may advise that you build a stock portfolio, buy a variable annuity, or invest in the firm's mutual funds. Or she may suggest that you go with one of the firm's recommended investment advisers who will manage your money for you.

A conscientious broker will lead you through a substantive conversation about how much money you have to invest, what you'll need the money for, and when you'll need it. You'll get commonsense investments tailored to your goals, responsibilities, and financial position. But let's face it, lots of brokers aren't conscientious. They'll push you through a short, introductory chat while boasting, "I understand the market [and you don't]. I can make you money." When they choose investments, however, their eyes are solely on the commish (commission), not on how well the products will perform for you.

Between the conscientious brokers and the unscrupulous ones, there's a group that's simply not too bright.

All brokers, even the conscientious, can be prisoners of their firms. If the firm wants something sold, it will scramble the sales force to sell it. Brokers usually have to do what they're told, even if they have their doubts. Otherwise they could lose their jobs. Greedy firms may not even tell their brokers how risky a particular product is. During the credit collapse of 2007–2009, plenty of brokers protested that they were being asked to foist bad securities on clients just to get them off the brokerage firm's books. Said their bosses, "Sell, or else."

You can make a lot of money on investments without ever having a stockbroker's name on your contact list. In fact, I think that investors like you and me shouldn't be buying individual stocks at all (see chapter 24). But if that's what you want, an honest, competent broker can be a great help.

Brokerage Firms Come in Three Main Types

The most common is the *traditional full-service broker.* Some are huge, international firms such as Morgan Stanley, JPMorgan Chase, Smith Barney, and big banks such as Bank of America and Wells Fargo. They offer every service and sell every financial product possible: retirement plans, dividend reinvestment plans, insurance, bank products, home mortgages, investment advisory accounts, credit cards. If your account is large enough, you'll have your own broker. You'll be charged top commissions and fees. Smaller investors might be offered online accounts at a lower cost, serviced by brokers at call centers. Some big firms won't pay brokers for handling accounts under $50,000. Others hit small accounts with higher fees.

Midsize full-service brokers, such as RBC Dain Rauscher and Edward Jones, offer a similar range of products as the giant firms. Small investors are more likely to get personal brokers, although some of these firms shunt them to call centers too. The only reason to choose a full-service brokerage firm—large or small—is that you like its product selections and investment research.

Successful brokers often leave big firms, register as *investment advisers* (page 1170), and open independent shops. They have access to the same types of financial products that big firms do but pay more attention to personal service. They may also offer financial planning for a fee. You'd choose an independent firm because you think that its brokers are freer to evaluate investments, discarding some of the crummy products that the brokers at big firms have to sell (although the independents might sell crummy products too). You still pay top price but perhaps with fewer nuisance fees. Some independents deal only with high-net-worth clients; others take smaller accounts too.

If you design your own strategy and pick your own stocks, you don't need an individual broker. Instead give your business to a *discount brokerage firm.* A discounter's principal job is to execute your orders to buy and sell. For this, it charges lower commissions than a full-service broker does. It also offers investment advice, in various forms, as well as Web sites loaded with investment tools, calculators, and access to stock research.

The original discounter, Charles Schwab & Co., headquartered in San Francisco, has transformed itself into something close to a full-service firm. Its commissions and fees are higher than those of most other discounters but lower than those of traditional firms. It offers investment help online, by phone, and through salaried brokers at offices around the country, as well as a ranking system for stocks that's intended to identify the better buys.

Boston-based Fidelity Investments is in the same price class as Schwab, with some trades costing more and some costing less. Fidelity offers a broad array of securities research from major firms. You can get investment "guidance" online, by phone, or in person at a branch office. The salaried brokers advise on using the Web site's do-it-yourself tools, developing an investment plan, or turning over your money for total management.

In the next lower price tier, you'll find E*Trade and TD Ameritrade. E*Trade offers a range of services similar to Schwab and Fidelity as well as investment recommendations through salaried advisers at its branches or by phone. TD Ameritrade, which charges a little less, also has advisers at local offices. Online, it will help you set up diversified investment portfolios based on exchange-traded funds.

Then there are the *deep discounters*—beloved of all dedicated stock traders. They specialize in order taking, although they offer other services too. Look at Interactive Brokers (for the most active traders), Scottrade, Firsttrade, and TradeKing. TradeKing also connects you with other traders so you can share ideas and shows you the tax implications of your trades.

But why pay anything at all? At Zecco (www.zecco.com), you get 10 online stock trades free each month, with accounts worth at least $25,000. Additional trades or trades in smaller accounts cost just $4.50 each. Zecco also offers a community, where you can share ideas with other traders and peek into their portfolios to see how they're doing. For more on communities, see page 866.

Big banks, such as Wells Fargo and Bank of America, also offer a limited number of free online trades to customers with accounts of sufficient size. You don't get the wide variety of stock research that's offered by the traditional discounters. Still, free is free.

The low-cost "direct" banks that serve their customers entirely online may offer brokerage services too. For example, take ING Direct's ShareBuilder account (www.sharebuilder.com). You invest a certain sum per month (or week or whatever) in the stocks of your choice, with the money coming out of your checking or savings account automatically. ShareBuilder does the trade for a commission of just $4.

At all discount brokers, you trade principally online or by phone. You can do IRA rollovers, buy 529 college savings plans, trade options, enter limit orders, and buy no-load mutual funds for no transaction fee—in short, everything that the average investor could want. Some firms are better than others for smaller accounts. Before signing up, compare services, commissions, fees, and the interest rate they pay on cash. Settle on a Web site you feel comfortable with. Why would you choose a discount broker? For the convenience and lower costs.

Online accounts are insured by the Securities Investor Protection Corporation (SIPC, page 801) just as traditional accounts are. The firms typically carry additional private insurance.

How to Decide Which Type of Brokerage Firm to Use

Use a deep discounter for executing one-time trades—for example, if you want to sell all the securities you inherited.

Use a deep discounter if you make your own investment choices and want nothing from a broker except fast service at a low commission. These sites also offer access to stock research. Or use Zecco free.

Use a midtier discounter if you want extra customer service such as guidance in setting up a portfolio.

Use a full-service broker if you seek advice on what to buy and sell.

The broker you pick doesn't have to be in your hometown. You can handle all your business by phone, Web, fax, and mail.

Don't use a broker at all if you don't know anything about picking stocks or other investments. Naive investors risk losing a lot of money if they fall into the hands of a manipulative salesperson. Deal with a stockbroker only if you know enough to judge the value of his or her advice.

Your Basic Brokerage Account

When you open an account, a full-service broker will ask for your full financial profile: savings, investments, liabilities, net worth, investment goals. Don't mislead the broker. He or she needs good information in order to give you good advice. The broker may run a credit check on you (and on your spouse, if you live in a community property state).

Check the form for accuracy and insist on a copy. The broker will include a simple, generic statement of your objectives, but feel free to add to it. You might write, "I want to keep my money safe and earn some income." Or "I'd like some growth, but I don't want to take much risk." Or "My long-term objective is to compound my money at an annual average of 8 percent. I am willing to take prudent risks but not highly speculative ones." Or "This is a retirement account. I am aiming for growth of 10 percent and understand that involves a high degree of risk." Or "This is my daughter's college account, and I'll need the money in eight years, when she's 18." Ask the broker to initial the statement. No offense should be taken as long as you're friendly and businesslike. The suitability of the broker's recommendations will be measured against your objectives and the financial profile you present.

If you're making a small purchase or sale, a discount broker may ask only for your name, address, and credit references. But if larger trades will go through your account, the discounter may want the same net-worth information that full-service brokers gather.

A *cash account* is for customers who don't want to get fancy. You plan to buy stocks or bonds and pay in cash by the settlement date (within three business days of making the trade). When you sell, you receive your money. That's all. It's the right account for people who rarely buy and sell.

A *margin account* is for people who expect to borrow money from their brokerage firm in order to buy securities. Margin accounts also let you sell short (page 883) and trade a wider variety of securities, such as options. How much can you borrow? Typically, up to 50 percent against the value of your stocks, convertible bonds, and certain mutual funds; 70 percent against corporate bonds; and 85 to 95 percent against your Treasuries, depending on the broker. You pay a variable rate of interest.

Brokers often open margin accounts for new customers as a matter of course. Don't let that happen unless you really intend to borrow or invest exotically. Once you have the account, you may find yourself borrowing even though you didn't mean to. For more on margin borrowing, see page 890.

A *discretionary account* lets the broker buy and sell without getting your permission. That may be the way you think you want your money managed. But it's an open invitation for him or her to earn extra commissions by stepping up trading in your account. Don't give a broker discretion! If you'll be out of the country for a while and want to keep on top of your account, carry your laptop or give your broker your international cell phone number, so that you can okay trades.

A *fee-based advisory account* puts your money under the firm's management. The broker makes suggestions about asset allocations and supervises the account, while investment advisers in the back room decide where to put your money. This is a discretionary account, but it's in the hands of professional investors rather than being run by your broker.

Don't congratulate yourself for choosing a "professional" account! It's probably run by a junior manager who buys and sells the same stocks for all the accounts under his control. For this, you'll pay 2 to 3 percent of your assets every year. Costs like that put a serious drag on your investment returns, leaving you well behind the gains of the market overall. You've probably guessed that fee-based accounts deliver large and continuing commissions to brokers, which is why they sell them so hard.

What's more, your fees don't cover all the investing you might do. Your broker can earn additional commissions and bonuses by selling you variable annuities or pieces of new issues that the firm underwrites. Trust me, if you want your money professionally managed *and* tailored to your needs, there are better ways (see chapter 32).

A *fee-based mutual fund advisory account* is the same as above, except that the managers invest your money in mutual funds—many of them the firm's own (expensive) funds. They might also offer portfolios of exchange-traded funds.

An *asset management account* brings together all your dealings with that particular institution: bank accounts, investment accounts, credit card balances, savings, whatever. Your assets, liabilities, and transactions are all reported on a single statement. You'll find these accounts at large full-service and discount brokerage houses and banks. Some mutual fund companies offer them too. Minimum deposit: in the $15,000 to $25,000 range.

These are margin accounts, so you can borrow against the securities. To make borrowing easy, the firm will probably note your "available credit" prominently on the statement and give you a checkbook and debit card. Beware, beware. That "available credit" is a loan against your securities. If you use your debit card to dip into this account at an ATM, you've taken a margin loan. If you don't repay, the margin loan compounds. If your stocks fall sharply, you'll get a "margin call," asking you to put up more cash or else be sold out. In short, these are not like bank loans—something that borrowers should be clear about. Don't borrow against your securities for consumer purchases. When that happens, you dissipate the net worth you are struggling to build. Borrow against securities only to make other investments, and then with full understanding of the risks.

A *joint account*—say, for husband and wife—allows each of you, separately, to give the stockbroker buy and sell directions. But any check issued from the account will be cut in both your names. If you're into a marital slugfest, your lawyer should notify your broker that any withdrawals from your account must have both signatures on the check. Find out what other steps should be taken to protect your half of the investments. (Spouses know how to forge each other's names!)

Brokerage house disclosure statements, signed when you open a new account, should outline all the risks you face—with options, commodities, stocks, and any other securities tradable through the account. Read everything. Get explanations for anything you don't understand. If you later complain that you were led down the garden path, the broker will whip out this statement to argue that you knew exactly what you were doing. (But even though you signed the statement, you can still pursue a legitimate claim. You can say that the broker didn't explain the risk in a particular investment or that the investment was too risky for someone in your circumstances—page 820.

A *confirmation slip* shows each buy and sell order—the security, the price, and the broker's commission. Sometimes the commission reads zero when, in fact, the broker has been paid (that happens with annuities and other packaged products). Brokers are paid for selling you everything except money market mutual funds.

It's important to keep the record straight as to who initiates each order. You place an *unsolicited order* when you pick a stock and ask your broker to buy it for you. An order is *solicited* when the broker calls you to recommend it. Your confirmation slip will show one or the other. Object immediately and in writing if a solicited order is erroneously marked unsolicited. That's often the mark of a broker trying to slip you a stock that's too risky for you. A 72-year-old widow might have a good case against a broker who suggested that she buy penny gold-mining stocks—but not if the broker's records show that buying the stocks were her idea. Insist that your record be corrected. If your broker blames the mistake on "computer glitches" more than once, switch brokers.

Your brokerage house will be covered by the Securities Investor Protection Corporation. If a firm fails and can't make all of its customers whole, SIPC steps in. It protects securities accounts worth up to $500,000 (including up to $100,000 in cash). Most brokerage houses buy private insurance that covers up to $150 million and more.

If a brokerage house fails, all accounts are usually moved to another firm within a week or two. There's hardly any break. If some of your securities are missing because of the firm's tangled record keeping, SIPC will usually replace them for you. You retain the continuing gains or losses in market value, just as if the securities had never been lost. If buying replacements is impractical, however, SIPC cashes you out for the value of your securities on the day of the failure.

Where Should You Keep Your Securities?

You have three choices:

1. Keep them at the brokerage firm—the right choice for investors who expect to buy and sell. When you sell, your broker needs those securities within three business days in order to complete the transaction.

The brokerage house will register your securities in the firm's own name, known as its *street name.* Its records, however, will show that those shares are yours. The companies whose stocks or bonds you own will send the brokerage firm all your mail—dividend or interest checks, proxies, annual reports, rights offerings, and so on. The firm puts the checks in your account and sends the mail on to you. For a fee, some firms will reinvest your dividends automatically in more of the company's shares. The broker should monitor your account for calls on your bonds (page 911), rights offerings (page 887), and tender offers (page 888) to buy your stock.

You also need to pay in three business days when you place an order to buy. For this reason, investors usually keep cash from previous sales in their broker's money market fund. That way it's right at hand. Alternatively, you can send a check by overnight mail or arrange to transfer funds from your bank account electronically. You often have to pay before you receive official confirmation of your order, so always take notes when you talk with your broker. If the "confirm" differs from what you expected, ask for a correction immediately and in writing.

If you don't buy and sell shares regularly but still keep them in a brokerage account, you may be assessed an inactive-account fee.

2. Keep your stocks and bonds on the books of a transfer agent in the Direct Registration System. These shares will be registered in your own name. You don't get a physical security. Instead your ownership is noted as a book entry in the agent's computers and on the computers of the company whose stock you hold. All dividend or interest checks, proxies, annual reports, rights offerings, and other communications from the company are sent directly to you. You can also sign up for the company's dividend reinvestment plan, where all dividends go toward the purchase of new shares (page 834); or its direct-purchase plan, which lets you buy shares from the company without going through a broker (page 835).

To register shares directly, simply tell your broker that that's what you want at the time of purchase. You can also tell the broker to transfer shares that you currently own in a street name into the Direct Registration System. When you want to sell, you supply the broker with your DRS account number and other information, and the stocks will be transferred to the brokerage firm electronically.

Direct registration is best for people who simply want to hold shares without a lot of buying and selling. The shares aren't in your brokerage account, so you shouldn't be hit with account maintenance fees or inactive-account fees. When you want to sell, you can transfer them to any broker you like.

Online broker alert: discount brokers may not let you use direct registration. Your only choices may be the firm's own street name or a paper stock certificate. A street name doesn't matter as long as there are no inactive-account fees.

3. Keep your securities yourself, in a home safe or a bank safe-deposit box. This is the most expensive, not to mention the riskiest. You will have to pay for the certificate. If you want to sell the shares, you have to send them to your broker by overnight mail (with fees if you miss the deadline, plus a possible loss on the trade). You're subject to fire and theft. You also run the risk that your heirs will lose the shares forever if you grow forgetful and never tell them about the safe-deposit box. If you lose the certificate, you might pay as much as 2 percent of its market value to replace it. Why the high price? Because the issuer has to buy insurance against the risk that you, or someone else, might find the securities and sell them. Replacement takes several weeks to several months. You cannot hold U.S. Treasury securities in certificate form. They're issued only as electronic book entries.

Broker Alert!

Brokers object to the warnings I give about business practices (and that's putting it lightly!). They care about their clients and feel that they do a good job for them. They say that they aren't affected by any conflicts of interest and I'm a rotter for suggesting otherwise.

In fact, I do believe that many brokers mean well. I believe they can help investors who know little or nothing about investing, never heard of financial planners (chapter 32), and are nervous about making money decisions—including mutual fund decisions—on their own. Good brokers create a balance of interests: enough selling to earn themselves a comfortable living while never straying beyond products suitable to their clients' needs.

Suitable, however is a tricky word. Is a high-commission product suitable when a lower-commission one would do just as well? Are high fees okay as long as the investor doesn't know about them? High fees and commissions reduce your long-term investment returns. Is that okay as long as you're happy with the advice?

Different people will answer those questions differently. Here I want to spell out the issues that you have to face if you're relying on a broker for advice.

Don't Trust Your Broker

Brokers sell the belief that you can trust them with your money. That's their primary product. If you have faith, you will take their word about how to invest.

You should *never* trust your broker, and I don't mean that personally. You can like your broker, think her smart, or find her helpful. You can ask for stock research or ideas. But trust should have nothing to do with your relationship. Like any other salesperson, she will offer you products. Like any other consumer, you should look at them skeptically, ask yourself if you need them, and consider the cost.

Your broker should not be your friend. Don't play golf together, chat about your kids, or invite your broker to parties. Keep the relationship arm's-length. Only then will you be able to look at his suggestions coolly or move your account if you're unhappy with the results.

Don't assume that because your broker belongs to your affinity group—a church or synagogue, a club, your ethnic group or gender—that he or she is wiser, kinder, and more interested in your welfare than other brokers are.

All too often, investors get trapped emotionally by their brokers. Because you've trusted and admired them, because you're friends, you're reluctant to think that something might be wrong. You don't want to hurt their feelings by challenging their performance or making complaints. It's hard to move your account, especially if you'll still see the broker in your social group.

Rule 1 for investors, then, is to keep their distance from their brokers. This is purely a financial relationship. If you're not satisfied, move on.

Rule 2 is to remember how little "trust" really means when the chips are down. Your broker wants you to treat his or her ideas as gospel. If it turns out that you were sold a pig in a poke, however, the broker will argue that the decision to buy was entirely up to you. If you trusted him, that's your problem. So sorry. Bye-bye.

Brokers Are (Often Reluctant) Commission Slaves

Even if brokers yearn to be serious students of the stock market, truly capable of giving advice, they haven't the time. They're expected to bring in tens of thousands of revenue dollars every day. To do that, they have to spend every minute on the phone, pitching current customers and bringing in new ones.

The firm "chains you to your desk in the morning and they're not going to release you until a certain quota has been reached," one broker said in a focus group for the National Endowment for Financial Education in Greenwood Village, Colorado. Exceeding the quotas is what wins brokers higher pay, awards, and vice presidencies. When a broker asks a colleague, "How are you doing?" he's not asking "Have your recommendations made money for your clients?" All he wants to know is "How much have you sold, and what commissions or other revenues have you racked up?" The more high-commission products a broker can induce you to buy, the more the broker earns—for himself and for his firm.

Three common ways that commissions bias brokers' recommendations:

1. They have to sell you something. They gain nothing by advising you to buy Treasury securities, keep your cash in money market funds, prepay your mortgage, or beef up your contributions to your 401(k). They might even suggest that you drop your 401(k) and invest with them instead. Not a good idea.

2. They get a regular income if you adopt an investment strategy that requires frequent purchases, such as writing *covered calls* (page 879) or investing in *Dow Dogs* (page 874). Covered calls appeal to conservative investors seeking income, but that's an expensive way to get it. Dow Dogs require an annual portfolio redo.

3. They praise the products that earn them the largest commissions or bonuses. In researching this question, I asked about the different commissions paid on different products. Here's a broker's reply: "Basically, the big bucks come from fee-based accounts (page 799). We get that annually! Got to build the fee-based book of business to reap the real rewards!!!" (Has your broker suggested a fee-based account lately?)

Don't Trust Your Firm's Research Department

Okay, so the broker is driven by commissions and fees. But what about the Famous Brokerage Firm's research department? Those workaholics slave over computer screens night and day to dope out what's happening to the companies they follow. When they praise a company, you can take it to the bank. Right?

Wrong. Analysts have their necessities too. They do terrific studies of the economy, an industry in general, and many stocks. They face conflicts, however, when talking about companies that are important to their firms.

Big firms have investment banking arms, which help companies raise money or find merger partners. They don't want bad reports on those clients or on companies they hope to gain as clients. After the tech stock bust of 2000, it turned out that famous analysts were telling the suckers (that is, the general public) to buy stocks they knew were dogs, while warning their big institutional clients to sell. To stop the cheating, the regulators (late, as usual) required the brokerage firms to separate their research and trading arms from their investment banking arms. In theory, preference is no longer shown to banking customers. Analysts' bonuses are now tied to the quality and accuracy of their research and stock prices. The firms also have to disclose the proportion of buy, hold, and sell recommendations it issues, which drastically lowered the number of buys.

But the conflicts don't go away. Important customers are still going to get a break. Here's a quick guide to analysts' recommendations. *Strong buy:* accumulate the stock. *Buy:* the stock isn't falling yet, but watch it. *Long-term buy:*

disaster this year, but maybe it will pick up later. *Hold/Neutral:* sell as fast as you can. *Sell:* the company failed last week. As Lily Tomlin has said, "No matter how cynical you become, it's never enough to keep up."

Brokers Take the Heat, but Management Lights the Fire

A brokerage firm is a hard taskmaster. Even a well-meaning broker can be driven to rogue practices by a firm that insists on high sales at any cost. New brokers and less successful brokers are especially vulnerable to this kind of pressure. Management sets quotas that brokers have to meet to keep their jobs. For example, they might have to produce at least $300,000 a year in revenue. In addition, firms may: (1) raise quotas unreasonably, which tempts brokers to churn accounts (page 820); (2) offer incentives, such as extra pay or status vacations, for selling mediocre products that the firm makes extra money on; (3) mislead brokers about the riskiness of a product they're asked to sell; (4) order brokers to sell a crummy block of shares that its savvier institutional customers have rejected; (5) demand that brokers sell fee-based advisory accounts, even to clients who many not need them; (6) create a climate of callousness by passing out perks and vice presidencies to big producers no matter how dirty their techniques.

Firms circulate each broker's production throughout the office to keep up the pressure for higher sales. It fires brokers who don't bring in enough accounts or squeeze enough commission income out of the accounts they have. Since sales are often reported on a monthly basis, some brokers push through as much business as they can at the end of the month in order to make the grade.

An Important Point About Fees

A 2.5 percent annual fee on an advisory account may sound like nothing. But let's say that account is earning a 7 percent return. Minus fees, that's down to 4.5 percent. Minus 3 percent inflation, you've got 1.5 percent in real returns. Minus capital gains taxes—well, you could be in minus territory. Fees on variable annuities may climb to 4 percent. Why would you pay, when you can get good mutual funds for less than 0.5 percent? And good investment management for 1 percent? Forests have been leveled for the paper used to study investment returns. Only one thing has any predictive value: *cost.* The less you pay, the better your possible return.

How Can Brokers and Their Firms Succeed if Their Customers Don't?

Many clients never learn that they're underperforming the market. That's because the reports you get from your broker don't show your percentage gain or loss. If you do figure it out and leave, well, there are always new customers coming along. After all, when you drop a stockbroker, where do you go? To another stockbroker, natch. And the broker you left gets some other broker's unhappy customer. It's just one big shuffle.

I should add that a broker needn't be self-interested to burn through your money. He might just be stupid. Here's the comment of a broker who lost an Oklahoma farm couple $200,000 by selling their municipal bonds and using the proceeds to trade options. "Hey, I'm sorry," he said. "I didn't know what I was doing."

How Can You Find a Good Stockbroker? (The Ideal Way)

I have raised all these conflicts of interest so that you'll know what you're up against if you ask a stockbroker for investment advice. That doesn't change the fact that many brokers do a good job for people and many investors want a broker's advice. So how can you find someone suitable?

1. Gather recommendations from associates whose investment objectives are similar to yours. Ask what they like and don't like about the broker, and what their successes and failures have been. (If they say "no failures," don't believe it. Get your recommendations from someone else.)

2. Call the office managers of the brokerage houses that interest you. Say that you're looking for an experienced stockbroker who entered the business not later than 1995. (That guarantees that he or she will have suffered through the bubble and the bust.) Give a brief summary of your resources and your investment objectives and ask for a recommendation. Tell the manager that you want a "good fit," not just the "broker of the day." The BOTD is the one in line for the next walk-in customer. Often, it's a new broker or one of the office's less successful brokers.

3. Telephone or e-mail the brokers on your list, explain that you're looking for someone to help with your investments, and make appointments to interview them by telephone. During the interview ask (and write down) how long they've been in business, what colleges they went to and when they graduated, where and when they passed the exams that qualified them as brokers, what other brokerage firms they've worked for, and why they left. Ask what kinds of investments they know best and which ones they're weak on. Ask what most of their clients buy. An income investor belongs with someone who buys a lot of bonds; a speculator needs a broker who loves new issues and hot stocks. A broker may claim that he or she is good at everything, but that's not possible. Brokers generally recommend the types of investments that, in their hearts, appeal to them the most. For that reason, you may find it helpful to have a broker whose way of life is similar to your own.

4. Tell the brokers about yourself, how much money you'll invest, and what you'll want the money for (college? retirement?). Ask what kinds of investments they'd suggest for someone like you. Take notes. If you feel that a broker is talking nonsense, or not taking you seriously, or not connecting with your needs, or showing off, or sounding impatient, cross him or her off your list.

Also cross off any kids—first, because they still believe the stuff they learned in training school about the virtues of all the firm's financial products; and second, because you don't want a neophyte learning his or her lessons on your money.* Kids on the fast track, with a big mortgage, a new BMW, and total faith in what they're selling, may push you toward risky investments that pay high commissions. Kids on the slow track may know so little and be so nervous about their new job that they don't advise you well. Research has shown that younger brokers and managers are more susceptible to hot stock market trends and less interested in balanced portfolios.

5. Ask each broker for the names of three satisfied customers with whom he or she has worked for at least three years. The broker may say, "That's confidential." You say, "Please get their permission to give out their names." Don't be intimidated by a broker who says that he or she doesn't do referrals. A broker who can't produce happy clients for you to call may not have any. When you talk to the clients, check what the broker has told you against their personal experience. Ask what they think the broker has done for them. You may get some surprisingly candid answers.

6. Check on the brokers you're interested in. Look at their CRD report (page 817), to see how long they've been registered as stockbrokers, what firms they've worked for, and whether any of their customers filed complaints against them. Make sure that the report jibes with what they told you.

All this checking may sound obsessive, but it isn't. You'd be astonished at how many lies are told, even by brokers at famous firms. Here's a story from

---

*An old joke says that brokerage firms pay $100,000 to train a new stockbroker and customers pay $1 million.

an ex-stockbroker, Mary Calhoun, of Watertown, Massachusetts, who now acts as an arbitrator and expert witness in arbitrations between investors and brokers. She says that when she started, a Merrill Lynch superbroker advised her, "Mary, never tell anyone you've been in business less than seven years!" If you find that a broker has misled you in any way, cross that name off. Anyone willing to tell you a small lie will tell you a whopper too.

7. Once you've finished with the phone work and have one or two favorites, set up personal interviews to see how you like them one-on-one. Answer all the questions that the broker is likely to have about you. Discuss how you might best work together. Get more specific about your goals and what the broker would recommend. Ask for a written proposal. If you have a substantial sum of money, don't give the broker all of it at once. Hold back to see how well he or she performs. Ask whether the broker offers discounts on sales commissions. Many do if your orders are large enough, especially if you came up with the investment idea. The broker knows that you can always take it to a discounter.

8. If you'll be asking the broker to research your own stock ideas, see how much help he or she is prepared to give. Some will just funnel you research reports from the firm's own analysts. Others will send information even on stocks the firm doesn't follow. Spend some time talking to the broker about this if getting stock research is important to you.

9. Ask what the broker will send you about stocks you already own. You should get updated research reports, company announcements, and the company's annual and quarterly reports.

10. Ask about commission rates, annual fees, transaction costs, and any other expenses. No fee should show up on any of your account statements that you haven't been told about in advance. Ask about the total costs of any packaged product such as unit trusts and variable annuities. If you pay 2.5 or 3 percent for a product or for a fee-based advisory account, you'll find it tough—maybe impossible—to make money, after inflation and taxes. Fees like that are just too high.

11. After the interviews, discuss the brokers' proposals with someone you trust. Do their strategies make sense for you? Does the advice sound honest and intelligent? Did you feel that you were treated well? Always remember that the broker isn't doing you any favors; you're doing the broker a favor by becoming a client. Walk away from anyone who seems to be talking down.

12. All this takes time, and it should. You want a long-term relationship with a broker and shouldn't blindly stab at the first one who comes along. If you're not happy with one of the brokers after the personal interviews, keep looking. You have nothing to lose by leaving your money in the bank or a money market mutual fund, even if the market is going up. Stocks, it is said, are like buses. If you miss one, another one will be by in just a few minutes, and it will be going the same way.

You may have noticed something missing from this list: I didn't ask whether you liked the broker and felt comfortable there. Liking a broker has nothing to do with it. You're not looking for a best friend. Some of the most treacherous brokers are the best and friendliest talkers. So keep focused. Look past the charming smile and think about what the broker says.

How Do You Find a Stockbroker (The Real Way)?

You bump into a broker on the golf course, at a dinner party, or at your church or temple. He or she mentions a couple of good stocks that went up 30 percent. You say, "Hey, will you handle my account?" Or your best friend says, "My broker earned me 30 percent last year" and you hit the phone, begging that broker to take you on. You won't have a clue whether the broker is really competent or will listen to what you say about the kinds of investments you want. (Or, for that matter, whether he or she *really* earned 30 percent for your friend—I suspect not, even though that might be what your friend believes.)

Even if you're stumbling into a brokerage relationship, use the checklist above as a guide. Your broker will treat you more seriously if he or she knows that you're thinking carefully about what you're doing.

Fifteen Ways to Keep Your Broker Flying Right

1. Talk to the broker about your investment goals—a retirement nest egg? retirement income? college for your children?—and how best to balance income, growth, and risk. These objectives should be written down on the new-account form, in words that satisfy you, on your first visit as a customer. Get a copy of the form and keep it with your records.

If the broker doesn't fill out a new-account form, or if you would like to be more specific, set down your objectives in a letter, ask the broker to initial it, and keep a copy. Those are his or her marching orders. If your letter says, "Prudent growth investments for my daughter's college education 10 years from now" and your broker puts you into stock-index options, you have proof that the investment wasn't suitable. Don't be afraid to present this letter. A good broker finds it helpful to know what your expectations are.

2. Read every word of the account agreement before signing it and get explanations for everything you don't understand. Refuse a margin account if you don't plan to buy on borrowed money. No point being tempted.

3. Confirm every verbal buy or sell order in writing or e-mail so there's no mistake (and keep a copy). Your e-mail to the broker should include your understanding of the investment's goals. If the broker has told you that an oil well deal is "safe for someone who needs income," repeat that promise in your note. If the hole comes up dry, that e-mail could help you win a settlement or an arbitration case. (Remember: a broker, when challenged, will always say that he or she explained all the risks and you understood them. Your note shows exactly what you thought you were buying. If more of these notes were written, more brokers would settle without giving you a hard time.)

4. Write down the following magic questions and keep them near the telephone. Ask each one of them every time your broker recommends an investment:

- *Why are you suggesting this?*
- *How does it meet the goals I outlined in the customer agreement?*
- *Will you send me a research report? Or a prospectus?*
- *What is the investment's past performance?*
- *If it's a stock, how high is the price-earnings ratio, compared with its historical range* (page 872)?
- *If this is a new or secondary stock offering, is your firm one of the underwriters* (meaning, one of the firms tasked with selling the stock to the public)? The law requires brokers to tell you. (They'll probably say, "Yes, that's why we know it so well," even if they're trying to offload a dog.) Beware.
- *Is the company an investment banking client of your firm?* (That signals a possible conflict of interest—see analysts, page 805.) If so, don't buy without seeing independent research on the stock from another firm. The broker should send the research, or you might find it online at Google Finance (http://finance.google.com//finance) or Yahoo/Finance (http://biz.yahoo.com) (look for "Analysts reports").
- *If it's an initial public offering of stock, is there a lockup, and how long does it last?* The lockup is the number of days, often 180, that insiders have to hold the stock before bailing out. The firm will try to keep the stock price up until that period ends. Then the price might fall. (For more on initial public offerings, see page 880).
- *How long do you recommend that I hold the stock?* If only for the short term, do you really want it? If the broker says it's a long-term hold but then comes

back in a year and suggests that you sell—well, you've learned something. He may be turning over your account for the commissions.

• *Can I sell whenever I want? Are penalties involved?* (An important question if you're being sold packaged products such as unit trusts or annuities.)

• *On a scale of 1 to 10, how would you rate the market risk?*

• *What are the commissions and other transaction costs? Are there any ongoing fees?*

• *What can go wrong?* (There is no investment that can't go wrong.)

• *If I don't choose this investment, what alternatives might you suggest?*

The answers should help weed out investments that are inappropriate for you. If you're interested, get the research material or prospectus and think about it for a day or two. Never tumble when a broker says, "It's now or never." First, that's rarely true. Second, if it is, say, "Never." Smart investors never buy sight unseen or buy when a broker is hustling them to a decision. (You run into the Dopeler Effect—the tendency of stupid ideas to seem smarter when they come at you rapidly.)

On the other hand, don't take a week to decide. By then the price may be higher than you ought to pay.

5. Always get a research report on a stock and read it before buying! Without it, the stock is only a name. The report tells you what the company does and something about the industry it's in. At the end of the report, you'll find some interesting disclosures, such as: Does the brokerage firm or the analyst own shares in the company being recommended, including shares bought prior to the public offering? Has the firm been paid by this company for investment banking services over the past 12 months? Is the analyst's pay partly based on how well the investment banking business does? "Yes" answers suggest bias— they're pitching the stock to help the client.

The research report also has to disclose what percentage of all the firm's ratings are buys, holds, and sells and the percentage of investment banking clients that fall into each category. You won't find many clients under "sell." Finally, you'll see a chart of the stock's historical price, showing the price when the firm started covering it, the dates of the various buy/hold calls it has made, and the price and *price targets* at the time (a price target is the analyst's guess—sheer guess—as to how high the price might move). Have the analyst's calls done well? Did the stock go in the expected direction? Does the analyst keep moving up the stock's target price without even advising that some of it should be sold? Maybe this is *not* the time to buy.

Few customers go to the trouble of reading all this stuff; they just say yes when the broker calls. Brokers sell more to clients who just say yes. They sell more carefully (and, I suspect, give better advice) to customers who ask questions and study a recommendation before they buy.

6. Check every slip that confirms a trade. Mistakes are sometimes made in writing up orders. The broker might enter the wrong stock symbol or write "buy" instead of "sell." He or she might write that the order was unsolicited (page 801), when that's not the case. If you don't catch the error right away (and confirm your order in writing), the broker may claim that there was no error, and it could be hard for you to prove otherwise.

7. Check your statements to make sure that checks are deposited in the correct account and in a timely manner.

8. When you call your broker about a mistake, follow up with a letter or e-mail. If the error isn't straightened out, call the firm's office manager and ask why. Send the manager a copy of the note you wrote to the broker. Any broker who is slow to correct a "mistake" may be covering up something.

9. Call (and write) immediately if an investment pitched as "safe" starts to go down or if you suddenly, and unexpectedly, take a loss that you can't afford. The broker might have misrepresented the purchase.

10. Keep written notes of every conversation with your broker, date them, and put them in a file. *This is the best advice on this page!* If the broker ever claims that you gave permission for a trade when you didn't or argues, falsely, that he or she fully explained a risky investment, your notes will prove otherwise. Good arbitrators give a lot of weight to contemporaneous notes, kept faithfully. There will be audiotapes of your phone conversations with your broker, which the firm may play at the arbitration (your lawyer should get copies). The notes, however, show what you understood. Good notes might even win an early settlement.

Incidentally, let the broker know that you're taking notes, as in "Just a minute, I'm writing this down." Stockbrokers tend to highlight the promise in any investment and glide over the risks—which might happen less often if they know that their comments are on the record.

11. If a broker recommends a fee-based account, ask for the total fee— the fixed annual fee plus the cost of the underlying investment—and write it down. Ask the broker why this is better for you than a regular transactions account. Write that down too. Ask yourself whether you might do better with a fee-only financial planner who's an investment adviser (chapter 32).

12. Ask for the costs—*all* the costs—of any packaged products, such as variable annuities, unit trusts, mutual funds, and anything else the broker sells.

13. Keep all paperwork: your new-account agreement, confirmations of trades, monthly statements, copies of the letters and e-mails you write to your broker, notes of conversations, literature about your investments. You never know what will help you win a settlement if you think you've been misled.

14. Keep track of the fees and commissions you pay each year. Commissions appear on each confirmation slip after a trade, but brokerage firms (being no dopes) don't normally aggregate them on your monthly statements. Only your broker knows the total—and should send it to you if you ask. You have to excavate fees on products sold with prospectuses. Ask your broker to list them for you and, yes, write them down. If you ever check the prospectus, you may discover that you didn't get the whole story.

15. Go for periodic portfolio reviews. Discuss the big picture to be sure that you and your broker still agree on your goals. Then ask the broker to show you your percentage return for the year (adjusted for purchases, sales, additions, withdrawals, dividends, and commissions), compared with the return of the stock market and bond market as a whole. Also, ask for your compounded average annual percentage investment return since your relationship began. Only a few firms disclose this routinely, probably for good reason, but you should insist. How else can you hold your broker accountable or see how good your own investment ideas really were? The data you need are right there on the broker's computer.

If your broker can't or won't compute your compounded average annual returns, do it yourself. You'll need a suitable computer program. For a guide to them all, subscribe to *Computerized Investing*, a publication from the American Association of Individual Investors ($24 a year, www.aaii.com/store). Most investment tools simply let you track your investments, showing your gain or loss and tax basis. Search for one that can figure your annual return.

If you suspect that a broker is churning or otherwise mishandling your account, check it out at Stockbroker Analysis (www.stockbroker-analysis.com; 239-243-9548). This firm analyzes your portfolio—unearthing your total investment gains and losses, gains and losses from trading, total costs, and net percentage returns compared with what your money could have earned if it had been invested in a pure stock or bond index. You'll also see what percentage of your investment you spent on commissions. It shouldn't be more than 1.5 percent on stocks and 1 percent on bonds, Stockbroker Analysis says. Cost: $175 if you scan or e-mail copies of your account yourself and $200 if you mail copies for Stockbroker Analysis to scan. Analyzing small subaccounts costs an additional $35 to $50.

To Fly Right Yourself . . .

- *Stick to your investment program.* By saying yes to what fits and no to what doesn't, you blaze a clear trail for your broker to follow.
- *Take responsibility for understanding everything you buy.* If, after two explanations, you still don't get it, skip it. No investment is so special that it's worth buying blind. Besides, if the broker can't explain it, maybe he or she doesn't understand it either. Or doesn't want *you* to understand it.
- *Don't whine, complain, or chew over opportunities lost.* Let the market bury its dead. This is always the first day of the rest of your investing life.
- *Don't deceive your broker about the size of your assets, where they're invested, and what other brokerage accounts you keep.* A good broker will make better recommendations if he or she knows the whole picture.
- *Take your losses like a man—er, person.* After market collapses, speculators who bought on margin sometimes try to walk away from legitimate debts they owe their brokers, forcing the brokers to go to court or arbitration to try to collect. Resist only if you were genuinely misled.
- *Don't succumb to fantasies.* You know in your heart that no investment is risk free. You know in your gut that no one can guarantee an extra-high return, be it in a stock or a money market mutual fund.
- *Be honest about your own investment results.* Most investors remember their winners, forget their losers, and never average the two together. So they haven't a clue how well they've actually performed. For easier tracking, get a good computer program (page 814). If you discover that you're underperforming the market average (which wouldn't be surprising), take the hint. Maybe you ought to be in an index fund.

How to Replace a Broker You Already Have

Maybe you're uncomfortable with the advice you're getting but not with the firm. In that case, tell the broker—politely—that the relationship isn't working. Call the office manager and ask to work with someone else (but don't accept a rookie). Interview the new broker just as you did (or should have done) before, and be candid about why the other one didn't work out. Your original broker shouldn't take offense. This sort of thing happens all the time.

Alternatively, you might want to move to another firm. That's normally easy. The new firm will send you a form from the Automated Customer Account Transfer Service (ACATS). You enter the details of your current account and send it back. Your new firm will tell your old firm to transfer the securities.

When they arrive, the new firm will check them before accepting and depositing them in your account. The entire process may take two to four weeks (sometimes more), depending on the types of securities you own. Avoid any buying or selling during this period. It will put a stick in the spokes.

There can be problems. Maybe you made an error on the form. Maybe you owe fees to your old firm that haven't been paid. Maybe you own stocks on margin, and the new firm doesn't want to accept them. The new firm may not accept nonstock securities, such as options or your old firm's name-brand mutual funds and unit trusts. You'll have to cash them in or leave them where they are. If you cash them in, you may owe exit fees or redemption penalties; if you leave them, you may be charged a $40 inactive-account fee every year. (These are good reasons to stay clear of broker-brand products in the first place.)

Individual Retirement Accounts may be slower to move than other securities, if you need to change the custodian. Fee-based advisory accounts could be more complicated too.

Don't ask the old firm to ship securities directly to you. That might take weeks of "misunderstandings," arguments, and tears. Besides, you want to keep the securities at your new firm anyway. They're safer there and on hand if you want to sell.

Before changing brokers, add four questions to the new-broker interview list: Which securities in my present portfolio would you sell? Why? What would you replace them with? Why?

An investor who wants to switch brokers can be easy pickings for a new broker intent on sales. It's easy to convince you that the old guy sold you rotten stocks. The more the new broker can get you to sell, the higher the commissions he or she will earn. But maybe you're holding a lot of good securities. Maybe the problem with your old broker was chemistry, not advice. If the new broker wants to replace what you have with substantially similar securities, shy away.

Sometimes your old broker will move to a new firm, taking you along. If he or she decides to revamp your portfolio after the move, it's because the new firm wants different things sold. This raises big questions in my mind: Is the broker saying that his or her old recommendations were no good? If so, why should you continue being a customer?

Cold Calls

The phone rings at dinnertime. "Hello, I'm from Famous Brokers, Inc. You've heard of us, of course." Or (a secretary's voice) "Please hold the phone for Mr. von Patter, our vice president."

You're getting a cold call. A stockbroker has your number and is hoping to hook you before you hang up. "Would you be interested in a rare opportunity? No? How about something medium-rare? How about conservative municipal bonds? You should buy now. This market is good."

Hang up. Say no, thanks, and good-bye. Don't even wait to hear the spiel. You've just read about how to find a broker. Don't settle for one who picked your number from a pack of cards.

Dishing the Dirt on Your Broker

Never start an association with a stockbroker and a brokerage house without first checking up on them. Do it even if you're dealing with a well-known firm. Big firms hire hyenas just as small firms do. A hyena who's a "big producer" (producing huge sales commissions) may be welcome almost everywhere, even though he or she eventually wipes the customers out.

You can learn a tremendous amount about your broker—at no cost—by tapping into the computerized Central Registration Depository (CRD) maintained jointly by the state securities regulators and the Financial Industry Regulatory Authority (FINRA).

The CRD contains the broker's employment history for the past 10 years—what firms he or she worked for, the reasons for leaving, and any years of self-employment or unemployment. It reveals black marks on the record, such as gambling convictions, crimes involving money and securities, fraud, bankruptcies, and unsatisfied judgments. You'll also find any investment-related civil actions and court judgments; arbitration and customer-complaint settlements of $10,000* or more; complaints alleging forgery, theft, or misappropriations within the past two years; pending consumer complaints alleging sales practice violations, with damages of $5,000 or more; and disciplinary actions for violating the rules of various regulatory bodies and exchanges. Similar information is recorded about the brokerage firm and its principals. These forms are supposed to be updated anytime there's new information—for example, an arbitration decision against the broker, a new complaint, or a change of employment.

To get all this information, access FINRA BrokerCheck at www.finra.org. Or call the BrokerCheck hotline at 800-289-9999 and ask for the information to be mailed. Here's what you're looking for:

---

*This may rise to $15,000 or $25,000.

- *Has the broker hopped around from one firm to another?* Maybe he or she churns through a book of customers and starts over somewhere else. If the broker goes from one small firm to another, maybe you're dealing with a specialist in penny stocks (page 956).
- *Did the broker leave his or her last firm during or after an arbitration award or disciplinary hearing?* That's not a good sign.
- *Is the broker enmeshed in personal troubles*—judgments, bankruptcies, lawsuits? At best, they will be distracting. At worst, the broker will feel pressed to churn your account in order to dig out of his or her financial hole.
- *How long has he or she been selling?* Rookie brokers may fudge on this point. You want someone who has been through both bad times and good and has some perspective. You also want someone who is truthful about his or her length of service.
- *What kinds of firms has the broker worked for?* You'll probably recognize the big national or regional names. But if you see a lot of firms you never heard of, maybe this broker isn't so hot.
- *What is the broker's disciplinary record?* The vast majority of brokers don't have one. That's the kind you want.

Warning: The broker may have had troubles that don't appear on the CRD. For example, lawyers often don't put the broker's name on an arbitration complaint, even if the broker sold deceptively. They name only the brokerage firm, which generally makes it easier to settle the case. The bad broker's record stays clean. If the broker is named but the case settles without a hearing, the agreement may state that it won't be reported to the CRD (this dodge has limits, but they're normally easy to get around). Some firms may not even report customer complaints, as the regulations require. One state official told me about visiting a firm and finding hundreds of complaints just stuffed in a file.

So there are some thieving brokers walking around whose records don't reveal the rotters they are. Your best hope of smoking them out is to avoid one who job-hops a lot.

How to Be a Smarter Customer

The more you know about investing, the better ideas you'll get from your broker and the smarter decisions you'll make about your own account. Brokers won't teach you. You're responsible for reaching a minimum level of competence yourself. Here are some ways to teach yourself about stocks and bonds:

- *Read.* Five good, classic books on securities analysis are *The Intelligent Investor* by Benjamin Graham, as revised by Jason Zweig and Warren Buffett; *The Battle for Investment Survival* by Gerald M. Loeb; *Stock Market Primer* by Claude N. Rosenberg Jr.; and *Stocks for the Long Run* and *The Future for Investors* by Jeremy Siegel. Prowl your library and bookstore for others. Look for general guides, not books that tout a particular system or guru or books addressing the investment fad or fear of the moment.

- *Subscribe and surf.* For business news, read *The Wall Street Journal,* the *Financial Times,* and Bloomberg.com. For news and features directed at investors, look at Forbes.com, Marketwatch.com, Finance.yahoo.com, Google.com/finance, MoneyWatch.com, and CNN Money.com. For mutual funds, nothing's better than Morningstar.com. For news and information about all aspects of personal finance, read *Kiplinger's Personal Finance* magazine, *Money* magazine, and *SmartMoney,* in print or online. But read them for general principles. Don't be lured away from your sensible long-term plan by hopping into every hot fund of the month!

  Serious students of long-term stock investing need the *Value Line Investment Survey*, a guide to public companies, their financial data, and the outlook for their stocks (www.valueline.com). As for Web chat groups, don't take them seriously. They're pocked with stock hypes posted by dishonest brokers and investors who hope to manipulate you to their profit. You knew that, of course. If you buy, you're hoping to go along for the ride. No tears here if you wipe out.

- *Join.* Try the American Association of Individual Investors (www.aaii.com, 800-428-2244, 625 North Michigan Avenue, Chicago, IL 60611). Members get the monthly *AAII Journal,* other investment information, and access to seminars on investing and financial planning. Or read AAII's *Computerized Investing,* a bimonthly publication on how to manage your investments by computer.

  Also try the National Association of Investors Corporation (www.betterin vesting.org, 877-275-6242, P.O. Box 220, Royal Oak, MI 48068), which helps people form investment clubs. Learning in a group is more fun and often more effective than learning on your own. An NAIC membership includes a subscription to the association's publication, *Better Investing Magazine,* as well as online stock and mutual fund analysis and other tools. You can also download free information on how to start and run an investment club.

- *Study.* Some schools and colleges offer adult education courses. When taught by personal-finance teachers, they can be a big help. But take care when you're studying with a stockbroker, insurance agent, or financial planner whose "courses" are indirect pitches for his or her services. Learn what you can from the course, but don't take it as gospel—especially if your "professor" is "teaching" a marvelously "safe, high-yield" investment.

■ *Experiment.* Start a "learning account," with real cash, at a discount brokerage firm. Use it to invest small amounts of money. Try out the ideas that you've read about in books and magazines. See if your stocks go up and, if they don't, how it feels to lose. Test your ability to make good decisions in the face of rapidly changing conditions. You can't learn on paper. You have to put real money at risk.

When Brokers Are Liable for Your Losses

When you lose money based on what a broker advised, you can sometimes force the brokerage firm to give it back. To collect, however, you have to be able to show that the broker handled your money in a way that's specifically illegal. (Stupidity is not a compensable offense.) Here's a list of the cardinal sins.

1. Unsuitable investments. The broker buys securities that contravene your stated goals or are too risky for someone in your position. Say, for example, that you tell the broker that all you have in the world is $50,000, which you need to live on. The broker says, "Sure," and puts you into an array of speculative or non-dividend-paying stocks. If you take major losses, the broker should be liable. It makes no difference that you approved the purchases. The broker should never have recommended them in the first place. It's also unsuitable for a broker to concentrate most of your money in two or three stocks, talk you into buying on margin, or buy you aggressive growth stocks if you're a widow who said she needs income.

It's harder to prove unsuitability than you might think. The broker might argue that you asked for more growth in your portfolio and knew what you were doing. There will be tapes of your conversations; you'll hear the broker telling you about the investment and yourself saying, "Yes, that sounds good." (That's why you shouldn't say yes until you've thought about it.) The arbitrator might decide that you should have known what you were doing even if you didn't. Only the egregious cases win.

Smart businesspeople will also find it hard to win. Arbitrators tend to think that if you can run a company successfully, you ought to be able to analyze what's going on in your securities accounts. That's totally wrong, of course. You can be the sharpest steak knife manufacturer in the country, with hundreds of employees, but that doesn't make you sophisticated about stocks and bonds. No matter. The stereotype is against you. The arbitrators will assume that you knew—or should have known—what you were doing.

2. Churning. You're being churned when securities, including mutual funds, are constantly bought and sold for your account solely to generate sales commissions. Sometimes so much money is siphoned off that it's almost impossible for you to come out ahead. There's no specific rule on how much trading is too much. What's fair in a speculator's account is excessive for novices with a limited amount of money. To find out what your broker is doing, add up the fees and commissions and any margin interest you paid over the past 12 months; using your monthly statements, find your average account value over the same 12 months; then divide your costs by the average value (if you bought on a margin, count only the equity in the account). The result is the percentage return you have to earn just to cover your costs. If it's higher than 3 percent, you are probably being churned.

You can also look at the turnover ratio in your account. This is the total equity value of all your purchases for the year divided by the average equity in your account. Three times is a definite red flag, although two times is too much for the average investor seeking moderate growth. You occasionally find churning in bank trust accounts too.

3. Unauthorized trading. The broker buys and sells without your prior permission. This happens more often than you might think and is one strong reason for keeping notes of your conversations. A broker may claim that you gave permission when you didn't.

4. Misrepresentation. A broker lies about an investment, conceals pertinent information, or plays down known risks. For example, say that your latest monthly statement shows a drop in the value of your account. Your broker might say, falsely, "That's a mistake; you're really making money. It's just that some of your options profits aren't posted yet." Another example: The broker may whisper that Red Inc. is about to merge and advise you to load up on it. He neglects to mention that the Justice Department is opposing the takeover. When you see that in the newspapers, he says that he has a friend at Justice who heard that the government will drop its case. That turns out to be a lie. The deal blows apart, and your stock heads south.

If you can prove any concealments or lies (ideally, from those notes you keep of your conversations with your broker), you may be able to recover your loss.

5. Overleverage. You're induced to borrow more against your securities than is consistent with your investment goals. Your broker may not have fully disclosed the risk of buying securities on margin or taken the time to see if you truly understood. If you didn't grasp the fact that a margin call could cost you some of your stocks, maybe you have a case. Margin buying is almost never consistent with conservative investment goals.

6. Falsification of documents. A broker might note on your new-account form or options agreement that you're richer than you really are. This can happen with brokers who peddle high-risk investments. To trade options, the firm might require you to have a net worth of $100,000, not counting your house. If you're worth less, the broker might put down $100,000 anyway and later claim that you supplied the false amount. Never sign a brokerage agreement that contains false numbers or blanks that a broker can fill in later.

Brokers have also been known to forge clients' signatures, which, of course, is illegal. The forgery may go undetected unless you pay close attention to your account statements. Look for any trading, checks, or cash releases to third parties that you didn't authorize.

7. Theft. A broker may actually lift money from your account. For example, your statement might say that your brokerage firm sent you $3,000 from your asset management account, but you never received the check. Or you might find that you suddenly own just 400 shares of Microsoft, when last month you owned 500 shares. A good brokerage firm will always restore losses from theft, but first you have to notice it. Untold millions of dollars are probably lost each year by people who don't read their brokerage house statements or don't understand what they read. (Adult children of elderly parents, take note.)

8. Unregistered securities or an unregistered broker or brokerage firm. You can recover your losses if your broker sells a stock, partnership, or any other security not registered for sale in your state, unless an exemption has been filed. Unregistered securities are typically over-the-counter stocks selling for $5 or less a share. By statute, most states entitle you to get all of your money back, plus interest and attorney's fees. That is, you can get your money if the firm hasn't gone bankrupt. Firms and brokers must also be registered to do business in your state.

9. Negligence. If your broker fails to act with due care—for instance, carrying through your orders to buy or sell—he or she may be liable for negligence. A broker may also be negligent for failing to tell you the bad news about a security.

The deadliest sin is incompetence, but it's hard to collect on. If your broker offered muddled advice and you took it, you'll usually have to swallow the loss. It's not illegal to be stupid.

If You've Been Cheated, Don't Make These Mistakes

• *Don't blame yourself.* The fault doesn't lie in your personal greed or innocence, nor is your loss a "lesson" or just one of investing's unlucky breaks. The broker has a duty to offer you securities that fit your needs and tolerance for risk and to describe them honestly. They don't have to be the best possible investments or the lowest-cost investments, but they have to be suitable. If the broker cheats, you have a right to be outraged. You have to accept investment risk, but acceptable risks don't include deception, fraud, and abuse.

■ *Don't walk away.* Demand reparations from the broker, the broker's office manager, and the president of the brokerage firm. Sometimes that works. If you get a form letter claiming that you knew the risks, your course of action will depend on how much you lost. A small loss might not be worth the expense of trying to collect, alas—although if you pester, the firm might throw you a bone. For a larger loss, go to arbitration (page 828) or mediation (page 827). The more noise you make, the more willing a firm might be to settle your case quickly, if it suspects it's in the wrong. Do your yelling on a blog, where you'll collect a community of wronged investors—all of them eager to spread the word. Favorite angry blog headlines: XYZ Company Sucks, or I Hate XYZ.

■ *Don't let the clock run out.* Industry arbitration forums generally don't accept claims based on transactions that are more than six years old. This is called the *subject matter* limit. It's different from statutes of limitations, which can be much shorter. The statutes limit the time you have for alleging specific violations, and although arbitration panels don't have to follow them, they usually do. Claims under federal law have to be challenged within one year from the date of discovery and no more than three years from the date of the transaction. State laws may give you a little longer. Nevertheless, any delay might jeopardize your claim. There's also a psychological statute of limitations. Arbitrators may hold it against you if you don't bring a claim immediately.

Many people are so nice that they don't want to offend their broker by complaining too much or closing their account. That's how an abusive broker gets to abuse you some more.

How to Get Action on Your Complaint

■ *Act immediately.* Call your broker the moment anything feels wrong. If you let a problem linger, your complaint may lose its credibility. This is especially important if a broker makes a transaction that you didn't authorize. If you don't object immediately, you may be deemed to have ratified the transaction.

■ *Don't yell.* Ask the broker for an explanation, and take notes. Ask for his or her explanation in writing, by either snail mail or e-mail. Tell the broker exactly how you want the problem corrected ("sell that stock and restore my money"). Send a letter or e-mail stating why the investment was unsuitable and reiterating your view of what should be done. If you don't get a written explanation from the broker, it's likely that his or her excuse won't wash. When a broker ducks you, it's always for a reason. *Keep a copy of all correspondence!*

- *Follow up.* If two weeks pass, nothing has changed, and the written explanation hasn't arrived, write or e-mail a short, polite note to the branch office manager (call the office and ask for the person's name). Include a copy of the note you sent to your broker and copies of records that prove your point. These might include monthly account statements, order confirmations, notes to your broker, and the written investment objectives that your broker started out with. State the rule that you think has been violated ("an unsuitable investment for someone in my position" . . . "misled me as to the risks in options" . . .). Ask for a specific remedy ("Restore my purchase price of $12,000 plus interest lost since 11/13/2008" . . . "Mark on the statement that this trade was solicited, not unsolicited" . . .). Make it clear that you are prepared to take this case further.

If another two weeks pass and still nothing happens, repeat the entire exercise with the president of the brokerage house.

The regrettable truth is that writing or e-mailing almost never works. I advise it only because sometimes the firm responds favorably, which would save you a lot of trouble. If it rejects your complaint, the written record might support a claim that the firm doesn't properly supervise its brokers. You might get a letter from the firm's lawyer falsely stating that if you go to arbitration and lose, you'll be liable for the broker's enormous legal fees. You won't, assuming that you aren't bringing a frivolous case. The firm is trying to scare you off and should be called on it. Proof of attempted intimidation might win you sympathy from an arbitration panel. Your broker might try to "guilt" you too. "What, you're complaining, when I'm knocking myself out to make money for you?" Or "How can you do this to me, we're such friends, you must have misunderstood me, this could damage my career." Those are standard ploys and a sign that your suspicions are right.

- *Call the cops.* If you get a letter from the firm's lawyer saying that you're wrong, the broker is right, and your claim is denied, don't fold your tent. Write a letter to the consumer protection office of your state's division of securities. You should also write if the broker simply fails to respond. Enclose copies of your letters to the broker and copies of the records that prove your claim. Sometimes your state's enforcers can solve your problem, usually within a few weeks. To find the office of your state securities commission, go to the North American Securities Administrators Association site at www.nasaa.org or call NASAA at 202-737-0900.

You can also contact the Office of Investor Education and Advocacy at the Securities and Exchange Commission. You'll find an investor complaint form at www.sec.gov/investor.shtml. You can fill it in online, mail it to the office at 100 F Street NE, Washington, DC 20549, or fax it to 202-772-9295. This is mostly a form-letter office. It will send inquiries to firms that investors complain about and forward your broker's response. Nevertheless, it's important to write. A large number of complaints about a particular broker or firm can trigger an investigation. For personal help, however, your best shot is your state securities office.

Bringing Up the Big Guns

When a broker does you wrong and the state securities office can't help, you have to go to arbitration (page 828). You can't sue in court. The brokerage agreement you signed requires you to arbitrate—and not just anywhere but through a specific industry process. Unfortunately, industry arbitration panels can be biased against individual investors. Even if your broker obviously screwed you, they may say it's your fault for not understanding what was going on.

Nevertheless, arbitration also produces judgments that are fair. Even if they are unfair, you may get at least some of your money back.

In theory, you don't need a lawyer to help you with your case. You can represent yourself. You'll have to tell what happened in a clear, orderly, and well-organized way, starting with the day you opened the account. If you appear in person, you should bring any relevant witnesses and documents to support your case. If you make your case by mail, you need copies of those documents and witness statements. You'll have to ask the brokerage firm for some of the documents you'll need, such as the detailed history of your account (getting this information is called the *discovery process*). You can't win just by saying that your broker did you wrong. The broker will say that the risks were fully explained and you understood them.

Unfortunately, investors without lawyers don't fare well. They win cases much less often than investors with lawyers do, and when they win, they get smaller amounts. There's also a Catch-22 at work: if you put on a good, solid legal case all by yourself, the arbitrators might decide that you're such a smart cookie, you should have known better than to make such a dumb investment, and rule against you. The process is, well, arbitrary.

So get a lawyer, if you can afford it. The other side will have lawyers who know exactly what they're doing. They can negotiate if they think you have a pretty good case. Or they can declare total war—dragging their feet to run up your expenses, papering you with motions, trying to hold the hearing far away from where you live, failing to produce documents that are crucial to your case, and twisting what you say when you testify. You need a lawyer, either to negotiate or to hammer them.

And I don't mean any old lawyer. You need someone experienced in securities arbitration, who knows the other side, what relevant documents it may be holding, and how to assess your shot at a settlement. Experienced lawyers can spot complaints that you didn't even know you had. For example, you might have charged that you were given an unsuitable investment without noticing that the broker was also churning your account. Or you might not think to ask for the brokerage firm's research reports on the stock you bought; maybe the broker went off on his or her own rather than following the firm's opinion. Good preparation—a lawyer's specialty—is critical. You need to get your "paper case" firmly in hand.

So how can you find a lawyer? No surprise here; it all depends on how much money is at stake.

▪ *For small claims:* If there's a law school in your city, call and ask if it runs a small-claims arbitration clinic. Your case will be handled by students but will be overseen by an experienced specialist. Fees are minimal. You'll also find clinics listed at the Web site of the Securities and Exchange Commission (www.sec .gov). Go to the site's search engine and enter "Arbitration/Mediation Clinics." If you aren't lucky enough to have a local clinic (there are only a handful of them around the country), call one of the free lawyer search services below, explain your situation, and ask for a lawyer who helps with cases in your price range. They might charge an hourly fee to refine your claims, help you get your documents together, and prepare your case. Still, it's sad but true that people who lose modest amounts of money usually cannot get help. If you think that the system is rigged against you, you're right.

▪ *For larger claims:* Three places maintain lists of arbitration lawyers. You can find names, free, at the Public Investors Arbitration Bar Association in Norman, Oklahoma (https://securelaba.org or 888-621-7484) or the National Association of Consumer Advocates in Washington, D.C. (www.naca.net or 202-452-1989). For a fee, the Securities Arbitration Commentator in Maplewood, New Jersey (http://sacarbitration.com or 973-761-5880), will send you a list of lawyers who've handled arbitration cases in the past year in the city nearest to you where arbitrations are heard. You can also get the sum they sought for clients and the actual award. At this writing, SAC charges a $75 fee plus $50 a name, although it's working on a free site. Call SAC and explain what you want, or query it at help@arbitrationrecords.com. SAC will respond with the number of names available, and you'll decide how much you want to spend.

With lawyers' names in hand, start with a phone call. Explain the circumstances, including your personal situation and the amount of money you lost. If the lawyer is interested, you'll arrange a meeting (or you'll mail the lawyer more information, if you live some distance away). He or she will explain the relevant legal issues and tell you whether your case appears strong or weak. If you become a client, you'll have to cover all expenses, win or lose. If you win, the lawyer typically takes one-third of the recovery. If you lose, you owe expenses only. Sometimes the arbitrators order the brokerage firm to pay your expenses, but that's rare.

Mediation—Try This First

Mediation can be a faster and simpler way of pursuing a settlement. It helps especially when your case is morally strong but legally flawed, the other side is liable but the damages are unclear, there's bad blood between the parties, or a pigheaded lawyer or client presses for more than the case is worth. As a neutral third party, the mediator can assess each side's strengths and weaknesses and serve as a reality check. Here's how the process works.

Both sides agree on a mediator, chosen from a list of experienced people whose professional backgrounds are disclosed.

The proceeding starts with a meeting where the adversaries and their lawyers present their evidence and their views. (You need evidence. It's not enough to say, "I told him to be conservative, so he shouldn't have bought those stocks.") Each side then retires to a separate room. The mediator speaks privately to each. He or she explains the relative merits of your case, probes for the kind of settlement you'd accept, and conveys (with permission) the irreducible needs of the other side.

Settlement offers and counteroffers are then carried back and forth. The mediator gradually moves the discussion forward and may lean on one side more than the other. But he or she can't dictate a deal. The parties reach a compromise themselves—typically during the mediation or just after. The process may take about a day.

There's no written award, only a voluntary settlement document that the mediator may or may not see. Unless you agree, mediation isn't binding. If you don't like the final offer, you're free to proceed with binding arbitration.

You'll find tons of information at FINRA's Web site, www.finra.org. Click on "Arbitration & Mediation" and then "Overview of Arbitration & Mediation." Filing for mediation costs $50 to $300 depending on the size of your claim (less if you've also filed for arbitration). The mediator's travel expenses and hourly fees will normally be split with the brokerage firm. For small cases, you might pay $50 an hour; for large ones, $500 an hour or more. You can request a mediator whose fees fall within a specified range.

You don't have to hire a lawyer but, again, will do much better if you have one. To win the maximum settlement, the case has to be prepared as well as a case that's going for arbitration—and, in fact, that's where failed mediations usually wind up. You can ask for mediation without filing an arbitration claim, but that makes it harder to gather the evidence you'll need (page 829). Many investors file for arbitration, wrestle documents from the other side, then go to mediation with evidence in hand. If mediation doesn't work, arbitration can proceed.

Arbitration: How to Take Your Best Shot

Arbitration is binding. You lay your case before a panel and abide by the result. About half of investors get an award of some sort, but often it's only a fraction of what they lost. It's rare to get all your money back, rarer to win attorney's fees, and even rarer to win punitive damages against a dirty-dealing broker. Although many arbitrators are fair minded, others are biased toward the industry; awards are inconsistent and sometimes capricious; and the arbitrators normally don't publish the reasoning behind their decisions. Nevertheless, when you signed the customer agreement with your broker, you agreed to settle disputes in an industry arbitration forum, which, for all its difficulties, is faster and cheaper than going to court. And you might even win! Here's how to give it your best shot:

- *Hire an experienced securities lawyer.* You'll be gravely disadvantaged without one. And don't choose a lawyer in general practice; choose one who is experienced in securities arbitrations (page 826).
- *Investigate the arbitrators.* If you're claiming a loss of more than $100,000, you'll have three arbitrators. At this writing, one of them has to belong to the securities industry, although that may change. Supposedly, industry arbitrators "understand" the issue better than anyone else and can "explain" it to the other arbitrators—in other words, help them see the dispute the broker's way. (That's like requiring a doctor to be on a medical malpractice jury so he can "explain" why a doctor might honestly cut off the wrong leg.) The other two are *public* arbitrators, meaning that they're supposed to have only a tangential relationship to the industry. But they can do substantial legal, accounting, and banking business with brokerage firms and still pass as "public" arbitrators. Another potential conflict of interest with public arbitrators: if they give an investor a big award, they'll be blacklisted by the lawyers for the brokerage firm. The firms

accept only arbitrators who, often enough, reject investors' claims or make only modest awards. Truly, these panels are stacked against you.

With losses of $25,000 or less, you get a single public arbitrator. With $25,001 to $100,000, you get a single arbitrator but can ask for three.

FINRA's computers generate random lists of industry and public arbitrators who have been through the industry's training program. Each side can strike off a certain number. That's where experience comes in. Your adversary's lawyers do this for a living. They'll know many of the arbitrators in the pool and will strike off those who appear to be too sympathetic to investors. Your own lawyer may know the pool too or can dig into the arbitrators' backgrounds to learn more about them. You too want to get rid of those whom you suspect of possible bias. If you're representing yourself, you can find out what those arbitrators have awarded in previous cases (or, more to the point, *not* awarded) by looking them up on the databank maintained by the Securities Arbitration Commentator. For each arbitrator, you pay $80 to learn what losses investors claimed in the cases they heard and what was actually awarded ($40 if you want only the award). But it's hard to draw conclusions without knowing what each case was about.

- *Gather the information needed to prove your case.* Arbitrators hear plenty of cases where it's the broker's evidence (even if flaky) against little more than the customer's word. Usually the broker is going to win such a contest by default. Even cases presented by a lawyer, unless it's an experienced arbitration lawyer, might not marshal enough facts.

For starters, you need the complete history of your account: the new-account agreement showing your objectives and financial situation, monthly and annual statements, and all the order confirmations. If you've misplaced any of these documents, the brokerage firm is supposed to supply them. You'll be in an especially good position if you kept a running record of your dealings with the broker, including contemporaneous notes of what the broker told you about each investment and copies of all your written instructions.

Ask for the firm's research on the securities in dispute. Did your broker misrepresent the investment? Ask for any information it distributed to brokers that described the investment and how to sell it. Brokers may rely on internal sales documents that don't explain the risks.

Ask for the broker's personnel file. Ask for copies of any other complaints against the broker. Get the broker's CRD file (page 817), which may disclose any prior disciplinary actions. Ask for any tapes—complete tapes—of telephone conversations between your broker and you.

Also ask for the parts of the firm's compliance and supervision manuals that relate to your situation. You need them to figure out whether your broker violated the firm's own rules. Do the rules say, "Don't concentrate a client's money in just two or three securities"? Do they say, "Recommend only the stocks that we do research reports on"? If your broker strayed off the reservation, this will help your case. The supervision manual will instruct the office manager on how brokers should be managed—instructions that, in your case, were probably not followed.

The brokerage firm is supposed to meet your reasonable requests for information. If it resists (and it almost always does), ask for help from your arbitrators. There may be a separate *discovery arbitrator* available to handle your requests. In theory, you're entitled to get the documents before the hearing so you can study them. In practice, documents may be produced, literally, at the hearing room door—by which time it's too late for you to analyze them. It's an extraordinary abuse of process. Without a lawyer, it may be hard to get anything useful out of the firm.

While the broker's lawyers are stonewalling, they will demand that you produce documents for them; for example, personal financial information and your investment history with any other brokerage firm. They'll be trying to prove that you're a sophisticated investor who knew exactly what you were doing.

If you think your case is complicated and may take more than one day in arbitration, write on your original claim form that you'd like the hearing to take place on consecutive days or within a short period of time. Otherwise the hearings might be scheduled weeks or months apart, giving the arbitrators time to forget the facts about your case. When you are contacted to schedule hearings, remind the caller that you asked for consecutive days.

■ *Line up witnesses.* Maybe you know other customers whom the broker similarly misled. Maybe you have another broker who can testify that you always asked only for conservative investments. Maybe someone at work overheard you discussing the investment with your broker and repeating the broker's claim that there was "no risk." Maybe you bragged to a friend that your broker got you a no-risk investment at a high interest rate. If this witness cannot be available in person, ask the arbitrators in advance for approval to put the person on a speakerphone during the hearing (and make sure there's a speakerphone available). An affidavit from the witness is less helpful and sometimes not permitted because he or she cannot be cross-examined.

If you want to call the firm's office manager or compliance officer as a witness and the firm refuses, ask your arbitrator to order it. A grandmother living on her income might want to ask those officers what they were doing while her broker sold her stock-index options. The firm's compliance manual doubtlessly says that they shouldn't have let such a sale stand.

■ *Try to settle the case.* FINRA reports that 44 percent of its arbitration cases were settled by the parties in 2006. The stronger your evidence and the more experienced your lawyer, the more likely the other side will make a deal. Ask for full damages. That includes your direct losses, compensation for the money you lost while your funds were tied up in this lousy investment (those are called *opportunity costs*), attorney's fees, the cost of filing the case, and interest from the day you filed the claim. But be prepared to compromise. Accepting a known sum usually beats the risk of going through arbitration and perhaps ending up with zero or only a slim award. Settlements commonly range from 20 to 80 cents on the dollar.

In your dealings with the brokerage house, don't shout, don't weep, don't accuse, don't tremble. Lay out your demands in a businesslike way and stick to them.

■ *Ask for a hearing in a convenient place.* Hearings should be held in a city near where you lived when you opened the account, since most of the evidence and witnesses will be there. If there are extenuating circumstances—for example, you're retired in Florida and cannot travel easily—ask to have the hearing near where you live now. To see what's possible, go to FINRA.org, click on "Arbitration & Mediation" and then on "Regional Offices and Hearing Locations."

Ordinary cases take a day, maybe two. But complicated cases may stretch over several months, making them almost as troublesome to pursue as a lawsuit.

If your damages come to $25,000 or less, you don't get a hearing unless you specifically ask for it. You can prosecute your case by sending a written claim plus statements from witnesses and supporting evidence. You'll get the decision in the mail. An "on-the-papers" case usually has better results if a lawyer helps you prepare it.

■ *Organize your narrative in advance and practice telling it.* Arbitrators are accustomed to hearing clients present their own cases and will generally do their best to help you along. Tell your story in an orderly way, starting with when you opened the account. Organize your presentation around the specific rules or laws you think the broker violated (page 820). Be as clear and forceful as you possibly can.

Typically, each side makes a brief opening statement. Then you present evidence and witnesses. The brokerage firm (which will always have a lawyer) will do the same. Each side will cross-examine the other. The arbitrators question both of you and listen to your closing arguments.

In general, investors complain that their broker soft-soaped them into thinking that a risky investment was safe or didn't act on their orders to sell an investment that subsequently declined. The broker replies that the customer knew exactly what he or she was doing and is sore only because the investment failed. The wealthier you are and the better established in your profession, the tougher it is to argue that you're a Wall Street innocent, even when you are. That's why notes of your conversations with your broker can be so important. They establish what you and the broker said to each other at the time.

In cases of flagrant abuse, you can ask for punitive damages. These are assessed when the broker's behavior is so outrageous that the conscience recoils from merely requiring that he or she give the money back. You don't stand much of a chance of winning punitives, however, especially when your claim is small. They were awarded in only 8 percent of the cases that requested them, according to a Securities Arbitration Commentator survey in 2007.

About 4 to 12 weeks after the hearing, you will receive a decision in the mail. Arbitrators go by what they think is fair, not by legal precedents. Normally, you get no explanation of the decision, which is incredibly frustrating. If you want an explanation, you and the brokerage firm, jointly, will have to request it at least 20 days before the first scheduled hearing date. The arbitrator who writes it will be paid an extra $400. If the brokerage firm won't agree to ask for the explanation, you're out of luck. Arbitration decisions usually cannot be appealed.

▪ Consider hiring a court reporter for your hearing. That gives you a record of what everyone said—a positive incentive to keep the arbitrators polite and restrict the number of whoppers your broker is prepared to tell. In the rare instance that there might be grounds for appeal, you can have a transcript made. Tapes are made of all arbitrations, but they're often inaudible, hence unusable to prove perjury or other misconduct.

▪ *When you win but lose.* If you win in arbitration but your brokerage firm goes out of business—as a small firm might—you're stuck. FINRA can't enforce payment of the award.

How Much Does Arbitration Cost?

At this writing, filing fees for FINRA arbitration range from $50 for claims of $1,000 or less to $1,800 for claims of more than $1 million. There's a partial refund if you settle more than 10 days before the hearing. That's just the door opener, of course. There are legal expenses, travel expenses for you and your witnesses, fees for a prehearing conference, fees for the arbitrators, and so on. The arbitrators can also order the loser to pay the winner's costs.

For More Information . . .

Everything you need is at FINRA's Web site, www.finra.org. Click on "Arbitration & Mediation" and then go to "Overview of Arbitration & Mediation."

For complaints against commodity brokers, the government-sponsored U.S. Commodity Futures Trading Commission (CFTC) runs a reparations program that is quick, cheap, and designed for investors to use without a lawyer (but get a lawyer if the loss is large). The CFTC employs administrative law judges for cases over $30,000 and judgment officers for smaller cases. It costs $125 to $250 to file, depending on the size of the case. The hearing may be conducted by telephone. Decisions can be appealed. There's also a "voluntary" procedure for $50 that's decided only on the paper record with no appeal. Common complaints concern unauthorized trading, churning, and failure to disclose risk. For more information and a complaint form, go to www.cftc.gov, click on "Customer Protection," and look for "Reparations Program."

The National Futures Association runs arbitration and mediation programs for complaints against commodity brokers (see www.nfa.futures.org for details and filing fees). But lawyers say that if the firm is a member of an exchange, you're better off using FINRA's forums. The NFA assigns arbitrators to your case and its panels are thought to be biased toward the industry.

Truth Breaks Out

A few years ago, I got a letter from a stockbroker that made a strong impression on me. I had written some newspaper columns that criticized certain shoddy sales practices, and mail from furious brokers was raining down on me. But this letter was different. Here's what it said:

> *I have been employed as a broker for the past 15 years. Most of those years have been with a major [brokerage] house. I must admit that at first your columns angered me as much as anyone who has ever had their lucrative employment threatened by an "outsider." But upon reflection, I am convinced you are right . . .*
>
> *The first thing a securities salesman learns is to gain the confidence of his customer. This enables the salesman to more easily sell the customer*

the products that pay the salesman the highest commission. All securities firms have different commission schedules for different investment products. Most firms will respond that their brokers are free to sell their customers any investment product they wish. But in practice, the broker-salesman is "encouraged" to sell the product most profitable to the firm and do it often. All securities firms also have formulas that indicate how often customers' money should turn over, and these are considered minimums. . . .

When I first entered the business, our firm had a broker who can truly be considered a "customer's man." He had the most clients, and the most money of his clients under his control, that I had ever heard of to that point. The firm's management took the view that he was not producing enough commissions. The broker said that we were in the middle of a bear market . . . and he was not going to squander his clients' money to produce commissions for the firm. The firm finally pressured the broker so much that he resigned.

We younger, hungrier brokers fell upon his book of clients like a pack of wolves, and tried everything to keep that book and generate commissions. But I don't think we kept a single one. . . .

I don't want you to conclude from what I have written that I am like that broker—far from it. I, too, have fallen prey to the siren's song of wealth and glamour that has been and is Wall Street. I have overtraded customer accounts, and bought for them "investments" that made more sense for me than them. I guess I wrote [to you] as a catharsis, and to clear my head and that of my colleagues of the siren's song.

The letter was signed "Anonymous Vice President, Investments, Major Investment Firm," with an invitation to write if I wanted the writer to disclose his name. How tragic to feel that your whole life has been built upon a fraud.

Buying Stocks Without Sales Commissions: The No-Load World

Many companies will sell you stocks directly without going through a stockbroker. There's no sales commission and sometimes no fees. At this writing, about 1,300 companies offer some version of this service, including some of the bluest of chips: Pfizer, Colgate-Palmolive, Home Depot, Wal-Mart Stores, Verizon. The plans are of three general types:

1. Dividend reinvestment plans (DRIPs). Your dividends will automatically be invested in additional shares. That's a good deal. If you get small dividend payments by check, you'll probably fritter them away. Reinvested, they'll eventually add up to real money. You might have to buy your first share through a broker.

2. Direct stock purchase plans (DSPs). Once invested in a DRIP, you can buy additional shares with cash, not just with your dividends. For a list of all these plans, the DRIPs, and the DSPs, see DirectInvesting.com (www.directinvesting .com). It also lists more than 480 companies that charge no investment fees.

3. No-load plans. More than 100 companies will sell you even the first share without going through a broker, although these plans generally charge fees. They're listed at NoLoad.info (www.noload.info), which describes many of the plans, indicates which have higher and lower fees, and links you with the place to buy.

Fee plans generally charge $5 to $15 on signing plus small service fees per share when you buy—a fraction of what the brokerage commission would be. Even so, fees at many companies have been creeping up. There may be charges each time you buy, charges for automatic purchases, and charges for reinvesting. A few companies charge $15 a year. For supersmall investors, including children's accounts, that's too much. Look for a company with a cheaper plan. You can invest as little as $10 and as much as $10,000 per month, depending on the company. Most let you buy a single share; a few require a minimum of 10, 25, or even 100 shares. You're usually charged the current market price, although some firms sell shares at a 3 to 5 percent discount when you reinvest your dividends.

DRIP, DSP, and no-load plans are strictly for investors who want to accumulate stock in a particular company and hold for the long term. You normally don't buy on the day that you place your order. Instead the company buys a block of shares weekly or monthly for all the investors who sent in their money during that time. Selling is slow too. A few companies let you put in a sell order by phone or online. Otherwise you have to write or fax written instructions. To get your money might take as long as 10 business days. There's usually a termination fee. If speed is an issue, check the company's redemption policy in the prospectus before you buy.

A few DRIPs and direct-purchase plans offer special services, such as Individual Retirement Accounts, automatic investment plans (they'll deduct as little as $25 a month from your bank account and use it to purchase shares), and loans against your shares.

If a company whose DRIP you want to join requires that you own at least one share, you can buy it from a stockbroker. Be sure to register it in your name through the Direct Registration System (page 802). Members of the National Association of Investors Corporation ($79 membership fee, www.betterinvesting.org) get one free stock purchase a month and pay $4.99 for each additional purchase.

Tax alert: If you buy shares at a discount, the discount is generally taxed as a dividend that year (although a 1994 private-letter ruling from the IRS has encouraged some companies to treat the discount as part of your capital gain when you sell). You're taxed on any commissions and fees that the company pays on your behalf (commissions are charged at institutional rates). Reinvested dividends are taxable, just as they are in mutual funds. You'll get a 1099 form at the end of each year. Check to see how any discounts you got were handled.

If you sell just part of your DRIP account, it can be the very devil to figure out your income taxes. Every dividend you received was used to buy shares, or fractions of shares, at a different price, and you'll have to work out the gains you made on all of them. Fortunately, there are three ways around this: (1) Die and leave the shares to your heirs. (2) Donate the shares to a charity and take a tax deduction. (3) Sell your entire account at once. In that case, you can figure your cost by adding up the amount of your initial purchase, all the dividends that were reinvested, and any additional investments that you made in cash. Those data are easy to find on the year-end statements the company sent. You saved every single statement, of course. Mmmmm, you didn't? Call the company to see if it can pull your chestnuts out of the fire.

Striking Gold in Old Stocks and Bonds

Maybe you own some mystery securities—stocks or bonds you inherited or bought years ago whose prices aren't listed anywhere online. Some of the companies have expired, others may be too small for the listing services to notice, yet others may have been purchased by larger companies. Here's how to find out if your securities have any value:

• *Call the information operator in the city where you last knew the corporation to be.* It may still be operating at the same old stand. If you get the telephone number, call the company and ask for its share price.

• *Write to the company at its last known address or hunt for it online.*

• *Search for its address in your public library.* Your library may subscribe to the Dun & Bradstreet Million Dollar Database, which lists 1,600,000 U.S. and Canadian corporations. If you find the address, call the company's treasurer, who will know what your securities are worth.

- *Ask your stockbroker, if you have one.* He or she might find the company in one of his or her databases, including the "pink sheets," which list thousands of small public companies.
- *Use a stock research service.* You can request help online or mail photocopies of the stock or bond certificates. Two companies to try: Spink Smythe & Co., www.spinksmythe.com, 800-622-1880, 145 West 57th Street, New York, NY 10019; $100 for each certificate. Or Old Company Stock and Bond Research Service, www.scripophily.net, 888-786-2576, PO Box 223795, Chantilly, VA 20153; at this writing $39.95. They'll tell you whether the security has value.
- *Don't throw out old stock or bond certificates until you've learned that the company formally went out of business.* Even moribund firms are sometimes brought to life again. Also find out if the certificates have any collector's value.

Investment Newsletters

To add to your knowledge of investing, you might subscribe to a range of print or online newsletters. You can buy almost any view of the market that appeals to you. There are market-timing letters. Growth stock letters. Psychic advisory letters. Mutual fund letters. Bond letters. Insider buying letters. Asset allocation letters. Technical analysis letters. Precious-metal letters. College professor letters. End-of-the-world letters. Letters that channel the spirit of Bernard Baruch. To publish a newsletter, you don't even have to register as an investment adviser.

Legitimate letter writers genuinely work at being good stock pickers for their customers. Others don't. The baddies may buy small-company stocks, then try to run up the price. They may have "consulting" relationships with the companies they tout (in other words, they're paid to promote). Newsletter editors aren't required to disclose these conflicts of interest explicitly, so you'll probably never know about them.

Because of their quirky unevenness, newsletters aren't for stock market innocents. You have to be able to tell the sound from the wacky, the honest from the spurious, the smart from the ordinary. Some letters are promoted with bogus claims. You might laugh off a writer who trumpets "874 percent on your money in eight months!" But what about one who claims 25 percent? Is that true or false?

A 1995 study of 237 investment letters done for the National Bureau of Economic Research found that less than a quarter of them beat the appropriate market index. What's more, they were lousy at market timing (yes, you've heard me say this before). Other studies have found only 20 percent or 12 percent beating the market over a decade.

Some letters with big reputations trade stocks furiously or make big-money bets on stock-index options. If you don't do the same, you won't match their investment returns. In general, letters that do well at all tend to succeed in only one kind of market environment and you have to know which.

But if you're savvy about securities and want fresh sources of ideas, letters can make interesting reading. To find some, subscribe to Hulbert Interactive at the Web site of Subscription-Offers.com (www.subscription_offers.com/invest ment/hulbert-interactive; $149 a year). It researches and rates the performance of investment newsletters and advisers; $99 a year. Or choose the monthly *Hulbert Financial Digest* newsletter, $59 by e-mail, $69 by snail mail. What's especially good about Mark Hulbert's data is that they're compiled in a uniform way. The publicity that the newsletters put out themselves covers various time periods (carefully chosen) and is generally unaudited, so investors can't compare their performance by themselves. Hulbert compares them over identical periods of time. Hulbert also deducts brokerage commissions, which gives a more realistic picture of what a market letter might do for you.

You want a letter with a good seven-year performance, Hulbert says. And you probably don't want to have to call a daily hotline for advice. When reading a new newsletter, think about whether you're willing to take the kinds of risks it recommends. If you plan to follow its model portfolio, test to see whether you can afford it. Some require multimillion-dollar investments. Most require at least $100,000. If you have less than that, Hulbert thinks you should look for a mutual fund letter instead. (Mutual funds are smart buys for bigger portfolios too.)

One drawback to letters: to hold their subscribers' interest, they have to keep finding new things to buy and sell. That's not the approach that long-term investors should take.

Another drawback: the editors can't time the market or pick stocks reliably. You're dreaming if you think that a good newsletter will make you rich.

A Final Word

Who really needs a stockbroker? The conventional answer is: you need one if you're a new investor or an inexperienced investor and don't know much about stocks.

To me, that answer is dead wrong. Stockbrokers are for active, savvy investors who want investment ideas and know how to evaluate what they hear.

Inexperienced investors are the very people who are least able to tell a good broker from a bad one and the most susceptible to bad advice.

I'd say: if you're a new or inexperienced investor, don't look for a stockbroker at all! You can't afford the learning experience. Start with a couple of no-load mutual funds and relax. Only a knowledgable investor can pick what's choice from a broker's patter and blow off the rest.

Like the SAT for college admissions, there ought to be an admissions test for opening a brokerage account. If you don't score above "innocent" on the verbal and math, a kindly investor protection angel would tell you that a stockbroker isn't for you.

Stocking Up

Still Your Ticket to the Future

Over the long term, crash or no crash, stocks beat the tar out of other investments. If you haven't yet noticed my preference for stock-owning mutual funds, you've been using this book as a doorstop.

After a massive market collapse, like the one in 2008–2009, you might want to swear off stocks. I understand completely. I was as rattled by the dreadful daily declines as everyone else. But you have to step back and take a look at history. There were stock market rallies even during the Great Depression. Over the long term, which can be 15 years or more, stocks are still the best investment for people saving for retirement or saving for college for young children.

There are extended periods when bonds do better than stocks, which is why you should own bonds too. Since 1926, however, U.S. stocks have exceeded the inflation rate by an average of 6.46 percent a year, with dividends reinvested. Intermediate-term government bonds have run only 2.23 percent over inflation, so, after taxes, bonds just barely keep up.

To protect yourself when stocks decline, you need to follow the age-appropriate diversification rules in chapter 21. Older people need a larger safety cushion than younger people do, but even in your 60s and 70s, you need some growth investments to pay for your older age. Stocks do grow over 10 or 15 years and more (and, in good times, over shorter terms). When you buy, you're investing in America's long-term future, and your own.

What Makes Stock Prices Rise and Fall?

Plain old supply and demand. Prices rise when more people want to buy a stock than want to sell it.

Stocks represent a claim on a particular company's future dividends and earnings. Over the short term, investors want to buy because:

1. They believe that the company's earnings will improve—because of a strong economy, a new product, new management, a new business strategy, and so on.

2. The market in general is moving up, creating enthusiasm for all kinds of shares. Investors become willing to pay more for every dollar of future expected earnings.

3. Interest rates drop, which makes stocks more attractive relative to bonds. (However, if it's early in what turns out to be a recession, stock prices and interest rates drop in tandem—for a while, at least. In the investing game, there are no guarantees.)

4. There's some special event, such as a takeover offer for the company or the hope of one.

A reversal of these conditions leads more people to sell the stock than buy it, which makes the price fall.

Over the long term, a different and more mysterious dynamic appears to be at work. Long periods of rising prices have been followed by long periods of flat or falling prices. At their peaks, markets overreach and self-destruct. Here's the postwar history:

- Stocks generally rose from 1946 to 1966 (21 fat years).
- From 1966 to 1982, stocks zigzagged up and down, with no net gain (17 lean years).
- From 1983 to 2000, stocks rose again (18 superfat years).
- Since 2000, they've dropped, climbed back to their 2000 peak, and at this writing dropped again (10 lean years so far).

In each cycle, prices at the bottom are higher than they were the last time around, and prices are higher at the peak. That reflects general economic growth, with some periods much more robust than others.

Panics aren't unusual, a perspective that's especially helpful for stock investors to remember. You've probably forgotten, but the 1980s and 1990s—two decades praised for their strong economic growth—were riddled with financial troubles. In the early eighties, interest rates reached 20 percent, the economy tanked, and the Federal Deposit Insurance Corporation had to rescue Continental Illinois National Bank and Trust Company, then the nation's seventh largest bank. In the late 1980s, the savings and loan industry collapsed as a result of irresponsible, unregulated lending. Housing starts plunged to their lowest levels since World War II. In 1990 the scandal-ridden junk bond industry fell apart, taking a major brokerage firm with it. In 1998 Russia defaulted on its debt, emerging Asia collapsed, and the government rescued a hedge fund judged to be too big to fail. Each time, stocks came back.

The 2007–2009 emergency is further-reaching than its predecessors and will probably take longer to cure. If history is any guide, we might face several more years of zigzagging stock market returns. That means periodic ups and downs in prices, with the market never rising much above its previous peak.

At some point, stocks will break loose and soar again, but you don't know when. Maybe soon, maybe not. There's nothing guaranteed about these cycles—or *apparent* cycles. Over the long run, however, holding diversified stock investments has always worked.

How do you invest in a zigzag market?

Here's what worked in the zigzag 1966–1982 period and might work now: (1) Dollar-cost averaging. You make regular investments in stocks; for example, through your 401(k). That way, you buy them cheaply as well as when they're expensive. Over the entire cycle, you improve your average return. (2) Reinvesting dividends, another form of dollar-cost averaging. (3) Diversifying. A mix of stocks and bonds performs better than stocks alone. (4) Going to cash—assuming that you presciently went to cash at the start of the cycle and not partway down. If you cashed out partway down, you lost.

Here's what didn't work in the 1966–1982 period: market timing. Investors tried to develop systems for knowing when to buy into the market and when to get out. None of them worked consistently.

In the 2000–?? zigzag market, investors have been looking for alternatives to traditional stocks and bonds. The alternatives haven't worked consistently either. The investments that generally ended in tears included hedge funds, buying and operating rental properties, and new types of debt securities with higher than average interest rates. Commodities had a good run and might come again. Gold worked if you bought it in 2000, but fell back after the buying panic during the price spike in 2008. For individuals, it's a high-risk play.

When we look back on this period, however, the best strategies will probably have been the usual ones: a diversified portfolio of stocks and high-quality bonds, rebalanced regularly. Investors who held to this approach through past bear markets, including deep ones, have enjoyed long-term success.

Some Definitions

When you buy the *common stock* of a corporation, you are buying an ownership share. A tiny slice of the company belongs to you, and you are owed a tiny slice of its dividends and earnings. Your interest in the company is known as *equity.* Stockholders are also referred to as *equity investors.*

The company's executives (who run the show) take one of two attitudes toward your profits: They might pay them out to you in quarterly dividends. Or they might keep the profits and reinvest them in the business. Many companies do some of both.

A *security* is a general word for a "paper" investment, such as stocks, bonds, or mutual funds. It doesn't include "hard" investments such as gold coins or real estate. In the old days, a security was a real piece of paper, showing that you owned a particular stock or bond. Nowadays, it's generally a computer blip with your name attached. Your proof of ownership is a mailed or e-mailed acknowledgment, after you buy. If you deal with a stockbroker, you will get a *confirmation* when you make a purchase or sale.

You buy a stock at the *asked*, or *offered*, price (the price the broker asks). You sell it at the *bid* price (the price the broker bids for it). The difference between the bid and the asked is the *spread,* and it's a cost, eroding the profits of investors who trade a lot.

A *trade* is an order to buy or sell. The buyer thinks the price of the stock is going up, the seller thinks it isn't. The function of a market is to bring buyers and sellers together at a price they both consider fair.

When you buy a *growth stock,* you aren't expecting dividends. You're expecting rapidly rising earnings. When you buy a *blue chip,* you expect more modest growth in earnings, sweetened by dividend increases. *Value stocks* are low-priced relative to their earnings, because the company or its industry is in trouble. When you buy value, you're betting on a turnaround.

An *income stock* focuses on delivering high and rising dividends. In general, the higher the dividend, the less the share price tends to fall in bear markets and the more slowly it tends to rise when markets go up. You usually have to trade income for growth.

Your bottom line is *total return*—your dividends plus your gain or loss on the price of the stock. Say, for example, that you bought a stock for $50 and saw it rise by $5 over the next 12 months, to $55. You also earned $2 in dividends. Your total return was $7, or 14 percent on your original $50 investment. On a total-return basis, an income investor with high enough dividend earnings might do better than someone who gambled solely on growth.

When economic growth slows down, you hear a lot about *defensive* or *non-cyclical* stocks. They're supposed to fall less in bear markets than other stocks do. Food stocks, traditional utilities, and pharmaceuticals are good examples. But they still go down. When growth turns up, you hear a lot about *cyclical* stocks, whose earnings tend to rise (and fall) when the economy does. Steel, housing, automobiles, and airlines are cyclical industries.

Small-company stocks are more *volatile* than big-company stocks. That means they rise and fall more rapidly in price and take wider swings. Shares trading at around $3 or less are called *penny stocks.* They'll reduce your $3 to pennies—count on it (page 956).

Among mutual funds, *active managers* pick and choose stocks that they think will beat the market average. *Passively managed* funds invest in stocks that mimic the average, believing, as do I, that the market average usually outperforms active managers, over time.

Your total investment pot—all your securities together—is your *portfolio.* Each general type of investment is called an *asset class.* Stocks, bonds, and commodities are asset classes.

You *diversify* by buying more than one type of investment. Asset classes that behave differently from one another—rising and falling at different rates and different times in the investment cycle—are called *noncorrelated investments.* That's what you need for true diversification.

Diversification doesn't necessarily win you higher investment returns. It does something more important: it reduces your risk. Your investment pot won't fall as far in bad markets as other people's will, which leaves you in a safer place. You'll feel better psychologically—less apt to panic and sell. Even better, you'll have more money on tap to catch the wave when the market goes up again.

Have I missed anything? Oh, yes . . . for those who forget: *Bull markets* rise. *Bear markets* fall. It's easy to keep them straight. In bear markets, you say, "Grrrrr."

How to Own Stocks

There are two ways of holding stocks. You can pick individual companies or you can buy mutual funds.

You should not—repeat, *not*—mess around with individual shares. What looks like a top company can wipe out almost overnight. Think AIG, Lehman

Brothers, Enron, Fannie Mae—the list goes on and on. By the time you read this, there will be dozens more. I make the case against owning individual shares on page 863.

Individuals should buy stocks through mutual funds, and not just any mutual funds. You should focus on either *no-load funds,* meaning funds sold directly by the fund company, with no sales commission, or *exchange-traded funds.* In chapter 22, I discuss funds in general and how to judge them. Here I'll run through the different types of stock funds that you might want to buy.

Buying Traditional Stock-Owning Mutual Funds

Classic, diversified, no-load mutual funds are dull, dull, dull. That's why I like them. You can make lots of money by buying and forgetting them and getting on with the rest of your life. Rightly used, mutual funds have almost no entertainment value. For thrills, I go to the racetrack. For my retirement, I buy boring mutual funds.

Even if you love the blood sport of buying individual stocks, use diversified mutual funds for your core holdings.

Regrettably, many investors treat their funds as if they were individual stocks. You might watch the market daily, follow quarterly performance reports, zap into funds on this year's "Top 10" lists, and zap out again if the fund declines. This traduces mutual funds' very reason for being. Only the money manager is supposed to trade. You're supposed to buy and hold. Jumping into and out of funds raises your cost of investing, increases your risk of buying and selling at the wrong time, and makes it almost impossible to keep up with the general stock market over time. It also drives you into the arms of investment advisers who help you trade, which is another expense.

Do yourself a favor and simplify your life. Go with the target date funds I recommend below. They're easy and low cost. You can buy them and never think about them again until you retire. The managers do all the diversification and rebalancing for you.

If you prefer to assemble your own diversified portfolio, accumulate no more than six or seven index funds, focused on different types of stocks. Your core stock fund should follow Standard & Poor's 500-stock index of leading U.S. companies. It's a growth-and-income fund. Most active fund managers who buy blue chips usually find that their performance can't keep up with the S&P, over time (for a discussion of active management versus indexing, see page 740).

Next add index funds that buy smaller stocks, especially small value stocks which have a history of yielding higher returns; real estate stocks, international stocks (they focus on developed countries), and emerging market stocks. The latest interesting addition: a commodities fund. For a full discussion of mutual funds in general, see chapter 22.

To simplify, you could buy a U.S. "total market" fund, which covers all types of large and small U.S stocks, and a "total international" fund, which buys the stocks of developed and developing countries.

Invest in them regularly, rebalance as markets change (page 710), then sit back and wait. That's how to become a mutual fund millionaire.

I'll discuss index-fund portfolios later. First, take a look at the simple and highly-effective all-in-one funds.

Target-Date Funds: Choose Once and Forget It

These are my favorites, the easiest investments in the universe. They're hugely popular among holders of 401(k)s and Individual Retirement Accounts. People who hear about them feel that little click in the mind that says, "Yes, this is going to work."

With a target-date retirement fund, you have to decide only one thing: when do you think you might retire? Pick a fund designed for approximately that retirement date (65 is a good age to settle on), put your money there, and forget about it. There are funds for retirement in 2010, 2015, 2020, 2025, 2030, 2035, 2040, 2045, 2050, and 2055, depending on the fund company you choose—and more years will be added as time goes on. Each fund owns a mix of stocks and bonds that is suitable for a person retiring roughly in that year. For example:

- *If you're in your 20s, 30s, or 40s*—retirement is far away. You'd pick a fund aimed at a year between 2030 and 2045. Funds invested for that many years own mostly stocks for long-term growth. They also own a small percentage of bonds, to limit your risk. If you were picking your own, separate investments, this is just what you'd want.

- *If you're in your 50s and 60s*—retirement is in view. You'd pick a fund aimed at the years between 2015 and 2025. They're still invested in stocks but keep a higher percentage of their money in bonds. The closer you get to your probable retirement date, the more conservative your fund becomes.

Target-date retirement funds run on automatic pilot. They gradually change their mix of investments as the years go by. Today a 2030 fund is heavily into stocks, including international and emerging-market stocks. Some funds include commodities. Ten years from now—when you're that much closer to retirement— your fund will own a somewhat smaller percentage of stocks and a slightly higher percentage of short- and intermediate-term bonds. You never have to rejigger your own investments as you age. The fund does that for you, all the time.

Your fund doesn't come to an end when the target date is reached. You can keep it for as many more years as you like. It's usually an appropriate mix of stocks and bonds, even for people who work past their expected retirement age.

As you grow even older—say, 80-plus—many target-date retirement funds become straight income funds, invested to yield dividends and interest while protecting your principal from risk. So they're still sleep-tight funds, with money managed in a suitable way.

More than half of large-company 401(k) plans offer target-date retirement funds, with more on the way. For investments outside a 401(k), including an Individual Retirement Account (IRA), you can find target-date funds at all the major mutual fund companies. Below are the three that invest at the lowest cost. Any of them is an excellent choice compared with the (probably) unplanned mix of stocks and bonds you might own now:

1. The Vanguard Group. 10 funds called Target Retirement funds. These are the lowest-cost funds by far. At this writing, they charge around 0.2 percent a year. They hold down expenses by investing through index funds (page 850). Low-cost funds give you better returns than similar high-cost funds because they leave more of your money in your account to grow (www.vanguard.com, 877-662-7447; there's a $10 annual fee on small accounts).

2. Fidelity Investments. 12 Freedom Funds, costing 0.5 percent to 0.8 percent, depending on the target year. You might think that it's no big deal to pay Fidelity an extra 0.5 percent a year, but the dollars mount up. If you invested $400 a month for 30 years in both Vanguard and Fidelity and the funds grew 8 percent a year, the Fidelity fund would cost you $52,748 more than Vanguard did (www.fidelity.com, 800-343-3548).

3. T. Rowe Price. 12 Retirement Funds, costing from 0.58 percent to 0.73 percent (www.troweprice.com, 800-638-5660).

Here is the most important thing to know about choosing a target-date fund: to achieve its purpose, it should be the only fund you own. At the very least, you should keep most of your money there. A target-date fund plots your investments carefully. For any age, the manager keeps an appropriate balance between the percentage of money you hold in stocks and the percentage you keep in bonds. If you own many other mutual funds, that careful plan goes down the drain. You'll wind up with too much or too little in stocks, depending on the market and on the funds you've picked. By concentrating your investments in a one-stop fund, your retirement money will always be arranged in an intelligent way.

"But wait a minute," you say, "I thought I was supposed to diversify. With just one fund, don't I have all my eggs in one basket?" Yes and no. It's one basket because you own a single fund. But your fund contains all the different kinds of assets that you ought to own: large and small U.S. stocks, real estate stocks, international stocks, U.S. government and corporate bonds, and, in some funds, commodities. With just one simple investment choice, you get it all.

One warning about target-date funds: some of them overload you with stocks and other risky securities when you're 65. On paper, a higher stock allocation provides more long-term growth during your retirement years and can lead to a larger inheritance for your kids. But such a fund will fall more in price when the stock market drops. That's dangerous if you'll depend on those savings for a regular retirement check. The withdrawals you make when the market is down may cause you to run out of money in your older age.

So check the percentage of stock that the fund plans to hold in the year you'll be 65 (it will be in the prospectus). A prudent allocation would be 45 percent stock or less, with the rest of the money in quality bonds. If the fund you're considering will be 50 or 60 percent in stocks when you're 65, skip it; it's too aggressive. You do need to own some stocks in retirement but not such a large percentage amount. Choose a fund that restricts its stockholdings to a more appropriate range regardless of its target year.

Target-date funds came in for a lot of criticism after the stock market crash of 2008. For some reason, people approaching retirement age expected them to be safe. But any investment portfolio that's 40 percent in stocks will fall 20 percent when the market loses half of its value—that shouldn't come as a surprise. Fortunately, there's a high percentage of bonds in target-date funds for older workers and retirees. That gives you something to live on while waiting for stocks to come back up.

Besides, what would you own if you weren't in a target-date fund? You'd have other stock-owning funds in your portfolio and they'd have behaved the same way.

When people lose money in midlife or later, they wish they had put all their investments in bonds. But switching entirely to bonds would greatly diminish the odds that your savings would last for life. Target-date funds recognize that fact, by keeping stocks in your investment mix.

I love target-date funds, as long as you choose your retirement year carefully. They do everything you need. They diversify your money. Choose appropriate assets for your age and situation. Hold down your costs. Save you from irretrievable mistakes. Limit your risk by keeping the proper balance between stocks and bonds, even when the market changes. If you hired an investment adviser to do these things for you, you'd pay 1 to 2 percent a year, plus the cost of the investments that the manager chose. A target retirement fund comes with built-in investment advice, and at a fraction of the price.

Life-Cycle Mutual Funds: Simple, with More Choice

Like a target-date fund, a life-cycle fund is fully diversified. This single investment gives you all the types of stocks and bonds you ought to own in a single package.

But life-cycle funds differ from target-date funds in one big way: you choose the specific mix of stocks and bonds that you want. A *growth* fund will hold around 75 percent of its money in stocks and 25 percent in bonds. A *moderate* fund usually puts 60 percent of its money in stocks and 40 percent in bonds. A *conservative* fund might drop to 25 percent stocks and 75 percent bonds and cash. There are other flavors too.

Life-cycle funds don't change their investments over time. A growth portfolio that's 75 percent in stocks will stay that way, give or take a few percentage points. When you're young, a growth portfolio is exactly the right choice. But when you hit 50, you might want to switch to a moderate mix. *Switching* means that you sell your first fund and buy a different one. You can do that tax free in a retirement account, such as a 401(k) or Individual Retirement Account. But if you're investing outside a retirement account, selling your first fund will trigger a tax on the profit you made. That's something to think about in advance. You should choose a portfolio that you're pretty sure you can live with for a very long time.

As you can see, a life-cycle fund requires more decisions than a target-date fund does: what type of investment mix to start with and when to switch to a more conservative mix. In general, you should choose your mix by age. Be aggressive in your 20s, 30s, and 40s, moderate in your 50s and 60s, conservative in your 70s and up. Don't bother "diversifying" by buying both an aggressive fund and a conservative one. Taken together, that gives you a moderate mix, so you might as well put all your money into the moderate fund right from the start.

The three mutual fund companies I've mentioned that offer low-cost target-date funds also sell life-cycle funds. As usual, costs matter. You pay the least for Vanguard's four life-cycle funds, called LifeStrategy Funds. (They're also based on indexed investing—see page 850.) Ascending the cost ladder, look at Fidelity's seven Asset Manager Funds, then T. Rowe Price's three Personal Strategy Funds.

For ease of use, life-cycle funds are my second choice. They require you to decide how much stock market risk you want to take (you may not necessarily know). Also, you have to pick the right time to switch from one fund to another. But they're simpler by far than trying to pick from the thousands of funds available. They're professionally diversified, and you can hold them a long time. They're also regularly rebalanced to keep your mix of stocks and bonds at the level you originally chose. Life-cycle funds will give you better returns, and at less risk, than you'd probably earn from the random mix of stocks and funds that you might otherwise buy yourself.

Index Funds: A Menu of Good Ingredients for a Diversified Portfolio

My personal investing choice is to keep things simple, which is a synonym for boring. Boring investing has had a remarkable record of success. Target-date mutual funds and life-cycle funds are boring. So is a portfolio of index funds. Index funds take more managing than the all-in-one funds. You have to choose your own mix of stocks and bonds and rebalance faithfully. But you don't have to worry about whether your manager will lose his or her touch or which stocks or industries to buy and sell. Your funds follow the markets as a whole.

For a full discussion of index funds, see page 745. When deciding which ones to buy, nothing is more important than cost.

When two different funds are following the same index, the one with the lower costs will always perform the best. Vanguard, which invented the index fund for individuals, used to hold the low-cost crown and still does for smaller investments. At this writing, it's charging 0.15 percent a year for its most popular funds, on a minimum investment of $3,000 ($1,000 for an IRA). In 2004, however, Fidelity elbowed into Vanguard's business. It's charging 0.1 percent a year for similar funds, on a $10,000 minimum.*

If you're working with a fee-only financial planner or investment adviser, he or she might use the passively managed index-y funds from Dimensional Fund Advisors in Santa Monica, California. They're an excellent suite of funds, available through advisers only.

Several other mutual fund families offer index funds. But beware the costs! I've seen index funds charging 1 percent and more, which is a total rip-off. Index funds don't need high "management" fees because they're not managed. *Never* buy an index fund with a sales charge; it's a waste of money.

For index investing, the following are the only funds you should be looking at. For most categories, I'm recommending just three fund families: Vanguard, Fidelity, and T. Rowe Price. T. Rowe Price is the most expensive of the three, but

---

*You'll still look to Vanguard if you have $100,000 or more. On accounts that size, it charges just 0.07 percent. You also get that low fee if you have at least $50,000 in a fund, have held it for at least 10 years, and are registered for online access to your accounts.

its fees are still low compared with the rest of the mutual fund world. All three companies publish excellent consumer education material, in print newsletters and online. Fidelity and T. Rowe Price offer just a few index funds. Vanguard, the inventor of the retail index fund, has a cornucopia of choices.

1. For funds that track the entire American stock market—big stocks and small stocks together. Fidelity's Spartan Total Market Index, Vanguard's Total Stock Market Index, or T. Rowe Price's Total Equity Index. These are the most widely diversified U.S. stock funds you can buy and my personal favorites. You are investing in the American economy as a whole.

2. For funds that track smaller stocks. Vanguard's Small-Cap Index Fund. If you want to specialize, you can choose a Small-Cap Value Index Fund or a Small-Cap Growth Index Fund.

3. Funds for international stocks. Every well-diversified investment plan should include some international stocks. You may think they're risky. But academic studies have proven that combining an international fund with a U.S. fund reduces your long-term risk with a good chance of raising your returns. That may not happen in any particular year, but it's true over many years. Your choices: Fidelity Spartan International Fund, which invests in the leading companies in the industrialized world (Europe, Australia, and the Far East, principally Japan); Vanguard Total International Stock Index Fund, which is even more diversified—investing in both the developed world and in the emerging markets of Eastern Europe, Southeast Asia, and Latin America. Or T. Rowe Price's International Equity Index, including some emerging-markets.

Vanguard recently introduced a Total World Stock Index Fund, which covers everything: U.S., international, and emerging-market. This might become the top one-stop index investment. Cost: 0.45 percent.

4. Funds for emerging markets. Vanguard's Emerging Markets Stock Index. Every diversified portfolio should own some emerging markets (page 978). Looking to the future, these are the countries that will grow the most.

5. An index fund for real estate diversification. There's only one: Vanguard's REIT Index Fund (*REIT* means real estate investment trust). REITs buy commercial real estate, such as shopping centers, apartment buildings, and hotels. They often do well when other stocks are doing poorly, so owning them reduces your total investment risk.

6. For bond index funds. Diversified bond funds invest in both government and corporate bonds. Vanguard's Total Bond Market Index Fund costs 0.2 percent a year. T. Rowe Price's U.S. Bond Index Fund charges 0.3 percent. Fidelity's U.S. Bond Index Fund charges 0.32 percent. Investors own bonds to provide liquidity and income and to limit their risk. The younger you are, the less you need bonds (although, for diversification, you need a few). Vanguard offers shorter-term bond index funds too, as well as indexed tax-exempt municipal bond funds.

7. A commodities index fund. *Commodities* covers agricultural and natural resources, such as oil, metals, timber, livestock, and grain. The best way to invest is through exchange-traded funds (page 785), which are cheaper and much more efficient than traditional mutual funds. Buy only the ETFs linked to the broadest commodity indexes, not the subindexes that specialize in just one type of good. Examples would be the PowerShares DB Commodity Index Tracking Fund, which contains six commodities (crude oil, heating oil, gold, aluminum, corn, and wheat); or iPath Dow Jones–UBS Commodity Index Total Return ETN, diversified over 23 commodities. For both, the management expense is 0.75 percent. Other commodity index ETFs that look diversified might actually be 70 percent or more in oils, with less emphasis on metals and agricultural products. Use a search engine to check on this before you buy. (Note that the iPath ETN—exchange traded note—is a debt security backed by the UBS bank. You have no claim on the underlying commodities. By contrast, with an ETF you have a claim on the commodities too. For more on ETNs and their risks, see page 962.)

In the world of traditional mutual funds, I'd suggest only Pimco's Commodity-RealReturn Strategy Fund. It's linked to a popular commodities price index and also invests in government bonds whose returns are adjusted for inflation. Its price is out of my usual range; broker-sold shares cost as much as 1.99 percent a year in fees. Alternatively, you could open an account at a mutual-fund "supermarket," such as those offered by Charles Schwab & Co. or Fidelity Investments. They let you buy funds from many different companies through a single source. At a supermarket, CommodityRealReturn costs 1.24 percent a year.

These seven types of funds—U.S. large-stock, U.S. small-stock, international stock, emerging-market, real estate, bond, and commodity—are all you need for a well-diversified investment plan. Vanguard has other index funds tracking all kinds of markets, but you could drive yourself crazy trying to choose among them. There's simply no point. The widely diversified funds that I've been talking about will give you everything you need.

That said, I'll mention two more types of index funds because they might interest you, or your company might offer them in your retirement plan:

1. Funds that track Standard & Poor's 500-stock index. They cover America's 500 leading companies, which represent more than 70 percent of the U.S. stock market. Personally, I prefer a total market fund, which includes these companies and adds smaller ones too. In many 401(k)s, however, the 500 fund may be the only stock index fund you can get—in which case, go for it. There's Fidelity Spartan 500 Index Fund, at 0.1 percent a year, and Vanguard's 500 Index Fund, at 0.15 percent.

2. An index fund for socially conscious investors. Look at Vanguard's FTSE Social Index Fund. It tracks the performance of 382 large and midsize U.S. companies whose policies are considered favorable to workers, consumers, and the environment. Expenses: 0.24 percent a year (for more on social funds, see page 858).

You can get two winning strategies for the price of one by using Vanguard's target-date funds or life-cycle funds. Both use low-cost indexing strategies to invest. The competing target and life-cycle funds, from Fidelity, T. Rowe Price, and other fund companies, rely on money managers to pick the stocks and bonds. Given the record, they'll have a tough time beating Vanguard's indexed approach, but you never know.

If you want to try actively managed funds, use broad index funds as your core. Then look for managers in more specialized areas. For example, you might own a total market fund, with a managed small-stock or emerging-markets fund on the side. If you go this route, compare the managed fund's performance with the matching index fund every year. After five years, go with the one that performed the best.

Avoid *enhanced* index funds. They try to tart up their performance by writing options or playing other nonindex games. Naturally, they charge more for this "service," which may or may not make you any money. Give enhanced and *index-plus* funds a pass. They contravene the very concept of indexing by adding the fallible judgment of a manager to the mix.

The General Types of Mutual Funds, for Indexers and Others

In the next few pages, I've listed the main types of stock-owning mutual funds, what they do, for whom they're designed, and the risks they run. Most of them are available as index funds as well as managed funds.

1. Growth funds invest in companies, mostly big or midsize, whose earnings are believed to be accelerating. Dividends are a low priority.

If all goes well: You get satisfying long-term performance. They're at their best when the market is zipping up. Most of your returns come from capital gains, with very little from dividends.

What to worry about: Bear markets are bad for their health. And yours too.

Who should buy: Long-term, performance-minded investors who can stomach larger than average market drops but don't want to run the even higher risk of investing in small-company funds.

2. Aggressive growth funds buy new issues (page 880) and small-growth companies whose earnings have been rising fast. These funds are usually a blur of buy and sell, hopping into stocks that are steaming up, hopping off stocks whose prices stall. Expenses are high and dividends slim.

If all goes well: Aggressive growth funds shine in strongly rising markets, especially when a lot of new issues are being offered. They usually bounce back strongly after a stock market drop.

What to worry about: They get creamed when markets fall or when the bubble bursts in a sector where stock performance has been the dizziest. The damage could be drastic if the fund owns stock in very small firms and has to sell to raise cash to meet shareholder redemptions. The fund's own selling could drive a stock price down. Investors have to be prepared to suffer.

Who should buy: Deluded market timers who think they know how to catch the upswings without being buried when stocks go down. Investors with nerve. Long-term investors who are gambling with 5 to 10 percent of their money and can ignore market drops. Over their holding period, they might get higher returns. *Might.*

3. Value funds buy good companies that are temporarily unwanted and unloved, on a long-term bet that their stocks will turn around. They follow the classic approach of the famous investor John Templeton, who said, "In selecting investments, look for the points of maximum pessimism." Buy what everyone else is selling or is afraid to touch. Most of the legendary investors are value investors.

If all goes well: You'll have a strong investment. Value stocks don't perform as well as growth stocks do when the market soars. But over full market cycles, they've matched or outperformed growth stocks historically. They also have higher dividend yields. On average, one-third of your return will probably come from dividends, with the rest from capital gains.

What to worry about: Bear markets, of course. But good value funds don't decline as much as growth funds do.

Who should buy: Long-term, performance-minded investors who like to buy cheap and want decent dividends too.

4. Small-company funds specialize in *small-capitalization*[*] stocks. Generally speaking, a stock is "small-cap" when its share price, multiplied by the number of shares outstanding, comes to less than $500 million (some managers set higher caps; up to $1 billion). Funds may specialize in small-growth stocks or small-value stocks or buy some of both. When small-cap funds start attracting a lot of money and can't find enough small stocks to buy, they start adding midsize ("midcap") companies too.

If all goes well: Historically, small caps have done better than large caps over long time periods. Small-cap value funds, in particular, have outperformed. But it costs more to buy and sell small stocks, so over shorter periods, beating the big-stock averages isn't guaranteed.

What to worry about: They're hammered in bad markets and may do worse than large-cap funds for several years in a row.

Who should buy: Long-term, performance-minded investors who don't scare easily and will hold for at least five years. It's not unreasonable to make small caps one-fifth or one-quarter of your portfolio.

5. Growth-and-income funds emphasize blue-chip companies that grow steadily (except in recessions, of course) and pay good dividends. An S&P index fund is a growth-and-income fund.

If all goes well: You get more current income than you would from growth funds, plus the potential for solid price appreciation. In some years, these funds have outdone the growth funds, thanks to the compounding effect of reinvested dividends.

What to worry about: What can I say? They're still stock funds, which means that they go down when the market does, although generally not by as much as the growth funds do. The dividends help cushion the drop.

Who should buy: Investors who like blue chips, want some income from their stocks, and don't demand aggressive performance in rising markets. They're an excellent choice for novice or conservative stock investors, investors who will hold only one fund, or investors who hold more aggressive funds and want to diversify.

6. Equity-income funds, income funds, and dividend-income funds concentrate on companies that pay high dividends even if they don't show terrific growth. Good examples would be certain electric utilities, some telephone companies, and real estate investment trusts. They may own bonds too.

---

*A stock's capitalization is its market price multiplied by the number of shares outstanding. Put another way, it's the value the market puts on the company as a whole at a given point in time.

If all goes well: You get somewhat more income than growth-and-income funds provide, although somewhat less growth. In declining markets, your losses shouldn't be as bad. Your income might keep up with inflation because these kinds of companies tend to keep raising their dividends.

What to worry about: That some of your companies will quit raising dividends, which would hurt the price of your fund.

Who should buy: Conservative investors who want more income from their money while staying invested for modest growth.

7. Balanced funds buy common stocks, preferred stocks (which pay higher dividends than the common), and bonds. They may allocate fixed percentages of their money to stocks and bonds—say, 60 percent stocks, 40 percent bonds. If that's the allocation you want, it's simple to let the fund do it for you.

If all goes well: Your fund emphasizes income without abandoning growth. When interest rates fall, balanced funds can grow smartly because both their stocks and their bonds should rise. In a bear market, their interest and dividends help support the price of the shares.

What to worry about: You're in trouble when interest rates rise. The value of your bonds will drop, and your stock might too.

Who should buy: Income investors who don't want to foreclose on their chances for some capital growth.

8. Tax-managed funds pay attention to what you receive after tax. They hold trading to a minimum, take only long-term gains, and harvest tax losses to offset gains. In my view, every manager should pay attention to taxes, but most of them don't. They play their trading games and leave the taxes to you. Index funds that follow broad indexes, such as the S&P and Wilshire 5000, are tax efficient too.

If all goes well: You'll have no, or minimal, capital gains distributions at the end of the year. You will, however, get your share of any taxable dividends that the fund receives.

What to worry about: Only the fund's performance. It's a rare year that taxes will be a problem.

Who should buy: Anyone with a taxable portfolio. Tax efficiency makes a big difference to your net gain.

9. Sector funds specialize in the stocks of a particular industry. For example, they might buy only housing stocks, airline stocks, health care stocks, biotechnology stocks, financial stocks—the sector list goes on and on. A fund will typically move up strongly when its industry gets hot, then stagnate or fall as buying interest moves to some other market sector.

If all goes well: You will pick exactly the sector that's about to move up and sell before it peters out. Then you'll hop to another sector that's about to move up. You'll do this successfully over and over. (Pinch me, I'm dreaming.)

What to worry about: You'll buy a fund after its big move up. As soon as you buy, it will go limp. You might catch the losses but not the gains.

Who should buy: Highly experienced investors who understand how various industries respond to changes in the economy and who have a good track record for picking individual stocks. Also long-term investors who have faith in certain industries, such as health care or energy.

10. Real estate funds buy companies connected to the trade, such as real estate investment trusts, home builders, and mortgage companies. They're sector funds with benefits—they've often moved up when other stocks are moving down. That is, until 2007, when the housing industry began to collapse. In the crash, all types of stocks declined together.

If all goes well: In normal markets, they offer mild diversification.

What to worry about: A year like 2007 or 2008. Single-industry funds pose a higher than usual risk when the economy turns against them.

Who should buy: Investors seeking a real estate diversification, especially at a time when the industry's stocks are particularly low.

11. Commodity funds can be an excellent diversification. Commodities generally move up when stocks move down, and vice versa. When stocks and commodities rise and fall in tandem, they move at different rates. Commodities also behave differently from bonds—another diversification plus—and are better than stocks as a hedge against inflation.

If all goes well: Global growth will put pressure on limited supplies of food, energy, and metals, pushing up prices. They'll continue to work as an excellent diversification and inflation hedge. Any disruptions in supplies hurts stocks but helps commodities.

What to worry about: These are volatile investments, so buckle your seat belt for a bumpy ride. When global growth slows or falls, commodities collapse.

Who should buy: Globally minded investors who understand the risks and rewards.

12. International funds. For foreign stocks. Every investor should consider them (see chapter 27).

13. Emerging-markets funds. The aggressive growth funds of the international world (see chapter 27). Volatile but well worth 5 percent of your portfolio or more.

Stock Investing for the Socially Committed

At the most recent count, $2.7 trillion was committed to socially responsible investing (SRI). You choose these stocks if your top concern is the impact that corporations have on society, through such things as employment practices, environmental behavior, corporate governance, community investing, product safety, policies on alternative energy, and respect for human rights. Some SRI funds address the moral concerns of specific religious groups, such as Catholics and evangelicals (seeking corporations considered pro-family and pro-life), and Muslims (avoiding interest-paying securities such as bonds).

SRI funds screen companies for the types of practices their investors love or hate. Typically, they reject some industries wholesale, such as tobacco, liquor, gambling, and weapons suppliers, as well as specific companies with poor records on the environment and other social criteria. Once they have a tentative "buy" list, they use traditional securities analysis to identify the stocks that they think will perform the best. Most of them are managed funds.

The standard objection to SRI is that this type of investing is likely to yield reduced returns. Advisers who work within a limited universe, the skeptics say, won't be picking all the best stocks.

Leave aside the question of whether any adviser can be relied upon to pick the best stocks. Years of research—especially by finance professor Meir Statman of Santa Clara University in California—show that you can have your conscience and good investments too. Sometimes SRI mutual funds run ahead of the general market; for example, in the 1990s, when they stocked up on consumer durables and techs. At other times SRI funds run behind, as was true during the 2003–2007 bull market, when they steered clear of the soaring oils, metals, and industrials. Over a market cycle, the SRIs and non-SRIs perform about the same. With either type of fund, your returns depend primarily on the classic metrics, such as investment style, sector allocations, and the amount of money invested abroad.

Some of the newer SRI mutual funds diversify across all industries, even traditional baddies such as metals and weapons. In those black-hat sectors, the managers look for the best of class—meaning, for example, companies with pollution problems that they're actively cleaning up (as opposed to the companies ignoring the stink).

For more information about social investing, go to the Social Investment Forum (www.socialinvest.org) or SocialFunds.com (www.socialfunds.com). They both list SRI mutual funds as well as some of the brokers and planners who specialize in the field. Two companies offer SRI index funds: Vanguard and

Calvert Investments. You'll find additional adviser names at First Affirmative Financial Network (www.firstaffirmative.com) and Progressive Asset Management (www.progressive-asset.com). The many boutique social investment firms include Boston Common Asset Management and Trillium Asset Management Corporation. Some large institutions, such as Wells Fargo, offer SRI managed accounts to wealthy investors.

For those who sneer at the choices of the social and religious funds, I offer an anti-SRI: the Vice Fund, founded in August 2002 and, at this writing, managing $180 million in assets. Vice doesn't make nice and doesn't diversify. It revels in global gambling, tobacco, liquor, and aerospace/defense. Since its inception, it has performed almost twice as well as the S&P 500.

In our hearts, didn't we know that would happen? Conscience is comforting, but in the real world, sin wins.

Investing in Stocks Through Exchange-Traded Funds

Exchange-traded funds, or ETFs, are mutual funds that trade like stocks. You buy and sell them through a broker, paying the usual sales commissions. Like traditional index funds, they follow a market index—either a broad index, such as the S&P 500, or a narrow index developed specifically for the ETF. For the details on how ETFs work and how they're different from traditional funds, see page 785. The question here is whether to choose traditional mutual funds or ETFs as your way of buying stocks. As always, it depends.

- *If you're a steady investor gradually building a retirement fund*—use traditional no-load mutual funds. They charge no commissions when you buy, which makes them the most efficient way to save. This is especially true for people making modest monthly investments. The flat-rate commission on each ETF purchase, ranging from $10 to $25 at discount brokerage houses, eats up your money fast.

- *If you're a disciplined investor who rebalances your portfolio regularly*—stick with no-load funds. If you rebalance with ETFs, you'll have to pay sales commissions every time you shift your investments around. Why would you do that? There's the cost of bid/asked spreads too (page 868).

- *If you're retired and drawing money out of your portfolio*—again, use no-load funds. No-loads don't charge for withdrawals. Selling portions of your ETFs will cost you bid/asked spreads and sales commissions.

- *If you're a steady investor building a retirement fund and working with a stockbroker*—compare the ETFs' commissions, spreads, and annual expenses with the commissions and expenses on the broker's traditional mutual funds.

The ETFs will almost certainly be cheaper. You also can sell ETFs anytime you want, whereas the broker's mutual funds might charge a penalty if you sell within five years. (Why are you still working with a broker?? Go buy low-cost, no-load mutual funds.)

▪ *If you want to grow your savings by reinvesting dividends*—choose a traditional mutual fund. You generally can't reinvest dividends in ETFs unless the broker provides a reinvestment service, and then there's usually a fee.

▪ *If you have a taxable account and a single large lump sum to invest*—consider a broad-based ETF that you'll buy and hold. ETFs pass their taxable dividends to investors every year, but you may not have to pay any capital gains taxes until you sell your shares. By contrast, traditional mutual funds pass along their realized capital gains to investors every year. (Note, however, that traditional index funds tied to the S&P 500-stock average and tax-managed funds rarely pass along capital gains. For a buy-and-hold investor, a Fidelity or Vanguard S&P fund is cheaper than an ETF, after counting commissions, and usually just as tax efficient.)

▪ *If you're an active trader*—use ETFs. They can be bought and sold throughout the day, just like any other stock. Trade through a discount broker to reduce your costs. Most traditional mutual funds discourage active trading.

▪ *If you want to take a flyer on a specific corner of the stock market*—ETFs are your game. There are hundreds of them. They invest in targeted indexes that represent types of products (medical devices, clean energy), industries (materials, health care), international sectors (Chinese real estate, global consumer staples), commodities (gold, global timber), countries (China, India, Israel), currency (Chinese yuan, Australian dollar), and investment strategies (midcap 400 value stocks, technical leaders).

These narrowly indexed ETFs are likely to produce taxable capital gains that have to be distributed to investors. The same is true of the few ETFs that are actively managed. They aren't as tax efficient as the ETFs based on broader indexes such as the S&P.

▪ *If you're harvesting tax losses*—ETFs keep you in the game. Say that you have losses in your real estate mutual fund but want to stay invested in that sector. If you sell the fund to nail down the loss for tax purposes, you're required to wait 31 days before buying it back. As an alternative, you could sell the fund and immediately buy a real estate ETF. That way, you get the tax loss without giving up your investment position. By the way, don't wait until year-end to take losses; take them during the year as they occur. If you wait until year-end, the stock may have recovered, costing you a tax deduction.

▪ *If you've settled on ETFs as an investment, which are the best ones to buy?*

For savers who will buy and hold, chose "Spiders" (*SPDRs,* for *Standard & Poor's Depository Receipts*). They mimic the S&P 500 and are the most widely traded ETF by far. Annual expense: 0.12 percent.

For traders, the favorite is "Qubes" (ticker symbol: QQQQ), which follows the speculative NASDAQ 100 index for high-tech stocks.

International investors like the MSCI Emerging Markets Index (EEM) and Vanguard Emerging Markets ETF (VWO) as an easy way of betting on the superior growth in the developing parts of the world. Vanguard's is the lowest cost.

Vanguard has a whole suite of ETFs called "Vipers." Here you can get a clear cost comparison between traditional funds and ETFs:

(1) Say that you're saving $1,000 a month. Vanguard's Large-Cap Index Fund charges 0.2 percent a year with no commission, so you'll pay less than $20. Vanguard's Large-Cap ETF, which follows the same index, charges just 0.07 percent a year, but you'll also pay $25 a month ($300 a year) in sales commissions. Ouch. Choose the index fund.

(2) Say that you're investing $100,000 all at once. The traditional fund costs you $200 a year. The ETF costs you $70 a year plus the onetime commission. The ETF wins by a mile.

Timing the Market

Timers try to get into the market by buying stocks ahead of an upswing or during its early stages. They'll take their profits just before the market drops down.

That's the dream. Here's the reality: in almost all cases, you'll miss the turns. Succeeding once doesn't mean that you'll succeed again. You'll sell too soon. You'll sell too late. Ditto when you buy. For more trashing of market timing, see page 696.

Aha, you say, even though I can't do it, my market-timing newsletter or adviser can. Not in my opinion. When letter writers get it right, it's luck, not science, which means that they won't reliably get it right again. Studies show that most market letter writers are fully invested at market peaks (they didn't get out in time) and heavily in cash at market bottoms (they didn't get back in time). You can do that yourself without paying for advice.

Be skeptical of the glorious records that many market timers publish. They're usually not audited. They ignore the effects of commissions and taxes. They may not be real (a 3-year-old newsletter may present 20 years of results to "prove" how well its system would have worked in the past—but systems developed in hindsight often stumble in real time). They might make false comparisons, such as setting their own investment record, including dividends, against the Dow Jones Industrial Average without dividends—something that you wouldn't know from the advertising pitch. Finally, you don't know how well the results compare with those of investors who bought and held, which would be the only fair test.

Even if a newsletter tells you to sell at just the right time, it may miss the moment when you should have bought back in. There's no point selling at $20, feeling like a genius as the market drops to $8, then not rebuying until the price has run up to $21. That turns you from genius into goat. You didn't rebuy because you kept thinking that the price was going to fall again and the market faked you out (*whipsawed* is the word). Remember: To make money, every timer has to make three right calls. You have to get in, then out, then in again.

But say that you subscribe to an investment site that you still believe in. Ask yourself whether you'll really follow every call. If you'll pick and choose among the buy/sell recommendations, forget it. That's no system at all. The commissions and taxes from trading also slice you up if you're investing in a taxable account.

As an experiment, devote a small part of your money to following a market timer while leaving the rest in a well-allocated selection of mutual funds. After two or three market turns, ask yourself: Did the gains on the good calls outweigh the losses on the bad ones? What's the effect on my long-term return of subtracting any commissions paid or taxes owed on capital gains? If your market-timed account isn't markedly higher than the funds you bought and held, timing isn't worth the effort it takes.

Still, some of you can't resist it. So I offer here a few simple ideas that shouldn't get you into too much trouble. They can work, although not consistently. They apply to the stock market overall, not to the shares of specific companies—so you have to be using ETFs or no-load mutual funds. Everybody knows these ideas, of course, so by the time you buy or sell, there may be no value left. (Another reason why timing strategies are a crock.) Anyway . . .

▪ *Buy during recessions.* That's when stocks are at their cheapest. But you have to buy midway through the recession—if you can identify it; even economists often can't. Toward the end of a business downturn, stocks are already leaping up. (The best time to sell, on average, comes about four months before a recession starts, so remember to count.)

▪ *Buy after a major stock market crash*—defined as a fast and sudden drop. That would be 2008, the worst single year ever in the market. After such an embarrassment, stocks typically bounce back by 50 percent. The key word here is *after*—you can't be sure when the crash is over.

▪ *If a smaller market crashes, buy that too.* Latin American markets toppled in

1995 during the Mexican peso collapse but later came roaring back. In 1997, currency crises hacked away at Southeast Asia—another buying opportunity. So was the Russian bond default in 1998. You may have to hold for a while in order to get your reward, but you'll have bought relatively cheaply.

■ *Buy or sell a stock group when you foresee a significant change in government policy.* If a war will wind down, so will defense stocks. If new sources of energy become a priority, their stocks will too.

■ *Sell when there's an inverted yield curve.* That's when short-term interest rates rise higher than long-term interest rates. Each of the recessions since 1970 was preceded by an inverted yield curve. When the curve is inverted only for a month or two, there may be no bear market. But if short rates keep climbing, or fall back and then climb again, stocks will fall—although not necessarily immediately. The yield curve inverted in 2006, and timers had more than a year to wait. Would you have stayed in cash all that time, or would you have given up and bought back in? Especially when Federal Reserve chair Ben Bernanke (echoing the previous chair, Alan Greenspan) said in a speech that the yield curve is no longer a sign of recession ahead? (The Fed isn't a good predictor either.)

■ *Earlier editions of this book gave some other selling and buying signals beloved of various market timers.* The market's behavior since the tech-stock bust in 2000 has overwhelmed them all. That's why market timing is so hard. A rule of thumb may work for a while, then suddenly not work—and no one posts a notice that it's going to change.

Research has proven beyond all doubt that your asset allocation accounts for almost all of your returns, with only a tiny role played by which stocks you bought and when you bought them.

The Case Against Buying Individual Stocks

As a long-term investor, you might think that your job is to find "great companies" and hold their stocks forever. But "great companies" don't necessarily last. The superstars of 1990 were has-beens by 2000. The leaders in 2000 soon saw their stocks collapse. In hindsight, you can always find stocks with wonderful long-term records. But you can't know in advance which ones they're going to be.

You take big risks when buying individual stocks. Here's a short list:

1. You overpay. A stock price is supposed to reflect the company's expected growth in future earnings and dividends. But when stocks are popular, people bid up their prices to unrealistic levels. In the late 1990s, tech stocks were selling for far more than they could ever deliver in earnings growth. Investors kept buying them anyway, based on the theory of "greater fool" (as in "I may be a fool to pay this high price, but I'll sell it to a greater fool who will pay even more"). Prices collapsed when the last fool decided not to play. Microsoft is a great company, but in 1999 it wasn't a great stock. After the 2008 collapse, it turned out that the famous financial stocks weren't even great companies.

2. You buy stocks that are in the news. That's where you hear about companies—and, of course, so does everyone else. Newsy stocks are more apt to be overpriced, compared with companies you've never heard of. You hear about underpriced stocks only after they've risen 50 percent (and they're newly in the news!). Stockbrokers like to sell newsy stocks because those are ones you're mostly likely to be interested in.

3. You buy and hold. That's what long-term investors are supposed to do. But business moves too fast today. Only a very few companies turn in splendid long-term results—mostly those in traditional businesses and paying dividends.* Others bite the dust. To keep a portfolio of good stocks, you have to weed them constantly—selling some and buying others. But even professionals don't do that well, including the smarties who run managed mutual funds. And neither do you and I (although we like to kid ourselves).

4. You don't know—and cannot know—what's going on in a company. If you own an individual stock, take this little test: How good is the business? What are the trends in profit margins, sales rates, and inventories? How competent are its top executives, what are their problems, and how are they handling them? Is the market share rising or falling in the company's various lines of business? What's the competition up to, at home and abroad? You probably can't answer these questions, and there's no reason you should. Without answers, however, you have no basis for deciding whether to buy, hold, or sell the stock. After the once-lordly Lucent tumbled, we discovered that it had made a wrong bet on fiber-optic technology and its management was a mess. Who knew until we read it in the newspapers and the stock was down 90 percent? And who ever heard of credit default swaps before 2008?

5. You don't diversify. To be properly diversified, you'd have to hold 50 or

---

*The 20 top performers in Standard & Poor's 500 index for 1957–2003, from *The Future for Investors* by Jeremy Siegel: Altria (formerly Philip Morris), Abbot Laboratories, Bristol-Myers Squibb, Tootsie Roll Industries, Pfizer, Coca-Cola, Merck, PepsiCo, Colgate-Palmolive, Crane, H.J. Heinz, Wrigley, Fortune Brands, Kroger, Schering-Plough, Procter & Gamble, Hershey Foods, Wyeth, Royal Dutch Petroleum, and General Mills. These aren't investment recommendations; some companies on this list have had troubles too. But notice that there's not a tech stock in the bunch. Each generation's tech stocks got blown away by something new.

more stocks in various industries and in companies of different sizes. Individuals can't do that. You hold just a few stocks, in popular companies. If one of those companies goes bad, it's hard to recover.

6. You have no idea how well your total stock portfolio has performed. Typically, you remember your winners, every single one of them. You forget your losers. You never average the two together. So you have no idea whether you've done as well as the market over time. Almost certainly, you're behind.

7. You are up against professionals who watch (or whose computer programs watch) the market 24/7. They're on the other end of your trades. Do you really think that you know more about a stock than they do?

Stocks have an entertainment value for people who like the game and have time on their hands. It's exciting to see a stock go up (I won't mention the down). If you love to play, set aside 5 percent of your investment fund and cheerio. But do yourself and your family a favor and keep your long-term, life-changing money in well-diversified mutual funds.

But If You Insist . . .

This isn't a book on securities selection (to say the least!). But if you want to dip your toe into buying individual stocks, the following sections provide a vocabulary and a look at the landscape. Most stocks move with the market, up and down, but they also have their own separate destinies. A stock might suddenly rise, stall, or slide in price while the rest of the market, or the rest of the stocks in its industry, are doing something else entirely. If one stock in a particular industry gets active—say, a home-building company misses its earnings forecast and investors sell—that's a sign that other stocks in that industry may soon face the same problems, even if they're showing no signs of it now. But not always. Every company is its own world.

All this means that picking stocks is more demanding of your time, knowledge, and persistence than picking mutual funds. Successful investors subscribe to printed and online investment publications, read company reports, analyze industries, and study market valuations. They devote many hours to study and research. They keep their eyes open to what's going on around them, how the world is changing, and what neighborhoods and nations need.

Don't Count Yourself a Stock Picker if You Merely Buy Stocks on the Advice of a Broker. Stockbrokers (or their firms' research departments) may have good ideas. But if you just nod and say, "Yes, yes," you aren't an investor, you're a sheep. As you've probably noticed, brokers pick bad stocks too, and they all cost the same to buy and sell. If you're going to invest in individual stocks, you need to develop a mind of your own.

Stock Picking and the New Online Communities

Instead of trusting their brokers for stock picks, some investors are turning to one another. For example, take Cake Financial (www.cakefinancial.com), a free Web site. Members post their stock and mutual fund portfolios for all to see (although not the amount of money invested). You benefit two ways. First, Cake tracks the performance of all your accounts, combined, so you can quickly see how you're doing compared with standard market indexes. (Are you beating the market? Probably not.) Second, the community becomes your source of fresh investment ideas. You can follow the actions of the most successful investors on the site, to see what and when they're buying and selling. There are lists of the most actively bought and sold stocks and "hidden gems." Members post questions to one another and share ideas in the hope of improving their performance. You'll find similar free communities at the brokerage firm sites Zecco (www.zecco.com) and TradeKing (www.tradeking.com). Value Forum (www.valueforum.com) charges a membership fee. Wikinvest (www.wikinvest.com) is a stock research site to which anyone can contribute.

The big question is whether all this sharing does any good. An index of the top holdings of Cake's top investors shows them to be more speculative than the general market—losing more money in declines and shooting up during recoveries. Generally speaking, that kind of volatility injures long-term returns. And why would you think that today's top investor will stay on his or her pedestal? Like any hot mutual fund, hot traders fade when the market suddenly moves elsewhere. Dude 2020, sweetlily, and the rest of the posters aren't any smarter than the professional managers of mutual funds, and no more likely to beat the market over time.

Still, there are people—and you may be one of them—for whom stocks are an obsession. You spend hours researching them and more hours trading. Alternatively, you want to trade but don't have the time to do the research. Community sites are a far better choice for ideas than the big public message boards at places like Yahoo! Finance, because the members aren't pumping penny stocks or wasting your time with useless comments. Instead, you see actual trades from people with good recent records, compared with those of the other investors on the site. And it's more fun.

A Mini-Tour of the Stock Markets

The markets, or exchanges, are where buyers meet sellers to trade stocks, bonds, options, and other financial instruments. The New York and NASDAQ exchanges are the largest, best regulated, and least subject to price manipulation. As markets and company size get smaller, prices get flakier and crooks find it easier to play games.

The New York Stock Exchange

Also known as the Big Board. It's the dominant exchange, where most of the biggest and best-known companies trade. Historically, it has been an *auction market,* where prices are set on the trading room floor by the competing bids of buyers and sellers. (That's the scene you see on TV, when stock prices plunge and traders in gray jackets stare at screens or hold their heads.) Nowadays, the NYSE is becoming more of an electronic market, where buyers and sellers are matched by computer. In 2007 it purchased the American Stock Exchange and renamed it NYSE Alternext. That's where more of the medium-size and smaller companies trade. It's also home to most ETFs.

NASDAQ (National Association of Securities Dealers Automated Quotations)

A purely electronic exchange. In general, it lists midsize and smaller companies, although it's home to some big financial and tech stocks too. Like the Big Board, it sets high governance and financial standards for the companies it accepts for trading. Because of its speedy execution system, the NYSE sends stocks to trade here too.

Electronic Trading Systems

These systems automatically match buy and sell orders for broker/dealers who subscribe to them. They're regulated by the Securities and Exchange Commission.

The Over-the-Counter Market

Also known as the OTC. There are no formal listings in this market, nor a particular place where buyers and sellers gather. It's a vast web of dealers who "make a market" in particular companies, most of them small or new. Market makers facilitate trades. They buy a company's shares as they come up for sale, at prices they determine, and sell the shares to other dealers at whatever markup they can get.

The *OTC Bulletin Board* (www.otcbb.com) provides prices electronically for thousands of stocks. Any company can participate, as long as it files current, audited financial reports with the SEC. Some of the Bulletin Board prices are firm; others are soggy (meaning that when you ask a dealer for a published price, he or she may suddenly change it); still others are blatantly manipulated.

Pink OTC Markets (pink sheets) quotes prices for all public companies, including those that don't even file financial statements and *shell companies* that are merely names with no business. Pink sheet companies are mostly small and *closely held,* meaning that there are just a few shareholders, including the owner. Mostly, they're penny stocks. Con games are easy in this market. If you get a phone call or e-mail about a pink sheet stock, hang up, delete.

A Mini-Tour of Buying and Selling

Here's how stock trading works:

You place an order to buy or sell a stock, with your stockbroker or through your online discount brokerage account. Individual investors generally give *market orders,* telling the broker to execute the order at the best price available at the time. A professional investor or serious trader may give a *limit order,* telling the broker to stay within a certain price, as in "Don't pay over twenty-five dollars for that stock" or "Sell if the share drops eighteen dollars." A *listed* share is one that trades on the NYSE or NASDAQ.

The brokerage firm enters your order on the exchange that it typically deals with for market orders of that size. A customer is found for the other side of your trade—not a particular, named customer, but a dealer who fills your order from inventory or a match found electronically.

You buy at the *asked,* or *offer,* price (the price the dealer offers). The seller on the other side of your trade sells at the *bid* price. The difference between the two is the *spread.* That's where the dealers' profits lie. If a stock is quoted at $10 asked and $9.95 bid, it has a five-cent or "nickel" spread. Large, actively traded shares have a tiny spread—less than a penny. *Thinly traded* shares— meaning companies where not a lot of stock changes hands in a particular day— have much wider spreads, especially if they're over the counter. The wider the spread, the greater the gain you need in order to make a profit. There has to be an awfully good reason to buy OTC stock with a wide spread; offhand, I can't think of one. You can find the spread on listed stocks and some OTC stocks on

Bloomberg.com (under "Market Data"/"Stocks") and Yahoo! Finance, as well as similar sites.

A *round lot* is 100 shares of stock, which is the ideal minimum order. Anything less is an *odd lot*. Odd-lot orders can be pooled before the stock exchanges open for the day and executed at the regular price. If you insist on buying or selling odd lots later in the day, you'll pay a surcharge.

Learn to invest by degrees. When you find a stock you like, buy 100 shares. If the company continues to do well, buy another 100 shares. Step into it gradually. If something bad happens, you can quit right there. With this system, you don't have to make an all-or-nothing buy decision, which helps investors who feel unsure.

In many cases, it's also smart to sell by degrees: 100 shares this week, 100 shares next week, and so on. When prices have been rising sharply, spaced sales are a way of taking profits without getting out of the stock entirely. Spaced sales also save you from making an all-or-nothing sell decision about a stock whose price has stalled or slipped. Many investors have trouble pulling the trigger on a loss. It's psychologically easier to sell a bit at a time, because you know you can always quit selling if you see a reason to hold the company longer.

As a general rule, you should think about selling any stock that drops 10 percent from its peak price. If the stock is volatile—meaning that it typically shows steep drops and gains—you might not sell until its slide reaches 15 percent. Investors who like to buy and hold might not sell at all if they think the company is sound. In fact, they might buy more. But if your stock drops 10 percent when the rest of the market doesn't, something is probably wrong.

To force yourself not to hang on to a deteriorating stock, enter a *stop-loss* order. That tells your broker to sell the stock automatically if it drops to a certain price. If the stock moves up, set a new stop-loss order at 10 percent below the new, higher price.

A stop-loss isn't a guarantee. In a free-falling market, your order may not be executed at the price you set. Normally, however, your broker will come pretty close.

Constant trading—buying and selling stock—costs a lot of money. Even with a discount broker, your commissions may come to 1 or 2 percent. If you turn over all of your stocks once a year, you might pay up to 4 percent. That means you'd have to gross 12 percent on your investments to net 8 percent, pretax. So the less you trade, the better your chance of making money.

If you're trading in a taxable account, there's even more incentive to buy and hold. Every time you sell at a profit, you owe a tax. Profits on stocks held for 12 months or less are called short-term capital gains and taxed in your highest marginal bracket. Long-term capital gains, on stocks held for more than 12 months, are much more lightly taxed.*

Sad Stories I Have Heard (Or, What It Takes to Break Even)

You bought a stock, and it's a dog. As soon as you bought it, the price started down. But you haven't sold, because you don't want to take the loss. You will wait until the price comes back.

You Are Cherishing Four Illusions
   1. You think that the price will come back soon because you couldn't have been so wrong. In fact, the price could stay down for years. It might never come back.
   2. You think that as long as you don't sell, you don't have a loss. But a "paper" loss is just as real as the other kind. The stock is worth less than you paid for it. Period.
   3. You think that there's only one way of earning back the money you lost: by holding on to the stock you lost it in. But you might earn your money back faster by selling the stock and reinvesting in something else.
   4. You think that gains come just as easily as losses.

   The falsity of this last point needs an illustration. When a stock drops from $50 to $25, you lose 50 percent of your money. To recover, however, your stock has to climb from $25 back up to $50—a rise of 100 percent. How many stocks do you buy expecting a 100 percent increase in price? Not very many.
   That's why it's so important to cut your losses before they get too deep. The farther your stock falls, the harder it becomes to earn the money back—not only with that stock but with any stock. Check out the bad news on page 871.

If You're Holding a Loser, Consider Selling for the Tax Loss

Capital losses are deductible in full against realized capital gains, and deductible at the rate of $3,000 a year against your ordinary income. If you still like the stock, you can buy it back after 30 days—perhaps at a lower price if the market

---

*In 2010, long-term capital gains are tax free in the 10 percent and 15 percent tax brackets. This may or may not be extended into later years, so check.

Table 22.

THE LONG ROAD BACK

When a Stock Drops by	The Gain You Need to Break Even Is
5%	5%*
10%	11%
15%	18%
20%	25%
25%	33%
30%	43%
35%	54%
40%	66%
45%	82%
50%	100%
55%	122%
60%	150%
65%	186%
70%	233%
75%	300%
80%	400%
85%	566%
90%	900%
95%	1,900%

*Rounded down from 5.2%. Even small losses require greater percentage gains in order to win your money back.

Source: American Association of Individual Investors.

is going down. If you rebuy before the 31st day, you can't take the tax loss. And that's all you'll hear from me about taxes and stock portfolios. If God had wanted me to be J. K. Lasser, He or She would have arranged it.

A Short List of Stock-Picking Points to Give You a Glimpse of What It Takes

Every stock picker has a system, but it can't be packaged and delivered. You start by trying this and that, and pretty soon you've cleared a path. Since there are thousands of stocks that rise over the long term, one path may work just as well as another. In that eclectic spirit, I offer some ways of helping stock pickers get started.*

Screening for Companies

You might start by attaching yourself to a major trend. Maybe something economic, like the rapid growth of the developing world. Maybe something demographic, like the growing need for health care for the elderly. Maybe something technological, like products for new energy industries. Or think about the industry you work in. What developments there are going to influence profit growth? (But don't confuse familiarity with knowledge. Research your own industry the same way you would an industry you know less about. Maybe the new developments aren't so hot.)

Once you've found a possible industry, ask: Is it growing? Are profit margins sustainable? Can prices be raised? Can competitors easily enter this industry, or will the leaders keep their franchise for a while? Does it have any political troubles? Is it a steady grower, even during recessions?

If you like the answers you get, start looking for promising companies within that industry. Ask: Is the company an industry leader? Does it control a unique product or service? Does it dominate a profitable market? Does it have some new products coming along? Has management done a good job of raising the company's earnings and profit margins?

This is what analysts call a *top-down approach.* You start with a big thought, then narrow your focus to companies that embody it.

You can also work from the *bottom up,* by screening stocks for certain financial characteristics. Ask: What companies are improving their profit margins from a low base? Growing their sales at increasing rates? Growing their operating income? Raising their dividends? Coming out of an earnings slide?

You wind up with a *thesis*: a specific reason to own that particular company. It's not enough just to say, "It's a great company." How would you know? (Remember Lucent and AIG?) You have to be expecting certain things to happen to spur the company's growth. For beginners, it's best to shop among high-quality companies, leaders in their industries, with above-average earnings growth and low debt.

---

*A top financial planner who read this chapter commented, "Mostly useless, Jane! Laymen can't pick stocks. Their choices wind up being all emotion." He's right, but you'll have to learn that yourself.

The P/E Ratio

Once you've got a likely company, ask: How popular has this company already become with investors? One measure is its *price/earnings (P/E) ratio.* It tells you how much you're paying for each dollar of earnings. When a company carries a high P/E, its earnings have usually risen rapidly and investors are betting that growth will accelerate some more. It's popular. You're joining a crowd. At companies with low P/Es, profits have grown more slowly or are in a slump. It's out of favor and unloved. One theory of investing says, "Pick low-P/E stocks." When they turn around and start getting noticed, they'll have a lot of room to rise.

To calculate a price/earnings ratio, you divide the current market price by the company's earnings per share for the past 12 months. Or save yourself the trouble and look up the ratio online, at sites such as Bloomberg.com and Yahoo! Finance. At this writing, P/Es in the 20 to 25 range and higher are generally considered rich. P/Es over 40 are ridiculous. A P/E of 15 is about average. A P/E under 10 is considered low—and perhaps a good buy if the company is sound. A P/E under 5 suggests a company in trouble or facing serious business risks. That could be a buying opportunity if you see improvement down the road.

The P/E is also known as a *multiple.* At a 15 P/E, a company is said to be selling at a multiple of 15 times earnings. Analysts may refer to "a multiple of 15 times *estimated earnings,*" meaning that they're judging the stock price by what they think the company will earn in the year ahead. A multiple of 15 times *trailing earnings* measures the price by its earnings over the past 12 months. Multiples of *current earnings* are a mix of past and forecast earnings. Make sure you know which multiple you're dealing with.

Every stock has its own P/E range. You should study its history before deciding whether it's selling at an attractive price. Every industry has its own P/E too. The high-tech industry sells at high multiples, while a cyclical industry such as steel sells at lower multiples. If one stock in an industry is selling at much higher multiples than its competitors, you should proceed cautiously. No company can grow faster than its industry forever.

One important point about P/E ratios: the concept of "high" or "low" is a floating one. The current value of any investment depends on what competing investments have to offer. Stocks sell at somewhat lower P/Es when interest rates are high (because bonds are attractive alternative investments) and at higher P/Es when interest rates are low (except in a recession, when both may be low at the same time). Stock pickers trying to use P/Es to time the market couple them with the market's "simple moving average"—at which point you're above my pay grade. Go to Google and look up P/E SMA.

The Dividend Yield

What is the company's *dividend yield*? To calculate it, divide the annual dividend by the stock's current price per share. Income investors look for dividends in the 5 percent range in industries that typically pay high yields, such as traditional utilities and real estate investment trusts. High-percentage dividends also can mean that a company's stock price has dropped, which appeals to *value investors.*

Historically, the market has generally favored value stocks. They sell at low prices compared with their *book value* (that's roughly what a company would be worth if it went out of business immediately) and other measures. But value investors have to distinguish between companies whose troubles are temporary (say, they need to be reorganized, but new management has a plan) and those that will stay in the pits for a while (they face serious problems, with no visible way out). A superhigh dividend might very well be cut.

One much-touted way of trying to get ahead of the market is called the Dow Dividend strategy (or Dow Dogs). You buy equal dollar amounts of the 10 highest-yielding stocks in the Dow Jones Industrial Average and hold them 12 months. Then you switch to the newest top 10. Or you buy the 5 highest yielders. Or you buy the 5 lowest-priced stocks with the 10 highest yields. There are many variations (Google again). Historically, focusing on high-dividend stocks (which are value stocks) and turning them over every year has generally beaten the market, provided that you're trading in a tax-deferred account. In taxable accounts, you don't do as well. And (horrors!) in some years, the 10 lowest yielders have been better buys.

Dividends get less attention in fast-rising markets. Growth investors aren't interested in them at all. But in flat markets, reinvested dividends make up a substantial portion of your total return. (For more on dividends, see page 878.)

Growth Versus Value

Growth investors look for companies whose earnings are growing faster than 15 percent a year. They're especially fond of smaller companies—"smaller" meaning sales in the $50 million to $500 million range, not penny stocks. Historically, such companies have grown faster than the giants; when they're good, they're very, very good. But giants can be growth stocks too. In some periods, they trounce the smalls.

Momentum has also been a favorite game of growth-stock investors. You look at how fast a stock is rising relative to its previous pace or to an independent index. A stock whose price rise has picked up speed is expected to have a further run. Like any other system, this one will work until it doesn't.

Value investors look for fallen angels—good companies that have fallen on hard times but are likely to recover. Maybe there was a management problem, a problem with a product or service, a problem in the industry, or unforeseen competition. A value company generally has a low P/E ratio, a low price relative to its book value, declining earnings and profit margins, and/or a high dividend yield. Other investors expect its price to go lower and its fortunes to get worse, and that could well happen. But value investors see a stock that's underpriced, compared with its potential, and likely to pay off big if the company's management turns it around. A value stock could also be a good company selling at a reasonable price, as opposed to an inflated price. To the classic great investors, such as Warren Buffett, CEO of Berkshire Hathaway, value investing *is* investing.

Reading the Charts Versus Kicking the Tires

Technical investors ("chartists") take their buying and selling clues from changes in the stock price, without regard for what the company does. They're looking for price patterns that they think will be predictive. *Fundamental investors* think that charting is voodoo. They inspect the industry and company, evaluate management, and read financial statements. Their investment decisions are based on how well they think the company is doing.

One popular, fundamental indicator is *earnings per share.* That's the company's total earnings divided by the number of shares outstanding. Investors like to see earnings per share heading steadily up (and plenty of companies "manage" their earnings to show exactly that). Stocks usually jump when earnings turn out to be better than analysts expected, even by only a penny. The new expectation is that those stocks will do better yet. They plunge, of course, if the earnings come in a penny short.

Don't automatically write off a stock whose earnings per share are down. In some cases, that's good news. For example, the company might have made a major investment that will produce higher earnings in the future. Or maybe a new, improved management group is writing off the mistakes of the old regime. You always have to know what the company is up to.

Following the Insiders

Some investors pick companies whose own officers are buying stock. Insiders tend to buy more than usual before large price rises in the stock and may sell more than usual before large price declines. Insider buying is generally a better signal than insider selling (executives sell for personal as well as investment reasons). But one or two purchases don't mean much. It's more significant if three or more insiders buy within a three-month period and no insider sells, opines the well-known market timer Martin Zweig. The best price gains come in the first six months after insiders start to purchase, with the biggest punch packed into the first month. So copycats have to move fast. Conversely, when insider selling turns out to have been a signal, the price decline tends to be gradual (except in cases of deception or fraud, when insiders bail in advance of a shocking earnings drop). A number of online newsletters follow insider buys and sells.

Following the Gurus

The Web makes it easy to piggyback for free on the stock-picking strategies of top professional investors. GuruFocus (www.gurufocus.com), for example, tracks the portfolios of about 40 famous managers, publishing their latest known picks and listing the stocks that appear to be consensus buys or sells. One warning: there's a lag before the portfolios become public. By the time you see the stock, the manager might already have sold.

Buybacks

What about *buybacks*, when companies announce major purchases of their own shares? One camp says that's good: top management thinks that the stock is cheap relative to the company's prospects. Another camp says that's bad: top management isn't clever enough to invest that money in ways that will make the company grow. It may be using buybacks simply to prop up the stock price.

Stocks and Taxes

For long-term holders, stocks can be a highly efficient investment in a *taxable account.* You have no annual expenses, as you do with mutual funds—only the brokerage commission, and you can use a discount broker. You choose when to sell and pay the capital gains tax. You can buy and hold stocks without ever selling at all, and pass the gains to heirs tax-free. You can sell losers toward year-end and use those losses to shelter capital gains and up to $3,000 in ordinary income each year. Top candidates for buy-and-hold: brand-name blue chips with a proven ability to grow and a history of increasing dividends every year. Some of these stocks can be bought directly from the company, allowing you to skip the brokerage commission entirely (page 834).

Stocks are not tax efficient inside a traditional Individual Retirement Account. All the gains in IRAs are taxed as ordinary income, not as capital gains. You can't deduct losses. IRAs are taxable to your heirs when you die.

Beginners should start buying stocks with no more than 5 or 10 percent of the money they've set aside for investment. Put the rest into well-diversified mutual funds. Educate yourself—see page 815 for some books and investor organizations to join. Focus on leading companies whose management keeps on showing good results. Study the stock, to reach an opinion on whether it's over-priced. Avoid OTC stocks. A stock is more than a piece of paper you trade; it's a real company, with prospects and plans. When good, farsighted management creates a good, farsighted strategy to grow a good company or rescue a troubled one, you've got a winner.

Can You Really "Hold for the Long Term"?

No, not when you buy individual stocks. Business is too fast today. A company that was a blue chip five years ago could be in the cellar now and might stay there for a long time. Think General Electric and Microsoft after 2000 and Pfizer during the 1980s and most of the 1990s. Think of the companies that suddenly went bankrupt or lost most of their value in a downturn—Enron, WorldCom, Lehman Brothers, Citigroup, AIG. Google rides the world today. Is there a competitor coming up that will eventually eat its lunch? Only a very few companies turn in splendid long-term results—mostly those in traditional businesses and paying dividends.

Once you enter the world of individual stock investing, you have to keep analyzing the companies you own. This isn't a spectator sport. If a stock has done well, will its run continue? Why do you think so? Should you replace it with a different stock that may be coming up? If a stock disappoints you, will you sell it? If not, why not? These are the challenges of buying stocks, and not even professional investors do it very well. If they did, they'd beat the market all the time and, of course, they don't.

There may be some "forever" stocks, but you can't identify them in advance. The only investment that you can buy and hold with confidence is an index fund, which participates in the market as a whole.

The Best Tip in This Chapter. Turn off the stock-tip TV shows that shoot you new investments all the time, and abandon any obsession with chat rooms online. Instead plant your garden or play with your dog. Your investment returns will automatically improve.

A Word About Inherited Stock. You didn't pick it, it was chosen for someone else—probably someone with very different goals from yours. It may be from Daddy's beloved company, but sell it if it doesn't fit. At the very least, sell enough so the stock makes up no more than 5 percent of your assets. If the company falters, you don't want your retirement to falter too.

Remember This About Any Stock Price!

The stock market *anticipates*. The current price generally contains all that investors know, or can reasonably guess, about a company's prospects over a reasonable holding period. On the day you buy, you have paid in full for the expected value of any new product or service that the company has announced. For the stock price to rise, prospects for that company have to improve beyond what investors now foresee. If expectations change, the stock price will decline without any immediate slump in the company's performance. The market is anticipating a slump to come.

Dividends

A dividend is your cut of any profits that the company distributes to shareholders. It's declared and usually paid quarterly.

Rapidly growing companies pay low dividends or none at all. Profits are reinvested in the business to help shareholder value grow. This pleases growth investors, who seek high capital gains.

Slower-growing companies, on the other hand, don't get the same high returns by reinvesting in their basic businesses. Sometimes they use their profits to buy other companies or buy back their own shares (for good or ill). But they also pay dividends to shareholders. This pleases investors who want income as well as reasonable growth.

If you're an income investor, look for companies that have paid dividends for 10 years or more and whose dividends usually rise every year, because rising dividends help pull the stock price up. Stagnating dividends suggest that the company isn't going anywhere.

Even growth investors should think about owning some dividend-paying stocks, for two reasons. First, they normally don't drop as far as growth stocks do when bear markets strike. That helps stabilize your portfolio. Second, dividend-paying stocks may deliver higher total returns (dividends plus capital gains) than growth stocks do. One smart use of dividends is to buy more of the company's stock. For companies with dividend reinvestment plans, see page 834.

Consider selling your shares, however, if your high-dividend company takes on a lot of debt. Dividends may be cut to help the company make its payments. Dividends also get cut when a company or industry restructures, as happened to many electric utilities, or when earnings fall substantially.

When timing your purchases and sales, watch out for stocks selling *ex-dividend*. That is the two-day period before the "date of record," which lists the names of all the company's shareholders. If you buy during those two days, you will not make the list, so you won't receive the dividend. If you sell any shares during that period, however, the dividend follows you because you are still the owner of record.

When a stock goes ex-dividend, the amount of the dividend per share is substracted from the price; the market price normally falls by that amount. If it doesn't, that means that the value of the stock has actually gone up.

All things being equal, you might as well buy when you can collect the dividend. A stock that's ex-dividend has an *x* next to its name in the stock tables. Some companies pay part of their dividends in the form of new stock rather than cash.

Covered Calls

Investors are always trying to squeeze more profit out of their stocks without taking more risk. That's a dubious proposition but a stockbroker's easiest sale.

Take covered calls. With this strategy, you buy stocks and sell (or "write") options against them. The investor who buys the option has the right to buy your shares if they rise to a specified price (the *strike price*) within a specified period of time. If the stock doesn't rise, you get to keep it along with the price (the *premium*) that the option buyer paid. If the stock does rise, you keep the premium and earn a modest gain on the stock, but the option buyer takes your stock (*exercises* the option) at the strike price and earns all further gains. In a market that generally goes up, you may be losing more on the upside than you're gaining by earning premium income.

A covered call strategy also involves higher brokerage fees. You pay to write the options and pay to replace any stock that's called away. Your broker likes that. You also pay taxes on your option income, as well as on your profits when the option is exercised—another cost.

Here's an alternative to writing covered calls: increase the amount of money you allocate to cash and bonds and also increase the amount you allocate to riskier stocks, such as value stocks and smaller stocks. Your cash and bonds will give you additional income and more downside protection; your riskier stocks maintain your exposure to the upside, maybe with improved returns.

The Truth About Stock Splits

Nouveau investors think that stock splits make their shares worth more. Wrong, wrong, wrong. After a stock split, a company is worth exactly the same as it was before. Your $120 stock might be split into two $60 shares or three $40 shares, but the total value remains $120. In a reverse split, four shares worth $5 each may be combined into a single $20 share. After a split, all prior financial information will be restated to reflect the changed number of shares outstanding.

So the news that "they're splitting the stock" should not be a clarion call to buy. On the other hand, the stock is definitely worth a look. Companies with high share prices usually don't split their stock unless they expect stronger growth and higher dividends. If that indeed happens, the stock price will rise. Studies show that a stock that has split tends to outperform the market for up to three years.

Sometimes, however, the company is just trying to drum up interest in the stock. Individual investors are more comfortable with share prices in the $50 range than in the $100 range, so they may be willing to buy a bit more if the stock splits down to a level they like. But all you get out of a ploy like this is a short market flurry. The price won't rise if the company's prospects remain unchanged.

Beware of a Low-Priced Company That Splits Its Stock

There's no reason for a $30 stock to split into two $15 pieces, except to hype itself to the innocent.

New Issues: For Rich Gamblers Only

Stock markets will careen from the heights of greed to the pits of fear and back again until the last syllable of recorded time. And whenever the greedometer hits new highs, *new issues* come pouring out.

A new issue is a private company whose shares are being sold to the public for the first time. It's often called an IPO, which means—depending on your view of these things—Initial Public Offering or It's Probably Overpriced.

Many IPOs are genuine businesses with real earnings and honest prospects. These are the only ones to entertain. Some are businesses with promise but launched at too rich a price. Some use the money they raise from the public merely to buy out the founder—and why would you, as an investor, want to do that? On the fringes of this market are the start-ups; two guys and an idea. The idea may be great, but there's no proof that they can turn it into a business. Beyond the fringe are the "blind pools": an entrepreneur raises money in order to buy (he assures you) a profitable business, but you don't know what that business is going to be. Don't just walk away from a blind pool. Run.

New issues bubble up on hope and hype. Speculators dream of copping a $10 stock that will be worth $50 within the week. The odds are better than even that an IPO will indeed go up over the first 30 days. But the biggest gains come on offering day, and what's your personal chance of getting your hands on such a hot stock? High if you're a big player, trade through a firm that's part of the underwriting syndicate, and give your broker a lot of business. Otherwise, low. The average Joe and Joan are there to take the mediocrities off the insiders' hands.

Even highfliers may tank within a very few months. Professor Jay Ritter of the University of Florida publishes reams of data on IPOs (http://bear.cba.ufl .edu/ritter). One of my favorite tables on his site shows average IPO prices on the day the stock comes out (big jump, for the insiders who hold it) compared with the three-year return for investors who buy and hold (market-adjusted losses, with especially big losses for the smaller issues). Other tables show that IPOs with positive returns may be underperforming the market in general.

It's fun to believe the new-issue hype, which is often stirred by the underwriters' own analysts. In-house analysts virtually have to recommend the stock, even if, privately, they think it's a dog. But longer-range studies consistently show that new issues do worse, on average, than Standard & Poor's 500-stock average. And that doesn't even count the trash issues offered at less than $5 a share.

So . . . don't buy IPOs. If one interests you, get the prospectus and watch the stock. If the company is real, with audited earnings increases, a reasonable P/E ratio, and genuine prospects, buy it later. You'll probably get it at less than the offering price. If it doesn't drop, forget it. Another stock will come along.

At the very least, don't buy until the *lockup period* has expired. That's the length of time the insiders have to hold the stock before they can sell—typically, 180 days. The underwriter will try to support the stock price during that period.

After that, the stock will be left to itself and often drops. Hot companies that go public at superhigh price-earnings ratios (100 times earnings isn't unusual) are unrealized losses just waiting to happen.

The *prospectus*—the legal document that accompanies the new issue of any stock, bond, or mutual fund—is chock-full of pertinent information and warnings about the company and is, unfortunately, the least read publication in America. Even *Undertaker's Weekly* has more fans.

Secondaries

You can also buy newly issued stocks from companies that are already public. For well-established companies, they're called *secondary offerings*. For new companies that went public a year or more ago, they're called *follow-ons*. Analyze them the way you'd look at ongoing companies, with particular reference to how they intend to use the new money they're raising. It should be used for expansion, not for paying off bank debt or enriching the founders by buying more of their shares.

Preferred Stocks: Old Dogs Don't Learn New Tricks

Preferred stocks sound tempting. They pay a fixed, high dividend, sometimes more than the same company's bonds. If common-stock prices rise, the preferreds will rise a little too. So you get a good income plus some hope of capital growth.

But a lot more is wrong with preferreds than right:

1. If you're interested in growth, you'll get far, far more of it from the common stock. The common may also pay dividends, and, unlike the preferred's, the common's dividend can rise.

2. If you're interested in income, bonds are safer. Preferreds have excellent payment records, but in a pinch the company could cancel your dividends for a while. With cumulative preferreds, unpaid dividends must be made up; with noncumulative preferreds, they don't.

3. If you're interested in preserving your principal, bonds are safer too. Preferreds fluctuate more in price and they don't "mature," so there's never a point when you can expect your capital back. Or they mature in 49 years, with no guarantee of principal if you sell prematurely.

4. There aren't a lot of high-quality preferreds. Most of them are from lower-quality companies. Big banks and big brokerage firms issue a lot of preferreds. Lehman Brothers preferreds, where are you now?

5. The moment a preferred succeeds—when prices are up and you're

reveling in your high dividend payments—the corporation may call in the shares. Not only will you lose the stock, but the call price may be at something less than market price.

6. When you sell, you may have to take a discount on the price. There's not a big market for preferreds.

There are angles to preferreds. Some have adjustable dividend payments that fluctuate with interest rates. Participating preferreds earn a portion of the company's profits in addition to the dividend. These gimmicks may or may not be to your advantage. You need a broker whose research department really understands preferreds.

Dividends on preferred stocks may be taxed at your ordinary income rate, not at the low rate available to dividends on common stock. For this reason, they're bought by conservative investors for tax-deferred retirement accounts or by retirees with low taxable incomes, looking for high yields. If you're interested, buy only companies with high-rated bonds (AA or better), so you'll have some assurance that the dividend will be paid. If the company fails, you stand ahead of common shareholders at the payment window, but that's no guarantee.

Convertible Preferreds: A Gambler's Game

These preferreds can be converted into common stock at a specified, higher price. While you hold them, you earn a fixed dividend—less than you'd get from bonds or regular preferreds but more than the common pays. If the stock price rises above the conversion price, you get an attractive capital gain. If the price of the common falls, however, your convertible is "hung." You can wait it out, but the company may call in your shares. You might be forced to convert at a loss. If what you want is a safe, high income, why would you run this risk? These stocks are for fun, not for real.

Selling Short: For Sophisticates Only

To *short* a stock is to make a bet that the price will fall.

Here's the Ideal Transaction

1. You borrow 100 shares of stock and sell them at today's price—say, $50. As collateral, you put up 50 to 100 percent of the stock's current market value, typically using your securities account plus a loan from your broker.

2. Over the following four weeks, the stock price plunges to $10.

3. At that point, you "cover" your short by buying 100 shares at $10 and returning them to your broker. Your gross profit is $40 a share.

4. From that you subtract your buying and selling commissions; any dividends paid by the stock during the time that you held it, which you owe to the owner; and the interest you owe on any money borrowed from the broker (known as a *margin loan*).

Here's What Can Go Wrong

1. The stock price can rise instead of fall. If you have to buy back the shares at $60, you'll lose $10 a share, plus commissions, plus interest on the margin loan. The higher the stock rises, the more money you lose.

2. If you put up only part of the price and the stock goes up instead of down, you might be asked for more collateral. That's known as a *margin call.* If you don't comply, part or all of your stock position will be sold, leaving you liable for any losses, plus commissions and loan interest. Note, too, that no short sale pays dividends.

The average investor can't stand the tension of having a short sale run the wrong way. It's different from owning a stock outright. When your own stock falls, you can comfort yourself with the thought that it will rise again. But when a stock rises, you can't feel sure that it will fall. You need a lot of experience (plus a fundamentally dark view of life) to get a kick out of a short sell.

The riskiest shorts are popular companies that are overpriced. Happy campers may drive those prices higher still. The safest shorts are stocks that already appear to be moving down.

To protect yourself, set a stop-loss limit. Tell your broker to close out your position if the stock rises by a certain amount, say 10 percent.

Remember: short sellers potentially have more to lose than other investors. If you buy a $10 company that goes bankrupt, you cannot be out any more than 100 percent of your investment, or $10. But say that you short a $10 stock and the price goes to $30 before you cover. You've lost $20, which is 200 percent of your investment.

A New (Scary, Bad) Way of Selling Short

You can buy an *inverse* exchange-traded fund. Whichever way the market moves each day, the ETF moves in the opposite direction. Some of these funds are designed to gain two or three times the market's daily loss. Unfortunately, they don't work the way you think they do. Effectively, they close out their positions each day, which locks in not only daily losses (good), but also daily gains (bad). When stocks fell 50 percent in 2008, you might have expected a gain of at least

50 percent from an inverse ETF. In fact, several of them gained only 4 percent. That's better than a loss, but not what you signed up for. These funds can be poison if they move against you. Forget 'em.

Free Money: Use It or Lose It

Some securities are like lottery tickets. For some special reason, your number comes up and you get a payoff you didn't expect. You get it, that is, if you're truly watching your investment (or your broker is)—for example, by reading your company's Web site regularly. If you miss an important announcement, you may lose money that should have been yours. For example:

Warrants

When you buy certain securities, such as new issues or the preferred stocks or bonds of speculative companies, they might come with *warrants*. They're a sweetener, to get you to buy an issue that otherwise looks like a dog. (It could still be a dog, but the warrants make it look like a more valuable dog.) Warrants give you the right to buy a certain number of the company's common shares at a specified, higher price.

Say, for example, you buy the low-rated bonds of Mongrel Inc. They come with a warrant giving you the right to buy shares in Mongrel at $5 anytime over the next five years. The current market price is $4. Those warrants are worth money. If the underlying stock moves up, they're worth more money. If the stock price exceeds $5, your warrants are said to be "in the money."

You can sell the warrants through a stockbroker if you don't want to use them to buy the stock, but they generally have an expiration date. If you do nothing, warrants eventually become worthless. And that's what happens when people don't pay attention. They forget about their warrants and let them expire, unsold and unused.

Warning: a predatory company might cut the ground from under its warrant holders. Just when the stock is moving up nicely and you're expecting jackpot gains, the company will call in the warrants at, say, 5 cents each. You have 30 days either to sell the warrants at the current, higher price or to exercise them and buy the stock. You won't lose money on the transaction, but you'll lose the future gains that, as a warrant holder, you expected and deserved.

If you don't hear about the redemption (by following your company's Web site or getting a call from your stockbroker), you'll wind up with warrants worth only a nickel apiece. It's a dirty trick. Those warrants were your reward for taking extra risk. The company breaks faith with you by taking them away. Moral:

don't bother buying new issues with warrants. The company may not allow you to reap the gains you gambled for.

Note to speculators: suppose that you own no warrants. You can still gamble on them by buying them through a broker. If the stock moves up smartly, you'll earn a higher percentage profit from the warrants than from the stock. If you're wrong, you'll also swallow a larger loss. If you buy and the company suddenly decides to redeem, you could lose money on the transaction, even if you were smart enough to buy a warrant that should have been worth a lot.

Spin-offs

A company might designate a subsidiary as an independent corporation. All current shareholders automatically get a piece. Your broker will be notified and the firm will report it on your monthly statement. It will also be fully discussed on your company's Web site. Read everything, to find out why the company was spun off. Maybe the business is a weak sister. Or maybe your company is changing its focus and getting rid of extraneous businesses even though they're sound. If you don't want to own the new company, it's smart to sell right away. If you think that the business is sound, it's a good time to buy.

Convertibles

A company in trouble may give its current bondholders some convertible preferreds to encourage them to hang on. The converts can be turned in for common stock at a fixed, higher price. If the company does well, so do you. But some investors never realize that they have this right, because they don't pay attention to their accounts. They could lose that extra capital gain.

Calls

A company calls a preferred stock or bond by ordering investors to turn it in for cash. If you don't get the word, you will lose money. You'll discover the call eventually because you'll stop getting dividends or interest. When you contact the company, you'll receive the securities' call value but lose the money you could have earned by turning in the securities earlier and reinvesting the proceeds. Some brokerage firms will turn in their customers' stock automatically.

You might lose even more if you ignore a call on convertible bonds or convertible preferred stocks. The call value may be considerably lower than the value of the underlying common stock. If you don't convert into the common stock by the call date or sell your security to someone else, all that extra value will go down the drain.

Class Actions

Sometimes the price of a stock suddenly collapses, and it turns out that management has been fudging. Maybe the financial statements mixed some fiction with the facts. That lapse will almost certainly trigger a class-action lawsuit on behalf of everyone who owned shares at the time. You'll get a notice about the lawsuit. Keep it. You'll get another notice if there's a settlement or judgment in the stockholders' favor. To collect your money, you'll have to make a phone call, fill in a form, and—sometimes—follow up to be sure that you get the check. People who don't open their brokerage house mail or can't be bothered filling out forms are giving up found money.

Stock Rights

When a company sells new shares, it might give first dibs—or rights—to its current stockholders. As an incentive to get you to buy, you'll be offered a discount on the price.

Say, for example, that your stock sells at $10 and you're offered the right to buy more at $9. If you exercise that right, you'll save $1 per share—the difference between your discounted buying price and the market price. If you don't want to buy any more stock, you can sell that right—probably for slightly less than $1, after commissions.

Either way, you have to act within a specified number of weeks, or your rights will expire. If your broker doesn't call you or you throw out your brokerage house mail without reading it, your rights will vanish into a landfill. You may actually lose money because, once the period for exercising the right expires, the company's share price may fall by the value of the rights that were issued. You have to exercise (or sell) your rights just to stay even.

Children can do their elderly parents a great kindness by keeping track of all these matters. Arrange for all mail relating to their brokerage accounts to come to you. A forgetful investor can easily lose substantial sums.

Your brokerage firm might handle your securities in your best interest—for example, by selling rights or warrants that would otherwise expire worthless— even if you give no instructions to do so. The profits go into your account. However, you cannot count on your broker's picking up every single offer. You have to pay attention too. Shareholders who register their stock under the Direct Registration System (page 802) will receive mail directly from the company, so they'll know that something is happening even if their broker drops the ball.

Mergers and Buyouts

Every year thousands of shareholders lose money because they don't respond to a tender offer for their stock. You can retrieve this money after the fact but will lose all the dividends and appreciation you could have earned in the meantime.

A *merger* is the voluntary combination of two companies under a new corporate name. Usually the shareholders of both companies turn in their old shares for those of the new entity.

A *takeover* is the friendly purchase of one company by another. The dominant company offers cash and/or securities to the shareholders of the company it buys.

A *hostile takeover* is an offer from a group that your company's management objects to. To avoid it, the company might restructure, sometimes offering you a big dividend. Or it might ask a more acceptable partner—a "white knight"—to bid for the company shares.

In a *leveraged buyout,* a management team or private equity firm makes an offer to buy most or all of the company's common shares. The buyers do it on borrowed money, or leverage. The company becomes privately owned, without a public market for its shares.

Tender Offers

These come from anyone who wants to buy some or all of your shares, usually at a higher price than you could get in the open market. You are being asked to *tender* (surrender) your shares.

Tender offers drive up the price of your shares, although not necessarily quite as high as the tender price. For example, a tender at $33.50 for a share that's selling for $25 might push the market price up to $32. The discount allows for the risk that the deal might fall through. The greater the risk, the larger the discount.

In some cases, however, the share price might jump higher than the offer—say, to $35. That shows that the pros expect a second bidder with a higher offer.

You have three ways of responding to a tender offer:

1. Sell your shares in the open market for a quick and easy profit. This is the surest way of making money. You'll get your profit even if, in the end, the tender fails.

2. If it's a hostile takeover, consider holding on to your shares for a while. You're betting that more offers will be made and the stock price will go even higher. Then you can sell. This, of course, is a gamble that you might lose.

3. Tender to the would-be buyer. The offer will probably be higher than the stock price. In a partial tender, where the buyer wants, say, only 50 percent of the shares, you'll have to respond within 10 days to ensure that at least some of your shares will be taken.

There are arguments against tendering. First, if the deal fails, you'll get your stock back and will have lost all the gains you could have made by selling your shares in the open market. Second, the value of the offer may not be firm. It might be announced at, say, $33.50 per share. But if that price includes preferred stock and bonds with payment gimmicks, the package may be cheaper than the bidder claims. Again, a fast sale might be a better option. But don't hang on to the shares very long. Your shares will become harder to sell as the bulk of the shares are tendered and the market for the remaining shares shrinks to the vanishing point.

After a merger or takeover, the stock price of the surviving company usually goes nowhere for a while or falls. So you might want to sell any shares you own and look around for a better stock. This is particularly true if the buying group loaded up your company with debt.

What If You Fail to Sell or Tender Your Shares? This can happen if: you don't read the financial news; you (or your elderly parent) have forgotten that you own the shares; your broker, who is holding the shares, neglected to inform you; or you've been asleep for 20 years.

In a partial tender, your untendered shares still have value in the open market. But if the buyout or takeover was for all the shares, there will no longer be a public market for the shares you kept.

The ultimate value of those untendered shares will depend on the deal. Companies that make all-cash offers will set aside that money for you. It won't earn any interest, so its value will be demolished by inflation. But it's there, somewhere, if you suddenly wake up and claim it.

You may be luckier if the tender offer included securities. Those abandoned securities will stay in your name, gaining or losing value as the market changes. Dividends will accrue, although they won't earn interest. If you call up the company in a couple of years and ask about your shares, you may find them worth a handsome sum.

But your company isn't a permanent lost-property office. After 3 to 7 years (longer, in some states), the money and securities due on untendered shares are turned over to the state as abandoned or unclaimed property. You can get them back, but your securities will probably have been sold, and from that point on you'll have earned no interest on the money.

When a brokerage firm holds your stocks, you may or may not be informed of tenders or impending expirations or redemption dates. A good firm will do so, but it's not required. Ask about this when you open an account.

If you're not prepared to follow your investments closely enough to keep track of such things as spin-offs, warrants, and tender offers, sell your shares and buy mutual funds.

What If Your Company Has a Near-Death Experience and Is Put on Government Life Support?

Sell immediately, if not sooner. Sell the moment the stock comes under suspicion. Don't wait around to see if the rumors are true. Don't plan on calling your broker in a couple of days. The likes of you and me can't afford to play with the big boys. They'll clean us out and move on to the next demolition. Someday that miserable stock will be a buy again, but you don't know when. Rescue what you can.

Buying on Margin

You buy securities *on margin* when you borrow some of the money from your stockbroker. Why do it? Because a lucky margin buyer will make a bigger profit than someone who buys the same stock for cash.

Suppose that you're interested in a $50 stock. For $5,000 cash, you'll get 100 shares. If you borrow another $5,000 from your broker, you'll get 200 shares.

If that stock rises $5 in price, the cash buyer earns $500—a 10 percent return on his investment. But the margin buyer earns $1,000—a 20 percent return on his own $5,000. He also earns double the dividends because he owns double the number of shares.

That's called *leverage*—increasing your profit by buying an asset with borrowed money. For stocks listed on the leading exchanges and certain major over-the-counter stocks, you can borrow up to 50 percent of the cost, depending on the broker. Smaller loans, or none at all, may be allowed against other OTC stocks.

Unfortunately, a successful margin investor does not get to take all the profits home. Besides sales commissions, you have to repay the loan plus interest.

Brokers charge around 1.5 to 2.5 percentage points over the *broker call rate,* which is the interest the broker pays on money borrowed from the bank. The interest expense compounds in your brokerage account, and you generally pay it when the securities are sold. (That amount is deductible against investment income earned from your various securities.)

On the downside, margin loans can kill you. If the share price drops by $5, the cash investor loses 10 percent, while the margin investor loses 20 percent. If the price drops by $12 a share, the cash investor is merely holding on to a loser. The margin buyer may have to put up more money or be partly sold out.

For the details on margin loans, see page 310. I want to restate only two points here:

1. Interest charges and sales commissions can easily eat up the profits on securities held on margin for many months Margin buyers make money only on securities whose price moves up fast.

2. If your stock drops too far in price, the broker will ask for more collateral in the form of cash or securities. That's what's known as a *margin call.* If you don't have the money, some of your securities will be sold to cover the debt. You usually get a margin call if the value of your interest in all the securities in your account, net of the debt, shrinks to 30 or 25 percent of market value. To make margin calls less likely, borrow less than the maximum 50 percent.

Reading an Annual Report

Where do you start? Not at the front. At the back, just ahead of the financial tables.

Read the report of the certified public accountant (CPA). This third-party auditor will tell you right off the bat if the report fairly represents the company's financial condition, according to "generally accepted accounting principles."

CPAs have been known to let some real howlers get by—in frauds such as the Enron and WorldCom failures, the abysmal disclosures by banks and other financial institutions discovered after the 2008 market crash, and, of course, the partnerships that invested with Bernie Madoff. But the auditors are the only numbers police that an investor has, so you might as well see what they have to say. If the CPA qualifies his or her opinion in any way or calls the report clean only if you take the company's word about a particular piece of business (which the CPA clearly didn't want to do), watch out. Doubts like these are usually settled behind closed doors, before the annual report is published. When they make it into print, it suggests that the company is a riskier investment than you might want.

Now go to the front, to the letter from the chairman. Usually addressed "to our stockholders," it reflects both the character and the well-being of the company. Is it stuffy or friendly? Straightforward or obfuscating? Proud or defensive? This letter should tell you how the business fared this year—its failures as well as its successes. Most important, it should tell you why. Candor builds confidence. Beware of sentences that start with phrases such as "Except for" and "Despite the." They're clues to problems. Think about selling any stock whose chairman barely mentions that earnings fell.

On the positive side, the chairman's letter should give you some insight into the company's future and its stance on the economic and political trends that affect its business. You want a savvy letter, not a lot of boring double-talk.

While you're still in the front of the report, look for what's new in each line of business. Is management getting the company in good shape to weather the tough and competitive years ahead?

Next go to the footnotes of the financial reports. These are worth a try even if you're not a numbers person, because they explain so much. A number that looks bad in the report itself may actually be good because of some special circumstance. A number that looks good may actually be bad.

For example, are earnings down? That's usually bad, but if it's only because of a change in accounting methods, that may be good; the company owes less tax and has more money in its pocket. Are earnings up? That's usually good, but maybe it's bad; there may have been a special windfall—such as the sale of a business—that won't happen again next year. Does the company own shares of another company? The balance sheet may list those shares at original cost, while the footnote says that they're worth twenty times that amount. Does the company have a huge deferred tax or pension liability? That means that the earnings aren't on as sound a footing as you might have thought. You need the footnotes to tell you whether the numbers in the main report present a fair picture of the company's finances.

If you're going to be a real stock picker, you can't avoid being a numbers person for very long. The key to a company's performance lies in its financial data, not in its press releases.

Start with the *balance sheet*. It's a snapshot of where the company stands at a single point in time. On the left are *assets,* everything the company owns. Things that can quickly be turned into cash are *current assets*. On the right are *liabilities,* everything the company owes. *Current liabilities* are the debts due in one year, which are paid out of current assets.

The right-hand side of the balance sheet also shows you the *shareholders' equity.* That's the difference between total assets and total liabilities. It is the presumed dollar value of what stockholders own. You want it to grow from year to year.

The amount by which current assets exceeds current liabilities is the *working capital.* You want to see a nice cushion here. It says that a company can pay its bills. If current assets are smaller than current liabilities, the company is running into trouble. A declining amount of working capital, over time, is also a red flag. Some analysts apply rules of thumb to the ratio between current assets and current liabilities—for example, that assets should be twice liabilities. That's known as a *current ratio.*

But holding that much working capital may not be a terrific idea. Why leave money sitting around that could be earning 20 or 30 percent if invested in the business? I raise this point to show you that "traditional" ratios aren't gospel. On the other hand, the stocks of companies with small amounts of working capital may be risky. What will management do if business contracts? It needs a clear strategy for paying its bills.

One important number to crunch is the company's *debt-to-equity ratio,* including its preferred stocks. You get it by dividing long-term liabilities by stockholders' equity.

A high ratio means that the company borrows a lot of money to spark its growth. That's okay if the company is in a strong growth industry such as high tech or a stable industry with reasonably predictable earnings—enough to cover debt service. One example of the latter would be a regulated utility. But high debt-to-equity ratios can bury a company that is vulnerable to cycles of boom and bust, such as brokerage firms, retailers, and steel companies. The boom years are fine. It's the bust years that kill you.

The second basic source of numbers is the *income statement,* or *statement of profit and loss.* It shows how much money the company made or lost over the year. You want the *operating income*—the income from the ongoing business—to be going up. Operating income, or operating profit, is the earnings before deducting for interest payments and taxes.

Most investors look first at the bottom-line number: *net earnings per share.* But it can fool you. The company's management might have boosted earnings by selling off a plant, changing the depreciation rules, or cutting the budget for research and advertising. (See the report's footnotes!) So don't get smug about net earnings until you've found out how they happened. This much-watched figure is often manipulated to make companies look better or worse than they really are.

The five-year *summary of operations* gives you more perspective. Look for

894 Making the Most of Your Money *Now*

net sales or *operating revenues.* This is the primary source of money received by the company.

Ask yourself: Are net sales or operating revenues going up at a faster rate from year to year? If not, is the company reducing the rate of rise in its costs? When costs rise faster than sales, profits get mushy. Also ask: Are sales going up faster than inflation? If not, the company's real unit sales are falling behind. And ask again: Have sales gone down because the company is selling off a losing business? If so, profits may be soaring—which is great! And one time more: What's happening to operating income (income from the business, excluding unusual gains or losses)? Is it rising faster than operating costs? If so, *net profit margins* are widening—that's usually investor heaven. Falling profit margins are not. Some companies help with this analysis by breaking out net profit margins for you.

You compute the net profit margin (after expenses) by dividing it by net revenues. It's an indication of how good the company is at cost control. The higher the net profit margin, the greater the percentage of sales that's being taken down to the bottom line.

As a savvy investor, however, you have to be sensitive to the many other variables that affect profit margins. Say, for example, that margins are rising because the company raised prices. "Great," you say, and hold on to the stock. Then the stock price falls, and you wonder why. It turns out that your company's competitors held prices level. So your own company's sales and profits fell. Professional investors anticipated that the price increase wouldn't take and promptly drove the stock price down. (I never promised you that analyzing a company was going to be easy.)

One way of following dividends is to divide them by the company's total earnings. What percentage is being paid out to shareholders? You should get a fairly stable percentage payout over the business cycle, with dividends rising as earnings improve.

That brings up the most important thing of all. One annual report, one chairman's letter, one ratio won't tell you much. You have to compare. Is the company's debt-to-equity ratio better or worse than it used to be? Better or worse than industry norms or your company's major competitors? Better or worse at this point in the economic cycle than it was last time? Are liabilities growing or shrinking? How do this year's footnotes and audit letter compare with last year's on the same topics? In company watching, comparisons are all. They tell you if management is staying on top of things.

Financial analysts work out many other ratios to tell them how the company is doing. You can learn more from specialized books on the subject. The Web is a font of information about corporations. You can check the financial reports that the company files with the Securities and Exchange Commission on the SEC's EDGAR (Electronic Data Gathering, Analysis, and Retrieval) database (www .sec.gov.edgar.shtml).

One thing you will never learn from an annual report is how much to pay for a company's stock. The company may be running well—but if investors expected it to be running better, the stock price might fall. The company might be slumping badly—but if investors see better days ahead, the stock price could rise.

You study the report to learn how well the company is handling its problems and opportunities and whether it appears to know the difference. You study the market to get a feel for its price.

When to Sell a Stock

You can hold a broad-based index mutual fund forever. You can also find good dividend-paying blue chips that get bluer every year. But many stocks should be sold from time to time as their potential peters out. Sometimes a whole industry gets into trouble because of competition or unfavorable market trends. Sometimes an individual company comes under pressure because of a crippling legal liability or a misjudged merger. Sometimes a stock just dies in the water while other industries pass it by.

In the Long Run, It Is More Important to Avoid Bad or Tuckered-Out Stocks than to Pick Good Ones!

Since the bias of the stock market is up, eliminating losers will, of itself, improve your performance.

The most amateurish of all mistakes is to hold on to a stinker because (you think) you couldn't have guessed so horribly wrong. Oh yes, you could. But there's nothing wrong with making mistakes. That happens all the time in professional investing. The error lies in not correcting your mistake by selling the stock while your loss is still small. Small losses can be canceled by small gains; big losses drag down your performance for years (page 871).

Consider Selling When . . .

- *There's no further reason to hold the company.* Here's where your buying thesis comes in. Think back to your original expectations for the company. Maybe they weren't fulfilled. Or maybe they were, but no exciting new developments are in sight. The decision to hold a stock is virtually the same as a decision to buy. Does this company look better to you than other companies you might own?

- *Your stock did just fine for two or three years, but its gains are now slowing.* It's not doing as well as other stocks you own or other stocks in the same industry.
- *Your company's industry will be hurt by a fundamental economic change.* For example, financial companies will come under greater regulation as a result of the 2008 financial collapse. They won't be able to gamble with so much borrowed money, which will put a lid on their profits. Any such companies will become a buy again when conditions change or when they adjust their business to the new realities.
- *The financial reports aren't looking quite so good.* This quarter's earnings are lower than last year's or lower than expected for two quarters running. Profit margins have stopped widening and started to narrow. One piece of bad news is usually followed by more bad news.
- *The stock price is down by 10 to 15 percent.*
- *In the annual letter from your company's chairman, he or she makes excuses for failing to reach last year's goals,* and you see no plan for pulling out of the slump.
- *Something odd is happening to the price.* Perhaps it jumped 20 percent soon after you bought it, with no apparent explanation—in which case, you might want to take your lucky profits and run. Or perhaps the price suddenly dropped by 8 percent. Maybe someone knows something you don't.
- *Something has happened to call the integrity of management into question.* If one little lie becomes public, you can be sure that the earnings were erected on lots of other lies.
- *You think that prices are too high for stocks in general (see market timing, page 696), and the stock isn't something that you want to hold forever.* Furthermore, your stock's price-earnings ratio has ballooned to a much higher level than normal.

Please note that I said "consider" selling. Some of these stocks may still be good long-term holds. So do your selling slowly, to see what happens—dumping 100 shares this week, 100 shares next week, taking some profits, and watching the price. You might decide to sell half and hold the rest.

Don't Sell a Stock Just Because It Has Risen a Few Points and You Don't Want to Lose the Profit

Maybe it will keep on going up. "Let your profits run," the old saw says. Sell it because you have a reason to sell.

Conversely, don't panic if the stock drops 5 points. That might be temporary. Consider selling if it drops by 10 to 15 percent (or if you have some other good reason to dump it). Short of that, sit back and wait. Or buy more. If you believe in the company, this is your chance to get more shares at a better price.

One Final Point

Smart shoppers will drive 50 miles to a factory outlet to buy a new coat at 40 percent off. But when stocks go on sale at a big discount because the stock market has gone down, many shoppers shy away. They feel safer buying stocks when they're expensive rather than when they're cheap. And then they wonder why they don't make any money.

Buying stocks cheaply is the best way of capturing the superior performance that the market delivers over time. So look at bear markets as if they were half-price sales and buy.

25

How to Use Bonds

Income Investing—The Right Way and the Wrong Way

**Seeking future security, people drop stocks and buy bonds.
Out of the frying pan, into the fire.**

Properly used, bonds are safe and solid investments. They pay regular income and protect wealth. But they're not without risk. Investors relying only on bonds for income may find themselves eaten up by inflation and taxes. Investors seeking safety may suffer capital losses. Bonds are essential to your investment plan, but you have to know how to play them right.

A Bond Is . . .

. . . a loan. You lend money to a government or corporation and earn interest on the funds. After a certain period of time, the borrower pays the money back. When you "buy" a bond (through a discount broker or full-service stockbroker), you are accepting an IOU. Some bonds are secured by company assets, giving you a claim on those assets if the company fails. Other bonds are unsecured. One class of bonds, called *zero-coupon,* pays no current interest; instead your interest builds up inside the bond and is paid at maturity.

Bonds come in several types: *Treasuries,* issued by the U.S. government; *governments,* issued by various U.S. government agencies such as Ginnie Mae (page 931); *corporates,* issued by corporations; *tax-exempt municipals,* issued by cities, states, and other municipal authorities; *international government or corporate bonds;* and *asset-backed securities,* issued to help finance auto, credit card, mortgage, and other loans. The complex products that got into trouble during the 2007–2009 credit crunch—things like *collateralized mortgage obligations* (CMOs, page 969)—are also asset-backed securities. Don't mess with them.

A Bond Is Not . . .

. . . a higher-rate certificate of deposit. Bond investors shoulder some risk. Usually your principal and interest are paid on time, but they might not be if the issuer goes bad. Furthermore, the bond's underlying value goes up and down as market conditions change. If you sell a bond before maturity, you might get less (or more) than you paid. A CD's value, by contrast, always remains the same.

A Bond Mutual Fund Is Not . . .

. . . like a bond. You can hold a bond until maturity or until it's redeemed by the company and get all your money back. But there's no special date when a mutual fund will return your original investment. The market value of the fund changes every day—sometimes rising, sometimes falling. How much you get when you sell your shares depends on market conditions at the time.

COBRAs Are Not Traditional Bonds

Many companies, including financial companies such as banks and brokerage firms, sell COBRAs, or Continuously Offered Bonds for Retail Accounts.* They may have fixed rates or variable rates. They mature in anywhere from 9 months to 30 years. They're packaged for easy sale to retail investors like you, with $1,000 minimums. It's easy to use them for laddered portfolios that pay a steady income stream. Some are noncallable, meaning that the company can't redeem them early if interest rates decline.

These notes, like most corporate bonds, aren't secured by any of the company's assets. If the company enters bankruptcy, your claims are so low on the list that you probably won't be repaid. If you want your money back before the notes mature, you may find them difficult to sell—especially if the company is having any sort of financial trouble. What makes these notes different from bonds is that there's no public trading market. The brokerage firm that sold you the notes maintains a market and probably will buy them back (at some discount from face value), but you can't count on it. One exception: if you die, your survivors can usually (not always) sell the notes back to the brokerage firm at face value. Check this point in the prospectus.

Best advice: if you like the convenience of these notes, stick with top-rated

---

*This is not to be confused with the COBRA health-insurance law.

AAA, AA, or A securities, fixed interest rates, and shorter terms. If only lower-grade notes are on offer, that tells you something. Extra risk.

Why Not Stick with a Bank CD Instead of Buying a Bond?

Why not, indeed? Certificates of deposit are the very best choice for people who want total simplicity, no fees, and guaranteed principal at all times.

But bonds have other advantages. Some are fully or partly tax free, whereas CDs are fully taxable. And they usually yield higher returns than comparable CDs.

What Are Bonds Good For?

Use high-quality bonds to:

1. Preserve your purchasing power. For this you want intermediate-term bonds (maturing in roughly five to seven years), with all the income reinvested. Your money won't grow very much, after taxes and inflation. But you'll hold on to the value of what you have. You could also buy Treasury Inflation-Protected Securities.

2. Reduce the risk of owning stocks. Bond prices tend to rise and fall at different times than stocks, and at different rates of speed. So if you own both stocks and bonds and average their performance together, you have a more stable portfolio than if you owned only one of them. Put another way, bonds secure your financial base so that you can afford to take the risk of stocks.

3. Provide income to live on. Bonds pay interest you can count on. But exactly how to invest for income isn't as clear-cut as you might think (page 920). You might want a mutual fund withdrawal plan (page 1142) instead of straight interest income from bonds.

4. Protect you in an emergency. If you lose your job or face some other financial emergency, you'll need your savings and investments to get you through. If you own only stocks and the stock market is down, you'll be selling at a loss to raise the funds you need. If you own bonds as well as stocks, however, you can sell the bonds instead—probably at no loss or just a little one. You'll be able to leave your stocks alone to recover when the market turns up again.

5. Improve the yield on money you'd otherwise keep in cash. Prudent investors hold cash for unexpected expenses or expenses they know they'll have in the next two or three years. Treasury bills, money market funds, or bank CDs are the safest places for your "prudence fund." But you can pick up a half point or even a full point in yield by switching to short-term (two-year) bond funds. When stocks tumble, short-term bond prices may also decline. But the drop may be small, provided that the fund is managed conservatively. If you have no emergency need for cash, you can hold your short-term bond fund until it recovers and earn more than if you had stuck with money market funds. If an emergency does overtake you at a time when bond prices are down, selling your short-term fund should result in only a modest loss.

For bonds and bond funds, I emphasize *conservative*—meaning yields in line with AAA to A securities. Funds with higher yields can be as risky as stocks.

Questions to Ask About Bond Mutual Funds

Higher-risk bonds come from companies or municipalities with financial troubles (or potential troubles). Troubled companies may default. Troubled municipalities will probably pay, but their credit rating and market price will fall. Bonds with longer terms are also higher risk, even if their credit quality is high. If you're looking for safety here are five questions to ask about any bond fund you buy:

What's the credit quality? You're shopping in the AAA to A range (page 918), not BBB or below. Ask the fund what its average credit quality is. No-load funds give their rating online. The lower the credit quality, the riskier the fund.

What's it investing in? Bond funds that look sedate on the outside might actually be managed by gunslingers. Those are the funds that dropped 10 percent or more in the crash of 2008. Some of them invested heavily in lower-rated issues (BBB-minus and below) or unrated bonds. That's something you can check in the prospectus or on the fund's online snapshot before you buy. What's harder to see are the exotic strategies that a manager might use—high leverage (borrowed money) and complicated derivatives that turn an apparently A-rated fund into a time bomb. These strategies are also disclosed in the prospectus but the average investor will have a hard time grasping what they mean. My advice: don't try, just run away. The risks aren't worth the slightly higher yields that these funds might pay.

What's the duration? For a full explanation of duration, see page 911. Short durations shield you from too much risk; long durations expose you to larger price swings and explain the sudden losses that can occur when interest rates go up. An optimal duration is three to four years. At that point on the spectrum, you've increased your yield without adding too much extra risk. A speculative duration is six years or longer. No-load bond funds show their durations in the snapshots they provide on their Web sites.

What's the volatility? This one is trickier. A bond fund may appear to have a short duration, but if interest rates drop, the duration may lengthen. The fund's price may plunge further than you believed it could. That's because the fund buys risky securities—the market's toxic waste. You can tell that a fund is risky if it yields markedly more than its peers. (Funds that buy mortgage-backed securities such as Ginnie Maes also have changing durations, not because they're especially risky but because that's the way those investments work. You simply have to be prepared for changes in price.)

What's the currency? Dollar-denominated bonds reflect only credit quality and interest rates. Foreign-currency bonds also reflect the changing value of the dollar in the world. They're a bet on currency changes, not a pure interest rate decision (page 976).

Try to evaluate all five risks. Alternatively, stick with classic, well-diversified bond mutual funds from the major no-load families, which don't take hidden risks and behave as expected in the market.

If You Want to Gamble on Riskier Bonds

Flip the advice in the previous paragraphs. Look at funds that buy bonds of lower credit quality, longer durations, or denominated in other currencies. You take on more risk—that is, more chance of higher returns than you'd get from more conservative bonds—but also the considerable chance of getting poor returns. High-yield bonds aren't for the "safe" part of your portfolio. They're always better bought in mutual funds—if, indeed, you want them at all (page 936).

Bonds Versus Bond Mutual Funds

Whether to buy a bond or a bond fund is often a tough call. Whereas stock investors clearly belong in mutual funds, many bond investors may be better off owning bonds individually. Here are the issues. You decide.

The Case for Buying Individual Bonds

1. You want a guarantee that you'll get your principal back plus a fixed investment return. You'll get it if you buy high-quality bonds and hold them to maturity. The holding period is critical. If you have to sell before maturity, you'll take a discount on the price—and the smaller your investment, the larger the discount. Best advice: buy Treasuries, or buy corporates or municipals rated A and up. Stick to 5- to 10-year terms, no longer. You'll get all your money back.

To test whether you're sure you can hold bonds to maturity, ask yourself this: Could I afford to keep them if I lost my job? Even if the value of all my other investments dropped? If the answer is yes, you're okay with individual, high-quality bonds. If the answer is no, go to mutual funds.

Mutual funds don't offer you a maturity date, so you aren't guaranteed a fixed return. You can't even be sure that, on the day you sell, you'll get all your principal back. You probably will—especially if you hold the fund for several years. Still, your true yield depends on the fund's market value at the time.

2. You want to minimize costs. Buy newly issued bonds. You'll get the same price that the big institutions pay, and the issuer swallows the sales commission. At maturity or when the bond is called (page 911), you can redeem it through the issuer's paying agent at no fee.

With mutual funds, on the other hand, you pay annual fees, the amount depending on the fund you choose. If you buy from a broker, you'll also pay sales commissions. These costs reduce your investment returns.

Warning: your costs go up if you buy older bonds out of a stockbroker's inventory. The broker will be eager to sell them because they carry lucrative price markups—up to 5 percent and sometimes more. Discount brokers' prices are expensive too. Mutual funds get much better prices on older bonds than you ever will. Note that if you work with a fee-only investment adviser (page 1175), he or she may buy you older bonds at wholesale prices. That works.

3. You don't need to diversify. You can't afford a lot of diversification when you buy individual bonds. That doesn't matter if you invest in Treasury securities. You should also be okay with municipals and corporates rated A or better that mature within 10 years or less—assuming that you can hold them for their full term.

The minimum investment on individual bonds is generally $5,000 for corporates and municipals and $100 on Treasury notes and bonds (for the latest on Treasuries, check Treasury Direct at www.treasurydirect.gov).

In *conclusion*, buy individual bonds if: (1) You'll buy only new issues; (2) you'll buy Treasuries or other top-quality bonds, so default won't be a worry; (3) you'll hold the bonds until maturity.

The Case for Buying Bond Mutual Funds

1. They're convenient. A professional manages your money and can buy bonds at wholesale prices. You don't have to think about which bonds to buy and whether you're getting a good price.

2. Your dividends can be reinvested automatically, earning the same yield that the bond fund pays. With most individual bonds, by contrast, you have to put your dividends into lower-yielding bank accounts or money market funds—that is, if your objective is to keep them safe. (The only individual bonds that let you reinvest at the same rate are zero-coupons; page 946.) Reinvestment options aren't material, however, if you plan to live on the income from your bonds.

3. You want to be diversified. Bond funds spread your money over many different issuers. This is critical to investors attracted by the higher yields on medium- to lower-grade bonds. Some of the lower-grade bonds may default. To minimize that potential loss, you need to own a piece of many different issues.

4. You can invest in corporates and municipals with small amounts of money. The initial purchase may be $1,000 to $3,000, after which you can make small, regular contributions. Even smaller contributions are accepted in an Individual Retirement Account or 401(k). But mutual funds aren't only for small investors. Individuals with large amounts of money buy them too.

5. You think that you probably could hold a 5- or 10-year bond to maturity, but aren't sure. Funds are for people who want access to their money at any time, without running the risk of having to sell at a discount.

6. You want to speculate on a decline in interest rates. When interest rates fall, bond values rise, and you could sell your fund shares for a capital gain. The value of individual bonds would increase too, but you wouldn't get as good a price if you tried to sell. Speculators should buy only no-loads. Gains melt away when you have to pay front-end or back-end sales commissions.

In conclusion, buy bond funds if: (1) You want to be well diversified—especially important when buying lower-quality bonds; (2) you have only a modest amount of money and want to earn more than Treasuries pay; (3) you have a lot of money and want it professionally managed at a low fee; (4) you want to make regular, small contributions; (5) you aren't sure of your holding period and want to be able to sell at current market value at any time; (6) you're speculating on a decline in interest rates (good luck!); (7) you want the advantage of automatic dividend reinvestment.

To Me, the Answer to the Question "Bonds or Funds?" Turns on These Two Points: (1) Do you demand, to a high degree of certainty, that by a specific date you will get all your capital back, in addition to all the interest you've earned—and will you hold until that date? If so, buy high-quality bonds, not funds. (2) Do you need a lot of flexibility, to sell anytime you might need the cash? If so, buy bond mutual funds.

If You Decide on Bond Mutual Funds: Bonds of similar types and credit quality behave pretty much alike. They pay similar rates of interest; their prices in the marketplace rise and fall by similar amounts. Bond-fund managers can't outperform their peers by making "smarter" choices within their bond universe. They outperform only by making riskier choices, which means there's also a chance that they'll underperform. Actively managed funds, where the manager chooses which bonds to buy, have a hard time competing with index funds, which passively follow a leading bond index—especially after costs.

Most likely, you buy bond funds not to gamble on higher yields but to reduce your risk. You can get both—better yields *and* lower risk—by choosing high-quality funds with rock-bottom expenses. Two no-load mutual fund companies offer especially low expenses on bond funds of all types: the Vanguard Group (www.vanguard.com) and Fidelity Investments (www.fidelity.com). I suggest that you limit your bond fund shopping to these two firms.

What About Closed-End Bond Funds? These are baskets of bonds, either corporate or municipal, assembled by an investment house and sold to the public. They trade like stocks, on a stock exchange, which means that you buy them through brokerage firms. The portfolio is professionally managed, so your bond investments change with time. You receive monthly or quarterly payouts of the fund's interest earnings; at the end of the year, you receive any realized capital gains. Closed-end funds are best for investors who buy and sell funds, seeking capital gains, not for investors seeking steady income. For more on closed-ends and how they work, see page 784.

What About Exchange-Traded Funds? ETFs are a form of mutual fund that's bought and sold like stocks, on a stock exchange. For an explanation of how they work, see page 859. They're not the best choice for people accumulating assets because you're always paying brokerage commissions. But they have charms for people seeking a combination of income and liquidity. You might use them instead of a bond ladder (page 921). They're also good for people speculating on lower interest rates.

Is There a Case for Buying Bonds in a Unit Trust? I'm skeptical, although unit trusts are widely sold for this purpose. Read more about them starting on page 958.

The Case for Owning No Bonds at All

There's *no* case for excluding fixed-income investments from your portfolio. Treasuries, in particular, are a hedge against the risk of seriously unpleasant times.

The Case for Owning a Higher Percentage of Bonds Than You Probably Do, if You're Young

You never know which type of financial asset will perform the best over the next five years—stocks, bonds, or cash. A particularly good time to buy bonds has been when stock dividends are low. As I write this, in 2009, bonds have out-performed stocks since 2000, a year when dividends were a puny 1.2 percent. Since then, they've doubled to 2.4 percent. Traditionally, a high dividend would be 5 percent.

Can bonds outperform again? Let me read you every investor's Miranda warning: past performance doesn't guarantee future results. But you never know. The easiest way to capture potential market gains in bonds is by owning mutual funds. As a diversified investor, you should own them anyway, because bonds are a safety net. Besides, have I said it before? You never know.

Three Absolutely Wrong Things to Do with Bonds

1. Do not—repeat, *not*—invest most of your retirement plan money in bonds when you're middle-aged. This is a waste of your precious youth. Adjusted for inflation and taxes, bonds give you only modest growth (and some-times negative growth). Middle-aged people need significant holdings of stocks. This is true even though stocks go through patches of poor returns. You never know when they'll turn up again.

2. You should not—repeat, *not*—buy tax-free municipal bonds without checking to see if they'll give you a competitive yield (page 941). They're a best buy when they're yielding about the same as taxable bonds; that's rare, but we saw it in 2007–2008. Under normal conditions, you'll profit if you're in the 25 percent tax bracket and up. In lower tax brackets, buy Treasuries or corporates.

3. You should not—repeat, *not*—put tax-free bonds into your tax-deferred Individual Retirement Account. You owe taxes on withdrawals from tradi-tional IRAs. If you use IRA money to buy munis, you'll be converting them into a taxable investment. Don't put them in Roth IRAs either. Roths accumulate tax free, so they're the place for corporate bonds and bond funds that would otherwise be taxable.

4. You should not—repeat *not*—put most or all of your money into long-term bonds and CDs when you retire, in order to live on the income. You may live 30 years or more, and over that time the purchasing power of your money—both interest and principal—will collapse. (For more on investing at retirement, see page 1142.) Around 40 percent of your money should be in stocks.

5. You should not—repeat *not*—pay any attention to this last piece of advice if you're scared of stocks, don't know anything about them, and can live on your pension, Social Security, and interest income. In this instance, you might not even want a bond mutual fund because it will occasionally show a loss.

People unwilling to tolerate occasional losses are candidates for tax-free bonds, Treasuries, and bank CDs. As the value of the fixed portion of your income shrinks, you can compensate by dipping into capital (the longer you live, the fewer years you have left, and the less capital you will need for future expenses).

Financial advisers can yammer away about optimal returns until they're blue in the face. What you deserve from your money more than anything else is the sense that you're secure.

For an explanation of how best to use bonds for income, jump to page 920. But you'll understand the strategy better if you first learn how bonds work.

The Bond Buyer's Mantra

Repeat after me:

Falling interest rates are good. When interest rates fall, bond prices rise. If I hold a bond mutual fund, its share price will go up.

Rising interest rates are bad. When interest rates rise, bond prices fall. If I hold a bond mutual fund, its share price will decline.

These basic principles of bond investing stand behind every paragraph of this chapter, so remember them.

If you buy individual bonds and hold to maturity, changes in market prices don't matter. When the bond matures, you will get your money back.

If you buy bond mutual funds and hold for long enough, you may also make money even if interest rates go up. That's because the fund keeps buying new bonds at those higher rates, and the extra interest eventually overcomes your loss of principal. In general, rising rates recoup your losses after about two years if you're holding a short-term fund; five years, for an intermediate-term fund; and eight years, for a long-term fund.

What's a Bond Worth?

Bonds have several values:

The Principal. When you put up $1,000 for a new bond, you will get $1,000 back on the day the bond matures. That's your principal. The bond's face value is known as *par.*

The Price. When you read that a bond costs 100, that means $1,000. It's "100 percent of the par value." When you read that a bond costs 95.25, that means $952.50, or 95.2 percent of the par value. To get the dollar price, you add a zero to the quote.

The Interest Payment. Most bonds pay interest semiannually on your money. The interest rate is called the *coupon.* A $1,000 bond paying $50 a year ($25 semiannually) has a coupon rate of 5 percent.

The Market Price. If you want to sell your bond before maturity, the price will depend on market conditions. Remember your mantra. If interest rates have risen since your bond was issued, your bond is worth less than it was when you bought it. If interest rates have fallen, your bond is worth more. This is the most critical fact about bond investing and the least understood. The interest payments that you get from your bond remain the same. But the market price continually adjusts, so your bond always yields the return that investors currently demand. This makes no difference if you plan to hold your bond until maturity. But it makes a big difference if you want to sell ahead of time or if you own a bond mutual fund.

The table on page 909 shows how the bond market works. The left-hand column shows how interest rates might change. The right-hand column shows the effect of these changes on the price of a particular bond.

Keeping It Simple

When you buy individual bonds, *always buy new issues!* These are bonds newly offered to the public by government bodies or corporations. The issuer pays the broker's commission. You get a prospectus explaining what the money is being raised for and what (if anything!) is backing your interest and principal payments. You want a well-backed bond.

New-issue bonds come at an honest market price. No one can monkey around with the stated yield. On the whole, new-issue transactions are simple, sweet, and clean.

This is really all you need to know about buying individual bonds.

Messing It Up

What gets you into trouble is buying older bonds. Dealers have huge inventories of these bonds, so one can be found that exactly serves your purpose. Older bonds are part of the so-called *secondary market.*

Table 23.

HOW BOND PRICES CHANGE

What Happens in the Market	What Happens to Your Bond
You buy a new 30-year bond. You pay its par value and earn a 6 percent coupon.	Your $1,000 bond, at 6 percent interest, pays you $60 a year.
Immediately, market conditions change. Newly issued bonds now have to pay 6.5 percent in order to attract investors.	The market value of your $1,000 bond drops to $934.* Its fixed $60 interest payment now produces a 6.4 percent current yield. You have an unrealized loss on your investment of $66. The bond is said to be priced at a *discount*.
Market conditions change again. Newly issued bonds now have to pay only 5.5 percent in order to attract investors.	The market value of your $1,000 bond rises to $1,073.* Its fixed $60 interest payment now produces a 5.6 percent current yield. You have earned $73 on your original investment. The bond is said to be priced at a *premium*.
Thirty (zzzz) years later . . .	You have collected a total of $1,800 in interest payments ($60 a year). The market value of your bond might have dropped to $900 in some years and risen to $1,100 in others. When the value was high, you could have sold for a profit. If you didn't, you'll redeem it for $1,000—earning the 6 percent annual return you bargained for.

* I'm rounding these numbers.

Source: The Vanguard Group, Valley Forge, Pennsylvania.

What's wrong with buying older bonds? In a word, price. All things being equal, an older bond costs more than a new one because of the dealer's markup—the additional sum that is added to the wholesale price. You won't find the markup on your confirmation statement. Any sales commission or transaction fee disclosed will represent only a portion of the real price you paid.

The biggest markups (and sales commissions) are usually on longer-term and zero-coupon bonds (page 945). There are also big markups on all the firm's garbage: bonds of poor credit quality or oddball bonds with virtually no resale market. The brokerage firm's rules might say that brokers aren't supposed to sell that stuff to retail investors, but they sometimes do.

A few years ago, it wasn't uncommon for brokers to charge excessive (hidden) markups even on garden-variety bonds. That pretty much ended when the Financial Industry Regulatory Authority introduced TRACE (Trade Reporting and Compliance Engine), which tracks all corporate bond transactions. Go to www.finra.org/marketdata and enter the name of the company whose bonds you're interested in. You'll get a list, along with the bonds' coupon interest rates, maturities, ratings, market prices, and current yields. Check any particular bond that your broker recommends. According to industry guidelines, firms are not supposed to charge a markup of more than 5 percent. Competition should drop the cost lower than that—say, $20 on a long-term bond and $10 on an intermediate bond. Still, there are rogue brokers out there. In 2007 FINRA fined Morgan Stanley $6.1 million for letting its brokers mark up bonds by as much as 16 percent.

Contrast this with what you pay for a Vanguard bond mutual fund—about 0.2 percent a year. From a cost point of view, funds are a much better buy than bonds on the secondary market.

If you're buying older municipal bonds, you can check their wholesale prices too. They're tracked by the Real-Time Transaction Reporting System, run by the Municipal Securities Rulemaking Board (MSRB), which regulates the muni market. There are two sites:

(1) Investinginbonds.com (www.investinginbonds.com), run by the Securities Industry and Financial Markets Association. Click on "Municipal Market At-A-Glance," and enter the state whose bonds you're interested in. You can sort by various criteria, including maturity, price, and yield. (SIFMA also offers TRACE data for corporate bonds, but the TRACE site is more complete.)

(2) The MSRB's Electronic Municipal Market Access (EMMA, at www.emma.msrb.com). Click on "Advanced Search" to sort by various criteria. You can even search for bonds of a particular type. For example, if you live in Kansas and want a sewer bond, you can enter the state and the word *sewer* to find out what's available.

Both sites provide the Official Statement issued with most bonds, explaining the terms of the deal and what the proceeds are being used for. You'll also find consumer information about investing in munis.

One more source of information: the Markets Data Center at *The Wall Street Journal* (http://online.wsj.com/public/us). There you'll find prices for the most widely traded bonds.

The Bond-Buying Buzzwords

Once you stray off the straight-and-narrow path of new-issue bonds, you land in a briar patch. A few of the terms listed here apply to every bond. But most of them describe the pricing of older bonds that are selling for more, or less, than their face value. To explain these terms, I'll use the examples I gave in the table on page 909, starting with a $1,000, 30-year bond paying 6 percent interest.

Coupon. The fixed-interest payment made on each bond. A $1,000 bond paying 6 percent a year has a $60 coupon. Put another way, its *coupon rate* is 6 percent. It is typically paid semiannually—$30 every 6 months.

Current Yield. The coupon interest payment divided by the bond's price. A new-issue $1,000 bond paying $60 a year has a current yield of 6 percent. If the price of the bond drops to $934, the current yield—still based on a $60 interest payment—would rise to 6.4 percent. (Remember your bondspeak: at $934, the price would be quoted at 93.4.)

Premium. The amount by which the bond's market value exceeds its par value. A $1,000 bond selling at $1,073 carries a $73 premium. Bond prices can go to premiums when interest rates fall.

Discount. The amount by which the bond's market value has fallen below the par value. A $1,000 bond selling at $934 is at a $66 discount. Bonds go to discounts when interest rates rise. If you buy at a discount and eventually realize a profit, that profit is taxed as ordinary income, not a capital gain.

Call. When the issuer decides to redeem a bond before its maturity date. For example, a bond maturing in January 2020 might be *called* in September 2010, and you'd have no choice but to surrender it. The earliest possible call date is usually specified in the bond contract. Some bonds are callable at any time. The *call price* is usually the par value plus a sweetener.

Term. Generally speaking, short-term bonds run for under 3 years. Intermediate-term bonds run up to 10 years. Long-term bonds go longer than that.

Duration. Duration doesn't affect you if you buy individual bonds and hold to maturity. It's a sophisticated measure for two groups of people: (1) investors who speculate in bonds—buying in hope of a price increase so they can sell at a profit; and (2) bond-fund investors wondering which of two similar funds carries the higher risk.

By *risk*, I mean how far the fund's price might drop when interest rates rise and bond prices decline. A general measure is the fund's maturity. Long-term bonds swing more in price than short-term bonds do (page 909). But what about two bond funds of the same average maturity? One might be riskier than the other because of the kinds of investments it makes.

That's where duration comes in. It estimates how violently a bond or bond fund will react to a change in interest rates. The shorter the duration, the less price change you can expect.

When you're looking at two bond funds with similar credit ratings, maturities, and yields, ask about duration (you'll find the duration on the Web sites of no-load funds; for load funds, ask your broker). If one fund has a noticeably higher duration, it carries more market risk. When you take higher risks, you should be rewarded with higher yields. Some bond funds have changing durations (see "What's the volatility?" page 901). They shouldn't be offered to individual investors in the first place (except for funds that invest in mortgages).

Yield to Maturity. What your bond would earn if you held it to maturity and reinvested each interest payment at the same yield paid by the bond itself. For example, if the broker says that your yield to maturity is 5.4 percent, that assumes that every single interest payment is reinvested at 5.4 percent. If you spend your interest income or reinvest it at a lower rate, as usually happens, you will earn slightly less. That's not a big deal if you buy the bond at par ($1,000). But if you buy an older bond, there may be a marked difference between the current yield and the yield to maturity. Because of this difference, you might be flimflammed into buying a bond that yields less than you think.

For example, say that new 10-year bonds are selling at 5.4 percent yields. Your broker calls you up one day and says, "Hey, I have this nice little number at 6 percent." "Great," you say. "Buy." You think that the bond is beating the market. But your broker doesn't mention that the bond costs $1,046, a $46 premium. At maturity, you will redeem the bond for $1,000, taking a $46 capital loss. Your yield to maturity, counting that loss, would be 5.4 percent. So you're getting less than your broker claimed. If the bond is called before maturity (as bonds selling at premiums often are), you might get less than 5.4 percent. You'd also get less if the broker charged you more than $1,046 for the bond.

The reverse is true when you buy a bond selling for less than its face value. Say that you pay $946 for a $1,000 bond. At maturity, you'll have a $54 gain. Counting that gain, the bond's yield to maturity will be higher than its current yield. Why would you deliberately buy a bond reporting a lower current yield? Because the issuer isn't likely to call it early. You accept less current income in hope of hanging on to the bond's high yield to maturity, including its built-in gain. (I say "in hope" because this strategy doesn't always work. If interest rates fall far enough, these bonds too may rise to premiums and be subject to a call.)

So . . . always check an older bond's price and yield on TRACE (page 910), to see if your broker is charging a fair price. Better yet, consider buying only newly issued bonds, not older ones.

Yield to First Call. This is what a bond will yield if the issuer calls it (repays it) at the earliest date the contract allows. It's also the yield that you will most likely get if you buy a bond that's selling at a premium (that is, over $1,000). In the previous section, I showed what the yield to maturity might be for a premium bond—that is, a bond selling for more than its $1,000 face value. But that was just an academic exercise. In real life, the issuer won't let you keep those bonds until maturity. They pay high current rates of interest, and the issuer will want to replace them with bonds paying lower rates. So the information you really need is the yield to the first date that these bonds can be called. That's your likeliest yield and holding period.

Continuing the example used in the previous section: If you paid $1,046 for the bonds and they were called the following year, your actual yield would be only 1.4 percent because of that $46 capital loss. That's something your broker probably forgot to mention. Anytime a broker offers you a bond with a high current yield, ask: (1) Is the bond selling above par (above $1,000), and if so, what is its yield to first call, and (2) is it a junk bond (page 936)? Most Treasuries cannot be called.

Yield to Worst. A bond may have several call dates, in which case you want to know the lowest possible yield that the bond can pay. This is called *yield to worst*. Always ask for it.

Tax Equivalent Yield. This applies to tax-free municipal bonds. It tells you what rate of return you'd have to earn on a taxable bond to equal what you're getting from the muni, in your tax bracket.

Total Return. Ultimately, this is the only return that matters. It's all the money you earn on the bond or bond fund, and it comes in two parts: (1) the annual interest and (2) the gain or loss in market value, if any.

For example, take a $1,000 bond with a 6 percent coupon, and assume that bond prices go up. If you sell that bond for $1,050, your total return that year (before brokerage commissions) is $110, or 11 percent—$60 from interest and $50 from the gain in the market price.

Or suppose that you pay $1,050 for a $1,000 bond with a $60 coupon, for a current yield of 5.7 percent. If you sell that bond one year later for only $1,000, you'll have taken a $50 loss. Your total return is $10, or 1.0 percent—$60 from the bond interest minus the $50 loss.

Out of all these yields, brokers have created so many sophisticated fiddles that I couldn't begin to understand them all. Nor would I want to. Just give me a nice new-issue bond and leave me alone. If you do buy an older bond from a broker, the only way to know what you're getting is to ask for the current yield, the yield to maturity, the yield to first call, and the yield to worst. If you buy and hold, you get something slightly less than the yield to maturity (because you probably couldn't reinvest your interest payments at the same rate you were getting from the bond). If you sell before maturity or your bond is called, your return will depend on the commission you pay, the call price, and market conditions at the time of sale.

Yields on Bond Mutual Funds

Bond mutual fund managers can fiddle too, to make you think that you're earning more than is actually the case. Because of their sorry abuse of the public in the past, the Securities and Exchange Commission (SEC) wrote a rule dictating how yields must be disclosed. All bond funds have to do that calculation in the same way, so that you can compare them.

The *SEC yield* is computed from the bond portfolio's average yield to maturity over the past 30 days, minus expenses and any sales loads. The yield is then annualized. This rule covers yields shown in advertising material, online disclosures, and automated quote services on the phone, but not what you're told in person by a stockbroker or financial planner. So ask the broker or fund salesperson specifically for the SEC yield. Any other yield may be misleading.

Beware the *distributed yield*. This yield calculation counts only the interest currently paid on the portfolio, not any built-in capital losses that come from buying bonds at a premium (page 911). Distributed yields look high when the actual yield you'll receive, after adjusting for losses, is much lower.

Here's what else the rules say you should receive: the *yield to average maturity*, which is the average maturity of all the bonds in the fund's portfolio; the *yield to average call*, if there's a good chance that bonds will be called before maturity; and the fund's *total return* for the latest 1-, 5-, and 10-year* periods. Funds with shorter life spans have to disclose their performance from the day

---

*Ask for the 3-year yield too. The 10-year yield is useless unless the fund's manager has remained the same.

they began. Total return is their interest income plus or minus any gains or losses in the value of their shares.

You cannot compute your actual yield from your dividend check. The check might not contain every penny of this term's interest income (some of it might be in your next check). It might also include income from writing options or capital gains distributions from bonds that were sold at a profit. You have to rely on the fund to tell you what it's yielding.

How Risky Are Bonds?

Bonds aren't as risky as stocks. But they're riskier than many investors realize—especially the longer-term bonds. Bond risk comes in several forms.

Market Risk From Interest Rates (Part One)

The market value of your bonds will rise and fall as interest rates go down and up. If you sell, you might get more than you originally paid or you might get less, just as would happen if you sold a stock. This matters only if (1) you sell your bonds before maturity or (2) you own a bond mutual fund. Anytime that you sell a mutual fund, the price is set by market rates.

Short-term bonds are safest (if they're conservatively invested) because they fluctuate the least in price. They also pay the lowest rates. Intermediate-term bonds come next. Long-term bonds fluctuate the most.

To minimize market risk, buy a "ladder" of short- to intermediate-term bonds, as explained on page 921.

Market Risk From Interest Rates (Part Two)

Two apparently similar bond funds can behave differently when interest rates change. A rise in rates may hurt one fund's price just a little bit while hurting another fund a lot. The difference may depend on the fund's duration (page 911). It might also depend on how each fund uses derivatives—complex securities where the price of one asset depends on the price change in another asset. Some derivatives increase a fund's market risk; other derivatives lower it. A fund yielding more than its peer group may be using derivatives in a speculative way.

Holding-Period Risk

The longer it takes for your bond to reach maturity, the greater the chance that you'll have to sell ahead of time. You risk losing money when you sell early because market prices might be down.

To minimize holding-period risk, don't buy 20- and 30-year bonds. The odds of your holding that long are small. The average income investor should buy short- to intermediate-term bonds, defined as lasting no more than 10 years.

Inflation Risk

As consumer prices rise, both your principal and interest lose purchasing power. Take that $1,000 bond with a coupon of 6 percent a year. After just five years of 3 percent inflation, your $1,000 principal will have a purchasing power of only $862, while your $60 interest check will buy only $52 worth of goods. Your standard of living has dropped by 14 percent. And what will happen over the next five years and the five years after that, if inflation persists?

To minimize inflation risk, buy Treasury Inflation-Protected Securities (TIPS, page 929). Their yield rises with the inflation rate.

To minimize inflation risk with corporate bonds, don't spend all the interest if you can avoid it. Instead, reinvest enough to counter the inflation rate. For example, suppose that you own a $1,000 bond and inflation is running at 3 percent. In order to maintain its purchasing power, your $1,000 principal needs to rise in value by $30. If you're earning $60 in interest, you should reinvest $30 (to bring your principal up to $1,030), pay the taxes due, and live on what's left. In a bond mutual fund, reinvestment is easy. If you own individual bonds, put that $30 into a bank or money market fund. Reinvest the whole $60 if you don't need the income to live on.

Call Risk

If interest rates fall, corporations and municipalities will call in their older, high-interest bonds and issue new ones at lower rates. Typically, you get 5 to 10 years' call protection from both corporations and municipalities. The call may come at par ($1,000) or par plus a little bit extra. But that's not much consolation. You will have been earning a high rate of interest. After the call, you'll have to reinvest at a lower rate.

Most bonds are called through a *refunding*. The company issues lower-coupon bonds and uses the proceeds to retire its higher-coupon debt. You may also be parted from some of your bonds, usually long-term municipals, by a *sinking fund*—a lottery system for retiring a certain number of bonds each year (in which case, no sweetener is paid). A special or extraordinary redemption can occur in specified circumstances, such as changes in the economics of a project that make it unworkable.

Calls used to be one of the normal hazards of bond investing that you could hedge against successfully. Now it's guerrilla war out there. Bond issuers tuck weasel words into the finest of print to deceive you and your broker about how early a call could come. One reason not to be a bondholder (or to buy a mutual fund and let the fund manager worry about it) is that so many corporations and municipalities are playing fast and loose with your call protection.

What do you lose when your bonds are called? If you bought at par, your principal is returned intact (sometimes with a little sweetener). But you lose the capital gain you earned when the bond's value rose. If you paid more than the call price, you suffer an early capital loss. When a convertible bond is called, you'll lose the higher price it might have been selling for in the open market. Calls also deprive you of high bond income that would have kept you sitting pretty for many years.

To eliminate call risk, buy newly issued U.S. Treasury notes and bonds. They are almost always callproof (or not callable until 25 years have passed, which, by me, is the same thing). Plenty of intermediate-term corporate and municipal bonds are also noncallable.

If you buy an existing bond, it's smart to choose one with low interest payments, selling at a discount from par value. Your yield to maturity will equal that of higher-coupon bonds, but your investment isn't as likely to be called. Or buy zeros that are callable only at par. If zeros are callable at their *accreted value*— meaning their original price plus all the interest earned to date—they're no better than garden-variety bonds.

Default Risk

The issuer might not pay the bond's principal and interest on time. For example, the company might go bankrupt, or its loans might have to be restructured. U.S. government bonds have no default risk. Municipals, even those of middling quality, rarely stumble. High-quality corporates are usually solid too. Low-rated bonds, especially corporates and those of developing countries, are the ones most likely to descend into default.

To minimize default risk, buy only higher-quality stuff. You will sacrifice some yield. A 10-year AAA bond might yield 0.5 percentage points less than a BBB-rated bond, depending on the market at the time. That's a pretty small price to pay compared with the risk of losing money. To avoid default risk in the muni market, you can buy insured bonds, giving up maybe 0.15 to 0.3 percent of the yield. But what's the point? Munis hardly ever default. In the credit crisis of 2007–2009, muni bonds turned out to be stronger than the insurers that supposedly guaranteed them. At this writing, there's only one AAA-rated insurer left. (For more on muni bond insurance, see page 942.)

The three most common bond-rating systems, from Standard & Poor's,

Moody's, and Fitch, are shown below. These systems aren't perfect. In 2007 the firms were caught giving high ratings to what turned out to be poor-quality securities. Those were complex securities, however. With occasional exceptions, ratings on plain-vanilla securities do a reasonable job of identifying risk. You can get free ratings on public companies by registering at these sites: Standard & Poor's (www.standardandpoors.com), Moodys.com (www.moodys.com), and Fitch Ratings (www.fitchratings.com).

Table 24.

WHAT BOND RATINGS MEAN (USUALLY)

	Standard & Poor's*	Moody's*	Fitch*	Risk
Investment-grade bonds	AAA	Aaa	AAA	Champagne, roses
	AA	Aa	AA	Good enough even for the queen
	A	A	A	Probably fine but down in class for a conservative investor
	BBB	Baa	BBB	Okay for now, but a daring buy for people who normally choose quality bonds
Junk bonds†	BB	Ba	BB	Junk with pretensions, or "junque"
	B	B	B	The real stuff, and risky as heck
	CCC	Caa	CCC	Junk that's showing its true colors
	CC	Ca	CC	Junk that smells like old fish heads
	C	C	C	Junk that isn't paying interest anymore; on life support
	D	C	DDD	Defaulted bonds: brain dead
				Unrated bonds: bonds that none of the major rating services have touched; probably low junk, although some small municipalities may be of high quality

* A plus (+) or minus (−) from S&P or Fitch indicates that, within its category, the bond is relatively strong or weak. Moody's designates a strong bond with the numeral 1.

† Buying individual junk bonds is much too risky for the average investor. Instead buy them in high-yield (junk) bond funds. Use this explanation of the ratings to check the fund's portfolio, to see how much of its assets are invested at various quality grades.

Credit Risk

If a company starts racking up losses or a municipality reveals huge unfunded pension obligations, the credit rating on its bonds will fall. As long as you hold those bonds, your interest payments stay the same (provided that the issuer doesn't default). But if you have to sell before maturity, you'll take a beating on the price. When a company's or municipality's finances improve, its credit rating rises, and so does the price of its bonds.

To minimize credit risk, check your bond's current safety rating and whether that rating is likely to change. Moody's publishes a "Watchlist." At S&P and Fitch, you look up the company to see if it's on credit watch.

Deception Risk

There are several ways of making you think you're earning more than is actually the case. Two examples:

1. A broker or planner may tell you that your fund's current yield (from interest and other income) is 7 percent. But that's only part of the story. If interest rates rose last year, your fund may have dropped in value—say, by 4 percent. So its total return—7 percent in income minus 4 percent in market losses—was actually only 3 percent. Quite a difference.

2. A unit trust might buy a three-year, A-rated $1,000 bond with an 8 percent coupon interest rate that has only one year left to run. It might be selling at a current yield of 7.8 percent, compared with only 5.5 percent on newly issued one-year bonds. The trust buys that bond in order to jack up its current yield. But it has to pay a fat $1,024 for it. When the bond is redeemed, the trust will take a $24 loss. As a result, the bond's actual yield to maturity is only 5.5 percent. Thus are customers duped. Salespeople are supposed to give you the current yield plus the yield to maturity, which would show what you'll really earn. Good ones do. Be sure to ask for it.

To minimize deception risk: Check bond prices on EMMA or TRACE (page 910). Check the bond fund's prospectus for the SEC yields and the annual total returns (page 772). You can use these yields to compare one fund with another.[*] Use discount brokerage sites, where yields are disclosed. Buy through fee-only investment advisers. Avoid unit trusts (page 958).

---

[*]Unfortunately, you can't compare bond fund returns with the rates on bank certificates of deposit. The calculations don't mesh.

A Bond Strategy for Income Investors

You are an income investor if you expect to live on the monthly checks that your capital produces. Instead of reinvesting your dividends and interest, you take the money and spend it. For bond buyers, there's a right way and a wrong way to go about this.

The Wrong Way to Get Income from Your Bonds

The wrong way, in my view, is to buy a lot of long-term bonds. This conclusion may surprise you because "long bonds" usually pay the highest interest rates. The year you buy them, you'll earn some real spending money, even after inflation and taxes.

So you love Year One. Year Two, however, isn't quite so terrific. Both your capital and your income lose purchasing power. By Year Three you are barely breaking even after taxes and inflation. By Year Four, you are probably in the hole. Each subsequent year, your bond income buys you less and less. How much less depends on the inflation rate.

- *If inflation holds steady or declines,* you'll get poorer slowly, losing a modest amount of purchasing power every year. For extra money, you may have to sell some bonds before maturity. If interest rates have fallen, the sale might yield a modest profit, but you'll take a loss if interest rates are up. Small amounts of municipal bonds may be virtually unsalable. Your money may still stretch over your lifetime, but you can't be sure. If your savings are small, the diminished real value of your bonds may force you to reduce your standard of living in later years.

- *If the rate of inflation rises,* the purchasing power of both your capital and your income will take a devastating hit. You will have to use up your money at a much faster rate than you had planned or cut back sharply on expenses.

- *If deflation occurs, and soon,* you'll be glad that you're collecting income from long-term bonds. In that case, your purchasing power would rise (provided that you owned noncallable Treasury bonds; corporates or municipals would be called by their issuers, robbing you of your high-interest income). But deflation is a way-outside bet. Americans lived through bouts of deflation in the 1870s, parts of the 1880s and 1890s, and the 1930s, but not since.

Why take any of these risks when you can pursue a sensible income strategy with intermediate-term bonds instead? The extra yield you get from long bonds may be in the 0.5 percent range. That's a pretty skinny bonus for putting your money at such hazard.

The Right Way to Get Income from Your Bonds

Buy a mixture of intermediate- and shorter-term bonds and ladder them. Here's why:

■ *They pay a reasonable income.* It's less than you'd get from a portfolio of long-term bonds, but usually just a tiny bit less.

■ *They give you inflation protection.* If interest rates rise, your maturing short-term bonds can be reinvested at a higher interest rate. That will preserve some of your purchasing power. Unlike the owners of long-term bonds, you're not chained to a fixed check.

■ *They protect you against the need to sell bonds before maturity, perhaps at a loss.* With the right mix of bonds, you always have some that are reaching their maturity date. That gives you fresh cash to use.

Historically, the total return on intermediate bonds—changes in principal plus interest—has been just as good as that on long-term bonds. Intermediates do a little better when inflation rises; long bonds do a little better when inflation falls. But the differences even out. So you can pursue this strategy without feeling that you're losing capital on the deal.

Here's how to carry it out:

Buy bonds with maturities of 1, 2, 3, 4, and 5 years—all the way up to 10 years. That's called laddering your investments. Altogether, your income might equal what you'd get from a 7-year bond. People with substantial assets will choose a ladder of municipals or Treasury securities, including zero-coupon Treasuries. It's generally assembled with the help of a stockbroker or other financial adviser. People with fewer assets can build this same ladder with bank certificates of deposit (page 67).

When your one-year bond (or CD) matures, you have a choice. If short-term interest rates are uncommonly high, you can increase your income by reinvesting for another one-year term. Alternatively (and this is the usual case), long-term rates will be higher. So you'd increase your income by reinvesting in a 10-year bond. This helps offset the hole that inflation has left in your purchasing power.

The following year, your two-year bond will come due. You'll again have a choice about where to reinvest for better returns—probably by buying another 10-year bond. Or you might fill in a particular bond maturity that's missing.

Eventually, you will have a ladder of 10-year bonds, some of which are maturing every year. Result: a decent income plus some inflation protection. Every year you will have fresh cash in hand. If you need money, it's there to spend. You won't be forced to raise it by selling bonds before maturity, perhaps at a loss. If you don't need money right now, you can reinvest for higher income if rates are up.

What can go wrong?

Being no dope, you have already spotted the crack in my ladder. If interest rates decline steeply, you lose. Every time one of your bonds matures, you might have to reinvest at a lower interest rate. In that case, you'd have been better off putting all your money in intermediate- or long-term bonds. But that's strictly hindsight. Standing here today, you don't know where interest rates will go.* You have to be ready for anything. The ladder gives you liquidity and choice.

Even if interest rates do decline, bond ladders don't have to lower your income right away. In the first year, for example, you would reinvest the proceeds of your one-year bond in a 10-year bond. Assuming that 10-year rates are higher, your income might rise, even if rates in general are coming down. The risk of reinvesting at lower rates may not arise until most of your bonds are in the 7- to 10-year range.

You might include some long-term bonds to hedge against the risk of declining rates. Hold them for the rest of your life. If they have to be sold at a loss before maturity, let your heirs do it. For them, it's free money anyway.

An alternative to laddering: buy bond exchange-traded funds (ETFs—page 785). You can get an intermediate-term ETF, paying the kind of interest rate that you're seeking in a bond ladder. At the same time, you have liquidity: you can sell the ETF at any time, at market rates. You pay a brokerage commission when you buy an ETF, and there's an annual fee. That compares with zero cost for a Treasury or CD ladder that you assemble yourself. On the other hand, an ETF is a onetime purchase—you don't have to keep managing it, as you do with a bond ladder (or paying a broker to manage it for you). Your income from the ETF will vary as interest rates rise and fall.

Two Critical Backstops for Income Investors

1. Don't put all of your money in bonds, regardless of their maturity. Going back to the table on page 719, you can see that adding stocks improves your returns while reducing risk. At older ages, you might keep 70 to 80 percent of your money in bonds, for the interest they produce, and put the remainder into stocks.

---

*The federal funds futures market tends to predict very short-term rates, if you follow that sort of thing. Futures trade on the Chicago Board Options Exchange. Prediction errors have been high, however, in the months that, in hindsight, precede recessions.

Which kinds of stocks? Income investors will probably go for equity-income mutual funds or blue-chip stocks with a history of dividend increases. But looking only at dividends is taking too narrow a view of how one can get income from stocks. Capital growth is a source of income too. As your stocks rise in value over time, sell some of the shares and spend the money. It makes sense to supplement bond interest with cash withdrawals from stock-owning mutual funds. For a simple, creative way of setting up such a withdrawal plan, see page 1142.

2. You might add some zero-coupon bonds (page 945) to the mix. The financial adviser who figured out the strategy I'm about to explain calls it his "nursing home bailout program." Pretend you're the client, and think about it this way.

"I'm sixty, I own my house, and statistics say I have twenty-four years to live. I want to live well.

"I'll divide my capital into money to spend and money to save. The spending money will be deployed partly in short- and intermediate-term bonds and partly in conservative dividend-paying, stock-owning, no-load mutual funds. My savings will go into twenty-four-year zero-coupon bonds and a small amount of stock-owning mutual funds.

"Over the next twenty-four years, I will consume every dime in my spending account—all the bonds and all the mutual funds. I'll tap the funds through annual cash withdrawals. I'll spend a certain percentage of my bonds as they mature. I have figured out a spending rate that gives me a reasonable chance of maintaining a steady standard of living.

"If I'm still breathing after twenty-four years, I will turn to my savings stash. There my stocks will have gained and my zeros will have matured. That gives me a fresh pot of capital to sustain the remainder of my life. If I have to enter a nursing home, my stocks, my zeros, and the value of my house should pay for quality care."

That's what I call a creative use of bonds!

Mutual Funds for Income Investors

Can you ladder with bond mutual funds? No, because most bond funds have no maturity date. For true ladders, you need individual bonds or bank CDs.

But you get a similar effect by owning a combination of short- and intermediate-term funds. Leave all your dividends in the funds to be reinvested. For the income you need, make regular, fixed withdrawals from each fund, once a year or on a monthly cash withdrawal plan. The fund company T. Rowe Price offers a "Smart Ladder" through its savings bank affiliate. With a single deposit, you get a product that provides the yields a five-year CD ladder would pay.

A Bond Strategy for Preserving Purchasing Power

If you don't need to live on the income from your bonds, you can use that money to maintain the purchasing power of your capital. Here's how:

Buy individual, high-quality, intermediate-term bonds—perhaps 5- to 10-year Treasuries. They're safe, and you owe no state or local income taxes on the interest. Reinvest every dime that you earn in more Treasury notes or in a money market mutual fund. You might pick a money fund fully invested in Treasuries, so state and local taxes won't be due on those dividends either. If you're in the 25 percent bracket or higher and investing outside a retirement plan, consider tax-free municipal bonds instead. One last option: buy zero-coupon bonds, maturing when you expect to use the money (page 945). Your interest will be reinvested automatically at the same rate of interest that you earn on the bond itself.

Don't buy your bonds all at once. Buy a few of them every few months, over the next 18 to 24 months. That way, you'll cover a range of interest rates.

With this strategy, your investment won't grow much in real terms, but your purchasing power will be preserved.

Can You Preserve Purchasing Power with Mutual Funds?

That depends on what happens to interest rates. Yes, if interest rates stay roughly level or decline. No, if interest rates rise substantially and you hold the fund for only a few years.

But mutual funds have an ace in the hole. You can reinvest small dividend payments at the same yield as the mutual fund returns, which is better than you'd get from a money market fund. If interest rates rise and you hold long enough, these reinvestments will offset the fund's decline in market price.

A Bond Strategy for Interest-Rate Speculators

Here's where long-term bonds come in. They're a terrific way to speculate on the direction of interest rates.

Suppose you're convinced that interest rates are going to drop. Remember your mantra: Falling interest rates are good. Falling interest rates mean profits. When interest rates fall, bond prices rise. To your mantra, add this corollary (no modern mantra is without its corollary): the longer the term of the bond, the bigger the profit when interest rates decline.

The following table shows exactly how much bigger. If you put $10,000 into Treasuries and interest rates drop one percentage point over the next 12 months, you'll pick up only $97 on a 1-year bill—a gain of less than 1 percent. But you'd get $1,637 on a 30-year bond, for a 16.4 percent gain. The potential gain on a 30-year zero-coupon bond is a huge 34 percent. Conversely, if interest rates rise, the longer-term bonds would lose the most.

The nerviest speculators buy Treasury bonds on margin, putting up 10 percent of the cost and borrowing 90 percent. They go for zeros, where the price swings are biggest. You can make huge profits if your timing is right and take huge losses if it isn't.

Take the 30-year zero shown in the table. Assume that you bought it on 90 percent margin, putting up 10 percent of the cost and borrowing 90 percent from your broker. If, over the next year, interest rates fell by 1 percentage point, you'd earn a 277 percent profit before costs—big-time leverage! But if rates rose 1 percentage point, you could potentially suffer as much as a 316 percent loss. (In the real world, you'd get margin calls and would probably bail out.)

Speculators should buy only Treasury bonds. Unlike corporates or municipals, most Treasuries cannot be called away from you if interest rates decline. They will pay today's rates for 25 years or more.

Can You Speculate with Mutual Funds?

Yes, but do it with exchange-traded Treasury funds. You can buy through any discount broker. In a typical market cycle, bond prices rise before stock prices

Table 25.

THE GAIN OR LOSS ON A $10,000 INVESTMENT

Treasury Security	When Interest Rates:	
	Fall by 1% *	Rise by 1%*
1-year	$ 97	$ −95
5-year	443	−421
10-year	798	−729
20-year	1,310	−1,110
30-year	1,637	−1,312
30-year zero	3,400	−2,527

* Assuming a 5.5 percent yield on all issues.

Source: The Vanguard Group, Valley Forge, Pennsylvania.

do. A speculator would swing first into long-term Treasury ETFs and then into stocks.

A Bond Strategy for Historians

Some investors get scared every time rates pop up, for fear that they portend a drift back to double-digit price increases. But that's not likely. From 1791 to 2007, U.S. prices rose at an annual compound rate of only 1.5 percent, and that included three periods of inflation greater than those we experienced in 1980.*

Inflationary spasms are usually followed by periods of disinflation or even deflation, when prices fall. In stable periods, long-term U.S. Treasury bonds yield around 5 percent. Here's the record of American price changes:

Table 26.

U.S. PRICES, 1792–2007*

Rate of Price Change	How Often Those Changes Took Place
Over 1%	56% of the time
Under 1%	19% of the time
Stability	25% of the time

* Annual compound rate.

Source: The Leuthold Group, Minneapolis.

A Bond Strategy for Losers

Not real losers, just losers in this calendar year. If interest rates rise and your bonds show a substantial loss, you can do a tax swap that actually leaves you better off. Here's how:

---

*Those periods were the 1790s, 1860s, and 1910s, computed on a moving-average basis. For this data, my thanks to investment adviser Steven Leuthold, who in 1980 published an insightful book, *The Myths of Inflation and Investing.* Among its little treasures was a 1,000-year history of consumer prices in the Western world. He found that prices rose about 61 percent of the time and fell about 39 percent of the time. The annual compound inflation rate ran at less than 1 percent—suggesting that, over time (sometimes over a lot of time), market economies stabilize themselves.

1. Sell the bonds to realize the loss.

2. Use the proceeds to buy other bonds at the market's current, lower prices. The swap extends the maturity of the investment, and your yield to maturity drops a bit (that's the price of the transaction). But you wind up with roughly the same interest income you had before.

3. Use the loss in bonds to tax-shelter any capital gains you took this year or to offset $3,000 of your ordinary income. Carry forward any additional losses and use them on future tax returns.

4. Be sure not to buy exactly the same bonds. If you do so within 30 days, you can't claim the loss.

Tax-loss swapping works with exchange-traded funds, just as long as you switch to a different ETF. You can also do it with mutual funds, as long as you buy a different fund (or park your money for 30 days before buying back the same fund). You'd do such a swap only if you owned no-load funds, because they have no sales charges. Sales charges could erase any taxes you saved.

Before hustling to sell a fund, find out if you really have a loss. If you bought several years ago and reinvested the dividends, the total value of your account may still be higher than it was at the beginning.

Where to Hold Your Bonds

Hold your long-term, fixed-income investments in a tax-deferred retirement account. That saves you from paying annual taxes on the interest that you earn. The full payment will grow and compound in your account. Withdrawals are taxed as ordinary income, just as they would be if you invested outside the account.

Decision Time: Which Bonds to Buy? How to Buy Them?

You now have (I hope) a theory of bonds. You know why you want them and how you'll use them. The next step is to choose the bonds that will serve you best.

When buying individual bonds, always look to the credit rating (page 918). AAA and AA are top quality, while A might be called a "business risk." BBB is on the very cusp of investment quality. One slip, and it's junk. Unfortunately, bond ratings aren't reliable, as we learned in the 2008 credit crash. Some AAA securities crumbled overnight. Still, they work for most issues and are the best we've got.

Treasury Bonds

No bond is safer than a Treasury. Other bonds pay higher interest rates, but Treasuries' strong advantages may matter more.

Treasuries, Defined. Medium-term Treasuries run from 2 to 10 years and are called notes. Minimum investment: $100. (Treasuries of 1 year or less, called bills, are generally for savers, not investors; see page 225.)

When I say that Treasuries are safe, I mean only that the interest and principal payments will always be made on time. Treasuries are exposed to the same market risk as any other bonds. If you sell before maturity, you might get more or less than you paid, depending on market conditions at the time. You have to hold to maturity to be sure of getting all your capital back.

Treasuries don't pay as much income as other bonds of comparable maturities, but the interest is taxed only at the federal level, not by states and cities. For people in high state tax brackets, Treasuries may yield more. Most Treasuries pay fixed rates. Some of them offer inflation adjustments.

Why You Might Want a Treasury

1. **You might want a bond with no credit risk.** Treasuries will never be downgraded or default.

2. **Treasury bonds are noncallable, at least for the first 25 years.** That's important if you're speculating on declining interest rates and win your bet. Most corporate and municipal bonds would be called away (page 911) and replaced with lower-rate securities.

3. **Treasuries are liquid.** If you have to sell before maturity, you get better prices on them than on other kinds of bonds.

4. **You can buy Treasuries from the Federal Reserve at www.treasury direct.gov,** paying no brokerage commission. For more on buying and selling, see page 228.

The Drawbacks

1. **In return for their safety and liquidity, Treasuries yield less than other bonds of comparable maturities.**

2. **Taxpayers in high brackets net a lower current income from Treasuries than they would from tax-exempt bonds.** But you might not care in view of Treasuries' other advantages, especially their immunity to call.

Treasury Inflation-Protected Securities (TIPS). These securities promise that inflation won't erode your purchasing power. Whether inflation goes up or down, you get a fixed, real return. Here's how that works:

When an issue of inflation-protected Treasuries is sold, the market sets a basic, fixed interest rate. The government credits additional interest, equal to the rise in the consumer price index. The inflation adjustment accrues semiannually and is applied to your principal. In other words, your principal grows. The fixed rate is paid on top. Your total return is the basic rate plus the inflation rate, no matter how high inflation runs.

As an example, say that new Treasuries pay 3 percent. If inflation is running at 3.5 percent, your total return would be 6.5 percent. If inflation rises to 5 percent, your total return that year would be 8 percent. After inflation, you're always left with that real return of 3 percent.

If the consumer price index ever dropped, your bond's principal would drop too, but never below the bond's face value. So you also get a bit of protection against deflation.

Both TIPS and fixed-rate Treasuries are priced to cover whatever future inflation rate the market currently expects. TIPS outperform when inflation turns higher *unexpectedly*. To see how much inflation is built into a TIPS bond today, compare its basic, fixed interest rate with the rate on a comparable fixed-rate Treasury. The difference between the two is the forecasted inflation rate for the term of the bond.

TIPS aren't a perfect hedge against inflation. If interest rates rise because real growth picks up, TIPS prices will fall. They're still bonds and behave like them. If you had to sell before maturity, you'd take a loss. Prices also fell during the 2008 panic when big investors dumped TIPS to raise cash. In a hyperinflation, the semiannual adjustment of your TIPS would lag the rapid rise in the price index. Still, TIPS are as close to a pure inflation hedge as you can get if you hold to maturity. You receive a real rate of return with no credit risk.

TIPS tax alert: if you hold individual TIPS, only the basic interest rate will be paid semiannually in cash. You don't get the inflation adjustment until you sell the bond or it matures. Even so, you're taxed on that inflation adjustment every year. There are two ways around this: (1) Hold your TIPS in a tax-deferred retirement fund, or (2) buy TIPS mutual funds or ETFs. They distribute the inflation adjustments monthly, in the form of dividends. You can reinvest the dividends in new shares.

If you choose a Treasury, should you buy . . .

. . . Individual Bonds? Absolutely yes. You don't need to diversify, because Treasuries carry no credit risk. So there's no point paying a mutual fund's annual management fee or the brokerage commission on an ETF. You can buy your Treasuries free from www.treasurydirect.gov. If you buy through a broker or commercial bank, you'll be charged its normal sales commissions.

You can also redeem your bond through TreasuryDirect at maturity, but not before. If you want to sell early, you'd have to ask for your Treasury to be transferred to something called the *commercial book-entry system,* to make it accessible to stockbrokers. Anyone who expects to sell before maturity (for example, interest rate speculators) should buy through a broker or bank.

Always buy newly issued Treasuries if you can get the maturity you want. When you buy existing bonds, the bank or broker who sells them will mark up the price. Treasuries are ideal for the ladder suggested on page 921. If you don't need current income, reinvest all the interest you earn in order to maintain the purchasing power of your capital.

If you're buying individual TIPS, hold them in a tax-deferred retirement fund.

. . . A Mutual Fund or ETF? No. Funds and ETFs charge annual fees. You'll net more money more securely by buying Treasuries individually. If you want a mutual fund invested in government-insured securities, go for one with higher yields, such as a fund that buys government agency issues, including Ginnie Maes. Don't fall for the funds that call themselves Treasury "Plus." They try for higher yields by pursuing fancy options programs, but they're often at the bottom of the performance lists. If ever there were a plain-vanilla investment, it's a Treasury bond.

One exception: consider a mutual fund or ETF if you're buying TIPS in a taxable account. They distribute the inflation adjustment monthly, which isn't true of individual TIPS (see above). TIPS mutual funds may also buy the inflation-protected bonds of corporations and other countries, in an effort to outperform straight Treasuries.

Ginnie Maes

A Ginnie Mae is a black-box investment whose workings you and I will never see. It's a fine, conservative bond with an appealing yield. But you have to treat it carefully. Very carefully.

Ginnie Maes, Defined. Ginnie Mae is short for Government National Mortgage Association. It's the highest-yielding government-backed security that you can get. New Ginnie Maes often yield 0.5 to 1 percentage point more than Treasuries of comparable maturities—and they're guaranteed by the full faith and credit of the U.S. government. Unfortunately, it takes at least $25,000 to buy a new issue. That's why so many investors buy their Ginnie Maes in the form of mutual funds or unit trusts (page 958).

A Ginnie Mae is a pool of individual mortgages insured by the Federal Housing Administration or guaranteed by the Department of Veterans Affairs. Your own mortgage might be in a Ginnie Mae. Every time you make a monthly mortgage payment, your bank might subtract a small processing fee and pass the remainder to the investors in that pool.

Each investor gets a pro rata share of every home owner's mortgage payment. When a home owner prepays a mortgage, the investors get a pro rata share of that too.

Important! Ginnie Maes work differently from bonds. When you buy a traditional bond, each semiannual check you get is pure interest income. At maturity you get your capital back. But with a Ginnie Mae, each monthly check is a combination of (1) interest earned and (2) a payback of some of the principal that you originally invested. At the end of the term, you'll get no capital back. It will have been paid to you already over the life of your investment.

Suppose, for example, that you get a check for $237. Of that amount, $229 might be interest; $8 might be principal. That's an $8 bit of your original investment, returned to you. If you're living on the income from your investments, what should you do with this check? You can spend up to $229 of it because that's interest income. But you must save the remaining $8. If you spend that $8, you are consuming your principal, which is something that few Ginnie Mae investors understand. The statement that comes with your check will tell you how much is interest and how much is principal.

Each month, the amount of principal in your check will be a speck higher and the amount of interest a speck less. Over the term of the Ginnie Mae, you will gradually receive all your principal back. If you spend every check you get, all your principal will be gone. Conversely, if you save every check, including the interest, you will preserve the purchasing power of your capital, after taxes and inflation.

Also important! If a broker says that the fund is "government guaranteed," that means only guaranteed against default. Principal and interest payments will always be made on time. But the feds don't insure your investment result. How much money you make on a Ginnie Mae, or a Ginnie Mae fund or unit trust, depends on investment conditions and how wisely you buy.

Why You Might Want a Ginnie Mae

1. You like its high current yield and its government-backed protection against default. Unlike Treasuries, Ginnie Maes are fully taxable by state and local governments as well as by the federal government. So you might choose them for the "safe" portion of your tax-deferred retirement fund. They're also worthwhile in states that have no income tax.

2. If you're living on your savings, Ginnie Maes deliver attractive income. They're especially good for people in low brackets who pay little or no income tax.

The Drawbacks for Investors in Individual Ginnie Mae Bonds and Unit Trusts. (The following list of risks is formidable, but plunge on. It has a happy ending.)

1. The size of your check varies every month, depending on how fast the mortgages are prepaid. This can disconcert an income investor. Some months you get more, some months you get less.

2. You have to keep track of how much of your check is interest and how much is principal. When the principal payment is small, the best way to reinvest it at a decent rate of return is to stow it in a money market mutual fund.

3. You may be deceived by your Ginnie Mae's high current rate of interest. A unit trust, for example, might be paying 7 percent because it is packed with older, high-rate mortgages for which the trust paid more than face value. But when those home owners refinance, the trust will take a loss. What you thought was an eight-year, 7 percent investment might turn into a three-year, 5 percent investment. Sic transit truth. Just as bad, you may never realize how small your return actually was because yields on Ginnie Maes are so tough to calculate.

4. Any yield that's promised on a Ginnie Mae is only an estimate. Not until all the mortgages are finally paid can it be said with certainty what you earned. And no one will bother doing that calculation for you. So you'll never know.

5. If you have to sell your Ginnie Mae before maturity, the odds are that you'll lose money. These securities tend to rise very little in good markets and to plunge in bad ones. You might get lucky, but you never know.

6. The happy ending: you can get around most of these problems by buying Ginnie Maes in mutual funds.

If you choose a Ginnie Mae, should you buy . . .

. . . An Individual Security? After that long list of drawbacks, how could I recommend an individual Ginnie Mae? In fact, I don't. Nor do I like the unit trusts (page 958). If you do buy an individual security, buy only a newly issued Ginnie Mae, for sale at face value. Then you can't be confused by a broker quoting a phony yield. Avoid at all costs a high-interest Ginnie Mae that sells for more than its face value. Its true yield, after all the mortgage prepayments, will be much lower.

Sometimes older Ginnie Maes are good deals—and they sell for less than $25,000 because some of their mortgage principal has already been repaid. But you can't easily tell the good deals from the bad, so the safest thing is to stay away. That's professional-manager territory.

. . . A Mutual Fund? In my view, this is the only way of buying Ginnie Maes. Leave it to the fund manager to worry about whether he or she is getting the right price. All your principal is reinvested for you, even those $8 bits. You can reinvest the income too. You get semiannual and annual reports of how well your fund is doing. Minimum investments are often $1,000 or so. As with any other mutual fund, however, share prices rise and fall. You risk losing money if interest rates rise. Check the prospectus to see if the fund buys any mortgages that don't carry a government guarantee.

You can find mortgage-backed ETFs, but they hold securities issued by Fannie Mae and Freddie Mac as well as Ginnie Mae. Mutual funds are better.

Other Government Securities

There's an alphabet soup of government agencies that raise money from the public. For bonds exempt from state and local taxes, look at those issued by the Federal Farm Credit System, which makes farm loans ($1,000 minimum investment), and the Federal Home Loan Banks, which make short-term loans to savings and loan associations ($10,000 minimum investment). Other agency securities are fully taxable. Check an agency's tax status before you buy.

Agency bonds aren't backed by the full faith and credit of the federal government, but they'd almost certainly be bailed out in a pinch. Many agency securities have a credit line with the Treasury. They yield a hair more than Treasuries—maybe an extra 0.25 or 0.35 percentage points. That's $25 to $35 a year on a $10,000 investment. If you're sure that you'll hold the note to term, maybe that extra fraction is worth it. But it's not if you might have to sell before maturity. You won't get quite as good a price for agency notes as you would for Treasuries.

How to get the right price on government securities: go to the *Wall Street Journal* online (http://online.wsj.com//public//us) and click on "Market Data Center," then on "Bonds, Rates & Credit Markets." You'll find a list of current wholesale prices.

Corporate Bonds

Corporates pay higher interest rates than Treasuries. That's because they're riskier. Business conditions may cause their quality ratings to drop, which lowers their market price. Some corporate bonds default. Still, they're much safer than stocks.

Corporates, Defined. These bonds represent loans made to corporations and come in a wide range of maturities. You need at least $5,000 to invest (that's five bonds at $1,000 each). You'll get the best price if you buy bonds newly issued to the public rather than older bonds sold out of the broker's inventory. Some corporate bonds are backed by some sort of collateral, such as equipment or real estate—although, in a bankruptcy, that collateral can be tough for bondholders to get their hands on. Most corporates are *debentures,* meaning that they're secured only by the executives' smiles. This section talks about high-quality, investment-grade corporates. For speculative (junk) corporates, rated BB and lower, see below.

Why You Might Want a Corporate

1. **You're investing with tax-deferred money in your retirement plan and want a higher interest rate than Treasuries pay.** Corporates are fully taxable by federal, state, and local governments.

2. **You're in the 15 percent federal tax bracket.** At that level, you will normally net more, after tax, from taxable corporate bonds than from tax-exempts.

The Drawbacks.

1. **You usually get only five-year call protection,** so if interest rates decline you won't enjoy your high interest rates for very long.

2. **The interest on corporate bonds is taxed by every government in sight: federal, state, and local.** That's why corporates are principally for low-bracket investors or tax-deferred retirement plans.

3. Corporates are hard to sell before maturity at a decent price unless you're selling large lots, in the range of $100,000 plus. The TRACE system has improved the pricing because it encourages competition. Still, if you buy individual bonds in smaller lots, you should plan on holding them until maturity.

4. The bond's credit rating could be cut, which would lower its market value. This matters principally to investors who might have to sell before maturity. Among the things that could hurt your bond's credit rating: the business goes bad, a takeover stuffs the company's balance sheet with debt, a regulatory commission doesn't let the utility raise its rates.

5. The company might default.

If you choose a corporate, should you buy . . .

. . . An Individual Bond? Possibly, if it's a chip so blue that you think it will never disappoint (rated AA or AAA), the bond is a new issue, you'll hold to maturity, and you're buying for a short or intermediate term. For small investors, COBRAs are a possibility (page 894)—again, top quality, blue, blue, blue. When you buy individual bonds, you are not diversifying, so buy only the very best. The major online brokerage sites let you screen bonds based on various criteria, such as rating, maturity, and yield. The minimum investment is $1,000, but brokers may not accept less than $5,000.

Corporate bonds can be riskier than they seem. A merger or takeover may reduce their quality rating. So would an erosion of the business. In a real crisis, bondholders can be wiped out, or mostly wiped out. When quality corporates are compared with supersafe Treasuries, corporates don't stand up as well. Treasuries can be bought without a sales commission, and the interest they pay is free of state and local income taxes. After tax, quality corporates may yield no more than Treasuries and might even yield less. So why accept the risk?

. . . A Mutual Fund? Absolutely yes. If you're going for corporates, a well-managed, diversified mutual fund is the best buy. Maximize your returns by choosing a no-load fund with low annual costs. The fund may include some of the higher-yielding government-backed securities, such as Ginnie Maes. It may also own some slightly lower-rated bonds to enhance your return and help cover its own expenses.

Warning: two "investment-grade" corporate bond funds may have very different portfolios—one of them heavy with AA and A securities, the other one heavy with BBBs. The fund with the BBBs will have higher yields. It will also rise and fall more in price when interest rates change. Check it out in the prospectus. No-load funds should show this online.

Corporate ETFs are less interesting. An ETF's principal selling point is the tax deferral it offers on capital gains taxes, and bond ETFs don't have much in the way of capital gains. You'll be paying brokerage commissions to buy and sell and not getting anything special in return.

What About Floating-rate Corporate Bonds?

Not worth it, in my view. These corporate bonds pay interest rates that change from time to time, in line with market rates. That's great if interest rates rise. But think about it: why would a company issue floaters when rates are low? No way—they bring them out when they think rates are high and are going to fall, so they'll be able to pay you less. As a civilian up against professionals, I wouldn't take the other side of that bet. Besides, floaters often come from companies with lower credit ratings.

If you want inflation protection, buy Treasury TIPS. The Treasury brings out bonds regularly, whether rates are low or high.

Corporate High-Yield (Junk) Bonds

These bonds, rated BB or lower, act more like stocks. Their price responds to changes in interest rates, but they also rise and fall in line with their company's stock. They produce more current income than higher-quality bonds but also lose more value in the marketplace when the companies that issue them get into trouble. Your total return may be no better than what you'd get with quality bonds, and at more risk. I'm not a fan.

Junk Bonds, Defined. I'm always astonished by the readers who tell me that they wouldn't touch junk with an 11-foot pole (which is the pole they reserve for investments they wouldn't touch with a 10-foot pole). Then they ask what I think of their high-yield bond fund.

They're so blinded by the emotional power of words (*junk* sounding bad, *high-yield* sounding good) that they can't accept that the two are one and the same. But the higher the yield to maturity, the junkier the credit rating. In the bond markets, there is no free lunch.

Corporate junk comes in two types: (1) "Fallen angels"—older bonds from good companies that have gotten into trouble. Perhaps management lost its touch, or perhaps the whole industry is in trouble. These bonds have a pretty good chance of recovering. (2) "Original issue"—new bonds from companies that have had poor quality ratings all along. Some are smaller firms with good potential but not yet ready for prime time. Some are firms with tons of debt already and unlikely to improve. Some rarely trade, due to lack of market interest. Some are true basket cases.

International junk comes from foreign companies whose financial supports are as mysterious to their sponsors as to everyone else.

Why You Might Want Junk Bonds. For the high yield, why else? When bought in good economic times, the average junk bond pays around 3 or 4 percentage points more than Treasury bonds. One problem: that's probably not enough to compensate you for the risk that the economy might sour, in which case your junk fund will drop in price—sometimes precipitously. What you gain in income, you may lose in market value. Ideally, you buy junk in more skeptical times, when the average bond yields 8 or 9 percentage points more than Treasuries. In other words, if you buy junk at all, you should treat it as a timing play, not as a permanent part of your portfolio.

The Drawbacks

1. If the company or project does badly, the bond will default and you'll lose your high interest income. In reorganization, you'd be lucky to get 40 percent of your principal back and might get much less. You might be forced to exchange your bonds for preferred stocks, whose value may sink so low that you'll lose even more of your money.

2. If the company or project does well, the issuer will call in its junk bonds and refinance the debt at a lower rate of interest. So you don't get to keep those lovely high yields. You endure all the risks, then are robbed of some of the rewards. Heads they win, tails you lose.

3. If you want to sell a small number of junk bonds before maturity, it is difficult to get a decent price. Many junkers aren't salable at all.

If you choose junk bonds, should you buy . . .

. . . An Individual Bond? No, no, a thousand times no. Junk is too risky. If you're bold enough to buy these bonds at all, you need to be able to afford a portfolio of them, in the hope that your winners will cover your losers. You also need a terrific bond analyst to buy them for you.

. . . A Mutual Fund? For the average investor, it's the only way to go. You are gambling that, with good management, the fund's high income will more than make up for the capital you'll lose through defaults or loss of market value, especially in recessions. That's not a good gamble. Academic studies have shown that, over the long run, high-yield bond funds do about the same as good-quality funds, while taking more risk along the way. You also need to reinvest those high dividends to make up for the losses your fund will take when some of its bonds lose value or default. If you spend the income, you're consuming your profits and leaving your losses to build up. In short, these funds aren't the bonanza that they appear looking only at their interest payouts. If you want an investment with higher risk, allocate a little bit more of your money to stocks and forget high-yield bonds.

Municipal Bonds

If you're in a middle tax bracket or higher, munis net you more income than you'd earn from taxable bonds. The other beauty of munis is that they almost never default.

Municipals, Defined. Municipal bonds are issued by cities, states, counties, or government entities. They pay less interest than taxable bonds but are exempt from federal tax. If you live in the state where the bond was issued, you're normally exempt from state taxes too. No state taxes the bonds of Puerto Rico, Guam, and the Virgin Islands, but most of them tax the interest on bonds issued by other states. If you own an out-of-state bond in a muni mutual fund, that portion of your dividends may be state-taxed. Municipal bonds issued for private activities are subject to the alternative minimum tax.

Munis come in the same short, medium, and long maturities as any other bonds. The minimum investment is $5,000, but brokers may not accept less than $20,000. You should be able to get 10-year call protection, although some munis sneak in calls after 5 years or less.

The Case for Owning Only Your Own State's Bonds and Bond Funds. You're exempt from state income taxes when you own your own state's bonds. Quality munis (rated AAA and AA) almost never default, so you probably aren't going to lose any money. In cities that levy income taxes, you might buy city bonds and duck local taxes too. If the state gets into trouble, the market value of all its bonds will drop. That doesn't matter, however, if you own the bonds primarily for income or plan to hold them to maturity. You'll almost certainly be paid on time.

If you're holding a single-state mutual fund, however, it matters a lot if that state's credit rating drops. The state will keep making its interest payments, so your income won't be hit. But the value of your fund shares will decline.

The Case for Diversifying into the Bonds of Other States. To say that munis rarely default doesn't mean they never do. At this writing, states and cities are facing large, unfunded liabilities for pensions and health care due to their future retirees. If they start to struggle, their credit ratings and market price will drop. It's possible that a municipality might declare bankruptcy. Supercautious investors own bonds of many states, just in case.

Where state and local taxes are superhigh, investors usually swallow the risk of owning only local bonds. Where taxes aren't so bad, however, check what diversification would cost. Your state will probably tax the income from out-of-state bonds—but how much is that, really, in dollar terms? A multistate bond fund might even yield more than your one-state fund, helping to offset the tax. For the calculation you need to compare multistate with one-state funds, see appendix 1 (page 1191).

If your state levies no income taxes—lucky you. You're free to diversify your investments with multistate bonds or bond funds.

Municipals Come in Several Types

1. General obligation (GO) bonds—backed by the taxes raised by the state or municipality. They are issued for public purposes such as building schools and waste-treatment plants. GOs are the very safest munis. I'm not aware of any defaults. Even so, a GO's credit rating may drop if the issuer's finances weaken. That won't matter to people holding GOs to maturity as long as the issuer pays. But it lowers the value of any tax-exempt mutual funds holding that issuer's bonds.

2. Revenue bonds—backed by revenues from the projects they were issued to finance. Some revenue bonds are of the highest quality, especially when they're issued for essential services. If the proceeds of the bond are used to build a water main, for example, the bond interest may be covered by the very money that residents pay to use the water. But revenue bonds used for lower-income housing, nursing homes, industrial development, and retirement developments can be the bond world's equivalent of the Irish Sweepstakes.

3. Industrial-development and pollution-control bonds—a form of revenue bond used to finance buildings and equipment that will be leased to private companies. The projects have to be for a public purpose. Revenues from the leases pay the bond interest, so their success depends on how well the private companies do. Defaults have been low so far, but these munis carry a higher degree of risk. Some municipalities have been caught issuing "tax-exempts" to raise money for purely private purposes. The feds reclassify them as taxable. Don't buy any bonds that aren't clearly for the public good.

4. Taxable municipals—revenue bonds issued principally for private purposes such as stadiums and shopping centers. They may be exempt from state and local taxes but not from federal tax. Individuals should handle them with care. They're often lower rated and won't pay off unless the enterprise succeeds.

5. Prerefunded municipals—higher-coupon bonds that, for complicated reasons, are effectively backed by U.S. Treasury securities. At the call date, these munis will be redeemed. If you own a muni that the issuer decides to prerefund, its credit quality and price will rise. At that point, you might want to sell the bond. If you hold to maturity, you will lose your capital gain. Alternatively, if the interest rate is rich enough, you might want to keep on collecting interest for as long as you can.

6. Serial bonds—where a portion of the issue comes due every year. That may or may not suit your financial plan. It's important to buy munis that will mature exactly when you'll want the money.

7. "Black-box" bonds—shorthand for bonds issued by state and local agencies to get around state debt-limit laws. They're called black box because no one, including the brokers who sell them, is exactly sure how reliably all these bonds are backed. In a budget crunch, would the issuing agencies have the authority to pay? Who knows? Because of these uncertainties, black-box bonds sell at higher yields than other munis. They're living proof that debt-limit laws make great applause lines for politicians but fundamentally don't work. When a government needs money, it will usually find ways to raise it. Individuals should avoid black boxes. Stick with old-fashioned general obligation bonds and soundly backed revenue bonds.

8. Zero-coupon municipals—see page 946.

9. Inflation-protected municipals—a small but growing market. There's a low, fixed interest rate paid in cash plus an inflation adjustment, payable at maturity. Because these are municipals, you owe no taxes on the interest that accrues.

10. High-yield municipals—with junk ratings of BB or lower. Munis get junk ratings if the project the bonds financed (such as a hospital or bridge) isn't earning enough revenue to cover the debt reliably. Cities and states with intractable budget deficits may also wind up in the junk heap. These munis are risky. They default much more often than low-rated corporates.

Are You in the Right Bracket for Tax-Free Municipals? For a tax-free bond to make any sense, you generally have to be in the 25 percent federal bracket or higher. Occasionally interest rates are high enough, relative to taxable bonds, to attract even those in the 15 percent bracket.

Here's a quick-check table for finding out whether tax-free or taxable bonds make more sense for you, compared with buying Treasuries. When making comparisons, always use bonds or bond mutual funds of equivalent durations and credit quality. Otherwise you might make the wrong choice.

To use this table, look down the left-hand column to find the yield of the tax-exempt bond or fund you're considering. Then read across to the column under your federal income tax bracket. That shows the taxable yield you'd need to match the return from the tax-exempt.

Table 27.

HOW TO CHOOSE BETWEEN TAXABLE
AND TAX-EXEMPT BONDS

	This Is the Minimum Yield You Need from a Treasury Security to Equal a Tax-Exempt, in the Following Tax Brackets					
If a Tax-Exempt Bond Yields:	10%	15%	25%	28%	33%	35%
3.0%	3.3	3.5	4.0	4.2	4.5	4.6
3.5	3.9	4.1	4.7	4.9	5.2	5.4
4.0	4.4	4.7	5.3	5.6	6.0	6.2
4.5	5.0	5.3	6.0	6.3	6.7	6.9
5.0	5.5	5.9	6.7	7.0	7.5	7.7
5.5	6.1	6.5	7.3	7.7	8.2	8.4
6.0	6.7	7.1	8.0	8.3	9.0	9.2
6.5	7.2	7.7	8.7	9.0	9.7	9.9
7.0	7.8	8.2	9.3	9.7	10.4	10.8
7.5	8.3	8.8	10.0	10.4	11.2	11.5
8.0	8.9	9.4	10.7	11.1	12.0	12.3
8.5	9.4	10.0	11.3	11.8	12.7	13.1
9.0	10.0	10.6	12.0	12.5	13.4	13.8

Source: David Kahn, RSM McGladrey, New York City.

Note that this table works only for Treasury securities, where no state and local taxes are owed. If you're considering a corporate bond, your break-even yield will be a little higher. A short calculation in appendix 1 (page 1191) shows you what a corporate would have to earn.

That appendix also provides calculations for (1) working backward from a taxable security to see what tax-exempt yield you'd need to beat it; (2) checking the taxable equivalent of tax-exempt securities whose yields don't show on this table; (3) finding tax equivalents for higher brackets than those shown here; and (4) finding out whether you'd net more from a mutual fund that owns only your own state's bonds or a higher-yielding fund containing the bonds of several states.

The Death (and Future Recovery?) of Municipal Bond Insurance. For years, retail investors have been choosing insured municipal bonds. If the issuer of the bonds defaults, the insurance company will make all the interest and principal payments as they come due. To make this work, the insurance company has to be rated AAA—meaning very safe. A municipal bond with a single-A rating rises to a AAA rating once it becomes insured. That reduces the interest rate that the issuer of the bond has to pay to attract investors. Insurance gives investors comfort.

Or rather, it used to give investors comfort. Some bond insurers failed during the 2007–2009 credit collapse, because they'd carelessly branched out into insuring high-risk mortgage securities. Other insurers lost their AAA credit ratings and dragged down the market value of the munis they insured. The municipal bonds themselves were fine—they kept paying interest and principal on schedule. They turned out to be safer and more reliable than the companies that supposedly guaranteed them.

At this writing, there's only one AAA-rated municipal bond insurance company—Berkshire Hathaway Assurance. But why would you want insured bonds? The cost of insurance subtracts anywhere from 0.15 percent to 0.3 percent from your yield, and the chance of default is virtually nil.

In 2007 Standard & Poor's studied uninsured munis issued by 10,260 borrowing units during the previous 20 years. There were zero—repeat, zero—defaults among those rated AAA or AA at any point during their life. Among the single As, only 0.16 percent defaulted and among the BBBs, only 0.29 percent. That's a far better record than you see in investment-grade corporate bonds, which are sold without insurance.

Note that the insurer does not guarantee the bond's market value. You are not reimbursed if you sell before maturity and lose money because the bond's rating is down or if you lose money in an insured bond mutual fund. You're protected only against nonpayment of interest and principal. That is, you *may* be protected, depending on whether the insurer survives.

Bond insurance may get another lease on life if a large municipal bond issuer defaults. But you don't have to worry about default if you stick with issues rated AAA or AA.

My take: Don't waste your money on insured munis or insured muni bond funds. Instead pick simple, uninsured, high-grade general obligation or revenue bonds or the mutual funds that buy them. Lower-grade issues yield more and hardly ever default but might cause you to worry during a period when government budgets come under pressure.

Why You Might Want Tax-Free Bonds. Why else but to keep your capital safe and earn a safe and steady tax-free income? If you don't need the income to live on, reinvest every interest payment in more bonds or in tax-free money market mutual funds. Otherwise your capital will lose purchasing power. If you expect to drop to a low tax bracket in retirement, time your munis to expire by retirement day. At that point, you'd want to reinvest the proceeds in Treasuries for a safe but higher yield.

The Drawbacks to Tax-free Bonds

1. **The liquidity is awful on small, individual holdings.** If you try to sell a $5,000 bond before maturity, you'll probably have to accept a discount ("haircut") of 2 to 3 percent. On a $10,000 bond, the haircut might run 1 to 1.5 percent. That's on top of brokerage commissions. In short, selling early wrecks your total return. To get decent prices, you have to sell in $100,000 lots.

2. **If you live in a state with budget problems, your risks compound.** Your bonds' credit ratings might be downgraded, which would lower their price. You'd wind up with a low return or even a loss if you had to sell before maturity. One or more of the low-grade bonds you bought might even default.

3. **Unlike Treasuries, munis can be called, generally after 10 years.** So you might get your principal back early. If interest rates have fallen, you will have to reinvest at a lower rate, which will lower the yield you earn on your capital.

4. **If you're subject to the *alternative minimum tax,* tell your broker about it.** The AMT taxes certain types of municipals, such as student loan bonds and some industrial-development bonds. Luckily for me, advanced tax advice is outside the mission of this book. See an accountant.

5. The amount of investor protection is pitiful. Municipalities are exempt from many of the laws on financial disclosure that rule corporations. Since 1995, they've been required to tell investors about changes in their financial condition—for better or worse. They're also supposed to disclose how much they expect to pay for their employees' future pensions and health care, and how well that obligation is funded. These disclosures should be zapped to depositories where brokers can check them. It's the issuers' obligation to report and the broker's obligation to check, so you won't unknowingly buy from an issuer in financial trouble.

Unfortunately for muni investors, these rules are generally unenforced. Many issuers don't provide reports or are chronically late, sometimes by several years. When you buy an older bond, the issuer might be in financial trouble but hasn't disclosed it yet (there's supposed to be a "distress notice" on file). This is yet another reason not to buy older bonds. You might pay a premium price for a bond whose future payments are at risk. By contrast, newly issued munis have been checked by the credit agencies, so you know what you're getting.

6. Funds labeled *dividend advantage* look appealing because they promise you extra yield. They do it by borrowing money to buy additional bonds. That looks great up front but can stick you with big losses whenever the market turns down.

How to Get a Good Price on Older Bonds. Newly issued bonds sell at par ($1,000 a bond). But older issues trade at more or less than par, depending on the market at the time. Sometimes brokers add extravagant markups when you buy and pay shameless, below-market prices when you sell.

There are two places to go to see if a broker's price is fair: Investinginbonds .com (www.investinginbonds.com; click on Municipal-Market-At-a-Glance) and the Municipal Securities Rulemaking Board's Electronic Municipal Market Access (www.emma.msrb.org). They both list the wholesale prices of bonds that are trading currently. To identify the bond, it helps to have its individual CUSIP number, issued by the Committee on Uniform Security Identification Procedures (the broker can give it to you).

If you choose a municipal bond, should you buy . . .

. . . An Individual Bond? Yes, if your state or city has a top credit rating, you can afford to diversify over four or five issues, and you are sure that you can hold the bonds until they mature. You pay no sales commission if you buy a new issue and escape the sales charges and continuing fees charged by mutual funds and unit trusts. At maturity, you will get all your capital back (assuming no defaults). That's a promise that mutual funds can't make because they have no maturity date.

The munis you choose should pass the following tests: (1) They're blue-chip quality, AAA or AA. (2) They're general obligation bonds or revenue bonds for an essential municipal service. (3) They mature within 10 years, so you're pretty sure of holding for the full term (which is not so likely with 30-year bonds). Alternatively, they are targeted to mature in exactly the year that you know you're going to want the money. (4) They don't have an early call date. (5) They're a new issue, so you get the same price that the professionals pay. If only an older bond fits the maturity you need, ferret out the markup to see if the price is fair (page 910). Don't buy a low-rated or unrated muni under the illusion that, since it's a "government issue," it's safe. It isn't.

. . . A Mutual Fund? Yes, if: (1) You want to be able to draw on your money without waiting for your bonds to mature. This is just as important for people with large amounts to invest as for small investors. (2) You aren't sure exactly when you might need to tap your principal: also important for investors of any size. Fund shares can be sold at any time, at a better price than individual bonds would bring if you had to liquidate them before maturity (although in either case, you could lose some of your principal if interest rates have risen). (3) You understand the market risk of the fund you chose. Some funds keep a high percentage of their money in high-quality bonds. Others concentrate on lower-quality A and BBB bonds. The latter yield more but could run into heavy weather if the market is roiled by rising interest rates or falling credit quality. Some of their bonds might slip from BBB down to junk, at great loss to their shareholders. These bonds would still be making interest payments, but their market price would fall. (4) You choose a no-load (no-sales-charge) fund with low expenses, so your yield doesn't go through a meat grinder.

Whenever there's a major default (Orange County, for example), prices of muni funds usually sag. That's almost always a buying opportunity.

There are municipal bond ETFs, but, for technical reasons, they're not as efficient as traditional muni mutual funds. They may find it hard to match the performance of the funds, and, of course, you pay brokerage commissions to buy and sell (including when you reinvest your dividends).

Zero-Coupon Bonds

Zeros are for extremists. You're either a wild speculator hoping for a quick capital gain or a careful planner who wants to lock in a fixed sum of money by a certain date.

Zeros, Defined. A zero bond has no current "coupon" or interest payment. Instead you buy the bond at a fraction of its face value and wait. The interest accumulates within the bond itself, usually compounded semiannually. At maturity, the bond is redeemed for its face value.

For example, suppose that in June 2010 you buy a 10-year, $1,000 Treasury zero yielding 4.75 percent. You'd have paid $625.35. The following year, the bond would be worth $655, thanks to accumulated interest. The year after that, you'd have $686. And so on up. (The bond's value also rises and falls in response to market conditions, but that's another story.) In June 2020, you'll redeem that zero for $1,000.

Most people who buy zeros go for Treasury bonds, although you might also be interested in municipal zeros. Corporate zeros are bought chiefly by institutions.

All the interest you earn will compound at the bond's own internal interest rate—in the previous example, 4.75 percent. A regular bond can't do that for you. With regular bonds, you get a dividend check every six months and have to reinvest the money as best you can (for example, in a money market fund).

You have to buy zeros through a full-service or discount brokerage firm; they aren't available through TreasuryDirect. Brokers call them STRIPS, meaning Separate Trading of Registered Interest and Principal of Securities. (Aren't you sorry you asked?) Zeros can also be backed by mortgage securities such as Ginnie Maes.

There are two ways of buying zeros. You can get them when they're newly issued, or you can turn to the secondary market and buy an older zero out of a brokerage firm's inventory. New issues are best. New-issue Treasury STRIPS can generally be had in a wide variety of maturities. Among tax-exempts, however, your choice will be more limited.

Whether you buy new issues or older ones, they should yield whatever Treasuries are yielding in the market now, for comparable maturities. Check the current yields at Investinginbonds.com.

Warning: stockbrokers tend to talk prices, not yields. For just $395, your broker might say, you'll have $1,000 in 20 years. What's the yield? On the surface, 4.75 percent, which might sound just fine for your particular purposes. But if the commission is $25 per STRIP, your net yield drops to 4.62 percent. Another broker might charge you $395 plus only $10 per STRIP, for a fatter net yield of 4.7 percent. So always ask about yield to maturity after commissions (the net yield should show on your confirmation slip). Compare that with what you might net if you bought from a discount broker. I comparison shopped a few years ago and found a difference of $34 per $1,000 between the highest and lowest offers. That's a difference in yield of 3.4 percent—not chicken feed.

Why You Might Want a Zero

1. You want to guarantee that you'll have a fixed sum of money in a certain year. By paying $625 in June 2007, for example, you knew for sure that you'll have $1,000 in July 2017. Zeros are good for covering fixed-dollar obligations, such as paying off your mortgage on the day you retire, repaying a balloon loan, or guaranteeing a future cash payout negotiated as part of a divorce.

2. You are speculating on falling interest rates. Recite your mantra: falling interest rates are good. When interest rates fall, bond prices rise. When rates decline, zeros move up faster in price than any other kind of bond. So they're the gambler's chip of choice.

3. You want to lock in a tax-exempt interest rate. Most Treasury and many muni zeros cannot be called prior to maturity. That's the only kind to buy. Noncallable munis yield a little less than callable ones do, but callable zeros may foil your investment goal.

The Drawbacks

1. If interest rates rise instead of fall, you'll lose more value in zeros than you would in other bonds if you have to sell before maturity. For proof, see table 25 on page 925. So buy only zeros that you're sure you can hold to term. If retirement is 15 years away, buy a 15-year zero, not a 30-year zero that you'll have to sell if you need to raise cash.

2. Income taxes are owed every year on the interest buildup inside a zero-coupon Treasury. But your bond doesn't pay any cash to help cover the tax. To avoid paying taxes on phantom income, put Treasury zeros into tax-deferred retirement plans. If you're using the zeros to fund a particular future payment, consider using tax-free municipal zeros.

If you buy an older zero rather than a new one, you'll complicate your tax return. In the year that you buy the zero, only part of the taxable interest belongs to you; the rest belongs to the seller. You'll need an accountant to sort it out.

3. Some zeros are callable. Your bonds might be snatched away after 5 or 10 years, when you had planned on holding them for 15. Early calls are doubly painful because a zero's big payoff comes during the final third of the bond's life. If a broker sold you a zero municipal priced at more than its current principal and interest value (it happens), you could lose principal on an early call.

If you choose a zero, should you buy . . .

. . . An Individual Bond? Yes, if you plan to hold until maturity. It's the cheapest way of buying these bonds, assuming that you get a good price. With zero-coupon Treasuries, you don't have to diversify. Most brokers' commissions run $5 to $10 per bond.

. . . A Mutual Fund? In most cases, no. The funds levy annual management fees, which reduce your yield. Buy a fund only if you're speculating on falling interest rates. It's cheaper to trade no-load mutual fund shares than to buy and sell zeros directly, and you'll get a fairer price on the bonds.

Unlike other bond mutual funds, zero-coupon funds have fixed maturity dates—for example, 2015, 2020, 2025, 2030, or 2035. On maturity day, all the bonds are redeemed and the investors paid. The further away the maturity date, the bigger your profit if interest rates fall and you sell before maturity. Conversely, the bigger your market losses if interest rates rise. But you suffer no loss if you hold the fund to maturity.

Convertible Bonds

Convertible bonds are widely marketed to conservative investors, especially retirees, as a "safer" way of participating in stock market growth. But they carry more risks than many buyers realize.

Convertibles, Defined. These bonds can be converted into a fixed number of the company's common shares. You can make the exchange when the common shares have risen to a certain price. While you're waiting, you earn interest, although not as much as you'd earn from that company's regular bonds.

When the stock price rises, the price of the convertible normally goes up too, although not as much. You can sell your converts at a profit if you'd rather not make the switch to stocks.

When the stock price falls, converts normally don't drop quite as far as the underlying stock. Like a bondholder, you can sit tight and collect a regular income.

Why You Might Want a Convertible. They pay higher dividends than the underlying stock. There's potential growth if the stock appreciates and somewhat less risk if the market falls. But there's more risk than you think. In a decline, converts drop almost as precipitously as stocks.

What they don't tell you: many converts come from smaller, low-rated companies. When the market drops, the convertibles don't decline as far as the underlying stock, but that may not be saying much. They may lose more value than blue-chip stocks. What's "safe" about that?

Furthermore, the convertibles market isn't as liquid as the market for bonds and stocks. If a lot of people want to sell, prices will drop more quickly than they would for other investments. That's another reason why converts don't give you as much bear market protection as you might expect.

The Drawbacks

1. **They pay less income than you'd get from regular bonds and offer less appreciation than you could get from stocks.** Conservative investors will accept that in return for offsetting gains. But you may not know about the other risks.

2. **A convert costs more than the underlying stock is currently worth.** So you're making a bet that the stock price will rise substantially. In the mid-1990s, you won that bet; after the turn of the century, you lost it. Pricing convertibles is a science too complex for the average investor. If you overpay, it might take years to make the money you expected. Your bond might even be called by the company before you've had time to earn a profit.

3. **Let's assume that you get lucky and the company's stock is running well.** Your convert is moving up in price, and you're collecting nice interest payments. Suddenly the bond might be called. That forces you to sell or convert to the stock, like it or not. If you weren't following your investment and heard about the call too late, you'll still get the call value of the bond, but you will lose the extra value that the bond had gained in the marketplace.

If you choose a convertible bond, should you buy . . .

. . . An Individual Bond? No. You don't know how much to pay for it, and the risk is high because so many converts are issued by companies with poor credit ratings.

. . . A Mutual Fund? Yes, if you absolutely must. Buy why not buy a balanced stock-and-bond fund rather than muddle along with a mediocre hybrid? Or why not a high-yield bond fund, since so many converts are from lower-quality companies too? As a class, high-yield funds tend to outperform converts.

International and Emerging-Market Bonds

See chapter 27.

Hey, Jane, You Forgot to Mention Money Funds . . .

No, I didn't. Money market mutual funds are not investments, they're variable-rate savings accounts. I love them for your ready cash (page 220). They're terrific parking places for funds awaiting investment somewhere else. They're ballast for a portfolio with too much risk, but they are not long-term investments in themselves.

When you stash most of your assets in a money fund, you are robbing yourself of growth. You'll appear to stay even with inflation, but, after tax, your purchasing power will slowly shrink. The investment alternative to money funds is a short-term one- or two-year bond fund. It pays a slightly higher yield with small risk to your ready cash, provided that the fund also has a short duration (page 911).

. . . And Tax-Deferred Annuities

Check them out on page 1071, along with all the other tax-deferred investment vehicles.

The Dialogue of Stocks and Bonds

Investors often act as if stocks and bonds live in separate worlds: one on Neptune and one on Mars, with orbits that will never cross. In fact, they are two sides of the same financial marketplace, always adjusting to each other's prices. Investors who follow their dialogue have a better feel for what's going on.

Stock and bond prices rise and fall approximately in tandem. If stock prices are booming while bonds are fading, something's wrong. Either bonds will perk up or stocks will turn down. Stock and bond prices do move in opposite directions for short periods of time. But they're never happy until they're once again on parallel tracks.

Bonds usually (but not always) lead stocks, which is why investors should pay attention to what the bond markets are doing. A spectacular example came in 1987. The bond market crashed in April and May, while stock investors were still reaching for the stars. Then, in October, stocks crashed too.

The mediator between stocks and bonds is interest rates. Their influence on the market cycle is crystal clear.

At the start of a typical cycle, interest rates rise and bond prices gradually decline. For a while, stock investors pay no attention. But eventually rates get so high that investors can't resist them. They move money out of stocks and into various fixed-income vehicles. Stocks start to fall. ("Usually," says Roy Neuberger of the investment firm Neuberger & Berman, "when both short-term and long-term rates start rising, they tell the stock investor one story: run for the hills.")

High interest rates also put a damper on business. The economy slinks into recession, and demand for new credit slows way down.

This is when the cycle turns. Slow credit demand means that interest rates have room to fall, which causes bond prices to rise. When rates have been low enough, long enough, professional investors switch some of their money out of interest rate investments and back into stocks. Stock prices bottom out and move sharply up. Bonds have led stocks once again.

Typically, however, market-timing investors don't yet believe that anything has changed. They sit through the first 30 or 40 percent of the rise in stocks without lifting a finger to invest, thus losing some of the market's fastest gains.

Why do stock investors wait so long to buy? Usually because the economy is in the pits. They forget that markets anticipate. Falling interest rates signal easier credit, which paves the way for recovery. Investors should anticipate too, or else stay in the market all the time.

Stocks and bonds have one more important relationship: they define the risks you choose to take and what your returns are likely to be. If you think you've been setting your investment sights too low, you'll reduce the percentage of bonds and other fixed-income investments you hold and raise your long-term commitment to stocks. If you think you've been taking unreasonable risks, you'll buy fewer stocks (or different ones), lower your holdings of long-term bonds, and move into short- and intermediate-term bonds. Either way, the balance you strike between stocks and bonds will determine the size of the nest egg you'll have when you come to the end of your working life.

26

The Call of the Wild

Some Absolutely Awful Investments

Wall Streeter Ray DeVoe called it the Crack of Doom. It's the point when you know for sure that not only are you going to lose money, but you are going to lose a lot more money than you can afford.

Quinn's First Law of Investing is never to buy anything whose price you can't follow online. An investment without a public marketplace attracts the fabulists the way picnics attract ants. Stockbrokers and financial planners can tell you anything they want because no one really knows what's true.

The First Corollary to Quinn's First Law says that even when the price is available online, you shouldn't buy anything too complex to explain to the average 12-year-old.

These rules proscribe some of Wall Street's most popular investments. They're "popular" not because you've been dying to own them but because brokers and planners press them upon you. Not coincidentally, they all carry higher sales commissions than surer, simpler investments do. I wouldn't touch any of them myself—and I hope that you'll avoid them too.

I won't even offer you "how-to" lists for finding gems among the dreck. Some gems exist, but they're not worth the time it takes to do the research or the risk that your broker will talk you into buying something that you shouldn't. What's more, today's diamonds may turn into zircons overnight.

Hedge Funds: For People with Money to Lose

The competition for "worst investment" is pretty stiff, but hedge funds definitely make the cut. Some hedge funds have earned spectacular returns, and naturally those are the ones you hear the most about. Thousands of other funds produce subpar gains or fail. Originally, these private investment funds were designed to "hedge" against different types of markets. They bought stocks "long" (to hold in case prices rose) and sold other stocks "short" (to make money if stocks declined). Both positions were held at once, in the hope of making money under any market scenario. That's what a hedge is supposed to do.

Today the hedge fund universe has exploded into dozens of styles. Traditional long/short funds are generally called *market neutral*. Those that use unconventional assets such as commodities, to try to earn gains in any weather, say they seek *absolute returns*. Another group of funds specializes in *arbitrage*—using computers to find tiny differences in securities that are virtually alike, then buying one and selling the other at the same time to lock in risk-free returns. Yet others buy *distressed securities*—stocks or bonds in the toilet. Or they're *event driven*—betting on certain types of corporate events such as mergers or spin-offs. *130/30 funds* hold long positions worth 130 percent of the portfolio and shorts worth 30 percent of the total. *Macro funds* make big bets on anything they want anywhere in the world.

In none of these funds, however, can you find out what they're really doing, because they don't have to tell you. You do know that they're taking high risks on borrowed money with virtually no government regulation.

Hedge funds peddle three ideas:

1. Because of their hedges, they're not as risky as other funds. *Wrong.* See their subpar average market performance, below. They abandoned traditional hedging to take higher risks and often lost.

2. Their managers are smarter than anyone else in the market and hence will make more money for investors. *Wrong.* Again, just look at their average performance. Some smart managers succeed brilliantly, and others don't. The brilliant managers may succeed in one market climate but not in another. Plenty of them aren't as smart as they think they are.

3. They bring stability to a portfolio because they're not correlated with other investments—they may hold steady while other parts of the market are going down. *Wrong, wrong, wrong.* Hedge fund prices swing wildly. Hundreds of funds went down in 1998 when Russia defaulted on its debt, and hundreds more vanished when the market plunged in 2007–2009. Without question, some funds succeed in their mission and swing against the market, or at least decline less than stocks as a whole, but then, "some funds" always do. There's no magic to a hedge. A 2006 study by Bernstein Wealth Management Research concluded that if your objective is to stabilize your investments, skip hedge funds and buy bonds.

During bull markets, affluent investors love to buy hedge funds—not only in the hope of profit but for their mystique. That's where the big boys play. Some brokerage firms put together "funds of hedge funds" and sell them in $15,000 or $20,000 lots to give bragging rights to wannabes.

Hedge funds may work for the superwealthy and large institutions that can spread millions of dollars over a group of managers they meet with and whose strategies they get to know. Large gains in a couple of their funds will (they hope) offset losses in the others.

Hedge funds do not work for the average affluent, and here's why:

1. Fees, fees, fees. The funds typically charge 1 to 2 percent a year plus 20 percent of the annual profits, including "paper" profits that might evaporate next year. They don't share in the losses—those are all yours. You pay yet another layer of fees if you diversify by buying a package of funds (a "fund of funds")—maybe 1.75 percent of assets or 1 percent plus 10 percent of the profits. Then add administrative fees and trading fees. Your fund has to be a huge winner just for you to net Treasury bill returns! Bernstein Wealth Management Research found that the funds with higher fees produced lower returns. Duh.

2. Risk, risk, risk. Hedge funds may have highly concentrated positions. They earn outsize gains when they win and suffer outsize losses when they lose.

3. Subpar average returns. The HRRX Global Hedge Fund Index is one of the benchmarks for hedge fund performance. From 2003 through 2008—a period that covers a rising market and a steeply falling one—the index did worse than *all* the major investment classes: U.S. stocks, international stocks, emerging market stocks, and fixed-income vehicles.

4. Phony, inflated investment returns, including the data cited above. Hedge funds aren't required to make their performance public. Disclosure is entirely voluntary. The funds that report are those trolling for investors or managing money for public pension funds. They typically stop reporting, however, if they're not doing well and expect to go out of business within a few months. The worst performances don't get into the public reports of average returns.

Furthermore—and this should amaze you—they're free to play games with their reports. For example, a hedge fund can carry illiquid assets on its books at the price it paid, not the current, estimated market price, which makes the fund seem more stable than it really is. It may fudge the value of illiquid investments to hide losses and boost its annual fee. The management company may start several small "incubator" funds with in-house money to see how they perform. Those with low returns are closed; those with higher returns are launched as new funds. When they launch, they "backfill" their public records by reporting their performance from the days when they were small and not managed as public funds.

The result of all this accounting hanky-panky? Returns that are *highly* over-stated. The hedge fund industry claimed an average return of 13.5 percent from 1996 through 2003. A 2004 study* found that, subtracting the fudges and failures and adjusting for fees, they actually earned just 9.7 percent, compared with 12.3 percent for Standard & Poor's stock average.

5. Disaster in falling markets. Hundreds of funds failed in 2008–2009 when the markets dropped, global credit dried up, and investors screamed for their money back. Many survived the storm, of course, including some of those specializing in short selling. But their gains failed to outweigh the losses in the rest of the industry. Some of the largest players had to fold. Various multiyear studies have found that over whole business cycles, hedge funds in general have underperformed the major stock averages.

6. High death rates. Of all the hedge funds active in 1996, fewer than 25 percent were still alive nine years later, according to a study published in 2005. These wipeouts don't show up in the performance averages either, but billions of investor dollars have gone down the tubes. The average life of hedge funds is only about five years. When you look at their reported records on Morningstar, it's unusual to see returns for more than two or three years.

7. Deceptive guarantees. You may think you're protected by a "high-water mark." If the fund's value drops, the managers don't get their 20 percent until the value recovers and rises past its previous high. Only problem: if the fund stays under water for a couple of years, the managers may decide it will never recover and shut it down. While you're nursing your losses, they'll move to a new fund—probably one of several they've been incubating privately. They'll pick one with hot performance, natch, open it to investors, and start raking in their 20 percent. This game helps explain why so many funds fail: their managers don't want to bother keeping them open in years when they can't rip the investors for anything more than management fees.

8. Locked-up money. You might not be able to withdraw your cash for six months, one year, or even more. Quarterly results may not be reported for several weeks. When you ask for the money, you may have to wait 30 to 90 days for the check. Favored investors may get "side letters" letting them get their money earlier—but that's not likely to include you. In a run on the funds, as

*"Hedge Funds: Risk and Return," by economist Burton Malkiel of Princeton University and Atanu Saha, a managing principal at the Analysis Group, a consulting firm.

happened during the 2008 credit collapse, the managers may suspend redemptions.

9. Extra taxes. Their trading practices can create a lot of short-term capital gains, taxable as ordinary income. Long/short funds might be managed for tax efficiency, but that's not so easy for other types of funds. Anyway, most hedge fund managers, including the long/shorts, don't pay much attention to taxes.

10. Dirty dealing. For a short period of time in 2006, the Securities and Exchange Commission required hedge funds to register, like other funds, and submit to SEC audits. The funds sued, and a court concluded that the SEC didn't have the authority to peek. So all is dark again. But during those few months of sunshine, the government found dirty practices all over the place: false asset valuations, reporting the results only of their better investments to the fund databases, and trading on inside information, to name just three. I can guarantee that those practices are still going on.

Some hedge funds turn into private-equity funds—pools of cash that buy and manage companies. They're for high rollers only.

A slew of mutual funds mimic hedge fund strategies (130/30, long/short, and so on and so forth) because that's the sexy thing to do. Like ladies of the night, they'll follow money anywhere. Don't buy hedge fund mimics, either.

Penny Stocks and Online Touts: For Suckers Only

Most of the penny stocks come from mystery companies, with an untested business, that sell for $3 or less per share. Not all cheap stocks are bad. Some are respectable companies that have fallen on *really* hard times. But almost all the rotten issues are cheap. They're peddled by phone by Hole-in-the-Wall Gangs who transfix their victims with the claim that the investment "cannot lose." Or they buy Google search words to con you on the Internet. If you type in "hot stocks" and sign up for one of the investment-tip services, you deserve all the losses you're going to take.

The "research" they give you on penny stock companies is usually paid for by the company itself. It writes a wonderful fairy tale about its future and hires an apparently "disinterested" print or online newsletter to pitch it to suckers. You'll read about a fabulous project under development, important patents pending, plans to partner with a major (unnamed) company, $1 billion markets that the company expects to get a share of. All baloney. Favorite types of "new products" deal with balding, erectile dysfunction, aging, weight loss, and other health issues—stuff you'd like to buy yourself if it were on the market and actually worked. You're blinded not only by your dreams of money but your dreams of being young and gorgeous all over again!

The online tip sheets deceive you in other ways. They boast about stocks they say they backed that subsequently rose in value 1,000 percent—but they pick the stocks after they rise and pretend that they recommended them all along. They get you excited about a subpenny stock worth $0.0004 cent a share that went to 0.72 cent, raising a $1,000 investment to $1.8 million in one month. (Do you really believe you could have sold your shares for that price? To whom?)

That brings me to pump-and-dump schemes. You buy a stock that the broker or the newsletter tipped, and it goes up! You buy another, and that goes up too! These guys, you tell yourself, really know what they're doing. Well . . . they do, but not in the way you think. What's really happening is that the market makers—all insiders—are selling their own stock to you at higher and higher prices that they pick out of thin air (the pump). They might even let you make some money on a small buy to get you to buy some more. After you've racked up larger "profits" and want to sell, you'll discover that no one wants to buy except at a price that's even less than the pennies you paid (the dump). Pump-and-dump stocks are also showing up as text messages and cell phone spam. You might get a phony "wrong number" call on your voice mail ("Hi, it's me, I just want to say that that stock I mentioned, Jumping Cow, got its government contract and will go through the moon when that's announced. But don't tell anyone, this is for your ears only"), or a similar "wrong address" e-mail.

Some investors think they're wise to these games and can make money by being first in, first out. Online scams take advantage of that attitude too. They tell you that a small company is preparing a big publicity campaign and that the buzz will drive up the price. Buy now, buy now, before "the public" hears! But who, I ask you, do you think "the public" is? Why would you imagine that something on the Internet is somehow secret? The whole pitch is false.

Some penny stock hustles are "blank checks" or "blind pools." (One state securities commissioner calls them "deaf pools," as in "Give me your money, and you'll never hear from me again.") You buy shares in a hollow company, or "shell," that does no business of its own. When it gets your money, it goes looking for small private companies to buy. Some of these companies are legitimate, such as a printer or a bakery. Others are frauds.

Always hang up on high-pressure penny stock brokers. Ignore stocks that don't trade on a major exchange (the exchanges set financial requirements for the stocks they list). Never hunt for hot-stock sites on the Internet. If this advice comes too late, sell your shares and rescue whatever money you can.

Unit Trusts: The Mystery Deals

Imagine a house with an elephant in the basement. It's been said that the animal holds up the house. Grateful for the constant support, the householders feed their elephant lavishly. But they never go down with a flashlight to see if the beast is as big as they thought.

That pretty much defines the bizarre faith engendered by unit investment trusts, a multibillion-dollar industry directed especially to conservative investors. You buy bond unit trusts for their "steady income" and "locked-in yields" and stock unit trusts because you believe in a particular investment strategy. Stockbrokers like to claim, based on *no* independent evidence, that the trusts do better than comparable mutual funds.

But no one has ever gone down with a flashlight to look. One academic study that tried to make the comparison gave up, because virtually no performance data are available for unit trusts. I know of no other major investment with so complete a blackout on how well (or poorly) participants are doing. Trust sponsors claim "transparency" because you get a list of the securities in the trust. But that's very different from having daily data on how that particular mix of securities is doing. There's simply no hard information on whether unit trusts are better than, the same as, or worse than competing mutual funds. Because of this blackout, and the temptation it offers to put weak securities in the trusts, I suspect the worst.

A unit trust is a fixed portfolio of stocks, bonds, or other securities. The sponsor assembles a package of them and sells them as new offerings. You buy an interest in the package for a minimum of $1,000 or $2,000. The trust is held, virtually unchanged, for anywhere from 6 months to 30 years. Securities are occasionally sold out of the trust, but normally, no new ones are added. At the end of the term, the remaining securities are sold and the proceeds distributed to the investors.

Unit trusts aren't cheap. The up-front sales commission runs in the area of 3 percent, with another 1.5 percent in the second year, plus an 0.5 percent "creation fee"—5 percent in all. Annual fees run in the 0.4 to 1 percent range. Brokers tell you that trusts are cheaper than mutual funds because they carry a lower annual fee. But the sales commissions on the trusts are generally higher, so this is a dubious claim.

Investors in a unit trust receive a pro rata share of its interest or dividends, mailed to them monthly, quarterly, or semiannually.

In a bond unit trust, you also receive a pro rata share of the proceeds as the bonds mature. For example, take a $20,000 investment in a municipal bond unit trust. Initially you might earn $50 a month in bond interest. Five years later, a block of those bonds may mature. You'd receive a $2,000 check representing your share of the proceeds. That $2,000 is a return of some of the capital you invested. After that, your monthly check might drop to $45 because there are fewer bonds in the trust. Each check specifies how much is interest and how much is principal.

Ginnie Mae unit trusts are a little more complicated. They invest in mortgages, so every check you get is a combination of mortgage interest and principal, the latter being a partial return of your own capital. Every time a home owner prepays a mortgage, the proceeds are distributed to the trust's investors (for more on Ginnie Maes, see page 931). Your entire investment plus interest will be gradually paid out over the term of the trust.

The distributions you receive from bond unit trusts usually cannot be reinvested in the trust itself. The sponsor arranges for them to be invested in a mutual fund. Distributions from equity unit trusts are generally reinvested in the trust itself.

You can switch to another trust within the same family, generally at a reduced sales charge. You may be able to sell your units back to the sponsor before maturity, at whatever it considers market price. If the sponsor isn't buying, you can redeem your shares from the trustee—in which case, shares may have to be sold to pay you off. After fees, you'll probably get less than the portfolio's net asset value.

Equity Unit Trusts: A Mistake, Four Ways

If your trust mimics the performance of a stock index, you are overpaying bigtime. You can get index mutual funds from Vanguard or Fidelity for 0.2 percent a year or less, and with no up-front sales charge. If you buy index performance through a unit trust, you're throwing away money.

If your trust holds stocks chosen by a manager, you're stuck with those decisions for the trust's entire term. A bad stock won't be sold, it will just sit there and rot. Better stocks won't be substituted. Some unit trusts follow short-term investment theories, such as Dow Dogs: buying the 10 highest-yielding Dow stocks at the end of each year.* In theory, these stocks outperform the general market average. In practice, sometimes they do, sometimes they don't. But notice the genius of the pitch: you have to buy a new unit trust, with a new sales charge, every year. Those costs will be hard for even good Dogs to overcome.

---

*Some Dog trusts buy the 10 Dow stocks with the lowest percentage price change over the previous year. There are lots of theories. Woof.

You also have to pay taxes on your annual gains, unless you hold the Dogs in a tax-deferred account.

With either type of trust, your return depends on what happens in the market over a fixed period of time. If your trust matures during a downturn, tough luck. You don't have the option of holding on. If you want to stay invested when the portfolio terminates, you can move your money into a new trust—again, paying a new sales charge and paying taxes on any gain. Why would you do that? Why not buy a regular mutual fund that you can hold as long as you like?

Finally, if your unit trust faces a lot of redemptions and securities have to be sold, the investors remaining in the trust could get hurt. The sales may lock in market losses or reduce the likelihood of future gains.

The Question for Bond Trust Investors Is Whether They Will Really Earn Those Lovely Yields They Read About in the Sales Literature

When you buy, you're quoted an "estimated current return," based on the bonds in the portfolio. The bonds aren't changed over the life of the trust, so you assume that that's what you'll get for the entire term.

Not likely.

To begin with, bond unit trusts rarely last until their maturity date. When the trust's principal value has shrunk to perhaps 25 or 20 percent of its opening value, the sponsor often sells the remaining securities and distributes the proceeds. That shag-end sale may bring a profit or a loss, depending on market conditions at the time. Some unit trusts have been dumping grounds for bonds that the sponsors otherwise couldn't sell. At liquidation, investors in these trusts would almost certainly take a loss.

Furthermore, you probably won't get the promised "steady stream of income," for the following reasons:

1. Some of the higher-interest bonds will probably be called before maturity or retired through a sinking fund. This usually lowers your final yield. The trusts try for call protection on their bonds of at least 5 years and sometimes 10. But that's a far cry from a "steady stream of income" on a 30-year trust. If long-term, guaranteed income is your objective, buy noncallable Treasury bonds instead.

2. Some securities will be sold out of the trust in order to cover early redemptions. If the amount of bonds sold exceeds the sum redeemed (as sometimes happens), the leftover money will be distributed to investors, returning a small share of their principal whether they want it or not. In choosing which securities to sell, the trusts try to hold your yield steady. Sometimes they can; sometimes they can't.

3. The credit quality of some bonds will slide. If a bad bond has to be sold out of the portfolio, you lose some of your principal. If a bond defaults, you lose interest and, generally, part of your principal (although some residual value will remain). Junk bond unit trusts are double trouble. Their better-quality bonds get called because those issuers will be able to borrow at lower rates. The poorer bonds remain in the trust. After the calls, you lose some of your "steady" income, and you're stuck with the issues most likely to default. Because of the trust's opaque structure, you'll never know.

4. Some trusts are smoke and mirrors (S&M). They pay a higher income than you'd get from other bond investments, which makes you think that you're earning a superior yield. But, in fact, you're earning a normal yield and are running an abnormal risk of loss. That happens because the trust buys a lot of older bonds that carry higher interest rates than are available today. You get more current income, but to get those high rates, the trust had to pay more than the $1,000 face value for the bonds—say, $1,100. They will almost certainly be called before maturity at their $1,000 value, leaving the trust with a $100 loss. After the call, your yield will drop.

But that's only step one in the deception. Step two is to disguise the loss. The trust does that by buying zero-coupon bonds. Zeros pay no current income; each year's interest is added to the value of the bond itself. The gains from the zeros are supposed to balance the losses you take on the bonds that are called.

That's the theory, anyway. In practice, these S&M trusts are time bombs. Follow what is going to happen: (1) You will lose some of your income when your high-rate bonds are called. (2) You will take a capital loss on the money used to buy those bonds. (3) The zeros will eventually cover that loss, but you'll have to wait until they mature 20 years from now. (4) If you sell early, you'll probably lose money. To be sure of coming out whole, you have to wait for the trust to liquidate. So much for the "high-yield" unit trust that was supposed to pay a steady income!

Shares in older bond unit trusts, which are widely sold, can run you into a similar trap. You're attracted by the high current income. But when those bonds are called, your income will drop, and you'll be left with a capital loss. You can spot this risk by asking the broker for two numbers: the trust's current yield and its estimated long-term return. If the long-term return is lower, it has been packed with older, higher-rate bonds.

Anytime a broker offers you a unit trust that apparently yields markedly more than the new bonds coming to market, laugh hysterically and change the subject. "If you want a high yield real bad, that's what you'll get," a friend of mine says. "A real bad high yield."

You Will Never Know What Your Bond Trust Actually Earned

You'll get a check when the trust is cashed out but no information on what your yield turned out to be. The sponsors say that the brokers have the tools to compute it if you ask. So ask—but who knows if your broker can actually figure it out? The sponsors should disclose it as a matter of course, but maybe they'd rather you didn't know.

Sophisticated Investors in Tax-Free Securities, Who Want a Fixed Income, Don't Buy Unit Trusts

They buy high-quality, new-issue, intermediate-term bonds instead. There's no up-front sales commission on these bonds, some are noncallable, you pay no annual management fee, and the income really is steady. Unit trusts, with their misleading yields, are pitched to smaller investors who know less about how the bond market works.

A unit trust invested in Treasury bonds (as some are) is a pure con. You're paying a 1 to 5 percent sales commission to buy securities that you can get yourself, commission free, through TreasuryDirect.

Exchange-Traded Notes: Brought to You by Wall Street's Financial Engineers

Exchange-traded notes track an underlying investment of any sort—typically a commodity index or obscure stock index. You trade them as if they were stocks. When you sell, you're paid by the sponsoring institution. So ETNs are basically IOUs: a particular sponsor's promise to pay. They're unsecured. When Lehman Brothers Holdings failed in 2008, the three ETNs it had created failed, too.

Sponsors tout ETNs as better than exchange-traded funds (ETFs) because your profits are taxed at the low capital gains rate rather than as ordinary income. But the IRS is examining that question, so lower taxes aren't a sure thing. How does stuff like this get sold? you wonder. Stockbrokers and commissioned planners, of course. Complex new investments always look like great ideas until the day they aren't.

Principal-Protected Notes: More Financial Engineering

With these notes, your money is said to be safe, and there's supposedly an upside: the investment is linked to some sort of index that can grow. When the notes mature, typically in 6 to 10 years, you get your money back plus any growth that has accrued. In short, the usual fantasy—total safety plus stocklike gains.

So here's the downside: You pay hidden fees. You earn no current interest or dividends. You'll lose money if you have to cash in the investment before the term is up. There's usually a cap on how much you're allowed to earn. You earn nothing if the index happens to be down on the day your note matures. The company backing these notes might fail. Any gains are taxed as ordinary income, not capital gains. Why bother with something like this? If you want safety plus growth, put some of your money into a bond or certificate of deposit and some of it into a stock-owning mutual fund.

Foreign Currencies: Lose Money Fast!

When the dollar plunges, investors get hot for foreign currency bets. The *forex* (foreign exchange) market lets you trade one currency for another: dollars for euros, euros for yen, yen for pounds, pounds for Icelandic kronur. It's the largest market in the world, open all the time, where prices change fast and by large amounts. As I write, there are pitches to newbies all over the Web: Buy a currency trading platform! Sign up for training courses! Free practice accounts! Just $500 to start investing, and then borrow to increase your stake! Wow!

No market is more unpredictable than currencies. You may be right that the dollar is dropping (or rising) over the long term, but the forex is a one-minute market where your stake can be slashed almost as soon as you've put up the money. You're betting against the world's most sophisticated traders, so any profits are dumb luck. Costs are high, both to buy and to unwind trades. You have to be watching your computer screen all the time.

If you love losing money, trade the forex. If you love making it, diversify away from the dollar by buying international stock and bond mutual funds.

Commodities Futures and Options: A Loser's Game

For those of you eager to make a hopeful bet on commodities, let me steer you to mutual funds (chapter 22). If losing money is your objective, try *commodities futures.*

Many an innocent has lost his or her life savings by hearing or seeing an infomercial touting futures. If winter is coming, the pitch is for oil ("prices will rise!"). These soulless opportunists seize the weather, the season, or the news and use it to separate unsophisticates from their money.

Those are the innocents. What shall I say about the guilty—experienced investors who open commodity futures accounts in the nutty belief that they can beat the game? They're on the road to learning Quinn's Second Rule of Investing: never buy anything that trades in a pit.

The "pits" are the arenas where futures contracts are bought and sold: a contract on June gold, a contract on December wheat, a contract on March soybeans. You put up perhaps 5 or 10 percent of the cost of the contract to bet on the price of a specific commodity on a specific future date. Prices are moved by rumor, politics, war, scientific discoveries, business announcements, economic developments, and international weather and crop reports, and they move fast. You can "go long" (a gamble that prices will rise) or "go short" (a gamble that prices will fall). Winners may earn many times their investment. But if prices run against you, you can lose far more money than you put up—perhaps tens of thousands of dollars more. In fact, you are liable for up to the contract's full value. Fortunes can be lost or made within a few days or even a few hours.

End of lesson. The only other thing you need to know is that an estimated 75 percent of commodities speculators lose money. I would bet that 99.9 percent of amateur commodities speculators lose money.

The record is probably no better for plungers who buy *options on futures*. A *call option* gives the holder the right to buy the underlying futures contract at a specified price within a specified time; it's a bet that the price will rise. A *put option* gives the holder the right to sell and is a bet that the price will fall. If you pay, say, $1,000 to buy an option and prices move in your direction, the value of your option will rise. But if prices run against you, you can never lose more than the $1,000 you put up.

There are two main differences between options on futures and futures themselves:

1. When you buy or sell a future, you are contracting to buy or sell the actual commodity. If you don't close out a purchase (at a profit, you hope) before the contract's delivery date, you'll literally have bought the farm. You'll own warehouse receipts for a silo full of soybeans or wheat. By contrast, when you buy an option on a future, you are buying the right to the contract's change in value over a limited period of time. If you don't sell or exercise your option, it will expire worthless.

2. With futures, you can lose much more than the money you put up. The same is true if you *sell* an option. Both carry unlimited risk. If you *buy* an option, however, your losses can't exceed your original investment. For this reason, brokers say that buying options is "safer," although the risk of losing 100 percent of my investment isn't on my comfort list. (Any kind of options trading is terrific for brokers. They earn up to 10 percent of your principal, depending on what commodity you buy, how many contracts, and the price per contract. How are you going to beat costs like that?)

You don't have a prayer of winning if you buy through the slickies who tout options on get-rich-quick radio and TV shows or online. (For information, call 800-555-GYPP.) The investments they sell are real enough, but their prices are grossly inflated. As much as 40 percent of your "investment" may be sliced off the top in sales commissions and hidden costs. Any price moves in your commodity would have to be huge to cover these expenses and yield a profit.

Any customer with a modest income and few assets who was fast-talked into buying options on futures has a good chance of winning a reparations case against the broker. There's no way these investments are suitable for anyone with a low net worth. For reparations and arbitration procedures, see page 828.

Stock-Index Options and Futures

You can book bets on stocks without ever owning one by buying and selling stock-index options and futures. They're a speculation on the future prices of some of the major market averages. If you know where the Standard & Poor's 500-stock index will be next month, here's the place to make your fortune. But, of course, you don't know, and there's the rub.

During the early years of the Great Bull Market, options players made astonishing profits on very small amounts of cash. But the morning after the 1987 crash, those same investors woke up to learn that they'd lost many times their original stake. An Indiana teacher who thought he was risking only $5,000 found himself $100,000 in debt (the firm settled this case in arbitration). A stockbroker in Oklahoma, after losing a large arbitration case, admitted to his clients that options confused him. "I never should have messed with them," he said. A Florida broker who suffered huge losses in his own account took his brokerage firm to arbitration, arguing that he was in over his head and his boss should have realized it. We got a rerun when the stock market bubble burst in January 2000.

Here's a glimpse of the complexities of stock-index trading, just to show you what you're up against.

Stock-Index Options, Defined: When you buy or sell these options, you're hoping to profit from the changing price of stocks. You're betting that a specific stock index will rise or fall by a specified amount within a limited period, typically one to four months. The cost of the option is known as its *premium.* You also have to pay brokerage commissions.

Buying a call is betting that the index will rise by at least a certain amount. *Buying a put* is betting that the index will fall by a certain amount. When you buy an option, your risk is limited to the money you put up.

When you sell an option, however, your risk is unlimited! Many investors and brokers fail to grasp this crucial difference. So, in their innocence, they hit on what seems like a "safer" way of playing a strong market than buying calls. They decide to sell puts, which are a bet that stocks won't fall over a specified period of time. But if you're wrong, you can lose far more than your original investment.

A winning option can be held until maturity and settled for cash, or it can be sold at a profit ahead of time. To cut your losses on a losing option, try to dispose of it before it expires. If you don't or can't, that money is gone. Options are offered on a variety of stock market indexes. The most popular is the Standard & Poor's 500, followed by Standard & Poor's 100 (100 blue-chip stocks).

Stock Futures, Defined: When you buy or sell futures, you are contracting to buy a particular commodity. In this case, the "commodity" is a stock market index, the most popular being the E-mini S&P 500-stock index—a contract one-fifth the size of the index as a whole. You put up about 10 percent of the contract as collateral. If stock prices move in the right direction (either up or down, depending on your bet), you can sell the contract at a profit. Or you can take a cash settlement at the end of the contract's term. Either way, you get your collateral back. If the market runs against you, you will be asked for more collateral. Your losses could be substantially more than you put up.

Options on Stock Futures, Defined: Here you're betting on whether the price of a stock futures contract will rise or fall. You can buy or sell calls (if you're expecting a rise) or puts (if you're expecting a decline). Either way, you will own a piece of paper that speculates on the changing worth of another piece of paper. If you're not with me, that's proof that you shouldn't be with an options broker, either.

The prices of options on futures swing more widely and wildly than the prices of options on the stock indexes themselves. So of these three super-risky investments, buying futures options combines the highest potential for gain with "limited" losses (only 100 percent of your investment could go down the drain).

A Conservative Use of Stock Index Options Is to Hedge Against an Anticipated Market Drop

If you own a large and diversified stock portfolio but don't want to sell for tax or other reasons, you can buy puts on an index that resembles your holdings. In a market decline, you'll lose on your stocks but make money on your puts. Your losses may not be fully covered by your gains, but at least you'll have limited the shock. If the market doesn't fall, you'll have paid a pretty penny for peace of mind.

A Speculative Use of Stock Index Options Is to Bet on Which Way the Market Will Move

Minor changes in the stock index produce big percentage gains or losses on the index options. But to win this game, you have to get three things right: (1) the market has to move in the right direction; (2) the index has to rise or fall by more than enough to cover your costs; and (3) the change has to come within a short and specified period. That's market timing with a vengeance. It shouldn't surprise you to hear that the majority of options buyers lose. But their brokers win. At a full-service firm, your combined buying and selling commissions generally run in the area of 5 to 8 percent of your invested capital, although they can go both lower and higher.

Just as you can speculate in puts and calls on the market as a whole, you can do so on individual stocks, such as General Electric or Microsoft.

A conservative use of options is to sell calls against blue-chip stocks you own—an action known as *writing covered calls.* If you own GE, for example, you can sell someone the right to buy it from you at a specified higher price (the "strike price"). The money you collect is called a *premium.* If GE doesn't rise above the strike price, you keep the premium and the stock—so you eat your cake and have it too. If the price does go up, your GE stock will be called away, costing you the capital gain. So you earn extra taxable income by writing options (after paying sales commissions) but will give up a lot of stock profits over time. You also pay additional commissions when you buy more stock to replace the shares that were called away.

A hugely high-risk use of options is to sell them against stocks you don't own, a strategy known as *writing naked calls.* Suppose that you write such a call against Microsoft. As long as the price of Microsoft doesn't rise above the strike price, you win. If it does, you lose. You would have to buy Microsoft in the open market, whatever its price, to deliver to the person who bought the call. Alternatively, you might write *naked puts.* As long as the stock doesn't drop below the strike price, you win. If it does, you will have to buy the stock for something more than its market price.

Some speculators substitute options for stocks. If you feel in your gut that GE will go up pretty soon, it's cheaper (and potentially more profitable) to buy a three-month call on the stock than to buy the stock itself. If the price rises enough, you win. If your gut was just registering indigestion, however, you'll be out the money. One popular game: buying calls on companies that announce stock splits in hope that the stock will jump in price.

To give your bet more time to work, speculators might consider buying *LEAPS—long-term equity anticipation securities.* These are options that can last for up to three years, giving you more time for the stock price to move your way. Longer-term options cost more than the short-term kind.

When the speculators are Wall Street pros, I couldn't care less. Professional investors are action junkies, and options are an easy fix. Ditto for economists and other interest rate experts who often gamble on Treasury bond futures. But no individual seriously trying to build net worth should use options, period. Even if you win at the start, you will lose in the end.

Chicken Funds: The Ultimate Plucking Machine

Chicken funds (structured as unit trusts, principal-protected notes, and other packaged investments) flourish after any stock market scare. Sponsors package a "safe" zero-coupon bond (page 945) with a speculative or growth investment such as stocks or real estate. Part of your money buys the zero, which returns your original investment after a specified period of time. The rest goes into the riskier side of the package. The pitch is "Come back to the market, my dear departed ones. I'm positive that your money will grow. To calm your nerves, I will guarantee that, whatever happens, you will get your money back."

Salespeople call chicken funds "balanced investments." I call them humbug. The zeros don't lower your investment risk.

Here's what's wrong with chicken funds:

Over five to eight years, the zero will mature—eventually repaying the money you originally put in. But it will have lost a lot of purchasing power. Also, you may have paid taxes every year on the interest building up inside the bond. To keep up with inflation and taxes and earn a real return on your money, you are counting on the other part of your investment—the stocks, commodities, or real estate—to succeed. So the zero hasn't shielded you from risk at all.

You're at double jeopardy if you want to sell. You'll lose money unless both parts of your packaged investment did well. Had you held, say, your stocks and your zeros separately, you'd be able to sell just one or the other, as market conditions dictate.

Markets Are Not "Safe." Zeros Will Not Make Them So.

When you buy a zero combined with any other kind of investment, you are really making a three-part bet: that your growth investments will succeed; that you will hold to maturity; or that interest rates will fall, so that if you sell before maturity, the zero will show a profit, not a loss. That's a lot of ifs. Furthermore, you pay a higher commission to buy zeros packaged with growth investments than if you bought them separately through a mutual fund or discount broker.

Collateralized Mortgage Obligations (CMOs)

CMOs have been touted to people who might otherwise buy Ginnie Maes. They're packages of AAA-rated mortgages, either government insured or privately insured. They offer higher rates of interest than Ginnie Maes and are supposed to pay out in a certain number of years. In fact, you can't count on receiving your money over the stated period of time—the payback period is always longer or shorter, depending on the rate at which home owners prepay their loans. Starting in 2008, you couldn't count on receiving your money at all, because of the high rate of defaults and foreclosures. In the previous edition of this book, I wrote that I was skeptical of fancy new ways of holding investments that worked okay the old way. I still am. For mortgage investments, stick with a Ginnie Mae or Ginnie Mae mutual fund.

A Few More Things You May Regret in the Morning

1. **Any new investment touted as "safe"** with a higher-than-normal yield.
2. **Any mutual fund calling itself Something Plus**—as in Government Plus. Such a name implies high yields at no increase in risk. That's never true. There is always risk. "Plus" means "We'll try to squeeze out some extra money by hedging with index options, zloty futures, and puts on silver shower curtains." That might work. Then again, it might not. Mark these mutual funds a minus. Ditto any fund calling itself "enhanced."

3. Anything hyped on late-night get-rich-quick TV shows. No-money-down real estate deals. Options on grain or oil futures. Penny stocks. Investment tapes and seminars of any kind.

4. Anything hyped online—by spam or in ads that turn up when you're surfing for something else.

5. Anything hyped by phone, by a salesperson you don't know. Even if the firm is honest, this is no way to pick an investment. If the firm is dishonest, you're being set up to lose serious money. The bigger the profit the broker promises and the greater the pressure to make a decision, the worse the investment is going to be.

6. Diamonds and other precious gems. Wholesale prices are rigged. Markups are huge, as are discounts when you try to sell. Published price indexes are unreliable. The price of any individual stone depends on subjective judgments about its "quality grade," which is an invitation to cheat. Even if the dealers all agree on a stone's grading and it's backed by a certificate from the Gemological Institute of America, you could still get burned by paying too much. True investment-grade stones are kept in their own soft bags, in vaults. Stones made into jewelry generally are of lesser grade and don't fluctuate so much in price. By the time a stone is set, it may retail for more than double the value of the gem itself.

7. Smaller stocks that trade over the counter in limited amounts. Brokers may take huge markups on these issues. You may need a 20 percent increase in price just to cover the overt and hidden costs. Buy a smaller OTC stock only for a sound, fundamental reason and plan to hold it a long, long time.

8. Rare, or *numismatic,* coins. These are strictly for specialists. Among coin collectors, the condition of a coin is critical, and you're in no position to judge. Two coins of the same apparent grade could sell for different prices, depending on who graded them. A coin might be graded up when you buy in order to make it more expensive. When you sell, a different dealer might grade it down, which lowers its price. Even the price of an "MS65" (MS meaning "mint state"), which is just about tops, will vary according to who certified it. Some quite ordinary coins are sold to the credulous at excessive prices. To buy well, you have to know your way around.

By all means, collect rare coins as a hobby. Start visiting dealers and auctions. Subscribe to *Coin World* at www.coinworld.com, which has reasonably good coin price indexes. If you really get smart about your hobby, your passion could become your investment. But plunge into it only for the interest, not for gain.

9. Collectibles of all kinds—stamps, art, porcelain, rare books, maps, antiques, rare wines, Oriental rugs, baseball cards, Mickey Mouse ears. None is worth a moment of your time, except for fun. They yield their treasure only to dedicated collectors or dealers, who study them, admire them, and understand their value. Buy a lithograph because you love it, not because you think it will make you rich.

Gold: The Ultimate Worry Bead

For some, it's a trauma defense. Let the Middle East mushroom into darkest night, let terrorists nuke downtown New York, there will be gold.

For others, it's the supreme inflation hedge. If the U.S. dollar is ever carted off in wheelbarrows, there will be gold.

But in practice, gold doesn't always work out so well. Take the trauma defense. Back when Lebanon first fell apart, rich people rushed to their banks to retrieve their gold, only to be robbed of it by gunmen at the door. The gold hoards of many Kuwaitis were similarly seized by Iraqi troops.

Gold can also be a bust as an inflation hedge, depending on the years you hold it. In 1974, with gold at $200 an ounce, it became legal again for Americans to own it. The price ran up to a peak of $873 in 1980, then collapsed to $253 in 1999. Over those years, gold bugs saw their investment fall well behind the inflation rate. Then the price moved up again, topping $1,000 in 2007 and again in 2008 before falling back. Only you, the reader, know where it is today. Maybe way up. But you can't rely on it as a handy defense against rising prices over specific time periods.

Gold will protect you against hyperinflation and a U.S. currency collapse. The question is whether you want to hedge against that risk.

The rich usually say yes. They can afford to sequester money in an asset that earns no interest and is subject to buying and selling panics. If the global economy fails to right itself and U.S. dollars lose their status and value, gold will be precious indeed. Those who share these fears might put 5 percent of their savings into gold ETFs (page 972) and treat it as a permanent holding.

Alternatively, you might treat gold as an ordinary investment—sometimes good, sometimes not. Opportunists buy when the price declines. They sell when a rising price catches public attention and folks line up to buy gold coins.

What moves the price of gold? Who knows? Demand may suddenly explode for a wide variety of geopolitical reasons, none of them predictable. In recent years, it has moved with the oil price, but that's not a fixed relationship. It often rises when the dollar plunges in value against various currencies, but again, not always. It's thought to move up on the expectation of higher inflation and move down on the expectation of level to lower inflation—that is, unless there's a competing inflation investment that looks even better. Investors may be perfectly happy in Treasury TIPS rather than gold.

Gold is a reasonable investment, unlike the rest of the things in this chapter. But neither is it an essential part of your portfolio unless you have substantial wealth. If you're still interested in owning gold—as a long-term "safety" holding or short-term speculation—here are the various ways to buy:

Gold-Mining Stocks, Mutual Funds, and Stock-Owning Exchange-Traded Funds

There are two ways of using these funds, one aggressive, one conservative:

Gunslingers swing into equities when they think that gold prices are going to rise. The stocks of gold-mining companies move up faster than gold itself. Conversely, the stocks suffer deeper losses when gold prices drop, so speculators may not own them long.

Conservative buyers might own a gold mutual fund or ETF for diversification. Gold stocks often go up when the rest of the market is going down, and vice versa. And unlike gold itself, the stocks pay dividends. To avoid the funds' roller-coaster price risks, invest a fixed amount of money regularly, every month, for several years. You'll wind up with a long-term precious-metals position at a reasonable average cost.

Gold Exchange-Traded Funds

This is the investment of choice, for both speculators and long-term hoarders. A sponsor holds large gold bars in various international banks and sells shares against them. The shares, in the form of ETFs, trade on a stock exchange and are expected to track the gold price minus the sponsor's costs. The two major ETFs: State Street Global Advisors' SPDR Gold Shares and Barclays iShares COMEX Gold Trust. Note that you don't own gold itself, you own a promise to pay backed by State Street or Barclays. If their credit rating were to decline, the value of your ETF would probably decline as well, even if the gold price was going up. On the other hand, if you want to own an interest in gold itself rather than in gold stocks, it's much cheaper and more convenient to buy an ETF than to invest in coins.

Gold Bullion Coins and Bars

These are for trauma strategists, who—not trusting ETFs—want to own gold itself, stored in a safe deposit box or private vault. *Bullion* coins have no numismatic interest. They're traded on the value of their gold content plus a small premium to cover distribution, manufacturing costs, and profits. Premiums depend on the weight of your coin and the size of your order. For a small order of one-ounce coins, you might pay 2 to 6 percent over the spot gold price, depending on the dealer, plus a 1 percent sales commission. There may also be a shipping charge. For spot prices, go to the Web site of the New York Mercantile Exchange (www.nymex.com) or sites such as TheBullionDesk.com (www .thebulliondesk.com).

Investors should stick with one-ounce coins. The smaller coins (half-ounce, quarter-ounce, and so on) are more heavily freighted with sales and manufacturing expenses, making it hard for buyers to earn a profit. You'll see small coins in jewelry, not in safe-deposit boxes. Of the many bullion coins now on the market, the most widely sold are the U.S.-minted American Eagle and American Buffalo, the Canadian Maple Leaf, the South African Krugerrand, the Australian Kangaroo, and the Chinese Panda.

Here are some rough cost data to help you gauge the fairness of the prices you're offered on a purchase of 5 to 10 gold coins: The U.S. and Canadian mints sell coins to primary wholesale dealers for the current auction price of gold plus 3 percent. The primary wholesalers mark up the price by about a half percentage point and sell to retailers. The lowest-cost retailers add another half point, so their coins sell at the price of gold plus 4 percent. Other retailers price up from there. So gold prices have to rise by 4 percent or more for you to break even after costs.

Costs are typically higher if you buy just one coin and lower on orders of 20 coins or more. You may owe sales taxes unless you can legally store your gold hoard out of state.

When you resell a coin, you might be offered 2 to 3 percentage points over the auction market price minus a 1 percent sales commission—but bids vary, so shop the online dealers such as Bullion Direct (www.bulliondirect.com), Goldmasters USA (www.goldmastersusa.com), Kitco (www.kitco.com), Monex Precious Metals (www.monex.com), and OnlyGold (www.onlygold.com). Besides price, compare the shipping charge and any other fees.

Bullion bars are generally fabricated for wealthy investors who buy their gold in major-league amounts. Small bars are poured too, sometimes by little-known companies whose bars may or may not be readily accepted for resale. To protect your investment, stick with the majors. The dominant small bars traded in the United States are made by Credit Suisse and PAMP SA, sealed in plastic, and sold with a certificate of authenticity (you'll need them in their original condition for resale). One-ounce bars sell for the gold price plus a premium of $7 to $10.

Silver Doesn't Carry the Same Cachet as Gold

The price may indeed go up in times of rising inflation and high political risk. But silver more often trades as an industrial metal, responsive to changes in industries such as photography, dentistry, and electronics. The coin of choice for silver investors is the one-ounce American Eagle. Investors can also buy silver bars.

Platinum coins have a modest following. Like silver, platinum is used primarily in jewelry and for industrial purposes (especially in auto antipollution devices). Prices jump around a lot. The jury is out on whether this metal will ever be considered a store of value. The commonest platinum coins are the American Eagle Platinum and Canadian Maple Leaf Platinum.

Four Other Bad Ideas Denounced Elsewhere in This Book

I'm mentioning them here to be sure you know that they're on the list. For tax-deferred variable annuities and equity indexed annuities, see chapter 29. For life settlements, see page 398. For initial public offerings, see page 880.

The Impossible Triple Play

Bad investments pretend to be all things to all people. "Buy me," they whisper, "and you'll get your three wishes: high growth, high income, and no risk of loss." Some throw in a fourth wish, tax avoidance, just for spice.

But no single investment fulfills all those hopes. When you go for high income, you give up some safety and growth. When you go for high growth, you give up some safety and income. When you go for safety, you lose growth and income. Any investment that promises all three is a fraud of some sort.

The financial press is loaded with warnings from saddened investors who fell for one slick promise too many. Study their stories. Better an object lesson than a learning experience.

27

Aimez-Vous Growth?

The Case for Putting More Money Abroad

**The question is no longer whether Americans should
invest abroad. It's only what to buy and how much.**

In this global economy, Americans should be investing abroad as comfortably as
they do at home. Thousands of you do already. But to some investors, foreign
markets still feel like too much of a gamble—especially when there's a recession on.

I'd like to change your mind. In fact, I'd like to move you from developed
markets (Europe, Japan) to the emerging ones, where the greatest growth will
be (Southeast Asia, Latin America).

There are four strong reasons for putting some of your money abroad:

1. To invest in some of the world's most powerful economic trends.
These include the competition for oil, global demand for other commodities
that lie in the hands of emerging countries, the development of Eastern Europe,
the consolidation and restructuring of Western Europe, Latin America's dra-
matic economic turnaround, the growth of consumer markets in Asia, the rise of
China and India, the spread of sophisticated global communication, and demand
for infrastructure such as roads and power lines. These trends will outlast the
financial panic of 2007–2009. Two-thirds of the world's investment opportunities now lie offshore.

2. To catch other countries' business cycles. Over the long term, leading
international companies do as well as similar companies in the United States.
But over the shorter term, their stocks rise and fall at different times or at different rates of speed. Potentially, you can improve your returns by having a piece
of the action, wherever it is.

3. To invest in currencies other than greenbacks. When you buy foreign stocks, you're exchanging dollars for foreign currencies. Sometimes dollar-based investments give you the best international returns, sometimes foreign currencies do. Owning both is a way of spreading risk.

4. To reduce the risk to your investments overall. This surprises many investors, who assume that foreign stocks carry greater risks. Individually, they may, but not in combination with U.S. stocks. Foreign markets may be strong when U.S. markets are weak, and vice versa. When one market declines, another may rise. During major U.S. market drops, such as the bursting bubble of 2000 or the financial panic of 2007–2009, foreign and U.S. markets usually drop in sync. But over time, the diversification thesis holds.

What's a Good International Asset Allocation?

Advisers suggest that you commit 20 to 30 percent of your portfolio to foreign stocks. Put the bulk of it into a large, well-diversified, stock-owning mutual fund, with perhaps 10 percent in emerging markets and 5 percent in an international small-company fund.

The Dollar Connection

When you buy foreign securities, two factors influence how much money you'll make or lose: (1) How well those particular foreign markets perform. Are stocks rising or falling? Are bond interest rates going up or down? Is the political or economic climate good or bad? These concepts are familiar to anybody who invests. (2) Which way the U.S. dollar moves. This is the unfamiliar part. The dollar connection leaves a lot of investors confused.

Sometimes the Dollar Declines on Certain International Currency Markets. The result: foreign securities rise in value, in dollar terms. As an example, take a $100 Japanese stock whose price in Japan remains unchanged. If the dollar drops by 5 percent against the Japanese yen, the dollar price of that stock will rise to $105. You will make money solely because of the currency change. The oversize international returns that U.S. investors earned during much of the first decade of this century came in part from the dollar's general decline.

Sometimes the Dollar Rises on Certain Foreign Markets. American currency is worth more, while foreign currency is worth less. Result: foreign securities fall in value, in dollar terms. If you buy a $100 Japanese stock and the dollar rises 5 percent against the yen, your stock will be worth $95. Your loss came from the currency, not from any weakness in the underlying stock.

Some Countries Peg Their Currencies to the Dollar, but That Doesn't Free You from Risk. These countries might loosen the peg, letting the dollar float (in these situations, it usually drops). Or they might repeg it at a lower rate.

Generally speaking, your foreign investments are helped by a falling dollar and hurt by a rising dollar. A country's stock exchange may be flying in local-currency terms but look depressed to a U.S. investor because the dollar is going up. When the dollar moves down again, U.S. investors will show much better returns.

But the relationship between currency and investment performance isn't exact. When the dollar rises against a national currency, that country's products get relatively cheaper for American consumers. Its exports, corporate profits, and stock prices usually go up, which offsets your losses from the unfavorable currency change. The reverse may happen when the dollar declines. That country's exports get more expensive, so its exports, profits, and stocks go down. Economic change offsets the effect of currency change.

Now you understand (I hope) why international investing needs to be a long-term proposition. Over the short term, currency change may dominate. Over the long term, however, the effects of currency cycles roughly cancel each other out—especially in well-diversified funds that invest in major markets. Long-term investors are hitched to international growth. Your capital gains will far outweigh the effects of short-term currency shifts.

It's quite another story, however, for people invested in single-country funds—especially in emerging markets. There, a government-sponsored currency devaluation could hurt your returns for a considerable period of time.

Investors in foreign-currency bonds also shoulder a risk. Your long-term returns are lower than you'll earn from stocks, so a negative currency change eats up proportionately more of your gain. In some years, your entire gain or loss comes entirely from currency fluctuation. Foreign bonds should be thought of as pure currency diversification—a bet against the dollar that should earn a competitive return over a long holding period. (The most widely traded emerging-market countries, such as Argentina, Brazil, and Russia, have debt denominated in dollars. In that case, there's no currency risk.)

Every investment gain or loss in foreign markets come in two parts: changes in the market itself and changes in currency values, if any. Both contribute to your total return.

Do Yourself a Favor: Buy Mutual Funds

It's hard to pick foreign stocks and bonds successfully. To do so, you have to follow foreign economies, politics, tax laws, financial news, and interest rates; the outlook for each foreign currency relative to the dollar; each company's growth, profitability, and prospects; and the vagaries of each foreign stock market. That's a lot. What's more, you have to do your research without access to as much financial information or stock market data as is available in the United States. There's less investor protection, less enforcement of securities laws, more stock manipulation, and more government interference than American markets tolerate.

Or you could buy mutual funds.

If ever there is an argument for mutual funds, it's for buyers of international securities. Sit back, relax, and leave the driving to them.

Which Type of Stock Fund?

International funds buy securities everywhere but the United States. For your first (or sole) foreign investment, this is the kind to own. Look for a big, diversified fund. It leans toward larger companies in the industrialized countries but usually allocates some money to emerging markets and smaller stocks too. With this investment, you stay in control of the portion of your total assets that you keep abroad. You also share in every type of international growth.

A growing number of international funds specialize in smaller stocks. They're more volatile than big, diversified funds but ought to deliver higher capital gains, long term. You can also buy value funds that look for distressed companies, hoping they'll recover and outperform.

Global funds buy stocks worldwide. As much as one-half of their assets could be invested in the United States. They'll beat the pure international funds when the American market is strong and underperform them when it's weak. At various times, you'll have different portions of your money invested abroad, depending on what the manager decides to buy.

Regional funds stick to a local group of countries, such as Europe or the Pacific Rim. They're bets on a particular part of the world, for those who think they know which part of the world is going to do the best. Some Pacific funds specifically exclude Japan, so they look good when Japan is in a funk. But they may trail when Japanese stock prices march up.

Emerging-markets funds buy stocks in the world's rising countries in Eastern Europe, Asia, and Latin America. They're more volatile than stocks in the developed world—meaning that they soar in rising markets and collapse in falling ones. On the other hand, the countries they invest in tend to be the fastest growing in the world. Their politics are reasonably stable, they're reforming their economies on free-market lines, and they have a positive balance of payments. The big international fund that you own may invest a small percentage of its money in emerging markets. If not, or if you want a higher exposure to these countries, buy an emerging-markets fund, shut your eyes to the deep drops when global shares decline, and plan to hold for a very long time. In my view, emerging markets should be part of every diversified portfolio. They're not optional anymore.

Frontier funds, the newest addition to the international list, buy stocks in corners of the world that you never thought of investing in before: Africa, the Caucasus, the Near East. The Gulf oil countries have been on the list too, but they may move to the "emerging" category. Frontier markets are wild, unpredictable, and poorly regulated, with small numbers of stocks, and subject to enormous economic, political, and currency risk. The reason to own them is globalization. Modern, commercial cultures are being created in places where they didn't exist before.

At this writing, only one mutual fund has ventured into these waters: T. Rowe Price's Africa & Middle East Fund. Exchange-traded funds will also be showing up. Frontier stocks are strictly for gamblers, but I'll mention in passing that some of these stocks have enjoyed stupendous growth.

International index funds beat the actively managed funds, on average. For a discussion, see page 851.

Single-country funds are generally closed-end (page 788). That frees their managers to invest in small stocks, private placements, and illiquid issues—commonplace in very small markets—without worrying about how to pay off investors who want to cash out. If you want to quit the investment, you simply sell the shares on a stock exchange. Like any other closed-end fund, these should generally be bought only when they trade at a deep discount to the value of the securities in the fund's portfolio (say, a discount of 10 to 15 percent or more). If you buy at a premium over the net asset value, you are usually setting yourself up for a loss. Ditto if you buy when the fund is first being offered to investors.

Even at a discount, any single-country fund carries extra risk. If that country's market or currency hits a downdraft, so does your investment—and the manager can't shift his or her money to a more profitable part of the globe. If a new closed-end fund for that particular country is introduced, investors may lose interest in the older fund, causing its price to drop.

Closed-ends are for people who want to roll the dice on a particular country. Don't even think about it unless you know that country well and have taken the time to study how its fund price moves.

Exchange-traded funds (page 859) follow a multitude of foreign indexes. If an ETF is a better buy for you than a traditional mutual fund, look for one that follows a broad market index. Examples would be Vanguard's FTSE All-World ex-US ETF (tracking all the world's major stock indexes except the one in the United States) or its Emerging Markets ETF. You can also bet on narrow segments, such as Chinese real estate, but you might as well buy a lottery ticket.

International Bond Funds

There's only one reason for a long-term investor to buy an international bond fund: you want to diversify against the dollar. If the dollar declines in value against the currencies represented by the bonds in the fund (euros, yen, and so on), the market price of your fund will rise. If the dollar rises against those currencies, the market price of your fund will fall. International bond funds are almost entirely currency plays, which makes them high risk.

You might be temped by a fund because it's paying a higher current interest rate than you can get from bond funds in the United States. That's not a good reason to invest.

There's no free lunch in the interest rate market. If a bond is paying 10 percent in U.S. dollar terms when similar American bonds are at 5 percent, it means that the market expects a 5 percent rise in the dollar against that particular currency, to equalize yields. You'll make extra money only if the market guessed wrong and the dollar doesn't rise that far. The market may indeed guess wrong, but you're betting against some of the best brains in the business.

International bond funds vary in how they handle currency shifts. Some adjust your dividends up and down as the dollar falls and rises. If you're living on this income, you'll find that your periodic payouts gyrate a lot. Other funds pay the full dividend and adjust for currency changes in other ways—maybe in the fund's net asset value or maybe in your individual tax basis. These changes aren't as noticeable if you're reinvesting dividends.

The funds may try to stabilize their dividend payouts by hedging currencies and placing other arcane bets. The cost of hedging normally makes only a minor difference to a fund's net asset value. On the other hand, one reason you invest abroad is for currency diversification, and hedging takes some or all of that away. If you haven't diversified against the dollar, you're losing one of the chief benefits of investing internationally.

Some advisers tout global bond funds instead of international funds because global funds include U.S. bonds. This limits your currency risk but also reduces your diversification. Surprisingly, a fund described as "international" might also buy U.S. securities, which defeats the very reason for owning them.

Over the long term, international diversification lowers the downside risk in a fixed-income portfolio. That's because bond prices rise and fall in different countries at different times, so you're usually getting good performance from at least part of your portfolio. For the average investor, however, the reduction in risk may be negligible. Owning international stocks is important; international bonds should be one of the last things you buy—if you buy them at all. In general, the potential reward is probably not worth the risk.

There's an interesting argument, however, for tossing some money at bond funds invested in emerging-market debt: they're more stable than they used to be. Assuming that these fast-growing countries gradually improve their credit ratings, you could get superior returns over the very long term. Play with a small amount of money (in your retirement account, if you have the option), and only if you're an experienced investor.

If you depend on your capital for a steady income, homegrown bonds are generally best. If you want to gamble on higher total returns (including capital gains), add foreign-currency bond funds to the mix. If you do choose a bond fund, make it a no-load (because you don't want sales charges cutting into your total return) or a closed-end fund selling at a decent discount.

Foreign-Currency Mutual Funds and Exchange-Traded Funds

Take care. Some of these investments advertise themselves as money market funds because they buy foreign money market instruments, such as short-term government securities and certificates of deposit. But the value of your shares isn't held at one dollar, as is the case with real money funds. Instead your investment will fluctuate with changes in the dollar value of foreign currencies.

Although these mutual funds and ETFs earn interest, they're almost entirely currency plays. Some buy just a single currency, some buy several. They'll do moderately well when the dollar declines and badly when it rises. Their expenses are high, which takes a big bite out of their potential yield.

The same is true of the principal-protected foreign-currency baskets offered by some brokerage houses. You buy for a specified term. The basket contains complex long and short positions in various currencies. At the end of the term, you're guaranteed your principal back plus a portion of the basket's gain, if any. These baskets are complex and riddled with fees. Your return could easily be less than you'd get from a bank account.

The Cost of Going Global

It costs more to buy foreign securities than American securities. You pay for currency conversion and face much higher expenses for completing transactions. There are often big markups on securities prices, especially in emerging markets. As a result, global and international funds charge higher annual fees than domestic funds. Investors should consider exchange-traded funds, which carry lower fees than traditional, managed mutual funds, or international index funds. This is especially true if you're buying bond funds or currency funds, where expenses can eat up the yield fast.

For how to account for foreign taxes paid by your fund, see page 784.

Foreign-Currency Bank Accounts

They're offered by a small number of banks. You can get interest-paying money market funds and certificates of deposit denominated in Japanese yen, Canadian dollars, British pounds, the euro, and other currencies. Interest is paid in those currencies, and so are the fees charged.

At present, these accounts are used principally by companies that do business abroad and by travelers locking up the cost of their foreign vacations. For example, if you're going to Germany six months from now and buy a six-month euro-denominated certificate of deposit, your vacation fund will be insulated from any changes in the value of the dollar. If you care.

Many U.S. Mutual Funds Invest a Small Portion of Their Money Abroad

Check your prospectus to see if your funds have the right to do so. Then check your semiannual reports to see if any foreign shares have actually been bought.

If all your funds together routinely keep around 20 percent of their assets in foreign stocks, you don't have to buy an international fund in order to diversify. Your American funds have done it for you.

But, but, but: one or two of your funds may change their minds and sell part of their positions. You'd then have less foreign diversification than you'd intended. Furthermore, U.S.-based managers may not have as much success with foreign stocks. If things go badly, they might cut and run rather than prowl the world for other opportunities.

For better control of your asset allocation, split your money between pure U.S. funds and pure international funds. Separate funds also make it easier to measure your managers' relative performance. An all-U.S. fund can be cleanly compared with a U.S. fund index. If it also contains international stocks, it's harder to judge how good your manager actually is.

Some Other Ways to Join the Parade

If you're interested in doing your own securities and currency research and love individual stocks despite the drawbacks (page 713), there are several other roads to foreign investing:

U.S. Multinational Corporations

Here's an armchair way for your money to travel. Look for major U.S. companies that earn a large percentage of their profits abroad. Just a few examples: IBM, Coca-Cola, Microsoft, Procter & Gamble, and McDonald's. Owning them gives you a stake in international growth as well as a minor currency play. Their foreign earnings are worth more when the dollar declines and less when the dollar rises. On the other hand, U.S. multinationals pretty much rise and fall with the S&P 500-stock index, so you aren't truly diversifying your overall investment risk.

Foreign Stocks Trading in the United States

You'll find the big names, such as BP, ING, Novartis, Nortel, Sony, Toyota, and UBS trading on the major U.S. exchanges or over the counter.

American Depositary Receipts (ADRs)

An indirect way of buying individual company stock, ADRs represent foreign shares that are held in the vaults of a custodian bank. You buy and sell them as if they were the stocks themselves. At this writing, more than 1,300 ADRs are offered to retail investors. Some are listed on the New York Stock Exchange, the NYSE Euronext, or on NASDAQ. Many trade through the pink sheets (page 868). You can also buy some through dividend reinvestment plans (page 834).

More than one-fourth of the ADRs are sponsored by the companies themselves. They give you American-style financial information (although not as quickly) and pick up the cost of administering the securities. The remaining ADRs are unsponsored, meaning that they're managed by a bank without company involvement. With unsponsored ADRs, you usually get no financial reports. The administrative cost (maybe 2 to 4 cents a share) is deducted from your dividends. Many ADRs represent 1 share each, but some represent bundles of 5 or 10 shares or fractions of a single share.

Many of the listed ADRs attract a lot of buyers. But pink sheet issues are often illiquid. When you sell them, you're apt to take a haircut on the price. Generally speaking, investors should stick with sponsored ADRs that are listed on NASDAQ or the U.S. exchanges and trade actively all the time. The trades settle in dollars. If the dividends are paid in a foreign currency, they're exchanged for dollars by the depository bank and sent to the investor.

Foreign Ordinary Shares

These are direct investments in individual stocks on foreign stock exchanges. You have access to thousands of shares that have no ADRs. The big brokerage firms, including the online discounters, offer a global investing service, although the costs are much higher than for speculations in U.S. shares. Not worth the price, it seems to me.

Individual Foreign Bonds

Absolutely not for the average buyer. They carry high minimum investments—often $25,000 to $50,000 or more. And it's tough to make money on them after paying all the costs: currency conversion, brokerage commissions, transaction fees, and the profit that brokerage houses tack on to the price. Bond lovers should buy mutual funds instead.

Follow the Growth

In 2008, a financial panic enveloped the world. Stocks in foreign, developed countries did no better than U.S. stocks. Stocks in emerging countries fell off a cliff. Then the emerging countries staged a comeback, with stocks rising much faster than anywhere else. Growth will reassert itself in those parts of the world. The diversification story hasn't changed.

28

Investment Real Estate—The New Winning Systems

Finding the Properties That Pay

Everyone said, "You can't lose money in real estate because they're not making any more of it."
Hmmmm. Where did everyone go wrong?

Of all the nonsense written about estate, the looniest says that it's a good long-term buy because they're not making any more of it. Of course they are. Builders put up new condominiums and housing developments. Big tracts of land are chopped into small ones. Run-down neighborhoods are rehabbed. Or, as in 2007–2009, a tidal wave of foreclosures overwhelms the market with properties for sale. If you invest in residential estate—the favorite of small investors—all these properties become your competitors. When too much new real estate gets made, prices fall.

After a housing bust, you might think that high-profit properties are stacking up in the streets, waiting for investors to buy them for a song. Buy now, hold, rent while you're waiting, and sell when prices jump back up.

Think again. Property is more reasonably priced than it was in 2006, but that doesn't mean you can easily make money on it. Investing in real estate—*true* investing—is a professional's game. It runs on cash flow, not on the gamble of selling the property for more than you paid. The amateurs who made money in the late 1990s and early 2000s did so by accident. The real estate boom lifted dumb investments as well as smart ones. Then it dumped the dumb ones into a sinkhole. It's always possible that you might catch another real estate wave, but that's speculating, not investing. If your game plan relies on prices going up, buy real estate mutual funds. Don't get your fingernails dirty.

To make money in real estate, strategically, you have to accomplish one of two things: (1) Buy the property at a true bargain price—meaning less than a typical discount from the Realtor's listed price, including the listed price of a foreclosed property. Or (2) upgrade the property to a higher use (hence a higher value). Successful investors find many ways of doing this. You'll find several of their strategies starting on page 987.

Before I go there, I want to say a word about two strategies that usually fail. They're highly popular with individual investors, so I want to discuss them before getting down to serious business.

How to Lose Money in Real Estate

There are two easy ways.

The most popular loser is the single-family rental house. You buy a house with a rent that won't cover its carrying cost—and that's almost every one of them, including houses bought out of foreclosure. You dip into your pocket to help cover the expenses, expecting to earn your money back, and more, by selling at a much higher price. This strategy worked fine from the late 1990s through 2006, when speculation lit a firecracker under housing values. But those gains have gone south. Even if home prices drift gently up—say, at 3 percent a year—most rental houses aren't good deals. After expenses, you'd probably do better with nice, quiet Ginnie Mae bonds (page 931). And Ginnie Maes never call to complain that the windows leak or the bulb in the back hall burned out.

You run into the same problems with rental condominiums, and there you've got a double risk. They get overbuilt fast, in popular condo areas, and seem to attract more speculators. In a poor market, a huge number of units can suddenly be for sale, dragging down prices or, almost as bad, preventing them from going up.

You might find a house whose rents exceed your mortgage payments and other expenses in one of the cities hardest hit by real estate bust. If the property offers a double-digit capitalization rate, jump on it (for how to calculate capitalization rates, see page 1001). But packs of other investors are looking there too, which means that you probably won't get a bargain price. You might even have to lower your rent to compete with all the other new rental properties on the market. Cash returns in the area of 3 to 6 percent aren't worth the risk you take or the effort you put in.

The other popular strategy that rarely works is the "cosmetic" fixer-upper.

You buy a house with a few minor problems and put some money into repairs. A few months later, you try to resell at a higher price. But every investor is looking for that same perfect fixer-upper, so you don't get a bargain on the purchase price. To make money after makeover expenses, you'll probably have to price it higher than similar houses in the neighborhood. As a result, you won't find a buyer right away, especially in an area with a high foreclosure rate. Months, or a year, could pass. To pick up some money, you'll eventually take a tenant whose rent won't cover your carrying costs. That brings you back to the failed strategy I mentioned first.

You May Not Even Realize That You Lost Money on a Property!

As long as you sell for more than you paid, it feels as if you came out ahead. That will encourage you to get into another terrible real estate deal. So do yourself a favor and find out the truth. Determine what you *really* made or lost on any venture you tried in the past, taking figures from your tax returns. Count all the expenses, including capital expenditures and transaction costs. Add in the value of your time (an expense you wouldn't have if you simply bought Ginnie Maes) and state your profits as an annual compounded rate of return. Even your boom-time gains were probably lower than you think. How would you have done without the luck of a once-in-a-lifetime real estate bubble?

Going forward, resolve not to buy into any new property without a business-like projection of what it will take to make an acceptable profit.

How to Make Money in Real Estate

Active real estate investing is a part-time or full-time job. You're a deal maker, an entrepreneur. You're running your own small business. The successful investor will:

- *Work up a personal investment system.* What kinds of properties do you intend to specialize in? (Specialists do better than generalists.) For some overlooked approaches, see page 992.
- *Spend a lot of time looking at the kinds of properties that interest you.* You might do 1 deal for every 50, or 100, or 1,000 you consider. You won't actually visit 1,000 properties, but you might look at 1,000 deeds in the courthouse. If even reading that sentence bores you, forget active real estate investing. Buy real estate mutual funds instead.
- *On a rental property, nail all the operating costs*—not just mortgage, taxes, and insurance but also advertising for tenants, repairs, utilities, trash hauling, maintenance of all kinds, reserves for repainting and replacements, fix-up costs

between renters, loss of rent during those periods, minimal cosmetic improvements (to maintain the property's value and make it rentable), and a dozen other things. Costs are so high compared with rents that you'll have to buy at a spectacularly bargain price to make this deal work.

- *Develop strict financial criteria to identify properties worth buying.* For example, you should have rules for how much you'll pay for a property—any property—relative to its fix-up costs, rents, and expenses (page 1001) and rules for the minimum projected profit that you'll accept. Investors who fail either lack sound criteria or lack the discipline to follow them. It does no good to buy the best property you can find if it doesn't meet your financial criteria. Don't grade on a curve! As one developer told me, "You make your money when you buy, not when you sell." Your number one criterion: *buy only properties that you can get for at least 20 percent below what you believe is their current market value.* That's not an easy job, but true real estate investing isn't easy and never was. It only looked that way because, during the boom, so many people made money by accident. To get a big discount, you'll have to search for sellers yourself. Lowball offers through real estate brokers rarely work.

- *Learn how to project a property's probable compounded annual rate of return.* It's not enough to say, "Wow, I'll net three thousand dollars a month." That might come to only a 3 percent return on the capital you invested. At that rate, you might as well keep your money in the bank. If you don't have a financial calculator, get one and learn how to use it.

- *Have a large enough line of bank credit to carry a good investment through a bad market or a period when it cannot be rented.* Otherwise you may be forced to sell at a giveaway price.

- *Look for properties that my friend Jack Reed* * *calls lepers.* Neither the seller nor other potential buyers see any extra value in them. But thanks to your X-ray vision, you do. You'll find some leper strategies below.

Four Good Investment Rules

- *Buy for at least 20 percent less than current market value.* That means finding a seller who's in a hurry, doesn't see the value hidden in his or her property, or

---

*Jack tracks down profitable investing strategies for his newsletter, *Real Estate Investor's Monthly* ($125; 342 Bryan Drive, Alamo, CA 94507). You can see a free copy on his Web site, www.johntreed.com. For nuts-and-bolts tutorials, I recommend one or more of his 20 invaluable real estate investing books, including *How to Get Started in Real Estate Investment,* and, for people doing lease-to-own options (page 990), *Single-Family Lease Options.*

doesn't want to go to the effort of mining it. When prices are falling, you can't be certain of current value, making your job even harder.

■ *Bargain properties have to be flipped—that is, fixed and resold immediately—to achieve the highest return.* But be warned that flips don't always work out. You may misjudge the property and overpay. When the property is vacant, vandals may strike. A buried heating oil tank in the yard may have sprung a leak, socking you with a cleanup cost. And that's just the start of the stories I've heard. The most successful flippers appear to be real estate brokers and the people who invest with them. Their line of work helps them find bargain properties. When the property's problems have been solved, their own salespeople stand ready to market it.

■ *Buy property that can be upgraded profitably (zoning change, subdividing, renovation).* These things take time, which means that you have to be able to pay the carrying costs—often for longer than you thought. The longer you have to hold, the higher the selling price you need to achieve your profit goals.

■ *Don't rely on future marketwide appreciation for making money.* If real estate prices rise, fine. But that's not what your strategy should depend on. Anything can happen during these postcollapse years: more recession, high inflation, rising interest rates, falling rents, falling prices, or, by some miracle, stability. Your business plan should provide for ways to make money even in a flat or declining market, thanks to a solid cash flow. As long as the property is earning enough, you can afford to wait until values rise.

How to Find Rental Properties That Pay

To succeed, you have to buy a property with upgrade potential or at a bargain price, not just a nice-looking property sold by a Realtor at an everyday price. Assuming that you follow through on those criteria, here are some strategies to try:

Buy Your Bargain Property in Working-Class Neighborhoods

Homes and apartment houses there are far less likely to be overpriced than they are in the classier sections of town. And working-class homes rise just as much in percentage value, maybe even more.

Live in a Low-Priced City and Watch for Periods of Low Confidence

These could occur during a recession or after a plant closing, assuming that jobs are likely to return.

Buy a Leper House with a Problem That Traumatizes the Seller and Prospective Buyers

Maybe asbestos was blown onto the ceiling. Maybe the foundation has dropped four inches and the floors tip. Whatever the problem, investigate the cost of solving it, then offer a low enough price to make the repair and guarantee yourself a substantial profit. The seller may accept, just to get the monster off his or her hands. (This strategy, incidentally, is a variant on buying a house that needs only cosmetic repairs. By going beyond cosmetics, you can truly get a bargain price—at least 20 percent under current market value minus cost of repairs.)

Buy a One-Bedroom House

Look for a detached house, not a condominium. There aren't many of these, but they're dandy investments. They sell cheaply because hardly anyone wants to own them. They rent dear because they appeal to single people and childless couples. If the house has an enclosed space that you can turn into a second bedroom inexpensively—an attic, a breakfast room, a sunporch, an attached garage—you may have a real winner. But check out the neighborhood before converting the garage. In some areas, houses without garages are tough to resell. And be sure that you can get the required permits.

Buy Two Houses on One Lot

One of them sits in the other's backyard. Few home owners want them, so the second house goes for about two-thirds off. But most tenants don't mind the arrangement. You get normal rents and a fine cash flow. Take a look at the profit potential in moving one of the houses to a lot of its own.

Buy a Two-Family House and Live in Half of it Yourself

It still has to meet your financial criteria. Assume that you yourself are paying a market rent as well as a half-share of the upkeep, and see if it still yields a double-digit capitalization rate (page 1001).

Lease Your House to a Renter with an Option to Buy

This strategy works especially well when rents are sagging and real estate prices are going nowhere. It has made investors a lot of money, but there are some legal risks. First, the good part:

You put an ad in the paper reading "$4,000 moves you in" or "Buy a house, no money down," depending on how much money (if any) you want up front. Usually it's 1 to 3 percent of the purchase price. You then strike a deal that will let the tenant buy the property at a fixed price, usually within one to three years. The tenant pays the monthly rent plus something more, which is credited toward his or her down payment. If the normal rent is $800 a month, the lease option rent might be $1,200, with $400 put toward the purchase price. Part of the up-front payment might also go toward the price. At the end of the term, the tenant can buy at the specified price, although he or she isn't required to.

You and your tenant-buyer sign a rental agreement and an option agreement. If the contract lasts longer than a year, consider annual increases for both the rent and the house price. Your local apartment association can supply a lease form, but there are no standard forms for the option sale. You'll need a real-estate lawyer to draw it up.

Lease options greatly improve your cash flow by paying you more than you'd get from rents. They bring you tenants who take especially good care of the house. And you often can set a purchase price at the high end of the going range. If the tenant ultimately can't buy, you get to keep all the extra money.

Fairness demands that you work only with tenants who will have a good shot at making the down payment and qualifying for a mortgage during the option period. It's dirty pool to take lease option money from people who obviously won't be able to buy. Even qualified buyers, however, often pass on the option rather than take it up.

Now the bad part: a lease option, if challenged, may be construed by a court to be a land-contract sale. Sales can lead to tax reassessments. They trigger the due-on-sale clause in your mortgage, giving the lender the option of ordering you to pay off the loan (lenders rarely hear or care about lease options, but they might). As a practical matter, these and similar risks are rarely encountered. Still, you should know they're there.

If Your House Has Some Extra Land

You own a little more land than the zoning requires but not enough to subdivide into a separate building lot. Try to sell that extra sliver to a neighbor for a garage, a swimming pool, or a green space for planting shrubs and trees. You'll still have to go through a formal subdivision.

Should You Invest in an Expensive Rental Property?

Expensive homes generally make poor real estate investments because rents fall well short of covering your costs. On the other hand, you may find a house you really like at a good price. So here's a strategy if you're getting older and own several homes in the midprice range: Sell the midprice homes and roll the profits into a high-cost home that you'd eventually like to live in, using a tax-free

1031 exchange (page 1003). Rent out the high-cost home for a while. Move into it later, making it your permanent residence. You've preserved the profits from your other houses, tax deferred, and acquired a house that suits you fine for the rest of your life.

Properties Just Waiting to Be Squeezed for Cash

Here are some properties that can be flipped:

A Teardown. Buy a house or a duplex that is going to be torn down. Don't pay any more than $1,000 for it. Hire a house mover to take it to another lot. You can generally sell the property for twice the money that you have in it (including all your expenses), if you do it right.

Absentee Owners. Do some research at the county records office. Write to everyone who owns land locally but lives somewhere else. Ask what they would sell their property for. Maybe 1 out of 200 will name a price that's half the real value because he or she doesn't know the going price of property in your town. That one you buy. (The flip side of this advice: if you ever receive such a letter, don't answer it before calling a local real estate agent to find out what the property is worth.)

Tax-Sale Redemptions. In some states, former owners have a right of redemption, during a limited time, if their homes were seized for nonpayment of local property taxes and sold at auction. Call or write such people if their houses sold for substantially less than market price. They usually have several months to redeem their homes for the sale price plus interest. If that's utterly beyond their means, you might make a deal. Put the redemption money into an escrow account; let the former owner use the account to redeem the house and sell it to you at the same low price; pay the former owner a reasonable fee for his trouble; and resell the house at full market value. (There is no flip side to this advice. For the former owner, it's all found money. He or she might even advertise for someone to do this deal with.)

Houses sold to satisfy federal tax delinquencies carry redemption rights all over the country.

Expiring Options. Look for people who are renting a house with an option to buy at something less than the current market value but who haven't the money to do the deal. You can buy their option, take over the house at the low option price, and resell for a higher price. Valuable real estate options are expiring all the time, unused. Where do you find them? Advertise: "We buy options to purchase real estate." Or write to the tenants of any real estate investor who does a lot of lease option deals. Or write to tenants against whom eviction notices have been filed, to see if they had an option on the house they're quitting. Or see if any lease option memoranda have been filed with the county clerk. Some investors buy valuable options and resell them to someone else rather than taking title to the property. You can do this deal with commercial properties too.

Tenancies in Common. A person who owns property as a tenant in common (page 85) may want out. But the other owners might refuse to sell and decline to buy the defector's interest. That person can sometimes start a lawsuit to require a sale. But he or she may be constrained by personal considerations or else may want the money fast. In this situation, an investor can often buy the defector's interest at a low price, then force a buyout or sale or wait until the other owner decides to sell or refinance voluntarily. You can advertise for these investments—"We buy the interests of tenants in common"—or go through deed records and compile a mailing list of tenants in common. Opportunities often arise when Great-Uncle Garrett leaves a plot of land to all three of his nephews, who hold different views on what should be done with it.

Probate Sales. Estates will sometimes (not often) sell real estate at a low price to buyers who pay cash. This usually happens when heirs are pressing for their money and aren't using a real estate agent. To find these properties, phone or send a letter to the executors of every estate filed for probate. You might send out hundreds of letters a month, leading to one deal every three months on the terms you want.

Clouded Titles. Attorneys, paralegals, and specialists in title searches, in particular, might invest in properties with clouded titles. The owners may be glad to sell at almost any price. Buy only when you can cure the title and resell the property for full market value. But don't buy if you've been advising the owner and have a fiduciary relationship, unless the owner gives up on the property. In that case, get a signed waiver releasing you from your duties and acknowledging your prior good-faith advice on how to handle the situation.

Houses Going into Foreclosure. Send a letter every 10 days to people whose houses are scheduled for foreclosure. Offer to buy immediately for cash. Not many people respond at first because they're still hoping to save their homes. But they become more interested once they accept the inevitability of the loss. Do a thorough title search before going through with the deal. The house may be encumbered by liens. The records don't always show how much is currently owed on the liens, so work with the owner to find out. The best foreclosure investors learn how to do these title searches themselves. Outside firms often don't get the job done in time.

One advantage of buying from the owner is that you usually get a low price. One risk is that the owner may go bankrupt, which could tie up the house in court. Some states have laws regulating preforeclosure sales, so check yours out.

Foreclosure Auctions. Foreclosure or trustee sales are a lot trickier than people think. You normally can't inspect the house in advance. You have to guess what it's like inside by its exterior condition. Some angry evictees trash the interior on their way out. The house has to be worth at least 30 percent more than the mortgage against it to make your risk worthwhile. The title may not be clean. In the frenzied market for mortgage securities during the bubble, mortgages sometimes were transferred improperly from one institution to another and you'll need to straighten out the paperwork. If there were liens on the house that the foreclosure wiped out, there's a risk that the lien holders who are wiped out by the foreclosure will complain that they hadn't been properly notified. If their claims are upheld, however, the deal is generally unwound with no great harm to the auction buyer. Don't spend money on fix-up costs before making sure that no viable liens (including IRS liens) exist.

Sales normally occur on the courthouse steps. Most states require a cashier's check in the exact amount of your bid, but some allow you to pay the owner 10 percent, to be followed soon by the whole amount. You shouldn't pay any more than 75 to 80 percent of the fair market value, as best you've been able to determine it. Get-rich-quick books often tout the bargains in foreclosure sales, but professionals say that a good house is hard to find. Maybe 1 deal in 20 makes any sense. New investors should generally buy after a foreclosure or before, not at a foreclosure auction.

Foreclosed Houses Held by a Bank. They're generally listed with a real estate agent, and you can see the inside. But these listings aren't bargains, they're at market price. You can offer 20 percent below market but probably won't even get a counteroffer. Bank foreclosure departments aren't marketers, they're owners trying to get a good price, and the real estate agents won't push them on your behalf. But keep offering. If the property continues not to sell, consider dropping your offer to 25 percent below market (houses lose value when they sit unoccupied). One day the bank may suddenly say yes. Investors get perhaps 1 out of every 25 properties they pursue this way, but that house will be a bargain.

Another option is to follow the foreclosure sales to learn which lenders end up owning particular properties you like. Try to call the bank officer in charge of those properties and offer 20 percent below market value. Because of the foreclosure glut, the officer might not take your call, referring you to a Realtor instead. If you do get someone on the line, describe the property, its condition, and the length of time it has been on the market, and offer 20 percent below market value. The officer will generally say no. Again, keep offering. You never know when you might get a yes, and in-person offers may work better than going through a real estate agent. Incidentally, if the bank says that a property has been sold, ask if the deal has actually closed. If not, keep calling. Sometimes those sales fall through.

How Much Leverage Should You Risk?

Real estate returns—both profits and losses—are greatly magnified by *leverage,* defined as the amount of cash you put toward the down payment compared with the property's price. The less cash you put down, the larger your mortgage and the higher your leverage. High leverage gives you more potential for profit if prices rise. Conversely, if prices fall, the higher your leverage, the larger your percentage loss.

Gains in market value (if any) are the sideshow. If you're hoping to flip the property, you have to reduce the gain by the money you spent on mortgage interest, insurance, taxes, fix-up costs, and selling expenses. If you're planning to rent, you need to look at the cash flow, which is the income you get from the property after all outlays for operating expenses, mortgage payments, and capital expenses such as replacing a roof. The lower your down payment, the bigger your mortgage and the larger your monthly payments. Even with a traditional down payment of 20 percent, it's almost impossible to cover all your costs with

Table 28.

HOW LEVERAGE WORKS

Cost of the House	Amount of Cash You Put Down	Increase (Decrease) in Value	Percentage Gain (Loss) on Your Cash
$200,000	$200,000	$6,000	3%
200,000	40,000	6,000	15%
200,000	20,000	6,000	30%
200,000	10,000	6,000	60%
200,000	10,000	(6,000) *	(60%) *

* Loss.

rents. You'll have *negative cash flow,* meaning that you'll be reaching into your pocket each month to help support your investing habit. If you put the minimum down, your cash flow problem is even worse. What happens if you lose your job or are forced into early retirement? If your salary was supporting your real estate investment, you may have to sell the property fast, maybe for 10 to 15 percent less than its actual value. When you have a big mortgage to repay, your profits may evaporate or turn into a loss.

The wise investor arranges for rents to cover his or her costs. Working backward, that almost always means buying the house at a bargain price. No bargain, no worthwhile profit over the long run.

Have You the Nerve to Be a Landlord?

Before buying any rental property—a single-family home, a duplex, a four-plex—ask yourself: Do I have the guts to evict? To demand the rent on time? To demand the rent at all if someone gives me a sob story? Can I throw out an illegal pet? A sweet mutt adored by a four-year-old? With cancer?

If you can't answer all these questions with a hard-boiled yes, don't even try to be a landlord. In this game, nice guys get their clocks cleaned. You may set out to be the first decent landlord in history and discover too late that you were merely incompetent. Buying any sad story, from any tenant, could cost you not only your profit but your principal and your credit rating too.

I don't mean to be harsh on tenants, having once been one myself. Most tenants are fine. They take care of your property and pay on time. Other tenants start out fine, then turn into monsters. They bounce checks. Make excuses. Break rules. When it becomes clear that you're going to evict, they may sell your stove and refrigerator, break all the windows, and punch holes in the walls.

Before even getting into this business, rent the movie *Pacific Heights* to see how bad landlording can be. It's only a mild exaggeration. Deliver an eviction notice if the rent is two days late. A salvageable tenant may be furious but will pay on time from that day forward. Bad tenants you want out sooner, not later. Good tenants won't be late, ever, unless by an honest mistake. An eviction notice will annoy them too, but they'll apologize.

Never take tenants without checking them out: a credit check, personal calls to the tenants' past two employers, and personal calls to the past two landlords, asking if they'd rent to these people again. (The current landlord might lie, just to get rid of them.) Insist on cash or money orders for the security deposit and the first month's rent; that gets rid of people who give bum checks and will hold the apartment until you can evict them. If bad tenants slip through your screen, move against them decisively. Enforce all rules to the letter. Demand cash or money orders from anyone who ever bounced a rent check. Evict anyone who violates the lease. *Grrrr.* If you think I'm being overly harsh, you're a landlord newbie.

The Accidental Landlord

Some home owners try to sell and can't (or can't sell for any price they will accept). So they move to a new house and find tenants for the old one. What happens?

If you have a recent mortgage, you probably can't charge enough rent to cover your expenses. So the house will keep on leaking money, although not as much as it would if it were vacant. As long as you're charging a fair market rent, you get a small tax break: all rental expenses, including depreciation, can be written off against rental income and, in some cases, against other income too (page 1002).

Don't let the house become a permanent rental! If that happens, you will owe a capital gains tax on the property when you sell. How do you hang on to the status of "temporary" landlord? Keep offering the house for sale, don't give a lease, and pray that you won't have to rent it for very long. Best advice: (1) Don't get into this box in the first place. Owning two homes can be Bankruptcy City. Sell your own house before buying another. If you take a new job in another city, live in a rented room until your house is sold, even if it means leaving your family behind. It's the lesser misery. (2) Sell on a lease-to-own option (page 990). You can usually strike a fair deal with an individual buyer who will pay a fair rent plus something extra toward the down payment. A professional real estate investor, however, who's aware of your anxiety, might offer only rent and demand that the entire payment go toward the purchase. Whatever you decide, try not to let the option run for more than a year or two. Never sign a lease option contract without the advice of an attorney who specializes in real estate. (3) Slash the price on your unsold house, just to get rid of it. It might be worth selling for less than its mortgage value if you have enough savings to cover the remaining debt. The amount you're earning on your savings may be less than the carrying costs on the house.

The Huge Risks in Raw Land

Generally speaking, it's not smart to buy land and sit on it, waiting passively for its price to rise. Prices may rise slowly, and in the meantime empty land devours money. You'll owe real estate taxes and maybe loan interest if you financed your purchase with the seller. There's almost never any rental income. (If it's a meadow, maybe you can get a farmer to hay it.)

Owners of raw land also face enormous political risks. For example, your town might decide that it's growing too fast and downzone your land from commercial to residential, or from multifamily to single-family use, or to a green space. That sharply reduces your property's value. Or a new town environmental officer might declare part of your property a wetland, which virtually prevents its use as a building lot. In some parts of the country, you may be unable to get water rights. Anything can happen to a piece of raw land, and most of what can happen is bad.

When a land deal is good, however, it is often very, very good. Consider investing when:

▪ *You have reason to believe that you can, within a reasonable period, make the land more valuable.* For example, you might subdivide it into building lots, get its zoning upgraded to higher-density use, or get a road approved for a plot that was previously inaccessible. Any of these changes will raise the land's value.

▪ *You believe that you have some inside information about where roads will go or where a major company plans to move.* In real estate, it is usually legal to trade on such tips. Your risk is that the tip was wrong or that, though right, it didn't affect the value of your property.

▪ *You can buy on an option.* With an option, you pay the owner for the right to purchase the land, at a stated price, within a certain number of months or years. During that period, you do the rezoning or subdividing and line up a buyer. Then you take possession of the land or assign the option to your buyer. If your plans don't work out, however, your option will expire. The landowner gets to keep both the improved property and your option money.

When You Do a Raw-Land Deal

The checklist is long. Can you build on the property? What are the town's environmental rules? What's the current zoning? How will water and electricity get to the site? Where will the town allow roads to be built? What about sewage systems? Can foundations be dug, or will a developer have to blast or pound in pilings to reach deep bedrock? Where does the town stand on development, politically? How fast does the planning board act on proposals brought before it? Arm yourself with a good *local* real estate lawyer. If you plunge into raw-land development, you are going to need one—especially one who knows the territory.

The Environmental Risks

Any real estate investor—from the owner of a single-family house to a major-league developer—potentially faces huge liabilities under the rapidly changing laws on environmental protection. You may say, "I have no problem with my property." But a year from now a new substance may be found to cause cancer and be added to the government's "horribles" list. Surprise! That substance may be in your roof. Unless you replace the roof, your investment will lose value.

You think this far-fetched? Consider the retired California couple who invested in a mortgage on a pear orchard. The borrower defaulted, and they foreclosed. Two fuel tanks were found buried on the property. To start, they had to pay $30,000 toward the cleanup, and the state could force them to spend $100,000 more. And consider the Indiana home owners who lived near an area where the state stored road salt. The salt got into the groundwater and contaminated the wells. The water was drinkable, but the home owners' pipes and appliances corroded. Their property values plunged.

And consider that nice piece of land you just bought. Fifty years ago, it might have been the site of a factory that left toxic chemicals in the soil. Or tomorrow night two guys in dark clothes may use it as a dump for leaky drums of industrial waste, leaving you financially liable and responsible for the cleanup. You're also in trouble if you own a building that's found to have asbestos or lead paint in it. The law may not force you to remove it. But few people will buy or finance the building as long as the asbestos is there, so your investment has been damaged.

Professional investors won't buy a commercial property anymore without first getting an environmental audit. The auditor tests the property for buried oil tanks, chemicals, pesticide residues, asbestos, and other substances that impair its value. Individuals should get audits too, especially if you're buying open land, land next to an old gasoline station, a commercial or industrial property, farmland, or an apartment building. In fact, your lender may require it. Probable price range for small investors: $500 to $30,000, depending on the property. Before rejecting the expense of an audit out of hand, think what you'd lose if you bought a contaminated piece of real estate that had to be cleaned up.

Three other reasons to check for toxic waste: (1) If you buy a property and waste crops up later, you may not be forced to pay for the cleanup as long as you made "all appropriate inquiry" before buying. "Appropriate" hasn't been defined, but an audit should do it. (2) Even if the government has to pay for cleaning up your property, it might not do the job for years. In the meantime, you're holding an asset that can't be sold for anything close to what you paid. (3) Anyone who buys your property will probably subject it to an environmental audit. If wastes are found, it may kill the deal and will certainly reduce its price.

In short, the risks of investing in real estate have risen sharply. The average investor has not yet caught up with these new environmental dangers, which could wreck any deal you do.

What It Takes for Success in High-Risk Conditions

Total Awareness, All the Time. You should follow real estate constantly, tracking the ever-changing political and financial risks. The new environmental hazards, for example, might persuade you to lean toward the shorter-term investing ideas. Some investors don't even want their names on a chain of title, lest they get hit for part of a property's cleanup costs. So they're finding ways to trade property interests without ever owning the real estate themselves. One idea: options. You can trade them without taking title to anything.

Patience. You may have to look at dozens of properties in person, and hundreds on paper, to find one that meets your investment specifications. Many a seller is lying in wait for an idiot who will overpay.

Tough-Mindedness. You have to be firm with tenants, firm with buyers, firm with sellers. Not mean, but firm. Real estate investing is a deal-making, business-to-business world with fewer rules than the average consumer is used to. Consumer laws provide some protections when you buy a house to live in but not when you buy one to rent out. That's why your investment criteria are so important, as is your discipline in following through.

Flexibility. A truly superior investor brings his or her technical knowledge of real estate contracts and finance to bear on a single critical point: the special needs of the person on the other side of the deal. What can you give him or her to secure the terms you want? If there's no way to reach your minimum requirements, bow out. Never do a deal just to do it or because you've already put in a lot of time.

Quick Decision Making. When you first think about real estate, take a lot of time to study up. Read some books on real estate finance. Learn about local property values. Analyze your area's economy: Are jobs and people moving in or out? Check the environmental hazards. Choose some investment niches to investigate. Set some yardsticks for yourself (page 1001). But once you step into the arena, be prepared to move quickly. No one leaves money lying on the table for very long. If you have to think and think and think and *think* about it, someone else will buy. The best deals go the fastest. You should buy the first acceptable deal (one that meets your criteria), not keep prowling for the "best" one.

An Iron Gut. In almost every deal, something goes wrong. Rehab estimates are off. Somebody dies. The town passes new laws that change the rules. Your lender reneges. The seller tries to change the terms. A tenant sets fire to an apartment. Most of the problems can be worked through. But it will take time, your nerves will fray, and you might not make as much money as you thought. That's how real estate investing goes. If you can't handle the drama, buy Ginnie Maes.

Time. Direct investing in real estate is a part-time or full-time business. To make money, you have to be personally involved: inspecting properties, evaluating prices, negotiating, arranging for tenants, seeing to repairs, going to zoning hearings, lining up financing, living your deal in a dozen ways. If you don't have the time, don't even think about trying to buy.

Clear Financial Yardsticks. Before you begin your real estate investment career, draw up some yardsticks for yourself. Measure every opportunity against them. If they fit, follow up. If they don't, move on. Find out quickly if a deal falls within your financial parameters, so you won't waste your time on something that can't produce a large enough return. These yardsticks will change as you gain experience, but they should always be written clearly on your cuff. They act as a discipline against the all-too-human tendency to buy that pretty house or lot just because it's there.

Some Financial Parameters

No set of financial parameters fits every investment or every investor. But here are some guidelines to start with:

- *A rental property will work only if you bought it at a bargain price* (20 percent under current market value) or you create value by rescuing a problem property. Buying at market price, just to rent, doesn't give you decent returns. Neither does buying at market price and making ordinary improvements.

- *Don't make improvements to a house or building you own unless* you can get $2 of increased market value out of every $1 you spend. You need to fix up a fixer-upper, but by just enough.

- *On rental properties that you plan to hold, focus on the capitalization rate,* which is the rate of return on your invested capital. You have a 10 percent cap rate if your net operating income comes to 10 percent of the price of the property. (Net operating income is the rental income from the property minus expenses such as insurance and repairs but before mortgage payments.) Many buyers go with low cap rates of 4 or 5 percent, counting, for their profit, on the property's future rise in value. But those are poor investments. Tougher-minded buyers won't accept cap rates lower than 10 percent and preferably 12 percent.

■ *Given all the risks in rental real estate, you should be shooting for a combined annual return of 25 percent,* in upgrading and/or bargain-purchase profits, marketwide appreciation, amortization, cash flow, and tax savings. To calculate a one-year rate of return, add the dollar amounts of those six items and divide by the money you invested, including the value of your acquisition time. There are fancier ways of calculating returns, but for individuals, this will do.

■ *Bargains are measured by the discount you can get from current market value.* Professionals demand discounts of at least 20 percent. If they can't get that price on a particular deal, they move to the next one.

■ *Have an exit strategy.* That's one of the big differences between professionals and amateurs. Amateurs buy with dreams of profit in their heads. When professionals buy, they already have a plan for getting out. Specifically, they need to see a way of reselling almost immediately for a profit. Their plans don't always work out, but quick resale should be a reasonable possibility. If you buy at a bargain price because the house has a cracked foundation, for example, a repair should get it right back on the market at a sizable increase in price.

■ *All things being equal, invest close to home, in neighborhoods you know*—but only if prices are reasonable there. If they're not, you have two choices: forget about real estate or buy in another part of the state or the country where you think you can make a profit. Long-distance rental-property ownership is feasible as long as you have some local help, although local help raises your costs. Real estate investing requires a close understanding of the pertinent laws in the state you choose.

As Little as Possible About Taxes

You Can Deduct Your Rental Costs, including depreciation, against your rental income from this and similar projects, within the limits allowed for passive losses (see page 607). Any excess expense can tax-shelter some of your regular income if you meet the income test. If you don't, all your unused tax deductions are allowed to accumulate. You can use them against taxable rental income in future years or to reduce the size of your taxable profit when you finally sell this or another investment property.

Investors in Raw Land Get Virtually No Deductions because land isn't depreciable. If you borrowed money to buy the land, you may or may not be able to write off the interest. Such interest can normally be deducted only if you own the property for trade or business; or, if it's an investment, only against income from other passive investments, such as stock dividends or the sale of a rental property. The interest on loans of up to $100,000 become deductible, however, if you borrowed on a home equity line of credit.

You Can Defer Paying Taxes When You Dispose of an Investment Property by doing a *1031 tax-free exchange.* Instead of selling the property, you exchange it for another one. You don't even have to do a direct two-way swap. You can set up a three-cornered trade (or more). For example, suppose you want Jennie's property, Jennie wants Cipa's, and Cipa wants Lynn's. You can each deed the house to the proper person, noting that the agreement is part of an overall plan to accomplish an exchange. Get help from a professional to do this right.

If You Don't Do a Tax-Free Exchange, You May Have a Taxable Gain Even if You Sell at a Nominal Loss. That's called a *phantom gain.* The depreciation deductions reduce your adjusted basis* in the property. You have a gain if you sell for more than your adjusted basis, even if it's less than you originally paid.

Can You Get Rich Buying Second Mortgages?

A second mortgage (mortgages are called trust deeds in some states) is a second loan against a home. It makes a tempting income investment because it pays a lovely yield and normally doesn't require property management, as direct real estate investing does. But you face huge risks if the borrower defaults.

When you buy a second mortgage, you are betting that the borrower is going to make his or her payments on time—as, in fact, most do. You advertise for these loans ("We buy second mortgages") or find them through real estate brokers and lawyers. They are usually bought at a discount from face value in order to increase your yield.

---

*Your adjusted basis amounts to your cost plus any improvements you made to the property minus all the depreciation deductions you have claimed or could have claimed, and—well, it goes on. See an accountant.

Before buying, put the borrower through a credit and employment check (don't count on the broker to do it for you). Some of these borrowers are perfectly sound, but others are flakes whom normal lenders wouldn't touch.

You want a loan that comes due within a short period—say, two or three years. It should be collateralized by real estate, usually by the property itself. The borrower should have substantial equity in the property and a history of making all payments on time. In general, the house should be worth at least 30 percent more than all the loans against it. Raw land should be worth at least 60 percent more because of the risk. Many investors won't buy second mortgages against raw land.

If the borrower defaults, he or she will probably default on the first mortgage too. If the first mortgager forecloses, your interest will almost certainly be wiped out. You might have to make monthly payments on the first mortgage yourself while you wait for the house to be sold, or bid on the house at the foreclosure auction yourself, in order to salvage your investment. Talk about these risks with a real-estate attorney before getting into second mortgages. Attorneys often invest in mortgages themselves, because they understand the process. Anyone who buys into second mortgages should have a substantial personal income or a large pool of assets, to support the investment if something goes wrong.

Can You Get Rich by Listening to Seminar Gurus?

In most cases, no—you can only get poor. Poor, by spending your hard-earned money on the windy, deceptive books and tapes they flog. Poor, if you try to follow their half-baked schemes, which will cost you money with small chance of reward. Really poor, if you can't afford the deals you get into. They set you up for default and maybe even bankruptcy. Many of these "geniuses" have wound up bankrupt themselves. A few have gone to jail.

I studied a group of guru TV programs once, talked to the gurus, and got their materials. I found them misleading, fantastical, false, and, in some cases, flatly illegal. The dream they sell—that you can buy profitable property with no credit, no job, no experience, even with a bankruptcy behind you—shouldn't pass anyone's first-round BS test. For terrific and detailed reviews of dozens of gurus, including their books, tapes, and seminars, visit John T. Reed's Web site at www.johntreed.com/Reedgururating.html. Some are recommended, many others aren't. You've been warned.

For the Passive Investor

If dealing with tenants or bidding at auction is harder work than you had in mind, consider the stocks of real estate investment trusts (REITs—pronounced *reets*)—or even better, a mutual fund that buys them. They're for potatoes who want to own properties without leaving their couches.

REITs do your investing for you. They're real estate management companies that buy, own, and manage properties that they intend to hold for the long term. They earn income from rents, leases, and the occasional capital gain.

By law (and to avoid being taxed), REITs have to pay out most of their earnings to their investors every year, in stock or cash. As a result, their yields are relatively high, attracting income investors. Be warned that dividends received from REITs are taxed in your ordinary income bracket. Dividends from other real estate stocks are normally taxed as capital gains. Qualified taxes paid on global funds, to other governments, are passed through to U.S. investors as tax credits.

Most REITs trade on a stock exchange. That means you can buy and sell at will. You're not locked in, as you would be with a real estate limited partnership. You invest through a discount or full-service stockbroker, paying normal brokerage commissions. A REIT's share price will rise and fall in line with its management success, dividend payouts, property values, and broader industry and stock-market trends.

Over the long term, REITs act as a proxy for the commercial real estate market. They follow a price path that's somewhat different from that of other stocks. For this reason, investors use them as a way of diversifying their portfolios. But just because a class of stocks is different doesn't mean that it carries less risk. When the market crashed in 2008–2009, REITs led the slide and fell further than the market as a whole. That's the danger of investing in a single industry. Its fortunes depend entirely on how that industry performs—and in 2008–2009, commercial real estate stank. You own it because you want a toehold in this portion of the economy. When the odor of real estate improves, REIT stocks do too.

Some REITs—called *unlisted, untraded,* or *private* REITs—don't trade on an exchange. They invest in real estate companies, and you're expected to leave your money there for 10 to 12 years. You earn attractive dividends. At the end of the period, the sponsor will list the REIT on an exchange so that you can sell, or liquidate the properties and distribute the proceeds. Only then will you know what your investment has actually earned. If you need the money before 10 or

12 years are up, you'll take a haircut on the price. That is, if you can get your money out at all.

You'd be wise to stay away from unlisted REITS, for several reasons. First, they're high cost. Counting sales commissions and other fees, you'll pay 11 to 16 percent up front. Put another way, out of every dollar you invest, only 84 cents may actually go into real estate. Second, these investments lock you in, so you give up flexibility. If you need your money early, you'll have to accept a discount from the shares' estimated value. The sponsor may have the right to let you out only for "hardship" reasons and to suspend redemptions at any time. Third, they harbor substantial conflicts of interest. The sponsor usually owns several companies that do business with the REIT, and at high fees. (Other REITs have conflicts too, but unlisted REITs appear to have more than most.) Fourth, you'll have paid more fees over the years than if you had invested in publicly traded REITs, so your returns probably won't be as good. In the end, how well you do depends on the sponsor's exit strategy. When the REIT finally goes public, what will it be worth? Less than you'd net from public REITs.

Reits Come in Three Types, but Only One of Them Matters

Equity REITs are the principal object of desire—your best long-term bet for dividends and growth. They own apartment buildings, hotels, community shopping centers, regional malls, outlet centers, industrial parks, office buildings, self-storage buildings, nursing homes, mobile home parks, and other properties. Some are regional, others are nationwide, but most specialize in certain types of properties. Speculative REITs raise money for unusual types of properties, such as private prisons, or properties they haven't even purchased yet. Blue-chip REITs are major real estate companies with long histories of superior management, rising dividends, and increasing profits. The newest direction: global REITs that invest in properties abroad.

REITs are tough for individuals to analyze. The key number is *funds from operations* (FFO)—generally defined as income after operating expenses and before depreciation and amortization. You want the FFO to grow. Publicly traded REITs disclose FFOs on their shareholder reports.

To check how the market assesses a REIT, compare its FFO to earnings. A high FFO-to-earnings ratio says that the REIT is expected to keep on growing at a high rate; a low ratio says it's in trouble (although it could improve). Different types of REITs carry different ranges of ratios, and you need to know where yours fits in.

Another question: Where are the dividends coming from? Are they fully covered by FFO (as they should be), or is the REIT paying its investors by taking loans, selling properties, or dipping into reserves? If any of the latter, avoid it; the dividends may not be sustainable. An especially high yield is always suspect. It means that the REIT has dropped in price—maybe because some of its properties are failing or because its dividend may be cut. Your dividend payment might also be partly a return of your own original capital, in which case you're not earning as much as you think.

Not that you can always tell what's going on with FFO. Some REITs fudge that number or structure themselves to benefit their sponsors more than their shareholders.

Mortgage REITs haven't as good a performance history as equity REITs. Instead of buying properties, they invest in mortgages (bad in 2008–2009) and, sometimes, construction loans. They may have some sort of equity participation, so they're not necessarily straight income investments. Still, they behave more like bonds than stocks, doing their best when interest rates are stable. If you want to diversify into real estate, mortgage REITs don't cut it.

Hybrid REITs combine equity and mortgage REITs. But for real estate participation, the equity side is the only one that counts.

REIT initial public offerings (IPOs)—companies selling stock for the first time—are always risky. Untested real estate companies will try to raise money for properties they haven't even bought yet. Well-established companies are more promising, although, like other IPOs, they might come to market overpriced. Best bet: don't chase a new REIT stock. See if its price settles back after a few months and consider it then.

But consider *secondary offerings*—new issues of stock from REITs that are public already. They're generally raising money to purchase more property. Their history tells you something about their likely success.

REITs Often Suffer from Conflicts of Interest. A mortgage REIT that lends to its sponsor has its sponsor's needs in mind, not yours. An equity REIT "advised" by a developer may be paying too high an advisory fee, lending money to the developer or buying his or her properties at too high a price. REITs that invest in nursing homes may be controlled by the homes' operators. Look for these interlocking relationships in the REIT's prospectus, proxy statement, and annual reports (get them all from your broker before investing). You want an independent REIT, preferably one whose management owns a significant portion of the stock. (That's in the proxy statement too.) Owner-managers are investing with you, not against you.

The Best Way to Buy REITs. Don't try to analyze these complex stocks. Instead let a smart mutual fund manager buy them for you. Cohen & Steers (www.cohenandsteers.com, 800-330-7348) offers the widest range of U.S. funds, global funds, and exchange-traded funds; its expenses are high, however, and you pay up-front sales charges. No-load Fidelity has both a U.S. and an international REIT (www.fidelity.com, 800-343-3548). No-load Charles Schwab has a global REIT, covering both U.S. and international real estate companies (www.schwab.com, 866-893-6699). Vanguard's REIT Index Fund is the low-cost choice (www.vanguard.com, 877-662-7447). For a full listing of REITs, mutual funds, and exchange-traded funds, go to REIT.com at www.reit.com. Check the expense ratio on any fund you consider. When you're investing for income, it's especially important to choose a fund that has low costs. Also, choose funds with long records, not the newer ones. For diversification, pick one U.S. fund and one international fund or a single global fund.

Buying Mortgages

Some investors buy second mortgages or deeds of trust from people who don't want to hold them anymore. For example, take a home owner who sells a house and takes back a note for part of the down payment. The buyer-borrower promises to pay over the next three or five years. After a while, however, the home seller wishes that he or she had cash instead. Enter an investor, who buys the note at a discount from its face value. Assuming that the borrower pays on time, these notes can yield a high rate of return.

Personally, I rank mortgages as my 21st favorite investment—roughly between unsecured loans to horseplayers and Chinese railway bonds. Here's what you face:

1. These borrowers aren't first-rate risks. If they were, they'd have had enough cash for the down payment or enough credit at the bank. Don't invest without running a credit check, to be sure that the borrower always pays all of his or her loans on time. Don't invest if the borrower put little or no money down on the home.

2. If you hold a second mortgage and the first mortgage goes into default, you may be wiped out. In foreclosure, the house may sell for enough to cover the first mortgage but not yours too. As a safety cushion, don't invest unless the house is worth at least 30 percent more than all the loans against it—and get your own appraisal to prove it.

3. If the first mortgage goes into default, the only way to save your

investment may be to make the payments yourself for a while, in hopes that the house can be sold for enough to cover both loans. If the house has value and goes to foreclosure, you might buy it yourself, repay the first mortgage holder, and hope to resell at a profit. (Investors in second mortgages need fat cash reserves.)

4. If the mortgage you're holding goes into default and you want to foreclose, it will trigger foreclosure on the first mortgage too. Out of the frying pan and into the fire.

5. A property that looks good now will lose a lot of value if the economy sours or a local plant shuts down. You limit these risks by buying notes with no more than two or three years to run.

6. The highest yields come from mortgages or deeds of trust on properties that would be tough to dispose of if the borrower didn't pay: raw land, cooperative apartments, vacation lots, mobile homes. In these cases, don't invest unless the property's appraised value is at least 50 percent more than all the loans against it.

The mortgage business is full of brokers who try to match investors with sellers in return for a finder's fee. A broker may assure you that he or she has checked out the deal thoroughly—which may be false. Either do all the checking yourself or invest with a well-established broker known for dotting the i's and crossing the t's. Lawyers are especially suited for making mortgage investments because they're not daunted by the idea (or price) of going to court. If a court fight would worry you, let me suggest a few peaceful Chinese railway bonds.

Why Buy Real Property at All?

Investors buy real estate to make a buck. They study the market, see an advantage, and go for it. But it's riskier than, say, a no-load stock-owning mutual fund. Real estate in general may do well, eventually. But if your particular property comes a cropper—because of an environmental hazard, a lawsuit, a difficult tenant, a change of zoning, a market collapse—your loss can be huge. You can't easily trade out of it, the way you can a stock. That's what makes REITs more attractive than, say, raw land.

The classic argument for owning property is diversification. Real estate prices may go up at a time when stocks are going down.

But if diversification is the only draw, the average investor needn't bother.

You may own your own home. You may also own a vacation home. Odds are that a substantial percentage of your net worth is tied up in these properties. Your next logical step would be stocks rather than another piece of property. What's more, stocks have greatly outperformed real estate prices over time.

The lure of real estate, however, isn't always logical. A devoted investor becomes obsessed by properties—tromping through them, judging them, reshaping them, haggling over them. They're not like mutual funds that you can buy and forget. You have to give real estate your soul.

RETIREMENT PLANNING

You will grow old. You will retire. Those twenty- and thirty-some-things dashing around the sidewalks and malls, cell phones to their ears, texting friends, are going to inherit the earth. Then they're going to grow old too.

Bummer.

There are two things you have to do.

First comes the one you hear most about: lay away money for yourself. That's pretty simple, as long as you actually *do* it. The only trick is starting when you're young. Steady, long-term investing matters more to your future than what you put your investments *in.*

The second thing is harder: when you retire, you have to figure out how to make your existing money last for the rest of your life. A ton of new products is coming to market, claiming to "solve" that problem for you. Will they really, and how do you choose? This is going to be one of the most interesting times of your life.

29

How to Retire in Style

The Tax-Deferred Route to Easy Street

**It's daring and challenging to be young and poor,
but never to be old and poor. Whatever resources
of good health, character, and fortitude you bring
to retirement, remember also to bring money.**

How much money will you need when you retire?

Plenty. As a very general rule of thumb, take the annual income you think you're going to need when you retire and multiply it by 25.

You can't be sure of "the number" because conditions always change. Maybe you'll have to retire earlier than you thought for reasons of health or because your company closed. Maybe the stock market will collapse the year you retire—think of how awful it was for people who left (or lost) their jobs in 2008, with retirement balances down by 40 percent or more. On the other hand, maybe you'll hit the jackpot and win a better life than you expected.

The stock market and the economy are beyond your control. What you *can* control is what you save today and where you save it. That's what to focus on.

The right place to save is a tax-favored account. The right amount to save is at least 10 percent of your earnings when you're young, moving to 15 percent by your late 30s. That's tough to do if you've already built a standard of living around a zero savings rate or maybe 3 percent in a 401(k). Cutting back on spending in order to save is always harder than never having raised your spending in the first place.

But what do you think is going to happen if you don't save? You'll still grow old. You'll still retire. Maybe you're counting on your kids to chip in the cash you failed to save for yourself? That will undermine your children's retirements too.

So get with the program. Your time is *now!*

An Important Word About Inflation

Do you know about Harvey? Harvey was America's most famous rabbit, a giant of his kind, a star of his own eponymous movie. He was invisible. Only his costar, Jimmy Stewart, could see him. But despite Harvey's handicap, his performance was so riveting that he stole the show. Rent the movie and make some popcorn for a fun night at home.

You might wonder what this has to do with a chapter on retirement savings, other than the fact that only gray-hares will remember the film at all. But I think of today's inflation as Harvey. It's always there, yet workers treat it as invisible when they think about how much money they hope to have when they retire.

For a comfortable income in retirement, you traditionally aim for 80 percent of your gross preretirement earnings. That's in the first year. In the second year, your purchasing power will have shrunk a bit and so will the value of fixed capital. In the third year, you'll start to notice it, and more so in the fourth. At a "mere" 3 percent inflation, every $100 you have now will be worth $74 in 10 years, so by then you'll be living on something around three-quarters of your preretirement income. If the inflation rate goes up, things get worse. At 5 percent inflation, for example, that $100 would be worth only $60 in 10 years. In the following decade, your standard of living could drop by another half. That's Harvey for you. Invisible but riveting.

An Important Word About Safety Versus Growth

You're told over and over that it's mighty important to invest your money for growth. I say it too. Long-term savings won't add up to much if you keep it all in a bank account. But as you approach middle age, aggressive strategies become risky. You're drawn to high-growth stocks because you're trying to win more retirement money fast (probably making up for money you didn't save before!). If stocks turn down sharply, however, your nest egg can be so badly bruised that your future retirement will be permanently impaired.

You can afford high-growth strategies when you have options—say, plenty of years to recover from a major loss or plenty of money, even if you lose some. Most of us, sniffing retirement, aren't in that situation. It pays to get more conservative financially as your working years advance—holding higher percentages of your money in bonds. Yes, you'll miss some nice stock markets, but so what? At this age, the cost of being wrong is just too great.

For Better, for Worse, and Then for Retirement

When you're married, you'll retire *together*—something that couples sometimes forget. You'll need a joint plan for saving and budgeting. A joint plan for deciding when to leave work (will one of you work longer than the other?). A joint plan for where you'll live, whether to downsize, and how to invest. When you sit down to talk about it, you may discover—to your surprise—that you have very different ideas about the future. Some of your conversations may be strained. But now's the time to talk it through. A successful older age begins much earlier, not only financially but emotionally too.

For Same-Sex Spouses and Domestic Partners

The following sections talk a lot about inheritance rights or survivor's benefits in pensions and retirement plans. Traditional spouses (man and woman) always have special rights. Same-sex spouses generally are left out in the cold.

That's because the federal ERISA law governs most retirement plans—traditional pensions, ESOPs, 401(k)s, 403(b)s, 457s, Individual Retirement Accounts, and others. ERISA is subject to the Defense of Marriage Act passed in 1996, which defines spouses as persons of the opposite sex. So even though same-sex marriages are recognized in a handful of states, that's good only for tax breaks and benefits provided by the state in question.

Federal law remains hostile. A same-sex spouse isn't eligible for your pension's joint and survivor annuity and has no right to be consulted if you want to borrow against your 401(k). You can't file a joint federal tax return. Social Security won't pay you spousal benefits on your mate's account. The law doesn't require a division of the pension in divorce.

Same-sex couples picked up a small break under the *inherited IRA* rules passed in 2006 (page 1062). Previously, the best tax breaks went only to a spouse of the opposite sex when the IRA owner died. Now substantial inheritance tax breaks go also to same-sex spouses, registered domestic partners, and other nonspouse heirs, including children and friends. In addition, you can now apply for a hardship withdrawal from your 401(k) on your partner's behalf—for example, to help pay medical bills. To qualify for equal treatment, partners have to be listed, by name, on the plan's beneficiary form.

Piling Up the Cash

You already have a base: your Social Security benefits. Yes, doubters, you *will* receive a check. Its size will rise annually, so you'll get inflation protection too. When Social Security is reformed, however, future payments may not replace as much of a retiree's earnings as do the checks that are mailed today—especially for higher-income people. You'll need more money, and here's where to get it:

■ *Take advantage of every tax-deductible, tax-deferred, tax-free corporate or individual retirement plan that comes your way.* If you haven't joined your company plan, do it now. If you're already in the plan but are putting away just 3 or 5 percent of your salary, raise that to 10 percent and, next year, to 15 percent. Company savings plans often (not always) match at least part of the money you put in. That's like finding gold in the street. All you have to do is bend over and pick it up.

If you don't have a company plan, start an Individual Retirement Account (page 1047). You can make automatic monthly contributions from your bank account to a plan offered by a mutual fund group.

■ *Don't lightly give up a job that pays a traditional pension.* When you're retired, there's nothing more comfortable than a monthly check in the mail. Unfortunately, corporate pensions are being steadily cut back (page 1017). Your traditional plan might be frozen and replaced with a plan that offers less. Even so, it's a valuable benefit to have. Public-sector pensions are often enshrined in state constitutions, so they're a surer bet.

■ *If you're saving for both retirement and college for your kids, put retirement first.* Your kids can borrow their way through school, but you can't borrow your way through old age. For a strategy that combines college and retirement savings, see page 684.

■ *Own your own home.* A paid-up home stabilizes your living costs. No monthly mortgage payments, no monthly rent. If you own the house or apartment long enough, it can give you extra equity to live on. For example, you might sell it, buy something smaller, and bank the surplus. Or you might take a reverse mortgage (page 1055). Homes started losing their value when the real estate bubble burst in 2007, but that doesn't invalidate home ownership. It's proof that when you own a home debt free, you're safe. Paying off the mortgage wasn't sexy during the credit boom. Now that's where satisfaction lies.

■ *Don't kid yourself about early retirement.* It takes a fortune to quit at 50 and keep yourself going for another 40 years. Maybe you have a fortune, thanks to a lucky strike in stock options, bonuses you've salted away, or a lifetime of maximizing your 401(k)—in which case, bon voyage. Otherwise you are likely to want some part-time earnings, even if you set your early-retirement date at 60. And no matter how much money you have, you can't afford to go without health insurance (chapter 13).

■ *Invest a substantial portion of your long-term retirement savings for growth.* That generally means stock-owning mutual funds. Don't be frightened by the sinkhole that opened under the market in 2008 and switch entirely into bonds. Bond funds have their place, even for younger people. But you're wasting your youth (by which I mean all the years under 60) if you get so frightened of stocks that you keep most of your retirement plan in fixed-income investments. Follow the rule of 110: subtract your age from 110, and use that number as the percentage of your financial investments to keep in the stock market. If you're 40 and subtract that number from 110, you get 70—meaning that 70 percent of your *long-term* money could be in stocks. Subtracting 50 from 110 gives you 60—so 60 percent could go into stocks. What's long term? Money that you don't intend to touch for 10 years or more. Any money you might need earlier should be in the bank, in money market funds, or in bonds.

■ *Even after retirement, keep a modest portion of your capital invested for growth.* At 70, you might want to be 40 percent invested in stock-owning mutual funds— maybe equity-income or growth-and-income funds. For asset-allocation suggestions, see pages 723–725. If you switch all your money into fixed-income investments at 60 or 65 and live on the interest, Harvey at any size will gradually eat you up.

Use the Web to estimate whether you're saving enough to live well when you retire. Your company's 401(k) administrator may provide a calculator. You'll also find calculators at Choose to Save (www.choosetosave.org), AARP (www.aarp.org) and Fidelity's myPlan (www.personal.fidelity.com/planning/retirement/content/myPlan/index.shtml). The answers you get from these sites will differ but all of them will probably show that you're nowhere close. Ignoring the facts won't help. Studies show that people who use the retirement calculators raise their savings rates, which will leave them better prepared when their paychecks finally stop.

Your Pension: If You're Lucky Enough to Have One

You *must* understand your corporate retirement plans. If you don't know how much of your retirement income is guaranteed and how much isn't, you won't have a clue as to what you ought to be saving now. By law, your employer has to send you a pension benefit statement at least once every three years (and annually, if you ask for it in writing), showing the size of your pension. At many large companies, you can track it online. Don't burst out laughing when you're young and see the numbers. Pensions always start small and build over time.

Corporate plans come in two basic types: defined benefit plans and defined contribution plans.

Defined Benefit Plans

Defined benefit is the fancy name for *pension*. For every year you work, you accumulate a specific benefit, which translates into a lifetime monthly income. Typically, you pay nothing into the plan. It is financed entirely by your employer. In corporate plans, your monthly pension check will be a fixed amount, so inflation will erode your income over time. In most government plans, you get cost-of-living adjustments—at either the current inflation rate or something slightly less.

Pension plans come in two main types:

Traditional plans calculate your pension based on your salary, your age, and the number of years you worked for the company. They're especially good for older workers and workers who stay with a company for a long time. Most of the time, extra weight is given to the size of your salary in the years just before you retire. Your benefit statement expresses your pension as a dollar amount per month.

The newer *hybrid plans* are designed to look more like savings or profit-sharing plans. Most of them are *cash-balance plans*. Typically, they give no special weight to age or how long you've been with the company. You're credited with a fixed amount of money for every year you work. Usually it's a percentage of pay—say, 5 percent—plus interest based on a specific index. Your benefit statement shows your pension as an accumulated account value—say, $50,000. You can take that amount with you if you leave for another job or leave it with the company and convert it into a lifetime income when you retire.

In 2009 nearly half the pension plans at larger companies were of the cash-value type, according to the consulting firm Hewitt, and their numbers are going up. They appeal to younger workers who move from job to job. But compared with traditional plans, they're not so good for workers who get above-average raises and are still with the company when they retire.

The hybrid called a *pension-equity plan* works like a cash-balance plan but gives some extra credits to longtime workers or workers hired in midcareer.

Just because you have a traditional pension plan doesn't mean that you can keep it. The trend today is for companies to freeze their plans—both the traditional ones and the newer hybrids—and transition to 401(k)s and similar plans.

That reduces the company's obligations to its workers and throws the responsibility for a successful retirement on you. A frozen plan might continue to operate for existing employees but not for new hires. Or it might stop adding new credits even for existing employees.

Some pension plans are being terminated. When that happens, your benefits to date are paid out immediately or replaced with an insurance company annuity. Neither choice is good for employees. You lose your future monthly income, and annuity payments are fixed. The annuity's safety depends on the solvency of the insurance company, backed up by limited state guaranty funds (page 403). You're not covered by the employer-funded Pension Benefit Guaranty Corporation (page 1021).

How to Get the Most from a Defined Benefit Plan

1. Don't job-hop too readily if you're middle-aged and have been in a traditional pension plan for many years. These plans weight their benefits, to pay proportionately more to the workers with the longest service. The odds are that your company will keep its promise to late-career workers. A new job offer would have to be markedly better before it's financially smart to quit.

As you move past 45, the more critical this risk-reward analysis becomes. If you're offered a job at another company, what potential promotions lie ahead? What retirement benefits are available? Will you earn enough to make up for the future pension credits you're leaving behind? Will your new company pay you a "signing bonus" to cover it? (That's possible if the job is important enough.)

If you're in a cash-balance plan, you don't have to think so hard about whether to leave. Usually there's no special benefit for longevity. Companies use the same pension-crediting formula for everyone, short-term and long-term workers alike.

2. Know your company's vesting schedule. You *vest* when the money in your pension account becomes yours to keep. In traditional plans, full vesting may come after you've been with the company for five years, or over a three- to seven-year period, depending on which approach your company chooses. In cash-value plans, you vest after three years. In that short period, you'll acquire only in a peanut payment. But money is money. If you're offered a new job three months before your existing credits will vest in full, it's worth playing for time so you can collect.

3. If you do quit your current employer, the plan may offer you two ways of taking your traditional vested pension benefits: in a lump sum or as a monthly pension for life when you retire.

The case for a lump sum: you can roll it into an Individual Retirement Account.

That preserves your tax shelter and gives you more flexibility, long term. If you die, your heirs will inherit the money. You cut the link with your company and don't have to keep it informed of your address. You're also protected against the risk of having your former company fail (your pension may not be fully protected by the Pension Benefit Guaranty Corporation). Do *not* take a lump sum and spend it, even if it's small. You will never make it up. You'd also have to pay taxes on the withdrawal, plus a 10 percent penalty if you're under 59½. Cash-balance plans almost always offer you a lump sum. Traditional plans are more likely to make you wait for lifetime annuity payments when you retire.

The case for leaving the benefit with the company: Sometimes it will pay you more. Here's why: when you have a traditional pension plan and take a lump sum, you don't get the full amount in cash. Instead the amount is *discounted*— that is, reduced—by a certain interest rate, known as a discount rate. Ask the employee benefits office what discount rate it uses (or what range of rates). You would have to invest your lump sum to yield at least that percentage gain per year, for as long as you live, to get as much monthly income as the pension would have paid. If the discount rate is low, you can probably do it. If the rate is high, however, it might be hard for your investments to generate the same amount of income that a pension would pay. In that case, it's better to leave the money with the company and take the monthly income when you retire. (If you're currently at retirement age, see page 1120.)

If you leave a traditional pension benefit with your company, it will be frozen at its current level, payable at your retirement age. If it's currently worth $1,100 a month in 15 years, when you're 65, that's what you'll get—even though in that future year, the purchasing power of the pension will have dropped significantly. Still, every retirement dollar counts. Keep a note in your personal files so you won't forget any small pensions due from previous employers.

Lump sums paid from cash-value plans aren't discounted. What you see is what you get. If an employee dies before retiring, the full amount in the plan is generally paid as a death benefit to the spouse. If you're not married (or your spouse waives his or her rights), most plans let you leave the benefit to someone other than your spouse.

If you die before activating your vested pension, your spouse will get a survivor's benefit—50 percent of what would have been your monthly benefit, payable for life. (For your spouse to be eligible, you generally have to have worked at the company for at least five years.) Other heirs, however, will usually get nothing.

Lump sums versus lifetime payouts: what your spouse has to think about. Your spouse has to consent, in a notarized statement, if you want to take your pension in a lump sum. That's because he or she is losing rights. As long as the benefit remains in the company plan, the spouse is entitled to a survivor's benefit if you die before the pension starts. The law also requires that he or she get a portion of your pension when you retire (a joint-and-survivor pension—page 1121), although these rights can be waived. If you take the money out of the plan and roll it into an Individual Retirement Account, a spouse's protection is lost. You can leave an IRA to anyone you want.

There's also the question of investment success. If you take out the money and invest it well, your spouse will be richer if you die. If you invest it badly, he or she might have been better off with half your traditional pension benefit for life.

4. If you leave the company, hate your new job, and return to the company you left, find out what happens when you rejoin the pension plan. You can pick up old pension and vesting credits as long as you weren't away for too many years.

What if you take a leave of absence due to a company-sanctioned sabbatical, an illness or disability, or to have (or adopt) a child? You'll get pension credits for up to 501 hours of service. You'll accrue no new benefits during the time you're gone, but the credits help you hang on to the pension level you've already earned.

5. Know what your retirement benefits are. As you approach middle age, or if you're thinking about a new job with another company, ask your current employee benefits office to estimate what your actual pension is likely to be. It's important to walk through the calculation step-by-step and check the assumptions the company is using. Pension administrators are only human and make mistakes (page 1067). Keep the benefit statements the company sends.

6. Find out to what extent your company integrates its plan with Social Security. With integration, you don't get a full pension check. Instead it's partly reduced by your Social Security benefit. If that sounds like a dirty trick, I agree—but the law allows it. Complex IRS rules govern the level of integration. In general, lower-paid workers will feel this cut more than their higher-paid counterparts. Ask your company for guidance on what your combined benefit is likely to be, so that you'll know how much extra you have to save.

7. If you divorce, your spouse is entitled to part of your pension or an equivalent sum. Laws governing the split depend on your state. See page 169.

8. Most workers' pensions are insured in full by the industry-funded Pension Benefit Guaranty Corporation (PBGC). If your plan fails, the insurance will cover your basic monthly payment, most early-retirement pensions, annuities for survivors, and most disability benefits. The maximum payment, for workers retiring at various ages, is listed at www.pbgc.gov (click on "Workers & Retirees"). It rises every year for workers in newly failed plans. In 2009 it came to $4,500 a month ($51,750 a year) for single workers retiring at 65 (less if you retired earlier or are married and took a joint-and-survivor benefit).

The PBGC doesn't cover every company benefit. If your pension plan failed, you'd lose the amount of your pension that exceeded the PBGC ceiling, so highly paid employees would be out some money. Nor does the insurance cover collateral benefits such as life and health insurance, vacation pay, severance pay, pay for disabilities that occurred after the plan terminated, and improvements made to the plan within the past five years.

To reduce failures, the Pension Protection Act of 2006 requires that pension plans be 100 percent funded over a seven-year period. That means that the plan must have enough assets to pay its current benefits.* Plans that fall below this level aren't as healthy as they should be. Companies have to disclose their pension funding levels every year to participants, beneficiaries, and unions. If your plan is less than 80 percent funded, it may face restrictions on paying benefits (such as not allowing lump sum withdrawals) until its health improves. Saving money separately in a 401(k) or similar plan diversifies your retirement risk.

State and local pensions aren't required to disclose their funding levels, and some are particularly weak. They're backed by taxing power, but municipal bankruptcies or taxpayer revolts might cut these benefits or require that you put in money.

There's no insurance coverage at all for the defined benefit plans of federal, state, or local governments, some plans run by churches and fraternal organizations, and the plans of professional-service employers (for example, doctors and lawyers) that haven't covered more than 25 active workers at any time. Nor does the PBGC insure defined contribution plans such as 401(k)s.

You're entitled to your vested benefits even if the company terminates the plan, merges, or goes out of business. The PBGC keeps a list of people who haven't claimed the pensions due them from failed plans. In April 2007, some $133 million was owed to 32,000 people (those are the last data available before this book was published). If you might be one of them, scour the "Pension Search Directory" at www.pbgc.gov.

9. Check into what stands behind your pension if you're classified as a highly compensated employee. In 2009 that was defined as someone whose 2008 salary was in excess of $105,000 or who owned at least 5 percent of the

---

*If the plan actually terminates, there might not be enough assets—but fully funded plans don't terminate.

company. Your future monthly retirement benefit probably exceeds the amount the PBGC insures. It may not even be fully contained in your company's tax-qualified pension plan. A significant portion might be in a Supplemental Executive Retirement Plan (SERP), also known as a top-hat plan, backed by nothing but your company's ability to pay. If your company fails, you get in line with its other creditors. Part of your pension might be uncollectible. Find out how much of your retirement fund is in the regular, tax-qualified retirement plan and how much is in a supplemental plan. Check your plan rules to see if you can take your SERP benefits in a lump sum if you leave the job.

Defined Contribution Plans

For employers, these plans are no-risk deals. Instead of promising you a specific lifetime pension, the company promises only to offer you a tax-deferred investment plan. You make regular contributions. The company usually adds some matching money itself, but that's optional. The size of your retirement fund, and the income it can generate, depends entirely on how well your investments do. The company takes no responsibility for the outcome.

Defined contribution plans include 401(k)s, stock bonus plans, employee stock ownership plans, employee Keogh plans (rarely used today), and Simplified Employee Pensions. None of these plans is insured by the Pension Benefit Guaranty Corporation. Company contributions, if any, might be in cash or in company stock. You might get a fixed and guaranteed percentage of your salary (known as a money purchase plan) or an optional contribution based on a percentage of salary or profits (known as a profit-sharing plan). The company might also match part of the contributions you make to a savings plan such as a 401(k). The assets in retirement plans are held in trust. If the company fails, all your money should still be there (barring fraud, from which no private plans, especially small ones, are ever perfectly secure—page 1035).

The money in these plans is all invested—sometimes at the company's discretion, sometimes at yours. The maximum you can contribute each year is linked to the inflation rate. By retirement, you can accumulate a sizable amount. At that point, you generally have three choices: take the money in a lump sum and roll it into an Individual Retirement Account, leave it with the company to manage for you, or turn it into a fixed monthly income for life.

How large will your retirement income be? Who knows? The size of your check depends on how much was contributed each year, the plan's expenses (always higher than the expenses of defined benefit pension plans), how well you invested those funds, and the state of the stock market at the time you leave the job. You bear all the risk. Maybe you'll retire on more than a defined benefit plan would have paid. On the other hand, maybe you'll get less—and with a shocking suddenness. Think of what happened to people who retired in 2007. After the 2007 and 2008 stock market dive, the money in their retirement plans might have been chopped by 40 percent.

How to Get the Most from a Defined Contribution Plan

1. The earlier you start saving, the better. A dollar saved today is worth more than a dollar saved tomorrow, thanks to the unflagging power of interest, dividends, and profits left alone to compound. Compounding is a true perpetual money machine. No force (except early withdrawals!) can ever stand in its way. (Yes, yes, I know that a dollar saved today is worth less tomorrow if the stock market collapses—but it's still worth more over time!)

2. Some companies perch a defined contribution plan on top of a defined benefit pension plan. Typically, the pension part will carry less and less of the load in the years ahead. The responsibility for producing a decent income for retirees will shift toward the riskier defined contribution plan. That means you should increase your own contributions just to keep your expected future benefit level. Check the current size of your total combined benefit in the plan documents: the summary plan description and your individual benefit statement. The company is required to give them to you (page 1069).

3. It's not costly to job-hop when you're backed by defined contribution plans. You can take your vested plan money with you. Your new employer will enroll you (or offer to enroll you) in its own defined contribution plan as soon as you're hired. All things being equal, 40 years of work under defined contribution plans should net you only a slightly smaller sum from a series of employers than you'd get if you stayed with a single one, assuming that you preserve each account and worked for each company long enough for the benefits to vest.

4. If you want to quit your job, find out your "escape date"—the earliest you can leave with your full retirement account in hand. Your own contributions, plus the money they earn, are always yours for the taking. Company contributions vest in full after three years or gradually over two to six years, depending on which schedule the company chooses.

5. Job switchers should reinvest their lump sum retirement plan payouts in an Individual Retirement Account or their new employer's 401(k) plan, if that's allowed. If you spend the money, that chunk of your retirement savings is permanently gone. You will never make it up. Besides losing that nest egg and the value of years of tax deferral, you will also have to pay income taxes on the payout plus a 10 percent penalty if you're under 59½. Spending even a dime of an early lump sum payout is just nuts.

6. Don't fail to contribute to these plans when they're offered. Major employers plan for their pensions to cover a certain percentage of your retirement pay, expecting the rest to come from Social Security and your 401(k) account. They assume you'll join the plan and contribute the maximum. If you don't, your nest egg will fall short. A rising number of companies now put you in the 401(k) automatically unless you deliberately opt out. Don't opt out. At companies without pension plans, a 401(k) may be all you've got.

7. You must learn something about investing—a new responsibility that many savers haven't accepted yet. Professionally run pension funds typically invest 60 percent of their money in stocks because over time they produce the largest returns. Yet many individuals still go for lower-yielding fixed-income investments. If you put all your 401(k) money into bond funds or stable-value funds, the size of your retirement account will disappoint you. Conversely, other workers overinvest in stocks, which kills them when the market drops.

Companies offer a good mix of stock funds, bond funds, and mixed-stock-and-bond funds from which to choose. The target retirement funds are a particularly good choice. For more on allocating 401(k) money, see chapter 21.

Defined contribution plans come in many varieties. Here's what you might be offered:

Employee Stock Ownership Plans (ESOPs)

Of all the defined contribution plans that you might be offered, an employee stock ownership plan is by far the riskiest. It's entirely, or substantially, invested in your company's stock. You get the stock free, which is nice. If the company does well—and many of them do—you can hit the jackpot. But you're not allowed to diversify into other investments until your reach 50 *and* have had 10 years of service. So you can't get out of company stock that is going nowhere. A few companies fail, leaving their ESOPs worthless. It's fine to have an ESOP if it's frosting on the cake but not if it's your company's only or primary retirement plan or if you're depending on the stock to pay your future bills.

Most ESOPs are found in private, closely held companies. In general, here's how they work:

The plan buys shares of the company's stock—typically, from an owner who wants to sell out. The company pays; no contributions are required from the employees. The shares are credited to individual employees according to a formula. Each year the plan may acquire additional shares, which helps increase the value of your account. There's a vesting schedule; you vest when the shares become yours to keep, even if you leave the firm. Depending on the plan, you might vest in all the shares in your account after 3 years or vest in them gradually over 6 years.*

Usually ESOPs borrow money to purchase company shares. Those shares are gradually allocated to employee accounts as the loan is repaid—typically, over 5 to 12 years. If the ESOP doesn't borrow money, the new shares are allocated when the company contributes them. It can contribute any number of shares it wants—including zero in a bad year—up to the limit the law allows.

You're entitled to the vested value of your account when you leave your job or if the company is sold. But nothing requires the company to give you the money right away. Some companies pay you over 2 or 3 years. Others stretch the payments over as many as 10 years. It all depends on why you left the company and the plan's rules.

If you retire, become disabled, or die, the company normally has to start paying you the following year, although it can stretch out the payments for 5 years more. The same is true if the company is sold. You're paid interest on the outstanding balance.

If you leave the company for any other reason, such as getting another job, the first payment can effectively be delayed for 6 years, with the remaining payments stretched over the next 5 years. (Accounts worth more than $985,000 in 2009 might have to wait as much as 10 years. That cutoff point rises with inflation every year.)

If there's a loan against the plan, payments can be delayed until the loan has been repaid, although generally no longer than 10 years (or 5 years if the employee died).†

As a practical matter, companies rarely make their employees wait that long, because it's a hassle to keep track of them and because it's not fair. But you shouldn't imagine that your ESOP benefits will go into your pocket right away. If you need the money to help pay current bills, tough luck.

Your plan will pay you either in cash or in shares that you can convert to cash. Distributions can be rolled tax free into an Individual Retirement Account,

---

*Under older rules, some plans vest all at once after 5 years or gradually over 7 years.
†This applies to C corporations that report income on their own tax returns, not S corporations that pass income through to their shareholders' personal returns.

including distributions to a surviving spouse.* If you don't roll them over, you'll owe income taxes on the money plus a 10 percent penalty if you're under 59½.

If you're over 59½, consider taking the shares directly and then selling them back to the company (or on the open market if it's a public company). That way, your profits are taxed at the low, long-term capital gains rate. (For more on this, see page 1036.)

Some ESOPs, especially the older ones, diversify. Stocks in other companies may make up 20 or 30 percent of the plan. The majority of ESOPs, however, are made up entirely of the company's own stock. If the shares are publicly traded, you know exactly what the market thinks they're worth. If your company is privately held, the shares are worth what an appraiser says they are, on your annual benefit statement.

New ESOPs are set up each year, not because employees are clamoring for them but because they offer management so much. ESOPs provide companies with special tax breaks, and they're a captive buyer for a retiring owner's personal shares.

Often employees have access to a backup retirement plan. About 70 to 75 percent of the companies with ESOPs offer 401(k)s, pensions, or some other type of account, according to studies by professors Joseph Blasi and Douglas Kruse of Rutgers University. Still, employees are generally far too dependent on their company's success. Workers earning under $40,000 have an average of 28.8 percent of their financial wealth tied up in company stock. That rises to 33.9 percent for workers earning $40,000 and more. That's far too much! Furthermore, some of the backup plans offer stock options and other forms of profit sharing, which tie you even more tightly to the company's financial success.

Ideally, you should hold no more than 5 percent of your retirement savings in company stock. And even then you're in good shape only if the rest of your retirement investments are well diversified.

When your ESOP overexposes you to company stock or you have only an ESOP as a retirement plan, it's a crummy deal, even if it's a wonderful company. No employee should be asked to stake his or her entire future on whether, at retirement, the company's stock will be up or down or whether it will have value at all. If you are stuck with such a plan, jump at a good job somewhere else that offers you broader retirement benefits. In the meantime, make superhuman efforts to save money for yourself—for example, by funding a traditional or

---

*Other heirs can transfer distributions into an *inherited IRA* but only if the plan allows—see page 1062.

Roth Individual Retirement Account. If your company fails or flags, that personal money might become your major retirement fund.

Anyone with an ESOP should fund other retirement plans to the max. Also, take full advantage of the escape hatches that your ESOP is required to offer by law:

1. When you reach 55 or older and have been in the plan for at least 10 years, you can demand that 25 percent of an ESOP account be invested in other assets. This switch can be made all at once or over 5 years, depending on what the company allows. Diversify, even if the company's stock is going up. The majority of companies with ESOPs are successful, but you can't predict in advance which ones will have poor results or when, exactly, a down year will occur.

If your company offers a 401(k) plan, you can put the money there. Alternatively, tell the ESOP to roll your partial payouts into an Individual Retirement Account, where you can invest them yourself. Either way, diversify to the fullest. It's the safest thing to do.

2. At age 60, you can order that half of your money be switched out of your company's stock into a broader range of investments. (That's 50 percent of the ESOP minus the percentage you took out before.)

3. Some companies let you diversify even earlier than the law requires. Jump at the chance.

4. At 62 you can start pulling money out of the plan entirely, even if you haven't retired. This might be a good time to start an Individual Retirement Account.

Some companies—typically larger ones—have folded their ESOPs into their 401(k)s and use them to match employee contributions. That makes it easy to diversify out of the ESOP and into broad-based mutual funds.

ESOP experts who read this section pointed out that ESOPs are better than having no employer-supported retirement plan at all. Agreed. ESOPs also cover all of a company's employees, whereas lower-paid workers in companies with 401(k)s might not sign up for the plan or, if they do, may not save much. Also agreed. Nevertheless, don't kid yourself: people depending on ESOPs are at much higher risk than people in diversified plans.

401(k) Savings Plans: For Employees, the Best Deal in Town

You'll find 401(k) salary deferral plans at almost every large company and many smaller ones. Details differ from firm to firm. But at bottom, they are all the same unbeatable deal.

Some younger workers don't contribute to 401(k)s because they "can't afford" to. In fact, you can. If you contribute, say, 5 percent of pay, you'll discover that you can live on the money that remains in your paycheck without even noticing the contributions that went into the plan. A 401(k) provides so much in tax savings and, usually, free employer contributions that it's crazy not to join. If you don't, you'll look back 10 years later and kick yourself. Many companies now sign up new employees automatically. You can opt out of the plan if you want, but staying in is the right thing to do.

People turn sour on 401(k)s when the stock market declines. But that's an investment problem, not a plan problem. Investments always have their ups and downs, and in 401(k)s, you can add bonds or stable-value funds to your mix. You *must* save for retirement somewhere. For employees, 401(k)s are your best shot.

Here are the answers to your questions about 401(k)s.

How Does the Plan Work?

There are two types of 401(k)s: a traditional plan and a Roth.

In a *traditional 401(k),* you agree that part of your salary will be set aside for your retirement, usually every year. That money is exempt from current federal income taxes (although not from Social Security taxes and, sometimes, local income taxes). Earnings on your contributions—interest, dividends, and capital gains—accumulate tax deferred. You are taxed only when you withdraw the funds. Traditional plans are good for people who want to save for retirement while preserving the largest possible net paycheck for themselves. When you leave the plan, you can roll the money into a traditional Individual Retirement Account

Your plan may also allow for after-tax contributions. You get no tax reduction for saving this money, but the earnings will accumulate tax deferred.

In a *Roth 401(k),* your contributions come from after-tax dollars. When you leave the plan, you can roll the money into a Roth Individual Retirement Account. None of your earnings will ever be taxed. This plan is a great choice for people who don't need a tax deduction in order to afford the contribution and people who fear that their tax rate may increase when they retire. My opinion: aim for the Roth. Tax-free compounding is a real gift.

How Do I Contribute?

By payroll deduction, which is doubtless why 401(k) plans work so well. The dollars slip into the plan without your seeing them go. You live on the net paycheck you receive, forgetting the portion that was set aside. Left alone, your 401(k) money sits there peacefully and, over time, will grow.

How Much Can I Put In?

Your own maximum pretax contribution is some percentage of salary (set by your company) up to a legal ceiling that rises with inflation every year. In 2009 it was $16,500.* If you're 50 and up, you can add an annual $5,500 "catch-up" contribution. Any after-tax contributions go on top of that.

Highly paid employees might not be able to save the full $16,500. The law prevents them from contributing a substantially higher percentage amount of their salary than lower-paid employees do, and the lower-paid might not be adding very much. Nevertheless, the higher-paid are still entitled to the $5,500 catch-up contribution.

The total maximum annual contribution to all of your company savings plans, including any after-tax dollars and anything your employer puts up, is 100 percent of your salary, up to $49,000 in 2009 plus the $5,500 catch-up for people 50 and older.

Whatever your ceiling, fund these plans to the absolute maximum of your ability. Start small if you must and step up your commitment every year. If you change jobs several times in your working life, this may be the only significant pool of retirement money you'll ever have.

Some companies let you sign up for automatic increases in your contributions, effective at the time of year that you normally get a raise. Always use this wonderful option. Employees often forget to increase their savings rate once they join a 401(k). Automatic increases do the right thing for your future while you sleep.

Does My Employer Contribute?

Usually, yes. You might get 25 or 50 cents—sometimes even $1—for every dollar you put in, up to a certain percentage of pay. Often the match is made

---

*This is the total, annual pretax contribution allowed, even if you work two jobs with two 401(k) plans or change jobs midyear.

with company stock instead of cash. This is free money, even if the stock goes down. Any employee who doesn't contribute in order to get the company match is throwing away a pile of assets. The employer's contributions always go into a traditional 401(k), even if your own contributions go into a Roth 401(k).

Matches are entirely optional, however. A company that's being squeezed financially will probably reduce or eliminate the match.

Can I Make Nondeductible Contributions to My Traditional 401(k)?

Yes, and here's a good reason for it. When you leave the company, you can roll those contributions into a Roth IRA. That allows your investment to compound tax free for life.

How Is 401(k) Money Invested?

Most plans offer you a wide range of investment choices. They may include U.S. stock-owning mutual funds, international stock funds, bond funds or fixed-interest contracts, the company's own stock, and an annuity that guarantees a future lifetime income. Target retirement funds provide a balance of stocks and bonds that's appropriate for your age. With a *managed account,* a manager picks the investments for you. For more on choosing mutual funds, inside and outside a retirement plan, see chapter 22.

Some companies stock their 401(k)s with *collective funds.* They're similar to mutual funds but aren't the "name" funds offered to retail investors. Instead they're large investment pools like those behind traditional pension plans. You don't get prospectuses and may get performance reports only once a quarter. On the other hand, expenses are low, which ought to improve your investment returns over the long run. Studies of pension funds show that, on average, they far outperform the selections individuals make in their 401(k)s.

Can I Switch from One Investment to Another?

Absolutely. Most plans let you change your investments at will, online or by phone. In some cases, you may be limited to a fixed number of switches per year. But constant tinkering is dumb. Your best strategy is to decide what percentage to keep in stocks and stick with it. Any change should depend on your personal goals, not what you think the market is going to do.

There are two exceptions to the open-switching rules. Some 401(k)s offer shares in illiquid real estate investments, such as apartment houses or shopping malls. The properties cannot be suddenly sold if a lot of participants want to retrieve their money all at once. In such a case your funds will be frozen, perhaps for a long time. Illiquid real estate is a terrible investment for 401(k)s to offer. If there's one in your plan, forget about it. If you want to have some real estate in your portfolio, choose a real estate investment trust. REITs own real estate stocks that are freely tradable on the marketplace.

The second potentially illiquid investment is a stable-value fund. It offers an attractive rate of interest, guaranteed by insurance contracts. But those contracts are long term. If your company goes bankrupt and the employees want to empty their 401(k) accounts, the stable-value fund won't have the cash on hand to meet the guarantees. It may take a while to get your money out, and you might get a lower interest rate than you were promised. Stable-value funds are far more dependable than illiquid real estate funds, but, in a pinch, they're not as accessible as bond funds or money market funds.

When Is My Money Invested?

Your employer has to put the money in the plan within 15 business days after the end of the month that your contribution was taken out of your paycheck. You should be able to track this online.

My Employer Just Changed My Plan! Is That Legal?

Some companies are trying to help employees who have made bad investment choices by "reenrolling" them in the 401(k). They move your money from the investments you had before into a *default* account that's better diversified. That saves you from holding too much of your 401(k) in company stock or too much in a no-growth money market fund. You might be reenrolled if your company adds new options to the plan or changes record keepers.

For most employees, the switch is probably a good deal. Some people, however, may have reasons to hold an undiversified mix of investments. For example, your 401(k) might be entirely in fixed-interest stable-value funds because you own stocks in an investment account outside the IRA. It's legal for the company to change your plan as long as you're notified in advance and given the option of keeping the mutual funds you have now. (Did you open your company's e-mail or read its newsletter?) Think about it before demanding to keep your old investments. Maybe the company's new choices are right.

What Does My Plan Cost?

Good question! You can see the expense ratio for the individual funds you've invested in (page 765), but the rest is a mystery. Large company plans may be charging only 0.3 percent, but small and midsize plans are usually soaked for more. A 2007 study by IMC, a consulting firm, concluded that as many as

10 percent of 401(k) plan participants are paying unreasonable fees and another 15 percent are paying fees characterized as high.

The employers themselves may not know how much their plans are costing them because of the confusing way that the plan servicers quote their prices. There are more than 80 ways that fees can be displayed and no easy way to add them up. At this writing, the Department of Labor is considering cost-disclosure rules so employers can compare prices and get a better deal. DOL should go further and require disclosure to consumers too. Employers have been shifting more of their own administrative expenses onto the plans, which raises your costs and reduces your returns. It's wrong for you to be left in the dark and wrong for you to be forced to swallow fees you can't control.

How Do I Know How My Investments Are Doing?

Once a quarter, you should get a report on the status of your account by mail or e-mail. If you don't, ask for it in writing; your employer is required to give it to you. Your plan may also give you continuous access to your account online, plus an 800 number, so you can check on how your investments are doing. My advice: don't check. Following daily fluctuations tempts you to try to jump into and out of stocks or switch to faster-moving mutual funds. That kind of trading will almost certainly depress your long-term returns.

Can I Make Cash Withdrawals from the Plan While I'm Still at Work?

As a practical matter, no, if you're under 59½. Most (but not all) 401(k) plans allow withdrawals in cases of hardship, such as needing money for medical bills, avoiding foreclosure, buying a house, college tuition, and other expenses. But you may have to prove an "immediate and heavy financial need" with no prospect of getting the money anywhere else. Once over that hurdle, you face other rules: limits on how much can be withdrawn; a six-month restriction before you can start making contributions again; and taxes and penalties on the money you take out.

Withdrawals are easier after 59½. At that point, few companies continue the hardship rule, and although you'll owe income taxes, no penalty is imposed.

But why would you want to take out money? You're not allowed to put it back. If you need cash, borrow it from the plan instead and use payroll deductions to repay the loan.

Can I Borrow from the Plan?

At most companies, yes. There is normally no credit check. Most plans allow loans for any purpose. Some restrict them to value-added purposes, such as buying a house, avoiding foreclosure, or paying college tuition. A few smaller plans permit no loans at all. For the pros and cons of borrowing against your retirement plan rather than from another source, see page 313. Never borrow just because you want something and the money is there.

Some plans offer debit cards connected to their 401(k)s. That makes it easy—too easy—to borrow. A debit card is convenient for someone in a multiemployer plan. But don't carry it around. It's for a serious hardship *only.*

How Much Can I Borrow?

The size of your loan depends on the value of your account. You can generally borrow half the vested account balance (including your employer's contribution) up to $50,000, whichever is less. Some plans impose lower maximums. If you already have one or more loans against your plan, your further borrowing is reduced. Some plans put a limit on the number of loans you can have at the same time.

Does My Spouse Have to Agree to the Loan?

Some plans require it, others don't. It's generally not required for loans of $5,000 or less.

What Are the Loan Terms?

You pay market interest rates, generally equal to the bank prime lending rate plus 1 or 2 percentage points. The interest isn't tax deductible. Most loans have to be repaid within 5 years. For loans taken out to buy a principal residence, 10 years may be allowed. Repayments are usually made by payroll deduction.

What If I Still Have a Loan When I Leave My Job?

You'll probably have to repay it within 60 days. A few companies give you a year or more. If you cannot repay (say, by getting a bank loan), the outstanding loan balance is treated as a withdrawal. You'll owe income taxes on the money and a 10 percent penalty if you're younger than 55 in the year that you leave the job. If you're 55 or older, you'll owe taxes but no penalty.

Is My Money Safe in a 401(k)?

Yes. Your investments may fall in value, but that's another story. Your account is housed in a trust, so no matter what happens to the company, your money is safe. Still, there are complications. If your company goes bankrupt, the plan could be orphaned, without a sponsor or fiduciary. There's no one to distribute the assets, so the accounts are not accessible. This happens mainly in smaller plans. The Department of Labor is responsible for protecting orphaned plans and finding a new fiduciary, but that could take time.

If you've been stuck in an orphaned plan and a new fiduciary finally sends you a check for the savings you accumulated, take care to roll it into an Individual Retirement Account or your current employer's 401(k) within 60 days. Otherwise it's considered a withdrawal. You'll owe taxes and penalties and won't be able put that money into another tax-protected retirement plan. For information on bankrupt plans, call the Labor Department at 866-444-3272.

I said that your money is safe, but it's not safe from fraud. In very small companies, especially disorganized ones, the owner may deduct your contribution from your paycheck and never put it into your 401(k) account. Check the quarterly statements to be sure that your contributions are actually getting into the plan. If you're not getting statements, ask for them. If you don't get them, quit putting money into the plan and start a Roth IRA instead. And report your company to the Labor Department.*

What if you lost money because your plan failed to follow your specific investment directions? The plan is liable for your losses, according to a 2008 Supreme Court decision *(LaRue v. DeWolff, Boberg & Associates Inc.)*.

Can I Take All My Money from the Plan If I Leave?

You can take every dime you contributed plus all the income you earned.

If your company matched your contributions, how much employer money you get depends on the plan's vesting schedule. Some plans give you none of the company match unless you've been in the plan three years, and then you get it all. Other plans vest your money gradually over a six-year period, starting in the second year. To avoid paying taxes on your 401(k) distributions, and to keep your cache intact, roll it into an Individual Retirement Account. You can also roll it into your new employer's retirement plan, if that's allowed. (If you die,

---

*Not that it will do anything for you. At this writing, it's deeply uninterested in enforcing the pension laws, but maybe it will improve.

however, your heirs may get better choices if the money is in an IRA—page 1039.)

I make an exception for appreciated stock that you got as a company match. *Don't* roll it into an IRA. Take the stock out of your plan and manage it so that your profit will be taxed at the low capital gains rate (see below).

Alternatively, you can leave your 401(k) in your old company's plan if you like its investment choices and if your account is worth more than $5,000. This is often an excellent option from a comfort point of view. Costs are low, you're working with familiar mutual funds, you may have access to a high-interest investment, and you're not at risk of handing over your money to someone who will manage it badly. If you stay with the company plan, find out how you change investments and what the rules are on taking out money. Keep the company up to date on your changes of address, and maintain a file on the plan so your heirs will know it's there.

Speaking of heirs, be sure that they know about all the options they have when they receive the 401(k) that you left them. Your spouse can roll the money into an Individual Retirement Account, where it will continue to grow tax deferred. Other heirs get that tax break only if they transfer the money into a special "inherited IRA." Otherwise, they'll have to take the cash, and pay taxes on it, within five years. For details, see page 1062. All 401(k)s, even small ones, are now required to offer this option.

You should also remove your money from the 401(k) if: (1) Your company is going to be sold or merged. The new company might change the plan's administrator and investment options. (2) If there's the slightest doubt about your company's financial soundness. Your 401(k) is tucked away in a separate trust, so you won't lose it if the company fails. Still, there might be delays in getting the money out. (3) If the company is small. Small companies usually don't offer a wide range of investments and often charge higher management fees than big companies do. You'll do better in an IRA.

If your account is worth $5,000 or less, you have to take it out of the plan. If you don't tell the company where to put it, the company will automatically roll it into an IRA.

What's the Tax-Saving Way of Taking Company Stock out of the Plan?

Here's a great strategy for employees who receive stock from a company—in an ESOP, 401(k), or similar plan—that has risen in value. Don't roll it into an Individual Retirement Account. If you do, your gain will be taxed as ordinary income when you take it out.

Instead have the shares transferred directly to a brokerage account and sell them. You'll owe ordinary income taxes on the value of the stock when it was originally put into your account (that's called your *basis*). But all the increase in value will be taxed at the low capital gains rate. This works best for people older than 59½. If you're younger, you owe a 10 percent penalty on the basis. You get this break both on free stock that you received from the company and any employer stock that you bought with your own 401(k) contributions. It's a great tax-saving strategy. Not enough people know about it.

How Long Does It Take to Get My 401(k) Money When I Leave?

Each plan has different distribution rules. In theory, it could hang on to your money until you reach 65. In practice, you'll be eligible to start withdrawals within a few weeks or at the end of the following calendar quarter, when the administrator values the plan. In the meantime, your money stays in the plan, in whatever investments you chose. Ask about the rules in advance, so you won't go nuts waiting.

Am I Taxed When I Leave the Plan?

You are not, as long as you roll the money into another qualified tax-deferred plan, such as an Individual Retirement Account. But unless you're careful, you can get stuck with taxes and penalties by accident! Here's how to avoid them:

Pick the IRA that you want before starting the rollover. Fill in the forms and ask the IRA representative how the check should be made out. Once that's done, tell your plan to send the check to the IRA directly. Result: no muss, no fuss, no tax. It's even okay to receive the check yourself as long as it's made out to the IRA trustee for the benefit of the IRA. You just pass the check along.

Do *not* have the check made out to you personally! If you do, here's what happens: (1) Your company usually withholds 20 percent for federal income taxes. (2) You deposit the remaining 80 percent into your new IRA account, but you're now 20 percent short. (3) You have to find a sum equivalent to the 20 percent withheld, to add to the IRA within 60 days. (4) If you don't, the missing amount will be treated as a withdrawal. You'll owe taxes on the money plus a 10 percent penalty if you're under 55. (5) If you spend part of the 80 percent, that's taxed as a withdrawal too. You preserve your tax shelter only on money switched to the IRA within 60 days.

There are three ways out of this mess: (1) Use other savings to replace the 20 percent that's missing from your IRA rollover; (2) borrow enough money to fill the 20 percent gap; or (3) file your tax return instantly, claim the withheld 20 percent as a tax refund, and hope the IRS sends the money in time for you to pop it back into the IRA. Better yet, don't let this happen in the first place.

Which Type of Individual Retirement Account Should I Choose?

For future investment, put the money in one of two places: (1) A mutual fund group that offers a diversified list of well-regarded stock and bond funds. You might start by depositing everything into the group's money market fund. Let it sit there in safety while you study the other investments. Later you can transfer the cash into the stock and bond funds you want. (2) A self-directed IRA account at a full-service or discount brokerage house. These IRAs let you buy individual stocks and bonds as well as mutual funds. They can also receive any company stock coming out of your plan. If you go with one of the mutual fund supermarkets (page 779); you can buy funds from different mutual fund groups through a single account. That saves a lot of paperwork.

In either case, be sure that the IRA lets your heirs use the special inherited IRA tax break outlined on page 1062.

If you're retiring and want to turn your 401(k) into a lifetime income, roll it into an immediate-pay annuity at an insurance company (page 1124).

Should I Roll the Money into an IRA If I'm Going to Make Some Withdrawals Pretty Soon?

That depends on how old you are. If you're 55 or older when you leave your job, withdrawals from your 401(k) are penalty free, so you might as well take the money you're going to need. If you roll it into an IRA, withdrawals won't be penalty free until you're 59½. Logical conclusion: those 59½ and older should switch to an IRA, taking out money later as needed. Those 55 to 59 should take the cash from their 401(k) that they're going to need up front and roll only the remainder into an IRA.

What Happens to My Money When I Retire?

You get it all. For your payout options, see page 1111.

What If I Divorce?

Your spouse is usually entitled to a share. Exactly how will depend on the rules of your state and the settlement you negotiate. See page 169.

What If I Die?

If you're married, your spouse gets the money automatically. Nevertheless, you should name your spouse as the beneficiary of the account, just to keep the record clean.

If you're married and want to name someone else as beneficiary, your spouse has to waive his or her rights in a notarized statement filed with the plan. That's especially important if you divorce or your first spouse dies and you've named, say, your children as beneficiaries. *If you remarry, your new spouse will inherit, no matter what the beneficiary form says*—unless the new spouse has formally waived his or her rights. If you do want that money to go to your kids, ask your new spouse to sign the waiver the moment you officially become husband and wife. Don't stall! Whip out the forms and a pen as soon as you say "I do." If you trip in the party tent, break your neck, and breathe your last, your new spouse will get all the 401(k) money, cutting out your children.

What if you divorced, didn't remarry, but never took your ex off your beneficiary form? Your ex will collect the money. In your separation agreement, your ex might have waived his or her right to your retirement plan but that doesn't matter. The beneficiary form trumps the separation agreement. To prevent this, change the plan beneficiary as soon as the separation agreement is signed.

A Really, Truly Important Note That Can Save Your Heirs Thousands of Dollars in Taxes!

Find out what happens to your 401(k) if you're holding it when you die. How does the plan distribute the money to your heirs?

Any heirs can take the money in cash, immediately, and pay the income taxes due. But unless the inheritance is small, they'd be wise to look for a way of taking the money tax deferred.

If the beneficiary is your spouse, he or she can roll the money into a personal IRA and let it continue to accumulate tax deferred. No taxes, no problem.

For other heirs (including same-sex spouses), the plan has to let the money be transferred into an inherited IRA. Inherited IRAs have special rules—see page 1062 for more details. They let your beneficiaries, even very young ones, inherit the money tax deferred (or tax free, if you have a Roth 401(k) and make withdrawals gradually over their lifetimes. Those many extra years of tax shelter can be worth hundreds of thousands of dollars to the people you leave behind.

Be sure that your beneficiaries know about the value of transferring money to an inherited IRA! Leave them a letter telling them about it, or copy this page and leave it with your final instructions. If the 401(k) is large, they won't want to miss this tax-saving chance.

How to Get the Most from a 401(k) Plan

1. Make the maximum contribution or as close to it as you can. A 401(k) with a company match is the richest deal you'll ever find. Saving is simple because the money comes out of your paycheck automatically. In an emergency, you can usually borrow some of the funds.

In theory, you might want to fund a tax-deferred 401(k) with just enough money to capture the employer match. Any additional savings could go into a Roth IRA outside the plan, where savings can grow tax free.

By this logic, you'd want to put everything into a Roth IRA if there's no company match. But will you really do it? Will you save regularly, month after month, no matter how many other expenses you have? I suspect not. The beauty of a 401(k) lies in the automatic contributions that come out of your paycheck. That discipline will build larger savings in the end.

If your company offers a Roth 401(k), that solves the problem. By investing there, you'll enjoy the simplicity of automatic contributions plus any employer match. When you leave the job, you'll be able to roll your account into a Roth IRA, where your earnings will grow tax free.

2. Invest a good part of your money in the plan's diversified stock-owning mutual funds rather than in fixed-income investments. For a discussion of appropriate asset allocation, see chapter 21. If your plan has a target-date mutual fund, consider it. These funds provide an appropriate allocation for someone your age.

3. Don't invest much of your 401(k) in your company's stock. Five percent is plenty. Don't invest in the stock at all if the company uses it to match your contribution. You don't want your job and your retirement riding on a single firm, even a firm you imagine to be a blue chip. Remember Enron, WorldCom, and Lehman Brothers—all beloved of their workers—RIP. If you get stock as a company match, swap out of it as fast as you can. By law, you must be able to switch into other 401(k) investments if you've been with the company for at least three years. Do it. Do it now.

4. If you have a lot of money in your 401(k), consult an accountant before transferring it out of the plan. You might want to put some money into a Roth IRA (page 1048) instead of a traditional IRA. These are complicated choices, relating to tax law and estate planning—way above a financial writer's pay scale. I just want to alert you that these possibilities exist. You pay income taxes on traditional 401(k) money that you switch into a Roth. If market conditions change within a limited period of time, you can undo the deal and recover the taxes paid.

Should I Make After-Tax Contributions If the Plan Allows It?

That depends on the tax laws, your tax bracket, how you plan to invest the money, and whether your employer will match what you put in. An employer match is free money you won't want to lose. All of the money in the plan will accumulate tax deferred.

If there's no employer match for after-tax contributions, fund a Roth IRA first. After that, if you still have money to spare, where you save will depend on how you want to invest. For buying taxable bond mutual funds or fixed-interest stable-value funds, use after-tax contributions to your 401(k). The 401(k) keeps the earnings tax deferred. If you're buying stock mutual funds, however, keep the money out of the 401(k). Outside the plan, your profits will be taxed at the low rate on capital gains. Inside the plan, they'll be taxed at the higher rate on ordinary income when you take out the money.

When you leave the company, the earnings on any assets you bought with after-tax money will be taxed immediately unless you roll them into an IRA or similar plan. Rolling the after-tax contributions into a traditional IRA complicates your taxes when you make withdrawals in the future. Every withdrawal, from any of your tax-deferred plans, will become partly taxable. You don't want that to happen. A better idea is to roll this money into a Roth IRA.

Is Yours a "SIMPLE" Plan?

Firms with 100 or fewer employees who earned at least $5,000 in the previous year can offer SIMPLE plans—short for Savings Incentive Match Plan for Employees. They can be either 401(k)s or Individual Retirement Accounts. They follow most of the rules for each. In 2009, qualified employees could contribute up to $11,500 a year plus a $2,500 catch-up for people 50 and older (these maximums will rise with the inflation rate). The company contributes too. It might match your contribution up to 3 percent of your total pay. Or it might contribute a flat 2 percent for all qualified workers, whether they've funded their plans or not.

You can also set up a SIMPLE if you're self-employed. You can put more money into a SIMPLE IRA than into a traditional IRA.

SIMPLE plans are completely portable. You can invest in the same kinds of stocks, bonds, and mutual funds that you'll find in other employee plans. You're vested immediately in the money that the company puts up, meaning that it's irrevocably yours. As with regular 401(k)s and IRAs, you owe income taxes on withdrawals plus a 10 percent penalty if you're under 59½.

Special Plans for the Self-Employed

Individual (Solo) 401(k)s: For the Largest Personal Contributions

A solo 401(k)—either a traditional plan or a Roth—is for people who work for themselves, with no employees or only a spouse as an employee. You can contribute 100 percent of your earnings up to $16,500, *plus* a profit-sharing contribution, *plus* a $5,500 catch-up contribution if you're 50 and older. The maximum comes to 25 percent of your W-2 earnings if you're incorporated or 20 percent of your net self-employment income if you operate as a sole proprietorship. Total potential contribution in 2009: $49,000, plus $5,500 in catch-up.

If you have money to spare, this is the plan you want. Anyone earning up to $200,000 can put far more into a solo 401(k) than into a SEP-IRA, your next-best choice (below). The maximums are adjusted for inflation every year. To see how much you can contribute compared with SEPs and SIMPLEs, go to the Solo 401k Calculator on the Web site of Beacon Capital Management Advisors, at www.solo401kcalculator.com.

Regular contributions aren't required, by the way. You can shrink them or stop them if business is bad, so it's great for people whose incomes are inconsistent. The plan can also provide for loans. When you quit work, you can roll your solo 401(k) into a traditional or Roth Individual Retirement Account.

The obvious candidates for solo 401(k)s are people who work for themselves full-time: consultants, artists, professionals, writers, or owners of other types of businesses.

Less obvious are employees who moonlight. Suppose, for example, that you work for a company that provides you with a 401(k), but you write detective novels on the side. The detective money is self-employment income, all of which can be whisked into a solo 401(k). Your personal contribution to your solo plan is limited by the amount you put into your company's 401(k). The 2009 maximum from earnings is $16,500 (plus $5,500) for both plans combined. But you can also add 20 or 25 percent of your business income to your solo plan as a profit-sharing contribution.

Solo 401(k)s are offered by some no-load mutual fund groups such as Fidelity and T. Rowe Price, discount brokers such as TD Ameritrade and Charles Schwab, insurance companies, and investment houses. I vote for the no-load groups and the discounters because you'll pay lower fees and mutual fund management expenses. For accounts worth more than $250,000, you have to file IRS Form 5500 or 5500EZ.

The SEP-IRA: For People Making Smaller Contributions

Simplified Employee Pensions (SEPs) are handled like Individual Retirement Accounts, which makes them cheap and easy to administer. You contribute a straight percentage of pay: up to 25 percent of your W-2 earnings if you're incorporated or 20 percent of your net self-employment earnings if you operate as a sole proprietorship or partnership. Maximum 2009 contribution: $49,000. No catch-up contributions are allowed for people 50 and up, nor can you take a loan against the plan. You might start out with a SEP-IRA and later convert to a solo 401(k) if you want to borrow or are in a position to contribute a larger amount than is allowed for a SEP.

SEPs can be used for income you get from moonlighting, if you have a job that already offers you a retirement plan.

If you have employees, they have to be included in the SEP. It's entirely employer funded. Employees pay nothing. You contribute the same percentage of pay to their accounts as you do to yours. You're allowed to change the percentage every year or even contribute zero, depending on how the business is doing. Employees must be included in the plan if they're at least 21, earned at least $550 during the year you made the SEP contribution (which would include part-timers), and worked for you in at least three of the past five years. SEP-IRAs vest right away. The employee can remove money from his or her SEP at any time.

Solo 401(k)s, SEPs, and Keoghs (below) have similar withdrawal rules: a 10 percent penalty for withdrawals before 59½, unless an exception applies (death, disability, and so forth), with mandatory withdrawals starting at 70½. For free tax information, go to www.irs.gov and download Publication 560 ("Retirement Plans for Small Business"). If you die or divorce, SEPs follow the IRA rules.

SEPs are available from no-load mutual fund groups, discount stockbrokers, regular stockbrokers, financial advisers, banks, and insurance companies. Commissioned salespeople might try to get you to put a tax-deferred annuity into your SEP, but don't do it. In this context, it's merely a more expensive way of buying mutual funds. For more on annuities, see page 1071. If, at retirement, you want to turn your nest egg into a lifetime income, you can use your SEP proceeds to buy an annuity then.

Keogh Plans: Out of Style and Out of Date, Except for the Very Well Paid

Since the advent of solo 401(k)s and SEP-IRAs, Keoghs have fallen out of style, except in special circumstances. Here's how the three types of Keoghs work:

- *A money-purchase Keogh*—resembles a SEP, except that you have to pick a percentage of income that you'll contribute every year and stick with it. So you lose flexibility. No point to that. These types of plans are out.

- *A profit-sharing Keogh*—resembles a SEP with the same maximum contribution. The Keogh costs more to administer, but businesses like it if they have employees. You can limit the amount of money that workers can take from the plan if they leave the job within a few years. You can also restrict withdrawals by current employees until age 59½. No withdrawal restrictions can be put on SEP-IRAs.

- *A defined benefit Keogh*—for older, high-income people who can afford large contributions. You pick the annual pension you want when you retire, then contribute whatever sums are needed to reach that goal. In 2009 you were allowed to fund a pension as large as $195,000 a year for life.

A defined benefit plan is expensive to maintain. Each year it has to be checked by an actuary. He or she will update it for any changes in the law, tell you how large a contribution you can make, and send you an impressive bill. But that's okay if you can tax-defer large amounts of income and gains on that income too. If your earnings drop, your Keogh can be stopped in its tracks and the money rolled into an Individual Retirement Account.

If you have employees, they have to be included in your Keogh. If you die or divorce, defined benefit Keoghs follow the pension rules; the other Keoghs follow the 401(k) rules.

SIMPLE 401(k)s and SIMPLE IRAs

These plans are useful for self-employed people with employees. The employees help fund the plan, and administrative costs are low. See page 1041.

Other Tax-Deferred Retirement Plans Not to Be Missed

403(b) Plans

Tax-deferred plans for employees of tax-exempt organizations, certain ministers, charitable or educational organizations, and cooperative hospital service organizations. They're similar to 401(k)s, with the same basic contribution limits: up to $16,500 in 2009, plus $5,500 for people 50 and older. If you've had 15 years of service with the same employer and contributed an average of less than $5,000 a year, you get an additional catch-up contribution: up to $3,000 a year, with a lifetime maximum of $15,000. Contributions and earnings are tax deferred. Most of the plans allow borrowing. You have to repay the loan within 5 years (longer, if you borrowed to buy your principal home). If you fail to repay on time, the outstanding balance is treated as a taxable withdrawal. Hardship withdrawals are allowed for severe financial distress.

A 403(b) is funded mostly with your own payroll deductions. Only a few employers make matching contributions. That makes it especially important to contribute the maximum to your plan. If your employer also provides a traditional state pension plan, you may be able to trade 403(b) credits for a larger monthly pension payment. If you participate in both a 403(b) and a 457 (see page 1046), you can make the maximum contribution to both.

As investments, most 403(b)s offer tax-deferred annuities. There are *fixed annuities,* with an interest rate that's attractive initially but may then drop to a lower rate. Or *variable annuities,* which let you put your money into stock funds, bond funds, and short-term money market instruments. In general, 403(b) annuities are lousy deals. They're larded with fees—on average, 2.25 percent, and often higher—that chop your investment returns. You may be drawn into annuities because you're approached by a colleague who is selling them on commission. Trust me, your colleague is doing you no favors.

Some 403(b) plans give you the option of investing in mutual funds. If I had my way, they'd be required for every plan! You pay less for mutual funds than you do for annuities. The optimal choice would be no-load (no-sales-charge) mutual funds, thanks to their rock-bottom costs. Your employer has a list of all the vendors your plan allows. If no-load mutual funds aren't included, press your employer to offer them. You'll find advice on how to do that at the excellent information site 403bwise (www.403bwise.com).

If you're unhappy with the investments you currently have in your 403(b), you can move your money to another approved vendor in the plan. If you're switching out of an annuity, however, you may be charged exit penalties on the contributions you made within the past 5 to 15 years. Ugh. That's another reason to hate annuities. You might be allowed to transfer 10 percent of the amount in the annuity penalty free once a year.

If you're not investing more than $5,000 a year and there's no employer match, consider skipping the 403(b) and funding a Roth IRA (page 1048) instead.

If you leave your job, you may be able to take the plan with you. Alternatively, transfer the assets into another 403(b) or roll them over into a 401(k) or an IRA. No annuity penalties should apply.

When you withdraw money from a 403(b), it's taxed as ordinary income, plus a 10 percent penalty if you're under 59½. There's no penalty, however, in certain, specified circumstances, such as disability, death, or taking qualified hardship withdrawals. There's also no penalty if you're 55 or older in the year that you leave your job.

You must start withdrawals when you reach 70½. If you divorce, 403(b)s follow the 401(k) rules. For more tax information, download IRS Publication 571 from www.irs.gov.

Congress authorized Roth 403(b)s in 2006. At this writing, not many plans offer Roths, but their number will grow. With this type of plan, you contribute after-tax dollars, and your earnings grow tax free. When you leave your job, you can roll the money into a Roth IRA (page 1048). Roths are especially good for higher-income people and people who think their tax rates will be higher when they retire.

Federal Thrift Savings Plan

For federal government employees. It's a form of 401(k) with excellent, well-diversified investment choices for serious long-term investors. It follows the 401(k) rules on contributions, tax deferral, and withdrawals. For information, see www.tsp.gov.

Section 457 Plans

These are offered to state and local government employees. Contribution limits for 2009: $16,500, plus $5,500 if you're 50 or older and the plan allows it. In the final three years before normal retirement age, you can often contribute up to twice the annual limit, or $33,000 in 2009. If you use the final-three-years option, you can't use the $5,500 catch-up too. You can participate in both a 403(b) and 457, making the full contribution to each.

There's rarely an employer match in a 457. If the employer does contribute, it reduces the amount you're allowed to put in. Loans are allowed if the plan permits. Hardship withdrawals may be allowed too. If you leave the government, you can roll the money into another 457, a 403(b), a 401(k) if the plan allows it, or an Individual Retirement Account.

A 457 isn't subject to the usual age limit on withdrawals. When you leave your job, you can take money out of the plan, paying taxes but no early-withdrawal penalties. Withdrawals must begin by age 70½.

If you die or divorce, 457s follow the 401(k) rules. For good information on these plans, see 457bwise (www.457bwise.com).

The Saver's Credit: Help for Lower Earners

Here's a helping hand for people who save for retirement even though their incomes are low. You get a credit on your federal income tax return if you contribute to certain types of retirement plans: 401(k), 403(b), SIMPLE, IRA, or salary deferral SEP. The credit ranges from 10 percent to 50 percent of contributions up to $2,000, with larger credits going to lower earners. You qualified in 2009 if your modified adjusted gross income, as an individual, didn't exceed $27,750; for a head of household, $41,625; for a married couple, $55,500. These cutoff points rise annually with inflation. A tax credit reduces your income tax dollar for dollar. To collect this credit, you have to be at least 18, not a full-time student, and not claimed as a dependent on someone else's tax return.

For the Latest Contribution Ceilings on Retirement Plans

Go to www.applebyconsultinginc.com, a site maintained by Denise Appleby of Appleby Retirement Consulting in Grayson, Georgia. It's a good place for checking the current inflation-adjusted limits on contributions to the various types of retirement plans. You'll also find tons of information on how the plans work and ideas for using them. Highly recommended!

Individual Retirement Accounts

There are two ways of using an Individual Retirement Account. First, as a way of making regular contributions to retirement savings. Second, as a vessel to receive any money you're rolling over from a 401(k) or similar employer plan. When you leave your job, you can roll an employee account of any size into an IRA.

How Much Can I Contribute to an IRA?

Individuals can put away up to $5,000 a year out of earnings or alimony in 2009. Two-income couples can save up to $10,000—$5,000 for each. One-income couples can also save up to $5,000 each if they file joint returns. In that case, the breadwinner funds a *spousal IRA* for the spouse at home. If you're 50 and older, you can save another $1,000—raising the maximum to $6,000 each, or $12,000 for a 50-plus couple. If your earnings as a couple are nominal, one or both IRAs might have to be smaller than $5,000. Interest and dividends don't count as earnings for making IRA contributions.

By the way, I mean it when I say that you can contribute *up to* $5,000 or $6,000. You don't need the full amount, as some savers believe. You can contribute a lesser amount. You can even skip a year (although that would be a pity). If you earn less than $5,000, you can contribute all of it to your IRA (net of expenses, if you're self-employed). That's handy for, say, a spouse who earns a small amount from a home business or part-time job.

You can contribute to more than one IRA in a single year. But the $5,000 (or $6,000) limit per person (double that for couples) applies to all your IRAs combined.

The rules are different when you're rolling over a lump sum payout from a retirement plan such as a 401(k). There's no ceiling on the amount of money you can roll into an IRA.

There are two types of IRAs: a traditional IRA and a Roth IRA.

All About Roth IRAs

Roth IRAs are terrific inventions. Your contribution is not tax deductible, but your earnings grow tax free. You can withdraw your own contribution from the Roth at any time, tax free and penalty free, so you have constant access to your money. Your heirs can inherit it income-tax free.

Roths are ideal for: (1) Savers who think their taxes may go up in the years ahead and want to shelter their money now. (2) Wealthy people who don't expect to use much of their retirement savings and want to leave it to their heirs. (3) People who seek flexibility—they want tax-free access to their money even though it's in a retirement plan. (4) People over 70½, still working, who want to keep contributing to a retirement plan. (5) People over 70½ who don't want to be forced to take money out of the IRA if they don't need it.

Who Can Start a Roth IRA?

In 2009, singles qualified for the full Roth contribution on an adjusted gross income of $150,000 or less, and marrieds with $166,000 or less. On higher incomes, the contribution gradually declined, phasing out at $120,000 for singles and $176,000 for marrieds. These limits rise annually with inflation, starting in 2010.

The Roth IRA Rules for People Making Regular Contributions

1. You get no tax deduction for the contribution. A Roth is funded with after-tax dollars.

2. At any time at all, you can take your own contribution out of the Roth IRA, tax free and penalty free. If you put $1,000 in today, you can take it out next week, no muss, no fuss. You money is always available if you happen to need it. That gives you tremendous flexibility. You can use the Roth as a combination emergency savings account (by investing some of the money in a money market fund) and tax-free retirement account (by investing the rest of the money for long-term gain).

3. The earnings on your contributions—interest, dividends, and capital gains—have to stay in the Roth for at least five years. After that, you can also withdraw the earnings tax free *if* you meet one of the following four circumstances:

- *You're over 59½.*
- *You want to use up to $10,000 of your IRA earnings to buy or build a first home* for yourself, your spouse, your child, your grandchild, or your parents. A first-time home buyer is defined as someone who hasn't owned a home during the past two years. (If you're married, your spouse can't have owned one either.) This $10,000 is a lifetime draw; you can take it all at once or in bits and pieces.
- *You're disabled.*
- *You've died, and your beneficiaries are receiving the money.*

4. Withdrawals exceeding your contributions are subject to income taxes if they don't meet one of the conditions listed above. They're also subject to a 10 percent penalty if you're under 59½.

5. The five-year holding period starts on the day that you open your first Roth. It doesn't change when you make additional contributions. If you open a second Roth, it's governed by the date you opened the first one.

6. As with other IRAs, you can make a contribution just before filing your tax return and apply it to the previous year. So $5,000 contributed in April 2010 can be counted in 2009. If this is your first contribution to a Roth, the start date for your five-year holding period would be January 2009. You've gained a year toward the time you can start withdrawing the earnings tax free.

7. You can keep contributing for as long as you like, even past 70½ (the cutoff age for traditional IRAs).

8. You don't have to make withdrawals at all if you don't want to. You can leave the money untouched, to accumulate for heirs.

9. You can roll your money from one Roth IRA into another one tax free, if you want to change the institution that holds the account.

10. If you have a Roth 401(k) or Roth 403(b) at work and leave the company, you can roll those savings into a Roth IRA to continue the tax-free growth.

The Rules for People Converting Money From a Traditional IRA or Other Plan into a Roth IRA. You can roll any amount of money from a traditional IRA, 401(k), or similar plan into a Roth IRA. The hitch is that you'll be taxed on the money you transfer, in your ordinary income bracket. Anyone who converts in 2010 can stretch out the taxes over the following two years. If you convert in 2011 and later, the tax will be due in the current year. No tax penalty is owed, however, even if you're under 59½. Once the funds are in the Roth, future earnings will accumulate tax free.

Is conversion a good idea? That depends. It's a good deal if: (1) You'll pay the taxes from other funds rather than take the tax money out of the IRA or 401(k). That moves all your assets to the Roth account to accumulate tax free. (2) You'll be in the same (or a higher) tax bracket when you retire. (3) You don't expect to need the money, so you don't want to be forced to start drawing it out at 70½. Most or all of the account can be left to your heirs tax free. It's even worth converting an IRA into a Roth on your deathbed if you're wealthy enough to be subject to estate taxes. You'll save far more in estate tax than you'll pay in income tax. To state the obvious, Roth conversions are great for people with plenty of money.

On the other hand, a Roth conversion probably isn't worth it if you have to take money out of your IRA or 401(k) to pay the tax; if you'll drop to a lower tax bracket when you retire; or if you're going to need to withdraw most of the IRA money during your retirement. For the average person, a Roth conversion probably won't work out.

You'll find lots of calculators on the Web that tell you, roughly, whether it's worth it to convert a traditional IRA or 401(k) into a Roth. Try 72t on the Net (www.72t.net) as well as the calculators that you find by using a search engine. If you decide to convert, call up the firm where you keep your traditional IRA and tell it to change the account. Presto, it's now a Roth. If you want to convert only part of your savings, the firm will roll that portion into a separate Roth account.

What if you convert your IRA or 401(k) to a Roth and then decide you made a mistake? You have a limited time to undo the transaction (it's called "recharacterization"). Simply call your IRA or 401(k) plan administrators, say you changed your mind, and ask them to put things back the way they were before. They'll tell you whether you've met the tricky tax deadlines. After a certain period of time, you're allowed to convert back to a Roth if it starts looking like a smarter move than it did before.

Adding to Your Converted Roth IRA. If you fall within the income limits for making regular Roth contributions, you can add to the Roth you established with money converted from other plans. If you don't fall within the income limits, here's a way around the problem:

Make a contribution to an Individual Retirement Account. You can start one if you're self-employed or if your employer doesn't offer a retirement plan. Even if your employer offers a plan, you can have a separate IRA if you fall within certain income limits (page 1053). From there, convert the IRA money into your Roth IRA. There are no income limits on people who want to do conversions.

Okay, You Converted to a Roth. Now You Want the Money Out. Here are the rules on withdrawing money that used to be in a traditional 401(k), 403(b), or IRA and that you converted to a Roth:

- *If you convert assets to a Roth when you're younger than 59½,* you have to hold them in the Roth for five years or until you reach 59½, whichever comes first. Each new conversion has its own five-year clock. If you withdraw the money earlier, you'll owe a 10 percent penalty.

- *If you convert assets to a Roth when you're 59½ or older,* you can withdraw them at any time, with no five-year holding period and no penalties. But you have to hold the account for five years before you can withdraw the earnings on those assets penalty free. Say that you converted $100,000 and have earned $5,000 in interest. You can tap the $100,000 right away but have to wait five years for the $5,000.

- *Don't worry about keeping track of what the earnings are.* By law, the first withdrawals from a Roth are assumed to come from your own contributions. When those are exhausted, your next withdrawals are assumed to come from assets you converted to the Roth. By that time, five years will probably have elapsed, making the earnings tax free too.

Solve your five-year problem. Start the clock! IRA expert Ed Slott[*] offers this smart idea: if you qualify for a Roth IRA, start one right now, with the

---

[*]Author of *The Retirement Savings Time Bomb . . . and How to Defuse It,* a must-read book for people who want to minimize taxes for themselves and their heirs when withdrawing money from an IRA. Make sure that your tax or investment adviser reads it too. It's full of ideas and details on how these strategies work.

minimum dollar amount that the mutual fund group or investment house allows. That starts the five-year clock running. If you leave your job and roll your 401(k) into the Roth, five years will already have passed. You'll be able to tap the money whenever you want.

If I Have a Choice, Should I Contribute to a Roth IRA or a company 401(k)?

Choose the 401(k) if the company matches some percentage of your contribution. *And* if payroll deduction is the only way you'll save. *And* if you want to be able to borrow against your plan. Money borrowed from a 401(k)—say, for college tuition—can be replaced, plus interest. Money withdrawn from an IRA can never be replaced.

Consider choosing the Roth IRA, however, if your employer doesn't contribute to your plan. You might use the Roth for the first $5,000 of your savings and put additional savings into the 401(k). A Roth is also good for savings in excess of the amount that the company will match. You can make Roth contributions automatic by having money deducted from your bank account. But please: if you find that you're not making regular monthly contributions to your Roth, return to the discipline of your 401(k) instead.

The same advice applies to savers with 403(b)s and other tax-deductible retirement accounts.

Always choose the company plan if it's a Roth 401(k) or Roth 403(b). You get the advantage of automatic payroll savings and a future of tax-free earnings too.

What's Best: A Roth IRA or a Traditional, Tax-Deductible IRA?

In my book, it's the Roth almost every time. When you're retired and earning money on your Roth investments, tax free, you'll be one happy pup. Even better, withdrawals from a Roth don't count toward your "income" when figuring whether your Social Security checks are taxable. Withdrawals from a regular IRA do.

Traditional, deductible IRAs are better only in limited circumstances. Among them: (1) You need the tax deduction in order to make the full IRA contribution—an exception that sounds sensible on paper but doesn't apply to many people in real life. With automatic payroll deductions, you can set aside more than you think. (2) You're contributing in your 50s and will withdraw the money at 59½. Over short holding periods—say, less than 10 years—the traditional IRA's tax deduction will probably be worth more than the Roth IRA's tax-free gains. (3) You will soon retire and will be in a low or zero tax bracket.

Should My Kids Use a Roth IRA?

Great idea, if your family can afford to use it as a tax-planning device. Roths have to be funded out of earnings. If your kids earn money over the summer, in a family business or even doing chores at home, they could put it into a Roth, and you could return the cash to them via an annual gift. They'd have to file a tax return but would probably owe no tax. When they grow up, or five years after starting the Roth, they'd be able to buy a home, using up to $10,000 of their IRA earnings plus their own contributions, tax free.

They could also tap a Roth for higher education expenses, such as tuition, books, and fees, drawing out their own contributions tax free. If they take any more to help pay tuition, that additional money will be taxed, but they won't be charged the usual 10 percent penalty.

If they leave their Roth money alone, it should grow to a mighty big sum by the time they retire.

All About Traditional IRAs

With a traditional IRA, your contribution is tax deductible and your earnings grow tax deferred. They're both taxed at your ordinary income rate when you take out the money. Anyone with earnings can open an IRA. There are no income limits unless you're also covered by another retirement plan.

Who's Eligible for a Traditional, Tax-Deductible IRA? You can fund an IRA if you're in one of three situations:

First, you're self-employed or work for a company that doesn't have a retirement plan. You can deduct up to $5,000 ($6,000, if you're 50 or older). If your spouse also has no plan, you can deduct a second $5,000 or $6,000. Traditional IRAs work well for people who need the tax deduction to be able to afford the contribution. (If you don't need the tax deduction, choose a Roth instead.)

Second, you're eligible for a deductible IRA if your company has a retirement plan but you don't participate. In a company with a defined contribution plan, such as a 401(k) or 403(b), you don't "participate" until money goes into the plan on your behalf. That may not occur during your first year on the job—in which case you'd be able to make a deductible IRA contribution. If your company has a traditional pension plan, however, you participate even if you're not vested yet.

Third, people who participate in company plans can have deductible IRAs if their adjusted gross incomes don't exceed a specified ceiling. The ceiling in 2009: for singles, $55,000 for the full contribution, phasing out at $65,000; for married couples filing jointly, $89,000, phasing out at $109,000. What if your spouse participates in a retirement plan and you don't? You could deduct a full $5,000 (or $6,000) IRA for yourself in 2009 if your combined incomes didn't exceed $166,000, phasing out at $176,000.

If you have a traditional 401(k) and leave the job, you'd usually roll your plan money into a traditional IRA. You pay no taxes on the transfer, and your savings continue to accumulate tax deferred. You could also roll that money into a Roth IRA. In that case, it would count as a conversion to a Roth on the money you transferred. If the taxes aren't large, the Roth would be the better choice—see page 1048.

How Does a Traditional IRA Compare with Other Tax-Deductible Investments?

1. Company 401(k) plans beat IRAs. Payroll deduction ensures that you contribute regularly, and there's often an employer match. The 401(k) permits substantially larger contributions and usually allows loans. Employees with modest earnings qualify for the Saver's Credit (page 1047).

2. For the self-employed, solo 401(k)s and SEP-IRAs beat IRAs too, because you can put more money into them.

3. The IRA wins if you have no 401(k) and can't afford to put any more than $5,000 aside. It's a cheap and simple way to save. If your earnings are small and you have other means of support, every penny of an annual paycheck of $5,000 or less can be stashed in an IRA to accumulate tax deferred. But—I've said it before—use the Roth IRA, not the traditional, tax-deductible IRA! The Roth's tax-free earnings are one of the best deals in town.

Should I Make After-Tax Contributions to an IRA? *No,* if you qualify for saving money in a Roth IRA. Choose the Roth instead.

Yes, if your income is above the Roth limit (page 1048) and you qualify for an IRA (page 1053). Add the money to the IRA and then roll it into the Roth, which high-income people can do starting in 2010.

No, if you simply want to invest. All your investment gains will be taxed as ordinary income when you take out the money. It's smarter to choose a low-cost mutual fund, where your gains will be taxed at the low capital gains rate.

A nondeductible IRA might be worthwhile if you use it to hold only bonds and other fixed-income investments. You'll owe ordinary income taxes on these earnings anyway, and in an IRA they accumulate tax deferred. The downside is that after-tax contributions complicate your tax returns. Every withdrawal, from any of your IRAs, becomes a mix of taxable and nontaxable money. That's something for your accountant to worry about, but you still have to keep the records.

Answers to Your Questions About Both Traditional IRAs and Roths

How Do I Set Up an IRA?　Decide where you want to invest your retirement money, then ask the institution for its IRA account forms. Fill out the papers, send in the money, and you're up and running.

For certificates of deposit, you'd go to a bank or credit union. For a diversified portfolio of mutual funds, you'd choose a no-load mutual fund group or discount brokerage house that runs a mutual fund supermarket (page 779). If you want individual stocks and bonds as well as mutual funds, use a discount brokerage house or a full-service broker.

Fees to open, maintain, and close an IRA account have dropped substantially as banking and investment institutions compete for your money. Compare all costs before you choose. You can have as many IRAs as you want—for example, one at a bank, one at a mutual fund group, and one at a brokerage firm. But whether you have one IRA or ten, your total annual contribution can't exceed your $5,000 or $6,000 ceiling (except for rollovers, which can be in any amount).

What If I Want to Invest in Assets Other Than Stocks, Bonds, and CDs?

For complicated assets, you need a *self-directed IRA* at an investment house or mutual fund complex that will act as trustee for these kinds of things. Some quick rules:

■ *Real estate.* You can buy an investment property with IRA assets. The IRA trustee pays the expenses and collect any rents or other income. The downside is that you're not diversified and will lose tax benefits such as depreciation. All the transactions have to be handled entirely by third parties, not by you or by any company you own. You're not allowed to lend the IRA money, sell it property, buy property it owns, use your own rental agent to find tenants for it, or hire your own company (or even use your own sweat equity) to fix up IRA properties for resale. Your IRA can't own your vacation home. You can't let a relative rent an apartment in a property the IRA owns. Those are all prohibited transactions. If you mess up, your IRA breaks apart. I mention all this because I see come-ons on the Web from people happy to sell you information on how to put your vacation house into an IRA. That's no skin off their nose but plenty off yours.

■ *Other businesses.* Some IRAs invest in movie or mining deals, own and lease private jets, or own prize bulls that earn their living as studs. As with real estate, you can't handle any portions of those businesses yourself. They all have to be managed by your IRA trustee who, I assure you, will charge you plenty.

- *Hard assets.* IRAs can hold American Eagle gold, silver, and platinum bullion coins, coins issued by a state, or certain gold, silver, platinum, and palladium bullion bars. (It's not clear whether American Buffalo coins qualify.) You can't buy and hold the coins yourself. They have to be bought by your IRA trustee and shipped to a depository. You can wreck your IRA by something as simple as keeping the coins in your own safe-deposit box.
- *No-nos.* IRAs aren't allowed to hold life insurance, art, gems, antiques, or collectibles such as numismatic coins. You can buy a tax-deferred variable annuity, but why would you want to? That's merely a more expensive way of buying stocks and bonds. Besides, your IRA is already tax deferred, so the annuity offers you nothing. Many financial planners put clients' IRA money into variable annuities because they earn attractive commissions on the sale. It's wrong, wrong, wrong.

Do not, incidentally, use your IRA to buy municipal bonds or muni mutual funds. You don't need tax deferral for these investments because they're tax exempt already. What's more, if you put them into a regular IRA, their interest becomes taxable at withdrawal.

- *Penalties for prohibited transactions.* If you get involved in managing properties owned by your IRA, keeping gold coins in your own safe-deposit box, or any other prohibited transaction, and the IRS finds out, you're nuked. Your IRA will be terminated. You'll have to pay income tax on its entire value, plus a 10 percent penalty if you're under 59½. Your whole IRA goes down, even if you bought the coins with only a small part of the money. If you plan to get involved in any of these investments, keep the self-directed IRA separate from other IRA funds.

How Do I Roll a Retirement Plan Distribution into an IRA? Maybe you retired. Maybe you quit your job to take another one. Either way, you might be entitled to a lump sum distribution from your employer's qualified retirement plan.

If you're happy with your employer's plan, consider leaving your money there. Alternatively, you can take your money and still preserve its tax shelter by rolling it into an IRA.

You can take the rollover in one of two ways:

1. The good way. This is the *direct rollover.* The money is paid directly into your new IRA (or into your new employer's qualified plan, if that's the option you want). Sometimes you never see the check; sometimes you receive it but it's made out to the trustee of the new IRA or plan so you have to mail it to the plan. All employers have to offer you direct rollovers.

2. The bad way. The check is made out to you personally and you deposit it in your new IRA. This triggers the withholding tax mess explained on page 1033. If you take the check personally, by mistake, be sure that it gets into your new IRA within 60 days. If you deposit it on the 61st day, it will be treated as a withdrawal. You'll have to take out the money, pay taxes on the whole amount, and add a 10 percent penalty if you're under 59½.

You can roll over all of the money or some of it as you choose. Anything that's not rolled over is subject to tax (and penalties, if you're under 59½).

With smaller checks, a rollover sometimes doesn't seem worth it. But $3,000 at an untaxed 6 percent a year grows to $9,621 in 20 years and $17,230 in 30 years, without your having to lift a finger. That's worth it.

Some retirement plan distributions cannot be rolled over into IRAs. Excluded are:

- *Any amount you're required to withdraw* because you've reached age 70½.
- *Any sums you've arranged to receive in installment or annuity payments.* These are defined as roughly equal payments, made at least once a year and scheduled to last for your lifetime, life expectancy, the lifetime or life expectancy of you and a beneficiary, or 10 years or more.

What If I Own Company Stock in My Retirement Plan? If the stock has risen in value, you'll save taxes if you *don't* roll over this portion of your assets. Instead ask the plan to distribute the stock directly to a brokerage account. Then sell it immediately, to diversify. You'll owe income taxes on the value of the stock when it was first put into your plan, but the rest of your gain will be taxed at the low capital gains rate. If you'd rolled this same stock into an IRA, you'd have owed ordinary income tax on all your gains.

Can I Change My IRA Investments? Yes, indeed. You can switch from one investment to another within the same institution or to another institution entirely.

Within the same institution, switching can be as easy as picking up the phone or going on your plan's Web site. To switch to another institution, you can either: (1) request a direct IRA-to-IRA transfer, which can be done as often as you want: or (2) have a check made out to you, which you must roll into the new IRA within 60 days. Done this way, each IRA can be rolled over just once a year.

Serious advice from Aunt Jane: *Don't* have the check made out to you! It's all too easy to forget to deposit the money into your new IRA in time! You're courting disaster. If the mail is late, you bring down the tax goblins on your head.

Sometimes you're thwarted by the institution you leave behind. It may drag its heels on transferring your investments. It may charge an exit fee. A few brokerage firms can actually prevent you from leaving because the agreement you originally signed locks up your money. Moral: don't open an IRA without first checking your escape routes. And get a list of all the fees.

I Have an IRA and Also an Investment Account Outside the Plan. How Should I Split My Investments Between Them? In theory, put bonds and other fixed-income investments into the IRA. The interest they pay is always taxed as ordinary income, so it's no disadvantage to keep them in the plan. Use the money you hold outside the IRA to invest in stocks. There your profits are taxed at the low capital gains rate, and you can write off capital losses against your ordinary income.

In practice, however, the division of assets shouldn't be so cut and dried. You need an allocation of bonds outside the IRA in case you suddenly need money at a time when the stock market has tanked. Having those bonds will save you from having to sell your stocks when they're down. Furthermore, you might drop into a lower income tax bracket when you retire. In that case, you might not pay much tax on the gains on any stocks you hold in your IRA—and you'll have deferred the tax for lo those many years. So mix it up a little. There are no firm rules.

Can I Make Early Withdrawals from an IRA? Yes, if you're willing to pay the price. First come income taxes. Second, there's usually a 10 percent penalty if you're under 59½. Third, if your IRA is in a bank certificate of deposit or annuity, you may owe an early-withdrawal penalty.

How Long Can I Contribute? For tax-deferred IRAs—as long as you have earnings, up to the year before you reach 70½. Then you have to stop. But you can keep on depositing up to $5,000 or $6,000 a year for an at-home spouse who is under 70½. For Roth IRAs, you can contribute as long as you have earnings.

Can I Borrow from, or against, an IRA? No dice. But if you have a truly short-term need for money—for example, a bridge loan while waiting for a mortgage to come through—you could tap your IRA through the rollover rule. No taxes are due if you take money out of your IRA, use it, then replace it within 60 days. You're allowed to do this once a year with each of your IRAs, including Roths. But you know what happens if you miss the deadline for putting the money back . . . Bridge loans are a high-risk gamble.

What If I Divorce? As part of the divorce agreement, some or all of the IRA money may go to your former spouse. Anything taken out of the account can be rolled into an IRA for your ex, tax free. The funds must be shifted to the new IRA within 60 days, or taxes and penalties will be due. Whether you split the IRA or not, be sure to take your ex off the beneficiary form. If you die without removing your ex's name, he or she will collect the money anyway.

How to Get the Most from an IRA

1. Put yourself on a regular contribution plan. Money should come out of your bank account automatically, in every pay period, and deposited in your IRA. You can set up the payments yourself online or ask the IRA trustee to arrange them for you. Just $416 a month or $208 twice a month gets you to $5,000 for the year. Savers who wait until the last minute will probably find that they don't have $5,000 on hand.

2. If you didn't make monthly contributions, all is not lost. You can open an IRA on the very eve of the day that your tax return is due (not including extensions), deposit up to the maximum for that year (assuming you have the money), and still deduct it from the previous year's income.

3. If you have a scattering of IRAs at many different institutions, consolidate them. They add to your paperwork and maybe to your maintenance fees. Better to have all the money under one roof—with a mutual fund group or in a self-directed IRA at a brokerage firm. You might also wring a higher return from a single lump sum (or from two lump sums, if you have both a traditional plan and a Roth) than from a clutch of separate, disorganized accounts. If you keep your IRA money in bank deposits, make sure that all your retirement accounts at any one financial institution don't exceed the federal deposit insurance limit. At this writing, retirement accounts are insured for up to $250,000 per depositor, per bank.

4. If you're a TWOI-some—two workers, one income—use a spousal IRA to build up the assets of the at-home spouse.

5. As a general rule, you shouldn't tap your IRA until retirement. If you're a home owner and need money, take a home equity loan instead. You will probably earn more on your IRA than you will pay for the home equity loan after tax. Even better, don't spend the money at all, or save for the purchase you want to make. Still, if you're in serious need of cash and under 59½, take a look at Loophole 9 on page 1064. It's a way of using your IRA funds without paying the 10 percent early-withdrawal penalty.

6. If you want to move your IRA from one institution to another, there are two different ways of getting the job done: transfers and rollovers. Which you choose will depend on your character and your needs.

A *transfer* is the sure and easy way. The new institution does most of the work, and every dime of your money is reinvested. The drawback is that transfers sometimes take weeks. That's damaging only when you want to make a particular investment right away. (Tip: ask your old institution if there's an exit fee and pay it promptly. That sometimes pushes things along.)

A *rollover* is usually the quicker way. Tell the old institution to close your account, which often can be accomplished within a few days. Ask it to mail you a check made out to your account at the new institution, then send the new institution the check by registered mail or overnight delivery. You have to complete the rollover within 60 days. If you miss the deadline, you'll have made a permanent withdrawal on which taxes and maybe penalties are due. If the check is accidentally made out to you personally, the rollover still works, as long as you make the 60-day deadline.

But again, Aunt Jane says, it's risky to assume that you'll make the 60-day deadline. What if you take sick and the check sits on your bureau? Play it safe and do the IRA-to-IRA transfer.

7. If you're moving to a mutual fund group and aren't yet sure which funds you want, put your IRA into its money market fund and choose investments later. If you dither around trying to pick a stock or bond fund, the 60-day deadline might get by.

Important Information About Inherited IRAs!

For spouses. If your spouse dies and you inherit his or her IRA—be it a Roth IRA or a traditional IRA—you'll receive it estate-tax free. You have three choices. You can treat the IRA as your own, telling the trustee to change the name on the account. You can roll it into a new IRA in your name, income-tax free. Or you can retitle the account as an inherited IRA. Which of the three you should choose depends on how old you are and how you want to invest.

If you're 59½ or older: If you're happy with the service you're getting on the account, leave it in place and retitle it in your name. You can keep the same investments or change them, as you like. If you're not happy with the service, you can roll the money into an IRA somewhere else.

If you're under 59½: Retitle the account as an "inherited IRA." That way, you can take out money without paying the 10 percent penalty on early withdrawals. The rules on retitling are very specific. Say that Steve Smith leaves his wife, Cora, an IRA worth $150,000. The account should be retitled, "Steve Smith IRA (deceased May 5, 2010) for the benefit of Cora Smith, beneficiary." If the IRA trustee or adviser errs and retitles it just plain "Cora Smith," it's now Cora's personal IRA. In that case, she'll be charged the 10 percent penalty for making withdrawals while she's underage.

When you reach 59½, retitle the account again, this time in your own name. That lets you defer withdrawals until you're 70½, if you have a traditional IRA and want to leave the money in the account to grow. Otherwise you might have to start making withdrawals earlier (see below). It also gives your beneficiaries maximum flexibility for timing their own withdrawals from the account if you should die.

Making withdrawals: You can take money out of the IRA at any time or leave it in the account to grow. The longer you leave it there, the more money you'll have in the future, thanks to years of tax-sheltered growth. The withdrawal rules vary, depending on the type of IRA you have:

■ *If you receive a traditional IRA, withdrawals are taxed as ordinary income.* If you retitle it as an inherited IRA and keep it that way, withdrawals have to start when your spouse would have reached 70½. If it's titled in your own name, however, you can wait until you yourself are 70½.

■ *If you receive a Roth IRA, withdrawals are tax free as long as your spouse established the account at least five years ago.* If not, you have to wait until the five-year mark has passed. There's no requirement that you ever take any money out. It can grow tax free for as long as you live. When you leave the money to your own beneficiaries, they too receive it income-tax free. They have to start making required withdrawals, but if they handle them right, the IRA can keep on growing for their lifetimes too (see below).

Naming a new beneficiary: As soon as you inherit an IRA, name new beneficiaries—for example, your kids. Once their names are on the account, they'll have the option of extending the tax shelter if you die. Make sure that your beneficiary designation meshes with what it says in your will. When you die, the beneficiary form rules (page 1062).

The "disclaimer" strategy: Here's an idea for wealthy people, where the spouse stands in line to inherit the IRA. After your death, he or she can refuse to accept (disclaim) all or part of the IRA. That money will then pass to the beneficiary next in line. It could be a trust that pays your spouse a lifetime income and then passes to your children. Or the IRA could pass to your children directly. If the children inherit, they could either retitle the IRA as an inherited IRA or disclaim to your grandchildren. The children would still have to take their minimum distributions, but the bulk of the IRA could be tax deferred (or continued tax free if it's a Roth) for generations.

This strategy gives your spouse options—either to take the IRA or to disclaim. If the spouse disclaims, it gets the money out of his or her estate. Don't try this at home! You need an expert to set it up.* All the contingent beneficiaries have to be listed on your IRA beneficiary form, or this disclaimer option won't work.

For IRA beneficiaries other than a spouse—for example, kids who inherit from a parent. You can take the money right away or over a limited number of years. If it's a traditional IRA, you'll owe income taxes when you make withdrawals. If it's a Roth IRA, you'll get the money tax free, provided that the Roth account has existed for at least five years. If it's newer than that, you have to wait for the five-year mark before you can take any money tax free. Nonspouse beneficiaries *do not* pay penalties for withdrawals made when they're younger than 59½.

But let's say that you want to save some or all of the IRA money for the future. You have a wonderful opportunity to keep it tax-sheltered for a lifetime. If you've inherited a traditional IRA, the earnings can continue to grow tax-deferred. With a Roth IRA, the earnings can accumulate tax free.

To reach this happy result, however, you have to get the paperwork right. One slip and the shelter will collapse, forcing you to take the money all at once.

You have to retitle the account as an "inherited IRA." For example, say that Dick Jones dies, leaving his IRA to his son Bernie. The account should be retitled, "Dick Jones IRA (deceased June 25, 2010) for the benefit of Bernie Jones beneficiary." If Dick has another son, Misha, and leaves half the IRA to each of them, Misha would title his half, "Dick Jones IRA (deceased June 25, 2010) for the benefit of Misha Jones beneficiary." All of the money goes into that account. Each year, you're required to withdraw a minimum amount, based on your life expectancy. But in midlife, the minimums are small. At 40, you'd have to withdraw only about $\frac{1}{44}$ of the amount; the next year, $\frac{1}{43}$ of the amount; and so on. You're leaving plenty of money in the IRA to accumulate tax free or tax deferred.

Now let's say that you die. You leave the IRA to your daughter. She too can retitle it as an inherited IRA. That doesn't start the clock on withdrawals again. Instead she completes the withdrawals that you were entitled to over your lifetime. The assets in that single account could eventually be stretched over 100 years or more.

---

*For a book describing the strategy, get *Retire Secure! Pay Taxes Later,* by James Lange.

You don't have to take the minimum withdrawal. You're allowed to take any amount you want, in any year. Choosing the minimum, however, preserves more money for your own old age.

If You Started the IRA, What Should You Do to Preserve the Account for Your Heirs?

1. Name one or more beneficiaries for every IRA account you own—not in your will but on the account's official beneficiary form. (Make sure that it jibes with the provisions in your will.) If your spouse is beneficiary, he or she can turn the money into a personal IRA. If you name someone other than a spouse, specify percentages—for example, "one-third to each of my three children." At your death, the children can ask the IRA trustee to split the account into three pieces. Each of them can either take the money or set up an inherited IRA of his or her own.

If you name the beneficiaries only in your will, not on the IRA beneficiary form, your kids lose the tax shelter. The IRA money will most likely go into your estate and have to be distributed more quickly after your death.

2. File the beneficiary forms with your plan trustee as well as with your lawyer or financial adviser, and in a place in your home where your heirs will find them.

3. If you've left your job but kept your 401(k) in the company investment plan, find out if it allows payouts through inherited IRAs. If not, roll the money into an IRA where that option is allowed.

Is My IRA Safe? Yes. By law, your investments are kept in a separate trust, not mixed with the assets of the investment company. If the company goes broke, your accounts are protected.

Protect Yourself from Financial "Advisers"! I'd guess that the majority of advisers—brokers, planners, call centers, insurance agents—know almost nothing about inherited IRAs and stretched-out payments. They might tell you to roll the money into an IRA of your own, which you can't do if you're not a spouse. They might say there's nothing to do except take the money and give up the tax shelter, which you now know is wrong. Once you've made a mistake, you're toast. You have to take the IRA money and pay the tax. I'll say it again: get the book *The Retirement Savings Time Bomb . . . and How to Defuse It.* It will help you figure out what to do and lead your adviser along.

Getting Away with It

It usually costs you an extra 10 percent if you're under 59½ and draw money out of a 401(k), SEP, Keogh, 403(b), or Individual Retirement Account. But you won't owe the penalty if you fit into one of the following loopholes:

1. You've left your job and are at least 55. This particular loophole works for all qualified retirement plans except IRAs and SEPs.

2. You're paying for qualified higher education expenses (for withdrawals from IRAs only).

3. You're withdrawing up to $10,000 from any IRA for a first home. If it's a Roth, you have to have held the IRA for at least five years.

4. You're dead, and the money is going to your beneficiary. (Not an ideal way to avoid a penalty . . .)

5. You're totally disabled.

6. The money is going to a divorced spouse pursuant to a court decree. To avoid penalties on IRAs and SEPs, transfer the funds into a new IRA.

7. You need the money for deductible medical expenses that exceed 7.5 percent of your adjusted gross income. But in this case, there's a catch. Making a withdrawal from a retirement plan increases your adjusted gross income, which reduces the size of the medical deduction you can take. Thank you, Uncle Sam.

8. You're withdrawing money from a traditional IRA because you've been unemployed for more than 12 weeks and need money to pay for health insurance for yourself and your family.

9. You set up a payment schedule for withdrawing the money, in substantial equal payments, over the rest of your life.

This last loophole—Loophole 9, or, officially, IRS rule 72(t)—sounds restrictive on the surface, but it's fabulously flexible and can help you solve a lot of problems. It applies not only to IRAs but also to all the other retirement plans.

Loophole 9: IRS Rule 72(t)

This escape route is so useful that I want to spend a few paragraphs telling you about it. It lets you avoid the 10 percent early-withdrawal penalty if you're under 59½. At any age, you can set up a regular withdrawal schedule that, if followed faithfully, would lead to "substantially equal" periodic payments for the rest of your life (or for the joint life expectancies of you and your spouse or another beneficiary).

Here's the beauty part: the payments *don't* have to last for life if your need for money is short term. Once you start withdrawing, you must keep to the schedule for at least five years *or* until you reach 59½, whichever period is longer. After that, you can change your mind. You might decide on larger withdrawals or smaller ones. Or you might take no more money at all. Mandatory withdrawal rules don't begin again until you pass 70½, except for Roth IRAs, where you're allowed to keep all the money in the plan for as long as you like.

I can think of several problems that Loophole 9 might solve. For example, you might tap the fund to help pay your bills for a few years if your income drops. Once your budget is back on track and you've met the 72(+) rules, you can stop the withdrawals and let your remaining money grow. Or you might have lost your executive job and replaced it with a job paying less. A withdrawal plan could provide the extra income you need.

This loophole works best for those in their mid-50s who may not have to use it for more than five years or so. Young people should forget it. Their monthly payments would be small and, once started, would have to continue at least until they reached 59½. That would pretty much run down the fund. There are penalties to ending the program ahead of time or changing the size of the payments you take out.

There Is One Immutable Law of Financial Planning That Loophole 9 Runs Up Against

God punishes anyone who uses loopholes. In this case, your trials are actuarial.

There is more than one way of calculating substantially equal payments, and the method chosen makes a huge difference to the size of your income. I ran one example for a 55-year-old woman. She had an IRA worth $150,000 that was earning a 6 percent rate of return. Depending on which calculation she chose, her first-year payment could have been as little as $5,068 or as much as $8,764. Alternatively, she could have divided her money into two separate $75,000 IRAs, drawn $2,534 or $4,383 a year from one of them, and left the other one alone. Or she could have split the IRAs into different sizes. The possibilities are endless. The IRS's free Publication 590, "Individual Retirement Arrangements," leads you through all the numbers. It's available online at www.irs.gov or by calling 800-TAX-FORM. If you find it too complicated (most people do), ask an accountant for help. If you get the size of your substantially equal withdrawals wrong, tax penalties may be due.

The Automatic IRA

At this writing, there's talk about creating an automatic IRA. It would be made available by all (or most) businesses that don't currently offer retirement plans. There's no requirement for employers to contribute, although they might. Your own contributions would be deducted from your paycheck automatically and invested according to your wishes. If an automatic IRA or similar plan is made available at your small company, by all means use it.

What Can Go Wrong with Retirement Plans?

Not much goes wrong with qualified retirement plans, I'm pleased to say. As a way of investing, they carry little risk. Abuses occur, but not a lot. The biggest danger is that you won't invest enough or won't invest well enough.

Nevertheless, there are some weaknesses in the system that you need to consider:

■ *Self-directed IRAs.* They're fine, as long as you're with financial institutions that offer traditional investments. But once you leave the reservation, they're a mixed bag. Independent pension administrators handle unusual and illiquid deals: real estate, venture capital, foreign exchange, alpaca farms, mortgage notes. You're hoping for a killing, and those kinds of hopes always come laced with killer fees. Your pension administrator may be linked financially with firms that manage the investments. Apparent high yields in the early years might mask bad accounting that doesn't show up for a long time. A hard-charging, hard-selling investment firm is a calamity you ought to see coming.

The terrible 2008 stock market decline might tempt you to try alternatives. But in the mid-2000s, the favorite alternative was high-yield mortgage and real estate investing, and look what happened to that. If you're wealthy, it doesn't hurt to put 5 percent of a large IRA into venture deals as long as you understand the business, don't mind the fees, and can absorb a loss. The average investor, however, will do better allocating an extra 5 percent to something safe.

■ *Company 401(k)s, 403(b)s, and other contributory plans.* Your company might give you poor or high-cost investment choices (school districts that offer insurance company 403(b)s, are you listening?). If you're investing less than $5,000 and your employer doesn't match your contribution, start a Roth IRA instead.

■ *Simple mistakes.* To catch errors in your account, check it online (or watch your quarterly statements). You want to be sure that all your contributions are getting into the plan. Also, check that you're getting the proper company match.

■ *Small companies that are poorly run may deduct money from your paycheck for the 401(k) and never deposit the money into your account.* If you're with a small company and don't get annual reports, call the plan trustee and ask for them. The law says you're entitled. If you get no satisfaction (the trustee may be the owner of the company), report the problem to the U.S. Department of Labor at 866-444-3272 and stop putting in money. Start a Roth IRA instead. The Pension Benefit Guaranty Corporation doesn't cover losses from fraud in contributory plans. If the company goes bankrupt, there's little or no hope of getting your money back.

• *Pension plans.* Your company can terminate its pension plan and put all your benefits to date into an insurance company annuity. If the insurance company fails (we're going far afield here, but all things are possible), you won't be covered by the Pension Benefit Guaranty Corporation. All the states have guaranty funds to act as safety nets for failed insurance companies. Pension annuities are typically covered for $100,000, but a few states insure for more. If employees lose money, they might successfully sue an employer that chose a risky insurance company, especially if some conflict of interest was involved. But the court battle will be expensive and long.

• *Mistakes in calculating pension checks.* They're checked by an outside auditor, but errors happen. Suspect a problem if your check is inexplicably less than your colleagues got or the money seems low for the number of years you worked. The risk is greatest if your company merged or was purchased and got a new pension plan administrator.

To catch obvious errors, check the annual statement that shows how much your traditional pension benefit has grown. You want to be sure that the company counted all your earnings and hours. What? You don't know how many hours you worked? That's why you should keep all your W-2 forms and year-end pay stubs. The company has records too, but they might get lost or mangled if your company is sold. It's good to be able to prove your work history in a pinch. Here are some of the less obvious errors that can affect a pension check:

• *If you worked past normal retirement age,* the extra months or years might not be figured in your benefit.

• *If you started out in a union plan and then moved to management,* your union credits might be forgotten. The same thing can happen to a worker moving from one division of a company to another, when the divisions have separate plans.

• *If your plan counts "all" compensation toward your pension,* it might forget to include your bonuses, overtime, and commissions.

• *If your pension is based on your five highest earning years,* the computer might assume that those are the last five years you worked, which isn't always the case.

- *If you ever worked part-time,* those years might be dropped from your pension calculation. You're generally covered if you work more than 1,000 hours a year. But some companies accept 500 hours or less, so check it out.
- *If you've been into and out of the workforce and your plan has a Social Security offset,* the company might overestimate your Social Security earnings, which reduces your pension check. Get a copy of your Social Security earnings history (page 1096), then ask the company what it assumed when it figured your check. If its assumptions were incorrect, show proof of your earnings. The company will refigure your pension, giving you a larger check.
- *If you leave with a lump sum,* all the errors that affect the calculation of monthly pension checks affect you too.
- *If the pension laws have changed,* your company may still be running by the old rules. For example, it may use an outdated interest rate table to calculate how much money you're owed.

If you think your pension check might be wrong, query the plan administrator in writing. E-mail is fine too, but don't do it by phone. If you haven't asked in writing, you haven't asked. Request all the factors used to calculate your payout, such as your earnings, the benefit formula, and the number of years you worked. The wrong birth date or hire date can make a big difference in what you get.

If you see nothing obviously wrong but still feel uncomfortable, you can ask an actuary for help. The American Academy of Actuaries (www.actuary.org) maintains a Pension Assistance List of actuaries who offer up to four hours of free help. They'll check the plan documents and your work history and calculate what your benefit should be. If they find an error, they'll help you prepare a letter to your plan.

The National Center for Retirement Benefits, in Northbrook, Illinois (www.ncrb.com; 800-666-1000) charges nothing to check out your pension, profit sharing, or 401(k) payment but takes 20 percent of any money it recovers. The fee drops to 15 percent of the recovery for handling 10 or more people from the same company. The firm handles private, union, and government plans with a few exceptions, such as plans that have gone bankrupt.

If you think you have a court case, contact the National Pension Lawyers Network (www.pensionaction.org/npln.htm). Lawyers typically charge one-third of the money you recover, plus expenses. Don't delay if you suspect you've been underpaid. You don't want the statute of limitations to cut off your claim.

For questions about your plan, the U.S. Administration on Aging maintains a Pension Counseling and Information Program that serves 22 states. For links, go to the Pension Rights Center (www.pensionrights.org). The center is an excellent source of information on what's happening to traditional pensions, pension freezes, and proposed retirement plan reform.

What Do You Know About Your Plan?

By law, there's a bunch of things that your company has to tell you. Even if you don't read them right away, keep them in a file. If a question ever comes up about the size of your benefit or what you're entitled to, the answers will be here.

The two most important pieces of information for you to have are: (1) an estimate of your future benefits and (2) an up-to-date summary plan description.

1. Individual benefit statement—at minimum, free once every three years, for traditional pension plans and cash-value plans. Workers can request it, in writing, once a year. Often it's available online. Traditional pension benefit statements tell you how large a monthly benefit you have accrued so far. Cash-value pension statements show the size of your accrued cash account. Profit-sharing plans and employee stock ownership plans have to send you an annual statement showing what the value of your share is worth. A 401(k) or similar plan has to disclose your performance at least quarterly. In most cases, these statements are also available online. Check all these reports carefully for mistakes and file them in your retirement plan folder at home.

People divorced from plan members and survivors of members who died, and who have a financial interest in the plan, can request a statement in writing once a year.

2. Summary plan description—free when you join the plan. This is more colloquially known as your plan handbook. It should also be available to you online. It describes your benefits and how they're figured, how you qualify for coverage, and how you get your money out. If you want to read the entire plan document, you can get a copy or examine it wherever it's kept, but it's written in cuneiform.

3. Summary of material modifications—free within seven months after the end of the plan year when the change was made. As a practical matter, companies usually announce significant changes right away. This document is a follow-up. Changes that could reduce your benefits at 65 have to be announced in advance.

4. Summary annual report—free once a year for people in 401(k)s and similar contributory plans. It provides information about the financial status of your plan.

5. Annual funding notice—free within four months after the end of the plan year. This notice is for participants in both traditional and hybrid pension plans. It tells you how well funded your plan is—meaning whether it has enough assets to pay the promised benefits. The funding notice also tells you how much money the plan gained or lost on its total investments last year. It's expressed in dollars, however, not as a percentage return, so this disclosure doesn't tell you much. The report also gives a dollar figure for administrative expenses paid by the plan and should show any financial transactions between the plan and people close to it.

Several problems with these various data: (1) The investments can be described so generally that you don't have a clue what the pension plan really buys. (2) It's often out of date. It needn't be filed until seven months after the end of the plan year. (3) Lots of expenses are left out. (4) It doesn't disclose the plan's percentage gain or loss. (5) Reports from small plans (fewer than 100 employees) provide even less detail and don't have to be audited if they meet certain IRS requirements. So who really knows? (6) You might discover that the plan is overweighted in, say, real estate. But there's nothing much you can do about it in plans that don't allow you to choose your own investments. You can complain, of course, and spread the word around the office. Might as well.

For more detailed information on what to look for in these documents, download the booklet "What You Should Know About Your Retirement Plan" from the Web site of the U.S. Department of Labor, www.dol.gov/ebsa/publications.

What If Your Boss Refuses to Distribute Reports?

This sometimes happens in very small plans where most of the money belongs to the honcho anyway. On paper, you're told to write to the plan administrator or trustee (send the letter by certified mail), but that may be the boss, who isn't cooperating anyway.

If you think that your money is being misappropriated, call the federal Employee Benefits Security Administration at 866-444-3272. An operator will refer you to the Labor Department office that handles complaints in your area. Try to get other employees to call too. EBSA doesn't have enough people to follow up on most complaints, but it does get money restored to some plans.

When EBSA writes to a company, it doesn't reveal who complained, although in offices with two doctors, a nurse, and a receptionist, it's not hard to figure out. Workers may put up with pension abuse for fear of losing their jobs. Best advice, if it's a 401(k): look for another job. In the meantime, quit contributing and start a Roth IRA instead.

You can get your plan's annual report (Form 5500) by submitting a written request to the U.S. Department of Labor, Employee Benefits Security Administration, Public Disclosure Facility, 200 Constitution Avenue NW, Washington, DC 20210. Among other things, it gives you the plan's total administrative expenses, lists the investments, tells you whether it has gained or lost money over the year, discloses any loans to company officers, and, for pension plans, shows how well the plan is funded. Every large company is required to file this tax form annually. Smaller companies file less often. If you're nearby, you can visit the Public Disclosure Room and copy the documents yourself. Otherwise EBSA will copy them for you at 15 cents a page (two to six pages, depending on the form, plus attached documents).

Even if you get the report, it may be couched in language that conceals what's really going on. Outside trustees or record keepers may know that something's wrong (for example, the plan might not receive a contribution that's due), but—astonishingly—no law requires them to tell the employees. One would think that's what trustees were *for.* For a booklet that helps you decipher Form 5500, go to www.dol.gov/esba/publications and download *Protect Your Pension.*

Aunt Jane's Single Most Important Secret for Accumulating Huge Pots of Money for Your Retirement, Revealed Here for the First Time

When you're due a payout from any retirement plan and you haven't yet retired, leave the money where it is or roll it into another plan. Don't spend it. Don't even think of spending it. Don't think even of spending part of it. Give it a kiss and forget about it.

The sum that you want to spend may seem small. But it's not just the loss of that money that hurts. It's the loss of all the money that that money would have earned over the next umpty-ump years, plus the loss of the shelter that protected that money from tax.

Steady deposits in tax-favored retirement plans are only the beginning of wisdom. You also have to leave that money alone.

Tax-Deferred Annuities

So potent are the words *tax deferral* that, in their presence, otherwise strong minds turn to pudding. Analysis flies out the window. Of all the unexamined premises of financial planning, one of the most dangerous is that tax deferral is always smart. It's not. Sometimes it's dumb.

Which brings me to tax-deferred annuities.

I am not speaking here of the retirement annuities bought by teachers and others for their tax-deferred 403(b) retirement savings plans.

The subject before us is retail tax-deferred annuities, bought by conservative savers with after-tax dollars. In certain limited circumstances, they make sense. But I'd guess that the majority of annuities are sold inappropriately, to the wrong people, at too high a price. The annuity hype comes from salespeople earning high commissions for roping you in. Beware, beware,

All retail annuities have three things in common: (1) You get no tax deduction for the money you put up. (2) Inside the annuity, your money compounds tax deferred. (3) At withdrawal, the earnings—including any capital gains—are taxed as ordinary income.

Beyond that, each annuity has its own cost structure (usually high!!), gimmicks (expensive), and rate of return (reduced by costs). You buy annuities from stockbrokers, financial planners, insurance agents, or mutual funds. But regardless of who makes the sale, an annuity is always backed by an insurance company.

Before we go further, some definitions:

An *immediate-pay annuity* pays you an income over your lifetime or for a fixed number of years, starting now (for the scoop on immediate-pay annuities, see page 1124). A *tax-deferred annuity*—the type that concerns us here—accumulates money for the future.

Tax-deferred annuities come in three types, depending on how you want to invest. A *fixed annuity* pays a fixed interest rate for a certain term. An *equity-indexed annuity* is loosely linked to the stock market's rise and fall, but with a guarantee that you'll always earn a fixed minimum rate (which can be pretty close to zero). A *variable annuity* offers you a menu of mutual funds, known as *subaccounts,* that are invested in stocks and bonds. You choose the investments you want. Variable annuities have been tricked out with various retirement income benefits (page 1084). A *single-premium deferred annuity* is bought with a single sum of money. The minimum purchase is generally $10,000, although buyers typically put up much larger sums. A *flexible-premium annuity* takes smaller or irregular amounts. You might pay $100 a month or dump in $1,000 every now and then. Due to extra fees, this is a particularly expensive way to buy.

When you decide to quit accumulating money and start spending it (known as the *payout phase*), annuities offer another range of choice. You can take guaranteed monthly payments for the rest of your life (that's called *annuitizing*). You can make periodic withdrawals. You can take the money in a lump sum. You can roll your savings into another annuity tax free.

Your insurance company typically imposes a penalty on withdrawals made before 7 to 15 years have passed. One exception: you're usually allowed to take 10 percent of your money each year, penalty free. There's a 10 percent tax penalty on withdrawals made before your reach 59½. If you die, your heirs, including your spouse, will owe income tax on any annuity money they inherit.

You Don't Date Annuities, You Marry Them

An annuity isn't a mutual fund that you buy today and sell tomorrow. Nor is it a certificate of deposit, ready for any new use at maturity. When you buy a tax-deferred annuity, you are making (or ought to be making) a 15- to 25-year commitment at minimum. That's because you could have chosen to buy those same mutual funds outside the annuity, in which case you'd have paid lower fees and lower taxes on your capital gains. It takes 15 to 25 years for the value of the annuity's tax deferral to overcome the disadvantage of its higher costs, and that's in higher tax brackets. In the lower tax brackets, it might never catch up.

My Bottom Line on Buying Annuities, Moved Up to the Top Line

- *Buy fixed annuities if you'd otherwise keep the money in a bank account* and the annuity pays the same or more than a certificate of deposit. You'll earn the interest tax deferred.
- *Buy immediate-pay annuities late in life if you start worrying that you might run out of money.* The annuity guarantees you an income for life.
- *Buy low-load tax-deferred annuities (page 1087) if you're in your early 50s or younger and won't touch the money for 30 years.* (But only after you've fully funded your 401(k) and opened a Roth IRA if you're eligible.) If you choose the annuities sold by commissioned brokers, planners, and insurance agents, buy no later than your early 40s. You need a lo-o-o-o-ong holding period to overcome their high costs and tax disadvantages. When choosing among low-loads, look for the one with the highest guaranteed minimum rate.
- *Buy low-load tax-deferred annuities for your young children, not to be touched until they retire.* (If your children have earnings, invest in a Roth IRA first for its lower cost and tax-free gains.)
- *Do not buy full-sales-charge, tax-deferred variable annuities if you're in your 50s or older*—which happens to be the ages that salespeople target. You're effectively buying mutual funds at an excessively high price and will pay higher taxes on the gains. (Dare I say it? The hidden sales commission typically ranges from 5 to 8 percent of the money you put up.)
- *Do not be seduced by the special, guaranteed income benefits attached to variable annuities.* The sales pitch suggests that your income from the annuity will rise in your later age. On paper, it can. In real life, it's unlikely because the annuity's

costs are so high. The odds are, you'll wind up with a fixed income instead. Adding insult to injury, your income will be lower than if you had bought a simple, fixed lifetime annuity in the first place.

▪ *Do not be seduced into buying a deferred annuity because you can turn it into a lifetime income later in life.* You don't need a deferred annuity for that purpose. You can buy a lifetime income whenever you want, with savings that you build up somewhere else. The annuity strategy makes sense only if you're in a high tax bracket *and* are investing assets that would otherwise be taxed at your ordinary income rate *and* know that you'll annuitize when you retire.

▪ *Use the free-look period.* If you're talked into buying an annuity and then have second thoughts, you typically have 10 days or more to rescind the sale without paying a surrender penalty. Don't hesitate to do so.

That's my summary. Now to explain the cost of annuities and how they work.

Buyer Beware: High Taxes and Fees

When you buy a tax-deferred annuity, the IRS saith:

1. Ordinary income taxes are owed on your tax-deferred earnings whenever you take out the money. This is true even for the gains on stock funds held in an annuity that otherwise would have been taxed at the low capital gains rate. Annuities *increase* your tax.

2. There is normally a 10 percent penalty on earnings withdrawn before age 59½. The penalty is waived only in limited circumstances, among which are death and disability. You can also dodge the penalty by setting up a lifetime withdrawal schedule.

3. If you annuitize—meaning, turn your tax-deferred savings into a lifetime income—part of each withdrawal is treated as taxable income. The rest is the nontaxable return of your own capital.

4. If you make occasional withdrawals, subject to no particular schedule, the entire withdrawal is treated as taxable income. Taxes are levied until you have taken all of the money earned on the principal you put up. After that, you can start withdrawing your original investment tax free.

5. If you die, your heirs will owe income taxes on the gains inside the annuity they inherit. If you died owning mutual funds instead, your heirs would inherit the gains income-tax free.

The insurance company saith:

1. Your average expenses, on commissioned variable annuities, will run in the area of 2.5 percent. That chops your investment performance. You can buy the same types of mutual funds outside an annuity for 0.5 percent or less. If you add guaranteed lifetime withdrawal benefits, your fees can climb to 3.75 percent.

2. You usually have to pay a surrender fee for quitting the annuity too soon. The first year, it's often 7 percent of the money withdrawn. In the second year, it's 6 percent, and so on, until, after 7 years, the penalty finally dribbles away. Some penalty periods last for only 5 years. Others last for 10 or even 15 years. With flexible annuities, new surrender fees may be attached to every deposit you make. Drawn-out exit fees are designed to lock customers in.

At the other end of the scale, a few annuities release you after only one year, with a penalty of six months' interest for leaving any earlier.

3. An annuity with a long-term lock-in doesn't cut you off from your cash entirely. Usually you can withdraw a portion of the policy's value every year (say, 10 percent) without paying a surrender fee. But you'll still owe income taxes on money you take out and a 10 percent tax penalty too if you're under 59½. If you think you might need to retrieve some funds, you shouldn't be buying a tax-deferred annuity in the first place.

4. A handful of insurers let you draw out money, without penalty, to cover the costs of a nursing home, terminal illness, or unemployment.

The Big Fakeroo

I'm troubled by the way annuities are frequently sold. You may be misled about what they are likely to yield, compared with an alternative.

The typical brochure extols the glories of tax deferral. On a slick little chart, you'll see a fat line zipping up to heaven. That represents how fast your money grows untaxed. Inching up from the very bottom of the chart is a thin, unhappy line. That supposedly shows the pitiful returns earned by simps who let their investments be taxed every year.

But those pretty charts may greatly exaggerate what annuities actually yield. Often, they "forget" the tax you owe when you cash in the annuity. So they're comparing apples to oranges: annuity returns pretax versus the after-tax return on stocks, bonds, or certificates of deposit. Once taxes are subtracted, the annuity doesn't look nearly as good. Better than a taxable investment, but not as much better as you think.

Many salespeople argue that there's no point showing the annuity's value after tax because that's not the way to take the money. Instead of cashing out all at once, you should annuitize—that is, turn your savings into a lifetime income, which stretches out your tax payments too. That may be true, but historically, the vast majority of investors don't annuitize. Even for those who will, the sales brochure is wrong because it doesn't account for the taxes you owe on the income you'll receive. After tax, your yield drops.

Fixed-Rate Deferred Annuities: For Conservative Savers

These investments pay about the same as short- to medium-term certificates of deposit. They're good for conservative savers who would otherwise keep their money in taxable CDs. They come in two types: the traditional, dinosaur product, where the insurance company can jerk you around, or the more transparent product, where you can see what's going on.

The transparent product is called a *CD-like annuity* or *multiyear guarantee annuity* (MYGA). You choose the period of time you want to invest—anywhere from 1 to 10 years. There's a different interest rate for each term, and it lasts for the entire period. At the end of the term, you can take your money without penalty, renew for another fixed term, or roll the money, tax free, into a different annuity that offers you a better rate (a 1035 exchange). Very simple, very clean. At the end of the term, the company will renew you automatically for the same term or (if the term was long) to a shorter, three-year term. If you want the money out, be sure to say so. Every time you re-up, the surrender period usually starts all over again.

If you cash out of a CD-like annuity before the term is up, your earnings will be adjusted. If interest rates have dropped since you bought the annuity, your cash value will go up; if rates have risen, your cash value drops. In either case, you may pay a surrender penalty too. (This is called a *market value adjustment.*)

By contrast, the dinosaur annuity, referred to in the listings as a *deferred annuity*, requires you to invest for longer terms (5 to 15 years). You get a fixed rate of interest for a certain period of time (usually only 1 year but sometimes longer). After that, the insurance company can raise or lower the rate, usually once a year. Typically the company sticks existing customers with lower rates while offering higher rates to the new customers at the door. If the existing customers are unhappy, tough luck. The company knows they're stuck. They face early-withdrawal penalties, perhaps for the annuity's entire term. The insurers do guarantee you a certain minimum interest rate—at this writing, in the 1.5 to 3 percent range. You can keep the annuity until you're 85 or 90 (at some companies, 105), if you're so inclined. But given its complexity and the opportunities for abuse, why would you buy it at all?

A dinosaur deferred annuity might attract you with a signing bonus—an extra 1 to 5 percent in the first year—to make itself look good or to cover the surrender fee on an existing annuity you've been talked into giving up. To cover that bonus, the insurance company is apt to pay low, noncompetitive interest rates in future years. It may also charge a surrender fee for a longer period.

Surrender fees are often handled as *rolling loads*. Every dollar you put in has to stay there for the full surrender period. For example, say that you make periodic payments over 10 years into an annuity with a 7-year rolling load and then withdraw the money. You can retrieve your older payments penalty free, but payments made during the past 7 years will carry a surrender charge.

CD-like annuities sometimes offer bonus interest rates too in the first year. But all the rates are spread out before you, for you to say yes or no. If you're in the market for a safe, no-surprises investment, stick with CD-like annuities. (By the way, they're called CD-*like* annuities as a result of misleading sales. They used to be called CD annuities, which made some buyers think that they were buying higher-interest bank CDs. They may still think so—it all depends on the salesperson.)

Who Might Want a Fixed-Rate, CD-like Annuity?

This investment works for people who put safety first and are satisfied with the modest tax-deferred interest rate. A likely buyer might be:

- *A conservative person in late middle age, saving for retirement,* who doesn't need current income from his or her capital, doesn't care that fixed-income investments may fall behind after taxes and inflation, and plans to keep the annuity virtually for life. You're treating this as "safety" money for your late old age. You won't make withdrawals until you absolutely have to.

- *A saver with plenty of growth investments* who wants a safe interest rate hedge and plans not to touch the money for many years.

- *A saver who normally won't budge out of certificates of deposit.* A fixed annuity may pay a little more interest, and it's tax deferred.

- *Someone with a high-cost, badly performing life insurance policy* who wants to transfer the cash value into an annuity in a tax-free exchange.

- *A saver who intends to turn the annuity into an income for life.* That way, your money remains tax deferred, not only while it's building up but also during the years when you are gradually drawing it out. This is the surest way of making any annuity pay.

- *Someone who's allergic to taxes at all costs.* But look first at municipal bonds. Their current yield may be a little less than what annuities pay. But that yield is good until maturity, whereas the interest rate on annuities will change. Furthermore, you'll eventually owe taxes on your annuity savings, while munis are permanently tax exempt. After tax, it will take a deferred annuity many, many years to equal the net income you'd get from a muni bond.

A Fee-only Planner Can Find You a Low-load Fixed Deferred Annuity, if that suits your objectives. Even some dinosaur types offer programs with low commissions and better guarantees. They're just not the ones that the average commissioned agent sells.

Don't Sit Tight in a Lousy Fixed Annuity that started out well but now pays a subpar interest rate. Look for a better company (page 917) and make a tax-free exchange.

How to Lower the Risk of Getting a Poor Fixed Annuity

1. Buy only CD-like, multiyear annuities that pay a fixed rate over a specified period of time. You know exactly what you're getting. At the end of the term, the insurance company has to offer you another good rate to keep your business. It can't play games with you.

2. Buy your CD-type annuities only from companies rated A+ and higher. And don't buy for the longest terms. Stay with shorter, three- to five-year terms. The companies offering these types of annuities aren't the familiar giants. Shorter terms give you some protection, in case your company's financial soundness rating starts to slip.

3. Here's what to look for if you decide to buy a dinosaur deferred annuity:

• *Don't buy an annuity advertising interest rates that are markedly above average.* They'll drop below average pretty soon.

• *Don't buy from a company whose exit fees are unreasonably high.* A standard surrender charge in the industry starts at 5 or 7 percent and declines by one percentage point every year. The baddies charge fees for 10 years or more. The baddies also tend to be companies with lower ratings for financial soundness.

• *Buy only from companies rated A++ and up.* Plenty of companies of this quality offer traditional annuities, so there's no need to settle even for one rated A+.

• *Make sure that your annual statement will show your annuity's yield as a percentage rate.* Some statements show only dollars earned, which can conceal many sins. If you see only dollars, ask your agent for a letter from the company disclosing the true percentage yield. You're entitled to know.

• *Find out what the people who bought this annuity (or a similar one) a few years ago received as a renewal rate.* You are looking for a company that pays both its old and new customers the same rate or pays the old customers only a tiny bit less. The rates paid on old deposits are readily available. In the course of researching this chapter, I spoke to two insurance company actuaries, both of whom pressed a button and called up all the rates on their computer screens. If the salesperson won't supply the information you asked for or claims it's too difficult to get, assume the worst. If he or she says that your particular annuity hasn't been sold for the past five years, ask for the rates on a similar contract. If the agent still says no, you say no, too.

Do you think that getting all these rates is too much trouble? Here's what one actuary said to me: "Tell your readers to make their agents disclose the annuity's past interest rate history. Many agents won't bother as long as their customers don't insist. And because of that, a lot of bad annuities get sold. But agents are a dime a dozen. If more people quit doing business with uncooperative agents, maybe this industry would start telling more truths."

The real truth is that none of this matters because you're not going to buy a dinosaur annuity anyway. I hope.

4. Look for an insurance company with a high rating for safety and soundness (page 406). Because ratings aren't always reliable, diversify your holdings. If you're going to put $300,000 into fixed annuities, spread it among three different companies. If you're investing less than $100,000, however, consider using only one *highly rated* company. Insurers pay lower interest rates on investments under $100,000.

5. Don't buy an annuity paying less interest than you can earn on a similar investment outside the annuity. The agent may assure you that, thanks to the tax deferral, the annuity will win. Maybe so—but not in your lifetime. As an example, consider a tax-deferred annuity paying 5 percent versus a taxable investment at 6 percent. It takes 30 years for the annuity to pull ahead if you're in a combined state and federal tax bracket of 35 percent.

6. Never buy without checking the competition. An insurance agent may say, "My Best Super American Plan pays the highest rate in the country," and that could be pure BS. How do you check? Read on.

How to Shop for a Fixed Annuity

Listings are all over the Web. I recommend Total Return Annuities.com (www .totalreturnannuities.com; 866-866-1999) for its useful consumer information. The annuities are listed by term and show the insurance company's financial soundness rating, the minimum purchase, the guaranteed interest rate, any bonus rate, and the *yield to surrender*, which is the yield that counts. A site called Annuity Advantage (www.annuityadvantage.com; 800-239-0356) uses the same data.

Go for the multiyear, CD-like annuities, not the traditional, dinosaur, deferred annuities. The dinosaurs don't have a *T. rex* looming over the quotes, but they might as well. They attract you by promising higher current rates, but their current yield to surrender is lower than you'll get on CD-like annuities, and it's not guaranteed. If you're approached by an agent, check his or her offer against the listings on the Web.

Be aware of commissions! Agents generally pitch dinosaur annuities because they pay the highest commissions. You don't see the commissions, but they probably amount to 5 percent of the money you put in, plus an additional 1 percent for the wholesaler. Junk annuities, with high interest rates up front and a certainty of low rates later, may pay 10 percent commissions. No knowledgeable person would touch that stuff. Many of the most aggressive companies, tempting you with the highest first-year interest rates, have mediocre ratings for financial soundness. They might as well raise a flag reading, "We can't afford to pay high interest very long." Commissions on CD-like annuities generally run at 1 or 1.5 percent plus 1 percent at the end of the rate-guarantee period, if you renew.

Beware the agent who claims that he or she is earning no commission. There is *always* a commission, except at low-load companies (page 1082) where salaried agents sell by phone. You don't see the commission because it doesn't come out of your investment up front. It's paid from the difference between what the insurer earns on its investments and the interest rate it pays to you, as well as from the surrender charge if you leave early.

Are Your Fixed Annuities Safe?

It depends. Fixed annuities are backed by bonds and other assets in the insurance company's general account. They're valued at the cash guaranteed in the contract plus any interest that has been credited. Failing insurance companies are placed into rehabilitation. If another insurer buys the business, your current interest rate should be good (although it might be nicked a little if the failed insurance company was unreasonably aggressive). If there's no buyer, you're protected up to the maximum supported by your state's insurance guaranty fund ($100,000 in 31 states, $300,000 in 15 others, and $500,000 in another 4). You might collect more than this if the company has enough assets, but recovery could take years. If you want to invest a lot of money, split it into more than one annuity, each one comfortably below the amount that your state guarantees. For your state's limits, see the Web site of the National Organization of Life & Health Insurance Guaranty Associations (www.nolhga.com, click on "State Associations").

Equity-Indexed Annuities—An "Investment" to Avoid!

Run, run, run from the investments known as *equity-indexed annuities* (EIA). All too often, they're sold deceptively, to people who don't understand how they work, by salespeople who are making a killing in commissions. Attorney generals in several states have brought and settled class-action lawsuits against companies that sell EIAs. FINRA, which regulates securities firms, has put out an investor alert (www.finra.org/investors). They're a major source of consumer complaints.

EIAs are contracts with insurance companies. They're sold to people—usually older people—who normally buy interest rate investments such as fixed annuities or bank CDs. These conservative investors would love to earn higher, stock market returns over the long term but wouldn't dream of putting any money at risk.

An indexed annuity is their grail. It combines the potential for stock market gains with little risk of principal loss. Every year, the insurance company credits you with interest, tax deferred, based on a complex formula loosely connected with how the stock market performs. If the market rises over a specified period of time, you make some money. If it doesn't, you're guaranteed some sort of minimal return. All profit, no loss (you think). How could anyone resist? Greedy salespeople may encourage new retirees to roll their entire 401(k) into the EIA.

But although the concept can be stated simply, the investment is complex, and salespeople may withhold certain critical information. For example, you'll probably have to hold the investment for 5 to 16 years—a problem if you're 75 and were sold a 16-year product. Your "minimum guaranteed return" is typically figured only on part of your investment, so you could still lose money overall. You face large penalties for withdrawing early. If you die before the EIA matures, your beneficiaries may get less than you put in. The fees are huge. Salespeople may show you, on paper, how super these annuities perform over periods when stocks do well, while glossing over how little you'll earn (or your risk of loss) if stocks decline.

The Securities and Exchange Commission has ordered stronger regulations for equity-indexed annuities issued on or after January 12, 2011. They will require more disclosure to consumers and supposedly provide you with better protection against deceptive sales. Will that solve the problem? No. Deceptive selling won't go away, and when did "disclosure" turn a bad investment into a good one?

EIAs sell themselves as a free lunch. You have nothing to lose, thanks to that minimum guarantee, and everything to gain if stocks go up. But just because

EIAs work out sometimes doesn't make them a good idea. You give up too much in flexibility in older age, pay a ton, will earn less than you imagine in a rising market, and could still lose money. In many tests, equity-indexed annuities don't perform any better than fixed annuities, due to the EIA's higher cost.

If you know all these things and decide to listen to the sales pitch anyway, here's what to ask:

1. If I put my money into this investment, how long do I have to keep it there? Generally, you commit to holding for 5 to 16 years. Don't even think of investing money that you might need over that period. (There are 1- to 3-year EIAs, which are a roll of the dice as far as the stock market is concerned.)

2. What do I earn over that time period? Even if you write it down, you'll still be confused. You're typically credited with anywhere from 60 to 100 percent of the price gain of the S&P 500 (or some other average). For example, if the market rises by 8 percent and your annuity gives you 75 percent of the gain, your contract will earn 6 percent. Insurers can generally change that percentage from year to year, so you're never sure how much you'll get. If the contract isn't profitable enough, they'll reduce the amount of gain they credit to customer accounts.

Don't imagine that a company that credits you with 100 percent of the year's market gain is giving you a better deal than one that credits you with less. That "100 percent" is a sales tool. They'll make up the money somewhere else.

There may also be a cap on what you're allowed to earn in a year when the stock market soars. The company can usually change the cap whenever it wants.

3. Am I credited with the dividends that the market pays? Answer: No. Losing dividends is significant. At this writing, they're averaging around 3.5 percent. Since 1926, they've accounted for 43 percent of the S&P's compounded gains. Losing dividends is *big*, in dollar terms.

4. You're often offered a signing bonus of 5 percent, sometimes up to 16 percent. That's a sure sign of a high-cost, low-yield, anticonsumer annuity. You'll more than pay for your "bonus" in reduced returns.

5. At the end of the term, how does the insurer figure your gain? This is confusing too. Some companies use the market price on the day the annuity matures. Some look at each policy anniversary date and pick the highest one. Some average the price over your annuity's final 12 months. Some credit a portion of each year's market gains, if any. Some give you 100 percent of the gain but deduct 1 percent for expenses. And there are other systems. There's no way of knowing in advance which one will pay the most. Everything depends on how the market performs over your particular holding period.

6. What if stock prices drop? You'll be credited with zero that year. If stock prices rise the following year but remain below the previous peak, some annuities credit you with a gain but others don't. Stocks can rise while your annuity earns nothing (the reverse can happen with certain types of annuities). The upside, in bear markets, is that your annuity didn't lose, which is the reason people buy it. I think you're giving up more than you realize for this peace of mind.

7. What if you want to quit the annuity early? Some insurers pay you only the guaranteed minimum return. Some credit you with all or part of your earnings to date but impose a surrender charge. You might lose money if you withdraw ahead of time. Some annuities let you take 10 percent of your money every year penalty free. Others will make the distribution but build a penalty into your ultimate return. You owe income taxes on the money you take out and a 10 percent penalty if you're under 59½.

8. What are the fees? Hard to tell. There are annual fees, usually up to 2.5 percent, and early withdrawal fees. Ask the salesperson to write them all down for you. Fees are deducted before the insurance company credits you with interest. The sales materials may claim "no commission" but of course you pay one, buried in the fees. Commissions run from 5 to 10 percent and sometimes as high as 15 percent of the money you put in.

9. How are you taxed? It's all ordinary income, even though it's linked to stocks. You don't get the low rate on capital gains.

10. What if the investment shows a loss when it matures? You receive the annuity's minimum guarantee. It's typically quoted as "1.5 percent," but 1.5 percent of what? You assume that it's 1.5 percent of the money you put in, but it's often not. It could be 1.5 percent of 90 percent of your investment. For 5- to 10-year holding periods, that works out to a guarantee of 0.43 to 1 percent a year. Assuming 3 percent inflation, you have a loss—not in nominal capital but in purchasing power. (If an annuity guarantees 6 percent, which sounds terrific, it might be 6 percent on only 30 percent of your investment—but you have to probe to find out.)

There's one risk here that I don't know how to evaluate. Insurers usually hedge their obligations to pay with a variety of financial instruments. In unusual markets (think 2008), these instruments can behave in unusual ways. Any unexpected losses will adhere to the insurer, not you. But the insurer may recoup by reducing the percentage of stock market growth with which it credits your contract. So be very clear about your minimum guarantee.

An Alternative to an Equity-Indexed Annuity. Divide your money between a fixed annuity and a stock-owning mutual fund in a way that guarantees that you'll get your total investment back plus a chance of capital gain. Here's an example of that strategy, with thanks to Peter Katt, a fee-only life insurance adviser:

Assume that you start with $100,000 to invest. Put $64,333 into a 10-year fixed annuity earning 4.5 percent. At the end of the term, you'll have your $100,000 back. Put the other $35,667 into a well-diversified stock-owning mutual fund. Over the term, the odds are that your stock fund will rise in value— so you'll lose nothing *and* will have a gain that's taxed at the low capital gains rate. If your stocks fall in value, you still have $100,000 and can hold the stocks for an even longer term, waiting for recovery.

A Word About the Brokers, Agents, and Financial Planners Who Sell Equity-Indexed Annuities. Some of them know how flaky this investment is and don't care. Others don't know—they simply trust what the insurance company told them. When they find out what happens to some of their customers, they're shocked and quit selling the product. I do blame salespeople for not understanding what they sell, but the ultimate responsibility for this toxic waste lies with the insurance companies and securities firms—a cynical crowd.

Variable Annuities—Bad Buys on Their Own, Risky with Income Guarantees

On the surface, variable annuities (VAs) seem heaven-sent to anyone who buys mutual funds. You generally start the annuity with $10,000 or $15,000, depending on the company. That money is invested in mutual funds—subaccounts, in annuityspeak—and accumulate tax deferred. There's the usual range of investment choices: U.S. stocks, international stocks, bonds, and a balanced stock-and-bond portfolio. You pick your own mix and can typically switch whenever the spirit moves you. Or you can ask the company to allocate your assets for you. Your money grows tax deferred.

The rage today is for VAs with income guarantees. You're promised a fixed, minimum income for life, with the chance that your income might rise if the stock market does well. Put another way, you can win, but you can't lose. Supposedly.

Why am I down on variable annuities? Because they cost too much, raise your taxes, deliver mediocre long-term returns, and are often sold deceptively. Is that enough to start with? I see a niche for low-load annuities (page 1087), but it's a small one.

I'll discuss the popular income-guarantee riders on page 1088. First let me explain the VA itself.

A variable annuity is a mutual fund investment in an insurance wrapper. You pay extra to buy your funds this way. Diversified U.S. stock funds often charge 1 percent (and less than 0.5 percent if you buy no-loads). Most variable annuities charge 2 percent or more.

Sales expenses and profits account for most of the extra cost. The rest is insurance. You're buying a built-in option to convert your annuity into a monthly lifetime income at some point in the future. That's money wasted. First, you might not want to convert to a lifetime income. Second, you can use ordinary savings to buy a lifetime income any time you want. The VA cost also includes a guarantee that if you die before a certain age (say, 75), your heirs will collect at least as much money as you originally invested, minus any money you've already taken out. This so-called benefit, however, is seldom needed or used. Over a typical annuity holding period, it's rare for the contract to wind up with less money than you started with years earlier.

The extra cost of a VA lowers your investment return. You'd be richer if you bought those same mutual funds outside the annuity. When you withdraw money from the annuity, it's taxed as ordinary income. Your gains in outside funds are taxed at the low capital gains rate. What's more, annuity holders lose their flexibility. If an emergency comes up and you need to take money out, you might pay a stiff penalty. If it's in outside mutual funds, you have access to the money all the time.

But, but, but—you say—inside the annuity, gains are tax deferred. True. But it takes 15 to 25 years for the value of the tax deferral to exceed the annuity's extra tax and investment cost. The higher your tax bracket, the more you lose by giving up the low capital gains rate, and the worse annuities look.

But, but, but—you say—my heirs get a money-back guarantee if I die early. Yes, and you pay for it excessively. You're depriving yourself of retirement income *just in case* the account shrinks in value *and* you die early *and* it's important to leave the original amount to your heirs. Is that a good trade-off, when you think it through?

So . . . Who Is a Variable Annuity Really For?

■ *Someone who buys in his or her 30s or early 40s, holds until 65 or 70, and turns the accumulated savings into an income for life.* With this strategy, you'll outperform investors who purchase their mutual funds outside the annuity. But do buyers like this actually exist?

■ *An active mutual fund trader who trades so often that he or she usually earns short-term capital gains, taxed at ordinary income rates.* There aren't a lot of these, either.

- *Someone making a large, long-term investment for a child or grandchild.* Instead of giving $10,000 cash, you might put it into a VA. When the child passes 59½, a lovely nest egg will await.

- *Someone, er, um, well . . . that's about it.* I can't think of anyone else for whom a VA works.

VAs do *not* work for people in their 50s to 70s, who will pay the high costs but can't hold the investment long enough to reap the benefits. In other words, they're wrong for most of the people who buy them today.

VAs sold to people in their 80s or higher, with long surrender periods, may be illegal transactions. The rules say that VA sales have to be "suitable" for the buyer. They're not suitable if the buyer is unlikely to outlive the surrender period or needs a regular income to cover bills. If you or a parent winds up in this situation, use the resources of your state insurance department or FINRA to try to get a refund. (Go to www.finra.org if you bought through a securities firm. If you bought from an insurance agent, find your state insurance office at www.naic.org.)

VAs get especially complicated if you have to enter a nursing home. A deferred annuity is counted as an asset that has to be spent before you can qualify for Medicaid.

Annuities invested in bond funds are just as problematic as those invested in stocks. With bonds, your tax rate is the same whether you buy the annuity or not. But the cost of the annuity depresses your returns. It might still take you 20 years to outperform a bond fund purchased outside the annuity.

If you already have a variable annuity, you generally shouldn't cash it in. You've paid the price; stick around for the investment gain. Start withdrawals as late as you can, and take the money over several years to keep the tax deferral running longer. If you annuitize—turn it into an income for life—it should beat an outside mutual fund if you exceed your life expectancy.

But be warned: anyone with an annuity is a sitting dupe. Within a few years, your broker or planner will probably suggest that you switch to another, "better" annuity, in a tax-free exchange. If you bite, you'll pay another commission (although, as usual, the commission is hidden so that you won't realize how much you've paid). The penalty period on withdrawals will start all over again—raising the risk that you'll have to pay for access to your own money if you need it to pay bills.

The Low-Load Annuity Advantage

If you think you're a candidate for an annuity, go low-load. Their costs are small, compared with the rest of the products on the market, and you can take out your money whenever you want, without paying a penalty. Low costs, total flexibility. Why would you look at anything else? It may take only 10 or 12 years for a low-load to start doing better than outside mutual funds, after tax.

Low-load annuities are available through fee-only financial planners. Here are five low loads you can buy yourself:

- The Vanguard Variable Annuity (www.vanguard.com; 877-662-7447).
- Fidelity Personal Retirement Annuity (www.fidelity.com; 800-544-2442).
- T. Rowe Price Deferred Variable Annuity (www.troweprice.com; 800-469-5304).
- Ameritas No-Load Variable Annuity (www.ameritasdirect.com; 800-555-4655).
- TIAA-CREF Intelligent Variable Annuity (www.tiaa-cref.org; 877-276-9429).

Taking Your Money out of an Annuity When You Retire

The insurance company gives you several options:

- *Take a lump sum.*
- *Take the money in a fixed number of guaranteed payments.* If you die before the term ends, a beneficiary can collect the remaining payments.
- *Take a fixed monthly income for life,* for yourself or yourself and a beneficiary.
- *Take a lifetime income,* including a guaranteed payment for a *period certain,* such as the first 10 years. If you die before the period is up, a beneficiary will collect the payments for the remaining term.
- *Take systematic withdrawals based on your life expectancy,* if your contract allows it. At 65 you will—on average—reach almost 85. So you draw on your annuity as if you had about 20 years to live. By 75, your life expectancy will have lengthened to almost 87, which changes the size of the monthly payments you can take. If the annuity also covers your spouse, payments can be jiggered to reflect your joint life expectancy. You can also take extra payments from time to time. If the value of your investment drops, however, the annuity may expire earlier than you expected. Note that your interest rate isn't locked in. If you're using a fixed annuity, it will change from year to year. If you have a variable annuity, you'll get whatever the contract earns.

- *Alternatively, when you first buy the annuity,* you can attach a flexible lifetime income rider, explained below.

The New, Attractive Nuisance:
Variable Annuities with Lifetime Income Options

This is a difficult subject to write about. On the one hand, the option sounds irresistible to baby boomers looking toward retirement. You get safety of principal, a guaranteed lifetime income, potential for growth in your investment, and access to your money if your circumstances change. Your income can rise but never fall. You always get at least 100 percent of your original investment back. If you die, any money remaining in the contract goes to your heirs.

What's not to like? Plenty, as I'll explain.

This is a simplified version of how these annuities work. The mechanics are far more complicated than the versions I'm giving here. Each contract has its own wrinkles, so the companies are hard to compare. The prospectus that "explains" how your future income and benefits are figured is incomprehensible (never a good sign). But in general, here's what you're being sold:

- *The guaranteed minimum lifetime withdrawal benefit*—by far the most popular choice today. It's for people who want to start withdrawing an income from their annuity right away or after a limited number of years. It's sold, especially, to new retirees who are rolling over an IRA or 401(k) account.

This benefit lets you withdraw a fixed percentage of your original investment each year—typically 5 percent but sometimes more—regardless of how well the investments in your annuity perform. That's not a 5 percent return *on* your investment, as some buyers think. It's a fixed-dollar payout from your annuity account. If you invest $100,000, for example, you'll get $5,000 a year (5 percent). Your annuity is invested in stocks and bonds. In a year when its value rises substantially, that $5,000 will be paid partly out of your investment earnings. In a year when your annuity's value rises only modestly or falls, $5,000 will be paid partly or entirely out of your original capital.

Your guaranteed lifetime monthly withdrawal amount might increase, but only if the value of your investments rises by more than a certain amount. You'll need a spousal rider if you want the withdrawals to last for your spouse's lifetime too. If you need more money, you can withdraw more than the guaranteed minimum at any time, but in that case you'll lose the lifetime-income guarantee.

If you die before your original investment has been returned, the remainder is paid to a beneficiary. (The death benefit is calculated in a variety of ways, depending on the contract.) You have to pay careful attention to how the annuity is titled if you want any benefits to go to your spouse—see page 1093.

What's not to like? Let me count the ways:

1. The fee$$$. You're probably paying 3.75 percent (or more!) for the annuity, plus the withdrawal option, plus the death benefit. You'll pay even more if you want your spouse to be able to collect the lifetime withdrawal too. Typically, the contract includes a minimum and a maximum fee. If you're paying the minimum, the insurer can increase it at any time (at this writing, costs are going up).

2. False hope of gain. You're expecting the market value of your annuity to rise, which would mean that your future monthly withdrawals could increase. That's called a *step-up* in the annuity world. But your chance of earning a step-up is poorer than you think. You're taking out, say, 5 percent a year in current income and paying 3.75 percent in fees. For your income to grow, the investments in your annuity have to earn *more than* 8.75 percent annually. If you do earn a step-up, your percentage fee might step up too.

You might earn that 8.75 percent over time if you invest your entire annuity in stocks. The salesperson will probably show you that scenario, to make the deal look good. More likely, you'll invest in a balanced portfolio of stocks and bonds, which is unlikely to yield the high returns you'll need. Basically, you're probably buying a fixed lifetime income at a much higher price than you'd pay if you bought a simple, old-fashioned, immediate-pay annuity. If you want to get out of the investment, you'll pay a surrender charge.

I priced a comparison between a VA with lifetime benefits and an immediate-pay annuity for a 66-year-old man—both of them guaranteeing $500 a month for life. The difference will surprise you. The fancy VA contract cost $109,900. The immediate-pay annuity cost only $66,900—for the same minimum benefit! Ah, you say, but VA gives you access to your money if you want it, while the immediate-pay annuity locks you in. I say that's a pretty high price to pay for access.

So . . . here's a better idea: Buy the immediate annuity for $66,900. Put the remaining $43,000 into a mix of money market funds and diversified stock-owning mutual funds. The money market funds give you ready access to cash. The stock funds give you long-term growth. The tax rate on the gains is much lower than you'd pay on gains in the annuity. *And* you get the same amount of guaranteed income for life.

▪ *The guaranteed minimum income benefit*—for people who want a future lifetime income, guaranteed. The insurance company promises that after a certain number of years, you can opt for a guaranteed minimum level of monthly payments, regardless of how well the market performs. For example, say that you're guaranteed 5 percent compounded annually over 10 years. When 10 years are up, you have two choices: (1) Take the actual dollar value of the annuity in a lump sum. It might be worth more or less than your guarantee (probably less, after annual expenses of 2.5 to 3 percent). (2) Turn the investment into a lifetime income (or an income for a fixed number of years), based on the 5 percent guarantee. The guarantee is good, even if the investments didn't perform that well, after expenses.

What's not to like? This rider is often sold deceptively. You think that if you annuitize, your payments will be based on a 5 percent return after expenses. Actually, you'll get less because of the way the insurance company prices the annuity. Your effective return might be something closer to 3 percent, but you'd have to be an actuary to figure it out. These deals are cheats. You might do better by cashing out and buying a lifetime annuity elsewhere. You might also decide—when the term comes to an end—that you don't want to annuitize after all. In either case, you'll have paid all those fees for nothing.

■ *The guaranteed minimum accumulation benefit*—for people who want absolute safety plus a chance for their money to grow. The insurance company guarantees that after 10 years, your annuity will be worth at least what you paid for it, even if your investments have declined in value.

What's not to like? The fee you pay for this rider is a waste of money. I asked Alexa Auerbach of Ibbotson Associates the following question: What's the chance that a well-diversified investor will lose money over 120 months (10 years), with dividends reinvested? She tested three portfolios—all Treasury bonds, all stocks (Standard & Poor's 500-stock index), and a 50-50 split between stocks and bonds—over 376 periods, starting in 1965. Guess what? You *never* would have lost any money, even in the worst month of the 2008 collapse. Most 10-year returns were in the triple digits. You're probably paying the insurance company for nothing.

Complaints filed with regulators about these annuities are riding high, sales materials are murky, and the products are hard to understand—not only by you but by the brokers and planners who sell them. Complicated products almost always disappoint, especially those that carry high sales commissions! I recommend *against*.

A Danger to the Insurance Industry? These new and untested guarantees are risky for insurance companies too. Back in 2002, two insurers got into serious trouble by selling variable annuities with a guaranteed death benefit. The stock market performed poorly, and the companies unexpectedly had to come up with more capital to support the contracts. No consumer lost money (fortunately), but the companies almost failed. Today's new, living-benefit contracts are even riskier to an insurer's health, not only due to market risk but because it's not expensive for consumers to withdraw extra money from the annuities. The industry could be courting trouble all over again. In fact, several insurers struggled during the 2008 market collapse. The companies offering the highest and best guarantees are usually the most vulnerable. They're already raising fees, which lowers the benefits that investors can expect.

You Shouldn't Think About Buying Even a Low-Load Variable Annuity Unless You Can Answer All of the Following Questions "Yes"

- *Have you put the maximum into your tax-deferred retirement plan?* That comes first because those contributions can be deducted from tax. You might also want to add any after-tax money that your plan accepts.
- *Have you funded a Roth IRA if* you're eligible?
- *Will you start young enough to make the annuity's tax deferral pay?* For regular annuities, you usually need a holding period of 15 years or more; for low-load annuities, 10 years or more.
- *Will you invest the annuity money entirely in stocks?* You need superior long-term gains to overcome the annuity's costs and yield a halfway decent return.
- *Will you leave the annuity alone until you reach 59½?* Prior withdrawals will cost you a 10 percent tax penalty.
- *Is this investment primarily for you rather than for your heirs?* If not, your heirs would rather you bought straight mutual funds. They'll owe income taxes on the deferred gains in inherited annuities. They could receive unrealized gains in mutual funds income-tax free.
- *Is your tax bracket high?* In low brackets, variable annuities may never outperform mutual funds outside the annuity.

Are Your Variable Annuities Safe?

Yes, if you mean safe from an insurance company failure. The assets are held in a separate account. The value of your annuity is based on the value of the assets behind it. Your lifetime-income guarantees should be good if your company is taken over by another insurer, but it's unclear what would happen if your company went into receivership.

If You Already Have an Annuity, Should You Switch to a New One?

Yes, if you're in a fixed-rate annuity and the insurer is stiffing you with a truly rotten rate—say, 3 percent in a 4.5 percent world. Switch to a CD-type annuity instead.

Yes, if you're in a high-cost variable annuity and will switch to a low-load annuity.

Probably, if you're in a high-cost variable annuity and keep all your money in its bond and fixed-income accounts. You might net more by switching to a fixed annuity, after costs.

Probably not, if you're in a fixed annuity and are tempted by the potentially higher returns you might get in a variable annuity sold by a broker. To get those higher returns, after costs, you have to hold the annuity for at least 15 years and often more. You also have to invest your annuity money entirely in stocks. Will you actually do that? If so, skip the broker and buy a low-load annuity.

No, if you're in a fixed annuity, like the interest rate, and aren't a risk taker. Stay where you are. There's nothing in a variable annuity that you really want. Don't switch to a new fixed annuity, either, just for a high first-year bonus rate. That bonus may raise your yield by only a minuscule amount over a 10-year holding period. What's more, insurers with eye-popping first-year rates on fixed deferred annuities might drop your rate into the cellar once they've got you in their clutches.

No, if you're near the end of the period when you'll owe surrender fees. From that point on, you'll be able to take out your money without penalty. If you buy another annuity, the penalty period will start all over again. Not surprisingly, this is just the moment when an agent is likely to approach you.

No, if the agent pitches you on a new variable annuity without explaining the costs and risks that this chapter talks about. I've spoken in generalities; the agent should lay out everything in dollars and cents. Also *no* if the agent has switched you before and proposes to do it again. You're being churned. That means your money is being turned over to earn the agent a commission, not to get you a better deal.

If You Do Switch Annuities, Do a 1035 tax-free exchange. The low-load annuity company, or your agent, will handle the paperwork.

If You Inherit an Annuity, How Are You Taxed?

If you inherit a tax-deferred annuity from your spouse, you have all the same withdrawal options that your spouse would have had. You can keep the annuity, switch to another one (in a tax-free exchange), or take the money out on whatever schedule the contract permits. Ordinary income taxes are due on the earnings when the money is withdrawn.

If you inherit an annuity and are not the spouse—say, you received it from your mother or a domestic partner—you have three options:

1. Take all the money, over no more than five years from the time you inherited. You're taxed when you take the money out. The first payments are treated entirely as taxable earnings. Once you've taken all the earnings, the final payments are a tax-free return of the capital originally invested in the contract.

2. Take systematic withdrawals based on your life expectancy, if your contract allows it. Each year, you take out the amount that's appropriate for your age or a larger amount if you need the money. This option stretches out your payments *and* gives you flexibility, although there's no guarantee that the money will last for life. As with the five-year payout, the first payments are treated as taxable earnings, with the final payments a tax-free return of capital.

3. Buy an immediate-pay annuity (either fixed or variable—page 1124). This choice gives you an income for life, no matter how long you live. It's also the most tax efficient. Part of each payment is taxable income, and part is a tax-free return of capital.

Have You Accidentally Disinherited Your Spouse? Or Left Your Spouse Without the Annuity Benefits He or She Expects?

Many a married couple is going to be in for a surprise. When one of you dies, the annuity may not behave the way you think. These contracts are complicated, with lots of moving parts. Unless you buy right—and title the annuity correctly—you might not get all the benefits that you thought you paid for. It's even possible that the money invested in the annuity will bypass your spouse and go to your kids. A 2007 study by Advanced Sales Corporation, a variable-annuity research firm, found that more than one-third of VAs are titled incorrectly and could create serious problems for heirs. One of those VAs may be yours.

To get the inheritance questions right, it helps to know the parties to the contract:

- *The contract owner*—the person who buys the annuity (that's you) and chooses the annuitant and the beneficiaries. There can be joint owners, or the annuity can be owned by a trust.

- *The annuitant*—the person on whose life the future payments are based. You can be both the owner and the annuitant, or someone else can be the annuitant. When payouts are made, the annuitant's life expectancy rules. If the owner dies, the annuitant's beneficiaries collect.
- *The beneficiary*—the person or persons entitled to inherit the money contained in the annuity if the owner or annuitant dies.

What can go wrong? Try these examples:

- *Say that you buy one of the hot, new annuities with minimum withdrawal benefits guaranteed for your single life.* That's the way that most annuities are sold. If you die, your spouse will get the value of the annuity (perhaps with a death benefit, depending on what the contract says). He or she will be able to keep the investment, letting it grow tax deferred. But your spouse will probably not be able to continue the lifetime withdrawals that you signed up for. That may come as an unwelcome surprise.

A quick example may be helpful here. Say that a husband invests $100,000 in an annuity, with a guaranteed withdrawal of at least $5,000 a year for life. Then he dies. The wife inherits the underlying investment at whatever value the contract assigns. She can keep the annuity, exchange it for another one, or withdraw the money—whatever she wants. But she cannot continue to withdraw $5,000 a year for life unless the annuity benefit includes a spousal continuation option.

The husband may have thought that his wife would get that monthly withdrawal because he named her as beneficiary. But all that does is give her the right to the contract's proceeds. Without a spousal continuation option, the wife is out of luck.

- *Say that you buy an annuity, naming yourself as owner, your spouse as annuitant, and your children as beneficiaries.* If you die, the money invested in the annuity goes to your children, not your spouse. Some contracts dictate that if your spouse dies, the children get the annuity money right away. You lose the investment you made.
- *Say that you buy the annuity, naming yourself as owner and your spouse as annuitant.* Then your spouse dies. In some contracts, the annuity has to be paid out to you. You can't continue it as a tax-deferred investment.
- *Say that you own an annuity and decide to put it into an irrevocable trust.* To do so, you have to retitle it, making the trust the owner. This particular change of ownership triggers income taxes and has to be recorded as a taxable gift as well. (It's safe, however, to put the annuity into a revocable, or living, trust.)

- *Say that you buy an annuity in the name of your revocable trust, with the proceeds payable to the trust.* When you die, the trust pays out to your spouse. Your spouse will owe taxes on the money immediately. The investment cannot be continued tax deferred.

These are only a few examples of the horrors that potentially await. So how do you preserve the annuity's options and proceeds tax deferred?

- *If you want to be sure that your spouse inherits,* both spouses should be named on the annuity as owners, as annuitants, and as primary beneficiaries. Your children or other heirs should be named as secondary beneficiaries, if both of you die.

- *If you buy an annuity with guaranteed lifetime withdrawal benefits* and want your spouse to have those benefits too, get a contract that allows for spousal continuation.

- *Don't mess around with putting annuities into trusts without talking to a lawyer* who specializes in the field.

- *On ordinary transactions, question the salesperson carefully:* What happens if I die or if my spouse dies? Can the annuity investment be continued? If not, who gets the proceeds? When are taxes paid? What do we need to do to get the money to the proper beneficiary? Write down exactly who should receive the annuity's proceeds if you die, and what should happen to any lifetime withdrawal benefits. Ask the salesperson to run it through the insurance company's legal department, so you'll know exactly how to fill out the beneficiary forms. Don't take the salesperson's word on what to do. He or she might have the right answer, but you can't be sure and should have written confirmation from the company. Don't buy if the salesperson balks.

Social Security

You *will* get a Social Security check when you retire. If you doubt me, just look around and count the votes. How many among us would vote to abolish Social Security's safety net? What would be the future of any politician who tried? There's a good deal of talk about privatizing Social Security, leaving beneficiaries to invest for themselves. But I wouldn't take bets on that—especially after the 2008 stock market collapse.

Nevertheless, Social Security probably won't be worth as much when today's fortysomethings retire as it was in the past. You'll still get rising benefits, but they may replace a smaller percentage of your working income than they do today. That's why it's so important to save more money for yourself. You won't get quite as much out of Social Security as your parents and grandparents did. But trust me, what you'll get, you'll need.

Chapter 30, on deploying your money at retirement, tells you how and when to claim Social Security benefits. The question here is how to create the largest benefit you can.

Here's How to Get the Most from Your Social Security Account

1. Pay your taxes! Kids who float from job to job may think it's clever to work "off the books." But like everyone else, they will eventually knock at Social Security's door. When figuring your benefit, Social Security looks at how many (or how few) years you officially held a job during the years you were old enough to work. If your record shows several years of zero participation in the Social Security system, your retirement check will be dragged down. It's sometimes fun to be young and poor but never to be old and poor. So pay those taxes every year.

2. Make sure that Social Security has a record of all your earnings to date. More often than you realize, payment records go awry. Your employer might err when reporting your earnings to Social Security or fail to report them at all. Social Security might err in transferring that record to your account. You might err when giving your Social Security number. In 2006 (latest number available), the Social Security Administration was sitting on a cumulative $745 billion[*] worth of reported wage credits—some of it dating back to 1937—whose owners have never been identified.

Social Security mails you a personal Social Security statement about three months before your birthday, every year. It shows your Social Security earnings record and what your benefits would be if you died or stopped working now. Check it for accuracy. You might see a zero in the most recent year, but that's only because Social Security hasn't posted your current earnings yet. If you see a zero for an earlier year when earnings ought to have been reported, call Social Security to see what to do about it. As long as you can prove that you were employed, you'll be given credit—even if your employer failed to make the required Social Security payments.

If you can't find your latest statement (or didn't get one), go to www.ssa.gov, click on "Your Social Security Earnings Statement," and request a copy online. In you're not online, call 800-772-1213 and follow the prompts.

3. Check the statement to see if you qualify for Social Security benefits at all, and if not, how close you've come. Your statement shows how many

---

[*] That's a big number, but it represented only 0.5 percent of all posted wages.

work credits you need in order to earn a retirement check and how many credits you've racked up so far. A woman who worked many years ago, then dropped out to have children or take care of an elderly parent, may find that—with just a couple more years of full- or part-time work—she'll qualify for a benefit. Having your own account may not matter if you can collect on the account of a present or former spouse (page 1134). But it matters a lot if you don't have that to fall back on.

4. Make your personal planning decisions in light of what Social Security is likely to pay. Here, too, the answers you get from your personal earnings statement will help. It discloses: (1) your estimated monthly retirement benefit (stated in today's dollars) at three different ages: 62, full retirement age (currently about 66), and 70; (2) the likely survivor benefits for your family if you die in the current year; and (3) what you might get in disability pay if you became totally and permanently disabled.

The deeper you move into middle age, the more critical this information becomes. Once you know how much income you can count on, you'll get a better fix on how much more you have to save.

5. Keep on truckin'. You can file for benefits as early as 62. But that permanently reduces your Social Security check—currently, by 25 percent. The older you are when you first file for benefits, the higher your benefits will be.

Looked at one way, early retirement makes sense. You collect a lot of money in those years between 62 and 66. If you wait until 66, you retire with a bigger check, but 10 or 12 years may pass before you make up for the 4 years of early-retirement pay you did without.

Looked at another way, however, early retirement makes no financial sense at all unless you're bored or ill or can't find work. On the job, you are earning more than your retired colleagues get, and your salary adds to the size of your future Social Security check.

Would You Be Better Off if Social Security Were Privatized?

Many people imagine that they'd have more money if they could ditch Social Security. "Just give me my contribution and my employer's, and I could invest for a higher income," they say. I doubt it. To begin with, you probably wouldn't invest it all. You'd spend some. Some would be thrown away on bad investments. You might be crushed in a bear market (think 2008). Some might invest too conservatively. In the end, you'd probably fail to build the enormous sum needed to pay yourself a Social Security–equivalent income that would keep up with the inflation rate for the rest of your life. And if you failed, what then?

Even if you could amass this money, many of your fellow citizens couldn't.

You might be okay, but a large group of seniors would be broke—just as they were before Social Security began. Welfare payments would soar.

Without Social Security, you'd also lose the survivor benefits paid to your spouse and children if you die. Those checks keep many struggling young families afloat. You'd also lose disability payments if you became so ill or badly injured that you couldn't work.

Despite all the scare stories you read, Social Security isn't in serious trouble. Everyone knows what it's going to take to keep the system going: a small additional payroll tax plus trimming future benefits in a modest way. Eventually it will get done. Compulsory Social Security protects part of everyone's old-age income from the hazards of life, and we should be grateful for it. Without it, large numbers of our elderly would live poor.

Making It Last

Still Living Rich at 99

**If you ever needed a plan for your money, you
need it now. You earned it. You saved it. Now
it's time to keep it safe and spend it well.**

Here you are, at the very lip of retirement or beyond. You have pretty much defined your future standard of living by the money you saved and invested. But it's not over yet! You still have plans to lay and choices to make. The stock market may have hurt you or helped you during these crucial pre- and post-retirement years. How you handle your pension and investments, and how fast you draw down your savings, will make a huge difference to your comfort for years to come. Managing retirement money seems daunting at first, but I'll show you ways to simplify.

Early Retirement: American Dream, American Nightmare

You may have no choice about when to retire. You may be laid off, or your company might close. You might get sick, or your spouse might and you have to stay home to provide care.

Or you might have an apparent choice. An early-retirement bonus might be offered to anyone willing to take the leap. If you say no, your job could continue as usual. But then again, it might not.

Or you might jump yourself, without being pushed. Some people point their entire savings and investment programs toward bailing out of the workforce at 55.

The Truth Is, You Can't Retire at 55

Correction: you probably can't.

It takes a tremendous amount of money to be able to quit early—far more than you think. Until you sit down with a calculator (or an accountant or financial planner), you won't appreciate how much capital you're going to need, especially when future inflation is factored in.

If you have no children to educate, own your home free and clear, have savings and secure investments worth $1 million or more, live modestly, and have employer-subsidized health insurance, maybe you can do it. If you're lucky enough to have a guaranteed pension, you can make it on less. Especially if you expect a large inheritance.

Short of that, you should figure on staying at work. Even if you retire early on an inflation-indexed government pension, you'll probably need another job.

The very earliest that most employees can even consider shaking loose—assuming that their company pays early retirement benefits—is 55. If you're due a pension, it will probably amount to half the size or less of what you'd receive at 65. Social Security doesn't start until 62, and then at a reduced rate (page 1133). By quitting work early, you'll have fewer years of earnings, which may reduce your Social Security benefit even more. You will get penalty-free access to your employee retirement plans, such as 401(k)s and 403(b)s. To tap an IRA, you have to wait until you're 59½ or else start lifetime withdrawals now.

But will this money really last for the rest of your life?

To Retire Early . . .

Here's what you need for the life of leisure you intend:

1. Health insurance, to carry you to 65 and Medicare. Corporations may provide health plans for retirees. If not, you can usually stay in the group plan, at your expense, for up to 18 months. After that, however, you will have to find your own individual plan. For more on finding health insurance in middle age, see page 430.

2. A pension. If early retirement is your overriding goal, it helps to work most of your life for an employer who offers a traditional pension as well as a 401(k). Job-hoppers can lose significant pension benefits. A government pension would serve you best, thanks to its cost-of-living increases. Corporate pensions usually come in fixed dollars that erode from the day you start collecting.

3. A major nest egg, invested in a mix of stocks and bonds. To feel reasonably sure that the money will last for 40 years, you should withdraw no more than 3 percent of the money the first year and add an inflation adjustment for each year after that. Keep to your program, even in years when the stock market goes up. You need your money to grow so that you can keep up withdrawals in years the market drops. For a 30-year retirement, start with a withdrawal of 4 percent. If you take 10 percent because you need the money . . . well, when you run out, I hope your kids will take you in.

4. No kids at home. All the expenses of raising and educating your children should be behind you. Your adult children should be *off your payroll!*

5. Life insurance if you're married. Your spouse may not be able to live on the reduced pension and Social Security left behind if you die first, especially if you're forced to eat into your capital. Perhaps you should convert your term insurance to whole life (chapter 12). If you bought an insurance policy years ago and believe it's "paid up," *please* check. A lot of these policies are actually busted. Their investments didn't accumulate enough cash to keep them going, so they're gradually running out. Your spouse may get only a fraction of what you'd planned—and maybe nothing at all. The time to find out is *now*.

6. No debt. Wind down your credit cards while you still have a paycheck and make a plan for getting rid of your mortgage either before you retire or soon after. If you still have a big mortgage, consider refinancing it over 30 years to bring down your monthly payments.

7. Low housing expenses. Consider selling your house, buying a smaller one or a condominium for cash, and investing the proceeds that remain. Or move to a lower-cost part of the country. Or move to Mexico or Costa Rica. One moneymaking idea, if you think you'd be a successful landlord: buy a two-family house, live in one half, and rent out the other half (but check the laws on rent control and eviction first—and see page 990). Or find a roommate to share expenses. Living on a sailboat works, as long as you're healthy enough to hoist the sails. You might sell your house, invest the proceeds, and move into a rental. That eliminates all those upkeep costs that make home owning such a money pit.

8. Low living expenses. Early retirees need simple tastes. Cheap entertainments. Only one car (or no car at all; use taxis, subways, and buses). Life in the country, where real estate taxes are low. I don't mean to make this sound like a downer, but you have to be very clear in your mind that—without successful stock options, a big inheritance, or a winning lottery ticket—quitting work means keeping to a slender budget.

9. A job! Forget "early retirement" in its classic, freebooting sense. Think about earning enough money to fill the gap between your retirement income (pension, interest, dividends) and your expenses so you can leave your capital alone to grow. Some companies rehire their own retirees for temporary work on specific projects. Many senior citizen centers keep lists of companies that seek older people for occasional work. If the job is covered by Social Security, so much the better. That beefs up the retirement benefit that you'll get at 62.

10. A spending and investment plan worked out with a fee-only financial planner. Don't try to doodle this by yourself on a yellow pad. Taxes, inflation, interest rates, the size of your savings, and the sources of your income all have a bearing on whether you can afford to retire. If you do quit work, you need to know quite specifically what your savings must yield to keep you afloat, how much you have to earn, what you can afford to spend, and where to cut back if the value of your investments falls. That's a job for a professional. If you spend too much in your early-retirement years, you'll eventually descend into poverty.

Beware the Financial "Adviser" Who Hustles You to Retire *Now*

It's a cynical game. An adviser (always a commissioned salesperson) will look at your 401(k) and other savings and tell you that you can afford to quit your job much earlier than you thought. He or she will show you high-yielding investments that seem to pay the very same income as you're earning at work. All you have to do is retire, pour your 401(k) money into an IRA, and let the adviser manage the money. You'll be put on a program of regular cash withdrawals, which seems to fulfill your dream.

It's a fake, of course. Typically, the adviser buys a costly variable annuity with the highest monthly payout option he or she can find. There's also a mix of aggressive mutual funds. Your withdrawal rate will be set at perhaps 8 or 9 percent of your total investment, with increases promised after five years. You imagine that the income will last for life. By the time you realize that it won't—that, in fact, you're going to run out of money—you've given up not only your job but most of your savings too.

Don't let anyone sell you an early-retirement scheme. It's not true that "anyone can retire early." Test your readiness with the rules of thumb you'll find in this chapter, and don't leave your job until you've asked a fee-only financial planner if it's going to work (page 1171).

Does Your Company Allow Phased Retirements?

Some companies let you step back from your current job into something less taxing. You're still on the payroll (and on the health insurance plan!), but your hours may be shorter or the projects longer term. You'll take a pay cut. But the company may let you start receiving part of your pension—called an *in-*

service distribution—if you're 62 or older (or normal early-retirement age if it's younger than 62). Phased retirements aren't common, but you may see more large companies offering this option as a way of keeping talent when the boomers start to retire en masse.

The Golden Boot

Not all early retirees have a choice.

You may arrive at work one morning to learn that your company has opened an early-retirement window for everyone 50 and up. Typically, you have 30 to 90 days to jump (or be politely shoved). If you leave, you'll get bonuses not normally available. Should you take the offer?

As you sit at your desk, with your heart beating a little faster, ask yourself the following three questions:

Question One: Do I really want to retire (or at least leave this job)?

If the answer is yes, see a fee-only financial planner and work out the arithmetic. This window may fit perfectly with your plans. If the answer is no . . .

Question Two: What happens if I stay?

In the bosses' minds, all employees are divided into "greenwood" and "deadwood." Some they want to keep and grow; others they want to chop away. But they can't walk down the hall saying, "You, you, and you, retire early!" without running afoul of the age discrimination laws. So it's up to you to guess their intent.

Take it for granted that deals have been offered indirectly to particular employees ("Congratulations, you're due for a double bonus next year and a vice presidency will be opening up"). If nothing like that has come your way, drop by your boss's office for a chat. What's the future of your department? Is your job subject to reorganization? What's your next promotion? Is your boss going to stay or go? If the vibes say "stay," you might want to chance it. Someone has to keep the shop open. If the vibes say "go," don't hesitate.* You might lose your job anyway, and without a good-bye bonus. To collect your bonus, you may have to sign an agreement not to sue under the Age Discrimination in Employment Act. Asking you to sign is legal.

Question Three: Where do I get advice?

Don't try to figure out the finances yourself. Your company's employee benefits office may have hired an explainer for the duration. Alternatively, see a fee-

---

*Always go if your new boss is 20 years younger than you are.

only financial planner (not a salesperson—page 1176) who can analyze the offer objectively. Anyone given the Golden Boot might be offered several incentives. Typically, they include a higher pension than you've actually earned; severance pay, based on your salary and years of service; a modest life insurance policy; and health insurance (partly at your expense) until you're eligible for Medicare. You'll get your 401(k) money and your vested pension, if any. If you have choices about your pension, the planner will help you make them.

Despite all these goodies, early retirees get the short end of the money stick. Even if you're 60 and are offered the pension of a 65-year-old, you'll lose five years of salary, which would have paid a lot more than the pension does. You also lose five years of earnings that would have bolstered your Social Security check. Still, a Golden Boot is a leg up for anyone with other work in mind. Taking this income as a base, you can write a book, start a business, or accept a lower-paying job that offers you more satisfaction.

The Early-Retirement Checklist Works for Later Retirees Too

With a later retirement, you'll be better off because you'll have built up more savings. Your 401(k) and any pension will be worth more too. You'll get a larger Social Security check. You may not need earnings from a part-time job. If you're 65, you can go directly to Medicare without having to shell out for private insurance. Still, go through your budget carefully. Happy retirements founder when you overspend.

If You're Married, Will You Retire at the Same Time?

Often the answer is no. And almost as often, the person who wants to keep working is the wife. She may be younger than her husband, or she may have been out of the workforce when the kids were young and now is happy to be back. The husband will have to figure out how to spend his time. (Hint: waiting around for his wife to come home and make dinner shouldn't be an option.)

There are lots of pluses when one of the couple keeps his or her job. Having a paycheck makes it easier to transition into a retirement budget. The retired spouse doesn't have to start taking Social Security right away—a delay that will raise your mutual income in the future (page 1134). The worker may have health insurance—worth its weight in gold. The retiree might get involved in volunteer work that will lead to new lives for both of you.

Getting It Together: Your Assets and Your Spending Plan

Early retirement or late, you now face the ultimate reality test. Your capital and life circumstances are pretty much known. What can be squeezed out of your resources? How much can you afford to spend each year so that you won't run out of money? And how should you spend it?

These simple questions involve some extraordinary choices, which will affect your personal comfort for the rest of your life. You'll have to decide:

- How much can you afford to spend?
- What's the best way of taking money out of your various tax-deferred retirement plans—lump sum, deferred payments, or lifetime annuity?
- How should your retirement savings be invested?
- Who should invest those savings for you?
- Should you keep your present house or sell it?
- What rate of inflation should you assume?
- When should you take your Social Security benefits?
- What do you do about health insurance if there's no retiree plan?
- How do you handle company stock or stock options?

None of these questions has just one answer. You'll need to test one set of possibilities against another to see how the alternatives play out. When you have only a couple of choices, you can often make the right decision yourself. But for complex and multiple choices, I don't recommend flying solo. God hasn't made enough erasers and yellow pads for you to work this out alone. If you make a mistake, you might run out of money in old age.

Fortunately, God is making more fee-only financial planners (page 1176). Go see one. Ask for advice. He or she can lay out every choice: What net income you'd get from various types of pension plan distributions. What your retirement plan rollover choices are. How much capital you can round up to invest. What investment yield you can expect from your capital. Whether it pays to sell your house. What inflation will do to your purchasing power. Whether you should look for a part-time job. Don't begrudge the expense of the analysis. At this stage of life, it's not only the best investment you could make, it will also save you a ton of money in the end.

Be sure to work with an adviser who charges flat fees for his or her time, not someone who sells financial products. Salespeople are biased toward lump sum withdrawals from retirement plans because that gives you money to buy the investments they sell, even when it's objectively better to leave your money with the company. They're also biased toward selling variable annuities (ugh!) because they pay such high commissions. You need a cooler head.

Once you've nailed down your income and assets, you have to shape a budget to match. Chapter 8 should help you go about it. When listing your outlays, don't look back at your old life, look ahead to your new one. The differences are going to surprise you.

Retirement spending is totally unlike workaday spending. That's why you can often live comfortably on 75 percent of what you earned before. Your house may be paid for. Your children are gone (one devoutly hopes). Fires may no longer burn in your breast for classier furniture, show-off cars, or drop-dead parties. You'll no longer need disability insurance if you have no earnings to replace. With sufficient savings (or no dependents), you won't need life insurance either, which saves you the price of the insurance premiums (although you may want to keep cash-value life or switch to no-lapse life—page 341). You'll buy more sneakers and tracksuits and fewer dresses and suits. Instead of keeping two cars, you may drop to one. You'll eat more meals at home and fewer out. You're not commuting. Your income taxes normally go down* and you won't owe Social Security or Medicare taxes. You'll ease back on holiday gifts. You'll have time to do things yourself that you used to pay other people to do for you. And finally—a big item—you're no longer putting money away for retirement. You've arrived.

Celebrating their freedom, the newly retired often travel. But after a while, that impulse usually quiets down. One essential expense is good health insurance, the cost of which will escalate even if your employer is paying part of the tab. Long-term care insurance needs to be in the budget too. Real estate taxes will rise—a consideration when you're deciding where you're going to live. Your everyday expenses, however, won't go up as much as you think and might even fall. The older you get, the less purchasing power you are likely to need. Your capital will last longer than you might think.

Once you have assembled all your financial resources and all your likely expenses, ask the planner or accountant the following question: "Assuming a reasonable investment return on my savings, and assuming that I want my income to keep up with inflation every year, how much can I afford to spend each year?"

---

*You'll need closer to 90 percent of what you earned before if your income taxes stay the same or rise.

The news might be good.

"Ms. Certain," an accountant might say, "assuming that your savings earn 6 percent and assuming that you want to maintain the purchasing power of a $45,000 income, your money will easily last until your death with a nice chunk left over for your heirs."

With that comforting knowledge, what might Ms. Certain do?

- She might feel free to donate some money to charity.
- She might roll her lump sum pension plan distribution into an IRA and leave it alone to grow.
- She might travel, throw parties, and live it up.
- She will most certainly relax. She knows for sure that, at life's end, she won't be a bag lady on the streets. If she has to enter a nursing home, she'll have enough money to pay the initial bills. Medicaid will carry her if her savings run dry.

On the other hand, the news may be bad.

"Mr. Hopeful," a planner might say, "assuming that your savings earn 6 percent and assuming that you want to maintain the purchasing power of a $45,000 income, you will run out of money in 14 years." That will startle Mr. Hopeful, whose life expectancy might be 24 years. But at least he knows his situation and can start to adjust.

- He might try to increase his return on investment by holding less money in bank savings accounts and more in bond funds and equity-income funds.
- He might take part-time work.
- He might reduce his expenses and live on less.
- He might sell his house, buy something smaller, and use the remaining equity to build up his nest egg.
- He might accept his son's invitation to move into the small apartment over the son's garage—if not now, then maybe 10 years from now.
- If he has a choice, he might change his mind about retiring and stay at work a little longer.

Knowing the limits of your savings gives you tremendous power over your future. You'll know what to do in order to make your retirement work.

For Do-It-Yourselfers

I recommend getting expert help at this critical time of your life. But if your finances are pretty simple, you can work out the budget and the investments yourself. You'll find a good Retirement Income Calculator at www.troweprice

YOUR RETIREMENT SPENDING PLAN

	YOUR PLAN	MY EXAMPLE
1. Social Security	$	$ 15,000*
Pension	$	0
Lifetime annuity	$	0
Earnings, part-time work	$	$ 14,000
Other income†	$	0
Total income	$	$ 29,000
2. First-year retirement expenses, including taxes	$	$ 45,000
3. Gap between income and expenses‡	$	$ 16,000
4. Total savings, in banks, Individual Retirement Accounts, mutual funds, and so on	$	$320,000
5. Percent of total savings needed to fill the gap between this year's income and this year's expenses	$	5%
6. The return on investment that your savings are earning	$	6%
7. Using the table on page 1110§, find out how long your savings will last.	$	20 years

* Social Security benefits rise with inflation, so this number has a small spending cushion built in.
† Don't count income from your savings. That is included later.
‡ If there isn't a gap, you're fine. Go read a murder mystery.
§ Assumes an annual 3 percent inflation rate. For other rates, see pages 1195–1200.

.com. Enter your age and some financial data, and the calculator tells you what you can afford to spend.

The worksheet above offers another approach. All calculations are pretax. If your money won't last as long as you will, you'll have to earn more income, cut spending, or—most probably—do both. Don't swing for the fences by switching to aggressive investments in the hope of creating a fortune in a fortnight. Home runs aren't that frequent. If you strike out, it will be even harder to pay the bills.

Get Real About Your Options!

Preretirees keep saying, "I need such-and-such amount of income from my investments," but if you start with what you think you "need" in the early years, you may run out of money later. The right question is "Given a certain amount of savings and a conservative allocation between stock and bond funds, how much can I afford to spend each year?" You have to match your spending to your resources, not to your desires.

You also have to match your gifting to your resources. While you still had a paycheck, maybe you were helping your grandchildren with tuition. When your paycheck stops, that might not be possible anymore. Don't make gifts that your retirement budget can't support! Explain to your children that things have changed. They'll understand, or should. You're protecting their future, as well as yours, by making sure that you can support yourself in your older age.

What really makes your money last is spending control. Budgets matter more than investments. If you've got a grip on your checkbook, you'll make it through.

How Much of Your Capital Can You Afford to Spend Every Year?

Table 29 on page 1110 shows how long your savings are likely to last in a world of 3 percent inflation. It assumes that you'll start by taking a certain percentage of your total savings. Each subsequent year, you'll take enough additional money to match that year's rise in the Consumer Price Index. For example, say you start with $1,000 in the first year. The second year, you'll take $1,030; in the third year, you'll take $1,060.90, and so on. In Appendix 2, starting on page 1193, you'll find tables with different inflation rates.

Notes to the table

1. Look up your probable life expectancy on the table in Appendix 4 (page 1205). Think about how long your parents and grandparents lived. Pick a likely life span for yourself. That's the period over which you need your money to stretch. Consider your spouse's life span too. To be careful, chart a course that will take at least one of you to age 95.

2. The average rate of return on your nest egg assumes that some investments earn more and some less. Over time, for example, your stock investments might earn 8 percent; your bond investments, 5 percent; and your money market mutual funds, 3 percent. Keep the money you need for 2 or 3 years' living expenses stashed in a money fund. Money you won't touch for 10 years or longer goes into stock funds. The money in between goes into bond funds.

3. Recalculate as inflation changes, based on the current value of your nest egg and the amount you need for expenses. The appendix contains tables for inflation rates from zero to 7 percent.

Table 29.

THE 3 PERCENT SOLUTION

Percentage of Capital Withdrawn In the First Year	WILL LAST THIS MANY YEARS, IF THE ORIGINAL WITH-DRAWAL RISES BY 3% ANNUALLY AND YOUR MONEY IS INVESTED AT THE FOLLOWING AVERAGE RATES OF RETURN									
	3%	4%	5%	6%	7%	8%	9%	10%	11%	12%
2%	50	67	158	#	#	#	#	#	#	#
3%	33	40	52	100	#	#	#	#	#	#
4%	25	28	33	42	71	#	#	#	#	#
5%	20	22	24	29	36	54	#	#	#	#
6%	16	18	19	22	25	31	44	#	#	#
7%	14	16	18	20	22	27	36	#	#	#
8%	13	13	14	15	16	18	20	24	30	#
9%	11	11	12	13	14	15	16	18	21	#
10%	10	10	10	11	12	13	14	15	17	19
11%	9	9	9	10	10	11	12	13	14	15
12%	8	9	9	9	9	10	10	11	12	13
13%	7	7	8	8	8	9	9	10	10	11
14%	7	7	7	7	8	8	8	9	9	10
15%	6	6	7	7	7	7	8	8	8	9

* Assumes a single withdrawal at the start of the year. All the numbers are rounded.

Source: David Kahn, RSM McGladrey.

4. What if it appears that your savings will run out before you do? You can lower your living expenses, raise the returns you're getting from your investment (a plausible answer for anyone holding every dime in cash), or try to earn more money.

To use the table above, add up all the capital on which you are free to draw: bank accounts, retirement plans, and other investments. Decide what percentage of your capital to withdraw this year and find that percentage in the left-hand column. Read across that line to the column showing the average rate of return your money is earning. That shows how many years your capital will last.

As an example, use the retirement spending plan shown in the preceding table and assume that the $320,000 nest egg earns an average of 6 percent pretax. You want $16,000 to help meet your expenses, or 5 percent of your total capital. At an initial 5 percent withdrawal rate, and allowing for a 3 percent average annual increase in the price of everything you buy, your money will last for 29 years. If that's not long enough, you'll have to reduce your spending or get a job. You've hit the wall. It's too late to kid yourself.

How to Take Money Out of Your Retirement Plans

Given a fixed and final retirement sum, the size of your income will depend on two things: (1) the kinds of retirement plans you have and (2) the system you choose for withdrawing the money. Some plans are easy; they offer you no choice at all. More likely, you will have several choices, some better than others. Here's how to get the most from your savings, taking it plan by plan:

Your Defined Benefit Plan

This is the classic pension plan, which pays you a taxable monthly income for the rest of your life. *Corporate pensions* are usually fixed. At retirement, your payment looks generous (or adequate, or stingy, as the case may be). Ten years later, it looks worse because price increases have eroded its purchasing power. Anyone tied to a corporate defined benefit plan had better come armed with a separate pool of savings and investments to make up for the pension's unstoppable losses to inflation. *Government pensions,* by contrast, often have annual cost-of-living adjustments, although the increases may be something less than the inflation rate.

Before you start withdrawals, there may be two choices you have to make:

1. Should the pension cover you alone or you and your spouse? You'll get a larger monthly check if you take the pension for your lifetime only. But at your death, the pension stops and your spouse gets nothing. That's okay as long as your spouse doesn't need your pension or if you have good reason to believe that your spouse will die first. But if your spouse will depend on that money, it should cover both your lives. A two-life pension (joint-and-survivor) isn't as big as one that lasts for your life alone, but at least your spouse won't be left empty-handed.

If you do opt for spousal protection, you generally face another choice: Should you leave your spouse the same size check you get as a couple or a smaller check? If this income is critical to your spouse's welfare, take the largest check your spouse can get. That means a smaller check for you as a couple, but it's better to cut back together than to leave your spouse struggling on too small an income after your death. The struggler won't remember you as fondly as you'd like.

2. Should you take your pension as a monthly income or in a lump sum? Generally, monthly payments are your only choice. But some employers offer the option of lump sums. By law, you have to be given a *relative value disclosure* showing the size of your potential lump sum payment compared with the monthly lifetime pension payment for you alone or jointly with your spouse. With these numbers in hand—making your options very clear—here's how to decide what to do:

• *If you want a lifetime monthly income, find out what the lump sum could buy if you bought an immediate-pay annuity* from an insurance company. You can make quick comparisons at ImmediateAnnuities.com (www.immediate annuities.com). If an insurance company will pay you more than the lifetime pension your company offers, take the lump sum and buy the annuity. It's a no-brainer. If not, choose the company pension.

Your choice may be dictated by your gender. Women, on average, live longer than men. Employers ignore this fact when figuring how large a pension you've earned. Women and men of equal ages, and with equal earnings and employment histories, receive the same amount. Insurance companies, however, take women's longer life spans into account. Given the same amount of money to invest in an annuity, women get smaller monthly payments from insurance companies than men, because women's payments have to stretch over more years. Bottom line: a woman might get more from a pension, while a man might get more from an insurance annuity. But you can't be sure, so check it out.

Also, compare the annuity's joint husband-and-wife benefits with those the pension pays. If your spouse will need income after you die, you want to find the largest future benefit you can. (For more on spouse protection, see page 1119.)

• *If you're highly dependent on this money, take a monthly pension (or an insurance annuity, if it pays more).* A pension lasts for life, even though it's eroded by inflation. If you take the lump sum and invest it, you might not be able to stretch it out. Your investments might not go well, or you might live a lot longer than you think.

• *If you're an inexperienced investor, take the monthly pension (or insurance annuity).* A financial planner might show you, on paper, that you'd get a higher income by investing the lump sum. But what if the planner's investments fail? You may not be able to judge whether you're getting good advice. And sometimes even good advice doesn't work out.

• *If your pension includes a cost-of-living adjustment, keep it!* That benefit will be priceless over future years.

• *If keeping the pension also gives you access to retiree health insurance, cling to it for life.*

• *If you doubt that your company is sound, take the lump sum,* unless your pension is fully insured by the Pension Benefit Guaranty Corporation (page 1021).

• *If you're a terrific investor or your money is in the hands of a fee-only planner with a good track record, consider the lump sum.* But first ask what *discount rate* of interest the company used when it figured your lump sum. That's the rate at which money is invested by your pension plan to provide you with an income for life. You'd have to invest your entire lump sum at that same rate for life just to match what you'd get from the company, guaranteed. To improve your income, you'd have to earn a higher rate of return. At this writing, the discount rate is low so taking the lump sum makes sense, unless you'd rather not, for safety reasons. If the discount rate rises, taking the pension might be the better choice.

• *If you have other sources of income, take the lump sum.* You can roll that money into a tax-deferred Individual Retirement Account and let it accumulate for your older age. That gives you inflation protection.

• *If you're rich enough not to need a pension, take the lump sum.* Roll it into an IRA and leave the money to your kids. Consider a Roth IRA, paying taxes now so that your kids can enjoy the future earnings tax free.

• *If your health is so poor that you don't expect to live very long, take the lump sum.* You can tap it for larger payments than you'd get from a pension, because it doesn't have to cover a full life expectancy.

• *You may decide on a lump sum solely because you need some quick money—* maybe to repay debts or to buy an RV for retirement travel. If your company allows it, consider taking that part of your pension in cash and the rest in monthly checks for the rest of your life.

• *If your spouse will need income after your death, be sure to take the joint-and-survivor annuity* (page 1126).

Is your pension "integrated" with Social Security? If it is, it will be partly reduced by the size of your Social Security benefit. When making that reduction, companies estimate what your benefit will be. If they estimate too high, they wind up paying you too little. Be sure that your company has the right Social Security benefit level (page 1068).

Your Defined Contribution Plan

Defined contribution is the umbrella name for 401(k)s, 403(b)s, 457s, stock-bonus plans, profit sharing, and employee stock ownership plans. At retirement, you are owed a lump sum of money. Period. Some of it will be money you contributed, some of it may be money from your employer. No promises have been made about the size of this sum or how long it will last. Maybe it will see you through a comfortable retirement. Then again, maybe it won't.

There are various ways of taking this money:

You Might Choose a Lifetime Annuity—a fixed monthly payment covering you alone or you and your spouse (or another beneficiary) for life. Your employer will buy the annuity from an insurance company.

Before accepting it, find out what your lump sum would buy if you purchased an annuity independently. Maybe another insurance company is offering a higher monthly income than your company will provide. If so, you can roll the lump sum from your retirement plan into the insurance annuity. For details on immediate-pay annuities, see page 1124.

If you die before collecting all the money you invested, the remainder goes into the general insurance pool. That's what makes annuities work. Some people die early, leaving money in the pool; others outlive their life expectancies and collect more than they invested. You buy lifetime annuities because you need the income and cannot predict how long you are going to live.

You Might Choose Periodic Installment Payments—an income that lasts for a specified number of years. You get higher payments than those you would receive from a lifetime annuity. But at the end of the period, those payments stop. Periodic payments suit someone who expects another source of income in the future (like a payout from a trust fund); someone with a comfortable investment portfolio that can be tapped when the annuity payments stop; or someone in poor health who doesn't expect to live very long. If you die before collecting all the money in your retirement fund, the remainder goes to a beneficiary.

You Might Leave Some or All of Your Money in the Company Plan—a good idea for people who won't need the income right away. You get professional money management at no extra charge and can make withdrawals as you need them (at times specified by the plan). It also makes sense to stay in the plan if you're 55 to 59½. At those ages, you can make penalty-free withdrawals from a 401(k), provided that you've left the company. If you roll the money into an Individual Retirement Account, you can't make penalty-free withdrawals until you pass 59½. To stay with the company, however, your total retirement account must be worth at least $5,000. Otherwise you'll be cashed out.

If the beneficiary of your plan is someone other than your spouse, make sure that he or she knows about "inherited IRAs" (page 1060). That strategy lets your beneficiary increase the value of the IRA by stretching out its tax shelter for a lifetime.

You Might Roll the Money into an Individual Retirement Account—so you can invest it yourself. For how to do it without tax complications, see page 1056. Penalties apply if you withdraw IRA money before 59½ unless you meet one of the exceptions on page 1059. Consider using a Roth IRA, so that future earnings will accumulate tax free (page 1048).

If your company has both a defined benefit plan and a defined contribution plan, play it this way:

1. Leave the money in the defined contribution plan to grow tax deferred, or else roll it into an IRA.

2. Live on your monthly defined benefit pension, Social Security, and other savings for as long as you reasonably can.

3. When inflation has eroded your fixed pension so much that you're feeling the pinch, start using the money in your defined contribution plan or IRA. That fund might have gained enough in value to restore or increase your purchasing power. You must start making withdrawals at age 70½.

The Lump Sum Withdrawal. If you decide to take all the money out of your pension or profit-sharing account, there are four things you can do with it:

1. Have the plan trustee roll some or all of the funds directly into a traditional Individual Retirement Account. You can tap the IRA as needed for living expenses, paying income taxes on the money you take. Or you can leave the money alone to grow tax deferred. There is usually a 10 percent penalty on withdrawals prior to age 59½.

If you're younger and need some money right away, you can use the 72(t) exception (Loophole 9, page 1065). That exception allows substantially equal withdrawals, starting at 55, at a rate set up to last a lifetime. No penalty is charged. If you find that you don't need all the money, you can stop the withdrawals after five years. The 72(t) exception is especially helpful to early retirees. You can tap your IRAs for income until you reach 62, when Social Security clicks in. After that, you can leave the IRA alone until a later age.

If you made after-tax contributions to your traditional 401(k), you can roll those over into an IRA too. In that case, however, any subsequent withdrawals from any of your IRAs will be partly a tax-free return of those contributions. It messes up your tax forms and probably isn't worth it. You can also choose not to roll over those pretax contributions. They can be reclaimed and invested in an after-tax account.

2. Roll the 401(k) into a Roth IRA. You'll pay taxes on the money, but your future earnings will grow tax-free. Also, you don't have to start taking withdrawals at 70½, if you don't want to. For more on Roth-ing, see page 1048.

3. Worst idea on this list: have the plan pay out the funds to you, then roll the money into an IRA yourself. Danger, danger. To avoid being taxed on the distribution, you have to complete the rollover within 60 days. If you miss the 60-day deadline—say, because the mail is late—you're sunk. All the money is taxable, no exceptions.

What's more, when a 401(k) plan distributes money directly to you, your employer generally has to withhold 20 percent for income taxes. That 20 percent will be treated as a taxable withdrawal unless you come up with an equal sum to add to the IRA within 60 days (page 1057).

If you want to have quick and temporary access to your 401(k) funds, roll the money directly into an IRA, withdraw some cash to cover that short-term need, and return it to the IRA within 60 days. That way, you don't face the 20 percent withholding. Still, you're running a big risk.

4. Ask if the company will give you some of the money in cash and roll the rest into an IRA. This gives a you a partial payout with no tax penalty if you're at least 55 (although 20 percent will be withheld for income taxes). What you don't take in cash glides into the IRA in a tax-free rollover.

Withdrawals From a Keogh Plan

There are two types of Keoghs, each with different withdrawal rules. With a *profit sharing* or *money-purchase Keogh* (page 1044), follow the rules that I just laid out for defined contribution plans. You can tap the Keogh, or not tap it, at any rate you like. Or you can take a lump sum. No withdrawals are required until you pass 70½. *Defined benefit Keoghs,* by contrast, work like any other traditional pension plan. You can take a monthly pension or roll the cash into an Individual Retirement Account if the plan allows lump sum distributions.

After That Magic Age . . .

Most of us will be drawing on our retirement plan as soon as, or shortly after, we leave the job. You should put off using it if you can, giving the account more time to accumulate tax deferred. But you can't put it off forever. At 70½, you hit the witching year. At that point, you have to set up a lifetime plan for gradually removing the money from your corporate and personal retirement accounts. Only Roth IRAs can continue untouched for the rest of your life.

The first withdrawal from an employer's plan generally has to occur by April 1 of the year following the later of (1) the year you reach 70½ or (2) the year you retire. If you're still working for the company past 70½, even part-time, you can put off withdrawals.*

The rule is slightly different for withdrawals from your own IRA or from employer plans when you own 5 percent of the company or more. In those cases, you have to start taking money no later than April 1 of the year following the year you reach 70½, whether you're retired or not.

After your first withdrawal, each year's required amount must be taken no later than the close of the calendar year. That could give you two payments the first year—one after reaching 70½, which you can defer until April of the following year; and one for 71, which must be completed by the end of December. If you take both payments in one year, you might be pushed into a higher bracket. In that case, it's better to take the first distribution earlier, so you'll pay less tax.

If you're still working, you can keep on contributing to 401(k)s, SEPs, Keoghs, and Roth IRAs after 70½, but not to tax-deferred IRAs.

How Much Do You Have to Take Out Each Year?

Enough so that if you continued at that rate, you would empty all your retirement plans over (1) your lifetime or (2) the joint lifetimes of you and your spouse, if your spouse is your beneficiary and he or she is more than 10 years younger. The IRS publishes Uniform Lifetime Tables showing your life expectancy. You can find them on the Web or consult the IRS's free Publication 590, *Individual Retirement Arrangements*—an indispensable guide to how these plans are taxed.

---

*Because of the stock market crash of 2008, the government allowed people with IRAs and 401(k)s to skip the required minimum withdrawal in 2009. You have to resume taking withdrawals in 2010.

How do you figure your withdrawals? It's easy—and I say this as one who's allergic to arithmetic. The steps are:

1. What was the value of your IRA last December 31? (Look at the December 31 before you turned 70½ if this is your first withdrawal.)

2. What is your life expectancy, according to the Uniform Lifetime Table? Use this table if you're solo or if your spouse is your beneficiary and is no more than 10 years younger than you are. If your spouse is more than 10 years younger, use the Joint Life Tables.

3. Divide the value of the IRA by your life expectancy. That gives you the minimum withdrawal for the current year.

4. Do this for each IRA and SEP-IRA you have (always excepting the Roth, where withdrawals are not required). Add up the results. That's the amount that must be withdrawn. You can take it from one IRA or from several as long as the total dollar amount is met.

5. Go through the same steps for each Keogh or other retirement plan you own. With Keoghs, the proper amount must be taken from each plan separately. You can't use extra withdrawals from one Keogh to cover money that ought to come out of another, as you can with IRAs. This argues for combining all your Keoghs into a single plan. Then you can cash in whichever investments seem the most appropriate.

6. Go through the same steps for your 401(k) if you're not working and the money is still in the company plan. Are you sure you want to keep it there?

If you can't figure out the proper withdrawals yourself, the trustee for your retirement plan will usually help. Many mutual funds offer automatic withdrawal services. There are calculators on Web sites. Or ask an accountant or qualified financial planner.

It Is Critical That You Take the Right Amount Each Year

If you withdraw too little, you'll be socked with a 50 percent penalty on the sum that you should have taken but didn't (unless you can convince the IRS that you were all thumbs with the life expectancy tables). Don't wait until the end of the year for the withdrawal. If there's a problem with the paperwork, or some sort of delay at the financial institution that's holding your money, you might miss the deadline.

What If I Die While I'm Making Withdrawals from My Plan?

- *If you have a regular pension or defined benefit Keogh.* The pension dies with you if you arranged to have it last for your lifetime only. If there's a beneficiary, he or she receives whatever payments you provided for. The same is true if you converted a 401(k), 403(b), or 457 into a lifetime annuity.

- *If you have a tax-deferred IRA or SEP-IRA and leave it to a spouse.* Your spouse can turn it into a personal IRA, withdrawing money as needed based on the usual IRA rules. No withdrawals are necessary if he or she is younger than 70½. A spouse older than that will have to make withdrawals based on his or her own age. (In both cases, however, the spouse has to complete the withdrawal you were required to make in the year of your death.) The spouse should be sure to put his or her Social Security number on the plan, so the taxable withdrawals are reported properly.

- *If you have a tax-deferred IRA, Roth IRA, or SEP-IRA and leave it to someone other than your spouse.* The beneficiary can use the inherited IRA rules (page 1060) to extend the tax-favored distributions over a lifetime, based on his or her age in the year after your death (use the Single Life Table). Of course, the money can always be withdrawn earlier, including in a lump sum, following the usual IRA rules. Withdrawals from Roths will be tax free.

- *If you have some other retirement plan.* The withdrawals or rollover rules are similar to those for a tax-deferred IRA or SEP, with one exception: your spouse cannot treat your plan as his or her own. However, he or she can roll the plan into a new IRA.

Spouse Protection

The law worries a lot about widows, and so it should. Wives usually live longer than their husbands and generally wind up with far lower incomes. So an automatic *survivor annuity* has been written into all defined benefit plans (the classic pension plans) and the lifetime-payout options offered by defined contribution plans, such as 401(k)s. It protects men as well as women, but, as a practical matter, women need it more. Here are the spouse protection rules for the various kinds of plans:

If You Die Before You Retire

Traditional, private pension plans have to offer a *preretirement survivor's annuity*. It's worth at least half of what your own lifetime benefit would have been if you had chosen to retire early.

Your spouse can waive this right, however. If he or she does and you live to retire, you'll have a larger pension check. But if you die, the pension goes right into the coffin with you. Your spouse gets nothing.

I once got a sad letter from a widow. She had waived her preretirement benefit thinking that it covered only the years before her husband retired—and, indeed, the company's form letter was none too clear on this point. When he died unexpectedly, she was horrified to learn that she had lost his "postretirement" pension too. Don't waive the preretirement benefit if you'll need your spouse's pension to live on. If you've already waived it and change your mind, it can be reinstated, provided that your spouse is still alive.

Public pension plans may have different rules, but they generally offer good spouse protection too.

At the Time You Retire

You have a choice: take a larger pension that lasts for your lifetime and then stops or a smaller pension that lasts for the lifetime of you and your spouse. By law, the default choice is the pension that covers your spouse (called a joint-and-survivor pension). He or she is entitled to a benefit worth at least 50 percent of yours, and up to 100 percent, if that's what you want and your plan allows it. If you die while collecting this pension, your spouse continues to get checks in the amount you signed up for.

Your spouse can waive this benefit too, which would give you a larger check each month. But when you die, the pension ends and your spouse gets nothing. That's okay as long as your spouse has an adequate income. If not, a single-life pension is a mistake. (Nevertheless, some insurance agents urge this choice upon you. "Take the larger pension," they say, "and protect your spouse with an insurance policy instead." That is almost always a bad idea. For the reasons, see page 1121.)

Some pension plans let you take your benefit in a single lump sum payout. Again, your spouse has to agree.

The protection here is absolute. In one case, a female executive was retiring and wanted to take the maximum pension lasting for her life alone. Her husband was in jail for assaulting her. She had to visit him to ask if he'd forgo his joint-and-survivor check, and he refused. Solution: divorce.

If You're the Spouse, When Might You Want to Sign Away Your Pension Rights?

Normally, I'd say "Don't do it!" You're going to need that income after your spouse is dead. But it's probably okay to sign away your rights if: (1) You have a good pension of your own. (2) You have so much money saved and invested that you don't need the pension to live on, even if the markets turn bad. (3) You're gravely ill and not likely to outlive your spouse.

The consent has to be in writing and notarized, so the company knows it's real. Think carefully before going ahead, because waiving the benefit at retirement is an irrevocable choice. Once a spouse says bye-bye to his or her share of the pension, it's gone forever. *Never* sign if you're doing it because money is short and you need a larger check today. If you're struggling already, what will you do if the pension stops?

If Yours Is a Profit-Sharing Plan, Including 401(k)s, 403(b)s, and Employee Stock Ownership Plans

Spouses are protected here too.

If you die before retirement and you're married, all vested benefits in profit-sharing accounts normally have to go to your spouse. Your spouse can waive the payout, however—for example, if you're in a second marriage and want the money to go to the children of your first marriage. The moment you remarry, your new spouse becomes the beneficiary of the plan, no matter what it says on the plan's beneficiary form or in your will. If you still want your children to get part or all of the money, your spouse has to waive his or her right to it by signing a notarized form and filing it with the plan.

If, at retirement, you decide to convert your plan into a lifetime income, your spouse still is protected. The annuity has to cover you both unless the spouse specifically agrees that the payments will cover your life only.

There's zero spouse protection, however, if you take all your money in a lump sum or roll it into an Individual Retirement Account. You can bestow an IRA on anyone you want.

With Plans You Set Up Yourself

IRAs and SEPs provide no protection for the spouse. You're not required to create a survivor annuity. The assets in the plan can be left to any beneficiary you name.

Keoghs mimic corporate plans. With a defined benefit or money-purchase Keogh, spouse protection is required, including the joint-and-survivor annuity.

With a profit-sharing Keogh, you follow the rules for corporate profit sharing plans such as 401(k)s.

Beware Pension Max!

One of the tragedies of our time is that so many spouses are being talked out of their pension protection by an army of insurance agents and financial planners. These salespeople believe—incorrectly—that they've found a better way. One of the names for their product is "pension maximization," or pension max for short.

They advise you, the worker, to take the higher, single-life pension. You use that extra income to buy a cash-value life insurance policy. If you die first, your pension ends, but the proceeds of the policy will create an income for your spouse. If your spouse dies first, you cancel the insurance and have that higher pension for the rest of your life.

Sounds neat—especially when it's laid out in a slick, computer-generated presentation. It looks as if pension max brings both you and your spouse out ahead.

Sadly, those presentations usually mislead. After paying for the policy, the couple may have less to live on after tax than if they had taken the joint-and-survivor pension. More distressingly, if the husband dies, the insurance policy may not be large enough to provide the promised income for the wife.

After I aired this opinion in a newspaper column, angry insurance reps peppered me with dissenting letters. I invited them to prove the glories of a pension max program started at retirement age. All told, 10 of them took up the challenge; their work was analyzed by 2 financial planners using two different systems.

Only one proposal worked passably well, and it turned out to be a ringer. It was constructed by a computer software company using a low-load life insurance policy that carried a minimal sales commission (page 371). All the proposals sent in by insurance agents were off the mark. Some ignored taxes, to make the couple's income look higher than would actually be the case. Some lowballed the amount of insurance needed, which gambled with the widow's future standard of living. Some suggested policies that cost more than the couple would gain in extra pension benefits. Some illustrated a program that started 10 years before retirement but didn't include those early costs in their "proof" of how well the idea worked.

A luckless client is not likely to find the holes in pension max proposals. I couldn't have found them either without expert help. Many a widow will discover the error only on learning she won't have all the income she'd counted on. (If this happens to you, consider suing the insurance agent and insurance company; that may be the only way of sending the industry a message.)

Even if a pension max proposal appears to work mathematically, the widow is taking a long list of other risks:

Income Risk. Inflation or unexpected expenses may eat away at your retirement income. At some point, you may no longer be able to afford the premium on the life insurance policy. The widow will lose the protection she had counted on.

Inflation Risk. Many government pensions and some private ones provide regular cost-of-living adjustments. Pension max proposals rarely offer enough life insurance to cover all that extra income. So the widow is shortchanged.

Investment Risk. Pension max is usually funded with universal or variable-life insurance, which is linked to changes in interest rates or stock prices. If rates or stocks fall, you may have to pay more for the coverage or accept a lower death benefit. If you decide to pay more, you'll lower your current standard of living. If you can't pay more, your widow may get less future income than you expected.

Longevity Risk. Even if the insurance policy isn't large enough to replace the husband's pension in full, pension max will work out if the husband lives long enough. After a few years, a smaller policy will be okay, because the widow herself has fewer years to live. But you're taking an awful risk. If the husband is hit by a truck the day after retirement, the widow's income will come up short.

Annuity Risk. Today a $500,000 cash-value life insurance policy might buy a 70-year-old woman a lifetime income of $3,700 a month. But if interest rates fall in the future, that sum will buy a widow something less. You cannot be sure that the insurance policy will provide the income needed.

Marital Risk. If the husband owns the policy and the marriage goes bad, he might cut off the wife by canceling the insurance or changing the beneficiary.

Management Risk. If the widow collects a lump sum, she may not have the knowledge and experience to manage it well. Instead of buying an annuity, she might be persuaded to put it into investments that cost her some of the money.

Health Insurance Risk. A widow who leaves her husband's pension plan may lose retiree health coverage. It is especially risky to leave public-sector pension plans, such as those for teachers and other state employees, because benefits are sometimes added later.

My bottom line: at retirement, no widow who will need the income should gamble on pension max. The presentation that she and her husband get from the planner or insurance agent probably doesn't tell the whole story. To check what the agent is saying, turn to Appendix 3, page 1201. There you'll find a list of additional risks plus a worksheet that you can use to test the honesty of the salesperson's proposal. Never buy pension max without running it through this worksheet. Odds are that the proposal either lowers your after-tax income as a couple or provides too little insurance protection for the surviving spouse, or both.

Immediate-Pay Annuities— Creating a Guaranteed Income for Life

When you finally retire, the size of your savings isn't the thing you focus on. You want to know how much income your savings will deliver. There are various ways of turning a lump sum into steady income, including regular withdrawals from an investment portfolio, living on interest and dividends, and mutual funds that make monthly payouts. The easiest and most certain way, however, is to buy a single-premium immediate-pay annuity.

You buy this annuity with a lump sum of money—$5,000 or $10,000 minimum, but typically $50,000 or more. In return you get a guaranteed income for life or for a specific period of time. That's it. Simple, clean, and low cost.

You can roll money into an immediate annuity, tax free, from a 401(k) or Individual Retirement Account. You can buy one with after-tax dollars that you saved in a bank or in other investments. If you've been saving money in a tax-deferred annuity, you can exchange it for an immediate-payout plan. One tip, for people who own tax-deferred annuities: don't automatically switch to an immediate-pay annuity offered by the same insurance company. Check what other companies are offering, which is easy on the Web. Another insurer may offer you a much better deal (page 1129).

Who Might Want an Immediate-Pay Annuity?

Anyone who needs a fixed income for life. If you're living entirely on your investments, you might want to turn part of that money into the equivalent of a guaranteed pension, in case your investments get into trouble. If you're older and starting to worry that your nest egg might run out, switching to an annuity assures you of an income for as long as you live.

An immediate-pay annuity does more than pay you a regular income you can count on. The checks will be larger than the amount you can prudently draw from your other investments and larger than you'd get from a variable annuity with lifetime benefits. By giving you an income you can count on, annuities also free you to invest more of your other money in a stock portfolio for growth.

Don't annuitize too early. Waiting until an older age keeps your options open. For example, you might contract an illness that shortens your life, in which case you'd rather have cash for immediate home care than a lifetime income. In general, men should start thinking about annuities at around age 70 to 75, and women at age 75 to 80. You might annuitize a portion of your money each year over five years. Each annuity will carry a different payment, depending on changes in interest rates, so you've diversified that risk. A gradual purchase also preserves your options because you can stop at any time.

The knock on immediate-pay annuities is that if you die too soon, the insurance company keeps what's left of your money. But is that so bad if it also protects you (and your spouse, if you're married) from running out of money? Buying a guarantee that you'll still be able to eat at 95 is more important than worrying about leaving something behind for your kids, whom you raised and educated and who now ought to be on their own. Besides, your kids may inherit your house and your other savings, so you're not leaving them with nothing.

Annuities are best bought by people in good health who might outlive their life expectancy. Longevity is how you beat the system. But they're also the right choice for anyone who wants a guaranteed income for life—especially if you're single or if your kids are unlikely to help you in older age. If you're not in perfect health, look for *impaired life* annuities, which pay higher monthly benefits than normal annuities do. A married couple, with one spouse ailing, might consider an annuity for the healthy spouse.

Immediate-pay annuities come in two types, fixed and variable:

With *immediate-pay fixed annuities,* you get a fixed-dollar payment, which means that inflation will erode your income over time. But if you start your immediate-pay annuity late in life, there are fewer years for this damage to occur. If you couple the annuity with a portfolio of stocks and bonds, you have the best of both worlds: a reliable income and a long-term growth investment.

With *immediate-pay variable annuities,* you're investing in a portfolio of stocks and bonds. Your payment is guaranteed for life but not its size. Initially, you'll get less per month than a fixed annuity would pay. In subsequent months, your payments will rise or fall, depending on how well your investments did.

If you want a guaranteed income that you can budget for, skip the variable annuity. Choose a fixed annuity instead, coupled with a separate portfolio of stocks and bonds for growth. If you can manage with variable payments, however, the variables might pay you a higher income over your lifetime, thanks to the general long-term rise in the value of stocks.

If you buy from an insurance agent, you'll pay higher fees for a variable than you would for a fixed annuity. Best advice: buy from one of the low-cost mutual fund groups, such as Vanguard, Fidelity, T. Rowe Price, or TIAA-CREF.

Here are the various types of monthly income you can buy. For how these payouts are taxed, see page 1127.

Single Life Annuity. You get a fixed monthly, quarterly, or annual income guaranteed to last for as long as you live. This arrangement pays you the highest possible monthly check for the money you put up. If you die before reaching your life expectancy, the insurer keeps the extra money. If you outlive your life expectancy, the insurer swallows the extra cost.

Joint-and-Survivor Annuity. Your fixed monthly income lasts for your lifetime and the lifetime of another annuitant, such as your spouse. The size of your check depends on what your spouse will receive after your death. Half your check? Two-thirds of your check? The same size check? The more you leave for the surviving spouse, the smaller your income while you're both still alive, and vice versa.

Inflation-Adjusted Annuity. You buy an income guaranteed to rise by a fixed amount—say, 3 percent—each year. This deal sounds better than it really is. You start with a much lower monthly income than you'd get from a regular annuity. It might take 20 years before the inflation adjustment starts producing a higher income that a fixed annuity would have paid, right from the start. On the other hand, you're protected from unexpectedly high inflation, if that's your principal fear.

Annuity for "Life or Period Certain." Your guaranteed income covers your lifetime or a fixed number of years, whichever is more. A typical choice is "life or 10 years certain." Under this arrangement, the insurer makes regular payments for at least 10 years—to you if you're alive or to a beneficiary if you die. If you die in the 11th year, your beneficiary gets nothing. But you yourself get payments for as long as you live. "Period certain" arrangements cost money. You get a smaller income than you would from straight life annuities. The longer the period, the smaller your monthly checks.

Most people who buy annuities choose the period certain. It galls them to think that they might drop dead the day after buying, leaving everything to the insurer. But so what? Once you're dead, why care, as long as your spouse has been provided for? Assuming you live for the period certain, your heirs get nothing from the annuity anyway. Consider providing separately for your heirs (say, by leaving them the house) and then buying a straight life annuity for yourself (or yourself and your spouse) alone.

Two variants on period certain are the *cash refund* annuity and the *installment refund* annuity, both of which guarantee enough payments to you or a beneficiary to match your full, original investment (your premium). The former pays your beneficiary in a lump sum, the latter makes installment payments. Either way, the contracts lower the size of your monthly income. You're putting your heirs' inheritance ahead of your own security. Are you certain that your heirs will support you if you discover, later in life, that the annuity income isn't enough? If not, forget 'em and buy the highest possible payment for yourself.

Payments for a Period Certain. You sign up for a fixed number of payments— level or rising—over a period of your choice (but not exceeding your life expectancy). You may outlive this income, so you'll need a source of support to fall back on. But if you die before getting all the money, the remainder goes to your heirs rather than to the insurance company. This can be a good alternative to a straight life annuity if you have other resources.

Do You Want "Longevity Insurance"?

You might call this a delayed fixed-income annuity. You buy it now but don't collect on it right away. In 20 or 25 years—usually, when you're 85—it begins to pay you a fixed income for the rest of your life. The payment is fixed on the day that you buy; it's not linked to how well your investments perform. You're insuring against the risk of outliving your other investments or having your other investments blow up.

The premiums for longevity insurance aren't high. That's because the insurer has to pay only if you live to a later age and enjoy many hale years after that. You can't take any money out of the contract in advance. If you die, your heirs normally get nothing. You can purchase a death benefit, so that they'll get some money if you die before starting to collect. But then, of course, the program won't be cheap anymore.

Consider longevity insurance if you're in good health, from a long-lived family, don't need the money you're putting into the contract, and have no kids to leave money to (or will leave them other assets, such as a house). You generally need to live into your mid-90s to make this investment pay. Of course, you might—and if you do, this extra money will be there.

How Annuity Payouts Are Taxed

When you buy an immediate-pay annuity with a lump sum of money:

■ *If the money was rolled over from a 401(k), IRA, or other qualified retirement plan:* No taxes are due on the rollover. Instead you'll be fully taxed on every withdrawal at your current, ordinary-income rate.

■ *If you bought the annuity with an after-tax lump sum:* Each payment is a mix of taxable income and a tax-free return of your original capital. At the end of the year, the insurer will send you a 1099R showing the amount of taxable income you received. The portion that's taxable is established by the IRS.

When you're holding a tax-deferred annuity and annuitize it (turn it into an immediate-pay annuity):

■ *If you take a lifetime annuity or payments over a fixed period:* Each payment is a mix of taxable income and a tax-free return of your original capital. At the end of the year, the insurer will tell you how much taxable income you received. If you started these payouts before reaching 59½ and they're projected to last for your lifetime, you're not subject to the 10 percent tax penalty on early withdrawals.

■ *If you take a lump sum withdrawal:* You're taxed all at once on all of your earnings over the years. There's also a 10 percent penalty if you're under 59½. Not a smart move.

■ *If you roll your lump sum into another insurance company's annuity:* You can use a tax-free 1035 exchange. Your insurance agent will show you how.

■ *If you make occasional withdrawals:* They are treated entirely as taxable income until you have taken out all the money that your investment ever earned. Any further withdrawals are a tax-free return of your original investment.

■ *If you die:* The tax depends on the type of annuity and its status.

1. If you're collecting income from a straight life annuity and die before recovering all the money you paid in, the loss is reported on your final tax return. (If you recover more than your original investment, it is taxed when you receive it, not after your death.)

2. If you're collecting income from an annuity designed to last for your lifetime or a period certain and you die before the period expires and leave the payments to a beneficiary, the beneficiary pays taxes on the income received.

3. If you're still accumulating money in the annuity and die, it passes to a beneficiary. The beneficiary normally has two choices: take the money as a lifetime income or withdraw it within five years. Either way, it's taxed. A married couple, however, can arrange for a joint annuity that continues to grow tax deferred even if one spouse dies. Do it this way: designate one spouse the owner and annuitant (the person who will receive the money); designate the other spouse as the contingent owner and beneficiary. If either spouse dies, the other can keep the contract growing.

How to Get the Most from Annuity Payouts

1. If you have a tax-deferred annuity, leave it alone as long as you can. Spend your nonannuity savings first.

2. Don't buy a straight lifetime annuity if you're not well. These products are for healthy people who worry about outliving their savings. But consider an impaired-risk immediate-pay annuity, which some companies offer. They assume shorter life spans, so your money will buy you a higher income per month. As with any immediate annuity, you are betting against the insurance company. It's betting you'll die; you're betting you'll live.

3. Consider installment payments or a systematic withdrawal program if you hope to leave some of your annuity money to heirs. But you get smaller payments than if you had chosen an income for life. If you guess wrong about your longevity, your money will run out.

4. Don't expect to get a higher monthly income by investing your money yourself and making regular withdrawals. You might beat the payout you'd get from the insurance company, after tax—but then again, you might not. And there's no guarantee that your money will last as long as you do.

5. Shop around. Pricing is transparent, and the best buy is easy to spot. The differences among companies can be considerable. As I write, I am looking at a price list for 15 companies. With $100,000, a 70-year-old man can buy an income as small as $793 or as large as $845 a month, depending on the company he chooses. For a woman, the range is $739 to $777.

6. Once you choose your insurance company, you are usually locked in for life, so take the time to choose carefully. A few insurers, however, let you stop payments in midstream and take some or all of the remaining money in cash.

How to Buy the Very Best Immediate-Pay Annuity

This is one of the easiest jobs in personal finance. First you look up the right Web site and then dial the right phone number. After that, the search for the best fixed-payment annuities takes 5 steps and 5 minutes:

1. The right Web site is ImmediateAnnuities.com. In the calculator on its site, enter your gender, age, state, and the amount of money you want to invest. You'll get price quotes for 11 different types of annuities. Click a box if you want a free report on the top 7 products in any of the categories. No salesperson will call. If you want help, call the agent, Hersh Stern, at 800-872-6684. You can buy through him or use the list as a benchmark when talking to your own insurance agent or financial planner.

Prices are usually quoted as "price per $1,000." A quote of $8.38 means that you'll get $8.38 a month for every $1,000 you invest. That's $838 a month on a $100,000 annuity. The best annuity is the one that will pay you the highest monthly income, from an insurance company with a top rating for financial safety and soundness (page 406). That's all there is to it.

2. Starting from the top of your list, find out if that company has good ratings from at least 3 of the 5 main insurance rating services (ratings should be on the insurers' Web sites, or search for the companies on the Web sites of the ratings agencies). To date, almost all immediate-pay annuities have been honored when an insurer failed, so you don't necessarily have to stick with AAA-rated companies. But for comfort—especially after the 2008–2009 financial collapse—you might not want to drop below AA. If the insurer with the highest monthly payout also meets your quality standards, go no further.

3. If you've been saving money in a tax-deferred annuity at a top-rated insurance company, ask that company for its quote on immediate-pay annuities. Insurers may give current customers better rates than they offer to customers buying in from the outside. On the other hand, they may not. Always check the quote against what you can get from ImmediateAnnuities.com.

4. Ask for an annuity quote from Low Load Insurance Services at www .llis.com, to see if you can find an even better rate. This company works primarily with financial planners and wants the planner's name when you ask for a quote. Readers of this book can enter Jane Bryant Quinn as the "advisor," and your request will be handled directly by LLIS staff. They'll ask whether you want a qualified or nonqualified annuity. A *qualified annuity* is purchased with money rolling out of a 401(k) or IRA. A *nonqualified annuity* is one that you're buying with after-tax savings. (P.S. I earn nothing from this.)

5. If you want an immediate variable annuity, rather than a fixed annuity, consider those offered by low-cost Vanguard, Fidelity, T. Rowe Price, and TIAA-CREF.

6. To spread your risk, you might buy annuities from two or more companies. The 2008–2009 financial collapse shows that you can't be too safe, especially in your retirement years.

The Charitable Alternative

Here's a way of earning an income from your money while serving others too. Forget about buying an annuity from a life insurance company and letting the insurer walk away with anything left over. Give that money to a charitable organization instead. A hospital. A social welfare agency. A college. A church. A community foundation. Many such organizations stand ready to pay you a lifetime income in return for cash and other types of gifts. You get a tax deduction too. If you give appreciated property, you'll save on capital gains taxes. For details, see page 140. You won't get as large a monthly income as insurance companies pay, but you'll have the pleasure of knowing that you've done some good.

Penguins and Predators

A few years ago, I visited Antarctica. I remember watching penguins, who had to enter the water to feed. One by one, they'd waddle down to the water's edge, forming a dithery little crowd, hesitating for long minutes before plunging in. On land they were safe; in the water, there were leopard seals that ate penguins for lunch.

New retirees are penguins. Awaiting them in the retirement waters are leopard seals: financial salespeople who want to lunch on their lump sum retirement payouts. As the boomer generation retires in larger numbers, more money will vanish into the seals' waiting jaws. Some employers become accomplices. They refer retirees to specific planners or invite a planner to give a preretirement course. But on what basis are these "teachers" chosen? Some may give good advice, while others are hustlers in disguise. You might also fall prey to one of the "free lunch" scams set up specifically for older people. More hustlers will pitch you on expensive and unsuitable products that pay high commissions— living trusts, deferred annuities, equity indexed annuities, costly reverse mortgages, and even fraudulent investments products. See the warnings about "free lunches" put out by FINRA, which regulates securities firms. Go to www.finra .org click on "Investors," then on "Investor Alerts," and then on "Frauds and Scams."

One danger of the 401(k) retirement system is that employees won't put aside enough money for themselves. Another danger is that once they've saved it, a leopard seal will snatch it away. You must take great care to protect your lump sum. If you don't leave your money in your employer plan, roll it into an IRA at a no-load mutual fund group (chapter 22). Initially, put it all into the money market fund, where it will be safe. Take a long time to test advisers or examine other mutual funds before deciding what to do with the money next.

When Should You Start Drawing Social Security?

That decision isn't always obvious. You have several choices, especially if you're married. Go over all the options with a Social Security representative before deciding when to claim your payment. He or she will lay out the dollar amounts of the benefits you can get, at various ages. For tons of current information plus a Retirement Estimator, go to Social Security Online at www.ssa.gov.

Full Retirement Age: A Date Everyone Needs to Know

You have to wait until your *full* retirement age to collect your full Social Security benefit. Full retirement age is 66 for anyone born between January 2, 1943, and December 31, 1954. For people born later than that, full retirement age creeps up by two months every year. It reaches 67 for people born on January 2, 1960, and later.

It's possible to start collecting benefits as early as 62, but if you do, your payment will be permanently reduced. Your spouse's payment will be smaller too if he or she collects benefits on your account.

If you wait until after your full retirement age to collect, your basic benefit rises by 8 percent for every year of delay. At 70, these increases stop, at which point you should file for your benefit right away.

All recipients get an increase each year, tied to the inflation rate. The purchasing power of your Social Security payment will never drop.

As a general rule, you get about the same amount of Social Security benefits whether you retire early or late, assuming that you live out your full life expectancy. Early retirements simply stretch out the money over a greater number of years.

But let me put in a plug for retiring late, if your life makes that possible. Your basic benefit will rise, thanks to the additional years you worked. The higher benefit will provide more income for your spouse, if he or she collects on your account. If you outlive your life expectancy, you'll collect more than if you had started your benefit at 62. If you don't live that long, you'll still have received a higher current income while you're alive and will leave a higher benefit for your spouse.

The size of your Social Security benefit is based on your highest 35 years of earnings, with past years indexed to reflect the rise in wage inflation. If you worked for fewer than 35 years, a zero is entered for the missing years, which reduces your payment.

The Earnings Limit

You're allowed to earn a limited amount of money from wages* without affecting the size of your Social Security benefit. (For up-to-date information on what the ceilings are, see Social Security Online.) If you retire early, your payment will be reduced by $1 for every $2 you earn above the annual limit. In the year you'll reach full retirement age, you're docked $1 for every $3 you earn above the limit (at this point, the limit will be higher than it was when you were 62). Starting with the month you actually reach full retirement age, you get the same Social Security payment no matter how much money you earn.

All is not lost if you started taking benefits early but earned enough money to exceed the Social Security earnings limit. When you reach 66, Social Security will recalculate your benefit to give you credit for the months when you were docked. At that point, your monthly benefit will rise.

If You're Divorced

A divorced spouse can collect on his or her ex's account provided that he or she is unmarried and the marriage lasted at least 10 years. This doesn't affect the benefits due a current spouse. Both spouses collect the full amount. For more on spousal benefits, see page 1134.

When to Start Benefits If You're Single

- *Retire at 62 only if you can live on a smaller payment or your health is poor.* Your benefit will be 25 percent less than if you had waited until your full retirement age. Your benefit will be further reduced if you're still working and earn more than a certain amount. But taking Social Security early will provide larger total payments to anyone who doesn't expect to reach his or her normal life expectancy. If you haven't saved enough money and had to leave your full-time job, you may have no option but to start benefits right away.
- *Retire at 63 to 65.* You'll get less than your full retirement benefit but more than you'd have if you retired at 62.
- *Wait until 66 and collect your full retirement benefit.* This is a great choice for older workers who haven't retired. You get your Social Security *and* you can

---

*"Earnings" do not include investment income.

earn all you want without reducing your Social Security benefits. It's like having two paychecks in the mail.

■ *Retire even later, if you're still working and in good health.* Your benefit rises for each year that you wait between ages 67 and 70. At 70, it tops out. At that point, claim your benefits right away. In general, single women should consider waiting if they can afford it. They have longer life spans than men, so they're more likely to profit by delaying their retirement and earning a higher monthly payment.

When to Start Benefits If You're Married

Here's where things get complicated. Your decision turns not only on your age and health but on your spouse's age and health; whether the spouse has a separate Social Security record; and, if so, whether the earnings on that record are low or high.

A worker with a steady, well-paid employment history will collect a benefit based on his or her personal earnings. A worker with a fitful job history, or with low earnings, will collect on that record plus something extra—the *spousal benefit*—based on his or her spouse's earnings. If you collect as a spouse, you'll receive up to 50 percent of your spouse's payment while you're both alive and up to 100 percent in survivor benefits when he or she dies. The amounts depend on how old each of you were when you retired. Social Security will automatically send you the largest payment for which you're eligible.

Here's a tip on what's best, in most cases, when you each have a Social Security record but the wife* will claim a spousal benefit:[†]

■ The husband should delay retirement as long as possible, even if he has a shorter life expectancy than his wife. That builds up a larger survivor benefit for his wife after his death. The wife should collect on her own earnings record at 62 and apply for the higher spousal benefit when her husband retires (or when she reaches 66, even if he hasn't retired). This system maximizes the amount you'll collect as a couple if the husband dies before his wife. If the wife dies first, she'll have collected benefits on her own earnings record that she might otherwise have missed. Thanks to his late retirement, the husband will have a higher payment for the rest of his life.

---

*These rules are the same for a husband with little or no Social Security earnings who applies for benefits on his wife's record. But using wife as *spouse* tells the story in its most typical way. I could use the word *spouse* everywhere, but you'd never figure out which spouse I was talking about. Try it and see!

[†]Calculated by Alicia Munnell and Mauricio Soto for the Center for Retirement Research at Boston College, Chestnut Hill, Massachusetts.

- If the wife has the higher Social Security earnings record, she should delay retirement in order to build up a larger payment for herself. The husband could start with his own benefit at 62 and then switch to the spousal benefit when he reaches 66.

The general rule for married couples, above, may not fit your situation. So here are the details for you to consider before claiming a Social Security payment:

If the wife has only a small earnings record of her own and will collect on her husband's benefit:

- *You can retire on your own benefit whenever you want, regardless of whether your husband has retired.* If you're younger than 66, your benefit will be reduced. When your husband retires, you can collect a spousal benefit based on his record. If you retired early, however, your spousal benefit will also be reduced.

- *You can claim a spousal benefit on your husband's record even if he hasn't retired, provided that he has reached the full retirement age.* He can file for benefits and delay their start. That lets you receive a payment while he works for a few more years. (Exception: an eligible divorced spouse can collect on his or her ex's record as soon as the ex is entitled to benefits, provided that they've been divorced for at least two years.)

- *If you and your husband retire early, the benefit is reduced for both of you.* At 62, his benefit will be 25 percent less than if he'd retired at 66. Your benefit will be only 35 percent of his. You're stuck with a permanently smaller benefit as a couple.

- *If you're much younger than your husband and he retires at 66, you should wait to claim spousal benefits until you're 66 as well.* That way, you'll get the full amount—50 percent of his retirement benefit while you're both alive and 100 percent of his benefit if he dies.

- *If your husband waits to retire until after 66, his payment will rise.* The maximum spousal benefit, however, stays at half of his benefit at 66. It does not rise to half of the higher benefit he gets when he retires at a later age.

- *If your husband retires at 62 and you wait until 66, you'll get 50 percent* of what would have been your husband's payment at his full retirement age.

- *Run these rules in reverse if the husband is the one with the small earnings record.*

If both spouses have substantial Social Security earnings of their own:

- *You can retire on your own benefit,* following the same rules you would if you were single.

- *A special tip: You can retire at 66 and collect a spousal benefit on your husband's record if he's retired.* At 70, switch to the benefit due from your own Social Security earnings record. It will be higher, thanks to the four years you waited to collect. Because this strategy is rarely used, not all Social Security personnel are familiar with it. They might say that you have to take the benefit based on your own earnings record, because it's higher than the spousal benefit. Ask to speak to a supervisor. To make this work, you have to ask for spousal benefits when you're at full retirement age.

If your husband is still working, he can file for benefits at 66 but delay their start. That lets you file for spousal benefits based on his record. When he eventually retires, he too can claim a higher payment.

If your husband dies, you have several choices for claiming your survivor benefit (the same rules apply to a husband whose wife dies first):

- *You can start your survivor (widow's) benefit as early as 60, drawing on his earnings record (50, if you're disabled).* The younger you are, the smaller the monthly payment. If you wait until 66, you can claim 100 percent of the benefit your husband was collecting when he died.
- *If you're currently receiving spousal benefits based on his record,* you will be switched to the higher survivor benefit automatically.
- *If you have your own substantial Social Security benefit, you could start with a widow's benefit at 60,* then switch to your own benefit at a later date—for example, at 66, when your full retirement payment will be due.
- *If your husband dies before starting to collect Social Security, you still get a survivor benefit.* The amount will be based on a complicated formula that you'll need a Social Security rep to calculate for you.

When you have an eligible child at home when you retire or die:
Your family is entitled to additional Social Security benefits. An *eligible* child (including a dependent stepchild) is one who's unmarried, under age 18, or under 19 if still in high school. A severely disabled child is eligible if the problem struck prior to age 22 and the child remains disabled.

You're subject to a maximum family benefit, no matter how many eligible children are in your family.

How Much Can Widows, Widowers, and Spouses Earn and Still Get Benefits?

All Social Security benefits are subject to the earnings limit explained on page 1133. Whether you receive benefits as a retiree, spouse, widow, widower, or child, your payment goes down if you exceed the limit. A 60-year-old widow or widower, employed at good wages, may find that she or he earns too much to collect a full widow's or widower's benefit. In that case, you'd be smarter not to claim it. Let it build up until you actually retire, when the payout will be larger. At age 66, you can claim the benefit and earn a high paycheck too.

What If You Earn More than the Social Security Limit?

When you work, your employer reports your earnings to Social Security. That's checked electronically against the benefits you got. If your earnings were higher than the limit, Social Security will ask for some money back. You can write a check or pay in installments by having your subsequent Social Security payments reduced.

Alternatively, you can report at the start of the year that you expect to exceed the earnings limit. Estimate how much extra you're likely to make. Your monthly payment will be adjusted accordingly—then readjusted when Social Security gets your final earnings report. If you earned less money than you originally thought, Social Security will restore any benefits due.

When You Have a Government Pension

Some federal, state, and local government jobs aren't covered by Social Security. You get a government pension instead. If you retire from the government and take a job that does provide Social Security benefits, your future benefit will be reduced.

If your spouse has Social Security and you qualify for a spousal benefit, don't expect to collect very much. You generally get only the amount of the Social Security benefit that exceeds two-thirds of your government pension. That's usually zero.

Can You Unretire?

Sure. If you quit work, start getting Social Security, and then take a job again, you can simply withdraw your claim.

Two things could happen.

1. You could repay all the Social Security money you've already received.

That cancels any reduction in benefits you took for retiring earlier than 66. You are treated as if you never retired at all. When you reapply, you will get your full retirement payment. Whether this is a good idea depends on how much you'll have to repay and how confident you are of getting that money back in the form of higher benefits over the years. If you live a long life, this will have been a great idea. If not, not.

2. You can simply report that you've returned to work. Depending on the size of your income, your benefit will be reduced or stopped. When you retire again, your retirement age will be refigured based on the number of Social Security payments you previously received. For example, if you retire at 62, receive the equivalent of six full Social Security payments, return to work, suspend benefits, then retire again at 66, you'll be treated as having retired at 65 and six months. You'll get less than your full retirement benefit but more than you got at 62. Payments for re-retirees aren't refigured until age 66, so if you re-retire earlier, you will have to wait.

Should You Take Benefits Early So That You Can Invest Them?

Not a good idea. There's no guarantee that you'll earn more on your investments than the increase you'll get from Social Security for delaying retirement a few more years. By claiming early, you also reduce any benefits you might leave to a spouse when you die. Finally, the probability is high that you'll spend those extra dollars rather than invest them.

Applying for Social Security Benefits

You can apply as early as three months before you want your benefits to start. Otherwise benefits generally start in the month when application is made. If you apply after 66, you can—if you want—claim back payments for up to six months.

Before okaying your benefits, the government will want your Social Security number, originals or certified copies of your birth certificate and the birth certificates of anyone else applying for benefits (no photocopies allowed), proof of citizenship or a green card if you were born outside the United States, and proof of how much money you made last year (W-2s or self-employment tax returns will do). If you don't have all these documents and can't get them, don't worry. Social Security will suggest some acceptable substitutes. All Social Security benefits are indexed to the inflation rate. You get your higher payments each January.

Apply for Medicare at 65. Its start date has remained unchanged, even though the full retirement age is going up.

How to Get Paid. Social Security wires your payment by direct deposit to your savings account or checking account, as you prefer. It can still be mailed if you don't have a bank account. Those without accounts can also have their payments loaded onto a debit card, in a program called Direct Express.

How to Talk to Social Security. You can apply for retirement benefits online at Social Security Online. If you'd rather deal in person, check the Web site to see if one of Social Security's 1,300 offices is anywhere near you. You can also look in the White Pages under U.S. Government. By phone, help is at 800-772-1213, from 7:00 a.m. until 7:00 p.m., Eastern time. At other times, you can call that number for automated help.

Social Security also provides a tremendous amount of consumer information and publications online. For publications, go to www.ssd.gov/pubs.

How Your Social Security Benefits Are Taxed. Retirees with middle incomes and up may owe federal income taxes on part of their Social Security benefits. There are two levels of tax:

1. At the first level (incomes of $25,000 to $34,000 for singles or $32,000 to $44,000 for marrieds filing jointly), up to 50 percent of your benefits are subject to tax.

2. At the second level (above $34,000 for singles or $44,000 for marrieds filing joint returns), you'll owe taxes on up to 85 percent of your Social Security benefits. That doesn't mean your tax rate is 85 percent, only that up to 85 percent of your benefits are taxed in your regular bracket. Some states also tax Social Security income, but most don't.

Every January you'll be mailed a Social Security Benefit Statement (Form SSA-1099) showing how much money you received. Use that to figure out whether any taxes are owed. When adding up your income, include half your Social Security benefits, municipal bond interest, and certain other nontaxable items.

How Should You Invest for Retirement?

The investment rules in chapter 21 are as good at 65 as at 35. But there are several points that retirees in particular should think about:

1. You are not dead! You will probably live for another 25 years or more, during which time inflation will nibble or chomp at any fixed income you receive. You might impoverish yourself if you put all your money in bonds, certificates of deposit, money market mutual funds, or other fixed-income investments. Your savings might run out in 10 or 15 years, leaving you at the mercy of welfare or your kids. You *must* keep some portion of your capital invested for growth—in stock-owning mutual funds. I don't care about the market crash. Stocks rebuild themselves over time.

2. It's too late for making crazy investments. This is no time to get aggressive with your portfolio. You can own a small amount of small-stock funds and emerging-market funds, but be sure you balance them with extra money allocated to Treasury bonds. That combination gives you growth while limiting your portfolio's downside in bad markets.

3. You need heart attack insurance. When the stock market crashes, you have to be able to wait it out. That means knowing for sure that you can pay your bills for several years into the future. So figure out how much money you need to draw from your savings every year for current expenses*—say, $10,000. Put twice that amount, or $20,000, into a savings account or money market mutual fund. That covers you for the next two years. Then put three times that annual amount into certificates of deposit—one $10,000 CD maturing in three years, another one maturing in four years, and a third one maturing in five years. Your basic expenses are now covered for five full years. Market declines will still be scary, but at least you'll know that no one can put you out on the street. Every year or so, take money out of your long-term investments and add it to your cash cache, so that you're always covered for the next five years of living expenses.

4. Paying taxes won't kill you. When investing, pursue an appropriate strategy and pay your taxes as they fall. If you look at the tax angle first and the investment angle second, you are going to make some lousy decisions. For example, if you're a low-bracket investor, municipal bonds will yield you almost nothing after inflation. If you're 75, you don't want a tax-deferred variable annuity with penalties for withdrawals over the next 15 years. If 25 percent of your money is in the stock of your former employer, sell it, pay the capital gains tax, and diversify.

---

*To figure this amount, determine your income from Social Security, pensions, and other regular sources. Subtract your essential expenses, for food, fuel, utilities, taxes, home upkeep, insurance, medications, and transportation. The gap between these two numbers is the amount you have to withdraw from savings every year.

5. It's too late to start from scratch. Hordes of entrepreneurs troll for new retirees who dream of beginning another life. They'll hold out a dream of riches if you'll just invest your severance pay or lump sum pension payout in their guinea hen farms or solar go-karts. Don't do it. You are holding the only serious money that you will ever have. If you want to start a business, grow it yourself out of personal experience and the contacts you have.

6. There's more than one way to skin a cat. "Income investors" usually focus on interest income—from bonds or certificates of deposit. But stock dividends are income too. With a portion of your money in dividend-paying stocks, you're getting income and some growth. Furthermore, growth in the value of your stocks can be income too. Whether you're getting 5 percent from the interest on a $10,000 bond or by selling 50 shares of a $10 stock, you're collecting $500 to spend.

Some Investing Rules of Thumb for Retirees

- *To find a comfortable allocation between stocks and bonds, subtract your age from 110.* That's the percentage of your assets to put into stocks. Say, for example, you're 65: 110 minus 65 leaves 45. Put 45 percent of your assets into stock-owning mutual funds.

- *The all-important 4 percent rule.* The first year you retire, withdraw no more than 4 percent of your total savings to help pay your bills. With $100,000 in savings, you'd take $4,000. In the second year, withdraw the original amount plus an amount equal to that year's inflation rate. With 3 percent inflation, you'd take $4,120. In the third year, withdraw the amount you took in the second year plus an additional sum to cover inflation. You're now up to $4,244. Continue this system, raising each new year's withdrawal by the current inflation rate. Tons of good research say that if you don't exceed these amounts, you can be reasonably sure that your nest egg will last for 25 years and possibly more than 30 years, depending on how you invest. For a 40-year retirement, start your withdrawal rate at 3 percent of your portfolio. If there's a bad bear market when your first retire, my commiserations—and see page 1149.

- *What about the new 5 and 6 percent rules?* Financial planners are trying to figure out how to squeeze more income from your retirement investments and still have the money last for 25 or 30 years. The studies that show it's safe to take more than 4 percent assume that you'll hold 65 to 75 percent of your money in stocks. You get more growth from these portfolios, wind up with more money in later age, and, potentially, leave more for heirs. On the other hand, your investments will also suffer more in the years that stocks decline—and in those years, you have to be prepared to reduce the amounts you withdraw. So it's not a steady 5 percent (plus inflation) withdrawal rate, it's more stop and start. To go this route, you have to have enough money and fortitude to get through bad markets without fear.

▪ *What if you're 80?* For a 20-year retirement period, starting with a 5 percent withdrawal is safe, with an additional amount added for inflation every year.

▪ *What kinds of stock funds should you buy?* That depends on your strategy. Over time, small-stock value funds should give you higher returns than funds invested in Standard & Poor's 500-stock index. The problem is that they're volatile. In a selling panic, their prices plunge. But consider pairing them with some S&P stocks for 35 percent of your money, with the other 65 percent invested in safe one-year Treasury bills. If the stock market drops, only about a third of your money will be at risk. What's more, the combination of small stocks and Treasuries provides the same expected return as a portfolio invested 100 percent in the large-company S&P stocks, and with less risk.

This approach might not be for you. You might prefer a more traditional allocation, such as 25 percent U.S. stocks, 25 percent international and emerging-market stocks, and 50 percent high-quality bonds. These are the kinds of decisions a fee-only planner (one who manages money) can help you make. Planners have computer programs that run the different options, showing you potential outcomes and likely risks.

▪ *Diversify out of any stock you hold in your former company.* If you want to keep some of it, don't let it exceed 5 percent of your portfolio.

▪ *If you invest in high-yield bond funds, treat them as part of your stock allocation, not your bond allocation.* They tend to rise and fall with stocks and the economy. By contrast, high-quality bonds tend to move in an opposite direction from stocks. Quality bonds are diversifiers; high-yield bonds are not.

Taking Withdrawals from Your Individual Retirement Account

Most likely, you'll start taking withdrawals when you retire or soon after. You decide the amounts you want (no more than 4 percent of the money, please—for safety's sake). When you reach 70½, strict withdrawal rules click in (page 1117). If you don't take the right amount, you face a humongous fine: 50 percent of the money you should have taken but didn't. The trustees of your IRA should remind you about withdrawals each year. Don't let it slip your mind.

Investment Strategies to Consider—
Inside and Outside an IRA

In plotting your retirement investment strategies, consider your savings as a whole. Some money may be in Individual Retirements Accounts and some in taxable accounts. Some may be in mutual funds and some in the bank. The strategies below don't pay attention to the types of account you have, only to the strategy as a whole. In general, your fixed-income investments should be concentrated in your IRA. Hold your stock fund investments outside the IRA, to get the low tax rate on capital gains.

It's hard to execute a sensible withdrawal strategy if you're holding individual stocks. When you need 4 percent from your portfolio, what should you sell? The pharma stock? The mining stock? The tech stock? Who knows? What's more, individual stocks may not be good for your financial health (see chapter 24). In retirement, convert your individual stocks into stock-owning mutual funds. Never mind the taxes. Mutual funds are better diversified, and they make it easier to create an income stream. Here are 14 ways of living on your money for life:

1. The Simple One-Pot Strategy

Invest your money in a mix of stock and bond mutual funds at a single mutual fund company. At 65, a reasonable allocation would be 45 percent diversified stocks, 55 percent short- and long-term bonds. At 70, consider 40 percent stocks and 60 percent bonds. For the stock portion, favor funds invested in U.S. dividend-paying stocks and international stocks from developed countries.

Reinvest all your dividends and ask your mutual fund company to rebalance your portfolio once a year (page 710). Also, ask the fund to put you on an automatic withdrawal plan. Once a year (or once a month if you prefer), your fund will send you a check in the dollar amount that you request. Follow the 4 percent withdrawal plan, explained on page 1141.

As you get older, shift more of your money into bonds and reconsider the amounts that you're taking from your investments every year. Is the 4 percent plan still working? At 80, you could start anew with 5 percent withdrawals, to stretch your money over another 20 years.

With this plan, you make your own investment decisions and get an inflation-adjusted payment that you can budget for. There's no guarantee that your payments will last for life, but the odds are reasonable. If your investments perform poorly, you'll have to reduce the amounts you take. If they perform well, you can recalibrate after a few years. A new start, even at 4 percent, might increase the dollars you can take.

2. An Even Simpler One-Pot Strategy

Three investment companies—the Vanguard Group, Fidelity Investments, and Charles Schwab—have developed *payout funds* for people in their retirement years. You invest a large chunk of money in a single payout fund. The manager allocates your investment among the company's stock and bond funds. You receive a monthly check, which varies in size, depending on how well the investments do. In bad markets, you'll get less, so you have to be prepared to reduce expenses. But you'd do that anyway if you were running your money yourself. In good markets, you'll have more to spend.

The funds have different objectives. Vanguard's and Schwab's are designed to provide payouts for life and leave something for your heirs. Fidelity's last for a specific number of years. None of these funds requires you to make your own decisions about the percentage of stocks or bonds to own. The professionals decide for you and rebalance automatically. They hope to grow your investment by enough to provide you with increasing monthly payments—if not immediately, then at some point in the future.

These payout funds are new, so they have no track record. There's also no guarantee that they'll last as long as you expect (for guarantees, buy a fixed annuity). What you have instead are three experienced investment companies using their best research to try to squeeze your nest egg for the highest payouts commensurate with your goals. If you change your mind about what they're doing, you can stop at any time and switch to some other type of investment. By the time you read this, other investment companies may be offering payout funds too. Look for the ones with the lowest costs.

Because your income is going to vary, you wouldn't depend on these funds for cash to cover your basic expenses. Instead they're for your discretionary income—travel, entertainment, a new car, gifts—spending you can expand or reduce, depending on how the market does. Here's how they work:

■ *The Vanguard Managed Payout Funds.* You start with a specified monthly payment. Every January the payment is reset for the following year, depending on how the investments performed in the previous year. You may get more or less than you did the year before.

The funds all maintain a higher allocation to stocks than you'd make yourself. That's because they have two objectives: first, to provide you with lifetime payouts, and second, to leave your heirs with at least as much as you originally invested. That takes an aggressive strategy. It works only because your monthly payments can be reduced after poorly performing years.

There are three funds: (1) Growth Focus, with the smallest payout and highest investment in stocks, is for people who'd like some income but are also eager to leave the most that they can to heirs. (2) Payout Distribution Focus, with the highest monthly payout and lowest (but still substantial) commitment to stocks, is for people primarily seeking a higher income for themselves. (3) Growth and Distribution Focus, an in-between fund, is for people interested both in income and in leaving an inheritance.

- *Fidelity Income Replacement Funds, with a Smart Payment Program.* These funds invest your money and send you monthly payments over a fixed number of years. You choose the term. It might be 8 years, 10 years, 12 years, and so on, all the way to 34 years. A target payment is set for the year. It may be higher or lower than the year before, depending on how the investments performed. The goal is to keep your payments rising with inflation, if not every year, then over the fund's entire term.

Fidelity offers you higher monthly payments than Vanguard does, because its funds aren't intended to leave a payment for heirs. At the end of the term, you'll have gotten all of your money back, plus all of the net earnings over the years. If you choose an extended term, these payments could cover you for life. But, of course, the longer the term, the lower the monthly payments will be.

- *Schwab Monthly Income Funds.* They offer you three levels of payout: Maximum (5 to 6 percent annually), Enhanced (4 to 5 percent annually), and Moderate (3 to 4 percent annually). The amount you receive may fluctuate from month to month, depending on how the market does. Again, there are no guarantees.

3. The Two-Pot Rebalancing Strategy

Invest your money in the same mix of stock and bond funds suggested above— say, 40 percent diversified stock funds and 60 percent bond funds. Put yourself on an annual 4 percent withdrawal plan. In year two, if stocks are worth more than 40 percent of your portfolio, take your 4 percent withdrawal, plus an inflation adjustment, from the stock portion of your investments. If the stocks are worth less than 40 percent of your portfolio, take your 4 percent withdrawal by selling bonds. Do the same in each subsequent year, always taking your money from the pot—either stocks or bonds—that exceeds your target allocation.

What if stocks are up but not by enough to cover your full 4 percent withdrawal? Take enough from each pot to get your investments back to the appropriate level—in this example, 40 percent stocks, 60 percent bonds.

With the two-pot plan, you're using your withdrawals to rebalance your portfolio back to its original target at the start of every year. This keeps your portfolio at a constant risk level and may improve your returns (see page 710 on the value of rebalancing). As you get older, change your targets—to 35 percent stocks and 65 percent bonds and, later, to 30 percent stocks and 70 percent bonds.

The drawback to this two-pot strategy, for some, is that you have to manage it yourself. It's easy if you run your own money by computer but harder for people who prefer a passive approach.

4. The Three-Pot Strategy

Divide your investments according to when you'll need the money. One pot for the cash you'll need within 5 years—saved in the bank, a money market mutual fund, or in laddered bonds or CDs. A second pot for money you won't need for at least 12 years—invested in well-diversified stock-owning mutual funds. A third pot for the money in between—invested in bond funds that can be sold to cover emergency expenses or drawn on for income when the stock market falls. To keep everything in balance, shift money from the stock pot to the bond pot or cash pot when the stock market is up.

5. A Higher-Payout Strategy

You might decide that the traditional 4 percent withdrawal rate isn't good enough. You want to start by drawing 5 or 6 percent from your portfolio, plus inflation adjustments in later years. That can work, under four conditions: (1) You invest 65 to 70 percent of your retirement portfolio in well-diversified stocks. (2) You follow the withdrawal rules in the Two-Pot Rebalancing Strategy, above. (3) You won't panic if stocks drop 50 percent in a vicious bear market. (4) You'll take no inflation increases in a year when the portfolio's total value declines and no make-up withdrawals in later years. In steep market declines, you'll skip withdrawals entirely for a few months.

This strategy takes a lot of management, not to mention emotional discipline and budget flexibility. Your money may run out in 10 or 15 years unless you're able to stop withdrawals during bad markets and live on other sources of income. Don't sell when stocks go down, or this plan won't work out. You have to be fully in the game when stocks rise again.

6. A Front-Loaded Strategy

Withdraw more from your retirement portfolio in the early years, intending to cut back in the later years. This requires careful planning. When you reach the cutback stage, your remaining portfolio has to be large enough so that a

4 percent withdrawal rate (plus an annual inflation adjustment) will pay for the standard of living you want. It doesn't hurt to build in a cushion too.

7. An Investments-Plus-Annuity Strategy

This approach provides you with a lot of security.

First, make sure that you have enough guaranteed lifetime income to cover your basic expenses: food, fuel, utilities, transportation, insurance, home upkeep, taxes, and medications. For some retirees, pension and Social Security do the trick. Others provide themselves with a rolling 5 or 10 years' worth of cash and laddered bonds to help pay the bills.

Next, use a substantial part of your savings to buy an immediate-pay lifetime annuity. That provides you with a regular income, guaranteed. Finally, invest the rest of your money in stocks and bonds to use for discretionary spending.

8. The Interest-and-Dividends-Only Strategy

Here you spend your interest and dividends instead of reinvesting them and never touch your principal. To succeed, you need a large portfolio of investments, generating lots of income, or enough outside income to cover your bills with only a small boost from your savings.

As long as you're not spending principal, you might raise the percentage of your investments devoted to stocks. A good choice would be funds that buy dividend-paying companies. In the 20 years ending in 2007, the dollar amount of dividends paid by companies whose stocks are in the S&P 500-stock average grew at an annual compounded rate of 5.9 percent, compared with an inflation rate of 3.1 percent.

The bond portion of your portfolio may or may not keep up with inflation. Bonds yield more income, initially, than dividend-paying stocks but don't have the growth potential.

Both dividends and interest will fall behind inflation, after tax. Eventually you will probably have to dip into your principal. With luck, however, the value of your stock portfolio will have grown, giving you more money to spend.

9. The Bond Ladder (or CD Ladder) Strategy

Use the fixed-income part of your portfolio to create an income stream, lasting any number of years you want. You can do it at the lowest cost with bank certificates of deposit or Treasuries bought through TreasuryDirect.gov.* For a 5-year

---

*Note that you can't use TreasuryDirect to buy bonds for an Individual Retirement Account. You have to use a broker instead. TreasuryDirect is only for individual purchases.

ladder, you might buy five certificates of deposit, maturing in 1 year, 2 years, 3 years, 4 years, and 5 years. For a 10-year ladder, consider a mix of Treasuries and CDs, with bonds and CDs maturing in alternate years. If you're working with a broker or planner, he or she can construct a ladder of corporate or municipal bonds. (This is the most expensive option, because of commissions or fees.)

What happens to each bond or CD at maturity depends on your goals. Did you construct the ladder to cover current expenses? Or are you simply keeping the money at hand in case of need?

To cover expenses, you'll spend the money from each CD as it comes due. In a 5-year ladder, replace it with a new, 5-year CD bought with other funds—for example, funds that you keep in an intermediate-term bond portfolio. Eventually, you'll have five 5-year CDs, with one maturing each year. That's 5 years worth of future expenses, guaranteed, invested at higher interest rates than you'd get from a savings account or money market fund.

If your objective is to keep money on hand for emergencies, don't spend the proceeds of the first CD when it comes due. Instead use the cash to buy a new 5-year CD. Do that each year, and, again, you'll wind up with five 5-year CDs, with one maturing annually. That gives you the flexibility to save or spend, depending on what's happening in your life.

The bond ladder should cover the portion of your savings that you've set aside for current or future expenses. The rest of your portfolio should be allocated to stocks and bonds, for long-term growth.

10. The Two-Act Strategy

Stage your retirement in two acts. For Act One, put 85 percent of your money into a portfolio of short- and intermediate-term bond funds and stock funds that specialize in companies that pay dividends. For Act Two, put the remaining 15 percent into a mix of 20-year Treasury Inflation-Protected Securities and well-diversified stock funds, including growth funds and emerging-markets.

Spend all of your Act One portfolio over the next 20 years—for example, by withdrawing ¹⁄₂₀ of the money every year. The market will produce many good years (despite the 2008–2009 gloom), so your future withdrawals should rise. Alternatively, invest your Act One money in Fidelity's 20-year Income Replacement Fund.

After 20 years, turn to your Act Two portfolio. Your stocks will have grown and your Treasuries will come due, giving you a second pot of money for your later age.

11. The Bear Market Strategy

If a bear market hits just before or shortly after you retire, don't pull all your money out of stocks. Hang in with the amount you allocated. After the bad market passes, you'll need stocks to make your portfolio grow again. But don't take as much money out of your portfolio as you originally intended. Spending too much during the early years of retirement is the main reason that retirees run out of money. Here are some strategies:

■ *Instead of starting your withdrawals at 4 percent of the portfolio, go down to 3 percent, plus an inflation adjustment each year.* Five years later, take another look. If your portfolio has recovered, raise your withdrawal rate to 4 percent, plus an annual adjustment.

■ *If you're already taking 4 percent and don't want to cut back,* don't take inflation adjustments for the next four years.

■ *Don't retire for another two or three years.* Or find a part-time job, so you won't have to withdraw as much from your savings. *Nothing* rescues a retirement faster than getting a few more years of income under your belt.

■ *The worst possible choice is to sell your stocks, switch to bonds and cash, but continue your withdrawals at the previous level.* You'd better hope that your kids will take you in.

12. The Deflation Strategy

What works in deflation, when consumer prices fall persistently for a year or more? (1) Intermediate- and long-term Treasury bonds, because they're safe and can't be called before maturity. (2) Bank CD ladders, for income and security. (3) Municipal bond ladders, using shorter-term munis that can't be called prior to maturity. (4) The stock market, which has performed well during *mild* deflations—especially traditional utilities and other dividend-paying stocks. Brief deflations don't pose a danger to the economy long term. Persistent deflations, however, are dangerous indeed.

13. The Save-Your-Spouse Strategy

When figuring what to do about retirement investments, don't consider your lifetime only. Look at how secure your spouse will be if you die first and your spouse lives to 95 or 100. For good spouse protection, consider:

■ *The joint-and-survivor annuity option for your pension,* so your spouse will have an income for life.

■ *Providing a lifetime annuity if money is likely to run short and you don't have a pension.* (Note that a variable annuity with lifetime benefits may not cover your spouse—page 1093.)

■ *Delaying Social Security until age 66 or even 70 if your spouse will draw benefits on your account.* This increases his or her future lifetime payments.

■ *Providing life insurance if your savings aren't sufficient.* That means converting a term policy into whole life or a whole-life into a no-lapse universal policy.

■ *Ensuring that a younger spouse has health insurance,* if you'll retire and go on Medicare at 65.

■ *Making your spouse a partner in your investment planning while you're still alive.* You want your spouse to be comfortable with managing the money when you're gone.

14. The Get-Help Strategy

I believe strongly in talking to a financial planner about deploying your retirement assets. There are many strategies. You need to play with what-if projections and figure out what works for you. See a fee-only planner (page 1176) or make use of the planning services at the major mutual fund groups. From time to time, recheck your decisions. Markets change, opinions change, life conditions change. You'll want to tap the best ideas, to see you through.

What If You're Afraid of Stocks?

Ignore all the previous advice. Some people haven't the temperament for stocks, don't care about the market, and would be scared stiff if they took a loss. The last thing in the world I want you to do is hand your money to a planner who invests in ways that alarm or confuse you. Leave your money in the bank and live on whatever you have, reducing your expenses as inflation eats into the value of your savings. Millions of people do exactly that. Or use your money to buy an immediate-pay annuity. At this point in life, your personal sense of security matters most.

In What Order Should You Spend from the Various Taxable and Tax-Deferred Accounts You Have?

In general, spend from your taxable accounts first, leaving your tax-deferred account alone to grow. Next, draw from your tax-deferred accounts such as traditional IRAs. Turn last to a Roth IRA, with its tax-exempt earnings. There are a couple of exceptions:

- *If your IRA is large and your income is low,* it pays to draw from the traditional IRA. Take as much as will be taxed in the lowest income brackets. You might be taxed in a higher bracket when you start making mandatory withdrawals at 70½.
- *If you're in a high tax bracket now but will be in a lower bracket in the future,* spend your Roth IRA first and your traditional IRA later, when it will be taxed at a lower rate.

Plan B—Don't Invest Without It

At retirement, you will see a fee-only planner (I hope!), set up an investment strategy, and develop a plan for withdrawing the monthly sum you need to pay your bills. Your plan should be stress-tested. How will it work if the stock market declines 50 percent or more? If it's a conservative plan, it will probably show that you have, say, a 90 percent chance of having your money last for life.

But what about that unruly 10 percent chance that your plan will fail? You need plan B. It tells you what to do if your investments become too small to support your lifestyle. You might have to sell your vacation house, work longer, defer all expensive vacations, and quit making annual gifts to your kids. If your portfolio sinks too far, you might have to sell most of your stocks and annuitize the money, to nail down enough guaranteed income to pay your basic bills. Whatever the strategy, think through plan B at the same time that you're setting up your original investment strategy. Remember: financial crises happen all the time, about one each decade. With luck, you'll never need plan B. If the worst happens, however, you and your spouse will have a survival exit plan.

When Should Retirees Give Up Stocks?

Never, if you're mentally active and well-to-do and can afford to outwait the market's cyclical declines. You probably won't have to use all your money during your lifetime. Even in your 80s, you can risk keeping some of your capital—maybe 20 to 30 percent—invested for growth. You may not get all the benefit, but your heirs will.

The advice changes if you expect to spend most of your savings during your lifetime. During early retirement, you still need stocks to increase the value of your capital and stay ahead of inflation. In late retirement, however, you can't afford the risk of a prolonged market downturn that would reduce the income you need to live on.

So take a look at your statistical life expectancy (page 1205) and modify it by your own state of health and the age your parents died. As you grow closer to that age (maybe five to seven years before), consider selling your remaining stock-owning mutual funds and moving entirely to fixed-income investments. Sell stocks even earlier if your health is poor. Keep two years' worth of living expenses in the bank or a money market mutual fund. With the rest of your capital, build a ladder of short- and intermediate-term bonds or certificates of deposit (page 1147). Spend all of the interest income from your fixed-income investments and as much principal as you need from each bond or CD that matures. The tables on page 1193 will help you determine how long your capital can last. Alternatively, invest in a lifetime annuity. If you own a house, you can access that capital by taking a reverse mortgage or selling and moving into an apartment or senior citizen complex.

Toward the end of your life, you shouldn't be saving money anymore. It's time to spend. These are the years you accumulated all those savings *for.*

Retiring on the House

How to Tap the Equity You've Built

31

**Your home is your piggy bank.
You have only to shake it and money will fall out.**

A lot of money rides on your house. It's usually your biggest asset. When you retire, should you pull out that money or leave it alone? Age in place or age someplace else?

These questions are bound up with where you'll live and may ultimately be swung by things that have nothing to do with money: your health, community ties, the weather, where your kids live, and your feelings about the house you're in. But the money issue has sharpened now that so many people have seen housing prices fall for a period of time. Should you sell right now while you know what your house is worth? Should you tap your home equity for cash? Or should you hang tight? Suddenly, in retirement, you've become a housing speculator.

Should You Move?

Don't move if you're happy in your house, can afford to keep it, and won't be financially affected by whether its value rises or falls. The money you have in home equities is not material to your welfare, at least not now. If you run short of cash sometime in the future, you can think about selling then.

But move sooner rather than later if you want to live somewhere else and depend on the current value of your house to buy the new house or condo you want. Maybe your house will be worth more next year—but then again, maybe it won't. Move, too, if you know that you'll want to age in a smaller place. It's easier to clean out a big house while you still have your health.

How to Make Money on a Move

1. Go to a lower-cost part of the country. Not only will a new house or condominium cost less, but your other living expenses will usually be lower too. That will leave you with more money to invest for a higher retirement income.

2. Stay in your community but trade down to a smaller place. You'll pay less for taxes, insurance, and upkeep and will have money left over to invest. Why be house poor in retirement? Shake loose some of that cash, save or invest it, and use the earnings to maintain your lifestyle.

3. Sell your house and rent. Home ownership is comfortable—no landlord, no rent. On the other hand, the cash you'll net from selling your house might appreciate faster in a diversified investment account than it will by staying locked up in your house. You'll be able to tap the money without borrowing against your home equity or taking an expensive reverse mortgage. Rents will rise, but so will insurance and property taxes for homeowners. Renters might be better off.

4. Move to a lower-cost part of the world. Even when the dollar declines, it can be cheaper to live in certain countries abroad. Your pension and Social Security checks will follow you, but Medicare won't. So check the local health services and whether a private policy will cover you both at home and abroad. Three other financial issues critical to expatriates are taxes (U.S. and foreign), the inheritance rules in the country you've moved to, and investments that hedge against a dollar decline.

5. If you're looking at continuing care communities, see page 478.

The Government Practically Pays You to Move

A beautiful pot of money lies locked up in your house, all of it reachable only if you decide to move. It's everything you paid into the house plus all of your gains over the years. Married couples can take up to $500,000 in profits untaxed; singles get up to $250,000. By profits, I mean any money you've made on the house after subtracting the price you originally paid, the cost of all home improvements over the years, and fix-up costs and real estate commissions when you sell. Most people will find that they can take their entire net profits tax free.

In some states, counter–tax breaks may encourage you not to sell. In California, for example, people who don't move pay lower property taxes than people who do. But that's the exception. For the majority of older Americans, moving—and downsizing—pays.

Alternatives to Moving

For many retirees, trading down to a less expensive house or condominium, or switching to rental housing, is so practical that it should top their list of retirement solutions. But if you want to hang on to your house despite the fact that money is short, you have several alternatives:

- *If you're still paying off your mortgage, you might refinance the loan over a new, 30-year period.* Your monthly payments will decline, leaving you with more to spend.

- *You might take in a roommate or a boarder.* A house too costly for one to maintain might be duck soup for two. Some mortgage lenders make special loans available to home owners who want to add a senior citizen apartment. But don't make a move without checking the following points: (1) Does your zoning allow you to take in boarders? (2) Are you subject to rent control laws? If so, your tenant might gain the right to occupy that apartment forever at a fixed or slowly rising rent. (3) Is the boarder covered by your liability insurance? (4) Have you taken a lesson in how business properties are taxed? For example, if you sell your house, you're taxed on the profit allocated to the portion of your house that was used as a rental apartment. (5) Are you offering a written lease? Without one, you may have no grounds for evicting a bad tenant. (6) Do you have the temperament to be a landlord (page 996)?

- *You might sell the house to one or more of your children and lease it back from them for life.* Here's how that deal works: (1) The children give you a 10 or 20 percent down payment. (2) You give them a mortgage for the rest of the money they owe. (3) The children send you a mortgage payment every month. (4) You pay your children a monthly rent, which, at the start, is less than the mortgage payment you receive. So holding the mortgage adds to your income. (5) The children pay the insurance and taxes. For them, the house is a rental property, so the mortgage interest, taxes, insurance, and depreciation are all deductible business expenses. Those deductions shelter their rental income and possibly some of their ordinary income, depending on how much money they make (page 606). (6) The children see to maintenance and repairs, which for them are also tax deductible. You usually pay the utility bills.

Work out this transaction with a lawyer. The house price, mortgage interest rate, and current and future rent must all be set at fair market value, or your children will lose their tax deductions.

You face some risks with a sale-leaseback. What if your child gets a divorce and has to sell the house as part of a property settlement? What if you and your child have a fight and he or she tries to drive you into a nursing home? Remember King Lear. What if you sold to two children together and they can't agree on the necessary repairs? You can also do a sale-leaseback with an outside investor, but that's even riskier. Outsiders could push you hard if they wanted their money out.

■ *You might reduce your expenses by using local programs available to low- or moderate-income home owners.* For example, you may be able to defer your real estate taxes or get a home repair loan that needn't be repaid until your house is sold. Ask about these and other forms of financial assistance at your local senior citizen center (find it through www.eldercare.gov).

■ *If you own your house free and clear, you might give it to a charity or an educational institution.* Talk to the charity about the kinds of arrangements it will make. You'll get an immediate tax deduction for the value of the gift and the right to live in the house for life. You pay the real estate taxes, insurance, and maintenance. At your death (and the death of your spouse, if the gift covers both of you), the house passes to the charity. This solution pays the most if you're older and your tax bracket is high.

■ *Your kids might kick in to help pay the expenses.* Try not to do this to them. They have troubles of their own.

■ *You might take a reverse mortgage—but only as a last resort.*

Reverse Mortgages: Money from Your Home

Reverse mortgages (also known as home equity conversions) let you tap the equity in your home without moving and without adding to your daily expenses. They feel like free money, easy to reach. For some retirement problems, they're the perfect solution. Unfortunately, they're being overhyped and deceptively sold. If misused, they can hurt your finances in the end. This section will help you decide whether or not a reverse mortgage is for you.

— Reverse Mortgages, Explained —

Reverse mortgages are loans against the equity you hold in your home. You can get one as early as age 62 (if you're married, you both have to be at least 62)—but resist. Financially, these loans are best for older people—typically 75 and up—with small incomes, paid-up homes (or homes that are almost paid up), and a life more pinched than it ought to be. Different lenders offer different programs. Generally speaking, the deal works like this:

1. A lender agrees to give you the loan. How much you can borrow has nothing to do with your income or credit history. It depends entirely on your age, the age of your spouse, how much equity you have in your home, current interest rates, and which reverse-mortgage program you choose. If you still have a mortgage against your home, you can use the proceeds to pay it off.

2. You pay little or no cash up front. All closing and insurance costs are included in the loan. (Warning: Those costs are high. *Very* high.)

3. You can take the money in one of several ways: a check a month, a fixed number of checks, a lump sum, a credit line that you can draw against at will, or a combination of these options. Borrowers especially like the credit line because it lets them use money as needed.

4. The lender charges interest on the loan, but you don't pay it currently. There are no monthly mortgage checks to write. The interest you owe builds up inside the loan, to be paid when the house is eventually sold. Every year, the amount you owe goes up, and by a lot.

5. You continue to pay the insurance and property taxes, as usual, and are responsible for keeping the house in good condition.

6. When the last surviving borrower(s)—say, you and your spouse—leave the house or die, the loan comes due. The house is sold. The lender gets its money out of the proceeds of the sale. Anything left over goes to you, if you're alive, or to your heirs. If it turns out that you borrowed more than the house is currently worth, the lender or insurance pool has to swallow the loss.

7. Each check looks and feels like income. But it isn't income, it's a loan. So it doesn't raise your income tax or reduce the size of your Social Security check. Nor will it hinder your access to programs for the low-income elderly in most states, as long as you borrow only enough to cover your expenses each month. That means no lump sum, unless it's spent in a single month, although monthly checks and credit lines are okay.

8. The older you are, the more you can borrow. For example, take a 75-year-old widow with $200,000 in home equity, borrowing at 7 percent interest. A reverse mortgage insured by the Federal Housing Administration (FHA) might pay her $782 a month for as long as she stays in the house. If she took out the loan at 85, she might get $1,228 a month.

9. You can get a reverse mortgage if you own a single-family home, a two- to four-unit property, a manufactured home, or a condominium. Some lenders accept New York City co-ops. Mobile home owners are usually out. You can also use a reverse mortgage to raise cash for buying a new home.

The Rewards

■ *With reverse mortgages, older people can usually stay in their homes as long as they're able,* thanks to the income the loan provides.

- *The loan proceeds can help meet the challenges of a longer life*—covering monthly bills if your savings run out or financing home health care so that you won't have to go to a nursing home.
- *The money also helps you keep the house in good repair* or helps you renovate for a downstairs bedroom or wheelchair access.

The Risks

- *A reverse mortgage may seduce you into keeping your house when you shouldn't.* It might be wiser to sell, save or invest your profits, and move to an apartment, condominium, or assisted-living home. Consider those options first and a reverse mortgage last. A reverse mortgage will cost you a chunk of your assets.
- *A salesperson might convince you to borrow as soon as you qualify, at age 62.* That's a big mistake. Younger borrowers get the lowest amount of cash and, over time, wind up with the largest loans. Your debt grows and grows as the interest owed builds up.
- *Worse, when you borrow early in your retired life, you use up your home equity too soon.* Without equity, you won't be able to buy a condo later in life. You won't have the cash to move into a quality home for assisted living. You'll have no money left to hire a health care aide whose visits could help keep you in your home. Maybe you thought your house would double in value, restoring the home equity you've taken out. Not likely. Save your reverse-mortgage option for later in life!
- *You pay huge effective rates of interest if you leave your house soon after taking out the loan* (maybe 50 percent a year in the first two years). That's because you pay closing costs and other fees up front while receiving the loan balance gradually, over time. If you're very long lived, however, you might wind up paying just 5 percent.
- *You may misunderstand the loan's permanence.* A "lifetime" loan doesn't necessarily last a lifetime. It lasts only as long as you stay in your home. The contract defines the end of that term, and you should study its every nuance. Can you spend 3 months in a nursing home and then return? Probably yes. How about 12 months? Probably not—if you're away 12 months, the lender can usually force a sale. Your house can also be sold if the lender decides that you're not keeping it in good condition.

Beware the Sales Pitches!

Salespeople earn large commissions on reverse mortgages—typically, up to 1 percent of the value of your home. So they come after you—by phone, mail, Web, TV, and highway billboard. Sample sales croons:

- *"Take the money for a cruise, buy an RV, or help your grandchild go to college."* Translation: "Spend, spend, spend. Never mind saving for the future."
- *"Use the proceeds to buy an annuity paying a lifetime income."* Reverse mortgage "workshops" are often run by salespeople whose chief interest lies in selling you a deferred annuity. They get you to take the loan and then wheel the money into a product that pays them a huge commission. To buy these expensive products, you have to take your reverse mortgage in a lump sum. That's the most expensive way to borrow and leaves you with no flexibility. And anyway, why bother? The reverse mortgage itself provides you with a monthly income, and at a lower cost than the annuity deal. If you want an income that will continue after you sell the house, consider buying an annuity then, not now. Proposals like these come very close to being scams.
- *"This loan gives you cash while you're waiting for your stocks to come back."* And you'll pay more in interest and fees than your stocks will ever earn.
- *"The value of your house is falling, grab the money while you can."* Translation: "I'm reading the headlines and know that this idea will scare you into doing what I want." In fact, you don't know if the value of your house will fall in the future. It might not. Second, you're still stripping valuable equity out of your house too soon. Don't do it! Wait until you're older and then decide.

The Reverse-Mortgage Programs

1. The most popular. The Home Equity Conversion Mortgage (HECM), insured by the Federal Housing Administration, accounts for more than 90 percent of the market. In 2009, you could borrow up to $625,500, depending on your age, current interest rates, and the value of your home. It's linked to the limits on loans that can be bought or guaranteed by Fannie Mae and Freddie Mac and is subject to change by Congress every year. For the latest, see the AARP Web site, www.aarp.org/money/personal/reverse_mortgages.

On any home within its lending limits, HECM gives you the largest loan. Even better, it offers a credit line that rises in the years ahead. That gives you more future borrowing power to help cover future bills.

Fees are higher than on competing loans because of the insurance that's included. It guarantees that you'll always have access to your credit line, even if the company managing your account goes out of business.

The HECM loan interest rate, however, is generally lower than you'll find elsewhere. For more on total loan costs, see TALC (page 1161).

For a quick-and-dirty look at how much you might be able to borrow with a HECM, use the Ibis Software calculator at www.rmc.ibisreverse.com.

2. Jumbo loans, for expensive homes. They're offered by a few private lenders and may provide more cash up front than you can get from HECM. They also charge more—much more—counting both interest rates and fees. This market changes constantly, so I've decided not to list specific products. If you live in an area of high-value homes, an insurance broker will know them (and pitch them to you). Alternatively, look for lenders on the Web site of the National Reverse Mortgage Lenders Association (www.reversemortgage.org). I predict that when you check the costs and the various limitations on these jumbo loans, you'll decide that HECM makes more sense.

3. The alternatives. If all you need is enough money for minor home repairs, your state or city may offer low-rate loans or grants for low- to moderate-income seniors. You might qualify for property tax abatements or for public benefits, such as Supplemental Security Income to help pay your bills. Go to www.elder care.gov to find agencies in your community that will help. You might also run your income and assets through www.aarp.org/quicklink to see what kinds of help you might have overlooked.

Finally, consult with your kids about reverse mortgages. They might decide that helping you with your bills is a better deal than losing their chance to inherit the equity in your home. On the other hand, they might not—the mortgage might look good to them. Either way, it's wise to include them in your thinking.

How to Get the Best Deal on a Reverse Mortgage

1. Choose a HECM. For most borrowers, it's the right loan.

2. Compare the HECM with one of the jumbo loans if you have an expensive house. Sometimes the jumbo wins. Often, however, you'll find that the HECM gives you all the cash you need, while saving you thousands of dollars in costs.

3. Look beyond the up-front cash the lender offers. A jumbo lender might provide a higher credit line at the start. But because HECM's credit line grows every year, HECM will probably provide you with much more money in the end. Your HEMC counselor (page 1161) can help you figure this out.

4. The most expensive way to borrow is by taking a lump sum up front.

You pay interest and fees on the whole amount, even though you intend to use only part of the money each month. Fixed monthly payments aren't much better because your income won't rise with inflation. The best option is taking the loan in the form of a credit line. That way, you can draw money as needed and will be charged interest only on the amounts you actually use. What's more, a HECM credit line rises every year, so your borrowing power—and future income—will go up.

5. Reverse mortgages carry all the fees of regular mortgages and then some. You might pay $15,000 to $20,000 up front.

6. Most of these loans charge variable interest rates, adjusted annually. HECM gives you three choices: (1) A loan with a rate that adjusts monthly. You get higher monthly payments and a lower initial interest rate than on the alternative choices. Over the life of the loan, however, the rate can rise by up to 10 percentage points. (2) A loan whose rate adjusts annually. You get smaller payments and a higher initial interest rate. The rate can rise by up to 2 points per year and 5 points over the life of the loan. (3) A loan with a rate that never changes, but there's a catch. You have to take the whole amount as a lump sum.

7. Finding the lowest-cost loan is tricky. Normal comparisons of rates and fees don't work. Reverse lenders are required to calculate a *Total Annual Loan Cost,* or *TALC rate,* based on all projected costs. The TALC rate is far from a perfect disclosure, but it lets you compare two loans in a reasonable way. Always ask for the TALC rate.

You can get a better, more customized cost estimate from a good reverse-mortgage counselor. The counselor should be working with special computer software developed for this purpose by the AARP. The program lets you enter specific interest rates, possible rates of home appreciation, and the rate at which you'll draw money from your credit line. That shows you how the costs of the various loans change over time.

8. If your home rises substantially in value or interest rates drop, you might want to refinance your reverse mortgage. You'll pay the closing costs all over again, so ask the mortgage counselor to show you, in real numbers, all the pros and cons.

What's This About a Counselor?

By law, you have to be counseled before taking a federally insured, HECM reverse mortgage, by a counselor approved by the U.S. Department of Housing and Urban Development. They're trained to take an impartial view. Good counselors show you the various borrowing options and their costs. (Be sure they're using that AARP-developed software!) They should also look at your personal situation, to help you decide whether to take this loan at all.

Reverse-mortgage lenders will rustle up a counselor for you—probably one who will encourage you to borrow. You can find your own counselor at the AARP-sponsored Web site HECM Resources (www.hecmre sources.org) or by calling HUD at 800-569-4287. They work by phone as well as in person. Their advice is free or low cost. HUD rules require the fee to be linked to your ability to pay, with a top of $125. No one can be refused counseling for not paying.

Call one of these counselors if you're considering a jumbo loan too. Take their advice seriously! The right decision will save you tens of thousands of dollars.

Where to Get Tons of Information

Go to www.aarp.org/money/personal/reverse_mortgages. You'll find great consumer information and advice as well as links to sources for HUD-approved counselors and reverse-mortgage lenders. You can download a free publication, "Home Made Money," or order a copy by calling 800-209-8085.

Also, stop by the lenders' trade association, the National Reverse Mortgage Lenders Association, at www.reversemortgage.org. And don't miss the warnings put out by FINRA, which regulates securities firms. Go to www.finra .org, click on "Investors," then on "Investor Alerts," and then on "Retirement Accounts."

Contemplating the Paid-up House

If you have enough cash to pay off the mortgage, should you or shouldn't you? This is one of those questions that can only be answered "It depends."

If you have enough income to live on, pay off the loan. A paid-up house stabilizes your living costs, saves you interest payments, and makes you feel secure. You don't give a hoot about locking up capital because you have all the income you need.

If your savings are earning substantially more than your mortgage interest rate, you might decide not to pay off the loan. But even in that situation, you might be happier without having mortgage bills roll in. By this time of life, you shouldn't have much of a mortgage left anyway.

If money is tight, however, hang on to your mortgage. If you pay off the loan, your precious liquidity will be lost. You'll be house rich but cash poor. You might even be forced to sell the house or take a reverse mortgage just to get your capital back out. For you, paying interest on a mortgage is the price of financial flexibility. You might even consider refinancing your existing mortgage into a new 30-year loan, in order to reduce the monthly payments.

If you paid off the mortgage and regret it, you can (1) try for a home equity credit line from your bank (hard to get, however, if your income is small); (2) sell your house, buy something smaller, and add the extra capital to your bank account; (3) sell your house and rent; (4) consider a reverse mortgage.

If you sell and buy a smaller place, should you take a mortgage or pay cash? Again, it depends on the size of your ready savings. Paying cash is best; it's no fun paying mortgage interest when you're retired. First and foremost, however, you must keep enough cash on hand to pay your future bills.

Should You Rent or Own?

In later life, sometimes it's smarter to quit being a homeowner. Consider selling your house, investing the proceeds for a higher retirement income, and renting an apartment. Here's how to look at the financial alternatives:

If You Buy a New House or Condo

1. Estimate the amount of money you'd have on hand if you sold your present house. Count your current savings and investments, plus the proceeds from the sale. Call that your pot.

2. Estimate how much a new home will cost. If you pay cash, subtract that total from your pot. If you'll take a mortgage, subtract the down payment. What's left is the money you have to live on. As a rough guide, assume that you'll use 4 percent of that money to help pay your annual bills.

3. Add up your monthly housing expenses—mortgage payment, if any, taxes, insurance, utilities, upkeep, and a reserve for repairs. Multiple by 12, to get the annual amount. If you itemize on your tax return, subtract the value of the deduction for real estate taxes and any mortgage interest. This is your net housing cost.

4. Subtract your net housing cost from the 4 percent you'll take from your pot. What's left is the net cash you'll have left over for other expenses.

If You Rent

1. Again, add up your total pot—savings, investments, and the proceeds from the sale of the house. Assume that you'll take 4 percent of that amount to help pay your annual bills.

2. Add up your monthly rental expenses—principally rent, utilities, and insurance and multiply by 12, to get the annual amount. This is your housing cost.

3. Subtract your housing cost from the 4 percent you're taking from your pot. What's left is the net cash you'll have left over for other expenses.

This rough comparison tells you which choice will give you a higher income right now. But it leaves things out. On the home-owning side of the ledger, your house might rise in value, which would provide more equity for your later years. Young retirees might want to own; older retirees might want to rent.

On the renter's side of the ledger lies a much larger pool of capital, thanks to all the money that was liberated from the house. With wise investing, that capital might gain more in value than if it were still tied up in your home. Rents will probably rise every year or so. But you can cover them with your investment gains or with that extra capital you have on tap. And remember: if you own, your insurance, upkeep, and real estate taxes will rise too.

So the question of renting versus owning is also answered "It depends." Work out the numbers and see how you feel about it. You'll also find rent-versus-buy calculators on the Web (use with many grains of salt!).

The Piggy Bank

Older people can count themselves lucky if they enter retirement with a home, especially a paid-up home. It's worth the effort when you're young if it points you toward freedom and financial flexibility as you age.

MAKING IT WORK

This book, I hope, has been moving you to make decisions. First you have to study and learn, then you have to follow up. A plan that stays in your head is a daydream. What adds to your wealth are the actions you take and whether you manage to take them in time.

At the end of this chapter, you'll find the broad principles that give shape to financial plans. Tackle them one after the other. Flesh them out with safe and sane financial products (many of which I've named in this book). You'll get more ideas as you go along.

Occasionally your goals will change, as successes and mistakes refine your knowledge of yourself. But having made one plan, you can easily make more and better ones. No activity is more comforting than drawing a circle around your finances and pronouncing them sound.

32

Be Your Own Planner . . . Or Find One You Trust

The Secret, Revealed

**You've been waiting for 31 chapters for the secret
to handling money well. Here it is: Use common
sense. The simplest choices are the best ones.
Impulse is your enemy, time your friend.**

Most families don't need professional investment advisers, especially if your assets are principally in retirement plans. Sensible management isn't hard! To be your own guru, you need only a list of objectives, a few simple financial products, realistic investment expectations, a time frame that gives your investments time to work, and a well-tempered humbug detector to keep you from falling for rascally sales pitches. Don't put off decisions for fear you're not making the best choice in every circumstance. Often, there isn't a "best" choice. Any one of several will work.

On the other hand, almost everyone can profit from a two-hour conversation with a *true* financial planner (see what I mean by "true" on page 1171). The planner can help you set priorities, align your spending and saving with your lifetime goals, spot things you've overlooked, and make other valuable suggestions.

I can think of some circumstances where a planner is a must. For example:

1. You earn good wages but cannot manage to save a dime. You need a reality check. Someone has to show you—in dollars and cents—how little you'll have when you retire unless you shape up. Most of us shape ourselves up. If you can't, get help.

2. You face a question that can be answered only by someone with technical expertise. For example, your company might have made you an early-retirement buyout offer and you want to examine your alternatives. Or, you're retiring and have several choices about how to handle the money in your retirement plan. That's a onetime decision with many tax and personal ramifications, and you want to get it right.

3. You're following your own plan—for savings, investments, and insurance—and wonder if an expert can improve it. Arrange for a meeting at an hourly fee. Make it clear that you want to talk about strategies and concepts, not sit through a sales pitch for financial products. (You shouldn't be with a "selling" planner in the first place.) Make no decisions until you've gone home and thought about it.

4. You have a substantial amount of money and lack the time, interest, and knowledge to manage it yourself.

5. You're not interested in planning, won't do it yourself, or are uncomfortable making decisions on your own. You start with a plan but don't have the discipline to keep it up. Find a planner and off-load the job.

6. You're pretending everything is fine even though you have only $5,000 in retirement savings and $25,000 in credit card debt. A planner can yank you out of denial and ease you onto a more productive path.

A talk with a planner will have one of three results: (1) You'll find a wonderful adviser who makes suggestions you're grateful for and whom you'll decide to work with on a continuing basis. These will almost certainly be fee-only planners—see page 1176. (2) You'll feel more confident that your personal decisions have generally been good ones and will continue managing your affairs yourself. You'll incorporate some of the planner's new ideas. (3) You'll run into a planner who makes you doubt your competence while urging you to rely on his or her advice. Or a planner who says that you'll do even better by buying the products (especially annuities) that he or she sells. In this last case, turn up the volume on your humbug detector. These planners earn commissions and plan to earn them from you.

Don't go near a broker or commissioned planner if you've just come into a lot of money (an inheritance, an insurance settlement, a lump sum retirement payout) and don't know what to do with it. Clients with loose cash and weak convictions are fresh meat, ready for roasting. A self-interested planner may urge you to buy high-commission investments that serve his or her objectives better than yours. Because you don't know much about investing, you won't know what's going on.

Before you set foot in the office of a stockbroker, insurance agent, or financial planner, learn the basics yourself. Sock your money into bank certificates of deposit or a money market fund, then study up. Read books. Work out your priorities. Take all the time you need to understand the tried-and-true principles of successful investing. Six months, one year, the wait doesn't matter. During that time, your money will quietly earn interest with no risk of loss and no risk of slipping into bad hands. The only expert that a novice can safely visit is a certified public accountant, for tax advice. That is, provided that the accountant doesn't sell financial products.

When you're ready to launch, you have two possible directions: (1) Try investing yourself, a little in this mutual fund, a little in that one (chapter 22). Give it a year, see how it feels, then invest some more. Don't worry about "missing the market." There's a new market every day. Once you've had some experience, you might discover you like it and keep going. Or you might decide that you want professional advice. (2) Turn to an investment adviser. You now know the language. You should be able to tell the difference between good and poor advice. That's what this long apprenticeship was for: to develop your ability to judge.

The Best Thing a True Planner Can Do for You

Help you set goals, prepare for life's potential shocks, then align your spending, saving, and investing to get you through. Picking investments is incidental compared with the importance of creating a framework for long-term success.

Which Kind of Professional to See

See a Certified Public Accountant (CPA)—for tax planning, tax form preparation, and small-business planning advice. Enrolled agents, who are licensed to represent you before the IRS, and public accountants, also have tax practices. Some CPAs have expanded their practice into personal financial planning (page 1178), earning a personal financial specialist (PFS) designation. It's a weaker designation than a CFP (page 1170), but the accounting profession intends to strengthen it.

See a Tax Attorney—for wills and estate planning. Any lawyer can provide an "I love you" will. That means "Everything to my spouse; if my spouse dies first, everything to the children (in trust, if they're minors); with my spouse's name on all beneficiary forms, such as 401(k)s and IRAs." For anything more complicated, see an attorney who specializes in estate planning.

See a Life Insurance Agent (Preferably a Low-Load Agent) or Fee-Only Life Insurance Planner—for a life insurance policy. For low-loads, see page 371. A chartered life underwriter (CLU) knows more about insurance than the average agent. Your attorney and insurance planner should work together if you want a policy to help pay estate taxes or buy your share of a closely held business. Term insurance you can buy yourself, online.

See a Health Insurance Agent—for health insurance, disability insurance, and long-term care policies.

See a Stockbroker—for help with buying stock, bonds, and mutual funds. (Although there are better ways. See page 793.) Many brokerage firms will also find you an investment adviser (typically for sums of $25,000 and up). The fee will be stiffer than if you went to a fee-only financial planner. Note that most brokers nowadays call themselves financial consultants, financial advisers, financial analysts, or vice presidents. They're all still stockbrokers, and their business is selling. They're not true planners or investment advisers.

See a Registered Investment Adviser (RIA)—for managing a large sum of money. Independent advisers set minimums in the $250,000 to $1 million range. They're *fiduciaries,* meaning that they have to put the interests of their clients ahead of their own. They also have to be registered with the state or the Securities and Exchange Commission and make a variety of disclosures—see page 1183.)

Titles such as "investment consultant" or "wealth manager" are self-awarded. Anyone can use them, whether they have expertise or not. I'd assume *not.* For personal money management, stick with RIAs. Anyone who charges you for investment advice and isn't an RIA could be breaking the law.

For an excellent explanation of the difference between brokers, advisers, and financial planners, including their services and differing legal obligations to customers, get the free brochure "Cutting Through the Confusion" on the Web site run by the North American Securities Administrators Association (www.nasaa.org). Click on Investor Education, then on Financial Education Resources.

See a "Planner"? *No.* Anyone can claim to be a financial planner. There are no rules. When scouting for a true planner, you're seeking specific professional and educational credentials. Plain old financial planners, without those credentials, are imposters.

See a Certified Financial Planner (CFP)—for advice on how your finances fit together: budgeting, saving, taxes, insurance, investing, college accounts, and retirement planning. There are two types of CFPs:

1. CFPs who sell financial products and charge commissions. They're qualified planners. But because they have to sell to make a living, their advice is inevitably biased, even if they don't mean it to be. They don't have a lot of time to spend on issues such as budgeting, getting out of debt, and retirement savings such as 401(k)s, which don't require you to buy something from them.

2. CFPs who sell no products and charge only fees. To my mind, these are the true planners. They engage you in personal discussions that help you sort out your priorities, align your budget with your goals, and arrive at a financial plan that works. Many fee-only planners are also Registered Investment Advisers and will manage your money, if that's what you want. Usually they invest it in low-cost, no-load mutual funds or exchange-traded funds. To qualify for money management services, you'll probably need an investment account in the $50,000 to $200,000 range, although some planners accept less. In a full-service shop, you'll also find accountants and tax attorneys, and will be given leads to insurance professionals.

See a Bank Trust Department—for handling a large trust for dependents after your death. Some trust departments have stellar investment records; others are mediocre and with customer service I'd call languid at best. Look for a bank that provides full reports of its investment performance (many of them don't), and look at a sample before signing up. You want to see your trust's percentage gain or loss compared with standard stock and bond indexes. Minimum trust: in the $200,000 to $500,000 range, depending on the institution. Big brokerage firms handle trust business too.

See the Web Sites of the Major No-Load Mutual Fund Groups—for useful consumer advice about allocating assets and making long-term investment decisions. They often have newsletters explaining different kinds of investments and helping do-it-yourselfers with college or retirement planning. You'll also find excellent materials at www.morningstar.com.

I have mixed feelings about the retirement-planning calculators available on the Web. You enter certain financial data and the calculators purport to tell you how much more you ought to be saving for your retirement. Their weaknesses are obvious. Some ask for data that are hard to get (if you have a pension, do you know how much it will pay when you retire?). Some ask for too little data to give you a meaningful result. You have to make loads of assumptions (What's the likely future inflation rate? How fast will your salary increase? What will you spend in retirement?)—as if you knew. A 1 percent change in your forecasted investment returns could add or subtract $200,000 from your projected retirement assets. What good is that? A couple of years ago, *Kiplinger's Personal Finance* magazine put a simple case through five prominent online calculators: a married couple, with a simple savings plan, wondered how much retirement income they could expect their growing nest egg to deliver. The answers differed wildly.

On the other hand, using an online calculator shows a commitment to finding out what you're going to need to retire on. The answers may be different, but they give you a general sense of whether or not you have enough. Usually you don't, and the numbers you see are a wake-up call. Research has shown that people who use these calculators save more money than people who don't.

Should I See a "Senior Specialist"?

No, no, no! State regulators warn that "senior specialists," "senior advisers," or "retirement advisers" have little expertise beyond marketing and selling. They probably earned their so-called credentials by taking a weekend course. They're trained to appeal to older people who might be susceptible to pitches for equity-indexed annuities, variable annuities, living trusts, and other products that pay high commissions. Typically, they'll advertise an "educational" seminar, with a name such as Senior Financial Survival Seminar or Senior Financial Safety Workshop. You'll get a free lunch and lectures from "experts" who claim to have nothing to sell. But of course they do. They'll offer to review your investments or estate plan "free," then advise you to switch into the products they offer. Don't do it! Throw away almost every business card that suggests you're dealing with someone especially trained to understand the kinds of investments older people need. For warnings from regulators on free-lunch seminars and the typical investments sold there, see the pages for individual investors at www .nasaa.org and www.sec.gov.

I said throw away *almost* every business card. There's one legitimate program that actually gives advisers some expertise. It's the Chartered Advisor for Senior Living (CASL) designation, offered by the American College in Bryn Mawr, Pennsylvania. Students cover various types of issues that older people face, including family relationships, investments, retirement income planning, estate planning, and health insurance. I wouldn't rely on only a CASL for senior planning, but a CASL plus a CFP would make your adviser well informed. The same warning applies to CASL planners as apply to CFPs: look for a fee-only planner, not one who sells products.

Other Financial Designations

There are hundreds of letters that financial advisers can put next to their names, many of them worthless. If you wonder about what stands behind a particular designation, go to www.finra.org and click on "Investor Information," then on "Professional Designations." You'll see who awards the title and how much study it takes. If you can't find it at FINRA, look it up on the Web. If the adviser can get a designation with just a few days of study—say, 30 hours—what does it say for his or her expertise? Not much. All it does is create apparently credible business cards for a hustler with something to sell.

What About "The Plan"?

Among most financial planners, The Plan is out of style. In theory, it's your starting point: a comprehensive tome—part customized, part boilerplate—that analyzes everything you've done so far and points to additions and changes that you ought to make. In professional hands, true plans cost a lot of money—typically $2,000 to $6,000. Clients haven't wanted to pay.

So most plans today amount to sales tools, promoted by stockbrokers, insurance agents, and planners who primarily sell products. The cost: anywhere from $250 to $2,500. You fill in a questionnaire about your finances. Back comes a computer-generated program, in hard covers, telling you what you lack. The analysis may well produce some good ideas. On the other hand, GIGO often rules: garbage in, garbage out. The program is designed to sell, not to explore alternatives. The questionnaire might not even consider your best investment options—for example, adding more money to your tax-deferred 401(k). The planner would rather you spent the money on products he or she has for sale.

As an experiment, I once purchased three of these commercial plans. My question to each salesperson was "Can I afford to retire?" The plans came up with radically different answers and were short of true planning ideas except for investments I should add. Those investments would have led me wrong.

What if you pay $1,500 for what turns out to be an unsuitable plan? Some clients execute it anyway because they don't want to "waste" the money they've already spent. That attitude plays into the planner's hands, who's ready to sell you products on the spot. I say: *walk away.* You're lucky that you've lost only the fee you paid up front and not all the rest of the money that might have followed.

When you work with a genuine planner, not a salesperson in disguise, a plan will evolve. Initially, you might get a miniplan addressing the question you came to ask—for example, "Am I saving enough for retirement?" or "What should I do with the money I've inherited?" If you keep working with that planner, you'll gradually address other issues, and a full-fledged blueprint will emerge. It won't be a plan in hard covers, it will be a comprehensive strategy for reaching your personal goals.

Goals-Based Planning

All planning should be based on what you want out of life. Start with your goals: a sufficient retirement income, college for your children, getting out of debt, a nice vacation every year, leaving a legacy for your heirs. A good planner will look at your current and projected income and assets, apply it to your goals, and see if your current savings are enough. If not, the discussions begin. What matters most? What could you downgrade? How much more could you save? Note that nothing involves buying financial products! This is entirely a mind game. You have to understand, deep in your soul, how your spending and saving affect what you'll be able to do. You might even call this *budget-based planning*. Having money tomorrow depends on what you spend today.

If you're doing your own planning, get out your trusty yellow pad. You'll find plenty of guidelines in the earlier chapters of this book. Define your financial objectives and estimate how much money you'll need for each. Set out a strategy for debt repayment and how you're going to raise your retirement savings. Implement your investment program with suitable mutual funds. It's important to write everything down. In your head, a plan is only a vague hope that things will turn out well. On paper, it's an action project that can be tested against your progress every year.

To help you with retirement saving, you'll find plenty of calculators on the Web. They'll give you a general idea of how much you should save to reach the retirement income you want or at what age your savings will run out if you don't improve. None will give you exactly the same answer; some are wide of the mark. Nevertheless, if they all say that you'll be flat broke somewhere between ages 71 and 76, you'll know what to do: work longer (if you can), save more, *and* plan to spend less after you retire.

What Matters Most When You're Looking for a Financial Planner?

You might expect me to say empathy, expertise, clear thinking, ability to explain, patience, delicacy in dealing with family issues, understanding your particular goals and financial position, investment smarts, honesty, responsiveness, and fidelity to the Boy Scout and Girl Scout oaths. Yes, you want every one of those things. But first and foremost, you want a planner who charges no sales commissions, only fees—that is, a *fee-only* planner. You pay for advice and perhaps money management, not for financial products.

Planners who charge commissions can make their living only if they sell you products. No matter how nice, no matter how smart, no matter that he or she is your friend, neighbor, or cousin, commissioned planners have to put their own interests first. They think, sincerely, that the stuff they sell is exactly what you need. How else would you expect them to think? But what you need is unbiased advice, and commissioned planners can't give it. Nor do they have the time to help you sort out your priorities and think your way through family issues. They have to sell.

So when you're shopping for a planner, ask how he or she is paid. If the answer is "I'm paid by fees" (because that's what people want), you have to unwind the answer. There's a big difference between *fee* and *fee only*. Here are the five ways advisers are generally paid.

1. Commission only. These planners don't make a cent unless they sell you something that carries a sales commission. They lean toward high-commission products, which presents a tremendous conflict of interest. You might not be able to see the commission because it's hidden in the product's fees (for example, inside your annual cost of a variable annuity). But trust me, the fees are there. If the planners say, "You pay nothing, I'm paid by the annuity company," laugh. *Of course* you pay.

2. Fee and commission, also called fee based. This is probably the most common arrangement. The planner charges a fee for certain services—for example, for drawing a simple plan or overseeing your investments—and also earns commissions on any products you buy. If commissions are deducted from the fee, the arrangement is called *fee offset*.

But make no mistake about it: sales commissions are the driving force and produce the same biases you see in commission-only planners. About half the planners disclose their commissions to clients, according to a study by the Securities and Exchange Commission. The rest leave you in the dark unless you press for information.

You can get good advice from a competent fee-and-commission planner, but it always comes with something to buy. In judging any proposed investment, keep in mind that it serves the planner's needs, probably ahead of yours. A bias toward high-commission products, such as variable annuities, is easy to spot. So is the bias away from investments that don't yield commissions, such as putting more money into your 401(k). More subtle is the bias to sell you something, anything, in cases where nothing but good advice would have served.

Some fee-based planners are in transition to a fee-only practice. They work in independent shops, not big brokerage houses. You can spot them by their interest in genuine planning—paying attention to your spending, saving, employee benefits, and personal goals. Even so, you're better off waiting until they finally cut the cord to sales commissions.

3. Fee-based managed accounts. I list these separately because they masquerade as fee only. A stockbroker oversees your account and makes recommendations while separate investment advisers manage your money. You pay a fixed percentage of assets. The total cost typically comes to 2 to 3 percent, and you get no additional financial planning services. What stops this arrangement from being fee only is that the broker can sell you commissioned products on the side—for example, variable annuities and unit trusts. Pass this arrangement by.

4. Salary and bonus (or commission). This is typical for planners who work at banks. They may also act as agents for insurance companies. In either case, they generally sell commissionable mutual funds and tax-deferred annuities and have the same biases as any other planners whose income depends on how much they sell.

5. Fee only. These planners charge only for their advice, accepting no other form of remuneration. Their fee structures vary—hourly charges, monthly or quarterly retainers, fees per job, or a percentage of the money they have under management. Typical money management fee: 1 percent (less for large portfolios). Some planners combine retainers with money management fees in the 0.3 percent range. Either way, the products that fee-only planners sell are entirely no-load—meaning that no sales commissions are attached. Of all the financial consulting arrangements, this is the cleanest.

Fee-only planners have conflicts of interest too. Say, for example, that you're leaving your job and have money invested in the company's 401(k). You can leave it there or roll it into an Individual Retirement Account. Often, it's best to leave the money where it is. But if the planner can persuade you to switch to the IRA, he or she will probably get the money to manage, at a fee of perhaps 1 percent a year. Or say that you're thinking of using a chunk of cash to pay down your mortgage. The planner might advise you to leave the money in your managed investment account, where, again, it will throw off a 1 percent fee. In the case of the mortgage prepayment, the planner's advice might be right financially. A true planner, however, should consider whether you'd be happier owning your home free and clear. You have to be on your toes when evaluating any planner's advice.

Some fee-only planners, especially certified public accountants, provide no ongoing help. They give you advice, then turn you loose. That's not too helpful unless you can implement the plan yourself. Otherwise you'll pay double: once for the plan and again for the services of a stockbroker or insurance agent (who might change the plan and charge you commissions of their own).

Incidentally, fees charged for tax and investment advice can be written off on your income tax return. They're part of that bagful of miscellaneous expenses that are deductible to the extent that they exceed 2 percent of your adjusted gross income. Sales commissions, however, are not deductible up front; they're used to reduce your taxable profits when you sell.

Which type of planner is more expensive: one who charges sales commissions or one who charges fees? On the surface, fee-only planners seem more expensive. You pay more for The Plan, if you want one—maybe up to $6,000. You pay hourly fees for analysis and advice (usually in the $75 to $200 range) or maybe quarterly retainers. You're charged a fixed percentage of any money the planner manages for you. So you're always getting bills. What you don't pay, however, is sales commissions. Any products that the planner buys will be no-load (no sales charge).

By contrast, fee-and-commission planners might charge $250 to $1,500 for The Plan, if you want one. That's often the only payment you will make out-of-pocket. The rest of the planner's compensation is indirect, from up-front sales charges or annual charges subtracted from your investments. Because you don't write separate checks to pay the commissions, you may not realize how large they are or how much you pay. Usually it's a lot.

Ask any planner you work with how much his or her services will cost. Fee-only planners will have brochures listing their prices. If the planner will manage your money, add the cost of the types of investments he or she recommends—for example, the annual fees charged by the mutual funds the planner chooses. The planner's fee plus the fees embedded in your investments are your total cost.

It's harder to suss out what a commissioned planner costs. There's the gross commission, of course—the total commission, shared by the planner and his or her firm. If you're buying stocks, the commission will show on your confirmation form. Next, you pay any listed fees. There are also the annual fees embedded in the financial products you buy—for example, in your mutual funds, unit trusts, or variable annuities. The planner's commission might come out of your investment up front or might be paid out of those product fees. It's not easy to excavate the fees. Your planner should give you a written list, including the commissions earned. Some planners try to put you off by saying, "I don't ask how much money you earn." That's totally irrelevant. You're asking for the price you're paying for products and services. You should know what you're being charged, including commissions, just as you'd expect to know the cost of anything else you buy. When you add up the price of dealing with commissioned planners, you may well find that they're more expensive than planners who charge only fees. They're especially expensive if they sell you products you don't need.

Don't let a commission- or fee-based planner tell you that his or her services are free or that there's no commission on a particular product. *Nothing* is free, even services that look free. If you want financial advice, you'll have to pay for it. Different systems of payment carry different incentives. Commissions encourage planners to sell whether you need the product or not. Fees encourage planners to be good enough to persuade you that their advice has value.

Six Places to Look When Shopping for a Fee-Only Planner

■ *National Association of Personal Financial Advisors* (www.napfa.org), about 1,270 planners in all states. To see if there are any near you, go to its Web site and type in your zip code. When names pop up, click on their profiles, where they announce their specialties. Some look for clients of high net worth. Others say they serve "middle income client needs." If you don't see the "middle income" phrase, e-mail local planners, explain the services you want, and ask if they offer advice by the hour or by the job. Some take hourly clients without advertising it. You can also get names of fee-only planners by mail. Call NAPFA at 800-366-2732.

■ *Garrett Planning Network,* a group of about 300 planners in 41 states. Look for their names at www.garrettplanningnetwork.com. They work on an hourly basis, with no minimum required. Fees range widely—at this writing, the majority charge $180 to $210 an hour. Middle-class clients are their specialty.

■ *Alliance of Cambridge Advisors,* a group of about 145 planners in 33 states, also specializing in middle-class clients. Look for their names at www.cambridge

advisors.com. They usually charge annual retainers covering all their services, although some of them might give you a onetime financial tune-up for a fee.

• *Personal Financial Planning Center* (www.pfp.aicpa.org), the site for certified public accountants who are personal financial specialists. Enter your zip code to get the names of local planners. Click on their names to see if they charge only fees. A few of these planners sell products on commission, so ask about it.

• *Certified Financial Planner Board of Standards (www.cfp.net).* Click on "Search for a Certified Financial Planner" to find CFPs in your area. Some will be "fee based" or "fee offset," others are "fee only." Go to their Web sites to find the true, fee-only planners.

• *Financial Planning Association.* The majority of these planners charge commissions, but the group includes some fee-only planners too. Go to Planner-Search at www.fpanet.org, search for local names, and inspect their listings. Those who advertise as "fee based" or "fee offset" charge commissions. You want the planners who are "fee only."

Most fee-only planners offer a get-acquainted session free. If you engage one, you'll sign a contract specifying what services the fee covers and how long the contract will last. If the planner is an investment adviser and will manage your money, decide whether it's to be on a discretionary basis. *Discretionary* means that the adviser makes the investment decisions, keeping you informed. *Nondiscretionary* means that you have to approve every transaction before it's made.

There aren't enough fee-only planners to help everyone who wants one, especially people with incomes and assets in the middle range. As a result, many middle earners wind up, by default, with stockbrokers or with fee-based planners who can charge commissions. Before taking this step, however, consider managing your investments yourself, following the principles in chapter 22 on mutual funds. It's easier than you think.

Alternatively, consider the retirement investment services offered by the major no-load mutual funds. They look at your assets and savings rate and give you a retirement investment plan. Here are three: T. Rowe Price (www.troweprice .com), an advisory planning service for $250, with regular checkups. You need at least $100,000, and it doesn't have to be in T. Rowe Price mutual funds. The Vanguard Group (www.vanguard.com), a financial planning service for Vanguard clients. Cost: $1,000 if you have less than $100,000 in Vanguard funds, $250 if you invest up to $500,000, and nothing for higher amounts. Fidelity Investments (www.fidelity.com), a portfolio advisory service for clients with $50,000 and up. You pay 1.1 percent of assets; less, if you have $200,000 or more. All three services come with monitoring or with regular checkups.

If you decide that you'd rather work with a fee-based adviser, be armed against the sales pitches. Stick with mutual funds, not individual stocks (page 713); avoid variable annuities (page 1084) and unit trusts (page 958); maximize your 401(k) investments before putting money into products that the planner sells (even though the planner claims that his or her products are better); and keep your investments simple. Be sure that the adviser takes you through the full planning checklist: setting goals, budgeting for debt reduction, maximizing your employee benefits, deciding how much term life insurance to buy, considering long-term care insurance, and reminding you to sign a will and a health care proxy. If your planner doesn't want to spend much time on anything other than investments, you're in the wrong place. Find someone else.

Whomever you work with, accept only advice that makes sense to you. If you're not sure about any of the investments or ideas the planner presents, you have only to mumble and hesitate until the session is over. Don't say yes when you're undecided. Never say yes under pressure, even of the most jovial sort. If you think you'd like to work with a particular planner but are a cautious type, start small. Add to your investment as you gain confidence in the planner's MO. If you don't gain confidence, quit.

Eighteen Ways of Looking for a Planner

There's no easy way to find a good planner. As in any other field, competence ranges from brilliant to dim. You can probably spot the dim, but working with mediocrities is risky too. They may steer you wrong because they don't see all the angles of the questions you pose or understand the risks in some of the products they sell so enthusiastically.

Here are some ways to find a planner—a *fee-only planner*—who's really good:

1. Turn back to page 807, where I list ways of finding a stockbroker. Most of those rules will also help you find a good financial planner, so I won't repeat them here. The Certified Financial Planner Board of Standards also has some tips. Gather your initial list of fee-only names from the Web sites that I've recommended and from friends or professional acquaintances such as accountants. Remind them that you want fee-only advisers, not those who are fee based.

2. Call or e-mail the people on your list, telling them why you're seeking

help and what services you need. For money management, ask about the minimum account requirement. If there seems to be a fit, ask for written material about the firm, including the state or federal ADV (that's the background check for investment advisers—page 1183). Read it before deciding to set up an interview.

3. In the written material, check out the planner's educational background. Here's what you want to see:

• *Higher education.* A college degree is a reasonable proxy for a mind that can tackle complex issues.

• *Evidence of planning expertise.* Look for the certified financial planner designation (CFP), awarded by the Certified Financial Planner Board of Standards to planners who have met its requirements and passed its test. The personal financial specialist designation (PFS) is given by the American Institute of Certified Financial Planners. The criteria are minimal, but the AICPA plans to beef it up. A number of colleges and universities, such as Texas Tech University in Lubbock, Texas, give financial planning degrees. The American College in Bryn Mawr, Pennsylvania, gives a chartered financial consultant designation, or ChFC. It identifies insurance agents who have studied financial planning with an emphasis on using life insurance products.

All these diplomas attest that the planner has passed a number of exams in areas such as goal setting, taxes, insurance, investments, and estate planning. But degrees and certificates are only a starting point. They don't say whether a particular planner is any good.

• *No kidding around.* If the business card says "Financial Planner," look for the CFP designation. If it's not there, you could be dealing with anyone: a stockbroker in hiding, an insurance agent with pretensions. You can tell who they are by the products they advise you to buy. People calling themselves "retirement planners" are often insurance agents. "Financial consultant," "financial adviser," and "registered representative" mean stockbroker. None of these salespeople is a planner in the sense you seek. Dump a "senior specialist" (page 1172) fast.

4. Decide on two or three planners to speak with in person. The opening interview should be free. Take a financial statement with you, showing your assets and liabilities, to give the planner a general idea of what he or she will have to do.

5. Ask about the planner's professional background. The basics should have been in the written material, but ask about previous employers and occupations. You want someone who has been practicing financial planning for 10 years or more, preferably at the same firm. Skip any new kids on the block, including career switchers who have been practicing for only a couple of years. They may turn out to be wonderful, but you want them to practice their new profession on someone else. Also skip any planner who has hopped around from firm to firm.

6. Ask what kinds of clients the planner has. Firms often specialize: in doctors, entrepreneurs, entertainers, teachers, or young, upper-middle-income families. The more experience the planner has with people like you, the better.

7. What are the planner's special areas of expertise? Which lawyers, accountants, or other specialists are on tap?

8. Does the planner sell financial products? (You trolled for fee-only planners, but check.) Does he earn referral fees for recommending you to particular specialists, such as insurance agents (fee-only planners shouldn't)? Is she involved in any other financial businesses, such as real estate, that she might recommend to you? You want to avoid planners with conflicts of interest.

9. Think about what the planner asks you. He or she should inquire not only into your finances but also your family, feelings about money, general knowledge of investments, personal goals, and way of life. If you're married, your spouse should attend at least the initial meeting, and the planner should elicit his or her feelings too. Planners who don't seem interested in you won't give you the best advice. You might take a list of objectives to the initial meeting and ask how the planner would approach them, one by one.

10. Think about how the planner answers the questions you pose. Does he or she seem open, straightforward, comfortable with issues, friendly, willing to explain? If the chemistry isn't right, the relationship won't work, no matter how bright the planner is. If you have any reservations, raise them on the spot, to see what the planner has to say.

11. Ask for professional references: lawyers, bankers, accountants. If you're refused, take your business elsewhere. Call each reference, ask what the relationship is, how long they've worked with the planner, and whether they can recommend him or her. Professionals don't put their names on the line for bad guys (unless, of course, the professionals are bad guys too).

12. Ask for the names of three clients you can speak with who have been with the planner for at least three years. Don't take no for an answer. When offered the names, don't fail to call. Ask how the planner is to work with, any problems they see, and how much better off they are thanks to what the planner did. In my experience, calls like these are incredibly useful. The clients are usually very fair in assessing the service they've been getting. (That is, unless you're with a sleazy operator, in which case the "clients" will be relatives. Your gut will probably tell you that something's wrong.)

13. If the planner will manage your money, discuss investment philosophy and approach. What kinds of investments does he like, and what might be his strategy for you? Also look at the performance reports that clients get. They should show the period's total, annualized return, net of all fees and expenses, compared with several standard indexes: Standard & Poor's 500 stock index, the Russell 2000 index of smaller stocks, the EAFE index of international stocks, Barclays Capital U.S. Aggregate Bond Index, 90-day Treasury bills, and consumer price inflation. That helps you keep track of your progress relative to the rest of the world. It also tells you how well the planner is performing relative to your goals.

14. Ask if the planner will acknowledge, in writing, if his or her relationship with you is one of a fiduciary. A fiduciary is an adviser required by law to put your interests first. Requiring this in writing will eliminate most questionable planners.

15. Ask the planner, "How are you paid?" This question is critical. The planner should hand over a schedule that discloses his or her compensation in full.

16. Find out how you can terminate the relationship. You should be free to quit at any time, with nothing owed beyond the end of the current month.

17. Don't pick a planner just because he or she is quoted in the newspapers. Reporters are looking for colorful quotes and comments and rarely check on whether the planners are any good. Courting the press is one way that planners advertise.

18. Don't pick a planner just because he or she gives investment seminars. That's advertising too. A San Francisco planner, Lawrence Krause, once told his trade secrets to the magazine *CALUnderwriter:* "You don't have to know as much as you think you have to know in running a seminar. All you have to know is more than your audience, and your audience doesn't know your subject. . . . You also have to remember that you're not there to educate. You're there to sell. The purpose of a seminar is twofold: one, to confuse your audience; and two, to create dependence. . . . As long as you are going to confuse them, do a good job of it. Then you ask for the order, so that they'll come to see you afterward."

Now you know.

The Background Check

Financial planners who handle investments have to register with the law as investment advisers. Here are the rules and what you can find out:

- *Investment advisory firms that handle $25 million or more in assets* have to register with the Securities and Exchange Commission (SEC).
- *Firms that handle less than $25 million* register with the states.
- *Individual advisers (investment adviser representatives, or IARs) are regulated by the states,* including those working for the larger firms.
- *The investment advisory firm has to make various disclosures.* Firms filing with the SEC fill in Form ADV (for "adviser"), parts 1 and 2.

Part 1 is for the regulators. It includes various disciplinary actions taken against the firm or its individual investment advisers.

Part 2 is for the public. It lists the firm's services and investment methods, the education and business backgrounds of the principals, whether the adviser conducts other types of financial businesses, and the way customers are charged. (Here's where you'll see if an adviser claiming to be fee only actually sells products on commission.) New customers have to be given a copy of the ADV part 2 or a brochure containing the same information. Ongoing clients have to be offered an updated copy every year. At this writing, the SEC has proposed expanding part 2 to include legal or disciplinary actions against the advisers, including, possibly, arbitrations and settlements of claims.

The firms also file a Schedule D for each individual adviser, giving the details of his or her disciplinary history, if any: criminal charges, civil actions, and regulatory proceedings. The firm doesn't have to give you the Schedule D. By law, it has to tell you only about any disciplinary actions taken against your adviser. But I wouldn't do business with a firm that didn't release its Schedule Ds.

The states have an equivalent ADV form with similar disclosures for the firms and advisers they regulate. They require advisers to demonstrate some minimal knowledge, such as an acquaintance with state and federal securities laws. The states may also have some operating requirements, such as bonding, minimum amounts of net capital, and rules on maintaining books and records. Their disclosures include arbitration claims against advisers in excess of $2,500.

You don't have to wait for an adviser to give you his or her ADV. You can find it yourself at the Investment Adviser Public Disclosure Web site. Go to www.adviserinfo.sec.gov. Click on "Investment Adviser Search" and enter the adviser's name. You'll get the full ADV, including part 1, with the disciplinary infractions, and Schedule D. The site covers advisers registered with the states as well as with the SEC.

Check what's checkable on the ADV (education, prior employment), to see if the planner is on the square. The regulators have no idea whether these documents tell the truth.

If the adviser has no ADV and is giving you investment advice, he or she may be breaking the law. That's not someone you should be working with.

■ *The ADVs let you look up the firm but not the background of the individual adviser, who is known as an Investment Adviser Representative.* If it's a small shop where the adviser *is* the firm, the ADV covers what you want to know. If you want to check the background of an adviser in a larger firm, check the CRD (below) or ask your state securities commission for a report. To find the commission, call the North American Securities Administrators Association (202-737-0900), or go to www.nasaa.org and click on "Contact Your Regulator." Some states are responsive, others slo-o-o-o-w.

■ *If your adviser is an employee of a brokerage firm, he or she should have a record at the Central Registration Depository* (CRD—page 817; go to www.brokercheck .finra.org). It will show the planner's past employment, where he or she is registered to sell securities, certain customer complaints, and infractions of various sorts. One hitch: firms don't always forward customer complaints to the CRD, as the rules require. If you make a complaint, send a copy to your state securities commission and to the Financial Industry Regulatory Authority (www.finra .org). They'll see that it's filed properly.

■ *The black holes.* There are three: (1) States may not have the budget or the will to enforce their own securities laws. (2) When a state licenses an adviser, it may not check to see if he or she has a disciplinary record in another state. (3) A state may not respond to your request for background information on a particular adviser.

When a Planner Does You Wrong

In the largely unregulated industry of financial planning, no formal body sets the rules and punishes rule breakers. You can file a complaint about CFPs at the Certified Financial Planning Board of Standards (www.cfp.net, or 800-487-1497) or complain to the Financial Planning, Association in Atlanta (www.fpanet .org, or 800-322-4237). But all they can do is yank the offender's professional certification or membership—hardly an onerous penalty, since he or she can go on practicing without it. If your planner is a member of an exchange, you can go to arbitration (page 828—see if arbitration is part of your customer agreement). Here's a sampling of the complaints typically brought against financial planners:

• putting clients into investments unsuitable for someone of their age and circumstances

- churning your account (that means buying and selling more often than necessary) to earn extra commissions
- failing to tell the truth about how large a fee the planner earned
- failing to diversify a client's investments to minimize risk
- exaggerating an investment's likely yield while failing to disclose the risks
- roping clients into outright frauds: nonexistent investments, Ponzi schemes, misrepresentations of every sort
- misrepresenting the tax benefits and investment outlook for tax-sheltered investments
- giving bad tax advice
- failing to disclose that the planner had a financial interest in the investment being sold
- failing to process a client's investments or insurance properly, leading to financial loss
- ignoring a client's specific investment instructions and goals

If you think you have grounds for a legal complaint against your planner, start by trying to work out a settlement. Sometimes a letter from a lawyer helps. If you're stonewalled, complain to the appropriate state regulator. For recalcitrant investment advisers, stockbrokers, or insurance agents who sell variable annuities or variable life, call your state's securities commission (find it at www.nasaa.org, 202-737-0900). For other insurance agents, call the state insurance commission (find it through www.naic.org). Occasionally they can help.

If your loss is large, you might be able to bring a lawsuit. More likely, your planner will have required you to sign an arbitration agreement, which generally requires your case to be heard in a forum dictated by the securities industry (page 824). To find a lawyer, contact the Public Investors Arbitration Bar Association (www.piaba.org, or 886-621-7484, in Norman, Oklahoma) or the National Association of Consumer Advocates (www.naca.net, or 202-452-1989, in Washington, D.C.).

Do You Need an Independent Investment Adviser?

A few sessions with a fee-only financial planner will benefit almost anyone. The planner can steer you toward mutual funds and asset allocations that are appropriate for your age and circumstances. With that advice, plus the explanations in this book's investment and retirement plan chapters, you can probably manage your IRA or 401(k) yourself. There's no need to pay extra for continuing investment advice.

There are some circumstances, however, when having a personal investment adviser makes sense. For example:

- You have a truly large pot of money—say, $10 million and up—and want someone to think continuously about how it should be deployed.
- You have only a modest pot of money but don't have the time to think about it yourself. Or you're all thumbs with money and not interested in learning.
- You face a lot of family complications, such as stepchildren, mixed inheritances, and some unfriendly family dynamics. You need a good planning mind to lead you through the minefields.

When looking for an investment adviser, consider fee-only financial planners with large amounts of money under management, or bank or brokerage house wealth management departments. As always, compare costs. Some banks and brokers hit you with fees at every turn, including fees for investing in their own high-cost mutual funds (or pooled trust funds, which amount to the same thing). Keep a close watch on how the account is handled. A bank trust officer can churn an account just as easily as a stockbroker can—perhaps more easily, if the account belongs to an orphan or to someone who's old and no longer paying a lot of attention.

To Protect Yourself

When doing business with a planner or investment adviser, proceed in the same orderly way that you would with a stockbroker (page 810), with written goals, notes of conversations, and so on. In a confrontation, you might find that the planner kept his or her own notes, which a court or arbitration board might consider more credible than your memory.

If the planner tells you that a specific investment carries little risk, ask for a letter confirming it. This sort of paper trail supports a winning claim. It may also encourage your planner to proceed with caution and exactitude. If your planner makes a move that differs from what you thought you'd agreed on, telephone immediately. If you don't like the explanation, send a letter reiterating how you want your money handled.

Yes, but . . . how do you avoid a crook like Bernie Madoff?

Madoff fooled the experts based on his sterling reputation, haughty self-confidence, trappings of wealth, and apparent ability to magic money out of the market year after year. The story of his $65 billion fraud is especially scary for individuals who understand how easily they, too, could have been taken in. They ask, "Who is it possible to trust?"

The answer is, "Trust no one." Instead, set up your account so that the manager can't get his or her hands on it.

Here's the single best question to ask any would-be financial adviser: "When I send you money to invest, whose name do I put on the check?" If the manager answers, "Make out the check to my firm" or a firm that the manager controls, walk away. The manager should not—repeat, *not*—hold the money that he or she is investing for you. Your account should be held by an independent custodian, such as State Street, TD Ameritrade, or some other third party. That's the name you should put on the check.

Why? Because it's the custodian's job to know where your money is at all times. Independent custodians hold your securities, collect interest and dividends, process trades, send you the confirmations of trades, receive any money you send into the account, disburse money at your direction, and compute your quarterly reports. They don't make any investment decisions. Your money manager tells the custodian what to buy and sell. But thanks to this separate relationship, your cash never passes through the manager's hands.

If you allow the manager to hold custody of the accounts, he or she has free rein. No one is there to check whether transactions actually went through or what the prices were. The manager might hire a respectable accounting firm to handle the annual audit, but the accountant will work with the data the manager produces. Auditors normally don't dig into whether the data were created honestly.

Some legitimate money managers insist on taking custody of your funds themselves because it simplifies reporting. An example might be a fund of hedge funds. But frankly, you don't need those kinds of expensive investments anyway. Plenty of dependable managers work only with independent custodians. That's the pool to fish in when you're trolling for investment help.

One warning: In the Madoff case, some banks signed on as custodians and then hired Bernie's firm as subcustodian. As a result, investors got their reports from Madoff rather than from the bank itself. If you see that happening with a custodian you hired, pull out immediately. Something smells.

The second best way of avoiding fraud is to disbelieve any manager who claims to earn steady or high market returns in good years and bad. No one does that. Even if God had been investing, he'd have lost money in the Flood!

Finally, be careful of someone who sells investments within your specific religious or ethnic group. Mormons have fallen for schemes pressed by fellow church members in the belief that a coreligionist wouldn't lie. Bernie Madoff looted the Jewish community. In my old hometown, a smart, preppy hedge fund guy hoodwinked college pension fund managers, maybe because they all wore bow ties. Never assume that a money manager must be okay because he or she is just like you.

I'll say it again—ensure that your account resides in the hands of an independent custodian. That's foolproof protection against a Bernie clone.

Aunt Jane's Last Recipe: A Do-It-Yourself Financial Plan

Over the next eight weeks, take the following nine steps to success:

1. Make a List of Specific Objectives

The list might read: "A college education for Emily and Joe, a down payment on a house, graduate school for Lydia, hockey camp for Josh next year, Temma's wedding, two weeks in France year after next, a retirement income worth $60,000 a year in today's dollars, pretax." Put down exactly what you want. Your objectives will change as your life does, but you should always know what you're working toward.

2. Draw Up a Spending Plan

This isn't a big deal. You've known about budgets all your life, and, if you've forgotten, there's always chapter 8.

3. Calculate What You Need to Save

This isn't a big deal either, once you've specified what you're aiming for. Ask yourself, "How much will each objective cost?" and "When am I going to need the money?" Then point your savings toward those goals. Plot short-term savings in your head. You want to go to France year after next? Take this year's price, divide by 24, and put away that much per month. Nothing complicated about it. Use Web calculators to estimate what you need to save for longer-term goals.

You'll have to coordinate your savings with your spending plan, which is the hard part. But if you didn't intend to try, you never would have bought this book. (You say your mother bought this book for you? Oh, well. Try anyway.)

4. Secure What You Have

This is your safety net: life, health, disability, homeowners insurance, and auto insurance. I've steered you toward inexpensive coverage, where it exists. Do-it-yourselfers can buy some policies on the Web.

5. Develop a Risk Plan

Decide on a prudent level of investment risk for someone of your age, goals, and circumstances. On this point, chapter 21 will help.

6. Follow Through with an Investment Plan

You will do splendidly with a few no-load mutual funds, chosen yourself and held long term, plus some Treasury securities, tax-exempts, or certificates of deposit.

7. Minimize Your Taxes

For savings, use a tax-deferred retirement plan (chapter 29) and, if you're in a high bracket, municipal bonds. What could be easier? If you have a high net worth, however, you'll have to deal with estate taxes, trusts, executive compensation contracts, and all the other tax entanglements that wealth is heir to. That's when you need professional help—and only the most experienced planners will do. Your outriders will include a clutch of specialized professionals: tax lawyer, accountant, actuary, investment adviser.

8. Maximize Your Retirement Plan

For how much to save, see chapter 29. When you actually retire, ask a fee-only planner about the best way to take withdrawals from your retirement plan. You can't afford to make mistakes. Chapter 30 gives you a look at the landscape. The planner can spell out the tax and investment implications of your various choices, and project a spending and investment plan to carry you through the rest of your life.

9. Get a Financial Checkup

Ask a fee-only planner to take a look at what you're doing and make suggestions.

That's it! The planning process from first sharpened pencil to final phone call. A project that you can handle, step by step, just by applying some basic, down-home common sense.

For generations, most Americans have managed their own money and done a pretty good job of it. You still can. The trick is to turn your back on today's insanely complex financial marketplace and buy the simple things that you can handle yourself. Trust me on this one. In the world of money, one or two clear and strong ideas, persisted in, will make you richer in the end.

Appendix 1

Taxable Versus Tax-Free Bonds

This worksheet helps you calculate which bond yields more in your personal tax bracket—a taxable bond or a tax-free municipal. On the left are the instructions, on the right an example of how the numbers work. I've picked an investor in the 35 percent federal and state bracket, looking at a tax-exempt bond yielding 5 percent. It turns out that he'd need a 7.69 percent taxable yield to equal his return from the tax-free bond.

When using this calculation, always use bonds, or bond funds, of equivalent credit quality and maturity. Otherwise, you won't have the right information. All percentages should be expressed as decimals.

Here's how to calculate the taxable equivalents of tax-free bonds, for interest rates and tax brackets not illustrated on the table on page 941.

	YOUR BRACKET	EXAMPLE
1. What is your maximum combined tax bracket (federal, state, and local), expressed as a decimal?	_____ %	0.35 (35%)
2. Subtract your maximum tax bracket from 1.00.	_____	0.65
3. What is the yield on the tax-free bond you're considering?	_____ %	0.05 (5%)
4. Divide the tax-free yield by the number on line 2. This gives you the taxable yield you'd need to net the same return you'd get from the tax-free bond.	_____ %	0.0769 (7.69%)

Here's how to calculate how much you'd need from a tax-free bond in order to match a taxable bond that you're considering:

	YOUR BRACKET	EXAMPLE
1. What is your maximum combined tax bracket (federal, state, and local), expressed as a decimal?	_____ %	0.35 (35%)
2. Subtract your maximum tax bracket from 1.00.	_____	0.65
3. What is the yield on the taxable bond you're considering?	_____ %	0.09 (9%)
4. Multiply the yield on line 3 by the number on line 2. This is the tax-free yield you need to earn the same net return you'd get from the taxable bond.	_____ %	0.0585 (5.85%)

Here's how to decide between a mutual fund specializing in the bonds of your state and a mutual fund containing the bonds of several states. You might assume that the single-state fund is always best because it's entirely tax exempt, but that's not necessarily so. If a multistate fund offers a higher yield, it might net you more despite the state tax on the out-of-state bonds. A multistate fund also carries less risk because its managers can diversify.

	YOUR BRACKET	EXAMPLE
1. What is your maximum state tax bracket?	_____ %	0.08 (8%)
2. What percentage of the interest from the multistate fund is taxable in your state? *	_____ %	0.80 (80%)
3. Multiply the tax bracket on line 1 by the percentage on line 2 to determine your effective state tax rate for this fund.	_____ %	0.064 (6.4%)
4. Subtract your effective state tax rate from 1.00.	_____ %	0.936
5. What is the average yield on the multistate tax-free fund you're considering?	_____ %	0.06 (6.0%)
6. Multiply the yield on line 5 by the number on line 4. This is the average yield you need from a mutual fund invested in the bonds of many states in order to match your return from the single-state fund.†	_____ %	0.0562 (5.62%)

* The interest on all out-of-state bonds except those from Puerto Rico and other U.S. possessions.
† This does not count the deduction you get on your federal tax return for the extra state taxes paid.
Source: David Kahn, RSM McGladrey, New York City.

Appendix 2

How Long Will Your Capital Last?

The following tables show how many years your capital will last at varying rates of withdrawal. For annual withdrawals of equal size, use the first table. The remaining tables assume that you'll take enough extra money each year to keep up with the inflation rate. At 4 percent inflation, for example, a first-year withdrawal of $5,000 grows to $5,200 the second year, $5,408 the third year, and so on.

To use these tables, choose a likely inflation rate, up to 7 percent (the table showing 3 percent inflation is on page 1110). In the left-hand column, find the percentage of your capital that you will withdraw in the first year. If you withdraw $5,000 from a $125,000 nest egg, for example, you have taken 4 percent. Read across to the pretax rate of return that you're expecting to earn on your money. Where those lines intersect, you will find the number of years your capital can last. I've assumed that the money is taken at the start of each year. The # symbol means that, at that rate of withdrawal, your capital will never be exhausted.

The source for all the tables in Appendix 2 is David Kahn, RSM McGladrey, New York City.

Table A-1.

ANNUAL WITHDRAWALS OF EQUAL SIZE

% of Original Capital Withdrawal Annually	WILL LAST THIS MANY YEARS IF INVESTED AT THE FOLLOWING AVERAGE RATES OF RETURN									
	3%	4%	5%	6%	7%	8%	9%	10%	11%	12%
2%	#	#	#	#	#	#	#	#	#	#
3%	119	#	#	#	#	#	#	#	#	#
4%	53	83	#	#	#	#	#	#	#	#
5%	29	37	62	#	#	#	#	#	#	#
6%	22	26	32	49	#	#	#	#	#	#
7%	18	20	23	28	40	#	#	#	#	#
8%	15	16	18	21	25	33	#	#	#	#
9%	13	14	15	17	19	22	28	#	#	#
10%	11	12	13	14	15	17	20	25	45	#
11%	10	10	11	12	13	14	16	17	22	32
12%	9	9	10	10	11	12	13	14	16	19
13%	8	8	9	9	10	10	11	12	13	15
14%	7	8	8	8	9	9	10	10	11	12
15%	7	7	7	8	8	8	9	9	10	11

Table A-2.

ASSUMING 1 PERCENT INFLATION

Percentage of Capital Withdrawal In the First Year	WILL LAST THIS MANY YEARS, IF THE ORIGINAL WITH- DRAWAL RISES BY 1% ANNUALLY AND YOUR MONEY IS INVESTED AT THE FOLLOWING AVERAGE RATES OF RETURN									
	3%	4%	5%	6%	7%	8%	9%	10%	11%	12%
2%	180	#	#	#	#	#	#	#	#	#
3%	53	111	#	#	#	#	#	#	#	#
4%	33	43	78	#	#	#	#	#	#	#
5%	25	29	36	59	#	#	#	#	#	#
6%	19	22	25	31	47	#	#	#	#	#
7%	16	18	20	23	27	38	#	#	#	#
8%	14	15	16	18	20	24	32	#	#	#
9%	12	13	14	15	16	19	22	28	#	#
10%	11	11	12	13	14	15	17	19	24	38
11%	9	10	10	11	12	13	14	15	18	21
12%	9	9	9	10	10	11	12	13	14	16
13%	8	8	8	9	9	10	10	11	12	13
14%	7	7	7	8	8	9	9	10	10	11
15%	7	7	7	7	8	8	8	9	9	10

Table A-3.

ASSUMING 2 PERCENT INFLATION

Percentage of Capital Withdrawal In the First Year	WILL LAST THIS MANY YEARS, IF THE ORIGINAL WITHDRAWAL RISES BY 2% ANNUALLY AND YOUR MONEY IS INVESTED AT THE FOLLOWING AVERAGE RATES OF RETURN									
	3%	4%	5%	6%	7%	8%	9%	10%	11%	12%
2%	68	167	#	#	#	#	#	#	#	#
3%	40	52	105	#	#	#	#	#	#	#
4%	28	33	43	75	#	#	#	#	#	#
5%	22	25	29	36	56	#	#	#	#	#
6%	18	19	22	25	31	45	#	#	#	#
7%	15	16	18	20	23	27	37	#	#	#
8%	13	14	15	16	18	20	24	31	#	#
9%	11	12	13	14	15	16	18	21	27	51
10%	10	10	12	12	13	14	15	17	19	23
11%	9	9	10	10	11	12	13	14	15	17
12%	8	8	9	9	10	10	11	12	13	14
13%	7	8	8	8	9	9	10	11	11	12
14%	7	7	7	8	8	8	9	9	10	10
15%	6	7	7	7	7	8	8	8	9	9

Table A-4.

ASSUMING 4 PERCENT INFLATION

Percentage of Capital Withdrawal In the First Year	WILL LAST THIS MANY YEARS, IF THE ORIGINAL WITH-DRAWAL RISES BY 4% ANNUALLY AND YOUR MONEY IS INVESTED AT THE FOLLOWING AVERAGE RATES OF RETURN									
	3%	4%	5%	6%	7%	8%	9%	10%	11%	12%
2%	40	50	67	150	#	#	#	#	#	#
3%	29	33	39	52	95	#	#	#	#	#
4%	22	25	28	33	42	68	#	#	#	#
5%	18	20	22	24	28	35	53	#	#	#
6%	15	16	18	19	22	25	30	42	#	#
7%	13	14	15	16	17	19	22	26	35	#
8%	11	12	13	14	15	16	18	20	23	30
9%	10	11	11	12	13	14	15	16	18	21
10%	9	10	10	10	11	12	13	14	15	16
11%	8	9	9	9	10	10	11	12	13	14
12%	8	8	8	8	9	9	10	10	11	12
13%	7	7	7	8	8	8	9	9	10	10
14%	6	7	7	7	7	8	8	8	9	9
15%	6	6	6	7	7	7	8	8	8	8

Table A-5.

ASSUMING 5 PERCENT INFLATION

Percentage of Capital Withdrawal In the First Year	WILL LAST THIS MANY YEARS, IF THE ORIGINAL WITH-DRAWAL RISES BY 5% ANNUALLY AND YOUR MONEY IS INVESTED AT THE FOLLOWING AVERAGE RATES OF RETURN									
	3%	4%	5%	6%	7%	8%	9%	10%	11%	12%
2%	35	41	50	67	145	#	#	#	#	#
3%	25	29	33	39	51	92	#	#	#	#
4%	20	22	25	28	33	42	66	#	#	#
5%	17	18	20	22	24	28	35	51	#	#
6%	14	15	16	18	19	22	25	30	41	#
7%	12	13	14	15	16	17	19	22	26	34
8%	11	11	12	13	14	15	16	18	20	23
9%	10	10	11	11	12	13	14	15	16	18
10%	9	9	10	10	10	11	12	13	13	15
11%	8	8	9	9	9	10	10	11	12	13
12%	7	8	8	8	8	9	9	10	10	11
13%	7	7	7	7	8	8	8	9	9	10
14%	6	6	7	7	7	7	8	8	9	9
15%	6	6	6	6	7	7	7	8	8	8

Table A-6.

ASSUMING 6 PERCENT INFLATION

Percentage of Capital Withdrawal In the First Year	WILL LAST THIS MANY YEARS, IF THE ORIGINAL WITH-DRAWAL RISES BY 6% ANNUALLY AND YOUR MONEY IS INVESTED AT THE FOLLOWING AVERAGE RATES OF RETURN									
	3%	**4%**	**5%**	**6%**	**7%**	**8%**	**9%**	**10%**	**11%**	**12%**
2%	31	35	41	50	67	139	#	#	#	#
3%	23	26	29	33	39	51	89	#	#	#
4%	19	20	22	25	28	33	41	64	#	#
5%	15	17	18	20	22	24	28	35	50	#
6%	13	14	15	16	18	19	21	25	30	40
7%	12	12	13	14	15	16	17	19	22	26
8%	10	11	11	12	13	14	15	16	17	20
9%	9	10	10	11	11	12	13	13	15	16
10%	8	9	9	10	10	10	11	12	12	13
11%	8	8	8	9	9	9	10	10	11	12
12%	7	7	8	8	8	8	9	9	10	10
13%	7	7	7	7	7	8	8	8	9	9
14%	6	6	6	6	7	7	7	8	8	8
15%	6	6	6	6	6	7	7	7	7	8

Appendix 2

Table A-7.

ASSUMING 7 PERCENT INFLATION

Percentage of Capital Withdrawal In the First Year	WILL LAST THIS MANY YEARS, IF THE ORIGINAL WITH-DRAWAL RISES BY 7% ANNUALLY AND YOUR MONEY IS INVESTED AT THE FOLLOWING AVERAGE RATES OF RETURN									
	3%	4%	5%	6%	7%	8%	9%	10%	11%	12%
2%	28	31	35	41	50	66	134	#	#	#
3%	21	23	26	29	33	39	51	86	#	#
4%	17	19	20	22	25	28	33	41	62	#
5%	15	16	17	18	20	22	24	28	34	48
6%	12	13	14	15	16	18	19	21	25	29
7%	11	12	12	13	14	15	16	17	19	22
8%	10	11	11	11	12	13	14	15	16	17
9%	9	9	10	10	11	11	12	13	13	15
10%	8	8	9	9	10	10	10	11	12	13
11%	7	8	8	8	9	9	9	10	10	11
12%	7	7	7	8	8	8	8	9	9	10
13%	6	7	7	7	7	7	8	8	8	9
14%	6	6	6	6	7	7	7	7	8	8
15%	6	6	6	6	6	6	7	7	7	7

Appendix 3

Pension Maximization: Will It Work for You?

At retirement, you have two ways of taking your pension: (1) *Lifetime only:* you get a higher monthly income, but it stops when you die. (2) *Joint-and-survivor:* you get a lower income, but it lasts for the lifetimes of you and your spouse.

A pension max salesperson will propose that you take the lifetime-only pension. To protect your spouse, you buy a life insurance policy. At your death, the proceeds of that policy can provide your spouse with a lifetime income.

This plan is potentially workable if: (1) your net lifetime pension, after paying the insurance premium, is greater than you would have received had you chosen the joint-and-survivor pension; *and* (2) after your death, the insurance proceeds are sufficient to buy your spouse a lifetime income at least equal to what the joint-and-survivor pension would have paid for life. Most proposals fail one or both of these tests.

The following worksheet will tell you whether a proposed plan will work or whether it puts your spouse at risk of running out of money. It was prepared by the late John Allen, J.D., of Allen-Warren in Arvada, Colorado. You and the salesperson should fill in the following blanks:

STEP ONE: *To see if a pension max scheme will improve your income as a couple, while you're both alive*

1. Your monthly pension, if paid for your life only. $_____
2. Your monthly pension after all taxes.* $_____
3. Your monthly pension as a couple if you take a joint-and-survivor option. $_____
4. The joint-and-survivor monthly pension after all taxes.* $_____

5. Your spouse's monthly pension after your death if you take the joint-and-survivor option. (This may or may not be the amount you reported on line 3.) $_____

6. Your surviving spouse's monthly pension after all taxes.* $_____

7. The midpoint between lines 5 and 6. Use this as a rough target for the monthly lifetime annuity payment your spouse ought to get if you choose pension maximization.† $_____

8. The size of the insurance policy needed to buy your spouse the appropriate annuity after your death. To calculate it, visit Immediate Annuities.com (www.immediateannuities.com). Enter your spouse's age in the year you'll retire‡ and the monthly income from Line 7. The calculator will tell you how much such an income will cost. $_____

9. The monthly life insurance premium required to buy the size policy shown on line 9. $_____

10. Subtract the monthly premium (line 9) from the after-tax income you'd get from a single-life pension (line 2). This gives you the disposable income that you, as a couple, would have left to live on. $_____

11. Compare this with the income you'd get from a joint-and-survivor pension, after tax (line 4). $_____

If your income after pension max is less than you'd get from a joint-and-survivor pension, stop here. It usually makes no sense to use the insurance scheme.

---

* Federal, state, and local. Don't estimate from a tax bracket. Calculate the actual tax.
† The midpoint includes a tax adjustment. A professional planner will be able to target the amounts in lines 6 and 7 exactly.
‡ Your plan should protect your spouse in the worst case—namely, if you die immediately after retiring.

===

STEP TWO: *If pension max provides you with more income as a couple, continue the calculation to see if it protects your spouse after your death.*

12. Your spouse's life expectancy, based on his or her age when you retire.* The number comes from the Life Expectancy Table on page 1205.

13. The portion of the spouse's annuity income that will be excluded from income taxes. This is called the Exclusion Ratio.† Carry it to three decimal places.   _____

14. Subtract the Exclusion Ratio from 1.000.   _____

15. Enter the monthly annuity income you targeted from line 7. $_____

16. Multiply line 14 by line 13. This tells you how much of the spouse's annuity income is subject to tax. $_____

17. Subtract income taxes‡ from the spouse's annuity income (line 14) and enter that income after tax. $_____

18. Enter the actual amount of net spousal income you need to protect (line 6). $_____

* For safety, refigure for 5, 10, and 20 years ahead. Each year the spouse lives, his or her life expectancy improves.
† To get the Exclusion Ratio: Multiply the spouse's monthly annuity income by 12. Multiply the result by the life expectancy (line 11). Divide the result into the size of the life insurance policy (line 8).
‡ Federal, state, and local. Don't just estimate from a tax bracket. Calculate the actual tax.

If line 17 is larger than line 16, you need more life insurance to protect your spouse. Redo the worksheet using a larger policy. If the cost of the larger policy reduces your income as a couple to less than you'd get from the joint pension, pension max doesn't work. *This is the usual case!*

If you start pension maximization earlier than retirement, you'll need a "present value" analysis. This recognizes that $1,000 spent on insurance today is worth much more than $1,000 received in higher pension benefits in the future. A present value analysis tells you whether those extra pension benefits are worth their cost. Don't buy from an insurance agent or planner who won't (or can't) do that calculation for you.

This worksheet does not consider the value of pensions with cost-of-living adjustments. You can simulate the analysis by estimating what your pension will be in 5, 10, and 20 years and using this sheet to see if the life insurance will indeed supply a comparable pension for the spouse.

The Risks of Choosing Pension Maximization

If your pension has a cost-of-living benefit, you will need to purchase a much larger amount of insurance in order to provide your spouse with a similar amount of income. And even that might not be enough if inflation explodes.

If you buy a universal life policy or an interest-sensitive whole-life policy and interest rates decline, your plan may not work out. You might have to pay a higher insurance premium or accept a lower death benefit. Ask the agent to show you what happens to the pension max plan if interest rates drop to the policy's minimum guaranteed rate.

If you buy a policy with a "vanishing premium" (page 392) and interest rates fall, your plan may not work out. You figured on paying premiums for a limited number of years but will have to pay them longer. That might reduce your standard of living.

At your death, annuity rates may have dropped. Your spouse may not be able to buy as high an income as you expected.

Inflation or unexpected expenses may eat away at your income. At some point in the future, you may not be able to afford the life insurance premiums. If you have to cancel the policy, and die, your spouse will lose that part of his or her income.

If you become forgetful, your insurance might lapse accidentally, leaving your spouse to do without. If the marriage goes bad and the husband owns the policy, he might cancel it or change the beneficiary.

Your spouse may get health benefits from your pension plan, which could be lost when you die and your pension stops. It is particularly unwise to sever all connection with a public-sector plan.

The Advantage of Pension Maximization

If your spouse dies first, the insurance can be canceled, leaving you with more disposable income.

If you want to continue paying for the insurance after your spouse dies, you'll have a larger estate to leave to your heirs (although, if leaving a larger estate is important to you, you can carry extra life insurance without using pension max).

If there's a divorce, the pension holder could cancel the policy (although the divorce settlement might require that the policy be kept in force).

If you and your spouse live for many years, you can—at some point—withdraw some cash from the policy. You will shrink the death benefit left for your spouse. But at later ages, less money is needed to provide the spouse with a lifetime income.

These advantages are speculative and don't begin to compensate for the disadvantages. You are gambling with your spouse's future security. Not a good idea.

Appendix 4

Life Expectancy

(Group Annuity Table)

These average life expectancies are used by insurance companies for their annuity business. The ages are on the high side, but it's better to plan conservatively. When applying the numbers to yourself, consider your family history and state of health. Many people live longer than these statistical averages show, and many die earlier. If you're in poor health or smoke, use a shorter life expectancy.

IF YOU'RE THIS OLD:	INSURERS THAT SELL ANNUITIES ASSUME THAT YOU WILL LIVE UNTIL THE FOLLOWING AGE:	
	MALE	FEMALE
45	84.0	86.3
46	83.9	86.2
47	83.9	86.2
48	83.9	86.2
49	83.8	86.2
50	83.8	86.2
51	83.8	86.2
52	83.8	86.2
53	83.7	86.2
54	83.7	86.2
55	83.7	86.2
56	83.7	86.3

Appendix 4

IF YOU'RE THIS OLD:	INSURERS THAT SELL ANNUITIES ASSUME THAT YOU WILL LIVE UNTIL THE FOLLOWING AGE:	
57	83.8	86.3
58	83.8	86.3
59	83.8	86.4
60	83.9	86.4
61	84.0	86.5
62	84.1	86.6
63	84.2	86.7
64	84.3	86.8
65	84.4	86.9
66	84.6	87.1
67	84.8	87.3
68	85.0	87.4
69	85.2	87.6
70	85.4	87.8
71	85.7	88.0
72	85.9	88.2
73	86.2	88.4
74	86.5	88.7
75	86.8	88.9
76	87.1	89.2
77	87.5	89.5
78	87.9	89.8
79	88.3	90.1
80	88.7	90.4
81	89.2	90.8
82	89.7	91.2
83	90.2	91.7
84	90.7	92.1
85	91.2	92.5
86	91.9	93.0
87	92.5	93.6
88	93.1	94.1

IF YOU'RE THIS OLD:	INSURERS THAT SELL ANNUITIES ASSUME THAT YOU WILL LIVE UNTIL THE FOLLOWING AGE:	
89	93.7	94.7
90	94.3	95.2
91	95.1	95.9
92	95.8	96.6
93	96.5	97.2
94	97.3	97.9
95	98.0	98.6
96	98.9	99.4
97	99.7	100.2
98	100.5	100.9
99	101.4	101.7
100	102.2	102.5

Source: The 2009 UP94 Pensioner Mortality Table with full projection, Ron Gebhardtsbauer, FSA, MAAA, Penn State University–Smeal College of Business.

Acknowledgments

Many wonderful experts contributed to this book. They took me through concepts, read drafts, corrected errors, and patiently dealt with dozens of e-mails as I tried to nail down fact after fact. All remaining errors are my own. Let me note right up front that not everyone agreed with all of my points of view, so they're off the hook! But, bless them, they helped anyway—and persuaded me to change some of my opinions, too. Many thanks to all.

For the chapters on retirement, Denise Appleby of Appleby Retirement Consulting, a fabulous expert on the technicalities of retirement plans (visit her Web site at www.applebyconsultinginc.com); Ed Slott, everyone's go-to guy for Individual Retirement Accounts and the author of *Parlay Your IRA into a Family Fortune* (www.edslott.com); David Wray, head of the Profit Sharing/401k Council of America and father of the 401(k) (www.psca.org); for pensions, Bob Leone, head of the defined benefit consulting group for Hewitt, the global consulting firm; for employee stock ownership plans, Corey Rosen, executive director of the National Center for Employee Ownership (www.nceo.org) and J. Michael Keeling, president of The ESOP Association; for Social Security, Mark Hinkle, the program's deputy press officer. Hersh Stern, publisher of the Annuity Shopper (www.annuityshopper.com), critiqued . . . well, I'll let you guess.

For the section on life insurance, thanks to my longtime friend Jim Hunt, insurance guru for the Consumer Federation of America, whose low-cost consumer advisory service could save every single reader from expensive life insurance mistakes (www.evaluatelifeinsurance.org); fee-only life insurance consultant Glenn Daily, who has guided me through many a thicket (wwwglenndaily.com); ditto fee-only insurance planner Peter Katt (www.peterkatt.com); ditto Judith and Mark Maurer of Low Load Insurance Sevices (www.llis.com); Joseph M. Belth, professor emeritus of insurance in the Kelley School of Business at Indiana University, editor of *The Insurance Forum* (www.theinsuranceforum.com) and one of the earliest consumer advocates in the field; Bob Barney, whose online term insurance site is a model of good consumer information (www.term 4sale.com); and Byron Udell, founder of AccuQuote (www.accuquote.com), another solid online service.

For auto and homeowners insurance, thanks to the tough-minded consumerist Robert Hunter, director of insurance for the Consumer Federation of America (go to www.consumerfed.org for tons of valuable information on all sorts of interesting subjects), and Jeanne Salvatore, a senior vice president at the Insurance Information Institute (www.iii.org), who can talk coverage in her sleep—and probably does.

On the gnarly subject of health insurance, special thanks to the experts at America's Health Insurance Plans who vetted (and sometimes argued with!) the chapter—all of it very helpful input. Thanks, too, to Jesse Slome, executive director of the American Association for Long-Term Care Insurance (www .aaltci.org) and Peter Ashkenaz, deputy director of the media relations group of the Centers for Medicare & Medicaid Services, who fact-checked the section on Medicare. For an insurance agent's perspective on individual policies, thanks to Scott Leavitt of Scott Leavitt Insurance & Financial Services, Boise, Idaho, and former president of the National Association of Health Underwriters (www .nahu.org, if you're looking for an agent).

On mortgages, my hand was held by Jack Guttentag, professor of finance emeritus at the Wharton School of the University of Pennsylvania (get his detailed advice on every aspect of mortgage borrowing at www.mtgprofessor .com); Keith Gumbinger, vice president at www.hsh.com, another indispensable consumer mortgage site; and Ken Scholen, the leading authority on reverse mortgages.

My bicoastal estate-planning team: attorney William Zabel of Schulte Roth & Zabel in New York City, author of *The Rich Die Richer and You Can Too,* with an excellent assist from attorney Jeffrey Herman; and, for a community property perspective, Charles A. Collier, Jr., now retired from Irell and Manella in Los Angeles and a past president of the American College of Trust and Estate Counsel.

The divorce and prenup pages were read by two partners in the law firm Pasternak & Fidis (www.pasternakfidis.com), domestic relations attorney Linda Ravdin and Marcia Fidis, a specialist in divorce taxation, estates, and trusts. Tax attorney Julian Block answered tax questions (www.julianblocktaxexpert.com). Attorney and consultant Randall McCathren, a national authority on auto leasing, advised me on that section (www.blcassociates.com). On investment real estate, who better than Jack Reed, author of more expert books on the subject than I can mention. You'll find them at his Web site, www.johntreed.com, with a good, free section for beginners.

On credit cards, my thanks to Gerri Detweiler, author of *The Ultimate Credit Handbook* and other valuable books. Gerri gives consumer tips at www.gerri detweiler.blogspot.com. And Robert McKinley, whose CardWeb.com (www .cardweb.com) amasses data on credit cards and helps you find good buys.

The assists on mutual funds came from John Woerth, principal for public relations at The Vanguard Group, and Steve Norwitz, vice president for public relations at T. Rowe Price. Marilyn Cohen, author the *The Bond Bible* and CEO of Envision Capital, clarified several bond questions for me. Stephen Meyerhardt and Joyce Harris of The Bureau of the Public Debt checked sections on U.S. Treasury securities and savings bonds. Another top savings bond source was Daniel J. Pederson of The Savings Bond Informer in Monroe, Michigan. Cecilia Gondor, executive vice president of Thomas J. Herzfeld Advisors, helped with closed-end mutual funds (www.herzfeld.com). Thanks, too, to one of the deans of financial planning, Harold Evensky of Evensky & Katz Wealth Management (www.evensky.com) and author of *Retirement Income Redesigned: Master Plans for Distribution*.

On college investing, I had valuable aid from Mark Kantrowitz, publisher of FinAid.org (www.finaid.org), the most popular site on the Web for tools and information about student aid; and three experts from The College Board (www .collegeboard.com): Jack Joyce, former director of information and training services and a walking encyclopedia on student aid; Sandy Baum, professor of economics at Skidmore College and the board's senior policy analyst; and Sandra Riley, who juggled the college-cost tables.

Speaking of tables, my deepest thanks to Alexa Auerbach and Mark Komissarouk, both of Morningstar, Inc. (www.morningstar.com), who provided all kinds of market performance data. And to David Kahn and Aaron Eidelman, managing directors of the accounting firm RSM McGladrey, and Rebecca Williams, also of McGladrey, who produced numbers even in the midst of their tidal wave of year-end tax planning.

A small army of researchers pitched in for various parts of the book—sometimes at the last minute. Many thanks to Vincent Bruce, Althea Chang, Amy Friedman, Miriam Leuchter, Joseph Robida, Tamar Snyder, Rebecca Tucker, and especially my longtime associate Dori Perrucci.

I'm grateful to all of my friends, who stayed friends even though I didn't show up for dinners ("Jane's in book jail again."). Thanks to my editor, Alice Mayhew, who pushed me through—firmly, but with a smile—and to Roger Labrie and the rest of the Simon & Schuster team. Thanks to my marvelous family, who have endured "Mom's working" yet one more time—Dave, Tammis, Hallee, Elias, Chris, Susan, Dana, Jesse, Tyler, Martha, Maisy, Hudson, Jordan, Matthew, Amanda, Justin, and Sue. And to Carll Tucker, author of the *The Bear Went Over the Mountain* (highly recommended!: www.carlltucker.com). We were married in the middle of my book struggle. I said, "I do" and then effectively vanished for twelve months, to finish up. Greater love hath no man.

Index

About the Author

Jane Bryant Quinn is the author of two previous editions of the bestselling *Making the Most of Your Money* and of *Smart and Simple Financial Strategies for Busy People*. Her career includes a popular column syndicated by *The Washington Post*, a biweekly column at *Newsweek* magazine, the CBS morning and evening news, and an online column at Bloomberg.com. For her latest opinions, you can visit her Web site, www.janebryantquinn.com. She lives with her husband in New York City.